ELEMENTS OF *Literature*

SIXTH COURSE

Literature of Britain
with World Classics

Florida Edition

This royal throne of kings,
this scepter'd isle . . .

— from *Richard II* by
William Shakespeare

HOLT, RINEHART AND WINSTON

A Harcourt Education Company

Austin • Orlando • Chicago • New York • Toronto • London • San Diego

CREDITS

EDITORIAL

Project Director: Kathleen Daniel
Managing Editor: Richard Sime
Senior Book Editors: Kristine E. Marshall, Mairead Stack
Editorial Staff: Abigail Winograd, Dennis Cooney, Robert Hoyt, Kathryn Rogers, Christopher LeCluyse, Megan Truex, Colleen Hobbs, Christy McBride, Michael Neibergall, Karen Kolar
Editorial Support: Laurie Muir, Dan Hunter, Ruth Hooker, Kelly Keeley, Margaret Sanchez
Editorial Permissions: Ann B. Farrar, Sacha Frey, Tracy DeMont, Mark Holland

Research and Development: Joan Burditt

Index: Robert Zolnerzak

PRODUCTION, DESIGN, AND PHOTO RESEARCH

Director: Athena Blackorby
Design Coordinator: Ruth Riley
Program Design: Kirchoff/Wohlberg, Inc.
Electronic Files: Banta Digital
Production: Dolores Keller
Photo Research: PhotoSearch, Inc.
Photo Research Coordinator: Mary Monaco
Manufacturing: RR Donnelley & Sons Company, Willard, Ohio

COVER

Cover Artist: Greg Geisler
Photo Credits: (front cover) Bodiam Castle, East Sussex, England, Roy Rainford/Robert Harding Picture Library; Sutton Hoo helmet, The Granger Collection, New York; sky, Jim Ong/SuperStock; Scottish thistle, W. Paton/Planet Earth Pictures and Grace Davies/Omni–Photo Communications; (back cover) Baron Carlo Marochetti's sculpture of Richard Coeur de Lion, photograph by Janet Balmforth, courtesy of Benedict Read
Quotation on Cover: From *Richard II,* Act II, Scene 1, by William Shakespeare

Printed in the United States of America

ISBN 0-03-067293-7   2 3 4 5 6 048 04 03

PROGRAM AUTHORS

Kylene Beers wrote the Reading Matters section of this book and developed the accompanying *Reading Skills and Strategies* component. A former middle school teacher, Dr. Beers has turned her commitment to helping readers having difficulty into the major focus of her research, writing, speaking, and teaching. A clinical associate professor at the University of Houston, Dr. Beers is also currently the editor of the National Council of Teachers of English journal *Voices from the Middle*. She is the author of *When Kids Can't Read: The Reading Handbook for Teachers Grades 6–12* and co-editor of *Into Focus: Understanding and Creating Middle School Readers*. She has served on the review boards of the *English Journal* and *The ALAN Review*. Dr. Beers is a recipient of the NCTE Richard W. Halle Award. She currently serves on the board of directors of the International Reading Association's Special Interest Group on Adolescent Literature.

Robert E. Probst established the pedagogical framework for the 1997, 2000, and the current editions of *Elements of Literature*. Dr. Probst is Professor of English Education at Georgia State University. He has taught English in Maryland and been Supervisor of English for the Norfolk, Virginia, Public Schools. He is the author of *Response and Analysis: Teaching Literature in Junior and Senior High School* and has contributed chapters to such books as *Literature Instruction: A Focus on Student Response; Reader Response in the Classroom; Handbook of Research on Teaching the English Language Arts; Transactions with Literature;* and *For Louise M. Rosenblatt.* Dr. Probst has worked on the National Council of Teachers of English Committee on Research, the Commission on Reading, and the Commission on Curriculum. He has also served on the board of directors of the Adolescent Literature Assembly and is a member of the National Conference on Research in Language and Literacy.

Robert Anderson wrote the special essay "Contemporary British Drama." Mr. Anderson is a playwright, novelist, screenwriter, and teacher. His plays include *Tea and Sympathy; Silent Night, Lonely Night; You Know I Can't Hear You When the Water's Running;* and *I Never Sang for My Father*. His screenplays include *The Nun's Story* and *The Sand Pebbles*. Mr. Anderson has taught at the Writer's Workshop at the University of Iowa, the American Theater Wing Professional Training Program, and the Salzburg Seminar in American Studies. He is a past president of the Dramatists' Guild, a past vice president of the Authors' League of America, and a member of the Theater Hall of Fame.

John Malcolm Brinnin wrote the biographies of poets in all collections as well as the Critical Comments on selected poems. He also wrote the special essays "Twentieth-Century British Poetry" and "T. S. Eliot: The Voice of an Age." Mr. Brinnin is the author of six volumes of poetry, which received many prizes and awards. He was a member of the American Academy and Institute of Arts and Letters. He was also a critic of poetry and a biographer of poets and was for a number of years director of New York's famous Poetry Center. His teaching career, begun at Vassar College, included long terms at the University of Connecticut and Boston University, where he succeeded Robert Lowell as Professor of Creative Writing and Contemporary Letters. Mr. Brinnin's books include *Dylan Thomas in America: An Intimate Journal* and *Sextet: T. S. Eliot & Truman Capote & Others*.

John Leggett wrote biographies for the fiction writers in "The Victorian Period" and "The Twentieth Century." He also wrote the historical introduction for "The Twentieth Century." Mr. Leggett is a novelist, a biographer, and a former teacher. He went to the Writer's Workshop at the University of Iowa in the spring of 1969, expecting to work there for a single semester. In 1970, he assumed temporary charge of the program, and for the next seventeen years he was its director. Mr. Leggett's novels include *Wilder Stone; The Gloucester Branch; Who Took the Gold Away?; Gulliver House;* and *Making Believe*. He also wrote the highly acclaimed biography *Ross and Tom: Two American Tragedies*.

SPECIAL CONTRIBUTORS

John Algeo wrote the essays "The English Language." Dr. Algeo was Professor of English at the University of Georgia at Athens. He is co-author, with Thomas Pyles, of *The Origins and Development of the English Language*.

Harley Henry wrote the historical introduction for "The Romantic Period." Dr. Henry is Professor of English at Macalester College in St. Paul, Minnesota. He has also been a senior Fulbright lecturer in Zimbabwe and a Redfield Visiting Professor at the University of Chicago. In addition to the Romantic Period, his teaching specialties include the literature of Zimbabwe; William Faulkner; American fiction from 1945 to 1960; and fiction about baseball.

Donald Gray wrote the historical introduction for "The Victorian Period." Dr. Gray is Professor of English at Indiana University, Bloomington. Dr. Gray has written essays on Victorian poetry and culture and has been editor of *College English*.

David Adams Leeming wrote the historical introduction for "The Anglo-Saxons" and "The Middle Ages" as well as the material on *Beowulf*. Dr. Leeming was for many years Professor of English and Comparative Literature at the University of Connecticut. He is the author of several books on mythology, including *Mythology: The Voyage of the Hero; The World of Myth;* and *Encyclopedia of Creation Myths*. For several years he taught English at Robert College in Istanbul, Turkey. He also served as secretary and assistant to the writer James Baldwin in New York and Istanbul. He has published the biographies *James Baldwin* and *Amazing Grace: A Biography of Beauford Delaney*.

C. F. Main wrote the historical introductions for "The Renaissance" and "The Restoration and the Eighteenth Century," the biographies of writers in those periods, the Critical Comments on *Macbeth,* and the special essay "Women Writers of the Restoration and the Eighteenth Century." Dr. Main was for many years Professor of English at Rutgers University in New Brunswick, New Jersey. He is the editor of *Poems: Wadsworth Handbook and Anthology* and has written reviews and articles on sixteenth-, seventeenth-, and eighteenth-century literature.

William V. Costanzo wrote the special essay "Film as Literature: More Than Meets the Eye." Dr. Costanzo is Professor of English and Film at Westchester Community College, State University of New York. He is active in the National Council of Teachers of English and has chaired the NCTE Commission on Media, the Committee on Film Study, and the Assembly on Media Arts.

Katharina M. Wilson wrote the special essay "The Example of a Queen: Elizabeth I." Dr. Wilson is Professor of Comparative Literature at the University of Georgia and the author of several books on early women writers. She is also the editor of encyclopedias and diverse anthologies of works by early women writers.

WRITERS

The writers prepared instructional materials for the text under the supervision of Dr. Probst and the editorial staff.

Ellen Ashdown
Former Teacher
Educational Writer and Editor
Tallahassee, Florida

Barbara Dodson
Editor and Creator of Educational Software
Los Gatos, California

Lynn Hovland
Former Teacher
Educational Writer and Editor
Berkeley, California

Carole S. Lambert
Educational Writer and Editor
Waterville, Maine

Mary E. McCurnin
Educational Writer and Editor
Tallahassee, Florida

Carroll Moulton
Former Teacher
Educational Writer and Editor
Southampton, New York

Elisabeth H. Piedmont-Marton
Former Teacher
Coordinator of the Writing Program
Austin, Texas

Carolyn C. Walter
Teacher and Educational Writer
Oak Park, Illinois

REVIEWERS AND CONSULTANTS

The reviewers evaluated selections and/or instructional materials. Consultants provided advice on current pedagogy.

Linda Ayers
Muncie Southside High School
Muncie, Indiana

Norma Bornarth
Broad Run High School
Ashburn, Virginia

Marilyn McHale Campbell
Formerly with Fairfax County
   Public Schools
Fairfax County, Virginia

Ada Castillo
Mission High School
Mission, Texas

Charlene Couvillon
Fort Walton Beach High School
Fort Walton Beach, Florida

Bonnie Fay
Poquoson High School
Poquoson, Virginia

Margaret Garrison
Peninsula High School
Gig Harbor, Washington

Katie Joyce
Southwest High School
Fort Worth, Texas

Aman B. Kay
Westbury High School
Houston, Texas

Daniel Leary
John Marshall High School
Cleveland, Ohio

Carole Matthews
Boulder High School
Boulder, Colorado

Kaye Price-Hawkins
English/Language Arts
   Consultant
Abilene, Texas

Shirley Ramey
Port Neches-Groves I.S.D.
Port Neches, Texas

Marilyn Schroer
Formerly with Fort Walton
   Beach High School
Fort Walton Beach, Florida

Cynthia Tryoff
Taft High School
San Antonio, Texas

Renee Wells
Port Neches-Groves I.S.D.
Port Neches, Texas

Scott Yamahata
Westchester High School
Los Angeles, California

Junko Yokota
National-Louis University
Evanston, Illinois

FIELD-TEST PARTICIPANTS

The following teachers participated in field testing of prepublication material for the series.

Janet Blackburn-Lewis
Western Guilford High School
Greensboro, North Carolina

Dana E. Bull
F. J. Turner High School
Beloit, Wisconsin

Maura Casey
Skyline High School
Oakland, California

Deborah N. Dean
Warner Robins Middle School
Warner Robins, Georgia

Gloria J. Dolesh
Friendly High School
Fort Washington, Maryland

Christina Donnelly
Parkdale High School
Riverdale, Maryland

Kay T. Dunlap
Norview High School
Norfolk, Virginia

Joseph Fitzgibbon
West Linn High School
West Linn, Oregon

Paul Garro
Taft High School
San Antonio, Texas

Suzanne Haffamier
Agoura High School
Agoura, California

Robert K. Jordan
Land O' Lakes High School
Land O' Lakes, Florida

Terry Juhl
Bella Vista High School
Fair Oaks, California

Elizabeth Keister
Blair Middle School
Norfolk, Virginia

Jane S. Kilgore
Warner Robins High School
Warner Robins, Georgia

Janet S. King
Reading High School
Reading, Pennsylvania

Cheryl L. Lambert
Milford Mill Academy
Baltimore, Maryland

Sarah A. Long
Robert Goddard Middle School
Seabrook, Maryland

Donna J. Magrum
Rogers High School
Toledo, Ohio

Nancy Maheras
Western High School
Las Vegas, Nevada

Mara Malone
Central High School
Baton Rouge, Louisiana

Margaret E. McKinnon
Roger L. Putnam Vocational-
   Technical High School
Springfield, Massachusetts

Lourdes J. Medina
Pat Neff Middle School
San Antonio, Texas

Joan Mohon
Todd County Central
   High School
Elkton, Kentucky

Terrence R. Moore
John Muir High School
Pasadena, California

Gayle C. Morey
Countryside High School
Clearwater, Florida

Beverly Mudd
Western High School
Las Vegas, Nevada

Jan Nichols
Apollo High School
Glendale, Arizona

Jeffrey S. Norton
Lewis and Clark High School
Spokane, Washington

Barbara Powell
Todd County Central High
   School
Elkton, Kentucky

Gloria S. Pridmore
Morrow High School
Morrow, Georgia

Dee Richardson
Moore High School
Moore, Oklahoma

Carole A. Scala
Southwest Middle School
Orlando, Florida

Barbara A. Slaughter
Lewis and Clark High School
Spokane, Washington

Barbara B. Smith
Dr. Phillips 9th-Grade Center
Orlando, Florida

Sister Eileen Stephens, CSJ
Cathedral Preparatory
   Seminary
Elmhurst, New York

Sally Thompson
Andrew Jackson Middle School
Suitland, Maryland

Blanca M. Valledor
G. Holmes Braddock Senior
   High School
Miami, Florida

Charla J. Walton
John C. Fremont Junior High
   School
Las Vegas, Nevada

William Ward
Roger L. Putnam Vocational-
   Technical High School
Springfield, Massachusetts

Lynn White
Tascosa High School
Amarillo, Texas

Noretta M. Willig
Baldwin High School
Pittsburgh, Pennsylvania

Deborah K. Woelflein
Merrimack High School
Merrimack, New Hampshire

CONTENTS IN BRIEF

The Victorian Period

The Twentieth Century

Resource Center

CONTENTS

The Anglo-Saxons 449–1066

Informational Text
pages 2, 4, 10, 18, 28, 39, 47, 49, 59, 61, 63

Collection 1

Songs of Ancient Heroes

The Middle Ages 1066–1485

Informational Text
pages 74, 76, 78, 86, 89, 93, 96,
100, 113, 126, 127, 149, 162,
167, 177, 181

Collection 2

The Gift of Story

☀ Selections with this icon are used as the basis for FCAT practice in *Florida Practice Tests*.

COMMUNICATIONS WORKSHOPS

The Renaissance 1485–1660

Informational Text
pages 192, 194, 206, 212, 216, 219,
221, 223, 236, 246, 250, 260, 271

Collection 3

Love, Death, and Time

Collection 4

Under a Hand Accursed

Informational Text
pages 282, 297, 330, 332, 340, 367,
368, 383, 384, 389, 399

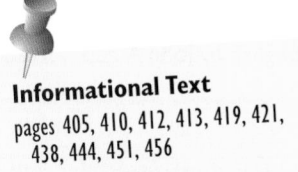

Collection 5

The Power of the Word

___

COMMUNICATIONS WORKSHOPS

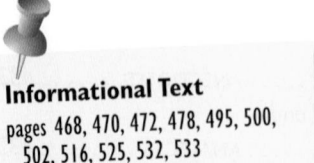

The Restoration and the Eighteenth Century 1660–1800

Collection 6

The Sting of Satire

Informational Text
pages 468, 470, 472, 478, 495, 500, 502, 516, 525, 532, 533

Informational Text
pages 543, 546, 552, 567, 571, 575,
578, 580, 583, 606, 609

Collection 7

An Appetite for Experience

The Romantic Period 1798–1832

The Romantic Period *by* Harley Henry   622

Time Line   624

London, 1802 *by* William Wordsworth   627

■ **A Closer Look**
   An Irresistible Bad Boy: The Byronic Hero   632
   The Lure of the Gothic   636

Informational Text
pages 622, 624, 626, 632, 636, 646,
648, 655, 666, 672, 682, 703, 704

Collection 8

The Power of Imagination

Informational Text
pages 724, 726, 733, 737, 738, 749, 759, 763, 770

Collection 9

The Quest for Beauty

COMMUNICATIONS WORKSHOPS

The Victorian Period 1832–1901

Informational Text
pages 782, 784, 788, 790, 798, 813, 816, 826, 832

Collection 10

Love and Loss

Informational Text
pages 849, 859, 868, 876, 896

Collection 11

The Paradox of Progress

COMMUNICATIONS WORKSHOPS

The Twentieth Century

Informational Text
pages 908, 910, 914, 920, 932, 938, 956, 974

Collection 12

The Center Cannot Hold

Informational Text
pages 980, 991, 993, 1006, 1012,
1037, 1040, 1046

Collection 13

The Transforming Imagination

COMMUNICATIONS WORKSHOPS

Informational Text
pages 1066, 1068, 1079, 1086, 1098, 1105, 1115

Collection 14

Ourselves Among Others

Informational Text
pages 1123, 1128, 1138, 1175

Collection 15

Clashes of Culture

Resource Center

SELECTIONS BY GENRE

Allegory

Analect, Anecdote, Axiom, and Proverb

Ballad, Song, and Riddle

Drama

Epic

FEATURES

Elements of Literature

The English Language

Across the Curriculum

Student Models

Writer's Workshops

SKILLS

Reading Skills and Strategies

Vocabulary

Language Workshops

Reading for Life

Learning for Life

Assessment

Elements of Literature on the Internet

TO THE STUDENT

Discover more about the stories, poems, and essays in *Elements of Literature* by logging on to the Internet. At **go.hrw.com** we help you complete your homework assignments, learn more about your favorite writers, and find facts that support your ideas and inspire you with new ones. Here's how to log on:

1. Start your Web browser and enter **go.hrw.com** in the location field.

2. Note the keyword in your textbook.

go.hrw.com
LEO 12-1

3. In your web browser, enter the keyword and click on GO.

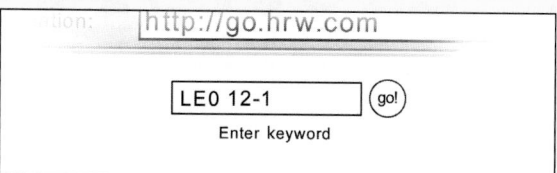

Now that you've arrived, you can peek into the palaces and museums of the world, listen to stories of exploration and discovery, or view fires burning on the ocean floor. As you move through *Elements of Literature,* use the best online resources at **go.hrw.com.**

Enjoy the Internet, but be critical of the information you find there. Always evaluate your

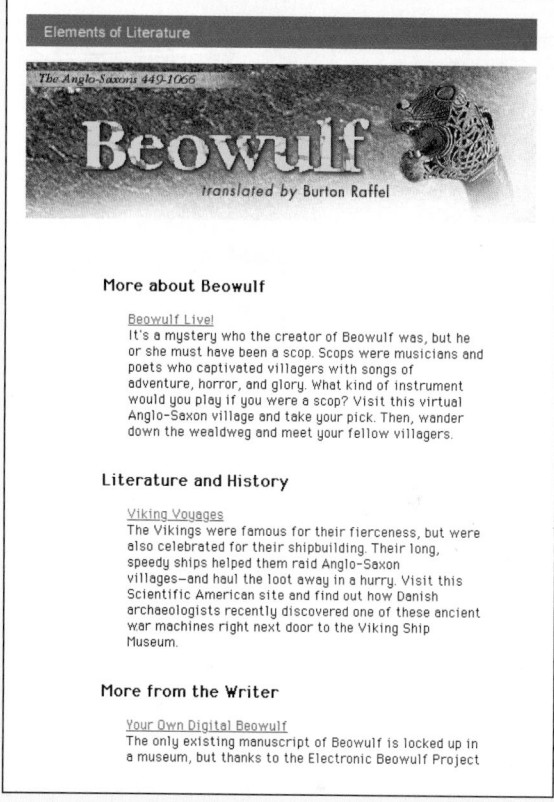

sources for credibility, accuracy, timeliness, and possible bias.

Web sites accessed through **go.hrw.com** are reviewed regularly. However, online materials change continually and without notice. Holt, Rinehart and Winston cannot ensure the accuracy or appropriateness of materials other than our own. Students, teachers, and guardians should assume responsibility for checking all online materials. A full description of Terms of Use can be found at **go.hrw.com.**

Building a Foundation for Success in Literature

Mastering the Sunshine State Standards
A Foundation for Reading

Reading Matters *By Dr. Kylene Beers*

Improving Your Comprehension

Improving Your Reading Rate

Preparing for FCAT and Other Standardized Tests
A Foundation for Test Taking

FCAT Test Smarts

Comparing Selections
FCAT Writing

Reading Matters

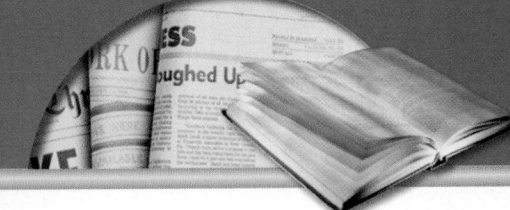

When the Text Is Tough

Remember the reading you did back in first, second, and third grades? Big print. Short texts. Easy words. Now in high school, however, the texts you read are often filled with small print, long chapters, and complicated plots or topics. Also, you now find yourself reading a variety of material—from your driver's ed handbook to college applications, from notes passed in the hall to graffiti printed on the wall, from job applications to income tax forms, from e-mail to e-zines, from classics to comics, from textbooks to checkbooks.

Doing something every day that you find difficult and tedious isn't much fun—and that includes reading. So, this section of this book is designed for you, to show you what to do when the text gets tough. Let's begin to look at some *reading* matters—because after all, reading *matters.*

READING UP CLOSE
♦ How to Use This Section

- **This section is for you.** Turn to it whenever you need to remind yourself about what to do when the text gets tough. Don't wait for your teacher to assign this section for you to read. It's your handbook. Use it.

- **Read the sections that you need.** You don't have to read every word. Skim the headings and find the information you need.

- **Use this information to help you with reading for other classes,** not just for the reading you do in this book.

- **Don't be afraid to *re-read* the information** you find in Reading Matters. The best readers constantly re-read information.

- **If you need more help, then check the index.** The index will direct you to other pages in this book with information on reading skills and strategies.

Improving Your Comprehension

Comprehension, your ability to understand what you read, is a critical part of the reading process. Your comprehension can be affected by many factors. Think about each of the following types of texts, and rate your comprehension of each from 1 (*never understand*) to 5 (*always understand*).

A) notes from your friends

B) e-mail messages from friends

C) college applications

D) job applications

E) magazines

F) computer manuals

G) Internet sites

H) school textbooks

I) novels you choose

J) novels your teachers choose for you

You probably didn't rate yourself the same for each type of text. Factors such as your interest level and the text's vocabulary level will cause your ratings to differ from text to text. Now, go back and look specifically at items *H, I,* and *J.* How did you rate there? If you think your comprehension of those materials is low, then you'll want to study the next few pages carefully. They are filled with tips to help you improve your comprehension.

READING UP CLOSE

♦ Monitoring Your Comprehension

Skilled readers often pay more attention to what they don't understand than to what they do. Here are some symbols you could put on self-adhesive notes to put onto texts as you are reading so you can keep up with what's confusing you. Decide how you would use each symbol.

Visualizing. The ability to visualize—or see in your mind—what you are reading is important for comprehension. To understand how visualizing makes a difference, try this quick test. When you get home, turn on a television to a program you enjoy. Then, turn your back to the television set. How long will you keep "watching" the program that way? Probably not long. Why not? Because it would be boring if you couldn't see what was happening. The same is true with reading: If you can't "see" in your mind what is happening on the page, then you probably will tune out quickly. You can improve your ability to visualize the text by practicing the following:

1. **Read a few sentences; then pause and describe what is happening on the page.** Forcing yourself to describe the scene will take some time at first, but will help in the long run.

2. **On a sheet of paper or a self-adhesive note, make a graphic representation of what is happening as you are reading.** For instance, if two characters are talking, draw two stick figures with arrows pointing between them to show yourself that they are talking.

3. **Discuss a scene or a part of a chapter with a buddy.** Talk about what you "saw" as you were reading.

4. **Read aloud.** If you are having trouble visualizing the text, it might be because you aren't really "hearing" it. Try reading a portion of your text aloud, using good expression and phrasing. As you hear the words, you may find it easier to see the scenes.

READING UP CLOSE

♦ Visualizing What You Read

Read the following from "The Death of Arthur" (p. 171) and discuss what you "see."

"So upon Trinity Sunday at night king Arthur dreamed a wonderful dream. And in his dream him seemed that he saw upon a chafflet a chair, and the chair was fast to a wheel, and thereupon sat king Arthur in the richest cloth of gold that might be made. And the king thought there was under him, far from him, an hideous deep black water, and therein was all manner of serpents and worms and wild beasts foul and horrible. And suddenly the king thought that the wheel turned up-so-down, and he fell among the serpents, and every beast took him by a limb. And then the king cried as he lay in his bed, "Help! help!" and then knights, squires and yeomen awakened the king and then he was so amazed that he wist not where he was."

Metacognition. Your attention wanders for a moment as you are reading something, but your eyes don't quit moving from word to word. After a few minutes, you realize you are several pages beyond the last point where you can remember thinking about what you were reading. Then you know you need to back up and start over. This ability to think about your thinking—or in this case, lack of thinking—is called **metacognition.**

Metacognition refers to your ability to analyze what you are doing as you try to make sense of texts. Consequently, a critical part of metacognition is paying attention to what you are reading. It's normal to find that your attention *sometimes* wanders while reading. If it always wanders, though, then try either of the following: (1) Keep paper and pen close, and jot notes as you read; (2) read for a set amount of time (five minutes), and then stop and review what's happened since the last time you stopped. Lengthen this time as you find yourself able to focus longer. Take the quiz below to see what your metacognition level is. The lower the score, the more you need to focus on staying focused.

READING UP CLOSE

♦ Measuring Your Attention Quotient

Take the following survey to see what your Attention Quotient is. The lower the score, the less you pay attention to what you are reading. The higher the score, the more you pay attention.

When I read, I . . .

1. let my mind wander a lot.

1	2	3
most of the time	sometimes	almost never

2. forget what I'm reading.

1	2	3
most of the time	sometimes	almost never

3. get confused and stay confused or don't even realize I am confused.

1	2	3
most of the time	sometimes	almost never

4. discover I've turned lots of pages and don't have a clue as to what I read.

1	2	3
most of the time	sometimes	almost never

5. rarely finish whatever I'm supposed to be reading.

1	2	3
most of the time	sometimes	almost never

• **Think-Aloud.** Comprehension problems don't appear only after you *finish* reading. Confusion occurs *as* you read. Therefore, don't wait until you complete your reading assignment to try to understand the text; instead, work on comprehending while reading by becoming an active reader.

Active readers **predict, connect, clarify, question,** and **visualize** as they read. If you don't do those things, you need to pause while you read to

- make predictions,
- make connections,
- clarify in your own thoughts what you are reading,
- question what you don't understand, and
- visualize the text.

Use the Think-Aloud strategy to practice your active-reading skills. Read a selection of text aloud to a partner. As you read, pause to make comments and ask questions. Your partner's job is to tally your comments and classify each according to the list above.

READING UP CLOSE

♦ *One Student's Think-Aloud*

Here's Steve's Think-Aloud for "Sonnet 130" (p. 229).

After reading entire sonnet once: "I don't get it. This is like he's saying the woman he loves is ugly. Why would he say these things?" **(Questioning)**

After reading sonnet a second time: "He isn't saying very nice things about her. But at the end he still says his love is rare, so I think he does love her." **(Commenting/Clarifying)**

After reading sonnet a third time: "You know, maybe this is a joke about love: like, it's always supposed to be perfect, you know—coral red lips and eyes like the sun—but that even if she doesn't have those things, he still loves her. I think it's those last two lines that are important, you know showing that love doesn't have to be perfect. This is like realizing that even if your car isn't the coolest car in the lot, it's your car, and so you still love it."

Questioning the Text. This scenario may be familiar: You've just finished reading one of the selections in this book. Then, you look at the questions that you'll be discussing tomorrow in class. You realize that you don't know the answers. In frustration, you decide to give up on the questions.

While giving up is one way to approach the problem, it's not the best approach. In fact, what you need to do is focus *more* on questions—and focus on them while reading the text, not just at the end. This doesn't mean memorizing study questions before you read so that as you are reading you are thinking only about those questions. What it means is constantly asking yourself questions about characters, plot, point of view, setting, conflict, and even vocabulary while reading. You'll find that the more you question the text while reading, the better you'll be able to answer the questions at the end of the text after reading.

READING UP CLOSE
◆ Asking Questions While Reading

Here is a list of questions you can use as you read literary selections. You should recopy this list on note cards and keep it close as you read.

Character Questions
1. Who is the central character? Is this character the narrator? What are the greatest strengths and greatest weaknesses of this character?
2. Is the narrator telling the story as it is happening or upon looking back? Can you trust this narrator? What if the narrator were a different character? How would the story change? What point of view does the narrator have—first person, limited third person, omniscient—and how does that point of view impact the narrator's authority?
3. Who are the other characters? What makes them important to the central character? What do their actions reveal about their personalities? How do your thoughts about the characters change as you read the story? Can you find specific points in the text where your feelings about characters shift? Could any character have been omitted from the story?
4. Which character do you like the best? What would that character like about you?

Plot, Setting, and Conflict Questions
1. What are the major events in the plot? Which events are mandatory for the story to reach the conclusion it does? What prior knowledge is necessary for understanding this plot?
2. How does the setting impact the story? Could you change the location or the historical context and have the same story? How does the author situate the reader in the setting? Is the setting believable?
3. What event creates the conflict? How is the conflict resolved? How does the central character react to the conflict? How do other characters react?

Re-reading and Rewording. The best way to improve your comprehension is simply to **re-read.** The first time you read something, you get the basic idea of the text. The next time you read, you revise your understanding. Try thinking of your first reading as a draft—just like the first draft of an essay. As you revise your essay, you are improving your writing. As you revise your reading, you are improving your comprehension.

Sometimes, as you re-read, you find some specific sentences or even passages that you just don't understand. When that's the case, you need to spend some time closely studying those sentences. One effective way to tackle tough text is to **reword** the text:

1. On a piece of paper, write the sentences that are confusing you.
2. Leave a few blank lines between each line you write.
3. Then, choose the difficult words and reword them in the space above.

While you wouldn't want to reword every line of a long text—or even of a short one—this is a powerful way to help you understand key sentences.

READING UP CLOSE

♦ One Student's Rewording

Thomas tried rewording some of "The Fall of Satan" (p. 441, lines 1–6). Because word order is as confusing as word choice, Thomas combined reordering with rewording. Open your book to page 441 and read the original lines there. See his changes below. Also note: He has combined a Think-Aloud (see page xxxviii of this section) with his rewording.

This first part seems backwards. Look, I think he's asking this muse—what's a muse? Okay, the side note says it's a muse of poetry; I think this is like a Greek mythology character—so I think he's asking this muse to sing, not a real song, but just to tell him something. So, it really could start by saying Heavenly Muse, tell me about "man's first disobedience, and the fruit of that forbidden tree." Well, that would be in the Garden of Eden. So he's saying to the Muse,

Tell me about when man first sinned in the Garden of Eden by eating the apple and that brought death to the world and all our problems because now we don't live in Eden, until Christ brings us back to that blissful—that would be like perfect—seat.

Summarizing Narrative Text. Understanding a long piece of text is easier if you can summarize chunks of it. If you are reading a **narrative,** or a story (including biography), then use a strategy called **Somebody Wanted But So (SWBS)** to help you write summaries of what you are reading.

SWBS is a powerful way to think about the characters in a narrative and to note what each did, what conflict each faced, and what the resolution was. As you write an SWBS statement for different characters or subjects within the same narrative, you are forcing yourself to rethink the narrative from different **points of view.**

Here are the steps for writing SWBS statements:

1. Write the words *Somebody, Wanted, But,* and *So* across four columns.
2. Under the *Somebody* column, write a character's name.
3. Then, under the *Wanted* column, write what that character wanted to do.
4. Next, under the *But* column, explain what happened that kept the character from doing what he or she wanted.
5. Finally, under the *So* column, explain the eventual outcome.
6. If you're making an SWBS chart for a long story or novel, you might need to write several statements at different points in the story.

READING UP CLOSE

♦ **One Student's SWBS Chart**

Read this SWBS statement of "A Voyage to Lilliput" from *Gulliver's Travels* (p. 488). This statement includes information up through the break on page 492. Try writing an SWBS statement from one of the Lilliputians' points of view.

Somebody	Wanted	But	So
Gulliver	wanted his freedom	but found himself to be a prisoner of very tiny people who were treating him well as long as he behaved,	so he did not try to break free of the ropes that held him.

Summarizing Expository Text. If summarizing the information in expository, or informative, texts is difficult, try a strategy called GIST.

Steps for GIST:

1. Choose three or four sections of text you want to summarize.
2. Read the first section of text.
3. Draw twenty blank lines on a sheet of paper.
4. Write a summary of the first section of text using exactly twenty words—one word for each blank.
5. Read the next section of text.
6. Now, in your next set of twenty blanks, write a new summary statement that combines your first summary with whatever you want to add from this second section of text. It's important to note that even though you've now read two sections of text, you still have only twenty blanks to fill, not forty.

Repeat this process one or two more times depending on how many more sections of text you have to read. When you are finished, you have a

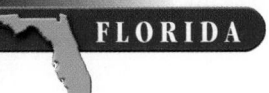
twenty-word statement that gives you the gist, or overall idea, of the entire text.

READING UP CLOSE

◆ One Student's GIST

Study the GIST statements for the first two columns of text from the informational piece "The English Language" found on page 609. Then try your hand at creating the third GIST.

GIST #1 (the first column)

In the eighteenth century some wanted the English language to stop changing but languages always change as the times change.

GIST #2 (adding the second column of information)

Changes in English occurred as English speakers came to North America and adapted old words, coined new words, borrowed words.

GIST #3 (adding the third column of information)

___ ___ ___ ___ ___ ___ ___ ___ ___

___ ___ ___ ___ ___ ___ ___ ___ ___ ___ ___

Question Maps. Most readers, at some point, will struggle with a text. Some readers find reading poetry a struggle, but they can breeze through computer magazines. Others find the technical language in computer magazines difficult but read poetry easily. It's not whether you struggle with texts that matters; instead, what matters is what you do when you struggle.

If you are an independent reader, then you know how to find the answers on your own—independently—to whatever causes you to struggle. If you are a dependent reader, you expect others to do the explaining for you. Dependent readers often say "I don't get it" and give up. Independent readers, by contrast, know what they don't get and then figure out how to get it.

If you think you are a dependent reader, then try using a Question Map like the one on the next page. As you complete the chart, you'll be mapping your way toward independent reading.

1. In the first column, **list your questions** as you are reading.
2. In the second column, **make notes about each question** as you write the question. For instance, jot down what made you think about the question or what page you are on in the text.
3. In the third column, **list possibilities for finding answers.** Remember that re-reading the text is always a good idea. Other

places to find answers include dictionaries (especially if you have questions about vocabulary), your own head (sometimes the text gives you part of the information and you must figure out the rest), or other parts of the book (especially if you are reading a science, math, or history book).

4. In the final column, **jot down answers to your questions** only after you've made notes about them and thought out where to find answers to them. If you can't answer your questions at this point, then it's time to see your teacher.

READING UP CLOSE

♦ One Student's Question Map

Here is a part of Denise's Question Map for "The Mark of the Beast" (p. 872).

Questions	Notes	Places to find answers	Answers
1. Why is Providence capitalized?	p. 872, 4th line	Ask teacher	making luck be like a person
2. Who is Hanuman?	p. 873, 4th line	Dictionary or encyclopedia	god in the Hindu religion

---

Smart Words. Sometimes you understand what you've read, but when it comes time to talk about or write about the selection, you can't find the words you want to help discuss the characters, theme, plot, or author's writing style. Here's a list of words that offer you springboards to discussion. They are beginning points—you still must be able to explain why you chose those words.

READING UP CLOSE

♦ Using Smart Words

Choose one of the selections you've read in *Elements of Literature* this semester and, using some of the words below, describe the plot, characters, theme, and author's writing style. Remember to explain your word choices with examples from the story.

Words to Describe the Plot

Positive	Negative
realistic	unrealistic
good pace from scene to scene	plodding
suspenseful	predictable
satisfying	frustrating
conclusion	conclusion
subplots make sense	confusing subplots
well-developed ideas	sketchy ideas

Words to Describe Characters

Positive	Negative
original	stereotyped
well-rounded	flat
dynamic—able to change	static—unable to change
well-developed	flawed

Words to Describe the Theme

Positive	Negative
subtle	obvious
unique	overworked
powerful	trivial
memorable	forgettable

Words to Describe the Author's Writing Style

Positive	Negative
descriptive, filled with figurative language	boring, no imagery
original	filled with clichés
lively, full of action	slow-moving
poetic or lyrical	plodding / jumpy

Improving Your Reading Rate

If your reading concerns are more about getting through the words than figuring out the meaning, then this part of Reading Matters is for you.

If you think you are a slow reader, then reading can seem overwhelming. But you can change your reading rate—the pace at which you read. All you have to do is practice. The point isn't to read so that you just rush over words—the I'mgoingtoreadsofastthatallthewordsruntogether approach. Instead, the goal is to find a good pace that keeps you moving comfortably through the pages. Why is it important to establish a good reading rate? Let's do a little math to see why your silent-reading rate counts.

MATH PROBLEM!
If you read 40 words per minute (WPM) and there are 400 words on a page, then how long will it take you to read 1 page? 5 pages? How long will it take if you read 80 WPM? 120 WPM? 200 WPM?

	1 page @400 words/page	5 pages @400 words/page
40 WPM	10 minutes	50 minutes
80 WPM	5 minutes	25 minutes
120 WPM	3 minutes	17 minutes
200 WPM	2 minutes	10 minutes

Reading Rate and Homework. Now, assume that with literature home-work, science homework, and social studies homework, in one night you have forty pages to read. If you are reading at 40 WPM, you are spending over six *hours* just reading the information; but at 120 WPM, you only spend about two hours. And at 200 WPM, you'd finish in one hour and twenty minutes.

Figuring Out Your Reading Rate. To determine your silent-reading rate, you'll need three things: a watch with a second hand, a book, and someone who will watch the time for you. Then, do the following:

1. Have your friend time you as you begin reading to yourself.
2. Read at your normal rate. Don't speed just because you're being timed.
3. Stop when your friend tells you one minute is up.
4. Count the number of words you read in that minute. Write down that number.
5. Repeat this process several more times using different passages.
6. Then, add the number of words together and divide by the number of times you timed yourself. That's your average number of words per minute.

Example

1st minute	180 words
2nd minute	215 words
3rd minute	190 words
	585 words ÷ 3 = 195 WPM

Reading Rate Reminders

1. **Make sure you aren't reading one word at a time with a pause between each word.** For instance, read the following rhyme. The first time you read it, pause between each word; but the second time, pause only where you see the slash marks. Hear the difference the phrasing makes?

   Mary had a little lamb. / Its fleece was white as snow. / Everywhere that Mary went / her lamb was sure to go./

   Word-at-a-time reading is much slower than phrase reading.

2. **Make sure when you are reading silently that you really are reading silently.** As you read, avoid moving your lips or reading aloud softly. Also, don't use your finger to point to words as you read. Instead use a bookmark to help yourself stay on the correct line while you practice your phrase reading.

3. **As you practice your fluency, remember that the single best way to improve your reading rate is simply to read more!** You won't get better at what you never do. Also, always remember, your rate will vary as your purpose for reading varies. Don't rush to read fast if that means understanding less.

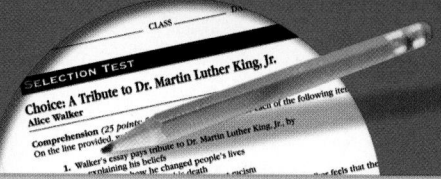

Comparing Selections

Read the passages "Inside a Blue Hole" and "To Save a Reef." Then, answer
the questions that follow.

Inside a Blue Hole
by Bill Belleville

© Stephen Frink/CORBIS

From the air, they can be stunning reliefs in the landscape—either as circular pools of cobalt blue in the shallow tropical banks, or as symmetrical ponds glowing like a clear sky inside the flat, monochromatic[1] terrain of the limestone islands of the wider Caribbean Basin.

Appropriately called blue holes, these geological accidents are no less appealing when confronted underwater in the marine environment. There, the uppermost rock walls of the holes often act as a base for scads of floating plankton[2] anchoring generations of corals, tunicates,[3] and bryozoans,[4] in turn drawing in fish—tiny schooling tropicals like chromis and sergeant majors, predators like snook, sharks, and barracudas, as well as spiny lobsters and assorted crabs. In the depths of the holes, it's possible for ancient caves to wind back into the crust for miles, sometimes connecting with other blue holes in land or sea.

1. **monochromatic:** single-colored.

2. **plankton:** microscopic plant and animal life that is eaten by nearly all aquatic animals.
3. **tunicates:** sea animals.
4. **bryozoans:** tiny water animals.

From "Inside a Blue Hole" by Bill Belleville from *Sea Frontiers*, August 1994, vol. 40. Copyright © 1994 by **International Oceanographic Foundation.** Reprinted by permission of the publisher.

When blue holes first found their way into popular travel literature a few decades ago, they were often described as mysterious and unknown. Their muddled natural history was ignored in favor of the melodrama of local legend and myth. The story goes, for instance, that on Andros in the Bahamas, the Lusca, a fearsome squidlike monster, lives in the bowels of the holes, reaching out for unwary native Androsians with its tentacles when the waters above the hole surge and boil. That myth grows out of true dangers associated with the blue holes. During swift tidal changes, whirlpools are spawned that surge and boil and hold the potential to pull unwary swimmers to the depths, Lusca or not.

Geologically, the origin of blue holes—also called ocean holes—is almost as fascinating as myth. Stripped of romantic spin, these phenomena were formed as sinkholes, much as were the sinks that periodically gobble up trees, houses, and cars throughout Florida. All sinks, including the sacred cenotes of the Yucatan, share a common crust called karst, a soft limestone in which a slightly acidic subsurface water flow carves caves, tunnels, and massive caverns under the surface. When new, these underground river systems contain the potable[5] water replenished by rainfall.

All sinks are originally formed when the roof of one of the caves collapses suddenly. Slightly acidic rainwater works on the limestone and other porous rock in the underground systems, slowly dissolving it. Around contemporary sinks on the mainland, the karst terrain is characterized by rolling hills and swales, artesian springs, and streams that sometimes vanish into the ground. The relief surrounding the geologically older ocean holes is far more subtle—eroded by tide and time.

In Florida and the lower southeastern United States, sinks present what cave explorer and videographer Wes Skiles calls "karst windows," providing direct access into the upper reaches of the Florida aquifer[6] for specially trained and equipped divers.

These blue holes can be grouped into several broad categories: Common, diver-accessible blue holes with tidal connections at relatively shallow depths between 10 and 50 feet; rare blue holes of extraordinary depth of hundreds of feet; hole basins filled with sediment and cut off both from the tide and cave access; and inland holes with a fresh-saltwater halocline connected to each other through an underground cave system.

Each has its own characteristics:

Common blue holes at relatively shallow depths almost always have tidal connections. Since there are simply more blue holes scattered in the shallow waters of the karst-rich Bahama banks, the Bahamas offer the best chance for sport divers to visit blue holes. And Andros, the largest island at 100-by-40 miles in size, probably has the most inland and ocean-sited holes. An airplane flight down the eastern coast of the island will reveal scores of blue holes punctuating the narrow shelf between the island and the 6,000-foot-deep abyss known as the Tongue of the Ocean. . . .

For sport divers, blue holes can be explored in two ways: by staying in the upper reaches of the hole under the recommended 130-foot depth and exploring the marine life on the walls and in the water column; and, by cave diving—with proper training and guidance—into the limestone caves found at the bottom of many blue holes.

Some blue holes have lost their tidal connections and become filled with sand and silt. A good example of this phenomenon is the prehistoric 600-meter-wide sink located inside the reef line five and a half miles off Key Largo in the Florida Keys. In this case, the

---

5. **potable:** drinkable.

6. **aquifer:** an underground layer of rock that holds water.

ancient blue hole is filled with fifty meters of sediment; little relief remains except for a scant outline of the hole's circumference when seen from the air. The presence of this sink and others like it doesn't bode well[7] for the biological health of the already-besieged reef system of the keys, according to E. A. (Gene) Shinn of the U.S. Geological Survey. Shinn indicates that Pleistocene[8]-era limestone under the reef system of the keys is riddled with the conduits[9] and caves of an ancient karst system. Thousands of septic tanks and shallow wells pump nutrient-rich wastewater into the soft limestone under the islands, allowing algae-stimulating nutrients to migrate laterally to the reefs through this system.

"Results of USGS studies," says Shinn, "indicated that ground waters beneath the reefs do contain nutrient levels many times higher than what is normal in seawater." Not surprisingly, the patch reef located just seaward of the Key Largo sink—once used as a dive site known as "Shark Reef"—is now dead. "The algae took that site away from us," says Laddie Akins, divemaster for Atlantis Dive Shop and director of the Reef Environmental Education Foundation. . . .

7. **bode well:** be a good sign or omen.
8. **Pleistocene:** an epoch beginning about 1.6 million years ago; it saw the rise of modern humans and toolmaking.
9. **conduits:** channels.

Understanding the Passage

1 What is the author's main purpose for writing this passage?
- **A.** to explain the benefits of diving into sinkholes
- **B.** to reveal the mystery behind the legend of the Lusca
- **C.** to describe how blue holes are being destroyed
- **D.** to describe the history and geology of blue holes

2 According to the passage, how does wastewater contribute to damage of the reef system?
- **F.** It contaminates the water, killing algae and other plant life.
- **G.** It causes blue holes to be filled with sand and silt, which kill the reefs.
- **H.** It contains nutrients that nourish algae, which damage the reefs.
- **I.** It destroys the soft limestone that carries nutrients to the reefs.

3 How do the final two paragraphs differ from the body of the passage?
- **A.** They broaden the topic to explain reef pollution.
- **B.** They summarize the passage by discussing the creation of blue holes.
- **C.** They conclude the passage by providing a description of blue holes.
- **D.** They narrow the topic by discussing one particular blue hole.

To Save a Reef

by Ted Levin

© Stephen Frink/CORBIS

The air is warm, the water warmer. The roll of the ocean is gentle. I float on the surface, face down, watching the pastel world of a Florida coral reef. Below us moves a phantasmagoria[1] of life: schools of sergeant majors; an orange-spotted filefish, lips puckered as though searching for a kiss; electric blue parrotfish; a slack-jawed barracuda, as shiny as polished silver. More than fifty yellowtail snappers—powder blue sprites, yellow striped, with deeply forked yellow tails— gather around me, then vanish into the rhythmic world of purple sea fans. Perfectly choreographed,[2] the fans sway to the pulse of the sea.

As a naturalist, I have explored and written about the Everglades for the past sixteen years. Now I am learning to appreciate how the health of the reef tract—a 220-mile-long, semicontinuous necklace of coral reefs that arcs along the Florida Keys from the state's southern tip out beyond the Dry Tortugas—is entwined with the Everglades, the Gulf of Mexico, and the Caribbean Sea. In 1997, for example, federal researchers found that disease on Florida's coral reefs had increased nearly threefold. The disease may be linked not only to the draining of the Everglades and our own infatuation with the Keys, but to polluted runoff from nearby and distant lands. . . .

"The Florida reef tract is downstream from everything," says biologist Steven Miller of the University of North Carolina at Wilmington. Yet here, six miles off the east coast of Key Largo, where he has taken me to see the reefs, even the water is a dazzling turquoise green. I see nothing that indicates this reef is under siege.

Miller's more educated eyes see trouble, however. We watch a pair of three-spot damselfish, 4-inch-long herbivores that create algae farms. First, they scrape a patch of coral. Then, over time, the fish feed on algae that grow on the damaged coral, and large numbers of the fish can destroy patches of coral. Damselfish populations were formerly held in check by predatory fish such as groupers and snappers. Says Miller, "Habitat destruction and overfishing have set in motion a population explosion of damselfish." . . .

1. **phantasmagoria:** a fast-changing scene.

2. **choreographed:** planned (usually a dance).

I quickly learn from Miller and others that in order to understand the problems facing the reefs, one must understand the nature of the reefs themselves. I'm not alone. Everyone on the Keys concerned about the subject—from dive-shop owners to tourists—is learning basic coral biology in order to comprehend what they can do to save the resource.

Reefs thrive on the shallow edge of tropical seas, most often off the eastern shore of continents where warm water currents brush the coast. Cold water kills reef-building coral, which is made up of colonies of tiny, jellyfish-like polyps. Each polyp—there may be billions in a large reef—absorbs calcium from the water and secretes a hard limestone skeleton. At night the polyps extend sticky, stinging tentacles from their skeletons to capture and consume small floating animals called zooplankton.

Low on the reef's food chain are algae, plantlike organisms that convert sunlight to food. Some live on coral skeletons. One type in particular, zooxanthellae, lives inside the tissue of the polyps. There the algae make up about half the weight of each fleshy polyp and are responsible for the beautiful color of coral.

Coral is the foundation of the reef community, providing the three-dimensional structure where fish and invertebrates live and feed. Some coral species are hard. Some are soft. Some branched. Some unbranched. Whatever the firmness and shape, every coral has a two-stage life cycle: the free-swimming larva and the stationary polyp. The larva is carried by currents, often far from the parent reef. If a larva settles on a hard, clean, silt-free bottom, it may survive to become part of a reef. If not, it dies. Once the larva has landed, the coral never moves again. . . .

In recent years, increased salinity in Florida Bay has been linked to seagrass die-offs, which are a likely source of nourishment for massive algal blooms. The greater salt content is the result of increased use of water on land to accommodate farming and housing developments. That means less water flowing through the Everglades into Florida Bay. Driven by tidal cycles and the wind, the soup-thick blooms have moved eastward, out across the reefs. Studies suggest that bay sediment[3] and algal blooms may have killed some of the already stressed coral colonies off the middle Keys.

Snorkeling near the northern end of the reef tract, I lift my head to listen to biologist Miller, who counts a flotilla of thirty-six fishing boats in the waters beyond us. He points out that visitation—whether by fishing boats, jet skis, snorkelers or divers—is one of the many problems that plague this lush and sensitive tropical community. . . .

The fate of Florida's coral reefs, however, is not "all gloom and doom," asserts Miller. In 1960, Florida set aside the world's first underwater park, John Pennekamp Coral Reef State Park. In 1975, Congress designated the nation's second national marine sanctuary off Key Largo. Six years later, the Looe Key National Marine Sanctuary protected a popular reef off Big Pine Key. In 1990, prompted by the grounding of three large ships on the coral reefs, Congress created the 2,800-square-nautical-mile Florida Keys National Marine Sanctuary. Portions of the sanctuary were set aside as reserves, as wildlife management areas, and for research. Channels have been marked in the shallows to protect seagrass beds from propellers, and moorings have been set to tie boats to, which eliminates anchor damage on the reef. . . .

---

3. sediment: matter that settles at the bottom of a liquid.

Understanding the Passage

4 What is the main idea of the passage?

F. With their vivid colors and diverse fish populations, coral reefs are spectacular natural phenomena.

G. By understanding the interconnectedness of nature, people can help save coral reefs.

H. Algae and bay sediment are two causes of coral death.

I. The state of Florida has taken steps, such as setting aside reserves, to save its coral reefs.

5 What is Steven Miller's opinion of boating in the Keys?

A. It provides visitors with opportunities to view the spectacular reefs.

B. It spurs people to protect coral reefs.

C. It causes too much damage to the reefs.

D. It should be outlawed by the state.

6 Why does the author compare his own view of the reef to Steven Miller's?

F. to show that the author is an authority on coral reefs

G. to show that damage to reefs may not be obvious to everyone

H. to show that reefs are dazzling to both experts and first-time visitors

I. to show that only biologists can really appreciate the complexity of reefs

Comparing the Passages

7 How is the structure of these passages similar?

A. Both present a thesis, or main idea, in the first paragraph.

B. Both conclude by summarizing the passage.

C. Both begin with a vivid description of their subject matter.

D. Both present information in chronological order.

8 What does the descriptive language the authors use tell you about their attitude
READ
THINK
EXPLAIN
toward their subjects? Compare the authors' attitude toward their subjects. Use details from the passages to support your response.

9 Both authors inform their readers about geological structures. Compare and contrast
READ
THINK
EXPLAIN
the types of information the authors provide. Use information and details from the passages to support your response.

FCAT Writing

At some point you and other Florida students participate in the FCAT Writing test. FCAT Writing is an "on-demand writing assessment." That means you will be asked to read a **writing prompt,** or assignment, and then plan and write your response within a given period of time—in this case, forty-five minutes. Therefore, you need to approach FCAT Writing with a plan of attack. Leave yourself approximately

- ten minutes to brainstorm, take notes, and outline your response

- thirty minutes to draft your response

- five minutes to edit your response

You will not know the prompt in advance, but you can prepare to respond by practicing, particularly in these two writing modes:

- **exposition**—give information, explain why or how, clarify a process, or define a concept

- **persuasion**—convince the reader that a given point of view is valid, or persuade the reader to take action

On the following pages you will find strategies that will help you feel confident in your response to the FCAT Writing prompt.

How to Read a Writing Prompt

An FCAT Writing prompt has two parts.

- The **Writing Situation** introduces the topic or concept you will write about, along with examples or definitions of the topic.

- **Directions for Writing** includes suggestions for how to get started, the kind of writing—expository or persuasive—you will do, and who your audience is.

Sample Prompts

Writing Situation: Your senior class wants to do a community service project.
Directions for Writing: Think about what your class might do in your community. Then, write to persuade your class to undertake the project of your choice.

Writing Situation: There are many jobs to choose from after you complete your education.
Directions for Writing: Think about the job that you would most like to do when you are finished with school. Now, explain why you chose this job.

Steps for Reading and Analyzing a Prompt

1. Determine your audience. Who are your readers? If your audience is not stated directly, assume it is the general population.

2. Look for CUE WORDS that tell you whether your task is to explain or to persuade.

3. State the task or purpose in your own words.

4. Take notes on your topic ideas.

Cue Words	Task or Purpose
Expository: *explain what, how, or why; define*	Give facts or ideas on a topic or concept, explain how to do something, or define a concept.
Persuasive: *convince, persuade, defend*	Take a point of view on the issue, and give reasons and evidence to support your opinion.

Expository Writing: Gathering and Organizing Ideas

Analyze the Prompt. Below is an analysis of the expository prompt on the opposite page.

> **Audience:** my classmates
>
> **Cue words:** explain why
>
> **Task/Purpose:** to choose and give reasons for the job I would most like to do when I have completed my education
>
> **Topic ideas:** I have always wanted to do something to help people. I thought about becoming a nurse, but I can't stand the sight of blood. I would most like to become a social worker.

Brainstorm Support. When doing expository writing, first consider your audience and purpose. Then, choose a specific topic.

Narrowing your topic may be easier if you freewrite on a piece of scratch paper.

Once you have narrowed your topic, you must help your audience understand the reasons why you think or feel as you do about your topic. Ask yourself the *5W-How?* questions (Who? What? When? Where? Why? How?) to brainstorm reasons.

Organize Your Explanation. An effective explanation must be well organized. Discussing more than one reason per paragraph, separating details from the reasons they support, or discussing one reason in more than one paragraph can make your explanation confusing. Avoid these problems by making an outline like the one below.

Main idea sentence: I would most like to become a social worker.

1. **Reason:** I am good with people.

   A. Detail: My friends and acquaintances always call on me when they're in trouble.

   B. Detail: Everyone tells me that I give good advice.

2. **Reason:** I would like to learn more about how to help people with various kinds of challenges.

   A. Detail: I would learn how to help people struggling with addiction problems and mental illness.

   B. Detail: I would learn how to help people deal with financial challenges and get out of debt.

3. **Reason:** Social workers do important work.

   A. Detail: Social workers help people find private and government programs to help them through hard times.

   B. Detail: Social workers act as mentors to their clients, encouraging them to grow and change.

When you are satisfied with your outline, you are ready to write your explanation. Remember to write an introduction that includes your topic sentence and a preview of your reasons and a conclusion that restates your topic sentence and sums up your reasons.

Persuasive Writing: Gathering and Organizing Ideas

Analyze the Prompt. Below is an analysis of the persuasive prompt on page lii.

Audience: my high school class

Cue word: convince

Task/Purpose: to give reasons that will persuade my high school class to undertake the community service project of my choice

Opinion notes: We could tutor elementary students or plant trees. There are many dilapidated houses in our area. <u>I think our class should help people repair their homes.</u>

Gather Support. When you have decided on your opinion, use the FUME key words to brainstorm reasons. Choose reasons that will be convincing to your particular audience. The support you use for a persuasive essay should be tailored to the audience. If you want people to take action, you must provide reasons that are important *to them*. Then, brainstorm FAD details to support your opinion. Then write your opinion statement.

FUME Reasons	FAD Support for Reasons
F = Fun: It would be fun to work together to make repairs.	**F = Fact:** Many people have an easier time opening up if they are working on a project than if they are attending a purely social event.
U = Useful: Our help will be useful to homeowners who can't afford to hire workers.	**A = Anecdote:** Mrs. Brown, an elderly lady who lives in our neighborhood, told me that her roof has leaked for years, but she doesn't have much money and doesn't know whom to call.
M = Meaningful: Repairing dilapidated houses will be meaningful to our neighborhood.	**D = Detail:** If our neighborhood looks better, it might inspire more people to care for their yards and keep the streets clean.
E = Educational: Repairing houses will teach us skills that will be useful later in life.	(Add a FAD detail.)
Opinion Statement: Our class should repair dilapidated homes in our neighborhood because it will be fun and educational as well as good for the community.	

Organize Your Essay. One good way to organize reasons in a persuasive essay is in order of their importance *to the audience.* You may want to start with your most important reason and work down to the least important, or you may prefer to start with your least important reason and work up to the most important.

Evaluating and Revising Your Response

Criteria

When you evaluate and revise, you improve your paper. The readers who evaluate FCAT writing use the four criteria below: focus, organization, support, and conventions. Practice evaluating and revising your writing according to these four criteria. Understanding them will help you improve all of your writing.

FOCUS: Main Idea Statement or Opinion Statement
If you do not have a statement of your concept, topic, or opinion, add one. If your statement is not clearly worded, rephrase it.

ORGANIZATION: Order and Transition
If the relationship between your ideas is not clear, rearrange them and add transition words such as *first, next, however, finally,* and *although.*

SUPPORT: Reasons/Examples and Elaboration
For expository writing that explains why or for persuasive writing, ask yourself,

- Do I have at least three reasons supporting my main idea or opinion statement? (If not, brainstorm more reasons.)

- Do I have at least one detail to elaborate each reason? (If not, use the **5W-How?** questions.)

CONVENTIONS: Sentence Structure and Mechanics
If all of your sentences follow the same simple subject-verb-object pattern, vary your structures, sprinkling your paper with a few compound and complex sentences and varying sentence beginnings. Check punctuation, spelling, and capitalization, and neatly mark corrections.

Scoring Rubric

Writing tests are usually scored on a point system. FCAT Writing, for example, is scored according to a six-point scale. (Responses that are illegible, incomprehensible, or blank are considered unscorable.)

5–6 Points: The writing focuses on the topic, and its organizational pattern provides for a logical progression of ideas. Effective use of transitional devices contributes to a sense of completeness. The support is consistently developed through ample use of specific details and examples. The writing demonstrates a mature command of language, and there is variation in sentence structure. The conventions of mechanics, usage, punctuation, and spelling are followed.

3–4 Points: The writing is focused but may contain ideas that are only loosely connected to the topic. An organizational pattern is present, but progression of ideas may not be logical. Development of support may be uneven. Word choice is adequate, and some variation in sentence structure is demonstrated. The conventions of mechanics, usage, punctuation, and spelling are generally followed.

1–2 Points: The writing addresses the topic but may include extraneous or loosely related ideas. It may have an organizational pattern but lack a sense of completeness or closure. Support may consist of generalizations or fragmentary lists. Limited or inappropriate word choice may obscure meaning. Frequent and blatant errors may occur in the basic conventions of sentence structure, mechanics, usage, and punctuation, and commonly used words may be misspelled.

The British Isles

LONDON

Dickens's House
Gray's Inn
Old Bailey
St. Paul's
The Tower
Tower Bridge
Thames River
Shakespeare Memorial
SOUTHWARK
British Museum
Covent Garden
Piccadilly Circus
Trafalgar Square
Westminster Abbey
Westminster Bridge
Big Ben and Parliament
Buckingham Palace

SHETLAND ISLANDS

ORKNEY ISLANDS

NORTH

Macduff
Dee R.
Cawdor
Culloden
Birnam Wood
Glamis
Dunsinane
Scone
Inverness
Loch Ness
Iona

HEBRIDES

SCOTLAND

UNITED KINGDOM*

Hadrian's Wall

Lake District

Haworth

Sherwood Forest

Liverpool

Coventry

Caernarfon

WALES

Tintern Abbey

Cardiff

ENGLAND

Sutton Hoo

Cambridge

Oxford

Cotswold Hills

Stratford-on-Avon

Avon R.

Bath

Glastonbury

Thames R.

Stonehenge

Quantock Hills

Tintagel

London

Runnymede

Canterbury

Dover

Hastings

Brighton

ENGLISH CHANNEL

FRANCE

NORMANDY

Calais

Le Havre

Cherbourg

NORTHERN IRELAND

Belfast

Dongal

Sligo

Galway

IRELAND

Shannon R.

Limerick

Killarney

Aran Islands

Blarney

Cork

Liffey R.

Dublin

IRISH SEA

Solway Firth

ATLANTIC OCEAN

Land's End

L. Kubinyi

*England, Scotland, Wales, and Northern Ireland

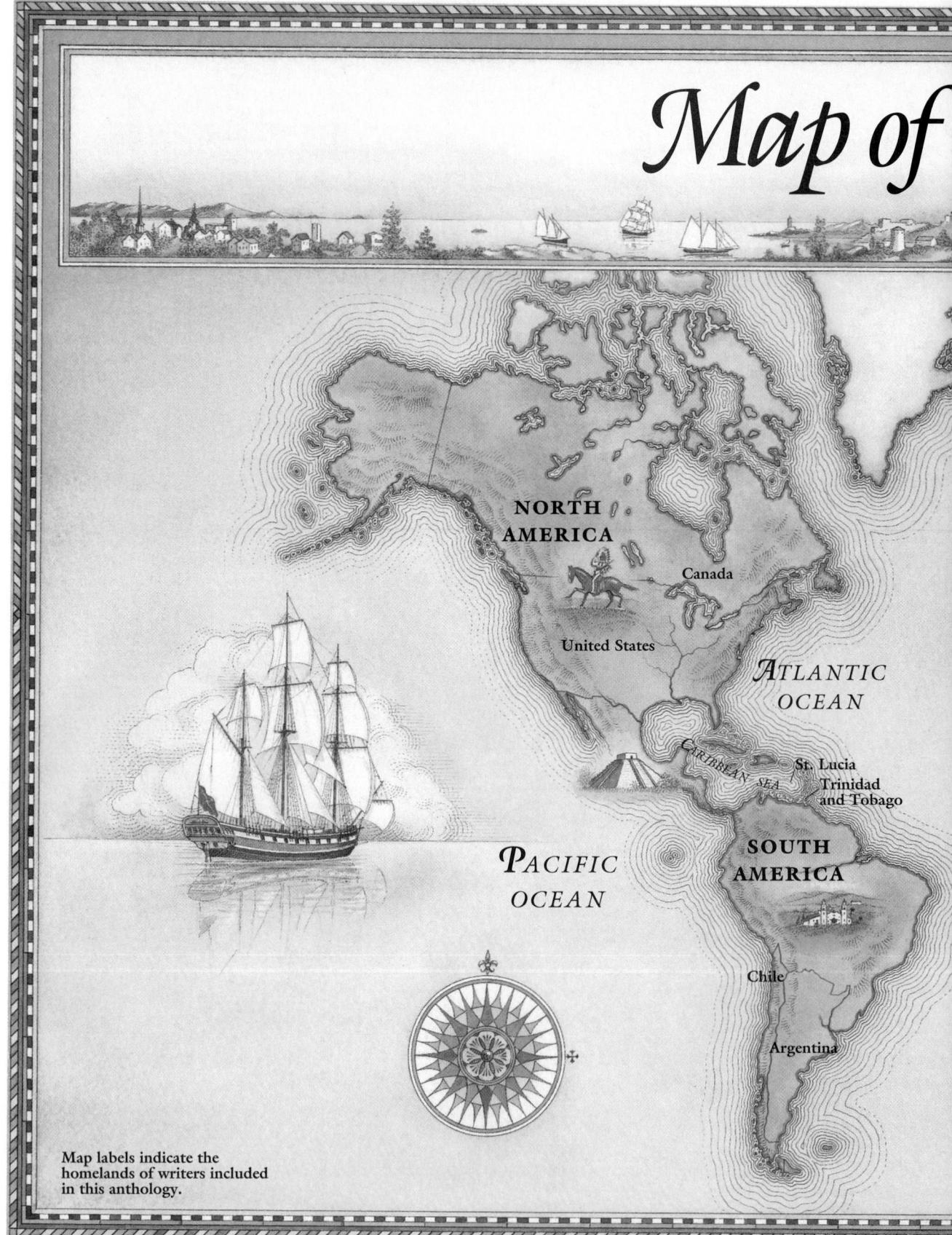

Map of

**NORTH
AMERICA**

Canada

United States

**ATLANTIC
OCEAN**

CARIBBEAN SEA

St. Lucia
Trinidad
and Tobago

**SOUTH
AMERICA**

**PACIFIC
OCEAN**

Chile

Argentina

Map labels indicate the
homelands of writers included
in this anthology.

the World

ARCTIC OCEAN

Russia

United
Kingdom
Denmark

Germany **EUROPE**
Maginot Line Ukraine

Russia

ASIA

France
Croatia
Romania
Italy

MEDITERRANEAN SEA

*Ancient
Mesopotamia*
Iraq   Iran

China

Japan

Algeria

Egypt

Saudi
Arabia

India

PACIFIC
OCEAN

AFRICA

Nigeria

Vietnam

Liberia

*A*TLANTIC
*O*CEAN

*I*NDIAN
OCEAN

Zimbabwe

AUSTRALIA

South
Africa

New
Zealand

L.Kubinyi

The Anglo-Saxons
449–1066

The Saxon Infantry (in chain mail, visor helmets, and shields) holds off the Norman attack. Detail from the Bayeux Tapestry (11th century).

The Anglo-Saxons

by **David Adams Leeming**

Anglo-Saxon England was born of warfare, remained forever a military society, and came to its end in battle.

—J. R. Lander

Aerial view of Stonehenge (c. 3000–1848 B.C.), located near Salisbury, England.

Page from the Book of Kells (8th century).

I solated from the European continent, rain-drenched and often fogged in, but also green and dotted with thatched cottages, quaint stone churches, and mysterious stone ruins, the island of Great Britain seems made for elves, legends, and poets. Yet if this land of mystery, beauty, and melancholy weather has produced Stonehenge, Robin Hood, and Shakespeare, it has also produced the theory of gravity, the Industrial Revolution, radar, penicillin, and the Beatles. We tend to associate the British with their monarchy and their former empire. But we should also remember that while most of the world suffered under various forms of tyranny, the English from the time of the Magna Carta (1215) were gradually creating a political system "by and for the people" that remains today a source of envy and inspiration for many nations. Although Americans rebelled against British rule in 1776, America would not be what it is today without the legacy of English common law—with its emphasis on personal rights and freedom. Nor would America be what it is today without the English parliamentary government, English literature, and the English language.

Stonehenge, consisting of large sandstone blocks and smaller bluestone pillars.

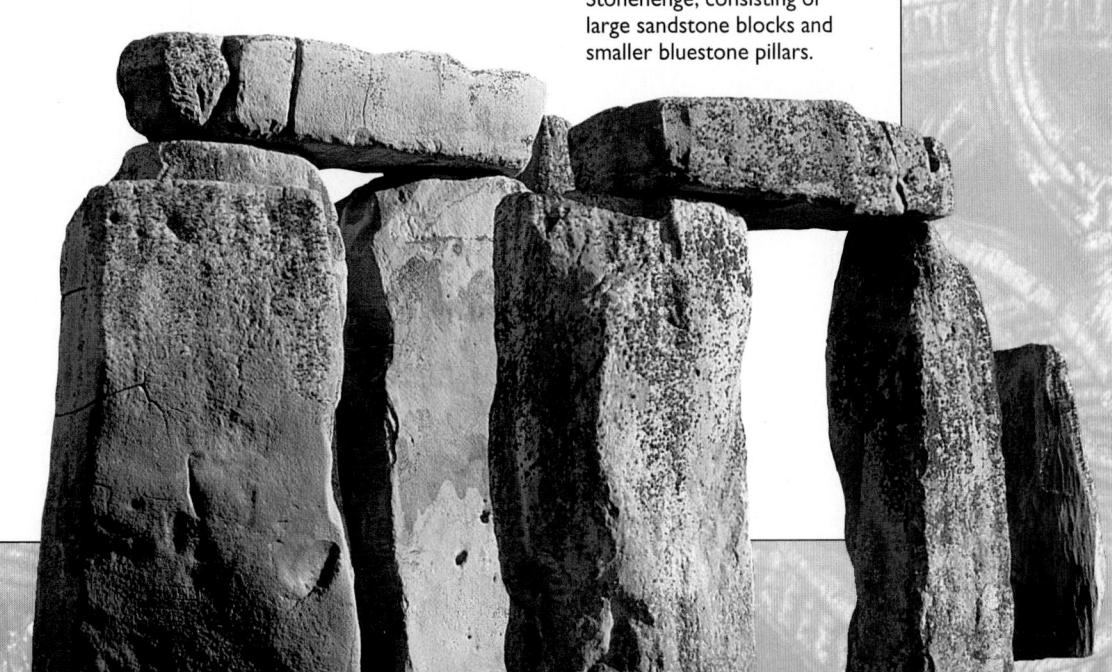

The Anglo-Saxons, 449–1066

LITERARY EVENTS

Roman poet Virgil born, 70 B.C.

Alexandria is center of Greek learning; library begun under Ptolemy, 307 B.C.

Throughout Europe, scrolls begin to be replaced by vellum books, c. 360

Roman poet Ovid writes *Metamorphoses*, c. 5

• King Arthur in battle. From a French manuscript.

In China, books printed by the late 500s

307–1 B.C.	A.D. 1–399	400–499	500–599

CULTURAL/HISTORICAL EVENTS

Celts called "Brythons" live in Britain, 300s B.C.

Julius Caesar invades Britain, 55 B.C.

Cleopatra VII becomes last queen of Egypt, 51 B.C.

Londinium (present-day London) founded by Romans as a supply port, c. 50

Queen Boadicea leads her eastern British tribe in an uprising against the Romans, 61

Christianity proclaimed lawful religion in the Roman Empire, c. 313

• Roman helmet.
© British Museum, London.

Roman legions withdraw from Britain, 409

Patrick brings Christianity to Ireland, 432

Angles, Saxons, and Jutes invade Britain, c. 449

Roman Empire falls to Germanic tribes, 476

Semilegendary King Arthur rules Celtic tribe, c. 516

Death of King Arthur at Battle of Camlann, 537

• Dome of the Rock, holy Muslim shrine in Jerusalem.

Widespread plague reaches Britain from Europe, 547

Buddhism introduced to Japan, 552

Saint Augustine converts Anglo-Saxon King Ethelbert and establishes monastery at Canterbury, 597

• Chinese sculpture of a seated Buddha (c. 650) from the T'ang dynasty.
The Metropolitan Museum of Art, Rogers Fund, 1919. (19.186). Photograph by Lynton Gardiner. © 1989 The Metropolitan Museum of Art.

Hymns produced by Caedmon, the earliest English Christian poet, c. 670

At Alexandria, Arabs discover the famous library with 300,000 papyrus scrolls, 640

Lyric poetry of the T'ang period promotes everyday use of Chinese language, 600s

Monks begin the Book of Kells, an illuminated manuscript of Latin Gospels, 760

Compilation of *Manyoshu* ("Collection of Ten Thousand Leaves"), Japanese anthology of about 4,500 poems, c. 759

The Venerable Bede, an English cleric, writes the *Ecclesiastical History of the English People*, 730

Beowulf first recorded, c. 700

• Crown of the Holy Roman Empire (10th century, with later additions).

Anglo-Saxon Chronicle begun, 891

Composition of the Poetic Edda, a famous cycle of Norse mythological poems, c. 850

Japanese court attendant Sei Shōnogan writes diary, *The Pillow Book*, c. 1000

In Japan, Lady Murasaki Shikibu writes the world's first novel, *The Tale of Genji*, c. 1000

The Exeter Book, a collection of English poetry, first copied, c. 975

Beginnings of the Arabian tales, *The Thousand and One Nights*, 900

600–699	700–799	800–899	900–1066

Paulinus is first Roman missionary to arrive in northern England, 601

Golden Age of T'ang dynasty begins in China, 618

Mohammed (b. 570), founder of Islam, begins to dictate the *Koran*, c. 625

Egyptian caliphs introduce the first organized news and postal service, 650

Synod of Whitby unites British Christian Church with Roman Church, 664

Moors invade Spain, 711

Pueblo period begins in southwestern North America, c. 750

Vikings invade Britain, beginning a century of invasions, 793

• Danes attacking an East Anglian town.

In France, Charlemagne crowned emperor of the West by Pope Leo III, 800

Decline of great Mayan civilization in Central America, 800s

Incas build fortress-city of Machu Picchu in Peru, c. 800

Algebra devised in Persia, c. 810

School of Astronomy founded at Baghdad, 813

Alfred the Great (849–899) becomes king of England, 871; he forces the Danes from Wessex, 878

Kingdom of Ghana in Africa flourishes, 900s

High King Brian Boru drives the Danes from Ireland at the Battle of Clontarf, 1014

Normans defeat Saxons; William the Conqueror becomes English king, 1066

• Mayan figure holding tortillas.

• Machu Picchu, Peru, lost city of the Incas.

This relatively small island of Great Britain has been invaded and settled many times: first by ancient people we call the Iberians, then by the Celts (kelts), by the Romans, by the Angles and Saxons, by the Vikings, and by the Normans. Whatever we think of as "English" today owes something to each of these invaders.

A small, isolated country, England is nevertheless the origin of a legal and political system that many other countries, including the United States, have since imitated. Over the centuries, English traditions and language have been reshaped by the island's invaders.

The Celtic Heroes and Heroines: A Magical World

When Greek travelers visited what is now Great Britain in the fourth century B.C., they found an island settled by tall blond warriors who called themselves Celts. Among these island Celts was a group called Brythons (or Britons), who left their permanent stamp in one of the names (Britain) eventually adopted by the land they settled.

The religion of the Celts seems to have been a form of **animism,** from the Latin word for "spirit." The Celts saw spirits everywhere—in rivers, trees, stones, ponds, fire, and thunder. These spirits or gods controlled all aspects of existence, and they had to be constantly satisfied. Priests called Druids acted as intermediaries between the gods and the people. Sometimes ritual dances were called for, sometimes even human sacrifice. Some think that Stonehenge—that array of huge stones on Salisbury Plain in Wiltshire—was used by the Druids for religious rites having to do with the lunar and solar cycles.

The mythology of the Celts has influenced English and Irish writers to this day. Sir Thomas Malory (page 169) in the fifteenth century, having time on his hands in jail, gathered together the Celtic legends about a warrior named Arthur. He mixed these stories generously with chivalric legends from the Continent and produced *Le Morte Darthur,* about the king who ultimately became the very embodiment of English values.

Early in the twentieth century, William Butler Yeats (page 978) used the Celtic myths in his poetry and plays in an attempt to make the Irish aware of their lost heroic past.

The Celtic stories are very different from the Anglo-Saxon tales that came later (see page 18), although it is the Anglo-Saxon myths that we tend to

A monk's cell (7th or 8th century) on Skellig Michael, off the coast of Kerry, Ireland.

All the Britons dye their bodies with woad, which produces a blue color, and this gives them a more terrifying appearance in battle. They wear their hair long, and shave the whole of their bodies except the head and the upper lip.

—Julius Caesar

study in school. Unlike the male-dominated Anglo-Saxon stories, the Celtic legends are full of strong women, like the tall and fierce and very beautiful Queen Maeve of Connacht (kân′ôt) in Ireland. Maeve once led her troops in an epic battle over the ownership of a fabulous white herd bull whose back was so broad fifty children could play upon it. Celtic stories, unlike the later, brooding Anglo-Saxon stories, leap into the sunlight (no matter how much blood is spilled). Full of fantastic animals, passionate love affairs, and fabulous adventures, the Celtic myths take you to enchanted lands where magic and the imagination rule.

The first British settlers were the Celts, a people whose daily lives were influenced by their magical religion. Their beliefs survive in Celtic mythology, which has influenced generations of later writers.

The Romans: The Great Administrators

Beginning with an invasion led by Julius Caesar in 55 B.C. and culminating in one organized by the emperor Claudius about a hundred years later, the Britons were finally conquered by the legions of Rome. Using the administrative genius that enabled them to hold dominion over much of the known world, the Romans provided the armies and organization that prevented further serious invasions of Britain for several hundred years. They built a network of roads (some still used today) and a great defensive wall seventy-three miles long. During Roman rule, Christianity, which would later become a unifying force, gradually took hold under the leadership of European missionaries. The old Celtic religion began to vanish.

Boadicea, queen of a Briton tribe, was flogged by the Romans after they had plundered her dead husband's property. She led the Britons to a fierce retaliation.

Boadicea's tribe, at once the most powerful and hitherto the most submissive, was moved to frenzy against the Roman invaders. They flew to arms. Boadicea found herself at the head of a numerous army, and nearly all the Britons within reach rallied to her standard. There followed an up-rush of hatred from the abyss, which is a measure of the cruelty of the conquest. It was a scream of rage against invincible oppression. . . . Her monument on the Thames Embankment opposite Big Ben reminds us of the harsh cry of liberty or death which has echoed down the ages.

—Winston S. Churchill

Hadrian's Wall, the seventy-three-mile defensive barrier built by the emperor Hadrian in about A.D. 122.

If the Romans had stayed, Londoners today might speak Italian. But the Romans had troubles at home. By A.D. 409, they had evacuated their troops from Britain, leaving roads, walls, villas, and great public baths, but no central government. Without Roman control, Britain was a country of separate clans. The result was weakness, which made the island ripe for a series of successful invasions by non-Christian peoples from the Germanic regions of Continental Europe.

Roman conquerors remained in Britain for more than four hundred years. They built roads and the walls that fended off attacks on Britain for several centuries. When the Romans finished withdrawing in A.D. 409, Britain was left without a centralized government—again susceptible to other invaders.

The Anglo-Saxons Sweep Ashore

This time the attack came from the north. In the middle of the fifth century, the invaders, Angles and Saxons from Germany and Jutes from Denmark, crossed the North Sea. They drove out the old Britons before them and eventually settled the greater part of Britain. The language of the Anglo-Saxons became the dominant language in the land which was to take a new name—Engla land, or England—from the Angles.

But the latest newcomers did not have an easy time of it. The Celts put up a strong resistance before they retreated into Wales in the far west of the country. There, traces of their culture, especially their language, can still be found. One of the heroic Celtic leaders was a Welsh chieftain called Arthur, who developed in legend as Britain's "once and future king."

At first, Anglo-Saxon England was no more politically unified than Celtic Britain had been. The country was divided into several independent principalities, each with its own "king." It was not until King Alfred of Wessex (r. 871–899), also known as Alfred the Great, led the Anglo-Saxons against the invading Danes that England became in any true sense a nation. The Danes were one of the fierce Viking peoples who crossed the cold North Sea in their dragon-prowed boats in the eighth and ninth centuries. Plundering and destroying everything in their path, the Danes eventually took over and settled in parts of northeast and central England.

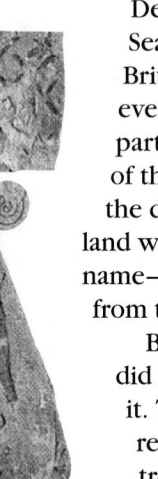

A picture stone (8th century) from Gotland showing a Viking ship under sail.

Statens Historiska Museer, Stockholm.

Gold and enamel jewel (9th century) thought to have belonged to King Alfred.

Ashmolean Museum, Oxford.

It is possible that even King Alfred would have failed to unify the Anglo-Saxons had it not been for the gradual reemergence of Christianity in Britain. Irish and Continental missionaries converted the Anglo-Saxon kings, whose subjects converted also. Christianity provided a common faith and common system of morality and right conduct; it also linked England to Europe. Under Christianity and Alfred, Anglo-Saxons fought to protect their people, their culture, and their church from the ravages of the Danes. Alfred's reign began the shaky dominance of Wessex kings in southern England. Alfred's descendants—Ethelfleda, a brilliant military leader and strategist, and her brother Edward—carried on his battle against the Danes.

The battle continued until both the Anglo-Saxons and the Danes were defeated in 1066 by William, Duke of Normandy, and his invading force of Normans from northwestern France.

The reemergence of Christianity and the role of Alfred the Great combined to unify Anglo-Saxon England. Alfred and his descendants fought the Danish invaders until the Norman Conquest in 1066.

What does "Anglo-Saxon England" mean?

Here are some key features of this age of warriors:

- Anglo-Saxon society developed from kinship groups led by a strong chief.
- The people farmed, maintained local governments, and created fine crafts, especially metalwork.
- Christianity eventually replaced the old warrior religion, linking England to Continental Europe.
- Monasteries were centers of learning and preserved works from the older oral tradition.
- English—not just the Church's Latin—gained respect as a written language.

The coronation of King Harold, from the Bayeux Tapestry (11th century).

Musée de la Tapisserie, Bayeux.

WOMEN IN ANGLO-SAXON CULTURE

Anglo-Saxon culture, with its emphasis on warfare, sounds as if it would be an inhospitable place for women. But women had rights in this society that were sharply curtailed after the Norman Conquest in 1066.

Evidence from wills first used during the later Anglo-Saxon period shows that women inherited and held property. Even when married, women still retained control over their own property. In fact, a prospective husband had to offer a woman a substantial gift (called the *morgengifu,* the "morning-gift") of money and land. The woman (not her family or her husband) had personal control over this gift; she could give it away, sell it, or bequeath it as she chose.

Christianity also offered opportunities for women. Women joined religious communities, and some women became powerful abbesses. These abbesses, usually women from noble families, were in charge of large double houses that included both a monastery and a nunnery. Hild (614–680), the abbess of Whitby (in present-day Yorkshire), was one of the most famous of these women. Hild accumulated an immense library and turned Whitby into a center of learning. Vikings sacked Whitby Abbey in the ninth century. The ruins of a monastery later founded at the same site still stand today, high atop cliffs overlooking the wild, gray North Sea.

Silver figurine (c. 9th–11th century) of Viking woman, from Grödinge, Söndermanland, Sweden. Statens Historiska Museer, Stockholm.

Anglo-Saxon Life: The Warm Hall, the Cold World

In 1939, in Sutton Hoo in Suffolk, England, archaeologists discovered a treasure that had been under the earth for thirteen hundred years. This enormous ship-grave contained the imprint of a huge wooden ship and a vast treasure trove—all of which had been buried with a great king or noble warrior. There was no trace left of the king or warrior himself, but his sword lay there, along with other meticulously decorated treasures of gold, silver, and bronze—his purse, coins, helmet, buckle, serving vessels, and harp. This grave can't help but remind us of the huge burial mound erected in memory of the king Beowulf.

Silver dish from the Sutton Hoo burial treasure (7th century).

As these Sutton Hoo ship treasures show, the Anglo-Saxons were not barbarians, though they are frequently depicted that way. However, they did not lead luxurious lives either, or lives dominated by learning or the arts. Warfare was the order of the day. As *Beowulf* shows, law and order, at least in the early days, were the responsibility of the leader in any given group, whether family, clan, tribe, or kingdom. Fame and success, even survival, were gained only through loyalty to the leader, especially during war, and success was measured in gifts from the leader. Beowulf, for instance, makes his name and gains riches by defeating the monsters who try to destroy King Hrothgar.

This pattern of loyal dependency was basic to Anglo-Saxon life. Such loyalty grew out of a need to protect the group from the terrors of an enemy-infested wilderness—a wilderness that became particularly frightening during the long, bone-chilling nights of winter. In most of England, the Anglo-Saxons tended to live close to their animals in single-family homesteads, wooden buildings that surrounded a communal court or a warm, fire-lit chieftain's hall. This cluster of buildings was protected by a wooden stockade fence. The arrangement contributed to a sense of security and to the close relationship between leader and followers. It also encouraged the Anglo-Saxon tendency toward community discussion and rule by consensus.

Anglo-Saxon life was dominated by the need to protect the clan and home against enemies. All groups, from family to kingdom, were organized around a leader who commanded absolute loyalty.

Reconstructed Anglo-Saxon village in West Stow, Suffolk, England. The communal hall is at the right.

The Anglo-Saxon Religion: Gods for Warriors

Despite the influence of Christianity, the old Anglo-Saxon religion with its warrior gods persisted. A dark, fatalistic religion, it had come with the Anglo-Saxons from Germany and had much in common with what we think of as Norse or Scandinavian mythology.

One of the most important Norse gods was Odin, the god of death, poetry, and magic. The Anglo-Saxon name for Odin was Woden (from which we have *Wednesday*, "Woden's day"). Woden could help humans communicate with spirits, and he was especially associated with burial rites and with ecstatic trances, important for both poetry and religious mysteries. Not surprisingly, this god of both poetry and death played an important role in the lives of people who produced great poetry and who also maintained a somber, brooding outlook on life.

The Anglo-Saxon deity named Thunor was essentially the same as Thor, the Norse god of thunder and lightning. His sign was the hammer and possibly also the twisted cross we call the swastika, which is found on so many Anglo-Saxon gravestones. (Thunor's name survives in *Thursday*, "Thor's day.")

Still another significant figure in Anglo-Saxon mythology is the dragon, which seems always, as in *Beowulf,* to be the protector of a treasure. Some scholars suggest that the fiery dragon should be seen as both a personification of "death the devourer" and as the guardian of the grave mound, in which a warrior's ashes and his treasure lay.

On the whole, the religion of the Anglo-Saxons seems to have been more concerned with ethics than with mysticism—with the earthly virtues of bravery, loyalty, generosity, and friendship.

National Museum, Reykjavik.

Coifi, the Anglo-Saxon chief priest, advises King Edwin to give up the old gods and accept the new religion of Christianity. Here is his argument.

Your Majesty, when we compare the present life of man on earth with that time of which we have no knowledge, it seems to me like the swift flight of a single sparrow through the banqueting hall where you are sitting at dinner on a winter's day with your thanes and counselors. In the midst there is a comforting fire to warm the hall; outside, the storms of winter rain or snow are raging. This sparrow flies swiftly in through one door of the hall, and out through another. While he is inside, he is safe from the winter storms; but after a few moments of comfort, he vanishes from sight into the wintry world from which he came. Even so, man appears on earth for a little while; but of what went before this life or of what follows, we know nothing. Therefore, if this new teaching has brought any more certain knowledge, it seems only right that we should follow it.

—The Venerable Bede, quoting Coifi in *Ecclesiastical History of the English People*

Despite the growth of Christianity, the Anglo-Saxon religion remained strong. Although it drew many of its deities and rites from Scandinavian mythology, the Anglo-Saxon religion was more concerned with ethics than with mysticism.

Three standing figures (Odin, Thor, and Freyr) in tunics, from a Viking tapestry (12th century).

The Bards: Singing of Gods and Heroes

The Anglo-Saxon communal hall, besides offering shelter and a place for holding council meetings, also provided space for storytellers and their audience. As in other parts of the ancient world (notably in Homeric Greece more than one thousand years earlier), skilled storytellers, or bards, sang of gods and heroes. The Anglo-Saxons did not regard these bards (called scops) as inferior to warriors. To the Anglo-Saxons, creating poetry was as important as fighting, hunting, farming, or loving.

The poets sang to the strumming of a harp. As sources for their improvisational poetry, the storytellers had a rich supply of heroic tales that reflected the concerns of a people constantly under threat of war, disease, or old age. We are told of the king in *Beowulf*:

> . . . sometimes Hrothgar himself, with the harp
> In his lap, stroked its silvery strings
> And told wonderful stories, a brave king
> Reciting unhappy truths about good
> And evil—and sometimes he wove his stories
> On the mournful thread of old age, remembering
> Buried strength and the battles it had won.
> He would weep, the old king.
>
> —Lines 2107–2114

Anglo-Saxon literature contains many works in this same elegiac strain. Poems such as "The Seafarer" (page 56), for example, stress the transience of a life frequently identified with the cold and darkness of winter. For the non-Christian Anglo-Saxons, whose religion offered them no hope of an afterlife, only fame and its reverberation in poetry could provide a defense against death. Perhaps this is why the Anglo-Saxon bards, uniquely gifted with the skill to preserve fame in the collective memory, were such honored members of their society.

> *The Anglo-Saxon bard's ability to recite poetic stories was considered as important a skill as fighting. Fame in the bard's mournful poetry—and a place in the community's memory—was a hero's only consolation against death.*

A knight, from a chess set carved from walrus ivory (12th century). British Museum, London.

A modern Argentine writer imagines the last Anglo-Saxon:

In a stable which is almost in the shadow of the new stone church, a man with gray eyes and gray beard, lying amidst the odor of the animals, humbly seeks death as one would seek sleep. The day, faithful to vast and secret laws, is shifting and confusing the shadows inside the poor shelter; outside are the plowed fields and a ditch clogged with dead leaves and the tracks of a wolf in the black mud where the forests begin. The man sleeps and dreams, forgotten. He is awakened by the bells tolling the Angelus. In the kingdoms of England the ringing of bells is now one of the customs of the evening, but this man, as a child, has seen the face of Woden, the divine horror and exultation, the crude wooden idol hung with Roman coins and heavy clothing, the sacrificing of horses, dogs, and prisoners. Before dawn he will die and with him will die, and never return, the immediate images of these pagan rites; the world will be a little poorer when this Saxon has died. . . .

—Jorge Luis Borges, *translated by* James E. Irby

Opening of *St. Matthew's Gospel*, from the Lindisfarne Gospels (7th century). Note the scribe's comments in the margins.

A Light from Ireland

Ireland had historical good luck in the fifth century. Unlike England and the rest of Europe, Ireland, isolated and surrounded by wild seas, was not overrun by the Germanic invaders. Then, in 432, the whole of Celtic Ireland was converted to Christianity by a Romanized Briton named Patricius (Patrick). Patrick had been seized by Irish slave traders when he was a teenager and had been held in bondage by a sheepherder in Ireland for six years. He escaped captivity, became a bishop, and returned to convert his former captors. His success was speedy and undying. From 432 to 750, while Europe and England sank into constant warfare, confusion, and ignorance, Ireland experienced a Golden Age. The Irish monks founded monasteries that became sanctuaries of learning for refugee scholars from Europe and England. Thus, it was in Ireland that Christianity, in the words of Winston Churchill, "burned and gleamed through the darkness."

The Christian Monasteries: The Ink Froze

In the death-shadowed world of the Anglo-Saxons, the poets or bards provided one element of hope: the possibility that heroic deeds might be enshrined in the society's memory. Another element of hope was supplied by Christianity. The monasteries served as centers of learning in this period, just as they would in the Middle Ages. In England the cultural and spiritual influence of monasteries existed right alongside the older Anglo-Saxon religion. In fact, the monasteries preserved not only the Latin and Greek classics but also some of the great works of popular literature, such as *Beowulf*.

Monks assigned to the monastery's scriptorium, or writing room, probably spent almost all their daylight hours copying manuscripts by hand. (Printing was still eight hundred years away in England.) The scriptorium was actually in a covered walkway (the cloister) open to a court. Makeshift walls of oiled paper or glass helped somewhat, but the British Isles in winter are cold; the ink could freeze. Picture a shivering scribe, hunched over sheepskin "paper," pressing with a quill pen, obeying a rule of silence: That's how seriously the Church took learning.

Latin alone remained the language of "serious" study in England until the time of King Alfred. During his reign, Alfred instituted the *Anglo-Saxon Chronicle,* a lengthy running history of England that covered the earliest days and continued until 1154. Partly because of King Alfred's efforts, English began to gain respect as a language of culture. Only then did the Old English stories and poetry preserved by the monks come to be recognized as great works of literature.

Christian monks preserved the literature of the ancient world as well as works of popular culture.

Here and there in the surviving manuscripts . . . we find the bored scribblings of the Irish scribes, who kept themselves awake by writing out a verse or two of a beloved Irish lyric—and so, by accumulation, left for our enjoyment a whole literature that would otherwise be unknown. . . . For the most part they enjoy their work and find themselves engrossed in the stories they are copying. Beneath a description of the death of Hector on the Plain of Troy, one scribe, completely absorbed in the words he is copying, has written most sincerely: "I am greatly grieved at the above mentioned death." Another, measuring the endurance of his beloved art against his own brief life span, concludes: "Sad it is, little parti-colored white book, for a day will surely come when someone will say over your page: 'The hand that wrote this is no more.'"

—Thomas Cahill

Quickwrite   Think about the importance of preserving a society's literature and language. Suppose that the monasteries had not preserved the classics of Greek and Latin literature. What might we have lost? Is there any possibility that our own literature and language could disappear from the earth? Write your thoughts on these questions.

(Opposite) Norse chessmen, carved from walrus ivory, found on Isle of Lewis, Scotland.

SONGS OF ANCIENT HEROES

from **Beowulf**
from **Gilgamesh**
"The Seafarer"

And sometimes a proud old soldier
Who had heard songs of the ancient heroes
And could sing them all through, story after story,
Would weave a net of words for Beowulf's
Victory, tying the knot of his verses
Smoothly, swiftly, into place with a poet's
Quick skill, singing his new song aloud
While he shaped it, and the old songs as well.

—*from Beowulf, translated by Burton Raffel*

Prow of the
Oseberg ship.

Beowulf

Beowulf is to England what Homer's *Iliad* and
Odyssey are to ancient Greece: It is the first great
work of the English national literature—the mythical
and literary record of a formative stage of English
civilization. It is also an epic of the heroic sources
of English culture. As such, *Beowulf* uses a host of
traditional motifs, or recurring elements, associated
with heroic literature all over the world.

The epic tells the story of Beowulf (his name may
mean "bear"), a Geat from Sweden who crosses the
sea to Denmark in a quest to rescue King Hrothgar
from the demonic monster Grendel. Like most early
heroic literature, *Beowulf* is oral art. It was handed
down, with changes and embellishments, from one
minstrel to another. The stories of *Beowulf,* like those
of all oral epics, are traditional ones, familiar to the
audiences who crowded around the harpist-bards in
the communal halls at night. The tales in the *Beowulf*

epic are the stories of dream and legend, of monsters and of god-fashioned weapons, of descents to the underworld and of fights with dragons, of the hero's quest and of a community threatened by the powers of evil.

By the standards of Homer, whose epics run to nearly 15,000 lines, *Beowulf* is relatively short—approximately 3,200 lines. It was composed in Old English, probably in Northumbria in northeast England, sometime between the years 700 and 750. The world it depicts, however, is much older, that of the early sixth century. Much of the poem's material is based on early folk legends—some Celtic, some Scandinavian. Since the scenery described is the coast of Northumbria, not Scandinavia, it has been assumed that the poet who wrote the version that has come down to us was Northumbrian. Given the Christian elements in the epic, this poet may also have been a monk.

The only manuscript we have of *Beowulf* dates from the year 1000 and is now in the British Museum in London. Burned and stained, it was discovered in the eighteenth century: Somehow it had survived Henry VIII's destruction of the monasteries two hundred years earlier.

Beowulf: People, Monsters, and Places

Beowulf: a Geat, son of Edgetho and nephew of Higlac, king of the Geats. Higlac is both Beowulf's feudal lord and his uncle.

Brecca: chief of the Brondings, a tribe, and Beowulf's friend.

Grendel: man-eating monster who lives at the bottom of a foul mere, or mountain lake. His name might be related to the Old Norse *grindill,* meaning "storm," or *grenja,* "to bellow."

Herot: golden guest-hall built by King Hrothgar, the Danish ruler. It was decorated with the antlers of stags; the name means "hart [stag] hall." Scholars think Herot might have been built near Lejre on the coast of Zealand, in Denmark.

Hrothgar: king of the Danes, builder of Herot. He had once befriended Beowulf's father. His father was called Healfdane (which probably means "half Dane"). Hrothgar's name might mean "glory spear" or "spear of triumph."

Unferth: one of Hrothgar's courtiers, reputed to be a skilled warrior. His sword, called Hrunting, is used by Beowulf in a later battle.

Welthow: Hrothgar's wife, queen of the Danes.

Wiglaf: a Geat warrior, one of Beowulf's select band, and the only one to help him in his final fight with the dragon. Wiglaf might be related to Beowulf.

Before You Read

FROM **BEOWULF**

Make the Connection

The Dragon Slayer

This is a story about a hero from the misty reaches of the English past, a hero who faces violence, horror, and even death to save a people in mortal danger. The epic's events take place many centuries ago, but this story still speaks to people today—perhaps because there are so many people in need of a rescuer, a hero. Beowulf is ancient England's hero. In other times, in other cultures, the hero takes the shape of King Arthur, or Gilgamesh, or Sundiata, or Joan of Arc. In twentieth-century America, the hero may be a real person, like Martin Luther King, Jr., or a fictional character like Shane in the Western novel. This hero-type is the dragon slayer, representing a besieged community facing evil forces that lurk in the cold darkness. And Grendel, the monster lurking in the depths of the lagoon, may represent all those threatening forces.

Quickwrite

Take notes on several contemporary fictional heroes from novels, films, or even comics or television. Pick one of them, and briefly analyze him or her using these questions:

- What sort of evil or oppression does he confront?
- Why does she do it? What's her motivation?
- For whom does he do it?

- What virtues does she represent?

Now discuss some of the heroes you and your classmates chose. Do they all seem to qualify as hero-types, or do some of them fall short in one way or another?

Elements of Literature

The Epic Hero

Beowulf, like all epic heroes, has superior physical strength and is supremely ethical. In his quest, he must defeat monsters that embody dark, destructive powers. At the end of the quest, he is glorified by the people he has saved. If you watch current events, particularly about people emerging from years of oppression, you will see this impulse toward glorification still at work. You might also see such glorification in the impressive monuments that are great tourist attractions in Washington, D.C.

Sutton Hoo helmet (7th century). Sutton Hoo ship treasure, Suffolk, England.
British Museum, London.

20 THE ANGLO-SAXONS

go.hrw.com
LEO 12-1

from Beowulf

translated by **Burton Raffel**

The Monster Grendel

1

... A powerful monster, living down
In the darkness, growled in pain, impatient
As day after day the music rang
Loud in that hall,° the harp's rejoicing

5 Call and the poet's clear songs, sung
Of the ancient beginnings of us all, recalling
The Almighty making the earth, shaping
These beautiful plains marked off by oceans,
Then proudly setting the sun and moon

10 To glow across the land and light it;
The corners of the earth were made lovely with trees
And leaves, made quick with life, with each
Of the nations who now move on its face. And then
As now warriors sang of their pleasure:

15 So Hrothgar's men lived happy in his hall
Till the monster stirred, that demon, that fiend,
Grendel, who haunted the moors, the wild
Marshes, and made his home in a hell
Not hell but earth. He was spawned in that slime,

20 Conceived by a pair of those monsters born
Of Cain, murderous creatures banished
By God, punished forever for the crime
Of Abel's death. The Almighty drove
Those demons out, and their exile was bitter,

25 Shut away from men; they split
Into a thousand forms of evil—spirits
And fiends, goblins, monsters, giants,
A brood forever opposing the Lord's
Will, and again and again defeated.

2

30 Then, when darkness had dropped, Grendel
Went up to Herot, wondering what the warriors
Would do in that hall when their drinking was done.
He found them sprawled in sleep, suspecting
Nothing, their dreams undisturbed. The monster's

35 Thoughts were as quick as his greed or his claws:
He slipped through the door and there in the silence

4. hall: guest-hall or mead-hall. (Mead is a fermented drink made from honey, water, yeast, and malt.) The hall was a central gathering place where Anglo-Saxon warriors could feast, listen to a bard's stories, and sleep in safety.

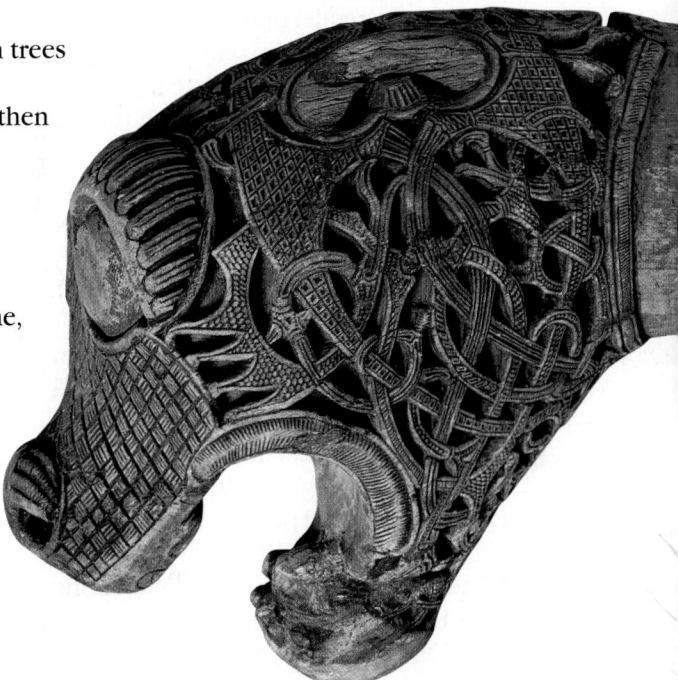

Animal head from Viking ship (c. 800).

University Museum of National Antiquities, Oslo, Norway. Photo by Eirik Irgens Johnsen.

Lines have been renumbered and do not correspond with the New American Library edition.

Snatched up thirty men, smashed them
Unknowing in their beds, and ran out with their bodies,
The blood dripping behind him, back
40   To his lair, delighted with his night's slaughter.
     At daybreak, with the sun's first light, they saw
How well he had worked, and in that gray morning
Broke their long feast with tears and laments
For the dead. Hrothgar, their lord, sat joyless
45   In Herot, a mighty prince mourning
The fate of his lost friends and companions,
Knowing by its tracks that some demon had torn
His followers apart. He wept, fearing
The beginning might not be the end. And that night
50   Grendel came again, so set
On murder that no crime could ever be enough,
No savage assault quench his lust
For evil. Then each warrior tried
To escape him, searched for rest in different
55   Beds, as far from Herot as they could find,
Seeing how Grendel hunted when they slept.
Distance was safety; the only survivors
Were those who fled him. Hate had triumphed.
     So Grendel ruled, fought with the righteous,
60   One against many, and won; so Herot
Stood empty, and stayed deserted for years,
Twelve winters of grief for Hrothgar, king
Of the Danes, sorrow heaped at his door
By hell-forged hands. His misery leaped
65   The seas, was told and sung in all
Men's ears: how Grendel's hatred began,
How the monster relished his savage war
On the Danes, keeping the bloody feud
Alive, seeking no peace, offering
70   No truce, accepting no settlement, no price
In gold or land, and paying the living
For one crime only with another. No one
Waited for reparation from his plundering claws:
That shadow of death hunted in the darkness,
75   Stalked Hrothgar's warriors, old
And young, lying in waiting, hidden
In mist, invisibly following them from the edge
Of the marsh, always there, unseen.
     So mankind's enemy continued his crimes,
80   Killing as often as he could, coming
Alone, bloodthirsty and horrible. Though he lived

Dragonhead from a Viking horse collar (detail) (10th century). Denmark.

National Museum, Copenhagen.

WORDS TO OWN

laments (lə·ments′) *n. pl.*: cries of grief.
reparation (rep′ə·rā′shən) *n.*: payment to compensate for wrongdoing.

In Herot, when the night hid him, he never
Dared to touch king Hrothgar's glorious
Throne, protected by God—God,
85 Whose love Grendel could not know. But Hrothgar's
Heart was bent. The best and most noble
Of his council debated remedies, sat
In secret sessions, talking of terror
And wondering what the bravest of warriors could do.
90 And sometimes they sacrificed to the old stone gods,
Made heathen vows, hoping for Hell's
Support, the Devil's guidance in driving
Their affliction off. That was their way,
And the heathen's only hope, Hell
95 Always in their hearts, knowing neither God
Nor His passing as He walks through our world, the Lord
Of Heaven and earth; their ears could not hear
His praise nor know His glory. Let them
Beware, those who are thrust into danger,
100 Clutched at by trouble, yet can carry no <u>solace</u>
In their hearts, cannot hope to be better! Hail
To those who will rise to God, drop off
Their dead bodies, and seek our Father's peace!

3

So the living sorrow of Healfdane's son°
105 Simmered, bitter and fresh, and no wisdom
Or strength could break it: That agony hung
On king and people alike, harsh
And unending, violent and cruel, and evil.
In his far-off home Beowulf, Higlac's
110 Follower° and the strongest of the Geats—greater
And stronger than anyone anywhere in this world—
Heard how Grendel filled nights with horror
And quickly commanded a boat fitted out,
Proclaiming that he'd go to that famous king,
115 Would sail across the sea to Hrothgar,
Now when help was needed. None
Of the wise ones regretted his going, much
As he was loved by the Geats: The omens were good,
And they urged the adventure on. So Beowulf
120 Chose the mightiest men he could find,
The bravest and best of the Geats, fourteen
In all, and led them down to their boat;
He knew the sea, would point the prow°
Straight to that distant Danish shore. . . .

104. Healfdane's son: Hrothgar.

110. Higlac's follower: Higlac is Beowulf's uncle and feudal lord.

123. prow (prou): front part of a boat.

- -

WORDS TO OWN
solace (säl′is) *n.:* peace.

- -

*Beowulf arrives in Denmark and is directed to Herot, the
mead-hall of King Hrothgar. The king sends Wulfgar, one of
his thanes (or feudal lords), to greet the visitors.*

The Arrival of the Hero

4

125   . . . Then Wulfgar went to the door and addressed
The waiting seafarers with soldier's words:
    "My lord, the great king of the Danes, commands me
To tell you that he knows of your noble birth
And that having come to him from over the open

130 Sea you have come bravely and are welcome.
    Now go to him as you are, in your armor and helmets,
    But leave your battle-shields here, and your spears,
    Let them lie waiting for the promises your words
    May make."
                    Beowulf arose, with his men
135 Around him, ordering a few to remain
    With their weapons, leading the others quickly
    Along under Herot's steep roof into Hrothgar's
    Presence. Standing on that prince's own hearth,
    Helmeted, the silvery metal of his mail shirt°
140 Gleaming with a smith's° high art, he greeted
    The Danes' great lord:
                    "Hail, Hrothgar!
    Higlac is my cousin° and my king; the days
    Of my youth have been filled with glory. Now Grendel's
    Name has echoed in our land: Sailors
145 Have brought us stories of Herot, the best
    Of all mead-halls, deserted and useless when the moon
    Hangs in skies the sun had lit,
    Light and life fleeing together.
    My people have said, the wisest, most knowing
150 And best of them, that my duty was to go to the Danes'
    Great king. They have seen my strength for themselves,
    Have watched me rise from the darkness of war,
    Dripping with my enemies' blood. I drove
    Five great giants into chains, chased
155 All of that race from the earth. I swam
    In the blackness of night, hunting monsters
    Out of the ocean, and killing them one
    By one; death was my errand and the fate
    They had earned. Now Grendel and I are called
160 Together, and I've come. Grant me, then,
    Lord and protector of this noble place,
    A single request! I have come so far,
    Oh shelterer of warriors and your people's loved friend,
    That this one favor you should not refuse me—
165 That I, alone and with the help of my men,
    May purge all evil from this hall. I have heard,
    Too, that the monster's scorn of men
    Is so great that he needs no weapons and fears none.
    Nor will I. My lord Higlac
170 Might think less of me if I let my sword
    Go where my feet were afraid to, if I hid
    Behind some broad linden shield:° My hands
    Alone shall fight for me, struggle for life
    Against the monster. God must decide
175 Who will be given to death's cold grip.
    Grendel's plan, I think, will be

139. mail shirt: armored garment made of interlocking metal rings.
140. smith's: metalworker's.

142. cousin: any relative.

172. linden shield: shield made from wood of the linden tree.

What it has been before, to invade this hall
And gorge his belly with our bodies. If he can,
If he can. And I think, if my time will have come,
180 There'll be nothing to mourn over, no corpse to prepare
For its grave: Grendel will carry our bloody
Flesh to the moors, crunch on our bones,
And smear torn scraps of our skin on the walls
Of his den. No, I expect no Danes
185 Will fret about sewing our shrouds,° if he wins.
And if death does take me, send the hammered
Mail of my armor to Higlac, return
The inheritance I had from Hrethel,° and he
From Wayland.° Fate will unwind as it must!"

185. shrouds: cloths used to wrap a body for burial.

188. Hrethel: Beowulf's grandfather, former king of the Geats.
189. Wayland: a smith celebrated for his skill in making swords and mail shirts.

5

190   Hrothgar replied, protector of the Danes:
      "Beowulf, you've come to us in friendship, and because
Of the reception your father found at our court.
Edgetho had begun a bitter feud,
Killing Hathlaf, a Wulfing warrior:°
195 Your father's countrymen were afraid of war,
If he returned to his home, and they turned him away.
Then he traveled across the curving waves
To the land of the Danes. I was new to the throne,
Then, a young man ruling this wide
200 Kingdom and its golden city: Hergar,
My older brother, a far better man
Than I, had died and dying made me,
Second among Healfdane's sons, first
In this nation. I bought the end of Edgetho's
205 Quarrel, sent ancient treasures through the ocean's
Furrows to the Wulfings; your father swore
He'd keep that peace. My tongue grows heavy,
And my heart, when I try to tell you what Grendel
Has brought us, the damage he's done, here
210 In this hall. You see for yourself how much smaller
Our ranks have become, and can guess what we've lost
To his terror. Surely the Lord Almighty
Could stop his madness, smother his lust!
How many times have my men, glowing
215 With courage drawn from too many cups
Of ale, sworn to stay after dark
And stem that horror with a sweep of their swords.
And then, in the morning, this mead-hall glittering
With new light would be drenched with blood, the benches
220 Stained red, the floors, all wet from that fiend's
Savage assault—and my soldiers would be fewer
Still, death taking more and more.
But to table, Beowulf, a banquet in your honor:

194. Wulfing warrior: The Wulfings were a Germanic tribe. Hrothgar's queen might have been a Wulfing.

Let us toast your victories, and talk of the future."
225 Then Hrothgar's men gave places to the Geats,
Yielded benches to the brave visitors,
And led them to the feast. The keeper of the mead
Came carrying out the carved flasks,
And poured that bright sweetness. A poet
230 Sang, from time to time, in a clear
Pure voice. Danes and visiting Geats
Celebrated as one, drank and rejoiced.

Unferth's Challenge

6

Unferth spoke, Ecglaf's son,
Who sat at Hrothgar's feet, spoke harshly
235 And sharp (<u>vexed</u> by Beowulf's adventure,
By their visitor's courage, and angry that anyone
In Denmark or anywhere on earth had ever
Acquired glory and fame greater
Than his own):
                    "You're Beowulf, are you—the same
240 Boastful fool who fought a swimming
Match with Brecca, both of you daring
And young and proud, exploring the deepest
Seas, risking your lives for no reason
But the danger? All older and wiser heads warned you
245 Not to, but no one could check such pride.
With Brecca at your side you swam along
The sea-paths, your swift-moving hands pulling you
Over the ocean's face. Then winter
Churned through the water, the waves ran you
250 As they willed, and you struggled seven long nights
To survive. And at the end victory was his,
Not yours. The sea carried him close
To his home, to southern Norway, near
The land of the Brondings, where he ruled and was loved,
255 Where his treasure was piled and his strength protected
His towns and his people. He'd promised to outswim you:
Bonstan's son° made that boast ring true.
You've been lucky in your battles, Beowulf, but I think
Your luck may change if you challenge Grendel,
260 Staying a whole night through in this hall,
Waiting where that fiercest of demons can find you."
     Beowulf answered, Edgetho's great son:
     "Ah! Unferth, my friend, your face

Anglo-Saxon gold buckle (7th century). Sutton Hoo ship treasure.
British Museum, London.

257. Bonstan's son: Brecca.

WORDS TO OWN
vexed (vekst) *adj.*: highly annoyed.

The Fury of the Northmen

When the fearsome Vikings began raiding England at the end of the eighth century, the church added a new prayer: "God, deliver us from the fury of the Northmen." Were these Scandinavian warriors—descended from the peoples of *Beowulf*—really such berserk destroyers? The fiercest ones were, indicated by the word *berserk* itself: In Old Norse, a *berserkr* was a "frenzied Norse warrior," so wild and fearless even his comrades kept clear.

Bear or bare? *Berserkr* literally means either "bear shirt" or "bare shirt," suggesting that these warriors wore bearskins or perhaps fought "bare"—without armor. Some say the berserkers were religious madmen, followers of Odin, god of death and war. Some say they ate mind-altering plants. Both may be true, because the berserker entered battle in a kind of fit, biting his shield, taunting death, and, like Beowulf, "If weapons were useless he'd use / His hands. . . . So fame / Comes to the men who mean to win it / And care about nothing else!" (lines 609–612).

Dragons from the sea. The Viking Age spanned the ninth through eleventh centuries, the European continent, and the Atlantic Ocean. Pushed by overpopulation, Vikings from Sweden, Norway, and Denmark struck out for new land. They

     Is hot with ale, and your tongue has tried
265 To tell us about Brecca's doings. But the truth
     Is simple: No man swims in the sea
     As I can, no strength is a match for mine.
     As boys, Brecca and I had boasted—
     We were both too young to know better—that we'd risk
270 Our lives far out at sea, and so
     We did. Each of us carried a naked
     Sword, prepared for whales or the swift
     Sharp teeth and beaks of needlefish.
     He could never leave me behind, swim faster
275 Across the waves than I could, and I
     Had chosen to remain close to his side.
     I remained near him for five long nights,

were farmers at home, but they were a warrior culture too, and they devastated England with nightmarish hit-and-run attacks. Even the name "Viking" comes from a telling phrase: For the Scandinavians, *to go a-viking* meant "to fight as a warrior or pirate."

The Vikings' extraordinary seafaring and shipbuilding skills, honed in their watery land of fiords, or narrow ocean inlets, gave them the advantage of making surprise attacks. The unique Viking warships were long (up to ninety-five feet, manned by thirty rowers), light and swift (to go farther on their provisions), and steady (built with a keel). Shallow-drafted, these dragon-prowed ships could be pulled onto a river shore, swiftly disgorging warriors wielding swords.

Unafraid of the unknown. But though the Vikings conquered peoples as far away as Spain and Russia (*Rus* was the Slavic word for Swedes), their motive was pure wanderlust as much as bloodlust. Expert in navigating by sun, stars, landmarks, and bird flights, the Vikings settled Iceland and Greenland and even explored North America—five hundred years before Columbus. That's why the United States once named a spacecraft *Viking:* to honor the human spirit that dared uncharted seas in the ninth century, and dares uncharted Mars in the twentieth.

Universitetets Oldsaksamling, Oslo.

Until a flood swept us apart;
The frozen sea surged around me,
280 It grew dark, the wind turned bitter, blowing
From the north, and the waves were savage. Creatures
Who sleep deep in the sea were stirred
Into life—and the iron hammered links
Of my mail shirt, these shining bits of metal
285 Woven across my breast, saved me
From death. A monster seized me, drew me
Swiftly toward the bottom, swimming with its claws
Tight in my flesh. But fate let me
Find its heart with my sword, hack myself
290 Free; I fought that beast's last battle,
Left it floating lifeless in the sea.

"Other monsters crowded around me,
Continually attacking. I treated them politely,
Offering the edge of my razor-sharp sword.
295 But the feast, I think, did not please them, filled
Their evil bellies with no banquet-rich food,
Thrashing there at the bottom of the sea;
By morning they'd decided to sleep on the shore,
Lying on their backs, their blood spilled out
300 On the sand. Afterwards, sailors could cross
That sea-road and feel no fear; nothing
Would stop their passing. Then God's bright beacon
Appeared in the east, the water lay still,
And at last I could see the land, wind-swept
305 Cliff-walls at the edge of the coast. Fate saves
The living when they drive away death by themselves!
Lucky or not, nine was the number
Of sea-huge monsters I killed. What man,
Anywhere under Heaven's high arch, has fought
310 In such darkness, endured more misery, or been harder
Pressed? Yet I survived the sea, smashed
The monsters' hot jaws, swam home from my journey.
The swift-flowing waters swept me along
And I landed on Finnish soil. I've heard
315 No tales of you, Unferth, telling
Of such clashing terror, such contests in the night!
Brecca's battles were never so bold;
Neither he nor you can match me—and I mean
No boast, have announced no more than I know
320 To be true. And there's more: You murdered your brothers,
Your own close kin. Words and bright wit
Won't help your soul; you'll suffer hell's fires,
Unferth, forever tormented. Ecglaf's
Proud son, if your hands were as hard, your heart
325 As fierce as you think it, no fool would dare
To raid your hall, ruin Herot
And oppress its prince, as Grendel has done.
But he's learned that terror is his alone,
Discovered he can come for your people with no fear
330 Of <u>reprisal</u>; he's found no fighting, here,
But only food, only delight.
He murders as he likes, with no mercy, gorges
And feasts on your flesh, and expects no trouble,
No quarrel from the quiet Danes. Now
335 The Geats will show him courage, soon

Two drinking horns (7th century).
Sutton Hoo ship treasure.

© British Museum, London.

WORDS TO OWN
reprisal (ri·prī′zəl) *n.*: punishment in return for an injury.

He can test his strength in battle. And when the sun
Comes up again, opening another
Bright day from the south, anyone in Denmark
May enter this hall: That evil will be gone!"

340   Hrothgar, gray-haired and brave, sat happily
Listening, the famous ring-giver sure,
At last, that Grendel could be killed; he believed
In Beowulf's bold strength and the firmness of his spirit.
      There was the sound of laughter, and the cheerful clanking

345 Of cups, and pleasant words. Then Welthow,
Hrothgar's gold-ringed queen, greeted
The warriors; a noble woman who knew
What was right, she raised a flowing cup
To Hrothgar first, holding it high

350 For the lord of the Danes to drink, wishing him
Joy in that feast. The famous king
Drank with pleasure and blessed their banquet.
Then Welthow went from warrior to warrior,
Pouring a portion from the jeweled cup

355 For each, till the bracelet-wearing queen
Had carried the mead-cup among them and it was Beowulf's
Turn to be served. She saluted the Geats'
Great prince, thanked God for answering her prayers,
For allowing her hands the happy duty

360 Of offering mead to a hero who would help
Her afflicted people. He drank what she poured,
Edgetho's brave son, then assured the Danish
Queen that his heart was firm and his hands
Ready:

      "When we crossed the sea, my comrades
365 And I, I already knew that all
My purpose was this: to win the good will
Of your people or die in battle, pressed
In Grendel's fierce grip. Let me live in greatness
And courage, or here in this hall welcome
My death!"

370   Welthow was pleased with his words,
His bright-tongued boasts; she carried them back
To her lord, walked nobly across to his side.
      The feast went on, laughter and music
And the brave words of warriors celebrating

375 Their delight. Then Hrothgar rose, Healfdane's
Son, heavy with sleep; as soon
As the sun had gone, he knew that Grendel
Would come to Herot, would visit that hall
When night had covered the earth with its net

380 And the shapes of darkness moved black and silent
Through the world. Hrothgar's warriors rose with him.
      He went to Beowulf, embraced the Geats'
Brave prince, wished him well, and hoped

That Herot would be his to command. And then
He declared:

385   "No one strange to this land
Has ever been granted what I've given you,
No one in all the years of my rule.
Make this best of all mead-halls yours, and then
Keep it free of evil, fight
390 With glory in your heart! Purge Herot
And your ship will sail home with its treasure-holds full." . . .

The feast ends. Beowulf and his men take the place of
Hrothgar's followers and lie down to sleep in Herot.
Beowulf, however, is wakeful, eager to meet his enemy.

The Battle with Grendel

8

Out from the marsh, from the foot of misty
Hills and bogs, bearing God's hatred,
Grendel came, hoping to kill
395 Anyone he could trap on this trip to high Herot.
He moved quickly through the cloudy night,
Up from his swampland, sliding silently
Toward that gold-shining hall. He had visited Hrothgar's
Home before, knew the way—
400 But never, before nor after that night,
Found Herot defended so firmly, his reception
So harsh. He journeyed, forever joyless,
Straight to the door, then snapped it open,
Tore its iron fasteners with a touch,
405 And rushed angrily over the threshold.
He strode quickly across the inlaid
Floor, snarling and fierce: His eyes
Gleamed in the darkness, burned with a gruesome
Light. Then he stopped, seeing the hall
410 Crowded with sleeping warriors, stuffed
With rows of young soldiers resting together.
And his heart laughed, he relished the sight,
Intended to tear the life from those bodies
By morning; the monster's mind was hot
415 With the thought of food and the feasting his belly
Would soon know. But fate, that night, intended
Grendel to gnaw the broken bones
Of his last human supper. Human
Eyes were watching his evil steps,
420 Waiting to see his swift hard claws.

Bronze plaque showing a
warrior killing a monster.

Statens Historiska Museer, Stockholm.

Grendel snatched at the first Geat
He came to, ripped him apart, cut
His body to bits with powerful jaws,
Drank the blood from his veins, and bolted
425 Him down, hands and feet; death
And Grendel's great teeth came together,
Snapping life shut. Then he stepped to another
Still body, clutched at Beowulf with his claws,
Grasped at a strong-hearted wakeful sleeper
430 —And was instantly seized himself, claws
Bent back as Beowulf leaned up on one arm.
    That shepherd of evil, guardian of crime,
Knew at once that nowhere on earth
Had he met a man whose hands were harder;
435 His mind was flooded with fear—but nothing
Could take his talons and himself from that tight
Hard grip. Grendel's one thought was to run
From Beowulf, flee back to his marsh and hide there:
This was a different Herot than the hall he had emptied.
440 But Higlac's follower remembered his final
Boast and, standing erect, stopped
The monster's flight, fastened those claws
In his fists till they cracked, clutched Grendel
Closer. The infamous killer fought
445 For his freedom, wanting no flesh but retreat,
Desiring nothing but escape; his claws
Had been caught, he was trapped. That trip to Herot
Was a miserable journey for the writhing monster!
    The high hall rang, its roof boards swayed,
450 And Danes shook with terror. Down
The aisles the battle swept, angry
And wild. Herot trembled, wonderfully
Built to withstand the blows, the struggling
Great bodies beating at its beautiful walls;
455 Shaped and fastened with iron, inside
And out, artfully worked, the building
Stood firm. Its benches rattled, fell
To the floor, gold-covered boards grating
As Grendel and Beowulf battled across them.
460 Hrothgar's wise men had fashioned Herot
To stand forever; only fire,
They had planned, could shatter what such skill had put
Together, swallow in hot flames such splendor
Of ivory and iron and wood. Suddenly
465 The sounds changed, the Danes started
In new terror, cowering in their beds as the terrible
Screams of the Almighty's enemy sang
In the darkness, the horrible shrieks of pain
And defeat, the tears torn out of Grendel's

Silver and gold brooch with amber ornaments (9th century). Roscrea, County Tipperary.

National Museum of Ireland, Dublin.

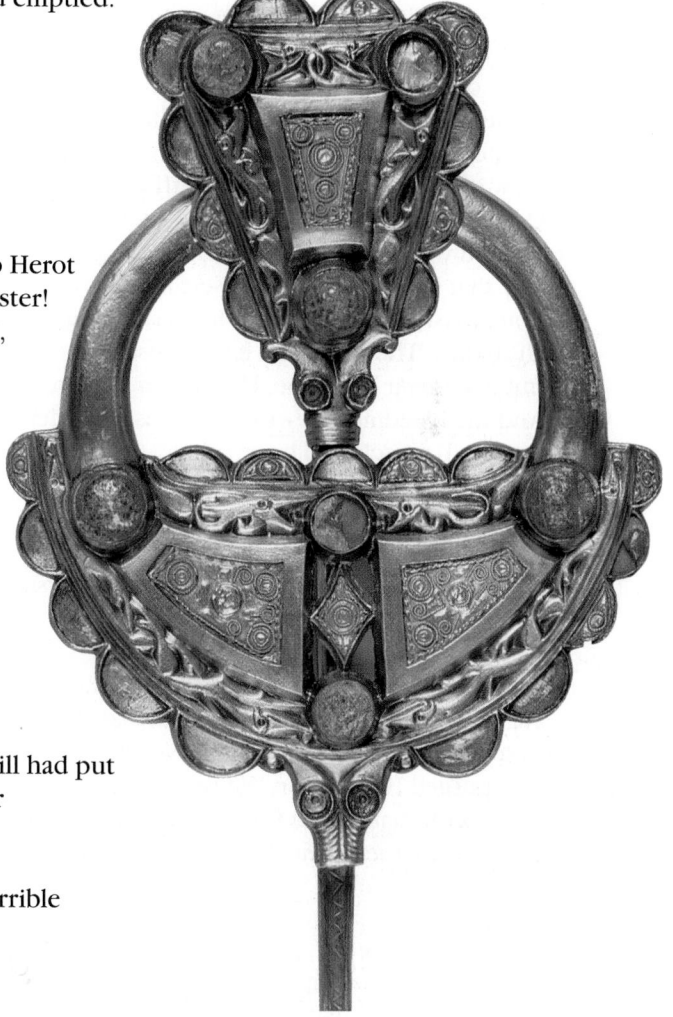

470 Taut throat, hell's captive caught in the arms
Of him who of all the men on earth
Was the strongest.

9

That mighty protector of men
Meant to hold the monster till its life
Leaped out, knowing the fiend was no use
475 To anyone in Denmark. All of Beowulf's
Band had jumped from their beds, ancestral
Swords raised and ready, determined
To protect their prince if they could. Their courage
Was great but all wasted: They could hack at Grendel
480 From every side, trying to open
A path for his evil soul, but their points
Could not hurt him, the sharpest and hardest iron
Could not scratch at his skin, for that sin-stained demon
Had bewitched all men's weapons, laid spells
485 That blunted every mortal man's blade.
And yet his time had come, his days
Were over, his death near; down
To hell he would go, swept groaning and helpless
To the waiting hands of still worse fiends.
490 Now he discovered—once the afflictor
Of men, tormentor of their days—what it meant
To feud with Almighty God: Grendel
Saw that his strength was deserting him, his claws
Bound fast, Higlac's brave follower tearing at
495 His hands. The monster's hatred rose higher,
But his power had gone. He twisted in pain,
And the bleeding sinews deep in his shoulder
Snapped, muscle and bone split
And broke. The battle was over, Beowulf
500 Had been granted new glory: Grendel escaped,
But wounded as he was could flee to his den,
His miserable hole at the bottom of the marsh,
Only to die, to wait for the end
Of all his days. And after that bloody
505 Combat the Danes laughed with delight.
He who had come to them from across the sea,
Bold and strong-minded, had driven affliction
Off, purged Herot clean. He was happy,
Now, with that night's fierce work; the Danes
510 Had been served as he'd boasted he'd serve them; Beowulf,

Eagle shield ornament (7th century).
Sutton Hoo ship treasure.
British Museum, London.

WORDS TO OWN
taut (tôt) *adj.:* stretched tight.
sinews (sin′yōōz) *n. pl.:* tendons or connective tissues.

A prince of the Geats, had killed Grendel,
Ended the grief, the sorrow, the suffering
Forced on Hrothgar's helpless people
By a bloodthirsty fiend. No Dane doubted
515 The victory, for the proof, hanging high
From the rafters where Beowulf had hung it, was the monster's
Arm, claw and shoulder and all.

10

And then, in the morning, crowds surrounded
Herot, warriors coming to that hall
520 From faraway lands, princes and leaders
Of men hurrying to behold the monster's
Great staggering tracks. They gaped with no sense
Of sorrow, felt no regret for his suffering,
Went tracing his bloody footprints, his beaten
525 And lonely flight, to the edge of the lake
Where he'd dragged his corpselike way, doomed
And already weary of his vanishing life.
The water was bloody, steaming and boiling
In horrible pounding waves, heat
530 Sucked from his magic veins; but the swirling
Surf had covered his death, hidden
Deep in <u>murky</u> darkness his miserable
End, as hell opened to receive him.
Then old and young rejoiced, turned back
535 From that happy <u>pilgrimage</u>, mounted their hard-hooved
Horses, high-spirited stallions, and rode them
Slowly toward Herot again, retelling
Beowulf's bravery as they jogged along.
And over and over they swore that nowhere
540 On earth or under the spreading sky
Or between the seas, neither south nor north,
Was there a warrior worthier to rule over men.
(But no one meant Beowulf's praise to belittle
Hrothgar, their kind and gracious king!) . . .

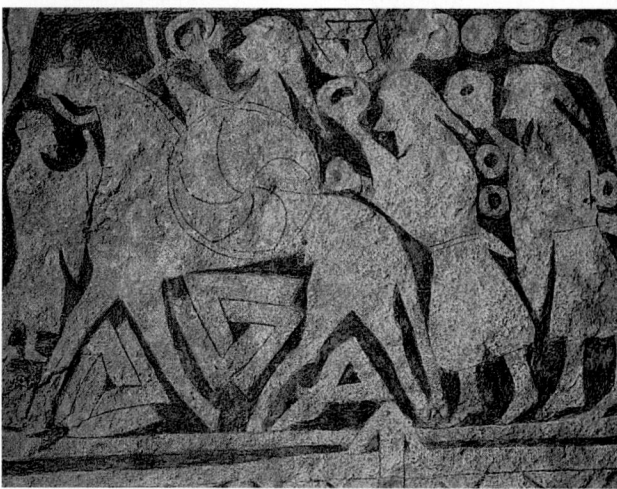

Detail of picture stone from Larbro, Gotland, Sweden.

Grendel's monstrous mother, in grief for her son, next
attacks Herot, and in her dripping claws she carries off one
man—Hrothgar's closest friend. The monster also carries off
Grendel's arm, which Beowulf had hung high from the
rafters. Beowulf is awakened and called for again. In one of

Words to Own
murky (mʉrk′ē) *adj.:* shadowy.
pilgrimage (pil′grim·ij) *n.:* journey made to a place of religious or historical interest.

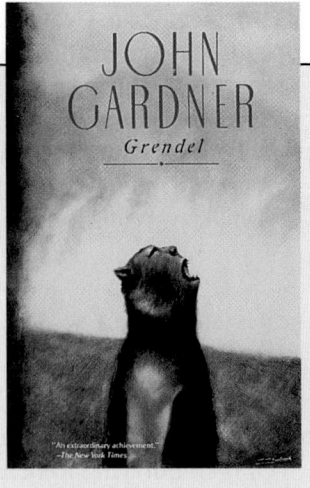

In his novel *Grendel* (1971), the contemporary American writer John Gardner (1933–1982) retells part of *Beowulf* from the point of view of the monster. In this excerpt, Grendel tells his own version of one of his raids on Hrothgar's hall.

from Grendel

John Gardner

I sigh, sink into the silence, and cross it like wind. Behind my back, at the world's end, my pale slightly glowing fat mother sleeps on, old, sick at heart, in our dingy underground room. Life-bloated, baffled, long-suffering hag. Guilty, she imagines, of some unremembered, perhaps ancestral crime. (She must have some human in her.) Not that she thinks. Not that she dissects and ponders the dusty mechanical bits of her miserable life's curse. She clutches at me in her sleep as if to crush me. I break away. "Why are we here?" I used to ask her. "Why do we stand this putrid, stinking hole?" She trembles at my words. Her fat lips shake. "Don't ask!" her wiggling claws implore. (She never speaks.) "Don't ask!" It must be some terrible secret, I used to think. I'd give her a crafty squint. She'll tell me, in time, I thought. But she told me nothing. I waited on. That was before the old dragon, calm as winter, unveiled the truth. He was not a friend.

And so I come through trees and towns to the lights of Hrothgar's meadhall. I am no stranger here. A respected guest. Eleven years now and going on twelve I have come up this clean-mown central hill, dark shadow out of the woods below, and have knocked politely on the high oak door, bursting its hinges and sending the shock of my greeting inward like a cold blast out of a cave. "Grendel!" they

the most famous verses in the epic, the old king describes where Grendel and his mother live.

11

545   . . . "They live in secret places, windy
       Cliffs, wolf-dens where water pours
       From the rocks, then runs underground, where mist
       Steams like black clouds, and the groves of trees
       Growing out over their lake are all covered
550   With frozen spray, and wind down snakelike
       Roots that reach as far as the water
       And help keep it dark. At night that lake
       Burns like a torch. No one knows its bottom,
       No wisdom reaches such depths. A deer,

squeak, and I smile like exploding spring. The old Shaper, a man I cannot help but admire, goes out the back window with his harp at a single bound, though blind as a bat. The drunkest of Hrothgar's thanes come reeling and clanking down from their wall-hung beds, all shouting their meady, outrageous boasts, their heavy swords aswirl like eagles' wings. "Woe, woe, woe!" cries Hrothgar, hoary with winters, peeking in, wide-eyed, from his bedroom in back. His wife, looking in behind him, makes a scene. The thanes in the meadhall blow out the lights and cover the wide stone fireplace with shields. I laugh, crumple over; I can't help myself. In the darkness, I alone see clear as day. While they squeal and screech and bump into each other, I silently sack up my dead and withdraw to the woods. I eat and laugh and eat until I can barely walk, my chest-hair matted with dribbled blood, and then the roosters on the hill crow, and dawn comes over the roofs of the houses, and all at once I am filled with gloom again.

"This is some punishment sent us," I hear them bawling from the hill.

My head aches. Morning nails my eyes.

"Some god is angry," I hear a woman keen.

"The people of Scyld and Herogar and Hrothgar are mired in sin!"

My belly rumbles, sick on their sour meat. I crawl through bloodstained leaves to the eaves of the forest, and there peak out. The dogs fall silent at the edge of my spell, and where the king's hall surmounts the town, the blind old Shaper, harp clutched tight to his fragile chest, stares futilely down, straight at me. Otherwise nothing. Pigs root dully at the posts of a wooden fence. A rumple-horned ox lies chewing in dew and shade. A few men, lean, wearing animal skins, look up at the gables of the king's hall, or at the vultures circling casually beyond. Hrothgar says nothing, hoarfrost-bearded, his features cracked and crazed. Inside, I hear the people praying—whimpering, whining, mumbling, pleading—to their numerous sticks and stones. He doesn't go in. The king has lofty theories of his own.

"Theories," I whisper to the bloodstained ground. So the dragon once spoke. ("They'd map out roads through Hell with their crackpot theories!" I recall his laugh.)

Then the groaning and praying stop, and on the side of the hill the dirge-slow shoveling begins. . . .

555 Hunted through the woods by packs of hounds,
A stag with great horns, though driven through the forest
From faraway places, prefers to die
On those shores, refuses to save its life
In that water. It isn't far, nor is it

560 A pleasant spot! When the wind stirs
And storms, waves splash toward the sky,
As dark as the air, as black as the rain
That the heavens weep. Our only help,
Again, lies with you. Grendel's mother

565 Is hidden in her terrible home, in a place
You've not seen. Seek it, if you dare! Save us,
Once more, and again twisted gold,
Heaped-up ancient treasure, will reward you
For the battle you win!"

Gundestrup cauldron.
National Museum, Copenhagen.

MAKING MEANINGS

First Thoughts

1. What **images** came to your mind as you read this part of the epic? Which image was most vivid?

Shaping Interpretations

2. In what specific ways does Herot **contrast** with the place where Grendel lives?

3. In lines 3–13, the poet describes the bard's songs in Hrothgar's hall. How does the content of the songs **contrast** with Grendel and his world?

Reading Check

a. Why does Herot remain empty for twelve years?

b. Why doesn't Grendel touch King Hrothgar's throne?

c. What do Hrothgar and his council do to try to save his guest-hall?

d. How is Beowulf taunted by the jealous Unferth? How does Beowulf reply?

e. Describe what happens to Grendel when he raids Herot and finds Beowulf in charge.

4. What significance can you see in the fact that Grendel attacks at night? What **images** describing Grendel might associate him with death or darkness?

5. Why do you think Grendel hates Herot? What **symbolic** meaning might underlie the confrontation between Grendel and Hrothgar?

6. Consider the tale-within-a-tale about Beowulf's swimming match with Brecca. What does this story contribute to your understanding of Beowulf's heroic **character** and of his powers?

7. Why do you think it's important to Beowulf and to his image as an **epic hero** that he meet Grendel without a weapon? What **symbolism** do you see in the uselessness of human weapons against Grendel?

8. What do you think of John Gardner's depiction of Grendel in the *Connections* on page 36? Do you feel any sympathy for Grendel? Why or why not?

Connecting with the Text

9. Review the notes you made before you read this part of *Beowulf*. Does Beowulf remind you of any heroes from history, current events, books, television, or movies? Who? What similarities do you notice among them? Just as important, how are they different?

Sigurd kills the dragon. Detail of carved portal of Hylestad stave church (12th century).

Universitetets, Oldsaksamling, Oslo.

A Collaboration Across 1,200 Years

D.J.R. BRUCKNER

European noblemen of a thousand years ago had much more exciting and intelligent entertainment than anything to be found now. Anyone who doubts that need only look in on Benjamin Bagby's astonishing performance of the first quarter of the epic poem *Beowulf*—in Anglo-Saxon, no less—tonight at the Stanley H. Kaplan Penthouse at Lincoln Center. . . .

From the moment he strode onstage on Sunday for the opening night, silencing the audience with that famous first word, "Hwaet!" ("Pay attention!"), until hell swallowed the "pagan soul" of the monster Grendel eighty minutes later, Mr. Bagby came as close to holding hundreds of people in a spell as ever a man has. As the epic's warriors argued, boasted, fought, or fell into the monster's maw, there were bursts of laughter, mutters, and sighs, and when Mr. Bagby's voice stopped at the end, as abruptly as it had

Benjamin Bagby reciting the story of Beowulf in Anglo-Saxon.

begun, there was an audible rippling gasp before a thunderclap of applause from cheering people who called him back again and again, unwilling to let him go.

Mr. Bagby—a Midwesterner who fell in love with *Beowulf* at twelve . . .—accompanies himself on a six-string lyre modeled on one found in a seventh-century tomb near Stuttgart. This surprisingly facile instrument underscores the meter of the epic verses and is counterpoint to Mr. Bagby's

voice as he recites, chants, and occasionally sings the lines.

. . . A translation is handed out to the audience, but after a while one notices people are following it less and just letting the sound of this strange and beautiful language wash over them. Perhaps not so strange, after all—enough phrases begin to penetrate the understanding that one finally knows deep down that, yes, this is where English came from.

—*The New York Times*, July 22, 1997

Carrying the sword Hrunting, Beowulf goes to the lake where Grendel's mother has her underwater lair. Then, fully armed, he dives to the depths of this watery hell.

The Monster's Mother

12

570 . . . He leaped into the lake, would not wait for anyone's
Answer; the heaving water covered him
Over. For hours he sank through the waves;
At last he saw the mud of the bottom.
And all at once the greedy she-wolf
575 Who'd ruled those waters for half a hundred
Years discovered him, saw that a creature

From above had come to explore the bottom
Of her wet world. She welcomed him in her claws,
Clutched at him savagely but could not harm him,
580 Tried to work her fingers through the tight
Ring-woven mail on his breast, but tore
And scratched in vain. Then she carried him, armor
And sword and all, to her home; he struggled
To free his weapon, and failed. The fight
585 Brought other monsters swimming to see
Her catch, a host of sea beasts who beat at
His mail shirt, stabbing with tusks and teeth
As they followed along. Then he realized, suddenly,
That she'd brought him into someone's battle-hall,
590 And there the water's heat could not hurt him,
Nor anything in the lake attack him through
The building's high-arching roof. A brilliant
Light burned all around him, the lake
Itself like a fiery flame.

                   Then he saw
595 The mighty water witch, and swung his sword,
His ring-marked blade, straight at her head;
The iron sang its fierce song,
Sang Beowulf's strength. But her guest
Discovered that no sword could slice her evil
600 Skin, that Hrunting could not hurt her, was useless
Now when he needed it. They wrestled, she ripped
And tore and clawed at him, bit holes in his helmet,
And that too failed him; for the first time in years
Of being worn to war it would earn no glory;
605 It was the last time anyone would wear it. But Beowulf
Longed only for fame, leaped back
Into battle. He tossed his sword aside,
Angry; the steel-edged blade lay where
He'd dropped it. If weapons were useless he'd use
610 His hands, the strength in his fingers. So fame
Comes to the men who mean to win it
And care about nothing else! He raised
His arms and seized her by the shoulder; anger
Doubled his strength, he threw her to the floor.
615 She fell, Grendel's fierce mother, and the Geats'
Proud prince was ready to leap on her. But she rose
At once and repaid him with her clutching claws,
Wildly tearing at him. He was weary, that best
And strongest of soldiers; his feet stumbled
620 And in an instant she had him down, held helpless.
Squatting with her weight on his stomach, she drew
A dagger, brown with dried blood and prepared
To avenge her only son. But he was stretched
On his back, and her stabbing blade was blunted

Battersea shield.
© British Museum, London.

625 By the woven mail shirt he wore on his chest.
The hammered links held; the point
Could not touch him. He'd have traveled to the bottom of the earth,
Edgetho's son, and died there, if that shining
Woven metal had not helped—and Holy
630 God, who sent him victory, gave judgment
For truth and right, Ruler of the Heavens,
Once Beowulf was back on his feet and fighting.

13

Then he saw, hanging on the wall, a heavy
Sword, hammered by giants, strong
635 And blessed with their magic, the best of all weapons
But so massive that no ordinary man could lift
Its carved and decorated length. He drew it
From its scabbard, broke the chain on its hilt,°
And then, savage, now, angry
640 And desperate, lifted it high over his head
And struck with all the strength he had left,
Caught her in the neck and cut it through,
Broke bones and all. Her body fell
To the floor, lifeless, the sword was wet
645 With her blood, and Beowulf rejoiced at the sight.
The brilliant light shone, suddenly,
As though burning in that hall, and as bright as Heaven's
Own candle, lit in the sky. He looked
At her home, then following along the wall
650 Went walking, his hands tight on the sword,
His heart still angry. He was hunting another
Dead monster, and took his weapon with him
For final revenge against Grendel's vicious
Attacks, his nighttime raids, over
655 And over, coming to Herot when Hrothgar's
Men slept, killing them in their beds,
Eating some on the spot, fifteen
Or more, and running to his loathsome moor
With another such sickening meal waiting
660 In his pouch. But Beowulf repaid him for those visits,
Found him lying dead in his corner,
Armless, exactly as that fierce fighter
Had sent him out from Herot, then struck off
His head with a single swift blow. The body
665 Jerked for the last time, then lay still. . . .

638. scabbard . . . hilt: A scabbard is a case that holds the blade of a sword; a hilt is a sword's handle.

Words to Own
loathsome (lōth′səm) *adj.*: disgusting.

*Beowulf carries Grendel's head to King Hrothgar and then
returns gift-laden to the land of the Geats, where he succeeds
to the throne. After fifty winters pass, Beowulf, now an old
man, faces his final task: He must fight a dragon who, angry
because a thief has stolen a jeweled cup from the dragon's
hoard of gold, is laying waste to the Geats' land. Beowulf
and eleven warriors are guided to the dragon's lair by the
thief who stole the cup. For Beowulf, the price of this last
victory will be great.*

The Final Battle

14

  . . . Then he said farewell to his followers,
Each in his turn, for the last time:
  "I'd use no sword, no weapon, if this beast
Could be killed without it, crushed to death
670 Like Grendel, gripped in my hands and torn
Limb from limb. But his breath will be burning
Hot, poison will pour from his tongue.
I feel no shame, with shield and sword
And armor, against this monster: When he comes to me
675 I mean to stand, not run from his shooting
Flames, stand till fate decides
Which of us wins. My heart is firm,
My hands calm: I need no hot
Words. Wait for me close by, my friends.
680 We shall see, soon, who will survive
This bloody battle, stand when the fighting
Is done. No one else could do
What I mean to, here, no man but me
Could hope to defeat this monster. No one
685 Could try. And this dragon's treasure, his gold
And everything hidden in that tower, will be mine
Or war will sweep me to a bitter death!"
  Then Beowulf rose, still brave, still strong,
And with his shield at his side, and a mail shirt on his breast,
690 Strode calmly, confidently, toward the tower, under
The rocky cliffs: No coward could have walked there!
And then he who'd endured dozens of desperate
Battles, who'd stood boldly while swords and shields
Clashed, the best of kings, saw
695 Huge stone arches and felt the heat
Of the dragon's breath, flooding down
Through the hidden entrance, too hot for anyone
To stand, a streaming current of fire
And smoke that blocked all passage. And the Geats'
700 Lord and leader, angry, lowered
His sword and roared out a battle cry,

Dragonesque brooch
(2nd century).
Romano-British.

© British Museum, London.

A call so loud and clear that it reached through
The hoary° rock, hung in the dragon's
Ear. The beast rose, angry,

703. **hoary** (hôr′ē): ancient.

705 Knowing a man had come—and then nothing
But war could have followed. Its breath came first,
A steaming cloud pouring from the stone,
Then the earth itself shook. Beowulf
Swung his shield into place, held it

710 In front of him, facing the entrance. The dragon
Coiled and uncoiled, its heart urging it
Into battle. Beowulf's ancient sword
Was waiting, unsheathed, his sharp and gleaming
Blade. The beast came closer; both of them

715 Were ready, each set on slaughter. The Geats'
Great prince stood firm, unmoving, prepared
Behind his high shield, waiting in his shining
Armor. The monster came quickly toward him,
Pouring out fire and smoke, hurrying

720 To its fate. Flames beat at the iron
Shield, and for a time it held, protected
Beowulf as he'd planned; then it began to melt,
And for the first time in his life that famous prince
Fought with fate against him, with glory

725 Denied him. He knew it, but he raised his sword
And struck at the dragon's scaly hide.
The ancient blade broke, bit into
The monster's skin, drew blood, but cracked
And failed him before it went deep enough, helped him

730 Less than he needed. The dragon leaped
With pain, thrashed and beat at him, spouting
Murderous flames, spreading them everywhere.
And the Geats' ring-giver did not boast of glorious
Victories in other wars: His weapon

735 Had failed him, deserted him, now when he needed it
Most, that excellent sword. Edgetho's
Famous son stared at death,
Unwilling to leave this world, to exchange it
For a dwelling in some distant place—a journey

740 Into darkness that all men must make, as death
Ends their few brief hours on earth.
    Quickly, the dragon came at him, encouraged
As Beowulf fell back; its breath flared,
And he suffered, wrapped around in swirling

745 Flames—a king, before, but now
A beaten warrior. None of his comrades
Came to him, helped him, his brave and noble
Followers; they ran for their lives, fled
Deep in a wood. And only one of them

750 Remained, stood there, miserable, remembering,
As a good man must, what kinship should mean.

Viking sword handles, embellished
with Viking Age motifs.
Statens Historiska Museer, Stockholm.

Detail of three-ringed gold collar
(6th century).

Statens Historiska Museer, Stockholm.

15

His name was Wiglaf, he was Wexstan's son
And a good soldier; his family had been Swedish,
Once. Watching Beowulf, he could see
755 How his king was suffering, burning. Remembering
Everything his lord and cousin had given him,
Armor and gold and the great estates
Wexstan's family enjoyed, Wiglaf's
Mind was made up; he raised his yellow
760 Shield and drew his sword. . . .
      And Wiglaf, his heart heavy, uttered
The kind of words his comrades deserved:
      "I remember how we sat in the mead-hall, drinking
And boasting of how brave we'd be when Beowulf
765 Needed us, he who gave us these swords
And armor: All of us swore to repay him,
When the time came, kindness for kindness
—With our lives, if he needed them. He allowed us to join him,
Chose us from all his great army, thinking
770 Our boasting words had some weight, believing
Our promises, trusting our swords. He took us
For soldiers, for men. He meant to kill
This monster himself, our mighty king,
Fight this battle alone and unaided,
775 As in the days when his strength and daring dazzled
Men's eyes. But those days are over and gone
And now our lord must lean on younger
Arms. And we must go to him, while angry
Flames burn at his flesh, help
780 Our glorious king! By almighty God,
I'd rather burn myself than see
Flames swirling around my lord.
And who are we to carry home
Our shields before we've slain his enemy
785 And ours, to run back to our homes with Beowulf
So hard-pressed here? I swear that nothing
He ever did deserved an end
Like this, dying miserably and alone,
Butchered by this savage beast: We swore
790 That these swords and armor were each for us all!" . . .

Together, Beowulf and the young Wiglaf kill the dragon, but the old king is fatally wounded. Beowulf, thinking of his people, asks to see the monster's treasure. Wiglaf enters the dragon's cave and finds a priceless hoard of jewels and gold.

16

    . . . Then Wiglaf went back, anxious
To return while Beowulf was alive, to bring him
Treasure they'd won together. He ran,
Hoping his wounded king, weak
795 And dying, had not left the world too soon.
Then he brought their treasure to Beowulf, and found
His famous king bloody, gasping
For breath. But Wiglaf sprinkled water
Over his lord, until the words
800 Deep in his breast broke through and were heard.
Beholding the treasure he spoke, haltingly:
    "For this, this gold, these jewels, I thank
Our Father in Heaven, Ruler of the Earth—
For all of this, that His grace has given me,
805 Allowed me to bring to my people while breath
Still came to my lips. I sold my life
For this treasure, and I sold it well. Take
What I leave, Wiglaf, lead my people,
Help them; my time is gone. Have
810 The brave Geats build me a tomb,
When the funeral flames have burned me, and build it
Here, at the water's edge, high
On this spit of land, so sailors can see
This tower, and remember my name, and call it
815 Beowulf's tower, and boats in the darkness
And mist, crossing the sea, will know it."
    Then that brave king gave the golden
Necklace from around his throat to Wiglaf,
Gave him his gold-covered helmet, and his rings,
820 And his mail shirt, and ordered him to use them well:
    "You're the last of all our far-flung family.
Fate has swept our race away,
Taken warriors in their strength and led them
To the death that was waiting. And now I follow them."
825   The old man's mouth was silent, spoke
No more, had said as much as it could;
He would sleep in the fire, soon. His soul
Left his flesh, flew to glory.

Gilded bronze and ivory casket.
National Museum, Copenhagen.

*Wiglaf berates the faithless warriors who did not go to the
aid of their king. With sorrow, the Geats then cremate the
corpse of their greatest king. They place his ashes, along with
all of the dragon's treasure, in a huge burial tower by the
sea, where it can be seen by voyagers.*

17

. . . And then twelve of the bravest Geats
830 Rode their horses around the tower,
Telling their sorrow, telling stories
Of their dead king and his greatness, his glory,
Praising him for heroic deeds, for a life
As noble as his name. So should all men
835 Raise up words for their lords, warm
With love, when their shield and protector leaves
His body behind, sends his soul
On high. And so Beowulf's followers
Rode, mourning their beloved leader,
840 Crying that no better king had ever
Lived, no prince so mild, no man
So open to his people, so deserving of praise.

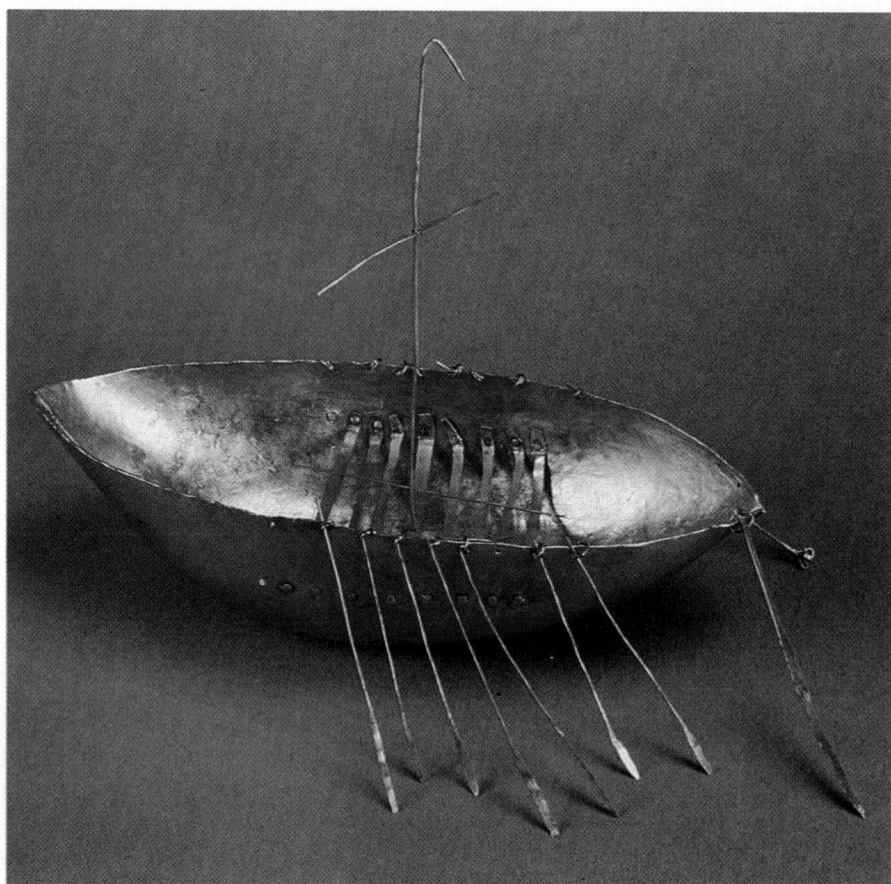

Gold boat (probably
1st century) found at
Broighter, County
Londonderry, Ireland.

National Museum of Ireland, Dublin.

Life in 999: A Grim Struggle

HOWARD G. CHUA-EOAN

Today's world is measured in light-years and Mach speed and sheathed in silicon and alloy. In the world of 999, on the eve of the first millennium, time moved at the speed of an oxcart or, more often, of a sturdy pair of legs, and the West was built largely on wood. Europe was a collection of untamed forests, countless mile upon mile of trees and brush and brier, dark and inhospitable. Medieval chroniclers used the word *desert* to describe their arboreal world, a place on the cusp of civilization where werewolves and bogeymen still lunged out of the shadows and bandits and marauders maintained their lairs.

Yet the forests, deep and dangerous as they were, also defined existence. Wood kindled forges and kept alive the hearths of the mud-and-thatch huts of the serfs. Peasants fattened their hogs on forest acorns (pork was crucial to basic subsistence in the cold of winter), and wild berries helped supplement the meager diet. In a world without sugar, honey from forest swarms provided the only sweetness for food or drink. The pleasures of the serfs were few and simple: earthy lovemaking and occasional dances and fests.

Feudal lords ruled over western Europe, taking their share of the harvests of primitive agriculture and making the forests their private hunting grounds. Poaching was not simply theft (usually punishable by imprisonment) but a sin against the social order. Without the indulgence of the nobility, the peasants could not even acquire salt, the indispensable ingredient for preserving meat and flavoring a culinary culture that possessed few spices. Though a true money economy did not exist, salt could be bought with poorly circulated coin, which the lord hoarded in his castle and dispensed to the poor only as alms.

It was in the lord's castle too that peasants and their flocks sought refuge from wolf packs and barbarian invaders. In 999, however, castles, like most other buildings in Europe, were made of timber, far from the granite bastions that litter today's imagined Middle Ages. The peasants, meanwhile, were relegated to their simple huts, where everyone—including the animals—slept around the hearth. Straw was scattered on the floors to collect scraps as well as human and animal waste. Housecleaning consisted of sweeping out the straw.

Illness and disease remained in constant residence. Tuberculosis was endemic, and so were scabrous skin diseases of every kind: abscesses, cankers, scrofula, tumors, eczema, and erysipelas. In a throwback to biblical times, lepers constituted a class of pariahs living on the outskirts of villages and cities. Constant famine, rotten flour, and vitamin deficiencies afflicted huge segments of society with blindness, goiter, paralysis, and bone malformations that created hunchbacks and cripples. A man was lucky to survive 30, and 50 was a ripe old age. Most women, many of them succumbing to the ravages of childbirth, lived less than 30 years. There was no time for what is now considered childhood; children of every class had to grow up immediately and be useful as soon as possible. Emperors were leading armies in their teens; John XI became Pope at the age of 21.

While the general population was growing faster than it had in the previous five centuries, there was still a shortage of people to cultivate the fields, clear the woodlands, and work the mills. Local taxes were levied on youths who did not marry upon coming of age. Abortion was considered homicide, and a woman who terminated a pregnancy was expelled from the church.

The nobility spent its waking hours battling foes to preserve its prerogatives, the clergy chanting prayers for the salvation of souls, the serfs laboring to feed and clothe everyone. Night, lit only by burning logs or the rare taper, was always filled with danger and terror. The seasons came and went, punctuated chiefly by the occurrence of plentiful church holidays. The calendar year began at different times for different regions; only later would Europe settle on the Feast of Christ's Circumcision, January 1, as the year's beginning.

Thus there was little panic, not even much interest, as the millennium approached in the final months of 999. For what terrors could the apocalypse hold for a continent that was already shrouded in darkness? Rather Europe—illiterate, diseased, and hungry—seemed grimly resigned to desperation and impoverishment. It was one of the planet's most unpromising corners, the Third World of its age.

— *from Time*

Beowulf Shrinklet

Hrothgar and Grendel could not get along;
the populace thought the killing was wrong.
  Beowulf, the hero from o'er the sea,
from monster or dragon he would not flee.
  "If treasure I wanteth," the hero thought,
"then I will journey to the great Herot."
  Grendel died at the end of the battle.
His mother enraged (and all but little)
  wanted revenge for her beloved son,
but the great bold hero ended her fun.
  For proof he carried the head and the
sword,
  and traveled back with troops for a reward.
  The great Beowulf returned to his home,
over the oceans on seaweed and foam.
  His conscience lived happily as the king.
He died at the hands of another thing.

—Calen Wood
Bakersfield High School
Bakersfield, California

MAKING MEANINGS

First Thoughts

1. Beowulf's story is an ancient one, more than one thousand years old. Did its age make it entirely alien to you, or did you find that it deals with issues or themes that seem relevant in our modern society as well? If so, what are they?

Reading Check

a. Describe how Beowulf manages to kill Grendel's mother.

b. Who comes to Beowulf's aid in his final battle with the dragon? Why does he help Beowulf?

c. What sad scene concludes the epic?

d. What happens to the dragon's hoard?

Shaping Interpretations

2. A hoarded treasure in Old English literature usually **symbolizes** spiritual death or damnation. How does this fact add significance to Beowulf's last fight with the dragon?

3. What details describe the dragon? Keeping those details in mind, explain what the dragon might **symbolize** as Beowulf's final foe.

4. Beowulf battles Grendel, Grendel's mother, and the dragon. What do these battles have in common, and what do they suggest Beowulf and his enemies might represent for the Anglo-Saxons?

5. Given what you know about the structure of Anglo-Saxon society, explain what is especially ominous about the behavior of Beowulf's men during the final battle. What does this suggest about the future of the kingdom?

6. The epic closes on a somber, elegiac note—a note of mourning. What words or **images** contribute to this **tone**?

7. Epic poetry usually embodies the attitudes and ideals of an entire culture. What values of Anglo-Saxon society does *Beowulf* reveal? What universal **themes** does it also reveal?

Extending the Text

8. How would we tell a hero story today? What would the **setting** be, what would the **enemy** be, and what **values** would the hero embody?

9. The *Connections* on page 47, "Life in 999: A Grim Struggle," describes daily life in late Anglo-Saxon England. How does this picture of daily life relate to what you've read in *Beowulf*—and to how you live today?

10. In the last episode of the epic, the leader's followers mourn his passing and praise his life. What qualities do we look for in leaders today—are they the same qualities Beowulf's people loved him for?

Challenging the Text

11. What do you think of the way women are portrayed in (or absent from) *Beowulf*?

Alliteration and Kennings: Taking the Burden off the Bard

The *Connections* on page 39 shows that the oral tradition is still alive and still a powerful way of communicating from poet to audience.

The Anglo-Saxon oral poet was assisted by two poetic devices, alliteration and the kenning.

Alliteration. Alliteration is the repetition of sounds in words close to one another. Anglo-Saxon poetry is often called alliterative poetry. Instead of rhyme unifying the poem, the verse line is divided into two halves separated by a rhythmical pause, or **caesura.** In the first half of the line before the caesura, two words alliterate; in the second half, one word alliterates with the two from the first half. Many lines, however, have only two alliterative words, one in each half of the poetic line. Notice the alliterative *g* and the four primary stresses in this Old English line from *Beowulf*:

God mid Geatum Grendles daeda

Kennings. The kenning, a specialized metaphor made of compound words, is a staple of Anglo-Saxon literature that still finds a place in our language today. *Gas guzzler* and *headhunter* are two modern-day kennings you are likely to have heard.

The earliest and simplest kennings are compound words formed of two common nouns: "sky-candle" for *sun*, "battle-dew" for *blood*, and "whale-road" for *sea*. Later, kennings grew more elaborate, and compound adjectives joined the compound nouns. A ship became a "foamy-throated ship," then a "foamy-throated sea-stallion," and finally a "foamy-throated stallion of the whale-road." Once a kenning was coined, it was used by the singer-poets over and over again.

In their original languages, kennings are almost always written as simple compounds, with no hyphens or spaces between the words. In translation, however, kennings are often written as hyphenated compounds ("sky-candle," "foamy-throated"), as prepositional phrases ("wolf of wounds"), or as possessives ("the sword's tree").

The work of kennings. Scholars believe that kennings filled three needs: (1) Old Norse and Anglo-Saxon poetry depended heavily on alliteration, but neither language had a large vocabulary. Poets created the alliterative words they needed by combining existing words. (2) Because the poetry was oral and had to be memorized, bards valued ready-made phrases. Such phrases made finished poetry easier to remember, and they gave bards time to think ahead when they were composing new poetry on the spot during a feast or ceremony. (3) The increasingly complex structure of the kennings must have satisfied the early Norse and Anglo-Saxon people's taste for elaboration.

Analyzing the text. As you examine these poetic devices, be sure to listen to the way they sound.

1. Read aloud the account of Beowulf's death (lines 791–828), and listen for the effects of the alliteration. Where are **vowels,** rather than consonants, repeated?

2. Look back over lines 233–391 from *Beowulf.* Locate at least two examples of kennings written as **hyphenated compounds,** two examples of kennings written as **prepositional phrases,** and two examples of kennings written as **possessives.** What does each kenning refer to?

3. Compile a list of modern-day kennings, such as *headhunter.*

4. Translators differ dramatically in how they rephrase the Old English to handle alliteration and the kennings. Here is a passage from a translation done many years before the Raffel translation. How does it compare with the corresponding lines (392–398) in Raffel's translation? Which translation sounds more modern? Which do you prefer to listen to?

> Now Grendel came, from his crags of mist
> Across the moor; he was curst of God.
> The murderous prowler meant to surprise
> In the high-built hall his human prey.
> He stalked neath the clouds, till steep before him
> The house of revelry rose in his path,
> The gold-hall of heroes, the gaily adorned.
> —*translated by* J. Duncan Spaeth

CHOICES: Building Your Portfolio

Writer's Notebook

1. Collecting Ideas for a Literary Analysis

At the end of this collection, you'll write a literary analysis. When you analyze a literary work, you usually focus on some element in the selection that interests you. You then analyze, or "take apart," the element to see how it works in the text. To start collecting ideas for an analysis, focus now on the **character** of Grendel, the monster. Look back over the passages in *Beowulf* that describe Grendel, and gather evidence on how he is described. Consider these questions: How does the storyteller, in the words he uses to describe the creature, also shape our feelings toward him? What accounts for Grendel's evil? What does Grendel seem to represent in the story? Save your work for later use.

Autobiographical Incident

2. Facing Monsters

Write a brief narrative in which you tell about a time when you, like Beowulf, faced an intense physical challenge, or were taunted over something you said or did, or had to overcome fear to do something that had to be done. Remember that a narrative tells of a series of related events. Give your narrative a strong ending.

Creative Writing

3. It's All in the Point of View

Just as John Gardner tried imagining this story from Grendel's point of view (see *Connections* on page 36), you might try retelling an episode from the perspective of one of the other characters, perhaps Grendel, his mother, the dragon, Hrothgar, or Beowulf's detractor, Unferth.

Speaking and Listening

4. Being a Bard

Retell an episode of *Beowulf* for your classmates, or, if it can be arranged, for a grade-school audience. Be faithful to the plot of the story, but feel free to change or adapt the content to fit your audience and your own storytelling talents. (See, for example, the story of *Beowulf* told in shrinklet format on page 48.) Plan an introduction to your story, and try to find ways of involving your listeners. For drama, use gestures, sound effects, and pauses.

Comparing Film and Epic

5. Movies and *Beowulf*

Movies, the cornerstone of American entertainment, often rely on familiar images: Heroes face villains to do battle in all kinds of places—from the ordinary to the strange. In a brief essay, compare and contrast *Beowulf* with some action movie you know well. Use the following questions to guide your comparison:

- Where does each hero come from?
- Who are the hero's trusted aides?
- What role does violence play in the story?
- How does the hero struggle against evil?
- Is the hero an outsider or a part of the community?
- What rewards or glory does the hero receive?

Mark Hamill as Luke Skywalker in *Star Wars* (1977).

Reading Skills and Strategies

VOCABULARY: USING CONTEXT CLUES

Sometimes you can determine the meaning of an unfamiliar word by looking for clues in the **context,** the surrounding words, phrases, and sentences. In fact, you've probably learned many words by using context clues. Below are some of the most useful types of context clues:

Restatement. A difficult word might be rephrased in slightly easier language. Restatements may be signaled by specific words or phrases: *that is, or, in other words.* Look at punctuation—dashes and parentheses also serve as signals. Often a restatement will be an **appositive** set off by commas or an item in a series.

> . . . keeping the bloody feud
> Alive, seeking no peace, offering
> No **truce,** accepting no settlement.
> —*Beowulf,* lines 68–70

A *truce* is something that would end a feud; it's a kind of settlement or a cease-fire.

Comparison. Compare unfamiliar words to familiar words that surround it. Sometimes specific words and phrases may also signal a comparison context clue: *like, as, similar to.*

> . . . but the swirling
> Surf had covered his death, hidden
> Deep in **murky** darkness his miserable
> End.
> —*Beowulf,* lines 530–533

Note all the words that have to do with obscuring from view: *covered, hidden deep, darkness. Murky* means "dark or gloomy, shadowy."

Contrast. An opposition might be set up. Certain key words and phrases signal a contrast context clue: *but, not, although, however, on the other hand.*

> . . . he can come for your people with no fear
> Of **reprisal;** he's found no fighting, here,
> But only food, only delight.
> —*Beowulf,* lines 329–331

Reprisal has to do with resistance, rather than acceptance or encouragement. A *reprisal* is punishment in return for an injury.

Synonym. You might find a word nearby that has the same or nearly the same meaning as the unknown word.

> He murders as he likes, with no mercy, **gorges**
> And feasts on your flesh.
> —*Beowulf,* lines 333–334

Notice the words *feasts on. To gorge* is to glut or to swallow greedily.

Example. Sometimes the text provides an example. Certain words and phrases help you spot example context clues: *such as, including, especially, namely.*

> **Scops,** such as the skilled storytellers who passed down the story of Beowulf, were honored members of Anglo-Saxon society.

Note the key words: *storytellers* and *Anglo-Saxon.* A *scop* is an Old English poet or bard.

Try It Out

Choose any five of the Words to Own from *Beowulf.* For each word, construct a sentence that gives the meaning of the word from its context. Use a different type of context clue for each sentence. To get started, use a chart like the one below. Ask a classmate to find the context clues in your sentences.

Word to Own	Context Clue	Example

A picture stone showing a Viking ship under sail.
Statens Historiska Museer, Stockholm.

Mesopotamia

Before You Read

THE HEAD OF HUMBABA

Background

The men and women who lived four thousand years ago would be astounded by the world we live in, and we, very likely, would be astounded by theirs. Obviously, the world has changed in countless ways. Science and technology have transformed the physical world we inhabit, and social and political evolution have altered the way we live. Nations, empires, religions, and languages have come and gone. People now have different beliefs, different worries, different problems.

So you would expect a story four thousand years old to have little to do with you or anything around you today. Your life is so different from the lives of the storyteller and his characters that you might have nothing in common, no shared experience. *Gilgamesh,* for instance, is such an ancient story—a poem, as all stories were in those days. The story was recorded on clay tablets around 2000 B.C. in Sumer, a part of ancient Mesopotamia.

Gilgamesh is the king of Uruk, an ancient Sumerian city. His great friend is Enkidu. Craving an adventure that will bring fame, Gilgamesh convinces Enkidu to journey with him to the cedar forest. There they confront the forest's guardian, the evil giant Humbaba.

Reading Skills and Strategies

Responding to the Text
As you read this adventure from the epic *Gilgamesh,* take notes on a separate piece of paper. Record your responses to what you're reading. Write down any questions you have about the text. Note any details that remind you of *Beowulf,* or of other monster-slaying stories.

Gilgamesh. Relief (8th century B.C.) from Temple of Sargon II. Khorsabad, Iraq.

Louvre, Paris.

(Map) World map by Ptolemy (A.D. 100?–165?). Shaded area indicates general location of Mesopotamia.

The Head of Humbaba

from Gilgamesh: A Verse Narrative

retold by **Herbert Mason**

At dawn Gilgamesh raised his ax
And struck at the great cedar.
When Humbaba heard the sound of falling trees,
He hurried down the path that they had seen
5 But only he had traveled. Gilgamesh felt weak
At the sound of Humbaba's footsteps and called to Shamash°
Saying, I have followed you in the way decreed;
Why am I abandoned now? Suddenly the winds
Sprang up. They saw the great head of Humbaba
10 Like a water buffalo's bellowing down the path,
His huge and clumsy legs, his flailing° arms
Thrashing at phantoms in his precious trees.
His single stroke could cut a cedar down
And leave no mark on him. His shoulders,
15 Like a porter's° under building stones,
Were permanently bent by what he bore;
He was the slave who did the work for gods
But whom the gods would never notice.
Monstrous in his contortion, he aroused
20 The two almost to pity.
But pity was the thing that might have killed.
It made them pause just long enough to show
How pitiless he was to them. Gilgamesh in horror saw
Him strike the back of Enkidu and beat him to the ground
25 Until he thought his friend was crushed to death.
He stood still watching as the monster leaned to make
His final strike against his friend, unable
To move to help him, and then Enkidu slid
Along the ground like a ram making its final lunge
30 On wounded knees. Humbaba fell and seemed
To crack the ground itself in two, and Gilgamesh,
As if this fall had snapped him from his daze,
Returned to life

6. Shamash (shä′mäsh′): the sun god. The god has been guiding the hero.

11. flailing: swinging.

15. porter's° A porter is a person who carries things.

And stood over Humbaba with his ax
35 Raised high above his head watching the monster plead
In strangled sobs and desperate appeals
The way the sea contorts under a violent squall.°

37. **squall:** sudden, brief storm.

I'll serve you as I served the gods, Humbaba said;
I'll build you houses from their sacred trees.
40 Enkidu feared his friend was weakening
And called out: Gilgamesh! Don't trust him!
As if there were some hunger in himself
That Gilgamesh was feeling
That turned him momentarily to yearn
45 For someone who would serve, he paused;
And then he raised his ax up higher
And swung it in a perfect arc
Into Humbaba's neck. He reached out
To touch the wounded shoulder of his friend,

50 And late that night he reached again
To see if he was yet asleep, but there was only
Quiet breathing. The stars against the midnight sky
Were sparkling like mica° in a riverbed.

53. **mica** (mī′kə): colored, translucent mineral.

In the slight breeze
55 The head of Humbaba was swinging from a tree.

FINDING COMMON GROUND

Review the notes you took as you read this ancient story. Did you find common ground between yourself and Gilgamesh and his friend? What other responses to the story did you record? Did you have any questions about the story—any details that you did not understand?

Read the story a second time, still taking notes. When you finish the second reading, review your understanding of the story. Are your questions answered? Do you have any different responses?

Now meet with other readers and compare notes.

• Is the text clear?

• Does it remind you of any details in Beowulf's story?

• Have you ever experienced any of Gilgamesh's feelings?

• Does the story have anything to say to people today?

Stone statues of Mesopotamian god Aby and his wife, from Tell Asmar (2600 B.C.).

Iraq Museum, Baghdad.

Before You Read

THE SEAFARER

Make the Connection

Has the Time of Heroes Passed?

In the PBS television series *The Power of Myth,* the television journalist Bill Moyers and the mythologist Joseph Campbell talk about heroes. At one point, Campbell says that as a child he had two heroes but now he has none. Here's a bit of the conversation that follows Campbell's comment:

Moyers: *We seem to worship celebrities today, not heroes.*
Campbell: *Yes, and that's too bad. A questionnaire was once sent around to one of the high schools in Brooklyn which asked, "What would you like to be?" Two-thirds of the students responded, "A celebrity." They had no notion of having to give of themselves in order to achieve something.*

Only a thousand years earlier, the poet who wrote "The Seafarer" addressed the same question: Has the time of heroes passed?

Quickwrite

Do you think we "worship celebrities today, not heroes"? And if we do, what effect does that have on what we value and whom we present to children as role models? Freewrite for a few moments to focus your thoughts on this question.

Elements of Literature

The Elegy

The dominant mood in Anglo-Saxon poetry is elegiac. As we have seen in *Beowulf,* this sense of sadness over the grimness and transience of earthly life is found in the heroic epic. It is also found in several Old English fragments and poems in which a bard laments the passing of better days and greater glories.

> An **elegy** is a poem that mourns the death of a person or laments something lost.
>
> *For more on the Elegy, see page 606 and the Handbook of Literary Terms.*

Background

"The Seafarer" is from the so-called Exeter Book, a manuscript of miscellaneous Anglo-Saxon poems dating from around A.D. 940, copied in A.D. 975, and now preserved at Exeter Cathedral in England. Though the manuscript survived the raids and fires of the centuries, the Exeter Book had not been well cared for. There are signs that its cover had been used as a chopping board; its pages had been marked by beer stains; and some had been partly burned. But today its "songs"—copied down by monks—are our chief source of Anglo-Saxon poetry.

The Anglo-Saxons were sea voyagers, and the northern seas were then, as now, especially cruel. The speaker in "The Seafarer" is an old sailor who drifted through many winters on ice-cold seas.

The Seafarer

translated by **Burton Raffel**

This tale is true, and mine. It tells
How the sea took me, swept me back
And forth in sorrow and fear and pain,
Showed me suffering in a hundred ships,
5   In a thousand ports, and in me. It tells
Of smashing surf when I sweated in the cold
Of an anxious watch, perched in the bow
As it dashed under cliffs. My feet were cast
In icy bands, bound with frost,
10   With frozen chains, and hardship groaned
Around my heart. Hunger tore
At my sea-weary soul. No man sheltered
On the quiet fairness of earth can feel
How wretched I was, drifting through winter
15   On an ice-cold sea, whirled in sorrow,
Alone in a world blown clear of love,
Hung with icicles. The hailstorms flew.
The only sound was the roaring sea,
The freezing waves. The song of the swan
20   Might serve for pleasure, the cry of the sea-fowl,
The death-noise of birds instead of laughter,
The mewing of gulls instead of mead.
Storms beat on the rocky cliffs and were echoed
By icy-feathered terns° and the eagle's screams;
25   No kinsman could offer comfort there,
To a soul left drowning in desolation.
          And who could believe, knowing but
The passion of cities, swelled proud with wine
And no taste of misfortune, how often, how wearily,
30   I put myself back on the paths of the sea.
Night would blacken; it would snow from the north;
Frost bound the earth and hail would fall,
The coldest seeds. And how my heart
Would begin to beat, knowing once more
35   The salt waves tossing and the towering sea!
The time for journeys would come and my soul
Called me eagerly out, sent me over
The horizon, seeking foreigners' homes.
          But there isn't a man on earth so proud,
40   So born to greatness, so bold with his youth,
Grown so brave, or so graced by God,
That he feels no fear as the sails unfurl,
Wondering what Fate has willed and will do.
No harps ring in his heart, no rewards,

24. **terns:** seabirds related to gulls.

45 No passion for women, no worldly pleasures,
   Nothing, only the ocean's heave;
   But longing wraps itself around him.
   Orchards blossom, the towns bloom,
   Fields grow lovely as the world springs fresh,
50 And all these admonish° that willing mind
   Leaping to journeys, always set
   In thoughts traveling on a quickening tide.
   So summer's sentinel, the cuckoo, sings
   In his murmuring voice, and our hearts mourn
55 As he urges. Who could understand,
   In ignorant ease, what we others suffer
   As the paths of exile stretch endlessly on?
                    And yet my heart wanders away,
   My soul roams with the sea, the whales'
60 Home, wandering to the widest corners
   Of the world, returning ravenous° with desire,
   Flying solitary, screaming, exciting me
   To the open ocean, breaking oaths
   On the curve of a wave.
                              Thus the joys of God
65 Are fervent° with life, where life itself
   Fades quickly into the earth. The wealth
   Of the world neither reaches to Heaven nor remains.
   No man has ever faced the dawn
   Certain which of Fate's three threats
70 Would fall: illness, or age, or an enemy's
   Sword, snatching the life from his soul.
   The praise the living pour on the dead
   Flowers from reputation: plant
   An earthly life of profit reaped
75 Even from hatred and rancor,° of bravery
   Flung in the devil's face, and death
   Can only bring you earthly praise
   And a song to celebrate a place
   With the angels, life eternally blessed
   In the hosts of Heaven.
80   The days are gone
   When the kingdoms of earth flourished in glory;
   Now there are no rulers, no emperors,
   No givers of gold, as once there were,
   When wonderful things were worked among them
85 And they lived in lordly magnificence.
   Those powers have vanished, those pleasures are dead.

50. admonish: scold mildly.

61. ravenous: very hungry.

65. fervent: passionate.

75. rancor (raŋˈkər): ill will.

The weakest survives and the world continues,
Kept spinning by toil. All glory is tarnished.
The world's honor ages and shrinks.
90 Bent like the men who mould it. Their faces
Blanch° as time advances, their beards
Wither and they mourn the memory of friends.
The sons of princes, sown in the dust.
The soul stripped of its flesh knows nothing
95 Of sweetness or sour, feels no pain,
Bends neither its hand nor its brain. A brother
Opens his palms and pours down gold
On his kinsman's grave, strewing his coffin
With treasures intended for Heaven, but nothing
100 Golden shakes the wrath of God
For a soul overflowing with sin, and nothing
Hidden on earth rises to Heaven.
             We all fear God. He turns the earth,
He set it swinging firmly in space,
105 Gave life to the world and light to the sky.
Death leaps at the fools who forget their God.
He who lives humbly has angels from Heaven
To carry him courage and strength and belief.
A man must conquer pride, not kill it,
110 Be firm with his fellows, chaste for himself,
Treat all the world as the world deserves,
With love or with hate but never with harm,
Though an enemy seek to scorch him in hell,
Or set the flames of a funeral pyre°
115 Under his lord. Fate is stronger
And God mightier than any man's mind.
Our thoughts should turn to where our home is,
Consider the ways of coming there,
Then strive for sure permission for us
120 To rise to that eternal joy,
That life born in the love of God
And the hope of Heaven. Praise the Holy
Grace of Him who honored us,
Eternal, unchanging creator of earth. Amen.

91. blanch: turn pale.

114. funeral pyre: pile (usually of wood) on which a dead body is burned. See the burial of Beowulf, page 46.

The Original Language and the Translator's Task

Here are the opening lines of "The Seafarer" in Old English. Following these lines is a translation by Kevin Crossley-Holland. Burton Raffel, whose very different translation is used on page 56, describes the special demands of verse translation: "Verse translation is a minor art, but a unique one. . . . The translator's only hope is to re-create something roughly equivalent in the new language, something that is itself good poetry and that at the same time carries a reasonable measure of the force and flavor of the original. . . ."

MÆg ic be me sylfum soðgied wrecan,
siþas secgan, hu ic geswincdagum
earfoðhwile oft þrowade,
bitre breostceare gebiden hæbbe,
gecunnad in ceole cearselda fela. . . .

I can sing a true song of myself,
Tell of my travels, of many hard times
Toiling day after day; I can describe
How I have harbored bitter sorrow in
     my heart
And often learned that ships are homes
     of sadness.

—*translated by* Kevin Crossley-Holland

MAKING MEANINGS

First Thoughts

1. What is your first impression of the speaker in this poem? What is his life like? What does he believe in and hope for?

Shaping Interpretations

2. What passages in the poem explain why the seafarer seeks the rigors of the sea rather than the delights of the land? Does he find what he looked for at sea?

3. Lines 58–64 suggest that the poet is beginning to talk about the glories of adventuring at sea, but then he changes direction. What does he turn his attention to over the next sixteen lines?

4. In line 80, the speaker begins to talk about the present state of the world—what does he think of it? How do these thoughts contribute to the poem's **elegiac tone**?

5. The poem ends with a statement of the poet's beliefs. What are they?

6. This short lyric is full of striking **metaphors**—for example, "frozen chains" in line 10. Select three of these metaphors, and explain what is being compared in each one. What emotional effect does each metaphor create?

7. What do you think the seafarer is searching for?

Connecting with the Text

8. In line 88, the poem's speaker says, "All glory is tarnished." Do you think this idea also applies to today's heroes and to present-day life? Explain your response.

Extending the Text

9. Could the sentiments expressed in this poem be applied to the homeless today? Find passages in the poem to support your answer.

CHOICES: Building Your Portfolio

Writer's Notebook

1. Collecting Ideas for a Literary Analysis

Earlier in this collection you may have begun collecting ideas for a literary analysis. One of the elements of literature that you can focus on in a literary analysis is tone.

Tone refers to the writer's or speaker's attitude. Tone is established by word choice. In poetry it can also be established by sound effects. Go through "The Seafarer" and list all the words and phrases and figures of speech that suggest an elegiac or mournful tone. Then read the poem aloud and note sounds that suggest a mournful tone or feeling. Save your work for possible use in the Writer's Workshop on page 67.

Comparing Texts Across Cultures

2. Ancient and Modern

Perhaps the most startling aspect of ancient literature is that it so often deals with emotions and thoughts similar to our own, despite the intervening centuries. Look, for instance, at this short poem by the American poet Robert Frost (1874–1963):

> ### Nothing Gold Can Stay
>
> Nature's first green is gold,
> Her hardest hue to hold.
> Her early leaf's a flower;
> But only so an hour.
> Then leaf subsides to leaf.
> So Eden sank to grief,
> So dawn goes down to day.
> Nothing gold can stay.
>
> —Robert Frost

Write a short essay comparing the thoughts expressed here and in "The Seafarer." What sentiments do they share? How do they differ? How do you feel about the main thrust of each poem?

Creative Writing

3. You Are a "Seafarer"

Create a "Seafarer" poem of your own, opening with the line "This tale is true, and mine." Write about your own or someone else's (old or young) aspirations, hopes, joys, and disillusionments. Try to incorporate alliteration and kennings in your poem, in true Anglo-Saxon style.

Critical Thinking

4. No Heroes? A Debate

"There are no heroes today." Do you agree or disagree with this statement? Refer to your responses to the Quickwrite on page 55. Take a position, and then gather evidence to support it—facts, reasons, and examples from life today. Think about what the opposing side might say and how you might respond to their ideas. Hold a debate, with each side allowed three minutes to present its ideas and two minutes to respond to the opposing side's remarks.

Visual Art

5. Depicting a Dilemma

Create a collage that visually represents the speaker's attitudes in "The Seafarer." Working with a partner or a group, put your imaginations to work, and gather images and words from newspapers and magazines. Remember that collages can also contain objects, such as feathers or shells or sand. Be prepared to explain why you included each element in the collage when you present it to your class.

A picture stone showing a Viking ship under sail.
Statens Historiska Museer, Stockholm.

Everyday Poetry: Anglo-Saxon Riddles

translated by **Burton Raffel**

In the Anglo-Saxon period, riddles were "everyday" poetry and intellectual exercises that entertained by puzzling. Like riddles in most cultures, the Anglo-Saxon riddle can be crude; it usually describes some household or farm object or some aspect of ordinary life. Ninety-five riddles are found in the Exeter Book.

The Anglo-Saxons must have whiled away many a long, dark winter evening by repeating riddles like these and having friends guess the answers. The answer to each riddle is below.

32

Our world is lovely in different ways,
Hung with beauty and works of hands.
I saw a strange machine, made
For motion, slide against the sand,
5 Shrieking as it went. It walked swiftly
On its only foot, this odd-shaped monster,
Traveled in an open country without
Seeing, without arms, or hands,
With many ribs, and its mouth in its middle.
10 Its work is useful, and welcome, for it loads
Its belly with food, and brings abundance
To men, to poor and to rich, paying
Its tribute year after year. Solve
This riddle, if you can, and unravel its name.

33

A creature came through the waves, beautiful
And strange, calling to shore, its voice
Loud and deep; its laughter froze
Men's blood; its sides were like sword-blades. It
swam
5 Contemptuously along, slow and sluggish,
A bitter warrior and a thief, ripping
Ships apart, and plundering. Like a witch
It wove spells—and knew its own nature,
shouting:
"My mother is the fairest virgin of a race
10 Of noble virgins: She is my daughter
Grown great. All men know her, and me,
And know, everywhere on earth, with what joy
We will come to join them, to live on land!"

47

A worm ate words. I thought that wonderfully
Strange—a miracle—when they told me a crawling
Insect had swallowed noble songs,
A night-time thief had stolen writing
So famous, so weighty. But the bug was foolish
Still, though its belly was full of thought.

Answers: 32. a ship; 33. an iceberg; 47. a bookworm.

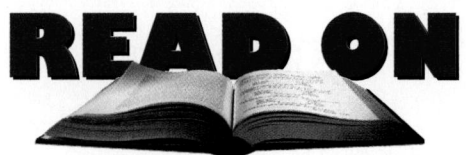

READ ON

A History Mystery

History and fiction merge in Rosemary Sutcliff's *The Eagle of the Ninth* (Farrar, Straus & Giroux). Travel back in time to Roman Britain, where eighteen-year-old Marcus Flavius Aquila, a centurion in the Roman army, attempts to solve the mystery of his father's disappearance and restore the family's honor.

Great Deeds of Ages Past

An exciting blend of narrative, poetry, and drama, *Sundiata* (Dearborn Trade Publishers) is the best-known African epic. It is the story of Sundiata, son of the king of Mali some eight hundred years ago. Passed down by griots, Africa's oral historians, the epic reflects the rich complexity of the ancient civilization of Mali.

Traveling Talk

Some of the most colorful English spoken today comes from a wide range of sources—American, Irish, Caribbean. How did the English language travel around the globe, and what happened to it during those travels? *The Story of English* (Viking Penguin), by Robert McCrum, et al., traces the continuing evolution of our language.

Beyond the Misty Mountains

Full of mythology, magic, and quiet humor, J.R.R. Tolkien's classic fantasy *The Hobbit* (Ballantine and Fawcett) follows the adventures of a comfort-loving Hobbit named Bilbo Baggins. Baggins is tricked by the wizard Gandalf into going on a hazardous quest to recover stolen treasure from the dragon Smaug. *The Lord of the Rings* trilogy continues the saga of Middle Earth.

The Storytelling Tradition of Ireland

The enchanting stories from the ancient oral tradition of Ireland, compiled by Jeremiah Curtin in the 1800s, have been gathered together in *Myths and Folk Tales of Ireland* (Dover). The book includes traditional fairy tales, as well as myths about the fabulous adventures of the great Celtic heroes Cucúlin and Fin MacCumhail.

The English Language

Old English: Where English Came From   *by John Algeo*

We have biological ancestors, from whom we inherit the tint of our skin, the shape of our skulls, and everything about our bodies. We also have cultural ancestors, from whom we inherit the society in which we live and especially the language we speak. We in the United States have diverse biological ancestors from whom we get our genes, but as English speakers, we share a common language. So in studying English and its history, we learn more about a legacy that all Americans can share.

Gold pectoral, or ornamental breastplate (c. 4th–5th century).

Out of the East: The Ancestor of English

Written records of English have been preserved for about 1,300 years. Much earlier, however, a people living in the east, near the Caspian Sea, spoke a language that was to become English. We call their language Proto-Indo-European because at the beginning of recorded history varieties of it were spoken from India to Europe. (*Proto-* means "the first or earliest form of something.")

The speakers of Proto-Indo-European were a vigorous sort who raised cattle and horses. They were fighters, farmers, and herders who used large wagons and built fortresses on hilltops. Eventually, they got the urge to travel and began spreading through Turkey, Iran, India, and most of Europe. In various places their language changed into those we now call Persian, Hindi, Armenian, Greek, Russian, Polish, Irish, Italian, French, Spanish, German, English, Dutch, Norwegian, Swedish, and a good many others. Such languages we call Indo-European.

Wanderlust: The Migrations

Speakers of Indo-European languages eventually wandered all over the earth and were the first human beings to travel into space and reach the moon.

Some early Indo-Europeans lived in what is now southern Denmark and northern Germany. Called Angles and Saxons, they were part of a large group of Germanic peoples living over much of northern Europe. About the middle of the fifth century (the traditional date is A.D. 449), the Anglo-Saxons migrated across the North Sea to the island of Britain and settled very happily in the green and fruitful land they found there.

The British Isles had already been inhabited by some distant Indo-European cousins of the Anglo-Saxons: the Britons, a Celtic people after whom the island was named. They had been conquered by the Romans, who were Indo-Europeans too, so all this jostling for space in the island was just one branch of the family trying to move in on another, rather like relatives from Chicago moving in with their kin in Florida for the winter.

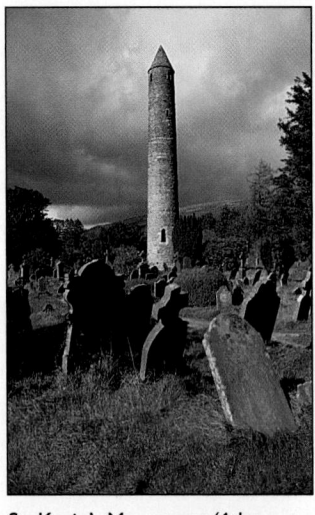

St. Kevin's Monastery (6th century), Glendalough, Ireland.

The Anglo-Saxons got a few words from the Romans in Britain, such as *castra* ("camp"), which can be seen in the names of many English cities (*Chester, Chesterfield, Dorchester, Gloucester, Lancaster, Manchester, Winchester,* and *Worcester*). They also found the cities that the Romans had built, with temples, waterworks, and public baths. They moved into the cities and admired the great buildings, but they never learned to share the Roman passion for bathing.

Meeting the Neighbors

When the Anglo-Saxons first arrived in Britain (which came to be called Engla land, England—the land of the Angles), they had very little to do with the Celts, whom they drove into the west where they still survive today as the Welsh (an Anglo-Saxon word that means "foreigner"). But another group of Celts, the Irish, later sent missionaries to the Angles. About the same time, in A.D. 597, the Roman church sent St. Augustine to do missionary work.

Although there is very little early Celtic influence on the English language—hardly more than a few place names, such as *London* and *Dover*—Latin, the language of the Christian church, was enormously influential. Even while the Anglo-Saxons were still living on the Continent, they had learned some Latin from Roman soldiers and merchants, including words like *mile, street, wall, wine, cheese, butter,* and *dish*. After the Anglo-Saxons settled in England and were converted, they borrowed many other Latin words concerned with religion and learning, such as *school, candle, altar, paper,* and *circle*.

Beginning near the end of the eighth century, other cousins, Northmen or Vikings from Scandinavia, invaded England. They were led by such memorably named worthies as Ivar the Boneless, son of Ragnar Shaggy-britches. It would be a mistake, however, to think of these Vikings as amusingly rough but lovable, like the comic-strip character Hagar the Horrible. They were fierce fighters and very nearly made England into another Scandinavian country. It was the English King Alfred the Great who defeated the Viking invaders and set about assimilating the Northmen into English life.

The influence of the Vikings' Norse language has been very great. Among the words borrowed are such common ones as *get, give, hit, kick, law, sister, skirt, sky, take, window, they, their,* and *them*.

What Tongue Is This?

Despite all the foreign influences, the language of the early English, which we call Old English or Anglo-Saxon, was clearly a Germanic tongue. An example of this language is the following short piece—a text that most readers of this book will know in a modern form:

> Fæder ūre, þū þe eart on heofonum, sī nama gehālgod. Tōbecume þīn rīce. Gewurðe þīn willa on eorðan swā swā on heofonum. Ūrne gedæghwāmlican hlāf syle ūs tō dæg. And forgyf ūs ūre gyltas, swā wē forgyfað ūrum gylltendum. And ne gelǣd þū ūs on costnunge, ac ālȳs ūs of yfele. Sōðlice.

This text is the Lord's Prayer from about the year 1000. It differs from the version we know in many ways. **Words** are different (*costnunge* instead of *temptation,* borrowed later from Latin). **Spellings and pronunciations** are different (*nama,* pronounced "nah-mah," instead of the present-day *name*). **Meanings** are different (*hlāf* in the sense of "bread," surviving today as *loaf*).

And **grammar** is different. Note the word order of *Fæder ūre* for *our Father* and the word ending, or case inflection, *–um* in *on heofonum* ("in heaven").

Old English grammar was different from ours in a number of other ways. For example, all **nouns** were one of three genders—masculine, feminine, or neuter—and the grammatical gender of a noun might have little to do with sex. Thus, of three words for "woman," *hlæfdige* was feminine, *wif* was neuter, and *wifmann* was masculine.

Adjectives had different forms depending on the gender, number, and case of the nouns they modified (*þæt tile wif* but *se tila wifmann*, both meaning "the good woman").

Whereas our **verbs** have two forms in the present tense (for example, *ride, rides*), Old English verbs had four: *ic ride* ("I ride"), *þū ridest* ("you ride"), *hē rideþ* ("he rides"), and *wē ridon* ("we ride").

Like other Indo-European languages, Old English used end-

> Beginning near the end of the eighth century, other cousins, Northmen or Vikings from Scandinavia, invaded England. They were led by such memorably named worthies as Ivar the Boneless, son of Ragnar Shaggy-britches.

ings on words to show how they relate to one another and how they are used in a sentence. For example, "The boy killed the dragon" was "Se cnapa slōh þone dracan," while "The dragon killed the boy" was "Se draca slōh þone cnapan." The words for "boy" and "dragon" change their forms, according to whether they are the subject or the object of the verb, and the word for "the" is different, depending on the function of the word it modifies. Today we rely solely on word order to show grammatical differences; Old English relied mainly on changes in word form.

Anglo-Saxon scribes wrote in a script they learned from Celtic missionaries. It was a pleasant-looking, rounded style of writing, as the sample below shows.

Occasionally, for special purposes, Old English writers used an altogether different alphabet, called the *futhorc,* composed of letters called runes, which they learned from their Germanic cousins while they still lived on

Detail from the Book of Kells (8th century).
The Board of Trinity College, Dublin. Photograph by The Green Studio Ltd, Dublin.

the Continent. These runes were probably used by the very early pagan English for magic and for monuments. They were straight, angular letters that were used for carving on wood.

Old English was mainly oral. Because writing was important business, it was usually reserved for Latin, the language of church services, books, education, and contact with other nations. To know Latin was to be learned. Not to know Latin was to be illiterate. It is small wonder that Latin came to have a greater and more lasting influence on English than any other language did.

An example of Insular script.

Words from Anglo-Saxon

We have come a long way since Anglo-Saxon times—in technology, in society, and in language. But much of the Anglo-Saxons' language, Old English, is still evident in our language.

Although today we have borrowed words from most of the world's languages, our basic vocabulary comes to us from Old English. Words like *heart, foot, head, day, year, earth, father, mother, son, daughter, name, east, full, hound, tooth, eat, weave,* and *sew* are survivals of Old English words (*heorte, fōt, hēafod, dæg, gēar, eorþe, fæder, mōdor, sunu, dohtor, nama, ēast, full, hund, toþ, etan, wefan,* and *siwan*). Indeed, all of those words come to us from Proto-Indo-European; thus, they have been part of our language for thousands of years.

Our **noun plural ending s** and **possessive ending 's** (as in *hounds, hound's*) come to us from Old English (*hundas, hundes*). So do the endings we use to **compare adjectives,** as in *darker, darkest* (*deorcor, deorcost*). The regular endings for the **past tense and past participle of our verbs,** as in *healed, has healed,* are from Old English (*hǣlde, hæfþ hǣled*), as are the vowel changes in verbs like *sing, sang, sung* (*singan, sang, sungen*). In many other ways, our English is recognizably the same as the oldest English of which we have any record.

Although we have lost most of the endings from Old English and have borrowed far more words from other languages than we have kept from Old English times, the heart of our speech is still the same. The preceding sentence consists entirely of words that have come to us from Old English, and its grammar would have been understood by an English speaker of the year A.D. 700. Despite its many changes, English has remained basically true to itself.

Try It Out

1. On a map of the world, locate the countries where the following **Indo-European languages** are spoken. Some languages are spoken in more than one country. What are at least three other languages that are used in more than one country?

Detail from the Book of Kells (8th century). The Board of Trinity College, Dublin. Photograph by The Green Studio Ltd, Dublin.

English	Icelandic
Russian	Irish
German	Spanish
Polish	Portuguese
Danish	French
Hindi	Italian

2. Using a good dictionary, look up the following **Anglo-Saxon prefixes** and **suffixes.** What does each word part mean? See how many common English words you can list using these word parts.

Prefixes	Suffixes
a-	-en
an-	-dom
be-	-hood
for-	-like
mis-	-ness
un-	-ward

3. Four of the following words are native words in **Old English,** four are **Latin** words borrowed into English very early (some while English speakers still lived on the Continent), and four are **Scandinavian** words borrowed as a result of the Norse invasions of England. Which words belong in each group? Check your work by looking at the **etymologies** in a college or unabridged dictionary.

belt	noon
brother	pillow
filly	pipe
horse	rug
house	skin
night	until

4. The Anglo-Saxons sometimes used an alphabet called *futhorc* or *futhark,* comprised of characters called **runes.** The first six letters of the runic alphabet—which spell out the word *futhorc*—looked like this:

ᚠᚢᚦᚨᚱᚲ or ᚠᚢᚦᚠᚱᚲ

Look up the entire runic alphabet in an encyclopedia. Working with a small group, write a brief phrase (such as an epitaph), and translate it into the runic alphabet. Compare your "translations" with those created by other groups in the class.

Writer's Workshop

The history
of the written
word is rich and
Page 1

EXPOSITORY WRITING

ANALYZING A LITERARY WORK

When you write an analysis of a literary work, you take the work apart to see how it creates meaning. The parts of a literary work that you examine in an analysis are those elements that form its structure. In some analyses you will focus on just one element—character in a short story, for example, or imagery in a poem.

Prewriting

1. **Getting started.** Unless you are assigned a literary work to analyze, your first step will be finding a work that interests you. Your best possibilities are the selections from *Beowulf* and "The Seafarer" in this collection because, presumably, you have read them carefully and talked about them in class. Review the notes you took for the Writer's Notebook assignments in this collection. Do any of your notes especially interest you? Is there some topic here that you can develop?

2. **Focus your analysis.** If you like, you can discuss all the basic elements of your literary work, but you might be better off narrowing your focus to just one or two prominent elements. Here are some possible focuses:

   • The symbolism of Grendel and Herot

   • The Christian elements in Beowulf's story

   • The heroic character of Beowulf as the deliverer of his people

   • The elegiac tone of *Beowulf* and "The Seafarer"

3. **Write a thesis statement.** Next, try out some thesis statements. Your thesis statement must be a sentence; it will be the controlling idea of your essay. You will have to experiment with a thesis statement. As you go along, you might find that a statement is just too broad (maybe it could be the subject of a whole book) or too narrow (you find you just don't have much to say about it).

   Thesis statement: In *Beowulf*, Grendel symbolizes evil while Herot symbolizes goodness.

4. **Gather support.** List all the evidence from the text that explains or supports your thesis statement. Most of your evidence will come from the text itself (this is your **primary source**). You might also want to quote from **secondary sources** that support your thesis statement. Cite specific lines from the text that support your main ideas; then, paraphrase, or state in your own words, what they say. Here is the start of a list of supporting details:

Technology HELP

See Writer's Workshop 2 CD-ROM. *Assignment: Interpretation.*

ASSIGNMENT
Write an essay in which you analyze a literary work or one of its key elements.

AIM
To read carefully to see how a literary element is used in a work, to explain how the element is used to reinforce meaning, and to supply convincing details to support your analysis.

AUDIENCE
Your teacher, classmates, or a literary magazine published by your school or an outside publisher.

Supporting details, lines 1–29:

Grendel: monster; living in darkness; demon; fiend.

Herot: music; songs about creation; singing heroes; happy people.

Paraphrase: Grendel is associated with all that is not good. He lives underground in darkness. He is called a demon and a fiend. Herot, on the other hand, is a happy place associated with song, creation, pleasure, great warriors.

Drafting

1. **Find a method of organization.** Here are two effective ways to organize your details:

    Chronological order. If you are writing about the development of a main character, you can organize your supporting details in the order in which they occur in the text.

    Order of importance. You might want to start out with a bang and introduce your strongest point first. Or you may reverse that and keep your most powerful point for the very end.

2. **Structure your analysis.** Traditionally, literary analyses take the following simple shape:

    An introduction that states your thesis, or main idea. Here, you must also cite the title and author of your text. You might want to summarize your text briefly. Remember: Do not tell the whole plot in tedious detail. You are writing an analysis, not a summary.

    A body that contains the most persuasive details you can find to support your thesis.

    A conclusion that sums up your main point. Try to find a strong way to conclude your essay.

Evaluating and Revising

1. Skim your text again. Have you cited the best details to support your thesis statement?

2. Check your quotations and the documentation of sources for accuracy. Have you used quotation marks properly?

3. Read your analysis aloud, or ask a peer to evaluate it. Is your ending strong? Do your sentences read smoothly?

▮ Evaluation Criteria

An analysis of a literary work
1. *cites the title and author*
2. *supplies a clear thesis statement*
3. *provides details to support the thesis statement*
4. *quotes accurately from the text, citing page and line numbers and using quotation marks*
5. *cites all secondary sources and uses quotation marks for sources quoted directly*
6. *organizes ideas clearly*
7. *has a strong ending*

Language Workshop H E L P

Sentence combining: page 69.

Language Workshop

The history
of the written
word is rich and

Page 1

SENTENCE COMBINING

Read aloud the following sentences. How do they sound?

> Beowulf neared the dragon's cave. He let out a loud battle cry. The dragon rose. The dragon approached Beowulf. It was angry that a man had come to this fearful place. The dragon breathed melting fire and scorching smoke. Beowulf firmly held his sword and shield.

Something holds this scene back, making it stiff: the jerky rhythm of the sentences, which share a basic subject-verb structure. Combining some sentences makes the flow smoother, the action more continuous, and the ideas clearer.

> Beowulf neared the dragon's cave, letting out a loud battle cry. The dragon rose and approached Beowulf, for it was angry that a man had come to this fearful place. While Beowulf firmly held his sword and shield, the dragon breathed melting fire and scorching smoke.

Strategies for Combining Sentences

1. **Turn sentences into phrases.** Often you can turn a short sentence (*He let out a loud battle cry*) into a phrase and insert it into another sentence.

   > Beowulf neared the dragon's cave, *letting out a loud battle cry.*

2. **Combine ideas.** When two or more sentences express similar ideas, you may be able to combine subjects, verbs, objects, or entire sentences with conjunctions like *and, but, or, for,* and *yet.*

   > The dragon rose *and* approached Beowulf, *for* it was angry that a man had come to this fearful place.

3. **Subordinate ideas.** When two or more sentences express related ideas, create one sentence with a main clause and a subordinate (dependent) clause. To show the relationship between the clauses, you must add a connecting word (such as *although, because, that, who,* or *while*). Placing the subordinate clause first adds even more variety.

   > *While Beowulf firmly held his sword and shield,* the dragon breathed melting fire and scorching smoke.

Writer's Workshop Follow-Up: Revision

Read aloud the essay you wrote for the Writer's Workshop on page 67. Do you hear any short, choppy sentences? Does the writing sound monotonous? Use the sentence-combining techniques you've just practiced to create dynamic action sequences, connect thoughts, and break up monotonous sentences. Read aloud your revisions to a peer reviewer: Do your combined sentences sound better? Do they make relationships between ideas clearer?

**Technology
H E L P**

See Language Workshop CD-ROM. *Key word entry: sentence combining.*

**Language Handbook
H E L P**

See Sentence Combining: page 1239.

Try It Out

Combine each pair of sentences below into one sentence.

1. The dragon's flaming breath scorched the shield. The shield melted at once.

2. Beowulf swung his sword at the fearsome dragon. Beowulf hit the dragon's impenetrable skin.

3. Then the dragon jumped away. It jumped with flames pouring out of its nostrils.

4. Beowulf faced the monster alone. Beowulf's sword had failed him.

Reading for Life

Evaluating a News Feature

Situation

In the Middle Ages, when people heard any news at all, they heard it randomly, from bards and other travelers. Today we can read many newspapers daily; we can also read electronically transmitted news almost instantaneously on the Internet. As we read news, we should apply analytic and evaluative strategies.

Strategies

What is the source of the news?

• Identify the ownership of the newspaper or the sponsorship of the Web site.

Is the news article signed? If it is, be aware of the writer's stance.

• Does the writer or reporter have a reputation for objectivity, or fairness, or is the writer known as an advocate of a certain political, social, or economic point of view?

Recognize the writer's motivation.

• Does the writer want to inform, entertain, or persuade readers? Does the writer have two or even more purposes?

Evaluate credibility and context.

• If the writer's credentials are not cited, how can you find out who he or she is?

• Does the writer present both sides of an issue? Does the

writer present facts that sufficiently support the main ideas and make the opinions believable?

• Does the writer present the information in a logical, convincing way, or does he or she appeal mainly to emotions?

Analyze the tone.

• What is the overall tone? Is it serious, sarcastic, or angry? Analyzing word choices and **connotations** can help you decide.

Using the Strategies

Use these questions to evaluate the extract from a newspaper column above.

1. Who or what is the writer's target?

2. Does this writer give a balanced presentation of the issues? Or does she want to convince you of *one* point of view?

3. Does the writer appeal mostly to your intellect or to your emotions?

4. How would you describe the writer's tone?

5. What words and phrases indicate the writer's tone?

6. On the basis of the writer's tone, what can you surmise about her politics?

Extending the Strategies

Analyze and evaluate a news article in a local or national newspaper or magazine.

What California Wrought All Over Itself

MOLLY IVINS

LOS ANGELES— . . . Perhaps I wrong the *Los Angeles Times*, but it seems to me that its recent retrospective on the 20th anniversary of Prop 13, California's original "tax revolt" initiative, was curiously flaccid. It was a throwback to that gutless form of journalism we used to excuse by calling it "objective"; one side said this and the other side says that, therefore we will give them both equal space. The much-maligned *San Francisco Chronicle* actually did a far better job than the august *Times* in its three-part series on the anniversary of Prop 13.

How much intelligence does it take to conclude that Prop 13 has been a disaster for the state? For that matter, how much objectivity does it take? The results of Prop 13 are easily quantified. The state has almost doubled in population since the early '60s. In the last two decades, it has built 20 new prisons but not one new campus of the University of California. Freeways, libraries, parks, and schools (above all the schools) are battered, dilapidated, shrunken. And in the eerie new politics of California that Shrag calls "neopopulist," the voters are about to respond by outlawing bilingual education. That'll help. . . .

—*from the Star-Telegram*
Austin, Texas
May 27, 1998

Proposition 13 was on the ballot in California in 1978. It called for a rollback in property taxes, which are the main source of school financing. The proposition was approved.

Learning for Life

Analyzing Groups

Problem

The early Anglo-Saxons found a sense of community in close-knit kinship groups. How do groups function in your world?

Project

Analyze the way a group that you belong to works. The group might be a family or one that you work with on projects at school. Or it might be a community group of some kind. What is the purpose of the group? How does the group solve problems? How do various people work within the group? What are the advantages and disadvantages of being part of a group?

Preparation

1. From the various groups to which you belong—at home, at school, at work, or through a religious or volunteer organization—choose one that has had a significant effect on you.
2. Determine the purpose of the group.
3. Analyze what the group members have in common, how they recognize and build on one another's strengths, and how their interrelationships affect the group's functioning.

Procedure

1. The next time the group gets together, observe how the members interact. How do they speak to and listen to one another, what roles do different members assume, and how does the group make decisions and work out compromises?
2. Jot down your impressions soon after the meeting. You don't need to use complete sentences—you might even sketch or doodle.

Presentation

Use one of the following formats (or another that your teacher approves):

1. **Say It in Pictures**
   Create a two-page photo-essay about the group for an illustrated magazine. Select photos that show how the group operates (be sure to include yourself in at least one), or take new ones if necessary. Write a caption to accompany each photo, and include a title that will draw readers into the essay. If you have access to desktop-publishing software, produce a camera-ready, or final, version of your photoessay.

2. **A Graphic Presentation**
   Present your analysis in the form of a graphic. (If you were working for a human resources group or a management consultant group, you would probably present your analysis this way.) Here are some possibilities: a flow chart showing how responsibilities are allocated and how projects are completed; a hierarchical chart showing the organization of the group and the responsibilities of various members; a problem-solution chart showing how problems are identified and resolved. Be sure to identify any glitches that you perceive in the ways the group functions.

3. **Talking About Community**
   With three to five other students, present a panel discussion on the various ways in which people build a sense of community. Panel members should represent a variety of groups, such as a family, a neighborhood organization, a sports team, a service club. Meet with the other panel members to phrase a discussion question, prepare a discussion outline, and elect a leader. Hold the discussion in front of an audience, such as the rest of the class or the parent-teacher organization.

Processing

What did you learn from this activity about how you and your classmates feel about groups and group projects? What are some of the needs met by groups in your community? Write a brief reflection for your portfolio.

Illumination from *Le Roman de Lancelot du Lac* (detail) (early 14th century). Guinevere, queen of Britain, and attendants watching a tournament from a tower. MS 806, fol.262.

The Middle Ages 1066–1485

The Middle Ages

by David Adams Leeming

At his most characteristic, medieval man was not a dreamer nor a wanderer. He was an organizer, a codifier, a builder of systems. He wanted "a place for everything and everything in the right place." Distinction, definition, tabulation were his delight. Though full of turbulent activities, he was equally full of the impulse to formalize them. War was (in intention) formalized by the art of heraldry and the rules of chivalry; sexual passion (in intention), by the elaborate code of love. . . . There was nothing which medieval people liked better, or did better, than sorting out and tidying up. Of all our modern inventions I suspect that they would most have admired the card index.
—C. S. Lewis

Illumination from a French manuscript of *Romance of the Rose* (15th century).
British Library, London.

In October 1066, a daylong battle near Hastings, England, changed the course of history. There, just ten miles from the channel dividing England from France, Duke William of Normandy, France, defeated and killed King Harold of England, the last of the Anglo-Saxon kings. So began the Norman Conquest, an event that radically affected English history, the English character, and the English language. Unlike the Romans, the Normans never withdrew from England.

Who was this William the Conqueror? He was the illegitimate son of the previous duke of Normandy, who was in turn a cousin of the English king called Edward the Confessor. Edward had died childless earlier in 1066, and Harold, the earl of Wessex, had been crowned the following day. But William claimed that the old king had promised the throne to him. Determined to seize what he considered rightfully his, William sailed the English Channel with an enormous army.

William was an efficient and ruthless soldier, but he wanted to rule the Anglo-Saxons, not eliminate them. Today, as a result, rather than a Norman, French-speaking England (and America), we find a culture and a language that combine Norman and Anglo-Saxon elements. To the Anglo-Saxons' more democratic and artistic tendencies, the Normans brought administrative ability, an emphasis on law and order, and cultural unity.

Norman warriors crossing the Channel in 1066, from a French manuscript (11th century). MS N.a. Lat. 1390, fol. 7.

© cliché Bibliothèque Nationale de France, Paris.

One of William's great administrative feats was an inventory of nearly every piece of property in England—land, cattle, buildings—in the Domesday Book. (The title suggests a comparison between William's judgment of his subjects' financial worth and God's final judgment of their moral worth.) For the first time in European history, people could be taxed based on what they owned.

Although the Normans did not erase Anglo-Saxon culture, they did bring significant changes to England. William and many of his successors remained dukes of Normandy as well as kings of England. The powerful Anglo-Norman entity they molded brought England into mainstream European civilization in a new way. For example, William divided the holdings of the fallen English landowners

October 14, 1066, was one of the decisive days of history. The battle itself was nip and tuck; the shift only of a few elements here or there, a gift of luck could have given the victory to the Anglo-Saxons. If Harold had won at Hastings and had survived, William would have had no choice but to renounce his adventure. There is little likelihood that anyone would have attempted a serious invasion of England during the next millennium—by water, at least. England would have strengthened its bonds with Scandinavia while remaining distrustful of the western Continent—even more distrustful than it is today. The native Anglo-Saxon culture would have developed in unimaginable ways, and William the Conqueror would be dimly known in history only as William the Bastard.

—Morris Bishop

The Middle Ages, 1066–1485

76 THE MIDDLE AGES

LITERARY EVENTS

• Scene from the *Story of Roland,* from Chartres Cathedral, France (13th century).

Death of Omar Khayyám, Persian poet and astronomer, 1131

French heroic poem, *Song of Roland,* written, c. 1100

In France, Chrétien de Troyes writes *Lancelot,* c. 1170s

In Spain, first mass production of paper, c. 1150

Marie de France, first known European woman to write narrative poetry, dies, c. 1216

Persian poet Saadi born, 1213

Beginnings of German epic poem, the *Nibelung-enlied,* c. 1200

1066–1099	1100–1149	1150–1199	1200–1249

CULTURAL/HISTORICAL EVENTS

King Edward the Confessor dies without heir, 1066

Duke of Normandy invades England, 1066

Domesday Book, a record of all land ownership in England, first compiled, 1086

Crusades begin, to free Jerusalem from Turkish control, 1095

Knights Templar, a religious order whose mission was to protect pilgrims to the Holy Land, founded, c. 1119

Construction begins on Cathedral of Notre Dame in Paris, 1163

Thomas à Becket murdered, 1170

Henry II invades Ireland, beginning nearly eight hundred years of British domination, 1171

Minamoto Yoritomo becomes first shogun (military ruler) of Japan, 1192

Mongol leader Genghis Khan invades China, 1211

English barons force King John to sign the Magna Carta, 1215

Pope Gregory IX begins the Inquisition, c. 1232

• A man and his wife on horse-back, the wife riding pillion (on a cushioned saddle), from a book of hours (c. 1500). British Library, London.

• From *Hours of the Duchess of Burgundy* (c. 1450).

Musée Condé.

Boccaccio writes the *Decameron*, 1349–1353

Geoffrey Chaucer born, c. 1343

Julian of Norwich, one of the first English women of letters, born, c. 1342

Petrarch crowned poet laureate in Italy, 1341

Development of Japanese Nōh plays, 1300s

Thomas Aquinas writes *Summa Theologica*, 1266–1273

Chaucer begins *The Canterbury Tales*, c. 1387

Entire Bible translated into English for first time by followers of John Wycliffe, 1380

Legendary hero Robin Hood appears in *Piers Plowman*, c. 1378

Sir Gawain and the Green Knight written, c. 1375

Margery Kempe, author of first autobiography in English, born, c. 1373

Dante Alighieri begins writing the *Divine Comedy*, c. 1307

Thomas Malory's *Le Morte Darthur* first printed by Caxton, 1485

William Caxton prints first book in English, c. 1475

First book printed with movable type by Gutenberg, 1455

In France, Christine de Pisan writes famous allegory, *Book of the City of Ladies*, 1405

Chaucer dies, 1400

1250–1299	1300–1349	1350–1399	1400–1485

First commoners allowed in British Parliament, c. 1250

Crusades end, 1270

• Marco Polo in Beijing.

Venetian traveler Marco Polo visits court of Kublai Khan in China, 1275

Edward I invades Scotland and declares himself king, 1296

Zimbabwe emerges as major trading empire, 1300s

Aztecs begin to establish empire in Mexico, 1325

Hundred Years' War between England and France begins, 1337

Black Death strikes England, 1348

English language used to open Parliament, 1362

• **Chinese porcelain jar (15th century), Hsuan-te (Xuande) period, Ming dynasty.**
The Metropolitan Museum of Art. Gift of Robert E. Tod, 1937. (37.191.1). Photograph by Schecter Lee. Photograph © 1986 The Metropolitan Museum of Art.

Ming dynasty begins 300-year rule of China, 1368

Peasants' Revolt in England, 1381

King Richard II deposed, 1399

Benin Kingdom in West Africa flourishes, 1400s

In France, Joan of Arc burned at the stake by the English, 1431

Inca Empire established in Peru, c. 1438

Italian inventor and artist Leonardo da Vinci born, 1452

War between the Houses of York and Lancaster (also called the Wars of the Roses), 1455–1485

Birth of Nicolaus Copernicus, European astronomer, 1473

Martin Luther born in Germany, 1483

First Tudor king, Henry VII, is crowned, 1485

• **Wooden helmet of an Aztec warrior.**
© British Museum, London.

An attack on a fortress, from a French manuscript (detail) (13th–14th century). MS Fr. 1604, fol. 57v.

among his own followers. These men and their families brought to England not only a new language—French—but also a new social system—feudalism—which displaced the old Nordic social structure described in *Beowulf.*

The Anglo-Norman entity that resulted from the Norman Conquest brought England into mainstream European civilization, which included feudalism.

Feudalism and Knighthood: Pyramid Power

More than simply a social system, feudalism was also a caste system, a property system, and a military system. Ultimately, it was based on a religious concept of hierarchy, with God as the supreme overlord. In this sense, even a king held land as a vassal

> . . . there was not one hide of land in England that he did not know who owned it, and what it was worth . . .
>
> —from The Anglo-Saxon Chronicle

A CLOSER LOOK

A TERRIBLE WORM IN AN IRON COCOON

If we hear the term "medieval period," we inevitably think of knights and their magnificent suits of armor. During the early Middle Ages, armor consisted of a helmet, a shield, and a relatively flexible mail shirt, or hauberk, made of countless riveted or welded iron rings. With the crossbow, however, came the need for more protection, so the knight was forced to compromise flexibility and mobility for self-defense.

Held together by rivets, leather straps, hinges, turning pins, buckles, and pegs, a suit of armor replaced mail as the warrior's chief protection. Knights wore a heavily padded undergarment of leather and a mail shirt under the armor, in addition to plate arm, leg, and foot pieces. Mail covered the neck, elbows, and

other joints, and gauntlets constructed of linked plates covered the hands. Some suits of armor weighed 120 pounds and contained 200 custom-fitted iron plates. The knight also carried a variety of weapons: lance, dagger, sword, battle-ax, and club-headed mace.

The threat of death in battle was bad enough, but the armor itself could also be fatal—causing death from suffocation, heart failure, even drowning. Battle during hot weather was particularly difficult. Since small slits in the helmet allowed only a limited line of vision and little ventilation, heatstroke—often deadly for the knight—was common. One anonymous poem describes the armored knight as "a terrible worm in an iron cocoon."

by "divine right." A king as powerful as William the Conqueror could stand firmly at the top of the pyramid. He could appoint certain barons as his immediate vassals, allotting them portions of his land in return for their economic or military allegiance—or both. In turn, the barons could appoint vassals of their own. The system operated all the way down to the landless knights and to the serfs, who were not free to leave the land they tilled.

The feudal system did not always work. Secure in a well-fortified castle, a vassal might choose not to honor his obligations to a weak overlord. The ensuing battles between iron-clad knights around moated castles account for one of the enduring images of the Middle Ages.

Yet the feudal system did carry with it a sense of form and manners that permeated the life, art, and literature of the Middle Ages. This sense of formalism came to life most fully in the institution of knighthood and in the related practice, or code, of chivalry.

We cannot think of the medieval period without thinking of knights. Since the primary duty of males above the serf class was military service to their lords, boys were trained from an early age to become warriors. Often, their training took place in houses other than their own, to be sure that the training was strict. When a boy's training was completed,

> The bond between lord and vassal was affirmed or reaffirmed by the ceremony of homage. The vassal knelt, placed his clasped hands within those of his master, declared, "Lord, I become your man," and took an oath of fealty. The lord raised him to his feet and bestowed on him a ceremonial kiss. The vassal was thenceforth bound by his oath "to love what his lord loved and loathe what he loathed, and never by word or deed do aught that should grieve him."
>
> —Morris Bishop

Only aristocratic knights could afford the huge cost of armor, a war horse, pack-horses, a mount to ride when not in battle, and servants. Because of the armor's weight and the complex fittings required to piece it together, a knight couldn't dress himself for battle. In fact, battles were usually scheduled to allow the warring knights time to be dressed. Servants stood by during battle in case the knight was unhorsed. An armored knight on his back was like an upside-down turtle trying to get on its feet. In this position, the knight was vulnerable to his adversary. If he fell into a shallow body of water, he could drown.

During the fifteenth century, the knight and his horse were considered invulnerable. But this role changed dramatically when the long-bow and later the musket ball came into war-fare. When his armor could no longer protect him in battle, the knight in shining armor became more of a courtier than a combatant. In the last years of their existence, knights participated in exhibitions rather than in warfare.

Chain-mail maker.
Stadtbibliothek,
Nürnberg.

A medieval knight in armor. MS 42130, fol. 202v.

he was "dubbed," or ceremonially tapped on his shoulder (originally a hard, testing blow). Once knighted, the youth became a man with the title "sir" and the full rights of the warrior caste.

Knighthood was grounded in the feudal ideal of loyalty, and it entailed a complex system of social codes. Breaking any one of those codes would undermine not only the knight's position but also the very institution of knighthood. Thus, in the story of *Sir Gawain and the Green Knight* (page 159), his code of honor binds Gawain to accept a challenge that he believes will bring him certain death.

Feudalism was a pyramid system based on a religious concept of hierarchy. Expected to serve as warriors, males above the serf class were trained as knights.

Women in Medieval Society: No Voice, No Choice

Since they were not soldiers, women had no political rights in a system that was primarily military. A woman was always subservient to a man, whether husband, father, or brother. Her husband's or father's social

Off for a day of haying, a peasant pushes his wife to work in a wheelbarrow. MS Lat. 1173, fol. 4v.
© cliché Bibliothèque Nationale de France, Paris.

standing determined the degree of respect she commanded. For peasant women, life was a ceaseless round of childbearing, housework, and hard fieldwork. Women of higher station were occupied with childbearing and household supervision. Such women might even manage entire estates while their men were away on business or at war, but the moment the men returned, the women relinquished their temporary powers.

Women in the Middle Ages had no political rights. A woman's social standing depended completely on her husband's or father's status.

> A woman is a worthy wight:
> She serveth a man both daye and nyght;
> Thereto she putteth all her might,
>   And yet she hathe but care and woe.
>
> —Anonymous (fifteenth century)

Chivalry and Courtly Love: Ideal but Unreal

Chivalry was a system of ideals and social codes governing the behavior of knights and gentlewomen. Among its precepts were adhering to one's oath of loyalty to the overlord and observing certain rules of warfare, such as never attacking an unarmed opponent. In addition, adoring a particular lady (not necessarily one's wife) was seen as a means of achieving self-improvement.

Noblewomen watching a tournament, from a German manuscript (c. 14th century). Cod. Pal. Germ. 848, Codex Manesse, fol. 52v.

Universitätsbibliothek, Heidelberg.

The idea that revering and acting in the name of a lady would make a knight braver and better was central to one aspect of chivalry, courtly love. Courtly love was, in its ideal form, nonsexual. A knight might wear his lady's colors in battle, he might glorify her in words and be inspired by her, but the lady always remained pure and out of reach. She was "set above" her admirer, just as the feudal lord was set above his vassal. Since such a concept flew in the face of human nature, it provided built-in drama for poets and storytellers, as the King Arthur sagas illustrate. When Sir Lancelot and Queen Guinevere, for example, cross the line between courtly and physical love, the whole social system represented by Arthur's Round Table collapses. Camelot crumbles.

Chivalry brought about an idealized attitude toward women, but it did little to improve their actual position. A woman's perceived value remained tied to the value of the lands she brought to a marriage. But chivalry did give rise to a new form of literature, the romance (page 167). The greatest English example of the genre is *Sir Gawain and the Green Knight.* Wandering minstrels told many other romances, but most of them were the equivalents of *dum-de-dum* doggerel verse today.

> **Chivalry led to an idealized attitude toward women and gave rise to a new form of literature, the romance.**

The New City Classes: Out from Under the Overlords

For the most part, medieval society centered around the feudal castle, but as the population grew, an increasing number of people lived in towns and cities. Eventually, those population centers would render the feudal system obsolete.

The development of the city classes—lower, middle, and upper-middle—is evident in the works of Geoffrey Chaucer (page 98). Many of his characters make

> We may still see on illumined screens the knight, with a change of clothing and locale. He has gone Western, but still he is the dextrous cavalier, vaulting to his saddle, the mighty fighter for virtue, ill educated but possessed of a salty wisdom, worshipful, faithful, and tongue-tied in the presence of good women.
>
> —Morris Bishop

The Middle Ages: Four Centuries of Change

These characteristics distinguished the Middle Ages:

- The Norman Conquest of England created a powerful Anglo-Norman entity and brought England into the mainstream of European civilization.
- The feudal system centralized military, political, and economic power in the Crown.
- The Roman Church transcended national boundaries and fostered cultural unity among Europeans.
- The rise of towns and cities freed people to pursue their own commercial and artistic interests.
- The Magna Carta weakened the political power of the Church and laid the groundwork for later English constitutional law.
- Exposure to Eastern civilization as a result of the Crusades broadened Europeans' intellectual horizons.
- The ideals of chivalry improved attitudes toward, but not the rights of, women.
- The rise of the yeoman class paved the way for democracy in England.
- The bubonic plague created a labor shortage that contributed to the end of feudalism and to the passing of the Middle Ages.

their livings outside the feudal system, and their horizons are defined not by any lord's manor but by such cities as London and Canterbury.

More important, the emerging merchant class had its own tastes in the arts and the ability to pay for what it wanted. Consequently, much medieval art is not aristocratic; it is middle class, even "people's art." The people of the cities were free, tied neither to the land nor to knighthood and chivalry. Their point of view was expressed in the ballads sung in alehouses and at firesides (page 90), in the mystery and miracle plays performed outdoors by the new guilds or craft unions, and even in the great cathedrals and municipal buildings that are synonymous with England to so many tourists today.

Gradually population centers shifted to the cities, where people lived and worked outside of the feudal system.

The Great Happenings

Against the backdrop of the feudal system imported from the Continent, several specific events radically influenced the course of English history, as well as English literature.

The Crusades: Ho! for the Holy Land. In Chaucer's *Canterbury Tales,* we meet a knight who has fought in "heathen" places—along the Mediterranean Sea and in North Africa. The knight's adventures in the fourteenth

Scene from *Passages d' Outremer* (detail) (15th century), depicting the Crusaders' attack, in 1153, on Ascalon, a Muslim-held city on the coast of the Holy Land. MS Fr. 5594, fol. 157v.

century were really an extension of the Crusades (1095–1270), a series of wars waged by European Christians against the Muslims, with Jerusalem and the Holy Land as the prize. Although the Europeans ultimately failed to hold Jerusalem, they benefited enormously from contact with the higher civilization of the Middle East. This contact with Eastern mathematics, astronomy, architecture, and crafts made possible the rich, varied life we find in Chaucer. If the Crusades produced Chaucer's fairly conventional Knight, they were also at least indirectly responsible for his lively Squire and elegant Prioress.

As a result of the Crusades, Christian Europe was exposed to the Middle East's sophisticated civilization.

The martyrdom of Thomas à Becket: Murder in the cathedral.

When Chaucer's pilgrims set out for Canterbury, their goal was the shrine of Saint Thomas à Becket (c. 1118–1170). Thomas, a Norman, had risen to great power as chancellor (prime minister) under his friend King Henry II (reigned 1154–1189). At that time, all Christians belonged to the Catholic Church. Even King Henry was a vassal—of the pope, the head of the Church and God's representative. The pope in those days was enormously powerful and controlled most of the crowned heads of Europe. By appointing his trusted friend Thomas as archbishop of Canterbury (head of the Catholic Church in England), Henry hoped to gain the upper hand in disputes with the Church. But the independent and often combative Thomas took the pope's side more than once, infuriating the king. In December 1170, Henry raged, "Will no one rid me of

Martyrdom of Thomas Becket, from an English psalter (detail) (13th century). MS W34, fol. 15v.

> Then the third knight inflicted a terrible wound as he lay, by which the sword was broken against the pavement, and the crown which was large was separated from the head; so that the blood white with the brain and the brain red with blood, dyed the surface of the virgin mother Church with the life and death of the confessor and martyr in the colors of the lily and the rose.
>
> —Thomas Grim, an eyewitness to Becket's death

this turbulent priest?" Taking his words literally, four of Henry's knights murdered Becket—right in his own cathedral. Public outrage at the murder led to devotion to St. Thomas the Martyr, and created a backlash against Henry, a significant setback for the monarchy in its power struggles with Rome.

At its worst, this setback led to the kinds of liberties taken by several of the clergymen in *The Canterbury Tales*—corruption that the state was in no position to correct. Thus, Chaucer's Monk lives a life of luxury without regard to the poor, his Friar chases women and money, and his Summoner and his Pardoner blackmail people with threats of eternal damnation.

Yet the medieval Church did have one positive effect: It fostered cultural unity—a system of belief and symbol that transcended the national cultures of Europe. The Church continued to be the center of learning. Its monasteries were the libraries and publishers of the time, and its language, Latin, remained the international language of educated Europeans. Its leader, the pope, was king of all kings—and his "kingdom" had no boundaries.

Public outrage at the political assassination of Thomas à Becket created a backlash against the English monarchy and weakened the king in his power struggle with Rome.

The Magna Carta: Power to (some of) the people. The event that most clearly heralded a return to older, democratic tendencies in England was the signing of the Magna Carta (the "Great Charter") by King John in 1215, at Runnymede. The vicious but pragmatic John was strongly backed by the pope, but the English barons forced him to sign the document. The signing was a defeat for central papal power. As aristocrats writing for aristocrats, the barons had no interest in the rights of the common people. But the Magna Carta later became the basis for English constitutional law, in which such rights as trial by jury and legislative taxation were established.

> No freeman shall be taken, or imprisoned, or outlawed, or exiled, or in any way harmed, nor will we go upon him nor will we send upon him, except by the legal judgment of his peers or by the law of the land.
>
> To none will we sell, to none deny or delay, right or justice.
>
> —Magna Carta, Clauses 39 and 40

In 1215, English barons forced King John to sign the Magna Carta as an effort to curb the Church's power. The document later became the basis for English constitutional law.

FLEAS, MONEY, AND GUNPOWDER: THE END OF AN ERA

The legendary pageantry, the codes of chivalry, the heroic quests undertaken by valiant knights in honor of fair ladies—these images come to mind at the mention of the Middle Ages. But what happened? Why did this period come to an end? Besides the plague's devastating effects, the development of a monetary system and the introduction of gunpowder contributed to changes in medieval England.

Before the eleventh century, few coins existed in England and western Europe. The English upper classes used gold and silver valued by weight, and foreign coins were usually melted down and transformed into ingots. Feudal lords made their own coins for use only on their property, and serfs used a barter system for purchases within the community. But the Crusades brought an economic change, for crusaders needed money that would be accepted in other lands. Silver was heavy, but gold coins were light and already in use throughout trade routes. The use of gold coins improved the peasants' buying and selling power; instead of the barter system, they were now able to earn gold in exchange for their labor or goods. The minting of coins was essential in the revival of England's economy.

Chivalric codes governed hand-to-hand combat during much of the Middle Ages. But the use of guns and gunpowder (and strategic military planning) changed all that. Discovered by the Chinese, gunpowder was introduced into English warfare around 1325. By 1346, warfare in the Western world had changed irreversibly. In

The Hundred Years' War (1337–1453): The arrow is mightier than the armor. What might be called the first national war was waged by England against France. Fought on the Continent, the Hundred Years' War was based on dubious claims to the throne of France by two English kings—Edward III (reigned 1327–1377) and Henry V (reigned 1413–1422).

This long war was militarily unsuccessful for the English. But it was an important factor in the gradual development of a British national consciousness. After the war, the English were no longer best represented by the knight in shining armor, an import from the Continent anyway. Instead, they were more accurately represented by the green-clad yeoman (small landowner) with his longbow. These English yeomen had formed the nucleus of the English armies in France. Their yard-long arrows could fly over castle walls and pierce the armor of knights. These small landowners now became a dominant force in the new society that grew out of the ruins of feudalism. The old ideals of chivalry lived on only in stories, such as the King Arthur tales retold by Sir Thomas Malory.

The English lost the Hundred Years' War with France, but by the war's end the yeomen (small landowners) who had formed the nucleus of the English armies had replaced the knights in armor. With this emergence of the yeoman class, modern, democratic England was born.

the landmark battle of Crécy, the French out-numbered the English. The English, aided by the longbow and by explosives, massacred their opponents. Over the next two hundred years, the cannon made the castle—previously impregnable—open to attack.

The rules of war and class had changed. Chivalry was at an end, and feudal obligation became a thing of the past. As a result, a free and prosperous middle class developed, revolutionizing the country's social and economic systems.

Battle of Crécy, from *Chroniques de Froissart* (detail) (14th century). English longbowmen are depicted overcoming French cross-bowmen.

© cliché Bibliothèque Nationale de France, Paris.

Coffin-Making and Burial During the Black Death, from Annales (14th century) by Giles de Mussis (10¾″ × 8″).
© Bibliothèque Royale Albert premier, Brussels.

> The character of the pestilence was appalling. The disease itself, with its frightful symptoms, the swift onset, the blotches, the hardening of the glands under the armpit or in the groin, these swellings which no poultice could resolve, these tumors which, when lanced, gave no relief, the horde of virulent carbuncles which followed the dread harbingers of death, the delirium, the insanity which attended its triumph, the blank spaces which opened on all sides in human society, stunned and for a time destroyed the life and faith of the world.
>
> —Winston Churchill

The Black Death. The Black Death, or bubonic plague, which struck England in 1348–1349, delivered another blow to feudalism. Highly contagious and spread by fleas from infected rats, the disease reduced the nation's population by a third—causing a labor shortage and inevitably giving the lower classes more leverage than ever before against their overlords. One long-term result was the serfs' freedom, which knocked out feudalism's last support. By the time King Henry VII's 1486 marriage reconciled the warring Houses of York and Lancaster, the Middle Ages were ending in England. Henry, a strong king, began the Tudor line that would lead to Elizabeth I. England's Renaissance was about to begin.

The Black Death caused a labor shortage, leading to the serfs' freedom and to the end of feudalism.

Quickwrite

Loyalty lay at the heart of the feudal system. The landowners extracted loyalty from their serfs, the lords expected loyalty from their knights, and the king demanded loyalty from everyone. Has loyalty remained as important in today's society? To whom, or to what, are you loyal, and why? Your answer might include institutions, like school or church, but does it also include ideas? Whom do you expect to be loyal to you, and in what ways? Jot down your thoughts on the issue to discuss with others in the class.

(Opposite) A master with his pupils, from the Chronicles of Hainault (15th century).

Collection 2

THE GIFT OF STORY

Ballads

Chaucer

Boccaccio

from ***Sir Gawain and
the Green Knight***

Malory

The stories people tell have a way of taking care of them. If stories come to you, care for them. And learn to give them away where they are needed. Sometimes a person needs a story more than food to stay alive. That is why we put these stories in each other's memory. This is how people care for themselves. One day you will be good storytellers. Never forget these obligations.

—Barry Lopez (American, 1945–   )

Before You Read

BALLADS

Make the Connection

The Sensational

THREE DEAD SONS VISIT MOTHER FOR DINNER . . . SLIGHTED WOMAN SPURNS LOVER'S DEATHBED REQUEST . . . MAIDEN HEADED FOR GALLOWS; FAMILY REFUSES HELP. These aren't the latest tabloid headlines or current soap opera summaries; they're the plots of medieval ballads. In the Middle Ages, just as today, certain forms of popular entertainment tended toward the sensational.

Since ballads were the poetry of the people, just as popular music is today, their subjects were predictably popular—domestic tragedy, false love, true love, the absurdity of husband-wife relationships, and the supernatural. Unlike today's music, the ballads were not copyrighted by a singer, but were passed down orally from singer to singer. Using a strong beat and repetition, the ballads were a gift of story passed from performer to performer, from generation to generation.

Quickwrite

Suppose a historian from the future were to analyze today's popular songs. How would the historian describe the music you and your friends enjoy? What subjects dominate the songs? (Are popular songs sensational the way the ballads are?) What inferences would the historian draw about us and our culture from the analysis of the songs and the stories they tell? Record your thoughts on these pop-music questions.

Elements of Literature

The Refrain

In concerts today a singer may invite the audience to "join in on the chorus." It's probable that a single singer sang the narrative portions of a ballad while the audience joined in on the **refrain.** The use of the refrain contributed to the song's rhythm and often reinforced its theme, but there was another practical reason for the refrain: It allowed the singer, who sang from memory and often improvised, time to think of the next verse.

> A **refrain** is a repeated word, phrase, line, or group of lines.
>
> *For more on Refrain, see the Handbook of Literary Terms.*

Background

The word *ballad* is originally derived from an Old French word meaning "dancing song." Although the English ballads' connection with dance has been lost, it is clear from their meter and their structure that the original ballads were composed to be sung to music.

The ballads as we know them today probably took their form in the fifteenth century, but they were not printed until three hundred years later when Sir Thomas Percy, Sir Walter Scott, and others traveled around the British Isles and collected them from the people who still sang them.

Illumination from a French manuscript of *Romance of the Rose* (detail) (15th century).
British Library, London.

This ballad is sung in different versions in several countries. The basic story of the song varies little, but Randall is variously known as Donald, Randolph, Ramsay, Ransome, and Durango. Sometimes his last meal consists of fish, sometimes snakes. The dialect of this version is Scottish. This ballad, like many others, is sung entirely as a conversation.

Lord Randall

"O where hae ye been, Lord Randall, my son?
O where hae ye been, my handsome young man?"
"I hae been to the wild wood; mother, make my bed soon,
For I'm weary wi' hunting, and fain° wald lie down."

5 "Where gat ye your dinner, Lord Randall, my son?
Where gat ye your dinner, my handsome young man?"
"I din'd wi' my true-love; mother, make my bed soon,
For I'm weary wi' hunting, and fain wald lie down."

"What gat ye to your dinner, Lord Randall, my son?
10 What gat ye to your dinner, my handsome young man?"
"I gat eels boil'd in broo;° mother, make my bed soon,
For I'm weary wi' hunting, and fain wald lie down."

"What became of your bloodhounds, Lord Randall, my son?
What became of your bloodhounds, my handsome young man?"
15 "O they swell'd and they died; mother, make my bed soon,
For I'm weary wi' hunting, and fain wald lie down."

"O I fear ye are poison'd, Lord Randall, my son!
O I fear ye are poison'd, my handsome young man!"
"O yes! I am poison'd; mother, make my bed soon,
20 For I'm sick at the heart, and I fain wald lie down."

4. fain: gladly.
11. broo: broth.

A knight and his lady feeding a falcon, from a German manuscript (detail) (c. 14th century). Cod. Pal. Germ., 848, Codex Manesse, fol. 249v.

Universitätsbibliothek, Heidelberg.

"Edward, Edward" is an international ballad, one found across northern Europe and brought to England and Scotland by travelers and sailors. Sir Thomas Percy, who compiled many of the popular ballads in the 1760s, found the same character in a Swedish ballad and also noted that another version of this ballad appeared with the title "Son Davie, Son Davie." Another collector changed the hero's name to Edward.

Edward, Edward

"Why does your brand sae drop wi' blude,°
    Edward, Edward?
Why does your brand sae drop wi' blude,
    And why sae sad gang ye,° O?"—
5 "O I hae kill'd my hawk sae gude,°
    Mither, mither;
O I hae kill'd my hawk sae gude,
    And I had nae mair° but he, O."

"Your hawk's blude was never sae red,
10   Edward, Edward;
Your hawk's blude was never sae red,
    My dear son, I tell thee, O."—
"O I hae kill'd my red-roan steed,
    Mither, mither;
15 O I hae kill'd my red-roan steed,
    That erst° was sae fair and free, O."

"Your steed was auld,° and ye hae got mair,
    Edward, Edward;
Your steed was auld, and ye hae got mair;
20   Some other dule ye dree,° O."—
"O I hae kill'd my father dear,
    Mither, mither;
O I hae kill'd my father dear,
    Alas, and wae is me, O!"

25 "And whatten penance will ye dree° for that,
    Edward, Edward?
Whatten penance will ye dree for that?
    My dear son, now tell me, O."—
"I'll set my feet in yonder boat,
30   Mither, mither;
I'll set my feet in yonder boat,
    And I'll fare over the sea, O."

"And what will ye do wi' your tow'rs and your ha',°
    Edward, Edward?
35 And what will ye do wi' your tow'rs and your ha',
    That were sae fair to see, O?"—

1. brand . . . blude: sword so drip with blood.

4. gang ye: go you.
5. gude: good.

8. nae mair: no more.

16. erst: before.

17. auld: old.

20. dule ye dree: grief you suffer.

25. whatten . . . dree: what punishment for sin will you suffer.

33. ha': hall; that is, ancestral home.

American Folk and Country and Western Music

When English, Scottish, Welsh, and Irish people left their homes to settle in America, the old ballads were part of their baggage. Some ballads have changed little since then. When researchers traveled through the southern Appalachian Mountains in the early 1900s to record the songs of the mountain people, they found them singing "John Randolph," a ballad markedly similar to "Lord Randall." On the other hand, "Streets of Laredo," which tells the story of a cowboy dying of a gunshot wound, retains the remnants of its British ancestry only in the line, "Oh beat the drum slowly and play the fife lowly." The fife and drum refer to a British military funeral. Even country and folk ballads written in this century tend to repeat the subjects and themes of the old medieval ballads. Consider:

- **ballads with supernatural elements,** such as the country and western song "Phantom 309" about ghost truck drivers;

- **ballads based on actual tragedies,** such as the country and western song "Ballad of the Green Berets" from the Vietnam War era and the folk songs "Birmingham Sunday" from the civil rights struggle of the sixties and "The Wreck of the Edmund Fitzgerald" about a twentieth-century sea tragedy;

- **ballads about domestic disasters,** such as the country and western song "The Grand Tour," about a singer who tours his home after his wife has left him.

"I'll let them stand till they doun fa',
    Mither, mither;
I'll let them stand till they doun fa',
40   For here never mair maun° I be, O."

40. maun: must.

"And what will ye leave to your bairns° and your wife,
    Edward, Edward?
And what will ye leave to your bairns and your wife,
    When ye gang owre the sea, O?"—
45 "The warld's room: let them beg through life,
    Mither, mither;
The warld's room: let them beg through life;
    For them never mair will I see, O."

41. bairns: children.

"And what will ye leave to your ain° mither dear,
50   Edward, Edward?
And what will ye leave to your ain mither dear,
    My dear son, now tell me, O?"—
"The curse of hell frae me sall ye bear,
    Mither, mither;
55 The curse of hell frae me sall ye bear:
    Sic° counsels ye gave to me, O!"

49. ain: own.

56. sic: such.

The story in this ballad exists in many versions in Europe, Asia, and the Middle East—perhaps illustrating the universal theme called the battle of the sexes. "Goodwife" and "goodman" are terms once applied to married men and women, something like "Mr." and "Mrs." today.

The story takes place around November 11—Martinmas, or the feast of St. Martin of Tours, which was usually celebrated with a big meal.

The Chef (15th century). Woodcut.

Get Up and Bar the Door

It fell about the Martinmas time,
    And a gay time it was then,
When our goodwife got puddings° to make,
    And she's boild them in the pan.

5 The wind sae cauld blew south and north,
    And blew into the floor;
Quoth our goodman to our goodwife,
    "Gae out and bar the door."

"My hand is in my hussyfskap,°
10   Goodman, as ye may see;
An° it should nae be barrd this hundred year,
    It's no be barrd for me."

They made a paction tween them twa,
    They made it firm and sure,
15 That the first word whaeer should speak,
    Should rise and bar the door.

Then by there came two gentlemen,
    At twelve o clock at night,
And they could neither see house nor hall,
20   Nor coal nor candle-light.

"Now whether is this a rich man's house,
    Or whether it is a poor?"
But neer a word ane° o them speak,
    For barring of the door.

25 And first they ate the white puddings,
    And then they ate the black;
Tho muckle° thought the goodwife to hersel,
    Yet neer a word she spake.

Then said the one unto the other,
30   "Here, man, tak ye my knife;
Do ye tak aff the auld man's beard,
    And I'll kiss the goodwife."

"But there's nae water in the house,°
    And what shall we do than?"
35 "What ails ye at the pudding-broo,°
    That boils into the pan?"

O up then started our goodman,
    An angry man was he:
"Will ye kiss my wife before my een,
40   And scad° me wi pudding-bree?"°

Then up and started our goodwife,
    Gied three skips on the floor:
"Goodman, you've spoken the foremost word,
    Get up and bar the door."

3. **puddings:** sausages, the black ones being made with blood.
9. **hussyfskap** (hu′zif·skep): household chores.
11. **an:** if.
23. **ane:** one.

27. **muckle:** much.
33. **but . . . house:** He probably wants water to soften the husband's beard.
35. **what . . . pudding-broo:** What's wrong with using the pudding broth?
40. **scad:** scald. **bree:** broth.

"Frankie and Johnny," one of the most famous of American ballads, comes out of the Midwest and the Mississippi River region. Like most ballads, it tells of love gone wrong.

Frankie and Johnny

words by **Boyd Bunch**

Frankie and Johnny were lovers
Oh, Lordy, how they could love.
They swore to be true to each other,
True as the stars above.
He was her man, but he was doing her wrong.

Frankie she was a good woman
As everybody knows.
Spent a hundred dollars
Just to buy her man some clothes.
He was her man, but he was doing her wrong.

Frankie went down to the corner
Just for a bucket of beer.
Said: "Mr. Bartender,
Has my loving Johnny been here?
He was my man, but he's a-doing me wrong."

"Now I don't want to tell you no stories,
And I don't want to tell you no lies.
I saw your man about an hour ago
With a gal named Nellie Bligh.
He was your man, but he's a-doing you wrong."

Frankie she went down to the hotel,
Didn't go there for fun.
Underneath her kimono
She carried a forty-four gun.
He was her man, but he was doing her wrong.

Frankie looked over the transom
To see what she could spy.
There sat Johnny on the sofa
Just loving up Nellie Bligh.
He was her man, but he was doing her wrong.

Frankie got down from that high stool,
She didn't want to see no more.
Rooty-toot-toot three times she shot
Right through that hardwood door.
He was her man, but he was doing her wrong.

Now the first time that Frankie shot Johnny,
He let out an awful yell.
Second time she shot him
There was a new man's face in hell.
He was her man, but he was doing her wrong.

"Oh, roll me over easy,
Roll me over slow.
Roll me over on the right side,
For the left side hurts me so."
He was her man, but he was doing her wrong.

Sixteen rubber-tired carriages
Sixteen rubber-tired hacks
They take poor Johnny to the graveyard—
They ain't gonna bring him back.
He was her man, but he was doing her wrong.

Frankie looked out of the jailhouse
To see what she could see.
All she could hear was a two-string bow
Crying, "Nearer my God to thee."
He was her man, but he was doing her wrong.

Frankie she said to the sheriff,
"What do you reckon they'll do?"
Sheriff he said, "Frankie,
It's the electric chair for you."
He was her man, but he was doing her wrong.

This story has no moral.
This story has no end.
This story only goes to show
That there ain't no good in men.
He was her man, but he was doing her wrong.

MAKING MEANINGS

Lord Randall
Edward, Edward
Get Up and Bar the Door

First Thoughts

1. The appeal of the ballads lies partly in what they don't tell you. What questions does each of these songs leave unanswered for you?

Shaping Interpretations

2. What is the emotional effect of the **refrain's** variation in the fifth stanza of "Lord Randall"?

3. Like many ballads, "Lord Randall" and "Edward, Edward" build up suspense with **incremental repetition:** the repetition of lines with a new element introduced each time to advance the story until a climax is reached. At what point in each ballad does the story reach a climax?

4. What could be the implications of Edward's last response to his mother in the final stanza of "Edward, Edward"?

5. How is the possibility of violence combined with ironic humor in "Get Up and Bar the Door"?

Extending the Texts

6. What popular songs or folk ballads do you know that focus on subjects like the ones in these three famous medieval ballads? Refer to your Quickwrite entry (page 90) for possible ideas.

September, calendar page from the Salting Manuscript, *Hours of Margaret de Foix* (c. 1470–1480).

Victoria and Albert Museum, London.

7. People often criticize the media today for glorifying violence. Do you think these ballads, including "Frankie and Johnny" (see *Connections* on page 95), glorify violence by singing about it? Why or why not? Is the issue the same? Discuss your responses.

ELEMENTS OF LITERATURE

Ballads: Popular Poetry

Ballads come from an oral tradition, so there are no strict rules dictating their form. However, a number of characteristics have come to be associated with ballads, and every ballad reflects at least some of them: **supernatural events; sensational, sordid, or tragic subject matter; a refrain;** and the **omission of details.** The ballad singers also used some of the following conventions:

• **incremental repetition,** to build up suspense. A phrase or sentence is repeated with a new element added each time, until the climax is reached.

• **a question-and-answer format,** in which the facts of a story are gleaned little by little from the answers. Again, this device builds up suspense.

• **conventional phrases,** understood by listeners to have meaning beyond their literal ones. "Make my bed soon" in "Lord Randall" is an example. Whenever a character in a ballad asks someone to make his bed, or to make her bed narrow, it means that the speaker is preparing for death.

• **a strong, simple beat,** with verse forms that are relatively uncomplicated. Ballads were sung for a general, rather than an elitist, audience. Only later, in the era of so-called literary ballads (more sophisticated poems that artfully evoked the atmosphere of the originals), did the rhyme scheme (*abcb*) and meter (a quatrain in which lines of four stresses alternate with lines of three stresses) of the ballad stanza become standard.

Giving an oral performance. With a small group, select a ballad and prepare it for performance. Have an audience **evaluate** your first performance according to **criteria** you all agree on (such as clarity of story, emotional appeal, and so on). Use your audience's evaluations to perfect your final performance.

CHOICES: Building Your Portfolio

Writer's Notebook

1. Collecting Ideas for a Comparison-Contrast Essay

In the Writer's Workshop on page 185, you'll write an essay in which you compare and contrast two or more pieces of literature or two or more elements in several pieces of literature. These ballads (including the American ballad "Frankie and Johnny") would make excellent subjects for your essay. To gather notes, refer to the ballad characteristics listed on page 96. Make a list of these characteristics and indicate where and how they are used in each ballad. Be sure to take notes on the subjects of the ballads. Save your notes for later use.

Research/Expository Writing

2. A Ballad Book

Find at least four American ballads and present them in a printed form that can be kept in the classroom for future reference. Write a brief introduction to each ballad, telling what you have learned about its origins.

Creative Writing

3. The Saddest Story

Try writing a folk ballad in four-line stanzas on a subject of your choice. Look for possible subjects in the newspaper or on television. Your ballad should tell a brief story, perhaps about some domestic or historic tragedy, and should include at least four ballad characteristics. You might imitate "Lord Randall" and "Edward, Edward," and tell your story in dialogue.

Expository Writing

4. Late-Breaking News!

Take one of the basic situations in these ballads, and retell it as a contemporary news story. Be sure to tell *what* happened, *where* and *when* it happened, *whom* it happened to, *why* it happened, and *how* it happened. Present your news story in print form, complete with headlines, or orally as a segment of a simulated television or radio newscast, complete with a lead.

Research/Comparing Versions

5. The Many Faces of Lord Randall

"Lord Randall" is supposed to have 103 known variations. Find one or two different versions to compare to the original "Lord Randall." (Or select another traditional ballad that exists in several versions.) In a

A musician, from a German manuscript (c. 14th century). Cod. Pal. Germ. 848, Codex Manesse, fol. 312r.

short essay, compare the ballad versions, noting similarities and differences. As part of your essay, try speculating on why certain details in the ballad might have been changed by subsequent singers.

Music/Cultural Comparisons

6. Bringing the Ballads to Life

If you play a musical instrument or sing, try performing some ballads from another culture for your classmates. Or you may collect recordings of the ballads and play them in class. Discuss the ways these ballads are like or unlike the traditional English ballads. For example, do ballads of other cultures have refrains? Do they emphasize feeling over thought?

Geoffrey Chaucer

(c. 1343–1400)

Geoffrey Chaucer (1400) by an unknown artist.

By Courtesy of the National Portrait Gallery, London.

Geoffrey Chaucer, often called the father of English poetry, made the English language respectable.

Ordinary people in Chaucer's England spoke the Anglo-Norman composite now called Middle English, a language that became the ancestor of Modern English. But in Chaucer's time the languages of literature, science, diplomacy, and religion were still Latin and French. Before Chaucer it was not fashionable for serious poets to write in English. People felt that English couldn't possibly convey all the nuances and complexities of serious literature. There were, it is true, some exceptions: The so-called Gawain poet (page 158) wrote in a northwestern dialect of English, and, of course, there were the popular ballads.

But the poets who wrote these works lacked the social stature of Chaucer. Chaucer was a well-known government official who served under three kings—Edward III, Richard II, and Henry IV. By composing in the **vernacular**—the everyday language spoken in London and the East Midlands—Chaucer lent respectability to a language that would develop into the medium for one of the world's greatest bodies of literature. In this sense, he was indeed the father of English poetry.

Friends in High Places

Not a great deal is known of Chaucer's life. He was born into a middle-class family in London in the early 1340s, not long after the beginning of the Hundred Years' War. We are told that his father was a wine merchant who had enough money to provide his son with some education. The young Chaucer read a great deal and had some legal training. He became a page to an eminent family from whom he received the finest training in good manners. As he advanced in his government career, he became attached to several noble patrons.

We know, too, that Chaucer was captured in France while serving as a soldier during the Hundred Years' War and that he was important enough to have the king contribute to his ransom. We also know that he married Philippa and had at least two children and that he was on several occasions sent to Europe as the king's ambassador. In 1367, he was awarded the first of several pensions for his services to the Crown. (On April 23, 1374, he was granted the promise of a daily pitcher of wine.) In 1385, he was appointed justice of the peace in the county of Kent, later becoming a member of Parliament. He continued to serve and to enjoy the king's protection.

Writing and Holding a Job

It seems clear that Chaucer was a relatively important government servant and that his work took precedence over his writing. (It would be as if a prominent adviser to the United States president were also a highly acclaimed poet.) Yet he wrote a great deal, and sometimes for personal advancement. In about 1369, for example, he composed his first important poem, *The Book of the Duchess,* in memory of his patron's wife, who had just died of the plague. But Chaucer's writing is just as clearly more than an attempt at political advancement or a passing fancy. Despite his government responsibilities, between 1374 and 1386, Chaucer managed to create several great allegorical poems, including the *House of Fame* and the *Parliament of Fowls,* and his poignant and amusing love story *Troilus and Criseyde.*

The Italian Connection

In 1372 and 1378, Chaucer traveled in Italy, where he was very likely influenced by the poems of Dante and Petrarch and by the stories of Giovanni Boccaccio (page 152). The connection between Boccaccio's collection of tales called the *Decameron* (c. 1348–1353) and Chaucer's *Canterbury Tales* (c. 1387–1400) is evident. Both use a framing device within which the characters tell their tales, and both include tales based on similar old plots. The framing device in the *Decameron* is a group of people who have fled the plague-ridden city of Florence and tell stories to while away their time in the country. Chaucer's frame is a religious pilgrimage during which each traveler is to tell four stories, two going out and two returning.

Chaucer began writing *The Canterbury Tales* in 1387, during a few years of unemployment when his patron was out of the country. Perhaps because he felt that he had lost his ability to find rhymes, he never completed all the stories. But the collection still must be considered one of the greatest works in the English language. *The Canterbury Tales* alone—even only the Prologue, where each traveler is described—would be sufficient to place Chaucer in the company of Shakespeare and Milton.

The Force of Personality

What is so great about *The Canterbury Tales?* In part, its greatness lies in Chaucer's language. But its greatness also comes from the sheer strength of Chaucer's spirit and personality. John Gardner, one of Chaucer's many biographers, offers a tribute to Chaucer's lasting power:

> In a dark, troubled age, as it seems to us, he was a comfortable optimist, serene, full of faith. For all his delight in irony—and all his poetry has a touch of that—he affirmed this life, to say nothing of the next, from the bottom of his capacious heart. Joy—satisfaction without a trace of sentimental simple-mindedness—is still the effect of Chaucer's poetry and of Chaucer's personality as it emerges from the poems. It is not

the simple faith of a credulous man in a credulous age: No poet has ever written better on the baffling complexity of things. But for all the foggy shiftings of the heart and mind, for all the obscurity of God's huge plan, to Chaucer life was a magnificent affair, though sadly transient; and when we read him now, six centuries later, we are instantly persuaded.

The End of the Old Alliterative Anglo-Saxon World

Chaucer used several metrical forms and some prose in *The Canterbury Tales,* but the dominant meter is based on ten syllables, with an unstressed syllable followed by a stressed syllable. We call this meter **iambic pentameter.** It is a rhythm that most closely matches the way English is spoken. You might hear this rhythm if you read aloud this line in Middle English (*swich* means "sweet"):

And báthĕd évĕry véyne ĭn swích lícŏur

When we read a line such as this, we experience a version of the meter that was to become the most popular metrical line in English. At a stroke, we have abandoned the old, alliterative world of the Anglo-Saxons and have entered the modern world of Shakespeare, Wordsworth, and even America's Robert Frost.

The Father in the Family Vault

Chaucer died on October 25, 1400, if we are to believe the date on his tombstone (which an admirer erected in Westminster Abbey in 1556). Chaucer was the very first of those many famous English writers who would be gathered into what we know as the Poets' Corner in Westminster Abbey—one of the great tourist sights in London today. "The Father of English poetry," notes Nevill Coghill, "lies in his family vault."

The Canterbury Tales:
Snapshot of an Age

The Canterbury Tales gives us a collection of good stories and a snapshot, a picture frozen in time, of life in the Middle Ages. To include the complete range of medieval society in the same picture, Chaucer places his characters on a pilgrimage, a religious journey made to a shrine or holy place. These pilgrims, like a collection of people on tour today, are from many stations and stages of life. Together they travel on horseback from London to the shrine of the martyr Saint Thomas à Becket at Canterbury Cathedral, about fifty-five miles to the southeast.

The *Tales* begin with a General Prologue, the first lines of which establish that this pilgrimage takes place in the spring, the archetypal time of new life and awakening. Fifty-five miles is a long journey by horseback, especially along muddy tracks that would hardly pass as roads today. An inn was always a welcome oasis, even if it provided few luxuries. The poet-pilgrim narrator, whom many consider to be Chaucer himself, starts out at the Tabard Inn in Southwark, a borough in the south of London, where he meets twenty-nine other pilgrims also bound for Canterbury. It is the host of the Tabard who suggests to the pilgrims, as they sit around the fire after dinner, that they exchange tales to pass the time along the way to Canterbury and back to London. The host's suggestion sets up Chaucer's frame story—the main story of the pilgrimage that includes each pilgrim's story.

As the Prologue progresses and we are introduced to the pilgrims, Chaucer's brilliant picture of life in late medieval England comes into focus. Here is what Nevill Coghill, one of Chaucer's translators, says about the Prologue:

Page from *The Canterbury Tales,* from the Ellesmere manuscript (15th century).

By permission of The Huntington Library, San Marino, California.

Pages from *The Canterbury Tales,* from the Ellesmere manuscript (15th century).

Chaucer, from the Ellesmere manuscript, fol. 153v.

In all literature there is nothing that touches or resembles the *Prologue.* It is the concise portrait of an entire nation, high and low, old and young, male and female, lay and clerical, learned and ignorant, rogue and righteous, land and sea, town and country, but without extremes. Apart from the stunning clarity, touched with nuance, of the characters presented, the most noticeable thing about them is their normality. They are the perennial progeny of men and women. Sharply individual, together they make a party.

At its most basic level, Chaucer's great work possesses an archetypal unity. As a pilgrimage story, it is one of the world's many quest narratives, and it moves appropriately from images of spring and awakening at the beginning of the Prologue to images of penance, death, and eternal life in the Parson's tale at the end of the work. The storytellers themselves are pilgrims, presumably in search of renewal at the Thomas à Becket shrine. Coming as they do from all walks of life, all social classes, they cannot help but represent "everyman," or all of us, on our universal pilgrimage through life.

Chaucer's Middle English is here translated into Modern English by Nevill Coghill. While this version is true to the spirit of Chaucer's original poem, you might attempt at least bits of the *Tales* in the wonderfully musical original.

Brief Pronunciation Guide to Middle English

Vowels

a: *ah,* as in *father.*

ai, ay, ei, ey: a long *a,* as in *pay.*

au, aw: *ow,* as in *house.*

oo: *oh,* as in *oat.*

e: at times, like a long *a,* as in *mate.* When a double *e* is used, it is always long. *Eek* is pronounced āk.

e: at times, like a short *e,* as in *men.*

The final *e* in Middle English is a separate syllable sounded like a final *ah: soote* rhymes with *soda.* But when the final *e* precedes a word that starts with a vowel or an *h,* it is not sounded. In "droghte of March," the final *e* in *droghte* is silent.

Consonants

g: hard *g,* as in *go,* except before *e* or *i* (in words borrowed from French) where it is sounded like *zh,* as in *garage. Pilgrimage* rhymes with *garage.*

gh, ch: like the German *ch,* as in *nicht.* (These sounds are usually silent in Modern English.) *Knight* is pronounced k·nicht'.

–tion, –cial: The *t* and *c* in such words are not blended with the *i* as they are in Modern English (as in the words *condition* and *special*). The *i* is sounded as a separate syllable. *Special* would have three syllables and *condition* four: kon·di·sē·ôn'. (*C* has the sound of *s* when it comes before *i.*)

Before You Read

FROM THE CANTERBURY TALES

Make the Connection

From Sketch to Portrait

If you went on a tour today, what types of people would you expect to meet? Most of Chaucer's pilgrims are the kinds of people he would have known and perhaps even observed many times riding toward Canterbury on the old pilgrimage road. Here in the *Tales* is a cross section of medieval life: the conservative military man, the talkative and often-married feminist, the lover, the barnyard humorist, the elegant and Frenchified nun, to name a few. Chaucer seems mainly to describe his travelers' appearances in what appear to be mere physical sketches. But a close reading shows that he has cleverly selected details that give us shrewd psychological portraits as well.

Quickwrite

Spend a few minutes describing a real or an imaginary person's appearance, from tip to toe. Try to show how certain details of the person's appearance suggest certain character traits (that she is miserly, that he is vain, that he wants to look like a popular rock star, and so on). Keep your notes.

Elements of Literature

Characterization

To create the portraits of his pilgrim characters—"nine and twenty in a company of sundry folk," Chaucer uses the methods of characterization that writers continue to use to this day. Like his contemporary counterparts, Chaucer reveals his characters

- by telling us directly what the character is like
- by describing how the character looks and dresses
- by presenting the character's words and actions
- by revealing the character's private thoughts and feelings
- by showing how other people respond to the character

Characterization is the process by which the writer reveals the personality of a character.

For more on Character, see the Handbook of Literary Terms.

Background

When Chaucer chooses to have each of his pilgrims tell a story on the way to Canterbury, he is using a popular literary device, the frame story. A **frame story** is a story that includes any number of different narratives. Chaucer uses the outer story of the pilgrimage to unite his travelers' individual tales, and the tales themselves have thematic unity as well. The hundred tales in Boccaccio's *Decameron* (page 154) and the roughly one hundred tales in *The Arabian Nights* are each set within a single fictional frame as well. The frame story is still used today. If you've read Amy Tan's *The Joy Luck Club,* you've read a modern frame story.

Chaucer reciting his poetry. Ms. 61, fr.

The Master and Fellows of Corpus Christi College, Cambridge.

Here bygynneth the Book of the Tales of Caunterbury.

Whan that Aprill with his shoures soote
The droghte of March hath perced to the roote
And bathed every veyne in swich licour
Of which vertu engendred is the flour,
5   Whan Zephirus eek with his sweete breeth
Inspired hath in every holt and heeth
The tendre croppes, and the yonge sonne
Hath in the Ram his half cours y-ronne,
And smale foweles maken melodye
10 That slepen al the nyght with open eye,
So priketh hem Nature in hir corages,
Than longen folk to goon on pilgrymages,
And palmeres for to seken straunge strondes,
To ferne halwes kouthe in sondry londes.
15 And specially, from every shires ende
Of Engelond, to Caunterbury they wende,
The holy, blisful martir for to seke
That hem hath holpen whan that they were seeke
Bifel that in that sesoun on a day
20 In Southwerk at the Tabard, as I lay
Redy to wenden on my pilgrymage
To Caunterbury with ful devout corage,
At nyght was come into that hostelrye
Wel nyne-and-twenty in a compaignye
25 Of sondry folk by aventure y-falle
In felaweshipe, and pilgrymes were they alle
That toward Caunterbury wolden ryde.
The chambres and the stables weren wyde,
And wel we weren esed atte beste;
30 And shortly, whan the sonne was to reste,
So hadde I spoken with hem everichon
That I was of hir felaweshipe anon;
And made forward erly for to ryse
To take oure wey ther-as I yow devyse.
35   But, nathelees, whil I have tyme and space,
Er that I ferther in this tale pace,
Me thynketh it acordant to resoun
To telle yow al the condicioun
Of ech of hem so as it semed me,
40 And whiche they weren, and of what degree,
And eek in what array that they were inne;
And at a knyght than wol I first bigynne.

Page from *The Canterbury Tales,* from the Ellesmere manuscript (detail) (15th century).

from The Canterbury Tales

Geoffrey Chaucer
translated by **Nevill Coghill**

The Prologue

When in April the sweet showers fall
And pierce the drought of March to the root, and all
The veins are bathed in liquor of such power
As brings about the <u>engendering</u> of the flower,
5   When also Zephyrus° with his sweet breath
Exhales an air in every grove and heath
Upon the tender shoots, and the young sun
His half-course in the sign of the *Ram°* has run,
And the small fowl are making melody
10   That sleep away the night with open eye
(So nature pricks them and their heart engages)
Then people long to go on pilgrimages
And palmers° long to seek the stranger strands
Of far-off saints, hallowed in sundry lands,
15   And specially, from every shire's end
Of England, down to Canterbury they wend
To seek the holy blissful martyr,° quick
To give his help to them when they were sick.
     It happened in that season that one day
20   In Southwark, at *The Tabard,* as I lay
Ready to go on pilgrimage and start
For Canterbury, most devout at heart,
At night there came into that hostelry
Some nine and twenty in a company
25   Of sundry folk happening then to fall
In fellowship, and they were pilgrims all
That towards Canterbury meant to ride.
The rooms and stables of the inn were wide:
They made us easy, all was of the best.
30   And, briefly, when the sun had gone to rest,
I'd spoken to them all upon the trip
And was soon one with them in fellowship,
Pledged to rise early and to take the way
To Canterbury, as you heard me say.
35   But none the less, while I have time and space,
Before my story takes a further pace,
It seems a reasonable thing to say

5. Zephyrus (zefʹə·rəs): in Greek mythology, god of the west wind.

8. Ram: Aries, first sign of the zodiac. The time is mid-April.

13. palmers: people who had visited the Holy Land and wore palm fronds to show it.

17. martyr: Saint Thomas à Becket (c. 1118–1170) was martyred at Canterbury, December 29, 1170.

WORDS TO OWN
engendering (en·jenʹdər·iŋ) *v.* used as *n.:* creation; production.

Miniature of John Lydgate and the Canterbury pilgrims leaving Canterbury, from a volume of Lydgate's poems (early 16th century). MS Royal 18 D II, fol. 148.

British Library, London.

What their condition was, the full array
Of each of them, as it appeared to me,
40 According to profession and degree,
And what apparel they were riding in;
And at a Knight I therefore will begin.
There was a *Knight,* a most distinguished man,
Who from the day on which he first began
45 To ride abroad had followed chivalry,
Truth, honor, generousness, and courtesy.
He had done nobly in his sovereign's war
And ridden into battle, no man more,
As well in Christian as in heathen places,

50 And ever honored for his noble graces.
    When we took Alexandria,° he was there.
He often sat at table in the chair
Of honor, above all nations, when in Prussia.
In Lithuania he had ridden, and Russia,
55 No Christian man so often, of his rank.
When, in Granada, Algeciras sank
Under assault, he had been there, and in
North Africa, raiding Benamarin;
In Anatolia he had been as well
60 And fought when Ayas and Attalia fell,
For all along the Mediterranean coast
He had embarked with many a noble host.
In fifteen mortal battles he had been
And jousted for our faith at Tramissene
65 Thrice in the lists, and always killed his man.
This same distinguished knight had led the van
Once with the Bey of Balat, doing work
For him against another heathen Turk;
He was of sovereign value in all eyes.
70 And though so much distinguished, he was wise
And in his bearing modest as a maid.
He never yet a boorish thing had said
In all his life to any, come what might;
He was a true, a perfect gentle-knight.°
75   Speaking of his equipment, he possessed
Fine horses, but he was not gaily dressed.
He wore a fustian° tunic stained and dark
With smudges where his armor had left mark;
Just home from service, he had joined our ranks
80 To do his pilgrimage and render thanks.
    He had his son with him, a fine young *Squire,*
A lover and cadet,° a lad of fire
With locks as curly as if they had been pressed.
He was some twenty years of age, I guessed.
85 In stature he was of a moderate length,
With wonderful agility and strength.
He'd seen some service with the cavalry
In Flanders and Artois and Picardy
And had done valiantly in little space
90 Of time, in hope to win his lady's grace.
He was embroidered like a meadow bright
And full of freshest flowers, red and white.
Singing he was, or fluting all the day;
He was as fresh as is the month of May.
95 Short was his gown, the sleeves were long and wide;

WORDS TO OWN
stature (stach′ər) *n.*: height.

51. Alexandria: city in Egypt captured by the Crusaders in 1365. In the next few lines, Chaucer is indicating the knight's distinguished and extensive career.

The Knight, from the Ellesmere manuscript, fol. 10r.

By permission of The Huntington Library, San Marino, California.

74. gentle-knight: In Chaucer's day, *gentle* meant "well bred and considerate."

77. fustian (fus′chən): coarse cloth made of linen and cotton.

82. cadet: soldier.

The Squire, from the Ellesmere manuscript, fol. 115v.

By permission of The Huntington Library, San Marino, California.

He knew the way to sit a horse and ride.
He could make songs and poems and recite,
Knew how to joust and dance, to draw and write.
He loved so hotly that till dawn grew pale
100 He slept as little as a nightingale.
Courteous he was, lowly and serviceable,
And carved to serve his father at the table.
　　There was a *Yeoman* with him at his side,
No other servant; so he chose to ride.
105 This Yeoman wore a coat and hood of green,
And peacock-feathered arrows, bright and keen
And neatly sheathed, hung at his belt the while
—For he could dress his gear in yeoman style,
His arrows never drooped their feathers low—
110 And in his hand he bore a mighty bow.
His head was like a nut, his face was brown.
He knew the whole of woodcraft up and down.
A saucy brace was on his arm to ward
It from the bow-string, and a shield and sword
115 Hung at one side, and at the other slipped
A jaunty dirk,° spear-sharp and well-equipped.
A medal of St. Christopher° he wore
Of shining silver on his breast, and bore
A hunting-horn, well slung and burnished clean,
120 That dangled from a baldrick° of bright green.
He was a proper forester, I guess.
　　There also was a *Nun,* a Prioress,
Her way of smiling very simple and coy.
Her greatest oath was only "By St. Loy!"°
125 And she was known as Madam Eglantyne.
And well she sang a service, with a fine
Intoning through her nose, as was most seemly,
And she spoke daintily in French, extremely,
After the school of Stratford-atte-Bowe;°
130 French in the Paris style she did not know.
At meat her manners were well taught withal;
No morsel from her lips did she let fall,
Nor dipped her fingers in the sauce too deep;
But she could carry a morsel up and keep
135 The smallest drop from falling on her breast.
For courtliness she had a special zest,
And she would wipe her upper lip so clean
That not a trace of grease was to be seen
Upon the cup when she had drunk; to eat,
140 She reached a hand sedately for the meat.
She certainly was very entertaining,
Pleasant and friendly in her ways, and straining
To counterfeit a courtly kind of grace,
A stately bearing fitting to her place,

The Canon Yeoman, from the
Ellesmere manuscript, fol. 194r.

By permission of The Huntington Library,
San Marino, California.

116. dirk: long dagger.

117. St. Christopher: patron saint
of travelers.

120. baldrick: belt slung over the
shoulder and chest to hold a sword.

124. St. Loy: Saint Eligius, known
for his perfect manners.

129. Stratford-atte-Bowe: Benedictine convent near London where inferior French was spoken.

The Prioress, from the Ellesmere
manuscript, fol. 148v.

By permission of The Huntington Library,
San Marino, California.

145 And to seem dignified in all her dealings.
As for her sympathies and tender feelings,
She was so charitably solicitous
She used to weep if she but saw a mouse
Caught in a trap, if it were dead or bleeding.
150 And she had little dogs she would be feeding
With roasted flesh, or milk, or fine white bread.
And bitterly she wept if one were dead
Or someone took a stick and made it smart;
She was all sentiment and tender heart.
155 Her veil was gathered in a seemly way,
Her nose was elegant, her eyes glass-gray;
Her mouth was very small, but soft and red,
Her forehead, certainly, was fair of spread,
Almost a span° across the brows, I own;
160 She was indeed by no means undergrown.
Her cloak, I noticed, had a graceful charm.
She wore a coral trinket on her arm,
A set of beads, the gaudies tricked in green,°
Whence hung a golden brooch of brightest sheen
165 On which there first was graven a crowned A,
And lower, *Amor vincit omnia.*°
   Another *Nun,* the secretary at her cell,°
Was riding with her, and *three Priests* as well.
   A *Monk* there was, one of the finest sort
170 Who rode the country; hunting was his sport.
A manly man, to be an Abbott able;
Many a dainty horse he had in stable.
His bridle, when he rode, a man might hear
Jingling in a whistling wind as clear,
175 Aye, and as loud as does the chapel bell
Where my lord Monk was Prior of the cell.
The Rule of good St. Benet or St. Maur°
As old and strict he tended to ignore;
He let go by the things of yesterday
180 And took the modern world's more spacious way.
He did not rate that text at a plucked hen
Which says that hunters are not holy men
And that a monk uncloistered is a mere
Fish out of water, flapping on the pier,
185 That is to say a monk out of his cloister.
That was a text he held not worth an oyster;
And I agreed and said his views were sound;
Was he to study till his head went round
Poring over books in cloisters? Must he toil
190 As Austin° bade and till the very soil?
Was he to leave the world upon the shelf?
Let Austin have his labor to himself.
   This Monk was therefore a good man to horse;

The Nun's Priest, from the Ellesmere manuscript, fol. 179r.

By permission of The Huntington Library, San Marino, California.

159. span: nine inches.

163. a set of beads . . . green: Beads are a rosary, or prayer beads and a crucifix on a string or chain. Every eleventh bead is a gaud, a large bead indicating when the Lord's Prayer is to be said.
166. *Amor vincit omnia* (ä′môr′ vin′chit ôm′nē·ä′): Latin for "Love conquers all."
167. cell: a small convent connected to a larger one.

177. St. Benet [Benedict] **or St. Maur** [Maurice]: Saint Benedict (c. 480–c. 547) was an Italian monk who founded numerous monasteries and wrote a famous code of regulations for monastic life. Saint Maurice was a follower of Benedict.

190. Austin: Saint Augustine (354–430), bishop of Hippo in North Africa. He criticized lazy monks and suggested they do some hard manual labor.

Greyhounds he had, as swift as birds, to course.°
195 Hunting a hare or riding at a fence
Was all his fun, he spared for no expense.
I saw his sleeves were garnished at the hand
With fine gray fur, the finest in the land,
And on his hood, to fasten it at his chin
200 He had a wrought-gold, cunningly fashioned pin;
Into a lover's knot it seemed to pass.
His head was bald and shone like looking-glass;
So did his face, as if it had been greased.
He was a fat and <u>personable</u> priest;
205 His prominent eyeballs never seemed to settle.
They glittered like the flames beneath a kettle;
Supple his boots, his horse in fine condition.
He was a prelate fit for exhibition,
He was not pale like a tormented soul.
210 He liked a fat swan best, and roasted whole.
His palfrey° was as brown as is a berry.
   There was a *Friar,* a wanton° one and merry,
A Limiter,° a very festive fellow.
In all Four Orders° there was none so mellow,
215 So glib with gallant phrase and well-turned speech.
He'd fixed up many a marriage, giving each
Of his young women what he could afford her.
He was a noble pillar to his Order.
Highly beloved and intimate was he
220 With County folk within his boundary,
And city dames of honor and possessions;
For he was qualified to hear confessions,
Or so he said, with more than priestly scope;
He had a special license from the Pope.
225 Sweetly he heard his penitents at shrift°
With pleasant absolution, for a gift.
He was an easy man in penance-giving
Where he could hope to make a decent living;
It's a sure sign whenever gifts are given
230 To a poor Order that a man's well shriven,°
And should he give enough he knew in verity
The penitent repented in sincerity.
For many a fellow is so hard of heart
He cannot weep, for all his inward smart.
235 Therefore instead of weeping and of prayer
One should give silver for a poor Friar's care.
He kept his tippet° stuffed with pins for curls,
And pocket-knives, to give to pretty girls.

194. course: to cause to chase game.

The Friar, from the Ellesmere manuscript, fol. 76v.

By permission of The Huntington Library, San Marino, California.

211. palfrey: horse.
212. wanton: here, jolly.
213. Limiter: a friar having the exclusive right to beg and preach in an assigned (limited) district.
214. Four Orders: The four orders of mendicant (beggar) friars are the Franciscans, the Dominicans, the Carmelites, and the Augustinians.

225. shrift: confession and absolution.

230. well shriven: well confessed and absolved (or forgiven) of sins.

237. tippet: hood or long sleeve (of his robe).

- -

WORDS TO OWN
personable (pur′sən·ə·bəl) *adj.*: attractive in appearance and personality.

- -

And certainly his voice was gay and sturdy,
240 For he sang well and played the hurdy-gurdy.°
At sing-songs he was champion of the hour.
His neck was whiter than a lily-flower
But strong enough to butt a bruiser down.
He knew the taverns well in every town
245 And every innkeeper and barmaid too
Better than lepers, beggars and that crew,
For in so eminent a man as he
It was not fitting with the dignity
Of his position, dealing with a scum
250 Of wretched lepers; nothing good can come
Of commerce with such slum-and-gutter dwellers,
But only with the rich and victual-sellers.°
But anywhere a profit might <u>accrue</u>
Courteous he was and lowly of service too.
255 Natural gifts like his were hard to match.
He was the finest beggar of his batch,
And, for his begging-district, paid a rent;
His brethren did no poaching where he went.
For though a widow mightn't have a shoe,
260 So pleasant was his holy how-d'ye-do
He got his farthing° from her just the same
Before he left, and so his income came
To more than he laid out. And how he romped,
Just like a puppy! He was ever prompt
265 To arbitrate disputes on settling days°
(For a small fee) in many helpful ways,
Not then appearing as your cloistered scholar
With threadbare habit hardly worth a dollar,
But much more like a Doctor or a Pope.
270 Of double-worsted was the semi-cope°
Upon his shoulders, and the swelling fold
About him, like a bell about its mould
When it is casting, rounded out his dress.
He lisped a little out of wantonness°
275 To make his English sweet upon his tongue.
When he had played his harp, or having sung,
His eyes would twinkle in his head as bright
As any star upon a frosty night.
This worthy's name was Hubert, it appeared.
280   There was a *Merchant* with a forking beard
And motley° dress; high on his horse he sat,
Upon his head a Flemish beaver hat
And on his feet daintily buckled boots.

240. hurdy-gurdy: lutelike instrument played by turning a crank.

252. victual-sellers: merchants, especially of food.

261. farthing: British coin worth one fourth of a penny but no longer in circulation.

265. settling days: days on which disputes could be settled out of court by independent negotiators. Though friars often acted as negotiators (for a fee), they were officially forbidden to do so.

270. semi-cope: capelike garment.

274. wantonness: here, pretense.

281. motley: multicolored.

Words to Own
accrue (ə·kro͞o′) *v.*: increase over time.

He told of his opinions and pursuits
285 In solemn tones, he harped on his increase
Of capital; there should be sea-police
(He thought) upon the Harwich–Holland ranges;
He was expert at dabbling in exchanges.
This estimable Merchant so had set
290 His wits to work, none knew he was in debt,
He was so stately in administration,
In loans and bargains and negotiation.
He was an excellent fellow all the same;
To tell the truth I do not know his name.
295 An *Oxford Cleric,* still a student though,
One who had taken logic long ago,
Was there; his horse was thinner than a rake,
And he was not too fat, I undertake,
But had a hollow look, a sober stare;
300 The thread upon his overcoat was bare.
He had found no preferment in the church
And he was too unworldly to make search
For secular employment. By his bed
He preferred having twenty books in red
305 And black, of Aristotle's° philosophy,
Than costly clothes, fiddle, or psaltery.°
Though a philosopher, as I have told,
He had not found the stone for making gold.°
Whatever money from his friends he took
310 He spent on learning or another book
And prayed for them most earnestly, returning
Thanks to them thus for paying for his learning.
His only care was study, and indeed
He never spoke a word more than was need,
315 Formal at that, respectful in the extreme,
Short, to the point, and lofty in his theme.
A tone of moral virtue filled his speech
And gladly would he learn, and gladly teach.
A *Serjeant at the Law* who paid his calls,
320 Wary and wise, for clients at St. Paul's°
There also was, of noted excellence.
Discreet he was, a man to reverence,
Or so he seemed, his sayings were so wise.
He often had been Justice of Assize
325 By letters patent,° and in full commission.
His fame and learning and his high position
Had won him many a robe and many a fee.
There was no such conveyancer° as he;
All was fee-simple° to his strong digestion,
330 Not one conveyance could be called in question.
Though there was nowhere one so busy as he,
He was less busy than he seemed to be.

The Clerk of Oxford, from the
Ellesmere manuscript, fol. 88r.

By permission of The Huntington Library,
San Marino, California.

305. Aristotle's (ar′is·tät′′lz):
Aristotle (384–322 B.C.) was a
Greek philosopher.
306. psaltery (sôl′tər·ē): stringed
instrument that is plucked.
308. stone . . . gold: Alchemists at
the time were searching for a stone
that was supposed to turn ordinary
metals into gold.

320. St. Paul's: London cathedral.
Lawyers often met outside it to discuss their cases when courts were
closed.

325. letters patent: letters from
the king permitting people to act as
judges at the Assizes, court sessions
held periodically.
328. conveyancer: person who
draws up a deed.
329. fee-simple: absolute ownership of real property; in other words,
either entirely right or entirely
wrong.

Places of Pilgrimage

Chaucer's pilgrims are hardly alone in their faith that visiting a holy site will have spiritual benefits. Besides Canterbury, many Christians of Chaucer's time made pilgrimages to Rome and to Jerusalem, both sites that the Wife of Bath, something of a professional pilgrim, had visited. Today, Christian pilgrims still travel to Jerusalem and Rome.

In ancient times, the Jews also made pilgrimages to Jerusalem during three major festivals: Pesah (Passover), Shavuot (Pentecost), and Sukkot (Tabernacles). These pilgrimages, associated with festivals that mark the Jews' escape from Egypt and journey to Israel, were expected of Jewish men.

For a follower of Islam, no place is more sacred than Mecca, located near the Red Sea in western Saudi Arabia. Mecca is the site of the Kaaba, a sacred, cube-shaped building made of stone, around which Muslim pilgrims must walk. Mohammed, the founder of Islam, decreed that all Muslims who are physically and financially able to make the trip must journey to Mecca at least once in their lifetime.

Varanasi, a city on the Ganges River in India and site of fifteen hundred temples, is visited by more than a million Hindu pilgrims each year. The Golden Temple, the main Hindu shrine there, is dedicated to the god Shiva. Pilgrims who worship at the Ganges at Varanasi believe they gain special merit in this life, and Hindus who die in Varanasi believe they are guaranteed release from endless rebirths.

The Grand Shrine of Ise, the most sacred site of Japanese Shinto pilgrimages, is located at Ise in Mie Prefecture, Japan. The shrines there are viewed as the dwelling place of two deities, the sun goddess Amaterasu and the agricultural god Toyuke. The history of Ise shrine dates back some two thousand years, but the actual buildings are always fairly new. By tradition, the shrines must be rebuilt in the same style every twenty-one years.

He knew of every judgment, case, and crime
Ever recorded since King William's time.°
335 He could dictate defenses or draft deeds;
No one could pinch a comma from his screeds°
And he knew every <u>statute</u> off by rote.
He wore a homely parti-colored° coat,

334. King William's time: William the Conqueror (c. 1027–1087) was king of England from 1066 to 1087.
336. screeds: tiresome, lengthy writings.
338. parti-colored: multicolored.

WORDS TO OWN
statute (stach′o͞ot) *n.:* law.

Girt with a silken belt of pin-stripe stuff;
340 Of his appearance I have said enough.
    There was a *Franklin*° with him, it appeared;
White as a daisy-petal was his beard.
A sanguine° man, high-colored and <u>benign</u>,
He loved a morning sop of cake in wine.
345 He lived for pleasure and had always done,
For he was Epicurus'° very son,
In whose opinion sensual delight
Was the one true felicity in sight.
As noted as St. Julian° was for bounty
350 He made his household free to all the County.
His bread, his ale were finest of the fine
And no one had a better stock of wine.
His house was never short of bake-meat pies,
Of fish and flesh, and these in such supplies
355 It positively snowed with meat and drink
And all the dainties that a man could think.
According to the seasons of the year
Changes of dish were ordered to appear.
He kept fat partridges in coops, beyond,
360 Many a bream and pike were in his pond.
Woe to the cook unless the sauce was hot
And sharp, or if he wasn't on the spot!
And in his hall a table stood arrayed
And ready all day long, with places laid.
365 As Justice at the Sessions° none stood higher;
He often had been Member for the Shire.°
A dagger and a little purse of silk
Hung at his girdle,° white as morning milk.
As Sheriff he checked audit, every entry.
370 He was a model among landed gentry.
    A *Haberdasher,*° a *Dyer,* a *Carpenter,*
A *Weaver,* and a *Carpet-maker* were
Among our ranks, all in the livery
Of one impressive guild-fraternity.
375 They were so trim and fresh their gear would pass
For new. Their knives were not tricked out with brass
But wrought with purest silver, which avouches
A like display on girdles and on pouches.
Each seemed a worthy burgess,° fit to grace
380 A guild-hall with a seat upon the dais.
Their wisdom would have justified a plan
To make each one of them an alderman;°
They had the capital and revenue,
Besides their wives declared it was their due.

341. Franklin: well-to-do landowner, but not of the nobility.

343. sanguine: ruddy-complexioned. In Chaucer's day this was considered a sign of a cheerful temperament; today the word signifies optimism.

346. Epicurus' (341–270 B.C.): Epicurus, an ancient Greek philosopher, taught that the goal of life is pleasure, which is achieved through virtue and moderation. Most people came to think of Epicureans as pleasure seekers.

349. St. Julian: patron saint of hospitality.

365. Justice at the Sessions: judge at a periodically held court meeting.
366. Member for the Shire: county representative in Parliament.
368. girdle: belt.

371. Haberdasher (hab′ər·dash′ər): seller of men's clothing and accessories.

379. burgess: citizen.

382. alderman: head of a guild and therefore a town council member.

WORDS TO OWN
benign (bi·nīn′) *adj.*: kind; gracious.

The Cook, from the Ellesmere manuscript, fol. 47r.

By permission of The Huntington Library, San Marino, California.

385 And if they did not think so, then they ought;
  To be called *"Madam"* is a glorious thought,
  And so is going to church and being seen
  Having your mantle carried, like a queen.
   They had a *Cook* with them who stood alone
390 For boiling chicken with a marrow-bone,
  Sharp flavoring-powder and a spice for savor.
  He could distinguish London ale by flavor,
  And he could roast and seethe and broil and fry,
  Make good thick soup, and bake a tasty pie.
395 But what a pity—so it seemed to me,
  That he should have an ulcer on his knee.
  As for blancmange,° he made it with the best.
   There was a *Skipper* hailing from far west;
  He came from Dartmouth, so I understood.
400 He rode a farmer's horse as best he could,
  In a woollen gown that reached his knee.
  A dagger on a lanyard° falling free
  Hung from his neck under his arm and down.
  The summer heat had tanned his color brown,
405 And certainly he was an excellent fellow.
  Many a draught of vintage, red and yellow,
  He'd drawn at Bordeaux, while the trader snored.
  The nicer rules of conscience he ignored.
  If, when he fought, the enemy vessel sank,
410 He sent his prisoners home; they walked the plank.
  As for his skill in reckoning his tides,
  Currents, and many another risk besides,
  Moons, harbors, pilots, he had such dispatch
  That none from Hull to Carthage was his match.
415 Hardy he was, prudent in undertaking;
  His beard in many a tempest had its shaking,
  And he knew all the havens as they were
  From Gottland to the Cape of Finisterre,
  And every creek in Brittany and Spain;
420 The barge he owned was called *The Maudelayne.*
   A *Doctor* too emerged as we proceeded;
  No one alive could talk as well as he did
  On points of medicine and of surgery,
  For, being grounded in astronomy,
425 He watched his patient closely for the hours
  When, by his horoscope, he knew the powers
  Of favorable planets, then ascendent,
  Worked on the images for his dependent.
  The cause of every malady you'd got
430 He knew, and whether dry, cold, moist, or hot;°
  He knew their seat, their humor and condition.
  He was a perfect practicing physician.
  These causes being known for what they were,
  He gave the man his medicine then and there.

397. blancmange (blə·mônzh′): French for "white food." In Chaucer's day this was a sweet dish containing diced chicken, milk, sugar, and almonds.

402. lanyard (lan′yərd): cord.

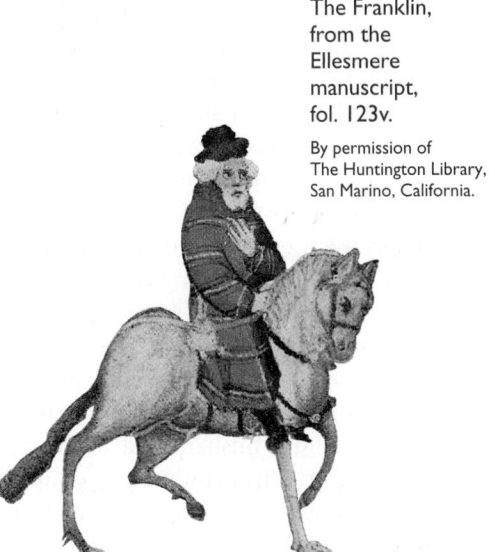

The Franklin, from the Ellesmere manuscript, fol. 123v.

By permission of The Huntington Library, San Marino, California.

430. dry . . . hot: the four humors, or fluids. People of the time believed that one's physical and mental conditions were influenced by the balance of four major fluids in the body—blood (hot and wet), yellow bile (hot and dry), phlegm (cold and wet), and black bile (cold and dry).

435 All his apothecaries in a tribe
Were ready with the drugs he would prescribe
And each made money from the other's <u>guile</u>;
They had been friendly for a goodish while.
He was well-versed in Aesculapius° too
440 And what Hippocrates and Rufus knew
And Dioscorides, now dead and gone,
Galen and Rhazes, Hali, Serapion,
Averroes, Avicenna, Constantine,
Scotch Bernard, John of Gaddesden, Gilbertine.
445 In his own diet he observed some measure;
There were no superfluities for pleasure,
Only digestives, nutritives and such.
He did not read the Bible very much.
In blood-red garments, slashed with bluish gray
450 And lined with taffeta, he rode his way;
Yet he was rather close as to expenses
And kept the gold he won in pestilences.
Gold stimulates the heart, or so we're told.
He therefore had a special love of gold.
455   A worthy *woman* from beside *Bath* city
Was with us, somewhat deaf, which was a pity.
In making cloth she showed so great a bent
She bettered those of Ypres and of Ghent.°
In all the parish not a dame dared stir
460 Towards the altar steps in front of her,
And if indeed they did, so wrath was she
As to be quite put out of charity.
Her kerchiefs were of finely woven ground;°
I dared have sworn they weighed a good ten pound,
465 The ones she wore on Sunday, on her head.
Her hose were of the finest scarlet red
And gartered tight; her shoes were soft and new.
Bold was her face, handsome, and red in hue.
A worthy woman all her life, what's more
470 She'd had five husbands, all at the church door,°
Apart from other company in youth;
No need just now to speak of that, forsooth.
And she had thrice been to Jerusalem,
Seen many strange rivers and passed over them;
475 She'd been to Rome and also to Boulogne,
St. James of Compostella and Cologne,
And she was skilled in wandering by the way.
She had gap-teeth, set widely, truth to say.
Easily on an ambling horse she sat

439. Aesculapius: in Greek and Roman mythology, the god of medicine. The names that follow were early Greek, Roman, Middle Eastern, and medieval medical authorities.

The Physician, from the Ellesmere manuscript, fol. 133r.

By permission of The Huntington Library, San Marino, California.

458. Ypres (ē′pr′) **and of Ghent:** Flemish centers of the wool trade.

463. ground: type of cloth.

470. church door: In Chaucer's day the marriage ceremony was performed at the church door.

WORDS TO OWN
guile (gīl) *n.*: sly dealings.

---

480 Well wimpled° up, and on her head a hat
As broad as is a buckler or a shield;
She had a flowing mantle that concealed
Large hips, her heels spurred sharply under that.
In company she liked to laugh and chat
485 And knew the remedies for love's mischances,
An art in which she knew the oldest dances.

    A holy-minded man of good renown
There was, and poor, the *Parson* to a town,
Yet he was rich in holy thought and work.
490 He also was a learned man, a clerk,
Who truly knew Christ's gospel and would preach it
Devoutly to parishioners, and teach it.
Benign and wonderfully <u>diligent</u>,
And patient when <u>adversity</u> was sent
495 (For so he proved in much adversity)
He hated cursing to extort a fee,
Nay rather he preferred beyond a doubt
Giving to poor parishioners round about
Both from church offerings and his property;
500 He could in little find sufficiency.
Wide was his parish, with houses far asunder,
Yet he neglected not in rain or thunder,
In sickness or in grief, to pay a call
On the remotest, whether great or small,
505 Upon his feet, and in his hand a stave.°
This noble example to his sheep he gave
That first he wrought, and afterward he taught;
And it was from the Gospel he had caught
Those words, and he would add this figure too,
510 That if gold rust, what then will iron do?
For if a priest be foul in whom we trust
No wonder that a common man should rust;
And shame it is to see—let priests take stock—
A shitten shepherd and a snowy flock.
515 The true example that a priest should give
Is one of cleanness, how the sheep should live.
He did not set his benefice to hire°
And leave his sheep encumbered in the mire
Or run to London to earn easy bread
520 By singing masses for the wealthy dead,
Or find some Brotherhood and get enrolled.°
He stayed at home and watched over his fold
So that no wolf should make the sheep miscarry.

The Parson, from the Ellesmere
manuscript, fol. 206v.

By permission of The Huntington Library,
San Marino, California.

480. wimpled: A wimple is a linen covering for the head and neck.

505. stave: staff.

517. benefice to hire: He did not hire someone else to perform his duties.

521. find . . . enrolled: He did not take a job as a paid chaplain to a guild.

WORDS TO OWN
diligent (dil′ə·jənt) *adj.:* careful and persistent in work.
adversity (ad·vʉr′sə·tē) *n.:* trouble; misfortune.

He was a shepherd and no mercenary.
525 Holy and virtuous he was, but then
Never contemptuous of sinful men,
Never disdainful, never too proud or fine,
But was discreet in teaching and benign.
His business was to show a fair behavior
530 And draw men thus to Heaven and their Savior,
Unless indeed a man were obstinate;
And such, whether of high or low estate,
He put to sharp rebuke, to say the least.
I think there never was a better priest.
535 He sought no pomp or glory in his dealings,
No scrupulosity had spiced his feelings.
Christ and His Twelve Apostles and their lore
He taught, but followed it himself before.
　　There was a *Plowman* with him there, his brother;
540 Many a load of dung one time or other
He must have carted through the morning dew.
He was an honest worker, good and true,
Living in peace and perfect charity,
And, as the gospel bade him, so did he,
545 Loving God best with all his heart and mind
And then his neighbor as himself, repined
At no misfortune, slacked for no content,
For steadily about his work he went
To thrash his corn, to dig or to manure
550 Or make a ditch; and he would help the poor
For love of Christ and never take a penny
If he could help it, and, as prompt as any,
He paid his tithes in full when they were due
On what he owned, and on his earnings too.
555 He wore a tabard smock° and rode a mare.
　　There was a *Reeve,*° also a *Miller,* there,
A College *Manciple*° from the Inns of Court,
A papal *Pardoner*° and, in close consort,
A Church-Court *Summoner,*° riding at a trot,
560 And finally myself—that was the lot.
　　The *Miller* was a chap of sixteen stone,°
A great stout fellow big in brawn and bone.
He did well out of them, for he could go
And win the ram at any wrestling show.
565 Broad, knotty, and short-shouldered, he would boast
He could heave any door off hinge and post,
Or take a run and break it with his head.

The Miller, from the Ellesmere
manuscript, fol. 34v.

By permission of The Huntington Library,
San Marino, California.

555. tabard (tab′ərd) **smock:** short
jacket.
556. Reeve: serf who was the
steward of a manor. He saw that
the estate's work was done and that
everything was accounted for.
557. Manciple (man′sə·pəl): minor
employee whose principal duty was
to purchase provisions for a college
or law firm.
558. Pardoner: minor member of
the Church who bought and sold
pardons for sinners.
559. Summoner: low-ranking
officer who summoned people
to appear in church court.
561. sixteen stone: 224 pounds.

WORDS TO OWN
disdainful (dis·dān′fəl) *adj.:* scornful.
discreet (di·skrēt′) *adj.:* cautious about one's words and actions.
obstinate (äb′stə·nət) *adj.:* unreasonably stubborn.

His beard, like any sow or fox, was red
And broad as well, as though it were a spade;
570 And, at its very tip, his nose displayed
A wart on which there stood a tuft of hair
Red as the bristles in an old sow's ear.
His nostrils were as black as they were wide.
He had a sword and buckler at his side,
575 His mighty mouth was like a furnace door.
A wrangler and buffoon, he had a store
Of tavern stories, filthy in the main.
His was a master-hand at stealing grain.
He felt it with his thumb and thus he knew
580 Its quality and took three times his due—
A thumb of gold, by God, to gauge an oat!°
He wore a hood of blue and a white coat.
He liked to play his bagpipes up and down
And that was how he brought us out of town.

585   The *Manciple* came from the Inner Temple;°
All caterers might follow his example
In buying victuals; he was never rash
Whether he bought on credit or paid cash.
He used to watch the market most precisely
590 And got in first, and so he did quite nicely.
Now isn't it a marvel of God's grace
That an illiterate fellow can outpace
The wisdom of a heap of learned men?
His masters—he had more than thirty then—
595 All versed in the abstrusest legal knowledge,
Could have produced a dozen from their College
Fit to be stewards in land and rents and game
To any Peer in England you could name,
And show him how to live on what he had
600 Debt-free (unless of course the Peer were mad)
Or be as frugal as he might desire,
And make them fit to help about the Shire
In any legal case there was to try;
And yet this Manciple could wipe their eye.

605   The *Reeve* was old and choleric° and thin;
His beard was shaven closely to the skin,
His shorn hair came abruptly to a stop
Above his ears, and he was docked on top
Just like a priest in front; his legs were lean,
610 Like sticks they were, no calf was to be seen.
He kept his bins and garners° very trim;
No auditor could gain a point on him.

The Manciple, from the Ellesmere manuscript, fol. 203r.

By permission of The Huntington Library, San Marino, California.

581. thumb . . . oat: In other words, he pressed on the scale with his thumb to increase the weight of the grain.

585. Inner Temple: one of the four legal societies in London comprising the Inns of Court. Only the Inns were permitted to license lawyers.

The Reeve, from the Ellesmere manuscript, fol. 42r.

By permission of The Huntington Library, San Marino, California.

605. choleric (käl′ər·ik): having too much choler, or yellow bile, and thus (supposedly) bad-tempered.

611. garners: granaries.

WORDS TO OWN
frugal (fro͞o′gəl) *adj.:* thrifty.

And he could judge by watching drought and rain
The yield he might expect from seed and grain.
615 His master's sheep, his animals and hens,
Pigs, horses, dairies, stores, and cattle-pens
Were wholly trusted to his government.
He had been under contract to present
The accounts, right from his master's earliest years.
620 No one had ever caught him in arrears.
No bailiff, serf, or herdsman dared to kick,
He knew their dodges, knew their every trick;
Feared like the plague he was, by those beneath.
He had a lovely dwelling on a heath,
625 Shadowed in green by trees above the sward.°
A better hand at bargains than his lord,
He had grown rich and had a store of treasure
Well tucked away, yet out it came to pleasure
His lord with subtle loans or gifts of goods,
630 To earn his thanks and even coats and hoods.
When young he'd learnt a useful trade and still
He was a carpenter of first-rate skill.
The stallion-cob he rode at a slow trot
Was dapple-gray and bore the name of Scot.
635 He wore an overcoat of bluish shade
And rather long; he had a rusty blade
Slung at his side. He came, as I heard tell,
From Norfolk, near a place called Baldeswell.
His coat was tucked under his belt and splayed.
640 He rode the hindmost of our cavalcade.
　　　There was a *Summoner* with us at that Inn,
His face on fire, like a cherubim,°
For he had carbuncles.° His eyes were narrow,
He was as hot and lecherous as a sparrow.
645 Black scabby brows he had, and a thin beard.
Children were afraid when he appeared.
No quicksilver, lead ointment, tartar creams,
No brimstone, no boracic, so it seems,
Could make a salve that had the power to bite,
650 Clean up, or cure his whelks° of knobby white
Or purge the pimples sitting on his cheeks.
Garlic he loved, and onions too, and leeks,
And drinking strong red wine till all was hazy.
Then he would shout and jabber as if crazy,
655 And wouldn't speak a word except in Latin
When he was drunk, such tags as he was pat in;
He only had a few, say two or three,
That he had mugged up out of some decree;
No wonder, for he heard them every day.
660 And, as you know, a man can teach a jay°
To call out "Walter" better than the Pope.

625. sward (swôrd): lawn.

The Summoner, from the Ellesmere manuscript, fol. 81r.

By permission of The Huntington Library, San Marino, California.

642. cherubim: in medieval art, a little angel with a rosy face.
643. carbuncles (kär′bun′kəlz): pus-filled skin inflammations, something like boils.

650. whelks: pus-filled sores.

660. jay: type of bird.

But had you tried to test his wits and grope
For more, you'd have found nothing in the bag.
Then *"Questio quid juris"*° was his tag.

665 He was a noble varlet° and a kind one,
You'd meet none better if you went to find one.
Why, he'd allow—just for a quart of wine—
Any good lad to keep a concubine
A twelvemonth and dispense him altogether!

670 And he had finches of his own to feather:
And if he found some rascal with a maid
He would instruct him not to be afraid
In such a case of the Archdeacon's curse
(Unless the rascal's soul were in his purse)

675 For in his purse the punishment should be.
"Purse is the good Archdeacon's Hell," said he.
But well I know he lied in what he said;
A curse should put a guilty man in dread,
For curses kill, as shriving brings, salvation.

680 We should beware of excommunication.
Thus, as he pleased, the man could bring <u>duress</u>
On any young fellow in the diocese.
He knew their secrets, they did what he said.
He wore a garland set upon his head

685 Large as the holly-bush upon a stake
Outside an ale-house, and he had a cake,
A round one, which it was his joke to wield
As if it were intended for a shield.

He and a gentle *Pardoner* rode together,

690 A bird from Charing Cross of the same feather,
Just back from visiting the Court of Rome.
He loudly sang *"Come hither, love, come home!"*
The Summoner sang deep seconds° to this song,
No trumpet ever sounded half so strong.

695 This Pardoner had hair as yellow as wax,
Hanging down smoothly like a hank of flax.
In driblets fell his locks behind his head
Down to his shoulders which they overspread;
Thinly they fell, like rat-tails, one by one.

700 He wore no hood upon his head, for fun;
The hood inside his wallet had been stowed,
He aimed at riding in the latest mode;
But for a little cap his head was bare
And he had bulging eye-balls, like a hare.

705 He'd sewed a holy relic on his cap;
His wallet lay before him on his lap,

664. *Questio quid juris* (kwest′ē·ō kwid yoo′ris): Latin for "I ask what point of the law [applies]." The Summoner uses this phrase to stall and dodge the issue.

665. varlet (vär′lit): scoundrel.

The Pardoner, from the Ellesmere manuscript, fol. 138r.

By permission of The Huntington Library, San Marino, California.

693. deep seconds: harmonies.

Words to Own
duress (doo·res′) *n.*: pressure.

Brimful of pardons° come from Rome, all hot.
He had the same small voice a goat has got.
His chin no beard had harbored, nor would harbor,
710 Smoother than ever chin was left by barber.
I judge he was a gelding, or a mare.
As to his trade, from Berwick down to Ware
There was no pardoner of equal grace,
For in his trunk he had a pillow-case
715 Which he asserted was Our Lady's veil.
He said he had a gobbet° of the sail
Saint Peter had the time when he made bold
To walk the waves, till Jesu Christ took hold.
He had a cross of metal set with stones
720 And, in a glass, a rubble of pigs' bones.
And with these relics, any time he found
Some poor up-country parson to astound,
In one short day, in money down, he drew
More than the parson in a month or two,
725 And by his flatteries and prevarication
Made monkeys of the priest and congregation.
But still to do him justice first and last
In church he was a noble ecclesiast.°
How well he read a lesson or told a story!
730 But best of all he sang an Offertory,°
For well he knew that when that song was sung
He'd have to preach and tune his honey-tongue
And (well he could) win silver from the crowd.
That's why he sang so merrily and loud.
735   Now I have told you shortly, in a clause,
The rank, the array, the number, and the cause
Of our assembly in this company
In Southwark, at that high-class hostelry
Known as *The Tabard,* close beside *The Bell.*
740 And now the time has come for me to tell
How we behaved that evening; I'll begin
After we had alighted at the Inn,
Then I'll report our journey, stage by stage,
All the remainder of our pilgrimage.
745 But first I beg of you, in courtesy,
Not to condemn me as unmannerly
If I speak plainly and with no concealings
And give account of all their words and dealings,
Using their very phrases as they fell.
750 For certainly, as you all know so well,
He who repeats a tale after a man
Is bound to say, as nearly as he can,
Each single word, if he remembers it,
However rudely spoken or unfit,

707. pardons: small strips of parchment with papal seals attached. They were sold as indulgences (pardons for sins), with the proceeds supposedly going to a religious house. Many pardoners were dishonest, and even loyal church members often ridiculed them.

716. gobbet: fragment.

728. ecclesiast (e·klē′zē·ast): practitioner of church ritual.

730. Offertory: hymn sung while offerings are collected in church.

755 Or else the tale he tells will be untrue,
The things pretended and the phrases new.
He may not flinch although it were his brother,
He may as well say one word as another.
And Christ Himself spoke broad in Holy Writ,
760 Yet there is no scurrility in it,
And Plato says, for those with power to read,
"The word should be as cousin to the deed."
Further I beg you to forgive it me
If I neglect the order and degree
765 And what is due to rank in what I've planned.
I'm short of wit as you will understand.

  Our *Host* gave us great welcome; everyone
Was given a place and supper was begun.
He served the finest victuals you could think,
770 The wine was strong and we were glad to drink.
A very striking man our Host withal,
And fit to be a marshal in a hall.
His eyes were bright, his girth a little wide;
There is no finer burgess in Cheapside.°

774. **Cheapside:** district of medieval London.

775 Bold in his speech, yet wise and full of tact,
There was no manly attribute he lacked,
What's more he was a merry-hearted man.
After our meal he jokingly began
To talk of sport, and, among other things
780 After we'd settled up our reckonings,
He said as follows: "Truly, gentlemen,
You're very welcome and I can't think when
—Upon my word I'm telling you no lie—
I've seen a gathering here that looked so spry,
785 No, not this year, as in this tavern now.
I'd think you up some fun if I knew how.
And, as it happens, a thought has just occurred
To please you, costing nothing, on my word.
You're off to Canterbury—well, God speed!

Chaucer, from the Ellesmere
manuscript, fol. 153v.

By permission of The Huntington Library,
San Marino, California.

790 Blessed St. Thomas answer to your need!
And I don't doubt, before the journey's done
You mean to while the time in tales and fun.
Indeed, there's little pleasure for your bones
Riding along and all as dumb as stones.

795 So let me then propose for your enjoyment,
Just as I said, a suitable employment.
And if my notion suits and you agree
And promise to submit yourselves to me
Playing your parts exactly as I say

800 Tomorrow as you ride along the way,
Then by my father's soul (and he is dead)
If you don't like it you can have my head!
Hold up your hands, and not another word."
    Well, our opinion was not long <u>deferred</u>,

805 It seemed not worth a serious debate;
We all agreed to it at any rate
And bade him issue what commands he would.
"My lords," he said, "now listen for your good,
And please don't treat my notion with disdain.

810 This is the point. I'll make it short and plain.
Each one of you shall help to make things slip
By telling two stories on the outward trip
To Canterbury, that's what I intend,
And, on the homeward way to journey's end

815 Another two, tales from the days of old;
And then the man whose story is best told,
That is to say who gives the fullest measure
Of good morality and general pleasure,
He shall be given a supper, paid by all,

820 Here in this tavern, in this very hall,
When we come back again from Canterbury.
And in the hope to keep you bright and merry
I'll go along with you myself and ride
All at my own expense and serve as guide.

825 I'll be the judge, and those who won't obey
Shall pay for what we spend upon the way.
Now if you all agree to what you've heard
Tell me at once without another word,
And I will make arrangements early for it."

830   Of course we all agreed, in fact we swore it
Delightedly, and made entreaty too
That he should act as he proposed to do,
Become our Governor in short, and be
Judge of our tales and general referee,

835 And set the supper at a certain price.

WORDS TO OWN
deferred (dē·furd′) v.: postponed.

We promised to be ruled by his advice
Come high, come low; unanimously thus
We set him up in judgment over us.
More wine was fetched, the business being done;
840 We drank it off and up went everyone
To bed without a moment of delay.
    Early next morning at the spring of day
Up rose our Host and roused us like a cock,
Gathering us together in a flock,
845 And off we rode at slightly faster pace
Than walking to St. Thomas' watering-place;
And there our Host drew up, began to ease
His horse, and said, "Now, listen if you please,
My lords! Remember what you promised me.
850 If evensong and matins will agree°
Let's see who shall be first to tell a tale.
And as I hope to drink good wine and ale
I'll be your judge. The rebel who disobeys,
However much the journey costs, he pays.
855 Now draw for cut and then we can depart;
The man who draws the shortest cut shall start."

850. if . . . agree: in other words, if you feel the same way in the evening (at evensong, or evening prayers) as you do in the morning (at matins, or morning prayers).

Pigskin binding by Doves Bindery for the Kelmscott *Chaucer* (1896).
Fitzwilliam Museum, University of Cambridge.

In this passage, Malcolm X describes his first visit to Mecca, the Muslim sacred city.

from The Autobiography of Malcolm X

Malcolm X, with Alex Haley

Mecca, when we entered, seemed as ancient as time itself. Our car slowed through the winding streets, lined by shops on both sides and with buses, cars, and trucks, and tens of thousands of pilgrims from all over the earth were everywhere.

The car halted briefly at a place where a *Mutawaf*[1] was waiting for me. He wore the white skullcap and long nightshirt garb that I had seen at the airport. He was a short, dark-skinned Arab named Muhammad. He spoke no English whatever.

We parked near the Great Mosque. We performed our ablution and entered. Pilgrims seemed to be on top of each other, there were so many, lying, sitting, sleeping, praying, walking.

My vocabulary cannot describe the new mosque that was being built around the Kaaba. I was thrilled to realize that it was only one of the tremendous rebuilding tasks under the direction of young Dr. Azzam, who had just been my host. The Great Mosque of Mecca, when it is finished, will surpass the architectural beauty of India's Taj Mahal.

Carrying my sandals, I followed the *Mutawaf*. Then I saw the Kaaba, a huge, black stone house in the middle of the Great Mosque. It was being circumambulated by thousands upon thousands of praying pilgrims, both sexes, and every size, shape, color, and race in the world. I knew the prayer to be uttered when the pilgrim's eyes first perceive the Kaaba. Translated, it is "O God, You are peace, and peace derives from You. So greet us, O Lord,

1. ***Mutawaf:*** guide for pilgrims visiting Mecca.

with peace." Upon entering the Mosque, the pilgrim should try to kiss the Kaaba if possible, but if the crowds prevent him getting that close, he touches it, and if the crowds prevent that, he raises his hand and cries out "Takbir!" ("God is great!") I could not get within yards. "Takbir!"

My feeling there in the House of God was a numbness. My *Mutawaf* led me in the crowd of praying, chanting pilgrims, moving seven times around the Kaaba. Some were bent and wizened with age; it was a sight that stamped itself on the brain. I saw incapacitated pilgrims being carried by others. Faces were enraptured in their faith. The seventh time around, I prayed two *Rak'a*, prostrating myself, my head on the floor. The first prostration, I prayed the Koran verse "Say He is God, the one and only"; the second prostration: "Say O you who are unbelievers, I worship not that which you worship. . . ."

As I prostrated, the *Mutawaf* fended pilgrims off to keep me from being trampled.

The *Mutawaf* and I next drank water from the well of Zem Zem. Then we ran between the two hills, Safa and Marwa, where Hajar wandered over the same earth searching for water for her child Ishmael.

Three separate times, after that, I visited the Great Mosque and circumambulated the Kaaba. The next day we set out after sunrise toward Mount Arafat, thousands of us, crying in unison: "Labbayka! Labbayka!" and "Allah Akbar!". . . Arriving about noon, we prayed and chanted from noon until sunset, and the *asr* (afternoon) and *Maghrib* (sunset) special prayers were performed.

Finally, we lifted our hands in prayer and thanksgiving, repeating Allah's words: "There is no God but Allah. He has no partner. His are authority and praise. Good emanates from Him, and He has power over all things."

Standing on Mount Arafat had concluded the essential rites of being a pilgrim to Mecca. No one who missed it could consider himself a pilgrim.

MAKING MEANINGS

First Thoughts

1. If you were the thirty-first pilgrim, which of your fellow travelers would you choose to travel next to? Which would you definitely try to avoid? Whose story would you be most interested in hearing?

Shaping Interpretations

2. Chaucer is a master at using physical details—eyes, hair, complexion, body type, clothing—to reveal **character.** Tell about at least three pilgrims whose inner natures are revealed by their outer appearances.

3. Clearly, Chaucer **satirizes** the Church of his time. Show how this is true by analyzing two characters connected with the Church. What "good" Church people does Chaucer include to balance his satire?

4. What aspects of society does Chaucer satirize in his portrayals of the Merchant? the Franklin? the Doctor? the Miller?

5. Which pilgrims do you think Chaucer idealizes?

6. In describing the pilgrims, what do you think Chaucer as the pilgrim-narrator has revealed about his own personality, biases, and values?

Extending the Text

7. Which of the pilgrims' professions or trades have survived in society today? Which of Chaucer's character types can still be seen in airports or pulpits, farms or classrooms, city streets or small towns?

8. When would people from all walks of life today travel together in large groups for a common purpose? How do you think the pilgrimage described in *The Autobiography of Malcolm X* (see **Connections,** page 126) is similar to, and different from, the journey that Chaucer's pilgrims undertake?

Reading Check

a. When, where, and for what purposes do the pilgrims gather?

b. What plan, which becomes the basis of the frame story, does the Host propose to the pilgrims?

c. Place each pilgrim within one of these three groups that comprised medieval society: the feudal system (related to the land), the Church, and the city (merchants and professionals).

d. In your own words, explain the pilgrim-narrator's plea in lines 745–762.

ELEMENTS OF LITERATURE

Imagery: The Revealing Detail

Chaucer is a master of **imagery,** language that appeals to the senses. Most images are visual, but imagery can also appeal to our senses of hearing, smell, taste, and touch. In a few vivid words, sometimes with a few added figures of speech, Chaucer has created a cast of characters as real to us today as the characters in the latest novel—more real, perhaps, because Chaucer's people exhibit all the essentials of human nature.

With twenty-nine pilgrims to introduce, Chaucer could not develop any character at length. He had to find a few well-chosen details to make immediate impressions. For example, Chaucer devotes only nine lines to the Cook, yet he found just one now-famous image to immortalize the Cook and his unfortunate appearance: The Cook has "an ulcer on his knee," an open sore caused either by a skin disease associated with a bad diet and poor hygiene or by an infectious or communicable disease. With this image in mind, would you be anxious to try the Cook's blancmange, even if it rated "with the best"? How does this detail make you feel about the Cook?

Chaucer also relied upon his readers' knowledge of physiognomy. Based on some of Aristotle's treatises, physiognomy compared varieties of people to animals and asserted that certain physical characteristics revealed one's personality type. Thus, when Chaucer's contemporaries read that the Wife of Bath had "gap-teeth, set widely, truth to say," they knew that the physiognomists believed that a gap between a woman's two front teeth indicated not only that she would travel far but also that she was bold and especially suited for love.

Analyzing Chaucer's imagery. The table below lists a few physical characteristics and their corresponding physiognomic interpretations. Choose a pilgrim who exhibits each characteristic. How does the physiognomic interpretation reinforce what you already know about the character's nature?

Think of what you know about the animals referred to in the chart. Can you make educated guesses as to why people would associate certain human characteristics with these particular animals?

Think also about this question: How do writers describe characters today? In stories (or movies) do any physical features automatically suggest something about character?

Physical Characteristic	Physiognomic Interpretation
ramlike appearance	strength
sowlike appearance	dirtiness
foxlike appearance	slyness
goatlike qualities	lechery
thin, fastidious type	bad temper, irritability
flaring or open nostrils	passion
pus-filled sores	lechery and drunkenness
high forehead	intelligence, breeding
white neck	looseness or immorality

gather information in a chart like the following one. Save your work for possible use later.

Element	Wife of Bath	Prioress
Appearance		
Personality		
Tastes		
Social position		
Life experiences		

Descriptive Writing

2. Creating a Character

Refer to the notes you made for the Quickwrite on page 103. Now that you have read descriptions of Chaucer's characters, you might have many more ideas of how to bring your own character to life. In an essay, describe your character. Remember that Chaucer tells us about such things as appearance, speech, mannerisms, profession, special interests, dislikes. Remember also that Chaucer doesn't necessarily tell us what he *thinks* of his characters; he lets his descriptions speak for themselves. You might want to imagine that your character has joined Chaucer's pilgrims, in a sort of time warp. If you wish, supply a drawing of your character.

Art/Character Study

3. A Canterbury Gallery

Chaucer uses words to create a picture of each pilgrim. Now it's your turn to go from words to pictures by creating a portrait of a pilgrim. Select one pilgrim, and draw an illustration of him or her. Or create a collage showing what you find most memorable and important about the pilgrim. You might want to create a class display of your illustrations or collages.

CHOICES:
Building Your Portfolio

Writer's Notebook

1. Collecting Ideas for a Comparison-Contrast Essay

For the Writer's Workshop on page 185, you will be writing an essay of comparison and contrast. Chaucer gives you plenty of characters to compare and contrast. You might find interesting subjects in the Wife of Bath and the Prioress—the only women Chaucer describes at any length. To gather notes for an essay comparing and contrasting these two women,

The story in "The Pardoner's Tale" has roots that are old and widespread. Avarice (or greed) as the root of evil is a theme that appears in stories of many lands. Starting from the Latin saying *"Radix malorum est cupiditas,"* translated loosely as "The love of money is the root of all evil," the Pardoner presents us with an *exemplum,* an anecdote or example inserted into a sermon to teach a moral lesson. As with every tale, Chaucer fits the story to the character of the storyteller.

Chaucer is a master of both **verbal** and **situational irony.** You use both types of irony all the time. You use verbal irony when you say one thing but mean another. For example, when a friend asks how you liked cleaning your room for three hours, you might reply, "It was a blast." Both of you know differently, of course. In situational irony, what actually happens is different from what you expect. You feel situational irony when it rains on the weather forecasters' picnic, or when the police officer's son turns out to be a criminal.

The Pardoner, from the Ellesmere manuscript, fol. 138r.

By permission of The Huntington Library, San Marino, California.

from The Pardoner's Tale

Geoffrey Chaucer
translated by **Nevill Coghill**

The Prologue

"But let me briefly make my purpose plain;
I preach for nothing but for greed of gain
And use the same old text, as bold as brass,
Radix malorum est cupiditas.°
5 And thus I preach against the very vice
I make my living out of—avarice.
And yet however guilty of that sin
Myself, with others I have power to win
Them from it, I can bring them to repent;
10 But that is not my principal intent.
Covetousness is both the root and stuff
Of all I preach. That ought to be enough.
  "Well, then I give examples thick and fast
From bygone times, old stories from the past.
15 A yokel mind loves stories from of old,
Being the kind it can repeat and hold.
What! Do you think, as long as I can preach
And get their silver for the things I teach,

4. *Radix malorum est cupiditas* (ra′diks ma·lō′rum est kōō·pi′di·tas): literally, "The root of evil is desire" (1 Timothy 6:10).

WORDS TO OWN
avarice (av′ə·ris) *n.:* too great a desire for wealth.
covetousness (kuv′ət·əs·nis) *n.:* the quality of craving wealth or possessions.

That I will live in poverty, from choice?
20 That's not the counsel of my inner voice!
No! Let me preach and beg from kirk° to kirk

21. kirk: Scottish for "church."

And never do an honest job of work,
No, nor make baskets, like St. Paul, to gain
A livelihood. I do not preach in vain.
25 There's no apostle I would counterfeit;
I mean to have money, wool and cheese and wheat
Though it were given me by the poorest lad
Or poorest village widow, though she had
A string of starving children, all agape.
30 No, let me drink the liquor of the grape
And keep a jolly wench in every town!
    "But listen, gentlemen; to bring things down
To a conclusion, would you like a tale?
Now as I've drunk a draft of corn-ripe ale,
35 By God it stands to reason I can strike
On some good story that you all will like.
For though I am a wholly vicious man
Don't think I can't tell moral tales. I can!
Here's one I often preach when out for winning;
40 Now please be quiet. Here is the beginning."

The Tale

In Flanders once there was a company
Of youngsters haunting vice and ribaldry,°

42. ribaldry (rib′əl·drē): vulgar language or humor.

Riot and gambling, stews and public-houses
Where each with harp, guitar, or lute carouses,
45 Dancing and dicing day and night, and bold
To eat and drink far more than they can hold,
Doing thereby the devil sacrifice
Within that devil's temple of cursed vice,
Abominable in superfluity,
50 With oaths so damnable in blasphemy
That it's a grisly thing to hear them swear.
Our dear Lord's body they will rend and tear.° . . .

52. Our . . . tear: Their oaths refer to "God's arms" and "God's blessed bones."

It's of three rioters I have to tell
Who, long before the morning service bell,
55 Were sitting in a tavern for a drink.
And as they sat, they heard the hand-bell clink
Before a coffin going to the grave;
One of them called the little tavern-knave
And said "Go and find out at once—look spry!—

WORDS TO OWN
carouses (kə·rouz′ez) *v.*: drinks and celebrates noisily.
abominable (ə·bäm′ə·nə·bəl) *adj.*: disgusting; hateful.
superfluity (sōō′pər·flōō′ə·tē) *n.*: excess.
blasphemy (blas′fə·mē′) *n.*: mockery of God.

---

60 Whose corpse is in that coffin passing by;
And see you get the name correctly too."
"Sir," said the boy, "no need, I promise you;
Two hours before you came here I was told.
He was a friend of yours in days of old,

65 And suddenly, last night, the man was slain,
Upon his bench, face up, dead drunk again.
There came a privy° thief, they call him Death,
Who kills us all round here, and in a breath
He speared him through the heart, he never stirred.

70 And then Death went his way without a word.
He's killed a thousand in the present plague,
And, sir, it doesn't do to be too vague
If you should meet him; you had best be wary.
Be on your guard with such an adversary,

75 Be primed to meet him everywhere you go,
That's what my mother said. It's all I know."
     The publican° joined in with, "By St. Mary,
What the child says is right; you'd best be wary,
This very year he killed, in a large village

80 A mile away, man, woman, serf at tillage,°
Page in the household, children—all there were.
Yes, I imagine that he lives round there.
It's well to be prepared in these alarms,
He might do you dishonor." "Huh, God's arms!"

85 The rioter said, "Is he so fierce to meet?
I'll search for him, by Jesus, street by street.
God's blessed bones! I'll register a vow!
Here, chaps! The three of us together now,
Hold up your hands, like me, and we'll be brothers

90 In this affair, and each defend the others,
And we will kill this traitor Death, I say!
Away with him as he has made away
With all our friends. God's dignity! Tonight!"
     They made their bargain, swore with appetite,

95 These three, to live and die for one another
As brother-born might swear to his born brother.
And up they started in their drunken rage
And made towards this village which the page
And publican had spoken of before.

100 Many and grisly were the oaths they swore,
Tearing Christ's blessed body to a shred;
"If we can only catch him, Death is dead!"
     When they had gone not fully half a mile,
Just as they were about to cross a stile,°

105 They came upon a very poor old man
Who humbly greeted them and thus began,
"God look to you, my lords, and give you quiet!"
To which the proudest of these men of riot
Gave back the answer, "What, old fool? Give place!

67. privy (priv′ē): secretive; furtive.

77. publican: tavern keeper; from *public house*, an inn or tavern.

80. tillage: working the land.

104. stile: steps used for climbing over a wall.

110 Why are you all wrapped up except your face?
Why live so long? Isn't it time to die?"
　　The old, old fellow looked him in the eye
And said, "Because I never yet have found,
Though I have walked to India, searching round
115 Village and city on my pilgrimage,
One who would change his youth to have my age.
And so my age is mine and must be still
Upon me, for such time as God may will.
　　"Not even Death, alas, will take my life;
120 So, like a wretched prisoner at strife
Within himself, I walk alone and wait
About the earth, which is my mother's gate,
Knock-knocking with my staff from night to noon
And crying, 'Mother, open to me soon!
125 Look at me, mother, won't you let me in?
See how I wither, flesh and blood and skin!
Alas! When will these bones be laid to rest?
Mother, I would exchange—for that were best—
The wardrobe in my chamber, standing there
130 So long, for yours! Aye, for a shirt of hair°
To wrap me in!' She has refused her grace,
Whence comes the <u>pallor</u> of my withered face.
　　"But it dishonored you when you began
To speak so roughly, sir, to an old man,
135 Unless he had injured you in word or deed.
It says in holy writ, as you may read,
'Thou shalt rise up before the hoary° head
And honor it.' And therefore be it said,
'Do no more harm to an old man than you,
140 Being now young, would have another do
When you are old'—if you should live till then.
And so may God be with you, gentlemen,
For I must go whither I have to go."
　　"By God," the gambler said, "you shan't do so,
145 You don't get off so easy, by St. John!
I heard you mention, just a moment gone,
A certain traitor Death who singles out
And kills the fine young fellows hereabout.
And you're his spy, by God! You wait a bit.
150 Say where he is or you shall pay for it,
By God and by the Holy Sacrament!
I say you've joined together by consent
To kill us younger folk, you thieving swine!"
　　"Well, sirs," he said, "if it be your design
155 To find out Death, turn up this crooked way

130. **shirt of hair:** Coarse shirts of woven horsehair were worn as penance. Here, the old man refers to such a shirt used to wrap his body for burial.

137. **hoary:** white.

WORDS TO OWN
pallor (pal′ər) *n.*: paleness.

Towards that grove, I left him there today
Under a tree, and there you'll find him waiting.
He isn't one to hide for all your prating.
You see that oak? He won't be far to find.

160 And God protect you that redeemed mankind,
Aye, and amend you!" Thus that ancient man.
    At once the three young rioters began
To run, and reached the tree, and there they found
A pile of golden florins° on the ground,

165 New-coined, eight bushels of them as they thought.
No longer was it Death those fellows sought,
For they were all so thrilled to see the sight,
The florins were so beautiful and bright,
That down they sat beside the precious pile.

170 The wickedest spoke first after a while.
"Brothers," he said, "you listen to what I say.
I'm pretty sharp although I joke away.
It's clear that Fortune has bestowed this treasure
To let us live in jollity and pleasure.

175 Light come, light go! We'll spend it as we ought.
God's precious dignity! Who would have thought
This morning was to be our lucky day?
    "If one could only get the gold away,
Back to my house, or else to yours, perhaps—

180 For as you know, the gold is ours, chaps—
We'd all be at the top of fortune, hey?
But certainly it can't be done by day.
People would call us robbers—a strong gang,
So our own property would make us hang.

185 No, we must bring this treasure back by night
Some prudent way, and keep it out of sight.
And so as a solution I propose
We draw for lots and see the way it goes;
The one who draws the longest, lucky man,

190 Shall run to town as quickly as he can
To fetch us bread and wine—but keep things dark—
While two remain in hiding here to mark
Our heap of treasure. If there's no delay,

164. florins: coins worth twenty-four pence. *Pence* is the British plural of *penny*.

The Three Living, The Three Dead, from the *Psalter and Prayer Book of Bonne of Luxembourg, Duchess of Normandy* (14th century), fol. 321v–322r. Grisaille, color, gilt, and brown ink on vellum (4 15/16" × 3 9/16"). French, Paris.

The Metropolitan Museum of Art.
The Cloisters Collection, 1969 (69.86). Photograph
© 1991 The Metropolitan Museum of Art.

When night comes down we'll carry it away,
195 All three of us, wherever we have planned."
　　He gathered lots and hid them in his hand
Bidding them draw for where the luck should fall.
It fell upon the youngest of them all,
And off he ran at once towards the town.
200 　　As soon as he had gone the first sat down
And thus began a parley with the other:
"You know that you can trust me as a brother;
Now let me tell you where your profit lies;
You know our friend has gone to get supplies
205 And here's a lot of gold that is to be
Divided equally among us three.
Nevertheless, if I could shape things thus
So that we shared it out—the two of us—
Wouldn't you take it as a friendly act?"
210 　　"But how?" the other said. "He knows the fact
That all the gold was left with me and you;
What can we tell him? What are we to do?"
　　"Is it a bargain," said the first, "or no?
For I can tell you in a word or so
215 What's to be done to bring the thing about."
"Trust me," the other said, "you needn't doubt
My word. I won't betray you, I'll be true."
　　"Well," said his friend, "you see that we are two,
And two are twice as powerful as one.
220 Now look; when he comes back, get up in fun
To have a wrestle; then, as you attack,
I'll up and put my dagger through his back
While you and he are struggling, as in game;
Then draw your dagger too and do the same.
225 Then all this money will be ours to spend,
Divided equally of course, dear friend.
Then we can gratify our lusts and fill
The day with dicing at our own sweet will."
Thus these two miscreants° agreed to slay
230 The third and youngest, as you heard me say.
　　The youngest, as he ran towards the town,
Kept turning over, rolling up and down
Within his heart the beauty of those bright
New florins, saying, "Lord, to think I might
235 Have all that treasure to myself alone!
Could there be anyone beneath the throne
Of God so happy as I then should be?"
　　And so the Fiend, our common enemy,
Was given power to put it in his thought
240 That there was always poison to be bought,
And that with poison he could kill his friends.
To men in such a state the Devil sends
Thoughts of this kind, and has a full permission

Death with his spear, from *The Pardoner's Tale*. MS Douce 322, fol. 19v.

229. miscreants (mis′krē·ənts):
criminals; literally, "unbelievers."

To lure them on to sorrow and perdition;°
245 For this young man was utterly content
To kill them both and never to repent.
   And on he ran, he had no thought to tarry,
Came to the town, found an apothecary°
And said, "Sell me some poison if you will,
250 I have a lot of rats I want to kill
And there's a polecat too about my yard
That takes my chickens and it hits me hard;
But I'll get even, as is only right,
With vermin that destroy a man by night."
255   The chemist answered, "I've a preparation
Which you shall have, and by my soul's salvation
If any living creature eat or drink
A mouthful, ere° he has the time to think,
Though he took less than makes a grain of wheat,
260 You'll see him fall down dying at your feet;
Yes, die he must, and in so short a while
You'd hardly have the time to walk a mile,
The poison is so strong, you understand."
   This cursed fellow grabbed into his hand
265 The box of poison and away he ran
Into a neighboring street, and found a man
Who lent him three large bottles. He withdrew
And deftly poured the poison into two.
He kept the third one clean, as well he might,
270 For his own drink, meaning to work all night
Stacking the gold and carrying it away.
And when this rioter, this devil's clay,
Had filled his bottles up with wine, all three,
Back to rejoin his comrades sauntered he.
275   Why make a sermon of it? Why waste breath?
Exactly in the way they'd planned his death
They fell on him and slew him, two to one.
Then said the first of them when this was done,
"Now for a drink. Sit down and let's be merry,
280 For later on there'll be the corpse to bury."
And, as it happened, reaching for a sup,
He took a bottle full of poison up
And drank; and his companion, nothing loth,°
Drank from it also, and they perished both.
285   There is, in Avicenna's° long relation
Concerning poison and its operation,
Trust me, no ghastlier section to transcend
What these two wretches suffered at their end.

244. perdition (pər·dish′ən): damnation.

248. apothecary (ə·päth′ə·ker′ē): druggist. Formerly, apothecaries prescribed drugs.

258. ere: before.

283. loth (lōth): reluctant; unwilling; alternate spelling of *loath*.

285. Avicenna's (av′i·sen′ə): Avicenna (980–1037), a famous Islamic philosopher and doctor, wrote several medical books.

- -

WORDS TO OWN
sauntered (sôn′tərd) *v.:* strolled.
transcend (tran·send′) *v.:* to exceed; surpass.

- -

Thus these two murderers received their due,
290　So did the treacherous young poisoner too. . . .

"One thing I should have mentioned in my tale,
Dear people. I've some relics in my bale
And pardons too, as full and fine, I hope,
As any in England, given me by the Pope.
295　If there be one among you that is willing
To have my absolution for a shilling°
Devoutly given, come! and do not harden
Your hearts but kneel in humbleness for pardon;
Or else, receive my pardon as we go.
300　You can renew it every town or so
Always provided that you still renew
Each time, and in good money, what is due.
It is an honor to you to have found
A pardoner with his credentials sound
305　Who can absolve you as you ply the spur
In any accident that may occur.
For instance—we are all at Fortune's beck°—
Your horse may throw you down and break your neck.
What a security it is to all
310　To have me here among you and at call
With pardon for the lowly and the great
When soul leaves body for the future state!
And I advise our Host here to begin,
The most enveloped of you all in sin.
315　Come forward, Host, you shall be the first to pay,
And kiss my holy relics right away.
Only a groat.° Come on, unbuckle your purse!"
　　"No, no," said he, "not I, and may the curse
Of Christ descend upon me if I do! . . ."

320　The Pardoner said nothing, not a word;
He was so angry that he couldn't speak.
"Well," said our Host, "if you're for showing pique,
I'll joke no more, not with an angry man."
　　The worthy Knight immediately began,
325　Seeing the fun was getting rather rough,
And said, "No more, we've all had quite enough.
Now, Master Pardoner, perk up, look cheerly!
And you, Sir Host, whom I esteem so dearly,
I beg of you to kiss the Pardoner.
330　　"Come, Pardoner, draw nearer, my dear sir.
Let's laugh again and keep the ball in play."
They kissed, and we continued on our way.

296. shilling: coin worth twelve pence.

307. beck: summons; in other words, subject to Fortune's will.

317. groat: silver coin worth four pence.

WORDS TO OWN
absolution (ab′sə·lo͞o′shən) n.: forgiveness.

MAKING MEANINGS

First Thoughts

1. How did you respond to the tale told by the Pardoner? How did you respond to the fact that it was told by a man of the Pardoner's character?

Shaping Interpretations

2. How do the tavern knave and the publican **personify** Death? What does the rioters' response to the description tell you?

3. What do you think the poor old man may **symbolize**?

4. Irony is a discrepancy between expectations and reality. How many layers of **irony** can you identify in this story?

5. Why is it ironic that the Pardoner preaches a story with this particular moral? How would you account for the psychology of the Pardoner: Is he truly evil, just drunk, or so used to cheating that he does it automatically?

6. What do you think Chaucer is **satirizing** in "The Pardoner's Tale"?

7. What **moral** does the Pardoner want us to draw from his tale? What moral do you think Chaucer wants you to draw from the Pardoner's tale?

Extending the Text

8. Do people with the Pardoner's ethics and tricks still exist today—in any field of life? Explain.

Reading Check

a. How does the Pardoner describe his own character and morals in his Prologue?

b. According to "The Pardoner's Tale," why are the three rioters looking for Death?

c. Where does the old man tell the three rioters to look for Death? How do they treat him?

d. Describe the rioters' plan for the gold and how it proves fatal to all three men.

e. Why do the Pardoner and the Host quarrel at the end of the tale? Who patches up their quarrel?

9. How would the Pardoner fill in the following personality profile?

Name: _____

Profession: _____

Last Book I Read: _____

Latest Accomplishment: _____

Why I Do What I Do: _____

Future Goals: _____

Quotation I Like Best: _____

CHOICES: Building Your Portfolio

Writer's Notebook

1. Collecting Ideas for a Comparison-Contrast Essay

You might find ideas for a comparison-contrast essay in "The Pardoner's Tale." (See the assignment in the Writer's Workshop on page 185.) The Pardoner is a clergyman who preaches against the very sins he is guilty of. If a contrast between the Pardoner and his tale interests you, take notes on all the ways the tale and its moral contrast with the Pardoner's own values. Save your notes for later use.

Drama/Pantomime

2. Hamming It Up

Working with a partner or a small group, present a dramatization or a pantomime of "The Pardoner's Tale." To dramatize, write speeches for each character and for a narrator who can fill in the story line. For a pantomime, have one person read Chaucer's text while the others act it out without words.

No one on the road to Canterbury is more real than the Wife of Bath (a married woman from the city of Bath, west of London). She is Chaucer's most vibrant and irrepressible character. Having outlived five husbands (and possibly looking for a sixth on this pilgrimage), she is witty, intelligent, opinionated, and sensual. The tale she tells belongs to the "marriage group," several tales that explore what men and women want and ought to do in marriage.

from The Wife of Bath's Tale

Geoffrey Chaucer

translated by Nevill Coghill

The Wife of Bath, from the Ellesmere manuscript, fol. 72r.

By permission of The Huntington Library, San Marino, California.

The Prologue

The Pardoner started up, and thereupon
"Madam," he said, "by God and by St. John,
That's noble preaching no one could surpass!
I was about to take a wife; alas!
5 Am I to buy it on my flesh so dear?
There'll be no marrying for me this year!"
    "You wait," she said, "my story's not begun.
You'll taste another brew before I've done;
You'll find it doesn't taste as good as ale;
10 And when I've finished telling you my tale
Of tribulation in the married life
In which I've been an expert as a wife,
That is to say, myself have been the whip.
So please yourself whether you want to sip
15 At that same cask of marriage I shall broach.
Be cautious before making the approach,
For I'll give instances, and more than ten.
And those who won't be warned by other men,
By other men shall suffer their correction,
20 So Ptolemy° has said, in this connection.
You read his *Almagest;*° you'll find it there."
    "Madam, I put it to you as a prayer,"
The Pardoner said, "go on as you began!
Tell us your tale, spare not for any man.
25 Instruct us younger men in your technique."
"Gladly," she said, "if you will let me speak,
But still I hope the company won't reprove me
Though I should speak as fantasy may move me,
And please don't be offended at my views;
30 They're really only offered to amuse." . . .

20. Ptolemy (täl′ə·mē) (A.D. 100?–165?): ancient geographer, astronomer, and mathematician from Alexandria, Egypt.
21. *Almagest:* word meaning "the greatest"; another title for Ptolemy's major work, *Mathematical Composition,* in which he argues that the earth is the center of the universe, a view held in Europe until 1543.

The Tale

When good King Arthur ruled in ancient days
(A king that every Briton loves to praise)
This was a land brim-full of fairy folk.
The Elf-Queen and her courtiers joined and broke
35 Their elfin dance on many a green mead,°
Or so was the opinion once, I read,
Hundreds of years ago, in days of yore.
But no one now sees fairies any more.
For now the saintly charity and prayer
40 Of holy friars seem to have purged the air;
They search the countryside through field and stream
As thick as motes° that speckle a sun-beam,
Blessing the halls, the chambers, kitchens, bowers,
Cities and boroughs, castles, courts and towers,
45 Thorpes,° barns and stables, outhouses and dairies,
And that's the reason why there are no fairies.
Wherever there was wont° to walk an elf
To-day there walks the holy friar himself
As evening falls or when the daylight springs,
50 Saying his matins° and his holy things,
Walking his limit round from town to town.
Women can now go safely up and down
By every bush or under every tree;
There is no other incubus° but he,
55 So there is really no one else to hurt you
And he will do no more than take your virtue.
   Now it so happened, I began to say,
Long, long ago in good King Arthur's day,
There was a knight who was a lusty liver.
60 One day as he came riding from the river
He saw a maiden walking all forlorn
Ahead of him, alone as she was born.
And of that maiden, spite of all she said,
By very force he took her maidenhead.°
65   This act of violence made such a stir,
So much petitioning to the king for her,
That he condemned the knight to lose his head
By course of law. He was as good as dead
(It seems that then the statutes took that view)
70 But that the queen, and other ladies too,
<u>Implored</u> the king to exercise his grace
So ceaselessly, he gave the queen the case
And granted her his life, and she could choose

35. mead: meadow.

42. motes: dust particles.

45. thorpes: villages.

47. wont (wänt): accustomed.

50. matins (mat′nz): morning prayers.

54. incubus (in′kyoo·bəs): evil spirit believed to descend on a sleeping woman and make her pregnant.

64. maidenhead: virginity.

WORDS TO OWN
implored (im·plôrd′) *v.*: begged.

Whether to show him mercy or refuse.
75   The queen returned him thanks with all her might,
And then she sent a summons to the knight
At her convenience, and expressed her will:
"You stand, for such is the position still,
In no way certain of your life," said she,
80 "Yet you shall live if you can answer me:
What is the thing that women most desire?
Beware the axe and say as I require.
   "If you can't answer on the moment, though,
I will concede you this: You are to go
85 A twelvemonth and a day to seek and learn
Sufficient answer, then you shall return.
I shall take gages° from you to extort
Surrender of your body to the court."
   Sad was the knight and sorrowfully sighed,
90 But there! All other choices were denied,
And in the end he chose to go away
And to return after a year and day
Armed with such answer as there might be sent
To him by God. He took his leave and went.
95   He knocked at every house, searched every place,
Yes, anywhere that offered hope of grace.
What could it be that women wanted most?
But all the same he never touched a coast,
Country, or town in which there seemed to be
100 Any two people willing to agree.
   Some said that women wanted wealth and treasure,
"Honor," said some, some "Jollity and pleasure,"
Some "Gorgeous clothes" and others "Fun in bed,"
"To be oft widowed and remarried," said
105 Others again, and some that what most mattered
Was that we should be cosseted° and flattered.
That's very near the truth, it seems to me;
A man can win us best with flattery.
To dance attendance on us, make a fuss,
110 Ensnares us all, the best and worst of us.
   Some say the things we most desire are these:
Freedom to do exactly as we please,
With no one to reprove our faults and lies,
Rather to have one call us good and wise.
115 Truly there's not a woman in ten score°
Who has a fault, and someone rubs the sore,
But she will kick if what he says is true;

87. gages: pledges.

Dijon Library, Dijon, France.

A scene from Virgil's *Aeneid*
(15th century). MS 493, fol. 74v.

106. cosseted (käs′it·id):
pampered.

115. ten score: two hundred.
A score is twenty.

WORDS TO OWN

concede (kən·sēd′) *v.:* grant.
extort (eks·tôrt′) *v.:* to get by threats or violence.

You try it out and you will find so too.
However vicious we may be within
120 We like to be thought wise and <u>void</u> of sin.
Others assert we women find it sweet
When we are thought dependable, discreet
And secret, firm of purpose and controlled,
Never betraying things that we are told.
125 But that's not worth the handle of a rake;
Women conceal a thing? For Heaven's sake!
Remember Midas?° Will you hear the tale?
    Among some other little things, now stale,
Ovid° relates that under his long hair
130 The unhappy Midas grew a splendid pair
Of ass's ears; as subtly as he might,
He kept his foul deformity from sight;
Save for his wife, there was not one that knew.
He loved her best, and trusted in her too.
135 He begged her not to tell a living creature
That he possessed so horrible a feature.
And she—she swore, were all the world to win,
She would not do such villainy and sin
As saddle her husband with so foul a name;
140 Besides to speak would be to share the shame.
Nevertheless she thought she would have died
Keeping this secret bottled up inside;
It seemed to swell her heart and she, no doubt,
Thought it was on the point of bursting out.
145   Fearing to speak of it to woman or man,
Down to a reedy marsh she quickly ran
And reached the sedge.° Her heart was all on fire
And, as a bittern° bumbles in the mire,
She whispered to the water, near the ground,
150 "Betray me not, O water, with thy sound!
To thee alone I tell it: It appears
My husband has a pair of ass's ears!
Ah! My heart's well again, the secret's out!
I could no longer keep it, not a doubt."
155 And so you see, although we may hold fast
A little while, it must come out at last,
We can't keep secrets; as for Midas, well,
Read Ovid for his story;° he will tell.
    This knight that I am telling you about
160 Perceived at last he never would find out
What it could be that women loved the best.
Faint was the soul within his sorrowful breast,

127. Midas: mythical king. Everything he touched turned to gold.

129. Ovid (43 B.C.–C. A.D. 17): Roman poet. Ovid's *Metamorphoses*, a collection of tales, includes one version of the Midas story.

147. sedge: grasslike plant.
148. bittern: type of wading bird.

158. read . . . story: In Ovid's version, it is Midas's barber, not his wife, who tells the secret to a hole in the ground. Reeds grow up in the hole and whisper the secret whenever the wind rustles them.

WORDS TO OWN
void (void) *adj.*: empty.

As home he went, he dared no longer stay;
His year was up and now it was the day.

165   As he rode home in a dejected mood
Suddenly, at the margin of a wood,
He saw a dance upon the leafy floor
Of four and twenty ladies, nay, and more.
Eagerly he approached, in hope to learn
170 Some words of wisdom ere he should return;
But lo! Before he came to where they were,
Dancers and dance all vanished into air!
There wasn't a living creature to be seen
Save one old woman crouched upon the green.
175 A fouler-looking creature I suppose
Could scarcely be imagined. She arose
And said, "Sir knight, there's no way on from here.
Tell me what you are looking for, my dear,
For peradventure° that were best for you;
180 We old, old women know a thing or two."

    "Dear Mother," said the knight, "alack the day!
I am as good as dead if I can't say
What thing it is that women most desire;
If you could tell me I would pay your hire."
185 "Give me your hand," she said, "and swear to do
Whatever I shall next require of you
—If so to do should lie within your might—
And you shall know the answer before night."
"Upon my honor," he answered, "I agree."
190 "Then," said the crone, "I dare to guarantee
Your life is safe; I shall make good my claim.
Upon my life the queen will say the same.
Show me the very proudest of them all
In costly coverchief or jeweled caul°
195 That dare say no to what I have to teach.
Let us go forward without further speech."
And then she crooned her gospel in his ear
And told him to be glad and not to fear.

    They came to court. This knight, in full array,
200 Stood forth and said, "O Queen, I've kept my day
And kept my word and have my answer ready."

    There sat the noble matrons and the heady
Young girls, and widows too, that have the grace
Of wisdom, all assembled in that place,
205 And there the queen herself was throned to hear
And judge his answer. Then the knight drew near
And silence was commanded through the hall.

    The queen gave order he should tell them all
What thing it was that women wanted most.
210 He stood not silent like a beast or post,
But gave his answer with the ringing word

Medieval knight
on horseback.

179. peradventure: perhaps.

194. coverchief . . . caul (kôl):
women's headgear. The coverchief
covered the entire head; the caul, a
small, netted cap, was sometimes
ornamented.

Of a man's voice and the assembly heard:
    "My liege° and lady, in general," said he,
"A woman wants the self-same sovereignty°
215 Over her husband as over her lover,
And master him; he must not be above her.
That is your greatest wish, whether you kill
Or spare me; please yourself. I wait your will."
    In all the court not one that shook her head
220 Or contradicted what the knight had said;
Maid, wife, and widow cried, "He's saved his life!"
    And on the word up started the old wife,
The one the knight saw sitting on the green,
And cried, "Your mercy, sovereign lady queen!
225 Before the court disperses, do me right!
'Twas I who taught this answer to the knight,
For which he swore, and pledged his honor to it,
That the first thing I asked of him he'd do it,
So far as it should lie within his might.
230 Before this court I ask you then, sir knight,
To keep your word and take me for your wife;
For well you know that I have saved your life.
If this be false, deny it on your sword!"
    "Alas!" he said, "Old lady, by the Lord
235 I know indeed that such was my behest,°
But for God's love think of a new request,
Take all my goods, but leave my body free."
    "A curse on us," she said, "if I agree!
I may be foul, I may be poor and old,
240 Yet will not choose to be, for all the gold
That's bedded in the earth or lies above,
Less than your wife, nay, than your very love!"
    "My love?" said he. "By heaven, my damnation!
Alas that any of my race and station
245 Should ever make so foul a misalliance!"
Yet in the end his pleading and defiance
All went for nothing, he was forced to wed.
He takes his ancient wife and goes to bed.
    Now peradventure some may well suspect
250 A lack of care in me since I neglect
To tell of the rejoicings and display
Made at the feast upon their wedding-day.
I have but a short answer to let fall;
I say there was no joy or feast at all,
255 Nothing but heaviness of heart and sorrow.
He married her in private on the morrow
And all day long stayed hidden like an owl,
It was such torture that his wife looked foul.
    Great was the anguish churning in his head
260 When he and she were piloted to bed;

213. liege (lēj): lord.
214. sovereignty (säv′rən·tē): power.

235. behest: command; order.

He wallowed° back and forth in desperate style.
His ancient wife lay smiling all the while;
At last she said "Bless us! Is this, my dear,
How knights and wives get on together here?

265 Are these the laws of good King Arthur's house?
Are knights of his all so contemptuous?
I am your own beloved and your wife,
And I am she, indeed, that saved your life;
And certainly I never did you wrong.

270 Then why, this first of nights, so sad a song?
You're carrying on as if you were half-witted
Say, for God's love, what sin have I committed?
I'll put things right if you will tell me how."
    "Put right?" he cried. "That never can be now!

275 Nothing can ever be put right again!
You're old, and so abominably plain,
So poor to start with, so low-bred to follow;
It's little wonder if I twist and wallow!
God, that my heart would burst within my breast!"

280   "Is that," said she, "the cause of your unrest?"
    "Yes, certainly," he said, "and can you wonder?"
    "I could set right what you suppose a blunder,
That's if I cared to, in a day or two,
If I were shown more courtesy by you.

285 Just now," she said, "you spoke of gentle birth,
Such as descends from ancient wealth and worth.
If that's the claim you make for gentlemen
Such arrogance is hardly worth a hen.
Whoever loves to work for virtuous ends,

290 Public and private, and who most intends
To do what deeds of gentleness he can,
Take him to be the greatest gentleman.
Christ wills we take our gentleness from Him,
Not from a wealth of ancestry long dim,

295 Though they bequeath their whole establishment
By which we claim to be of high descent.
Our fathers cannot make us a <u>bequest</u>
Of all those virtues that became them best
And earned for them the name of gentlemen,

300 But bade us follow them as best we can.
    "Thus the wise poet of the Florentines,
Dante° by name, has written in these lines,
For such is the opinion Dante launches:
'Seldom arises by these slender branches

305 <u>Prowess</u> of men, for it is God, no less,

261. **wallowed:** tossed and turned.

Opening page of the *Tale of the Wife of Bath* (c. 1898) from the Kelmscott *Chaucer*.

302. **Dante:** Dante Alighieri (dän′tā a′lə·gyer′ē) (1265–1321), Italian poet who wrote *The Divine Comedy*. (See page 392.)

WORDS TO OWN
bequest (bē·kwest′) *n.*: gift left by means of a will.
prowess (prou′is) *n.*: outstanding ability.

Wills us to claim of Him our gentleness.'
For of our parents nothing can we claim
Save <u>temporal</u> things, and these may hurt and maim.
   "But everyone knows this as well as I;
310 For if gentility were implanted by
The natural course of <u>lineage</u> down the line,
Public or private, could it cease to shine
In doing the fair work of gentle deed?
No vice or villainy could then bear seed.

315 "Take fire and carry it to the darkest house
Between this kingdom and the Caucasus,°
And shut the doors on it and leave it there,
It will burn on, and it will burn as fair
As if ten thousand men were there to see,
320 For fire will keep its nature and degree,
I can assure you, sir, until it dies.
   "But gentleness, as you will recognize,
Is not annexed in nature to possessions.
Men fail in living up to their professions;°
325 But fire never ceases to be fire.
God knows you'll often find, if you inquire,
Some lording° full of villainy and shame.
If you would be esteemed for the mere name
Of having been by birth a gentleman
330 And stemming from some virtuous, noble clan,
And do not live yourself by gentle deed
Or take your father's noble code and creed,
You are no gentleman, though duke or earl.
Vice and bad manners are what make a churl.°

335 "Gentility is only the renown
For bounty that your fathers handed down,
Quite foreign to your person, not your own;
Gentility must come from God alone.
That we are gentle comes to us by grace
340 And by no means is it bequeathed with place.
   "Reflect how noble (says Valerius)°
Was Tullius surnamed Hostilius,°
Who rose from poverty to nobleness.
And read Boethius,° Seneca° no less,
345 Thus they express themselves and are agreed:
'Gentle is he that does a gentle deed.'
And therefore, my dear husband, I conclude
That even if my ancestors were rude,
Yet God on high—and so I hope He will—
350 Can grant me grace to live in virtue still,

- -

WORDS TO OWN

temporal (tem′pə·rəl) *adj.*: limited to this world; not spiritual.
lineage (lin′ē·ij) *n.*: ancestry.

- -

316. Caucasus (kô′kə·səs): mountain range in southeastern Europe, between the Black Sea and the Caspian Sea; in other words, far away.

324. professions: promises.

327. lording: alternate form of *lord.*

334. churl: ill-mannered person.

341. Valerius (və·lir′ē·əs): first-century A.D. Roman writer who compiled historical anecdotes that public speakers could use.
342. Tullius (tul′ē·əs) **surnamed Hostilius** (hos·til′ē·əs): Tullius Hostilius, legendary king of Rome who rose from humble origins.
344. Boethius (bō·ē′thē·əs) (c. A.D. 480–c. 524): Roman philosopher. In his *Consolation of Philosophy,* he argues that rank is no guarantee of honorable conduct. **Seneca** (sen′i·kə) (c. 4 B.C.–A.D. 65): Roman philosopher whose works were popular in the Middle Ages.

A gentlewoman only when beginning
To live in virtue and to shrink from sinning.
    "As for my poverty which you reprove,
Almighty God Himself in whom we move,
355 Believe, and have our being, chose a life
Of poverty, and every man or wife
Nay, every child can see our Heavenly King
Would never stoop to choose a shameful thing.
No shame in poverty if the heart is gay,
360 As Seneca and all the learned say.
He who accepts his poverty unhurt
I'd say is rich although he lacked a shirt.
But truly poor are they who whine and fret
And covet what they cannot hope to get.
365 And he that, having nothing, covets not,
Is rich, though you may think he is a sot.°
    "True poverty can find a song to sing.
Juvenal° says a pleasant little thing:
'The poor can dance and sing in the relief
370 Of having nothing that will tempt a thief.'
Though it be hateful, poverty is good,
A great incentive to a livelihood,
And a great help to our capacity
For wisdom, if accepted patiently.
375 Poverty is, though wanting in estate,
A kind of wealth that none calumniate.°
Poverty often, when the heart is lowly,
Brings one to God and teaches what is holy,
Gives knowledge of oneself and even lends
380 A glass by which to see one's truest friends.
And since it's no offense, let me be plain;
Do not rebuke my poverty again.
    "Lastly you taxed me, sir, with being old.
Yet even if you never had been told
385 By ancient books, you gentlemen engage
Yourselves in honor to respect old age.
To call an old man 'father' shows good breeding,
And this could be supported from my reading.
    "You say I'm old and fouler than a fen.°
390 You need not fear to be a cuckold,° then.
Filth and old age, I'm sure you will agree,
Are powerful wardens over chastity.
Nevertheless, well knowing your delights,
I shall fulfill your worldly appetites.
395   "You have two choices; which one will you try?
To have me old and ugly till I die,
But still a loyal, true, and humble wife
That never will displease you all her life,
Or would you rather I were young and pretty

366. sot: fool.

368. Juvenal (jōō′və·n'l)
(c. A.D. 60–c. 140): Roman satirist.

376. calumniate (kə·lum′nē·āt′):
slander.

389. fen: swamp.
390. cuckold (kuk′əld): man
whose wife has been unfaithful
to him.

400 And chance your arm what happens in a city
   Where friends will visit you because of me,
   Yes, and in other places too, maybe.
   Which would you have? The choice is all your own."
      The knight thought long, and with a piteous groan

405 At last he said, with all the care in life,
   "My lady and my love, my dearest wife,
   I leave the matter to your wise decision.
   You make the choice yourself, for the provision
   Of what may be agreeable and rich

410 In honor to us both, I don't care which;
   Whatever pleases you suffices me."
      "And have I won the mastery?" said she,
   "Since I'm to choose and rule as I think fit?"
   "Certainly, wife," he answered her, "that's it."

415 "Kiss me," she cried. "No quarrels! On my oath
   And word of honor, you shall find me both,
   That is, both fair and faithful as a wife;
   May I go howling mad and take my life
   Unless I prove to be as good and true

420 As ever wife was since the world was new!
   And if to-morrow when the sun's above
   I seem less fair than any lady-love,
   Than any queen or empress east or west,
   Do with my life and death as you think best.

425 Cast up the curtain, husband. Look at me!"
      And when indeed the knight had looked to see,
   Lo, she was young and lovely, rich in charms.
   In ecstasy he caught her in his arms,
   His heart went bathing in a bath of blisses

430 And melted in a hundred thousand kisses,
   And she responded in the fullest measure
   With all that could delight or give him pleasure.
      So they lived ever after to the end
   In perfect bliss; and may Christ Jesus send

435 Us husbands meek and young and fresh in bed,
   And grace to overbid them when we wed.
   And—Jesu hear my prayer!—cut short the lives
   Of those who won't be governed by their wives;
   And all old, angry niggards of their pence,°

440 God send them soon a very pestilence!

A man and woman on horseback, from *The Devonshire Hunting Tapestries* (detail). Arras 1425–50.

Victoria and Albert Museum, London.

439. niggards (nig′erdz) **of their pence:** stingy persons.

WORDS TO OWN
suffices (sə·fis′iz) *v.:* satisfies.
pestilence (pes′tə·ləns) *n.:* plague.

Worn Out

My grandmother's hands
looked like leaves
carved where her veins
stood green.

Her strong fingers were rough.
Her skin gripped her bones,
crinkled and wrinkled,
textured and worn.

Those hands worked.
Ten fingers knitted scarves for the
    winter cold,
gardened strawberries and snapdragons
and cooked meals on her old stove
while a blue flame swooned
below the burner's glow.
Her hands scrubbed.
Her calloused hands scrubbed
dusty memories off the walls.

Her hands toiled and twisted
the stubborn lid off the jar of homemade
raspberry jam.
Her fingers clenched the stubborn lid
until her face would seize her bones and cling
while the veins in her hands would jump and
    string,
beneath the worn folds of her skin.

Her bones showed from the inside out
pointing up from beneath, supporting her
    skin
and revealing the mechanics inside.

Her hands left her behind,
protesting time and clutching will.

—Stephanie Bailey
Taylorsville High School
Salt Lake City, Utah

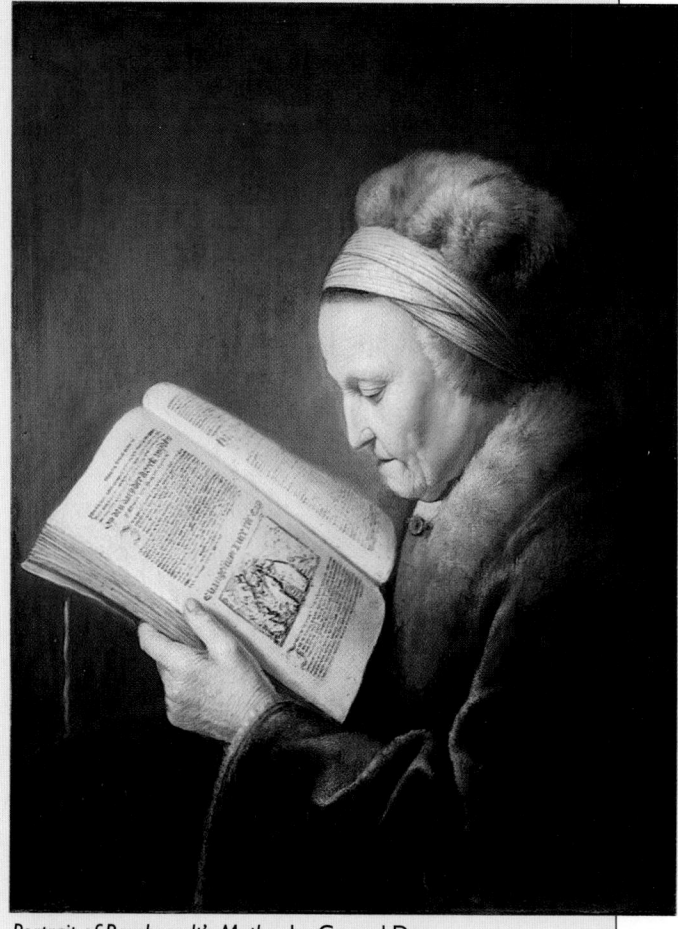

Portrait of Rembrandt's Mother by Gerard Dou.
Rijksmuseum Foundation.

MAKING MEANINGS

First Thoughts

1. What did you think of the Wife of Bath's opinion about what women want most? If she were asked what men want most, how do you suppose she would respond?

Shaping Interpretations

2. The knight's quest is to find out what women want. What **irony** do you see in this?

3. In lines 276–278, the knight moans about having the old woman for his wife. How does she respond to each objection he raises?

4. How does the knight's response to the choice given him by the old woman show that he's learned his lesson about what women want?

5. What opinions does the Wife of Bath express in the tale? What do all her opinions and her tale itself tell you about her **character**?

6. Look at the various things the Wife of Bath, in her tale, says people think women want. What do you think of those proposed answers?

> **Reading Check**
>
> a. What were the knight's crime, his original sentence, and his second sentence?
>
> b. What bargain do the knight and the old woman strike?
>
> c. What payment for her help does the old woman demand, and what is the knight's response?
>
> d. What final choice does the old woman offer the knight at the end of the tale? What is his response?

Extending the Text

7. What do you think contemporary men and women think about what the other wants most out of life or from a relationship? Do you think they would agree, or do they have different wishes and expectations of one another?

8. How would the Wife of Bath fit into contemporary society? What social trends would she support or reject?

Challenging the Text

9. Consider the way this story begins and ends. How does the knight get into trouble, and how do things turn out for him? Does the story satisfy or trouble you, and are there any elements that bother you?

ELEMENTS OF LITERATURE

Couplets: Sound and Sense

Chaucer's favorite rhyme scheme in *The Canterbury Tales* is the **couplet,** two consecutive lines of poetry that rhyme: "When good King Arthur ruled in ancient *days* / (A king that every Briton loves to *praise*)." (When he was growing old, Chaucer complained that his faculty of rhyming was leaving him, which may be the reason he never finished *The Canterbury Tales*.) Nevill Coghill, the translator of the tales used here, followed Chaucer's rhyme scheme, though he did not always use Chaucer's own rhyming words.

Analyzing Chaucer's rhymes. Look closely at these aspects of Chaucer's rhyme.

1. **Read aloud** parts of the Prologue to see how the couplets animate the survey of the pilgrims. Find some rhymes that are humorous.

2. Find what you think are the equivalents of these words in the Middle English version of the Prologue (page 104): *flower, breath, eye, courage,* and *condition.* The pronunciation of these words has changed since the Middle Ages. According to the words they're rhymed with in the Prologue, how would each of these words have been **pronounced** in Chaucer's day?

3. Identify at least two couplets in the Wife's tale that use **half rhymes** (also called **approximate rhymes**), words that share similar but not identical sounds.

Translating Chaucer. Compare the couplets Coghill uses in his translation of the first forty-two lines of the Prologue with the couplets Chaucer uses in his original. Then try to translate these original lines of the Prologue yourself, perhaps using more of Chaucer's original couplets.

Choices: Building Your Portfolio

Writer's Notebook

1. Collecting Ideas for a Comparison-Contrast Essay

The Wife of Bath is one of Chaucer's most interesting characters. For the comparison-contrast essay you will write for the Writer's Workshop on page 185, you might want to compare the outspoken Wife with a modern-day woman. Take notes on the Wife's opinions, values, and experiences. What does her story reveal about her? How do her opinions, values, and experiences compare with those of a woman today? Is the Wife of Bath a "modern woman" or is she medieval in her outlook? How would today's woman answer the question "What do women want?" You might even take notes on what the Wife of Bath would be doing if she were alive today. Be aware that in this exercise you will be analyzing the influences of a **historical context** on a work. You might find the influences minor. Save your notes.

Analyzing Character

2. Characters to Probe

Whom do you find more interesting, the Pardoner or the Wife of Bath? In an essay of several paragraphs, explain your response to one of these pilgrims and then analyze the person's character. Before you write, review the methods of characterization presented on page 103. Use specific details from the text to support your analysis.

Creative Writing

3. Inventing a Frame

Write a prologue to your own frame story. Begin by deciding what kind of journey or other experience will bring your characters together. Will they meet in a bus station? at an airport? on a summer visit? Maybe your characters are survivors of a storm or accident and are waiting for rescue. List four characters who are sharing this experience. In a prologue, introduce your characters. Describe each character from tip to toe, including details of appearance that suggest each character's traits. (Notice how the student writer of "Worn Out" on page 148 describes her grandmother.) You may write in prose or try your hand at rhymed couplets like Chaucer's. Devote at least six lines to each character. If you are so inspired, provide an illustration of each of your characters.

Visual Art

4. Illustrating

The illuminated manuscript was a popular art form of the Middle Ages. Its pages contained highly decorated initial letters or words or miniature pictures such as those shown on pages 100, 101, and 102. Select a passage from either "The Wife of Bath's Tale" or "The Pardoner's Tale," and write it out with illustrations, as if it were a modern illuminated manuscript.

Dramatization

5. Bring a Pilgrim to Life

Choose a pilgrim other than the Wife of Bath or the Pardoner. Dress as the character, and present a reading of his or her tale to your classmates. At the end of your reading, explain why you chose this character and why you think the tale was suited to its teller.

Research: Art/Music

6. Re-Seeing Chaucer

Artists William Blake (1757–1827) and William Morris (1834–1896) created their own versions of Chaucer's pilgrims, and Nevill Coghill, a translator of Chaucer, also wrote song lyrics for the musical *Canterbury Tales* (1968). Find copies of these works and evaluate them. Do they adhere to the original *Tales* or offer a new interpretation?

Reading Skills and Strategies

VOCABULARY: ANALYZING WORD PARTS

When a word is unfamiliar or difficult to understand, you can often discover its meaning by examining the word's parts. These parts make up the **structure** of the word, which may consist of a **root**, a **prefix**, and a **suffix**.

Roots. Words are built upon a base, or root, which contains the core of the word's meaning. Many words in the English language have Latin or Greek roots. The root *-scribe-* or *-script-*, for instance, comes from Latin and means "to write." Notice that the following words contain this root and that all relate to writing: *inscription, manuscript, postscript, prescribe, scribble, scripture.*

Prefixes. Affixes are word parts that can be attached to a root to modify its meaning. A **prefix** is an affix that is placed *before* the root; it can have a general meaning or several meanings. For instance, *a–,* derived from Old English, means "in, on, of, up, to," as in "ashore." The Latin and Latin-French meaning for *a–* is "from, off, away," as in "averse," and the Greek meaning is "lacking, without," as in "amoral." Here are some examples:

Prefixes	Meanings	Examples
a–, ab–, abs–	from, off, away	abide, absolution
be–	around, about	befall, bequest
co–, col–, com–, con–, cor–, syn–	with, together	concede, synchronize
ex–, e–, ef–	away from, out	exhale, extort
en–, em–, in–	in, into, within	encourage
super–	over, above, extra	superfluity, supervisor

By adding a prefix to a root, a new word is formed with the combined meanings of both. Notice that the word *submarine* is composed of the prefix *sub-,* meaning "below," and the root *-marine-,* meaning "water." Prefixes with different spellings but the same meaning often originate in different languages. In this sentence, the prefixes *quint-* (Latin) and *penta-* (Greek) both mean "five": The *quint*et played in a concert hall shaped like a *penta*gon.

Suffixes. A **suffix** is an affix that is placed *after* the root to modify the root's meaning. The plurals of nouns, tenses of verbs, and comparative and superlative forms of adjectives and adverbs are created by suffixes such as *-ed* or *-s.* A word's meaning and its part of speech can be changed by other suffixes, sometimes called **derivational suffixes.** The word *glory* is a noun. Notice what happens with the addition of various suffixes: glori*fication* (noun); glori*fy* (verb); glori*ous* (adjective); glori*ously* (adverb). Here are some examples:

Suffixes	Meanings	Examples
–ous (adjective)	marked by, given to	efficacious, virtuous
–ic (adjective or noun)	dealing with, caused by	classic, choleric
–ence (noun)	act, condition, fact	pestilence, reverence
–ize (verb)	make, cause to be	energize, sterilize

Try It Out

Each of the following words is from *The Canterbury Tales.* Use a dictionary to determine the root and affix(es) of each word, and show how the structure of each word contributes to the word's meaning.

1. diligent
2. obstinate
3. covetousness
4. superfluity
5. transcend

Silver and gold portable sundial (10th century).

Canterbury Cathedral, Kent.

Italy

Giovanni Boccaccio

(1313–1375)

Giovanni Boccaccio is one of Italy's foremost writers. Raised in Florence, Boccaccio later studied business in Naples, but he soon transferred his ambitions from banking to literature. In his first prose romance, Boccaccio describes meeting a lovely woman named Fiammetta, with whom he falls immediately in love. Scholars have hotly argued about this woman's real identity—and even whether she existed at all. Fiammetta reappears in many of Boccaccio's later works, which often explore the theme of love. It is Fiammetta who tells the story of Federigo's falcon in the *Decameron*.

The two great subjects of the stories in the *Decameron* are love and the corruption of the clergy. Many of the *Decameron's* stories are adaptations of popular folk tales, fables, anecdotes, and even jokes that Boccaccio might have overheard on the bustling streets of medieval Naples. Boccaccio's stories have served as both a source and a model for many writers who followed him, among them Chaucer, Shakespeare, and Milton.

Boccaccio (15th century) by Andrea del Castagno.
Uffizi, Florence.

(Map) Old map showing a portion of the Mediterranean Coast.

Before You Read

FEDERIGO'S FALCON

Make the Connection

The Pain of Love

Few experiences are more painful than falling in love with someone who couldn't care less. We get over it—most of us—and it never—well, almost never—does us serious damage. But while we're suffering, we suffer intensely. It's hard to think about anything else; we can't do our work; food, if we bother to eat, is tasteless; we find ourselves staring into space, missing everything going on around us. Worst of all, we're likely to do something so foolish that we make matters even worse.

But you never know how it will all turn out. In the most painful moments, when you think that things can't possibly get worse, they very well might. Or they might, surprisingly, turn around. . . .

Reading Skills and Strategies

Evaluating Historical Context

As you read this medieval love story, take notes on the ways the characters are like—and unlike—the characters in love stories today, or even the people you know in actual life. Keep movies and TV shows in mind too. Consider the ways in which a work's **historical context** can influence its meaning. Can historical context also be unimportant?

Background

"Federigo's Falcon" is part of the *Decameron,* a collection of tales written in fourteenth-century Italy shortly after a devastating plague struck Florence. The stories are grouped loosely within a frame tale about ten wealthy young Florentines who flee to a villa in the country to escape the plague-ravaged city.

To pass the time, the young people decide that for each of ten days (*decameron* is derived from the Greek words for "ten" and "day") they will elect a king or queen, who, in turn, will choose a theme that the others must use to tell a story. "Federigo's Falcon" is the ninth story told on the fifth day, a day devoted to telling stories with happy endings.

Detail from Frederick II's *Treatise on Falconry.*
Ms. Pal. Lat. 1071 fol. 5v.

Apostolic Library, Vatican City, Rome.

Federigo's Falcon
from the Decameron

Giovanni Boccaccio
translated by **Mark Musa and Peter Bondanella**

There was once in Florence a young man named Federigo, the son of Messer[1] Filippo Alberighi, renowned above all other men in Tuscany for his prowess in arms and for his courtliness. As often happens to most gentlemen, he fell in love with a lady named Monna[2] Giovanna, in her day considered to be one of the most beautiful and one of the most charming women that ever there was in Florence; and in order to win her love, he participated in jousts and tournaments, organized and gave feasts, and spent his money without restraint; but she, no less virtuous than beautiful, cared little for these things done on her behalf, nor did she care for him who did them. Now, as Federigo was spending far beyond his means and was taking nothing in, as easily happens he lost his wealth and became poor, with nothing but his little farm to his name (from whose revenues he lived very meagerly) and one falcon which was among the best in the world.

More in love than ever, but knowing that he would never be able to live the way he wished to in the city, he went to live at Campi,[3] where his farm was. There he passed his time hawking whenever he could, asked nothing of anyone, and endured his poverty patiently. Now, during the time that Federigo was reduced to dire need, it happened that the husband of Monna Giovanna fell ill, and realizing death was near, he made his last will. He was very rich, and he made his son, who was growing up, his heir, and, since he had

loved Monna Giovanna very much, he made her his heir should his son die without a legitimate heir; and then he died.

Monna Giovanna was now a widow, and as is the custom among our women, she went to the country with her son to spend a year on one of her possessions very close by to Federigo's farm, and it happened that this young boy became friends with Federigo and began to enjoy birds and hunting dogs; and after he had seen Federigo's falcon fly many times, it pleased him so much that he very much wished it were his own, but he did not dare to ask for it, for he could see how dear it was to Federigo. And during this time, it happened that the young boy took ill, and his mother was much grieved, for he was her only child and she loved him enormously. She would spend the entire day by his side, never ceasing to comfort him, and often asking him if there was anything he desired, begging him to tell her what it might be, for if it were possible to obtain it, she would certainly do everything possible to get it. After the young boy had heard her make this offer many times, he said:

"Mother, if you can arrange for me to have Federigo's falcon, I think I would be well very soon."

When the lady heard this, she was taken aback for a moment, and she began to think what she should do. She knew that Federigo had loved her for a long while, in spite of the fact that he never received a single glance from her, and so, she said to herself:

"How can I send or go and ask for this falcon of his which is, as I have heard tell, the best that ever

---

1. **Messer** (mes′ər): title of address similar to *sir.*
2. **Monna** (mō′nə): In Italian, *Monna* is an abbreviation for *Madonna* (mə·dän′ə), a formal title for a woman, similar to *madam.*
3. **Campi** (käm′pē): small town set in the mountains northwest of Florence. *Campi* literally means "fields."

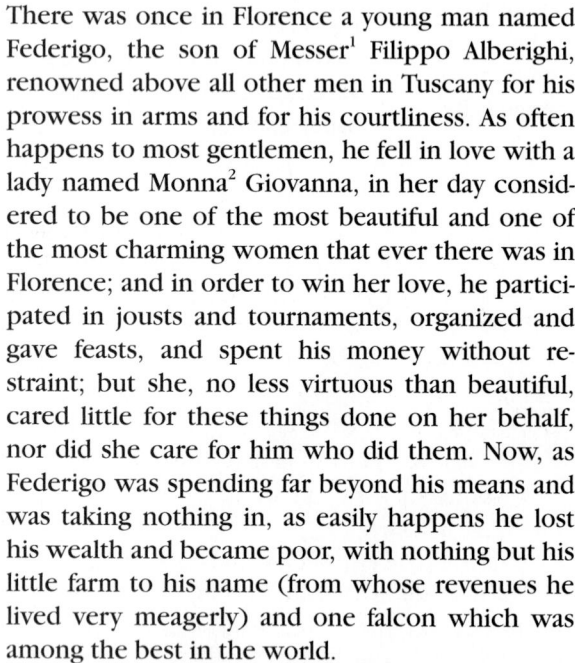

(Above) From an illuminated manuscript (detail) (14th century). MS Bodl. 264, fol. 123v.
The Bodleian Library, Oxford.

flew, and besides this, his only means of support? And how can I be so insensitive as to wish to take away from this gentleman the only pleasure which is left to him?"

And involved in these thoughts, knowing that she was certain to have the bird if she asked for it, but not knowing what to say to her son, she stood there without answering him. Finally the love she bore her son persuaded her that she should make him happy, and no matter what the consequences might be, she would not send for the bird, but rather go herself for it and bring it back to him; so she answered her son:

"My son, take comfort and think only of getting well, for I promise you that the first thing I shall do tomorrow morning is to go for it and bring it back to you."

The child was so happy that he showed some improvement that very day. The following morning, the lady, accompanied by another woman, as if going for a stroll, went to Federigo's modest house and asked for him. Since it was not the season for it, Federigo had not been hawking for some days and was in his orchard, attending to certain tasks. When he heard that Monna Giovanna was asking for him at the door, he was very surprised and happy to run there. As she saw him coming, she greeted him with feminine charm, and once Federigo had welcomed her courteously, she said:

"Greetings, Federigo!" Then she continued: "I have come to compensate you for the harm you have suffered on my account by loving me more than you needed to; and the compensation is this: I, along with this companion of mine, intend to dine with you—a simple meal—this very day."

To this Federigo humbly replied: "Madonna, I never remember having suffered any harm because of you. On the contrary, so much good have I received from you that if ever I have been worth anything, it has been because of your merit and the love I bore for you; and your generous visit is certainly so dear to me that I would spend all over again that which I spent in the past; but you have come to a poor host."

And having said this, he received her into his home humbly, and from there he led her into his garden, and since he had no one there to keep her company, he said:

"My lady, since there is no one else, this good woman here, the wife of this workman, will keep you company while I go to set the table."

Though he was very poor, Federigo, until now, had never before realized to what extent he had wasted his wealth; but this morning, the fact that he found nothing with which he could honor the lady for the love of whom he had once entertained countless men in the past gave him cause to reflect. In great anguish, he cursed himself and his fortune and, like a man beside himself, he started running here and there, but could find neither money nor a pawnable[4] object. The hour was late and his desire to honor the gracious lady was great, but not wishing to turn for help to others (not even to his own workman), he set his eyes upon his good falcon, perched in a small room; and since he had nowhere else to turn, he took the bird, and finding it plump, he decided that it would be a worthy food for such a lady. So, without further thought, he wrung its neck and quickly gave it to his servant girl to pluck, prepare, and place on a spit to be roasted with care; and when he had set the table with the whitest of tablecloths (a few of which he still had left), he returned, with a cheerful face, to the lady in his garden, saying that the meal he was able to prepare for her was ready.

The lady and her companion rose, went to the table together with Federigo, who waited upon them with the greatest devotion, and they ate the good falcon without knowing what it was they were eating. And having left the table and spent some time in pleasant conversation, the lady thought it time now to say what she had come to say, and so she spoke these kind words to Federigo:

"Federigo, if you recall your past life and my virtue, which you perhaps mistook for harshness and cruelty, I do not doubt at all that you will be amazed by my presumption when you hear what my main reason for coming here is; but if you had children, through whom you might have experienced the power of parental love, it seems certain to me that you would, at least in part, forgive me. But, just as you have no child, I do have one, and I

---

4. **pawnable:** able to be given as security in return for a loan of money or goods.

lose him. And therefore I beg you, not because of the love that you bear for me, which does not oblige you in the least, but because of your own nobility, which you have shown to be greater than that of all others in practicing courtliness, that you be pleased to give it to me, so that I may say that I have saved the life of my son by means of this gift, and because of it I have placed him in your debt forever."

When he heard what the lady requested and knew that he could not oblige her since he had given her the falcon to eat, Federigo began to weep in her presence, for he could not utter a word in reply. The lady, at first, thought his tears were caused more by the sorrow of having to part with the good falcon than by anything else, and she was on the verge of telling him she no longer wished it, but she held back and waited for Federigo's reply after he stopped weeping. And he said:

"My lady, ever since it pleased God for me to place my love in you, I have felt that Fortune has been hostile to me in many things, and I have complained of her, but all this is nothing compared to what she has just done to me, and I must never be at peace with her again, thinking about how you have come here to my poor home where, while it was rich, you never deigned to come, and you requested a small gift, and Fortune worked to make it impossible for me to give it to you; and why this is so I shall tell you briefly. When I heard that you, out of your kindness, wished to dine with me, I considered it fitting and right, taking into account your excellence and your worthiness, that I should honor you, according to my possibilities, with a more precious food than that which I usually serve to other people; therefore, remembering the falcon that you requested and its value, I judged it a food worthy of you, and this very day you had it roasted and served to you as best I could; but seeing now that you desired it in another way, my sorrow in not being able to serve you is so great that I shall never be able to console myself again."

August: Departure for the Hunt with Falcons, from the calendar for the *Très riches heures du duc de Berry* by the Limbourg brothers. MS 65 / 1284, fol. 8v.

Musée Condé, Chantilly, France.

cannot escape the common laws of other mothers; the force of such laws compels me to follow them, against my own will and against good manners and duty, and to ask of you a gift which I know is most precious to you; and it is naturally so, since your extreme condition has left you no other delight, no other pleasure, no other consolation; and this gift is your falcon, which my son is so taken by that if I do not bring it to him, I fear his sickness will grow so much worse that I may

And after he had said this, he laid the feathers, the feet, and the beak of the bird before her as proof. When the lady heard and saw this, she first reproached him for having killed such a falcon to serve as a meal to a woman; but then to herself she commended the greatness of his spirit, which no poverty was able or would be able to diminish; then, having lost all hope of getting the falcon and, perhaps because of this, of improving the health of her son as well, she thanked Federigo both for the honor paid to her and for his good will, and she left in grief, and returned to her son. To his mother's extreme sorrow, either because of his disappointment that he could not have the falcon, or because his illness must have necessarily led to it, the boy passed from this life only a few days later.

After the period of her mourning and bitterness had passed, the lady was repeatedly urged by her brothers to remarry, since she was very rich and was still young; and although she did not wish to do so, they became so insistent that she remembered the merits of Federigo and his last act of generosity—that is, to have killed

Couple, from an illustrated manuscript of the *Decameron* (c. 14th century).

© cliché Bibliothèque Nationale de France, Paris.

such a falcon to do her honor—and she said to her brothers:

"I would prefer to remain a widow, if that would please you; but if you wish me to take a husband, you may rest assured that I shall take no man but Federigo degli Alberighi."

In answer to this, making fun of her, her brothers replied:

"You foolish woman, what are you saying? How can you want him; he hasn't a penny to his name?"

To this she replied: "My brothers, I am well aware of what you say, but I would rather have a man who needs money than money that needs a man."

Her brothers, seeing that she was determined and knowing Federigo to be of noble birth, no matter how poor he was, accepted her wishes and gave her in marriage to him with all her riches. When he found himself the husband of such a great lady, whom he had loved so much and who was so wealthy besides, he managed his financial affairs with more prudence than in the past and lived with her happily the rest of his days.

FINDING COMMON GROUND

Federigo and Monna Giovanna live in fourteenth-century Italy. But we share with them some basic human problems. In your reading notes, you may have commented on some of the lovers' difficulties listed here:

- Federigo loves someone who doesn't love him.
- Giovanna must cope with a dying son's wish.
- Giovanna has to ask a favor of someone she has ignored and rejected.
- Federigo has to deal with the discovery that a noble gesture was actually a terrible mistake.

Try to find some contemporary examples of these lovers' problems. Working with a small group, think about how the lovers in this story might be treated by a contemporary writer or filmmaker. How are the problems faced by Federigo and Monna Giovanna both similar to and different from the problems faced by lovers today? How would their story differ if it were retold—as, say, the story of Joan and Fred—and reset in the world of today? Make a list of the differences and similarities that most intrigue you. What actors would you cast to play Giovanna and Federigo in a movie? Present your findings to other groups in your class.

Before You Read

FROM SIR GAWAIN AND THE GREEN KNIGHT

Make the Connection

Finding a Hero

One of the great works of medieval literature, this story was probably written around 1375, at a time when the old ideals of knightly conduct—courage, loyalty, and courtesy—were beginning to erode. Perhaps, as in our own age, people then were looking forward to the future but were also feeling nostalgic for values that had once defined their lives.

Quickwrite

Are we living in a heroic age? Or do most people feel that there are no genuine heroes today? What do we demand of our heroes today? Do a quick survey of your classmates or of people outside school. Keep your survey results, and think about today's heroes as you read about the severe testing of a hero at King Arthur's court.

Elements of Literature

The Romance

Romances (or at least works with some of the trappings of romances) are still being written today. They take the form of novels, movies, even comic strips. Strictly speaking, a **romance** is a narrative set in a world of pure wish fulfillment, where the ordinary laws of nature are suspended and where idealized and superhuman heroes fight and almost always conquer the forces of evil. The basic narrative pattern of the romance is the **quest,** in which the hero undertakes a perilous journey in search of something of value.

> From the thirteenth century onward, **romance** was a term applied to a verse narrative which traced the adventures of a brave knight or other hero who had to overcome danger for love of a noble lady or high ideal.
>
> For more on the Romance, see page 167 and the Handbook of Literary Terms.

Background

As *Sir Gawain and the Green Knight* opens, King Arthur and the knights of the Round Table are feasting. Suddenly an enormous green stranger bursts into the hall. King Arthur greets the Green Knight and asks him to state his business. The Green Knight, after a few scornful words about the manliness of King Arthur's knights, says he only wishes to play a New Year's game. He challenges any knight there to agree to "exchange one blow for another"—he will even give that knight his gisarme (gi·zärm'), his two-bladed ax. The stranger says he will stand for the first blow; the knight must agree to let the Green Knight have *his* turn in a year and a day. Gawain accepts the challenge—no other knight except Arthur himself has dared to, and Gawain refuses to let the king give up his life.

Gawain hefts his ax and chops off the giant green head. But the Knight never falters. He picks up his green head, repeats his challenge, and gallops off with the head in his arms.

Just before Christmas the next year, Gawain sadly sets off on the long journey to honor his pledge. One day he comes upon a beautiful castle. The lord of the castle invites him to rest a few days and then suggests an odd "game." The lord says that he will go hunting each day and whatever he wins in the hunt he will give to Gawain. In return, Gawain must give anything he has won that day to the lord.

Each day when the lord goes off hunting, his beautiful young wife tries to seduce Gawain. For two days, Gawain accepts only kisses, and true to his bargain, he gives the lord the kisses when he returns from hunting. But on the morning of the third day, the lady not only kisses Gawain but also makes him accept a magical green girdle, or sash. She says that if he wears the sash, he cannot be killed.

When the lord returns from the hunt, Gawain gives him the kisses but keeps the sash a secret.

Now it's New Year's Day. Gawain sets off to find the Green Chapel and the dreaded Green Knight. Snow and sleet have fallen, and howling winds have piled up drifts of snow. Gawain leaves the castle with the green sash wrapped around his armor. He is certain he is headed for his death.

from Sir Gawain and the Green Knight
translated by John Gardner

He put his spurs to Gringolet,° plunged down the path,
Shoved through the heavy thicket grown up by the woods
And rode down the steep slope to the floor of the valley;
He looked around him then—a strange, wild place,
5 And not a sign of a chapel on any side
But only steep, high banks surrounding him,
And great, rough knots of rock and rugged crags
That scraped the passing clouds, as it seemed to him.
He heaved at the heavy reins to hold back his horse
10 And squinted in every direction in search of the Chapel,
And still he saw nothing except—and this was strange—
A small green hill all alone, a sort of barrow,°
A low, smooth bulge on the bank of the brimming creek
That flowed from the foot of a waterfall,
15 And the water in the pool was bubbling as if it were boiling.
Sir Gawain urged Gringolet on till he came to the mound
And lightly dismounted and made the reins secure
On the great, thick limb of a gnarled and ancient tree;
Then he went up to the barrow and walked all around it,
20 Wondering in his wits what on earth it might be.
It had at each end and on either side an entrance,
And patches of grass were growing all over the thing,
And all the inside was hollow—an old, old cave
Or the cleft of some ancient crag, he couldn't tell which
25   it was.
                  "Whoo, Lord!" thought the knight,
                  "Is *this* the fellow's place?
                  Here the Devil might
                  Recite his midnight mass.

30 "Dear God," thought Gawain, "the place is deserted enough!
And it's ugly enough, all overgrown with weeds!
Well might it amuse that marvel of green
To do his devotions here, in his devilish way!
In my five senses I fear it's the Fiend himself

1. Gringolet: Gawain's horse.

12. barrow: grave mound.

Sir Gawain strikes off the head of the Green Knight in King Arthur's presence, from an English manuscript (c. 15th century). MS Cotton Nero A.X., fol. 94v.

By permission of the British Library, London.

35 Who's brought me to meet him here to murder me.
   May fire and fury befall this fiendish Chapel,
   As cursed a kirk° as I ever yet came across!"
   With his helmet on his head and his lance in hand
   He leaped up onto the roof of the rock-walled room

37. kirk: Scottish for "church."

40 And, high on that hill, he heard, from an echoing rock
   Beyond the pool, on the hillside, a horrible noise.
   Brrrack! It clattered in the cliffs as if to cleave them,
   A sound like a grindstone grinding on a scythe!°
   Brrrack! It whirred and rattled like water on a mill wheel!

43. scythe (*sīth*): long-handled cutting tool.

45 *Brrrrrack!* It rushed and rang till your blood ran cold.
   And then: "Oh God," thought Gawain, "it grinds, I think,
   For me—a blade prepared for the blow I must take
                              as my right!
              God's will be done! But here!
50   He may well get his knight,
              But still, no use in fear;
              I won't fall dead of fright!"

   And then Sir Gawain roared in a ringing voice,
   "Where is the hero who swore he'd be here to meet me?
55 Sir Gawain the Good is come to the Green Chapel!
   If any man would meet me, make it now,
   For it's now or never, I've no wish to dawdle here long."
   "Stay there!" called someone high above his head,
   "I'll pay you promptly all that I promised before."
60 But still he went on with that whetting noise a while,
   Turning again to his grinding before he'd come down.
   At last, from a hole by a rock he came out into sight,
   Came plunging out of his den with a terrible weapon,
   A huge new Danish ax to deliver his blow with,
65 With a vicious swine of a bit bent back to the handle,
   Filed to a razor's edge and four foot long,
   Not one inch less by the length of that gleaming lace.
   The great Green Knight was garbed as before,
   Face, legs, hair, beard, all as before but for this:
70 That now he walked the world on his own two legs,
   The ax handle striking the stone like a walking-stave.°
   When the knight came down to the water he would not wade
   But vaulted across on his ax, then with awful strides
   Came fiercely over the field filled all around
75   with snow.
              Sir Gawain met him there
              And bowed—but none too low!
              Said the other, "I see, sweet sir,
              You go where you say you'll go!

80 "Gawain," the Green Knight said, "may God be your guard!
   You're very welcome indeed, sir, here at my place;

Sir Gawain, from *Le Roman de Lancelot du Lac* (detail) (c. 15th century). MS 805, fol. 48.

The Pierpont Morgan Library, New York.

71. walking-stave (stāv): staff.

You've timed your travel, my friend, as a true man should.
You recall the terms of the contract drawn up between us:
At this time a year ago you took your chances,
85 And I'm pledged now, this New Year, to make you my payment.
And here we are in this valley, all alone,
And no man here to part us, proceed as we may;
Heave off your helmet then, and have here your pay;
And debate no more with me than I did then
90 When you severed my head from my neck with a single swipe."
"Never fear," said Gawain, "by God who gave
Me life, I'll raise no complaint at the grimness of it;
But take your single stroke, and I'll stand still
And allow you to work as you like and not oppose
95   you here."
          He bowed toward the ground
          And let his skin show clear;
          However his heart might pound,
          He would not show his fear.

100 Quickly then the man in the green made ready,
Grabbed up his keen-ground ax to strike Sir Gawain;
With all the might in his body he bore it aloft
And sharply brought it down as if to slay him;
Had he made it fall with the force he first intended
105 He would have stretched out the strongest man on earth.
But Sir Gawain cast a side glance at the ax
As it glided down to give him his Kingdom Come,°
And his shoulders jerked away from the iron a little,
And the Green Knight caught the handle, holding it back,
110 And mocked the prince with many a proud reproof:°
"*You* can't be Gawain," he said, "who's thought so good,
A man who's never been <u>daunted</u> on hill or dale!
For look how you flinch for fear before anything's felt!
I never heard tell that Sir Gawain was ever a coward!
115 *I* never moved a muscle when *you* came down;
In Arthur's hall I never so much as winced.
My head fell off at my feet, yet I never flickered;
But you! You tremble at heart before you're touched!
I'm bound to be called a better man than you, then,
120   my lord."
          Said Gawain, "I shied once:
          No more. You have my word.
          But if my head falls to the stones
          It cannot be restored.

Sir Gawain is tempted by the lady of the castle, from an English manuscript (c. 15th century). MS Cotton Nero A.X., fol. 129.

By permission of the British Library, London.

107. his Kingdom Come: life after death.

110. reproof: rebuke; scolding.

WORDS TO OWN
daunted (dônt′ed) *adj.*: intimidated.

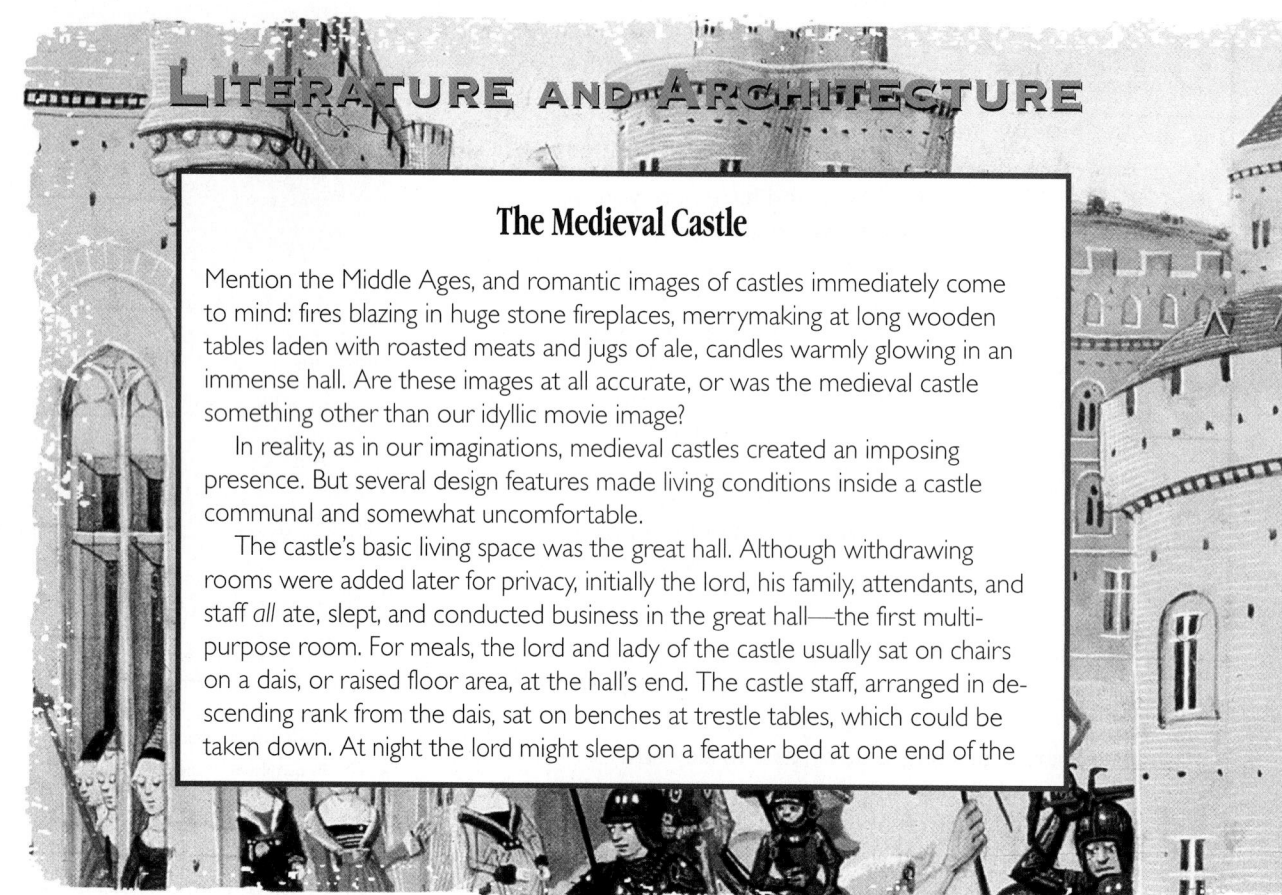

The Medieval Castle

Mention the Middle Ages, and romantic images of castles immediately come to mind: fires blazing in huge stone fireplaces, merrymaking at long wooden tables laden with roasted meats and jugs of ale, candles warmly glowing in an immense hall. Are these images at all accurate, or was the medieval castle something other than our idyllic movie image?

In reality, as in our imaginations, medieval castles created an imposing presence. But several design features made living conditions inside a castle communal and somewhat uncomfortable.

The castle's basic living space was the great hall. Although withdrawing rooms were added later for privacy, initially the lord, his family, attendants, and staff *all* ate, slept, and conducted business in the great hall—the first multi-purpose room. For meals, the lord and lady of the castle usually sat on chairs on a dais, or raised floor area, at the hall's end. The castle staff, arranged in descending rank from the dais, sat on benches at trestle tables, which could be taken down. At night the lord might sleep on a feather bed at one end of the

125 "But be brisk, man, by your faith, and come to the point!
     Deal out my doom if you can, and do it at once,
     For I'll stand for one good stroke, and I'll start no more
     Until your ax has hit—and that I swear."
     "Here goes, then," said the other, and heaves it aloft
130 And stands there waiting, scowling like a madman;
     He swings down sharp, then suddenly stops again,
     Holds back the ax with his hand before it can hurt,
     And Gawain stands there stirring not even a nerve;
     He stood there still as a stone or the stock of a tree
135 That's wedged in rocky ground by a hundred roots.
     O, merrily then he spoke, the man in green:
     "Good! You've got your heart back! Now I can hit you.
     May all that glory the good King Arthur gave you
     Prove <u>efficacious</u> now—if it ever can—
140 And save your neck." In rage Sir Gawain shouted,

WORDS TO OWN
efficacious (ef'i·kā'shəs) *adj.*: effective.

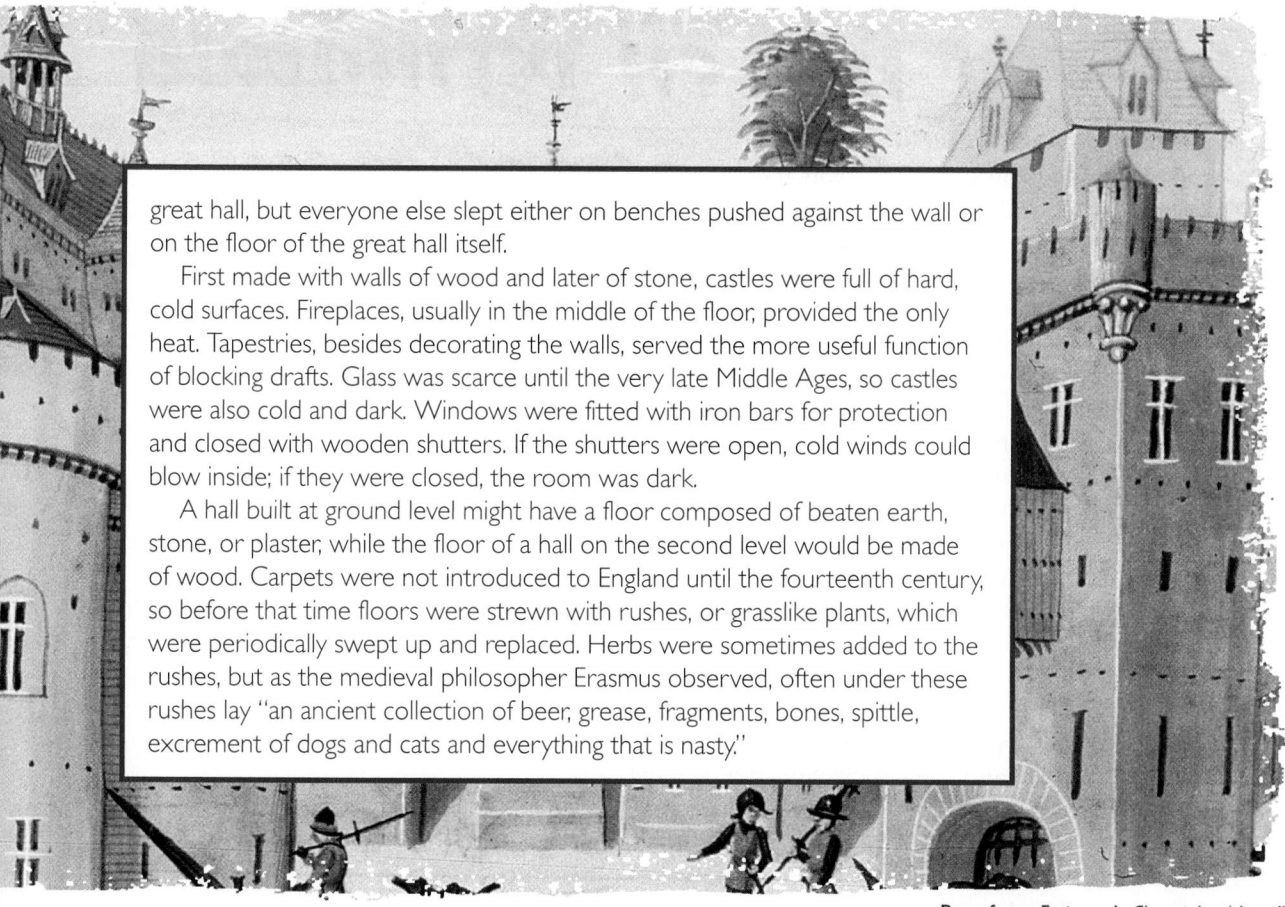

great hall, but everyone else slept either on benches pushed against the wall or on the floor of the great hall itself.

First made with walls of wood and later of stone, castles were full of hard, cold surfaces. Fireplaces, usually in the middle of the floor, provided the only heat. Tapestries, besides decorating the walls, served the more useful function of blocking drafts. Glass was scarce until the very late Middle Ages, so castles were also cold and dark. Windows were fitted with iron bars for protection and closed with wooden shutters. If the shutters were open, cold winds could blow inside; if they were closed, the room was dark.

A hall built at ground level might have a floor composed of beaten earth, stone, or plaster, while the floor of a hall on the second level would be made of wood. Carpets were not introduced to England until the fourteenth century, so before that time floors were strewn with rushes, or grasslike plants, which were periodically swept up and replaced. Herbs were sometimes added to the rushes, but as the medieval philosopher Erasmus observed, often under these rushes lay "an ancient collection of beer, grease, fragments, bones, spittle, excrement of dogs and cats and everything that is nasty."

Page from *Froissart's Chronicles* (detail). MS Fr. 2643, fol. 226v.

© cliché Bibliothèque Nationale de France, Paris.

"*Hit* me, hero! I'm right up to here with your threats!
Is it *you* that's the cringing coward after all?"
"Whoo!" said the man in green, "he's wrathful, too!
No pauses, then; I'll pay up my pledge at once,
145   I vow!"
          He takes his stride to strike
          And lifts his lip and brow;
          It's not a thing Gawain can like,
          For nothing can save him now!

150 He raises that ax up lightly and flashes it down,
And that blinding bit bites in at the knight's bare neck—
But hard as he hammered it down, it hurt him no more
Than to nick the nape of his neck, so it split the skin;
The sharp blade slit to the flesh through the shiny hide,
155 And red blood shot to his shoulders and spattered the ground.
And when Gawain saw his blood where it blinked in the snow
He sprang from the man with a leap to the length of a spear;
He snatched up his helmet swiftly and slapped it on,
Shifted his shield into place with a jerk of his shoulders,

160 And snapped his sword out faster than sight; said boldly—
And, mortal born of his mother that he was,
There was never on earth a man so happy by half—
"No more strokes, my friend; you've had your swing!
I've stood one swipe of your ax without resistance;
165 If you offer me any more, I'll repay you at once
With all the force and fire I've got—as you
                                        will see.
                    I take one stroke, that's all,
                    For that was the compact we
170   Arranged in Arthur's hall;
                    But now, no more for me!"

The Green Knight remained where he stood, relaxing on his ax—
Settled the shaft on the rocks and leaned on the sharp end—
And studied the young man standing there, shoulders hunched,
175 And considered that staunch° and doughty° stance he took,
Undaunted yet, and in his heart he liked it;
And then he said merrily, with a mighty voice—
With a roar like rushing wind he reproved the knight—
"Here, don't be such an ogre on your ground!
180 Nobody here has behaved with bad manners toward you
Or done a thing except as the contract said.
I owed you a stroke, and I've struck; consider yourself
Well paid. And now I release you from all further duties.
If I'd cared to hustle, it may be, perchance, that I might
185 Have hit somewhat harder, and then you might well be cross!
The first time I lifted my ax it was lighthearted sport,
I merely feinted and made no mark, as was right,
For you kept our pact of the first night with honor
And abided by your word and held yourself true to me,
190 Giving me all you owed as a good man should.
I feinted a second time, friend, for the morning
You kissed my pretty wife twice and returned me the kisses;
And so for the first two days, mere feints, nothing more
                                        severe.
195   A man who's true to his word,
                    There's nothing he needs to fear;
                    You failed me, though, on the third
                    Exchange, so I've tapped you here.

"That sash you wear by your scabbard° belongs to me;
200 My own wife gave it to you, as I ought to know.
I know, too, of your kisses and all your words
And my wife's advances, for I myself arranged them.

175. staunch (stônch): steadfast.
doughty (dout′ē): courageous.

199. scabbard (skab′ərd): case that holds the blade of a sword.

WORDS TO OWN
feinted (fānt′id) v.: pretended to strike.

It was I who sent her to test you. I'm convinced
You're the finest man that ever walked this earth.

205 As a pearl is of greater price than dry white peas,
So Gawain indeed stands out above all other knights.
But you lacked a little, sir; you were less than loyal;
But since it was not for the sash itself or for lust
But because you loved your life, I blame you less."

210 Sir Gawain stood in a study° a long, long while,
So miserable with disgrace that he wept within,
And all the blood of his chest went up to his face
And he shrank away in shame from the man's gentle words.
The first words Gawain could find to say were these:

210. stood in a study: stood thinking deeply.

215 "Cursed be cowardice and covetousness both,
Villainy and vice that destroy all virtue!"
He caught at the knots of the girdle° and loosened them
And fiercely flung the sash at the Green Knight.
"There, there's my fault! The foul fiend vex it!

217. girdle: sash.

220 Foolish cowardice taught me, from fear of your stroke,
To bargain, covetous, and abandon my kind,
The selflessness and loyalty suitable in knights;
Here I stand, faulty and false, much as I've feared them,
Both of them, untruth and treachery; may they see sorrow
225   and care!
        I can't deny my guilt;
        My works shine none too fair!
        Give me your good will
        And henceforth I'll beware."

230 At that, the Green Knight laughed, saying graciously,
"Whatever harm I've had, I hold it amended
Since now you're confessed so clean, acknowledging sins
And bearing the plain penance of my point;
I consider you polished as white and as perfectly clean

235 As if you had never fallen since first you were born.
And I give you, sir, this gold-embroidered girdle,
For the cloth is as green as my gown. Sir Gawain, think
On this when you go forth among great princes;
Remember our struggle here; recall to your mind

240 This rich token. Remember the Green Chapel.
And now, come on, let's both go back to my castle
And finish the New Year's revels with feasting and joy,
                        not strife,
        I beg you," said the lord,
245   And said, "As for my wife,
        She'll be your friend, no more
        A threat against your life."

Sir Gawain and the Green Knight (1952) by Dorothea Braby. Golden Cockerel Press.

Rare Books and Manuscripts Division, New York Public Library. Astor, Lenox, and Tilden Foundations.

Holding Out for a Hero

words by **Dean Pitchford**

Where have all the good men gone,
And where are all the gods?
Where's the street-wise Hercules to fight the rising odds?
Isn't there a white knight upon a fiery steed?
Late at night I toss, and I turn, and I dream of what I need.

Chorus:
I need a hero.
I'm holding out for a hero 'til the end of the night.
He's gotta be strong,
And he's gotta be fast,
And he's gotta be fresh from the fight.
I need a hero.
I'm holding out for a hero 'til the morning light.
He's gotta be sure,
And it's gotta be soon,
And he's gotta be larger than life.

Somewhere after midnight,
In my wildest fantasy,
Somewhere just beyond my reach,
There's someone reaching back for me.
Racing on the thunder and rising with the heat,
It's gonna take a superman to sweep me off my feet.

Chorus

Up where the mountains meet the heavens above,
Out where the lightning splits the sea,
I could swear there is someone somewhere, watching me.

Through the wind and the chill and the rain,
And the storm and the flood,
I can feel his approach
Like a fire in my blood.

Chorus

King Arthur's Wood
(c. late 19th century)
by Elizabeth Adela
Stanhope Forbes.

MAKING MEANINGS

First Thoughts

1. What do you think of the way the Green Knight and his wife trick and seduce Gawain? Do people today endure similar trials to test their values? Discuss.

Shaping Interpretations

2. "A man who's true to his word, / There's nothing he needs to fear." The Green Knight says this to Gawain after he reveals how Gawain has been tricked. What do you think of this idea?

3. In what ways is Sir Gawain a superhuman **romance hero**? In what ways is he weak or flawed, just as a real person might be?

4. Describe the **symbolic** use of the color green in this story. (Green usually symbolizes hope; it is associated with the appearance of new life in the plant world.)

5. What **images** make the setting of the confrontation seem demonic? Do you think there is any **symbolism** suggested by this setting? Explain.

6. If you read the complete story of Gawain and the Green Knight, you will learn that King Arthur's wicked half sister, Morgan Le Fay, sent the Green Knight to test Gawain. What do you think—did Gawain prove himself to be a good knight or not? Do you think sexual morality is as important in Arthur's court as honesty and courage? Discuss your opinions.

7. How would you describe the writer's **tone** in this story? Is he entirely serious, or do you find moments of humor? Find passages in the story to support your responses.

Reading Check

a. Where does Gawain find the Green Knight, and what is the Knight doing?

b. What happens with the first and second strokes of the Green Knight's ax?

c. What happens the third time?

d. Who does the Green Knight turn out to be?

e. How does the Knight finally evaluate Gawain's character?

Extending the Text

8. Do you think people long to find heroes like Gawain today? Do you think the singer of "Holding Out for a Hero" (see *Connections*, page 166) is thinking of a Gawain type? Why?

9. This story has been read as an **allegory,** or symbolic story, of Christian redemption. From this point of view, who would be the sinner and who would be the Christ figure? What would be the terms of salvation?

10. Compare the romantic triangle in this story— the two men and the woman—with romantic triangles in contemporary fiction or movies.

ELEMENTS OF LITERATURE

Romances: Wishes Fulfilled

Romances are often too incredible for some modern readers, too lacking in the realistic details of life we have come to expect of literature. Yet in *Sir Gawain and the Green Knight,* we feel the gripping reality of sexual temptation and of life in the medieval castle.

The **romance** has a simple, inevitable plot: A hero battles an evil enemy and ultimately wins. As part of the story, the hero undertakes a **quest.** The quest usually has three stages: a dangerous journey, a central test or ordeal to determine if the hero truly has the qualities of a hero, and a return to the point from which the journey began.

In *Gawain* we have the model of the chivalric hero whose honor is being tested. This is a serious romance whose purpose is clearly to teach a moral lesson. Yet the hero does not have unlimited powers. Gawain is a human being who, like all of us, is limited in his moral and physical strength.

Elements of Romance

- **a near-perfect hero**
- **an evil enemy**
- **a quest**
- **a test of the hero**
- **supernatural elements**
- **good vs. evil**
- **female figures who are usually maidens (in need of rescue), mothers, or crones**

Romances are still a popular form found in today's novels, movies, television shows, and comics. The *Indiana Jones* movies and the *Star Trek* TV episodes are essentially romances, as are these books, which you may have read: C. S. Lewis's *The Chronicles of Narnia,* many of Lloyd Alexander's books, Brian Jacques's *Redwall* series, J.R.R. Tolkien's *The Lord of the Rings,* and L. Frank Baum's *The Wizard of Oz.*

Romances are traditionally set in the past, which is where the Wife of Bath sets her story: "When good King Arthur ruled in ancient days." Today, romances may also be set in the future, as in the *Star Wars* movies. Through this journey to a remote time or place, the hero learns something of value.

Comparing romances. As part of a group, discuss the Gawain story as a romance. Next, expand your discussion to include other works, using a chart like the one below. Present your ideas to the rest of the class, using specific examples to support your conclusions.

Work	Romance Elements
Sir Gawain	
Beowulf	
"The Wife of Bath's Tale"	
Current movie or TV show	
Novel	

CHOICES:
Building Your Portfolio

Writer's Notebook
1. Collecting Ideas for a Comparison-Contrast Essay

WORK IN PROGRESS

When you write your essay of comparison and contrast for the Writer's Workshop on page 185, you might want to compare one of these medieval stories with a modern story. *Sir Gawain and the Green Knight* would be a good medieval story to use as part of your comparison-contrast. Take notes now on the ways Gawain's experiences are like or unlike the tests that the modern hero must undergo. Be sure to note how each story uses the elements of romance listed on page 167. If your modern story is far from a romance, note how it distorts the romance elements. Save your notes.

Expository Writing
2. Gawain Goes to Hollywood

When the elements of a romance story (or myth) are adapted to a more modern setting, we say that the story has been "displaced." In two or three paragraphs, discuss how *Sir Gawain* might be displaced into a contemporary movie or TV show. Think about the story's **plot, characterization,** and **theme.**

Expository Writing
3. The Game of Love

In the twelfth century, rules governing the "game" of love were actually set down by a court of love in France. Four of the rules are listed below. Do you agree or disagree with these "rules"? Have the rules of love changed? In an essay, explain your position.

iii No one can be bound by a double love.
xiv The easy attainment of love makes it of little value; difficulty of attainment makes it prized.
xvii A new love puts to flight an old one.
xix If love diminishes, it quickly fails and rarely revives.

Critical Thinking / Speaking
4. Roles for Women

In romance literature, women are often represented as (a) maidens, (b) mothers, (c) temptresses, or (d) crones. Is that true in *Sir Gawain*? Do these character roles for women still exist today? Prepare a panel discussion on this issue. Defend your ideas with specific evidence from current fiction and movies, as well as from *Sir Gawain*.

Sir Thomas Malory

(1405?–1471)

The historical identity of Sir Thomas Malory, the author of Britain's most famous work on King Arthur, is almost as uncertain as the identity of the hero of his *Le Morte Darthur*. All we know for sure about Malory is that he was a knight familiar with chivalric romances who was writing in the years 1469–1470. We know this from a sort of postscript that appears in the manuscript of Malory's work that William Caxton printed in 1485. In this postscript, Malory also asks his readers to pray for his deliverance, suggesting that he was in prison during some of the time he was writing his stories about Arthur.

Since the fifteenth century, scholars have been trying to find out more about the actual person who wrote the work Caxton entitled *Le Morte Darthur*. At one time as many as five different "historical" Malorys were proposed. However, most scholars have come to accept the Thomas Malory born in Warwickshire as the most likely author of *Le Morte Darthur*.

This Warwickshire Malory served in France during the Hundred Years' War and apparently fought at the siege of Calais in 1436. A few years later he married a woman named Elizabeth, who bore him a son. Sir Thomas was elected to Parliament at least once and died in 1471, perhaps from the plague.

The record of this aristocratic war hero, however, also contains a series of arrests for theft, burglary, and assault, including the robbing of an abbey in which he supposedly broke eighteen doors and roughed up the monks.

But the charges against Malory were merely accusations, and there is no record of any trials or convictions. The late fifteenth century was a time of great political partisanship and civil disorder, so it is very possible that Malory's imprisonment was politically motivated. He might have backed the wrong side in a political conflict.

The Arthur in Malory's work is not the historical sixth-century general who helped his fellow Britons defend themselves against the invading Saxons. No, Malory's Arthur is a consolidation of later legends that developed in England and on the Continent. Using Celtic and Continental sources, Malory created a mythic Arthur who later became the very embodiment of British values.

Le Morte Darthur, coming as it does at the end of the fifteenth century, serves as a kind of literary swan song to the feudal order of the Middle Ages, with its castles, knights, and chivalric codes. Malory's readers lived in a different world. Cities were growing, and money and competition were replacing the old feudal ways of barter and mutual obligation. Something in the chivalric order that Malory portrayed, however, seems to have answered a longing in his audience for a more orderly world.

In Malory's mythic form, Arthur has the mysterious birth typical of the romance hero. His childhood initiation—pulling a magic sword from a rock—points to his kinship with such mythic and romance heroes as the Greek Theseus and the German Siegfried. His strange death, departure, and promised return also place him among other "once and future kings"—heroes whose return is always hoped for.

The Arthurian tales were carried into the Elizabethan Age. They were resurrected in the nineteenth century by Alfred, Lord Tennyson, in his group of poems called *Idylls of the King* (see pages 802 and 826). Tennyson brought Arthur and his knights back at a time when the English nation, embarked upon empire, needed a reminder of its heroic past and special destiny.

The Arthurian legend was revived yet again in the twentieth century by T. H. White in his best-selling book *The Once and Future King* (1958). Though White's treatment of the Arthurian material is ironic (in keeping with an ironic age), it still inspired the 1960s musical play and movie *Camelot*, which captures the romantic imagination of another generation struggling with disillusion and social disorder.

Before You Read

THE DEATH OF ARTHUR

Make the Connection

Heroes That Never Die

People have always hated to let go of their heroes. In fact, many cultures tell stories in which the hero promises to return in an hour of need to help the people once again. How do we try to keep our heroes alive? We build statues to them and record their portraits on canvas, coins, and film. But most of all we tell those stories—stories that we hope will keep our heroes and their values alive in the memories of future generations.

Elements of Literature

The Romance Hero

Malory's Arthur is in many ways the archetypal, or typical, romance hero. He is born under mysterious circumstances, grows up in obscurity, and undergoes a childhood initiation involving a magic weapon. In his maturity he fights to defeat evil and promote peace. Throughout his life he is aided by magic weapons and wise mentors. Mysterious events surround his departure from this world, suggesting that he may return when his people need him the most.

If you remember your old myths and fairy tales, you'll recognize these elements of Arthur's story. Even movies and cartoons today use these archetypes of the romance hero. (Check out the story of Superman's origins.)

A **romance hero** is a larger-than-life figure who usually has mysterious origins and in the course of his life performs extraordinary deeds with the aid of magic forces.

Reading Skills and Strategies

Using Context Clues

Malory tells his story of Arthur in the language of the fifteenth century, which is full of archaic expressions. When we say a word is **archaic,** we mean it is not in use. Many of the archaic words in the story are footnoted. When you come across other archaic words that are strange to you, search each word's context—the words surrounding it—to see if you can find a clue to its meaning. It is in part the strangeness of the archaic language that gives this story its magic. "Oddly enough," the American writer John Steinbeck once said of Malory's tales, "I knew the words from whispering them to myself."

Background

Malory's *Le Morte Darthur* contains a series of tales about the birth, education, adventures, and death (or disappearance) of King Arthur. In the early tales, Arthur persuades his knights to unite in the fellowship of the Round Table and dedicate themselves to the chivalric code of honor. For a while, Arthur's vision is realized, and justice prevails in the kingdom. But human frailties, including Arthur's own, gradually corrupt the fellowship of the Round Table. Worst, perhaps, is the betrayal of Lancelot, Arthur's best knight, who falls in love with Queen Guinevere. Arthur and his Round Table become vulnerable to evil forces, personified by Sir Mordred, who is Arthur's illegitimate son.

In the last episode of Malory's manuscript, Arthur meets his wicked son in battle.

Arthur mortally wounded, from *Roman du Saint Graal* (early 14th century). Add. 10294 fol. 93.

British Art Library, London.

The Death of Arthur
from Le Morte Darthur

Sir Thomas Malory

So upon Trinity Sunday at night king Arthur dreamed a wonderful dream. And in his dream him seemed that he saw upon a chafflet[1] a chair, and the chair was fast to a wheel, and thereupon sat king Arthur in the richest cloth of gold that might be made. And the king thought there was under him, far from him, an hideous deep black water, and therein was all manner of serpents and worms and wild beasts foul and horrible. And suddenly the king thought that the wheel turned up-so-down, and he fell among the serpents, and every beast took him by a limb. And then the king cried as he lay in his bed, "Help! help!" and then knights, squires and yeomen awaked the king, and then he was so amazed that he wist not where he was.

And then so he awaked until it was nigh day, and then he fell on slumbering again, not sleeping nor thoroughly waking. So the king seemed verily that there came sir Gawain unto him with a number of fair ladies with him. So when king Arthur saw him he said, "Welcome, my sister's son, I weened ye had been dead! And now I see thee on live, much am I beholden unto Almighty Jesu. Ah, fair nephew, what been these ladies that hither be come with you?"

"Sir," said sir Gawain, "all these be ladies for whom I have foughten for, when I was man living. And all these are tho[2] that I did battle for in righteous quarrels, and God hath given them that grace at their great prayer, because I did battle for them for their right, that they should bring me hither unto you. Thus much hath given me leave God for to warn you of your death: for and ye fight as to-morn[3] with sir Mordred, as ye both have assigned, doubt ye not ye shall be slain, and the most party of your people on both parties.[4] And for the great grace and goodness that Almighty Jesu hath unto you, and for pity of you and many mo[5] other good men there shall be slain, God hath sent me to you of his special grace to give you warning that in no wise ye do battle as to-morn, but that ye take a treatise[6] for a month day. And proffer you largely,[7] so that to-morn ye put in a delay. For within a month shall come sir Lancelot with all his noble knights, and rescue you worshipfully and slay sir Mordred and all that ever will hold with him."

Then sir Gawain and all the ladies vanished, and anon the king called upon his knights, squires, and yeomen, and charged them wightly[8] to fetch his noble lords and wise bishops unto him. And when they were come the king told them of his avision,[9] that sir Gawain had told him and warned him that and[10] he fought on the morn, he should be slain. Then the king commanded sir Lucan the Butler and his brother sir Bedivere the Bold, with two bishops with them, and charged them in any wise to take a treatise for a month day with sir Mordred: "And spare not. Proffer him lands and goods as much as ye think reasonable."

So then they departed and came to sir Mordred where he had a grim host of an hundred thousand men, and there they entreated sir Mordred long time. And at the last sir Mordred was agreed for to have Cornwall and Kent by king Arthur's days; and after that all England, after the days of king Arthur.

Then were they condescend[11] that king Arthur and sir Mordred should meet betwixt both their hosts, and every of them should bring fourteen persons. And so they came with this word unto Arthur. Then said he, "I am glad that this is done." And so he went into the field.

---

1. **chafflet:** scaffold.
2. **tho:** those.
3. **for . . . to-morn:** if you fight tomorrow.
4. **most . . . parties:** most part of your people on both sides.
5. **mo:** more.
6. **treatise:** treaty or truce.
7. **proffer you largely:** make generous offers.
8. **wightly:** quickly.
9. **avision:** dream.
10. **and:** if.
11. **condescend:** agreed.

And when king Arthur should depart he warned all his host that and they see any sword drawn, "look ye come on fiercely and slay that traitor, sir Mordred, for I in no wise trust him." In like wise sir Mordred warned his host "that and ye see any manner of sword drawn, look that ye come on fiercely and so slay all that ever before you standeth, for in no wise I will not trust for this treatise." And in the same wise said sir Mordred unto his host: "for I know well my father will be avenged upon me."

And so they met as their appointment was, and were agreed and accorded thoroughly. And wine was fetched, and they drank together. Right so came out an adder of a little heath bush, and it stung a knight in the foot. And so when the knight felt him so stung, he looked down and saw the adder; and anon he drew his sword to slay the adder, and thought none other harm. And when the host on both parties saw that sword drawn, then they blew bemes,[12] trumpets and horns, and shouted grimly, and so both hosts dressed them[13] togethers. And king Arthur took his horse and said, "Alas, this unhappy day!" and so rode to his party, and sir Mordred in like wise.

And never since was there never seen a more dolefuller battle in no Christian land, for there was but rushing and riding, foining[14] and striking, and many a grim word was there spoken of either to other, and many a deadly stroke. But ever king Arthur rode throughout the battle[15] of sir Mordred many times and did full nobly, as a noble king should do, and at all times he fainted never. And sir Mordred did his devoir[16] that day and put himself in great peril.

And thus they fought all the long day, and never stinted till the noble knights were laid to the cold earth. And ever they fought still till it was near night, and by then was there an hundred thousand laid dead upon the earth. Then was king Arthur wood wroth[17] out of measure, when he saw his people so slain from him. And so he looked about him and could see no mo of all his host and good

knights left, no mo on live but two knights: t'one was sir Lucan de Butler and his brother sir Bedivere; and yet they were full sore wounded.

"Jesu mercy!" said the king, "where are all my noble knights become? Alas, that ever I should see this doleful day! For now," said king Arthur, "I am come to mine end. But would to God," said he, "that I wist now where were that traitor sir Mordred that hath caused all this mischief."

Then king Arthur looked about and was ware where stood sir Mordred leaning upon his sword among a great heap of dead men. "Now, give me my spear," said king Arthur unto sir Lucan, "for yonder I have espied the traitor that all this woe hath wrought."

"Sir, let him be," said sir Lucan, "for he is unhappy.[18] And if ye pass this unhappy day ye shall be right well revenged upon him. Good lord, remember ye of your night's dream and what the spirit of sir Gawain told you to-night, and yet God of His great goodness hath preserved you hitherto. And for God's sake, my lord, leave off this, for, blessed be God, ye have won the field. For yet we been here three on live, and with Sir Mordred is not one of live. And therefore if ye leave off now, this wicked day of Destiny is past!"

"Now tide[19] me death, tide me life," said the king, "now I see him yonder alone, he shall never escape mine hands! For at a better avail shall I never have him."

"God speed you well!" said sir Bedivere.

Then the king got his spear in both his hands, and ran toward sir Mordred, crying and saying, "Traitor, now is thy death-day come!"

And when sir Mordred saw king Arthur he ran until him with his sword drawn in his hand, and there king Arthur smote sir Mordred under the shield, with a foin of his spear, throughout the body more than a fathom. And when sir Mordred felt that he had his death's wound he thrust himself with the might that he had up to the burr of king Arthur's spear, and right so he smote his father, king Arthur, with his sword holding in both his hands, upon the side of the head, that the sword pierced the helmet and the tay[20] of the

12. **bemes:** bugles.
13. **dressed them:** prepared to come.
14. **foining:** lunging.
15. **battle:** battalion.
16. **devoir:** knightly duty.
17. **wood wroth:** mad with rage.

18. **unhappy:** unlucky for you.
19. **tide:** betide.
20. **tay:** edge.

brain. And therwith Mordred dashed down stark dead to the earth.

And noble king Arthur fell in a swough to the earth, and there he swooned oftentimes, and sir Lucan and sir Bedivere oft-times hove him up. And so weakly betwixt them they led him to a little chapel not far from the sea, and when the king was there, him thought him reasonably eased.

Then heard they people cry in the field. "Now go thou, sir Lucan" said the king, "and do me to wit[21] what betokens that noise in the field." So sir Lucan departed, for he was grievously wounded in many places. And so as he yode[22] he saw and hearkened by the moonlight how that pillers[23] and robbers were come into the field to pill and to rob many a full noble knight of brooches and bees[24] and of many a good ring and many a rich jewel. And who that were not dead all out, there they slew them for their harness and their riches.

When sir Lucan understood this work he came to the king as soon as he might, and told him all what he had heard and seen. "Therefore by my rede,"[25] said sir Lucan, "it is best that we bring you to some town."

"I would it were so," said the king, "but I may not stand, my head works so. Ah, sir Lancelot!" said king Arthur, "this day have I sore missed thee! And alas, that ever I was against thee! For now have I my death, whereof sir Gawain me warned in my dream."

Then sir Lucan took up the king t'one party and sir Bedivere the other party. And in the lifting up the king swooned, and in the lifting sir Lucan fell in a swoon, that part of his guts fell out of his body, and therewith the noble knight his heart burst. And when the king awoke he beheld sir Lucan, how he lay foaming at the mouth and part of his guts lay at his feet.

"Alas," said the king, "this is to me a full heavy sight, to see this noble duke so die for my sake, for he would have holpen me that had more need of help than I! Alas, that he would not complain him, for his heart was so set to help me. Now Jesu have mercy upon his soul!"

Bedivere returning Excalibur to the lake upon the death of Arthur, from *Roman du Saint Graal* (early 14th century). Add. 10294 fol. 94.

Then sir Bedivere wept for the death of his brother.

"Now leave this mourning and weeping, gentle knight," said the king, "for all this will not avail me. For wit thou well, and I might live myself, the death of sir Lucan would grieve me evermore. But my time hieth fast," said the king. "Therefore," said king Arthur unto sir Bedivere, "take thou here Excaliber,[26] my good sword, and go with it to yonder water's side. And when thou comest there, I charge thee throw my sword in that water, and come again and tell me what thou seest there."

"My lord," said sir Bedivere, "your commandment shall be done, and lightly[27] bring you word again." So sir Bedivere departed. And by the way

21. **do me to wit:** let me know.
22. **yode:** walked.
23. **pillers:** plunderers.
24. **bees:** bracelets.
25. **rede:** advice.

26. **Excaliber:** Arthur's sword, given to him by the mysterious Lady of the Lake.
27. **lightly:** quickly.

he beheld that noble sword, and the pommel and the haft was all precious stones. And then he said to himself, "If I throw this rich sword in the water, thereof shall never come good, but harm and loss." And then sir Bedivere hid Excaliber under a tree. And so as soon as he might he came again unto the king and said he had been at the water and had thrown the sword into the water.

"What saw thou there?" said the king.

"Sir," he said, "I saw nothing but waves and winds."

"That is untruly said of thee," said the king, "and therefore go thou lightly again, and do my commandment. As thou art to me lief[28] and dear, spare not, but throw it in."

Then sir Bedivere returned again and took the sword in his hand; and yet him thought sin and shame to throw away that noble sword. And so eft[29] he hid the sword and returned again and told the king that he had been at the water and done his commandment.

"What sawest thou there?" said the king.

"Sir," he said, "I saw nothing but waters wap and waves wan."

"Ah, traitor unto me and untrue," said king Arthur, "now hast thou betrayed me twice! Who would ween that thou that hast been to me so lief and dear, and also named so noble a knight, that thou would betray me for the riches of this sword? But now go again lightly; for thy long tarrying putteth me in great jeopardy of my life, for I have taken cold. And but if thou do now as I bid thee, if ever I may see thee, I shall slay thee mine own hands, for thou wouldst for my rich sword see me dead."

Then sir Bedivere departed and went to the sword and lightly took it up, and so he went unto the water's side. And there he bound the girdle about the hilts, and threw the sword as far into the water as he might. And there came an arm and an hand above the water, and took it and cleight it, and shook it thrice and brandished, and then vanished with the sword into the water.

So sir Bedivere came again to the king and told him what he saw. "Alas," said the king, "help me hence, for I dread me I have tarried over long."

Then sir Bedivere took the king upon his back and so went with him to the water's side. And when they were there, even fast by the bank hoved a little barge with many fair ladies in it, and among them all was a queen, and all they had black hoods. And all they wept and shrieked when they saw king Arthur.

"Now put me into that barge," said the king. And so he did softly, and there received him three ladies with great mourning. And so they set them down, and in one of their laps king Arthur laid his head.

And then the queen said, "Ah, my dear brother, why have ye tarried so long from me? Alas, this wound on your head hath caught over much cold!" And anon they rowed fromward the land, and sir Bedivere beheld all tho ladies go froward him. Then sir Bedivere cried and said,

"Ah, my lord Arthur, what shall become of me, now ye go from me and leave me here alone among mine enemies?"

"Comfort thyself," said the king, "and do as well as thou mayest, for in me is no trust for to trust in. For I must into the vale of Avilion[30] to heal me of my grievous wound. And if thou hear nevermore of me, pray for my soul!"

But ever the queen and ladies wept and shrieked that it was pity to hear. And as soon as sir Bedivere had lost the sight of the barge he wept and wailed, and so took[31] the forest and went all that night.

And in the morning he was ware, betwixt two holts hoar,[32] of a chapel and an hermitage. Then was sir Bedivere fain, and thither he went, and when he came into the chapel he saw where lay an hermit groveling on all fours, fast thereby a tomb was new graven. When the hermit saw sir Bedivere he knew him well, for he was but little tofore Bishop of Canterbury that sir Mordred flemed.[33]

"Sir," said sir Bedivere, "what man is there here interred that ye pray so fast for?"

"Fair son," said the hermit, "I wot not verily but by deeming. But this same night, at midnight,

---

28. **lief:** beloved.
29. **eft:** again.

30. **Avilion:** legendary island, sometimes identified with the earthly Paradise.
31. **took:** took to.
32. **holts hoar:** old thickets.
33. **flemed:** banished.

here came a number of ladies and brought here a dead corpse and prayed me to inter him. And here they offered an hundred tapers, and they gave me a thousand besants."[34]

"Alas," said sir Bedivere, "that was my lord king Arthur, which lieth here graven in this chapel." Then sir Bedivere swooned. And when he awoke he prayed the hermit that he might abide with him still, there to live with fasting and prayers: "For from hence will I never go," said sir Bedivere, "by my will, but all the days of my life here to pray for my lord Arthur."

"Sir, ye are welcome to me," said the hermit, "for I know you better than ye ween that I do: for ye are sir Bedivere the Bold, and the full noble duke sir Lucan de Butler was your brother." Then sir Bedivere told the hermit all as ye have heard tofore, and so he beleft with the hermit that was beforehand Bishop of Canterbury. And there sir Bedivere put upon him poor clothes, and served the hermit full lowly in fasting and in prayers.

Thus of Arthur I find no more written in books that been authorized, nother more of the very certainty of his death heard I never read. But thus was he led away in a ship wherein were three queens; that one was king Arthur sister, queen Morgan le Fay, the tother was queen of North Wales, and the third was the queen of the Waste

34. besants: *bezants*, gold coins of Byzantium.

Lands. Also there was dame Ninive, the chief lady of the lake, which had wedded sir Pelleas, the good knight; and this lady had done much for king Arthur. And this dame Ninive would never suffer sir Pelleas to be in no place where he should be in danger of his life, and so he lived unto the uttermost of his days with her in great rest.

Now more of the death of king Arthur could I never find, but that these ladies brought him to his grave, and such one was interred there which the hermit bore witness that sometime was Bishop of Canterbury. But yet the hermit knew not in certain that he was verily the body of king Arthur; for this tale sir Bedivere, a knight of the Table Round, made it to be written.

Yet some men say in many parts of England that king Arthur is not dead, but had by the will of our Lord Jesu into another place. And men say that he shall come again, and he shall win the Holy Cross.[35] Yet I will not say that it shall be so, but rather I would say: here in this world he changed his life. And many men say that there is written upon his tomb this verse:

HIC IACET ARTHURUS, REX QUONDAM REXQUE FUTURUS.[36]

And thus leave I here sir Bedivere with the hermit that dwelled that time in a chapel besides Glastonbury, and there was his hermitage. And so they lived in prayers and fastings and great abstinence.

And when queen Guenevere understood that king Arthur was dead and all the noble knights, sir Mordred and all the remnant, then she stole away with five ladies with her, and so she went to Amesbury. And there she let make herself a nun, and weared white clothes and black, and great penance she took upon her, as ever did sinful woman in this land. And never creature could make her merry, but ever she lived in fasting, prayers, and alms-deeds, that all manner of people marvelled how virtuously she was changed.

35. Holy Cross: cross on which Jesus was crucified.
36. Latin for "Here lies Arthur, the once and future king."

Head of a Woman (c. 1450) by Pesellino.
Board of Trustees of the National Museums and Galleries on Merseyside (Walker Art Gallery, Liverpool).

MAKING MEANINGS

First Thoughts

1. Does Arthur remind you of any other **romance heroes**—think of your other readings as well as heroes in popular culture. Discuss the connections.

Shaping Interpretations

2. Fill in this graphic to show how Malory uses other romance motifs.

Romance Motif	Arthur Story
Faithful follower	
Wise old man	
Dreams	
Number 3	
Magic	
Tests of follower	
Betrayal	

Reading Check

a. What does Arthur dream on Trinity Sunday?

b. How is the truce between Arthur and Mordred disturbed?

c. What is Sir Lucan's advice to Arthur? What does Arthur do?

d. What happens between Arthur and Mordred?

e. Where does Bedivere take the wounded king? What happens to Bedivere?

3. What mysterious details surround Arthur's last hours? What possibility do these details and the inscription on Arthur's tomb suggest?

Extending the Text

4. What aspects of this story do you think would appeal to people living at the beginning of the twenty-first century? Or do you think that people need different kinds of heroes today? Why?

5. Many people over the centuries have hunted for Arthur's tomb. According to this story, what should archaeologists look for in their search for Arthur's grave? (Do you think he really existed?)

CHOICES:
Building Your Portfolio

Writer's Notebook

1. Collecting Ideas for a Comparison-Contrast Essay

How does Malory's Arthur, a hero out of medieval romance, compare and contrast with Beowulf, a hero from a different, much older society? Read and review the Anglo-Saxon epic, starting on page 21, and take notes on how the two heroes are both alike and different. Consider each hero's quest, powers, failings, enemies, allies, and achievements or tasks left undone. Save your notes for possible use in the Writer's Workshop on page 185.

Creative Writing

2. Translating Malory

Many writers have translated the stories of Arthur and his knights. Try your hand at translating this story of Arthur's death. You will have to translate the **archaic words** and correct the **archaic punctuation,** but try to keep the power of the story and the excitement of the action. Before you start your translation, decide who your audience will be: children or adults? If you used context clues to guess at the meanings of some of the archaic words as you read, be sure to check your guesses in a dictionary.

Art

3. Arthur in Art

The Arthurian legends have inspired as many visual artists as literary ones. Choose a scene from Malory's account of the death of Arthur, and draw or paint what you see in your mind's eye. Descriptions like that of the hand emerging from the lake or of Arthur being carried off in the barge are particularly suited to visual representation.

The Weaving of Women's Tales

By God, if women had but written stories . . .

— Geoffrey Chaucer, from *The Wife of Bath's Prologue*

I n early Britain, women helped with family and community life, managed estates in their husbands' absence, and pored over books in stone-walled convents. They also composed important works of literature, yet scholars have only recently begun to recognize these women's literary contributions.

The Anglo-Saxon Period: Nameless Voices

Since poems in Anglo-Saxon Britain were composed and transmitted orally, the names of their original authors—whether female or male—have long been obscured. All literary works were generally attrib-

uted to the traveling bard (usually male) who recited them. Now, however, many scholars attribute such well-known poems as "The Wife's Lament" and "Wulf and Eadwacer" to women. In these lines from "The Wife's Lament," an anonymous poem, a wife expresses her grief at being banished from her home by her husband (something husbands were permitted to do).

> Our lips had smiled to swear hourly
> That nothing should split us—save dying—
> Nothing else. All that has changed:
> It is now as if it had never been,
> Our friendship. I feel in the wind
> That the man dearest to me detests me.
> I was banished to this knoll knotted by woods
> To live in a den dug beneath an oak.
> Old is this earthen room; it eats at my heart.
>
> —*from* "The Wife's Lament"

No doubt, the names of other women who composed oral works (such as lullabies, elegies, and work songs) were also lost when the works were written down by scribes. One prominent exception to this standard of anonymity was Lioba, a young Wessex nun whose elegant prose was a powerful force in the Church's efforts to convert the Continent.

Anglo-Saxon women also expressed themselves artistically in other (anonymous) ways. Many wove intricate tapestries that recorded the details of their domestic lives amid scenes of men in battle. Others produced beautiful illuminated manuscripts in a few

Timarete painting a portrait, from Giovanni Boccaccio's *De claris mulieribus* (Of famous women), France (2nd half of 15th century). M. 381, fol. 33v.

The Pierpont Morgan Library, New York.

female *scriptoria,* monasteries devoted to copying religious writings. Wealthy women often acted as patrons, commissioning poets and artists to produce works illustrating family history.

The Middle Ages: Court or Cloister

Only two avenues were open to women with literary ambitions in the Middle Ages: the luck to be born into an aristocratic family (girls in such families were sometimes educated alongside their brothers) or service in the Church.

Most women wrote in English rather than in Latin, the formal language used for religious, legal, and political purposes. Women writing in the vernacular wrote mostly about domestic or personal affairs—everyday matters not considered serious or weighty at the time they were written. For both these reasons, few writings by women were preserved in monastery vaults.

For the most part, only in the Church did women have access to the education, economic support, and freedom from family responsibilities necessary for sustained writing. But when women did produce religious writings, they didn't usually fit the accepted mode of orthodox religious works. Women's writings were often more subjective and personal in style. (Today, ironically, we *do* value such personal writing and would probably find the kind of philosophical tract admired in the twelfth century rather dull.)

Julian of Norwich (c. 1342–?)

One of the first English women of letters was a recluse who lived alone in a small cell attached to St. Julian's Church in Norwich. In her only surviving work, *A Book of Showings,* Julian described the sixteen visions of God, or "showings," that she experienced during a critical illness shortly after she turned thirty.

Julian first recorded her revelations in short versions soon after they occurred and in longer versions some twenty years later. Julian's apology to her readers in the short version—"God forbid that you should say or take me for a teacher . . . for I am a woman, ignorant, weak, and frail"—is omitted in the longer version. Perhaps this is a sign that she

no longer needed to pretend an inferiority she did not feel.

Julian's visions and reflections revealed a loving, nurturing God. Indeed, the central image in Julian's meditations became "God the Mother."

> As truly as God is our Father, so truly is God our Mother, and he revealed that in everything, and especially in these sweet words where he says: I am he; that is to say: I am he, the power and goodness of fatherhood; I am he, the wisdom and the lovingness of motherhood; I am he, the light and the grace which is all blessed love; I am he, the Trinity; I am he, the unity; I am he the supreme goodness of every kind of thing; I am he who makes you to love; I am he who makes you to long; I am he, the endless fulfilling of all true desires. For where the soul is highest, noblest, most honorable, still it is lowest, meekest, and mildest.
>
> —Julian of Norwich, *from A Book of Showings*

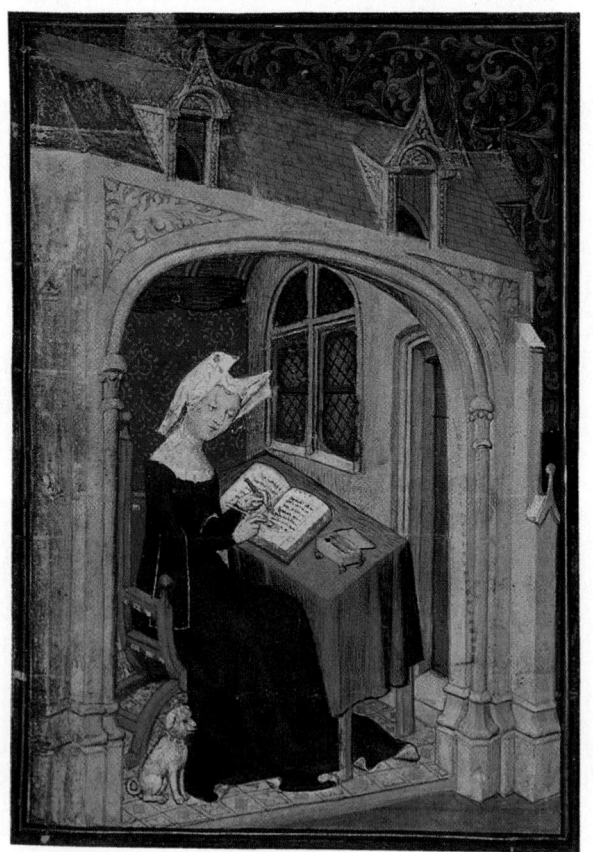

Christine de Pisan, writing, from *The Collected Works of Christine de Pisan* (15th century). French, MS Harley 4431, fol. 4. By permission of the British Library, London.

Margery Kempe (1373?–?)

The first autobiography in English, *The Book of Margery Kempe,* was dictated by a woman who could probably neither read nor write. Beginning with a religious conversion after the birth of her first child, Margery dictated her lively recollections to two scribes over many years. (The first scribe— thought to be Margery's own son—was nearly illiterate himself, and the work had to be done again with a second.) Although Margery refers to herself almost exclusively as "the creature" rather than "I" (as though to underscore her status as a creation of God), the *Book* projects the voice of a strong-willed, independent personality. In fact, Margery has been compared to Chaucer's vigorous Wife of Bath.

Like Chaucer's pilgrim, Margery was not affiliated with any convent or religious house. At forty, having by this time given birth to fourteen children, Margery made a pact of celibacy with her husband. In the following lines, Margery describes her life of penance.

Writing a letter, from *Les épitres d'Ovide* (detail) (early 16th century). MS Fr. 875, fol. 23v.
© cliché Bibliothèque Nationale de France, Paris.

> She gave herself up to great fasting and great watching; she rose at two or three of the clock, and went to church, and was there at her prayers unto the time of noon and also all the afternoon. Then she was slandered and re-proved by many people, because she kept so strict a life. She got a haircloth from a kiln, such as men dry malt on, and laid it in her kirtle as secretly and privily as she might, so that her husband should not espy it. Nor did he, and she lay by him every night in his bed and wore the haircloth every day, and bore children in the time.
>
> —Margery Kempe,
> from *The Book of Margery Kempe*

Dressed entirely in white, Margery traveled extensively in the Holy Land and to shrines in Britain and on the Continent. She made these pilgrimages despite the intolerance and disapproval of her peers. Her plain-spoken declarations of faith and frequent episodes of loud sobbing (she wept daily for fifteen years in sympathy with Christ's suffering) weren't readily understood by others. Indeed, one town even threatened to burn Margery at the stake as a heretic. She also was abandoned—in circumstances risky for a woman traveling alone—by several pilgrimage parties.

Margery's manuscript was widely read in the late Middle Ages but then was lost for centuries before resurfacing in an attic of the British Butler-Bowdon family in 1934. We can only wonder how many other women's writings await a similar rediscovery.

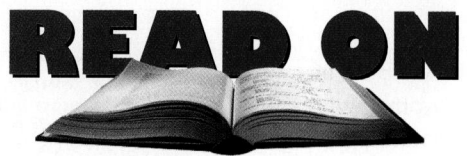

Stories That Save a Life

Perhaps you have been entranced by the story of Sindbad's fantastic voyages—just one of the many tales in *The Arabian Nights,* a framework of stories that dates back to the eighth century (translated by Husain Huddawy, W. W. Norton). Princess Scheherazade, whose husband wants to murder her, saves her own life by telling a dazzling variety of tales (fables, fairy tales, romances, and comic and historical anecdotes), stopping each night at the most suspenseful moment. Since her husband wants to hear what happpens next, he cannot bear to kill his gifted storyteller.

Different Lives in a Different Time

What was a woman's life like in the Middle Ages? The answer depends largely on where she lived and what social class she belonged to. In *Women in the Middle Ages* (Barnes & Noble), Frances and Joseph Gies examine the daily lives of women in the nobility, in religious orders, in the emerging trade classes, and in the peasantry.

Pilgrims in Outer Space

Join earthling Arthur Dent and his trusty sidekick from Betelgeuse, Ford Prefect, on a cosmic (and comic) quest through the galaxy. In *The Hitchhiker's Guide to the Galaxy* (Pocket Books), by Douglas Adams, you may "finally learn once and for all the plain and simple answer to all these nagging little problems of Life, the Universe, and Everything!" (First book of a four-volume series.)

A Lasting Hero

Early manuscripts mention a certain Arthur who led the Britons against the Anglo-Saxon invaders. Enlarged through legend, Arthur was eventually transformed into a romantic hero. Many writers have used the Arthurian legend to explore the grand themes of love, loyalty, and betrayal.

Arthur in our time. The English author T. H. White wrote his version of the Arthurian legend, *The Sword in the Stone* (G. P. Putnam's Sons), before World War II, when England once again needed a hero to shore up its national pride. He later expanded this story into a four-part novel, *The Once and Future King,* that explores the problems of war, justice, and national identity. And though White views Arthur's quest as a tragedy, he balances this somber theme with humorous characters and comic fun.

Magical stories made modern. Since his boyhood, the American writer John Steinbeck had been fascinated with Sir Thomas Malory's *Le Morte Darthur.* Realizing that difficult spelling and archaic words repelled modern readers, Steinbeck rewrote Malory's stories in plain, present-day language. In *The Acts of King Arthur and His Noble Knights* (Farrar, Straus and Giroux), the wonder of the original tales shines on.

Middle English: The Language in Transition *by John Algeo*

The history of English is divided into three long periods: Old English (before 1066), Middle English (1066–1485), and Modern English (1485 to the present). To be sure, all English speakers did not go to bed on the night of December 31, 1065, speaking Old English and wake up on the morning of January 1, 1066, saying "Let's talk Middle English now!" Language change is slower and subtler than that. And speakers are seldom aware of changes in their own lifetimes.

Some important changes in pronunciation and grammar happened shortly before 1066, however. Then, in 1066, the Normans conquered England, eventually causing extensive changes in vocabulary. The pre-1066 language looks like a foreign tongue, but by the end of the Middle English period it was quite similar to today's English.

What Happened to the Endings?

In Old English, as in the other Germanic languages, people tended to pronounce words with a strong accent on the first syllable but to rush over the following ones. Unstressed vowels consequently lost their distinctive sounds and were pronounced all alike, as a

The Scriptorium in the Tower of the Monastery of Tavara, from a Spanish manuscript (13th century). M. 429, fol. 183.

The Pierpont Morgan Library, New York.

Opening of *St. Luke's Gospel*, from the *Lindisfarne Gospels* (7th century). Cotton MS Nero D.IV, fol. 139.

Endings and Order

The change in the pronunciation and spelling of vowels had some far-reaching effects on English grammar. Old English nouns had changed their endings to show various things. For example, the Old English word for "door" as the subject of a sentence was *duru,* but as the direct object, it was *dure.* The plural "doors" was *dura.* After the unstressed vowels had fallen together, all three forms became *dore,* with a schwa sound at the end.

The loss of vowel distinctions meant that English speakers had to find other ways of indicating grammatical meanings, or they had to do without such information.

Effects on gender. For gender, Middle English decided to do without. Today almost no one is sorry that English replaced grammatical with natural gender. Instead of talking about "the door . . . she," "the roof . . . he," and "the wife . . . it," we use *he* for males, *she* for females, and *it* for things without gender.

Effects on plural forms. For number, Middle English came to rely on a few plural endings. Old English had many ways of marking the plural of a noun. A few of these survive in Modern English irregular plurals such as *tooth/teeth, ox/oxen,* and *child/children.* Other Old English plural forms, such as *dura* (doors) from *duru* (door), no longer exist. Middle English used the ending *–es* (from Old English *–as*) for most of its plurals. Thus, Old English

schwa (ə)—the sound in the last syllable of our word *cola.*

The misspellings that began to turn up in manuscripts show that unstressed vowel sounds merged in late Old English. Scribes sat at their desks all day long, tracing out letter shapes on parchment. About the year 1000, scribes had a great deal of trouble in remembering how the endings of words ought to be spelled. They hesitated about writing *stanas* or *stanes* (stones), *comon* or *coman* (they came). Their indecision shows that the scribes had ceased to pronounce the vowels of those endings differently from one another. Eventually, the scribes gave up trying to spell the endings differently and just used the letter *e* to write the unstressed vowel: *stanes, comen.* When that happened, the language became what we call Middle English.

hund/hundas became Middle English *hound/houndes,* and Old English *dura* was replaced by Middle English *doores.* Today we have only one regular ending, *–s,* as in *hounds* and *doors.*

Effects on case endings. Instead of case endings to show the functions of nouns in a sentence, Middle English came to rely on word order. In Middle English, "The knave slough [killed] the dragon" means something quite different from "The dragon slough the knave"; and that difference is signaled only by the order of the words. The difference from Old English, where word order was much less critical, is profound.

Uninvited Guests

Shortly after the unstressed vowels had come to be pronounced as schwas, a political event occurred that had important consequences for the English language. In 1066, William, duke of Normandy, invaded England with an army of soldiers from France. He defeated the English defenders, led by King Harold, at the Battle of Hastings.

Under William the Conqueror (as he came to be called), French became the language of government, law, education, and upper-class life. English continued to be spoken, of course, by most people: servants, craftsmen, farmers, foresters—the sturdy yeomanry of the land. But

All English speakers did not go to bed on the night of December 31, 1065, speaking Old English and wake up on the morning of January 1, 1066, saying "Let's talk Middle English now!"

French was the language of the rulers. England—once in danger of becoming an outlying part of Scandinavia—now seemed likely to become a province of France.

The two peoples—Vikings from Scandinavia and Normans from France—were in fact related. The Normans were, as their name suggests, not really French, but Scandinavians from the north who had settled in the western regions of France. They acquired the language of their new home, although they never learned to speak it like the native French people. To elegant Parisians, the Normans always sounded strange, foreign, and provincial.

Thus, the conquerors of Anglo-Saxon England were not at all refined emissaries of a higher civilization who brought culture to primitive England. On the contrary, they were a wild bunch only a few generations removed from their piratical ancestors.

In the long run, however, the Norman Conquest was probably a blessing. English was left to itself, to develop and grow without interference by scholars or government officials. The common folk of the early Middle English period were quite untroubled by traditions of spelling or preconceived notions of what their language ought to be like. So they spoke naturally— letting the vowels fall together and giving up the many grammatical endings of Old English, with no sense that they were losing anything of importance. And they were right.

The Battle and the Triumph

For several hundred years, England was a bilingual country. French was spoken by the upper classes among themselves, it was used in law courts and government, and it was used for literature. English was spoken by the lower classes for all the ordinary purposes of daily life— selling grain, buying dishes, scolding children, squabbling with neighbors, and loving the family.

For a time, no one could have said whether French or English would win out as the national language of England. However, several factors tipped the balance to English. Not the least important was the fact that most people spoke English. Also, the Normans in England got into a squabble with France, called the Hundred Years' War. The conflict intensified a feeling of patriotism for things English— especially the English language.

The English language thus gradually reasserted its place in the national life. In the second half of the fourteenth century, about three hundred years after the Conquest, English had again become the primary language in England. This was symbolized by a bill passed in Parliament in 1362 requiring that all law cases be conducted in English instead of in French.

At that time there was no standard English. Instead, people used the English of their native area. With the reestablishment of English as a language of government, however, the dialect of London (the capital city) quickly became a model to be followed.

In the fourteenth century, literature in English was revitalized. Chaucer, one of our greatest writers, wrote for the English royal court, using the London dialect. The anonymous author of *Sir Gawain and the Green Knight* produced his courtly tale in a northwestern dialect for country gentry. As the language flowered, so did the literature, with the same exuberance and variety.

Both a Borrower and a Lender Be

When English speakers started to use English again to talk about things they had discussed in French for three hundred years, they were literally at a loss for words. They knew no English words for many governmental, legal, military, and artistic things. The simplest thing was to borrow the French terms. And that is just what sensible English speakers did.

Examples of French borrowings are *baron, castle, chancellor, country, duke, government, noble, prince, royal, state; attorney, court, crime, judge, jury, prison; army, captain, corporal, lieutenant, sergeant, soldier; juggler, literature, magic, melody, poetry, sport.* Animals on the hoof looked after by English-speaking workers were, and still are, called by native English names: *cow, hog, sheep, calf, deer.* But when they were slaughtered and served up on the table as food, they were given the French names that the invading nobility used: *beef, pork, mutton, veal, venison.* Thus, our vocabulary continues to echo the English-worker/French-ruler dichotomy of six hundred years ago.

Since the fourteenth century, English has borrowed words from many languages, so English now has one of the richest and most international vocabularies in the world. In turn, English has become a major source of loanwords to other languages. That is another benefit of the Norman Conquest that William and his bully boys could not have imagined or understood.

Try It Out

1. **First recorded usages.** Many new words came into English during the Middle English period. Just before the definition of a word, *Merriam-Webster's Collegiate Dictionary,* Tenth Edition, gives the date or century when the word was first recorded in use. Find that date or century for each of these words. What language did each come from?

army	gentleman	justice
royal	castle	guide
master	servant	chief
herb	roast	soldier

2. **Word origins.** In each group below, one word was used in Old English, one is a Middle English loan from French, and one is a Modern English loan from French. What origin do you think each word has? Check your guesses in a dictionary.

   a. chair, chaise lounge, stool
   b. table, tableau, tablet
   c. (wheel) barrow, car, automobile

"Period. New paragraph."

©1998 Carl Rose from cartoonbank.com. All Rights Reserved.

Writer's Workshop

The history
of the written
word is rich an
Page 1

EXPOSITORY WRITING

A COMPARISON-CONTRAST ESSAY

Every day you look at people, places, experiences, and things and **compare** them (find similarities) and **contrast** them (find differences). Such thinking strategies help you evaluate alternatives and make decisions, ranging from what movie to rent to what college to attend. These skills also help you talk and write about literature. In this workshop you will write a **comparison-contrast essay** analyzing the likenesses or the differences, or both, in two literary works or in selected elements of two literary works.

Technology HELP

See Writer's Workshop 2 CD-ROM. *Assignment: Expository Writing.*

Prewriting

1. **Check your Writer's Notebook.** You can compare and contrast just about any two texts or elements of texts as long as they are alike or different in at least one significant way. As a topic for your comparison-contrast essay, consider following up on some of the notes you may have saved in your Writer's Notebook. For example, you may have notes on Chaucer's Prioress and Wife of Bath or on Gawain and a modern hero or on King Arthur and Beowulf.

WORK IN PROGRESS

2. **Gather your details.** Once you have decided on the texts you will compare and contrast, go through each text and note similarities and differences. Self-sticking note pads are handy for this. After you have skimmed your texts at least twice to look for details, put the details in some sort of graphic form for easy reference.

There are many kinds of graphics. One that is commonly used is the **Venn diagram,** like the one shown on the left below, in which the differences between the two texts can be cited in the outer part of the circles and the similarities can be cited where the circles overlap. **Outlines** and **charts** are also useful. The writer who is using the chart on the right below will focus on character. The specific features of a character (perhaps "has magical powers; is heroic, flawed, realistic," and so on) will be listed down the side; the two titles will be listed at the top.

ASSIGNMENT
Write an essay comparing and/or contrasting two or more texts or literary elements. The texts may be stories, poems, essays, dramas, or screenplays.

AIM
To inform; to analyze; to evaluate.

AUDIENCE
Your teacher, your classmates, or readers of a student literary magazine.

Title A   Title B

(Similarities)

Character	Title A	Title B
Feature 1:		
Feature 2:		
Feature 3:		

**Communications
Handbook
H E L P**

*See Taking Notes and
Documenting Sources;
Proofreading.*

3. **Plan your essay.** Decide how you will organize your ideas, and then make an outline. You can present your information using either the **block** or the **point-by-point** method of organization. With the block method you first discuss *all* the relevant features of one subject and then cover the same features of the other subject. With the point-by-point method, you take up *one* feature at a time and discuss it in terms of one subject and then in terms of the other. Here is an example of an outline for each method:

Block Method	**Point-by-Point Method**
Subject 1: Beowulf	**Feature 1:** quest
Feature 1: quest	Subject 1: Beowulf
Feature 2: powers	Subject 2: Arthur
Feature 3: achievements	**Feature 2:** powers
Subject 2: King Arthur	Subject 1: Beowulf
Feature 1: quest	Subject 2: Arthur
Feature 2: powers	**Feature 3:** achievements
Feature 3: achievements	Subject 1: Beowulf
	Subject 2: Arthur

Drafting

1. **Introduce your subjects.** In your **introduction,** be sure to identify the titles and authors of the works you are discussing and give any background information your readers may need. Include a **thesis statement,** which alerts your readers to what you are comparing and/or contrasting and gives some indication of what your analysis has led you to conclude.

> **Thesis statement:** Although both Beowulf and Arthur die bravely, pessimism and disintegration overcome Beowulf's community after his death, whereas there are clear suggestions of rebirth and renewal after Arthur's death.

2. **Support your generalizations.** In the **body** of your essay, present the information you outlined, using the block or point-by-point method of organization. Add specific details, examples, and quotations from the text or from authoritative outside sources to back up your assertions of similarities and differences.

3. **Draw conclusions.** In the last paragraph, write a **conclusion,** summing up your insights, evaluation, or response to your subjects. You may also want to leave your readers with a question or comment, which may motivate them to go back to the works and reevaluate them for themselves.

Evaluating and Revising

Peer evaluation. Working with a classmate who has read your draft, apply each of the criteria in the list at the left to your work, and revise as necessary.

❚ *Evaluation Criteria*

A good comparison-contrast essay

1. identifies what is being compared, gives necessary background information, and includes a thesis statement in the introduction

2. compares and/or contrasts at least two features, either by the block or the point-by-point method of organization

3. supports general statements with specific examples and quotations from the text or from outside sources

4. draws a conclusion from the similarities and/or differences presented

5. quotes accurately from the text and documents all quotations carefully

AGREEMENT: COMMON PROBLEMS

Here's a draft essay about one character from *The Canterbury Tales*.

> The pilgrims who meet by chance at the Tabard Inn is an unlikely collection of travelers. The Friar, along with the similarly well-fed Nun, are among the most outlandish of the pilgrims. Still, the Miller remains my favorite. His knotty shoulders and wart-tipped nose makes quite a vivid picture. Either his wide, black nostrils or his furnace-door mouth are the detail that best suggests the Miller's volatile temper. It's also hard to imagine that a man who can break a door with his head can also play the mournful-sounding bagpipes, but I guess I've just never seen one.

While the writer uses strong, vivid details, she has trouble with some sticky subject-verb combinations. *All* writers, even professionals, encounter the grammatical problems in this paragraph, but these problems can be mastered.

1. *Subject-verb agreement* means that a singular subject takes a singular verb and plural subjects take plural verbs. A subject's number is **not** changed by a following phrase or clause.

   The **pilgrims** who meet by chance at the Tabard Inn **are** an unlikely collection of travelers.

2. In formal usage, a singular subject followed by a parenthetical phrase such as *along with . . .* , *as well as . . .* , or *in addition to . . .* remains singular.

   The **Friar,** along with the similarly well-fed Nun, **is** among the most outlandish of the pilgrims.

3. A *compound subject* is two or more subjects having the same verb. A compound subject joined by *and* usually takes a plural verb, even if one subject is singular.

   His knotty **shoulders and** wart-tipped **nose make** quite a vivid picture.

4. When a compound subject is joined by *or* or *nor,* the verb agrees with the subject closer to the verb.

   Either his wide, black **nostrils or** his furnace-door **mouth is** the detail that best suggests the Miller's volatile temper.

Writer's Workshop Follow-Up: Proofreading

Reread the essay you wrote for the Writer's Workshop on page 185, checking for agreement problems. Have you maintained subject-verb agreement in each sentence? After you check for agreement in your essay, ask a peer reviewer to look over your paper for agreement problems; then make any necessary corrections.

Technology
H E L P

See Language Workshop CD-ROM. *Key word entry: agreement.*

Language Handbook
H E L P

See Agreement, page 1223.

Try It Out

Choose the word that creates correct agreement in each sentence.

1. Neither the Squire nor the Doctor (seem, seems) as gallant as the Knight.

2. The Nun's rosary beads and brooch (was, were) brightly polished.

3. We wonder how the Oxford Cleric, as well as his twenty volumes of philosophy, (was, were) carried by a horse "thinner than a rake."

4. If any of the pilgrims' character sketches (reveal, reveals) Chaucer himself, the description of the Host is closest.

Reading for Life

Analyzing a Film or Play Review

Situation

Imagine that you've just seen a videotape of the Oscar-winning film *Braveheart*, about a thirteenth-century Scottish hero, William Wallace. You want to compare your opinion of the film with that of a professional film critic. Here are strategies you should follow.

Strategies

Note the title of the review.

- The title may suggest the critic's general opinion and the tone of the review.

Recognize specific elements that the critic evaluates.

- These elements usually include the plot, the screenplay or script, direction, and actors' performances, as well as such elements of film as cinematography, special effects, the soundtrack, and editing.

Recognize the critic's criteria, or standards.

- Critics often compare the elements of one film or play with those of another film or play. They might use a production they consider excellent as a standard by which they judge the production they are reviewing.

Compare the critic's criteria with your criteria.

- Be aware of your own standards of excellence. They may differ from the critic's.

Another Highland Fling

RICHARD SCHICKEL

Braveheart is too much, too late. Gibson, who directs himself in Randall Wallace's screenplay, starts with certain disadvantages vis-à-vis Rob Roy [another film]: Sir Walter Scott never wrote a novel about William Wallace, and no one named a cocktail after him either. Got a real name-recognition problem here. Got a real length problem too. *Braveheart* runs almost three hours, and though it's full of incident, including several big and expertly staged battle sequences, it really doesn't have enough on its mind to sustain our full attention over that span. Freedom, Wallace keeps telling everyone, is a good thing, worth dying for. Tyranny, on the other hand, is a bad thing. . . .

But we know all that; it's what historical movies have taught us over the years. What you need in this situation is world-class villainy, somebody full of wicked surprise to break up the banalities. This *Braveheart* lacks. . . .

The other problem with *Braveheart* is its unhappy ending. After all that time, you want and expect evil to be confounded. What you get instead is the hero being tortured to death. The suspense is this: Will he crack, cry out in pain, thus robbing posterity of an inspiring example of masochism—sorry, heroism? Come on. That's Mel Gibson the wild horses are trying to pull apart. Of course he's going to die stoically. Everybody knows that a non-blubbering clause is standard in all movie stars' contracts. Too bad there isn't one banning self-indulgence when they direct.

—*from* Time, May 19, 1995

Be aware of the critic's tone.

- Notice the critic's choice of words and how they reveal his or her attitude toward the film.

Evaluate the review.

- Whether or not you agree with the review, decide if it is comprehensive, informative, fair, and convincing.

Using the Strategies

Answer these questions about the review above.

1. What elements of the film does the critic address?

2. What are some of the criteria that the critic uses to assess *Braveheart*?

3. What is the critic's **tone**? What words and phrases contribute to that tone? (Consider the title of the review.)

4. Does the critic convincingly support his opinions? Explain your judgment.

Extending the Strategies

- List the elements that *you* particularly look for when you watch a film.

- Compare your opinion of a film you've seen recently with a professional critic's opinion of that film.

Learning for Life

Evaluating Technological Advances

Problem

During the Hundred Years' War, the development of armor-piercing arrows made knighthood obsolete. How will advances in technology affect today's occupations?

Project

Investigate how emerging technology is expected to change an occupation that interests you. How will the demand for workers be affected? How will education and training requirements, as well as job tasks, change?

Preparation

1. Choose an occupation that interests you: one you're thinking of pursuing or simply one you're curious about.

2. Use the *5W-How?* questions (*Who? What? When? Where? Why? How?*) to gather information with a focus.

3. Use print and electronic sources for most of the information you need. You might also consult community groups such as trade or professional organizations.

Procedure

1. To get an overview of the occupation, start with the *Dictionary of Occupational Titles* and the *Occupational Outlook Handbook.* (Both are government publications, and both are available on-line in certain databases.)

2. In addition to using standard sources such as the card catalog and indexes for newspapers, magazines, and databases, consider checking with special-interest newsgroups on the Internet. (Moderated newsgroups are more reliable than unmoderated ones.)

3. Keep in mind that the sources you use should be not only reliable but also relevant, recent, and representative. Remember, too, to document all your sources.

Presentation

Use one of the following formats (or another that your teacher approves):

1. **Traveling Graphics**

   Create a traveling exhibit using hand-drawn or computer-generated **graphics** to display your findings. For example, you could use bar charts to show current and future job openings or qualifications. Include documentation of your sources, and give your exhibit a catchy title. Display your exhibit on Career Day at your school.

2. **Future Expectations**

   Write a job description detailing the tasks and responsibilities an employee in the occupation will be expected to carry out. Use present-tense action verbs (for example, "using an interferometer, a virtual-reality designer measures . . ."), and be as specific as possible. Make your job description accessible to a wider audience by adding a glossary of technical terms arranged in alphabetical order. With classmates who have also chosen this option, compile a booklet of job descriptions, or create a page for your school's database system.

3. **Sharing Interests**

   Give an informal talk reporting your findings to a school- or community-based group that shares your interest in the occupation. For example, students in an earth sciences class might enjoy learning how emerging technology is expected to affect the knowledge and skills required of meteorologists. You may prepare visuals (charts, graphs, and so on) to augment your presentation.

Processing

Did doing this activity confirm or deflate your interest in the occupation? Did it change your views about the kind of education and training you would need, and if so, how? Write a brief reflection for your portfolio.

The Renaissance
1485–1660

A Fête at Bermondsey (c.1570) by J. Hoofnagel. Oil on panel.

191

The Renaissance

by **C. F. Main**

O England! model to thy inward greatness,
Like little body with a mighty heart . . .
— *William Shakespeare*

Tower of London and shipping, with Charles, duke of Orleans, seated in the Tower writing, from the *Poems of Charles Duke of Orleans and Other Works* (c. 1500), Roy 16 F II fol. 73.

W hat do you think people living a hundred years from now will call the age we live in today? Will they say we lived in the Space Age, the Age of Computers, the Age of Anxiety, the Age of Violence? We might be given a label we can't even imagine.

Just as we don't know what people of the future will think of us, the people of Europe living in the 1400s, 1500s, and 1600s didn't know that they were living in the Renaissance. Historical periods—the Middle Ages, the Renaissance, the Romantic period—are historians' inventions, useful labels for complex phenomena. The Middle Ages in England did not end on a certain night in 1485, when King Richard III's naked body, trussed up like a turkey, was thrown in an unmarked grave. And the English Renaissance did not begin the moment a Tudor nobleman was crowned King Henry VII. The changes in people's values, beliefs, and behavior that marked the emerging Renaissance occurred gradually. Much that could be called "medieval" lingered on long after the period known as the Middle Ages was past. Historical periods cannot be rigidly separated from one another, but they can be distinguished.

Beginning in the late 1400s, the English Renaissance marked changes in people's values, beliefs, and behavior.

Rediscovering Ancient Greece and Rome

The term *renaissance* itself is a French word meaning "rebirth." It refers particularly to renewed interest in classical learning, which means the writings of ancient Greece and Rome. In the long period of the Middle Ages, most European scholars had forgotten the Greek language, and they used a form of Latin that was very different from the Latin of ancient Rome. Very few ordinary people could read. Those who could read were encouraged to concentrate on texts promoting Church doctrine. But in the Renaissance, people discovered the marvels hidden away in old Greek and Latin classics—books that had been tucked away on the cobwebbed shelves of monasteries for hundreds of years. Now people learned to read Greek once more and reformed the Latin that they read, wrote, and spoke.

> Knowledge is power.
> —Francis Bacon, 1597

Some people became more curious about themselves and their world than people in general had been in the Middle Ages, so that gradually there was a renewal of the human spirit—of curiosity and creativity. New energy seemed to be available for creating beautiful things and thinking new, even daring, thoughts. Today we still use the

World map drawn in a fool's head (detail) (1590). Based on *Ortelin's Atlas*, 1570.

© cliché Bibliothèque Nationale de France, Paris.

The Renaissance, 1485–1660

LITERARY EVENTS

• Martin Luther's sermon (detail) (16th century) from a triptych by Lucas Cranach.

Book licensing laws introduced in England, 1538

Spanish priest Bernardino de Sahagún begins compiling exhaustive Aztec encyclopedia in Mexico, 1529

Niccolò Machiavelli's *The Prince* written, 1513

Thomas More's *Utopia* published, 1516

William Shakespeare, the Bard of Avon, born, 1564

Tottel's Miscellany (including poems of Wyatt and Surrey) published, 1557

Edmund Spenser publishes first three books of *The Faerie Queene,* 1590

Christopher Marlowe's *Doctor Faustus* written, 1588

Okuni, a former priestess, forms first kabuki theater company in Japan (in 1629, Okuni and all other women banned from the kabuki stage), c. 1586

In France, Montaigne begins his *Essais,* 1572

1485–1515	1516–1540	1541–1565	1566–1590

CULTURAL/HISTORICAL EVENTS

Richard III is killed in battle, 1485

John Cabot explores northeast coast of North America, 1497

Vasco da Gama reaches India via Cape of Good Hope, 1498

Leonardo da Vinci paints *Mona Lisa,* c. 1503

Henry VIII crowned king of England, 1509

Balboa crosses Isthmus of Panama and sights Pacific Ocean, 1513

Martin Luther posts his ninety-five theses on church door in Wittenburg, Germany, beginning the Protestant Reformation, 1517

First Africans taken to Americas as slaves, 1517

Magellan leads first expedition to circumnavigate the globe, 1519–1521

Hernando Cortés conquers Mexico, destroying Aztec empire, 1521

In India, Babur conquers Delhi and founds Mogul dynasty, 1526

Henry VIII proclaims himself head of the Church of England, c. 1533

Michelangelo paints *The Last Judgment* on altar wall of the Sistine Chapel, 1534–1541

Polish astronomer Nicolaus Copernicus publishes theory that planets orbit the sun, 1543

Mary Tudor—"Bloody Mary"—reigns, restoring papal authority in England, 1553–1558

Elizabeth I becomes queen of England, 1558

English navy defeats Spanish Armada, 1588

• *Nicolaus Copernicus* (detail) (1575). German School.

• *Mona Lisa* (c. 1503) by Leonardo da Vinci.

• Hernando Cortés (1485–1547), Spanish explorer, meeting Montezuma II (c. 1480–1520), Aztec emperor.

Shakespeare's sonnets published (written c. mid-1590s), 1609

Ben Jonson writes *The Masque of Blackness* and *Volpone,* 1605–1606

Shakespeare writes *King Lear* and *Macbeth,* 1605–1606

Cervantes publishes Part I of *Don Quixote* (Part II published in 1615), 1605

Globe Theatre built in London, 1599

In London, outbreak of plague forces theaters to close, 1593–1594

Newspapers first published in London, 1621

Francis Bacon's *Novum Organum* (New Instrument) published, 1620

Aemilia Lanier publishes her book of poetry, *Salve Deus Rex Judaeorum,* 1611

King James Bible published, 1611

John Donne's *Holy Sonnets* written, 1610–1611

• Lithograph showing the arrival of the Pilgrims in Massachusetts Bay (1620).

• English astrolabe (1559), a navigational instrument, made for Queen Elizabeth I by Thomas Gemini.

John Milton begins *Paradise Lost,* c. 1658

American poet Anne Bradstreet's *The Tenth Muse Lately Sprung Up in America* published in London, 1650

Puritans close all theaters in England, 1642–1660

1591–1610   1611–1640   1641–1660

British East India Company founded for trade with Asia, 1600

Gunpowder Plot, an attempt by Guy Fawkes and others to blow up Parliament and assassinate James I, averted, 1605

First permanent English settlement in North America established at Jamestown, Virginia, 1607

In Italy, Galileo is first to study sky with telescope, 1609

The *Mayflower* lands at Plymouth Rock, Massachusetts, 1620

English physician William Harvey explains the circulation of blood, 1628

Taj Mahal built near Agra, India, c. 1632–c. 1649

Japan expels all Europeans, 1639

• Taj Mahal.

English Civil Wars fought, 1642–1651

Manchus proclaim Ch'ing dynasty in China, 1644

Charles I beheaded, 1649

Dutch establish settlement in South Africa, 1652

Oliver Cromwell rules England as lord protector, 1653–1658

Jews legally readmitted to England (after being expelled in 1290), 1655

Puritan Commonwealth ends; monarchy restored with Charles II, 1660

• The World Map (c. 1540), from the *Portolan Atlas of the World* by Battista Agnese of Venice.

Ladies and Gentlemen Dancing in a Sumptuous Interior by Paulus Vredeman de Vries (1567–c. 1630). Christie's, London.

God made man and woman at the close of the creation, to know the laws of the universe, to love its beauty, and to admire its greatness. He bound his human creatures to no fixed place, to no prescribed form of work, and by no iron necessity, but gave them freedom to will and to love. "I have set thee," says the Creator, "in the midst of the world, that thou mayest the more easily behold and see all that is therein. I created thee a being neither heavenly nor earthly, neither mortal nor immortal only, that thou mightest be free to shape and to overcome thyself. Thou mayest sink into a beast or be born anew to the divine likeness. To thee alone is given a growth and a development depending on thine own free will."

—Pico della Mirandola (1463–1494), *On the Dignity of Humanity*

term "Renaissance person" for an energetic and productive human being who is interested in science, literature, history, art, and other subjects. (In America, Virginia's Thomas Jefferson, author of the Declaration of Independence, is referred to as a "Renaissance man.")

Fifteenth-century scholars rediscovered the writings of ancient Greece and Rome. At this same time, people became more curious about themselves and their world.

It All Began in Italy: A Flourish of Genius

The new energy and creativity were first observable in Italy, where considerable wealth had been generated from banking and trade with the East. The Renaissance began in Italy in the fourteenth century and lasted into the sixteenth. Thinking about just a few of the extraordinary people who flourished in this period—artists such as Leonardo da Vinci and Michelangelo, explorers such as Christopher Columbus, or scientists such as Galileo—reminds us how remarkably rich this period was, and how much we owe to it.

Almost everyone in Europe and Britain at this time was Roman Catholic, in name anyway, so the Church was very rich and powerful, even in political affairs—in ways we would probably object to today. Many of the popes were lavish patrons of artists, architects, and scholars.

Pope Julius II, for example, commissioned the artist Michelangelo to paint gigantic scenes from the Bible on the ceiling of the Sistine Chapel, a small church in the pope's "city" that was called, as it is today, the Vatican. Lying on his back on a scaffold, Michelangelo painted the Creation, the fall of Man and Woman, Noah's flood, and other Biblical and mythological subjects. His bright, heroic figures, which are still admired by thousands of visitors to Rome each year, show individual human beings who are noble and capable of perfection. This optimistic view of human nature was also expressed by many other Renaissance painters and writers.

The Renaissance began in fourteenth-century Italy, where the Catholic Church financed many intellectual and artistic endeavors.

Humanism: Questions About the Good Life

Refreshed by the classics, the new writers and artists were part of an intellectual movement known as **humanism.** The humanists went to the old Latin and Greek classics to discover new answers to such questions as "What is a human being?" "What is a good life?" and "How do I lead a good life?" Of course, Christianity provided complete answers to these questions, answers that the Renaissance humanists accepted as true. Renaissance humanists found no essential conflicts between the teachings of the Church and those of an ancient Roman moralist like Cicero. They sought instead to harmonize these two great sources of wisdom: the Bible and the classics. Their aim was to use the classics to strengthen, not discredit, Christianity.

The Outdoor Concert (detail) (16th century) by the Italian School.

Hotel Lallemand, Bourges, France.

> Some books are to be tasted, others to be swallowed, and some few to be chewed and digested.
> —Francis Bacon, 1625

The humanists' first task was to recover accurate copies of these ancient writings. Their searches through Italian monasteries turned up writers and works whose very existence had been forgotten. Their next task was to share their findings. And so they became teachers, especially of the young men who would become the next generation's rulers—wise and virtuous rulers, they hoped. From the Greek writer Plutarch, for instance, these humanist teachers would learn that the aim of life is to attain virtue, not success or money or fame, because virtue is the best possible human possession and the only source of true happiness.

An intellectual movement known as humanism began to use the Latin and Greek classics, combined with traditional Christian thought, to teach people how to live and how to rule.

Printing Shop (1580s) by Jan van der Straet. Engraving.

The New Technology: A Flood of Print

The computer has radically transformed how we get information today. Similarly, the printing press transformed the way information was exchanged during the Renaissance. Before this, all books were laboriously written out by hand—you can imagine how difficult and expensive this was and how few books were available.

The inventor of printing with movable type was a German named Johannes Gutenberg (1400?–1468). He printed the first complete book, an immense Latin Bible, at Mainz, Germany, around 1455. From there, the art and craft of printing spread to other cities in Germany, in the Low Countries (the Netherlands, Belgium, and Luxembourg), and in northern Italy. By 1500, relatively inexpensive books were available throughout western Europe. In 1476, printing reached England, then regarded as an

Bookbinder (16th century).

island remote from the centers of civilization. In that year, William Caxton (1422?–1491), a merchant, diplomat, and writer who had been living in the Low Countries, set up a printing press in Westminster (now part of London). In all, Caxton's press issued about one hundred different titles, initiating a flood of print in English that is still increasing.

> **Gutenberg's printing press helped spread the new knowledge, making more books available to more people than ever before.**

Two Friends—Two Humanists

When you hear people speak of humanism, you may hear the name Erasmus. Desiderius Erasmus (1466?–1536) is today perhaps the best known of all the Renaissance humanists. Erasmus was a Dutch monk, but he lived outside the monastery and loved to travel, visiting many of the countries in Europe, including Italy, France, Germany, and England. He belonged, then, to all Europe. Because he wrote in Latin, he could address his many writings to all the educated people of western Europe.

On his visits to England, Erasmus taught Greek at Cambridge University and became friendly with a number of important people, among them a young lawyer named Thomas More (1477?–1535). More and Erasmus had much in common: They both loved life, laughter, and classical learning, and they both were dedicated churchmen, though they were impatient with some of the Church's corrupt practices at that time.

Like Erasmus, More wrote in Latin—poems, pamphlets, biographies, and his famous treatise on human society, *Utopia* (yoō·tō′pē·ə) (1516). This book became immediately popular, and it has been repeatedly translated into English and many other languages. Hundreds of writers have imitated or parodied it, and it has given us a useful adjective for describing impractical social schemes: *utopian*. More himself was far from impractical; he held a number of important offices, rose to the

Erasmus of Rotterdam (detail) (c. 1523) by Hans Holbein the Younger. Oil on wood (42 cm × 32 cm). Louvre, Paris.

Sir Thomas More (detail) (16th century) by Hans Holbein the Younger.

© The Frick Collection, New York.

Here, reduced to a small list, are the major characteristics of that great era called the Renaissance:

- People expanded their worlds by reading classical Greek and Roman writers rather than only religious writings that promoted Christian doctrine.
- Humanism spread, focusing attention on human life here and now, as well as on eternal life.
- A new technology—printing—made books widely available.
- A growing merchant class, rich with wealth plundered from the Americas, began to challenge the power of the bishops and the pope.
- The spread of scholarly Latin throughout Europe made possible the sharing of ideas.

very top of his profession, was knighted, and, as Lord Chancellor, became one of the king's chief ministers. More continues to fascinate people today. The play *A Man for All Seasons,* by Robert Bolt, later made into a movie (available on videotape), is about More and his tragic stand-off with King Henry VIII over a matter of law (see page 202). You might notice that many lawyers and politicians today hang a picture of Thomas More in their offices (the famous Holbein portrait is shown on page 199).

Desiderius Erasmus and Thomas More, humanists and close friends, helped shape European thought and history.

The Reformation: Breaking with the Church

While the Renaissance was going on throughout Europe, there occurred in some countries another important series of events called the

> Superstition, idolatry, and hypocrisy have ample wages, but truth goes a-begging.
> —Martin Luther, *Table Talk*, published in 1569

Reformation. In England these two vast movements were closely related, and their forces were felt by all English writers. Although the exact nature of the Reformation varied from country to country, one feature was common to all Reformers: They rejected the authority of the pope and the Italian churchmen. In England, conflicts with the papacy had occurred off and on over the centuries, but adjustments had always been made on both sides. By the 1530s, an open break with the Roman Church could no longer be avoided.

By then, a number of circumstances made such a break possible. Strong feelings of patriotism and national identity made the English people resent the financial burdens imposed on them by the Vatican—the pope, after all, was a foreign power in far-off Italy. Moreover, new religious ideas were coming into England from the Continent, especially from Germany. There, a monk named Martin Luther (1483–1546) had founded a new kind of Christianity, based not on what the pope said, but on a personal understanding of the Bible. Like any institution that has been around for a long time and that has ignored corruption within its ranks, the Church needed reform. Right at home in England, humanists like More and Erasmus were ridiculing old superstitions, as well as the ignorance and idleness of monks and the loose living and personal wealth of priests and bishops.

Strong feelings of patriotism and new ideas coming from the Continent encouraged people to question the authority of the Catholic Church and to object to the financial burdens imposed on them by the pope in Rome.

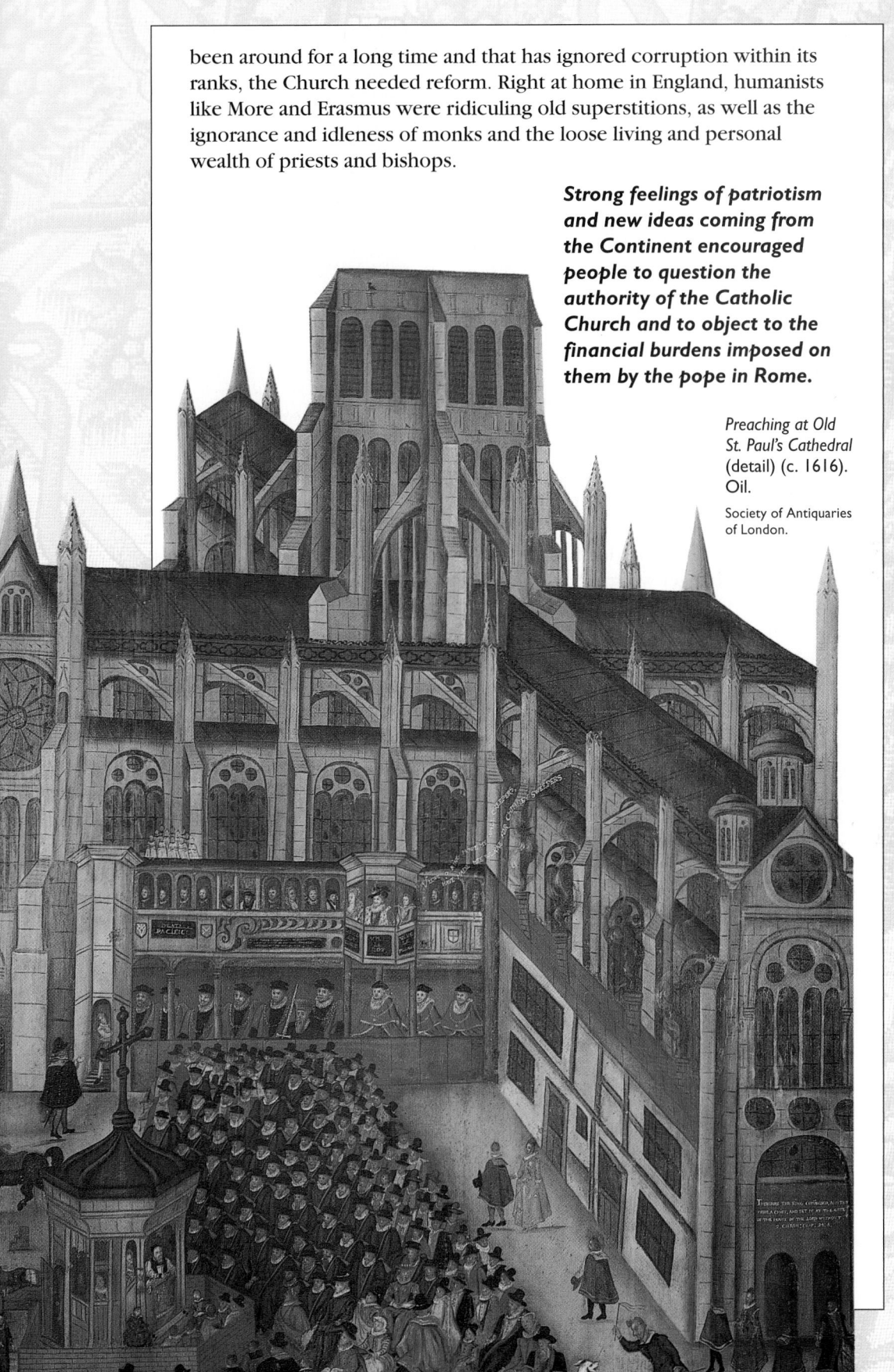

Preaching at Old St. Paul's Cathedral (detail) (c. 1616). Oil.

Society of Antiquaries of London.

King Versus Pope: All for an Heir

The generations-old conflict between the pope and the king of England came to a climax when Henry VIII wanted to get rid of his wife of twenty-four years. Divorce was not allowed, especially for kings (until recently, that was still true in Britain), so Henry needed a loophole. He asked Pope Clement VII to declare that he, Henry, was not properly married to his Spanish wife, Catherine of Aragon, because she had previously been wedded—for all of five months—to his older brother Arthur, now dead. (It was against Church law to marry a dead sibling's spouse; the Biblical basis for the law is in Leviticus.)

Henry had two motives for wanting to get rid of Catherine. First, although she had borne him a princess, she was too old to give him the male heir that he thought he must

Catherine of Aragon
(16th century) by M. Sittou.
Kunsthistorisches Museum, Vienna.

have. (Catherine had lost five babies.) What is more, another younger woman had won Henry's dangerous affections: The king now wished to marry Anne Boleyn, who had been his "favorite" for several years. (Henry had earlier seduced Anne's sister.) The pope was not able to grant Henry the annulment of his marriage, even if he had wanted to, because the pope was controlled by Queen Catherine's nephew, the emperor of Spain. And so, upon receiving the pope's refusal in 1533, Henry simply declared himself head of the English Church. He then appointed a new archbishop of Canterbury, who obligingly declared Henry's marriage to Catherine invalid.

With Catherine packed away under house arrest—since she refused to accept the annulment of her marriage—Henry closed all of England's monasteries and sold the rich buildings and lands to his subjects. While the vast majority of his subjects agreed with Henry's changes in the Church, some of them did not. The best known of all those who remained loyal to the pope was Sir Thomas More, now the Lord Chancellor of England. More felt he could not legally recognize his friend Henry as head of the Church. For More's stubbornness, Henry ordered that his Lord Chancellor be beheaded. It wasn't the first—or last—time that Henry executed a friend.

This was the very beginning of Protestantism in England. Many people were dissatisfied with the new church for reasons just the opposite of More's. They felt that it was not reformed enough, that it was merely a copy of Catholicism, as in

> . . . reminding us of a point in astronomy, which is that the longer the days are the farther off is the sun and yet the hotter; so is it with our love, for although by absence we are parted it nevertheless keeps its fervency, at least in my case and hoping the like of yours . . .
>
> —King Henry VIII, in a letter to Anne Boleyn, 1528

> This hath not offended the king.
>
> —Sir Thomas More, drawing his beard aside as he placed his head on the block, 1535

some respects it was. These dissidents, known as Puritans, Baptists, Presbyterians, Dissenters, and Nonconformists, wanted to get rid of many things they called "popish," such as the bishops, the prayer book, the priest's vestments, and even the church bells and the stained-glass windows. Some of them said that religion was solely a matter between the individual and God. This idea, which is still the foundation of most Protestant churches, is directly traceable to the teachings of those Renaissance humanists who emphasized the freedom of all human beings.

In 1531, refused an annulment by the pope, Henry VIII broke with the Catholic Church in Rome and declared himself head of the English Church. This marked the beginning of the Protestant Reformation in England.

The Great Harry (detail) (1546) from the Anthony Roll manuscript.

The Pepys Library, Magdalene College, Cambridge.

Henry VIII: Renaissance Man and Executioner

The five Tudor rulers of England are easy to remember: They consist of a grandfather, a father, and three children. The grandfather was Henry VII (1457–1509), a Welsh nobleman who seized the throne after England was totally exhausted by the long and bloody struggle called the Wars of the Roses. (Both factions involved used a rose as their emblem, one red, one white.) Henry VII was a shrewd, patient, and stingy man who restored peace and order to the kingdom; without these, there could never have been a cultural Renaissance.

His son Henry VIII (r. 1509–1547) had six wives: After Catherine of Aragon and Anne Boleyn, there were Jane Seymour, Anne of Cleves, Catherine Howard, and Catherine Parr. The fates of these unfortunate women are summarized in a jingle:

> Divorced, beheaded, died,
> Divorced, beheaded, survived.

The sexual intrigues of the court trapped several of Henry's wives: The king could play around, but he couldn't tolerate being suspicious of his wives' fidelity. The price paid by two young wives was heavy. Like Thomas More, Anne Boleyn and Catherine Howard lost their heads on the chopping block.

Despite his messy home life, Henry VIII was a very important figure. He created the Royal Navy, which put a stop to foreign invasions of England and provided the means for this island kingdom to spread its political power, language, and literature all over the globe. If we overlook his use of the sword against his enemies (and friends), Henry VIII himself deserves the title "Renaissance man." He wrote poetry and played many different musical instruments well; he was a champion athlete and a hunter; and he patronized the new humanistic learning. But in his old age, Henry was also coarse, dissolute, arrogant, and an unregenerate womanizer. He died without knowing that the child he ignored because she was female would become the greatest ruler England ever had.

Henry VIII's rule was bold and bloody. He increased England's strength and ensured its security by building up the Royal Navy, but those close to the king paid a high price.

An Allegory of the Tudor Succession: The Family of Henry VIII (c. 1589–1595) by the British School, possibly after Lucas de Heere. Oil on panel (45″ × 71¾″).

Yale Center for British Art, Paul Mellon Collection, New Haven.

The Boy King and Bloody Mary

Henry VIII was survived by three children: Mary, daughter of the Spanish princess, Catherine of Aragon; Elizabeth, daughter of Anne Boleyn, a lady-in-waiting at the court; and Edward, son of noblewoman Jane Seymour, who died twelve days after her son's birth. According to the laws of succession, the son had to be crowned first, and so at age nine the son of Henry and Jane Seymour became Edward VI (r. 1547–1553). An intelligent but sickly boy, he ruled in name only while his relatives wielded the actual power.

When Edward died of tuberculosis, he was followed by his half-Spanish half-sister Mary (r. 1553–1558). Mary was a devout, strong-willed Catholic determined to avenge the wrongs done to her mother. She restored the pope's power in England and ruthlessly hunted down Protestants.

Had she lived longer, and had she exercised better judgment, Mary might have undone all her father's accomplishments. But she made a strategic error when she burned about three hundred of her subjects at the stake. She further lost the support of her people when she married Philip II, king of Spain, a country England was beginning to fear and hate. (Mary was thirty-seven and Philip only twenty-six.) Mary's executions earned her the name "Bloody Mary." When Mary died of a fever, childless, her sister Elizabeth became queen.

Mary Tudor succeeded her father Henry VIII. Immediately, she killed Protestants and reversed her father's policies: She restored the pope's power in England.

Elizabeth: The Virgin Queen

Elizabeth I (r. 1558–1603) was one of the most brilliant and successful monarchs in history. Since she inherited a kingdom torn by fierce religious feuds, her first task was to restore law and order. She reestablished the Church of England and again rejected the pope's authority, and the pope promptly excommunicated her. To keep Spain appeased, she pretended that she just might marry her widowed brother-in-law, King Philip.

Philip was the first of a long procession of noblemen, both foreign and English, who wanted to wed her. But Elizabeth resisted marriage all her life and officially remained "the Virgin Queen" (thereby giving the American colony Virginia its name). She knew that her strength lay in her independence and her ability to play one suitor off against another. "I am your anointed Queen," she told a group from Parliament who urged her to marry. "I will never be by violence constrained to do anything. I thank God I am endued with such qualities that if I were turned out of the realm in my petticoat, I were able to live in any place in Christendom."

Mary Tudor (16th century) by an unknown artist.
Musée Condé, Chantilly, France.

Fain would I climb, yet fear I to fall.
—Sir Walter Raleigh to Elizabeth I, scratched on a windowpane

If thy heart fails thee, climb not at all.
—Elizabeth's reply, scratched underneath

Portrait of Queen Elizabeth I within the Armada Jewel (16th century) by Nicholas Hilliard.
The Victoria and Albert Museum, London.

THE GLASS OF FASHION

They displayed their new costumes from ten to twelve o'clock in the morning, strolling up and down the center aisle of St. Paul's Church. They insisted on rich fabrics: velvet, taffeta, gold brocade, and fur. They wore the finest silk stockings and cork platform shoes. They curled their hair, perfumed their gloves, and (if daring) wore makeup. They showed off favorite jewels—pearls, perhaps—in earrings, bracelets, and designs sewn all over their clothes. The men in the Renaissance were peacocks indeed!

Exquisite excess. Women also dressed flamboyantly in the Renaissance. Elizabeth I herself owned eighty wigs and three thousand gowns at her death.

In the 1580s and 1590s, the Renaissance silhouette was ridiculously exaggerated. Starched linen neck ruffs stretched from shoulder to shoulder. Shoulders themselves were extended with "wings" that make even the most exaggerated of today's shoulder pads look like cotton balls. Hoop skirts (called farthingales) could be four feet wide at the hips, and men's full, thigh-length pants were padded to what critics called "monstrous and outrageous greatness." Women corseted their waists into painful narrowness while men stiffened doublets (an upper garment) with pasteboard and stuffed them with horsehair, rags, or even bran in order to achieve what was called a peascod belly. A man's silhouette was

Portrait of Elizabeth Vernon, countess of Southampton (c. 1610) by an unknown artist.
By permission of the Duke of Buccleuch, Kettering, England.

Portrait of a lady said to be Lady Style (detail) (16th century) by the circle of William Larkin.
Christie's, London.

Portrait of a nobleman said to be the 7th earl of Shrewsbury in garter robes (detail) (16th century) by Paul van Somer.
Christie's, London.

narrowest at the bottom, where stockings and garters worn above the knee made even shapely legs look better.

Symbols and signals. In the Renaissance, intricate pattern (like poetry's "artificiality") was also a must. Braids, bows, spangles, and lace covered the luxurious fabrics, and slashed sleeves and doublets allowed embroidered underclothes to peek through. Colors were rich and bold—red, gold, black, and white was a favorite combination.

Colors and designs also had symbolic meanings: Green meant love, white and tawny together showed patience in adversity, a pansy represented sadness, a snake flattery, and so on. Queen Elizabeth often wore white and black together—both colors symbolized chastity. Whole trea-

tises were devoted to color and to defining "emblems" such as rainbows, clouds, worms, and flies.

Reading T-shirts. How will historians of dress read the clothes we wear today? Are bodices embroidered with flies so strange when viewed against the sort of printed T-shirts available by the hundreds in any shopping mall? What messages do our clothes send out to the world, and what will they tell the future?

Lettice Knollys, daughter of Sir Henry Knollys, wife of 4th Lord Paget (detail) (16th century) by the English School.

Manor House, Stanton Harcourt, Oxon, England.

An unknown lady in a masque costume (detail) (c. 1615).

City of Bristol Museum and Art Gallery, Bristol, England.

Mary Denton, née Martyn, age 15 in 1573 (detail) (16th century) by the circle of George Gower.

York City Art Gallery, York, England.

Gilbert Talbot, 7th earl of Shrewsbury, age 40 (detail) (16th century) by William Seger.

Christie's, London.

Execution of Mary, Queen of Scots (16th century) by an unknown Dutch artist.

A truly heroic person, Elizabeth survived many plots against her life. Several of these plots were initiated by her cousin, another Mary—Mary Stuart, Queen of Scots. As Elizabeth had no children, Mary was heir to England's throne because she, too, was a direct descendant of Henry VII. But Mary, a Catholic, was eventually deposed from her throne in Protestant Scotland. Put under house arrest, she lived as a royal exile in England, carefully watched by her cousin Elizabeth. Elizabeth endured Mary and her plots for twenty years and then, a true daughter of her father, sent her Scottish cousin to the chopping block.

> *Like her father, Elizabeth quickly and efficiently settled disorder both in her kingdom and in her own household. She once again rejected the pope and reestablished the Church of England. Elizabeth's intelligence and independence made her reign one of the most successful in England's history.*

The Spanish Armada Sinks: A Turning Point in History

King Philip of Spain, ever watchful for an excuse to hammer at England, used Mary's execution as an excuse to invade England. He assembled a vast fleet of warships for that purpose: the famous Spanish Armada. In 1588, England's Royal Navy, assisted greatly by nasty weather in the Irish Sea, destroyed the Armada. This victory assured England's and all of northern Europe's

... Then she, lying very still upon the block, one of the executioners holding her slightly with one of his hands, she endured two strokes of the other executioner with an axe, she making very small noise or none at all, and not stirring any part of her from the place where she lay: and so the executioner cut off her head, saving one little gristle, which being cut asunder, he lift up her head to the view of all the assembly and bade God save the Queen. Then, her dress of lawn falling from off her head, it appeared as gray as one of threescore and ten years old, polled very short, her face in a moment being so much altered from the form she had when she was alive, as few could remember her by her dead face. Her lips stirred up and down a quarter of an hour after her head was cut off ...

—Robert Wynkfielde, an eyewitness to the execution of Mary, Queen of Scots, 1587

(Opposite) *English Ships and the Spanish Armada, August 1588* (detail). English School. Oil.

National Maritime Museum, London.

To be a king and wear a crown is more glorious to them that see it than it is pleasure to them that bear it.

—Elizabeth I, 1601

independence from the powerful Catholic countries of the Mediterranean. It was a great turning point in history and Elizabeth's finest moment. If Spain had prevailed, history would have been quite different: All of North America, like most of South America, might be speaking Spanish instead of English.

In 1588, the English Royal Navy defeated the Spanish Armada. This stunning sea victory assured England's independence from the powerful Catholic countries of the Mediterranean.

As for her face, it is and appears to be very aged. It is long and thin and her teeth are very yellow and unequal, compared with what they were formerly, so they say, and on the left side less than on the right. Many of them are missing so that one cannot understand her easily when she speaks quickly. Her figure is fair and tall and graceful in whatever she does; so far as may be she keeps her dignity . . .

—André Hurault, French ambassador, writing about Elizabeth I, 1597

A Flood of Literature

What is the connection between these political events and English literature? With their own religious and national identity firmly established, the English started writing as never before. After the defeat of the Armada, Elizabeth became a beloved symbol of peace, security, and prosperity to her subjects, and she provided inspiration to scores of English authors. They represented her mythologically in poetry, drama, and fiction—as Gloriana, Diana, the Faerie Queene, and Cynthia. Literary works that did not directly represent her were dedicated to her because authors knew she was a connoisseur of literature and a person of remarkably wide learning.

Elizabeth encouraged and inspired many writers. With the era of peace and prosperity that followed the defeat of the Spanish Armada, the English started writing as never before.

Decline of the Renaissance: A Dull Man Succeeds a Witty Woman

Elizabeth died childless, so her second cousin, James VI of Scotland, was her successor. James was the son of Elizabeth's cousin Mary whom Elizabeth had beheaded years before. As James I of England (r. 1603–1625), he lacked Elizabeth's ability to resolve (or postpone) critical issues, especially religious and economic ones. James was a spendthrift where Elizabeth had been thrifty; he was thick-tongued and goggle-eyed where she had been glamorous and witty; he was essentially a foreigner where she had been a complete Englishwoman.

James I tried hard. He wrote learned books in favor of the divine right of kings and against tobacco, he patronized Shakespeare, he sponsored a new translation of the Bible, and he was in many respects an admirable man and a benevolent, peaceful ruler. Yet his relationship with many of his subjects, especially with pious, puritanically minded merchants, went from bad to worse.

The difficulties of James's reign became the impossibilities of his son's. Charles I (r. 1625–1649) turned out to be remote, autocratic, and self-destructive. Some of his most powerful subjects had him beheaded in 1649. For the next eleven years, England was ruled by Parliament and the Puritan dictator Oliver Cromwell, not by an anointed king. When Charles's self-indulgent son returned to power eleven years later, in 1660, England had changed in many important ways.

Of course the Renaissance did not end in 1660 as Charles II returned from exile in France, just as it had not begun at any specific date. Renaissance values, which were primarily moral and religious, gradually eroded, and Renaissance energies gradually gave out. The last great writer of the English Renaissance was John Milton, who lived on into an age in which educated people were becoming more worldly in their outlook. Scientific truths were soon to challenge long-accepted religious beliefs.

The English Renaissance was over.

The political climate in England began to change after Elizabeth's death. The end of the English Renaissance is usually marked by the return of the exiled king in 1660. By this time, more political and secular values were beginning to challenge the accepted doctrines of religion.

> All my possessions for a moment of time.
> —Elizabeth I's last words, 1603

Bird's-eye view of London, from the *Atlas Civitatis Orbis Terrarum* (c. 1574) by Georg Braun. Map L85c #27.

By permission of The Folger Shakespeare Library, Washington, D.C.

JEWISH LIFE IN ENGLAND: EXPULSION AND RETURN

As you read the literature of Renaissance England, you'll notice that many selections use Christian imagery or are about Christian topics. Certainly, all the writers in these collections were Christian. But what about Jewish life in England?

The most famous Jewish character in Renaissance literature is Shylock, the money-lender in Shakespeare's play *The Merchant of Venice* (c. 1596–1598). Shylock is portrayed as cruel and greedy, a man incapable of mercy. In Shakespeare's play, Shylock is a usurer, which means that he lent money at interest, something commonly done by banks today. But charging interest on borrowed money (called usury) was considered sinful by the Christian church. (Many usurers charged exorbitant interest, and a small loan might ruin a poor widow and her family.) Since Jews were usually not allowed to own land, they became the people who handled money.

With Shylock, Shakespeare presents us with a complicated character who is at once a stereotype and a persecuted individual. Stereotypes like this one of the greedy moneylender were used to justify

relentless persecution of the Jews. Without a homeland, Jews had been moving for most of their history. Expelled from many European cities and countries, Jewish refugees streamed into cities that already housed more Jews than their rulers wanted. Some cities, such as Venice (the setting for *The Merchant of Venice*), dealt with Jews by segregating them in ghettos and charging them extra taxes.

There were a few Jews in Shakespeare's England, although English Jews had been banished centuries before by King Edward I in 1290—because of controversy over their purchase of land. (Ownership of land by people considered "outsiders" was alarming then, as it still is in some places.) Some individual Jews probably continued to practice their religion in secret, but it wasn't until the middle of the seventeenth century, under the rule of Oliver Cromwell, that Jews were officially allowed to return to England.

Initial Word-Panel Illumination Showing a Marriage Ceremony, **from the** *Hamburg Halakhah Miscellany.* **Padua (1467–1477). The Hebrew letters mean "all." Codex Hebrew 337 (Scrin 132) fol. 75v. Vellum (6″ × 4½″).**

Staats und Universitätsbibliothek, Hamburg.

Quickwrite The humanists of the Renaissance were concerned with a question that we still ask ourselves today. "What is a good life?" they wondered. How would you answer this same question? What's the good life for you? Will you have a good life if you're rich, or if you're famous, or if you're able to do some good for someone, or if you have power, or if most of your days are simply happy? Write down your thoughts on this complex question. What do you think has influenced the way you define "the good life"?

since feeling is first

since feeling is first
who pays any attention
to the syntax of things
will never wholly kiss you;

wholly to be a fool
while Spring is in the world

my blood approves,
and kisses are a better fate
than wisdom
lady i swear by all flowers. Don't cry
—the best gesture of my brain is less than
your eyelids' flutter which says

we are for each other:then
laugh,leaning back in my arms
for life's not a paragraph

And death i think is no parenthesis

—E. E. Cummings
(American, 1894–1962)

Sir Thomas Wyatt
(1503–1542)

Sir Thomas Wyatt was a courtier of Henry VIII and spent much of his life traveling abroad as an ambassador for the king. The life of anyone who worked for the king could be dangerous as well as glamorous: Twice Henry had Wyatt imprisoned on charges that were probably false, and twice Wyatt managed to regain the king's favor. Besides being a diplomat, Wyatt was also a literary innovator who helped to change the nature of English poetry. Up to Wyatt's time, poetry was still essentially medieval in matter and manner, subject and form. Wyatt greatly admired Italian poetry, and he brought a new kind of poem, the love sonnet, to England from Italy. His English sonnets are actually adaptations of Italian sonnets.

Aside from his sonnets, Wyatt wrote many delightful lyrics modeled on English dance-songs, but he never had any of his works printed and publicly distributed. Wyatt had no

Sir Thomas Wyatt (16th century) by an unknown artist. Oil on panel (18½″ diameter).

ambition to be known as a "clerk," or a learned man of letters, the sort of person who published books. As a courtier he was expected to compose songs and verses, just as he was expected to do battle for his king, joust in tournaments, dance, and carry on intrigues with the ladies. And so Wyatt circulated his poems privately among his friends, in handwritten copies. Not until fifteen years after Wyatt's death did most of his poems appear in print. In 1557, an enterprising printer named Richard Tottel published *Songs and Sonnets,* an anthology containing ninety-seven of Wyatt's poems. This book, now called *Tottel's Miscellany,* has a rather bad reputation today because Tottel "improved" the poems by changing many words so that the poems sounded smoother to his ears. To make certain that we read Wyatt's words, rather than Tottel's, scholars had to search out the handwritten copies of the poems that predated their publication.

Before You Read
WHOSO LIST TO HUNT

Make the Connection

Wounded by Love

The battle of the sexes, Cupid's arrow, the thrill of the chase, conquered by love, a good catch: why do so many metaphors for love suggest a contest between hunter and prey? With your classmates, discuss love as a "hunt." Two questions to consider are these: Who inflicts the wounds in love—the pursuer or the pursued? Who is the one conquered?

Quickwrite

What do you think of the idea of love as a "hunt"? Take notes on your responses.

Background

According to traditional gossip, Wyatt wrote this poem about his longing for Anne Boleyn, a beautiful young woman at court. When he noticed that no less a person than King Henry was also attracted to Anne, he gave up the pursuit to whoever else wanted to "hunt" her. Whether or not the story is true, Anne did become the second of Henry's six queens. Wyatt adapted the poem from an Italian sonnet by Francis Petrarch (1304–1374). He also took from Petrarch's commentators the story about Julius Caesar's tame deer (line 13), whose collars were inscribed *Noli me tangere* (Latin for "touch me not"), warning hunters not to molest Caesar's property.

Whoso List to Hunt

Sir Thomas Wyatt

Whoso list° to hunt, I know where is an hind,°
But as for me, alas, I may no more.
The vain travail° hath wearied me so sore
I am of them that farthest cometh behind.
5 Yet may I, by no means, my wearied mind
Draw from the deer, but as she fleeth afore,
Fainting I follow. I leave off therefore,
Since in a net I seek to hold the wind.

Who list her hunt, I put him out of doubt,°
10 As well as I, may spend his time in vain.
And graven with diamonds in letters plain
There is written, her fair neck round about,
"*Noli me tangere,* for Caesar's I am,
And wild for to hold, though I seem tame."

1. **list:** archaic for "desires." **hind:** female deer
(rhymes with *kind*).
3. **travail:** hard work.
9. **put him out of doubt:** assure him (that he).

Anne Boleyn (late 16th century) by an unknown
artist. Oil on panel (21⅜″ × 16⅜″).
By Courtesy of the National Portrait Gallery, London.

MAKING MEANINGS

First Thoughts

1. Do you think this poem, specific as it is, describes attitudes and experiences still common in life today? Why or why not?

Shaping Interpretations

2. Given the background information you've just read, who is the hind in this poem and who is Caesar? Who is the **speaker**?

3. What warning does the speaker give potential hunters of the woman?

4. What **image** does the speaker use to show he's finally decided the chase is hopeless?

5. The speaker says the hind may seem tame but is "wild for to hold." Do you think he's referring to the woman herself or to Caesar's claim on her? Explain.

Connecting with the Text

6. If you were King Henry and you came upon this poem, how might you feel about its author? If you were Anne Boleyn, how might you react to the poem?

7. How do you feel about Wyatt's description of love as a hunt or a conquest? (Refer to your Quickwrite notes.)

ELEMENTS OF LITERATURE

Poetic Meter: Giving Form to Feeling

Poetic **meter** is a regular pattern of stressed and unstressed syllables. It is a rhythmic "beat"—like the steady pulse that draws you into dance music. Meter's basic unit is the **foot:** A foot consists of one stressed syllable and one or more unstressed syllables (mú·si·căl). The four basic metrical feet are

1. **iamb** (˘ ´), as in *relief*
2. **trochee** (´ ˘), as in *apple*
3. **anapest** (˘ ˘ ´), as in *introduce*
4. **dactyl** (´ ˘ ˘), as in *broccoli*

Poets also use two other metrical devices: the **spondee** (´ ´), or double stress, and the **caesura** (‖), or pause.

The analysis of a poem's meter is called **scansion.** When you scan a poem, you identify the type of foot (or feet) used in each line, and then you count them. **Dimeter** means two feet per line; **trimeter,** three; **tetrameter,** four; **pentameter,** five; and **hexameter,** six. This line from Wyatt's poem is **iambic pentameter** (it has five iambs):

Since in a net I seek to hold the wind.

Scanning poetry. Few poems are written in a meter that remains exactly regular throughout. The perception of meter may also vary from reader to reader, depending on which parts of phrases or sentences the reader thinks are most heavily stressed. Generally, however, readers can easily identify the dominant metrical pattern used in a poem.

1. Each of the following ordinary phrases uses one type of metrical foot. Identify the metrical foot in each.
   a. Best of all, victory!
   b. I bought a car today.
   c. Look for hidden pitfalls.
   d. in the cool of the night

2. Does Wyatt's "Whoso List to Hunt" show regular iambic pentameter? Scan three or four lines of the poem. What metrical patterns do you identify in these lines? Is the meter irregular in any of these lines? Explain.

CHOICES: Building Your Portfolio

Writer's Notebook

1. Collecting Ideas for an Interpretive Essay

When you write an essay about literature, a good starting point can be your own responses. Reflect on "Whoso List to Hunt" for a few minutes, writing freely about any personal connections you can make to the poem—experiences or feelings that you've had, or perhaps that you've witnessed in others. Try to find the one word or phrase from the poem that most strongly affects your feelings. Save your notes for use in the Writer's Workshop on page 275.

Creative Writing

2. A Woman's Place

What does the concept of love in this poem suggest about the position of women in Wyatt's time? How do you respond to the woman's statement "Caesar's I am"? How do you think *she* feels about her situation? Write a paragraph from the point of view of the "hind," and give her response to the situation described in the poem.

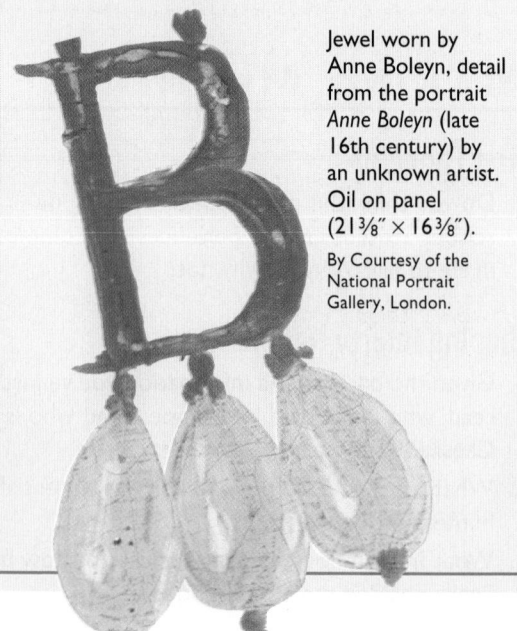

Jewel worn by Anne Boleyn, detail from the portrait *Anne Boleyn* (late 16th century) by an unknown artist. Oil on panel (21⅜″ × 16⅜″).

By Courtesy of the National Portrait Gallery, London.

Edmund Spenser

(c. 1552–1599)

The Granger Collection, New York.

Spenser—unlike such gentlemanly writers as Wyatt, Surrey, Sidney, and Raleigh—regarded himself primarily as a poet. Upon graduating from Cambridge University, he served as personal secretary to the earl of Leicester, then the favorite of Queen Elizabeth. In Leicester's household, Spenser became acquainted with several other poets and wrote his first book, *The Shepheardes Calender* (1579), a set of twelve pastoral poems, one for each month. Literary historians recognize 1579 as the date when the great age of Elizabethan literature began.

In 1580, Spenser and his new wife went to Ireland in the service of the English government. Except for two or three visits to England, he was to spend the rest of his life in that war-torn country. English troops had invaded and conquered Ireland, but the Irish did not regard themselves as conquered. They particularly resented people like Spenser, who was given an Irish castle and a vast estate in County Cork. Thirty miles away, Sir Walter Raleigh was the proprietor of an even vaster estate than Spenser's. When Raleigh was in Ireland, the two poets met and discussed their works in progress: Raleigh's *The Ocean to Cynthia* and Spenser's *The Faerie Queene*. Raleigh was so impressed with the latter that he persuaded Spenser to accompany him to London in 1589, and there in the following year Books I–III of *The Faerie Queene* were published.

In 1591, Spenser returned to Ireland, where conditions remained very unsettled and dangerous. But he managed to continue work on *The Faerie Queene* and other poems. When his first wife died, Spenser married Elizabeth Boyle, an Anglo-Irish woman living in Cork. Spenser's sonnet sequence *Amoretti* and his marriage hymn *Epithalamion* (both 1595) can be read autobiographically as records of his intense devotion to his wife. In 1596, Books IV–VI of *The Faerie Queene* appeared, along with another marriage song called *Prothalamion*.

As the century drew to a close, the Irish intensified their efforts to expel the English from their land. During one of their raids, Spenser's castle was burned and his infant son killed. Spenser himself escaped to London, where he died suddenly in 1599. He was given a splendid funeral and burial in the part of Westminster Abbey that has become known as the Poets' Corner. He lies near Chaucer, a poet who provided much of his inspiration.

Chaucer, Spenser, and Milton—these three were long regarded as England's greatest nondramatic poets. Of the three, Spenser is perhaps the least highly regarded today. Our age does not itself produce long poems of very high quality, and Spenser's fame depends mainly on the enormously long *Faerie Queene,* which despite its unfinished state runs about 33,000 lines. This poem is such a characteristic product of the Renaissance that some people find it has little to say to our own time. Moreover, Spenser's language is such a hybrid of Chaucerian and Elizabethan English that even when the work was brand new some purists objected to it. The dramatist and poet Ben Jonson, for instance, said Spenser "writ no language." But Spenser's special language is just right for his subject matter, and all the objections to him are easily overlooked by readers who want to lose themselves in the glorious world of imagination. They will always love Spenser.

Make the Connection

The Power of Paradox

Anyone who's been in love understands **paradox:** an apparent contradiction that is somehow true. Love makes you blissful and miserable. It's frightening and healing. It's physical and spiritual. It's incredibly fragile and yet so strong it seems deathless. In short, love is a potent puzzle that we never solve.

Quickwrite

Poets search for images to express the complex experience of falling in and out of love. How would you describe these two feelings: intense desire and loss of interest? Try to find a special image that represents each feeling. (Spenser uses fire and ice.)

Background

Spenser's *Amoretti* ("little love poems") is a sequence of eighty-nine sonnets recording a man's two-year courtship of a woman named Elizabeth (perhaps Spenser's courtship of his bride, Elizabeth Boyle). In Sonnet 30, Spenser uses, in an original way, the convention of the burning man and the icy lady. Sonnet 75 uses another convention, the writer's "eternizing conceit": Submit to my love, and I'll make you famous and even immortal through my writing. But again Spenser gives this old notion a new twist.

from Amoretti

Sonnet 30

Edmund Spenser

My love is like to ice, and I to fire;
How comes it then that this her cold so great
Is not dissolved through my so hot desire,
But harder grows the more I her entreat?
5 Or how comes it that my exceeding heat
Is not delayed° by her heart frozen cold,
But that I burn much more in boiling sweat,
And feel my flames augmented manifold?°
What more miraculous thing may be told
10 That fire which all thing melts, should harden ice,
And ice which is congealed° with senseless cold,
Should kindle fire by wonderful device?°
Such is the power of love in gentle mind,
That it can alter all the course of kind.°

6. **delayed:** tempered.
8. **augmented manifold:** increased in many ways.
11. **congealed:** thickened.
12. **device:** trick.
14. **kind:** nature.

Unknown Man with Flame Background (16th century) by Nicholas Hilliard.

Ham House, Surrey, England.

Sonnet 75

Edmund Spenser

One day I wrote her name upon the strand,°
But came the waves and washèd it away;
Again I wrote it with a second hand,
But came the tide, and made my pains his prey.
5 "Vain man," said she, "that doest in vain assay,°
A mortal thing so to immortalize,
For I myself shall like to this decay,
And eke° my name be wipèd out likewise."
"Not so," quod° I, "let baser things devise°
10 To die in dust, but you shall live by fame:
My verse your virtues rare shall eternize,
And in the heavens write your glorious name.
Where whenas death shall all the world subdue,
Our love shall live, and later life renew."

1. **strand:** beach.
5. **assay:** try.
8. **eke:** archaic for "also."
9. **quod:** quoth; said. **devise:** plan.

Portrait of an Unknown Lady
(16th century) by Nicholas Hilliard.
Victoria and Albert Museum, London.

MAKING MEANINGS

Sonnets 30 and 75

First Thoughts

1. How would you feel if someone in love with you had written these poems? Does your gender affect your response? How?

Shaping Interpretations

2. What **paradoxes** can you find in Sonnet 30? How would you explain them?

3. Fire and ice poems are meant to be clever, but in Sonnet 30, the **speaker** also says something serious about the power of love. What is it?

4. In what sense is the love of the two people in Sonnet 75 still alive today?

5. In Sonnet 75, what **image** does Spenser use for love's impermanence?

Extending the Texts

6. Some attitudes toward love and toward men and women have changed since these sonnets were written. Do you find the speaker's feelings dated or still relevant? Why?

ELEMENTS OF LITERATURE

Petrarchan and Spenserian Sonnets

Renaissance poets wrote with one eye on the past—they made new poems built on older forms and reflecting older themes. Wyatt's sonnets are adaptations or translations of sonnets written by the Italian Francesco Petrarca (1304–1374), known in English as Francis Petrarch. Petrarch addressed many love poems to a woman identified only as Laura, a proud woman of ideal virtue and beauty who remains totally indifferent to the poet. The poet-lover alternately burns with desire and freezes in Laura's cold disdain.

Sonnets in the Petrarchan manner contain many ingenious comparisons, which in time became known as **Petrarchan conceits.** A **conceit** is a fanciful comparison of two apparently very different things. Love may be compared to a baited hook, for instance, or being in love may be described as plowing water, an obviously futile effort. Petrarchan sonneteers also shape their emotion within a strict structure: fourteen lines of rhymed iambic pentameter, organized in two stanzas, one of eight lines (an **octave**) and one of six lines (a **sestet**). The rhyme in the octave is *abbaabba* and in the sestet usually *cdecde.*

In most Italian sonnets, the octave describes a situation, and the sestet describes a change in the situation. This change is called the **turn.** Sometimes the octave presents a problem and the sestet a solution or even another viewpoint. Sometimes the sestet intensifies the octave's problem with no solution. The possibilities are endless.

Two **English sonnet** forms—the Spenserian and Shakespearean sonnets—originated in the Renaissance. Like the Petrarchan sonnet, both forms use iambic pentameter, but they both differ from the Petrarchan sonnet in having three 4-line stanzas (**quatrains**) and a concluding couplet. The rhyme scheme of the *Amoretti* sonnets is original with Spenser: *abab bcbc cdcd ee.* Since it demands four words for two of the rhymes, only a clever rhymer can manage it.

Analyzing sonnets. Look back now at the sonnets by Wyatt and Spenser.

1. In what line is the **turn** of Wyatt's "Whoso List to Hunt" (page 215)? Does the turn show a logical or an emotional shift?

2. Identify the **rhyming words** in Spenser's Sonnets 30 and 75.

3. Make up your own **Petrarchan conceit** for the experience of love or for a loved one's appearance.

Writer's Notebook

1. Collecting Ideas for an Interpretive Essay

If you could talk to Spenser about one of these sonnets (whether to praise, challenge, argue, or just question), which would you focus on? Choose one, and then jot notes as you reread it carefully. Speak to Spenser directly about his ideas, words, feelings, sounds—anything. Save your dialogue for possible use with the Writer's Workshop assignment on page 275.

Creative Writing

2. Images of Love

In Sonnet 30, what images suggest desire and indifference? In Sonnet 75, what images suggest love's impermanence? Make a love's listing of your own, of the things that love, in all its variations, can be compared to. You could open your lines like this:

Love's passion is like _____ .

Be sure to check the images you jotted down in your Quickwrite notes before you read Spenser's poems.

Pair of English leather gloves (early 17th century).

Gift of Philip Lehman, "in memory of my wife, Carrie L. Lehman." Courtesy, Museum of Fine Arts, Boston.

The Faerie Queene: England Through the Looking Glass

In Spenser's long, complex, and unfinished poem *The Faerie Queene,* the word *faerie* does not mean a wee, airy creature dancing among the flowers. Rather, *faerie* suggests grand, heroic beings whose superhuman powers come from their own virtue and piety. The Faerie Queene herself (who does not even appear in the existing poem) is Gloriana, an idealized portrait of Queen Elizabeth, and her realm is at once the England that Spenser loved and a strange, imaginary country.

The poem is a romantic or chivalric **epic.** Unlike the classical epics of Virgil and Homer, romantic epics have an open form, with multiple characters and multiplying plots spreading out in all directions. The marvels, knights, ladies, battles, tournaments, enchantments, dragons, giants, dwarfs, and demons derive from the medieval romances of chivalry, such as the tales of King Arthur.

But its lively stories are only the surface of *The Faerie Queene.* Spenser's moral purposes are especially evident. In a letter to Raleigh, Spenser said that he intended his work to be an **allegory:** Each leading character in the twelve projected books was to embody one virtue or quality; taken together, they would characterize a truly noble person. The heroes or heroines of the six completed books exemplify holiness, temperance, chastity, friendship, justice, and courtesy.

The poem is a tremendous feat of rhyming: Each nine-line iambic stanza has only three rhymes— *ababbcbcc.* The last line's extra foot makes it hexameter. This line, called an **alexandrine,** often sums up a stanza or finishes it off with a striking image. This verse form, which Spenser created for *The Faerie Queene,* is now called the **Spenserian stanza.**

Trying to experience Spenser's immense poem by reading only a few verses is like trying to experience the ocean by looking at a teacup of sea water. However, the three stanzas that follow, describing the hideous Duessa, show Spenser's delight in heroic violence and the gusto with which he describes ugliness.

The Rainbow Portrait of Queen Elizabeth (16th century) by Federico Zuccaro.
Hatfield House, Hertfordshire, England.

As this part of the story from Canto VIII of Book I opens, a knight has been rescued from the clutches of a foul female creature called Duessa, or Falsehood. The knight is ordered by his traveling companion, Una, or Truth, to disrobe Duessa—not a tempting prospect.

Oral reading. Reading aloud will immediately help solve most of the problems posed by Spenser's unusual spellings. Pronounce the words more or less exactly as they are spelled. Paying attention to the rhymes will help.

"The Fowle Duessa"

from The Faerie Queene

Edmund Spenser

So as she bad, that witch they disaraid,
    And robd of royall robes, and purple pall,°
    And ornaments that richly were displaid;
    Ne sparèd they to strip her naked all.
5   Then when they had despoild her tire and call,°
    Such as she was, their eyes might her behold,
    That her misshapèd parts did them apall:
    A loathly, wrinckled hag, ill favoured, old,
Whose secret filth good manners biddeth not be told.

10 Her craftie head was altogether bald,
    And as in hate of honorable eld,°
    Was overgrowne with scurfe and filthy scald;°
    Her teeth out of her rotten gummes were feld,°
    And her sowre breath abhominably smeld;
15   Her drièd dugs,° like bladders lacking wind,
    Hong downe, and filthy matter from them weld;°
    Her wrizled° skin as rough, as maple rind,°
So scabby was, that would have loathd all womankind. . . .

Which when the knights beheld, amazd they were,
20   And wondred at so fowle deformèd wight.
    "Such then," said Una, "as she seemeth here,
    Such is the face of falsehood, such the sight
    Of fowle Duessa, when her borrowed light
    Is laid away, and counterfesaunce° knowne."
25 Thus when they had the witch disrobèd quight,
    And her filthy feature° open showne,
They let her goe at will, and wander wayes unknowne.

2. **pall:** mantle.

5. **tire and call:** attire and headgear.

11. **eld:** old age.
12. **scald:** scabs.
13. **feld:** fallen.

15. **dugs:** breasts.
16. **weld:** ran.
17. **wrizled:** wrinkled. **rind:** bark.

24. **counterfesaunce:** hypocrisy.

26. **feature:** appearance.

Shakespeare's Sonnets: The Mysteries of Love

Shakespeare. The name calls to mind characters in the great plays, who have come to life on stages around the world: *Hamlet, Macbeth, Romeo and Juliet, King Lear, Othello.* Yet had Shakespeare written no plays at all, he would still have an immense reputation as a poet for his *Sonnets* (1609). There are 154 sonnets altogether, their speaker is male, and their chief subject is love. Beyond these three points, however, there is little agreement, only questions:

Is the sonnets' speaker a dramatic character invented by Shakespeare, like Romeo, Macbeth, or Hamlet, or is he the poet himself? The speaker does call himself Will a few times, and he does make puns on his name, but is there any evidence that Will is the speaker in all the sonnets? If the sonnets are about the real man Shakespeare, then who are the real people behind the characters the sonnets mention: the rival poet, the beloved young man who may be the subject of many of the first 126 sonnets, or the beautiful and exciting dark-complexioned woman of some later sonnets?

Is the order in which the sonnets were originally published (probably without Shakespeare's consent) the correct or the intended sequence? Could they be arranged to tell a more coherent story? *Should* they be so arranged?

And in the 1609 publication, who is the "Mr. W. H." mentioned as the "only begetter" of the sonnets: the young man? someone else?

These and dozens of other questions about the sonnets have been asked and answered over and over again—but never to everybody's satisfaction. We have hundreds of conflicting theories, but no absolutely convincing answers.

About the individual sonnets, though, if not the whole sequence, agreement is perfect: They are among the supreme utterances in English. They say profound things about important human experiences, and they say them with great art.

Maids and winged hearts (detail) from *Emblèmes et Devises d'Amour* (early 16th century) by Pierre Sala. Stowe 955 fol. 12b–13.

British Library, London.

The Sonnets' Form

Each of Shakespeare's sonnets has its formal organization established by the rules of the sonnet form. Each sonnet also has a logical organization of ideas, also established by the sonnet form. Here is how Shakespeare structured Sonnet 18 to make these two organizations cooperate in a way that seems natural, not forced.

Logical organization   **Sonnet 18**   Formal organization

A question and tentative answers

Shall I compare thee to a summer's day? — a
Thou art more lovely and more temperate. — b   First quatrain
Rough winds do shake the darling buds of May, — a
And summer's lease hath all too short a date. — b

Sometime too hot the eye of heaven shines, — c
And often is his gold complexion dimmed; — d   Second quatrain
And every fair from fair sometime declines, — c
By chance, or nature's changing course untrimmed. — d

The turn

But thy eternal summer shall not fade, — e
Nor lose possession of that fair thou owest, — f   Third quatrain
Nor shall Death brag thou wander'st in his shade — e
When in eternal lines to time thou grow'st. — f

A final answer

So long as men can breathe, or eyes can see, — g   Couplet
So long lives this, and this gives life to thee. — g

In the English sonnet form known as the **Shakespearean sonnet,** the fixed requirements are fourteen iambic pentameter lines divided into three quatrains and a couplet, with the rhyme scheme *ababcdcdefefgg.* (See page 219 for Spenserian and Petrarchan forms.)

The logical organization of ideas, of course, varies from sonnet to sonnet. Here in Sonnet 18, the first line's question is followed by negative answers: The speaker's beloved does have some resemblances to a summer's day, but only superficial ones. The first two quatrains concentrate on the summer day's imperfections rather than on the loved one.

Then comes the **turn,** a shift in focus or thought. Here the speaker turns from the faulty summer's day to the beloved, and by the end of the third quatrain, the speaker has entirely abandoned the opening comparison. Like most literary terms, the word *turn* is a metaphor; the speaker, figuratively speaking, is "turning" from one thing to another.

In an Italian sonnet, divided into an eight-line octave and six-line sestet, the turn usually occurs after the octave. Sonnet 18, with its turn after line 8, follows this pattern, but in an English sonnet, the final couplet is often a second turn of great impact: a final summary or explanation of all that came before. In this sonnet, the couplet says, perhaps with some exaggeration, that by being addressed in this poem, the beloved person has become immortal.

(For Shakespeare's biography, see page 289.)

Make the Connection

The Heart of the Matter

Earlier (page 212), we asked the humanist's question, "What is the good life?" A related question may be equally difficult, and that is "What is the happy life?" What is it that makes us happy, that lets us look back over years receding into the past, and ahead to the inevitable conclusion, without sorrow or despair? Wealth hasn't answered the question satisfactorily for many people. Power always seems to dwindle away or be wrenched out of our hands in an instant. Fame evaporates faster than the early morning fog. If there is any answer to this question, for many people it is love. Time passes and death is inescapable, but love, if we are fortunate enough to find it or create it, sustains us through it all.

In these four sonnets, Shakespeare speculates about what love is, and what it does to us and for us.

Quickwrite

People warn you not to confuse infatuation with love: Having stars in your eyes makes for a wonderful glow but blurry vision. Eventually, a warm glow comes up against a reality check—and sometimes it doesn't pass. What distinguishes love from infatuation? Write freely for a few minutes trying to identify a few qualities of each, or of the people you've seen enjoying—or suffering from—each.

go.hrw.com
LEO 12-3

In this sonnet, the speaker describes how he rids himself of such ugly emotions as envy, self-pity, self-hatred, and the dismal feeling of certainty that everybody else is luckier than he is.

Sonnet 29

William Shakespeare

When, in disgrace° with Fortune and men's eyes,
I all alone beweep my outcast state,
And trouble deaf heaven with my bootless° cries,
And look upon myself and curse my fate,
5 Wishing me like to one more rich in hope,
Featured like him, like him° with friends possessed,
Desiring this man's art,° and that man's scope,°
With what I most enjoy contented least;
Yet in these thoughts myself almost despising,
10 Haply° I think on thee, and then my state,
Like to the lark° at break of day arising
From sullen° earth, sings hymns at heaven's gate;
　　For thy sweet love remembered such wealth brings
　　That then I scorn to change my state with kings.

1. **disgrace:** out of favor.
3. **bootless:** useless; futile.
6. **one . . . him . . . him:** three different men whom the speaker envies.
7. **art:** literary ability. **scope:** power.
10. **haply:** by chance.
11. **lark:** English skylark, a bird whose song seems to pour down from the sky.
12. **sullen:** gloomy.

Henry Percy, 9th earl of Northumberland.

Rijksmuseum, Amsterdam.

In several sonnets, the speaker emphasizes the difference between his age and his beloved's: He is much older, and so presumably will die first. In Sonnet 73, the speaker dwells on his advanced years. This sonnet is rich in striking metaphors, with each quatrain developing a single metaphor.

Sonnet 73

William Shakespeare

That time of year thou mayst in me behold
When yellow leaves, or none, or few, do hang
Upon those boughs which shake against the cold,
Bare ruined choirs° where late the sweet birds sang.
5 In me thou see'st the twilight of such day
As after sunset fadeth in the west,
Which by and by black night doth take away,
Death's second self, that seals up all in rest.
In me thou see'st the glowing of such fire,
10 That on the ashes of his youth doth lie
As the deathbed whereon it must expire,
Consumed with that which it was nourished by.°
    This thou perceivest, which makes thy love more strong,
    To love that well which thou must leave ere long.

4. choirs: parts of a church or cathedral in which services are held. The landscape of Shakespeare's England was dotted with church ruins resulting from Henry VIII's abolition of monasteries.

12. consumed . . . nourished by: choked by the ashes of the wood that once fed its flame.

An October Afterglow (detail) (19th century) by John Atkinson Grimshaw.

Christie's, London.

MAKING MEANINGS

Sonnets 29 and 73

First Thoughts

1. Obviously, the **speakers** in these two sonnets are in love, but what other emotions do you hear in their voices? Do you hear joy, sorrow, or something else?

Shaping Interpretations

2. Like many of the sonnets, Sonnet 29 is actually a single sentence. In the long introductory clause, what does the speaker say he envies?

3. The main clause of Sonnet 29 begins the **turn.** Where is it? How does the speaker's **tone,** or attitude, change after the turn?

4. In Sonnet 73, what four **metaphors** does the speaker use to describe himself? What contrast is implied between the speaker and his beloved?

5. Find the **turn** of Sonnet 73. What is its logical relationship to what comes before?

6. How do the seasonal and daily **images** in Sonnet 73 contribute to the poem's **tone?**

7. In Sonnet 73, the idea of line 12 is somewhat compressed. **Paraphrase** it in your own words, after you have thought about what originally fed ("nourished") the speaker's fires—fires that are now choked ("consumed").

Extending the Texts

8. If you wrote a contemporary version of Sonnet 29 ("When I failed the quiz and left my lunch at home . . ."), what would you replace Shakespeare's complaints with? Look at his list of problems, and see if you can come up with a contemporary version.

9. What people today could you imagine being the speakers of these sonnets?

Challenging the Text

10. In Sonnet 29, what do you think is the effect of devoting so many lines to the speaker's mental problems and so few to their cure?

Perhaps the most famous of Shakespeare's sonnets, Sonnet 116 defines true love metaphorically as a "marriage of true minds." Such love is completely firm against all "impediments," a word taken from the priest's remarks to those attending a Church of England wedding: "If any of you know cause or just impediment why these persons should not be joined together . . ."

Sonnet 116

William Shakespeare

Let me not to the marriage of true minds
Admit impediments. Love is not love
Which alters when it alteration finds,
Or bends with the remover to remove.
5 Oh no! It is an ever-fixèd mark°
That looks on tempests and is never shaken.
It is the star to every wandering bark,°
Whose worth's° unknown, although his height be taken.°
Love's not Time's fool, though rosy lips and cheeks
10 Within his bending sickle's compass° come.
Love alters not with his brief hours and weeks,
But bears it out° even to the edge of doom.°
    If this be error and upon me proved,
    I never writ, nor no man ever loved.

5. mark: seamark; a prominent object on shore that serves as a guide to sailors.
7. bark: boat.
8. worth's: value's. **height be taken:** altitude measured to determine a ship's position.
10. compass: range; reach.

12. bears it out: survives. **doom:** the Last Judgment; the final judgment at the end of the world.

The Bradford Table Carpet, detail of scenes of rural life (late 16th century). Embroidered on linen canvas with colored silks. English.
Victoria and Albert Museum, London.

This sonnet ridicules the fashionable, exaggerated metaphors some of Shakespeare's fellow poets were using to describe the women they loved: Your eyes are suns that set me on fire, your cheeks are roses, your breasts are snowballs. Such metaphors, known as **conceits,** are traceable to Petrarch, but by 1600 they had become, through overuse, tiresome or laughable. (Note that the word *mistress* in this poem simply meant "girlfriend" in the Renaissance.)

Sonnet 130

William Shakespeare

My mistress' eyes are nothing like the sun,
Coral is far more red than her lips' red.
If snow be white, why then her breasts are dun,°   **3. dun:** brown.
If hairs be wires, black wires grow on her head.
5   I have seen roses damasked,° red and white,   **5. damasked:** streaked.
But no such roses see I in her cheeks.
And in some perfumes is there more delight
Than in the breath that from my mistress reeks,°   **8. reeks:** is exhaled.
I love to hear her speak, yet well I know
10   That music hath a far more pleasing sound.
I grant I never saw a goddess go,°   **11. go:** walk.
My mistress, when she walks, treads on the ground.
    And yet, by Heaven, I think my love as rare
    As any she belied° with false compare.°   **14. belied:** misrepresented. **compare:** comparison.

MAKING MEANINGS

Sonnets 116 and 130

First Thoughts

1. Do you agree with Sonnet 116's definition of love? Why or why not?

2. In Sonnet 130, how do you picture the speaker's mistress?

Shaping Interpretations

3. What **metaphors** does Sonnet 116 use to describe the steadiness of love? How is time **personified** in this poem?

4. In Sonnet 116, between which lines does the **turn**—the change in **moods**—occur? How would you speak these lines to convey the change in mood?

5. What does the final **couplet** add to the message of Sonnet 116?

6. Sonnet 130 could have been written by someone who had read too many Petrarchan sonnets. How does the **speaker** poke fun at them?

7. Do you think the speaker's mistress in Sonnet 130 is actually unattractive? Why or why not?

8. Why is the **couplet** in Sonnet 130 absolutely necessary to keep the sonnet from being mis-understood?

9. If you came upon these two sonnets without knowing they were by the same writer, would you infer, from the attitudes expressed, that they were by one writer or two? Why?

Extending the Texts

10. Which of these four Shakespearean sonnets do you think could be read at a wedding? Could any of them be part of a funeral service? Explain.

CHOICES: Building Your Portfolio

Writer's Notebook

1. Collecting Ideas for an Interpretive Essay

When you write about literature, repeated readings are a basic step in finding new insights and writing topics. Choose the sonnet that you're most drawn to, and read it again, slowly. Then try reading it aloud, and copy it out on a piece of paper. For each reading, make notes on the words and ideas that affect you most strongly. For each reading, note at least one new detail you didn't see before. (You might want to highlight passages with a different color marker for each reading.) Save your work for possible use with the Writer's Workshop on page 275.

Comparing and Contrasting Tones

2. What Makes Tone?

Identify two sonnets in which you detect tones or moods. Compare and contrast the sonnets by focusing on each speaker's tone. Discuss how word choice, figurative language, imagery, and sound effects work together to create a very specific tone for each poem.

Comparing Poems Across Cultures

3. Love's the Same?

Look back at the modern love poem by the American poet E. E. Cummings on page 213. Write a brief essay in which you compare that poem with one of Shakespeare's sonnets. Do you think the poems reflect different cultures and historical contexts? Before you write, you might gather the details for your comparison in a chart like the following:

	Poem 1	Poem 2
Message		
Figurative language		
Form		
Tone		

Creative Writing

4. The Mistress Answers Back

Sonnet 130 is written from the male speaker's point of view. But how would his mistress reply? Write your own sonnet (or just a few verses) to a boyfriend, using this as a beginning: "My boyfriend's eyes are . . . "

Creative Writing

5. Mocking Modern Love

Sonnet 130 is a witty parody of love poems popular in Shakespeare's day. Write your own parody of modern love songs expressed in one style of popular music: country, heavy metal, alternative rock, and so on. Listen to several examples of the style first, paying attention to melody, rhythm, story line, imagery, and tone.

Visual Art

6. Being Moody

Create an emotionally suggestive illustration for each sonnet, using only two colors and one visual image in each illustration. The image may be a real object, such as a lark, or an abstract pattern, such as a heart shape. Combine colors and image creatively to convey the feelings you find in the poem.

Panel Discussion

7. Love in Our Time

In our own time—in art, entertainment, and ads—romantic love is exalted as a pinnacle of human happiness (especially, in the media, love with someone gorgeous, trim, and trendy). But what of people who never find a partner—or a perfect one? Are they losers? Is romantic love essential for happiness? In a panel discussion, critique our culture's messages about love, using examples. Be sure to look back at your Quickwrite notes (page 225) for your ideas about what true love is.

Before You Read

THE PASSIONATE SHEPHERD
THE NYMPH'S REPLY
TO THE VIRGINS
TO HIS COY MISTRESS

Make the Connection
Love's Logic

You have heard it before. On the radio or in a music video, a lead singer appeals passionately to a woman to be his love, although the specific lyrics vary. What you may not know is that people have heard this message for centuries. The "invitation to love" is an old poetic tradition. It was especially common in Renaissance England. Along with descriptions of all the delights that await a hesitant young woman, the Renaissance poet pressures her with what may really be the oldest "line" in the world: "We are all going to die, so take your pleasures now."

Quickwrite

What current love songs can you think of—in any popular music style? Look for songs sung by an impatient suitor to a specific lover who hasn't quite committed herself or himself—or not in the way the singer wants. If you can, find the words, or transcribe them. Listen to the songs as closely as you can. How is love treated in popular music today? Take notes on all your reflections.

Elements of Literature
Carpe Diem

The poems that follow reflect an ancient theme the Romans called *carpe diem* (kär′pe dē′em), meaning "seize the day." *Carpe diem* is a call to live life to the fullest right now: "Let us eat and drink, for tomorrow we die," as the Roman poet Horace said. *Carpe diem* poems are the literary counterpart of the human skull that was sometimes part of the decor at wild Roman parties— a grisly reminder of the fate none of us can escape.

Carpe diem, literally "seize the day," is a literary theme that urges living in the present moment, especially in pleasurable pursuits.

For more on Carpe Diem, see the Handbook of Literary Terms.

Embroidered picture of a woman, possibly personifying Summer (detail) (late 17th century). Satin embroidered with silk, metal thread, and beads. English.

By Courtesy of the Board of Trustees of the Victoria and Albert Museum, London.

Christopher Marlowe

(1564–1593)

Reputed portrait of Christopher Marlowe (1585). French School. Oil.

The Master and Fellows of Corpus Christi College, Cambridge, England.

Marlowe belonged to the first generation of Elizabethan dramatists. His career ended about the time Shakespeare's began, although he was only two months older than Shakespeare. The son of a shoemaker in Canterbury, Marlowe won scholarships to the King's School in Canterbury and then to Cambridge University. While still a student, he translated some love poems by Ovid, the Roman poet. The poems were declared too erotic by the Bishop of London, who had the books burned.

After completing his studies, Marlowe apparently became a spy. Elizabeth's government maintained an elaborate espionage system to keep track of Roman Catholics, but just what spying Marlowe did for the government remains uncertain. It *is* certain that Marlowe had only six more years to live when, at twenty-three, he came down to London from Cambridge. He also associated with a number of other recent university graduates living near the London theaters and supporting themselves by writing plays and pamphlets. Excitement and danger were part of their lives. Marlowe himself was jailed for his involvement in a street fight that ended with one man murdered.

Another brush with the law came when Marlowe's roommate, a fellow dramatist named Thomas Kyd, accused him of making scandalous, seditious, and atheistic speeches. Marlowe was arrested. A few days before the case was to be heard, he went with some rather shady characters down the Thames to a tavern in Deptford. After supper the men got into a violent fight over the bill; Marlowe was stabbed above the eye and died instantly. The court acquitted his assailant on the grounds of self-defense, though it is very possible that all the testimony in this case was fabricated and that Marlowe was assassinated for reasons not yet discovered. Theories about Marlowe's life and death are abundant; there are even a few people today who believe, without any evidence, that Marlowe wasn't murdered but lived on to write all of Shakespeare's plays for him.

All of Marlowe's dramatic poems are tragedies: *Dido, Queen of Carthage* (written with Thomas Nashe); *Tamburlaine; The Jew of Malta; The Massacre at Paris; Edward II;* and *Doctor Faustus.* Marlowe's greatest tragic heroes have been called "overreachers": self-driven, power-hungry men who refuse to recognize either their limitations as human beings or their responsibilities to God and their fellow creatures. Tamburlaine seeks power through military conquest; Barabbas, the Jew of Malta, through money; Faustus, through knowledge. They all want to be more than mere men, and only death can put an end to their monstrous ambitions. To express these grandiose themes, Marlowe created wild and soaring poetry, like nothing ever heard before on the stage. Although Marlowe did not write Shakespeare's plays, he showed Shakespeare what was possible in dramatic poetry.

This poem is part of two literary traditions. It is part of the *carpe diem* tradition, and it is a **pastoral,** from *pastor,* the Latin word for "shepherd." Pastoral works are set in an idealized countryside, and their characters are often blends of the naive and the sophisticated. The most famous of English pastorals, Marlowe's poem has often been set to music, and several poets have written answers or sequels to it.

The Passionate Shepherd to His Love

Christopher Marlowe

Come live with me, and be my love,
And we will all the pleasures prove°
That valleys, groves, hills, and fields,
Woods, or steepy mountain yields.

5 And we will sit upon the rocks,
Seeing the shepherds feed their flocks
By shallow rivers, to whose falls
Melodious birds sing madrigals.°

And I will make thee beds of roses,
10 And a thousand fragrant posies,
A cap of flowers, and a kirtle,°
Embroidered all with leaves of myrtle.

A gown made of the finest wool
Which from our pretty lambs we pull,
15 Fair linèd slippers for the cold,
With buckles of the purest gold.

A belt of straw and ivy buds,
With coral clasps and amber studs,
And if these pleasures may thee move,
20 Come live with me, and be my love.

The shepherd swains° shall dance and sing
For thy delight each May morning.
If these delights thy mind may move,
Then live with me, and be my love.

2. prove: experience.

8. madrigals: complicated songs for several voices.

11. kirtle: dress, gown, or skirt.

21. swains: young boys.

Shepherd and Shepherdess with Cupid in Pastoral Landscape (detail) (17th century). Embroidered textile. Colored silk and isinglass on canvas (10¼" × 14").

The Metropolitan Museum of Art. Gift of Irwin Untermyer, 1964. (64. 101. 1313). Photograph ©1977 The Metropolitan Museum of Art.

Sir Walter Raleigh

(1552?–1618)

Raleigh is one of the most colorful figures of a very colorful age. A handsome, expensively dressed, and probably arrogant man, at the peak of his success he was Queen Elizabeth's confidential secretary and captain of her guard. He fought brilliantly for England in France, Spain, Ireland, and America. He was passionately devoted to the cause of colonizing the Americas, and to advertise its products he became one of the first bold Englishmen to smoke tobacco and grow potatoes.

In his rise to power, Raleigh made many enemies, some of whom saw their chance to destroy him when the queen died. They poisoned King James's mind against him, and—on trumped-up evidence—he was convicted of treason. Raleigh was sentenced to death in 1603, though his execution was not carried out until 1618.

Imprisoned in the Tower of London during this long interval, he conducted chemical experiments and wrote a *History of the World* that runs from Adam and Eve to the establishment of the Roman Empire. He also dreamed of another expedition to Guiana, on the northern coast of South America; he had explored Guiana earlier in his life and believed it contained vast hoards of gold and jewels. In 1617, still under a death sentence, he was allowed to undertake his last voyage to Guiana. It turned out to be a disaster. The English obtained no treasure, and the Spanish killed many of Raleigh's men, including his beloved son. Very ill with fever, Raleigh sailed home to face a certain and shameful death. But according to the verdict of history, the shame is King James's, not Raleigh's. Raleigh was sacrificed to satisfy the Spanish, who were clamoring for his death as a condition for maintaining peaceful relations with England. The English, who hated and feared the Spanish, had not forgotten Raleigh when they deposed and beheaded James's son, King Charles I, in 1649.

In his speech on the scaffold, Raleigh described himself as "a seafaring man, a soldier, and a courtier." Although he did publish his *History,* he did not think of himself as a writer. He was carefree with his poems; only about thirty-five of them have survived, and they have been slowly assembled by literary researchers through the past four centuries. His most ambitious poem is *The Ocean to Cynthia,* one of the hundreds of literary works that Queen Elizabeth's subjects wrote to express their love and devotion. It survives only in fragments. This is unfortunate, because Raleigh's poems have considerable merit. They are powerful, outspoken, even blunt, and suffused with the courage of a man who was always ready to accept without self-pity whatever life might bring him. He could have been thinking of himself when he wrote in his *History,* "There is no man so assured of his honor, of his riches, health, or life, but that he may be deprived of either or all, the very next hour or day to come."

Here is Raleigh's reply to Marlowe's "Passionate Shepherd." Elizabethan London was a small place, and Raleigh's and Marlowe's paths must have crossed more than once. Other poets, including John Donne and Robert Herrick, replied to Marlowe, but Raleigh wrote the best answer. His speaker is identified as a "nymph," which means a young woman. Like her creator, she has a strong character.

The Nymph's Reply to the Shepherd

Sir Walter Raleigh

If all the world and love were young,
And truth in every shepherd's tongue,
These pretty pleasures might me move
To live with thee and be thy love.

5 But Time drives flocks from field to fold,°
When rivers rage and rocks grow cold,
And Philomel° becometh dumb;
The rest complains of cares to come.

The flowers do fade, and wanton° fields
10 To wayward winter reckoning yields;
A honey tongue, a heart of gall°
Is fancy's spring, but sorrow's fall.

Thy gowns, thy shoes, thy beds of roses,
Thy cap, thy kirtle, and thy posies.
15 Soon break, soon wither, soon forgotten,
In folly ripe, in reason rotten.

Thy belt of straw and ivy buds,
Thy coral clasps and amber studs,
All these in me no means can move
20 To come to thee and be thy love.

But could youth last and love still breed,
Had joys no date, nor age no need,
Then these delights my mind might move
To live with thee and be thy love.

5. fold: pen where sheep are kept in winter.

7. Philomel: the nightingale.

9. wanton: luxuriant.

11. gall: a bitter substance.

Embroidered wall hanging of the Morell family, Constanz, East Switzerland (detail) (1601).
Schweizerisches Landesmuseum, Zurich.

MAKING MEANINGS

First Thoughts

1. Rate the shepherd and the nymph on the persuasiveness of their arguments, using a scale of 0 to 10 (with 10 being most persuasive). Be ready to justify your ratings.

Shaping Interpretations

2. Describe the life that the shepherd envisions with his love. How will they be dressed? How will they spend their time?

3. In **pastoral** writing, the harsh realities of country life do not exist. Which details of the shepherd's description seem distinctly idealistic? What realistic, gritty details of a shepherd's life can you imagine?

4. In her reply, what flaws does the nymph find in the shepherd's idyllic vision? What are her conditions for living with him?

5. What is the **tone** of the nymph's reply?

Extending the Texts

6. How do you think a modern young woman would respond to the shepherd's invitation?

7. Idyllic escape with a loved one still has a strong appeal, whether the retreat is a remote island or a mountaintop hideaway. How is this romantic escape motif used today in literature, television, movies, and advertising?

LITERATURE AND TECHNOLOGY

The Clock Starts Ticking

School bells, alarm clocks, time clocks, schedules: in our time-conscious, time-driven world, life ticks by—even on our wrists. But this sense of time, so natural to us, isn't natural. It began as the medieval age shifted to the first modern age: the Renaissance.

From dawn to dusk. Not until the fourteenth century, with the invention of the mechanical clock, did church towers across Europe and England start ringing out the day's twenty-four hours. While simple clocks and signal bells had been around for many years, such *public* precision was unknown—and simply hadn't been needed. Before the explosion of urban commerce, daily life moved by the natural rhythms of daybreak and nightfall, planting and harvest. People saw their lives as part of an endless continuum; bells pealed only for prayer, gatherings, and disaster.

The beat of life. But to produce more and more goods, people wanted not just to mark time, but to *use* it. That's why the brilliant idea of a mechanical clock filled a new need and changed life forever. Earlier water clocks, which kept time by steadily filling a vessel marked with measuring lines, were technically sophisticated but cumbersome—and in cold winters they froze.

The new clock revolutionized timekeeping by using falling weights to power gears (spoked wheels). The crucial technology, though, was the escapement, a controlling device that alternately caught and released the final wheel's spokes: It produced a steady, regular revolution and an endless, repeating ticktock. The passing of time was now audible.

Do you have the time?   Time became elaborately visible too, and not only because the gears could move hands. In the late Middle Ages, churches, kings, and rich merchants commissioned turret clocks that tracked astronomical and hourly changes with moving figures (automata) depicting, for example, the sun and moon, jousting knights, and the Twelve Apostles.

Then, for the first time, clocks came indoors. Miniaturization allowed "chamber clocks" for the nobility and the merchant classes. Finally, in the sixteenth century, a small, personal, spring-driven clock appeared: the first watch. In Queen Elizabeth's extensive collection of watches, one ring watch came equipped with an alarm: A small prong emerged to scratch her finger.

Keeping time.   By the Renaissance, a whole new concept of time had emerged, mirroring and feeding humanism. Time was personal and finite, and timekeeping meant just that: controlling a precious commodity. *Ticktock.* To us, the pressure of time is often depressing, but not to the new moderns. Renaissance humanists and artists were driven but invigorated. They could be masters of time, seizing the day, reaching for fame's immortality through art.

Works of the first spring-driven clock (c. 1524) by Joseph Zech.
Society of Antiquaries of London.

Robert Herrick
(1591–1674)

We first hear of Herrick as an apprentice to his uncle, a London goldsmith and jeweler; it is pleasant to think that the future poet may have acquired his taste for small, beautiful things in his uncle's workshop. Herrick apparently lacked ambition and drive, since he did not enter the university until he was twenty-two, a very late age in those days, and he did not leave it until he was twenty-nine. For the next few years, he had no regular occupation, but enjoyed himself in London as a member of Ben Jonson's circle of young friends. At some point, he was ordained a priest, but the serious part of Herrick's life did not begin until he was thirty-nine.

Herrick was then called to a parish in Dean Prior, in Devonshire, far from London, in the West Country, which Londoners habitually regarded as wretched and barbaric. According to some of Herrick's poems, this was an intolerable exile; according to others, it was heaven on earth. At any rate, Herrick's stay in Dean Prior came abruptly to an end in 1647 with the arrival of the Parliamentary Army, which deprived him of his parish and substituted in his place a clergyman of a more puritanical stripe. (It would not be easy to find a less puritanical priest than Herrick.) When the king was restored some thirteen years later, so was Herrick, and he lived on at Dean Prior until he died at the age of eighty-three.

While deprived of his parish and living in London, Herrick published a fat little volume containing about 1,400 poems. The book was called *Hesperides, or the Works Both Human and Divine of Robert Herrick, Esq.* (1648). Less than a fourth of the poems fit into the "divine" category, and these are mainly witty verses on Biblical characters and events. All the rest of the poems are definitely "human," though the book's last line— "Jocund his Muse was; but his Life was chaste"—shows that Herrick's life was a bit less lively than his poetry. The word *Hesperides* in the title is borrowed from classical mythology; it is the collective name for the nymphs who live in a garden where they watch over a tree that bears golden apples. The title implies that Herrick's book is a garden full of precious things.

Herrick borrowed more than his title from classical antiquity. He was so steeped in Latin poetry that he frequently wrote his poems as if he were an ancient Roman, imposing pagan customs, creeds, and rituals on the English countrypeople and his own household. He imitated the Latin love poets, especially Catullus, when he addressed poems to beautiful women with such classical names as Julia, Corinna, Perilla, Anthea, and Electra.

Herrick also wrote about his small house, his spaniel named Tracy, the royal family in far-off London—whatever came into his mind. Altogether, his poems give us a picture of "Merrie England," which is not so much the England of any particular time or place, but an ideal, pastoral state where sadness is momentary and pleasure innocent.

Robert Herrick (18th century) by Schiavonetti.

By Courtesy of the National Portrait Gallery, London.

The first line of this little lyric, Herrick's most popular poem, has been a metaphorical part of our language ever since the nineteenth century, when Herrick was "discovered" by people interested in Renaissance literature. Instead of courting one woman, as in most *carpe diem* poems, Herrick addresses all "virgins," or young women. As you read, remember that Herrick was a priest.

To the Virgins, to Make Much of Time

Robert Herrick

Gather ye rosebuds while ye may,
    Old Time is still a-flying;
And this same flower that smiles today,
    Tomorrow will be dying.

5 The glorious lamp of heaven, the sun,
    The higher he's a-getting,
The sooner will his race be run,
    And nearer he's to setting.

That age is best which is the first,
10   When youth and blood are warmer;
But being spent, the worse, and worst
    Times still° succeed the former.

Then be not coy,° but use your time;
    And while ye may, go marry:
15 For having lost but once your prime,
    You may forever tarry.°

12. still: always.

13. coy: cold; inaccessible; aloof.

16. tarry: delay; linger.

Spring (detail) (1595) by Lucas van Valkenborch.

Christie's, London.

239

Andrew Marvell

(1621–1678)

Marvell, whose very English name should be accented on its first syllable, like *marvelous*, was the son of a clergyman, who sent him to Cambridge University. There he must have received an excellent education, because the poet John Milton, who was not easily impressed by other men's learning, said that Marvell was "well read in the Greek and Latin classics." After receiving his B.A., he traveled for several years to Holland, France, Italy, and Spain. There is, surprisingly, no record of Marvell's having been involved in the great upheaval of the 1640s. He seems to have survived the Civil Wars without allying himself with either the Royalists or the Parliamentarians. About 1650, he became a tutor to Mary Fairfax, an heiress and a daughter of Sir Thomas Fairfax, who had served as lord general of the Parliamentary armies. The Fairfaxes had several large estates, one of them at a place called Nun Appleton, and there Marvell wrote a remarkable long poem, "Upon Appleton House." But he did not publish this or any of the other poems that are so highly regarded today. In the best Renaissance fashion, he wrote only for his friends' and his own entertainment.

After leaving the Fairfax household, where presumably he wrote his best poems, Marvell became tutor to a ward of Oliver Cromwell, the lord protector and virtual dictator of England in the 1650s. Then, in 1657, he became assistant to John Milton, who needed help in carrying out his duties as Latin secretary to the Council of State because he was blind. Marvell

Andrew Marvell (c. 1655–1660) by an unknown artist. Oil on canvas (23 ½" × 18 ½").
By Courtesy of the National Portrait Gallery, London.

became active in politics, serving as member of Parliament for his native city, Hull, from 1659 until his death. When King Charles II was restored and the Commonwealth government dissolved in 1660, Marvell somehow had enough influence with the Royalists to save Milton's life. At this point in his career, Marvell began to publish verse satires against his political opponents and prose pamphlets on issues of the day. But his lyric poems remained in manuscript until after his death, when his housekeeper, calling herself Mary Marvell and claiming to be his wife, sold them to a publisher, who brought them out.

Marvell's posthumous volume, called *Miscellaneous Poems*, made little impression when it appeared in 1681. Styles in poetry had changed after 1660, so that Marvell's witty, ingenious metaphors must have seemed old-fashioned to readers who admired the lucid, rational poems of the Restoration writers. Today we are in a better position to appreciate Marvell. To many judicious critics, his poems seem to sum up much that is admirable in Renaissance lyric poetry. Like Jonson, he is a master craftsman, always in control of his materials. His poems have the precision, urbanity, and lightness of touch associated with the "sons of Ben." Many of Marvell's poems are also, under their graceful surfaces, deep and thoughtful, like Donne's. No wonder that Marvell is sometimes called the "most major" of the minor poets in English.

This poem is the most famous "invitation to love" in English. Nobody has ever assumed that Marvell, a bachelor, was writing to a
particular woman. But the poem is a much deeper poem than
others of its kind. Its speaker dwells on the details of human mortality with morbid exactitude, to make his beloved feel that even
immoral behavior while alive is preferable to being good but dead.
The title could be rephrased as "To his cold, standoffish girlfriend"; at the time, *mistress* did not mean a sexual partner.

To His Coy Mistress

Andrew Marvell

Had we but world° enough, and time,
This coyness,° Lady, were no crime.
We would sit down, and think which way
To walk, and pass our long love's day.
5 Thou by the Indian Ganges' side
Shouldst rubies find; I by the tide
Of Humber° would complain.° I would
Love you ten years before the Flood,°
And you should, if you please, refuse
10 Till the conversion of the Jews.°
My vegetable° love should grow
Vaster than empires and more slow;
An hundred years should go to praise
Thine eyes, and on thy forehead gaze;
15 Two hundred to adore each breast,
But thirty thousand to the rest;
An age at least to every part,
And the last age should show your heart.
For, Lady, you deserve this state,°
20 Nor would I love at lower rate.
    But at my back I always hear
Time's wingèd chariot hurrying near;
And yonder all before us lie
Deserts of vast eternity.
25 Thy beauty shall no more be found,
Nor, in thy marble vault, shall sound
My echoing song; then worms shall try
That long-preserved virginity,
And your quaint honor turn to dust,
30 And into ashes all my lust:
The grave's a fine and private place,
But none, I think, do there embrace.
    Now therefore, while the youthful hue
Sits on thy skin like morning dew,
35 And while thy willing soul transpires°
At every pore with instant fires,

1. **world:** geographical space.
2. **coyness:** reluctance to make a commitment.

7. **Humber:** muddy river in Marvell's hometown of Hull;
here, ironically compared to the grand Ganges in India.
complain: utter complaints about not being loved.
8. **Flood:** Noah's flood, described in Genesis.
10. **conversion of the Jews:** Christians once believed that
all Jews would be converted to Christianity immediately before the Last Judgment.
11. **vegetable:** plantlike; having the power to grow very
large, like oak trees.

19. **state:** ceremony.

Two Lovers (detail)
(15th century) from
an Italian slipware plate.
© British Museum, London.

35. **transpires:** breathes out.

Now let us sport us while we may,
And now, like amorous birds of prey,
Rather at once our time devour
40 Than languish in his slow-chapped° power.
Let us roll all our strength and all
Our sweetness up into one ball,
And tear our pleasures with rough strife
Through the iron gates of life;
45 Thus, though we cannot make our sun
Stand still, yet we will make him run.

40. slow-chapped: slow-jawed. Time is seen as consuming life.

MAKING MEANINGS

To the Virgins, to Make Much of Time
To His Coy Mistress

First Thoughts

1. Herrick and Marvell have similar objectives but different approaches. How do you react to the two poems and poets? Is one more persuasive than the other? How are their arguments both similar and different?

Shaping Interpretations

2. The sun appears in both "To the Virgins" (line 5) and "To His Coy Mistress" (line 45). How does each poet use the sun? How would you **paraphrase** the last two lines of Marvell's poem to his coy mistress?

3. What does each poet say about time and its effects on youth and beauty? A famous **image** of time appears in couplet form in Marvell's poem, in lines 21–22. What does he compare time to? What does this image make you see?

4. What does the **speaker** in "To the Virgins" say about marriage? How do you think the speaker in Marvell's poem feels about marriage?

5. Marvell's poem contains both **hyperbole** (see page 245) and **understatement.** Find examples of each rhetorical device. What does each device contribute to the poem's effect on the reader?

6. Where in his poem does Marvell seem to be making fun of certain kinds of love poems? Where do you spot echoes of Shakespeare's Sonnet 130 (page 229)?

Extending the Texts

7. Do you think there are echoes of Herrick's poem in contemporary media? Does the **speaker** in this poem hold any values that are shared by modern advertisements, television shows, or popular songs? What are they?

Challenging the Texts

8. What do these two poems imply about the relationship between men and women? Would a modern woman (or man) be likely to challenge any assumptions apparently held by the writer, or by the speaker in each poem? What might they challenge, what might they agree with, and why?

CHOICES:
Building Your Portfolio

Writer's Notebook

1. Collecting Ideas for an Interpretive Essay

Choose a *carpe diem* poem that you would like to write about. Before you start to analyze the poem, read it aloud at least once. Freewrite briefly about your initial reaction to the poem. Then try to state its theme in your own words. Now read it again, this time looking for other elements to focus on—perhaps figures of speech, imagery, or sound effects. Make notes on these elements of the poem, and their effects on you. Save your notes for possible use with the Writer's Workshop on page 275.

Comparing and Contrasting Poems

2. Probing Poems

In an essay, compare and contrast at least two of the *carpe diem* poems by Marlowe, Raleigh, Herrick, and Marvell. You might collect your data in a chart like the following one:

Element	Poem 1	Poem 2
Personal reaction Theme Images Figures of speech Sounds Tone		

Comparing Poems

3. Donne Answers Back

The poet John Donne (1572–1631) wrote "The Bait," a poem that was clearly inspired by Marlowe's "Passionate Shepherd." Locate Donne's poem (it's commonly found in poetry anthologies). In a brief essay, explain whether this poem is an answer to Marlowe's poem, an imitation of it, or neither. Remember to provide specific references to both poems.

Comparing Poems Across Cultures

4. The Moment Passes

In a brief essay, compare the following poem by the American poet Dorothy Parker (1893–1967) to one of the *carpe diem* poems you've just read.

Unfortunate Coincidence

By the time you swear you're his,
    Shivering and sighing,
And he vows his passion is
    Infinite, undying—
Lady, make a note of this:
    One of you is lying.

—Dorothy Parker

Creative Writing

5. Silent No More

Write an answer to either (a) the speaker of "To the Virgins," taking the point of view of an older woman, or (b) the speaker of "To His Coy Mistress," beginning your answer with the words "Had we but world enough and time." Your response may be poetry or prose, but give it a title.

Music/Literature

6. Seize the Song

Write your own *carpe diem* song in any musical style. You might write songs that can be paired, as Marlowe's and Raleigh's are. You might try to imitate the melancholic, romantic tone of some of the poems you've read, or you might adopt the more modern style of today's songs, which are sometimes romantic, sometimes plaintive, sometimes humorous. You might also refer to the Quick-write notes you made for the exercise on page 231.

Art/Literature

7. Picturing a Poem

Create a collage to illustrate one of the poems you've just read. Find elements for your collage that pick up images in the poem. Be sure to add to your collage the phrase in the poem you think is most important.

Panel Discussion

8. As Time Goes By

Hold a panel discussion in which you exchange views on the gender traits you infer were characteristic of the sixteenth century. Compare these traits with gender traits you find in modern novels, movies, and TV shows. Have things changed in the relations between men and women? Or are these relations in many ways the same? You might also address this question: Are gender traits fixed by genes, or are they learned? Can they be changed?

John Donne
(1572–1631)

Donne (a Welsh name pronounced "dun") wrote learned, passionate, argumentative poetry, most of which he never published, since he was never ambitious to be known publicly as a poet. His first aim in life was to be "courtier"—that is, a member of the queen's government. But he had a serious handicap: He was born into a prominent Roman Catholic family, being descended from no less a person than Sir Thomas More, the Lord Chancellor whom Henry VIII had beheaded in 1535.

When Donne was only eleven years old, he was already studying at Oxford. Catholic boys went to the university very young, to avoid the oath of allegiance to the queen, whom the pope had excommunicated. Barred from taking a degree because of his religion, Donne returned to his native city of London and in his late teens became a law student at Lincoln's Inn, one of the Inns of Court where lawyers were trained. He had no financial worries since his father, a prosperous iron merchant, had died when Donne was four and left him some money. He now became "Jack" Donne, a handsome, well-dressed youth who devoted his mornings to heavy reading in philosophy and foreign literature and his afternoons to circulating in society. A friend described him as being "a great visitor of ladies, a great frequenter of plays, a great writer of conceited verses."

After various adventures, such as taking part in two naval expeditions against Spain, Donne became private secretary to Sir Thomas Egerton, lord keeper of the great seal. This was an important post, the starting point of a brilliant career in government, for by now Donne had abandoned his Catholicism and spent his inheritance. But he blasted all his

John Donne (c. 1595) by an unknown artist.
Private Collection.

hopes and ambitions when, in 1601, he secretly married seventeen-year-old Anne More (no relation). Marriage with a minor, without her father's consent, was then a serious crime against both church and state. As soon as Anne's father heard about it, he had Donne arrested, jailed, and dismissed from his position. In jail, Donne wrote his shortest poem:

> John Donne,
> Anne Donne,
> Undone.

Though he was not kept in prison long, Donne never did recover his position, and for years he and Anne had to live off the bounty of friends and relatives. They certainly needed help since they eventually had twelve children, five of whom died in infancy.

In the early 1600s, Donne continued to read voraciously and to write poetry for private circulation and prose for public consumption. He wrote against the Church of Rome so effectively that he became known as an important defender of the Church of England. And so the new king, James I, persuaded Donne to become a clergyman in 1615. His brilliant, theatrical sermons immediately won him advancement in the Church, and he rose to be dean of St. Paul's, the principal cathedral of England, in London.

Thus, Jack Donne became the Reverend Dr. John Donne. He preached outdoors before the cathedral, and he preached at court before the king, always with great effect, for he put into his sermons the same passion and inventiveness that he put into his poems. He died full of years and honors, and a portrait showing how he looked in his death shroud can still be seen in St. Paul's.

Make the Connection

Love's Illusions

Unlike the multitude of Renaissance songs idealizing women, the following song satirizes women, using **hyperbole** (hī·pʉr′bə·lē), or extreme exaggeration. Imagine a lover who has fallen hard for the Perfect Woman once too often—and now takes a hard view of perfection.

Quickwrite

Think about songs popular today. Do most of them celebrate faithfulness and joy in a loved one, or do most complain about infidelity and betrayal? Jot down your general impression of today's popular love songs and their lyrics. You might begin by thinking of one or two songs you know fairly well and discussing them with examples.

Background

Donne's love poems are collectively known as his "Songs and Sonnets," but the title is misleading: Most of the poems are too intellectually demanding to be called songs, and none is a sonnet by formal definition. The following poem was indeed a song, however, because one manuscript includes musical accompaniment.

Song

John Donne

Go, and catch a falling star,
   Get with child a mandrake° root,
Tell me, where all past years are,
   Or who cleft° the devil's foot,
5 Teach me to hear mermaids° singing,
Or to keep off envy's stinging,
      And find
      What wind
Serves to advance an honest mind.

10 If thou be'st born to strange sights,
   Things invisible to see,
Ride ten thousand days and nights,
   Till age snow white hairs on thee,
Thou, when thou return'st, wilt tell me
15 All strange wonders that befell thee,
      And swear
      Nowhere
Lives a woman true, and fair.

If thou find'st one, let me know,
20   Such a pilgrimage were sweet;
Yet do not, I would not go,
   Though at next door we might meet,
Though she were true, when you met her,
And last, till you write your letter,
25   Yet she
     Will be
False, ere I come, to two, or three.

2. mandrake: plant whose forked root is said to resemble a human being's torso and legs.
4. cleft: split.
5. mermaids: the sirens of Greek mythology. The song of these sea nymphs lured sailors to crash their ships on rocky shores.

MAKING MEANINGS

First Thoughts

1. What is your reaction to this poem: Is it offensive to women, funny, both, or something else?

Shaping Interpretations

2. To whom is this **speaker** talking? What do you think might have occasioned the poem?

3. In the second stanza, what does the speaker say his listener will discover about a woman both "true and fair"?

4. In the last stanza, what does the speaker say he will not do? Why?

5. What **hyperbole** does the speaker use to make his points?

6. How would you describe the speaker's **tone**? List at least three words that reveal his attitude. Do you think he is being serious?

Connecting with the Text

7. How would you respond to Donne's challenge in this poem?

Extending the Text

8. What examples of **hyperbole** do you see in love songs, whether modern or from other times? How do the sentiments in Donne's song compare with those in love songs? (Refer to your Quickwrite notes for ideas.)

Challenging the Text

9. Could this poem be revised slightly to be about the faithlessness of men? How?

ELEMENTS OF LITERATURE

Metaphysical Poetry

In the nineteenth century, Samuel Coleridge described Donne's inventiveness as a "forge and fire-blast" that could twist "iron pokers into true-love knots." In the 1590s, when Donne started writing, this blazing poetic style was truly revolutionary.

Most poets then aimed for sweet, smooth, musical-sounding verse. But Donne would have none of it. "I sing not siren-like, to tempt, for I am harsh," he says in one poem. The new style he forged came to be called, by later critics, **metaphysical poetry**—a term that reflected its intensity of intellect, its self-conscious invention, and its bold emotion.

For the most part, Donne based the rhythm and sounds of his poems on colloquial—that is, spoken—English. "For God's sake hold your tongue and let me love," he begins one poem. The speaker in his poems frequently sounds blunt and angry, or he broods to himself, or he seems to be thinking out loud. At times the speaker almost seems to be lecturing the woman he is addressing.

Whatever his tone, Donne's speaker is always using his brains and bringing into the poems ideas from books, especially books of philosophy and theology. He also brings in images from everyday activities and trades and from learned disciplines like law, medicine, and science. Reading a metaphysical poem is frequently like figuring out the solution to a riddle—or trying to untangle a complicated knot.

To their critics, metaphysical poets were show-offs. They were accused of writing poems just to display their learning and wit.

Responding to the metaphysical poets. The seventeenth-century poet and critic John Dryden, who disliked it, said metaphysical poetry "perplexed the minds of the fair sex with nice speculations of philosophy." How do you feel about this kind of intellectual poetry? Can you see a connection between the metaphysical poets' imagery and the art by Escher, below?

Bond of Union (1956) by Maurits Cornelius Escher.

A VALEDICTION: FORBIDDING MOURNING

Make the Connection

Hard Partings

Leaving someone you love for a long time is never easy, but if this poem is autobiographical—as Izaak Walton, Donne's friend and biographer, claimed—Donne was trying to ease a parting of great pain. The poem is typical of Donne's poetry in having a dramatic occasion, a particular situation, on which the poem is spoken. Here, the speaker, a man about to take a long journey, says goodbye ("valediction") to the woman he loves, telling her not to cry or feel sad ("forbidding mourning").

Quickwrite

If you were leaving for a long time, what would you say to someone you love who is left behind? If you were the one left, what would you want to hear? Take notes on your thoughts.

Elements of Literature

Metaphysical Conceits

This poem contains the most famous of all **metaphysical conceits.** These are odd and surprising figures of speech in which one thing is compared with another thing that is very much unlike it. The metaphysical poets—as their name suggests— used such conceits for an analytic and psychological investigation of love and life. Here are some examples of these unusual conceits: A lover's tears are newly minted coins; the king's court is a bowl-

Mrs. Pemberton (16th century) by Hans Holbein the Younger.

The Victoria and Albert Museum, London.

ing alley; a man is a world; lovers are holy saints. In this poem, the lovers are said to be the two prongs of a compass, the kind used to draw circles in geometry.

Metaphysical conceits are especially complex and ingenious figures of speech that make surprising connections between two seemingly dissimilar things.

For more on Conceit, see the Handbook of Literary Terms.

Background

Walton said Donne wrote the poem for his wife when he left for a diplomatic mission to France. She urged him not to go because she was pregnant and unwell, but he felt obligated to the mission's leader, Sir Robert

Drury. Two days after arriving in Paris, Donne had a vision which he described to Sir Robert: "I have seen my dear wife pass twice by me through this room, with her hair hanging about her shoulders, and a dead child in her arms." A messenger sent back to England returned with the news that "Mrs. Donne . . . after a long and dangerous labor . . . had been delivered of a dead child" on the very day Donne had the vision.

In reading the poem, notice that the entire first stanza is a **simile** introduced by *As* and followed by *So*. The dying men in the stanza are not part of the dramatic situation, but only offered as an analogy to the lovers' separation.

A Valediction: Forbidding Mourning

John Donne

As virtuous men pass mildly away,
   And whisper to their souls, to go,
Whilst some of their sad friends do say,
   The breath goes now, and some say, no:

5 So let us melt, and make no noise,
   No tear-floods, nor sigh-tempests move,
'Twere profanation° of our joys
   To tell the laity° our love.

Moving of th' earth° brings harms and fears,
10   Men reckon what it did and meant,°
But trepidation of the spheres,°
   Though greater far, is innocent.°

Dull sublunary° lovers' love
   (Whose soul° is sense°) cannot admit
15 Absence, because it doth remove
   Those things which elemented° it.

But we by a love, so much refined,
   That ourselves know not what it is,
Interassurèd of the mind,
20   Care less eyes, lips, and hands to miss.

Our two souls therefore, which are one,
   Though I must go, endure not yet
A breach,° but an expansion,
   Like gold to airy thinness beat.

25 If they be two, they are two so
   As stiff twin compasses are two,
Thy soul the fixed foot, makes no show
   To move, but doth, if th' other do.

And though it in the center sit,
30   Yet when the other far doth roam,
It leans, and hearkens after it,
   And grows erect, as that comes home.

Such wilt thou be to me, who must
   Like th' other foot, obliquely° run;
35 Thy firmness° makes my circle just,°
   And makes me end, where I begun.

7. profanation: lack of reverence.
8. laity: laypersons; here, those unable to understand the "religion" of true love.
9. moving of th' earth: earthquake.
10. meant: "What does it mean?" was a question ordinarily asked of any unusual phenomenon.
11. trepidation of the spheres: irregularities in the movements of remote heavenly bodies.
12. innocent: unobserved and harmless compared to earthquakes.
13. sublunary: under the moon, therefore subject to change.
14. soul: essence. **sense:** the body with its five senses; that is, purely physical rather than spiritual.
16. elemented: comprised; composed.

23. breach: break; split.

34. obliquely: off course.
35. firmness: fidelity. **just:** perfect. A circle symbolizes perfection, hence wedding rings.

MAKING MEANINGS

First Thoughts

1. Were your reactions to this poem different in any way from your reactions to the preceding *carpe diem* poems? If so, how, and why?

Shaping Interpretations

2. How would you paraphrase the **simile** in lines 1–8?

3. The **speaker** tells his wife that their love is different from that of other couples. What difference does he see, and how does he express it?

4. Why do you think Donne refers to irregular events on earth and in the spheres in lines 9–12? What kind of event is like the separation of lovers?

5. How would you explain the **conceit** Donne uses in lines 25–36? What does it suggest about the nature of love?

6. Why does the speaker insist that the lovers— obviously two people—are actually one?

7. What impression did you form of the writer as you read and discussed this poem? What sort of man is he?

8. Do you think this poem comforted Mrs. Donne? Why, or why not?

Challenging the Text

9. Samuel Johnson, writing in the eighteenth century, disapproved of metaphysical conceits as "the discovery of occult resemblances in things apparently unlike. . . . The most heterogeneous ideas are yoked by violence together." Do you agree or disagree with Johnson? Do the conceits in this poem work well for you? Why, or why not?

Portrait of a lady with a large ruff, an armillary sphere in the background (16th century), by the English School.

Johnny van Haeften Gallery, London.

Before You Read
MEDITATION 17

Make the Connection

Last Partings

There is one valediction that everyone must make: one parting and passage that time holds in store for all of us, whether we prepare ourselves for the journey or not. In 1624, prompted by a serious illness, Donne wrote a series of meditations. The opening of this one refers to the practice, in Donne's time, of ringing church bells to announce the death of a parish member.

Reading Skills and Strategies

Using Context Clues

Donne's meditation will probably contain words that are unfamiliar to you. In many cases, using **context clues** will help you guess at the meanings of these words. For example, if you did not know precisely what the word *toll* means, you would be able to make a pretty good guess, from the first sentence, that it has to do with ringing a bell. (You would be able to figure, also from context, that it does not mean the payment due for using bridges and tunnels and highways.) Always check your guesses on word meanings in a dictionary. The word *toll*, for example, does mean "to ring a bell," but it also has strong **connotations** associated with death. For instance, we would not say a bell *tolled* for a wedding. (Even the sound of the verb *toll* is mournful.)

A Wooded Landscape at Evening (detail) (19th century) by Carl Bondel.
Bonhams, London.

Meditation 17

John Donne

Nunc lento   Now, this bell tolling softly
sonitu dicunt,   for another, says to me,
Morieris.   Thou must die.

Perchance he for whom this bell tolls, may be so ill, as that he knows not it tolls for him; and perchance I may think myself so much better than I am, as that they who are about me, and see my state, may have caused it to toll for me, and I know not that. The Church is catholic, universal, so are all her actions; all that she does belongs to all. When she baptizes a child, that action concerns me; for that child is thereby connected to that Head[1] which is my Head too, and engrafted into that body, whereof I am a member. And when she buries a man, that action concerns me: All mankind is of one Author, and is one volume; when one man dies, one chapter is not torn out of the book, but translated[2] into a better language; and every chapter must be so translated; God employs several translators; some pieces are translated by age, some by sickness, some by war, some by justice; but God's hand is in every translation; and his hand shall bind up all our scattered leaves[3] again, for that Library where every book shall lie open to one another: As therefore the bell that rings to a sermon, calls not upon the preacher only, but upon the congregation to come; so this bell calls us all: but how much more me, who am brought so near the door by this sickness. There was a contention as far as a suit[4] (in which both piety and dignity, religion and estimation,[5] were mingled), which of the religious orders should ring to prayers first in the morning; and it was determined, that they should ring first that rose earliest. If we understand aright the dignity of this bell that tolls for our evening prayer, we would be glad to make it ours, by rising early, in that application, that it might be ours, as well as his, whose indeed it is. The bell doth toll for him that thinks it doth; and though it intermit[6] again, yet from that minute, that that occasion wrought upon him, he is united to God. Who casts not up his eye to the sun when it rises? but who takes off his eye from a comet when that breaks out?[7] Who bends not his ear to any bell, which upon any occasion rings? but who can remove it from that bell, which is passing a piece of himself out of this world? No man is an island, entire of itself; every man is a piece of the continent, a part of the main;[8] if a clod be washed away by the sea, Europe is the less, as well as if a promontory were, as well as if a manor of thy friends or of thine own were; any man's death diminishes me, because I am involved in mankind; and therefore never send to know for whom the bell tolls; it tolls for thee. Neither can we call this a begging of misery or a borrowing of misery, as though we were not miserable enough of ourselves, but must fetch in more from the next house, in taking upon us the misery of our neighbors. Truly it were an excusable covetousness if we did; for affliction[9] is a treasure, and scarce any man hath enough of it. No man hath affliction enough that is not matured, and ripened by it, and made fit for God by that affliction. If a man carry treasure in bullion, or in a wedge of gold, and have none coined into current monies, his treasure will not defray[10] him as he travels. Tribulation is treasure in the nature of it, but it is not current money in the use of it, except we get nearer and nearer our home, Heaven, by it. Another man may be sick too, and sick to death, and this affliction may lie in his bowels, as gold in a mine, and be of no use to him; but this bell, that tells me of his affliction, digs out, and applies that gold to me; if by this consideration of another's danger I take mine own into contemplation, and so secure myself by making my recourse[11] to my God, who is our only security.

---

1. **Head:** Christ.
2. **translated:** spiritually carried across from one realm to another.
3. **leaves:** pages.
4. **contention . . . suit:** argument that went as far as a lawsuit.
5. **estimation:** self-esteem.
6. **intermit:** cease.
7. **comet . . . out:** Comets were regarded as signs of disaster to come.
8. **main:** mainland.
9. **affliction:** suffering.
10. **defray:** pay for.
11. **making my recourse:** turning for aid.

MAKING MEANINGS

First Thoughts

1. Are there any ideas in Donne's meditation that you find puzzling or hard to accept or understand? Why?

Shaping Interpretations

2. Several of Donne's **metaphors** suggest something about the relationship of people to one another. Look at those metaphors—what do they imply about society?

3. Why does the speaker feel that affliction is a treasure? In what ways is tribulation like money?

4. How would you explain what Donne means by saying "the bell . . . tolls for thee"?

5. What do you think Donne's **main ideas** are in this meditation? Do you agree with them all?

6. How would you describe the speaker's **tone:** depressed, angry, resigned, or something else? What beliefs and values do you think account for the tone?

Extending the Text

7. Which lines from Meditation 17 do you think are particularly relevant to life today: in your community, in the United States, or in the "global community"?

8. Ernest Hemingway found a title for a novel in Donne's meditation. What would you predict *For Whom the Bell Tolls* (1940) is about? Can you find two or three other phrases in the meditation that would make good titles? Which ones?

READING SKILLS AND STRATEGIES

Using Context Clues

Context clues can be found in several places: (1) The unfamiliar word might be defined in an appositive; (2) the sentences surrounding the unfamiliar word might give you a clue to its meaning; (3) the structure of the word itself might help you figure out what it means. (See also Reading Skills and Strategies on page 51.)

Locate where Donne uses the following words. Use context clues to help you guess at what Donne uses each word to mean. Check all your guesses in a dictionary.

perchance	promontory	covetousness
catholic	aright	bullion
engrafted	wrought	

The Ruins of Holyrood Chapel (c. 1824) by Louis Jacques Mandé Daguerre.

Before You Read

DEATH BE NOT PROUD

Make the Connection

Defeat or Triumph?

Although death is inescapable, it is not, for everyone, an invincible victor. For those who believe in immortality—as Donne firmly did—death is merely an episode in the progress of the soul, the moment of its delivery from the confines of the body to eternal life.

Quickwrite

Use the words *Defeats* and *Triumphs* as two headings. Under each head, write down the ways you think some deaths could be seen as triumphs and others as defeats.

Background

In Donne's collected poems, which are grouped by type,

"Death Be Not Proud" is one of nineteen "Holy Sonnets" included in the category of "Divine Poems." Because Donne never published the "Holy Sonnets," and because they are arranged in different ways in contemporary manuscripts and in books printed after his death, we do not know the order in which he wanted us to read them.

Death Be Not Proud

John Donne

Death be not proud, though some have callèd thee
Mighty and dreadful, for thou art not so,
For those whom thou think'st thou dost overthrow,
Die not, poor Death, nor yet canst thou kill me.
5 From rest and sleep, which but thy pictures° be,
Much pleasure,° then from thee, much more must flow,
And soonest our best men with thee do go,
Rest of their bones, and soul's delivery.°
Thou art slave to fate, chance, kings, and desperate men,
10 And dost with poison, war, and sickness dwell,
And poppy,° or charms° can make us sleep as well,
And better than thy stroke; why swell'st° thou then?
One short sleep past, we wake eternally,
And death shall be no more; Death, thou shalt die.

5. pictures: images. A sleeping person can resemble a dead person.
6. much pleasure: That is, rest and sleep give much pleasure.
8. rest . . . delivery: Death gives the body rest and delivers the soul from the bondage of the body.
11. poppy: opium. **charms:** magic; hypnotism.
12. swell'st: swell with pride.

MAKING MEANINGS

First Thoughts

1. Did you find any of your Quickwrite ideas in Donne's poem? Did any of his taunts to Death seem surprising or highly original to you? If so, which ones?

Shaping Interpretations

2. According to the poem, why shouldn't Death be proud? Whom must Death serve as a slave?

3. Explain how rest and sleep are the "pictures" of Death (line 5).

4. How does the sonnet resolve its **paradoxes,** or seeming contradictions: that those who die do not die and that Death itself will die?

5. What is the speaker's **tone** in this poem—how does he feel toward Death? What words reveal his attitude?

Connecting with the Text

6. How would you respond to Donne's mockery of Death?

Extending the Text

7. John Gunther used this poem's opening words as the title of a book he wrote about the death of his teenage son. What attitude toward this personal tragedy does the father's choice of title suggest?

Still Life—Vanitas (1623) by Pieter Claesz. Oil on wood.

The Metropolitan Museum of Art, Rogers Fund, 1949 (49.107).
Photograph ©1979 The Metropolitan Museum of Art.

CHOICES: Building Your Portfolio

Writer's Notebook

1. Collecting Ideas for an Interpretive Essay

In questions following Donne's "Song," Meditation 17, and "Death Be Not Proud," you were asked to interpret the speaker's **tone**. Take one of these works, and look for at least three details that support your interpretation of tone. Look for word choice, sound effects, and direct statements. Save your work for possible use in the Writer's Workshop on page 275.

Comparing and Contrasting Poems

2. Thinking About Goodbyes

Richard Lovelace's "To Lucasta, on Going to the Wars" (page 264) is also a valediction poem addressed to a beloved woman. Read Lovelace's poem. Then, in an essay, compare and contrast Lovelace's farewell with Donne's "A Valediction: Forbidding Mourning." Focus on the consoling arguments that the speakers use to comfort the one left behind.

Analyzing Metaphors

3. Meditating on Metaphors

In a brief essay, take two of the metaphors in Meditation 17, and show how Donne uses them to make his points. Be sure to explain the terms of each metaphor and to show how Donne extends them.

Creative Writing

4. Stretching the Truth

Imitate the first stanza of Donne's "Song" by constructing some hyperbolic statements of your own to show the impossibility of something. You might want to respond to the points Donne raises in "Song."

Creative Writing

5. Just Before Parting

Suppose that you, like Donne, are leaving a loved one behind for a long, possibly dangerous journey. Write your own "valediction" in a brief letter. Be sure to refer to the opinions you expressed in the Quickwrite on page 247.

Art and Literature

6. Picturing Death

In "Death Be Not Proud," Donne forcefully personifies Death. How do you picture Death from his words and images? Draw or paint an illustration of Death to accompany Donne's poem.

Technology

7. Love in a High-Tech World

If Donne were writing today, he might have chosen a computer and modem, rather than a geometer's compass, as a conceit for the "connectedness" of lovers. Think of a high-tech conceit you could use to express a love relationship. Collaborate with one or two classmates, and express your ideas in a poem, sketch, video, or mixed-media performance. Remember that, to be effective, a conceit must have apt points of comparison.

Ben Jonson
(1572?–1637)

Although Jonson was christened Benjamin, he was, and is, always known as Ben. He was probably born in the same year as his friend John Donne, and if his friend William Shakespeare had never existed, Jonson would probably be regarded as the chief dramatist of the age.

Ben's father died before he was born. His stepfather, a bricklayer, intended to make him into a bricklayer too, but while still a boy, Jonson became acquainted with William Camden, scholar and headmaster of the superb Westminster School. Camden enrolled young Ben in his school and educated him at his own expense.

Jonson never attended a university, but he had an immense knowledge of Latin literature and a small acquaintance with Greek. He was no mere pedant or bookish recluse. After leaving Westminster, Ben joined the English army and fought against the Spanish in Flanders. There, while the two massed armies watched, he engaged in single combat with the Spanish champion and killed him. Back in England, he became a playwright and an actor, specializing in loud and roaring parts. He had two brushes with the law: once when he killed a fellow actor in a duel and escaped hanging by demonstrating that he could read, and once when he went to prison for making derogatory remarks about Scotland in a play. In short, Jonson was very much a part of the tough, violent life of the time—a complete Londoner, holding forth at

Benjamin Jonson (early 17th century) after Abraham van Blyenberch. Oil on canvas (18½″ × 16½″).
By Courtesy of the National Portrait Gallery, London.

the Mermaid Tavern, where his witty combats with Shakespeare and others are mentioned in contemporary writings.

Gradually, Jonson became known as a dramatist. He was particularly good at devising masques (elaborate, expensively mounted productions) for the court of King James. Jonson also wrote tragedies and comedies for the public theaters.

Jonson's attitude toward his writing was different from Donne's and Shakespeare's; Jonson was more like today's writers, who are, for the most part, eager for public notice. In 1616, Jonson astonished the reading public by publishing a number of his plays and poems under the title *Works*, a label traditionally reserved for more intellectual subjects, such as theology and history. But Jonson believed that poems and plays *are* serious works of art, as serious in their own way as history and theology, and as worthy of high regard.

At the height of his career, Jonson was a sort of literary dictator in London—opinionated and crusty but admired by a number of younger writers, who became known as the "tribe of Ben" or the "sons of Ben." They stood by Jonson in his old age, when he was sick and poor and neglected because his blunt and forthright manner had made him many enemies. Jonson was buried near Chaucer in Westminster Abbey, in what later became known as the Poets' Corner. His inscription required only four words: "O rare Ben Jonson."

Make the Connection

The Bonds of Love

When you hear the word *love*, do you first think of romantic love? If you do, this is a natural response. But the ties of love also bind us powerfully to family, to friends, even to pets. And one of love's ironies is that a strong bond of love, so strengthening and fulfilling, also opens us to heartache when it is cut.

Quickwrite

What does the word *bond* mean to you? With a few classmates, brainstorm meanings, connotations, and associations (don't think only of love). You may want to create a cluster diagram to show your ideas. Afterward, look up *bond* in the dictionary, and compare what you find with your brainstormings.

Elements of Literature

The Epigram

Both of Jonson's poems you will read were published in his *Epigrams* (1616), a classical form Jonson favored in contrast to both Elizabethan romanticism and metaphysical complexity. For the ancients, an **epigram** was written to give permanence to an event or observation; it was pointed, polished, and striking—like engraving on a monument. Jonson's epigrams (which are short poems) often show a two-part structure, the first part establishing the mood or the event, the second making a pithy point.

Background

This poem is about Jonson's son, Benjamin, who died of the plague on his seventh birthday. (Jonson and his wife also lost a daughter, Mary, in infancy.) The name *Benjamin* in Hebrew means "a child of the right hand" and, ironically, connotes "a lucky, clever child."

On My First Son

Ben Jonson

Farewell, thou child of my right hand, and joy;
   My sin was too much hope of thee, loved boy:
Seven years thou wert lent to me, and I thee pay,°
   Exacted° by thy fate, on the just° day.
5 Oh, could I lose all father° now! for why
Will man lament the state he should envy—
To have so soon 'scaped world's and flesh's rage,
   And if no other misery, yet age?
Rest in soft peace, and asked, say, "Here doth lie
10   Ben Jonson his best piece of poetry;
For whose sake henceforth all his vows be such
   As what he loves may never like too much."

3. thee pay: pay thee back.
4. exacted: forced. **just:** exact. Loans were often made for exactly seven years.
5. father: sense of fatherhood; the need to mourn like a father.

Portrait of a boy
(16th century)
by Robert Peake
the Elder.

Christie's, London.

Make the Connection

Love's Tributes

Part of loving is telling—acting on that burning desire to reveal your heart's devotion. In this short lyric, the speaker addresses Celia, telling her—exuberantly—how much he loves her.

Quickwrite

It isn't easy to find ways to talk about love. How do characters in movies and television shows manage it? Think of one or two characters, and try to recall how each expresses, explains, or describes his or her feelings. Jot down some of those contemporary expressions of love.

Background

Jonson once said that he always wrote out his poems in prose before turning them into verse, just as his master Camden had taught him to. At times, it must be admitted, the prose that he versified was not his own but someone else's. Jonson crafted this poem out of five different prose passages that he found in the *Epistles* of the Greek philosopher Philostratus (A.D. 170?–245). This poem has a very famous tune that many people still know.

Throughout his life, Jonson's enemies taunted him for once being a bricklayer. In a sense, he remained a bricklayer all his creative life, a builder whose tiniest construction, like this song, is solid and seamless.

Song: To Celia

Ben Jonson

Drink to me only with thine eyes,
    And I will pledge with mine;
Or leave a kiss but in the cup,
    And I'll not look for wine.
5 The thirst that from the soul doth rise
    Doth ask a drink divine;
But might I of Jove's nectar° sup,
    I would not change° for thine.
I sent thee late a rosy wreath,
10   Not so much honoring thee
As giving it a hope, that there
    It could not withered be.
But thou thereon didst only breathe,
    And sent'st it back to me;
15 Since when it grows, and smells, I swear,
    Not of itself but thee.

7. Jove's nectar: Jove, more commonly called Jupiter, is the supreme god in Roman mythology. Nectar was the drink that kept the gods immortal.
8. change: exchange.

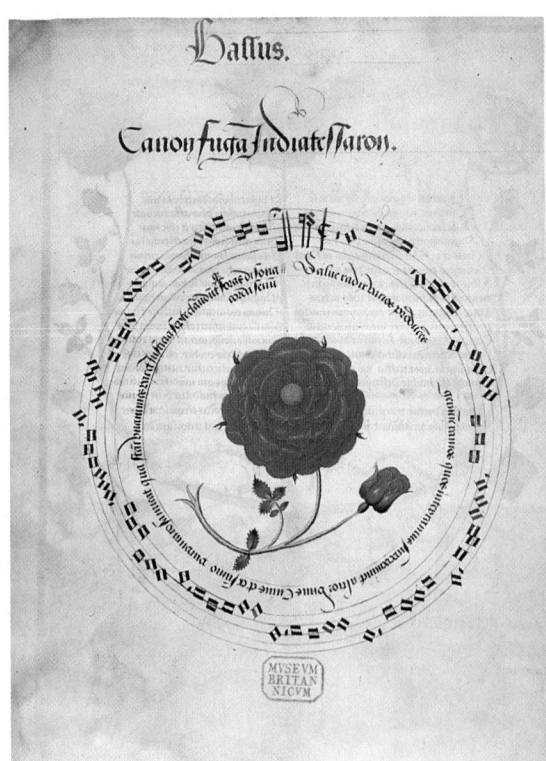

Motets (16th century) by Richard Sampson. Roy 11 E XI fol. 2v Canon, with circular staves and rose at center.

British Library, London.

MAKING MEANINGS

On My First Son
Song: To Celia

First Thoughts

1. What to you is the most important single line in each of Ben Jonson's poems? Why? Does your response to each poem relate to what you wrote for your Quickwrites before you read each poem? How?

Shaping Interpretations

2. In "On My First Son," why can the early death of a boy named Benjamin be regarded as **ironic**?

3. In "On My First Son," what comfort does Jonson suggest is possible in lines 7–8? Do you feel he's comforted?

4. In "To Celia," what do you think it means to "drink" and "pledge" with the eyes?

5. What does "thine" refer to in line 8 of "To Celia"?

6. How would you **paraphrase** lines 9–16 of "To Celia"?

7. These two poems are about two very different situations. Is there, nonetheless, anything that they share—any attitudes or beliefs? If you didn't know they were both by Jonson, would there be any reason to believe that they were written by the same person?

8. Jonson borrowed some of the features of "On My First Son" from Latin works: the direct address to the dead boy in line 9 and the first three words of the **epitaph,** or inscription, "Here doth lie . . . ." But the idea that his son is his best poem is original with Jonson. What do you think of this statement?

Connecting with the Text

9. What seemingly insignificant object—like the wreath returned by the speaker's beloved in "To Celia"—is nevertheless priceless to you because of the associations it evokes? Why is it priceless to you?

CHOICES:
Building Your Portfolio

Writer's Notebook
1. Collecting Ideas for an Interpretive Essay

Suppose you want to interpret a piece of art in this collection (perhaps the unusual painting on page 254). Your first step is to take notes on all the details you see in the painting: specific objects, colors, movement, a story perhaps. Look closely and write freely. Save your notes for the Writer's Workshop on page 275.

Explaining a Response
2. Rebutting Jonson

In "On My First Son," Jonson resolves never again to love so strongly, because his loss is unbearable. What do you think of Jonson's resolution? What effect could it have on him? In a paragraph, answer these questions.

Explaining a Response
3. Everyday Living

In one or two paragraphs, explain how the hard existence described in "Give Us This Day Our Daily Bread" (see *Connections* on page 260) corresponds to your previous notion of life in the late 1500s. Conclude by noting some aspects of Renaissance life you'd like to research.

Creative Writing
4. What Is Love?

In "To Celia," Jonson implicitly defines love as the soul's thirst (line 5). Elaborate on this definition in a paragraph (or a poem, if you like), or create a different definition based on your own metaphor.

Music
5. Crooning About Love

Write a love song of your own that begins with Jonson's first two lines in "To Celia."

Three Peasants (detail) (16th or 17th century) by Albrecht Dürer. Oil on panel.

Kunsthistorisches Museum, Vienna.

Had he not crossed paths with the scholar William Camden, Ben Jonson might have spent his life laying brick rather than composing poetry. Most young people of the age—those who didn't come from wealthy families or didn't acquire generous patrons—had difficult, exhausting lives. For them, witty conceits praising adored ladies were as foreign as the moon—and life was consumed with making ends meet.

Give Us This Day Our Daily Bread

Joseph Papp and Elizabeth Kirkland

You are living in England in the late years of the sixteenth century. Like most people, you live with your family in the countryside, eking out a meager existence as best you can. If you're lucky, your father is a yeoman farmer who owns enough land to support his family, or a "husbandman" who has less property but supplements his income by wage earning.

The land you live in is full of contradictions. A woman, Queen Elizabeth, rules the nation, while within the family, men still rule women. A highly educated elite enjoys the fruits of literature, while many people can't even read. The government invests huge sums of money in voyages of exploration and wars with other nations, while science and medicine remain in an appallingly primitive state. In London, the royal court glitters with jewels and finery, while misery reigns in rural hovels. Rich young men wander around Europe for fun, while in England, thousands of homeless people wander from parish to parish, begging and stealing to survive.

The gap between the rich and the poor seems to have widened in the 1570s and 1580s; wealth and power are concentrated in the hands of the few, and many people can't even find a job.

You come from a family of laborers. You don't have much land at all, hardly even a vegetable garden you can call your own, and you are completely dependent on whatever wages you can get by harvesting other people's crops and doing odd jobs around the village. There is no money for such "extras" as education or nice clothes or red meat. In fact, your father's daily income, even when combined with yours, barely covers the cost of feeding you and your brothers and sisters; thank goodness your mother is able to bring in a few extra pennies from her spinning.

Your dependent status as a tenant makes your perch in life still more precarious. To an unjust and unscrupulous landlord, profit is more important than principles, and yours feels no obligation to look out for your best interests. If he decides to "enclose" the land—to stop using it for farming and turn it into grazing pastures for sheep—he has endless means of forcing you out: He might make you give up your lease, or renew it only at great expense, or, most commonly, charge you exorbitant rent.

While your family has been struggling against these odds and worrying about how to make ends meet from day to day, larger forces have been at work that are going to affect you drastically. First, England has been undergoing a huge increase in population. The two-and-a-half million English people who were alive when your grandparents were born will practically have doubled by the time your grandchildren die. This unprecedented population growth is already being translated into inflated prices, as too many people chase after scarce resources. It also means that wages stay unacceptably low; with so many laborers on the job market, farmers and other employers can easily find people willing to work for the pathetically low wages they offer if you're not interested.

Getting and spending have been a constant battle, and staying on the winning side has depended on plentiful harvests, which bring the twofold benefit of jobs and low grain prices. But in recent years the battle has become a losing one: The heavy rains of the last two summers have ruined the harvests, the population has been growing faster than the crops, and famine has begun to cast its long, thin shadow across your life.

Grain—whether you eat the oatmeal cakes of northern England or the coarse wheat bread of the southerners—is a staple of your diet and, if you have no land and have to buy all your grain on the market, your single biggest expense. When prices shoot up, as they do in bad harvest years, it spells disaster for many a citizen; the Carriers in Shakespeare's *Henry IV Part 1* remember a comrade who "never joyed since the price of oats rose. It was the death of him." You try to find cheaper kinds of grain than your usual

wheat, supplementing your diet with stomach-filling peas and beans—but even the prices of these are rising now, and you begin to realize, horrifying though it is, that there aren't many alternatives. Starvation seems inevitable.

You wonder how you and your family are going to cope with the steady advance of such hunger, the hair falling out and the skin turning gray and the bleak prospect of watching your fellow villagers "starving and dying in our streets and in the fields [because] of lack of bread," as a contemporary in the northern town of Newcastle writes.

To make matters worse, there has been an economic recession too, mainly because of a slump in the cloth trade that your mother had been depending on for her livelihood. Many people rely on the cloth and wool trades for their living, and now, "the deadness of that trade and want of money is such that they are for the most part without work, and know not how to live," as an official of one parish reports.

—*from Shakespeare Alive!*

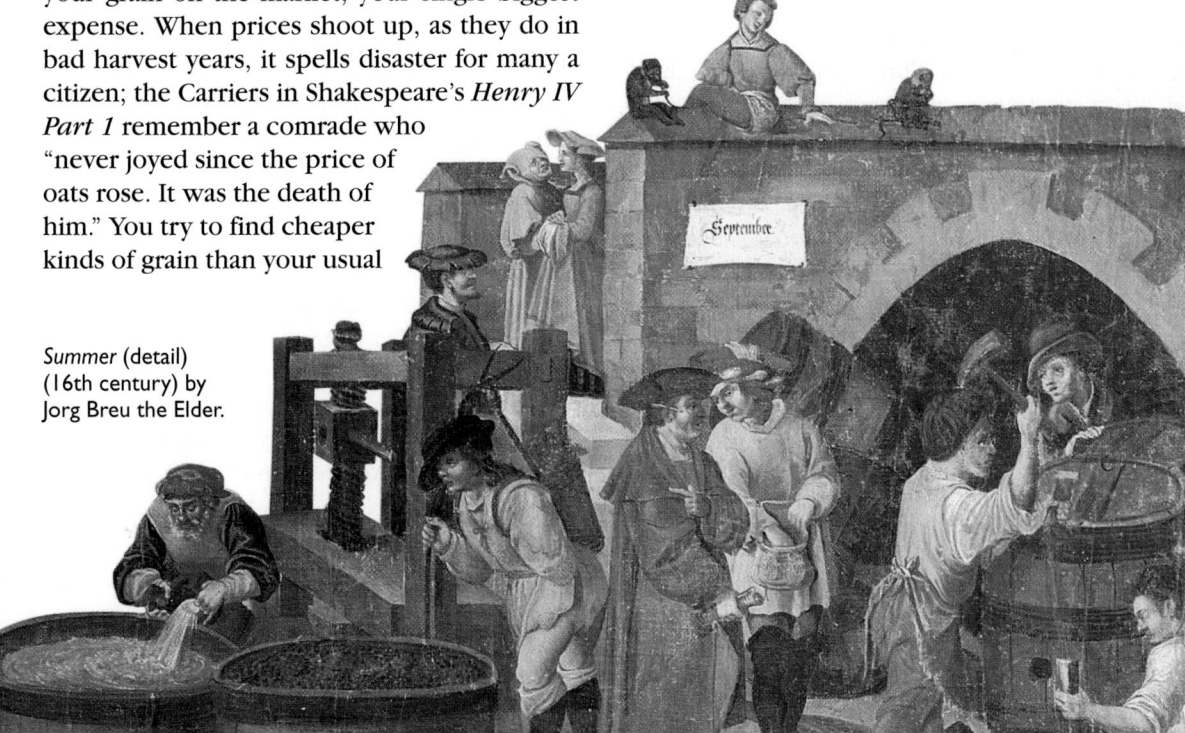

Summer (detail) (16th century) by Jorg Breu the Elder.

Sir John Suckling
(1609–1642)

Richard Lovelace
(1618–1657)

Sir John Suckling (detail) (17th century) by an unknown artist. Oil on panel (34.3 cm × 28.6 cm). By Courtesy of the National Portrait Gallery, London.

I t is convenient to consider these two poets together because they were Royalists; that is, they supported King Charles in the Civil Wars of the 1640s. Because of their politics, they are sometimes called Cavalier poets, "Cavalier" being the nickname for a supporter of the king, as "Roundhead" is for a supporter of Parliament. But these poets had more than politics in common; they shared a common literary goal, which was to write poems that sound like elegant conversation. In the next century, Alexander Pope, looking back at the work of the poets of the mid–seventeenth century, referred to them as "the mob of gentlemen who wrote with ease." Pope should have said that they *seemed* to write with ease, because he knew better than most people how hard it is to make any kind of writing, and especially poetry, sound easy and at the same time be technically accomplished.

John Suckling was born rich, but he gambled away his money and spent a lot of it on extravagant clothes. Suckling's military career included service as a gentleman soldier on the Continent and as the commander of a troop of cavalry fighting in Scotland for King Charles. He plotted unsuccessfully to deliver one of the king's chief advisers from the Tower of London; then he fled to France. There, at the age of thirty-three, he died—by suicide or murder (accounts vary). Suckling's poems, which were mostly published after his death, tend to be lighthearted, as was his life. Dryden praised him, saying that he had "the conversation of a gentleman." He is said to be the inventor of cribbage, a card game.

Lovelace (pronounced "love-less"), besides being very handsome, was altogether a more serious person than the playboy Suckling. Like his fellow Cavalier poets, he was very rich, at least at the beginning of his life. He was also a connoisseur of music, painting, and horsemanship. While still a student at Oxford, he made such an impression on King Charles and Queen Henrietta Maria, who were visiting the university, that the royal couple ordered the authorities to confer on him the Master of Arts degree at once. Lovelace became an ardent Royalist, and when the Civil Wars broke out, he fought bravely for King Charles. The Roundheads caught him twice and imprisoned him both times. His last days were sad, his health and fortune ruined in the service of a lost cause.

Richard Lovelace (detail) (17th century) by Wenceslaus Hollar. By Courtesy of the National Portrait Gallery, London.

go.hrw.com
LEO 12-3

Before You Read

WHY SO PALE AND WAN
TO LUCASTA
TO ALTHEA

Make the Connection

Knights Ride Again

Cavalier, cavalry, chivalry: the common root of all three words is the Latin word for "horse," *caballus*. All three also share, in their earliest uses, the dual meanings of "horseman" and "knightly behavior." Thinking about these two ideas gives you a way of understanding the Cavalier poets, who saw themselves as modern-day knights. They adopted the chivalrous code of intense loyalty to a leader, to God, and to one beloved woman. But they were also boisterously masculine, pleasure-loving, worldly, and cynical.

Quickwrite

After you read each poem, write out your immediate responses. If you could ask each poet one question, what would it be? What idea would you challenge each poet about?

Elements of Literature

Tone

The Cavalier poets' attitudes toward women, warfare, honor, and the other matters that concerned them shaped the tone of their poetry vividly. In these three poems, you'll hear the tone of voice strongly, and it will let you know how each poet feels about his subject. Try to read these poems as if you were listening to someone speaking aloud.

> **T**one is the attitude a writer takes toward the reader, a subject, or a character.
>
> *For more on Tone, see the Handbook of Literary Terms.*

In Renaissance literature, young men suffer horribly from unrequited love. Part of the convention is that the women whom the men admire show no pity. In fact, they ignore pleas for attention so firmly that the men become "pale and wan"—that is, sickly looking—like the young fellow whom the speaker of this poem is so irritated with.

Why So Pale and Wan, Fond Lover?

Sir John Suckling

Why so pale and wan, fond lover?
    Prithee, why so pale?
Will, when looking well can't move her,
    Looking ill prevail?
5   Prithee, why so pale?

Why so dull and mute, young sinner?
    Prithee, why so mute?
Will, when speaking well can't win her,
    Saying nothing do't?
10   Prithee, why so mute?

Quit, quit, for shame; this will not move,
    This cannot take her.
If of herself she will not love,
    Nothing can make her:
15   The devil take her!

An Unknown Youth Leaning Against a Tree Among Roses (16th century) by Nicholas Hilliard.

Victoria and Albert Museum, London.

The English Civil Wars are the backdrop to this poem. Like John Donne's "A Valediction: Forbidding Mourning" (page 248), the poem takes the form of a lover's goodbye to his beloved. Unlike Donne's, Lovelace's speaker is full of noble sentiments. It is tempting to identify Lovelace himself with this speaker, for the poet was an idealist about king and country, ready to sacrifice his happiness, fortune, and life in their service.

To Lucasta, on Going to the Wars

Richard Lovelace

Tell me not, sweet, I am unkind,
    That from the nunnery°
Of thy chaste breast and quiet mind
    To war and arms I fly.

5 True, a new mistress now I chase,
    The first foe in the field;
And with a stronger faith embrace
    A sword, a horse, a shield.

Yet this inconstancy is such
10   As you too shall adore;
I could not love thee, dear, so much,
    Loved I not honor more.

2. nunnery: literally, a convent for nuns; here, a metaphor for a pure, safe place.

George Clifford, 3rd earl of Cumberland (16th century) by Nicholas Hilliard.

National Maritime Museum, London.

Like "To Lucasta, on Going to the Wars," this poem follows the fashion, set by Sir Philip Sidney and Ben Jonson, of giving the women in poems classical names. Whether real women are hidden behind the names Lucasta and Althea, we do not know, nor does it matter, for there is little or no connection between having a love affair and the ability to write a good poem. We do know that Lovelace was imprisoned during the Civil Wars, and it seems likely that a man as attractive as he was would be visited by a female admirer.

To Althea, from Prison

Richard Lovelace

A Man Holding a Hand from a Cloud (miniature) (16th century) by Nicholas Hilliard.

Victoria and Albert Museum, London.

When Love with unconfinèd wings
    Hovers within my gates,
And my divine Althea brings
    To whisper at the grates;
5 When I lie tangled in her hair
    And fettered to her eye,
The gods° that wanton° in the air
    Know no such liberty.

When flowing cups run swiftly round,
10 With no allaying Thames,°
Our careless heads with roses bound,
    Our hearts with loyal flames;
When thirsty grief in wine we steep,
    When healths and drafts go free,
15 Fishes that tipple in the deep
    Know no such liberty.

When, like committed linnets,° I
    With shriller throat shall sing
The sweetness, mercy, majesty,
20 And glories of my King;°
When I shall voice aloud how good
    He is, how great should be,
Enlargèd° winds that curl the flood°
    Know no such liberty.

25 Stone walls do not a prison make,
    Nor iron bars a cage:
Minds innocent and quiet take
    That for an hermitage.°
If I have freedom in my love,
30 And in my soul am free,
Angels alone, that soar above,
    Enjoy such liberty.

7. gods: In many seventeenth-century versions of this poem, "gods" is replaced by "birds." **wanton:** frolic.

10. allaying Thames (temz): That is, the wine is not diluted with water from the Thames River.

17. committed linnets: caged birds.

20. my King: Charles I, king of England from 1625 to 1649.

23. enlargèd: released. **flood:** sea.

28. hermitage: holy refuge.

MAKING MEANINGS

Why So Pale and Wan, Fond Lover?
To Lucasta, on Going to the Wars
To Althea, from Prison

First Thoughts

1. Imagine Suckling and Lovelace discussing their conceptions of love. What would they agree and disagree on?

Shaping Interpretations

2. In "Why So Pale and Wan, Fond Lover?" what advice does the speaker give the pale lover? What is his **tone,** and how does it differ from Lovelace's in "To Lucasta" and "To Althea"?

3. In "To Lucasta," how does the speaker use **metaphors** of love to describe war? What do you think of these romantic ways of talking about war?

4. The speaker in "To Lucasta" implies two **paradoxes:** that his inconstancy (line 9) is really constancy and that to be loyal he must be disloyal. According to the speaker, how could these seemingly contradictory statements be true?

5. What evidence can you find in "To Lucasta" for believing that Lucasta has the same values as the speaker and will therefore not whine or scold him for losing her?

6. In "To Althea," what comparison is made in each stanza's final two-line **refrain**? What is different about the last comparison?

7. How would you explain line 6 in "To Althea"?

8. In "To Althea," what is the famous **paradox** stated in lines 25–26? What makes the jailed speaker free?

9. What does "To Althea" imply about what *does* make a prison? Do you agree or disagree?

Extending the Texts

10. Again, we have three poems either addressed to women or about a woman's treatment of a man. But the women's feelings are unknown. What do you imagine a modern woman's response would be to each speaker?

CHOICES:
Building Your Portfolio

Writer's Notebook

1. Collecting Ideas for an Interpretive Essay

Paraphrasing is a useful technique for preparing to write about any literary work. To **paraphrase,** you put a literary text into your own words. Paraphrasing helps you to check your own understanding of the work, particularly your understanding of metaphors or paradoxes, and your reading of any unusual syntax. Paraphrasing helps you identify places where your understanding is solid, or places where you need to think more about the text's meaning. Paraphrase any one of the three poems by the Cavalier poets. Save your work for possible use in the Writer's Workshop on page 275.

Analyzing a Poem's Relevance

2. The Poem Across Time

Does "To Althea, from Prison"—a poem about liberty and bondage—have any relevance to late-twentieth-century life? In a brief essay, give your opinion, referring to actual world conditions or events and citing specific passages from the poem to support your views.

Challenging the Texts

3. Face to Face

Suppose you could face these poets, say on a talk show. In a brief essay, list the questions you would ask. What challenges would you make to the poets' ideas or values? Be sure to refer to the notes you made in the Quickwrite on page 263.

Creative Writing

4. A Modern Lucasta

Write out a modern Lucasta's answer to a man who delivered this poem to her as he set off to war.

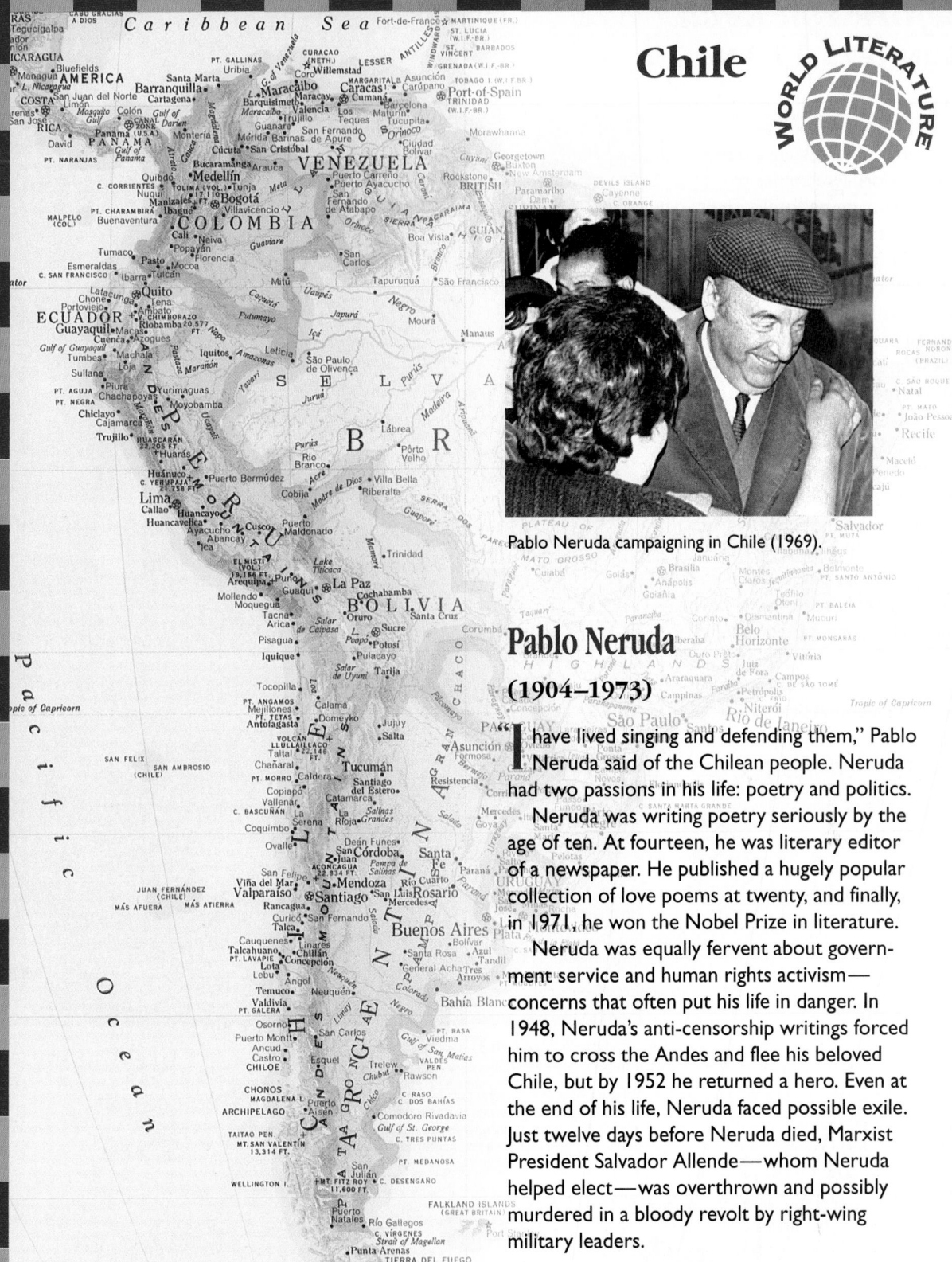

Pablo Neruda campaigning in Chile (1969).

Pablo Neruda

(1904–1973)

"I have lived singing and defending them," Pablo Neruda said of the Chilean people. Neruda had two passions in his life: poetry and politics. Neruda was writing poetry seriously by the age of ten. At fourteen, he was literary editor of a newspaper. He published a hugely popular collection of love poems at twenty, and finally, in 1971, he won the Nobel Prize in literature.

Neruda was equally fervent about government service and human rights activism—concerns that often put his life in danger. In 1948, Neruda's anti-censorship writings forced him to cross the Andes and flee his beloved Chile, but by 1952 he returned a hero. Even at the end of his life, Neruda faced possible exile. Just twelve days before Neruda died, Marxist President Salvador Allende—whom Neruda helped elect—was overthrown and possibly murdered in a bloody revolt by right-wing military leaders.

Before You Read
SONNETS 17 AND 79

Make the Connection

Mention the Renaissance poets, and the word *love* comes to mind almost immediately. Their sonnets resonate with the passion born of true love. But the Renaissance does not hold exclusive rights to this often mysterious emotion. Poets in modern times have also explored the experience of love.

The sonnets you are about to read were originally written in Spanish by the famous Chilean poet Pablo Neruda. You may not have had the experience Neruda describes in his sonnets. The speaker and his beloved are mature; they have probably been intimately connected for a long time.

Be sure to listen to these sonnets read aloud in Spanish to hear the special music they create in their original language.

Quickwrite

How does the love of older people differ from youthful love? Or does it? Take notes on your responses.

The Lover's Rock (1963) by David Alfaro Siqueiros. Mixed media on masonite (80 cm × 60 cm).

Private Collection. Courtesy of Galería Arvil, Mexico City, Mexico. Reproduction authorized by: Instituto Nacional de Bellas Artes y Literatura, Mexico. © Estate of David Alfaro Siqueiros/ SOMAAP Mexico/Licensed by permission of the British Library.

Sonnet 17

Pablo Neruda

translated by **Stephen Tapscott**

I do not love you as if you were salt-rose, or topaz,
or the arrow of carnations the fire shoots off.
I love you as certain dark things are to be loved,
in secret, between the shadow and the soul.

5 I love you as the plant that never blooms
but carries in itself the light of hidden flowers;
thanks to your love a certain solid fragrance,
risen from the earth, lives darkly in my body.

I love you without knowing how, or when, or from where.
10 I love you straightforwardly, without complexities or pride;
so I love you because I know no other way

than this: where *I* does not exist, nor *you,*
so close that your hand on my chest is my hand,
so close that your eyes close as I fall asleep.

Soneto 17

No te amo como si fueras rosa de sal, topacio
o flecha de claveles que propagan el fuego:
te amo como se aman ciertas cosas oscuras,
secretamente, entre la sombra y el alma.

5 Te amo como la planta que no florece y lleva
dentro de sí, escondida, la luz de aquellas flores,
y gracias a tu amor vive oscuro en mi cuerpo
el apretado aroma que ascendió de la tierra.

Te amo sin saber cómo, ni cuándo, ni de dónde,
10 te amo directamente sin problemas ni orgullo:
así te amo porque no sé amar de otra manera,

sino así de este modo en que no soy ni eres,
tan cerca que tu mano sobre mi pecho es mía,
tan cerca que se cierran tus ojos con mi sueño.

Sonnet 79

Pablo Neruda

translated by **Stephen Tapscott**

By night, Love, tie your heart to mine, and the two
together in their sleep will defeat the darkness
like a double drum in the forest, pounding
against the thick wall of wet leaves.

5   Night travel: black flame of sleep
that snips the threads of the earth's grapes,
punctual as a headlong train that would haul
shadows and cold rocks, endlessly.

Because of this, Love, tie me to a purer motion,
10   to the constancy that beats in your chest
with the wings of a swan underwater,

so that our sleep might answer all the sky's
starry questions with a single key,
with a single door the shadows had closed.

Soneto 79

De noche, amada, amarra tu corazón al mío
y que ellos en el sueño derroten las tinieblas
como un doble tambor combatiendo en el bosque
contra el espeso muro de las hojas mojadas.

5   Nocturna travesía, brasa negra del sueño
interceptando el hilo de las uvas terrestres
con la puntualidad de un tren descabellado
que sombra y piedras frías sin cesar arrastrara.

Por eso, amor, amárrame al movimiento puro,
10   a la tenacidad que en tu pecho golpea
con las alas de un cisne sumergido,

para que a las preguntas estrelladas del cielo
responda nuestro sueño con una sola llave,
con una sola puerta cerrada por la sombra.

FINDING COMMON GROUND

Before you discuss these poems, check your Quickwrite notes. Even if, after listening to the poems' speakers, you did not say, "Those could be *my* words," you may have said "Yes!" to some ideas, moods, feelings, and images. Then again, you may have some arguments to pick with Neruda or his speakers: Your ideas about love may not always mesh with theirs. What is your reaction? Here are some other questions you might want to discuss:

- What do you think Sonnet 17 means about love being dark and secret?

- What do you think of the ideas that love completes people and that it unites them so that they seem as one person? Have you encountered that idea in other poems in this collection? Where?

- Could you relate to the fear of night in Sonnet 79? Do you think love is the answer?

- What was your favorite **image** in each poem?

- Does Neruda use complex **metaphors** that remind you of the metaphysical poets' love of complex and unusual comparisons? Point out one or two examples.

- Do Neruda and the Renaissance poets hold similar notions about love, or are they very different?

- Do you find in Neruda's poems a conviction that love conquers time—as you find in Renaissance poetry?

- Where do your thoughts on love fall— close to Neruda or to the Renaissance poets?

Use your notes to discuss with classmates what you think romantic love is, what it means to people today, and what it has meant in ages past.

The English Language

The Birth of Modern English

*by **John Algeo***

The Modern English period can be dated from 1485, when Henry VII, the first Tudor king of England, came to the throne. The House of Tudor brought peace to the land, introduced the Reformation and Renaissance to England, helped to promote a pride in things English, and began the spread of our language all over the world. Just ten years before, in 1475, William Caxton had printed the first book in English. That event might also be taken as marking the beginning of the Modern period, for printed books were to help unify and spread English and make the opportunity to read and write readily available to all English-speaking people.

Aerial map and view across the Thames from the South Bank, with St. Paul's and London Bridge (c. 1730) by J. B. Homans.

The Language Changes That Made Modern English

When William Caxton printed the first books in English, he tried to make them look as much like handwritten manuscripts as he could. The shapes of the letters in his type font, the spellings he used, his choice of words and sentence structures—all suggested the manuscript writing of an earlier time. Because printing was a new-fangled invention, Caxton wanted his printed books to look as much as possible like the manuscripts that people were familiar with. Yet, despite his efforts, it is clear that the language of the late 1400s and early 1500s was a new form of English.

English during the first part of the Modern period, when it still resembled Middle English in some ways and had not yet reached the form we recognize as our own, is known as Early Modern English. That term embraces English from about 1485 through the mid-1700s.

Grammatical differences between Middle and Modern English were not very great. Middle English had already lost many of the inflections of Old English. The few it kept and passed on to Early Modern English are mainly ones we still have today: the plural ending *–s* and the possessive ending *–'s* for nouns; the comparative and superlative endings *–er* and *–est* for adjectives; and the verb endings for the past tense (*–ed*), past participle (*–ed* or *–en*), present participle (*–ing*), and the third-person singular of the present tense (*–s*). In place of that *–s,* Early Modern English also had an ending we no longer use, *–eth,* and in addition one for the second-person singular, *–est* (as in "he thinketh" and "thou thinkest").

Because British explorers, merchants, and settlers had an itch to travel, and scratched it vigorously, the English language has never been the same.

Shifting Vowels

The greatest change between Middle and Early Modern English was in the pronunciation of the "long" or tense vowels, illustrated by these words (given in their present-day spellings): *bite, feet, cane, mouse, boot, load.* In Middle English times, the vowels of these words had been pronounced as follows: *bite* like "beet," *feet* like "fate," *cane* like "khan" or "con," *mouse* like "moose," *boot* like "boat," and *load* like "laud" or "(out–) lawed." The sentence *See the same old moon in the cloudy sky* would have sounded in Middle English something like "Say the sahm awld moan in the cloody skee."

If we could go back to Chaucer's London by a time-travel machine, our first impression would be that some language other than English was being spoken. After a while, however, we would probably get used to it and decide that it was English after all, although pronounced very oddly.

No one knows why these changes (called the Great Vowel Shift) happened—many such big changes in language are inexplicable. However, something rather similar is going on in some varieties of English today. In New York City, Philadelphia, and various other places, especially in the middle part of the East Coast and westward from there, words like *bad, cab,* and *fan* sound something like "behd," "kehb," and "fehn." If that kind of change should become general and extend to other words and other parts of the country, two hundred years from now, people may be pronouncing *See the same old moon in the cloudy sky* something like "Sigh the seem oold mown in the clawdy skay." Stranger things have happened in the history of languages, and that change is no more improbable than was the Great Vowel Shift five hundred years ago.

Lagging Spelling

Ever since 1475, when books were first printed in English, we have had a tendency to keep our spelling unchanged, whatever happens to our pronunciation. Therefore, our spelling tends to become further and further out of line with the way we say words. When Caxton started printing books, he used a spelling for English that was already old-fashioned; and we have done little to modernize it since.

Ever since English first began to be printed, people have worried about the failure of our spelling to match our pronunciation. Many proposals have been made to reform English spelling, ranging from simply omitting silent letters, as in *tho* for *though* and *thru* for *through,* to more thorough reforms: "Wun sistem uv spelling wood seek tu eeliminaet awl iregguelarity." There have been even more radical suggestions, such as abandoning the Latin alphabet altogether and adopting a new one. One example is called the Shaw alphabet, designed for a contest set up by the twentieth-century writer George Bernard Shaw in his will. An example of the Shaw alphabet follows.

ꟿꟿꟿꟿꟿꟿ
(Shaw alphabet sample)

Serious spelling reform has little chance of success. English speakers have been remarkably faithful to the spellings that were decided upon during the Early Modern English period. We seem unlikely to change them now.

O Brave New World: The Spread of English and Foreign Influences

The reign of Queen Elizabeth I saw the beginning of the extension of English to the far corners of the world. The British established colonies in North America—in a land they called Virginia after the Virgin Queen and later in New England and many other places. Exploration, settlement, and commerce all led to the borrowing of words from many other languages.

French contributed *bigot, bombast, duel, explore, jaunty, moustache, shock,* and *vogue.* From Italian came *balcony, cameo, design, duo, fugue, grotto, portico, stanza, trill,* and *violin;* from Spanish or Portuguese, *alligator, apricot, banana, brocade, corral, hammock, renegade,* and *tobacco;* from Indian languages of Central America and the Caribbean, by way of Spanish, *avocado, cannibal, chocolate, maize, potato,* and *tomato;* from Dutch, *cruise, deck, freight, keel, skipper, smuggle, yacht, duffel, spool, knapsack, easel, etch,* and *landscape.*

The adventures of British explorers, merchants, and settlers during the Early Modern English period enriched our vocabulary immensely. Because they had an itch to travel, and scratched it vigorously, the English language has never been the same.

The New Learning: Classical Influences

While English was picking up words from languages abroad, it did not neglect the classical languages, Latin and Greek. The literature, art, philosophy, history, and culture of Rome and Athens were taken as ideals during the Renaissance. Naturally, modern European languages, including English, also borrowed words from Latin and Greek.

Manuscript map of Raleigh's Virginia (c. 1585) by John White.

© British Museum, London.

Among many other words, English borrowed from Latin *abdomen, area, compensate, delirium, editor, gradual, imitate, janitor, medium, orbit, peninsula, quota, series, strict, superintendent, ultimate, urban,* and *urge.* From Greek, usually by way of Latin and sometimes other intermediate languages, came *aristocracy, barbarous, chaos, comedy, cycle, drama, epoch, history, mystery, rhythm, theory, tragedy,* and *zone.*

The Rise of Standard English

Languages come in many varieties. A standard language is one that is used widely throughout a country and enjoys the respect of both those who use it and those who do not. It is typically the language of government and education.

The Early Modern English standard language was the result of several influences. The law clerks who recorded the proceedings of courts and who maintained the legal archives of England set a pattern of language usage that others followed. Especially important was the usage of the Court of Chancery, presided over by the Lord High Chancellor of England: Consequently, the widely used and prestigious form of Early Modern English is sometimes called Chancery Standard.

The introduction of the printing press, as already noted, helped to spread the new standard written language throughout England, making it available to all literate English speakers. Literacy was also increasing at this time. English people were reading the Book of Common Prayer (first published during the reign of Queen Elizabeth's brother and predecessor, King Edward VI) and the Authorized Version of the Bible (popularly known as the King James Bible because it was published during the reign of Elizabeth's successor, King James I). The phrases and rhythms of those two books, prayer book and Bible, were powerful influences in shaping the ideal of language to which English speakers looked during the Renaissance and for centuries after.

Try It Out

1. **Pronouncing words.** The fact that some words are pronounced in more than one way today is a sign that our language is still in the process of change. How do you pronounce the following words? Look in a dictionary to see if other pronunciations are listed.

   brooch   garage   roof
   creek   mature   which

2. **Investigating spellings.** Although our spelling is more consistent than that of the Renaissance, some words still have more than one possible spelling. What other spellings can the following words have?

   adviser   descendant
   cater-cornered   finicky
   collectible   mama
   cozy   parakeet

3. **Locating etymologies.** During the Renaissance, English borrowed words from many foreign languages. From what language does each of the following words come? Look up the words in a dictionary that gives **etymologies,** or word origins.

   balcony   landscape
   brocade   mustache
   canoe   scientific
   catastrophe   volcano

4. **Analyzing influences on English.** The standard English of the Renaissance was based on the language used by the government in law courts and was spread by the printing press. What influences affect the way we talk and write today?

5. **Translating Shaw's alphabet.** Using the following key, write the passage in the Shaw alphabet on page 273 in conventional spelling.

THE SHAW ALPHABET READING KEY
The letters are classified as Tall, Deep, Short, and Compound.
Beneath each letter is its full name; its sound is shown in **bold** type.

Tall:	peep	tot	kick	fee	thigh	so	sure	church	yea	hung
Deep:	bib	dead	gag	vow	they	zoo	meaSure	judge	woe	ha-ha
Short:	loll	mime	if	egg	ash	ado	on	wool	out	ah
	roar	nun	eat	age	ice	up	oak	ooze	oil	awe
Compound:	are	or	air	err	array	ear	lan	yew		

BUILDING YOUR PORTFOLIO

Writer's Workshop

The history
of the written
word is rich an

Page 1

EXPOSITORY WRITING

AN INTERPRETIVE ESSAY

One way you can make sense of any experience, including the experiences of reading literature, viewing movies, and looking at art, is by **interpreting** it—explaining its meaning in your own words. In this Writer's Workshop, you'll write an interpretive essay about a work of literature, film, or art.

Prewriting

1. **Check your Writer's Notebook.** By doing the Writer's Notebook activities in this collection, you may have already done much of the prewriting for an interpretive essay. Check back over your Writer's Notebook entries. You can add to or change what you did in your Writer's Notebook, or you can proceed with the prewriting activities that follow.

2. **Act and react.** If you still don't have a subject, go to a library, bookstore, or video store and find a work that's new to you and that you won't mind reading or viewing more than once. You might instead choose two different works, or two versions of a work (for example, a novel and its movie adaptation), to **compare and contrast.** Read or view each work carefully.

   Usually, your first reaction to a work is a personal one: delight or dismay, liking or loathing. Take a few minutes to take notes on your response, and don't worry about whether your response is "correct": No two people are likely to respond to any work in precisely the same way.

3. **Dig deeper.** To interpret the work for your readers, you need to move beyond personal response to **analysis**—reading (or viewing) the work critically to determine what its parts, or elements, are and how they work together to express some meaning about experience. The charts below show the elements to look for in poetry and in art.

Elements of Poetry

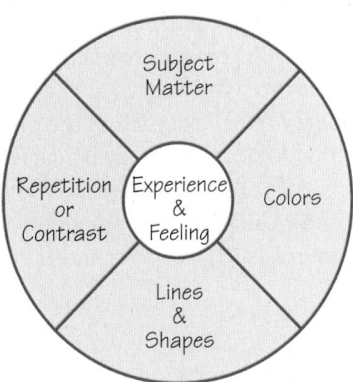

Elements of Art

Technology HELP

See *Writer's Workshop 2* CD-ROM. *Assignment: Interpretation.*

ASSIGNMENT
Write an essay interpreting a literary work, a movie, or a piece of art.

AIM
To inform; to explain; to persuade.

AUDIENCE
Your classmates or members of reading, film, or art groups.

Try It Out
Working with a partner or a small group, identify the literary elements used in one of the following:
1. an episode of a TV sitcom or soap opera
2. a popular song

Strategies for Elaboration: Analyzing a Work

Use the following strategies to analyze the elements of the work you've chosen.

- Read or view the work again, noting things you missed the first time. New insights may occur to you on a second reading or viewing.
- If you are writing about a piece of art, take notes on these elements: colors, details emphasized, overall tone or mood. Do you "read" a story into the painting? If you are writing about a portrait, look closely at what the person is wearing or holding. What background has the artist given the subject? What has the artist omitted from the portrait? If there are several people in a painting, what are their relationships (are they, for example, indifferent to one another, or are they warm and loving)?
- Freewrite on the connection you see between the work and its title.
- For a short written work, make a copy for yourself and use different colors of markers to highlight the various literary elements.
- Compare your ideas about the work with the ideas of others who are familiar with it. Their interpretations may differ from yours, but their ideas may help you clarify your own thinking.

The Elements of Film

See Film as Literature, pages 1012-1016.

4. **Find a focus.** In the space of a short essay, it would be difficult to analyze all the elements of a work. To make your interpretation manageable, look back at your personal response and your critical-reading notes. Which elements struck you most strongly? How do those elements help bring out the theme or the writer's or artist's meaning? Choose the ones that seem most significant to you. (More than three may prove unwieldy.) For example, you might focus on how diction and imagery help develop the theme of a poem or on how point of view affects the theme of a short story or on how color affects the feeling you have for a painting.

5. **Stake your claim.** In a sentence or two, state your opinion about the relationship between the elements you've chosen and the work's theme or meaning. This preliminary thesis statement will make a useful guide for planning your paper. Keep in mind, though, that you may decide to change it as you gather information to support your opinion and begin drafting your paper.

Communications Handbook
H E L P

See Evaluating the Credibility of Sources; Taking Notes and Documenting Sources.

6. **Search for support.** Since your thesis is an opinion, not a cut-and-dried fact, your readers expect you to back it up with reasons and evidence. Your reasons, which serve as the major points or claims of your essay, explain *why* you believe each of the elements you've chosen helps reveal the work's theme or meaning. Evidence for each of your reasons consists of ideas, quotations, and details from or about the work. Most evidence comes from the work itself (the *primary source*), but some may come from *secondary sources* such as books and articles about the work or its author.

Thesis Statement: In Sonnet 30, Edmund Spenser's imagery underscores his theme—that the speaker and his love are in direct opposition to each other.

Major Point: Spenser uses images of fire and ice, of hot and cold.

Evidence to Prove Major Point: In line 1, Spenser says, "My love is like to ice, and I to fire." In lines 5–6, he says, "Or how comes it that my exceeding heat / Is not delayed by her heart frozen cold."

Strategies for Elaboration: Gathering Support

Use the following strategies to gather the information you'll need to support your thesis statement.

- Read or examine the work again with your thesis statement and major points in mind.
- Be sure to copy quotations exactly. For a written work, include the page numbers for quotations from a work of fiction or the line numbers for quotations from a work of poetry.
- If you draw on secondary sources, avoid plagiarism by noting the author, title, and date and place of publication so that you can credit your sources.
- Review your notes to make sure that all your evidence is directly related to your thesis statement.

7. **Get organized.** The easier your ideas are to follow, the more likely your readers will accept them. To organize your material, look again at your thesis statement and your main points. Assessing the kinds of details you've chosen to support your thesis can help you choose a sensible order for your ideas.

- If you're focusing on diction and imagery, you might group related ideas in **logical order,** with points about diction in one group and points about imagery in a second group.

- For a thesis on character, you might arrange examples in **chronological order** to show how a character changes during the story. Or you could use **order of importance,** moving from your most important point to your least important one (or vice versa).

- If you're **comparing and contrasting** two works, you could treat each of the elements of one work first and then turn to those of the other work, or you could alternate between the works as you discuss each element.

Communications Handbook
H E L P

See Proofreading.

■ *Evaluation Criteria*

An effective interpretive essay

1. *includes an introduction that identifies the title and author (or artist or director) of the work and gives necessary background information about it*
2. *includes a clear and precisely worded thesis statement*
3. *identifies major points that support the thesis*
4. *for each major point, gives ample, specific, and relevant supporting evidence*
5. *is clearly and consistently organized*
6. *has a conclusion that reinforces the thesis of the essay*

Language Workshop
H E L P

Literary present:
page 279.

Revision
S T R A T E G I E S

Does your conclusion round
out your essay smoothly? If
not, add a sentence or two
using different forms of the
key words in your thesis
statement. Ask a writing
partner to give feedback on
your conclusion.

Drafting

1. **The introduction: setting the stage.** In your introduction, identify the work's title and author or artist (for a film, the title and either the director or the leading actor or both), and state your thesis. Provide just enough background information about a story or poem or movie so that your readers will be able to follow your ideas, but avoid summarizing the entire work. Remember that your readers are primarily interested in your insights about the work. If you are interpreting a piece of art, describe carefully in your introduction exactly what you see in the painting. Help your reader see the work too.

2. **The body: building your case.** As you develop the body of your essay, take one or more paragraphs to state each of your major points and to present the evidence that supports it. Use quotations from a literary work where they help you make a point especially well.

3. **The conclusion: wrapping it up.** Create a satisfying conclusion by stepping back once again to the focused overview you presented in your introduction. Don't just summarize your major points; instead, restate your thesis in a way that echoes the ideas in your introduction and provides your essay with a satisfying, forceful closure.

Evaluating and Revising

As you read your or your partner's draft, evaluate these points:

- Is there enough background information about the work so that the reader can follow the ideas?

- Does the thesis statement make the focus clear?

- Is there enough evidence to make the thesis convincing? Are the supporting details directly related to the thesis?

- Does the ending tie the ideas together and reinforce the thesis?

SENSE THROUGH TENSE: THE LITERARY PRESENT

When you talk or write about literature or film or art, you should use what is called the **literary present.** Thus, do not say "In Act V Lady Macbeth tried to wash the blood from her hands." Instead, say

"In Act V Lady Macbeth **tries** to wash the blood from her hands."

The present tense is used because, in the world of literature, Lady Macbeth is forever and always washing that blood from her hands. In the same way, you would not say of the beautiful miniature on page 218: "The young man sat amid devouring flames." Instead you would say

"The young man **sits** amid devouring flames."

Forever and always, that young man will be staring out from the burning flames. When you write about a writer's purpose or technique, you don't say "In Sonnet 75, Spenser's speaker asserted the eternal nature of his love." Instead, because the speaker in the sonnet will forever be asserting the nature of his love, you write

"In Sonnet 75, Spenser's speaker **asserts** the eternal nature of his love."

Here's an important distinction to keep in mind: When you quote directly from a work, use the same tense the author uses, whatever it may be. However, when you paraphrase the writer's ideas or draw your own conclusions about the work, use the literary present.

ORIGINAL (*past tense*)	One day I **wrote** her name upon the strand, But **came** the waves and **washèd** it away.

—Edmund Spenser, Sonnet 75

PARAPHRASE (*literary present*)	The speaker in Edmund Spenser's Sonnet 75 **writes** his beloved's name in the sand, but the waves **erase** it.
CONCLUSION (*literary present*)	In line 5 of Sonnet 75, Spenser **uses** the word *vain* in two different senses: *conceited* and *fruitlessly.*

Writer's Workshop Follow-Up: Proofreading

Look back at the interpretive essay you wrote for the Writer's Workshop beginning on page 275. Have you used the literary present correctly? Check to make sure that in direct quotations you've used the same tense the writer used. Then, check again, changing any verbs in your paraphrases of the work and in your own conclusions to the literary present. You might begin by focusing on one or two paragraphs: Circle each verb, and determine whether its tense is correct in that context.

Technology HELP

See Language Workshop CD-ROM. *Key word entry: verb tenses.*

Language Handbook HELP

See Tenses and Their Uses, pages 1225–1226.

Try It Out

Change the verbs that should be in the literary present in the following sentences.

1. The speaker in Spenser's Sonnet 75 proposed to immortalize his beloved's virtues.

2. Twice the speaker had written her name in the sand, and twice the waves erased her name.

3. Protesting, the woman pointed out that she herself "shall like to this decay."

4. The speaker insisted that the woman "shall live by fame."

Reading for Life

Reading a Consumer Report

Situation

A Renaissance person might have written a sonnet for someone he or she loved, but you've decided to give a practical gift. You want to make sure you get the best quality at a price you can afford, so you consult a product review in a magazine or on-line. As you read, apply these strategies in order to **evaluate the data** and **make a decision.**

Strategies

Notice how the report is presented.

- It may consist of running text, a chart or other graphic display, or both.

Recognize the criteria used in the evaluation.

- If there is a chart, the criteria may be indicated in the title as well as in the column headings.
- Consider other criteria— your special requirements or those of the person you're buying the gift for.

Interpret abbreviations.

- Some abbreviations may be self-explanatory (such as *P* for "poor" and *E* for "excellent"). Others may be explained in footnotes.

Recognize the structure of the comparison.

- Notice how the items are arranged—for example, from best to worst or from most expensive to least expensive.

Key no.	Brand	Price	Score	Fit	Features	Construction	Claimed volume	Books held
			0 P F G VG E 100					
1	RAYtote	$48		■ (M,L)	■		2200 cu. in.	59
2	Lugger	45		■ (S,M,L)	■	◻	1670	49
3	Rugged Gear	50		◻ (M,L)	◻	◻	2200	48
4	Mountain Climber	42		■ (M,L)	■		1700	52
5	Alpine Able	29		▨ (S,M)	◻		1875	52
6	Eagle's Peak Sierra with Lining	50		▨ (S,M)	◻		1500	49
7	Heavy Hiker	48		■ (S,M)	◻	■	1874	50
8	Total Tote	38		▨ (S,M)	▨	■	1586	47
9	Trail Tough	33		▨ (S,M)	◻	■	1910	53
10	Eagle's Peak Sierra	40		▨ (S,M)	◻	■	1500	49

■ Excellent ◻ Very good ▨ Good ▧ Fair ☐ Poor

Check other sources.

- In stores, read information provided by the manufacturer. Also read product descriptions in other print and electronic sources. Take notes and compare this information with what you find in a consumer report.

Using the Strategies

Answer these questions about the chart above.

1. In this chart from a product review of backpacks, what are the criteria for comparison?
2. What do the abbreviations *S*, *M*, and *L* stand for?
3. What can you conclude about quality in relation to price?
4. Which product would be a good choice if you were looking for a compact but sturdy pack for short hikes?
5. Which product presumably gives you the most room at the lowest price?

Extending the Strategies

- Identify a product you are interested in purchasing, and investigate it in a consumer report. Describe specific criteria you want your purchase to meet.
- Identify other specific sources of information you might check before choosing a particular product.

Collection 4

UNDER A HAND ACCURSED

Shakespeare

Dante

Fate has given this man a spirit
Which is always pressing onwards, beyond control,
And whose mad striving overleaps
All joys of the earth between pole and pole.
Him shall I drag through the wilds of life
And through the flats of meaninglessness,
I shall make him flounder and gape and stick
And to tease his insatiableness
Hang meat and drink in the air before his watering lips;
In vain he will pray to slake his inner thirst,
And even had he not sold himself to the devil
He would be equally accursed.

—Johann Wolfgang von Goethe, *from Faust*
(German, 1749–1832)

(Background) Orson Welles in his film production of *Macbeth* (1948).

The Renaissance Theater

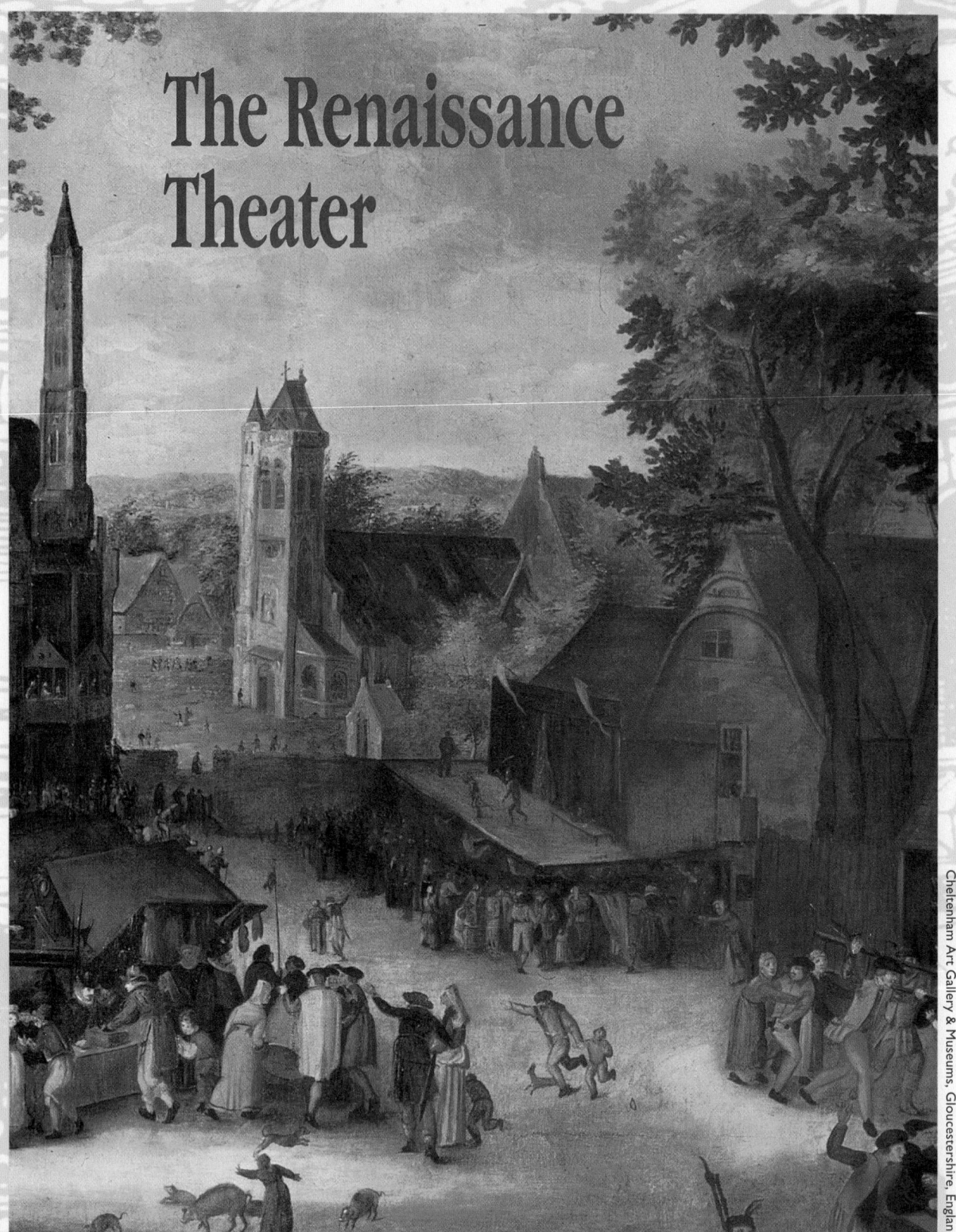

A Flemish Fair (detail) (late 16th to early 17th century) by David Vinckboons.

Drama as Teacher: The Forerunners

Even before the Renaissance, the English had been writing and performing plays for several centuries. Some scholars believe that medieval drama evolved from church ceremonies such as the dialogue songs performed at Easter Eve services. In these tiny playlets, three women would appear at a door representing the tomb of Christ and guarded by an angel. The angel would ask in Latin, "Whom do you seek?" and then he would announce the Resurrection.

From this obscure beginning, drama moved out of the churches and into the marketplaces of towns. There, in the 1300s and 1400s, various workers' guilds cooperated in staging cycles of plays that dramatized the whole history of the human race as then understood: its creation by God, its fall through the wiles of Satan, its life in Old Testament times, its redemption by Christ, and its final judgment at the end of the world. Parts of four cycles of these plays have been preserved, and they are named after the towns where they probably originated: York, Chester, Coventry, and Wakefield. Gradually, the plays became less religious, often relying on *deus ex machina* (an artificial device arbitrarily used to resolve a plot), and comedy was incorporated into them. The wife of Noah, for instance, makes a great fuss about entering the ark and is carried kicking and screaming aboard. Comic scenes like this one provide an early example of English skill in mixing the comic with the serious in drama. The most notable play of the period just before the Renaissance is *Everyman,* based on a Dutch original (see page 451).

Several kinds of plays, then, were written and produced before the Renaissance: **miracle** and **mystery plays** that taught people stories from the Bible and saints' legends; **moralities** that taught people how to live and die; and, starting in the early 1500s, a new kind of play called an **interlude.** Interludes were one-act plays, some of them indistinguishable from moralities, others rowdy and farcical. With the interludes the playwrights stopped being anonymous. Even before the new humanist learning came in, there were strong dramatic traditions that the great Renaissance playwrights knew about.

Globe Playhouse (detail) (c. 1599–1613) by C. Walter Hodges.

Representation of a Mystery Play (detail) (1825) by David Jee.

By permission of the British Library, London.

KEY

a   Main entrance
b   The yard
c   Entrance to lowest gallery
d   Entrance to staircase and upper galleries
e   Corridor serving the different sections of the middle gallery
f   Middle gallery ("Twopenny Rooms")
g   "Gentlemen's Rooms" or "Lords' Rooms"
h   The stage
j   The hanging being put up round the stage
k   The "hell" under the stage
l   The stage trap, leading down to the hell
m   Stage doors
n   Curtained "place behind the stage"
o   Gallery above the stage, used as required sometimes by musicians, sometimes by spectators, and often as part of the play
p   Backstage area (the tiring house)
q   Tiring-house door
r   Dressing rooms
s   Wardrobe and storage
t   The hut housing the machine for lowering enthroned gods, etc., to the stage
u   The "heavens"
w   Hoisting the playhouse flag

Old Traditions, New Theaters

By the mid–sixteenth century, the art of drama in England was three centuries old, but the idea of housing it in a permanent building was new. Even after theaters had been built, plays were still regularly performed in improvised spaces when acting companies toured the provinces or presented their plays in the large houses of royalty and nobility.

In 1576, James Burbage, the father of Shakespeare's partner and fellow actor Richard Burbage, built the first public theater and called it, appropriately, the Theater. Shortly thereafter, a second playhouse, called the Curtain, was erected. Both of these were in a northern suburb of London, where they would not offend the staid residents of London proper. Then came the Rose, the Swan, the Fortune, the Globe, the Red Bull, and the Hope— far more public theaters than in any other European capital.

The Globe: "This Wooden O"

The Globe is the most famous of the public theaters because the company that Shakespeare belonged to owned it. Many of his plays received their first performances there. It was built out of timbers salvaged from the Theater, which was demolished in 1599. Unfortunately, the plans for the Globe have not survived, though there still exist old, panoramic drawings of London in which its exterior is pictured. But the most important sources of information about the theater's structure are the plays themselves, with their stage directions and other clues.

Most scholars now accept as accurate the reconstruction of the Globe published by C. Walter Hodges, whose drawing appears on this page. Notice that the theater has three main parts: the building proper, the stage, and the tiring house, or backstage area, with the flag flying from its peak to indicate that there will be a performance that day.

Globe Playhouse
(c. 1599–1613) by
C. Walter Hodges.

A wooden structure three stories high, the building proper surrounded a spacious inner yard open to the sky. It was probably a sixteen-sided polygon. Any structure with that many sides would appear circular, so it is not surprising that Shakespeare referred to the Globe as "this wooden O" in his play *Henry V.* There were probably only two entrances to the building, one for the public and one for the theater company. But there may have been another public door used as an exit, because when the Globe burned down in 1613, the crowd escaped quickly and safely.

General admission to the theater cost one penny; this entitled a spectator to be a groundling, which meant he or she could stand in the yard. Patrons paid a little more to mount up into the galleries, where there were seats and a better view of the stage. The most expensive seats were chairs set right on the stage along its two sides. People who wanted to be conspicuous rented them, though they must have been a great nuisance to the rest of the audience and the actors. A public theater held a surprisingly large number of spectators—three thousand, according to two contemporary accounts. Since the spectators must have been squeezed together, it is no wonder that the authorities always closed the theaters during plague epidemics.

Up Close and Personal

The stage jutted halfway out into the yard, so that the actors were in much closer contact with the audience than actors are in modern theaters. Thus, every tiny nuance of an actor's performance could affect the audience. The actors were highly trained, and they could sing, dance, declaim, wrestle, fence, clown, roar, weep, and whisper. Large, sensational effects were also plentiful. Spectators loved to see witches or devils emerge through the trapdoor in the stage, which everybody pretended led down to Hell, just as everybody pretended that the ceiling over part of the stage was the Heavens. This ceiling was painted with elaborate suns, moons, and stars, and it contained a trapdoor through which angels, gods, and spirits could be lowered on a wire and even flown over the other actors' heads.

Behind the Scenes

The third part of the theater was the tiring (from *tire,* an archaic form of "attire") house, a tall building that contained machinery and dressing rooms and that provided a two-story back wall for the stage. Hodges's drawing of the Globe shows that this wall contained a gallery above and a curtained space below. The gallery had multiple purposes, depending on what play was being performed: Spectators could sit there, musicians could perform there, or parts of the play could be acted there—as if on balconies, towers, hills, and the like. The curtained area below the gallery was used mainly for "discoveries" of things prepared in advance and hidden from the audience until the proper time. In Shakespeare's *Merchant of Venice,* for example, the curtain is drawn to reveal three small chests, one of which hides the heroine's picture. Apparently, this curtained area

Globe Theater at Bankside (detail) (17th century). Watercolor.

© British Museum, London.

was too small, too shallow, and too far out of the sight of some spectators to be used as a performance space. If a performer were "discovered" behind the curtains (as Marlowe's Dr. Faustus is discovered in his study), he would quickly move out onto the stage to be seen and heard better. When large properties such as thrones, beds, desks, and so on were pushed through the curtains onto the stage, the audience would know at once that the action was taking place indoors. When the action shifted to the outdoors, the property could be pulled back behind the curtain.

The Power of Make-Believe

Renaissance audiences took for granted that the theater cannot show "reality": Whatever happens on the stage is make-believe. When the people in the audience saw actors carrying lanterns, they knew it was night, even though the sun was shining brightly overhead. Often, instead of seeing a scene, they heard it described, as when Shakespeare has a character exclaim over a sunrise,

> But look, the morn in russet mantle clad
> Walks o'er the dew of yon high eastward hill.

—Hamlet, Act I, Scene 1, lines 166–167

When a forest setting was called for, there was no painted scenery imitating real trees, bushes, flowers, and so on. Instead, a few bushes and small trees might be pushed onto the stage, and then the actors spoke lines that evoked images in the spectators' minds. In *As You Like It,* Rosalind simply looks around and announces, "Well, this is the forest of Arden." As the theatrical historian Gerald Bentley put it, Renaissance drama was "a drama of persons, not a drama of places."

Pomp and Pageantry

The scenery may have been kept to a minimum, but the theaters themselves were ornate. The interiors were painted brightly, with many decorations, and the space at the rear of the stage could be covered with colorful tapestries or hangings. Costumes were rich, elaborate, and expensive. The manager-producer Philip Henslowe once paid twenty pounds (then an enormous sum) for a single cloak for one of his actors to wear. Henslowe's lists of theatrical properties mention chariots, fountains, dragons, beds, tents, thrones, booths, and wayside crosses, among other things.

The audience also enjoyed the processions—religious, royal, military—that occurred in many plays. These would enter the stage from one door, cross the stage, and then exit by the other door. A few quick costume changes as the actors passed through the tiring house could double and triple the apparent number of people in a procession.

Music Most Eloquent

When people went to the London theater, they expected not only to see a tragedy or comedy acted but also to hear music, both vocal and instrumental. Trumpets announced the beginning of the play and important arrivals and departures within the play. High up in the gallery, musicians played between acts and at other appropriate times during the performance. And scattered throughout most of the plays, especially the comedies, were songs.

The songs in Shakespeare's plays are the best of this kind that have come down to us, for Shakespeare excelled in lyric and in dramatic poetry. He included a great variety of songs in his plays: sad, happy, comic, thoughtful songs, each one adapted to the play and scene in which it occurs and to the character who performs it. Some of the songs advance the dramatic action, some help establish the mood of a scene, and some reveal character. Like this invitation to love (from the comedy *Twelfth Night*), all of these songs are fresh and spontaneous, not contrived and artificial.

> O mistress mine, where are you roaming?
> O, stay and hear, your true love's coming,
>   That can sing both high and low.
> Trip no further, pretty sweeting;
> Journeys end in lovers meeting,
>   Every wise man's son doth know . . .
>
> What is love? 'tis not hereafter;
> Present mirth hath present laughter;
>   What's to come is still unsure.
> In delay there lies no plenty;
> Then come kiss me, sweet and twenty;
> Youth's a stuff will not endure.

Lady Masquer (detail) (c. 1610) by Inigo Jones.

Unfortunately, most of the original music for Shakespeare's songs has been lost. But just as the plays themselves have inspired many composers of music for opera, orchestra, and ballet, so have the songs from the plays been set to music right up to the present.

Varying the Venue

The acting companies performed in two other kinds of spaces: in the great halls of castles and manor houses, and in indoor, fully covered theaters in London.

For performances in a great hall, a theater company must have had a portable stage. In these buildings, the usual entertainment was a bear being attacked by dogs. The bear pits were vile places, but their temporary stages could easily accommodate any play except for scenes requiring the use of Heavens overhanging the stage.

Something like this stage may also have been used in private theaters like the Blackfriars, which Shakespeare's company, the King's Men, acquired in 1608. One great advantage of the Blackfriars—a disused monastery that was entirely roofed over—was that the company could perform there in cold weather and, since artificial lighting always had to be used, at night. Thus, the King's Men could put on plays all during the year, increasing profits for the shareholders, among them Shakespeare.

(Below) Aerial view of the new Globe Theatre on London's South Bank.

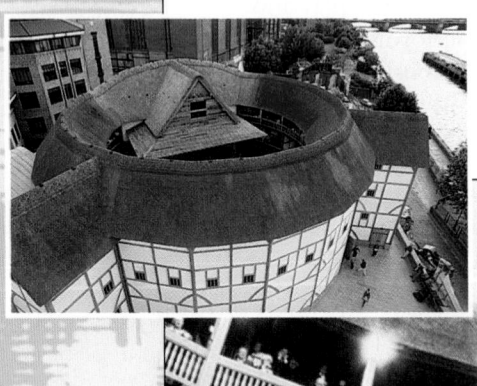

(Below) A 1997 production of Shakespeare's *Henry V* at the new Globe Theatre, London.

William Shakespeare

(1564–1616)

Every literate person has heard of Shakespeare, the author of more than 36 remarkable plays and more than 150 poems. Over the centuries, these literary works have made such a deep impression on the human race that all sorts of fancies, legends, and theories have been invented about their author. There are even those who say that somebody other than Shakespeare wrote the works that bear his name, although these deluded people cannot agree on who, among a dozen candidates, this other author actually was. Such speculation is based on the misconception that little is known about Shakespeare's life; in fact, Shakespeare's life is better documented than the life of any other dramatist of the time except perhaps for Ben Jonson, a writer who seems almost modern in the way he publicized himself. Jonson was an honest, blunt, and outspoken man who knew Shakespeare well; for a time the two dramatists wrote for the same theatrical company, and Shakespeare even acted in Jonson's plays. Often niggardly in his judgments of other writers, Jonson published a poem praising Shakespeare, asserting that he was superior to all Greek, Roman, and English dramatists, predicting that he would be "not of an age, but for all time." Jonson's judgment is now commonly accepted, and his prophecy has come true.

The Years in Stratford-on-Avon

Shakespeare was born in Stratford-on-Avon, a historic and prosperous market town in Warwickshire, and was christened in the parish church there on April 26, 1564. His father was John Shakespeare, a merchant once active in the town government; his mother—born Mary Arden—came from a prominent family in the county. Presumably, for seven years or so, William attended the Stratford grammar school, where he obtained an excellent education in Latin, the Bible, and English composition. (The students had to translate Latin works into English and then turn them back into Latin.) After leaving school, he may have been apprenticed to a butcher, but because he shows in his plays very detailed knowledge of many different crafts and trades, speculators have proposed a number of different occupations that he could have had. At eighteen, Shakespeare married Anne Hathaway, the twenty-six-year-old daughter of a farmer living near Stratford. They had three children, a daughter named Susanna and twins named Hamnet and Judith.

Flower Portrait of William Shakespeare (detail) by an unknown artist. Oil.

From the Royal Shakespeare Company Collection with the permission of the Governors of the Royal Shakespeare Theater, London.

Anne Hathaway's cottage in
Shottery, a mile outside Stratford.

We don't know how the young Shakespeare
supported his family, but according to tradition,
he taught school for a few years. The two
daughters grew up and married; the son died
when he was eleven.

Off to London

How did Shakespeare first become interested
in the theater? Presumably, by seeing plays.
We know that traveling acting companies frequently visited Stratford, and we assume that he
attended their performances and that he also
went to the nearby city of Coventry, where a
famous cycle of religious plays was put on every
year. But to be a dramatist, one had to be in
London, where the theater was flourishing
in the 1580s. Exactly when Shakespeare left
his family and moved to London (there is no
evidence that his wife was ever in the city) is
uncertain; scholars say that he probably arrived
there in 1587. It is certain that he was busy
and successful in the London theater by 1592,
when a fellow dramatist named Robert Greene
attacked him in print and ridiculed a passage in
his early play *Henry VI*. Greene, a down-and-out
Cambridge graduate, warned other university
men then writing plays to beware of this mere
actor who was writing plays—an "upstart crow
beautified with our feathers." Greene died of
dissipation just as his ill-natured attack was being
published, but a friend of his named Henry
Chettle immediately apologized in print to
Shakespeare and commended Shakespeare's acting and writing abilities and his personal honesty.

From 1592 on, there is ample documentation
of Shakespeare's life and works. We know
where he lived in London, at least approximately when his plays were produced and
printed, and even how he spent his money.
From 1594 until his retirement in about 1613,
he was a member of one company, which also
included the great tragic actor Richard Burbage
and the popular clown Will Kemp. Although
actors and others connected with the theater
had a very low status legally, in practice they
enjoyed the patronage of noblemen and even
royalty. It is a mistake to think of Shakespeare
as an obscure actor who somehow wrote great
plays; he was well known even as a young man.
He first became famous as the author of a best-
seller, an erotic narrative poem called *Venus and
Adonis* (1593). This poem, as well as the more
serious poem *The Rape of Lucrece* (1594), was
dedicated to a rich and extravagant young
nobleman, the earl of Southampton. The dedication of *Lucrece* suggests that Shakespeare and
his wealthy patron were on very friendly terms.

Emma Thompson (left) in Kenneth Branagh's film
production of *Much Ado About Nothing* (1993).

Shakespeare's Early Plays:
Variety and Prosperity

Among Shakespeare's earliest plays are the
following, with the generally but not universally

accepted dates of their first performances: *Richard III* (1592–1593), a chronicle or history play about a deformed usurper who became king of England; *The Comedy of Errors* (1592–1593), a rowdy farce about mistaken identity, based on a Latin play; *Titus Andronicus* (1593–1594), a blood-and-thunder tragedy full of rant and atrocities; *The Taming of the Shrew, The Two Gentlemen of Verona,* and *Love's Labor's Lost* (all 1593–1595), three agreeable comedies; and *Romeo and Juliet* (1594–1595), a poetic tragedy about ill-fated lovers—the Shakespeare play still most frequently taught in schools. The extraordinary thing about these plays is not so much their immense variety—each one is quite different from all the others—but the fact that they are all regularly revived and performed on stages all over the world today.

Years of Prosperity

By 1596, Shakespeare was beginning to prosper. He had his father apply to the Heralds' College for a coat of arms that the family could display, signifying that they were "gentlefolk," or people of high social standing. On Shakespeare's family crest is a falcon shaking a spear. To support this claim to gentility, Shakespeare bought New Place, a handsome house and grounds in Stratford, a place so commodious and elegant that the queen of England once stayed there after Shakespeare's daughter Susanna inherited it. Shakespeare also, in 1599, joined with a few other members of his company, now called the Lord Chamberlain's Men, to finance a new theater—the famous

Richard Easton and Hal Holbrook in *King Lear* (1993).

Globe—on the south side of the Thames. The "honey-tongued Shakespeare," as he was called in a book about English literature published in 1598, was now earning money as a playwright, an actor, and a shareholder in a theater. By 1600, Shakespeare was regularly associating with members of the aristocracy, and six of his plays had been given command performances at the court of Queen Elizabeth.

During the last years of Elizabeth I's reign, Shakespeare completed his cycle of plays about England during the Wars of the Roses: *Richard II* (1595–1596), both parts of *Henry IV* (1596–1597), and *Henry V* (1599). Also in this period he wrote the tragedy *Julius Caesar* (1599)—and the comedies that are most frequently performed today: *A Midsummer Night's Dream* (1595–1596), *The Merchant of Venice* (1596–1597), *Much Ado About Nothing* (1598–1599), *As You Like It* (1598–1600), and *Twelfth Night* (1600–1601). And finally at this time he wrote or rewrote *Hamlet* (1600–1601), the tragedy that, of all his tragedies, has provoked the most varied and controversial interpretations from critics, scholars, and actors. Shakespeare indeed prospered under Queen Elizabeth; according to an old tradition, she asked him to write *The Merry Wives of Windsor* (1600–1601) because she

Mel Gibson and Helena Bonham-Carter in Franco Zeffirelli's film production of *Hamlet* (1990).

Christopher Walken (top) and Raul Julia in *Othello,* New York Shakespeare Festival (1991).

wanted to see the merry, fat old knight Sir John Falstaff (of the Henry plays) in love.

Shakespeare prospered even more under Elizabeth's successor, King James of Scotland. Fortunately for Shakespeare's company, as it turned out, James's royal entry into London in 1603 had to be postponed for several months because the plague was raging in the city. While waiting for the epidemic to subside, the royal court stayed in various palaces outside London. Shakespeare's company took advantage of this situation and, since the city theaters were closed, performed several plays for the court and the new king. Shakespeare's plays delighted James, for he loved literature and was starved for pleasure after the grim experience of ruling Scotland for many years. He immediately took the company under his

patronage, renamed them the King's Men, gave them patents to perform anywhere in the realm, provided them with special clothing for state occasions, increased their salaries, and appointed their chief members, including Shakespeare, to be grooms of the royal chamber. All this patronage brought such prosperity to Shakespeare that he was able to make some very profitable real estate investments in Stratford and London.

Shakespeare's "Tragic Period": Beyond Experience

In the early years of the seventeenth century, while his financial affairs were flourishing and everything was apparently going very well for him, Shakespeare wrote his greatest tragedies: *Hamlet* (already mentioned), *Othello* (1601–1602), *King Lear* (1605), *Macbeth* (1605–1606), and *Antony and Cleopatra* (1606–1607). Because these famous plays are so preoccupied with evil, violence, and death, some critics feel that Shakespeare must have been unhappy and depressed when he wrote them. Moreover, such critics find even the comedies he wrote at this time more sour than sweet: *All's Well That Ends Well* (1602–1603) and *Measure for Measure* (1604). And so, instead of paying tribute to Shakespeare's powerful imagination, which is everywhere evident, these critics invent a "tragic period" in Shakespeare's biography, and they search for personal crises in his private life. When they cannot find these agonies, they invent them. To be sure, in 1607, an actor named Edmund Shakespeare, who may well have been William's younger brother, died in London. But by 1607, Shakespeare's alleged "tragic period" was almost over. It is quite wrong to assume a one-to-one

Glenn Close and Alan Bates in Franco Zeffirelli's film production of *Hamlet* (1990).

correspondence between writers' biographies and their works, because writers must be allowed to imagine whatever they can. It is especially wrong in the case of a writer like Shakespeare, who did not write to express himself but to satisfy the patrons of the theater that he and his partners owned. Shake-

Denzel Washington in Kenneth Branagh's film production of *Much Ado About Nothing* (1993).

speare must have repeatedly given the audience just what it wanted; otherwise, he could not have made so much money from the theater. To insist that he had to experience and personally feel everything that he wrote about is absurd. He wrote about King Lear, who cursed his two monstrous daughters for treating him very badly; in contrast, what evidence there is suggests that he got along very well with his own two daughters. And so, instead of "tragic" we should think of the years 1600–1607 as glorious, because in them Shakespeare's productivity was at its peak. It seems very doubtful that a depressed person would write plays like these. In fact, they would likely make their creator feel exhilarated rather than sad.

The Last Years: Continued Diversity

In about 1610, Shakespeare decided that, having made a considerable sum from his plays and theatrical enterprises, he would retire to his handsome house in Stratford, a place he had never forgotten, though he seems to have kept his life there rather separate from his life in London. His retirement was not complete, for the records show that after he returned to Stratford he still took part in the management of the King's Men and their two theaters: the Globe, an octagonal building opened in 1599 and used for performances in good weather, and the Blackfriars, acquired in 1608 and used for indoor performances. Shakespeare's works in this period show no signs of diminished

creativity, except that in some years he wrote one play instead of the customary two, and they continue to illustrate the great diversity of his genius. Among them are the tragedies *Timon of Athens* (1607–1608) and *Coriolanus* (1607–1608) and five plays that have been variously classified as comedies, romances, or tragicomedies: *Pericles* (1607–1608), *Cymbeline* (1609–1610), *The Winter's Tale* (1610–1611), *The Tempest* (1611–1612), and *The Two Noble Kinsmen* (1612). His last English history play, *Henry VIII* (1613), contained a tribute to Queen Elizabeth — a somewhat tardy tribute, because, unlike most of the other poets of the day, Shakespeare did not praise her in print when she died in 1603. (Some scholars argue, on very little evidence, that he was an admirer of the earl of Essex, a former intimate of Elizabeth whom she had beheaded for rebellion.) During the first performance of *Henry VIII*, in June of 1613, the firing of the cannon at the end

Kenneth Branagh in his film production of *Henry V* (1989).

of Act I set the Globe on fire (it had a thatched roof), and it burned to the ground. Only one casualty is recorded: A bottle of ale had to be poured on a man whose breeches were burning. Fortunately, the company had the Blackfriars in which to perform until the Globe could be rebuilt and reopened in 1614.

Shakespeare's last recorded visit to London was made with his son-in-law Dr. John Hall in November 1614, though he may have gone down to the city afterward because he continued to own property there, including a building very near the Blackfriars Theater. Probably, though, he spent most of the last two years of his life at New Place, with his daughter Susanna Hall (and his granddaughter Elizabeth) living nearby. He died on April 23, 1616, and was buried under the floor of Stratford Church, with this epitaph warning posterity not to dig him up and transfer him to the graveyard outside the church—a common practice in those days to make room for newer corpses:

> Good friend, for Jesus' sake forbear
> To dig the dust enclosèd here!
> Blest be the man that spares these stones,
> And curst be he that moves my bones.

Patrick Stewart and Anjanue Ellis in *The Tempest,* New York Shakespeare Festival (1995).

Shakespeare's Genius: Imagination and "Soul"

What sort of man was Shakespeare? This is a very hard question to answer because he left no letters, diaries, or other private writings containing his personal views; instead, he left us plays, and in a good play the actors do not speak for the dramatist but for the

Laurence Olivier in his film production of *Henry V* (1944).

Trying to identify Shakespeare the man in his plays is like looking at a very dim portrait under glass: The more you peer at it, the more you see only yourself.

characters they are impersonating. We cannot, then, say that Shakespeare approved of evil because he created murderers or advocated religion because he created clergymen; we cannot say that he believed in fatalism because he created fatalists, or admired flattery because he created flatterers. All these would be naive, contradictory reactions to the plays. Shakespeare's characters represent such a vast range of human behavior and attitudes that they must be products of his careful observation and fertile imagination rather than extensions of himself. A critic named Desmond McCarthy once said that trying to identify Shakespeare the man in his plays is like looking at a very dim portrait under glass: The more you peer at it, the more you see only yourself.

A Complete Man of the Theater

One thing is certain: Shakespeare was a complete man of the theater who created works specifically for his own acting company and his own stage. He had, for instance, to provide good parts in every play for the principal performers in the company, including the come-

Mel Gibson in Franco Zeffirelli's film production of *Hamlet* (1990).

dians acting in tragedies. Since there were no actresses, he had to limit the number of female parts in his plays and create them in such a way that they could readily be taken by boys. For instance, although there are many fathers in the plays, there are very few mothers: While boys could be taught to flirt and play shy, acting maternally would be difficult for them. Several of Shakespeare's young women characters disguise themselves as young men early in Act I— an easy solution to the problem of boys playing girls' parts. Shakespeare also had to provide the words for songs because theatergoers expected singing in every play; furthermore, the songs had to be devised so that they would exhibit the talents of particular actors with good voices. Since many of the plays contain many characters, and since there were a limited number of actors in the company, Shakespeare had to arrange for doubling and even tripling of roles: That is, a single actor would have to perform more than one part. Since, of course, an actor could impersonate only one character at a time, Shakespeare had to plan his scenes carefully, so that nobody would ever have to be on stage in two different roles at the same time. A careful study of the plays shows that Shakespeare handled very masterfully all these technical problems of dramaturgy.

Never Out of Print

Although the plays are primarily performance scripts, from earliest times the public has wanted to read them as well as see them staged. In every generation, people have felt that the plays contain so much wisdom, so much knowledge of human nature, so much remarkable poetry that they need to be pondered in private as well as enjoyed in public. Most readers have agreed with what the poet John Dryden said about Shakespeare's "soul": The man who wrote the plays may be elusive, but he was obviously a great genius whose lofty imagination is matched by his sympathy for all

Dear Miss Disdain (Beatrice from *Much Ado About Nothing*) (late 18th to early 19th century) by Louise Jopling.

Glenn Close and Mel Gibson in Franco Zeffirelli's film production of *Hamlet* (1990).

kinds of human behavior. Reading the plays, then, is a rewarding experience in itself; it is also an excellent preparation for seeing them performed on stage or on film.

Shakespeare's contemporaries were so eager to read his plays that enterprising publishers did everything possible, including stealing them, to make them available. Of course, the company generally tried to keep the plays unpublished because they did not want them performed by rival companies. Even so, eighteen plays were published in small books called quartos before Shakespeare's partners collected them together and published them after his death. This collection, known as the "first folio" because of its large size, was published in 1623. Surviving copies of this folio are regarded as valuable treasures today. But, of course, the general reader need not consult any of the original texts of Shakespeare because his works never go out of print; they are always available in many different languages and many different formats. The plays that exist in two different versions (one in a quarto and one in the folio) have provided scholars with endless matter for speculation about what Shakespeare actually intended the correct text to be. Indeed, every aspect of Shakespeare has been, and continues to be, thoroughly studied and written about by literary and historical scholars, theater and film people, experts in many fields, and amateurs of every stripe. No wonder that he is mistakenly regarded as a great mystery.

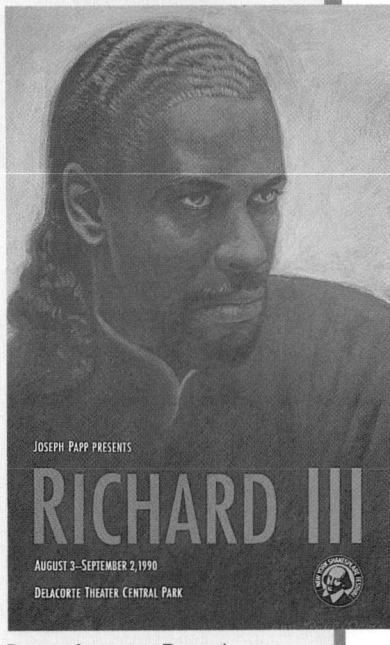

Poster featuring Denzel Washington in *Richard III* at the New York Shakespeare Festival (1990).

Laurence Olivier and Anna Calder-Marshall in the Mobil Showcase Network production of *King Lear* (1984).

The Tragedy of Macbeth:
The Sources of the Play

Orson Welles in his film production of *Macbeth* (1948).

Poster for *Macbeth,* featuring Raul Julia, at the Public Theater, New York (1990).

S hakespeare's play *Macbeth* conforms to the general rule of Renaissance tragedies, in which the drama had to be about real people whose deeds are recorded in history. (Renaissance comedies, on the other hand, concerned the imaginary doings of fictitious characters.) Shakespeare took the main events of Macbeth's career as king of Scotland (1040–1057) from Raphael Holinshed's *Chronicles of England, Scotland, and Ireland* (1577), the book that provided Shakespeare with historical material for many of his plays. But there are striking differences between his account of Macbeth and Holinshed's. The historical Macbeth had a much more legitimate claim to King Duncan's throne than Shakespeare's Macbeth did. The historical Macbeth gained the throne with the help of other nobles dissatisfied with King Duncan, and he ruled rather successfully. In contrast, Shakespeare's Macbeth has no supporters except his wife, whose strong and ambitious nature Shakespeare develops from a brief statement in the history. And in the play, the reign of Macbeth and his wife brings nothing but violence and disaster to Scotland.

© 1989 Paul Davis. Courtesy of the artist.

A witch placing a crown on Macbeth's head in the Faux-Real production of *Htebcam* (1994) ("Macbeth" spelled backward).

One explanation for these changes to Holinshed's story is that Shakespeare wanted to explore—from a safe distance—the events and attitudes of his own time. Contemporary audiences have all but lost sight of the scandal that was a backdrop for the play: the Gunpowder Plot of 1605, in which several Catholic zealots plotted to blow up King James I and his Protestant Parliament. Garry Wills, a professor and political columnist, says that for its Elizabethan audience, *Macbeth* was a thriller. (For Wills, the Gunpowder Plot would compare to a plan to bomb the U.S. Capitol building during a presidential address.) The threat to an anointed king, and the perceived evil behind it, was relived in Macbeth's complete threat to the social order in a Scotland of the distant past.

Shakespeare altered his source text, in ways both small and large, in order to pay homage to his own king and country; his changes were

Ellen Terry as Lady Macbeth (detail) (1888–1889) by John Singer Sargent. Tate Gallery, London.

The three witches in Roman Polanski's film production of *Macbeth* (1971).

intended for an audience of his *particular* moment in history. If he ever saw it, *Macbeth* must have pleased King James, the patron of Shakespeare's company. Since James had recently survived the Gunpowder Plot, he was especially interested in attacks on kings. James always defended the idea that he ruled by divine right. Moreover, he was a Scot and claimed to be a direct descendant of Banquo, to whom the third witch says, "Thou shalt get kings, though thou be none." For these reasons, scholars have for a long time thought of *Macbeth* as a play written for a command performance at court, though there is absolutely no proof that it was. James refused to sit through long plays, and this royal shortcoming has even been used to explain the fact that *Macbeth* is one of Shakespeare's shortest plays.

We can also say that Shakespeare made many changes in Holinshed's story because he was much more interested in psychological truth than in historical fact. And in this sense, *Macbeth* is also about *real* people, men and women tempted by ambition and power, caught up in a web of wants and needs. In playing out these real feelings and desires, Shakespeare's Macbeth transcends the historical Macbeth and gives us a portrait and a play for all times. As the critic Sylvan Barnet notes, "When one reads or sees *Macbeth,* one cannot help feeling that one is experiencing a re-creation or representation of what a man is, in the present, even in the timeless."

The Banquet (detail) by an unknown artist, from Act III, Scene 4, of *Macbeth* at London's Princess Theatre (1853).

Victoria and Albert Museum, London.

Before You Read

MACBETH

Make the Connection

Crime and Consequence

Have you ever wondered how just one action—whether tremendous or trivial—might affect the entire course of your life? Could one selfish impulse lead to a chain of decisions you will reflect on with the greatest anguish? The seeds of tragedy often lie in the most insignificant or excusable actions. And though Shakespeare's tragic hero Macbeth does not commit petty or insignificant crimes, his great ambition and corrosive guilt compel our understanding.

In *Macbeth,* a brave and intelligent man deliberately murders one of his fellowmen—his friend, his kinsman, his guest, his king—and then he must immediately, as a consequence of his first murder, kill two other innocent men. After that, he cannot turn away from his evil course: It leads him to further appalling crimes and finally to disgrace, alienation, isolation, despair, violent death, and decapitation.

Quickwrite

In *Macbeth,* the hero's lust for power brings absolute destruction on himself and his family. Think of people in actual life and in fiction who are obsessed with power. What are the typical consequences of such extravagant ambition? Jot down your thoughts on these questions.

Elements of Literature

Tragedy

Macbeth is a **tragedy:** a kind of play in which human actions have inevitable consequences, in which the characters' bad deeds, errors, mistakes, and crimes are never forgiven or rectified. By contrast, the characters in a comedy do not live under this iron law of cause and effect; they can do whatever they please as long as they amuse their audience, and as long as the funny mess they have made is easily cleaned up at the end of the play. But in a tragedy, an ill-judged action will remorselessly lead to a catastrophe, usually but not necessarily a death or multiple deaths.

A **tragedy** is a literary work depicting serious events in which the main character, who is often high-ranking and dignified, comes to an unhappy end.

For more on Tragedy, see the Handbook of Literary Terms.

The Tragedy of Macbeth

William Shakespeare

CHARACTERS

Duncan, king of Scotland

Malcolm
Donalbain } his sons

Macbeth
Banquo
Macduff
Lennox
Ross } noblemen of Scotland
Menteith
Angus
Caithness

Fleance, son to Banquo

Siward, earl of Northumberland, general of the English forces

Young Siward, his son

Seyton, an officer attending on Macbeth

Son to Macduff

An English Doctor

A Scottish Doctor

A Porter

An Old Man

Three Murderers

Lady Macbeth

Lady Macduff

A Gentlewoman attending on Lady Macbeth

Hecate

Witches

Apparitions

Lords, Officers, Soldiers, Attendants, and Messengers

Setting: Scotland; England

From Roman Polanski's film production of *Macbeth* (1971).

ACT I

Scene 1. *An open place.*

Thunder and lightning. Enter three WITCHES.

First Witch.
    When shall we three meet again?
    In thunder, lightning, or in rain?
Second Witch.
    When the hurlyburly's done,
    When the battle's lost and won.
Third Witch.
5   That will be ere the set of sun.
First Witch.
    Where the place?
Second Witch.   Upon the heath.
Third Witch.
    There to meet with Macbeth.
First Witch.
    I come, Graymalkin.°
Second Witch.
    Paddock° calls.
Third Witch.   Anon!°
All.
10   Fair is foul, and foul is fair.
    Hover through the fog and filthy air.   [*Exeunt.*]

Scene 2. *A camp.*

Alarum within.° Enter KING DUNCAN, MALCOLM, DONALBAIN,
LENNOX*, with* ATTENDANTS, *meeting a bleeding* CAPTAIN.

King.
    What bloody man is that? He can report,
    As seemeth by his plight, of the revolt
    The newest state.
Malcolm.   This is the sergeant
    Who like a good and hardy soldier fought
5   'Gainst my captivity. Hail, brave friend!
    Say to the king the knowledge of the broil°
    As thou didst leave it.
Captain.   Doubtful it stood,
    As two spent swimmers, that do cling together
    And choke their art.° The merciless Macdonwald—
10   Worthy to be a rebel for to that
    The multiplying villainies of nature
    Do swarm upon him—from the Western Isles°
    Of kerns and gallowglasses° is supplied;
    And Fortune, on his damnèd quarrel smiling,
15   Showed like a rebel's whore: but all's too weak:
    For brave Macbeth—well he deserves that name—
    Disdaining Fortune, with his brandished steel,

? **2.** *This scene, played against thunder and lightning, sets the mood of the play. The witches might have made their appearance through the trapdoor on the stage. Thunder would have been produced by rolling cannonballs in the area above the stage. How could these actresses (actors in Shakespeare's day) convey a sense of menace?*

8. Graymalkin: the witches' attendant, a gray cat.

9. Paddock: toad. **Anon!:** Soon!

Alarum within: trumpets offstage.

6. broil: quarrel.

? **7.** *The captain is bloody and could be carried in or supported by others. How would he speak his lines?*

9. choke their art: hinder each other's ability to swim.

12. Western Isles: a region of West Scotland comprising the Outer Hebrides.

13. kerns and gallowglasses: lightly armed Irish soldiers and heavily armed soldiers.

"What bloody man is that?"

Which smoked with bloody execution,
Like valor's minion° carved out his passage
20 Till he faced the slave;
Which nev'r shook hands, nor bade farewell to him,
Till he unseamed him from the nave to th' chops,°
And fixed his head upon our battlements.

King.
O valiant cousin! Worthy gentleman!

Captain.
25 As whence the sun 'gins his reflection°
Shipwracking storms and direful thunders break,
So from that spring whence comfort seemed to come
Discomfort swells. Mark, King of Scotland, mark:
No sooner justice had, with valor armed,
30 Compelled these skipping kerns to trust their heels
But the Norweyan° lord, surveying vantage,°
With furbished arms and new supplies of men,
Began a fresh assault.

King.   Dismayed not this
Our captains, Macbeth and Banquo?

19. **minion:** favorite.

22. **unseamed . . . chops:** split him from navel to jaws.

? 23. *Notice how this horrible action is described by a messenger, not shown on stage. What did Macbeth do to the rebellious Macdonwald?*

25. **'gins his reflection:** rises.

31. **Norweyan:** Norwegian. **surveying vantage:** seeing an opportunity.

Captain.   Yes;

35 As° sparrows eagles, or the hare the lion.
    If I say sooth,° I must report they were
    As cannons overcharged with double cracks;
    So they doubly redoubled strokes upon the foe.
    Except° they meant to bathe in reeking wounds,
40 Or memorize another Golgotha,°
    I cannot tell—
    But I am faint; my gashes cry for help.

King.

    So well thy words become thee as thy wounds;
    They smack of honor both. Go get him surgeons.

                          [*Exit* CAPTAIN *attended.*]

[*Enter* ROSS *and* ANGUS.]

    Who comes here?
45 **Malcolm.**   The worthy Thane° of Ross.
    Lennox.

    What a haste looks through his eyes! So should he look
    That seems to° speak things strange.
Ross.   God save the king!
King.

    Whence cam'st thou, worthy thane?
Ross.   From Fife, great king;
    Where the Norweyan banners flout the sky
50 And fan our people cold.
    Norway himself,° with terrible numbers,
    Assisted by that most disloyal traitor
    The Thane of Cawdor, began a dismal conflict;
    Till that Bellona's bridegroom,° lapped in proof,°
55 Confronted him with self-comparisons,°
    Point against point, rebellious arm 'gainst arm,
    Curbing his lavish° spirit: and, to conclude,
    The victory fell on us.
King.   Great happiness!
Ross.   That now
    Sweno, the Norways' king, craves composition;°
60 Nor would we deign him burial of his men
    Till he disbursèd, at Saint Colme's Inch,°
    Ten thousand dollars to our general use.
King.

    No more that Thane of Cawdor shall deceive
    Our bosom interest:° go pronounce his present° death,
65 And with his former title greet Macbeth.
Ross.

    I'll see it done.
King.

    What he hath lost, noble Macbeth hath won.   [*Exeunt.*]

---

35. As: No more than.

? 35. *This line can be delivered in several ways. How do you imagine the captain speaks it?*

36. sooth: truth.

39. Except: unless.

40. memorize another Golgotha: make the place as memorable as Golgotha, where Christ was crucified.

? 44. *Duncan can be played in several ways: as a strong but aging king; as a frail old man; as a kind but foolish old man who doesn't understand what's going on. As the play goes on, decide how you interpret Duncan's character.*

45. Thane: Scottish title of nobility.

47. seems to: seems about to.

51. Norway himself: that is, the king of Norway.

54. Bellona's bridegroom: Bellona is the goddess of war. Macbeth, who is a great soldier, is called her mate. **lapped in proof:** clad in armor.

55. self-comparisons: countermovements.

57. lavish: insolent; rude.

59. composition: peace terms.

61. Saint Colme's Inch: island off the coast of Scotland.

64. bosom interest: heart's trust. **present:** immediate.

? 67. *As you read, notice how later events relate to the king's words. How would you have him say these lines?*

Scene 3. *A heath.*

Thunder. Enter the three WITCHES.

First Witch.
    Where hast thou been, sister?
Second Witch.
    Killing swine.
Third Witch.
    Sister, where thou?
First Witch.
    A sailor's wife had chestnuts in her lap,
    And mounched, and mounched, and mounched. "Give me,"
5   quoth I.
    "Aroint thee,° witch!" the rump-fed ronyon° cries.
    Her husband's to Aleppo gone, master o' th' *Tiger:*
    But in a sieve° I'll thither sail,
    And, like a rat without a tail,
10   I'll do, I'll do, and I'll do.
Second Witch.
    I'll give thee a wind.
First Witch.
    Th' art kind.
Third Witch.
    And I another.
First Witch.
    I myself have all the other;
15   And the very ports they blow,°
    All the quarters that they know
    I' th' shipman's card.°
    I'll drain him dry as hay:
    Sleep shall neither night nor day
20   Hang upon his penthouse lid;°
    He shall live a man forbid:°
    Weary sev'nights nine times nine
    Shall he dwindle, peak,° and pine:
    Though his bark cannot be lost,
25   Yet it shall be tempest-tossed.
    Look what I have.
Second Witch.
    Show me, show me.
First Witch.
    Here I have a pilot's thumb,
    Wracked as homeward he did come.

[*Drum within.*]

Third Witch.
30   A drum, a drum!
    Macbeth doth come.

---

6. Aroint thee: begone.
rump-fed ronyon: fat-rumped, scabby creature.
8. But . . . sieve: Witches were believed to have the power to sail in sieves.

15. ports they blow: harbors they blow into.

17. card: compass.

20. penthouse lid: eyelid.
21. forbid: cursed.

23. peak: grow pale.

All.

> The weird sisters, hand in hand,
> Posters° of the sea and land,
> Thus do go about, about:
> 35   Thrice to thine, and thrice to mine,
> And thrice again, to make up nine.
> Peace! The charm's wound up.

[*Enter* MACBETH *and* BANQUO.]

Macbeth.

> So foul and fair a day I have not seen.

Banquo.

> How far is't called to Forres?° What are these
> 40   So withered, and so wild in their attire,
> That look not like th' inhabitants o' th' earth,
> And yet are on't? Live you, or are you aught
> That man may question? You seem to understand me,
> By each at once her choppy° finger laying

33. Posters: travelers.

? 38. *What words is Macbeth echoing here? Why, given the weather, does Macbeth think the day is "fair"?*

39. Forres: a town in northeast Scotland and site of King Duncan's castle.

? 39. *What should Banquo do as he sees the witches? How should his voice change between the words* Forres *and* What?

44. choppy: chapped; sore.

"All hail, Macbeth! Hail to thee, Thane of Glamis!"

From the Stratford Festival production of *Macbeth* (1983).

45 Upon her skinny lips. You should° be women,
And yet your beards forbid me to interpret
That you are so.
Macbeth.   Speak, if you can: what are you?
First Witch.
All hail, Macbeth! Hail to thee, Thane of Glamis!
Second Witch.
All hail, Macbeth! Hail to thee, Thane of Cawdor!
Third Witch.
50 All hail, Macbeth, that shalt be king hereafter!
Banquo.
Good sir, why do you start, and seem to fear
Things that do sound so fair? I' th' name of truth,
Are ye fantastical, or that indeed
Which outwardly ye show? My noble partner
55 You greet with present grace and great prediction
Of noble having and of royal hope,
That he seems rapt withal:° to me you speak not.
If you can look into the seeds of time,
And say which grain will grow and which will not,
60 Speak then to me, who neither beg nor fear
Your favors nor your hate.
First Witch. Hail!
Second Witch. Hail!
Third Witch. Hail!
First Witch.
65 Lesser than Macbeth, and greater.
Second Witch.
Not so happy,° yet much happier.
Third Witch.
Thou shalt get° kings, though thou be none.
So all hail, Macbeth and Banquo!
First Witch.
Banquo and Macbeth, all hail!
Macbeth.
70 Stay, you imperfect° speakers, tell me more:
By Sinel's death I know I am Thane of Glamis;
But how of Cawdor? The Thane of Cawdor lives,
A prosperous gentleman; and to be king
Stands not within the prospect of belief,
75 No more than to be Cawdor. Say from whence
You owe° this strange intelligence?° Or why
Upon this blasted heath you stop our way
With such prophetic greeting? Speak, I charge you.

[WITCHES *vanish.*]

Banquo.
The earth hath bubbles as the water has,
80 And these are of them. Whither are they vanished?

45. should: must.

? 51. *Banquo's words give a clue as to how Macbeth reacts to the witches. What is Macbeth doing? When Banquo asks, "Are ye fantastical," whom is he addressing?*

57. rapt withal: entranced by it.

? 61. *What does Banquo ask the witches?*

66. happy: lucky.

67. get: beget.

70. imperfect: incomplete.

? 71. *Sinel is Macbeth's father. What do you think Macbeth's tone is here? Is he overeager? or just casually curious?*

76. owe: own; have.
intelligence: information.

? Stage direction. *The witches on Shakespeare's stage would have vanished through the trap-door. Is Banquo, in his next speech, intrigued or disturbed? How does Macbeth feel?*

Macbeth.
>Into the air, and what seemed corporal° melted
>As breath into the wind. Would they had stayed!

Banquo.
>Were such things here as we do speak about?
>Or have we eaten on the insane root°
85   That takes the reason prisoner?

Macbeth.
>Your children shall be kings.

Banquo.   You shall be king.

Macbeth.
>And Thane of Cawdor too. Went it not so?

Banquo.
>To th' selfsame tune and words. Who's here?

[*Enter* ROSS *and* ANGUS.]

Ross.
>The king hath happily received, Macbeth,
90   The news of thy success; and when he reads°
>Thy personal venture in the rebels' fight,
>His wonders and his praises do contend
>Which should be thine or his. Silenced with that,
>In viewing o'er the rest o' th' selfsame day,
95   He finds thee in the stout Norweyan ranks,
>Nothing afeard of what thyself didst make,
>Strange images of death.° As thick as tale
>Came post with post,° and every one did bear
>Thy praises in his kingdom's great defense,
>And poured them before him.

100 **Angus.**   We are sent
>To give thee, from our royal master, thanks;
>Only to herald thee into his sight,
>Not pay thee.

Ross.
>And for an earnest° of a greater honor,
105   He bade me, from him, call thee Thane of Cawdor;
>In which addition,° hail, most worthy thane!
>For it is thine.

Banquo.   What, can the devil speak true?

Macbeth.
>The Thane of Cawdor lives: why do you dress me
>In borrowed robes?

Angus.   Who was the thane lives yet,
110   But under heavy judgment bears that life
>Which he deserves to lose. Whether he was combined
>With those of Norway, or did line° the rebel
>With hidden help and vantage, or that with both
>He labored in his country's wrack, I know not;
115   But treasons capital,° confessed and proved,
>Have overthrown him.

---

81. corporal: corporeal (bodily, physical).

84. insane root: henbane, believed to cause insanity.

90. reads: considers.

97. Nothing . . . death: killing, and not being afraid of being killed.
98. post with post: messenger with a message.

104. earnest: pledge.

106. addition: title.

112. line: support.

115. capital: deserving death.

Macbeth (*aside*). Glamis, and Thane of Cawdor:
The greatest is behind. (*To* ROSS *and* ANGUS.) Thanks for
 your pains.
 (*Aside to* BANQUO.) Do you not hope your children shall be
  kings,
 When those that gave the Thane of Cawdor to me
 Promised no less to them?

120 **Banquo** (*aside to* MACBETH). That, trusted home,°
 Might yet enkindle you unto the crown,°
 Besides the Thane of Cawdor. But 'tis strange:
 And oftentimes, to win us to our harm,
 The instruments of darkness tell us truths,

125 Win us with honest trifles, to betray 's
 In deepest consequence.
 Cousins,° a word, I pray you.
 Macbeth (*aside*). Two truths are told
 As happy prologues to the swelling act
 Of the imperial theme.—I thank you, gentlemen.—

130 (*Aside.*) This supernatural soliciting
 Cannot be ill, cannot be good. If ill,
 Why hath it given me earnest of success,
 Commencing in a truth? I am Thane of Cawdor:
 If good, why do I yield to that suggestion

135 Whose horrid image doth unfix my hair
 And make my seated heart knock at my ribs,
 Against the use of nature? Present fears
 Are less than horrible imaginings.
 My thought, whose murder yet is but fantastical,

140 Shakes so my single° state of man that function
 Is smothered in surmise, and nothing is
 But what is not.°
 Banquo. Look, how our partner's rapt.
 Macbeth (*aside*).
 If chance will have me king, why, chance may crown me,
 Without my stir.
 Banquo. New honors come upon him,

145 Like our strange° garments, cleave not to their mold
 But with the aid of use.
 Macbeth (*aside*). Come what come may,
 Time and the hour runs through the roughest day.
 Banquo.
 Worthy Macbeth, we stay upon your leisure.
 Macbeth.
 Give me your favor.° My dull brain was wrought

150 With things forgotten. Kind gentlemen, your pains
 Are registered where every day I turn
 The leaf to read them. Let us toward the king.
 (*Aside to* BANQUO.) Think upon what hath chanced, and at
  more time,

117. *"Behind" here means "to follow." How should this important aside be spoken? What is Macbeth's mood?*

120. trusted home: trusted all the way.

121. enkindle . . . crown: arouse in you the ambition to become king.

126. *How does this speech show Banquo as part of the conscience of the play?*

127. Cousins: This word is used frequently by Shakespeare to mean "fellows" or "kindred friends" of some sort.

Stage direction. *When a character is delivering an aside, the director or the playwright must arrange for the others on stage to be involved in some way so that it would be natural for them not to notice the character delivering the aside. Where should Macbeth go on stage to deliver this important aside? What do you think he meant by the "swelling act" in line 128? Where are Banquo, Angus, and Ross?*

137. *What do you suppose Macbeth is thinking of that makes his seated (fixed) heart knock at his ribs in an unnatural way?*

140. single: unaided; weak.

142. nothing . . . not: Nothing is real to me except my imaginings.

142. *What might Macbeth do as Banquo notices him brooding?*

145. strange: new.

145. *What does Banquo compare Macbeth and his new honors to? Is Banquo's mood different from Macbeth's?*

149. favor: pardon.

The interim having weighed it, let us speak
Our free hearts each to other.

155 **Banquo.**   Very gladly.
Macbeth.
Till then, enough. Come, friends.   [*Exeunt.*]

Scene 4. *Forres. The palace.*

Flourish.° Enter KING DUNCAN, LENNOX, MALCOLM, DONALBAIN,
and ATTENDANTS.

King.
Is execution done on Cawdor? Are not
Those in commission yet returned?
Malcolm.   My liege,
They are not yet come back. But I have spoke
With one that saw him die, who did report
5 That very frankly he confessed his treasons,
Implored your highness' pardon and set forth
A deep repentance: nothing in his life
Became him like the leaving it. He died
As one that had been studied in his death
10 To throw away the dearest thing he owed°
As 'twere a careless trifle.
King.   There's no art
To find the mind's construction in the face:
He was a gentleman on whom I built
An absolute trust.

[*Enter* MACBETH, BANQUO, ROSS, *and* ANGUS.]

O worthiest cousin!
15 The sin of my ingratitude even now
Was heavy on me: thou art so far before,
That swiftest wing of recompense is slow
To overtake thee. Would thou hadst less deserved,
That the proportion° both of thanks and payment
20 Might have been mine! Only I have left to say,
More is thy due than more than all can pay.
Macbeth.
The service and the loyalty I owe,
In doing it, pays itself.° Your highness' part
Is to receive our duties: and our duties
25 Are to your throne and state children and servants;
Which do but what they should, by doing everything
Safe toward° your love and honor.
King.   Welcome hither.
I have begun to plant thee, and will labor
To make thee full of growing. Noble Banquo,
30 That hast no less deserved, nor must be known
No less to have done so, let me enfold thee
And hold thee to my heart.

Flourish: of trumpets.

? 8. *What does this famous line mean: "nothing in his life / Became him like the leaving it"?*
10. owed: owned.

? 12. *What irony would you feel here? What does Duncan fail to realize about another face?*

19. proportion: greater amount.

23. pays itself: is its own reward.

27. safe toward: safeguarding.

? 32. *You know Macbeth's thoughts. How do you feel about him as the king lavishes praise on him? Is the king's reception of Banquo even warmer? How might Macbeth react here?*

"We will establish our estate upon Our eldest, Malcolm."

From Roman Polanski's film production of *Macbeth* (1971).

Banquo.   There if I grow,
    The harvest is your own.
King.   My plenteous joys,
    Wanton in fullness, seek to hide themselves
35 In drops of sorrow. Sons, kinsmen, thanes,
    And you whose places are the nearest, know,
    We will establish our estate upon
    Our eldest, Malcolm, whom we name hereafter
    The Prince of Cumberland: which honor must
40 Not unaccompanied invest him only,
    But signs of nobleness, like stars, shall shine
    On all deservers. From hence to Inverness,°
    And bind us further to you.
Macbeth.
    The rest is labor, which is not used for you.°
45 I'll be myself the harbinger,° and make joyful
    The hearing of my wife with your approach;
    So, humbly take my leave.
King.   My worthy Cawdor!
Macbeth (*aside*).
    The Prince of Cumberland! That is a step
    On which I must fall down, or else o'erleap,
50 For in my way it lies. Stars, hide your fires;
    Let not light see my black and deep desires:
    The eye wink at the hand;° yet let that be
    Which the eye fears, when it is done, to see.   [*Exit.*]
King.
    True, worthy Banquo; he is full so valiant,
55 And in his commendations° I am fed;
    It is a banquet to me. Let's after him,
    Whose care is gone before to bid us welcome.
    It is a peerless kinsman.   [*Flourish. Exeunt.*]

35. *There's a clue in this line that shows how moved the king is. What is the king doing at the words "drops of sorrow"?*

42. Inverness: Macbeth's castle.

43. *Who is to inherit Duncan's crown?*

44. The rest . . . you: When rest is not used for you, it is labor.

45. harbinger: sign of something to come.

52. wink . . . hand: be blind to the hand's deed.

53. *Where in this speech do we begin to hear Macbeth talk in terms of darkness?*

55. his commendations: praises of him.

Scene 5. *Inverness. Macbeth's castle.*

Enter Macbeth's wife, LADY MACBETH, *alone, with a letter.*

Lady Macbeth (*reads*). "They met me in the day of success;
and I have learned by the perfect'st report they have more in
them than mortal knowledge. When I burned in desire to
question them further, they made themselves air, into which
5   they vanished. Whiles I stood rapt in the wonder of it, came
missives° from the King, who all-hailed me 'Thane of Cawdor'; by which title, before, these weird sisters saluted me,
and referred me to the coming on of time, with 'Hail, king
that shalt be!' This have I thought good to deliver thee, my
10   dearest partner of greatness, that thou mightst not lose the
dues of rejoicing, by being ignorant of what greatness is
promised thee. Lay it to thy heart, and farewell."

Glamis thou art, and Cawdor, and shalt be
What thou art promised. Yet do I fear thy nature;
15   It is too full o' th' milk of human kindness
To catch the nearest way. Thou wouldst be great,
Art not without ambition, but without
The illness° should attend it. What thou wouldst highly,
That wouldst thou holily; wouldst not play false,
20   And yet wouldst wrongly win. Thou'dst have, great Glamis,
That which cries, "Thus thou must do" if thou have it;
And that which rather thou dost fear to do

? **Stage direction.** *As you picture Lady Macbeth reading
this letter, try to imagine what she
would be doing on stage and what
her mood would be, especially at
the words "Thane of Cawdor."*

6. missives: messengers.

? **13.** *What does Lady Macbeth
do with the letter? Whom is
she addressing here with "thou"
and "thy"? How would you explain
"th' milk of human kindness"?*

18. illness: wickedness; evil
nature.

"My dearest love, / Duncan comes
here tonight."

From the Stratford Festival production of
Macbeth (1983).

Than wishest should be undone. Hie thee hither,
That I may pour my spirits in thine ear,
25 And chastise with the valor of my tongue
All that impedes thee from the golden round
Which fate and metaphysical° aid doth seem
To have thee crowned withal.

[*Enter* MESSENGER.]

What is your tidings?
Messenger.
The king comes here tonight.
Lady Macbeth.   Thou'rt mad to say it!
30 Is not thy master with him, who, were't so,
Would have informed for preparation?
Messenger.
So please you, it is true. Our thane is coming.
One of my fellows had the speed of him,°
Who, almost dead for breath, had scarcely more
Than would make up his message.
35 **Lady Macbeth.**   Give him tending;
He brings great news.   [*Exit* MESSENGER.]
The raven himself is hoarse
That croaks the fatal entrance of Duncan
Under my battlements. Come, you spirits
That tend on mortal° thoughts, unsex me here,
40 And fill me, from the crown to the toe, top-full
Of direst cruelty! Make thick my blood,
Stop up th' access and passage to remorse,
That no compunctious visitings of nature°
Shake my fell° purpose, nor keep peace between
45 Th' effect and it! Come to my woman's breasts,
And take my milk for gall,° you murd'ring ministers,°
Wherever in your sightless° substances
You wait on nature's mischief! Come, thick night,
And pall° thee in the dunnest° smoke of hell,
50 That my keen knife see not the wound it makes,
Nor heaven peep through the blanket of the dark,
To cry "Hold, hold!"

[*Enter* MACBETH.]

Great Glamis! Worthy Cawdor!
Greater than both, by the all-hail hereafter!
Thy letters have transported me beyond
55 This ignorant present, and I feel now
The future in the instant.
Macbeth.   My dearest love,
Duncan comes here tonight.
Lady Macbeth.   And when goes hence?
Macbeth.
Tomorrow, as he purposes.

26. *What do you guess the "golden round" is?*
27. metaphysical: supernatural.

33. had . . . him: had more speed than he did.

36. *Who is the raven she refers to as being hoarse? Why does she call him a raven?*

39. mortal: deadly.

43. compunctious . . . nature: natural feelings of compassion.
44. fell: savage.
46. gall: a bitter substance; bile. **murd'ring ministers:** agents of murder.
47. sightless: invisible.
49. pall: cover with a shroud, a burial cloth. **dunnest:** darkest.

52. *How has Lady Macbeth reinforced the witches' statement: "Fair is foul, and foul is fair . . ."?*

57. *Is their passion for each other as great as their passion for power? If you feel it is, how might a director illustrate it here?*

Lady Macbeth.   O, never
          Shall sun that morrow see!
60   Your face, my thane, is as a book where men
          May read strange matters. To beguile the time,°
          Look like the time; bear welcome in your eye,
          Your hand, your tongue: look like th' innocent flower,
          But be the serpent under't. He that's coming
65   Must be provided for: and you shall put
          This night's great business into my dispatch;°
          Which shall to all our nights and days to come
          Give solely sovereign sway and masterdom.
Macbeth.
          We will speak further.
Lady Macbeth.   Only look up clear.°
70   To alter favor ever is to fear.°
          Leave all the rest to me.   [*Exeunt.*]

Scene 6. *Before Macbeth's castle.*

Hautboys° and torches. Enter KING DUNCAN, MALCOLM, DONAL-
BAIN, BANQUO, LENNOX, MACDUFF, ROSS, ANGUS, *and* ATTENDANTS.

King.
          This castle hath a pleasant seat;° the air
          Nimbly and sweetly recommends itself
          Unto our gentle senses.
Banquo.   This guest of summer,
          The temple-haunting martlet,° does approve°
5   By his loved mansionry° that the heaven's breath
          Smells wooingly here. No jutty,° frieze,
          Buttress, nor coign of vantage,° but this bird
          Hath made his pendent bed and procreant° cradle.
          Where they most breed and haunt, I have observed
          The air is delicate.

[*Enter* LADY MACBETH.]

10 **King.**   See, see, our honored hostess!
          The love that follows us sometime is our trouble,
          Which still we thank as love. Herein I teach you
          How you shall bid God 'ield° us for your pains
          And thank us for your trouble.
Lady Macbeth.   All our service
15   In every point twice done, and then done double,
          Were poor and single business to contend
          Against those honors deep and broad wherewith
          Your majesty loads our house: for those of old,
          And the late dignities heaped up to them,
          We rest your hermits.°
20 **King.**   Where's the Thane of Cawdor?
          We coursed° him at the heels, and had a purpose

---

61. beguile the time: deceive people of the day.

66. dispatch: management.

❓ 69. *How is Macbeth feeling?*
69. clear: undisturbed.
70. To alter . . . fear: To show an altered face is dangerous.

Hautboys: oboes.

1. seat: situation; setting.

4. martlet: a bird that builds nests in churches. **approve:** prove.
5. mansionry: nest (dwelling).
6. jutty: projection.
7. coign of vantage: advantageous corner (of the castle).
8. procreant: breeding.
❓ 9. *This scene contrasts strongly with the previous one. Again, what irony do you feel as Duncan admires the castle? How do you imagine Lady Macbeth acts as she now enters to greet her guests?*
13. 'ield: reward.

20. We rest your hermits: We'll remain dependents who will pray for you.
21. coursed: chased.

"See, see, our honored hostess!"

From Roman Polanski's film production of *Macbeth* (1971).

To be his purveyor:° but he rides well,
And his great love, sharp as his spur, hath holp° him
To his home before us. Fair and noble hostess,
We are your guest tonight.

25 **Lady Macbeth.**   Your servants ever
Have theirs, themselves, and what is theirs, in compt,°
To make their audit at your highness' pleasure,
Still° to return your own.

King.   Give me your hand.
Conduct me to mine host: we love him highly,
30 And shall continue our graces toward him.
By your leave, hostess.   *[Exeunt.]*

Scene 7. *Macbeth's castle.*

Hautboys. Torches. Enter a SEWER,° *and diverse* SERVANTS *with dishes and service, and pass over the stage. Then enter* MACBETH.

Macbeth.
If it were done when 'tis done, then 'twere well
It were done quickly. If th' assassination
Could trammel up the consequence, and catch,
With his surcease,° success; that but this blow
5 Might be the be-all and the end-all—here,
But here, upon this bank and shoal of time,

---

22. **purveyor:** advance man.
23. **holp:** helped.

26. **in compt:** in trust.

28. **Still:** always.

? **31.** *How do you imagine the scene ends?*

Sewer: butler.

? **1.** *This is one of Shakespeare's great soliloquies, in which Macbeth voices his indecision and possibly his conscience. What are his conflicts?*

4. **his surcease:** Duncan's death.

We'd jump° the life to come. But in these cases
We still have judgment here; that we but teach
Bloody instructions, which, being taught, return
10   To plague th' inventor: this even-handed° justice
Commends° th' ingredients of our poisoned chalice
To our own lips. He's here in double trust:
First, as I am his kinsman and his subject,
Strong both against the deed; then, as his host,
15   Who should against his murderer shut the door,
Not bear the knife myself. Besides, this Duncan
Hath borne his faculties° so meek, hath been
So clear° in his great office, that his virtues
Will plead like angels trumpet-tongued against
20   The deep damnation of his taking-off;°
And pity, like a naked newborn babe,
Striding the blast, or heaven's cherubin horsed
Upon the sightless couriers° of the air,
Shall blow the horrid deed in every eye,
25   That° tears shall drown the wind. I have no spur
To prick the sides of my intent, but only
Vaulting ambition, which o'erleaps itself
And falls on th' other——

[*Enter* LADY MACBETH.]

                              How now! What news?
Lady Macbeth.
He has almost supped. Why have you left the chamber?
Macbeth.
Hath he asked for me?
30   **Lady Macbeth.**   Know you not he has?
Macbeth.
We will proceed no further in this business:
He hath honored me of late, and I have bought
Golden opinions from all sorts of people,
Which would be worn now in their newest gloss,
Not cast aside so soon.
35   **Lady Macbeth.**   Was the hope drunk
Wherein you dressed yourself? Hath it slept since?
And wakes it now, to look so green° and pale
At what it did so freely? From this time
Such I account thy love. Art thou afeard
40   To be the same in thine own act and valor
As thou art in desire? Wouldst thou have that
Which thou esteem'st the ornament of life,°
And live a coward in thine own esteem,
Letting "I dare not" wait upon° "I would,"
Like the poor cat i' th' adage?°
45   **Macbeth.**   Prithee, peace!
I dare do all that may become a man;
Who dares do more is none.

7. jump: risk. (Macbeth knows he will be condemned to hell for the sin of murder.)

10. even-handed: impartial.
11. Commends: offers.

17. faculties: powers.
18. clear: clean.

20. taking-off: murder.

23. sightless couriers: winds.

25. That: so that.

[?] **26.** *Macbeth says he has no spur to prick the sides of his intent. Is that true?*

37. green: sickly.

42. ornament of life: crown.

44. wait upon: follow.

45. poor . . . adage: saying about a cat who wants fish but won't wet its paws.

Lady Macbeth.   What beast was't then
That made you break° this enterprise to me?
When you durst do it, then you were a man;
50   And to be more than what you were, you would
Be so much more the man. Nor time nor place
Did then adhere,° and yet you would make both.
They have made themselves, and that their fitness now
Does unmake you. I have given suck, and know
55   How tender 'tis to love the babe that milks me:
I would, while it was smiling in my face,
Have plucked my nipple from his boneless gums,
And dashed the brains out, had I so sworn as you
Have done to this.
Macbeth.   If we should fail?
Lady Macbeth.   We fail?
60   But° screw your courage to the sticking-place,°
And we'll not fail. When Duncan is asleep—
Whereto the rather shall his day's hard journey
Soundly invite him—his two chamberlains
Will I with wine and wassail° so convince,°
65   That memory, the warder of the brain,
Shall be a fume, and the receipt of reason
A limbeck only:° when in swinish sleep
Their drenchèd natures lie as in a death,
What cannot you and I perform upon
70   Th' unguarded Duncan, what not put upon
His spongy officers, who shall bear the guilt
Of our great quell?
Macbeth.   Bring forth men-children only;
For thy undaunted mettle° should compose
Nothing but males. Will it not be received,
75   When we have marked with blood those sleepy two
Of his own chamber, and used their very daggers,
That they have done't?
Lady Macbeth.   Who dares receive it other,
As we shall make our griefs and clamor roar
Upon his death?
Macbeth.   I am settled, and bend up
80   Each corporal agent to this terrible feat.
Away, and mock the time° with fairest show:
False face must hide what the false heart doth know.

                                        [*Exeunt.*]

---

48. break: disclose; reveal.

52. adhere: suit.

? 54. *How does Lady Macbeth try to intimidate her husband in this speech? Watch what she says about herself in the next lines. There has been some question as to whether "We fail?" (line 59) should be a question. How does the meaning change if the line is spoken as a statement?*

60. But: only.   **sticking-place:** the notch in a crossbow.

64. wassail: drinking. **convince:** overcome.

67. the receipt . . . only: The reasoning part of the brain would become like a **limbeck** (or still), distilling only confused thoughts.

? 72. *"Quell" is murder. What are Lady Macbeth's plans?*
73. mettle: spirit.

81. mock the time: deceive the world.
? 81. *Should Macbeth pause here? How should these key words be spoken?*
? 82. *How is this yet another echo of the witches' words in Scene 1?*

MAKING MEANINGS

Act I

First Thoughts

1. What are your impressions of Lady Macbeth at the end of Act I? What is her relationship with Macbeth (beyond being his wife)? What details in this act support your impressions?

Reading Check

a. In Scene 1, where do the witches plan to meet again, and why?

b. What news about Macbeth does the bloodstained captain bring to the king in Scene 2?

c. What does the king determine to do for Macbeth? Why?

d. What do the witches tell Macbeth and Banquo in Scene 3?

e. In what lines do you discover Lady Macbeth's plans for Duncan when he visits the castle?

Shaping Interpretations

2. In the very first scene of a play, a dramatist must tell the audience what kind of play they are about to see. What does the brief opening scene of *Macbeth* reveal about the rest of the play? How does the weather reflect the human passions revealed in the rest of the act?

3. How does the witches' prophecy of Macbeth's coming greatness act as a temptation for him?

4. Explain the **paradox,** or the apparently contradictory nature, of the witches' greeting to Banquo in Scene 3: "Lesser than Macbeth, and greater." How is this paradox true?

5. How does Banquo's reaction to the witches differ from Macbeth's? What do you think Macbeth's reaction suggests about his **character**?

6. One of the most interesting parts of any serious play is what goes on in the characters' minds. What **conflict** rages in Macbeth after he hears the witches' prophecy? What **resolution** to this conflict does Macbeth express in his aside, in Scene 4, lines 48–53?

7. Find details in the play that point to temperamental **contrasts** between Macbeth and his wife. Who is more single-minded and logical? Who is more argumentative and sensitive? Which one wins the argument? The chick

8. What **irony** would the audience feel as they watch Duncan enter the castle and hear him praise its peacefulness?

Extending the Text

9. One critic has said that the witches are "in some sense representative of potentialities within" Macbeth. How could that statement be explained? Is there any evidence in this act that Macbeth has wanted to be king before? Explain your answer.

READING SKILLS AND STRATEGIES

The Melody of Language: Blank Verse

Almost all of *Macbeth* is written in **blank verse,** or unrhymed iambic pentameter, a form of poetry that comes close to imitating the natural rhythms of English speech. An **iamb** is a metrical foot that has one unstressed syllable followed by one stressed syllable. (Each of the following is an iamb: *Macbeth, success, to win.*) **Pentameter** means that each line of verse has five feet, so one line of iambic pentameter has five iambs. Read this line aloud to hear the meter:

> **Banquo:** Good sír, why dó you start, and seém to feár . . .

Examining blank verse. Some lines in *Macbeth* are irregular, with fewer feet or with feet that are not iambs. The play even has a few prose passages, indicated by lines that are set full measure.

1. Scan one major speech by Macbeth and one by Lady Macbeth anywhere in Act I. What variations in iambic pentameter do you find? Why do you think these variations exist—how do sound and sense relate to each other?

2. Do the witches speak in blank verse? Why do you suppose Shakespeare wrote their speeches in this way?

3. Find a prose passage in Act I. Why do you think Shakespeare chose to use prose in this passage?

ACT II

Scene 1. *Inverness. Court of Macbeth's castle.*

Enter BANQUO, *and* FLEANCE, *with a torch before him (on the way to bed).*

Banquo.
How goes the night, boy?

Fleance.
The moon is down; I have not heard the clock.

Banquo.
And she goes down at twelve.

Fleance.   I take't, 'tis later, sir.

Banquo.
Hold, take my sword. There's husbandry° in heaven.
5   Their candles are all out. Take thee that too.
A heavy summons° lies like lead upon me,
And yet I would not sleep. Merciful powers,
Restrain in me the cursèd thoughts that nature
Gives way to in repose!

[*Enter* MACBETH, *and a* SERVANT *with a torch.*]

                              Give me my sword!
10   Who's there?

Macbeth.
A friend.

Banquo.
What, sir, not yet at rest? The king's a-bed:
He hath been in unusual pleasure, and
Sent forth great largess to your offices:°
15   This diamond he greets your wife withal,
By the name of most kind hostess; and shut up°
In measureless content.

Macbeth.   Being unprepared,
Our will became the servant to defect,°
Which else should free have wrought.

Banquo.   All's well.
20   I dreamt last night of the three weird sisters:
To you they have showed some truth.

Macbeth.   I think not of them.
Yet, when we can entreat an hour to serve,
We would spend it in some words upon that business,
If you would grant the time.

Banquo.   At your kind'st leisure.

Macbeth.
25   If you shall cleave to my consent, when 'tis,°
It shall make honor for you.

Banquo.   So° I lose none
In seeking to augment it, but still keep
My bosom franchised° and allegiance clear,°
I shall be counseled.

4. husbandry: economizing.

6. summons: call to sleep.

14. largess to your offices: gifts to your servants' quarters.

16. shut up: concluded.

18. to defect: to insufficient preparations.

25. cleave . . . 'tis: join my cause, when the time comes.

26. So: provided that.

28. franchised: free (from guilt). **clear:** clean.

Macbeth.   Good repose the while!

Banquo.

30   Thanks, sir. The like to you!

[*Exit* BANQUO, *with* FLEANCE.]

Macbeth.

Go bid thy mistress, when my drink is ready,
She strike upon the bell. Get thee to bed.

[*Exit* SERVANT.]

32. *What is to happen upon the ringing of the bell?*

Is this a dagger which I see before me,
The handle toward my hand? Come, let me clutch thee.

35   I have thee not, and yet I see thee still.
Art thou not, fatal vision, sensible°
To feeling as to sight, or art thou but
A dagger of the mind, a false creation,
Proceeding from the heat-oppressèd brain?

36. sensible: perceptible to the senses.

40   I see thee yet, in form as palpable°
As this which now I draw.
Thou marshal'st me the way that I was going;
And such an instrument I was to use.
Mine eyes are made the fools o' th' other senses,

45   Or else worth all the rest. I see thee still;
And on thy blade and dudgeon° gouts° of blood,
Which was not so before. There's no such thing.
It is the bloody business which informs°
Thus to mine eyes. Now o'er the one half-world

50   Nature seems dead, and wicked dreams abuse°
The curtained sleep; witchcraft celebrates

40. palpable: obvious.

41. *What does Macbeth do at this moment? If you were directing the play, would you suspend a dagger in front of Macbeth during this speech? Why or why not?*

46. dudgeon: hilt.   **gouts:** large drops.

48. informs: gives shape.

50. abuse: deceive.

"Is this a dagger which I see before me,
The handle toward my hand?"

From the Stratford Festival production of
Macbeth (1983).

Pale Hecate's° offerings; and withered murder,
Alarumed° by his sentinel, the wolf,
Whose howl's his watch, thus with his stealthy pace,
55   With Tarquin's° ravishing strides, towards his design
Moves like a ghost. Thou sure and firm-set earth,
Hear not my steps, which way they walk, for fear
Thy very stones prate of my whereabout,
And take the present horror from the time,
60   Which now suits with it.° Whiles I threat, he lives:
Words to the heat of deeds too cold breath gives.

[*A bell rings.*]

I go, and it is done: the bell invites me.
Hear it not, Duncan, for it is a knell
That summons thee to heaven, or to hell.   [*Exit.*]

52. Hecate's: Hecate (hek′it), goddess of sorcery.

53. Alarumed: called to action.

55. Tarquin's: Tarquin was a Roman tyrant who raped a woman named Lucrece.

60. now suits with it: now seems suitable to it.

64. *Trace in this soliloquy a vision, a call to action, and a leave-taking. What should you be feeling as an audience as Macbeth exits?*

Scene 2.   *Macbeth's castle.*

Enter LADY MACBETH.

Lady Macbeth.
That which hath made them drunk hath made me bold;
What hath quenched them hath given me fire. Hark! Peace!
It was the owl that shrieked, the fatal bellman,
Which gives the stern'st good-night.° He is about it.
5   The doors are open, and the surfeited grooms
Do mock their charge with snores. I have drugged their
        possets,°
That death and nature do contend about them,
Whether they live or die.
Macbeth (*within*).   Who's there? What, ho?
Lady Macbeth.
Alack, I am afraid they have awaked.
10   And 'tis not done! Th' attempt and not the deed
Confounds° us. Hark! I laid their daggers ready;
He could not miss 'em. Had he not resembled
My father as he slept, I had done't.

[*Enter* MACBETH.]

                                My husband!
Macbeth.
I have done the deed. Didst thou not hear a noise?
Lady Macbeth.
15   I heard the owl scream and the crickets cry.
Did not you speak?
Macbeth.   When?
Lady Macbeth.   Now.
Macbeth.   As I descended?
Lady Macbeth. Ay.

3. *What sound would you hear here? In this soliloquy, who are the "them" and who is "He"?*

4. stern'st good-night: The owl's call is supposed to portend death. The bellman was a person who rang a bell outside a condemned person's cell the night before his execution, to warn him to confess his sins.

6. possets: bedtime drinks.

11. Confounds: ruins.

13. *How should Lady Macbeth say this last line, which reveals why the plans have changed? Do you think she is beginning to show remorse?*

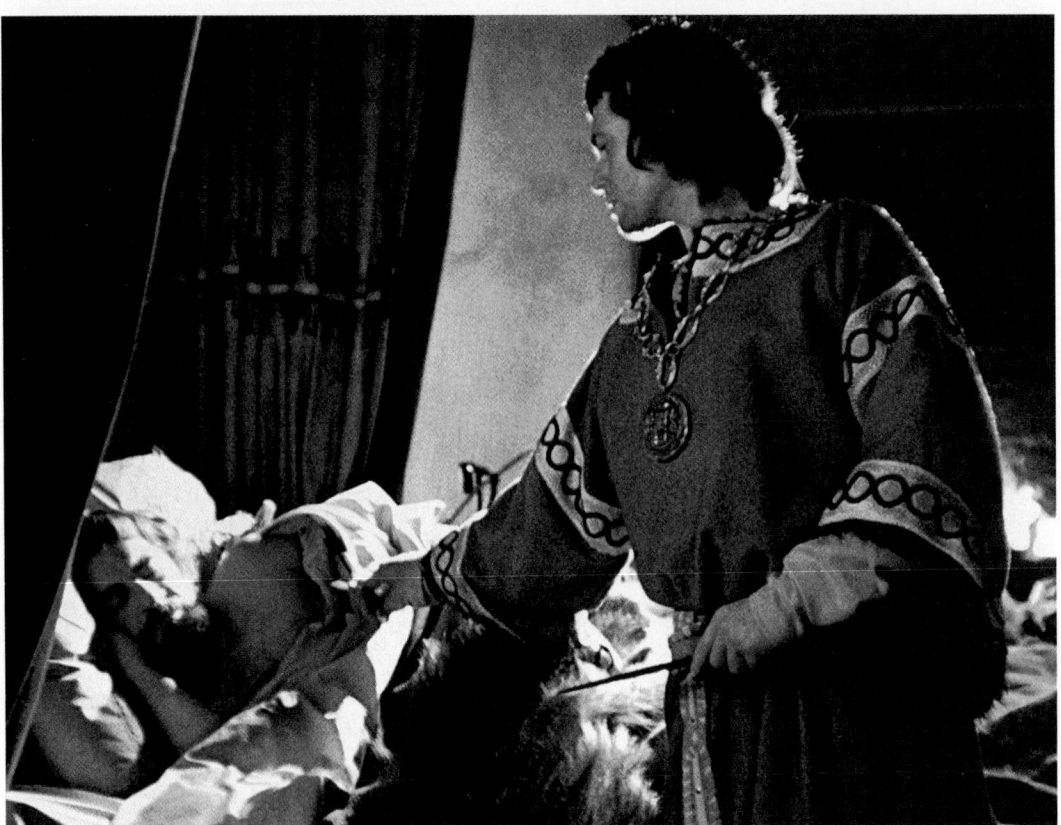

Macbeth pointing the dagger at Duncan in Roman Polanski's film production of *Macbeth* (1971).

Macbeth. Hark!
Who lies i' th' second chamber?
Lady Macbeth.   Donalbain.
20 **Macbeth.** This is a sorry sight.
Lady Macbeth.
A foolish thought, to say a sorry sight.
Macbeth.
There's one did laugh in 's sleep, and one cried "Murder!"
That they did wake each other. I stood and heard them.
But they did say their prayers, and addressed them
Again to sleep.
25 **Lady Macbeth.**   There are two lodged together.
Macbeth.
One cried "God bless us!" and "Amen" the other,
As they had seen me with these hangman's hands:
List'ning their fear, I could not say "Amen,"
When they did say "God bless us!"
Lady Macbeth.   Consider it not so deeply.
Macbeth.
30 But wherefore could not I pronounce "Amen"?
I had most need of blessing, and "Amen"
Stuck in my throat.
Lady Macbeth.   These deeds must not be thought
After these ways; so, it will make us mad.

? **33.** *Is Lady Macbeth fighting for control here?*

Macbeth.
    Methought I heard a voice cry "Sleep no more!
35   Macbeth does murder sleep"—the innocent sleep,
    Sleep that knits up the raveled sleave° of care,
    The death of each day's life, sore labor's bath,
    Balm of hurt minds, great nature's second course,°
    Chief nourisher in life's feast——

Lady Macbeth.   What do you mean?

Macbeth.
40   Still it cried "Sleep no more!" to all the house:
    "Glamis hath murdered sleep, and therefore Cawdor
    Shall sleep no more: Macbeth shall sleep no more."

Lady Macbeth
    Who was it that thus cried? Why, worthy thane,
    You do unbend your noble strength, to think
45   So brainsickly of things. Go get some water,
    And wash this filthy witness from your hand.
    Why did you bring these daggers from the place?
    They must lie there: go carry them, and smear
    The sleepy grooms with blood.

Macbeth.   I'll go no more.
50   I am afraid to think what I have done;
    Look on 't again I dare not.

Lady Macbeth.   Infirm of purpose!
    Give me the daggers. The sleeping and the dead
    Are but as pictures. 'Tis the eye of childhood
    That fears a painted devil. If he do bleed,
55   I'll gild the faces of the grooms withal,
    For it must seem their guilt.   *[Exit. Knock within.]*

Macbeth.   Whence is that knocking?
    How is 't with me, when every noise appalls me?
    What hands are here? Ha! They pluck out mine eyes!
    Will all great Neptune's ocean wash this blood
60   Clean from my hand? No; this my hand will rather
    The multitudinous seas incarnadine,°
    Making the green one red.

[Enter LADY MACBETH.]

Lady Macbeth.
    My hands are of your color, but I shame
    To wear a heart so white. *(Knock.)* I hear a knocking
65   At the south entry. Retire we to our chamber.
    A little water clears us of this deed:
    How easy is it then! Your constancy
    Hath left you unattended.° *(Knock.)* Hark! more knocking.
    Get on your nightgown, lest occasion call us
70   And show us to be watchers.° Be not lost
    So poorly in your thoughts.

---

36. raveled sleave: tangled thread.

38. second course: sleep (the less substantial first course is food).

? **41.** *Who else complained about sleep? In what way has Glamis "murdered sleep"?*

? **46.** *What is the "filthy witness"? What actions are the couple engaged in here? In the next line, Lady Macbeth discovers the daggers. Why is she so alarmed at seeing them in her husband's hands? How could Macbeth have been carrying them so they weren't visible before?*

? **55.** *What will Lady Macbeth do to the grooms if Duncan bleeds enough?*

61. incarnadine: make red.

? **63.** *Based on this speech, what does Lady Macbeth look like?*

68. Your . . . unattended: Your firmness has deserted you.

70. watchers: that is, up late.

? **71.** *What is Macbeth acting like?*

"My hands are of your color, but I shame
To wear a heart so white."

From the Stratford Festival production of
Macbeth (1983).

Macbeth.

To know my deed, 'twere best not know myself.

[*Knock.*]

Wake Duncan with thy knocking! I would thou couldst!

[*Exeunt.*]

Scene 3. *Macbeth's castle.*

Enter a PORTER. *Knocking within.*

Porter. Here's a knocking indeed! If a man were porter of hell
gate, he should have old° turning the key. (*Knock.*) Knock,
knock, knock! Who's there, i' th' name of Beelzebub?°
Here's a farmer, that hanged himself on th' expectation of
5   plenty. Come in time! Have napkins enow° about you; here
you'll sweat for 't. (*Knock.*) Knock, knock! Who's there, in
th' other devil's name? Faith, here's an equivocator,° that
could swear in both the scales against either scale; who
committed treason enough for God's sake, yet could not
10   equivocate to heaven. O, come in, equivocator. (*Knock.*)
Knock, knock, knock! Who's there? Faith, here's an English
tailor come hither for stealing out of a French hose:° come
in, tailor. Here you may roast your goose.° (*Knock.*) Knock,

Stage direction. *In the theater, this sharp, loud knocking
is frightening. In the next line,
what might Macbeth wish the
knocking could awake in himself?*

Stage direction. *Note that
the porter is drunk. What
would he be doing during this
long speech while the knocking
persists?*

2. have old: grow old.

3. Beelzebub: the Devil.

5. enow: enough.

7. equivocator: The porter means
a Jesuit (who allegedly used false
arguments in his zeal for souls).

12. French hose: tightfitting
stocking.

13. goose: iron used by a tailor for
pressing.

15   knock; never at quiet! What are you? But this place is too cold for hell. I'll devil-porter it no further. I had thought to have let in some of all professions that go the primrose way to th' everlasting bonfire. (*Knock.*) Anon, anon! (*Opens an entrance.*) I pray you, remember the porter.

[*Enter* MACDUFF *and* LENNOX.]

Macduff.
     Was it so late, friend, ere you went to bed,
20   That you do lie so late?
     Porter. Faith, sir, we were carousing till the second cock:° and drink, sir, is a great provoker of three things.
     Macduff. What three things does drink especially provoke?
     Porter. Marry, sir, nose-painting, sleep, and urine. Lechery, sir,
25   it provokes and unprovokes; it provokes the desire, but it takes away the performance: therefore much drink may be said to be an equivocator with lechery: it makes him and it mars him; it sets him on and it takes him off; it persuades him and disheartens him; makes him stand to and not stand
30   to; in conclusion, equivocates him in a sleep, and giving him the lie, leaves him.
     Macduff. I believe drink gave thee the lie° last night.
     Porter. That it did, sir, i' the very throat on me: but I requited him for his lie, and, I think, being too strong for him, though
35   he took up my legs sometime, yet I make a shift to cast° him.
     Macduff. Is thy master stirring?

[*Enter* MACBETH.]

     Our knocking has awaked him; here he comes.
     Lennox.
     Good morrow, noble sir.
     Macbeth.   Good morrow, both.
     Macduff.
     Is the king stirring, worthy thane?
     Macbeth.   Not yet.
     Macduff.
40   He did command me to call timely° on him:
     I have almost slipped the hour.
     Macbeth.   I'll bring you to him.
     Macduff.
     I know this is a joyful trouble to you;
     But yet 'tis one.
     Macbeth.
     The labor we delight in physics° pain.
     This is the door.
45   **Macduff.**   I'll make so bold to call,
     For 'tis my limited service.°   [*Exit* MACDUFF.]
     Lennox.
     Goes the king hence today?

21. second cock: about 3 A.M.

32. gave thee the lie: pun meaning "called you a liar" and "stretched you out, lying in bed."

35. cast: here, a pun meaning "to cast in plaster" and "to vomit" (cast out).

? **36.** *All the time this humorous bantering is going on, what do we know these king's men are about to discover?*

40. timely: early.

44. physics: cures.

46. limited service: appointed duty.

Macbeth.   He does: he did appoint so.

Lennox.
    The night has been unruly. Where we lay,
    Our chimneys were blown down, and, as they say,
50   Lamentings heard i' th' air, strange screams of death,
    And prophesying with accents terrible
    Of dire combustion° and confused events
    New hatched to th' woeful time: the obscure bird
    Clamored the livelong night. Some say, the earth
    Was feverous and did shake.

55 **Macbeth.**   'Twas a rough night.

Lennox.
    My young remembrance cannot parallel
    A fellow to it.

[*Enter* MACDUFF.]

Macduff.
    O horror, horror, horror! Tongue nor heart
    Cannot conceive nor name thee.

Macbeth and Lennox.   What's the matter?

Macduff.
60   Confusion now hath made his masterpiece.
    Most sacrilegious murder hath broke ope
    The Lord's anointed temple,° and stole thence
    The life o' th' building.

Macbeth.   What is't you say? The life?

Lennox.
    Mean you his majesty?

Macduff.
65   Approach the chamber, and destroy your sight
    With a new Gorgon:° do not bid me speak;
    See, and then speak yourselves. Awake, awake!

[*Exeunt* MACBETH *and* LENNOX.]

    Ring the alarum bell. Murder and treason!
    Banquo and Donalbain! Malcolm! Awake!
70   Shake off this downy sleep, death's counterfeit,
    And look on death itself! Up, up, and see
    The great doom's image! Malcolm! Banquo!
    As from your graves rise up, and walk like sprites,
    To countenance° this horror. Ring the bell.

[*Bell rings. Enter* LADY MACBETH.]

Lady Macbeth.
75   What's the business,
    That such a hideous trumpet calls to parley°
    The sleepers of the house? Speak, speak!

Macduff.   O gentle lady,
    'Tis not for you to hear what I can speak:

? 47. *How must Macbeth be feeling?*

52. combustion: tumult; uproar.

? 54. *In Elizabethan times, people often believed that nature mirrored terrible things happening to human beings, especially to kings. How did this weather mirror what was happening to the king in Macbeth's castle?*

? 55. *A single line, but full of irony. How would Macbeth say it?*

62. Lord's anointed temple: body of the king.

? 63. *How would you explain Macduff's metaphors?*

66. Gorgon: creature from Greek mythology whose face could turn an onlooker to stone.

74. countenance: be in keeping with.

76. parley: conference of war.

The repetition, in a woman's ear,
Would murder as it fell.

[*Enter* BANQUO.]

80   O Banquo, Banquo!
Our royal master's murdered.
Lady Macbeth.   Woe, alas!
What, in our house?
Banquo.   Too cruel anywhere.
Dear Duff, I prithee, contradict thyself,
And say it is not so.

[*Enter* MACBETH, LENNOX, *and* ROSS.]

Macbeth.

85   Had I but died an hour before this chance,
I had lived a blessèd time; for from this instant
There's nothing serious in mortality:°
All is but toys. Renown and grace is dead,
The wine of life is drawn, and the mere lees°
90   Is left this vault° to brag of.

[*Enter* MALCOLM *and* DONALBAIN.]

Donalbain.
What is amiss?
Macbeth.   You are, and do not know't.
The spring, the head, the fountain of your blood
Is stopped; the very source of it is stopped.
Macduff.
Your royal father's murdered.
Malcolm.   O, by whom?
Lennox.

95   Those of his chamber, as it seemed, had done't:
Their hands and faces were all badged° with blood;
So were their daggers, which unwiped we found
Upon their pillows. They stared, and were distracted.
No man's life was to be trusted with them.
Macbeth.

100   O, yet I do repent me of my fury,
That I did kill them.
Macduff.   Wherefore did you so?
Macbeth.
Who can be wise, amazed, temp'rate and furious,
Loyal and neutral, in a moment? No man.
The expedition° of my violent love
105   Outrun the pauser, reason. Here lay Duncan,
His silver skin laced with his golden blood,
And his gashed stabs looked like a breach in nature
For ruin's wasteful entrance: there, the murderers,
Steeped in the colors of their trade, their daggers

? **82.** *The emphasis on Lady Macbeth's gentleness and fairness when we know the foulness underneath might well merit a snicker from the audience. The snicker might be expected to grow into a laugh when she says, "What, in our house?" These are difficult moments to act. How do you think Lady Macbeth should be behaving?*

87. mortality: life.

89. lees: dregs.
90. vault: pun on "wine vault" and the "vault of heaven."

? **94.** *Macbeth and Lady Macbeth might well look at each other at this moment. Does Lennox draw the conclusion they wanted him to draw: that the servants killed Duncan?*
96. badged: marked.

104. expedition: haste.

110 Unmannerly breeched with gore.° Who could refrain,°
That had a heart to love, and in that heart
Courage to make 's love known?
Lady Macbeth.   Help me hence, ho!
Macduff.
    Look to the lady.
Malcolm (*aside to* DONALBAIN). Why do we hold our tongues,
That most may claim this argument for ours?°
Donalbain (*aside to* MALCOLM).
115 What should be spoken here,
Where our fate, hid in an auger-hole,°
May rush, and seize us? Let's away:
Our tears are not yet brewed.
Malcolm (*aside to* DONALBAIN). Nor our strong sorrow
Upon the foot of motion.°
Banquo.   Look to the lady.

[LADY MACBETH *is carried out.*]

120 And when we have our naked frailties hid,°
That suffer in exposure, let us meet
And question° this most bloody piece of work,
To know it further. Fears and scruples° shake us.
In the great hand of God I stand, and thence
125 Against the undivulged pretense° I fight
Of treasonous malice.
Macduff.   And so do I.
All.   So all.
Macbeth.
    Let's briefly° put on manly readiness,
    And meet i' th' hall together.
All.   Well contented.

[*Exeunt all but* MALCOLM *and* DONALBAIN.]

Malcolm.
    What will you do? Let's not consort with them.
130 To show an unfelt sorrow is an office°
    Which the false man does easy. I'll to England.
Donalbain.
    To Ireland, I; our separated fortune
    Shall keep us both the safer. Where we are
    There's daggers in men's smiles; the near in blood,
    The nearer bloody.
135 **Malcolm.**   This murderous shaft that's shot
    Hath not yet lighted, and our safest way
    Is to avoid the aim. Therefore to horse;
    And let us not be dainty of° leave-taking,
    But shift away. There's warrant° in that theft
140 Which steals itself° when there's no mercy left.

[*Exeunt.*]

110. **unmannerly breeched with gore:** unbecomingly covered with blood, as if wearing red trousers. **refrain:** check oneself.

114. **That . . . ours:** who are the most concerned with this topic.

116. **auger-hole:** unsuspected place.

119. **Our tears . . . motion:** We have not yet had time for tears, nor to express our sorrows in action.

120. **naked frailties hid:** poor bodies clothed.

122. **question:** discuss.
123. **scruples:** suspicions.

125. **undivulged pretense:** hidden purpose.

127. **briefly:** quickly.

130. **office:** function.

138. **dainty of:** fussy about.
139. **warrant:** justification.
140. **steals itself:** steals oneself away.

Scene 4. *Outside Macbeth's castle.*

Enter ROSS *with an* OLD MAN.

Old Man.
  Threescore and ten I can remember well:
  Within the volume of which time I have seen
  Hours dreadful and things strange, but this sore° night
  Hath trifled former knowings.°

Ross.   Ha, good father,
5 Thou seest the heavens, as troubled with man's act,
  Threatens his bloody stage. By th' clock 'tis day,
  And yet dark night strangles the traveling lamp:°
  Is't night's predominance,° or the day's shame,
  That darkness does the face of earth entomb,
  When living light should kiss it?

10 **Old Man.**   'Tis unnatural,
  Even like the deed that's done. On Tuesday last
  A falcon, tow'ring in her pride of place,°
  Was by a mousing° owl hawked at and killed.

Ross.
  And Duncan's horses—a thing most strange and certain—
15 Beauteous and swift, the minions° of their race,
  Turned wild in nature, broke their stalls, flung out,°
  Contending 'gainst obedience, as they would make
  War with mankind.

Old Man.   'Tis said they eat° each other.

Ross.
  They did so, to th' amazement of mine eyes,
  That looked upon't.

  [*Enter* MACDUFF.]

20   Here comes the good Macduff.
  How goes the world, sir, now?

Macduff.   Why, see you not?

Ross.
  Is't known who did this more than bloody deed?

Macduff.
  Those that Macbeth hath slain.

Ross.   Alas, the day!
  What good could they pretend?°

Macduff.   They were suborned:°
25 Malcolm and Donalbain, the king's two sons,
  Are stol'n away and fled, which puts upon them
  Suspicion of the deed.

Ross.   'Gainst nature still.
  Thriftless° ambition, that will ravin up°
  Thine own life's means!° Then 'tis most like
30 The sovereignty will fall upon Macbeth.

---

3. **sore:** grievous.
4. **trifled former knowings:** made trifles of former experiences.

7. **traveling lamp:** sun.
8. **predominance:** astrological supremacy.

12. **tow'ring . . . place:** soaring at her summit.
13. **mousing:** normally mouse-eating.

15. **minions:** darlings.
16. **flung out:** lunged wildly.

18. **eat:** ate.

24. **pretend:** hope for.
suborned: bribed.

28. **Thriftless:** wasteful. **ravin up:** greedily devour.
29. **own life's means:** parent.

from On the Knocking at the Gate in *Macbeth*

Thomas De Quincey

From my boyish days I had always felt a great perplexity on one point in *Macbeth*. It was this: The knocking at the gate which succeeds to the murder of Duncan produced to my feelings an effect for which I never could account. The effect was that it reflected back upon the murderer a peculiar awfulness and a depth of solemnity; yet, however obstinately I endeavored with my understanding to comprehend this, for many years I never could see *why* it should produce such an effect.

. . . At length I solved it to my own satisfaction; and my solution is this: —Murder, in ordinary cases, where the sympathy is wholly directed to the case of the murdered person, is an incident of coarse and vulgar horror; and for this reason—that it flings the interest exclusively upon the natural but ignoble instinct by which we cleave to life: an instinct which, as being indispensable to the primal law of self-preservation, is the same in kind (though different in degree) amongst all living creatures. This instinct, therefore, because it annihilates all distinctions, and degrades the greatest of men to the level of "the poor beetle that we tread on," exhibits human nature in its most abject and humiliating attitude. Such an attitude would little suit the purposes of the poet. What then must he do? He must throw the interest on the murderer. Our sympathy must be with *him* (of course I mean a sympathy of comprehension, a sympathy by which we enter into his feelings, and are made to understand them—not a sympathy of pity or approbation). In the murdered person, all strife of thought, all flux and reflux of passion and of purpose, are crushed by one overwhelming panic; the fear of instant death smites him "with its petrific mace."[1] But in the murderer, such a murderer as a poet will condescend to, there must be raging some great storm of passion—jealousy, ambition, vengeance, hatred—which will create a hell within him; and into this hell we are to look.

In *Macbeth*, for the sake of gratifying his own enormous and teeming faculty of creation, Shakespeare has introduced two murderers: and, as usual in his hands, they are remarkably discriminated: but—though in Macbeth the strife of mind is greater than in his wife, the tiger spirit not so awake, and his feelings caught chiefly by contagion from her—yet, as both were finally involved in the guilt of murder, the

1. **petrific mace:** stone club. This is an allusion to Milton's *Paradise Lost* (Book X, line 294), in which Death wields a "mace petrific."

Macduff.
   He is already named,° and gone to Scone°
   To be invested.°
Ross.   Where is Duncan's body?
Macduff.
   Carried to Colmekill,°
   The sacred storehouse of his predecessors
   And guardian of their bones.
35 **Ross.**   Will you to Scone?
Macduff.
   No, cousin, I'll to Fife.

31. named: elected.   **Scone** (skōōn).
32. invested: installed as king.

33. Colmekill: Iona Island, the ancient burying place of Scottish kings. (It was founded by St. Colm.)

murderous mind of necessity is finally to be presumed in both. This was to be expressed; and, on its own account, as well as to make it a more proportionable antagonist to the unoffending nature of their victim, "the gracious Duncan," and adequately to expound "the deep damnation of his taking off," this was to be expressed with peculiar energy. We were to be made to feel that the human nature—i.e., the divine nature of love and mercy, spread through the hearts of all creatures, and seldom utterly withdrawn from man—was gone, vanished, extinct, and that the fiendish nature had taken its place. And, as this effect is marvellously accomplished in the *dialogues* and *soliloquies* themselves, so it is finally consummated by the expedient under consideration; and it is to this that I now solicit the reader's attention. If the reader has ever witnessed a wife, daughter, or sister in a fainting fit, he may chance to have observed that the most affecting moment in such a spectacle is *that* in which a sigh and a stirring announce the recommencement of suspended life.

. . . All action in any direction is best expounded, measured, and made apprehensible, by reaction. Now, applying this to the case in *Macbeth:* Here, as I have said, the retiring of the human heart and the entrance of the fiendish heart was to be expressed and made sensible. Another world has stepped in; and the murderers are taken out of the region of human things, human purposes, human desires. They are transfigured: Lady Macbeth is "unsexed"; Macbeth has forgot that he was born of woman; both are conformed to the image of devils; and the world of devils is suddenly revealed. But how shall this be conveyed and made palpable? In order that a new world may step in, this world must for a time disappear. The murderers and the murder must be insulated—cut off by an immeasurable gulf from the ordinary tide and succession of human affairs—locked up and sequestered in some deep recess; we must be made sensible that the world of ordinary life is suddenly arrested, laid asleep, tranced, racked into a dread armistice; time must be annihilated, relation to things without abolished; and all must pass self-withdrawn into a deep syncope[2] and suspension of earthly passion. Hence it is that, when the deed is done, when the work of darkness is perfect, then the world of darkness passes away like a pageantry in the clouds: The knocking at the gate is heard, and it makes known audibly that the reaction has commenced; the human has made its reflux upon the fiendish; the pulses of life are beginning to beat again; and the reestablishment of the goings-on of the world in which we live first makes us profoundly sensible of the awful parenthesis that had suspended them.

2. **syncope** (siŋ′kə·pē): unconsciousness.

Ross.   Well, I will thither.
Macduff.
    Well, may you see things well done there. Adieu,
    Lest our old robes sit easier than our new!
Ross.
    Farewell, father.
Old Man.
40   God's benison° go with you, and with those
    That would make good of bad, and friends of foes!
                  [*Exeunt omnes.*]

40. **benison:** blessing.

Critical Comment

Macbeth's Porter

Why does Macbeth's comic porter—speaking a gross, drunken rigmarole—appear in Scene 3, right after the murder of Duncan? Is this not a monstrous interruption?

One way to account for the scene is to remind ourselves that Shakespeare was writer-in-residence to a company of actors and therefore bound to provide parts for every member in every play—even a part for the chief comedian in a tragedy. But this is not a satisfactory explanation because it was not characteristic of Shakespeare merely to do what was expected of him as a professional writer; he always did something more, almost making a virtue out of theatrical necessity. And so, as a second explanation of the porter's scene, some critics have argued that it is designed to provide **comic relief** from the tense aftermath of Duncan's murder. But this also is not a convincing reason, because the scene actually increases tension rather than relieves it. As Macbeth and his wife stand whispering about the evil thing they have done, they—and the audience—are startled to hear a loud and totally unexpected knocking on the main gate of the castle. Even a hardened criminal would be startled by the coincidence of these events, and Macbeth and his wife are mere beginners in crime. While they hastily retreat into their bedroom, the porter (a word meaning "door tender") shuffles on stage to answer the knocking at his leisure, thus prolonging the interval between the murder and its discovery and greatly increasing suspense. And, after all, suspense is what makes drama interesting.

Theatergoers in Shakespeare's day were accustomed to comic porters; they were familiar figures in miracle plays, in which they kept the gates of hell. They were expected to be droll and at the same time sinister. "Who's there, i' th' name of Beelzebub?" asks Macbeth's porter, referring to one of the chief devils and implying that the castle is a place the Devil occupies. And indeed it already has become hell, which is as much a state of mind as a particular place. Lady Macbeth has called for the "smoke of hell" in Act I, and Macbeth has been unable to say "Amen" when Duncan's men cried "God bless us!" in Act II. To cut out the porter's scene, as many directors have done (and also many editors of school texts), is to weaken the fabric of the play.

Mervyn Blake as the porter in the Stratford Festival production of *Macbeth* (1983).

MAKING MEANINGS

Act II

First Thoughts

1. What was your reaction to the murder of Duncan? Why do you think Shakespeare decided to murder Duncan and his guards offstage?

Reading Check

a. In Scene 1, Macbeth asks Banquo to meet him later for "some words." What incentive does he offer Banquo? How does Banquo reply?

b. Describe the vision that Macbeth has at the end of Scene 1. What details foreshadow the action to come?

c. In Scene 2, as Macbeth kills Duncan, what does Lady Macbeth hear? What does Macbeth hear?

d. Why, according to Lady Macbeth, was she unable to kill Duncan herself? Which tasks related to the murder does she perform?

e. In Scene 2, how does Macbeth respond to Lady Macbeth's suggestion that he go wash the "filthy witness" from his hands?

f. In Scene 3, what is the porter pretending as he goes to open the gate?

g. Why has Macduff come?

h. What reason does Macbeth give for killing Duncan's two guards?

i. Where do Duncan's sons decide to go?

j. In Scene 4, whom does Macduff suspect of Duncan's murder?

Shaping Interpretations

2. Though Macbeth encounters no actual opposition until long after Duncan is murdered, Shakespeare must **foreshadow** some trouble for him and, to build up **suspense,** must start one character edging toward suspicion of Macbeth. Who is this character, and what inkling does he give of his dissatisfaction with Macbeth?

3. In Act I, Scene 7, Lady Macbeth seemed to be planning to murder Duncan herself. But at the last moment, in Act II, Scene 2, she is unable to wield her dagger. Consider the reason she gives, and decide what her actions and explanation reveal about her **character.**

4. In Scene 3, when Duncan's corpse is discovered, Macbeth utters a hypocritical lament beginning, "Had I but died. . . ." But is it really hypocritical? The critic A. C. Bradley argues that, although the speech is meant to be a lie, it actually contains "Macbeth's profoundest feelings." Explain this apparent contradiction. How does Macbeth feel about having murdered Duncan? What clues tell you how he feels?

5. Lady Macbeth's fainting spell, like everything else she has done so far, has a purpose. What message do you think she wants her fainting spell to convey?

6. Macduff becomes an important character in the three remaining acts. Describe how Shakespeare **characterizes** him in Scenes 3 and 4.

7. What would you say is the **mood** of Act II? What **images** and actions help to create this mood? Why might images of blood and water appear in Scene 2? What do they **symbolize?**

Extending the Text

8. A terrible murder is committed in this act. How do various characters respond to the violence? How would people today, say, react to the news that a ruler has been assassinated in cold blood and that a nation is in political chaos?

Challenging the Text

9. Review De Quincey's interpretation of the porter's scene in the ***Connections*** on page 330; review also the Critical Comment on page 332. What purpose do you see for this scene? Is it just for **comic relief,** or does it have other dramatic functions? Give reasons for your interpretation.

10. In some productions of *Macbeth,* Scene 4 is cut. Why would this be done? Is there any dramatic purpose for keeping it? Why do you think the Old Man is included in the scene?

ACT III

Scene 1. *Forres. The palace.*

Enter BANQUO.

Banquo.
Thou hast it now: king, Cawdor, Glamis, all,
As the weird women promised, and I fear
Thou play'dst most foully for't. Yet it was said
It should not stand° in thy posterity,

5   But that myself should be the root and father
Of many kings. If there come truth from them—
As upon thee, Macbeth, their speeches shine—
Why, by the verities on thee made good,
May they not be my oracles as well

10 And set me up in hope? But hush, no more!

[*Sennet*° *sounded. Enter* MACBETH *as king,* LADY MACBETH,
LENNOX, ROSS, LORDS, *and* ATTENDANTS.]

Macbeth.
Here's our chief guest.
Lady Macbeth.   If he had been forgotten,
It had been as a gap in our great feast,
And all-thing° unbecoming.
Macbeth.
Tonight we hold a solemn supper, sir,
And I'll request your presence.

15 **Banquo.**   Let your highness
Command upon me, to the which my duties
Are with a most indissoluble tie
For ever knit.
Macbeth.
Ride you this afternoon?
Banquo.   Ay, my good lord.
Macbeth.

20 We should have else desired your good advice
(Which still° hath been both grave and prosperous°)
In this day's council; but we'll take tomorrow.
Is't far you ride?
Banquo.
As far, my lord, as will fill up the time

25 'Twixt this and supper. Go not my horse the better,°
I must become a borrower of the night
For a dark hour or twain.
Macbeth.   Fail not our feast.
Banquo.
My lord, I will not.
Macbeth.
We hear our bloody cousins are bestowed°

30 In England and in Ireland, not confessing

---

4. stand: continue.

10. *What would you say Banquo's mood is? Is he envious or thoughtful and troubled?*
Sennet: trumpet.

13. all-thing: altogether.

21. still: always.   **grave and prosperous:** weighty and profitable.

25. Go not my horse the better: unless my horse goes faster than I expect.

29. are bestowed: have taken refuge.

Their cruel parricide, filling their hearers
With strange invention.° But of that tomorrow,
When therewithal we shall have cause of state
Craving us jointly.° Hie you to horse. Adieu,
35 Till you return at night. Goes Fleance with you?

Banquo.
Ay, my good lord: our time does call upon 's.

Macbeth.
I wish your horses swift and sure of foot,
And so I do commend you to their backs.
Farewell.   [*Exit* BANQUO.]
40 Let every man be master of his time
Till seven at night. To make society
The sweeter welcome, we will keep ourself
Till supper-time alone. While° then, God be with you!

[*Exeunt* LORDS *and all but* MACBETH *and a* SERVANT.]

Sirrah, a word with you: attend° those men
45 Our pleasure?

Attendant.
They are, my lord, without the palace gate.

Macbeth.
Bring them before us.   [*Exit* SERVANT.]
To be thus° is nothing, but° to be safely thus—
Our fears in Banquo stick deep,
50 And in his royalty of nature reigns that
Which would be feared. 'Tis much he dares;
And, to° that dauntless temper° of his mind,
He hath a wisdom that doth guide his valor
To act in safety. There is none but he
55 Whose being I do fear: and under him
My genius is rebuked,° as it is said
Mark Antony's was by Caesar. He chid the sisters,
When first they put the name of king upon me,
And bade them speak to him; then prophetlike
60 They hailed him father to a line of kings.
Upon my head they placed a fruitless crown
And put a barren scepter in my gripe,
Thence to be wrenched with an unlineal hand,
No son of mine succeeding. If 't be so,
65 For Banquo's issue have I filed° my mind;
For them the gracious Duncan have I murdered;
Put rancors° in the vessel of my peace
Only for them, and mine eternal jewel°
Given to the common enemy of man,°
70 To make them kings, the seeds of Banquo kings!
Rather than so, come, fate, into the list,°
And champion me to th' utterance!° Who's there?

---

32. invention: lies.

34. us jointly: our joint attention.

❓ **35.** *Macbeth has asked three important questions in this scene. What are they? How do you think he would ask them?*

❓ **42.** *Notice that Macbeth uses the "royal we"; that is, he speaks of himself as "we," as a representative of all the people. Why do you think he wants to be alone?*

43. While: until.

44. attend: await.

48. thus: king. **but:** unless.

52. to: added to. **temper:** quality.

56. genius is rebuked: guardian spirit is cowed.

❓ **63.** *What is an "unlineal hand"? What is a "barren scepter"? What is eating at Macbeth now?*

65. filed: defiled; dirtied.

67. rancors: bitter enmity.

68. eternal jewel: immortal soul.

69. common enemy of man: Satan.

71. list: battle.

72. champion me to th' utterance: fight against me till I give up.

❓ **72.** *Why exactly is Macbeth so angry? What has he given up in order to make Banquo's sons kings?*

[*Enter* SERVANT *and two* MURDERERS.]

Now go to the door, and stay there till we call.

[*Exit* SERVANT.]

Was it not yesterday we spoke together?

Murderers.

It was, so please your highness.

75 **Macbeth.**   Well then, now
Have you considered of my speeches? Know
That it was he in the times past, which held you
So under fortune,° which you thought had been
Our innocent self: this I made good to you
80 In our last conference; passed in probation° with you,
How you were borne in hand,° how crossed; the instruments,°
Who wrought with them, and all things else that might
To half a soul° and to a notion° crazed
Say "Thus did Banquo."

First Murderer.   You made it known to us.

Macbeth.

85 I did so; and went further, which is now
Our point of second meeting. Do you find
Your patience so predominant in your nature,
That you can let this go? Are you so gospeled,°
To pray for this good man and for his issue,
90 Whose heavy hand hath bowed you to the grave
And beggared yours forever?

First Murderer.   We are men, my liege.

Macbeth.

Ay, in the catalogue ye go for° men;
As hounds and greyhounds, mongrels, spaniels, curs,
Shoughs, water-rugs° and demi-wolves, are clept°
95 All by the name of dogs: the valued file°
Distinguishes the swift, the slow, the subtle,
The housekeeper, the hunter, every one
According to the gift which bounteous nature
Hath in him closed,° whereby he does receive
100 Particular addition, from the bill°
That writes them all alike: and so of men.
Now if you have a station in the file,
Not i' th' worst rank of manhood, say 't,
And I will put that business in your bosoms
105 Whose execution takes your enemy off,
Grapples you to the heart and love of us,
Who wear our health but sickly in his life,°
Which in his death were perfect.

Second Murderer.   I am one, my liege,
Whom the vile blows and buffets of the world
110 Hath so incensed that I am reckless what
I do to spite the world.

74. *What do you imagine the murderers would be like: the all-too-common "hit men" of contemporary movies? Or could they simply be officers who have a grudge against Banquo? (They have been portrayed in many ways.)*

78. held you / So under fortune: kept you from good fortune.

80. probation: review.

81. borne in hand: deceived. **instruments:** tools.

83. soul: brain.   **notion:** mind.

88. gospeled: so meek from reading the Gospel (of Jesus).

91. *What techniques is Macbeth using on the murderers? Does it remind you of the way Lady Macbeth goaded him into killing Duncan?*

92. go for: pass as.

94. Shoughs, water-rugs: shaggy dogs and long-haired water dogs. **clept:** called.

95. valued file: classification by valuable traits.

99. closed: enclosed.

100. bill: list.

107. who wear . . . life: who are "sick" while he (Banquo) still lives.

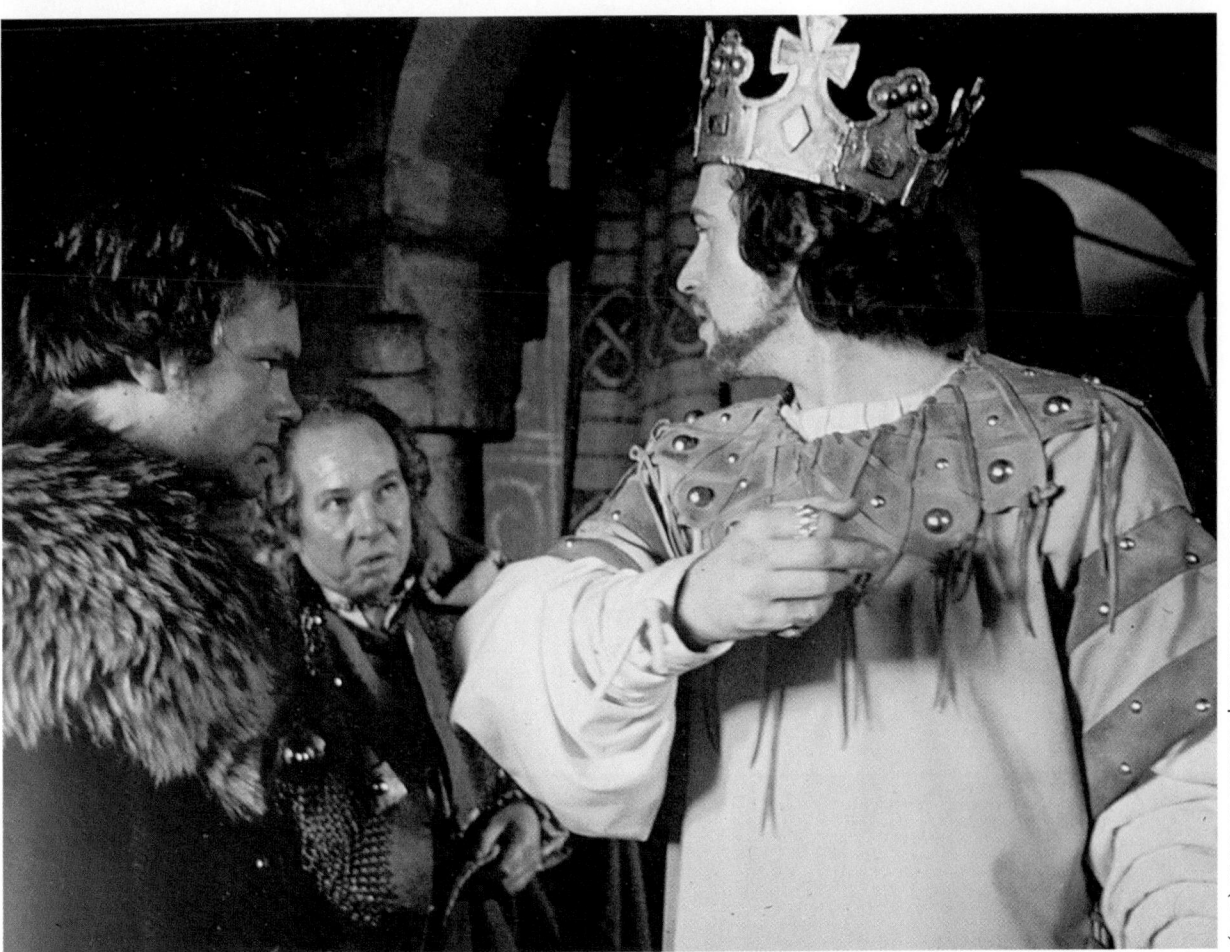

"It is concluded: Banquo, thy soul's flight,
If it find heaven, must find it out tonight."

First Murderer. And I another
So weary with disasters, tugged with fortune,
That I would set° my life on any chance,
To mend it or be rid on't.
Macbeth. Both of you
Know Banquo was your enemy.
115 **Both Murderers.** True, my lord.
Macbeth.
So is he mine, and in such bloody distance°
That every minute of his being thrusts
Against my near'st of life:° and though I could
With barefaced power sweep him from my sight
120 And bid my will avouch° it, yet I must not,
For° certain friends that are both his and mine,
Whose loves I may not drop, but wail his fall
Who I myself struck down: and thence it is
That I to your assistance do make love,
125 Masking the business from the common eye
For sundry weighty reasons.

113. **set:** risk.

116. **distance:** quarrel.

118. **near'st of life:** vital spot.

120. **avouch:** justify.
121. **For:** because of.

? 126. *How is Macbeth justifying to the murderers the fact that he has to ask them to do the job of killing Banquo?*

From Roman Polanski's film production of *Macbeth* (1971).

Second Murderer.　　　　We shall, my lord,
　　Perform what you command us.

First Murderer.　　　　　　Though our lives——
Macbeth.
　　Your spirits shine through you. Within this hour at most
　　I will advise you where to plant yourselves,
130　　Acquaint you with the perfect spy° o' th' time,
　　The moment on't; for't must be done tonight,
　　And something° from the palace; always thought°
　　That I require a clearness:° and with him—
　　To leave no rubs° nor botches in the work—
135　　Fleance his son, that keeps him company,
　　Whose absence is no less material to me
　　Than is his father's, must embrace the fate
　　Of that dark hour. Resolve yourselves apart:°
　　I'll come to you anon.
Murderers.　　　　We are resolved, my lord.
Macbeth.
140　　I'll call upon you straight. Abide within.

130. perfect spy: exact information.

132. something: some distance. **thought:** remembered.

133. clearness: freedom from suspicion.

134. rubs: flaws.

138. apart: alone (make up your minds by yourselves).

? **140.** *What has Macbeth arranged with the murderers? What is his mood here? Does Lady Macbeth have any part in arranging these next murders?*

"Gentle my lord, sleek o'er your rugged looks."

From Roman Polanski's film production of *Macbeth* (1971).

It is concluded: Banquo, thy soul's flight,
If it find heaven, must find it out tonight.   [*Exeunt.*]

Scene 2. *The palace.*

Enter LADY MACBETH *and a* SERVANT.

Lady Macbeth.
Is Banquo gone from court?
Servant.
Ay, madam, but returns again tonight.
Lady Macbeth.
Say to the king, I would attend his leisure
For a few words.
Servant.   Madam, I will.   [*Exit.*]
Lady Macbeth.   Nought's had, all's spent,
5   Where our desire is got without content:
'Tis safer to be that which we destroy
Than by destruction dwell in doubtful joy.

[*Enter* MACBETH.]

How now, my lord! Why do you keep alone,
Of sorriest fancies your companions making,
10   Using those thoughts which should indeed have died
With them they think on? Things without° all remedy
Should be without regard: what's done is done.
Macbeth.
We have scorched° the snake, not killed it:
She'll close° and be herself, whilst our poor malice°
15   Remains in danger of her former tooth.
But let the frame of things disjoint,° both the worlds° suffer,
Ere we will eat our meal in fear, and sleep
In the affliction of these terrible dreams
That shake us nightly: better be with the dead,
20   Whom we, to gain our peace, have sent to peace,
Than on the torture of the mind to lie
In restless ecstasy.° Duncan is in his grave;
After life's fitful fever he sleeps well.
Treason has done his worst: nor steel, nor poison,
25   Malice domestic,° foreign levy,° nothing,
Can touch him further.
Lady Macbeth.   Come on.
Gentle my lord, sleek° o'er your rugged° looks;
Be bright and jovial among your guests tonight.
Macbeth.
So shall I, love; and so, I pray, be you:
30   Let your remembrance apply to Banquo;°
Present him eminence,° both with eye and tongue:
Unsafe the while, that we must lave°
Our honors in these flattering streams

7. *What reversal of attitudes is taking place here?*

11. without: beyond.

12. *This scene can be played in several ways. Is Lady Macbeth hostile to her husband and angry with him? Or can she be shown to have some tenderness in this scene?*

13. scorched: slashed.

14. close: heal.   **malice:** enmity; hatred.

16. frame of things disjoint: universe collapse.   **worlds:** heaven and earth.

22. ecstasy: frenzy.

25. Malice domestic: domestic war (civil war).   **foreign levy:** exaction of tribute by a foreign country.

26. *What do you picture the couple doing in this scene? Are they sitting together? Are they close, or is there a distance between them?*

27. sleek: smooth.   **rugged:** furrowed.

30. Let . . . Banquo: That is, focus your thoughts on Banquo.

31. eminence: honors.

32. lave: wash.

LITERATURE AND COMPUTERS

The Bard and the Database

In literary circles it's known as the "Authorship Question": Did William Shakespeare, the actor from Stratford-on-Avon, really write the greatest poetry the world has ever known?

This question has been around since the 1700s, and over the years people have proposed as many as fifty-eight various writers as possible authors of Shakespeare's plays and poems, ranging from Sir Francis Bacon to Sir Walter Raleigh to Queen Elizabeth I herself.

Matching Shakespeare. Hoping to apply some twentieth-century computer technology to this seventeenth-century problem, Professor Ward Elliott of Claremont McKenna College near Los Angeles created a database of Renaissance literature, including the King James Bible, all of Shakespeare's poetry, and material from twenty-seven of the most promising candidates, and embarked upon his "Matching Shakespeare" study. Elliott's plan was first to identify Shakespeare's unique style

---

And make our faces vizards° to our hearts,
Disguising what they are.
35 **Lady Macbeth.**   You must leave this.
Macbeth.
O, full of scorpions is my mind, dear wife!
Thou know'st that Banquo, and his Fleance, lives.
Lady Macbeth.
But in them nature's copy's not eterne.°
Macbeth.
There's comfort yet; they are assailable.
40 Then be thou jocund. Ere the bat hath flown
His cloistered flight, ere to black Hecate's summons
The shard-borne° beetle with his drowsy hums
Hath rung night's yawning peal, there shall be done
A deed of dreadful note.
Lady Macbeth.   What's to be done?
Macbeth.
45 Be innocent of the knowledge, dearest chuck,°
Till thou applaud the deed. Come, seeling° night,
Scarf up° the tender eye of pitiful day,
And with thy bloody and invisible hand
Cancel and tear to pieces that great bond

---

34. vizards: masks.

? **35.** *With what degree of urgency must Lady Macbeth say this line?*

38. nature's copy's not eterne: That is, they won't live forever.

42. shard-borne: carried on scaly wings.

45. chuck: chick (a term of endearment).
46. seeling: eye-closing; blinding.
47. Scarf up: blindfold.

through computer analysis and then to compare this to the styles of various writers to see if any matched up.

Elliott's "Matching Shakespeare" study applied dozens of different linguistic tests, but five conventional tests and a powerful new one proved most accurate. The conventional tests measured features like the number of relative clauses and hyphenated compound words and length of words and sentences, and the new test used a pattern recognition technique.

And the real Shakespeare is. What have the tests shown? Did Shakespeare write Shakespeare? Based on his studies, Elliott believes that he has been able to eliminate all the principal candidates. Every writer failed at least one of the conventional tests, with some failing four or five. On the other hand, Shakespeare's writings all fell within a consistent profile. Although the study does not definitively prove that it was Shakespeare himself who wrote the works attributed to him, Elliott (along with most reputable scholars) feels that it does demonstrate that one individual *did* write them all.

Why has such a fuss been made about the authorship of Shakespeare's works? In part, it's because people cannot believe that someone who led such a seemingly ordinary life could have been such a genius. Shakespeare still confounds all the scholarly detectives who continue to debate the "Authorship Question."

50   Which keeps me pale! Light thickens, and the crow
     Makes wing to th' rooky° wood.
     Good things of day begin to droop and drowse,
     Whiles night's black agents to their preys do rouse.
     Thou marvel'st at my words: but hold thee still;
55   Things bad begun make strong themselves by ill:
     So, prithee, go with me.   [*Exeunt.*]

51. rooky: full of rooks, or crows.

Scene 3. *Near the palace.*

Enter three MURDERERS.

First Murderer.
   But who did bid thee join with us?
Third Murderer.   Macbeth.
Second Murderer.
   He needs not our mistrust; since he delivers
   Our offices and what we have to do
   To the direction just.°
First Murderer.   Then stand with us.
5   The west yet glimmers with some streaks of day.
     Now spurs the lated° traveler apace

1. *The identity of the Third Murderer is not made clear. Whom would you name as possible suspects?*

4. He needs . . . just: We need not mistrust him (the Third Murderer) since he describes our duties according to our exact directions.

6. lated: belated.

"O, treachery! Fly, good Fleance, fly, fly, fly!"

From Roman Polanski's film production of *Macbeth* (1971).

To gain the timely inn, and near approaches
The subject of our watch.
Third Murderer.   Hark! I hear horses.
Banquo (*within*). Give us a light there, ho!
Second Murderer.   Then 'tis he. The rest
10   That are within the note of expectation°
Already are i' th' court.
First Murderer.   His horses go about.
Third Murderer.
Almost a mile: but he does usually—
So all men do—from hence to th' palace gate
Make it their walk.

[*Enter* BANQUO *and* FLEANCE, *with a torch.*]

Second Murderer.
A light, a light!
Third Murderer. 'Tis he.
15 **First Murderer.**   Stand to't.

10. within . . . expectation: on the list of expected guests.

Banquo.
It will be rain tonight.
First Murderer.   Let it come down.

[*They set upon* BANQUO.]

Banquo.
O, treachery! Fly, good Fleance, fly, fly, fly!

[*Exit* FLEANCE.]

Thou mayst revenge. O slave!   [*Dies.*]
Third Murderer.
Who did strike out the light?
First Murderer.   Was't not the way?°
Third Murderer.
20 There's but one down; the son is fled.
Second Murderer.
We have lost best half of our affair.
First Murderer.
Well, let's away and say how much is done.   [*Exeunt.*]

Scene 4. *The palace.*
Banquet prepared. Enter MACBETH, LADY MACBETH, ROSS, LENNOX,
LORDS, *and* ATTENDANTS.

Macbeth.
You know your own degrees;° sit down:
At first and last, the hearty welcome.
Lords.
Thanks to your majesty.
Macbeth.
Oneself will mingle with society°
5 And play the humble host.
Our hostess keeps her state,° but in best time
We will require° her welcome.
Lady Macbeth.
Pronounce it for me, sir, to all our friends,
For my heart speaks they are welcome.

[*Enter* FIRST MURDERER.]

Macbeth.
10 See, they encounter° thee with their hearts' thanks.
Both sides are even: here I'll sit i' th' midst:
Be large in mirth; anon we'll drink a measure°
The table round. (*Goes to* FIRST MURDERER.) There's blood
     upon thy face.
Murderer.
'Tis Banquo's then.
Macbeth.
15 'Tis better thee without than he within.°
Is he dispatched?

19. *What would the murderers be doing as the light goes out?*
19. way: thing to do.

21. *Disposal of bodies is always a problem for directors of Shakespeare's plays. How would you have Banquo's body carried off? By whom?*

22. *This scene, so necessary to the play, is often called the play's turning point or technical climax. What have been Macbeth's good fortunes so far?*

1. degrees: ranks.

2. *This crucial scene is often called the dramatic climax of the play; it is tremendously exciting when staged well. Notice where Macbeth's subjects become aware of his capacity for irrational behavior.*

4. society: the company.

6. keeps her state: remains seated in her chair of state.

7. require: request.

10. encounter: meet.

12. measure: goblet.

15. thee . . . within: outside you than inside him.

"Never shake / Thy gory locks at me."

From the Stratford Festival production of *Macbeth* (1983).

Murderer.   My lord, his throat is cut;
    That I did for him.
Macbeth.   Thou are the best o' th' cutthroats.
    Yet he's good that did the like for Fleance;
    If thou didst it, thou art the nonpareil.
Murderer.
20   Most royal sir, Fleance is 'scaped.
Macbeth (*aside*).
    Then comes my fit again: I had else been perfect,
    Whole as the marble, founded° as the rock,
    As broad and general as the casing air:°
    But now I am cabined, cribbed,° confined, bound in
25   To saucy° doubts and fears.—But Banquo's safe?
Murderer.
    Ay, my good lord: safe in a ditch he bides,
    With twenty trenchèd° gashes on his head,
    The least a death to nature.
Macbeth.   Thanks for that.
    (*Aside.*) There the grown serpent lies; the worm° that's fled
30   Hath nature that in time will venom breed,
    No teeth for th' present. Get thee gone. Tomorrow
    We'll hear ourselves° again.   [*Exit* FIRST MURDERER.]

? **20.** *How would Macbeth react to this line?*

22. founded: firmly based.
23. broad . . . casing air: unconfined as the surrounding air.
24. cribbed: penned up.
25. saucy: insolent.

27. trenchèd: trenchlike.

29. worm: serpent.

32. hear ourselves: talk it over.

Lady Macbeth.   My royal lord,
You do not give the cheer.° The feast is sold
That is not often vouched, while 'tis a-making,
35 'Tis given with welcome. To feed were best at home;°
From thence, the sauce to meat° is ceremony;
Meeting were bare without it.

[*Enter the* GHOST OF BANQUO, *and sits in Macbeth's place.*]

Macbeth.   Sweet remembrancer!°
Now good digestion wait on appetite,
And health on both!
Lennox.   May't please your highness sit.
Macbeth.
40 Here had we now our country's honor roofed,°
Were the graced person of our Banquo present—
Who may I rather challenge for unkindness
Than pity for mischance!°
Ross.   His absence, sir,
Lays blame upon his promise. Please't your highness
45 To grace us with your royal company?
Macbeth.
The table's full.
Lennox.   Here is a place reserved, sir.
Macbeth.
Where?
Lennox.
Here, my good lord. What is't that moves your highness?
Macbeth.
Which of you have done this?
Lords.   What, my good lord?
Macbeth.
50 Thou canst not say I did it. Never shake
Thy gory locks at me.
Ross.
Gentlemen, rise, his highness is not well.
Lady Macbeth.
Sit, worthy friends. My Lord is often thus,
And hath been from his youth. Pray you, keep seat.
55 The fit is momentary; upon a thought°
He will again be well. If much you note him,
You shall offend him and extend his passion.°
Feed, and regard him not.—Are you a man?
Macbeth.
Ay, and a bold one, that dare look on that
Which might appall the devil.
60 **Lady Macbeth.**   O proper stuff!
This is the very painting of your fear.
This is the air-drawn dagger which, you said,
Led you to Duncan. O, these flaws° and starts,
Imposters to° true fear, would well become

33. cheer: sense of cordiality.

35. The feast . . . home: The feast seems sold (not given) when the host fails to welcome the guests. Mere eating is best done at home.

36. meat: food.

? **37.** *Lady Macbeth has summoned her husband to her area of the stage. What mood is she in?*

? **Stage direction.** *The ghost is crucial to this scene. From what you read here, should the ghost be imagined? Or should it actually appear on stage? How should it look, if so?*

37. remembrancer: reminder.

40. our . . . roofed: our nobility under one roof.

43. Who . . . mischance: whom I hope I may reprove because he is unkind rather than pity because he has encountered an accident.

? **46.** *When Macbeth says this line, what does he see?*

? **49.** *How should Macbeth ask this question? Whom should he be talking to?*

? **51.** *According to Macbeth's speech here, what is the ghost doing? Does anyone else see the ghost? How should the others be acting?*

? **53.** *Do you think this is true? Or is Lady Macbeth desperately trying to cover for her husband?*

55. upon a thought: as quick as a thought.

57. extend his passion: lengthen his fit.

? **58.** *Where do you think Lady Macbeth has taken her husband so that she can whisper this intimidating line?*

63. flaws: gusts; outbursts.

64. to: compared with.

65   A woman's story at a winter's fire,
    Authorized° by her grandam. Shame itself!
    Why do you make such faces? When all's done,
    You look but on a stool.

Macbeth.   Prithee, see there!
    Behold! Look! Lo! How say you?
70   Why, what care I? If thou canst nod, speak too.
    If charnel houses° and our graves must send
    Those that we bury back, our monuments
    Shall be the maws of kites.°   [*Exit* GHOST.]

Lady Macbeth.   What, quite unmanned in folly?
Macbeth.
    If I stand here, I saw him.

Lady Macbeth.   Fie, for shame!
Macbeth.
75   Blood hath been shed ere now, i' th' olden time,
    Ere humane statute purged the gentle weal;°
    Ay, and since too, murders have been performed
    Too terrible for the ear. The time has been
    That, when the brains were out, the man would die,
80   And there an end; but now they rise again,
    With twenty mortal murders on their crowns,°
    And push us from our stools. This is more strange
    Than such a murder is.

Lady Macbeth.   My worthy lord,
    Your noble friends do lack you.

Macbeth.   I do forget.
85   Do not muse at me, my most worthy friends;
    I have a strange infirmity, which is nothing
    To those that know me. Come, love and health to all!
    Then I'll sit down. Give me some wine, fill full.

[*Enter* GHOST.]

    I drink to th' general joy o' th' whole table,
90   And to our dear friend Banquo, whom we miss;
    Would he were here! To all and him we thirst,°
    And all to all.°

Lords.   Our duties, and the pledge.
Macbeth.
    Avaunt! and quit my sight! Let the earth hide thee!
    Thy bones are marrowless, thy blood is cold;
95   Thou hast no speculation° in those eyes
    Which thou dost glare with.

Lady Macbeth.   Think of this, good peers,
    But as a thing of custom; 'tis no other.
    Only it spoils the pleasure of the time.

Macbeth.
    What man dare, I dare.
100   Approach thou like the rugged Russian bear,
    The armed rhinoceros, or th' Hyrcan° tiger;

---

66. Authorized: vouched for.

? 68. *What could the actor playing Banquo do here in mockery of Macbeth?*

? 70. *What action is Macbeth engaged in here? What is his tone?*

71. charnel houses: vaults containing bones.

73. our . . . kites: Our tombs shall be the bellies of rapacious birds.

? 75. *Whom is Macbeth talking to?*

76. purged . . . weal: cleansed the state and made it gentle.

81. mortal . . . crowns: deadly wounds on their heads.

? 85. *What impression is Macbeth trying to create?*

91. thirst: desire to drink.

92. all to all: Let everybody drink to everybody.

? 93. *Whom is Macbeth talking to now? According to this speech, what might the ghost be doing?*

95. speculation: sight.

101. Hyrcan: of Hyrcania (near the Caspian Sea).

Take any shape but that, and my firm nerves°
Shall never tremble. Or be alive again,
And dare me to the desert° with thy sword.
105 If trembling I inhabit then, protest me
The baby of a girl.° Hence, horrible shadow!
Unreal mock'ry, hence!   [*Exit* GHOST.]
                    Why, so: being gone,
I am a man again. Pray you, sit still.
Lady Macbeth.
You have displaced the mirth, broke the good meeting,
With most admired° disorder.
110 **Macbeth.**   Can such things be,
And overcome us° like a summer's cloud,
Without our special wonder? You make me strange
Even to the disposition that I owe,°
When now I think you can behold such sights,
115 And keep the natural ruby of your cheeks,
When mine is blanched with fear.
Ross.   What sights, my lord?
Lady Macbeth.
I pray you, speak not: he grows worse and worse;
Question enrages him: at once, good night.
Stand not upon the order of your going,°
But go at once.
120 **Lennox.**   Good night; and better health
Attend his majesty!
Lady Macbeth.   A kind good night to all!

                    [*Exeunt* LORDS.]

Macbeth.
It will have blood, they say: blood will have blood.
Stones have been known to move and trees to speak;
Augurs and understood relations° have
125 By maggot-pies and choughs and rooks brought forth°
The secret'st man of blood. What is the night?°
Lady Macbeth.
Almost at odds with morning, which is which.
Macbeth.
How say'st thou, that Macduff denies his person
At our great bidding?
Lady Macbeth.   Did you send to him, sir?
Macbeth.
130 I hear it by the way,° but I will send:
There's not a one of them but in his house
I keep a servant fee'd.° I will tomorrow,
And betimes° I will, to the weird sisters:
More shall they speak, for now I am bent° to know
135 By the worst means the worst. For mine own good
All causes° shall give way. I am in blood
Stepped in so far that, should I wade no more,

102. **nerves:** sinews.

104. **desert:** lonely place.

106. **If . . . girl:** If then I tremble, proclaim me a baby girl.

[?] 108. *How "brave" should Macbeth appear to be with all the "brave" talk in these lines? What is his mood when he says "I am a man again"?*

110. **admired:** amazing.

[?] 110. *Lady Macbeth and her husband converse in private again. What would the other guests be doing?*

111. **overcome us:** come over us.

113. **You . . . owe:** You make me wonder what my nature is.

[?] 117. *What clue here would tell the actor playing Macbeth how he is to be behaving?*

119. **Stand . . . going:** Do not insist on departing in your order of rank.

[?] 122. *Read this speech carefully, and decide how Macbeth would deliver it: Slow? Fast? What is his mood?*

124. **Augurs . . . relations:** auguries (omens) and comprehended reports.

125. **By . . . forth:** by magpies, crows, and rooks (telltale birds) revealed.

126. **What . . . night:** What time of night is it?

[?] 127. *Is the old fire still present in Lady Macbeth? Or is she suddenly tired and broken?*

130. **by the way:** incidentally.

132. **fee'd:** that is, paid to spy.

133. **betimes:** quickly.

134. **bent:** determined.

136. **causes:** considerations.

"Come, let's make haste; she'll soon be back again."

Returning were as tedious as go o'er.
Strange things I have in head that will to hand,
140   Which must be acted ere they may be scanned.°
Lady Macbeth.
  You lack the season of all natures,° sleep.
Macbeth.
  Come, we'll to sleep. My strange and self-abuse°
  Is the initiate fear that wants hard use.°
  We are yet but young in deed.   [*Exeunt.*]

Scene 5. *A witches' haunt.*

Thunder. Enter the three WITCHES, *meeting* HECATE.

First Witch.
  Why, how now, Hecate! you look angerly.
Hecate.
  Have I not reason, beldams° as you are,
  Saucy and overbold? How did you dare
  To trade and traffic with Macbeth
5   In riddles and affairs of death;

140. *Does the prospect of a new adventure animate Macbeth? Or is he spent and exhausted?*
140. may be scanned: can be examined.
141. season . . . natures: seasoning (preservative) of all living creatures.
142. self-abuse: delusion.
143. initiate . . . use: beginner's fear that lacks hardening practice.
144. *How might Lady Macbeth react to this last line?*
Scene 5. Macbeth *was published in the first folio in 1623, seven years after Shakespeare had died. Some people think that this scene was written by someone else because the play was short and needed fleshing out. After you read the scene, decide if you think it "sounds" like the rest of the play.*
2. beldams: hags.

And I, the mistress of your charms,
The close contriver° of all harms,
Was never called to bear my part,
Or show the glory of our art?
10 And, which is worse, all you have done
Hath been but for a wayward son,
Spiteful and wrathful; who, as others do,
Loves for his own ends, not for you.
But make amends now: get you gone,
15 And at the pit of Acheron°
Meet me i' th' morning: thither he
Will come to know his destiny.
Your vessels and your spells provide,
Your charms and everything beside.
20 I am for th' air; this night I'll spend
Unto a dismal and a fatal end:
Great business must be wrought ere noon.
Upon the corner of the moon
There hangs a vap'rous drop profound;°
25 I'll catch it ere it come to ground:
And that distilled by magic sleights°
Shall raise such artificial sprites°
As by the strength of their illusion
Shall draw him on to his confusion.°
30 He shall spurn fate, scorn death, and bear
His hopes 'bove wisdom, grace, and fear:
And you all know security°
Is mortal's chiefest enemy.   [*Music and a song.*]
Hark! I am called; my little spirit, see,
35 Sits in a foggy cloud and stays for me.   [*Exit.*]

[*Sing within,* "Come away, come away," *etc.*]

First Witch.
Come, let's make haste; she'll soon be back again.

                                                    [*Exeunt.*]

Scene 6. *The palace.*

Enter LENNOX *and another* LORD.

Lennox.
My former speeches have but hit your thoughts,°
Which can interpret farther. Only I say
Things have been strangely borne.° The gracious Duncan
Was pitied of Macbeth: marry, he was dead.
5 And the right-valiant Banquo walked too late;
Whom, you may say, if't please you, Fleance killed,
For Fleance fled. Men must not walk too late.
Who cannot want the thought,° how monstrous
It was for Malcolm and for Donalbain
10 To kill their gracious father? Damnèd fact!°

7. close contriver: secret inventor.

15. Acheron: river of Hades.

24. profound: heavy.

26. sleights: arts.
27. artificial sprites: spirits created by magic arts.

29. confusion: ruin.

32. security: overconfidence.

1. My . . . thoughts: My recent words have only coincided with what you have in your mind.
3. borne: managed.

8. cannot . . . thought: cannot help but think.
10. fact: evil deed.

How it did grieve Macbeth! Did he not straight,
In pious rage, the two delinquents tear,
That were the slaves of drink and thralls° of sleep?
Was not that nobly done? Ay, and wisely too;
15   For 'twould have angered any heart alive
To hear the men deny't. So that I say
He has borne all things well: and I do think
That, had he Duncan's sons under his key—
As, an 't° please heaven, he shall not—they should find
20   What 'twere to kill a father. So should Fleance.
But, peace! for from broad words,° and 'cause he failed
His presence at the tyrant's feast, I hear,
Macduff lives in disgrace. Sir, can you tell
Where he bestows himself?

Lord.   The son of Duncan,
25   From whom this tyrant holds the due of birth,°
Lives in the English court, and is received
Of the most pious Edward° with such grace
That the malevolence of fortune nothing
Takes from his high respect.° Thither Macduff
30   Is gone to pray the holy king, upon his aid°
To wake Northumberland° and warlike Siward;°
That by the help of these, with Him above
To ratify the work, we may again
Give to our tables meat, sleep to our nights,
35   Free from our feasts and banquets bloody knives,
Do faithful homage and receive free° honors:
All which we pine for now. And this report
Hath so exasperate the king that he
Prepares for some attempt of war.

Lennox.   Sent he to Macduff?

Lord.
40   He did: and with an absolute "Sir, not I,"
The cloudy° messenger turns me his back,
And hums, as who should say "You'll rue the time
That clogs° me with this answer."

Lennox.   And that well might
Advise him to a caution, t' hold what distance
45   His wisdom can provide. Some holy angel
Fly to the court of England and unfold
His message ere he come, that a swift blessing
May soon return to this our suffering country
Under a hand accursed!

Lord.   I'll send my prayers with him.

                                     [*Exeunt.*]

13. **thralls:** slaves.

19. **an 't:** if it.

21. **for . . . words:** because of frank talk.

? 24. *Lennox is sometimes called the "ironic" character of the play. Do you agree? What tone would he use in this speech?*

25. **due of birth:** birthright.

27. **Edward:** Edward the Confessor (reigned 1042-1066).

29. **nothing . . . respect:** does not diminish the high respect in which he is held.

30. **upon his aid:** to aid him (Malcolm).

31. **To wake Northumberland:** that is, to arouse the people in an English county near Scotland. **Siward:** earl of Northumberland.

36. **free:** freely granted.

41. **cloudy:** disturbed.

43. **clogs:** burdens.

? 49. *This is basically an "information" scene. Can you summarize what it tells you about the plot?*

MAKING MEANINGS

Act III

First Thoughts

1. What title would you give to Act III?

Reading Check

a. In the short **soliloquy** that opens Scene 1, what does Banquo reveal that he knows about Macbeth? What does he decide to do?

b. How and why does Macbeth arrange Banquo's murder? How is Lady Macbeth involved in the murder?

c. In Scene 3, who escapes the murderers?

d. Describe what happens in Scene 4 when Ross, Lennox, and the other lords invite Macbeth to share their table. What does Macbeth do? What does Lady Macbeth do?

e. Macduff does not appear at all in Act III. Where is he, and why?

f. By Scene 6, what opinion do Lennox and the other lord hold of Macbeth?

Shaping Interpretations

2. Why do you suppose Shakespeare did not have Macbeth kill Banquo with his own hands, as he killed Duncan and his two guards? What can you infer about Macbeth's changing **character** after seeing how he engages in this complex plan involving professional murderers?

3. The relationship between Macbeth and Lady Macbeth has changed in several ways since they became rulers of Scotland. Find details in this act that reveal some of these changes. What reasons can you suggest for these changes?

4. In Scene 2, Macbeth describes his surroundings by saying, "Light thickens, and the crow /

Makes wing to th' rooky wood." How can these remarks also be seen as a **metaphorical** commentary on the events of the play? What other remarks by Macbeth function in this way?

5. In Shakespeare's tragedies, a **turning point** usually occurs in the third act. At this moment, something happens that moves the action ever downward to its tragic conclusion. How is Fleance's escape a **turning point** in this play?

6. How does the banquet scene blur the clear-cut and common-sense distinction that most of us make between the real and the imaginary? In what other scenes has this distinction also been blurred?

7. At the beginning of Scene 2, Lady Macbeth quietly tells herself, "Nought's had, all's spent, / Where our desire is got without content." What does she mean? At this point, would her husband agree?

8. Nobody except Macbeth sees Banquo's ghost. In some productions of the play, the ghost does not appear onstage; in others it does. If you were the director, which would you choose? What effect is created by having Banquo appear at the banquet, made up as a ghost? What is gained by having it appear as though no person motivates Macbeth's terrifying behavior?

Extending the Text

9. After his vision of Banquo's ghost in Scene 4, Macbeth finally accepts that "blood will have blood." What does this phrase mean? Is it relevant to today's world? How?

Challenging the Text

10. Shakespeare never reveals the identity of the Third Murderer, introduced in Scene 3. Who do you think the murderer is? Do you think the introduction of this Third Murderer is a flaw in the play? Explain your response.

ACT IV Scene 1. *A witches' haunt.*

Thunder. Enter the three WITCHES.

First Witch.
    Thrice the brinded° cat hath mewed.
Second Witch.
    Thrice and once the hedge-pig° whined.
Third Witch.
    Harpier° cries, 'Tis time, 'tis time.
First Witch.
    Round about the caldron go:
5   In the poisoned entrails throw.
    Toad, that under cold stone
    Days and nights has thirty-one
    Swelt'red venom sleeping got,°
    Boil thou first i' th' charmèd pot.
All.
10   Double, double, toil and trouble;
    Fire burn and caldron bubble.
Second Witch.
    Fillet° of a fenny° snake,
    In the caldron boil and bake;
    Eye of newt and toe of frog,
15   Wool of bat and tongue of dog,
    Adder's fork° and blindworm's° sting,
    Lizard's leg and howlet's° wing,
    For a charm of pow'rful trouble,
    Like a hell-broth boil and bubble.
All.
20   Double, double, toil and trouble;
    Fire burn and caldron bubble.

 Stage direction. *This scene usually begins in darkness. In Shakespeare's day, the caldron might have risen through the trapdoor. How would you have the witches act: gleeful? lamenting?*

1. brinded: brindled.

2. hedge-pig: hedgehog.

3. Harpier: an attendant spirit like Graymalkin and Paddock in Act I, Scene 1.

8. Swelt'red . . . got: venom sweated out while sleeping.

12. Fillet: slice. **fenny:** from a swamp.

16. fork: forked tongue. **blindworm's:** legless lizard's.
17. howlet's: owl's.

"I conjure you, by that which you profess, Howe'er you come to know it, answer me."

From the Stratford Festival production of *Macbeth* (1983).

Third Witch.
Scale of dragon, tooth of wolf,
Witch's mummy,° maw and gulf°
Of the ravined° salt-sea shark,
25   Root of hemlock digged i' th' dark,
Liver of blaspheming Jew,
Gall of goat, and slips of yew
Slivered in the moon's eclipse,
Nose of Turk and Tartar's lips,
30   Finger of birth-strangled babe
Ditch-delivered by a drab,°
Make the gruel thick and slab:°
Add thereto a tiger's chaudron,°
For th' ingredients of our caldron.

All.
35   Double, double, toil and trouble;
Fire burn and caldron bubble.

Second Witch.
Cool it with a baboon's blood,
Then the charm is firm and good.

[*Enter* HECATE *and the other three* WITCHES.]

Hecate.
O, well done! I commend your pains;
40   And every one shall share i' th' gains:
And now about the caldron sing,
Like elves and fairies in a ring,
Enchanting all that you put in.

[*Music and a song:* "Black Spirits," *etc.*]

[*Exeunt* HECATE *and the other three* WITCHES.]

Second Witch.
By the pricking of my thumbs,
45   Something wicked this way comes:
    Open, locks,
    Whoever knocks!

[*Enter* MACBETH.]

Macbeth.
How now, you secret, black, and midnight hags!
What is't you do?
All.   A deed without a name.
Macbeth.
50   I conjure you, by that which you profess,
Howe'er you come to know it, answer me:
Though you untie the winds and let them fight
Against the churches; though the yesty° waves
Confound° and swallow navigation up;

---

23. **Witch's mummy:** mummified flesh of a witch.   **maw and gulf:** stomach and gullet.
24. **ravined:** ravenous.

31. **drab:** harlot.
32. **slab:** slimy.
33. **chaudron:** entrails.

[?] *This exciting scene has five major sections, each with its own intensity. See if you can identify them when you're finished.*

[?] **48.** *How has Macbeth's attitude toward the witches changed since his earlier encounters with them?*

53. **yesty:** foamy.
54. **Confound:** destroy.

55   Though bladed corn be lodged° and trees blown down;
    Though castles topple on their warders' heads;
    Though palaces and pyramids do slope°
    Their heads to their foundations; though the treasure
    Of nature's germens° tumble all together,
60   Even till destruction sicken,° answer me
    To what I ask you.

First Witch.   Speak.

Second Witch.   Demand.

Third Witch.   We'll answer.

First Witch.
    Say, if th' hadst rather hear it from our mouths,
    Or from our masters?

Macbeth.   Call 'em, let me see 'em.

First Witch.
    Pour in sow's blood, that hath eaten
65   Her nine farrow;° grease that's sweaten°
    From the murderer's gibbet° throw
    Into the flame.

All.   Come, high or low,
    Thyself and office° deftly show!

[*Thunder.* FIRST APPARITION: *an Armed Head.*°]

Macbeth.
    Tell me, thou unknown power——

First Witch.   He knows thy thought:
70   Hear his speech, but say thou nought.

First Apparition.
    Macbeth! Macbeth! Macbeth! Beware Macduff!
    Beware the Thane of Fife. Dismiss me: enough.

                        [*He descends.*]

Macbeth.
    Whate'er thou art, for thy good caution thanks:
    Thou hast harped° my fear aright. But one word more——

First Witch.
75   He will not be commanded. Here's another,
    More potent than the first.

[*Thunder.* SECOND APPARITION: *a Bloody Child.*]

Second Apparition.
    Macbeth! Macbeth! Macbeth!

Macbeth.
    Had I three ears, I'd hear thee.

Second Apparition.
    Be bloody, bold, and resolute! Laugh to scorn
80   The pow'r of man, for none of woman born
    Shall harm Macbeth.   [*Descends.*]

---

55. bladed . . . lodged: grain in the ear be beaten down.

57. slope: bend.

59. nature's germens: seeds of all life.

60. sicken: sicken at its own work.

? **61.** *These exchanges are spoken rapidly. Do the witches now see Macbeth as a participant in evil?*

65. farrow: young pigs. **sweaten:** sweated.

66. gibbet: gallows.

? **67.** *What are the witches doing all during this scene?*

68. office: function.

Armed Head: helmeted head.

? **71.** *Why does the helmeted head deliver this message? How does the form of the apparition support the warning the apparition gives?*

74. harped: hit upon; struck the note of.

Macbeth.
Then live, Macduff: what need I fear of thee?
But yet I'll make assurance double sure,
And take a bond of fate.° Thou shalt not live;
85 That I may tell pale-hearted fear it lies,
And sleep in spite of thunder.

[*Thunder.* THIRD APPARITION: *a Child Crowned, with a tree in his hand.*]

                                    What is this,
That rises like the issue° of a king,
And wears upon his baby-brow the round
And top of sovereignty?°

All.   Listen, but speak not to't.
Third Apparition.
90 Be lion-mettled, proud, and take no care
Who chafes, who frets, or where conspirers are:
Macbeth shall never vanquished be until
Great Birnam Wood to high Dunsinane Hill
Shall come against him.   [*Descends.*]
Macbeth.   That will never be.
95 Who can impress° the forest, bid the tree
Unfix his earth-bound root? Sweet bodements,° good!
Rebellious dead, rise never, till the Wood
Of Birnam rise, and our high-placed Macbeth
Shall live the lease of nature,° pay his breath
100 To time and mortal custom.° Yet my heart
Throbs to know one thing. Tell me, if your art
Can tell so much: shall Banquo's issue ever
Reign in this kingdom?
All.   Seek to know no more.
Macbeth.
I will be satisfied.° Deny me this,
105 And an eternal curse fall on you! Let me know.
Why sinks that caldron? And what noise° is this?

[*Hautboys.*]

First Witch. Show!
Second Witch. Show!
Third Witch. Show!
All.
110 Show his eyes, and grieve his heart;
Come like shadows, so depart!

[*A show of eight* KINGS *and* BANQUO, *last* KING *with a glass° in his hand.*]

Macbeth.
Thou art too like the spirit of Banquo. Down!
Thy crown does sear mine eyelids. And thy hair,

82. *Macbeth takes the child's message to mean he need not fear Macduff. Nonetheless, why should the second apparition's message be approached with caution?*

84. take . . . fate: get a guarantee from fate (that is, he will kill Macduff and thus will compel fate to keep its word).

87. issue: offspring.

89. round . . . sovereignty: that is, crown.

93. *What does the third apparition prophesy? What must be Macbeth's mental state at this point?*

95. impress: conscript; draft.
96. bodements: prophecies.

99. lease of nature: natural life span.
100. mortal custom: natural death.

102. *What is Macbeth's mood? How might his tone change when he asks about Banquo's issue, or children?*

104. satisfied: that is, fully informed.

106. noise: music.

Stage direction. *A parade of eight Stuart kings passes before Macbeth. These are the kings of Banquo's line. The last king holds up a mirror (**glass**) to suggest an infinite number of descendants. Banquo appears last. According to the next speech, how does Banquo act toward Macbeth?*

Thou other gold-bound brow, is like the first.

115 A third is like the former. Filthy hags!
Why do you show me this? A fourth! Start,° eyes!
What, will the line stretch out to th' crack of doom?°
Another yet! A seventh! I'll see no more.
And yet the eighth° appears, who bears a glass
120 Which shows me many more; and some I see
That twofold balls and treble scepters° carry:
Horrible sight! Now I see 'tis true;
For the blood-boltered° Banquo smiles upon me,
And points at them for his.° What, is this so?

First Witch.
125 Ay, sir, all this is so. But why
Stands Macbeth thus amazedly?
Come, sisters, cheer we up his sprites,°
And show the best of our delights:
I'll charm the air to give a sound,
130 While you perform your antic round,°
That this great king may kindly say
Our duties did his welcome pay.

[*Music. The* WITCHES *dance, and vanish.*]

Macbeth.
Where are they? Gone? Let this pernicious hour
Stand aye accursèd in the calendar!
Come in, without there!

[*Enter* LENNOX.]

135 **Lennox.**   What's your grace's will?
Macbeth.
Saw you the weird sisters?
Lennox.   No, my lord.
Macbeth.
Came they not by you?
Lennox.   No indeed, my lord.
Macbeth.
Infected by the air whereon they ride,
And damned all those that trust them! I did hear
140 The galloping of horse.° Who was't came by?
Lennox.
'Tis two or three, my lord, that bring you word
Macduff is fled to England.
Macbeth.   Fled to England?
Lennox.
Ay, my good lord.
Macbeth (*aside*).
Time, thou anticipat'st° my dread exploits.
145 The flighty purpose never is o'ertook
Unless the deed go with it.° From this moment

116. Start: that is, from the sockets.
117. crack of doom: blast (of a trumpet) at Doomsday.
119. eighth: King James I of England (the present king).
121. twofold . . . scepters: coronation emblems.
123. blood-boltered: matted with blood.
124. his: his descendants.
124. *What does Banquo look like? What must be Macbeth's mental state now?*
127. sprites: spirits.

130. antic round: grotesque, circular dance.

136. *How would the mood on stage change as Lennox appears? What crucial information does he give Macbeth?*

140. horse: horses (or horsemen).

144. anticipat'st: foretold.
146. The flighty . . . it: The fleeting plan is never accomplished unless an action accompanies it.

The very firstlings of my heart° shall be
The firstlings of my hand. And even now,
To crown my thoughts with acts, be it thought and done:
150 The castle of Macduff I will surprise;°
Seize upon Fife; give to th' edge o' th' sword
His wife, his babes, and all unfortunate souls
That trace him in his line.° No boasting like a fool;
This deed I'll do before this purpose cool:
155 But no more sights!—Where are these gentlemen?
Come, bring me where they are.   [*Exeunt.*]

Scene 2. *Macduff's castle.*

Enter Macduff's wife LADY MACDUFF, *her* SON, *and* ROSS.

Lady Macduff.
    What had he done, to make him fly the land?
Ross.
    You must have patience, madam.
Lady Macduff.   He had none:
    His flight was madness. When our actions do not,
    Our fears do make us traitors.
Ross.   You know not
5   Whether it was his wisdom or his fear.
Lady Macduff.
    Wisdom! To leave his wife, to leave his babes,
    His mansion and his titles,° in a place
    From whence himself does fly? He loves us not;
    He wants the natural touch:° for the poor wren,
10   The most diminutive of birds, will fight,
    Her young ones in her nest, against the owl.
    All is the fear and nothing is the love;
    As little is the wisdom, where the flight
    So runs against all reason.
Ross.   My dearest coz,°
15   I pray you, school° yourself. But, for your husband,
    He is noble, wise, judicious, and best knows
    The fits o' th' season.° I dare not speak much further:
    But cruel are the times, when we are traitors
    And do not know ourselves; when we hold rumor
20   From what we fear,° yet know not what we fear,
    But float upon a wild and violent sea
    Each way and move. I take my leave of you.
    Shall not be long but I'll be here again.
    Things at the worst will cease,° or else climb upward
25   To what they were before. My pretty cousin,
    Blessing upon you!
Lady Macduff.
    Fathered he is, and yet he's fatherless.

147. firstlings . . . heart: that is, first thoughts, impulses.

150. surprise: attack suddenly.

153. trace . . . line: are of his lineage.

156. *By this speech, how does Macbeth show he has fallen ever deeper into evil? How different is Macbeth now from the reluctant murderer of the first part of the play? Why does Macbeth want to murder Macduff's children?*

Stage direction. *In many productions, the mood of this scene contrasts dramatically with the previous scenes of horror. How would you stage this domestic scene to suggest the vulnerability of Lady Macduff and her children?*

7. titles: possessions.

9. wants . . . touch: that is, lacks natural affection for his wife and children.

14. coz: cousin.

15. school: control.

17. fits . . . season: disorders of the time.

17. *How could Ross show his fear in line 17?*

20. hold . . . fear: believe rumors because we fear.

24. cease: cease worsening.

Ross.
    I am so much a fool, should I stay longer,
    It would be my disgrace° and your discomfort.
    I take my leave at once.   [*Exit* ROSS.]

30 **Lady Macduff.**   Sirrah,° your father's dead:
    And what will you do now? How will you live?
Son.
    As birds do, mother.
Lady Macduff.   What, with worms and flies?
Son.
    With what I get, I mean; and so do they.
Lady Macduff.
    Poor bird! thou'dst never fear the net nor lime,°
35   The pitfall nor the gin.°
Son.
    Why should I, mother? Poor birds they are not set for.
    My father is not dead, for all your saying.
Lady Macduff.
    Yes, he is dead: how wilt thou do for a father?
Son. Nay, how will you do for a husband?
40 **Lady Macduff.** Why, I can buy me twenty at any market.
Son. Then you'll buy 'em to sell° again.
Lady Macduff.
    Thou speak'st with all thy wit, and yet, i' faith,
    With wit enough for thee.°
Son.
    Was my father a traitor, mother?
45 **Lady Macduff.** Ay, that he was.
Son. What is a traitor?
Lady Macduff. Why, one that swears and lies.°
Son. And be all traitors that do so?
Lady Macduff. Every one that does so is a traitor, and must be
    hanged.
50 **Son.** And must they all be hanged that swear and lie?
Lady Macduff. Every one.
Son. Who must hang them?
Lady Macduff. Why, the honest men.
Son. Then the liars and swearers are fools; for there are liars
55   and swearers enow° to beat the honest men and hang up them.
Lady Macduff. Now, God help thee, poor monkey! But
    how wilt thou do for a father?
Son. If he were dead, you'd weep for him. If you would not, it
    were a good sign that I should quickly have a new father.
60 **Lady Macduff.** Poor prattler, how thou talk'st!

[*Enter a* MESSENGER.]

Messenger.
    Bless you, fair dame! I am not to you known,
    Though in your state of honor I am perfect.°

---

29. It . . . disgrace: That is, I would weep.

? 30. *In taking his leave, how would Ross show affection for Lady Macduff and her young son? Would you have Ross be younger or older than Lady Macduff?*

30. Sirrah: here, an affectionate address to a child.

? 31. *How would you have Lady Macduff act in this scene? Frightened? Bitter? Loving? Resigned?*

34. lime: birdlime (smeared on branches to catch birds).

35. gin: trap.

41. sell: betray.

43. for thee: for a child.

47. swears and lies: takes an oath and breaks it.

55. enow: enough.

62. in . . . perfect: That is, I am fully informed of your honorable rank.

I doubt° some danger does approach you nearly:
If you will take a homely° man's advice,
65 Be not found here; hence, with your little ones.
To fright you thus, methinks I am too savage;
To do worse to you were fell° cruelty,
Which is too nigh your person. Heaven preserve you!
I dare abide no longer.   [*Exit* MESSENGER.]
Lady Macduff.   Whither should I fly?
70 I have done no harm. But I remember now
I am in this earthly world, where to do harm
Is often laudable, to do good sometime
Accounted dangerous folly. Why then, alas,
Do I put up that womanly defense,
75 To say I have done no harm?—What are these faces?

[*Enter* MURDERERS.]

Murderer.
Where is your husband?
Lady Macduff.
I hope, in no place so unsanctified
Where such as thou mayst find him.
Murderer.   He's a traitor.
Son.
Thou li'st, thou shag-eared° villain!
Murderer.   What, you egg!

[*Stabbing him.*]

Young fry° of treachery!
80 **Son.**   He has killed me, mother:
Run away, I pray you!   [*Dies.*]

[*Exit* LADY MACDUFF, *crying* "Murder!"
followed by MURDERERS.]

Scene 3. *England. Before the king's palace.*

Enter MALCOLM *and* MACDUFF.

Malcolm.
Let us seek out some desolate shade, and there
Weep our sad bosoms empty.
Macduff.   Let us rather
Hold fast the mortal° sword, and like good men
Bestride our down-fall'n birthdom.° Each new morn
5 New widows howl, new orphans cry, new sorrows
Strike heaven on the face, that° it resounds
As if it felt with Scotland and yelled out
Like syllable of dolor.°
Malcolm.   What I believe, I'll wail;
What know, believe; and what I can redress,

63. doubt: fear.
64. homely: plain.

67. fell: fierce.

? **69.** *Some readers think that this messenger has been sent by Lady Macbeth. Is there any support for this theory? Would it be within her character? What must Lady Macduff do when she hears this terrible message?*

? **75.** *What would Lady Macduff and her son do as they see the murderers enter the room?*

79. shag-eared: hairy-eared.

80. fry: spawn.

3. mortal: deadly.
4. Bestride . . . birthdom: protectively stand over our native land.
6. that: so that.

8. Like . . . dolor: similar sound of grief.

The cistern of my lust, and my desire
All continent° impediments would o'erbear,
65 That did oppose my will. Better Macbeth
Than such an one to reign.

Macduff.   Boundless intemperance
In nature° is a tyranny; it hath been
Th' untimely emptying of the happy throne,
And fall of many kings. But fear not yet
70 To take upon you what is yours: you may
Convey° your pleasures in a spacious plenty,
And yet seem cold, the time° you may so hoodwink.
We have willing dames enough. There cannot be
That vulture in you, to devour so many
75 As will to greatness dedicate themselves,
Finding it so inclined.

Malcolm.   With this there grows
In my most ill-composed affection° such
A stanchless° avarice that, were I king,
I should cut off the nobles for their lands,
80 Desire his jewels and this other's house:
And my more-having would be as a sauce
To make me hunger more, that I should forge
Quarrels unjust against the good and loyal,
Destroying them for wealth.

Macduff.   This avarice
85 Sticks deeper, grows with more pernicious root
Than summer-seeming° lust, and it hath been
The sword of our slain kings.° Yet do not fear.
Scotland hath foisons to fill up your will
Of your mere own.° All these are portable,°
90 With other graces weighed.

Malcolm.
But I have none: the king-becoming graces,
As justice, verity, temp'rance, stableness,
Bounty, perseverance, mercy, lowliness,
Devotion, patience, courage, fortitude,
95 I have no relish of° them, but abound
In the division of each several crime,°
Acting it many ways. Nay, had I pow'r, I should
Pour the sweet milk of concord into hell,
Uproar° the universal peace, confound
All unity on earth.

100 **Macduff.**   O Scotland, Scotland!
Malcolm.
If such a one be fit to govern, speak:
I am as I have spoken.

Macduff.   Fit to govern!
No, not to live. O nation miserable!
With an untitled° tyrant bloody-sceptered,

64. continent: restraining.

66. *Why do you think Malcolm is drawing attention to his vices? What could he hope to accomplish?*
67. nature: man's nature.

71. Convey: secretly manage.
72. time: here, people.

77. ill-composed affection: evilly compounded character.
78. stanchless: never-ending.

84. *How do you imagine Malcolm delivering this speech? How could his delivery affect Macduff's response?*
86. summer-seeming: youthful, or transitory.
87. sword . . . kings: the cause of death to our kings.
89. foisons . . . own: enough abundance of your own to satisfy your covetousness. **portable:** bearable.

95. relish of: taste for.
96. division . . . crime: variations of each kind of crime.

99. Uproar: put into a tumult.

104. untitled: having no right to the throne.

105　When shalt thou see thy wholesome days again,
　　　Since that the truest issue of thy throne
　　　By his own interdiction° stands accursed,
　　　And does blaspheme his breed?° Thy royal father
　　　Was a most sainted king: the queen that bore thee,
110　Oft'ner upon her knees than on her feet,
　　　Died° every day she lived. Fare thee well!
　　　These evils thou repeat'st upon thyself
　　　Hath banished me from Scotland. O my breast,
　　　Thy hope ends here!

Malcolm.　　　　　　　　Macduff, this noble passion,
115　Child of integrity, hath from my soul
　　　Wiped the black scruples,° reconciled my thoughts
　　　To thy good truth and honor. Devilish Macbeth
　　　By many of these trains° hath sought to win me
　　　Into his power; and modest wisdom° plucks me
120　From over-credulous haste: but God above
　　　Deal between thee and me! For even now
　　　I put myself to° thy direction, and
　　　Unspeak mine own detraction;° here abjure
　　　The taints and blames I laid upon myself,
125　For° strangers to my nature. I am yet
　　　Unknown to woman, never was forsworn,
　　　Scarcely have coveted what was mine own,
　　　At no time broke my faith, would not betray
　　　The devil to his fellow, and delight
130　No less in truth than life. My first false speaking
　　　Was this upon myself. What I am truly,
　　　Is thine and my poor country's to command:
　　　Whither indeed, before thy here-approach,
　　　Old Siward, with ten thousand warlike men,
135　Already at a point,° was setting forth.
　　　Now we'll together, and the chance of goodness
　　　Be like our warranted quarrel!° Why are you silent?

Macduff.
　　　Such welcome and unwelcome things at once
　　　'Tis hard to reconcile.

[*Enter a* DOCTOR.]

Malcolm.
140　Well, more anon. Comes the king forth, I pray you?

Doctor.
　　　Ay, sir. There are a crew of wretched souls
　　　That stay° his cure: their malady convinces
　　　The great assay of art;° but at his touch,
　　　Such sanctity hath heaven given his hand,
　　　They presently amend.°

145　**Malcolm.**　　　　　　　　I thank you, doctor.

[*Exit* DOCTOR.]

---

107. interdiction: curse; exclusion.

108. breed: ancestry.

111. Died: that is, prepared for heaven.

[?] 114. *How might the tone change here? How has Macduff proved himself?*

116. scruples: suspicions.

118. trains: plots.

119. modest wisdom: prudence.

122. to: under.

123. detraction: slander.

125. For: as.

135. at a point: prepared.

137. the chance . . . quarrel: May our chance of success equal the justice of our cause.

[?] 137. *Where should Malcolm pause in this line? Should he act puzzled, or matter-of-fact?*

142. stay: await.

143. convinces . . . art: defies the efforts of medical science.

145. presently amend: immediately recover.

Macduff.
What's the disease he means?

Malcolm.   'Tis called the evil:°
A most miraculous work in this good king,
Which often since my here-remain in England
I have seen him do. How he solicits heaven,
150 Himself best knows: but strangely visited° people,
All swoll'n and ulcerous, pitiful to the eye,
The mere° despair of surgery, he cures,
Hanging a golden stamp° about their necks,
Put on with holy prayers: and 'tis spoken,
155 To the succeeding royalty he leaves
The healing benediction. With this strange virtue°
He hath a heavenly gift of prophecy,
And sundry blessings hang about his throne
That speak° him full of grace.

[*Enter* ROSS.]

Macduff.   See, who comes here?
Malcolm.
160 My countryman; but yet I know him not.
Macduff.
My ever gentle° cousin, welcome hither.
Malcolm.
I know him now: good God, betimes° remove
The means that makes us strangers!
Ross.   Sir, amen.
Macduff.
Stands Scotland where it did?
Ross.   Alas, poor country!
165 Almost afraid to know itself! It cannot
Be called our mother but our grave, where nothing°
But who knows nothing is once seen to smile;
Where sighs and groans, and shrieks that rent the air,
Are made, not marked;° where violent sorrow seems
170 A modern ecstasy.° The dead man's knell
Is there scarce asked for who, and good men's lives
Expire before the flowers in their caps,
Dying or ere they sicken.
Macduff.   O, relation
Too nice,° and yet too true!
Malcolm.   What's the newest grief?
Ross.
175 That of an hour's age doth hiss the speaker;°
Each minute teems° a new one.
Macduff.   How does my wife?
Ross.
Why, well.
Macduff.   And all my children?

---

146. evil: scrofula, called "the king's evil" because it allegedly could be cured by the king's touch.

150. strangely visited: oddly afflicted.

152. mere: utter.

153. stamp: coin.

156. virtue: power.

159. speak: proclaim.

? **Stage direction.** *Ross is Macduff's countryman. What news do you anticipate he brings with him?*

161. gentle: noble.

162. betimes: quickly.

166. nothing: no one.

169. marked: noticed.
170. modern ecstasy: ordinary emotion.

174. relation / Too nice: tale too accurate.

175. That . . . speaker: The report of the grief of an hour ago is hissed as stale news.
176. teems: gives birth to.

? **176.** *Does Ross look at Macduff on this line, or does he turn away?*

Ross.   Well too.

Macduff.

The tyrant has not battered at their peace?

Ross.

No; they were well at peace when I did leave 'em.

Macduff.

180   Be not a niggard of your speech: how goes't?

Ross.

When I came hither to transport the tidings,
Which I have heavily° borne, there ran a rumor
Of many worthy fellows that were out;°
Which was to my belief witnessed° the rather,
185   For that I saw the tyrant's power° afoot.
Now is the time of help. Your eye in Scotland
Would create soldiers, make our women fight,
To doff their dire distresses.

Malcolm.   Be't their comfort
We are coming thither. Gracious England hath
190   Lent us good Siward and ten thousand men;
An older and a better soldier none
That Christendom gives out.°

Ross.   Would I could answer
This comfort with the like! But I have words
That would° be howled out in the desert air,
Where hearing should not latch° them.

195 **Macduff.**   What concern they?
The general cause or is it a fee-grief
Due to some single breast?°

Ross.   No mind that's honest
But in it shares some woe, though the main part
Pertains to you alone.

Macduff.   If it be mine,
200   Keep it not from me, quickly let me have it.

Ross.

Let not your ears despise my tongue forever,
Which shall possess them with the heaviest sound
That ever yet they heard.

Macduff.   Humh! I guess at it.

Ross.

Your castle is surprised;° your wife and babes
205   Savagely slaughtered. To relate the manner,
Were, on the quarry° of these murdered deer,
To add the death of you.

Malcolm.   Merciful heaven!
What, man! Ne'er pull your hat upon your brows;
Give sorrow words. The grief that does not speak
210   Whispers the o'er-fraught heart,° and bids it break.

Macduff.

My children too?

---

179. *What is the double meaning of this line?*

182. heavily: sadly.
183. out: up in arms.
184. witnessed: attested.
185. power: army.

192. gives out: reports.

194. would: should.
195. latch: catch.

197. fee-grief . . . breast: that is, personal grief belonging to an individual.

203. *Macduff's pain becomes visible. How should we see it?*

204. surprised: suddenly attacked.

206. quarry: heap of slaughtered game.

210. Whispers . . . heart: whispers to the overburdened heart.

211. *How full, or soft, a voice would you have Macduff use in this line?*

Ross.   Wife, children, servants, all
   That could be found.
Macduff.   And I must be from thence!
   My wife killed too?
Ross.   I have said.
Malcolm.   Be comforted.
   Let's make us med'cines of our great revenge,
215   To cure this deadly grief.
Macduff.
   He has no children. All my pretty ones?
   Did you say all? O hell-kite!° All?
   What, all my pretty chickens and their dam°
   At one fell swoop?
Malcolm.
   Dispute° it like a man.
220 **Macduff.**   I shall do so;
   But I must also feel it as a man.
   I cannot but remember such things were,
   That were most precious to me. Did heaven look on,
   And would not take their part? Sinful Macduff,

? **216.** *How would Macduff say this line: "He has no children"?*

217. hell-kite: hellish bird of prey.

218. dam: mother.

220. Dispute: counter.

? **220.** *Is Malcolm being critical or encouraging here?*

"Bring thou this fiend of Scotland and myself;
Within my sword's length set him."

From the Stratford Festival production of *Macbeth* (1983).

225 They were all struck for thee! Naught° that I am,
Not for their own demerits but for mine
Fell slaughter on their souls. Heaven rest them now!

Malcolm.
Be this the whetstone of your sword. Let grief
Convert to anger; blunt not the heart, enrage it.

Macduff.
230 O, I could play the woman with mine eyes,
And braggart with my tongue! But, gentle heavens,
Cut short all intermission;° front to front°
Bring thou this fiend of Scotland and myself;
Within my sword's length set him. If he 'scape,
Heaven forgive him too!

235 **Malcolm.**   This time goes manly.
Come, go we to the king. Our power is ready;
Our lack is nothing but our leave.° Macbeth
Is ripe for shaking, and the pow'rs above
Put on their instruments.° Receive what cheer you may.
240 The night is long that never finds the day.   [*Exeunt.*]

225. Naught: wicked.

232. intermission: interval.
front to front: forehead to forehead (that is, face to face).

237. Our lack . . . leave: We need only to take our leave.

239. Put . . . instruments: arm themselves.

Critical Comment

The King's Evil

In Act IV, Scene 3, Malcolm and Macduff, exiled from Scotland, discuss the characteristics of a good king and praise King Edward, who has given them political asylum in England. Edward, a saintly monarch known to history as "the Confessor," was believed to have the gift of healing any of his subjects who suffered from an ailment known as the king's evil, a kind of scrofula or tuberculosis of the lymphatic glands and primarily a disease of children. Long before Shakespeare's time, the custom of being touched by the king was abandoned, but King James revived the practice and his successors continued it for a century or so. The eighteenth-century writer Samuel Johnson, scrofulous as a child, was one of the last English people to receive the royal touch.

Edward the Confessor (detail of the Wilton Diptych).

The National Gallery, London.

The conversation between Malcolm and Macduff not only compliments King James indirectly, but also implicitly condemns Macbeth, a kingly killer rather than a healer of children. Edward cures evil; Macbeth *is* evil.

Hecate: Queen of the Night

Hecate (here pronounced in two syllables, with the accent on the first: hek´it) is a figure from Greek mythology, a queen of the night and protector of witches and enchanters. This character comes from books, unlike the witches, who were based on older, usually widowed women, whose solitary lives placed them at the margins of Scottish society. Every theatergoer would find the witches believable, and every educated person would know that King James had written an important treatise called *Daemonologie,* asserting that witches "are channels through which the malignity of evil spirits might be visited upon human beings."

Most Shakespearean scholars believe that the scenes involving Hecate (Act III, Scene 5; Act IV, Scene 1) were written by somebody other than Shakespeare and introduced into *Macbeth* at some time before 1623, when the play was first printed. This other writer has never been positively identified, although some people think he was Thomas Middleton (d. 1627), a contemporary of Shakespeare and a fellow writer for the King's Men. Two songs, the first beginning with the words "Come away" (Act III, Scene 5) and the second with "Black Spirits" (Act IV, Scene 1), were also added to the Hecate scenes, and these songs are indeed by Middleton, the complete texts of them occurring in his thriller *The Witch.*

And so the practice of adding things to *Macbeth* began very early, and it has continued throughout most of the play's long stage history. The supernatural elements seem to invite directors to devise spectacles and take liberties, especially with the witches, who have been flown on wires in some productions and whose parts have been played by ballet dancers in others.

Macbeth holding out his hand to the three witches.

From the Stratford Festival production of *Macbeth* (1983).

MAKING MEANINGS

First Thoughts

1. What effect did the brutal murders of Lady Macduff and her son have on you? Have your feelings for Macbeth changed from the opening of the play until now? How do you account for your reactions?

Reading Check

a. What ingredients go into the witches' stew? What **symbolic** purpose does this vile concoction serve?

b. What has Macbeth come to ask the witches, and how do they answer?

c. Describe the three apparitions Macbeth sees when he visits the witches. What does each apparition tell him?

d. Which nobleman does Macbeth plan to murder after talking with the witches? How is his plan foiled?

e. At the end of Scene 1, what does Macbeth vow? How is his vow carried out in Scene 2?

f. According to the conversation between Malcolm and Macduff in Scene 3, what has happened to Scotland during Macbeth's reign?

g. What faults does Malcolm claim to have?

h. How does Macduff respond to each of Malcolm's three "confessions"?

Shaping Interpretations

2. In this act, Macbeth seeks out the witches, just as they initiated the encounter in Act I. How has Macbeth's situation changed since he last talked with the witches? How has his moral **character** deteriorated? Find lines and actions that support your interpretation.

3. Do you think the witches have caused any of these changes, directly or indirectly? Explain your reasons for thinking as you do.

4. In Scene 1, the eight kings appear in what was called in Shakespeare's day a **dumb show**—an interpolated brief scene in which nothing is said. What is the point of this particular dumb show?

5. In Scene 2, the lines spoken by Macduff's wife and son illustrate Shakespeare's great skill at **characterization**. Using only a few words, he brings the woman and the child to life. How would you describe Lady Macduff? How would you describe the boy?

6. Both the murderer and Lady Macduff herself call Macduff a traitor. In what sense does each mean it? Do you think Macduff is a traitor, in either sense?

7. In Scene 3, Malcolm deliberately lies to Macduff. What does this behavior, and the reason for it, reveal about Malcolm?

Extending the Text

8. In Scene 3, Malcolm and Macduff decry the chaos that Macbeth's rule has brought to Scotland, as if Macbeth's disorder has become Scotland's. Does that happen today—does the weakness or the evil of a nation's leader become that of a nation itself? Explain your response.

Challenging the Text

9. The murder of Macduff's small son is one of the most pitiful and shocking scenes in Shakespeare. Do you think it might have been better to have it reported after the fact rather than to have shown the carnage on stage? What would be lost and what would be gained by this change?

ACT V Scene 1. *Dunsinane. In the castle.*

Enter a DOCTOR *of physic and a waiting* GENTLEWOMAN.

Doctor. I have two nights watched with you, but can perceive
no truth in your report. When was it she last walked?

Gentlewoman. Since his majesty went into the field, I have
seen her rise from her bed, throw her nightgown upon her,
5 unlock her closet,° take forth paper, fold it, write upon't,
read it, afterwards seal it, and again return to bed; yet all this
while in a most fast sleep.

Doctor. A great perturbation in nature, to receive at once the
benefit of sleep and do the effects of watching!° In this
10 slumb'ry agitation, besides her walking and other actual performances,° what, at any time, have you heard her say?

5. **closet:** chest.

9. **effects of watching:** deeds of
one awake.

11. **actual performances:** deeds.

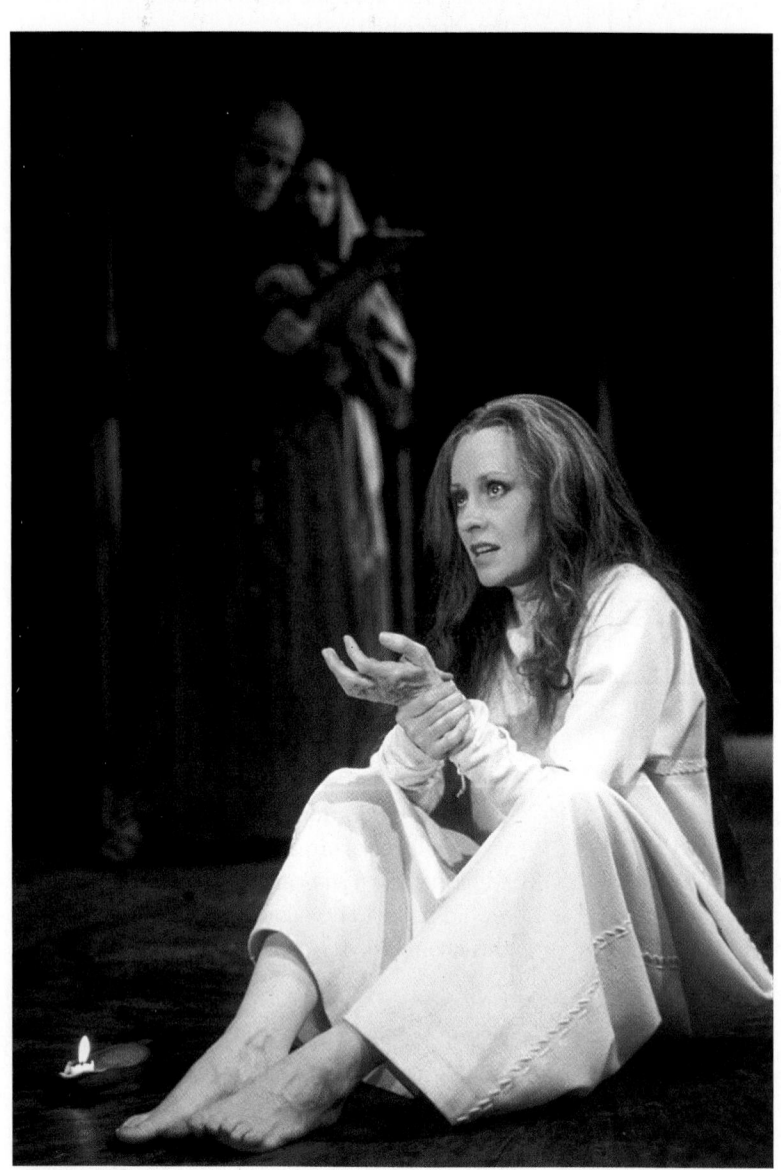

"Out, damned spot! Out, I say!"
From the Stratford Festival production of
Macbeth (1983).

Gentlewoman. That, sir, which I will not report after her.

Doctor. You may to me, and 'tis most meet° you should.

Gentlewoman. Neither to you nor anyone, having no witness
15   to confirm my speech.

[*Enter* LADY MACBETH, *with a taper.*]

Lo you, here she comes! This is her very guise,° and, upon
my life, fast asleep! Observe her; stand close.°

Doctor. How came she by that light?

Gentlewoman. Why, it stood by her. She has light by her con-
20   tinually. 'Tis her command.

Doctor. You see, her eyes are open.

Gentlewoman. Ay, but their sense° are shut.

Doctor. What is it she does now? Look, how she rubs her
hands.

25   **Gentlewoman.** It is an accustomed action with her, to seem
thus washing her hands: I have known her continue in this a
quarter of an hour.

Lady Macbeth. Yet here's a spot.

Doctor. Hark! she speaks. I will set down what comes from
30   her, to satisfy° my remembrance the more strongly.

Lady Macbeth. Out, damned spot! Out, I say! One: two: why,
then 'tis time to do't. Hell is murky. Fie, my lord, fie! A soldier, and afeard? What need we fear who knows it, when
none can call our pow'r to accompt?° Yet who would have
35   thought the old man to have had so much blood in him?

Doctor. Do you mark that?

Lady Macbeth. The Thane of Fife had a wife. Where is she
now? What, will these hands ne'er be clean? No more o'
that, my lord, no more o' that! You mar all with this starting.

40   **Doctor.** Go to,° go to! You have known what you should not.

Gentlewoman. She has spoke what she should not, I am sure
of that. Heaven knows what she has known.

Lady Macbeth. Here's the smell of the blood still. All the perfumes of Arabia will not sweeten this little hand. Oh, oh, oh!

45   **Doctor.** What a sigh is there! The heart is sorely charged.°

Gentlewoman. I would not have such a heart in my bosom for
the dignity° of the whole body.

Doctor. Well, well, well——

Gentlewoman. Pray God it be, sir.

50   **Doctor.** This disease is beyond my practice.° Yet I have known
those which have walked in their sleep who have died holily
in their beds.

Lady Macbeth. Wash your hands; put on your nightgown;
look not so pale! I tell you yet again, Banquo's buried. He
55   cannot come out on 's° grave.

Doctor. Even so?

Lady Macbeth. To bed, to bed! There's knocking at the gate.

---

13. meet: suitable.

16. guise: custom.

17. close: hidden.

? 20. *Why must Lady Macbeth have light by her continually?*

22. sense: powers of sight.

? 28. *After setting down the taper on a table, what does Lady Macbeth do with her hands?*

30. satisfy: confirm.

34. to accompt: into account.

? 35. *What does she think is still on her hands?*

? 37. *Who is the Thane of Fife?*

40. Go to: an exclamation.

? 43. *What action is suggested by this line?*

45. charged: burdened.

47. dignity: worth; rank.

50. practice: professional skill.

55. on 's: of his.

? 55. *Whom does she think she is speaking to here?*

Come, come, come, come, give me your hand! What's done cannot be undone. To bed, to bed, to bed!

[*Exit* LADY MACBETH.]

60 **Doctor.** Will she go now to bed?

Gentlewoman. Directly.

Doctor.

Foul whisp'rings are abroad. Unnatural deeds
Do breed unnatural troubles. Infected minds
To their deaf pillows will discharge their secrets.
65 More needs she the divine° than the physician.
God, God forgive us all! Look after her;
Remove from her the means of all annoyance,°
And still° keep eyes upon her. So good night.
My mind she has mated° and amazed my sight:
I think, but dare not speak.

70 **Gentlewoman.**   Good night, good doctor.

[*Exeunt.*]

*

Scene 2. *The country near Dunsinane.*

Drum and colors. Enter MENTEITH, CAITHNESS, ANGUS, LENNOX, SOLDIERS.

Menteith.

The English pow'r° is near, led on by Malcolm,
His uncle Siward and the good Macduff.
Revenges burn in them; for their dear° causes
Would to the bleeding and the grim alarm°
Excite the mortified° man.

5 **Angus.**   Near Birnam Wood
Shall we well meet them; that way are they coming.

Caithness.

Who knows if Donalbain be with his brother?

Lennox.

For certain, sir, he is not. I have a file°
Of all the gentry: there is Siward's son,
10 And many unrough° youths that even now
Protest° their first of manhood.

Menteith.   What does the tyrant?

Caithness.

Great Dunsinane he strongly fortifies.
Some say he's mad; others, that lesser hate him,
Do call it valiant fury: but, for certain,
15 He cannot buckle his distempered° cause
Within the belt of rule.°

Angus.   Now does he feel
His secret murders sticking on his hands;
Now minutely revolts upbraid° his faith-breach.
Those he commands move only in command,
20 Nothing in love. Now does he feel his title

59. *Once again there is a sudden dramatic change. What echo from the past brings it about? How do you think Lady Macbeth leaves the stage?*

65. divine: priest.

67. annoyance: injury.
68. still: continuously.
69. mated: baffled.

70. *What do the doctor and gentlewoman know? Why won't they speak out?*

1. pow'r: army.

3. dear: heartfelt.
4. alarm: call to arms.
5. mortified: half dead.

5. *Where have you heard about Birnam Wood before?*

8. file: list.

10. unrough: beardless.
11. Protest: assert.

15. distempered: swollen with disease.
16. rule: self-control.

18. minutely revolts upbraid: rebellions every minute rebuke.

Hang loose about him, like a giant's robe
Upon a dwarfish thief.
Mentieth.   Who then shall blame
His pestered° senses to recoil and start,
When all that is within him does condemn
Itself for being there?
25 **Caithness.**   Well, march we on,
To give obedience where 'tis truly owed.
Meet we the med'cine° of the sickly weal,°
And with him pour we, in our country's purge,
Each drop of us.°
Lennox.   Or so much as it needs
30 To dew° the sovereign° flower and drown the weeds.
Make we our march towards Birnam.

[*Exeunt, marching.*]

Scene 3. *Dunsinane. In the castle.*

Enter MACBETH, DOCTOR, *and* ATTENDANTS.

Macbeth.
Bring me no more reports; let them fly all!
Till Birnam Wood remove to Dunsinane
I cannot taint° with fear. What's the boy Malcolm?
Was he not born of woman? The spirits that know
5 All mortal consequences° have pronounced me thus:
"Fear not, Macbeth; no man that's born of woman
Shall e'er have power upon thee." Then fly, false thanes,
And mingle with the English epicures.
The mind I sway° by and the heart I bear
10 Shall never sag with doubt nor shake with fear.

[*Enter* SERVANT.]

The devil damn thee black, thou cream-faced loon!°
Where got'st thou that goose look?
Servant.
There is ten thousand——
Macbeth.   Geese, villain?
Servant.   Soldiers, sir.
Macbeth.
Go prick thy face and over-red° thy fear,
15 Thou lily-livered boy. What soldiers, patch?°
Death of° thy soul! Those linen° cheeks of thine
Are counselors to fear. What soldiers, whey-face?
Servant.
The English force, so please you.
Macbeth.
Take thy face hence.   [*Exit* SERVANT.]
     Seyton!—I am sick at heart,
20 When I behold—Seyton, I say!—This push°

---

23. **pestered:** tormented.

27. **med'cine:** that is, Malcolm.
weal: commonwealth.

29. **Each . . . us:** that is, every last drop of our blood.

30. **dew:** bedew; water (and thus make grow).   **sovereign:** royal; also, remedial.

31. *The "falling action" of a Shakespearean play is usually swift. How does this scene show that the hero's enemies are now rallying to crush him? What group is shown in this scene?*

3. **taint:** become infected.

5. **mortal consequences:** future human events.

9. **sway:** move.

11. **loon:** fool.

12. *Macbeth is in an extreme state of agitation. Which of the apparitions' prophecies is he relying on? How would you stage his treatment of the servant, which follows?*

14. **over-red:** cover with red.
15. **patch:** fool.
16. **of:** upon.   **linen:** pale.

20. **push:** effort.

Will cheer me ever, or disseat° me now.
I have lived long enough. My way of life
Is fall'n into the sear,° the yellow leaf,
And that which should accompany old age,
25 As honor, love, obedience, troops of friends,
I must not look to have; but, in their stead,
Curses not loud but deep, mouth-honor, breath,
Which the poor heart would fain deny, and dare not.
Seyton!

[*Enter* SEYTON.]

Seyton.
What's your gracious pleasure?
30 **Macbeth.**   What news more?
Seyton.
All is confirmed, my lord, which was reported.
Macbeth.
I'll fight, till from my bones my flesh be hacked.
Give me my armor.
Seyton.   'Tis not needed yet.
Macbeth.
I'll put it on.
35 Send out moe° horses, skirr° the country round.
Hang those that talk of fear. Give me mine armor.
How does your patient, doctor?
Doctor.   Not so sick, my lord,
As she is troubled with thick-coming fancies
That keep her from her rest.
Macbeth.   Cure her of that.
40 Canst thou not minister to a mind diseased,
Pluck from the memory a rooted sorrow,
Raze out° the written troubles of the brain,
And with some sweet oblivious° antidote
Cleanse the stuffed bosom of that perilous stuff
Which weighs upon the heart?
45 **Doctor.**   Therein the patient
Must minister to himself.
Macbeth.
Throw physic° to the dogs, I'll none of it.
Come, put mine armor on. Give me my staff.
Seyton, send out.—Doctor, the thanes fly from me.—
50 Come, sir, dispatch.° If thou couldst, doctor, cast
The water° of my land, find her disease
And purge it to a sound and pristine health,
I would applaud thee to the very echo,
That should applaud again.—Pull't off, I say.—
55 What rhubarb, senna, or what purgative drug,
Would scour these English hence? Hear'st thou of them?

21. **disseat:** unthrone (with word-play on *cheer*, pronounced *chair*).

22. *What mood is Macbeth in now?*

23. **sear:** withered.

35. **moe:** more. **skirr:** scour.

37. *Who is the doctor's patient?*

42. **Raze out:** erase.
43. **oblivious:** causing forgetfulness.

47. **physic:** medical science.

50. **dispatch:** hurry.
51. **cast/The water:** literally, analyze the urine.

56. *Lines 47–56 contain almost a roller coaster of emotions. Can you cite some?*

Doctor.
Ay, my good lord; your royal preparation
Makes us hear something.
Macbeth. Bring it° after me.
I will not be afraid of death and bane°
60 Till Birnam Forest come to Dunsinane.
Doctor (*aside*).
Were I from Dunsinane away and clear,
Profit again should hardly draw me here. [*Exeunt.*]

Scene 4. *Country near Birnam Wood.*

Drum and colors. Enter MALCOLM, SIWARD, MACDUFF,
Siward's son YOUNG SIWARD, MENTEITH, CAITHNESS,
ANGUS, *and* SOLDIERS, *marching.*

Malcolm.
Cousins, I hope the days are near at hand
That chambers will be safe.°
Menteith. We doubt it nothing.°
Siward.
What wood is this before us?
Menteith. The Wood of Birnam.
Malcolm.
Let every soldier hew him down a bough
5 And bear't before him. Thereby shall we shadow
The numbers of our host, and make discovery°
Err in report of us.
Soldiers. It shall be done.
Siward.
We learn no other but° the confident tyrant
Keeps still in Dunsinane, and will endure°
Our setting down before't.
10 **Malcolm.** 'Tis his main hope,
For where there is advantage to be given°
Both more and less° have given him the revolt,
And none serve with him but constrainèd things
Whose hearts are absent too.
Macduff. Let our just censures
15 Attend the true event,° and put we on
Industrious soldiership.
Siward. The time approaches,
That will with due decision make us know
What we shall say we have and what we owe.°
Thoughts speculative their unsure hopes relate,
20 But certain issue strokes must arbitrate:°
Towards which advance the war.° [*Exeunt, marching.*]

58. **it:** the armor.
59. **bane:** destruction.
❓ 60. *Is Macbeth truly coura-geous here? Or would you suggest that he is merely coasting on a kind of false bravery lent to him by the witches' prophecies?*

2. **That . . . safe:** that a man will be safe in his bedroom. **nothing:** not at all.

❓ 5. *Stop and describe what the soldiers are to do here and why.*
6. **discovery:** Macbeth's scouts.
❓ 7. *Malcolm seems to have more authority at this point in the play. Can you find specific instances where his new authority could be dramatized?*
8. **no other but:** nothing but that.
9. **endure:** allow.
11. **advantage . . . given:** afforded an opportunity.
12. **more and less:** high and low.

15. **just . . . event:** true judgments await the actual outcome.
18. **owe:** own. The contrast is be-tween "what we shall say we have" and "what we shall really have."
20. **certain . . . arbitrate:** The definite outcome must be decided by battle.
21. **war:** army.

"Tomorrow, and tomorrow, and tomorrow
Creeps in this petty pace from day to day,
To the last syllable of recorded time."

From Orson Welles's film production of *Macbeth* (1948).

Scene 5. *Dunsinane. Within the castle.*

Enter MACBETH, SEYTON, *and* SOLDIERS, *with drum and colors.*

Macbeth.

Hang out our banners on the outward walls.
The cry is still "They come!" Our castle's strength
Will laugh a siege to scorn. Here let them lie
Till famine and the ague° eat them up.
5 Were they not forced° with those that should be ours,
We might have met them dareful,° beard to beard,
And beat them backward home.

[*A cry within of women.*]

What is that noise?

Seyton.

It is the cry of women, my good lord.   [*Exit.*]

Macbeth.

I have almost forgot the taste of fears:
10 The time has been, my senses would have cooled
To hear a night-shriek, and my fell° of hair
Would at a dismal treatise° rouse and stir
As life were in't. I have supped full with horrors.
Direness, familiar to my slaughterous thoughts,
Cannot once start° me.

4. **ague:** fever.
5. **forced:** reinforced.
6. **met them dareful:** that is, met them on the battlefield boldly.
? 7. *Macbeth should contrast with Malcolm now. How should he be acting?*

11. **fell:** pelt.
12. **treatise:** story.

15. **start:** startle.

[*Enter* SEYTON.]

15   Wherefore was that cry?

Seyton.
    The queen, my lord, is dead.

Macbeth.
    She should° have died hereafter;
    There would have been a time for such a word.°
    Tomorrow, and tomorrow, and tomorrow
20   Creeps in this petty pace from day to day,
    To the last syllable of recorded time;
    And all our yesterdays have lighted fools
    The way to dusty death. Out, out, brief candle!
    Life's but a walking shadow, a poor player
25   That struts and frets his hour upon the stage
    And then is heard no more. It is a tale
    Told by an idiot, full of sound and fury,
    Signifying nothing.

[*Enter a* MESSENGER.]

    Thou com'st to use thy tongue; thy story quickly!

Messenger.
30   Gracious my lord,
    I should report that which I say I saw,
    But know not how to do't.

Macbeth.   Well, say, sir.

Messenger.
    As I did stand my watch upon the hill,
    I looked toward Birnam, and anon, methought,
    The wood began to move.

35 **Macbeth.**   Liar and slave!

Messenger.
    Let me endure your wrath, if't be not so.
    Within this three mile may you see it coming;
    I say a moving grove.

Macbeth.   If thou speak'st false,
    Upon the next tree shalt thou hang alive,
40   Till famine cling° thee. If thy speech be sooth,°
    I care not if thou dost for me as much.
    I pull in resolution,° and begin
    To doubt° th' equivocation of the fiend
    That lies like truth: "Fear not, till Birnam Wood
45   Do come to Dunsinane!" And now a wood
    Comes toward Dunsinane. Arm, arm, and out!
    If this which he avouches° does appear,
    There is nor flying hence nor tarrying here.
    I 'gin to be aweary of the sun,
50   And wish th' estate° o' th' world were now undone.
    Ring the alarum bell! Blow wind, come wrack!
    At least we'll die with harness° on our back.   [*Exeunt.*]

17. should: inevitably would.
18. word: message.

? **28.** *A scene that began in defiance changes with the great speech beginning "She should have died hereafter." What is Macbeth's new mood? Does Macbeth speak only for himself here, or for the general human condition?*

? **35.** *What is Macbeth thinking of now?*

40. cling: wither.   **sooth:** truth.
42. pull in resolution: restrain confidence.
43. doubt: suspect.

47. avouches: asserts.
50. th' estate: the orderly condition.
52. harness: armor.

? **52.** *Macbeth ends the scene in a state of great emotion. How would you characterize his mental state?*

Scene 6. *Dunsinane. Before the castle.*

Drum and colors. Enter MALCOLM, SIWARD, MACDUFF, *and their* ARMY, *with boughs.*

Malcolm.
　Now near enough. Your leavy° screens throw down,
　And show like those you are. You, worthy uncle,
　Shall, with my cousin, your right noble son,
　Lead our first battle.° Worthy Macduff and we°
5　Shall take upon 's what else remains to do,
　According to our order.°
Siward.　　　　　　　　　　Fare you well.
　Do we° but find the tyrant's power° tonight,
　Let us be beaten, if we cannot fight.
Macduff.
　Make all our trumpets speak; give them all breath,
10　Those clamorous harbingers of blood and death.
　　　　　　　　　[*Exeunt. Alarums continued.*]

1. **leavy:** leafy.

4. **battle:** battalion.　**we:** Malcolm uses the royal "we."

6. **order:** plan.

7. **Do we:** if we do.　**power:** forces.

"Make all our trumpets speak; give them all breath,
Those clamorous harbingers of blood and death."

From the Stratford Festival production of *Macbeth* (1983).

Scene 7. *Another part of the field.*

Enter MACBETH.

Macbeth.
They have tied me to a stake; I cannot fly,
But bearlike I must fight the course.° What's he
That was not born of woman? Such a one
Am I to fear, or none.

2. course: bout; round. (He has in mind an attack of dogs or men upon a bear chained to a stake.)

? **4.** *What is Macbeth desperately clinging to now?*

[*Enter* YOUNG SIWARD.]

Young Siward.
What is thy name?
5   **Macbeth.**   Thou'lt be afraid to hear it.
Young Siward.
No; though thou call'st thyself a hotter name
Than any is in hell.
Macbeth.   My name's Macbeth.
Young Siward.
The devil himself could not pronounce a title
More hateful to mine ear.
Macbeth.   No, nor more fearful.
Young Siward.
10   Thou liest, abhorrèd tyrant; with my sword
I'll prove the lie thou speak'st.

[*Fight, and* YOUNG SIWARD *slain.*]

Macbeth.   Thou wast born of woman.
But swords I smile at, weapons laugh to scorn,
Brandished by man that's of a woman born.   [*Exit.*]

[*Alarums. Enter* MACDUFF.]

Macduff.
That way the noise is. Tyrant, show thy face!
15   If thou be'st slain and with no stroke of mine,
My wife and children's ghosts will haunt me still.
I cannot strike at wretched kerns,° whose arms
Are hired to bear their staves.° Either thou, Macbeth,
Or else my sword, with an unbattered edge,
20   I sheathe again undeeded.° There thou shouldst be;
By this great clatter, one of greatest note
Seems bruited.° Let me find him, Fortune!
And more I beg not.   [*Exit. Alarums.*]

17. kerns: foot soldiers (contemptuous).
18. staves: spears.
20. undeeded: that is, having done nothing.
22. bruited: reported.

[*Enter* MALCOLM *and* SIWARD.]

Siward.
This way, my lord. The castle's gently rend'red:°
25   The tyrant's people on both sides do fight;
The noble thanes do bravely in the war;
The day almost itself professes° yours,

24. gently rend'red: surrendered without a struggle.
27. itself professes: declares itself.

And little is to do.

Malcolm. We have met with foes

That strike beside us.°

Siward. Enter, sir, the castle.

[*Exeunt. Alarum.*]

Scene 8. *Another part of the field.*

Enter MACBETH.

Macbeth.

Why should I play the Roman fool, and die

On mine own sword? Whiles I see lives,° the gashes

Do better upon them.

[*Enter* MACDUFF.]

Macduff. Turn, hell-hound, turn!

Macbeth.

Of all men else I have avoided thee.

5 But get thee back! My soul is too much charged°

With blood of thine already.

29. **That . . . us:** that is, who deliberately miss us.

2. **Whiles . . . lives:** so long as I see living men.

5. **charged:** burdened.

"I have no words: / My voice is in my sword, thou bloodier villain / Than terms can give thee out!"

From Roman Polanski's film production of *Macbeth* (1971).

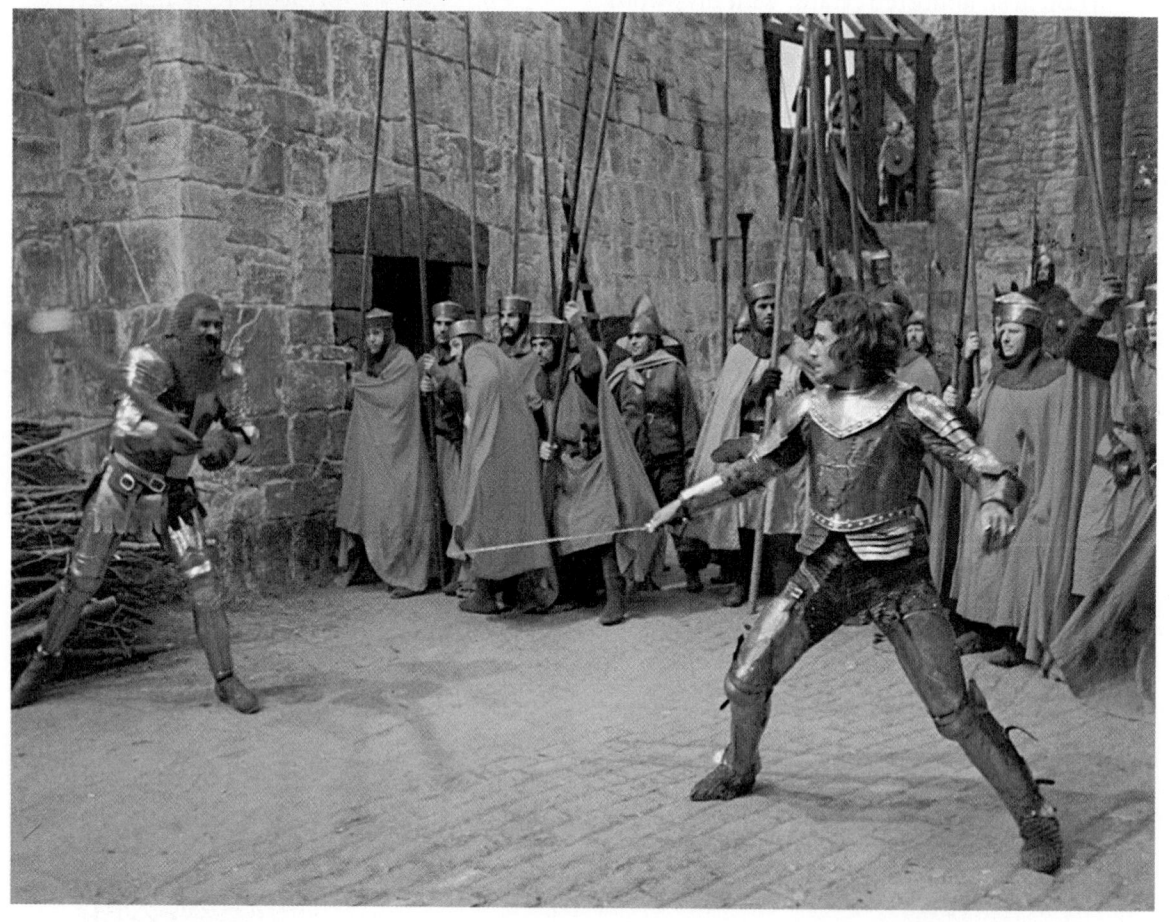

Macduff.   I have no words:
  My voice is in my sword, thou bloodier villain
  Than terms can give thee out!°   [*Fight. Alarum.*]
Macbeth.   Thou losest labor:
  As easy mayst thou the intrenchant° air
10 With thy keen sword impress° as make me bleed:
  Let fall thy blade on vulnerable crests;°
  I bear a charmèd life, which must not yield
  To one of woman born.
Macduff.   Despair° thy charm,
  And let the angel° whom thou still hast served
15 Tell thee, Macduff was from his mother's womb
  Untimely ripped.
Macbeth.
  Accursèd be that tongue that tells me so,
  For it hath cowed my better part of man!°
  And be these juggling fiends no more believed,
20 That palter° with us in a double sense;
  That keep the word of promise to our ear,
  And break it to our hope. I'll not fight with thee.
Macduff.
  Then yield thee, coward,
  And live to be the show and gaze o' th' time:°
25 We'll have thee, as our rarer monsters° are,
  Painted upon a pole,° and underwrit,
  "Here may you see the tyrant."
Macbeth.   I will not yield,
  To kiss the ground before young Malcolm's feet,
  And to be baited° with the rabble's curse.
30 Though Birnam Wood be come to Dunsinane,
  And thou opposed, being of no woman born,
  Yet I will try the last. Before my body
  I throw my warlike shield. Lay on, Macduff;
  And damned be him that first cries "Hold, enough!"

                    [*Exeunt, fighting. Alarums.*]

[*Reenter fighting, and* MACBETH *slain. Exit* MACDUFF,
  with MACBETH. *Retreat and flourish.° Enter, with drum
  and colors,* MALCOLM, SIWARD, ROSS, THANES, *and* SOLDIERS.]
Malcolm.
35 I would the friends we miss were safe arrived.
Siward.
  Some must go off;° and yet, by these I see,
  So great a day as this is cheaply bought.
Malcolm.
  Macduff is missing, and your noble son.
Ross.
  Your son, my lord, has paid a soldier's debt:
40 He only lived but till he was a man;
  The which no sooner had his prowess confirmed

8. terms . . . out: words can
describe you.

9. intrenchant: incapable
of being cut.

10. impress: make an
impression on.

11. vulnerable crests: heads
that can be wounded.

13. Despair: despair of.

14. angel: that is, fallen angel;
fiend.

? **16.** *What is the meaning
of lines 15–16? How do they
relate to the prophecy?*

18. better . . . man: manly spirit.

20. palter: equivocate.

24. gaze . . . time: spectacle of the
age.

25. monsters: freaks.

26. Painted . . . pole: pictured on
a banner set by a showman's booth.

29. baited: assailed (like a bear by
dogs).

Retreat and flourish: trumpet call
to withdraw, and fanfare.

36. go off: die (theatrical
metaphor).

In the unshrinking station° where he fought,
But like a man he died.

Siward.   Then he is dead?

Ross.

Ay, and brought off the field. Your cause of sorrow
45   Must not be measured by his worth, for then
It hath no end.

Siward.   Had he his hurts before?

Ross.

Ay, on the front.

Siward.   Why then, God's soldier be he!
Had I as many sons as I have hairs,
I would not wish them to a fairer death:
And so his knell is knolled.

50   **Malcolm.**   He's worth more sorrow,
And that I'll spend for him.

Siward.   He's worth no more:
They say he parted well and paid his score:°
And so God be with him! Here comes newer comfort.

[*Enter* MACDUFF, *with Macbeth's head.*]

Macduff.

Hail, king! for so thou art: behold, where stands
55   Th' usurper's cursèd head. The time is free.°
I see thee compassed° with thy kingdom's pearl,
That speak my salutation in their minds,
Whose voices I desire aloud with mine:
Hail, King of Scotland!

All.   Hail, King of Scotland!

[*Flourish.*]

Malcolm.

60   We shall not spend a large expense of time
Before we reckon with your several loves,°
And make us even with you. My thanes and kinsmen,
Henceforth be earls, the first that ever Scotland
In such an honor named. What's more to do,
65   Which would be planted newly with the time°—
As calling home our exiled friends abroad
That fled the snares of watchful tyranny,
Producing forth the cruel ministers°
Of this dead butcher and his fiendlike queen,
70   Who, as 'tis thought, by self and violent hands°
Took off her life—this, and what needful else
That calls upon us,° by the grace of Grace
We will perform in measure, time, and place:°
So thanks to all at once and to each one,
75   Whom we invite to see us crowned at Scone.

[*Flourish. Exeunt omnes.*]

42. unshrinking station: that is, place at which he stood firmly.

52. parted . . . score: departed well and settled his account.

? 53. *What character traits does Malcolm show in this scene? How is old Siward like a military man to the end?*

? Stage direction. *Macduff enters with Macbeth's head on a pole. A great shout goes up. What is Macduff's tone in the next speech?*

55. The time is free: The world is liberated.

56. compassed: surrounded.

61. reckon . . . loves: reward the devotion of each of you.

65. What's . . . time: What else must be done that should be newly established in this age.

68. ministers: agents.

70. self . . . hands: her own violent hands.

72. calls upon us: demands my attention.

73. in . . . place: fittingly, at the appropriate time and place.

? 75. *Scone (skōōn) is a village in Scotland. For centuries, all Scottish kings were crowned in Scone on the Stone of Destiny. The stone was taken to England in 1296 and was returned to Scotland, to Edinburgh Castle, in 1996. How would you have the characters exit? Who would exit last?*

Soliloquies and Asides

Renaissance playwrights had two useful devices for revealing to an audience or reader a dramatic character's inmost thoughts and feelings: soliloquies and asides.

A **soliloquy** is a meditative kind of speech in which a character, usually alone on stage and pretending that the audience is not present, thinks out loud. Everybody understands that the speaker of a soliloquy tells the truth freely and openly, however discreditable that truth may be. For instance, in his famous soliloquy beginning "To be or not to be," Shakespeare's Hamlet admits to the audience that he is thinking of committing suicide.

Asides are much shorter than soliloquies, but just as truthful. **Asides** are a character's private comments on what is happening at a given moment in a play. They are spoken out of the side of the mouth, so to speak, for the benefit of the audience; the other characters on stage pretend that they do not hear them. For example, Macbeth's asides in Act I, Scene 3, tell us that he cannot put the witches' prophecies out of his mind.

Macbeth's tragic decline can be best traced in his solo speeches—his asides and soliloquies. The most important of these, which are what make the play so interesting psychologically, occur as follows:

Act I, Scene 3, lines 130–142
Act I, Scene 4, lines 48–53
Act I, Scene 7, lines 1–28
Act II, Scene 1, lines 33–64
Act III, Scene 1, lines 48–72
Act IV, Scene 1, lines 144–156
Act V, Scene 3, lines 19–29
Act V, Scene 5, lines 9–15

The early soliloquies show Macbeth's indecision and his fierce inner conflict; then, after he succumbs to evil, they show the terror in his soul and his inability to recover his lost innocence. At times they even show that he is reconciled to his murderous career, especially after the second set of prophecies gives him a false sense of security. But finally the soliloquies show his despair and loss of feeling about, and interest in, life itself. All these changing states of mind are expressed in powerful images that help the audience share Macbeth's suffering. In contrast, we see Lady Macbeth mainly from the outside, though an attentive reader can find speeches in which she also reveals feelings. In *Macbeth,* the inner spiritual catastrophe parallels the outer physical catastrophe.

Nicholas Pennell as Macbeth in the Stratford Festival production of *Macbeth* (1983).

The Mystery of Evil

Macbeth fascinates us because it shows, perhaps more clearly than any of Shakespeare's other tragedies, how a character can change as a result of what he does. *Macbeth* also shows that crime does not pay, but that smug cliché is not very relevant to the play: Macbeth is "caught" as soon as he understands the witches' prophecy, and his mental anguish begins before he commits any crimes.

At the start of the play, the mere thought of committing a murder terrifies Macbeth, although he is no novice at carving up men in battle. But it is one thing to fight openly, quite another to kill stealthily. His wife says her great warrior-husband Macbeth is "too full o' th' milk of human kindness." Shakespeare apparently wants us to think of Macbeth as a good man and to feel sympathetic toward him even after he becomes a murderer. When Duncan's body is found, Macbeth does not feel excited about becoming king; instead, he mutters to himself, "The wine of life is drawn." He can't enjoy his kingly state; he is too terrified by what he is doing. "Full of scorpions is my mind," he says to his wife. He lives in such constant terror that by the end of the play he is numb to all feeling—even to the death of his beloved wife. A "dead butcher," Malcolm calls him: an automatic killer.

Lady Macbeth's deterioration is different from her husband's but just as dramatic. Legally, she is only an accomplice, never an actual murderer. But she is the first to decide that Duncan must die; Macbeth wavers right up to the last moment. After the first murders, she exerts immense self-control over herself while he surrenders to his nerves. But she does eventually crack under the strain. Malcolm might not have called her a "fiendlike queen" after her death had he known how much she suffered from pangs of conscience. Both Macbeth and his wife are moral beings who excite our pity rather than our contempt or disgust.

But why do they commit their crimes? The customary answer to this question—that they are ambitious—leads only to another question: Why are they so ambitious that they are willing to commit such crimes? Ultimately, these questions are unanswerable, because evil is as mysterious as it is real. Shakespeare makes no attempt to solve the mystery; instead, in *Macbeth,* he uses language to make it even more mysterious. The world of *Macbeth* is filled, from beginning to end, with mysterious and repulsive images of evil.

The Imagery: Darkness, Night, Blood

First of all, there are the witches. The play opens with the three witches performing their sinister rites and chanting, "Fair is foul, and foul is fair," blurring the differences between these opposites. Macbeth's first speech joins the same opposites, as though they were synonyms: "So foul and fair a day I have not seen." Macbeth's speech thus establishes a connection between himself and the witches even before he meets them.

Shakespeare's audience would have immediately recognized the witches as embodiments of evil in league with Satan himself. Several times they refer to themselves as the "weird sisters"—*weird* here meaning maliciously and perversely supernatural, possessing harmful powers given them by evil spirits in the form of nasty pet animals such as old gray tomcats and toads. English and Scottish witches are not to be regarded as the Fates of Greek mythology whose baleful influence could not be resisted. Rather, they are tempters of a kind that Shakespeare's contemporaries believed they should always avoid. One of the witches seems to foretell Macbeth's future by saying, "All hail, Macbeth, that shalt be king hereafter!" After an inner struggle, and under the influence of his wife's goading, Macbeth chooses to make "hereafter" happen immediately. Nowhere in the play do the witches *cause* Macbeth to make this wicked decision. Rather, he voluntarily surrenders himself, following a visionary dagger—a manifestation of his decision—that leads him into Duncan's bedroom. Having once given in to evil, Macbeth is thereafter under the control of evil forces stronger than his own moral sense.

Shakespeare expresses these evil forces in images of darkness, night, and blood. He has Banquo call the weird sisters "instruments of darkness," linking them to the thick gloom that pervades the whole play and provides a cover under which evil can do its work. Even in daylight Macbeth and his wife invoke the night: "Come, thick night," Lady Macbeth cries as part of her prayer asking evil spirits to "unsex" her. Macbeth also calls for night to come, to blindfold "the tender eye of pitiful day" so that the killers he has hired can safely murder innocent Banquo and his son.

By setting many of the violent scenes at night and by making the scenes in *Macbeth* "murky," full of "fog and filthy air," and pierced by the cries of owls, Shakespeare suppresses all the pleasant associations night might have, especially as the time for refreshing sleep. Just as he commits his first murder, Macbeth thinks he hears a horrible voice crying, "Macbeth does murder sleep"; thereafter, he becomes an insomniac and his wife a sleepwalker. Darkness, voices, ghosts, hallucinations—these are used to express Macbeth's and his wife's surrender to evil and their subsequent despair.

Evil in *Macbeth* takes the form of violence and bloodshed. Right after the opening scene with the witches, a man covered with gashes appears before King Duncan, who asks, "What bloody man is that?" Between this scene and the final one, in which Macbeth's bleeding and "cursèd" head is displayed on a pike, human blood hardly stops running. Images of blood appeal not only to our sense of sight but also to our sense of touch (Macbeth's bloody and secret murders are "sticking on his hands" in the last act), and even to our sense of smell ("Here's the smell of the blood still," Lady Macbeth moans in Act V as she holds out her "little hand"). Such imagery is designed to make us feel moral revulsion, not just physical disgust: Bloodshed leads only to more bloodshed.

The Poetry: Expressing the Dark Night

All this imagery reminds us that *Macbeth* is a poem as well as a play—a dramatic poem sharing many of the characteristics of lyric poetry. The most obvious of these is **meter,** here the unrhymed iambic pentameter or **blank verse** that Shakespeare's predecessor Christopher Marlowe established as the appropriate medium for tragedy. Poetry is to tragedy as singing is to opera: It elevates and enhances the emotional impact of the experience being communicated. Indeed, without the poetry there could be no tragedy, because without it Shakespeare could not have expressed the dark night into which Macbeth's soul sinks. And a tragic poet is much more concerned with states of mind and feeling than with physical action. Macbeth shares with Shakespeare's other great tragic heroes—Hamlet, Lear, Othello—the ability to express in eloquent, moving language whatever he is feeling. One of the most famous speeches of this kind occurs when, near the end of his bloody career, Macbeth sums up what life means to him:

> Out, out, brief candle!
> Life's but a walking shadow, a poor player
> That struts and frets his hour upon the stage
> And then is heard no more. It is a tale
> Told by an idiot, full of sound and fury,
> Signifying nothing.
>
> —Act V, Scene 5, lines 23–28

The bitter nihilism of these metaphors suggests that Macbeth is already dead in spirit, although his body must undergo a last battle. By murdering Duncan, he has murdered more than sleep: He has destroyed himself.

Nothing is impervious to **parody,** not even the high seriousness of a play like Shakespeare's *Macbeth.* In the following piece from *Twisted Tales from Shakespeare,* Richard Armour presents another view of the three weird sisters. You and your classmates might want to write a parody of your own.

Macbeth and the Witches

Richard Armour

Three witches, extremely weird sisters, are having a picnic amidst thunder and lightning somewhere in Scotland. Judging from their appearance, they were placed one-two-three in the Edinburgh Ugly Contest.

"When shall we three meet again in thunder, lightning, or in rain?" asks one of them. They hate nice weather and are happiest when they are soaking wet and their hair is all stringy.

"When the hurly-burly's[1] done, when the battle's lost and won," another replies. A battle

is going on between the forces of Duncan, the King of Scotland, and some Norwegians, assisted by the rebel Thane of Cawdor. At the moment it's looking good for Duncan, because two of his generals, Macbeth and Banquo, have cunningly put bagpipes into the hands of the enemy, who are blowing their brains out.

The witches hear some dear friend[2] calling and depart. "Fair is foul, and foul is fair," they comment philosophically as they leave. This must have been pretty upsetting to any moralists, semanticists, or baseball umpires who chanced to overhear them.

Shortly afterward, the battle having been won by Macbeth and the weather having turned bad enough to be pleasant, the witches meet again.

"Where hast thou been, Sister?" asks one.

"Killing swine," the second replies. All three of them have been busy doing similar diverting things, and one of them happily shows the others the thumb of a drowned sailor which she is adding to her thumb collection.[3]

---

1. See also hurdy-gurdy, hunky-dory, and okey-dokey.

2. A cat and a toad. Witches have to make friendships where they can.
3. In a comedy, this would be considered tragic relief.

The three witches and Lady Macbeth (in front) from the Faux-Real production of *Htebcam* (1994).

Macbeth and Banquo come by at this point, on their way to inform the King that they have defeated the rebels. They would rather tell him in person than render a report in triplicate.

"Speak, if you can," says Macbeth boldly to the hags. "What are you?" He rather thinks they are witches but would like to hear it from their own skinny lips.

The witches start hailing.[4] They hail Macbeth as Thane of Glamis and Thane of Cawdor and say he will be King Hereafter. Not to leave Banquo out, they hail him as "lesser than Macbeth, and greater." (The witches are masters of gobbledyspook.) He won't be a king, they say, but he'll beget kings, and now they have to begetting along.

Macbeth knows he is Thane of Glamis, but has no idea (or didn't have until now) of becoming Thane of Cawdor or King Hereafter. "Stay, you imperfect speakers, tell me more," he commands. But the witches, perhaps not liking the way he refers to their elocution, vanish into thin air, making it slightly thicker.

While Macbeth is meditating about what the witches have forecast for him, a couple of the King's henchmen, straight from a busy day of henching, ride up. They bring word that Duncan is liquidating the Thane of Cawdor and giving his title to Macbeth, it being an inexpensive gift. (Duncan, as King of Scotland, was Scotcher than anybody.)

"Look how our partner's rapt," remarks Banquo, noticing that Macbeth, stunned with all the good news, acts as if he has been struck on the noggin. But Macbeth is only lost in thought and will find his way out presently. Thus far the witches have been batting 1,000, and Macbeth is beginning to take more than a casual interest in Duncan's health.[5]

4. Until now it has been raining.
5. Henceforth, when he says "How are you?" to the King, it will be a bona fide question.

[These are Richard Armour's footnotes.]

MAKING MEANINGS

Act V

First Thoughts

1. How do you feel about what happens to Macbeth's body after he is dead?

Reading Check

a. Why, according to the doctor, is Lady Macbeth walking in her sleep?

b. In Scene 2, what opinion of Macbeth do the Scottish lords now hold?

c. When does Lady Macbeth die?

d. What is Macbeth's plan for dealing with the attacking troops? Why has he been forced to choose this plan?

e. What changes in his personality does Macbeth describe in Scene 5, lines 9–15?

f. In the speech in Scene 5 that begins "Tomorrow, and tomorrow, and tomorrow . . ." (lines 19–28), how does Macbeth describe life? What metaphors does he use?

g. How are the prophecies proclaimed by the three apparitions in Act IV, Scene 1, fulfilled in Act V?

h. At the end of the play, what has become of Macbeth? Who becomes King?

Shaping Interpretations

2. Theatrically, the spectacle of Lady Macbeth walking in her sleep is one of the most striking scenes in the play. It is entirely Shakespeare's invention, not found or suggested in his source. Why do you suppose Shakespeare has her walk in her sleep? How is this scene related to the remarks that Macbeth makes about sleep in Act II, Scene 2, just after he kills Duncan?

3. In the sleepwalking scene, Lady Macbeth refers to many of her waking experiences. For example, the words "One: two" may refer to the moment in Act II, Scene 1, when she struck the bell

Lady Macbeth holding a candle in a dark hallway.
From the Stratford Festival production of *Macbeth* (1983).

Connecting with the Text

7. What are your reactions to the idea expressed by Macbeth that life "is a tale / Told by an idiot, full of sound and fury, / Signifying nothing" (Scene 5, lines 26–28)? Explain your response.

Challenging the Text

8. Sometime shortly after 1660, a playwright named William Davenant (who claimed to be a natural son of Shakespeare) added another sleepwalking scene to *Macbeth*: He had the ghost of Duncan chase Lady Macbeth about the stage. How might this scene change the way audiences perceive Lady Macbeth's character? Might it make the other ghosts in the play seem any more or less real? What might the scene add to the play, and what might it take away?

The Play as a Whole

Shaping Interpretations

1. "Nothing in his life / Became him like the leaving it," says Malcolm in Act I, referring to the traitorous Thane of Cawdor. Malcolm also says that this Thane of Cawdor threw away the dearest thing he owned. How might these two statements also apply to Macbeth? Could these lines apply to any people in actual life?

2. One of the **themes** of *Macbeth* centers on evil, which Shakespeare saw as a force beyond human understanding. Do you think Shakespeare also saw evil as stronger than the forces of good? Support your answer with events from the play.

3. The philosopher Aristotle argued that a bad man cannot be the principal character of a tragedy. Does Shakespeare keep you from losing all sympathy for Macbeth in spite of Macbeth's increasing viciousness? Was there a point at which you lost sympathy for Macbeth? If so, where?

4. One critic has observed that part of Macbeth's tragedy is the fact that many of his strengths are also his weaknesses. Explain this apparent contradiction in Macbeth's **character.** What are his strengths? Which ones also work against him?

5. Think of a single event, at any time during the course of the play, that could have averted Macbeth's tragic end. What would this event be?

signaling Macbeth to go kill Duncan. Find traces of other experiences in what she says while sleepwalking.

4. At the end of Act IV, Malcolm says, "The night is long that never finds the day." In what metaphorical sense does he use the terms *night* and *day*? How does his remark **foreshadow** the outcome of the play?

5. The last act of *Macbeth* contains the play's **climax**—the most emotional and suspenseful part of the action—the moment when the characters' conflict is finally resolved. Which part of Act V do you consider the climax? Explain.

6. Shakespeare gave most of his **tragic heroes** an impressive dying speech in which they say something significant about their own life and death. Although he did not write such a speech for Macbeth, which speech of Macbeth's do you think serves in the play as his dying speech? Why do you select this speech rather than some other one?

How could it have come about? How would it affect the outcome of the play?

6. **Internal conflicts** rage within Macbeth, as well as **external conflicts** with other characters. Explain some of the play's main conflicts, and trace their **resolution.**

Extending the Text

7. What modern figure, real or fictional, had a downfall, like Macbeth's, that came after an attempt to gain great power? How is this modern figure like Macbeth, and how different? Would this modern figure make a good **tragic hero**? Refer to your Quickwrite notes (see page 300) as you answer this question.

Challenging the Text

8. Think about the quotation from Goethe on page 281. Do you think Macbeth himself has the free will to control his own destiny? Or is he controlled by fate?

9. Do you think people should **parody** a great tragic play like *Macbeth,* the way Richard Armour does in "Macbeth and the Witches" (see *Connections* on page 386)? Why or why not?

ELEMENTS OF LITERATURE

Imagery and Figurative Language

Macbeth's poetry is rich in imagery and figurative language that help to create atmosphere and reveal character and theme.

1. Powerful images in the play contrast the natural and the unnatural, as in Lady Macbeth's speech in Act I, Scene 7, lines 54–59:

. . . I have given suck, and know
How tender 'tis to love the babe that milks me:
I would, while it was smiling in my face,
Have plucked my nipple from his boneless gums,
And dashed the brains out, had I so sworn as you
Have done to this.

Francesca Annis and Jon Finch in Roman Polanski's film production of *Macbeth* (1971).

a. What unnatural sounds and events are reported in Act II, Scenes 2–4? Look at the **context** of these images. What mood do they create?

b. Look at the witches' scenes. What would you say is the emotional effect of each scene? Besides the witches themselves, what unnatural images occur in these scenes?

2. We hear about sleep and sleeplessness throughout the play. How is sleep described in these figures of speech?

a. **First Witch**. . . . I'll drain him dry as hay:
Sleep shall neither night nor day
Hang upon his penthouse lid; . . .

—Act I, Scene 3, lines 18–30

b. **Macbeth.** Methought I heard a voice cry "Sleep no more!
Macbeth does murder sleep"—the innocent sleep,
Sleep that knits up the raveled sleave of care,
The death of each day's life, sore labor's bath,
Balm of hurt minds, great nature's second course,
Chief nourisher in life's feast—

—Act II, Scene 2, lines 34–39

3. Choose one of the following images, and find three speeches (from different scenes in the play) in which the image occurs:

blood   darkness   disease   planting

Look back at the **context** of each speech (what happens just before and after): What is the emotional effect of each one?

CHOICES: Building Your Portfolio

Writer's Notebook

1. Collecting Ideas for a Cause-Effect Essay

With cause and effect, we often work backward: We are first aware of the effect and then we search for the cause(s). For Thomas De Quincey, the porter scene in *Macbeth* produced a certain effect, "a peculiar awfulness and a depth of solemnity." In the *Connections* essay on page 330, De Quincey explores the cause of this increased tension. What scenes in *Macbeth* had a strong emotional effect on you? Go back to the play and find the words and actions that caused this effect. Save your work for the Writer's Workshop on page 459.

(WORK IN PROGRESS)

Analyzing a Character

2. Monster or Not?

Lady Macbeth is sometimes regarded as a monster, ruthlessly ambitious and fiendishly cruel. What clues can you find in the play suggesting that Shakespeare did not want us to judge her so severely? In an essay, analyze her character as it is revealed through her words and actions and her relationship with Macbeth.

Analyzing the Writer's Purpose

3. Probing Shakespeare's Mind

When Macbeth discovers how Macduff entered the world (Act V, Scene 8), he also discovers that the witches are "juggling fiends" who have given him a false sense of security. Why do you think Shakespeare shows Macbeth taken in by their prophecies? What might Shakespeare be implying about Macbeth's **character**? about the witches' powers? Is he suggesting that Macbeth might be a victim of mysterious evil forces? Write your answer in one or two paragraphs.

Analyzing Tragedy

4. A Tragic Structure

Traditionally, critics have thought of the following as the classic elements of a Shakespearean tragedy: (a) a **protagonist,** the **tragic hero,** a man of high estate, whose desires or conflicts set the action in motion; (b) an **antagonist** who blocks this protagonist; (c) a **rising action** in which **complications** develop, leading in the third act to a **turning point**; (d) a **falling action** that inexorably leads to a tragic **climax;** (e) a **resolution,** in which the social order that had been torn asunder by the action is restored. In an essay, analyze *Macbeth*, showing how the play does or does not follow this tragic pattern.

Creative Writing

5. Macbeth Today

Rewrite the banquet scene (Act III, Scene 4), when Macbeth sees Banquo's ghost. Change the setting to a modern time and place, and let the characters speak in today's language. For example, Lady Macbeth might explain that Macbeth is suffering from stress. The Scottish lords might be cabinet members. Provide a list of characters that includes a phrase describing each character.

Oral Interpretation

6. Say the Soliloquy

With a small group, select one of Macbeth's soliloquies and "perform" it in the way a choir interprets a song: Vary voice pitches, volume, tempo, rhythm, meter, and tone. Repeat key lines as a refrain, and use echoing words, vocal sound effects, harmony, and chanting to accentuate and enhance the words.

Art

7. Bring a Scene to Life

Sketch the set and costumes you would provide for at least one scene of *Macbeth*. In set design, you must indicate placement of furniture and describe lighting. Costume sketches must describe materials and colors.

Reading Skills and Strategies

VOCABULARY: MAPPING MEANINGS

If you draw on your own personal knowledge and experience when learning a new word, the word more readily becomes a part of your working vocabulary. **Mapping** is a vocabulary-building strategy that encourages active participation. Mapping works like this: First, you see a new word used in a sentence. Before you look up the dictionary definition, you use **context clues** to guess at the word's meaning. After you look the word up in the dictionary, you use the word in a sentence of your own and become familiar with its different forms. Here's an example of mapping:

corporal ▶ Banquo: Whither are they vanished?
Macbeth: Into the air, and what
seemed **corporal** melted
As breath into the wind.

▼

Your guess: Something solid. **Context** suggests corporal is something that doesn't melt like breath. Corpse, a dead body, is a word that sounds similar. Perhaps there's some relation.

▼

Definition: of the body; bodily.

▼

Your sentence: Corporal punishment in schools has often been the subject of heated debates.

Other forms:

corpo-rally (adv.)

Here are some helpful suggestions for using mapping as one of your vocabulary-building strategies:

1. Have you heard the word before? Maybe you've heard a word that sounds similar to it.
2. Are there any context clues in the sentence?
3. Try substituting your guess for the word. Does it make sense in the context?
4. Many words have **multiple meanings.** When you look up the word in the dictionary, make sure you read all the definitions. Select the one that fits best; make sure that it's the right part of speech. *Corporal,* for example, can also refer to an officer in the army. But that definition doesn't work here, and, besides, it's a noun. You're looking for an adjective in this context.
5. Think about the other forms of the word for a few moments. You might also want to use them in some sentences.

Try It Out

In each sentence below, the vocabulary word is given in boldface. Using the mapping example for the word *corporal* as a guide, draw your own map for each of the following words.

1. **Macbeth.** . . . Thou sure and firm-set earth,
   Hear not my steps, which way they walk, for fear
   Thy very stones **prate** of my whereabout,
   And take the present horror from the time,
   Which now suits with it.

   —Act II, Scene 1, lines 56–60

2. **Lady Macbeth. Infirm** of purpose!
   Give me the daggers. The sleeping and the dead
   Are but as pictures. 'Tis the eye of childhood
   That fears a painted devil.

   —Act II, Scene 2, lines 51–54

3. **Macbeth.** . . .Will all great Neptune's ocean
   wash this blood
   Clean from my hand? No; this my hand will rather
   The **multitudinous** seas incarnadine,
   Making the green one red.

   —Act II, Scene 2, lines 59–62

4. **Macduff.** Confusion now hath made his
   masterpiece.
   Most **sacrilegious** murder hath broke ope
   The Lord's anointed temple, and stole thence
   The life o' th' building.

   —Act II, Scene 3, lines 60–63

WORLD LITERATURE

Italy

Dante Alighieri

(1265–1321)

Dante Alighieri (dän′tä a′lə·gyer′ē) decided to write his masterpiece, *The Divine Comedy,* in Italian rather than in Latin, and thus became the father of Italian literature. Dante was born in Florence, but his involvement in the violent politics of his city led to his banishment for life—Dante was warned that he would be burned at the stake if he were ever found in Florence again.

The Divine Comedy, completed during Dante's exile, is the supreme and culminating work of medieval thought. Many people consider this complex, symbolic poem to be the greatest poem ever written in any language. In three sections, Dante tells of an imaginary journey that takes him through Hell, Purgatory, and Heaven. In the course of his journey, Dante gives expression to nearly every major intellectual conception achieved in the Middle Ages.

Dante and His Poems (detail)
(1465) by Domenico di Michelino.
Duomo, Florence.

(Map) Old map showing the Mediterranean Coast.

Before You Read

FROM THE INFERNO OF DANTE

Background

If you had to name the three most evil people of all time, who would be on your list? The sinner at the pit of Hell in Dante's *Inferno* is Judas Iscariot, who suffers the greatest torment of all because he betrayed Jesus Christ to the Romans. The other two "worst" sinners whom Dante puts in the very jaws of Satan may come as a surprise— although you have probably met them in Shakespeare: Brutus and Cassius, the conspirators of ancient Rome who plotted the assassination of Julius Caesar. Another surprise is Dante's description of the worst part of Hell: Instead of a burning pit of fire and brimstone, the bottom of Hell is a ghastly, windswept lake of ice.

Dante's journey to Hell takes place in the first part of his long epic poem, *The Divine Comedy*. (The epic is a comedy in the sense that it has a happy ending.) Led by the poet Virgil, who, for Dante, symbolized human reason, Dante travels to the Inferno down through a kind of deep funnel that bores into the center of the earth. Around this abysmal cavity run nine ledges, or circles, which grow ever narrower as the cavity bores deeper into the earth. On each circle a certain kind of sin is punished. The sins of the flesh are on the upper circle, where punishment is mildest. Sins of anger are in the middle, and sins against reason are on the lowest circles, where torment is greatest.

Dante in the Valley of Terrors (late 19th to early 20th century) by William Frank Calderon.

From the Inferno, Dante ascends gradually through Purgatory. Then Virgil turns his traveler over to a woman named Beatrice ("blessed") who leads Dante into Paradise, where he is granted a blissful vision of God and salvation. What Dante learns of sin from visiting the agonies of Hell, of renunciation in witnessing the trials in Purgatory, and of joy in sharing the glories of Paradise will turn him from error forever.

As this part of *The Inferno* opens, Dante and his guide approach the last circle of Hell. It is dominated by the gigantic winged figure of Satan, frozen in ice.

Quickwrite

How do you envision Hell? Freewrite a description of what you think Hell might be like.

from The Inferno of Dante

Dante Alighieri
translated by **Robert Pinsky**

Canto 34

"And now, *Vexilla regis prodeunt*
    Inferni°—therefore, look," my master said
    As we continued on the long descent,

"And see if you can make him out, ahead."
5   As though, in the exhalation of heavy mist
    Or while night darkened our hemisphere, one spied

A mill—blades turning in the wind, half-lost
    Off in the distance—some structure of that kind
    I seemed to make out now. But at a gust

10 Of wind, there being no other shelter at hand,
    I drew behind my leader's back again.
    By now (and putting it in verse I find

Fear in myself still) I had journeyed down
    To where the shades were covered wholly by ice,°
15   Showing like straw in glass—some lying prone,

And some erect, some with the head toward us,
    And others with the bottoms of the feet;
    Another like a bow, bent feet to face.

When we had traveled forward to the spot
20   From which it pleased my master to have me see
    That creature° whose beauty once had been so great,

He made me stop, and moved from in front of me.
    "Look: here is Dis," he said, "and here is the place
    Where you must arm yourself with the quality

25 Of fortitude." How chilled and faint I was
    On hearing that, you must not ask me, reader—
    I do not write it; words would not suffice:

I neither died, nor kept alive—consider
    With your own wits what I, alike denuded
30   Of death and life, became as I heard my leader.

2. *Vexilla regis prodeunt / Inferni*: Latin for "The banners of the king of Hell advance." These words perversely echo a well-known Latin hymn.

14. where . . . ice: This is Judecca (jōō·dek′ə), the final division of Cocytus (kō·sīt′əs) and the innermost part of Hell. Judecca is named for Judas Iscariot, who betrayed Jesus.

? **7–18.** *What comparisons does Dante use to help you visualize what the narrator sees?*

21. creature: Satan. Dante also calls him by the names Lucifer, Beelzebub, and Dis. Before Satan rebelled against God and was cast down from Heaven, he was an angel of tremendous beauty.

The emperor of the realm of grief protruded
　　From mid-breast up above the surrounding ice.
　　A giant's height, and mine, would have provided

Closer comparison than would the size
35　　Of his arm and a giant. Envision the whole
　　That is proportionate to parts like these.

If he was truly once as beautiful
　　As he is ugly now, and raised his brows
　　Against his Maker—then all sorrow may well

40　Come out of him. How great a marvel it was
　　For me to see three faces° on his head:
　　In front there was a red one; joined to this,

Each over the midpoint of a shoulder, he had
　　Two others—all three joining at the crown.
45　　That on the right appeared to be a shade

Of whitish yellow; the third had such a mien
　　As those who come from where the Nile descends.
　　Two wings spread forth from under each face's chin,

Strong, and befitting such a bird, immense—
50　　I have never seen at sea so broad a sail—
　　Unfeathered, batlike, and issuing three winds

That went forth as he beat them, to freeze the whole
　　Realm of Cocytus that surrounded him.
　　He wept with all six eyes, and the tears fell

55　Over his three chins mingled with bloody foam.
　　The teeth of each mouth held a sinner, kept
　　As by a flax rake: thus he held three of them

In agony. For the one the front mouth gripped,
　　The teeth were as nothing to the claws, which sliced
60　　And tore the skin until his back was stripped.

"That soul," my master said, "who suffers most,
　　Is Judas Iscariot; head locked inside,
　　He flails his legs. Of the other two, who twist

With their heads down, the black mouth holds the shade
65　　Of Brutus: writhing, but not a word will he scream;
　　Cassius is the sinewy one on the other side.

31. *Who is the "emperor of the realm of grief"?*

41. three faces: grotesque perversion of the Trinity.

Inscription over Hell Gate (late 18th to early 19th century) by William Blake.
Tate Gallery, London.

But night is rising again, and it is time
 That we depart, for we have seen the whole."
 As he requested, I put my arms round him,

70 And waiting until the wings were opened full
 He took advantage of the time and place
 And grasped the shaggy flank, and gripping still,

From tuft to tuft descended through the mass
 Of matted hair and crusts of ice. And then,
75 When we had reached the pivot of the thighs,°

Just where the haunch is at its thickest, with strain
 And effort my master brought around his head
 To where he'd had his legs: and from there on

He grappled the hair as someone climbing would—
80 So I supposed we were heading back to Hell.
 "Cling tight, for it is stairs like these," he sighed

40–68. *Reread the description of this "emperor of grief" and try to draw what you see. After you read lines 69–80, stop and explain whose wings and flank and hair the narrator is referring to.*

75. pivot of the thighs: This midpoint of Satan's body is also the center of the earth. At this spot Virgil turns himself upside down because henceforth the travelers must journey *up* Satan's legs in order to reach the surface of the Southern Hemisphere.

The Triumph of Death (c. 1562) by Pieter Bruegel the Elder. Oil on panel. Prado, Madrid.

Like one who is exhausted, "which we must scale
    To part from so much evil." Then he came up
    Through a split stone, and placed me on its sill,

85 And climbed up toward me with his cautious step.
    I raised my eyes, expecting I would see
    Lucifer as I left him—and saw his shape

Inverted, with his legs held upward. May they
    Who are too dull to see what point I had passed
90   Judge whether it perplexed me. "Come—the way

90. *Can you infer what point it is that they have just passed?*

Is long, the road remaining to be crossed
    Is hard: rise to your feet," the master said,
    "The sun is at mid-tierce."° We had come to rest

In nothing like a palace hall; instead
95   A kind of natural dungeon enveloped us,
    With barely any light, the floor ill made.

93. mid-tierce: Formerly, tierce was the period from 6:00 to 9:00 A.M. (the first third of the day), so mid-tierce is about 7:30 A.M. In Hell, the sun is never consulted in telling time, but now that Dante and Virgil have emerged from Hell, the sun is used for that purpose.

"Before I free myself from the abyss,
    My master," I said when I was on my feet,
    "Speak, and dispel my error: where is the ice?

100 And how can he be fixed head-down like that?
    And in so short a time, how can it be
    Possible for the sun to make its transit

From evening to morning?" He answered me,
    "You imagine you are still on the other side,
105   Across the center of the earth, where I

Grappled the hair on the evil serpent's hide
    Who pierces the world. And all through my descent,
    You were on that side; when I turned my head

And legs about, you passed the central point
110   To which is drawn, from every side, all weight.
    Now you are on the opposite continent

Beneath the opposite hemisphere to that
    Which canopies the great dry land therein:
    Under the zenith of that one is the site

115. Under the zenith . . . slain: Under the zenith, or highest point, of the Northern Hemisphere's sky— a point reached directly through the earth and thus "opposite" where Dante and Virgil now stand—is the city of Jerusalem, the site where Jesus Christ, "the Man," was slain.

115 Whereon the Man was slain° who without sin
    Was born and lived; your feet this minute press
    Upon a little sphere whose rounded skin

Forms the Judecca's other, outward face.
    Here it is morning when it is evening there;
120   The one whose hair was like a ladder for us

Is still positioned as he was before.
    On this side he fell down from Heaven; the earth,
    Which till then stood out here, impelled by fear

Veiled itself in the sea and issued forth
125   In our own hemisphere. And possibly,
    What now appears on this side° fled its berth

And rushing upward left a cavity:
    This hollow where we stand." There is below,
    As far from Beelzebub as one can be

130   Within his tomb, a place one cannot know
    By sight, but by the sound a little runnel°
    Makes as it wends the hollow rock its flow

Has worn, descending through its winding channel:
    To get back up to the shining world from there
135   My guide and I went into that hidden tunnel;

And following its path, we took no care
    To rest, but climbed: he first, then I—so far,
    Through a round aperture I saw appear

Some of the beautiful things that Heaven bears,
140   Where we came forth, and once more saw the stars.

126. What now appears on this side: The island of Mount Purgatory, the pinnacle at which a sinner makes a total renunciation of sin, is apparently formed out of the inner earth displaced by Lucifer's fall. Climbing this peak will be the next leg of Dante's journey.

131. runnel: stream. This rivulet may derive from the river Lethe, the river of forgetfulness in classical mythology.

140. *As he does in the* Purgatorio *and* Paradiso, *Dante ends the* Inferno *with the word* stars. *What do you think the stars symbolize? How does the end of this Canto contrast with the other sights the travelers have seen?*

FINDING COMMON GROUND

Evil has fascinated artists and poets of every age. Certainly, of the three sections of *The Divine Comedy,* Hell is by far the most fascinating place—for readers, that is. Discuss Dante's particular vision of Hell with other students, and see if you can arrive at a consensus on this question: "What acts deserve the worst torments of Hell?" (Review your Quickwrite notes before you begin.)

• What do you think Judas, Brutus, and Cassius may have in common? What sins did all three commit?

• Brutus and Cassius have leading roles in Shakespeare's *Julius Caesar,* but Dante clearly did not regard them as heroes (and neither did Shakespeare). What do you think Dante's attitude would have been toward Shakespeare's *Macbeth?*

Do you think Macbeth would have occupied a place in Dante's Hell? Cite support from the play to explain your answer.

• In a memorable line, Dante describes his terror in the lowest depths of Hell by saying "I neither died, nor kept alive" (line 28). What do you think he means in this verse? Why would such a fate be especially terrifying?

• Suppose Dante were writing today: What categories of "sin" would he find especially prevalent in the modern world? Keep in mind the kinds of sins he felt merited the worst punishment. What kinds of punishments would be especially suitable for the offenders?

Shakespeare's Language

by John Algeo

Shakespeare's language is an early form of Modern English, basically the same kind of English we speak. But we need glosses, or explanations, for some words and phrases because English has changed during the past four hundred years.

Speaking the Speech: Shakespeare's Pronunciation

The actors who pronounced Shakespeare's lines on the stage of the Globe Theater would not have sounded like modern actors, American or British. We need not be concerned with the details of their pronunciation, but some differences are obvious even from the written text of the plays. For example, Shakespeare's contemporaries, like English speakers today, used a great many contractions. But they contracted words in different ways than we do.

Shakespeare liked to contract the pronouns that begin with vowels (*us* and *it*), as the following examples show:

... we / Shall take upon's what else remains to do ...

... To mend it, or be rid on't [of it].

... for't must be done to-night.

What is't that moves your Highness?

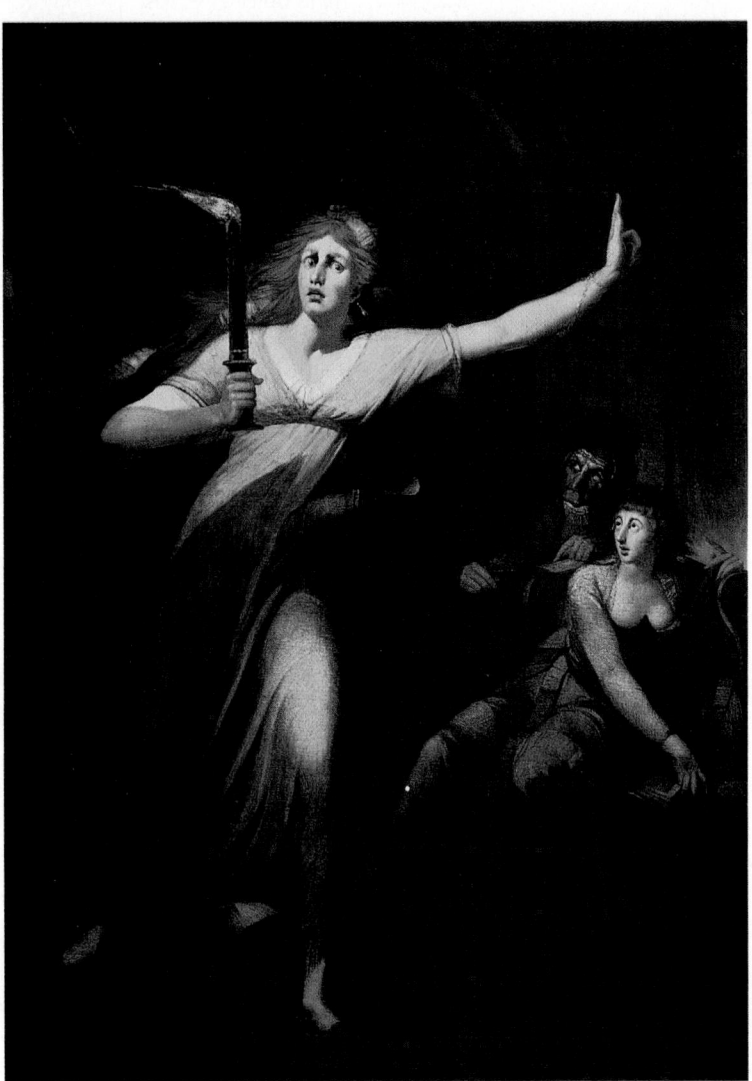

Lady Macbeth Sleepwalking (late 18th to early 19th century) by Henry Fuseli.

Louvre, Paris.

Shakespeare also frequently omitted unstressed syllables from the middle of words (as we still do in words like *fam'ly*):

... o'er the rest ...

... will these hands ne'er be clean?

... my near'st [nearest] of life ...

Thou marvel'st at my words ...

A whole syllable could be omitted from the beginning of a word if it was unstressed (as in the use of *'cause* for *because*, an omission we still make today):

. . . 'cause he fail'd . . .

Point against point, rebellious arm 'gainst arm . . .

. . . 'Twixt this and supper.

. . . if he 'scape . . .

I 'gin to be aweary of the sun . . .

Some of Shakespeare's words are stressed on different syllables from those we would now accent. For example, in "Stop up th' access and passage to remorse," the iambic rhythm of the line shows us that Shakespeare pronounced "acCESS," rather than "ACcess," as we would.

Other words have changed their forms in various ways since Shakespeare's day. In *Macbeth*, we find *murther* for *murder*, *afeard* for *afraid*, *aweary* for *weary*, and *alarum* for *alarm*.

Shakespeare's Grammar

Although Shakespeare's grammar is essentially the same as ours, it differs in numerous minor ways.

Shakespeare could use *which* where we use *who* to refer to a person: ". . . the slave / Which ne'er shook hands." He could also use *the which*, especially with broad or unstated antecedents: "He only liv'd but till he was a man; / The which [his manhood] no sooner had his prowess confirm'd, . . . / But like a man he died." Shakespeare could also use the pronoun *who* in an indefinite sense, for which

we use *the one who:* "Who was the thane, lives yet."

In present-day English, we use *mine* as a pronoun and *my* to modify a noun: "It's mine" but "It's my book." Shakespeare used both forms to modify nouns: *mine* before words beginning with a vowel, and *my* before words beginning with a consonant, just as we use *an* and *a* today ("an orange," "a lemon"): "Ha! they pluck out *mine* eyes. / Will all great Neptune's ocean wash this blood / Clean from *my* hand?"

Today, we generally use only a single pronoun for the person or people we talk to: *you* (with its possessives *your* and *yours*). Shakespeare had a choice between *th-* forms (*thou, thee, thy, thine*) and *y-* forms (*ye, you, your, yours*). *Thou* and *ye* were subject forms, like *I; thee* and *you* were object forms, like *me*.

Th- forms were used in talking to one person with whom the speaker was intimate (wife, husband, bosom buddy) or to whom the speaker was socially superior (child, servant, subject). *Y-* forms were used in talking to several persons, or to one person who was a social equal but not an intimate friend, or who was a superior (parent, boss, king). In the singular, *th-* forms showed intimacy or superiority; *y-* forms showed equality or servility.

Shakespeare made careful use of the different **connotations** of *th-* and *y-* forms. When Macbeth and Banquo meet the weird sisters (Act I, Scene 3),

they address the witches with *y-* forms because the two soldiers are in awe of these supernatural women; the witches, however, use *th-* forms for Macbeth and Banquo, thereby asserting their superiority over the mere mortals.

Macbeth and Banquo normally address one another with *y-* forms because, though equals, they are not intimates. At the beginning of Act III, however, when Banquo is thinking about the foul deeds that Macbeth has obviously used to come to the throne, he uses *th-* forms for Macbeth, since he regards Macbeth's murderous actions as having made a moral inferior of him. Banquo can think what he wants, but when Macbeth actually appears, Banquo addresses him with *y-* forms again. For Banquo to have called King Macbeth *thou* to his face would have been an insulting breach of etiquette.

The verb in Shakespeare's day had a special ending, *–st*, to go with *thou* as a subject, thus: "thou know'st," "thou didst," and "thou hast." It also had an alternative ending, *–th*, for the third-person singular ending, *–s*, that we still use today. Shakespeare could use "he knows" or "knoweth," "he does" or "doth," and "he has" or "hath." The two forms meant the same thing, although the *–s* ending was more common, and the *–th* probably sounded rather formal or old-fashioned even in Shakespeare's day. Sometimes Shakespeare used the two together—"The

> In some respects, Shakespeare's vocabulary was more complex than ours.

earth hath bubbles, as the water has"—with no apparent difference in meaning.

Shakespeare could omit the helping verb *do* in questions and negative sentences where we must have it:

Live you? [Do you live?]

Ride you this afternoon? [Do you ride this afternoon?]

Fail not our feast. [Don't fail (to be at) our feast.]

He loves us not. [He doesn't love us.]

On the other hand, Shakespeare could use an unstressed *do* where we cannot:

. . . swimmers, that do cling together . . .

. . . such things here as we do speak about . . .

His wonders and his praises do contend . . .

. . . the earth / Was feverous, and did shake.

Shakespeare had a wider choice of past participles than we do in standard English today, although some of Shakespeare's forms have survived even today in nonstandard speech:

I have spoke. [for *spoken*]

And his great love . . . hath help him. [for *has helped*]

Shakespeare could use forms of *be* instead of *have* to make a perfect tense of verbs indicating motion: "They *are* not yet *come* back."

Where we would say "Come on, *let's go* to the king," Shakespeare has simply "Come, *go we* to the King." Shakespeare's *go we* is an old first-person command that is more direct than the *let's go* form we now prefer.

In both Shakespeare's English and ours, noun phrases may consist of a determiner (like *the, a, my*), an adjective, and a noun: *the old house*. However, in short expressions used to address a person, Shakespeare could put the adjective first: "Gentle my Lord" [for "My gentle Lord"] and "Gracious my Lord" [for "My gracious Lord"].

Some of what we consider "mistakes" today are also found in Shakespeare. They are actually old ways of using English that have fallen out of favor in standard English; for example:

There's daggers in men's smiles . . . [There *are* daggers]

Who I myself struck down . . . [*Whom* I myself struck down]

. . . ask'd for who . . . [for *whom*]

Macbeth and the Witches (late 18th to early 19th century) by Henry Fuseli. Petworth House, Petworth, Sussex, England.

Shakespeare's Words

In some respects, Shakespeare's vocabulary was more complex than ours. We commonly use three words for location: *here, there,* and *where.* Shakespeare had nine, because in addition to those three, six others were available that are now rare, if not archaic: *hence, thence, whence* ("from here, from there, from where") and *hither, thither, whither* ("to here, to there, to where"):

> Whence cam'st thou, worthy Thane? [Where did you come from?]
>
> I will thither. [I will go (to) there.]
>
> Whither should I fly? [Where should I fly to?]

Shakespeare uses other words that are now rare or obsolete:

> I say sooth . . . [I tell the truth; we still have *sooth* in the form *soothsayer* ("truth teller").]
>
> This diamond he greets your wife withal [with] . . .
>
> Send out moe [more] horses. [In Early Modern English, *moe* referred to number, *more* to size.]

In Shakespeare's plays, some of the words that strike us as "fancy" were fancy even when he used them. They were "inkhorn terms"—words borrowed from the classical languages and used for their mouth-filling and impressive sounds, as well as for their subtleties of meaning. Just after he has stabbed King Duncan, Macbeth says that his hand will never be clean again, but will rather

> The multitudinous seas incarnadine . . .

"But the script says, 'Lay on Macduff.'"

He means that the blood on his hands would "make the many seas red," but the word *multitudinous* seems to mean far more than the short word *many,* and the literal meaning of *incarnadine* ("to turn into the blood-red color of raw flesh") is especially appropriate to Macbeth's actions and state of mind. Shakespeare was using fancy words—but for a purpose.

The trickiest words in Shakespeare, however, are those that look familiar but have different meanings than their present-day versions. They are false friends that make us think we understand what the language means, while in fact indicating something different from what we expect. Here are a few examples:

> Sweno, the Norways' king, craves composition [agreement, peace terms] . . . .
>
> Are ye fantastical [illusory, imaginary], or that indeed / Which outwardly ye show [seem, appear]?
>
> Say from whence / You owe [own, have] this strange intelligence [information].

> Sleep, that knits up [straightens out] the raveled sleave [tangled thread] of care. . . . [The image of reknitting the sleeve of a sweater that has unraveled makes sense, but is wrong.]

Because of differences like these between Shakespeare's English and ours, it takes some effort for us to read his plays and poetry. What we can get from the reading, however, is well worth the effort.

Try It Out

Find an example in Shakespeare's sonnets (pages 225–229) of each of the following:

a. A contraction that we would not use today

b. An "inkhorn term"

c. A word pronounced differently from the way we pronounce it today

d. *Thy* where we would use *your*

e. *Thou, thee,* or *thine* (notice who is talking to whom)

f. The *–th* and *–st* forms of verbs

g. A negative like "They try not" (instead of "They don't try")

h. An unemphatic statement like "They do try" (instead of "They try")

i. An unusual form of a verb (like "I have spoke")

j. A word we no longer have or no longer use with the same meaning

(Opposite) *St. Jerome* (detail) (15th century) by Domenico Ghirlandaio. Chiesa di Ognissanti, Florence.

Bacon
from **The King James Bible**
Worlds of Wisdom
Milton

A word is dead
When it is said,
Some say.
I say it just
Begins to live
That day.

—Emily Dickinson
   (American,
   1830–1886)

Sir Francis Bacon

(1561–1626)

From his earliest days, Francis Bacon knew that he was an important person. When he was about nine, Queen Elizabeth asked him how old he was, and he is said to have replied, "Two years younger than your Majesty's happy reign." A boy who speaks like this will go far, and Bacon went far. He rose in his chosen profession, the law, until he reached the very top and became Lord Chancellor of England and lord keeper of the great seal, an office that his father, Sir Nicholas Bacon, had also held. He was elevated to the peerage, the British nobility who could govern as members of the House of Lords, and he amassed a large fortune, though he was often in debt because of his extravagant lifestyle. At the height of his political career, he was found guilty of taking bribes and banished to his country estate, where he devoted himself full time to thinking and writing about new ways to discover knowledge.

Bacon once wrote a now-famous letter to his uncle, Lord Burghley, Elizabeth's secretary of state, in which he said, "I have taken all knowledge to be my province." Of course, he did not master all knowledge, but he did make important contributions to many different branches of knowledge: political science, economics, biology, physics, music, architecture, botany, constitutional law, industrial development, philosophy, religious thought, mythology, astronomy, chemistry, landscape gardening, and literature.

Sir Francis Bacon, Viscount of St. Albans (detail) (late 16th to early 17th century) by Paul van Somer. Oil.
Private Collection.

But he is most famous for his vision of humanity's future, when knowledge would be based on verifiable experimentation, and science would be separate from theology.

Bacon's best-known literary works, the *Essays,* are intended to help people get ahead in life. Bacon was the first Englishman to use the word *essay* to designate a brief discourse in prose. He took the word from the French writer Montaigne (män·tän′). But, whereas Montaigne's delightful *essais* are mainly about a fascinating person, Montaigne himself, Bacon writes instead about humanity in general.

Bacon had embarked on a new career as a practicing scientist when death overtook him. One wintry day, he descended from his carriage carrying a dead chicken, to freeze it in the snow and thereby test the preservative powers of cold. Today this seems like a painfully obvious thing to do, but nobody had tried it in a systematic way before 1626. Suddenly, in the midst of the experiment, Bacon took a chill. His servants carried him into nearby Highgate, the house of the earl of Arundel. In poor health most of his life, Bacon died there of complications resulting from exposure.

In all his works, Bacon's aim was to make the world better. As the destroyer of old Aristotelian ways of thinking and as the stimulator of "modern" ones, Bacon has no equal.

Before You Read
OF STUDIES

Make the Connection
Why Read?

Two popular sayings present contrasting points of view about the relationship of books and learning to life. According to one axiom, "Knowledge is power." According to the other, more cynical saying, "It's not *what* you know but *whom* you know." Bacon himself coined the first saying, but he would probably have agreed with both views, since he was extremely learned and also very well connected to powerful people.

Elements of Literature
Parallel Structure

Bacon's sentences have been studied for centuries as models of **parallel structure**—the repetition of words, phrases, or sentences that have the same grammatical structure. Parallelism makes a passage rhythmic and memorable. Bacon also uses it to present contrasting ideas. Reading aloud and paying attention to punctuation and parallel structure will help you make sense of Bacon's long, complex sentences.

Reading Skills and Strategies

Identifying the Main Idea

Bacon's essay is only one paragraph in length, but it is packed with ideas. As you read, take notes. Jot down statements that seem important to you. Often you will find **key statements** at the beginning and end of essays like this one. Those key statements often contain the main idea of the essay.

A Still Life with Books (detail) (17th century) by Charles E. Bizet d'Annonay.

Musée de l'Ain, Bourg-en-Bresse, France.

Of Studies

Sir Francis Bacon

Studies serve for delight, for ornament, and for ability. Their chief use for delight is in privateness and retiring;[1] for ornament, is in discourse; and for ability, is in the judgment and disposition of business. For expert men can execute, and perhaps judge of particulars, one by one; but the general counsels, and the plots and marshalling of affairs, come best from those that are learned. To spend too much time in studies is sloth;[2] to use them too much for ornament is affectation;[3] to make judgment wholly by their rules is the humor[4] of a scholar. They perfect nature and are perfected by experience; for natural abilities are like natural plants that need pruning by study; and studies themselves do give forth directions too much at large, except they be bounded in by experience. Crafty men contemn[5] studies; simple men admire[6] them; and wise men use them: For they teach not their own use; but that is a wisdom without them[7] and above them, won by observation. Read not to contradict and confute;[8] nor to believe and take for granted; nor to find talk and discourse; but to weigh and consider. Some books are to be tasted, others to be swallowed, and some few to be chewed and digested: That is, some books are to be read only in parts; others to be read, but not curiously;[9] and some few to be read wholly, and with diligence and attention. Some books also may be read by deputy, and extracts made of them by others; but that would be only in the less important arguments, and the meaner sort of books; else distilled books are like common distilled waters,[10] flashy[11] things.

Reading maketh a full man; conference[12] a ready man; and writing an exact man. And therefore, if a man write little, he had need have a great memory; if he confer little, he had need have a present wit;[13] and if he read little, he had need have much cunning, to seem to know that[14] he doth not. Histories make men wise; poets witty;[15] the mathematics subtle; natural philosophy deep; moral grave; logic and rhetoric able to contend. *Abeunt studia in mores.*[16] Nay, there is no stond[17] or impediment in the wit but may be wrought[18] out by fit studies: like as diseases of the body may have appropriate exercises. Bowling is good for the stone and reins;[19] shooting for the lungs and breast; gentle walking for the stomach; riding for the head; and the like. So if a man's wit be wandering, let him study the mathematics; for in demonstrations, if his wit be called away never so little, he must begin again: If his wit be not apt to distinguish or find differences, let him study the Schoolmen;[20] for they are *cymini sectores.*[21] If he be not apt to beat over[22] matters, and to call one thing to prove and illustrate another, let him study the lawyers' cases; so every defect of the mind may have a special receipt.[23]

1. **privateness and retiring:** privacy and leisure.
2. **sloth:** laziness.
3. **affectation:** artificial behavior designed to impress others.
4. **humor:** whim.
5. **contemn:** despise.
6. **admire:** archaic for "marvel at."
7. **without them:** separate from them; outside them.
8. **confute:** dispute.
9. **curiously:** carefully.
10. **common distilled waters:** homemade concoctions.
11. **flashy:** superficial; vapid.
12. **conference:** conversation; discussion.
13. **present wit:** ability to think fast.
14. **that:** what.
15. **witty:** imaginative.
16. ***Abeunt . . . mores:*** Latin for "Studies help form character," from Ovid's (43 B.C.– c. A.D. 17) *Heroides.*
17. **stond:** stoppage.
18. **wrought:** worked.
19. **stone and reins:** archaic for "kidney stones and the kidneys."
20. **schoolmen:** medieval philosophers.
21. ***cymini sectores:*** Latin for "hairsplitters"; literally, "dividers of cumin seed."
22. **beat over:** thoroughly discuss.
23. **receipt:** remedy.

Axioms
from the Essays
Sir Francis Bacon

Men fear death as children fear to go in the dark; and as that natural fear in children is increased with tales, so is the other.

—"Of Death"

Revenge is a kind of wild justice, which the more man's nature runs to, the more ought law to weed it out.

—"Of Revenge"

The virtue of prosperity is temperance; the virtue of adversity is fortitude.

—"Of Adversity"

He that hath wife and children hath given hostages to fortune.

—"Of Marriage and Single Life"

There was never proud man thought so absurdly well of himself as the lover doth of the person loved: And therefore it was well said, *That it is impossible to love and to be wise.*

—"Of Love"

They that deny a God destroy man's nobility, for certainly man is of kin to the beasts by his body, and if he be not of kin to God by his spirit, he is a base and ignoble creature.

—"Of Atheism"

A principal fruit of friendship is the ease and discharge of the fullness and swellings of the heart.

—"Of Friendship"

A man's own observation, what he finds good of, and what he finds hurt of, is the best physic [medicine] to preserve health.

—"Of Regiment of Health"

As the baggage is to an army, so is riches to virtue.

—"Of Riches"

No man prospers so suddenly as by others' errors.

—"Of Fortune"

There is no excellent beauty that hath not some strangeness in the proportion.

—"Of Beauty"

God Almighty first planted a garden. And indeed it is the purest of human pleasures.

—"Of Gardens"

Men in great place are thrice servants: servants of the sovereign or state, servants of fame, and servants of business.

—"Of Great Place"

It were better to have no opinion of God at all than such an opinion as is unworthy of him.

—"Of Superstition"

If English-speaking people living before our time read anything, they read the English Bible. And if they read nothing themselves, they regularly heard the Bible read in Church. For nearly four centuries, most writers in English have been influenced, consciously or unconsciously, by the English Bible. They have quoted it, echoed it, paraphrased it, alluded to it, imitated it, and retold its fascinating stories over and over.

Everyday English speech is full of words and phrases from the English Bible: "loving kindness," "tender mercy," "long suffering." We "cast pearls before swine" and "wait until the eleventh hour" before acting. We speak of the "wisdom of Solomon" and the "patience of Job." Many Biblical words (such as *scapegoat*) are by now so embedded in our language that we use them without knowing we are using Biblical language.

But even when the King James Bible was first published, its language sounded old-fashioned. The translators had preserved much of the style of William Tyndale, a Bible translator who had been dead for more than seventy years—years in which the language had changed rapidly. In 1611, English people were beginning to address each other as "you," but the new Bible kept the archaic verb forms and the old second-person pronouns *thou, thy, thine,* and *thee.*

Over the years, the language of the King James Bible has become even more distant from ordinary English. For some readers, this remoteness makes it more moving and evokes more sublime feelings than does a Bible in the vernacular. The King James Bible stands with Shakespeare as an exemplar of English when the language was, as many people believe, more flexible and eloquent than at any other time, and more capable of stirring people's hearts and minds.

Title page of the Holy Bible (detail) (1611). Printed by Robert Barker, London.

The Pierpont Morgan Library, New York. PML 5460.

Title page of the Holy Bible (detail) (1611). Printed by Robert Barker, London.

The Pierpont Morgan Library, New York. PML 5460.

Before You Read

FROM GENESIS

Make the Connection

How and Why

The first book of the Bible is called Genesis, which means "coming into being." Genesis opens with two accounts of creation: Chapter I emphasizes the cosmos or universe; Chapter 2 looks at the earth and humanity. Although Moses is traditionally thought of as the author of Genesis, many Biblical scholars now say that two different writers recorded these two creation accounts, which may well be regarded as complementary. Both narratives are very spare and simple but elevated in style.

Besides telling us how the physical universe we know came into being, the first chapters of Genesis deal with how and why human beings were created, and especially, in Chapter 3, why individual members of the human race must suffer and die, and why the history of the whole race has been so bloody and troubled.

Elements of Literature

Imagery

The ancient writers of the Bible were addressing an unsophisticated people. To appeal to their audience, they used a pictorial style rich in **imagery** to tell the story of the primordial origins of the whole human race. Through the centuries, many artists have interpreted scenes from Genesis.

Reading Skills and Strategies

Responding to the Text

As you read this selection from Genesis, and other Biblical selections here, keep a piece of paper handy. Record questions, responses, even memories evoked by these old texts. You might be reading these texts for the first time, or you might have read them or heard them many times in your childhood. Whatever your past experiences with the Bible, you'll find some of these passages striking strong emotional and intellectual responses.

Creation of Adam (detail) (1508–1512) by Michelangelo. Fresco.
Sistine Chapel, Vatican Palace, Rome.

brought her unto the man. And Adam said, "This is now bone of my bones, and flesh of my flesh: She shall be called Woman, because she was taken out of Man." Therefore shall a man leave his father and his mother, and shall cleave[16] unto his wife: And they shall be one flesh. And they were both naked, the man and his wife, and were not ashamed.

Now the serpent[17] was more subtil[18] than any beast of the field which the LORD God had made. And he said unto the woman, "Yea, hath God said, 'Ye shall not eat of every tree of the garden'?" And the woman said unto the serpent, "We may eat of the fruit of the trees of the garden: But of the fruit of the tree which is in the midst of the garden, God hath said, 'Ye shall not eat of it, neither shall ye touch it, lest ye die.'" And the serpent said unto the woman, "Ye shall not surely die: For God doth know that in the day ye eat thereof, then your eyes shall be opened, and ye shall be as gods, knowing good and evil." And when the woman saw that the tree was good for food, and that it was pleasant to the eyes, and a tree to be desired to make one wise, she took of the fruit thereof, and did eat, and gave also unto her husband with her; and he did eat. And the eyes of them both were opened, and they knew that they were naked; and they sewed fig leaves together, and made themselves aprons. And they heard the voice of the LORD God walking in the garden in the cool of the day: And Adam and his wife hid themselves from the presence of the LORD God amongst the trees of the garden. And the LORD God called unto Adam, and said unto him, "Where art thou?" And he said, "I heard thy voice in the garden, and I was afraid, because I was naked; and I hid myself." And he said, "Who told thee that thou wast naked? Hast thou eaten of the tree, whereof I commanded thee that thou shouldest not eat?" And the man said, "The woman whom thou gavest to be with me, she gave me of the tree, and I did eat." And the LORD God said unto the woman, "What is this that thou hast done?"

And the woman said, "The serpent beguiled me, and I did eat." And the LORD God said unto the serpent, "Because thou hast done this, thou art cursed above all cattle,[19] and above every beast of the field; upon thy belly shalt thou go, and dust shalt thou eat all of the days of thy life: And I will put enmity[20] between thee and the woman, and between thy seed and her seed; it shall bruise thy head, and thou shalt bruise his heel." Unto the woman he said, "I will greatly multiply thy sorrow and thy conception;[21] in sorrow thou shalt bring forth children; and thy desire shall be to thy husband, and he shall rule over thee." And unto Adam he said, "Because thou hast hearkened unto[22] the voice of thy wife, and hast eaten of the tree, of which I commanded thee, saying, 'Thou shalt not eat of it': Cursed is the ground for thy sake; in sorrow shalt thou eat of it all the days of thy life; thorns also and thistles shall it bring forth to thee; and thou shalt eat the herb of the field; in the sweat of thy face shalt thou eat bread, till thou return unto the ground; for out of it wast thou taken: For dust thou art, and unto dust shalt thou return." And Adam called his wife's name Eve; because she was the mother of all living. Unto Adam also and to his wife did the LORD God make coats of skins, and clothed them.

And the LORD God said, "Behold, the man[23] is become as one of us, to know good and evil: and now, lest he put forth his hand, and take also of the tree of life,[24] and eat, and live forever": Therefore the LORD God sent him forth from the garden of Eden, to till the ground from whence he was taken. So he drove out the man; and he placed at the east of the garden of Eden cherubims,[25] and a flaming sword which turned every way, to keep the way of[26] the tree of life.

—Genesis 1–3

16. **cleave:** be faithful.
17. **serpent:** traditionally understood to be the form assumed by Satan to tempt Eve. Satan is also identified with the angel Lucifer, who revolted against God and was expelled from Heaven.
18. **subtil:** subtle.

19. **cattle:** animals.
20. **enmity:** hostility.
21. **conception:** pains in childbearing.
22. **hearkened unto:** listened and obeyed.
23. **man:** both man and woman.
24. **tree of life:** the first indication that the tree granting everlasting life is prohibited to humanity.
25. **cherubims:** large, fierce angels, quite unlike the modern idea of a cherub.
26. **keep the way of:** prevent access to.

A Beam of Protons Illuminates Gutenberg's Genius

MALCOLM W. BROWNE

The birth of modern printing four centuries ago is cloaked in obscurity, but with the help of the cyclotron used to develop the atomic bomb, scientists are wresting long-forgotten secrets from Gutenberg Bibles and other antique documents to reconstruct the technology of the Renaissance.

In cooperation with scholars at New York City's Pierpont Morgan Library and elsewhere, a group of researchers at the Davis campus of the University of California has learned that Johann Gutenberg of Mainz, Germany, was an even greater inventor and innovator than historians had known. At Davis, physicists and historians have pioneered a technique capable of probing the atoms making up paper, parchment, and ink, thereby opening a new dimension of history to exploration.

The German invention of movable type around 1450 is one of the farthest-reaching technological achievements in history. Movable type, which could be assembled rapidly and put on a printing press, permitted the mass production of books and documents. Literacy, traditionally reserved to churchmen, scholars, scribes, and aristocrats, spread swiftly to the masses and forever changed the nature of society.

Paradoxically, however, the earliest printers left no written descriptions of their monumental achievement. According to Paul Needham, curator of printed books and bindings at the Morgan Library (which owns three Gutenberg Bibles), no one knows what Gutenberg's printing press looked like.

But Dr. Needham and the cyclotron team at Davis have learned a great deal about how Gutenberg and his associates worked and what materials they used.

Directing the cyclotron analyses of old documents is Thomas A. Cahill, head of the Crocker Nuclear Laboratory at Davis. "One of the most remarkable things we discovered in our five-year study," Dr. Cahill said in an interview, "was that Gutenberg's genius extended to the formulation of inks as well as the development of movable type. Other printers of the late 15th century and printers even today tend to use inks based on oils and carbon black. But for Gutenberg, nothing but the best would do. We found within a few seconds of our first analysis of his ink that it is unusually rich in compounds of lead and copper. Lead and copper were Gutenberg's signature, and their presence in the ink on a document is as convincing a sign of his agency as his own hand would be."

Dr. Cahill believes the high levels of copper and lead in Gutenberg's inks account for the fact that the printing in his books remains as fresh, glossy, and black as it was when it came off his press. Bibliographers regard the Gutenberg Bible, printed between 1454 and 1456, as one of the most perfectly printed books ever, rarely matched in quality even in modern times.

Gutenberg's most famous work is his "forty-two-line Bible," so called because nearly every column of type in its 1,286 pages is forty-two lines long. Some of the forty-two-line Bibles were printed on paper and others on vellum, but experts regard the workmanship in all of them as superb. The left and right margins of each of the two columns on each page are perfectly squared off, and Gutenberg avoided hyphenation by inconspicuously squeezing his type together or spreading it out.

Dr. Cahill and Richard N. Schwab, a history professor at Davis, began applying the cyclotron to historical problems in the early 1980s as an outgrowth of the Crocker Laboratory's work on air pollution. The cyclotron accelerates a narrow beam of protons that pierces a sample, and protons collide with some of the atoms in the sample along the way. When this happens, the atoms emit X-rays, whose varying energies match the specific types of atoms from [which] they were emitted. A detector measures these energies, and with this data a computer can determine the types and quantities of the elements present in the substance being studied.

The analysis of Gutenberg documents required still subtler techniques, Dr. Cahill said. Although the signatures of Gutenberg inks depend on their copper and lead content, the quantities of these and other metals varied appreciably from one batch of ink to another. Gutenberg's workers evidently compounded their inks according to a general recipe but may have been sloppy in their measuring. Similarly, the cyclotron can detect differences among the atomic signatures of various batches of paper (often bearing different watermarks) that Gutenberg used. A single Bible often contains pages from several different batches of paper that were printed at separate times.

By calculating how various inks and papers were combined in each volume, Dr. Cahill and his associates were able to reconstruct Gutenberg's manufacturing process step by step. "There were times when we could almost hear Gutenberg's press creaking," Dr. Cahill said.

This led to the realization that Gutenberg's workshop was much more sophisticated than many scholars had supposed, he said. The shop evidently employed a team of typesetters, all working simultaneously on separate batches of pages, carefully calculating space and text to make certain the assembled volume would come out exactly right.

These separately composed sections fit together almost seamlessly, but there are a few exceptions. One of the rare visible flaws occurs in the middle of Psalm 79, according to Dr. Needham of the Morgan Library.

"The compositor setting the type up to that point was probably sitting next to the compositor who was setting subsequent pages," he said. "One can see that the planning was not quite perfect, because the first compositor found himself in trouble on his last page, stuck with too much space and too little text. He eliminated abbreviations and stretched out his lines, but even so he came up short, and that page has only forty-one lines."

—*from The New York Times,* May 12, 1987

Page from Johann Gutenberg's 42-line Latin Bible (1453–1456) printed at Mainz.

The Granger Collection, New York.

MAKING MEANINGS

First Thoughts

1. How do you feel about the world that was lost when Adam and Eve sinned?

Shaping Interpretations

2. What characteristics or qualities of God does the Genesis narrative emphasize? (In your answer, consider the phrases "and it was so" and "it was good.")

3. How does this narrative explain the Sabbath—the day of rest?

4. How does this narrative view God's human creations? According to Genesis, what is our purpose on earth?

5. The name Adam relates to the Hebrew *adamah,* meaning "of the soil." How does Adam's creation from dust **foreshadow** his ultimate fate?

6. What aspects of the human condition does the story of Adam and Eve account for?

7. Scholars have speculated about the meaning of the tree of knowledge of good and evil. Read the text carefully, and decide what you think this tree **symbolizes** and exactly what happened as a result of Adam and Eve's eating of its fruit.

8. How does the writer of Genesis picture Paradise? In *your* imagination, what would a paradise be like?

9. What responses and questions did you note as you read Genesis? If you wish, share your notes in class.

Extending the Text

10. According to Genesis, what traits are characteristic of the human creation? Do you think these traits are still manifested in human life today? Are they totally negative traits, positive traits, or a mixture?

Psalms: Worship Through Poetry

The Bible is full of poetry. Every book of it contains poems or fragments of poems inserted into the prose text, and much of the prose itself is highly rhythmical. One book, the Psalms, consists entirely of poems, some of which were set to music and sung during worship services in the ancient temple in Jerusalem. The book of Psalms preserves 150 of these songs, a fraction of the total number that the ancient Hebrews knew and sang. Psalms were used as hymnals and included songs appropriate for many types of worship: thanksgiving, lament, praise, and devotion. Modern scholars now agree that the psalms were written by many authors over many centuries, but seventy-three of the psalms are said to be "for David" or "concerning David," the heroic Hebrew king.

In English, a collection of psalms is called a psalter (the *p* is silent as in the word *psalm* itself). (In Hebrew, the name for the collection is *Tehillim*, or "songs of praise.") There have been dozens of English psalters besides the one in the King James Bible, but none of them has lasted so well and so long. King James's translators did not try to impose rhyme on their versions because there is no rhyme in the originals. Instead, they imitated such Hebrew poetic devices as **repetition** and **parallel structure** (the use of sentences or phrases similar in structure):

> Let the floods clap their hands,
> Let the hills be joyful together.
> —Psalm 98:8

The psalmists were fond of saying essentially the same thing twice, in different words ("thy rod and thy staff" in Psalm 23). The King James Bible uses the numbering of the ancient Hebrew manuscripts; some other Bibles use a different numbering derived from a Greek translation of the Hebrew, and these Bibles have an extra psalm, number 151.

Biblical poetry, then, is much like modern free verse in that it does not have rhyme and meter but it does have other patterns of repetition, balance, antithesis, and parallelism. Metaphors and similes abound, and so do images drawn from nature and everyday experience:

> My God, in him will I trust.
> Surely he shall deliver thee from the snare of the fowler,
> And from the noisome pestilence.
> He shall cover thee with his feathers,
> And under his wings shalt thou trust:
> His truth shall be thy shield and buckler.
> Thou shalt not be afraid for the terror by night;
> Nor for the arrow that flieth by day;
> Nor for the pestilence that walketh in darkness;
> Nor for the destruction that wasteth at noonday.
> —Psalm 91:2–6

(Above left) Illuminated "P" (detail) (c. 1500) from a Flemish Bible.

Victoria and Albert Museum, London.

Before You Read
PSALM 23

Make the Connection

The Lord Is . . .

This song of trust, affirming the speaker's faith and confidence in God, is probably the best-known religious poem in the Western world. The opening verses, comparing God to a shepherd, use the kind of pastoral imagery found throughout the Bible. Then the metaphors in the psalm change, and the Lord becomes a host providing a banquet for the speaker, whose enemies watch him enviously as he eats, not daring to harm him. Among the rich and varied images of the poem, there is also a suggestion of the speaker as a pilgrim traveling through a dangerous world.

Quickwrite

This song was sung by a pastoral people, so the comparison of the Lord to a shepherd is appropriate. The world is very different for most people today. What metaphors would you use to describe the comforting presence of God?

Psalm 23

The LORD is my shepherd; I shall not want.
He maketh me to lie down in green pastures:
He leadeth me beside the still waters.
He restoreth my soul:
5 He leadeth me in the paths of righteousness for his name's sake.°
Yea, though I walk through the valley of the shadow of death,
I will fear no evil: For thou art with me;
Thy rod and thy staff they comfort me.
Thou preparest a table before me in the presence of mine enemies:
10 Thou anointest my head with oil; my cup runneth over.
Surely goodness and mercy shall follow me all the days of my life:
And I will dwell in the house of the LORD forever.

5. his name's sake: That is, he will live up to his name as shepherd.

Shepherds. Bas-relief on the lintel over the west portal of Chartres Cathedral.

Cathedral, Chartres, France.

Make the Connection

Captivities

This is a song of entreaty on the occasion of a national catastrophe: Many Israelites are being held captive in Babylon. This lament over a remembered home has been recited by many captives in the thousands of years since it was first sung in ancient Babylon.

Quickwrite

What other experiences in the history of the world might have inspired people to beg for release from captivity or even to seek vengeance on their captors? Take notes on your thoughts.

Background

In the sixth century B.C., Nebuchadnezzar, king of Babylonia, conquered Jerusalem and deported most of the Israelites to Babylon, a great ancient city, which is now a ruin, on the Euphrates River south of Baghdad. The speaker of Psalm 137 is a captive Israelite, bitterly lamenting his people's exile. The Babylonians have asked their captives to sing to entertain them, but what do the captives have to sing about?

Psalm 137

By the rivers of Babylon, there we sat down, yea, we wept,
When we remembered Zion.°
We hanged our harps
Upon the willows in the midst thereof.
5 For there they that carried us away captive required of us a song;
And they that wasted us required of us mirth,
Saying, "Sing us one of the songs of Zion."
How shall we sing the LORD's song
In a strange land?
10 If I forget thee, O Jerusalem,
Let my right hand forget her cunning.
If I do not remember thee,
Let my tongue cleave° to the roof of my mouth;
If I prefer not Jerusalem above my chief joy.
15 Remember, O LORD, the children of Edom° in the day of Jerusalem;
Who said, "Raze it,° raze it, even to the foundation thereof."
O daughter of Babylon,° who art to be destroyed;
Happy shall he be, that rewardeth thee
As thou hast served us.
20 Happy shall he be, that taketh
And dasheth thy little ones against the stones.

2. Zion: a hill in Jerusalem that is often a symbol for the whole of Israel.

13. cleave: adhere; stick.
15. children of Edom: The Edomites, neighbors of the Israelites, rejoiced when the Israelites' kingdom was conquered and most of its population deported.
16. Raze it: Level it to the ground.
17. daughter of Babylon: the Babylonian people.

Jeremiah Lamenting over Jerusalem.

MAKING MEANINGS

Psalms 23 and 137

First Thoughts

1. How do you think Psalm 23 could be used to provide solace to the singer of Psalm 137?

Shaping Interpretations

2. In Psalm 23, how does the singer extend the **metaphor** comparing God to a shepherd?

3. The second metaphor in Psalm 23 compares God to a generous host. (In the ancient Middle East, it was a sign of hospitality to anoint a guest's head and dusty feet with oil.) How does the speaker extend this metaphor of God as a gracious host and the singer as his guest?

4. The speaker in Psalm 137 is both homesick and vengeful. Which lines convey these emotions most vividly to you? How did you react to the final line?

Connecting with the Text

5. Psalm 23 is often read at funerals or memorial services. Why do you think people find it consoling? (Refer to your Quickwrite notes for page 422.)

6. Both psalms are full of vivid **imagery.** What pictures does each song put in your mind?

Extending the Text

7. On what occasion might Psalm 137 be sung? What relevance does this lament have for people today? (You might want to refer to your Quickwrite notes for page 423.)

Before You Read

THE PARABLE OF THE GOOD SAMARITAN

Make the Connection

Profound Truths

A **parable** is a very short anecdote that teaches a moral or religious lesson. In the Christian Bible, instead of speaking abstractly and philosophically, Jesus often teaches his followers by means of parables. On the surface, parables seem to be simple stories. Looked at closely, they concern the profound truths and moral laws on which human happiness depends. Perhaps you know some parables from other traditions.

Quickwrite

To test your Biblical knowledge, write down quickly what you think a Good Samaritan is.

Background

To understand this parable, you have to know that it is set in a totally Jewish context. According to Jewish law, the priest and the Levite (a member of the priestly tribe) would be considered legally unclean if they touched a dead person. Samaritans were people from Samaria who had a mixed ancestry and a mixed religion. They used the Torah of the Hebrew Bible as their scriptures, but the Israelites to the south frowned on the Samaritans' mixed religious practices. The lawyer is questioning Jesus.

The Parable of the Good Samaritan

And, behold, a certain lawyer stood up, and tempted him, saying, "Master, what shall I do to inherit eternal life?" He said unto him, "What is written in the law? how readest thou?" And he answering said, "Thou shalt love the Lord thy God with all thy heart, and with all thy soul, and with all thy strength, and with all thy mind; and thy neighbor as thyself." And he said unto him, "Thou hast answered right: This do, and thou shalt live." But he, willing to justify himself, said unto Jesus, "And who is my neighbor?" And Jesus answering said, "A certain man went down from Jerusalem to Jericho, and fell among thieves, which stripped him of his raiment,[1] and wounded him, and departed, leaving him half dead. And by chance there came down a certain priest that way: And when he saw him, he passed by on the other side. And likewise a Levite, when he was at the place, came and looked on him, and passed by on the other side. But a certain Samaritan, as he journeyed, came where he was: And when he saw him, he had compassion on him, and went to him, and bound up his wounds, pouring in oil and wine,[2] and set him on his own beast, and brought him to an inn, and took care of him. And on the morrow when he departed, he took out two pence, and gave them to the host, and said unto him, 'Take care of him; and whatsoever thou spendest more, when I come again, I will repay thee.' Which now of these three, thinkest thou, was neighbor unto him that fell among the thieves?" And he said, "He that showed mercy on him." Then said Jesus unto him, "Go, and do thou likewise."

—Luke 10:25–37

1. **raiment:** clothing.
2. **oil and wine:** ancient medicine.

The Good Samaritan
(1633) by Rembrandt
van Rijn.

MAKING MEANINGS

First Thoughts

1. According to the **parable,** how are you
   supposed to answer the question "Who is my
   neighbor?" In actuality, how would you answer
   the question?

Shaping Interpretations

2. Jesus asks the lawyer at the beginning what
   the law says about eternal life. What does the
   law say?

3. Why does the lawyer press on and ask another
   question: Who is my neighbor?

4. According to the parable, what happened to the
   man who journeyed from Jerusalem to Jericho?

5. Why is it **ironic** that the priest and the Levite
   ignore the wounded man, but the Samaritan
   helps him?

Extending the Text

6. What Good Samaritans do you know of
   in the world today? How does your
   response compare with the notes you took
   for the Quickwrite on page 425?

Challenging the Text

7. If you were writing an updated version of this
   parable, which details would you change to
   make it relevant to life in our society today?

8. Do you think this parable makes a point that is
   still important today? Talk about its relevance at
   the end of the twentieth century.

CHOICES: Building Your Portfolio

Writer's Notebook

1. Collecting Ideas for a Cause-Effect Essay

The effects of disobedience are the focus of the opening chapters of Genesis. This tendency to disobedience is one of many characteristics fundamental to human nature. Jot down some notes about another human trait, such as loyalty or ambition. You could ask yourself why: Why are some people loyal or ambitious? Or you could ask yourself what if: What if all competition were removed from society so that ambition was stifled? Save your notes to use in the Writer's Workshop on page 459.

Creative Writing

2. A Parable for Today

Try writing your own parable to illustrate a practical lesson about life today. First, identify the moral or spiritual truth you want to illustrate. Then, think of an everyday event that happened to you or someone you know that could illustrate this lesson. The parables in the Christian Bible find lessons in a poor woman who loses a coin, a dishonest employee who cheats his boss, bridesmaids who are asleep when the wedding party arrives, and a father who welcomes back a son who has been so wasteful he becomes the Biblical equivalent of a homeless person.

Comparing Translations

3. Same Psalm, Different Words

The version of Psalm 23 below appeared in a psalter translated by the Massachusetts Puritans and published in the *Bay Psalm Book* (1640). Write an essay comparing it to the version in the King James Bible. Tell which version you prefer and why.

Oral Interpretation

4. Making a Psalm Sing

Prepare a group of the psalms for oral recitation. As you prepare for your presentation, pay particular attention to the way the psalms use **repetition** and **parallel structure** to create rhythm. How many speakers will you assign to each psalm? The psalms were originally sung to the accompaniment of a harp. Will you provide any background music to dramatize your interpretations?

Research / Speaking

5. The Inventive Renaissance

In the *Connections* article "A Beam of Protons Illuminates Gutenberg's Genius" (page 419), you read about Gutenberg's innovations. What other remarkable inventions or technological innovations date from the Renaissance? Who are the people behind these creations? Select one person or invention to write about, and present your findings in a brief oral report.

Psalm 23

The Lord to me a shepherd is; want therefore shall not I.
He in the folds of tender grass doth cause me down to lie.
To waters calm me gently leads, restore my soul doth he;
He doth in paths of righteousness for his name's sake lead me.
5 Yea, though in valley of death's shade I walk, none ill I'll fear,
Because thou art with me; thy rod and staff my comfort are.
For me a table thou hast spread in presence of my foes;
Thou dost anoint my head with oil; my cup it overflows.
Goodness and mercy surely shall all my days follow me.
10 And in the Lord's house I shall dwell so long as days shall be.

Worlds of Wisdom

Before You Read

Background

From age to age, from culture to culture, human beings have wrestled with the same problems and questions: How should we live? How can we be happy? What is justice?

Although the pieces of world wisdom that follow come from a wide variety of sources in Africa and Asia, they have two features in common. First, the forms represented here—prophecy, fable, parable, anecdote, and proverb—all spring from the oral tradition. Second, just as with the wisdom literature in the Hebrew Bible, many of these pieces have religious contexts.

The **Koran,** the holy book of Islam, contains God's revelation to Mohammed by the angel Gabriel. The text was first written down in Arabic in the middle of the seventh century.

The text of **The Panchatantra,** the most famous Sanskrit collection of fables from ancient India, probably dates from 100 B.C. to around A.D. 400. According to tradition, this anthology was created as a practical manual in statecraft for young princes.

The parables illustrating the insights of **Zen Buddhism** are drawn from a philosophical and religious tradition within Buddhism that originated in China and then flowered in Japan starting in the twelfth century.

The poet **Saadi,** whose real name was Musharrif Od-Din Muslih Od-Din, lived in thirteenth-century Persia (now Iran). As a follower of Sufism, a mystical sect of Islam, he believed in the holiness of all creation. His witty, practical sayings and lush lyrics made him one of Persia's best-loved poets.

Taoism (dou'iz'əm), another Eastern tradition of religion and philosophy, developed in China shortly after the time that Buddhism first began in India, during the last centuries B.C.

Confucius, the founder of yet another Chinese philosophical system, left no written works. After his death in around 479 B.C., his disciples gathered his sayings in a collection known as the *Analects.*

For many centuries, the **Jabo** people of Liberia in West Africa have relied on proverbs in many key aspects of their social life and legal proceedings.

Reading Skills and Strategies

Connecting with the Texts

As you read the pieces that follow, jot down notes on the ones that connect with something in your own background or in today's world. (You might also copy down quotes that you especially like.)

(Map) The world, from Mercator's *Atlas* (c. 1595).

Night

from the Koran

translated by **N. J. Dawood**

In the Name of Allah, the Compassionate, the Merciful

By the night, when she lets fall her darkness, and by the radiant day! By Him that created the male and the female, your endeavors have different ends!

For him that gives in charity and guards himself against evil and believes in goodness, We shall smooth the path of salvation; but for him that neither gives nor takes and disbelieves in goodness, We shall smooth the path of affliction. When he breathes his last, his riches will not avail him.

It is for Us to give guidance. Ours is the life of this world, Ours the life to come. I warn you, then, of the blazing fire, in which none shall burn save the hardened sinner, who denies the truth and gives no heed. But the good man who purifies himself by almsgiving[1] shall keep away from it: and so shall he that does good works for the sake of the Most High only, not in recompense[2] for a favor. Such men shall be content.

1. **almsgiving:** performing deeds of charity.
2. **recompense:** repayment.

Leaf from a Koran (11th century) in Kufic calligraphy. Iranian. Ink, colors, gold on paper.

The Metropolitan Museum of Art, Rogers Fund, 1940 (40.164.2a). Photograph ©1989 The Metropolitan Museum of Art.

Shell-Neck, Slim, and Grim
from The Panchatantra

translated by Arthur W. Ryder

A Pair of Wild Fowls (detail) (1600–1625) attributed to Manṣūr, Imperial Mughal.

Collection Navin Kumar, New York.

In a certain lake lived a turtle named Shell-Neck. He had as friends two ganders whose names were Slim and Grim. Now in the vicissitudes[1] of time there came a twelve-year drought, which begot ideas of this nature in the two ganders: "This lake has gone dry. Let us seek another body of water. However, we must first say farewell to Shell-Neck, our dear and long-proved friend."

When they did so, the turtle said: "Why do you bid me farewell? I am a water dweller, and here I should perish very quickly from the scant supply of water and from grief at loss of you. Therefore, if you feel any affection for me, please rescue me from the jaws of this death. Besides, as the water dries in this lake, you two suffer nothing beyond a restricted diet, while to me it means immediate death. Consider which is more serious, loss of food or loss of life."

But they replied: "We are unable to take you with us since you are a water creature without wings." Yet the turtle continued: "There is a possible device. Bring a stick of wood." This they did, whereupon the turtle gripped the middle of the stick between his teeth, and said: "Now take firm hold with your bills, one on each side, fly up, and travel with even flight through the sky, until we discover another desirable body of water."

But they objected: "There is a hitch in this fine plan. If you happen to indulge in the smallest conversation, then you will lose your hold on the stick, will fall from a great height, and will be dashed to bits."

"Oh," said the turtle, "from this moment I take a vow of silence, to last as long as we are in heaven." So they carried out the plan, but while the two ganders were painfully carrying the turtle over a neighboring city, the people below noticed the spectacle, and there arose a confused buzz of talk as they asked: "What is this cartlike object that two birds are carrying through the atmosphere?"

Hearing this, the doomed turtle was heedless enough to ask: "What are these people chattering about?" The moment he spoke, the poor simpleton lost his grip and fell to the ground. And persons who wanted meat cut him to bits in a moment with sharp knives.

"And that is why I say:
  To take advice from kindly friends
    Be ever satisfied:
The stupid turtle lost his grip
    Upon the stick, and died."

---

1. **vicissitudes:** unpredictable changes.

Zen Parables

compiled by **Paul Reps**

The Moon Cannot Be Stolen

Ryokan, a Zen master, lived the simplest kind of life in a little hut at the foot of a mountain. One evening a thief visited the hut only to discover there was nothing in it to steal.

Ryokan returned and caught him. "You may have come a long way to visit me," he told the prowler, "and you should not return empty-handed. Please take my clothes as a gift."

The thief was bewildered. He took the clothes and slunk away.

Ryokan sat naked, watching the moon. "Poor fellow," he mused, "I wish I could give him this beautiful moon."

Temper

A Zen student came to Bankei and complained: "Master, I have an ungovernable temper. How can I cure it?"

"You have something very strange," replied Bankei. "Let me see what you have."

"Just now I cannot show it to you," replied the other.

"When can you show it to me?" asked Bankei.

"It arises unexpectedly," replied the student.

"Then," concluded Bankei, "it must not be your own true nature. If it were, you could show it to me at any time. When you were born, you did not have it, and your parents did not give it to you. Think that over."

The Gates of Paradise

A soldier named Nobushige came to Hakuin, and asked: "Is there really a paradise and a hell?"

"Who are you?" inquired Hakuin.

"I am a samurai," the warrior replied.

"You, a soldier!" exclaimed Hakuin. "What kind of ruler would have you as his guard? Your face looks like that of a beggar."

Nobushige became so angry that he began to draw his sword, but Hakuin continued: "So you have a sword! Your weapon is probably much too dull to cut off my head."

As Nobushige drew his sword, Hakuin remarked: "Here open the gates of hell!"

At these words the samurai, perceiving the master's discipline, sheathed his sword and bowed.

"Here open the gates of paradise," said Hakuin.

Square dish (Edo period, early 18th century) by Ogata Kenzan and Ogata Korin. Stoneware with underglaze and enamel decoration.

The First Principle

When one goes to Obaku temple in Kyoto, he sees carved over the gate the words "The First Principle." The letters are unusually large, and those who appreciate calligraphy[1] always admire them as being a masterpiece. They were drawn by Kosen two hundred years ago.

When the master drew them he did so on paper, from which workmen made the larger carving in wood. As Kosen sketched the letters, a bold pupil was with him who had made several gallons of ink for the calligraphy and who never failed to criticize his master's work.

"That is not good," he told Kosen after the first effort.

"How is that one?"

"Poor. Worse than before," pronounced the pupil.

Kosen patiently wrote one sheet after another until eighty-four First Principles had accumulated, still without the approval of the pupil.

Then, when the young man stepped outside for a few moments, Kosen thought: "Now is my chance to escape his keen eye," and he wrote hurriedly, with a mind free from distraction: "The First Principle."

"A masterpiece," pronounced the pupil.

---

1. calligraphy: the art of beautiful handwriting.

Sayings of Saadi

translated by **Idries Shah**

Portrait of a dervish (early 17th century), Turkish. Colors on paper (8⅝″ × 4³/₁₆″).

The Metropolitan Museum of Art, New York. The Cora Timken Burnett Collection of Persian Miniatures and Other Persian Art Objects. Bequest of Cora Timken Burnett, 1956 (57.51.30). Photograph ©1978 The Metropolitan Museum of Art.

The Unfed Dervish

When I see the poor dervish[1] unfed
My own food is pain and poison to me.

Information and Knowledge

However much you study, you cannot know
    without action.
  A donkey laden with books is neither an
    intellectual nor a wise man.
  Empty of essence, what learning has he—
  Whether upon him is firewood or book?

The Elephant Keeper

Make no friendship with an elephant keeper
If you have no room to entertain an elephant.

Safety and Riches

Deep in the sea are riches beyond compare.
But if you seek safety, it is on the shore.

The Fox and the Camels

A fox was seen running away in terror. Someone asked what was troubling it. The fox answered: "They are taking camels for forced labor." "Fool!" he was told, "the fate of camels has nothing to do with you, who do not even look like one." "Silence!" said the fox, "for if an intriguer were to state that I was a camel, *who* would work for my release?"

1. dervish: Muslim monk dedicated to a life of poverty.

Taoist Anecdotes

translated and edited by **Moss Roberts**

Gold, Gold

Many, many years ago there was a man of the land of Ch'i who had a great passion for gold. One day at the crack of dawn he went to the market—straight to the gold dealers' stalls, where he snatched some gold and ran. The market guards soon caught him. "With so many people around, how did you expect to get away with it?" a guard asked.

"When I took it," he replied, "I saw only the gold, not the people."

—Lieh Tzu

Laozi (detail) from *Homage to the First Principle*, a Yüan dynasty wall painting.

Courtesy of the Royal Ontario Museum, Toronto.

A Clever Judge

In the days when Ch'en Shu-ku was a magistrate in Chienchou, there was a man who had lost an article of some value. A number of people were arrested, but no one could discover exactly who the thief was. So Shu-ku laid a trap for the suspects. "I know of a temple," he told them, "whose bell can tell a thief from an honest man. It has great spiritual powers."

The magistrate had the bell fetched and reverently enshrined in a rear chamber. Then he had the suspects brought before the bell to stand and testify to their guilt or innocence. He explained to them that if an innocent man touched the bell it would remain silent, but that if the man was guilty it would ring out.

Then the magistrate led his staff in solemn worship to the bell. The sacrifices concluded, he had the bell placed behind a curtain, while one of his assistants secretly smeared it with ink. After a time he took the suspects to the bell and had each one in turn extend his hands through the curtain and touch the bell. As each man withdrew his hands, Shu-ku examined them. Everyone's hands were stained except for those of one man, who confessed to the theft under questioning. He had not dared touch the bell for fear it would ring.

—Chang Shih-nan

from The Analects of Confucius

translated and annotated by **Arthur Waley**

The Master said, "Yu, shall I teach you what knowledge is? When you know a thing, to recognize that you know it, and when you do not know a thing, to recognize that you do not know it. That is knowledge."

The Master said, "Even when walking in a party of no more than three I can always be certain of learning from those I am with. There will be good qualities that I can select for imitation and bad ones that will teach me what requires correction in myself."

Tzu-kung asked, saying, "Is there any single saying that one can act upon all day and every day?" The Master said, "Perhaps the saying about consideration: 'Never do to others what you would not like them to do to you.'"

Portrait of Confucius based on ancient traditions. Relief from the stele in the Pei Lin de Siganfou.

Jabo Proverbs

translated by **George Herzog**

As the sky extends over all, so do words that have been spoken.

One doesn't throw the stick after the snake has gone.

Daring talk is not strength.

It is not the person who looks at you with sparkling eyes when you speak who understands your words; but the one who bends his head down, he is the one who really understands.

FINDING COMMON GROUND

You probably recognized some ways you could apply these insights to life today. Looking over your reading notes and thinking back over the selections, jot down some responses to the following questions, or talk about them with a small group.

- How could these insights be applied to life today? Are any of them hopelessly outdated? Why?

- Wisdom literature often uses **metaphor** and conveys its moral or message indirectly. Did you understand what all these bits of wisdom mean? Talk about the advice that you found difficult or obscure.

- These selections cover a wide range of topics, including good works, greed, foolishness, self-discipline, anger, guilt, prudence, true knowledge, friendship, and practical foresight. Did you disagree with any of this worldly wisdom? Why?

Grebo face mask from the Ivory Coast.
Wood, paint (27½″ high).

The Metropolitan Museum of Art, New York.
The Nelson A. Rockefeller Collection.

John Milton

(1608–1674)

Early in his life, John Milton resolved to be a great poet. His teachers and his parents encouraged him in this ambition because they believed, as Milton said later in his life, that he "might perhaps leave something so written to aftertimes as they should not willingly let it die." Time has confirmed his parents' and his teachers' confidence in him: Milton's *Paradise Lost,* his major epic, is one of the most brilliant achievements in English poetry and perhaps the richest and most intricately beautiful poem in the world. Posterity has not let *Paradise Lost* die.

Milton was fortunate in his parents. His father, a musician and prosperous businessman, had Milton educated at St. Paul's School (which he loved) and Cambridge University (which he hated). Indulged in every way by his parents, Milton spent the next eight years after college (1632–1640) continuing his education by himself, since he firmly believed that a poet must be a person of learning, familiar with ancient and contemporary philosophy, history, languages, and literatures. He made a leisurely tour of Italy, whose language and culture he had long admired, and there he visited many interesting people, including the astronomer Galileo. Throughout this period, he wrote poems in English, Latin, Greek, and Italian. Some of these he collected and published in 1645. It has become customary to refer to them as Milton's "Minor Poems," but they would not be minor if anyone else had written them.

An Early, Brilliant Career

The two outstanding poems of Milton's early career are known today by their short titles: *Comus* and *Lycidas. Comus* is a masque, an elaborate pageant of the sort that Ben Jonson was famous for writing. *Comus* was presented at Ludlow Castle in 1634, for and by the earl of Bridgewater's family. It opens with two brothers and a sister—played by the earl's children—lost in a forest. The sister, separated from her brothers, is invited by a flashy magician named Comus to join his troupe and live a life of pleasure. But the girl is able to resist all his seductions because her heart is pure. *Comus* gave Milton an early opportunity to dramatize an idea he firmly believed in: Human beings have been given the ability and freedom to choose between good and evil, and so long as they choose the good they will remain strong and free.

Just as *Comus* surpasses all other Renaissance masques by the beauty of its language and the depth of its thought, so does *Lycidas* surpass all other pastoral elegies written in English. An **elegy** celebrates the memory of a dead person; this poem remembers Edward King, a fellow student of Milton's who was shipwrecked and drowned in the Irish Sea in 1637. The elegy is called pastoral because it imitates some ancient elegies by using imagery of shepherds and their flocks. Milton and Edward King (renamed Lycidas), both of whom had been preparing for careers in the Church, are the young shepherds feeding their flock. Milton changed his mind about the Church, and King—a most promising youth—was killed. To lament this loss, Milton harmonizes the classical and Christian views of death, in a way characteristic of Christian humanists. But the poem is more about life than death because it celebrates a human being's capacity to create something significant, even in a short lifetime.

Milton's Political Activity: Intelligent Devotion

In the 1640s, an ongoing struggle between King Charles and his Parliament came to a head. Milton, believing that a poet must be active in the life of his time, entered the paper warfare that accompanied the conflict and started publishing prose works—some of them very elaborate and a few of them very insulting—in support of the Parliamentary Party. For this reason, some people have referred to Milton as a Puritan, but this is a label that has only limited application to a person of Milton's stature. If he shared some of the Puritans' ideas and attitudes, such as their extreme dislike of kings and bishops, he also differed greatly from them in other important ways. For instance, he advocated divorce for incompatible married couples, and he argued that the press should be free from government censorship and interference. Although we take these freedoms for granted, most people in the seventeenth century, particularly most Puritans, considered them dangerously radical.

During part of this period, Milton served in the government of England under Oliver Cromwell, who, with the title of lord protector, ruled England after the Parliamentary Party had won the Civil Wars and executed King Charles.

As Latin secretary to the Council of State, Milton was responsible for all correspondence with foreign countries, Latin then being the language of diplomacy.

But Milton's eyesight was gradually failing. By 1652, he could only distinguish day from night; otherwise, by the age of forty-four, before he had finished his life's work, Milton was totally blind. Among the few poems he wrote during this time is the following sonnet about the calamity of his middle age:

On His Blindness

When I consider how my light is spent
  Ere half my days in this dark world and wide,
  And that one talent which is death to hide
  Lodged with me useless, though my soul more bent
To serve there with my Maker, and present
  My true account, lest He returning chide,
  "Doth God exact day-labor, light denied?"
  I fondly ask. But Patience, to prevent
That murmur, soon replies, "God doth not need
  Either man's work or His own gifts. Who best
  Bear His mild yoke, they serve Him best. His state
Is kingly: Thousands at His bidding speed,
  And post o'er land and ocean without rest;
  They also serve who only stand and wait."

The Blind Milton Dictating Paradise Lost *to His Daughters* (19th century) by Michaly von Munkacsy. Oil.

Collection of the New York Public Library, New York. Astor, Lenox, and Tilden Foundations.

go.hrw.com
LE0 12-5

All for Nothing

To Milton, the ideal government was a republic in which the most capable, intelligent, and virtuous men would serve as leaders. To establish and maintain such a government in England, he had devoted most of his intelligence and energy for twenty years. Then suddenly, in 1660, the cause for which he had worked so hard became totally discredited; the English recalled their dead king's son from exile and crowned him as King Charles II. Overnight, Milton found himself stripped of his possessions and under arrest as a traitor. Fortunately, influential friends, including the poet Andrew Marvell, intervened, and Milton was allowed to go into retirement rather than to the scaffold. From then on, he lived in seclusion with his three daughters and his third wife, his first two wives and only son having died. By reading aloud to him, his daughters enabled him to carry on the studies he thought necessary for a poet.

> **A**dam and Eve are the heroes of Milton's epic, and they represent us all.

Milton's Great Epic: *Paradise Lost*

Being a poet, in Milton's view, meant imitating the great writers of antiquity, the epic poets Homer and Virgil and the Greek dramatists Aeschylus, Sophocles, and Euripides. Because those writers chose subjects drawn from their own nation's history, Milton first pondered various English subjects for his works, especially King Arthur and the knights of the Round Table. But finally, after years of thinking and reading, Milton decided that King Arthur's exploits were mainly fictitious, and so he settled on subjects drawn from the Bible. Milton thought the Bible alone contained everything people needed to know for the practice of true religion; he rejected not only the Roman Catholic Church and the Church of England, but also all the sects—Puritan or otherwise—that had sprung up in England since the Reformation began. While the Christian religion was the most important matter in his life, to Milton religion involved only God, God's Word (the Bible), and each individual human being.

Milton published *Paradise Lost* twice: first in a ten-book version in 1667 and then in twelve books in 1674, the year of his death. It's no exaggeration to say that Milton in one way or another worked on this epic all his life. He made many different plans and even once thought of it as a tragedy with Satan, the fallen archangel transformed into the chief devil, as its protagonist. In the finished poem, Satan is still very conspicuous. The first two books are devoted mainly to him, he appears frequently in Books III through X, and Milton lavishes on him some of his most glorious writing. It's not surprising, then, that many readers have regarded Satan as the secret hero of the poem, especially since he receives no such grand treatment in the Bible. Milton was "of the Devil's party without knowing it," asserted the poet and artist William Blake. But this argument is convincing only to those who concentrate on certain parts of the poem and ignore the rest of it. Moreover, in literary works, evil frequently seems more interesting than good, and if any part of *Paradise Lost* fails from a literary point of view, it is Milton's portrayal of God.

In *Paradise Lost,* Milton took relatively few verses from the Bible, mainly from Genesis, and developed them into a 10,565-line poem. He used the conventions and devices of the classical epic to make the poem a work of art; he used his great learning and wide experience of human affairs to make the poem profound. Although the poem ranges back and forth between Hell and Heaven, the most important action takes place on Earth, where the first human beings, Adam and Eve, are given the choice of obeying or disobeying God. They choose, as everybody knows, to disobey, and having done so, they accept their punishment and make the best of the life that is left to them. They are the heroes of Milton's epic, and they represent us all.

Paradise Lost: Milton's Epic

At the very beginning of *Paradise Lost,* Milton describes the content of his epic as "things unattempted yet in prose or rhyme" (line 16). His allusions to Homer, Virgil, Dante, and a host of lesser epic poets leave no doubt that Milton wanted *Paradise Lost* to sum up and also surpass all previous epics. The quality that would set Milton's epic apart, of course, was that it dealt with great deeds on a cosmic scale at the dawn of Creation—rather than with earthly matters.

There is a formal, set way to begin an epic. At the outset, an epic poet does two things: The speaker invokes the Muse (one of the nine Greek goddesses who inspire poets and other practitioners of the arts and sciences) to speak or sing through the poet; and the speaker states the subject of the poem. Milton does both these things in the first, complicated sentence (lines 1–16) of *Paradise Lost.* Grammatically, this sentence begins in line 6 with the command "Sing, Heavenly Muse." "Sing," says Milton, and now we move back to line 1, "Of man's first disobedience," which is Adam and Eve's first act of disobedience against God, who has forbidden them to eat the fruit of a particular tree in Eden (see the selection from Genesis, page 416). The result, or "fruit," of their disobedience is expulsion from and loss of Paradise, another name for the Garden of Eden. Yet all is not lost, because a "greater Man" (line 4), Jesus Christ, has restored the possibility of Paradise to the human race.

Milton calls this argument "great" (line 24), for he is attempting to resolve a dilemma that has puzzled many people throughout the ages. On the one hand, we are told that through his Eternal Providence (line 25) God takes loving care of creation; on the other hand, we know that there are many very bad things in the world, such as war, crime, poverty, disease, oppression, and injustice. In *Paradise Lost,* Milton asserts that God is not responsible for these evils; instead, Adam and Eve's disobedience to God "Brought death into the world, and all our woe" (line 3). God gave Adam and Eve the freedom to choose between good and evil, and the strength to resist evil; yet they chose evil, and their offspring—all of us—have suffered the effects of their choice ever since.

This explanation is not original to Milton; many Christians have accepted it for centuries. Yet a reader need not accept this traditional explanation of the evil in the world in order to enjoy and admire the poem. (Indeed, some readers have found evidence in the poem that Milton himself did not really believe it.) The poem is rich enough to provide support for many different interpretations.

Reading *Paradise Lost*

Milton decided to write his epic in his native language and in Shakespeare's meter, which is **blank verse,** or unrhymed iambic pentameter. Though blank verse was the usual meter in dramatic poetry, it was not used at all for nondramatic poems in Milton's day and for long after. Most of Milton's sentences are long, and many of them are not in normal word order (subject-verb-object). Also, his vocabulary includes words not used in ordinary prose today. (Unfamiliar proper nouns are explained in the notes, but they still have to be understood in their context.)

In Milton's heroic, optimistic view of life, goodness was not goodness unless it resulted from a struggle to overcome evil. God purposely let Satan escape from Hell and establish himself on Earth, not only so that Satan's deeds would damn him further but also so that human beings would have something to fight against—and with God's help triumph over. In one of his prose tracts, *Areopagitica* (1644), Milton describes life as a race in which good must compete with bad. Virtue, he says, is not virtue unless it is won in the "dust and heat" of the conflict with evil. And so, when Adam and Eve lose Paradise, they also gain something: the opportunity to prove themselves in the real world. The Archangel Michael, who comes to dispossess them of their perfect garden, tells them how to live in the new, imperfect world. Practice good deeds, he says, and patience, temperance, faith, and love, and

> then wilt thou be not loath
> To leave this Paradise, but shalt possess
> A Paradise within thee, happier far.

—*Paradise Lost*, Book XII, lines 585–587

The Fallen Angels Entering Pandemonium, from *Paradise Lost*, Book I, by John Martin (exhibited 1841).

Tate Gallery, London

JOHN MILTON 439

Before You Read

THE FALL OF SATAN

Make the Connection

Evil on an Epic Scale

Why does evil exist? What is the source of its power to fascinate? The struggle of good versus evil is central to *Paradise Lost*—in this case, the conflict exists on a truly epic scale, as Satan first rebels (in Book I) against God and then (in Book IX) ensnares Adam and Eve to do likewise. In Milton's epic, and in the Bible, this original choice of evil over good explains the burdens of humanity and our fateful tendency to misuse our reason and freedom to let pride override fear of God.

Reading Skills and Strategies

Monitor Your Reading Strategies

Milton wrote in the 1600s, and on first reading, you may be daunted by his style. As you read Milton, you will find it helpful to identify areas of difficulty and apply strategies to deal with them. For example, Milton often **omits words** and **inverts syntax,** wrenching some of his sentences out of the usual subject-verb-complement order. If you are having problems finding the **subject and verb** in one of his long or inverted sentences, reread it until you can locate these core sentence parts. If you are stalled by an unfamiliar word, try using **context clues** to figure it out. Make use of the **glossary** printed at the right of the poem. Answer the **side questions** to help you summarize key ideas as you go along.

Above all, **read the text aloud** and pay attention to the pauses signaled by the punctuation.

Milton is challenging—just as many good things are. But when you have solved the puzzles posed by Milton's style, you should be hooked by this exciting story of the primal battle between the forces of good and the forces of evil.

The Angel of Divine Presence
(late 18th to early 19th century)
by William Blake. Watercolor.
Fitzwilliam Museum, University of Cambridge.

The Fall of Satan
from Paradise Lost
John Milton

Of man's first disobedience, and the fruit
Of that forbidden tree, whose mortal taste
Brought death into the world, and all our woe,
With loss of Eden, till one greater Man°
5   Restore us, and regain the blissful seat,
Sing, Heavenly Muse,° that on the secret top
Of Oreb, or of Sinai,° didst inspire
That shepherd,° who first taught the chosen seed°
In the beginning how the Heavens and Earth
10 Rose out of Chaos; or if Sion hill°
Delight thee more, and Siloa's brook° that flowed
Fast by the oracle of God, I thence
Invoke thy aid to my adventurous song,
That with no middle flight intends to soar
15 Above the Aonian mount,° while it pursues
Things unattempted yet in prose or rhyme.
And chiefly thou, O Spirit,° that dost prefer
Before all temples the upright heart and pure,
Instruct me, for thou know'st; thou from the first
20 Wast present, and with mighty wings outspread
Dove-like sat'st brooding on the vast abyss
And mad'st it pregnant: what in me is dark
Illumine, what is low raise and support;
That to the height of this great argument
25 I may assert Eternal Providence,
And justify the ways of God to men.
        Say first, for Heaven hides nothing from thy view,
Nor the deep tract of Hell, say first what cause
Moved our grand parents° in that happy state,
30 Favored of Heaven so highly, to fall off
From their Creator, and transgress his will
For one restraint,° lords of the world besides?°
Who first seduced them to that foul revolt?
The infernal Serpent;° he it was, whose guile,
35 Stirred up with envy and revenge, deceived
The mother of mankind, what time his pride
Had cast him out from Heaven, with all his host
Of rebel angels, by whose aid aspiring
To set himself in glory above his peers,°
40 He trusted to have equaled the Most High,
If he opposed; and with ambitious aim
Against the throne and monarchy of God,
Raised impious war in Heaven and battle proud

? 1–6. *After you finish this invocation to the Muse, sum up what the subject of Milton's story will be.*

4. one greater Man: Christ.

6. Heavenly Muse: Urania, the muse of astronomy and sacred poetry. Milton hopes to be inspired by Urania, just as Moses was divinely inspired to receive and interpret the word of God for the Hebrews.
7. Oreb . . . Sinai: alternative names for the mountain where Moses received heavenly inspiration.
8. shepherd: Moses. **chosen seed:** the Hebrews.
10. Sion hill: Zion, a hill near Jerusalem on which the Temple was built.
11. Siloa's brook: stream that flowed past the Temple, "the oracle of God," on Sion hill.
15. Aonian mount: in Greek mythology, Mount Helicon, the home of the Muses. Milton intends to write an epic greater than those of the classical Greek poet Homer and the classical Roman poet Virgil.
17. Spirit: the Holy Spirit; divine inspiration.

? 26. *According to this line, what is Milton's purpose? How would you paraphrase this purpose?*

29. grand parents: Adam and Eve.

32. one restraint: the command not to eat of the fruit of the tree of knowledge. **besides:** in every other way.
34. Serpent: Milton anticipates Satan's final form.

39. peers: equals; the other archangels.

With vain attempt. Him the Almighty Power
45 Hurled headlong flaming from the ethereal sky
With hideous ruin and combustion down
To bottomless perdition,° there to dwell
In adamantine° chains and penal° fire,
Who durst° defy the Omnipotent to arms.
50 Nine times the space that measures day and night
To mortal men, he with his horrid crew
Lay vanquished, rolling in the fiery gulf,
Confounded though immortal. But his doom
Reserved him to more wrath; for now the thought
55 Both of lost happiness and lasting pain
Torments him; round he throws his baleful eyes,
That witnessed huge affliction and dismay
Mixed with obdurate° pride and steadfast hate.
At once as far as angels ken° he views
60 The dismal situation waste and wild:
A dungeon horrible on all sides round
As one great furnace flamed, yet from those flames
No light, but rather darkness visible
Served only to discover sights of woe,
65 Regions of sorrow, doleful shades, where peace
And rest can never dwell, hope never comes
That comes to all; but torture without end
Still urges,° and a fiery deluge, fed
With ever-burning sulfur unconsumed:
70 Such place Eternal Justice had prepared
For those rebellious, here their prison ordained
In utter darkness, and their portion set
As far removed from God and light of Heaven
As from the center thrice to the utmost pole.°
75 O how unlike the place from whence they fell!
There the companions of his fall, o'erwhelmed
With floods and whirlwinds of tempestuous fire,
He soon discerns, and weltering° by his side
One next himself in power, and next in crime,
80 Long after known in Palestine, and named
Beelzebub.° To whom the Arch-Enemy,
And then in Heaven called Satan,° with bold words
Breaking the horrid silence thus began:
     "If thou beest he—but O how fallen! how changed
85 From him, who in the happy realms of light
Clothed with transcendent brightness didst outshine
Myriads though bright—if he whom mutual league,
United thoughts and counsels, equal hope
And hazard in the glorious enterprise,
90 Joined with me once, now misery hath joined
In equal ruin: into what pit thou seest
From what height fallen! so much the stronger proved
He with his thunder;° and till then who knew

28–44. *What questions does Milton ask, and how does he answer them?*

47. perdition: damnation.
48. adamantine (ad′ə·man′tin): unbreakable. **penal:** punishing.
49. durst: dared.

54–56. *What torments Satan in Hell?*

58. obdurate: stubborn; unrepentant.
59. ken: can see.

61–74. *Here starts a description of Hell. As you read, note the details as Milton describes them. Which aspect of Hell would be the hardest to bear?*

68. still urges: always afflicts.

74. center . . . pole: three times the distance from Earth, or "center," to the outermost point in the universe. In Milton's cosmos, Earth is the center of ten concentric spheres.
78. weltering: rolling about.

81. Beelzebub (bē·el′zə·bub′): next in power to Satan; described as prince of the devils in Matthew 12:24.
82. Satan: Hebrew for "adversary" or "opposer."

91. *How has Beelzebub, Satan's former comrade, changed?*
93. He . . . thunder: God.

The force of those dire arms? Yet not for those,
95 Nor what the potent Victor in his rage
Can else inflict, do I repent or change,
Though changed in outward luster, that fixed mind
And high disdain, from sense of injured merit,
That with the Mightiest raised me to contend,
100 And to the fierce contention brought along
Innumerable force of spirits armed
That durst dislike his reign, and, me preferring,
His utmost power with adverse power opposed
In dubious battle on the plains of Heaven,
105 And shook his throne. What though the field be lost?
All is not lost; the unconquerable will,
And study° of revenge, immortal hate,
And courage never to submit or yield:
And what is else not to be overcome?
110 That glory never shall his wrath or might
Extort from me. To bow and sue for grace
With suppliant knee, and deify his power
Who from the terror of this arm so late
Doubted° his empire, that were low indeed,
115 That were an ignominy° and shame beneath
This downfall; since by fate the strength of gods
And this empyreal substance° cannot fail,
Since through experience of this great event,
In arms not worse, in foresight much advanced,
120 We may with more successful hope resolve
To wage by force or guile eternal war
Irreconcilable to our grand Foe,
Who now triumphs, and in the excess of joy
Sole reigning holds the tyranny of Heaven."
125   So spake the apostate° Angel, though in pain,
Vaunting° aloud, but racked with deep despair;
And him thus answered soon his bold compeer:°
    "O Prince, O Chief of many thronèd Powers,
That led the embattled Seraphim° to war
130 Under thy conduct, and in dreadful deeds
Fearless, endangered Heaven's perpetual King,
And put to proof his high supremacy,
Whether upheld by strength, or chance, or fate;
Too well I see and rue the dire event,°
135 That with sad overthrow and foul defeat
Hath lost us Heaven, and all this mighty host
In horrible destruction laid thus low,
As far as gods and heavenly essences
Can perish: for the mind and spirit remains
140 Invincible, and vigor soon returns,
Though all our glory extinct, and happy state
Here swallowed up in endless misery.
But what if he our Conqueror (whom I now

Illustration from *Paradise Lost* (17th century). Engraving.

107. study: pursuit.
114. doubted: archaic for "feared for."
115. ignominy (ig′nə·min′ē): dishonor.
117. empyreal (em·pir′ē·əl) **substance**—heavenly—and therefore indestructible—substance of which all angels (including Satan) are made.

? **93–124.** *What details in Satan's speech show that he feels that he and God are opposing generals of two armies? Does Satan admit defeat?*

125. apostate: guilty of abandoning one's beliefs. Satan is an apostate.
126. vaunting: boasting.
127. compeer: companion; equal. Now Beelzebub speaks.
129. Seraphim: highest order of angels.

134. event: archaic for "outcome."

Censoring the Word

Most of us tend to associate censorship with either foreign dictatorships or the issue of obscenity. For the authorities of seventeenth-century England, however, the power of the word was great—potentially so great that freedom of speech and freedom of the press were unknown. Newspapers, books, and pamphlets were all subject to strict censorship.

Keeping a wary eye. Even in Elizabethan times, the government had kept a wary eye on literary activity, especially on drama. Plays and players had to be licensed, and playwrights were careful to avoid offending the powerful. For example, in his play *Henry IV*, Shakespeare changed the name Sir John Oldcastle to Sir John Falstaff to avoid offending the Oldcastle family, friends of Queen Elizabeth.

Government control of the press had its origins in the rise of newspapers and journalism early in the seventeenth century. Oliver Cromwell, a Puritan and the lord protector of England, banned all unofficial periodicals in 1655. After the Restoration of King Charles II in 1660, so-called licensing laws were regularly enacted by Parliament. The laws forbade publishing any material contrary to the doctrine of the Church of England or scandalous to the government. Penalties were stiff: fines, imprisonment, and sentencing to the pillory, where the offender was fastened to a wooden board with holes for the head and hands.

A censor's who's who. The list of writers who ran afoul of the licensing laws reads like a "who's who" of seventeenth-century literature.

In 1605, Ben Jonson was arrested and in danger of having his nose and ears slit for his coauthorship of *Eastward Hoe*. The play contained disrespectful remarks

Of force° believe almighty, since no less
145 Than such could have o'erpowered such force as ours)
Have left us this our spirit and strength entire
Strongly to suffer and support our pains,
That we may so suffice° his vengeful ire,
Or do him mightier service as his thralls°
150 By right of war, whate'er his business be,
Here in the heart of Hell to work in fire,
Or do his errands in the gloomy deep?
What can it then avail,° though yet we feel
Strength undiminished, or eternal being
155 To undergo eternal punishment?"
    Whereto with speedy words the Arch-Fiend replied:

144. of force: of necessity.

148. suffice: archaic for "satisfy."
149. thralls: slaves.

153. avail: be of help or advantage.

? 128–155. *What does Beelzebub think of their situation? How is Beelzebub different from Satan?*

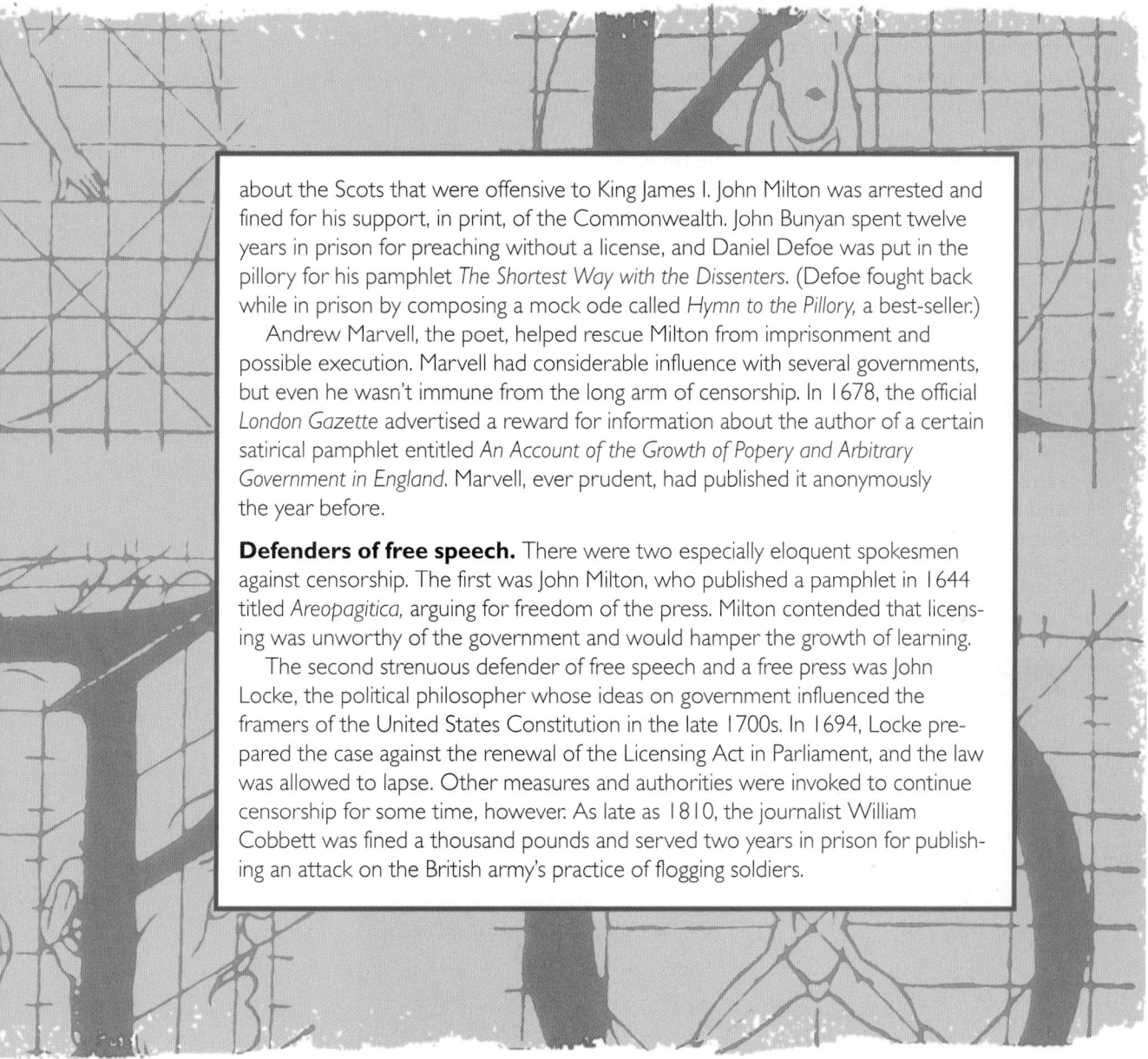

about the Scots that were offensive to King James I. John Milton was arrested and fined for his support, in print, of the Commonwealth. John Bunyan spent twelve years in prison for preaching without a license, and Daniel Defoe was put in the pillory for his pamphlet *The Shortest Way with the Dissenters*. (Defoe fought back while in prison by composing a mock ode called *Hymn to the Pillory*, a best-seller.)

Andrew Marvell, the poet, helped rescue Milton from imprisonment and possible execution. Marvell had considerable influence with several governments, but even he wasn't immune from the long arm of censorship. In 1678, the official *London Gazette* advertised a reward for information about the author of a certain satirical pamphlet entitled *An Account of the Growth of Popery and Arbitrary Government in England*. Marvell, ever prudent, had published it anonymously the year before.

Defenders of free speech. There were two especially eloquent spokesmen against censorship. The first was John Milton, who published a pamphlet in 1644 titled *Areopagitica,* arguing for freedom of the press. Milton contended that licensing was unworthy of the government and would hamper the growth of learning.

The second strenuous defender of free speech and a free press was John Locke, the political philosopher whose ideas on government influenced the framers of the United States Constitution in the late 1700s. In 1694, Locke prepared the case against the renewal of the Licensing Act in Parliament, and the law was allowed to lapse. Other measures and authorities were invoked to continue censorship for some time, however. As late as 1810, the journalist William Cobbett was fined a thousand pounds and served two years in prison for publishing an attack on the British army's practice of flogging soldiers.

"Fallen Cherub, to be weak is miserable,
Doing or suffering:° But of this be sure,
To do aught° good never will be our task,
160 But ever to do ill our sole delight,
As being the contrary to his high will
Whom we resist. If then his providence
Out of our evil seek to bring forth good,
Our labor must be to pervert that end,
165 And out of good still° to find means of evil;
Which ofttimes may succeed, so as perhaps
Shall grieve him, if I fail not, and disturb
His inmost counsels from their destined aim.
But see the angry Victor° hath recalled

158. doing or suffering: whether active or passive.
159. aught: anything whatever.

? **159–162.** *What does Satan vow? Would you say this is the essence of evil? Explain.*

165. still: always.

169. angry Victor: God.

170 His ministers of vengeance and pursuit
    Back to the gates of Heaven; the sulfurous hail
    Shot after us in storm, o'erblown hath laid
    The fiery surge, that from the precipice
    Of Heaven received us falling, and the thunder,
175 Winged with red lightning and impetuous rage,
    Perhaps hath spent his shafts, and ceases now
    To bellow through the vast and boundless deep.
    Let us not slip° the occasion, whether scorn
    Or satiate° fury yield it from our Foe.
180 Seest thou yon dreary plain, forlorn and wild,
    The seat of desolation, void of light,
    Save what the glimmering of these livid flames
    Casts pale and dreadful? Thither let us tend
    From off the tossing of these fiery waves,
185 There rest, if any rest can harbor there,
    And reassembling our afflicted powers,
    Consult how we may henceforth most offend
    Our Enemy, our own loss how repair,
    How overcome this dire calamity,

178. slip: lose.
179. satiate: satisfied.

Satan in His Original Glory
(late 18th to early 19th century)
by William Blake.

Tate Gallery, London.

190 What reinforcement we may gain from hope,
    If not, what resolution from despair."
        Thus Satan talking to his nearest mate
    With head uplift above the wave, and eyes
    That sparkling blazed; his other parts besides,
195 Prone on the flood, extended long and large,
    Lay floating many a rood,° in bulk as huge
    As whom the fables name of monstrous size,
    Titanian or Earth-born, that warred on Jove,
    Briareos or Typhon,° whom the den
200 By ancient Tarsus held, or that sea-beast
    Leviathan,° which God of all his works
    Created hugest that swim the ocean stream:
    Him haply slumbering on the Norway foam,
    The pilot of some small night-foundered° skiff,
205 Deeming some island, oft, as seamen tell,
    With fixèd anchor in his scaly rind
    Moors by his side under the lee, while night
    Invests° the sea, and wishèd morn delays:
    So stretched out huge in length the Arch-Fiend lay
210 Chained on the burning lake; nor ever thence
    Had risen or heaved his head, but that the will
    And high permission of all-ruling Heaven
    Left him at large to his own dark designs,
    That with reiterated crimes he might
215 Heap on himself damnation, while he sought
    Evil to others, and enraged might see
    How all his malice served but to bring forth
    Infinite goodness, grace, and mercy shown
    On man by him seduced, but on himself
220 Treble confusion, wrath, and vengeance poured.
        Forthwith upright he rears from off the pool
    His mighty stature; on each hand the flames
    Driven backward slope their pointing spires, and rolled
    In billows, leave in the midst a horrid vale.
225 Then with expanded wings he steers his flight
    Aloft, incumbent° on the dusky air
    That felt unusual weight, till on dry land
    He lights, if it were land that ever burned
    With solid, as the lake with liquid fire;
230 And such appeared in hue, as when the force
    Of subterranean wind transports a hill
    Torn from Pelorus,° or the shattered side
    Of thundering Etna,° whose combustible
    And fueled entrails thence conceiving fire,
235 Sublimed° with mineral fury, aid the winds,
    And leave a singèd bottom all involved°
    With stench and smoke: such resting found the sole
    Of unblest feet. Him followed his next mate,
    Both glorying to have scaped the Stygian° flood

? **169–191.** *Satan thinks of himself merely as a defeated general. What does he now propose?*

196. rood: an old unit of measure varying locally from about six to eight yards.

198–200. Titanian . . . Typhon: In an epic simile, Milton compares Satan to the Titans and Giants of Greek mythology. Briareos, a hundred-handed Giant, helped Zeus (Jove) battle the Titans. Typhon, a hundred-headed serpent-monster from Cilicia (near Tarsus), attacked heaven and was imprisoned by Zeus.
201. Leviathan: Biblical sea monster, either a reptile or a whale.
204. night-foundered: overtaken by night.
208. invests: covers.

? **209–220.** *What are God's plans for Satan?*

226. incumbent: lying.

? **230–238.** *Read this important epic simile carefully. Notice the natural forces that Satan is compared with. How does this description of Satan contrast with Blake's image on page 446?*

232. Pelorus: headland in Sicily, Italy; now called Cape Faro.
233. Etna: volcano in Sicily, Italy.

235. sublimed: vaporized.
236. involved: enveloped.
239. Stygian (stij'ē·ən): of or like the river Styx; infernal, hellish. In Greek mythology, the river Styx encircles the underworld.

240 As gods, and by their own recovered strength,
Not by the sufferance° of supernal° power.
"Is this the region, this the soil, the clime,"
Said then the lost Archangel, "this the seat
That we must change for Heaven, this mournful gloom
245 For that celestial light? Be it so, since he
Who now is sovereign can dispose and bid
What shall be right: farthest from him is best,
Whom reason hath equaled, force hath made supreme
Above his equals. Farewell, happy fields,
250 Where joy forever dwells! Hail, horrors! hail,
Infernal world! and thou, profoundest° Hell,
Receive thy new possessor; one who brings
A mind not to be changed by place or time.
The mind is its own place, and in itself
255 Can make a Heaven of Hell, a Hell of Heaven.
What matter where, if I be still the same,
And what I should be, all but less than he
Whom thunder hath made greater? Here at least
We shall be free; the Almighty hath not built
260 Here for his envy, will not drive us hence:
Here we may reign secure, and in my choice
To reign is worth ambition, though in Hell:
Better to reign in Hell than serve in Heaven.
But wherefore let we then our faithful friends,
265 The associates and copartners of our loss,
Lie thus astonished° on the oblivious° pool,
And call them not to share with us their part
In this unhappy mansion, or once more
With rallied arms to try what may be yet
270 Regained in Heaven, or what more lost in Hell?"

241. sufferance: permission.
supernal: heavenly.

251. profoundest: lowest; deepest.

? **254–255.** *Satan and Beelzebub land in Hell. How would you paraphrase what the proud Satan says in these lines? Do you agree?*

? **263.** *What do you make of this declaration? What do you predict Satan will do next?*

266. astonished: dazed.
oblivious: causing forgetfulness.

The Fall of Satan (1825) (detail) by William Blake. Illustration for *The Book of Job.*
Tate Gallery, London.

MAKING MEANINGS

First Thoughts

1. How did you react to Milton's portrait of Satan? What **images** describing Satan or words spoken by Satan made the greatest impression on you?

Shaping Interpretations

2. According to Milton, how is the rebellion of Satan and the angels against God connected with "man's first disobedience" and the origin of evil in the world? How does Milton explain the existence of evil in a world created by a loving God?

3. Reread Milton's first description of Hell (lines 53–74). How is hell both a psychological state and a physical place? What do you make of the poet's use of **paradox** in the phrase "darkness visible" (line 63)?

4. In his opening speech, Satan vows never to "repent or change" (line 96). Nevertheless, do you catch any hint of longing in this speech for the angels' former state? How might this yearning be related to Milton's mention of "the thought . . . of lost happiness" in lines 54–55?

5. Beelzebub reminds Satan that even in Hell the evil angels may be unwittingly serving God's

---

Reading Check

a. Whom does Milton call upon at the outset (lines 1–16)? What question does he ask about Adam and Eve (lines 27–33)?

b. What is Milton's **purpose** in writing this epic story?

c. Why was Satan cast out of Heaven?

d. In his first speech, what does Satan tell Beelzebub that he will never do? What course does he favor instead?

e. According to Milton in lines 210–220, who allows Satan the freedom to pursue his evil intentions?

f. In his last speech, what does Satan claim are the advantages of life in Hell?

---

purposes. How does Satan reply to this objection in lines 157–168?

6. In lines 210–220, Milton offers a solemn assurance that despite all Satan's power and grandeur, the devil is still subject to God's purposes. How do these lines contribute a level of **dramatic irony** to Satan's ringing assertion of freedom in his final speech (lines 242–270)?

7. Discuss why some people see Milton's Satan as a heroic figure. How do you feel about this heroic depiction of Satan?

8. What **images** in the story helped you to see and smell Hell?

Connecting with the Text

9. Perhaps the most famous verses of this passage are in Satan's last speech (lines 254–255):

> The mind is its own place, and in itself
> Can make a Heaven of Hell, a Hell of Heaven.

In your experience, is this an accurate description of what the mind can do?

Extending the Text

10. Do people today use the arguments and rationalizations used by Satan and his old crony Beelzebub in their dialogue (lines 143–168)? If so, how?

READING SKILLS AND STRATEGIES

Reading Milton's Poetic Language

Analyzing epic similes. The word *as* in Milton's epic tells us that a simile is coming, an elaborate **epic simile,** in which something in the poem is compared to something quite outside the poem—often an animal, sometimes a human being or human action. These epic similes allowed Milton to bring into his epic a variety of non-Biblical material. Note the **analogies,** or similarities between two unlike things, that the similes are based on.

1. What epic similes are used to describe Satan's bulk in lines 196–208? What is compared to what? How are these things alike?

2. What epic simile describes Satan's landing on dry land in lines 230–237? What is compared to what? How are these things alike?

Reading irregular syntax. To accommodate the demands of his meter, Milton often uses irregular syntax in which the sentences do not follow the normal subject-verb-complement order. In addition, Milton's sentences are long, and often words are omitted which have to be supplied by the reader.

1. In lines 76–78, what are the **subject,** the **verb,** and the **direct object**? What additional words should be supplied in lines 78–81 to make sense of the rest of this sentence?

2. Using normal English syntax, how would you rephrase lines 157–162?

Reading blank verse. Milton uses **blank verse,** or unrhymed iambic pentameter, to give his epic an exalted tone. Iambic pentameter means that each line of the poem has ten syllables, with five strong stresses alternating with five weaker stresses (the lines begin with an unstressed syllable and end with a stressed one). An **iamb** is an unstressed syllable followed by a stressed one, as in the word *refér.*

1. Scan lines 251–253 to show that they are written in iambic pentameter.

2. Choose a passage to read aloud so that you can hear the beat of the iambs. Where does Milton vary the meter to give his verse variety and to prevent a singsong rhythm?

CHOICES: Building Your Portfolio

Writer's Notebook

1. Collecting Ideas for a Cause-Effect Essay

In *Paradise Lost,* Milton argues that God is not responsible for the evils of our world. Rather, Adam and Eve's disobedience, their misuse of reason and freedom, caused these evils. What do you think is one of the biggest evils that exists in the world today? What are its causes? What are its effects? As you note your ideas, draw from your own experience, but also consider other sources, such as historical evidence. Save your work to use in the Writer's Workshop on page 459.

Paraphrasing a Text

2. Paraphrasing Milton

Choose one of the long speeches in this excerpt from *Paradise Lost:* for example, lines 84–124 (Satan), 128–155 (Beelzebub), 157–191 (Satan), or 242–270 (Satan). Write a prose paraphrase of the speech you select. You'll have to supply words that Milton omits and use normal English syntax.

Analyzing a Character

3. Analyzing the Arch-Fiend

In a brief essay, discuss Milton's characterization of Satan. Examine Satan's appearance, his actions, his words, and his effect on others. Where does Milton directly characterize Satan? Is Satan a heroic figure from any perspective? Open with a general statement summing up the character of the Arch-Fiend.

Creative Writing

4. A Fallen Angel Dialogue

Milton originally planned *Paradise Lost* as a drama. Working with a small group, try recreating the opening scene of the poem as a dramatic dialogue between Satan and Beelzebub. Start by compressing the two characters' speeches. How will you incorporate Milton's background narration and descriptive details into your dialogue?

Comparing Texts/Art

5. Two Hells

Another famous description of Hell and its overlord appears in the selection from *The Inferno* of Dante on page 394. Prepare two lists, one for Milton and one for Dante, and compare their images of Satan and his infernal domain. If you wish, draw the two underworlds—they are dramatically visual.

Allegory: Telling Two Stories at Once

Modern photographers sometimes create striking effects by superimposing one image on another to produce a double exposure. In the same way, writers sometimes use the literary form known as **allegory** to tell two stories at once. Allegories are usually used for teaching. In an allegory, characters, settings, and events stand for abstract ideas. Allegories thus have two meanings: a literal meaning and a symbolic one.

Allegories were especially popular during the Middle Ages. Around 1509, an enduringly relevant play called *Everyman* used the techniques of allegory to teach people the value of good deeds. Everyman (who stands for exactly what his name indicates) is summoned by Death to give an account of his life. Everyman asks his friends, who have allegorical names such as Fellowship, Beauty, and Strength, to go with him, but only Good Deeds stays with him to the end. *Everyman* is periodically dusted off and revived for the stage today. It still gets good reviews.

The Renaissance produced two masterly allegories. Edmund Spenser's *The Faerie Queene* is a long, rich allegory about the adventures of characters who embody such things as holiness, chastity, truth, falsehood, hypocrisy, and despair. (See page 221.) John Bunyan's allegorical novel *The Pilgrim's Progress from This World to That Which Is to Come* (1678), commonly called *The Pilgrim's Progress,* was such a success that, like many filmmakers today, he produced a second part.

The Perils of Piety

The narrator of *The Pilgrim's Progress* is a dreamer. Asleep, he dreams about a man called Christian who lives with his family in a city called Destruction. Besides living in a city with this appalling name, Christian has another problem: On his back he bears an immense burden that he cannot get rid of. It is like a part of himself. And so he decides to leave home and go on a "progress," or journey, to a wonderful place that he has heard of called the Celestial City. On this trip, described through most of the book, he has a few pleasant experiences, such as his visit to House Beautiful and the Delectable Mountains, but most of his adventures are unpleasant and even dangerous. He falls into the Slough (a mudhole; rhymes with "cow") of Despond, he climbs the Hill Difficulty, he fights a dragon-like monster called Apollyon, and he is arrested and unjustly punished in a place called Vanity Fair. His most insidious encounters are with characters who try to distract him from his progress: Mr. Worldly Wiseman, Talkative, Little-Faith, and Ignorance. Finally, all these obstacles overcome, Christian enters the Celestial City, where he will dwell eternally in bliss and where he is eventually joined by his wife,

Christian Reading in His Book
(late 18th or early 19th century)
by William Blake.

Title page of *The Pilgrim's Progress* by John Bunyan.

Christiana, and their children. Bunyan describes their journey in the second part of *The Pilgrim's Progress.*

In the following excerpt, Christian and his companion, Hopeful, have been imprisoned in the dungeon of Giant Despair's Doubting Castle. Goaded by his wife, Diffidence, the giant has starved them, beaten them mercilessly, and urged them to kill themselves. Christian and Hopeful talk about what to do.

Christian: "Brother," said Christian, "what shall we do? The life that we now live is miserable. For my part I know not whether it is best to live thus, or to die out of hand. 'My soul chooseth strangling rather than life,'[1] and the grave is more easy for me than this dungeon. Shall we be ruled by the Giant?"

Hopeful: "Indeed our present condition is dreadful, and death would be far more welcome to me than thus forever to abide; but yet let us consider, the Lord of the country to which we are going hath said, 'Thou shalt do no murder': no, not to another man's person; much more then are we forbidden to take his counsel to kill ourselves. Besides, he that kills another can but commit murder upon his body; but for one to kill himself is to kill body and soul at once. And moreover, my brother, thou talkest of ease in the grave; but hast thou forgotten the hell whither for certain the murderers go? For 'no murderer hath eternal life,'[2]

etc. And let us consider again that all the law is not in the hand of Giant Despair. Others, so far as I can understand, have been taken by him, as well as we; and yet have escaped out of his hand. Who knows but that God that made the world may cause that Giant Despair may die? Or that at some time or other he may forget to lock us in? Or but he may in short time have another of his fits before us, and may lose the use of his limbs? And if ever that should come to pass again, for my part, I am resolved to pluck up the heart of a man,[3] and to try my utmost to get from under his hand. I was a fool that I did not try to do it before; but however, my brother, let's be patient, and endure a while. The time may come that may give us a happy release; but let us not be our own murderers." With these words Hopeful at present did moderate the mind of his brother; so they continued together (in the dark) that day, in their sad and doleful condition.

Well, toward evening the Giant goes down into the dungeon again, to see if his prisoners had taken his counsel; but when he came there he found them alive; and truly, alive was all; for now, what for want of bread and water, and by reason of the wounds they received when he beat them, they could do little but breathe. But, I say, he found them alive, at which he fell into a grievous rage, and told them that, seeing they had disobeyed his counsel, it should be worse with them than if they had never been born.

At this they trembled greatly, and I think that Christian fell into a swoon; but coming a little to himself again, they renewed their discourse about the Giant's counsel; and whether yet they had best to take it or no. Now Christian again seemed to be for doing it, but Hopeful made his second reply as followeth:

Hopeful: "My brother," said he, "rememberest thou not how valiant thou hast been heretofore? Apollyon could not crush thee, nor could all that thou didst hear, or see, or feel, in the Valley of the Shadow of Death. What hardship, terror, and amazement hast thou already gone through, and art thou now nothing but

---

1. **My soul . . . life:** quotation from Job 7:15.
2. **no murderer . . . life:** quotation from 1 John 3:15.

3. **pluck . . . man:** be brave.

fear? Thou seest that I am in the dungeon with thee, a far weaker man by nature than thou art; also this Giant has wounded me as well as thee, and hath also cut off the bread and water from my mouth; and with thee I mourn without the light. But let us exercise a little more patience; remember how thou playedst the man[4] at Vanity Fair, and wast neither afraid of the chain, nor cage, nor yet of bloody death. Wherefore let us (at least to avoid the shame that becomes not a Christian to be found in) bear up with patience as well as we can."

Now night being come again, and the Giant and his wife being in bed, she asked him concerning the prisoners, and if they had taken his counsel. To which he replied, "They are sturdy rogues, they choose rather to bear all hardship than to make away themselves." Then said she, "Take them into the castle yard tomorrow, and show them the bones and skulls of those that thou hast already dispatched, and make them believe, ere a week come to an end, thou also wilt tear them in pieces, as thou hast done their fellows before them."

So when the morning was come, the Giant goes to them again, and takes them into the castle yard, and shows them, as his wife had bidden him. "These," said he, "were pilgrims as you are once, and they trespassed in my grounds, as you have done; and when I thought fit, I tore them in pieces, and so within ten days I will do you. Go, get you down to your den again"; and with that he beat them all the way thither. They lay therefore all day on Saturday in a lamentable case, as before. Now when night was come, and when Mrs. Diffidence and her husband the Giant were got to bed, they began to renew their discourse of their prisoners; and withal the old Giant wondered that he could neither by his blows nor his counsel bring them to an end. And with that his wife replied, "I fear," said she, "that they live in hope that some will come to relieve them, or that they have picklocks about them, by the means of which they hope to escape." "And sayest thou so, my dear?" said the Giant; "I will therefore search them in the morning."

Well, on Saturday about midnight they began to pray, and continued in prayer till almost break of day.

Now a little before it was day, good Christian, as one half-amazed, brake out in this passionate speech: "What a fool (quoth he) am I, thus to lie in a stinking dungeon, when I may as well walk at liberty! I have a key in my bosom called Promise, that will (I am persuaded) open any lock in Doubting Castle." Then said Hopeful, "That is good news, good brother; pluck it out of thy bosom and try." Then Christian pulled it out of his bosom, and began to try at the dungeon door, whose bolt (as he turned the key) gave back, and the door flew open with ease, and Christian and Hopeful both came out. Then he went to the outward door that leads into the castle yard, and with his key opened that door also. After, he went to the iron gate, for that must be opened, too; but that lock went damnable hard, yet the key did open it. Then they thrust open the gate to make their escape with speed, but that gate, as it opened, made such a creaking that it waked Giant Despair, who, hastily rising to pursue his prisoners, felt his limbs to fail, for his fits took him again, so that he could by no means go after them. Then they went on and came to the King's highway, and so were safe because they were out of his jurisdiction. . . .

—John Bunyan, *from The Pilgrim's Progress*

Next to the Bible, *The Pilgrim's Progress* has been the most widely read of all English books. What accounts for Bunyan's enormous appeal? He wrote for people who believed that every human being is engaged in a continuous battle against forces of evil that, while powerful, are not as powerful as God. And so Bunyan told his readers what they most wanted to hear: how, with God's help, they could defeat evil and attain eternal life. He expressed his message in language familiar to his readers, drawn from their daily experiences and from the Bible, folk tales, and popular literature. In Bunyan's literary double exposure, his readers recognized their own lives made surprising and interesting.

4. **thou playedst the man:** you were brave.

Reading Skills and Strategies

VOCABULARY: DISTINGUISHING MULTIPLE MEANINGS OF WORDS

Many words have, over time, accumulated more than one meaning. One word that has developed more than one meaning is *humor:*

> To spend too much time in studies is sloth . . . to make judgment wholly by their rules is the **humor** of a scholar.

> —Sir Francis Bacon, *from* "Of Studies"

Bacon uses the word *humor* to mean a person's general disposition or temperament. But if we say "My sister has a great sense of humor," we are referring to her ability to appreciate what is funny or amusing. These two definitions are related, however; they share the same origin and so are found under the same entry in the dictionary.

Using the dictionary. Arrangements of definitions may vary from dictionary to dictionary. In some dictionaries, the most frequently encountered meaning appears as the first definition, specialized senses follow, and rare, archaic, and obsolete senses are listed at the end. In other dictionaries, definitions are arranged in order from the oldest sense to the most recent.

Distinguishing word origins. Some words not only have different meanings but also have different origins. The fact that such words are spelled identically is an accident. Take the word *mean,* for example:

> Some books also may be read by deputy, and extracts made of them by others; but that would be only in the less important arguments, and the **meaner** sort of books . . .

> —Sir Francis Bacon, *from* "Of Studies"

The following chart shows the different meanings and **etymologies,** or origins, of *mean.*

Word	Origin	Present Meanings
1. mean	Old English *mænan:* to mean, tell, complain	to have in mind; intend; propose
2. mean	Old English *(ge)mæne:* plentiful, common	low in value; poor; inferior; stingy; miserly; bad-tempered
3. mean	Latin *medius:* middle	halfway between extremes; medium; average

Sometimes two meanings of the word can be used with different, but equally strong and relevant effects:

> . . . the thought
> Both of lost happiness and lasting pain
> Torments him; round he throws his **baleful** eyes,
> That witnessed huge affliction and dismay
> Mixed with obdurate pride and steadfast hate.

> —John Milton, *Paradise Lost,* Book I, lines 54–58

Baleful can mean "wretched" as well as "evil." Milton uses the multifaceted nature of language to complicate our image of Satan.

Try It Out

Using a dictionary, look up the **origin** and different **meanings** of each word listed below. Then use each word in two different **contexts** to illustrate two of the word's different meanings.

1. light   **2.** mind   **3.** bear   **4.** arm   **5.** fast

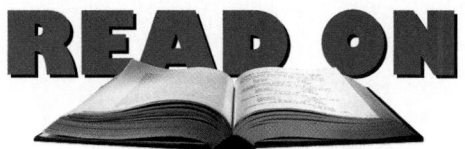

Love and War

The filmmaker Kenneth Branagh has brought a lively new perspective to some of Shakespeare's plays. *Henry V* (1989), about the warrior-king who led the attack on Agincourt in the early fifteenth century, is packed with action and adventure. The confused lovers in *Much Ado About Nothing* (1993), played by Branagh and Emma Thompson, spar and spark against a sunny Italian landscape. Both films are available on video.

Motorcycle Meditations

Part travelogue, part meditation, part rambling discourse, Robert Pirsig's *Zen and the Art of Motorcycle Maintenance* (Bantam Books) is above all an inquiry into human values. While taking an extended motorcycle trip, Pirsig pursues the same questions that intrigued Francis Bacon, John Milton, and the writer(s) of Genesis: What is the nature of the universe, and what is our place in it? How should we conduct our lives?

The Bard's Background and Playground

People flocked to Renaissance London in droves, where the theater was a major attraction. Shakespeare was an integral part of this world, but there's been a tendency to divorce the man from his background. *Shakespeare of London* (Penguin) by Marchette Chute and *Shakespeare Alive!* (Bantam Books) by Joseph Papp and Elizabeth Kirkland help bring the legend back to life, placing Shakespeare in the theatrical and social context where he thrived.

A Crisis of Conscience

Scholar, ambassador, Lord Chancellor, family man—Sir Thomas More had it all. But then King Henry VIII changed everything by deciding to divorce his wife, which meant breaking with the pope—an action More opposed. More's decision to follow his personal beliefs rather than his political interests serves as the basis for Robert Bolt's play, *A Man for All Seasons* (Vintage/Random House), also a 1966 film starring Paul Scofield and Orson Welles, as well as a 1988 made-for-television movie with Charlton Heston, John Gielgud, and Vanessa Redgrave. (Both versions are available on videotape.)

Love Is . . .

In *The Love Poems of Robert Herrick and John Donne* (Barnes & Noble), the works of two of the most well-known Renaissance poets come gloriously together. Even though both poets write about love, their ideas and style differ. The editor, Louis Untermeyer, notes that "Donne plunges the reader into emotion with nervous desperation," while Herrick "is all delicacy and delight." Donne's metaphysical passion and Herrick's spirited banter make this collection a complete exploration of the power of love.

The English Language

The Growth of Modern English

by John Algeo

During the seventeenth century, interest in the English language grew rapidly. English scholars vigorously studied the grammar, vocabulary, and style of written English.

The First Grammars and Dictionaries

The first grammars of English appeared shortly before the end of the sixteenth century. These small books imitated widely used Latin grammars and were intended to help English-speaking students learn Latin and foreigners learn English. The first such grammar was William Bullokar's *Pamphlet for Grammar* (1586). Although it would not compare well with the best grammars of our language written today, four hundred years later, it was no small achievement for its day. To write a grammar of a language for which there were no other grammar books was an accomplishment.

By the end of the seventeenth century, a great many grammar books had been written, and more continued to appear through the eighteenth and nineteenth centuries. Difficult as it may be for some of us to understand today, English speakers were fascinated by grammars of their language. Popular as grammar books were, however, readers and writers of English were even more interested in dictionaries.

The first English dictionary appeared at the beginning of the seventeenth century. In 1604, Robert Cawdrey published *A Table Alphabeticall . . . of Hard Usuall English Wordes*. As that title suggests, the earliest dictionaries made no effort to list all the words in the English language. Rather they were simply lists of "hard" words—learned, often borrowed words—that a reader might come across but that would be difficult for the ordinary person to understand.

The first dictionaries gave only a familiar synonym for each hard word. Gradually, dictionaries began to expand the number of words they listed and the kinds of information they included about each word. Definitions increased from single-word synonyms to fuller descriptions of meaning. In the eighteenth century, efforts were made to include all the words of the language and to define all their uses. New sorts of information added to the entry for a word included its etymology (origin and history), its part of speech, quotations illustrating its use, and its pronunciation.

As English dictionaries increased the number of words they included and the information they gave about each word, they became better and better. Today, English has the best dictionaries of any language on earth. The greatest of English dictionaries is the *Oxford English Dictionary* in twenty large volumes. It attempts to trace the history of all English words from their first appearance in the language until today. The biggest dictionary a high school student is likely to need is one like the *Webster's Third New International Dictionary,* and for most ordinary uses, smaller desk dictionaries serve very well.

The Battle of Styles: Ornate vs. Plain

The seventeenth century was an age of social unrest. In England, the Cavaliers, who supported the king and the established Anglican church, were opposed by the Puritans, who supported Parliament and a congregational form of church. The Cavaliers dressed elegantly, ate with gusto, attended the theater, and generally lived a high life. Puritans, on the other hand, dressed and ate plainly, thought the theater was wicked, and generally lived sober, God-fearing, dull lives. There was bound to be trouble between them. And so there was, with

go.hrw.com
HRW
LEO 12-English Language

the Puritans eventually gaining control of Parliament, executing the king, closing the theaters, and establishing a military and church dictatorship in England.

The difference in lifestyles between the Cavaliers and the Puritans was echoed in a difference in language styles: an ornate style versus a plain style. However, there was by no means a simple equivalence between Cavaliers and ornate style on the one hand and Puritans and plain style on the other. Indeed, in some cases, it was the other way around.

The ornate style used many words borrowed from foreign languages and learned words, thus creating what were scornfully called "inkhorn terms." An inkhorn was a container made from the horn of an animal and was used to hold ink for writing with a quill pen. **Inkhorn terms** were words that scholars might use in writing, but that seemed out of place in ordinary conversation. It was such inkhorn terms that were listed in the dictionaries of "hard" words.

Another aspect of the ornate style was called **euphuism** (after Euphues, a character in two books by John Lyly, who used alliteration, balanced expressions, antitheses, fantastic similes, mythological allusions, and other verbal tricks to create an artificial elegance of language). An example is the following sentence, in which Euphues cites some proverbs

> Popular as grammar books were, readers and writers of English were even more interested in dictionaries.

against rash and excessive action: "The vine watered with wine is soon withered, the blossom in the fattest ground is quickly blasted, the goat the fatter she is the less fertile she is; yea, man the more witty he is the less happy he is."

Still another aspect of the ornate style was the **metaphysical conceit,** an extended and exaggerated metaphor, such as that in Donne's poem "A Valediction: Forbidding Mourning."

Plain style, on the other hand, valued simplicity and clarity. It came to be favored especially by those with scientific interests, something that is natural enough. If you are going to describe a scientific experiment or observation, you are less interested in having people admire your cleverness with language than in having them understand what you did or saw. Scientists try not to intrude personally into the object of study. Their work and their language are supposed to be impersonal and public.

In the metaphysical or euphuistic ideal, on the other hand, the reader sees the world through the highly personal eyes of the writer. The aim is to surprise the reader by revealing the world in a fresh way. Thus, the two styles, contrasting sharply in their aims, contrast also in their techniques.

The plain style was promoted especially through the work of the Royal Society. Founded in

the second half of the seventeenth century, the Royal Society is one of the oldest organizations in Europe for "improving natural knowledge," that is, promoting scientific study. Members of the Society did much to combat the excesses of ornate style. As a result of their work and example, today the plain style is the unchallenged ideal for good prose.

What Is Style?

Although a plain style is our ideal today, we still find other kinds of style in use. What makes a style?

When we talk or write, we have a choice of ways to express our meaning. For example, if we want to mention our male parent, we can call him father, dad, papa, sire, pater, pop, my old man, or various other names. Obviously, those words, although they all mean the same thing in that they can all refer to the same person, are very different from one another in how they are used. If you are filling out an employment questionnaire, you are not going to be asked, "What is your daddy's name?" If you are telling a friend why you can't use the family car tonight, you are probably not going to say, "My sire is using it."

The options we take in talking or writing determine the style of our language. **Style** is the choice we make among alternative ways of saying the same thing. Among the elements that make up a style are options like these:

1. **Short and simple versus long and complex**

sentences. A sequence of short, simple sentences is likely to seem childish or simple-minded, but many long, complex ones are likely to seem confused.

2. **Active versus passive verbs,** as in "The Puritans chopped off King Charles's head" (active) versus "King Charles's head was chopped off" (passive). Passive verbs are especially useful for telling that something happened without telling who did it. They are favorites of scientific and bureaucratic writers, but many other people find them mealy-mouthed.

3. **Direct versus qualified statements.** Direct statements tell the facts just as they are. Qualified statements add words like *perhaps, possibly, it seems, it would appear, it is likely that, generally, make an effort to,* and so on. Writers may think that using qualifications will get them off the hook if they say something wrong. But readers find the result wishy-washy.

4. **Noun- versus verb-centeredness.** We can *agree* on something, or *reach an agreement* about it. We can *wash* the car, or *give it a wash*. We can *decide* to go, or *come to a decision* to do so. We can *promise* our friends something, or *make a promise to* them *about* it. When we put the main meaning into the verb, we have a more direct and forceful sentence, but

putting the main meaning into a noun after the verb lets us emphasize it.

5. **Plain versus fancy words.** Plain words like *newspaper, home, watery,* and *to run* are more comfortable than fancy words like *periodical, domicile, aqueous,* and *to course.* There are times, to be sure, when we want our language to be fancy. The danger in using fancy words, however, is that we will use them not quite right, and the result will be, not fancy, but unintentionally funny.

Try It Out

1. **Using a dictionary.** The English dictionary began its development during the seventeenth century with lists of "hard" words and their meanings. Look at the entry for a word in a modern desk dictionary. You may choose any word you like, but the following are suggestions:

atom   dwarf   hopefully
map   sphinx   learn

What different kinds of information does the entry give you about the word? To start off, you will find the spelling and pronunciation of the word. What else? (You will find somewhat different kinds of information in the entries for various words and for the same word in various dictionaries.)

2. **Recognizing allusions.** Allusions, or references, to the King James Bible and the Book of Common Prayer abound in the English lan-

guage. What do the following expressions mean? Find the passage in which each expression was originally used (it is indicated in parentheses).

a. My brother's keeper (Genesis 4:9)
b. A stranger in a strange land (Exodus 2:22)
c. A land flowing with milk and honey (Exodus 3:8)
d. Pride goes before a fall. (Proverbs 16:18)
e. Put one's house in order (2 Kings 20:1; Isaiah 38:1)
f. Escape by the skin of one's teeth (Job 19:20)
g. The meek shall inherit the earth. (Psalm 37:11)
h. Cast your bread upon the waters (Ecclesiastes 11:1)
i. Beat swords into plowshares (Isaiah 2:4)
j. Feet of clay (Daniel 2:33)

3. **Comparing styles.** Compare the style either of John Donne's "A Valediction: Forbidding Mourning" (page 248) and Ben Jonson's "Song: To Celia" (page 258), or of the King James account of the temptation and fall of Adam and Eve (page 416) and Milton's account of the fall of Satan in *Paradise Lost* (page 441). Note differences in vocabulary, length and complexity of sentences, repeated versus varied patterns of language, simple and direct statements versus involved and indirect ones, and the use of descriptive adjectives and adverbs. Which work is in plain style? Which is ornate?

BUILDING YOUR PORTFOLIO

Writer's Workshop

The history
of the written
word is rich an

Page 1

EXPOSITORY WRITING

ANALYZING CAUSES AND EFFECTS

Thomas De Quincey wondered for years why the knocking at the gate after Duncan's murder had such a solemnly awful effect, and playgoers debate to this day what drove Macbeth and Lady Macbeth to such bloody abandon. Analysis of **causes** and **effects** in both literature and life is never ending.

Prewriting

1. **Checking your Writer's Notebook.** By doing the Writer's Notebook activities on pages 390, 409, 427, and 450, you may have already completed the prewriting for an essay that analyzes causes and effects. Check back over your Writer's Notebook entries. You can repeat any activity to add to or improve what you've already done, or you can proceed with the prewriting activities that follow.

2. **Finding a topic.** The two questions that cause-and-effect writing answers are *Why?* and *What's the result?* You do not have to answer both in your essay, though you may—for example, De Quincey explains why Shakespeare "invented" the knocking at the gate and also describes its emotional and theatrical effect (page 330). To find a topic to write about, consider

   • **events:** occurrences, such as Macduff's leaving his family in *Macbeth*

   • **situations,** or **phenomena:** ongoing conditions, such as increasing vandalism in a community

   • **trends:** changes over time, such as the availability of CD-ROM technology

3. **Literature or life?** Like De Quincey, you may want to explain something that intrigues (or irritates or moves) you in a poem or play: *Why does Macduff leave his family? What are the effects of this event, in the play or on the audience?* You may also pose a "What if?" question and predict plausible results: *What if Lady Macbeth had not gone mad?* Or you might extend a literary work: *How will Banquo's son react when Malcolm is crowned?*

   For a real-life topic, you'll write best about something that concerns you or stirs your curiosity: *Why are daytime talk shows so popular? What will happen when your TV is also a computer? Why is your advanced math class three-fourths male?*

Technology HELP

See Writer's Workshop 2 CD-ROM. *Assignment: Cause and Effect.*

ASSIGNMENT
Write an essay analyzing the causes and/or effects of an event, situation, or trend.

AIM
To explain causes, effects, or both; to persuade your readers.

AUDIENCE
Your classmates or people affected by the subject.

Notice that your topic may have a broad or a personal focus. Also consider more abstract speculation. For example, *Macbeth* brings up the traits of ambition, leadership, and dominance, suggesting topics such as *What creates a good leader? What are the effects of friendship with a bold, dominant person?*

4. **Mapping the possibilities.** A visual map of ideas can open your mind to many perspectives. One technique is to begin by writing and circling a statement of your topic (the event, situation, or trend). Analyze it. What produced it? What happened (or might happen) because of it? Then write down *any* possibilities, showing the connections with arrows. You might discover a chain of causes and effects: *A causes B, B causes C,* and so on. Stimulate your thinking with the Strategies for Elaboration on the left.

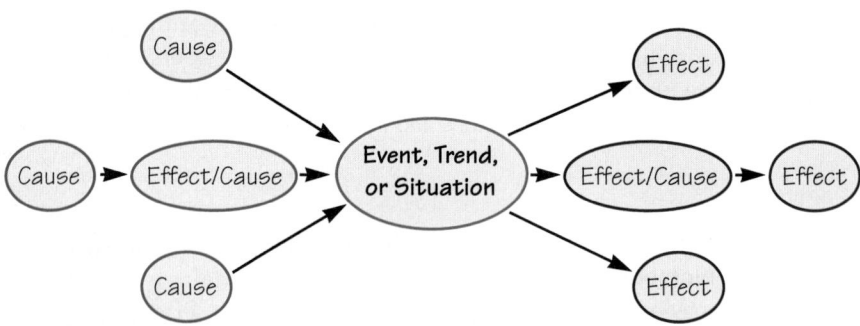

5. **Identifying a thesis.** After generating ideas, assess them. First, have you mapped out the situation or event to your satisfaction? If not, you need more ideas or another topic. Next, decide on a thesis for your essay: a statement of your topic that clearly indicates if you'll discuss causes, effects, or both.

6. **The evidence, please.** In this paper, you are conjecturing, or advancing an explanation. You must convince your readers that the causes or effects you propose are *plausible and likely*—and that means providing solid evidence or support. Stating your opinion isn't enough.

FoxTrot

by Bill Amend

FOXTROT ©1994 Bill Amend. Reprinted with permission of UNIVERSAL PRESS SYNDICATE. All rights reserved.

To compile your evidence, you might use a two-column chart. On the left, write the causes or effects you've chosen from your map. To the right of each one, write all your ideas for evidence, as well as objections and counterarguments.

Topic: *Why do Donalbain and Malcolm keep silent and flee in fear right after their father's murder?*

Causes	Supporting Evidence
shock	They feel "strong sorrow" but tears aren't "brewed" yet— too soon. **Objection?** They're thinking pretty well for being in shock. **Counterargument:** Yes, but shock suspends horror; people function "normally," and then they collapse.
suspicion	Macduff raised the question of why Macbeth killed the guards. Malcolm: Fake grief is easy if there's a motive.

Communications Handbook HELP

See Taking Notes and Documenting Sources.

7. **Being believable.** Choosing evidence also means considering who's reading it. What support will your audience find compelling, thought-provoking, or in line with its interests? And no matter who your readers are, you must come across as reasonable and trustworthy. You don't have to be stiffly serious; you might even be funny about the effects of forbidding off-campus lunches, for example. Your **tone,** however, must convey assurance and conviction.

Drafting

1. **The introduction.** Your essay should open in a way that will capture your readers' attention, while also quickly getting to what you're explaining. Always describe or define the situation clearly, in as much detail as your readers need. Classmates will need minimal scene setting for Malcolm and Donalbain's escape in *Macbeth*, but if your topic is the potential effects of televising court proceedings, readers will need sufficient data and information to see and understand current and past court situations. Also include your thesis statement.

2. **The body.** Redraw your cause-effect map to use as a good guide for writing. Take the causes or effects you've settled on, determine their order, number them, and redraw the map with numbers included. Refer to this map as you write your draft. Here are some general rules and tips for organizing the body of your essay:

   • Discuss causes before effects.

   • Use chronological order for cause-effect chains and for some topics spread out over time.

   • Otherwise, choose an arrangement that's easy to follow and persuasive: least/most important, least/most familiar, personal/social concerns, concrete/abstract explanations.

Revision
S T R A T E G I E S

To improve your opening and closing, read them together. (Skip everything else.) Could you link them in some way? Is one stronger or clearer than the other? Why? If necessary, add or cut details.

Communications Handbook
H E L P

See Proofreading.

- Answer objections to a cause or effect along with the cause or effect.
- Bring up alternative explanations either before or after your own. ("Before" gets them out of the way; "after" lets you refer to your better ideas.)

3. **The conclusion.** Write a conclusion that sums up your explanation of causes and/or effects. You might also refer to your introduction.

Evaluating and Revising

1. **Peer review.** Read like a skeptic, someone who's tough to convince and itching to find a legitimate flaw. (But when the explanation's good, admit it and point out why.) Look for sound logic. Beware of

   - **oversimplification:** having too few causes or effects to explain the situation, or mistaking a contributing cause for a necessary one

   - **the *post hoc, ergo propter hoc* fallacy ("after this, therefore because of this"):** assuming that if A preceded B, then A must have caused B

2. **Self-evaluation.** If you do get objections from reviewers, answer them calmly. Put a check mark on your paper by each spot where you include one of the features given in the Evaluation Criteria to the left. Then go back and revise your paper to include any of the features you didn't find.

"Your Majesty, according to our study the shoe was lost for want of a nail, the horse was lost for want of a shoe, and the rider was lost for want of a horse, but the kingdom we lost because of overregulation."

Language Workshop

The history
of the written
word is rich and

Page 1

EFFECTIVE TRANSITIONS: CONNECTING IDEAS

An essay that speculates about causes and effects delves into relationships. When you write, you're leading readers not just to see the facts or events *X, Y, Z,* but exactly how *X, Y,* and *Z* are connected. If readers must labor to understand the links, you won't be very convincing. Thus, **transitions,** ways to connect ideas, are extremely important in cause-effect writing. Notice how the boldface words in the following paragraph make it easy to follow; they create coherence both by connecting words and thoughts and by stating relationships.

> Immediately after their father's murder, Malcolm and Donalbain don't even cry. **The two brothers** speak to no one and hastily leave Scotland in fear—**even though** the obvious murderers are dead. Are **they two** cold, uncaring **children**? Or are there **other explanations** for **this behavior**? One **explanation** is simple: shock. Malcolm himself asks, "Why do we hold our tongues . . . ?," **so** we know he is not just **upset and confused.**

Techniques for Creating Effective Transitions

1. Use a pronoun, noun, or synonym to refer to a word or phrase used earlier. Notice how *the two brothers* and *children* refer to Malcolm and Donalbain and how *this behavior* and *upset and confused* are related.

2. Repeat a word used earlier. For example, *they two* refers to "the two brothers," and *explanation* refers to "other explanations."

3. Use transitional expressions that express relationship. In the paragraph above, *even though* and *so* link ideas. Here are some other examples of transitional expressions:
   - cause-effect: *as a result, because, consequently, since, therefore*
   - time: *after, eventually, finally, immediately, meanwhile, next, then*
   - importance: *first, last, mainly, most important, primarily*

Writer's Workshop Follow-Up: Revision

Take another look at the cause-effect essay you wrote for page 459. Have you implied a link that you need to state directly? Have you signaled to the reader what is important or in what sequence events occurred? Have you used pronouns and nouns to add variety and to refer to previous words and ideas? Working with a writing partner, underscore the transitions you've used. Then, go back and add transitions to make your sentences and paragraphs flow as clearly and smoothly as possible.

Technology HELP

See Language Workshop CD-ROM. *Key word entry: transitions.*

Try It Out

Turn these sentences into a clear paragraph by inserting logical, effective transitions. You may combine sentences, add words and phrases, and replace words and phrases with better ones.

For three years now the Panthers have made it all the way to state championships. And they have lost in the first round. The Panthers have obviously been good. Why do they keep losing here? One explanation leaps out when you study the stats. In each game either three or four fouled out in the first half. The best are on the bench, not on the floor. First, that's simply demoralizing for others. The opposing team gets more free shots.

Reading for Life

Analyzing and Creating Graphics

Situation

You've been impressed by the power of the word and have volunteered to tutor students in reading. In an effort to motivate your students, you want to show them rates of literacy in various parts of the world. You've gathered information and have decided to display it in a graph or table.

Strategies

Analyze your data, and choose an appropriate kind of graph or table in which to display it.

- Make sure you know exactly what your data show. All data on a single subject should be displayed in the same format.

- Choose a **line graph, bar graph, pie graph,** or **statistical table.** A **line graph** shows changes in one or more entities across time. A **bar graph** compares two or more entities in relation to quantity and time. For example, a bar graph might show population figures for several countries over two years. A **pie graph** shows percentages of a whole. A pie graph might show the percentages of people in a single country who practice different religions. In a **statistical table,** similar kinds of data are displayed in columns. A statistical table might show the populations of various cities within a country.

```
Rates of Literacy for Various Countries,
   1985 and 1998, in percentages

Democratic Republic of Congo (formerly Zaire):
   1985, 40%; 1998, 72%
India: 1985, 36%; 1998, 52%
Indonesia: 1985, 64%; 1998, 86.3%
Japan: 1985, 99%; 1998, 99.9%
Kenya: 1985, 40%; 1998, 69%
People's Republic of China: 1985, 75%; 1998, 73%
Saudi Arabia: 1985, 15%; 1998, 65%
South Africa: 1985, 77%; 1998, 76%
Sudan: 1985, 20%; 1998, 32%
United Kingdom: 1985, 99%; 1998, 99%
United States: 1985, 99%; 1998, 97.9%
```

Graph the information.

- Find a line, bar, or pie graph or a statistical table to use as a model. For a line or bar graph you'll need to create a horizontal axis that shows periods of time and a vertical axis that shows numbers or percentages. For a pie graph you'll need to scale segments of the graph to the quantities you're displaying. For a statistical table you'll need to label the columns.

Label the graph or table.

- Arrange data in a logical order, and label every part of the graph so that readers can recognize the information and interpret its meaning. Provide a title for the entire graph, and if necessary, provide a key that explains any special symbols, colors, or abbreviations.

Using the Strategies

1. Which two kinds of graphic formats would best display the data in the box above?

2. At what increments would you mark the percentages of literacy rates on a bar graph?

3. How could you best display the growth in literacy in each country for the two periods?

4. If you also had data on the population of each country, how could you change your graph or table to include that information?

Extending the Strategies

- Create a graph or table to display information about people in your community, state, or nation, such as their ethnic identification, level of education, or religious affiliation.

- Find and interpret graphic displays of information on a subject that interests you.

Learning for Life

A New Curriculum

Problem

The term *Renaissance person* is still used to describe someone who is skilled and knowledgeable in many areas—the arts and the sciences. Thomas Jefferson, the third president of the United States, was called a Renaissance man. Jefferson was a skilled writer, statesman, musician, inventor, architect, and philosopher. What would a person need to *know* and be able to *do* to be considered a Renaissance person today? How should we educate children to be "Renaissance people"?

Project

Identify a real person, or create an imaginary one, who exemplifies the characteristics of a modern-day Renaissance person. Suggest educational innovations to produce "Renaissance people."

Preparation

1. Working with a small group, brainstorm to generate a list of the areas in which a person of the twenty-first century should be skilled and knowledgeable.

2. Taking each area in turn, work together to establish the criteria necessary to qualify as a new Renaissance person. Be as specific as you can. If one area is languages, for example, should the person be able to speak, read, and write more than one language? Are two languages sufficient? Make it a group decision.

3. Review the curricula in all major subject areas in your school. Form a committee to study them, and make recommendations.

Procedure

1. Decide whether you'll develop your presentation around a real person or create an imaginary character. If you decide on a real person, someone may come to mind immediately, or you may need to do some research. To create an imaginary character, you can draw on the methods of direct and indirect characterization you've studied in this book, and in your composition text.

2. Think, too, about whether you'll approach this activity straightforwardly or handle it with humor. Deciding now which mode of presentation you'll use (see below) can help you choose the approach you prefer.

Presentation

Use one of the following formats (or another that your teacher approves):

1. **Write a Proposal**

   Focus on your study of the school's curricula, and write a proposal for revised curricula for all major areas. Open with an overview of your proposal and a summation of your recommendations. Describe in your introduction the kind of learning a Renaissance person of the twenty-first century will require.

2. **Coming to Life**

   Stage a one-person show depicting the Renaissance person you've chosen or created. Your production can be as simple or elaborate as you like. Present your show live, or arrange to have a friend videotape it to show at a schoolwide assembly or a school-board meeting.

3. **Images and Essences**

   Create a collage that conveys the multifaceted characteristics of a Renaissance person of today. Combine various objects and materials such as photographs, scraps of material, words—anything you find meaningful—using shapes, colors, and textures to capture the person's essence.

Processing

Did doing this activity change your ideas about what should be taught in the schools? Did it make you want to be a modern-day Renaissance person? Write a reflection for your portfolio.

The Restoration and the Eighteenth Century
1660-1800

Coronation Procession of Charles II to Westminster from the Tower of London (detail) (1661) by Dirck Stoop.

The Restoration and the Eighteenth Century

by C. F. Main

There are seven groups in English society
1. *The Great, who live profusely.*
2. *The Rich, who live very plentifully.*
3. *The Middle Sort, who live well.*
4. *The Working Trades, who labor hard, but feel no want.*
5. *The Country People, Farmers, etc., who fare indifferently.*
6. *The Poor, that fare hard.*
7. *The Miserable, that really pinch and suffer want.*

—*Daniel Defoe*

Southwark Fair (18th century) by William Hogarth.
Tate Gallery, London.

From 1660 to 1800, people from England and Europe were pouring into North America. These eager voyagers not only sought freedom from religious and political persecution; they also saw money to be made in the American continent's rich lands and forests—in furs, tobacco, and logs for British sailing ships. They also began transporting Africans for use as slave labor in the Americas. In 1775, these Colonies rebelled against British rule and eventually won their freedom. The United States was a raw, vigorous, brand-new nation. Across the Atlantic, things were very different.

In 1660, England was utterly exhausted by nearly twenty years of civil war. By 1700, it had lived through a devastating plague and a fire that left more than two thirds of Londoners homeless. By the middle of the eighteenth century, however, England had settled into a period of calm and order, at least among the upper classes. Despite the loss of the American Colonies, the reinvigorated British military forces established new settlements around the globe. And though life for many was wretched, the middle class grew. Throughout this long period in a very old nation with tastes much more refined than raw, British men and women also produced many brilliant works of philosophy, art, and literature.

This long period of time in England—from 1660 to 1800—has been given several labels: the Augustan Age, the Neoclassical period, the Enlightenment, and the Age of Reason. Each of these labels applies to some characteristics of these 140 years, but none applies to all.

> I would have been glad to have lived under my woodside, and to have kept a flock of sheep, rather than to have undertaken this government.
>
> —Oliver Cromwell, speaking to Parliament, 1658

> We, therefore, the Representatives of the United States of America, in General Congress, Assembled, . . . do, in the Name, and by Authority of the good People of these Colonies, solemnly Publish and Declare, . . . that all political Connection between them and the State of Great-Britain, is and ought to be totally dissolved. . . .
>
> —Declaration of Independence, July 4, 1776, Philadelphia

> Nothing of importance happened today.
>
> —Diary entry reportedly made by King George III, July 4, 1776

In contrast to the vital Colonies of North America, England was exhausted by war and disease in 1660. But by the end of the eighteenth century, England had transformed itself.

Augustan and Neoclassical: Comparisons with Rome

Many people liked to find similarities between England in this period and ancient Rome, especially during the reign of the emperor Octavian (63 B.C.–A.D. 14). When he became emperor, Octavian was given the high-sounding name *Augustus,* meaning "the exalted one." Augustus restored peace and order to Rome after Julius Caesar's assassination. Similarly, the Stuart monarchs of England restored peace and order to England after the civil wars that led up to the execution of King Charles I in 1649, and that continued even after the king was dead.

The Execution of King Charles I at White-hall, London, January 30, 1649. Woodcut.

The Granger Collection, New York.

The Restoration and the Eighteenth Century, 1660–1800

LITERARY EVENTS

1660–1669

In France, Jean-Baptiste Molière's *The Misanthrope* first performed, 1666

London theaters re-open; actresses appear on stage for the first time in England, 1660s

Samuel Pepys begins his diary, 1660

1670–1689

Aphra Behn publishes *Oroonoko,* an early anti-slavery novel, 1688

Poems of Bashō help popularize haiku poetry in Japan, 1680s

John Dryden's *All for Love, or The World Well Lost* first produced, 1678

John Bunyan publishes *The Pilgrim's Progress,* Part 1 (Part 2 appears in 1684), 1678

1690–1709

First issue of **Addison** and **Steele**'s *The Tatler* printed (*The Spectator* is begun in 1711), 1709

In Mexico, Sor Juana Inés de la Cruz publishes *Respuesta a Sor Filotea* (Reply to Sister Philotea), a defense of women's intellectual rights, 1691

1710–1739

Swift publishes *A Modest Proposal,* protesting English treatment of Irish poor, 1729

Jonathan Swift publishes *Gulliver's Travels,* 1726

Daniel Defoe publishes *Robinson Crusoe,* 1719

Alexander Pope writes *The Rape of the Lock,* 1712

CULTURAL/HISTORICAL EVENTS

1660–1669

Charles II proclaimed king of England (crowned in 1661), 1660

In Massachusetts, John Eliot translates the Bible into Algonquian, 1661

Plague claims more than 68,000 people in London, 1665

Great Fire destroys much of London, 1666

• *The Great Fire of London* (1666) by an unknown artist.

1670–1689

Ashanti empire formed in Africa, c. 1670s

English Test Act bans Roman Catholics from public office, 1673

James II, king of England, 1685–1688, tries to re-establish Catholic Church

Newton publishes *Philosophiae Naturalis Principia Mathematica* (Mathematical Principles of Natural Philosophy), 1687

"Glorious Revolution": James II succeeded by Protestant rulers William and Mary, 1688

1690–1709

• **Turtle-shaped Ashanti emblem** (17th or 18th century) from Ghana. Gold.

John Locke publishes *An Essay Concerning Human Understanding,* 1690

English Parliament enacts Penal Laws, depriving Irish Catholics of civil rights, 1695

England, Wales, and Scotland politically unified as Great Britain, 1707

1710–1739

George I, a German who could not speak English, becomes king of England, 1714

In England, Lady Mary Wortley Montagu introduces Turkish practice of inoculation against smallpox, 1718

• **Newton's reflecting telescope** (1688). Royal Society, London.

• Frontispiece of Phillis Wheatley's *Poems on Various Subjects, Religious and Moral* (1773).

In France, **Voltaire** publishes *Candide,* 1759

Samuel Johnson publishes his *Dictionary of the English Language,* 1755

Thomas Gray publishes "Elegy Written in a Country Churchyard," 1751

Samuel Richardson publishes *Pamela, or Virtue Rewarded,* 1740

African American poet Phillis Wheatley's *Poems on Various Subjects, Religious and Moral* published in London, 1773

Oliver Goldsmith publishes *The Vicar of Wakefield,* 1766

Wordsworth and **Coleridge** publish *Lyrical Ballads,* 1798

Mary Wollstonecraft publishes *A Vindication of the Rights of Woman,* 1792

James Boswell's *The Life of Samuel Johnson* published, 1791

Olaudah Equiano, once held in slavery in Colonial America, publishes his autobiography in Britain, 1789

| 1740–1764 | 1765–1779 | 1780–1800 |

George III, crowned king of England, 1760, becomes known as the king who lost the American Colonies

In France, Denis Diderot begins work on the *Encyclopédie,* 1747

Benjamin Franklin invents the lightning rod, 1752

Catherine II ("Catherine the Great") becomes czarina of Russia, 1762

• *Catherine the Great* (1762–1769) by Vigilius Erichsen.

British Parliament passes Stamp Act for taxing American Colonies, 1765

Mozart writes *Symphony No. 1* at age nine, 1765

• Teapot reading "Stamp Act Repeal'd" (English, 1766).

Boston Tea Party protests tax on tea, 1773

American Revolution begins, 1775

James Watt develops the steam engine, 1780s

• French Revolution button (c. 1789–1793) translating to "Liberty or Death." Brass with miniatures painted on ivory.

French Revolution begins with storming of the Bastille, 1789

British crush Irish nationalist rebellion led by Theobald Wolfe Tone, 1798

Rosetta stone (key to deciphering Egyptian hieroglyphics) found in Egypt, 1799

Napoleon heads revolutionary government in France, 1799

King Charles II of England (c. 1675) by (school of) Nicholas Dixon. Vellum.

Fitzwilliam Museum, University of Cambridge, England.

The people of both Rome and England were weary of war, suspicious of revolutionaries and radicals, and ready to settle down, make money, and enjoy life. The Roman Senate had hailed Augustus as the second founder of Rome; in 1660, the English people brought back the son of Charles I from his exile in France, crowned him as King Charles II, and hailed him as their savior. As a warning to revolutionaries, they dug up the corpse of Oliver Cromwell, who had ruled England between Charles I and Charles II, and cut off its head. The monarchy was restored without shedding a drop of blood.

In this age, many English writers consciously modeled their works on the old Latin classics, which they had studied in school and university. These writings that imitate Latin works were called neoclassical—"new classical." The classics, it was generally agreed, were valuable because they represented what was permanent and universal in human experience. All educated people knew the Latin classics better than they knew their own English literature.

> **With the restoration of the king, England likened itself to Augustan Rome: Both had entered a period of calm and order after an era of political turmoil.**

Reason and Enlightenment: Asking "How?"

Labels like the "Age of Reason" and the "Enlightenment" reveal how people were gradually changing their view of themselves and the world. For instance, Shakespeare, the greatest writer of the Renaissance, expressed a commonly held view when he described the unusual events that preceded the assassination of Julius Caesar—"a tempest dropping fire" and "blue lightning." These unnatural events, says a character in the play *Julius Caesar,* are "instruments of fear and warning." For centuries people had believed that before a great public disaster like the assassination of a ruler, the earth and sky gave warnings. People believed that unusual events such as earthquakes, comets, and even babies born with malformations had some kind of meaning, and that they were sent as punishment for past misdoings or as warning of future troubles. People did not ask, "*How* did this unusual event take place?" but "*Why* did this unusual event take place, and what does it *mean*?"

Gradually, during the Enlightenment, people stopped asking "Why?" questions and started asking "How?" questions, and the answers to those questions—about everything from the workings of the human body to the laws of the universe—became much less frightening and superstitious.

A Scene from "The Beggar's Opera" (c. 1728) by William Hogarth. Oil. Collection of Paul Mellon, National Gallery, Washington.

By 1664, wigs and makeup were the rage for men and women. Powdered and stuffed with horsehair, women's headdresses grew to enormous proportions. Jewels, flowers, ribbons, plumage, and even fruit decorated these monstrous structures—reaching two to three feet in height. Men also wore their hair in pigtails—tied with a bow and powdered. In 1795, a tax was created to generate income from the rich—a guinea on every powdered head. Cosmetics were made from ingredients such as borax, vinegar, bread, eggs, and pigeon wings. Black patches, or fake beauty marks, were an important fashion accessory.

The wealthy divided the year between London, country estates, and health resorts. A whirlwind of masked balls, dances, and formal dinner parties, known as the London season, ended by the first week in June. Summers were often spent in seaside towns and at freshwater springs. Daniel Defoe described one trendy health resort: "[The attendants] present you with a little floating dish like a basin, in which the lady puts her handkerchief and a nosegay, of late the snuffbox is added, and some patches; through the bath occasioning a little perspiration, the patches do not stick as kindly as they should."

It was a careless, pleasure-seeking time centered on dancing, dining, drinking, theatergoing, card playing, and gambling. As is always the case with fashion, change was inevitable. By the end of the eighteenth century, the lifestyle of the wealthy leaned toward simplicity and sobriety.

Embroidered casket (c. 1665). Lady Lever Art Gallery, Port Sunlight, England.

For instance, the astronomer Edmond Halley (1656–1742) took the terror out of celestial phenomena by calculating when they were going to occur. He computed, with "immense labor," he said, the orbit of the comet that still bears his name. He predicted it would appear in 1758, 1834, 1910, and 1986—and it did. And how did he know it would reappear at seventy-six-year intervals? Because that was the time it took to complete its orbit. Such a reasonable, mathematical explanation made no connection at all between the comet and human affairs.

> The truth is, the science of Nature has been already too long made only a work of the brain and the fancy: It is now high time that it should return to the plainness and soundness of observations on material and obvious things.
>
> —Robert Hooke

Natural phenomena were increasingly explained by scientific observation as people began to ask how things happened in the natural world.

The Birth of Modern English Prose: Stripping Down

In 1662, to answer questions about the universe, King Charles II chartered a group of philosophers: the Royal Society of London for the Promotion of Natural Knowledge. Among other things, its members called for a kind of writing that was precise, exact, and not decorated with the elaborate metaphors or odd allusions of their predecessors. Above all, these new scientists wanted to shorten the endless sentences of their predecessors. And so in this age was born what we think of as modern English prose.

While the Royal Society affected the course of English prose, the "founder and first true master" of modern English prose was John Dryden (1631–1700), an all-around man of letters. Because of his influence, the era in which Dryden lived is often referred to as the "age of Dryden." In the *Essay of Dramatic Poesy* (1668), a major critical work, Dryden sought to "vindicate the honor of our English writers." He also wrote comedies, as well as the best tragedy of the day, *All for Love* (1677), a neoclassical version of Shakespeare's *Antony and Cleopatra*. Among Dryden's achievements in poetry were perfecting the technique of English poetry, regularizing meter, and making diction precise. He was a master of explaining ideas, of reasoning in verse. Dryden set the standards that most of the poets of the next century aspired to.

Under the influence of the Royal Society and John Dryden, English prose became more precise, exact, and plain.

Changes in Religion: More Questions

The new scientific and rational explanations of phenomena gradually began to affect some people's religious views. If comets were not sent by God to warn people, perhaps God didn't interfere at all in human affairs. Perhaps the universe was like an immense piece of clockwork, set in motion by a Creator who more or less withdrew from this perfect mechanism and let it run by itself. Such a view, part of a complex of ideas known as Deism, could make people feel self-satisfied and complacent,

Interior of Henry VII's Chapel, Westminster Abbey (c. 1750) by Canaletto.

Museum of London.

especially if they believed, as Alexander Pope noted in his long poem *Essay on Man* (page 524), that "Whatever is, is right." Some philosophers even argued that "In this best of all possible worlds, . . . all is for the best"—a view that the French writer Voltaire ridiculed in his novel *Candide* (1759). (See page 538.) But, other than a tiny minority of "enlightened" rationalists and materialists, most people, including great philosophers and scientists like Sir Isaac Newton (1642–1727) and John Locke (1632–1704), remained religious. Christianity in its various forms continued to exercise an undiminished power over almost all Europeans in this period, just as it had in the Middle Ages and the Renaissance.

> Nature and Nature's laws lay hid in night:
> God said, Let Newton be! and all was light.
>
> —Alexander Pope, epitaph
> intended for Sir Isaac Newton

The new science influenced religion: A movement called Deism viewed the universe as a perfect mechanism, which God had built and left to run on its own.

Covent Garden with St. Paul's Church (detail) (18th century) by Balthasar Nebot.

Guildhall Art Gallery, London.

Religion and Politics: Repression of Minority Sects

Religion determined people's politics in this period. Charles II reestablished the Anglican Church as the official church of the country, which it continues to be in England to this day. (In the United States, this denomination is called the Episcopal Church.) With the approval of Parliament, the king attempted to outlaw all the various Puritan and Independent sects—dozens of them, all happily disagreeing among themselves—that had caused so much uproar during the preceding thirty years. Persecution of these various sects continued throughout the eighteenth century.

> A brave world, sir, full of religion, knavery, and change: We shall shortly see better days.
>
> —Aphra Behn

When Charles II reestablished the Anglican Church as the official church of the country, other sects were outlawed and persecuted.

The Bloodless Revolution: Protestants from Now On

Charles II had a number of illegitimate children, but no legal heir. When he died in 1685, he was succeeded by his brother James II, a practicing Roman Catholic. Most English people were utterly opposed to James. After all, it was widely believed that Roman Catholics had not only set fire to London and caused other disasters, but were actively plotting to hand the country over to the pope. When James's queen produced a little boy—a Catholic heir—pressure on the royal family became so great that, in 1688, they suddenly fled to France. Thus, the so-called Glorious (bloodless) Revolution (1688) was accomplished. James II was succeeded by his Protestant daughter, Mary, and her Dutch husband,

William of Orange. Ever since, the rulers of England have been, at least in name, Anglicans.

> *During the "Glorious Revolution," Charles's Roman Catholic successor was forced into exile, and Protestant rule resumed with the ascension of William of Orange and Mary to the throne.*

Addicted to the Theater

For more than twenty years, while the Puritans held power, the theaters in England were closed. During the exile of the royal court in France, Charles had become addicted to theatergoing, so one of the first things he did after regaining his throne was to repeal the ban on play performances, imposed in 1642.

After the reestablishment of the monarchy, these major events occurred in the arts and sciences:

- With King Charles II's return to the throne and a period of increased stability, writers drew on the "new classical" style of Roman, Greek, and Latin models.

- Thinkers in this Age of Reason emphasized logic, scientific observation, and factual explanation. These rational explanations affected some people's religious views.

- Literary tastes turned to wit and satire to expose excesses and moral corruption.

- In journalism, the periodical essay developed, commenting on public manners and values.

- To satisfy the reading tastes of a developing middle class, writers began to experiment with long fictional narratives called novels.

- Theaters closed by the Puritans reopened, and female actors were now included on the stage; drama during the Restoration was witty, bawdy, and cynical.

- By the end of the period, the excesses of the rich and the onset of industrialization turned people's taste to an appreciation of nature and simplicity.

The First Opera House in the Haymarket (18th century) by William Capon.

Guildhall Library. Corporation of London.

and women are naturally good (that is, the notion that if society is reformed, people will automatically do what is right).

> **The commanding figure at the end of the eighteenth century was Dr. Samuel Johnson, a man of conservative and traditional beliefs. He questioned the optimistic assumption that the future would be better than the past.**

Searching for a Simpler Life

By the time of Johnson's death in 1784, the world was changing in disturbing and profound ways. The Industrial Revolution was turning English cities and towns into filthy, smoky slums. Across the English Channel, the French were about to murder a king and set their whole society on a different political course. The eighteenth century was closing, and—just as at the end of the twentieth century, people sensed that a new era was about to begin—people in England knew that the age of elegance, taste, philosophy, and reason was over.

As a reflection of all this change, writers were developing new interests. Appalled at the industrial blight, they were turning to external nature and writing about the effect of the natural landscape on the human psyche. Disgusted with the excessive focus on the upper classes and "good taste," they were looking back at the past and searching out the simple poems and songs composed by nameless, uneducated folk poets. They were even becoming interested in the literary possibilities of the humble life and were trying to enter into the consciousness of the poor and simple. Nothing could be less Augustan than these tendencies. In short, a new literary age was already beginning during the lifetime of the last great representative of the older age.

> **At the end of the century, as industrialization mushroomed, writers returned to nature and folk themes for inspiration.**

Quickwrite

During the eighteenth century, there was a great shift in the way most people thought about the world. Natural phenomena were more and more being explained by the new method of rational, scientific observation. The Renaissance love of the pastoral was abandoned, in favor of eighteenth-century tastes in fashion and art that ran to the artificial and highly formal. What are the prevailing philosophies and tastes in your world? What changes in people's thinking—about religion, science, fashion, art, politics, the environment, or anything else—have you seen during your lifetime?

(Opposite) *"Well-a-day! Is this my son Tom!"* (detail) (18th century) by Samuel Hieronymous Grimm.

British Library, London.

Before You Read

FROM GULLIVER'S TRAVELS

Make the Connection

Reforming the World

The way some people see it, the world stands in urgent and constant need of reform. Some would-be reformers write editorials or preach sermons. Others use a different weapon to stress the need for change: the stinging criticism of satire. What do you see in today's society that you think should be reformed?

Reading Skills and Strategies

Identifying the Writer's Stance

As you read Swift's story and essay, keep in mind that he is a reformer, a person who believes there is something seriously wrong with people and institutions as they are. As you read, take notes. Note the objects of his disapproval. Jot down words, phrases, and situations he uses to convey his feelings. Look for instances where he **overstates** or **underplays** details in order to make a point. After your reading, use your notes as you discuss how Swift's urge to reform affects the **tone** of his writing.

Elements of Literature

Irony

Swift, like all satirists, wants to make his readers recognize the gap between things as they are and things as they ought to be. To get his audience to feel this contrast, Swift constantly resorts to **irony** to sharpen the sting of his satire.

Irony is a pointed contrast between reality and expectations. There are three types of irony: **Verbal irony** is a contrast between what is said and what is actually meant; **situational irony** is a contrast between what is expected to happen and what actually does happen; and **dramatic irony** is a contrast between what a character knows and what the reader or audience knows.

For more on Irony, see the Handbook of Literary Terms.

Lilliputians examining the man-mountain's possessions. Illustration from *Gulliver's Travels* (1726).

The full title that Swift gave his most famous book is *Travels into Several Remote Nations of the World. In Four Parts. By Lemuel Gulliver, First a Surgeon, and then a Captain of Several Ships.* Immediately upon publication, it was a sensational success. It seemed so convincing that some readers went about claiming that they had heard of, or even met, its author. But Gulliver is, of course, a figment of Swift's imagination.

The book seems to be a true account of actual adventures because Swift includes many realistic-sounding details and even maps of the places Gulliver visits. The first part, describing the visit to Lilliput, opens with an account of Gulliver's early life: his birth, parentage, and schooling. After studying medicine, Gulliver becomes a ship's doctor and embarks on a long voyage; when the ship breaks up in a storm, he manages to swim ashore and, exhausted, falls into a deep sleep. What could be more convincing?

from Gulliver's Travels

from Part 1: A Voyage to Lilliput

Jonathan Swift

I lay down on the grass, which was very short and soft, where I slept sounder than ever I remember to have done in my life, and, as I reckoned, above nine hours; for when I awaked, it was just daylight. I attempted to rise, but was not able to stir: For as I happened to lie on my back, I found my arms and legs were strongly fastened on each side to the ground; and my hair, which was long and thick, tied down in the same manner. I likewise felt several slender ligatures[1] across my body, from my armpits to my thighs. I could only look upward; the sun began to grow hot, and the light offended my eyes. I heard a confused noise about me, but in the posture I lay, could see nothing except the sky.

In a little time I felt something alive moving on my left leg, which advancing gently forward over my breast, came almost up to my chin; when bending my eyes downward as much as I could, I perceived it to be a human creature not six inches high, with a bow and arrow in his hands, and a quiver at his back. In the meantime, I felt at least forty more of the same kind (as I conjectured) following the first. I was in the utmost astonishment, and roared so loud, that they all ran back in a fright; and some of them, as I was afterward told, were hurt with the falls they got by leaping from my sides upon the ground. However, they soon returned, and one of them, who ventured so far as to get a full sight of my face, lifting up his hands and eyes by way of admiration, cried out in a shrill, but distinct voice, *Hekinah degul:*[2] The others repeated the same words several times, but then I knew not what they meant. I lay all this while, as the reader may believe, in great uneasiness: At length, struggling to get loose, I had the fortune to break the strings, and wrench out the pegs that fastened my left arm to the ground; for, by lifting it up to my face, I discovered the methods they had taken to bind me, and at the same time with a violent pull, which gave me excessive pain, I a little loosened the strings that tied down my hair on the left side, so that I was just able to turn my head about two inches. But the creatures

2. Hekinah degul: This and other examples of the Lilliputian (lil′ə·pyo͞o′shən) tongue are mainly nonsense words. Swift was very fond of puns, pig Latin, and other kinds of word games.

- -

WORDS TO OWN
conjectured (kən·jek′chərd) *v.:* reasoned; guessed.

- -

1. ligatures: ties or bonds.

Gulliver awakens in Lilliput (c. 1880), illustration by an unknown artist.

some of them attempted with spears to stick me in the sides; but, by good luck, I had on me a buff jerkin,[3] which they could not pierce. I thought it the most prudent method to lie still, and my design was to continue so till night, when, my left hand being already loose, I could easily free myself: And as for the inhabitants, I had reason to believe I might be a match for the greatest armies they could bring against me, if they were all of the same size with him that I saw. But fortune disposed otherwise of me.

When the people observed I was quiet, they discharged no more arrows; but, by the noise increasing, I knew their numbers were greater; and about four yards from me, over against my right ear, I heard a knocking for above an hour, like that of people at work; when turning my head that way, as well as the pegs and strings would permit me, I saw a stage erected, about a foot and a half from the ground, capable of holding four of the inhabitants, with two or three ladders to mount it: From whence one of them, who seemed to be a person of quality, made me a long speech, whereof I understood not one syllable. But I should have mentioned, that before the principal person began his oration, he cried out three times, *Langro dehul san* (these words and the former were afterward repeated and explained to me). Whereupon

ran off a second time, before I could seize them; whereupon there was a great shout in a very shrill accent, and after it ceased, I heard one of them cry aloud, *Tolgo phonac;* when in an instant I felt above an hundred arrows discharged on my left hand, which pricked me like so many needles; and besides, they shot another flight into the air, as we do bombs in Europe, whereof many, I suppose, fell on my body (though I felt them not), and some on my face, which I immediately covered with my left hand. When this shower of arrows was over, I fell a-groaning with grief and pain, and then striving again to get loose, they discharged another volley larger than the first, and

3. **buff jerkin:** short, closefitting leather jacket, often without sleeves.

immediately about fifty of the inhabitants came and cut the strings that fastened the left side of my head, which gave me the liberty of turning it to the right, and of observing the person and gesture of him who was to speak. He appeared to be of a middle age, and taller than any of the other three who attended him, whereof one was a page who held up his train, and seemed to be somewhat longer than my middle finger; the other two stood one on each side to support him. He acted every part of an orator, and I could observe many periods of threatenings, and others of promises, pity, and kindness.

I answered in a few words, but in the most submissive manner, lifting up my left hand, and both my eyes to the sun, as calling him for a witness; and being almost famished with hunger, having not eaten a morsel for some hours before I left the ship. I found the demands of nature so strong upon me, that I could not forbear showing my impatience (perhaps against the strict rules of decency) by putting my finger frequently on my mouth, to signify that I wanted food. The *Hurgo*[4] (for so they call a great lord, as I afterward learnt) understood me very well. He descended from the stage, and commanded that several ladders should be applied to my sides, on which above an hundred of the inhabitants mounted and walked toward my mouth, laden with baskets full of meat,[5] which had been provided and sent thither by the King's orders, upon the first intelligence[6] he received of me. I observed there was the flesh[7] of several animals, but

Gulliver in Lilliput, illustration by Gennady Spirin.

Reprinted by permission of Philomel Books from *Gulliver's Travels in Lilliput*, retold by Ann Keay Beneduce, illustrations ©1993 by Gennady Spirin.

could not distinguish them by the taste. There were shoulders, legs, and loins, shaped like those of mutton, and very well dressed, but smaller than the wings of a lark. I ate them by two or three at a mouthful, and took three loaves at a time, about the bigness of musket bullets. They supplied me as fast as they could, showing a thousand marks of wonder and astonishment at my bulk and appetite.

I then made another sign that I wanted drink. They found by my eating, that a small quantity would not suffice me; and being a most ingenious

---

4. Hurgo: This Lilliputian word is perhaps a partial anagram (a word formed by rearranging the letters of another word) of the English word *rogue*. It would be characteristic of Swift to call a "great lord" a rogue.
5. meat: archaic for "food."
6. intelligence: news.
7. flesh: meat.

people, they slung up with great dexterity one of their largest hogsheads,[8] then rolled it toward my hand, and beat out the top; I drank it off at a draft, which I might well do, for it hardly held half a pint, and tasted like a small wine of Burgundy, but much more delicious. They brought me a second hogshead, which I drank in the same manner, and made signs for more, but they had none to give me. When I had performed these wonders, they shouted for joy, and danced upon my breast, repeating several times as they did at first, *Hekinah degul.* They made me a sign that I should throw down the two hogsheads, but first warned the people below to stand out of the way, crying aloud, *Borach mivola,* and when they saw the vessels in the air, there was an universal shout of *Hekinah degul.* I confess I was often tempted, while they were passing backward and forward on my body, to seize forty or fifty of the first that came in my reach, and dash them against the ground. But the remembrance of what I had felt, which probably might not be the worst they could do, and the promise of honor I made them, for so I interpreted my submissive behavior, soon drove out those imaginations. Besides, I now considered myself as bound by the laws of hospitality to a people who had treated me with so much expense and magnificence. However, in my thoughts, I could not sufficiently wonder at the intrepidity of these <u>diminutive</u> mortals, who durst venture to mount and walk on my body, while one of my hands was at liberty, without trembling at the very sight of so prodigious a creature as I must appear to them.

After some time, when they observed that I made no more demands for meat, there appeared before me a person of high rank from his Imperial Majesty. His Excellency, having mounted on the small of my right leg, advanced forward up to my face, with about a dozen of his retinue. And producing his credentials under the Signet Royal,[9] which he applied close to my eyes, spoke about ten minutes, without any signs of anger, but with a kind of determinate resolution; often pointing forward, which, as I afterward found, was toward the capital city, about half a mile distant, whither it was agreed by his Majesty in council that I must be conveyed. I answered in few words, but to no purpose, and made a sign with my hand that was loose, putting it to the other (but over his Excellency's head for fear of hurting him or his train) and then to my own head and body, to signify that I desired my liberty. It appeared that he understood me well enough, for he shook his head by way of disapprobation, and held his hand in a posture to show that I must be carried as a prisoner. However, he made other signs to let me understand that I should have meat and drink enough, and very good treatment. Whereupon I once more thought of attempting to break my bonds; but again, when I felt the smart of their arrows, upon my face and hands, which were all in blisters, and many of the darts still sticking in them, and observing likewise that the number of my enemies increased, I gave tokens[10] to let them know that they might do with me what they pleased. Upon this, the *Hurgo* and his train withdrew, with much civility and cheerful countenances.

Soon after I heard a general shout, with frequent repetitions of the words, *Peplom selan,* and I felt great numbers of people on my left side relaxing the cords to such a degree, that I was able to turn upon my right, and to ease myself with making water; which I very plentifully did, to the great astonishment of the people, who conjecturing by my motions what I was going to do, immediately opened to the right and left on that side, to avoid the torrent which fell with such noise and violence from me. But before this, they had daubed my face and both my hands with a sort of ointment very pleasant to the smell, which in a few minutes removed all the smart of their arrows. These circumstances, added to the refreshment I had received by their victuals and drink, which were very nourishing, disposed me to sleep. I slept about eight hours, as I was afterward assured; and it was no wonder, for the physicians, by the Emperor's order, had mingled a sleeping potion in the hogshead of wine. . . .

10. **gave tokens:** signaled.

8. **hogsheads** (hôgz′hedz′): barrels.
9. **Signet Royal:** royal seal; the seal used as a signature to mark documents as official.

WORDS TO OWN
diminutive (də·min′yoo·tiv) *adj.*: very small.

My gentleness and good behavior had gained so far on the Emperor and his court, and indeed upon the army and people in general, that I began to conceive hopes of getting my liberty in a short time. I took all possible methods to cultivate this favorable disposition. The natives came by degrees to be less apprehensive of any danger from me. I would sometimes lie down, and let five or six of them dance on my hand. And at last the boys and girls would venture to come and play at hide-and-seek in my hair. I had now made a good progress in understanding and speaking their language. The Emperor had a mind one day to entertain me with several of the country shows, wherein they exceed all nations I have known, both for dexterity and magnificence. I was diverted with none so much as that of the rope dancers,[11] performed upon a slender white thread, extended about two foot, and twelve inches from the ground. Upon which I shall desire liberty, with the reader's patience, to enlarge a little.

This diversion is only practiced by those persons who are candidates for great employments, and high favor, at court. They are trained in this art from their youth, and are not always of noble birth, or liberal education. When a great office is vacant, either by death or disgrace (which often happens), five or six of those candidates petition the Emperor to entertain his Majesty and the court with a dance on the rope, and whoever jumps the highest without falling, succeeds in the office. Very often the chief ministers themselves are commanded to show their skill, and to convince the Emperor that they have not lost their faculty. Flimnap, the Treasurer, is allowed to cut a caper on the straight rope, at least an inch higher than any other lord in the whole empire. I have seen him do the summerset[12] several times together upon a trencher[13] fixed on the rope, which is no thicker than a common packthread[14] in England. My friend Reldresal, principal Secretary for Private Affairs, is, in my opinion, if I am not partial, the second after the Treasurer; the rest of the great officers are much upon a par.

These diversions are often attended with fatal accidents, whereof great numbers are on record. I myself have seen two or three candidates break a limb. But the danger is much greater when the ministers themselves are commanded to show their dexterity; for, by contending to excel themselves and their fellows, they strain so far, that there is hardly one of them who hath not received a fall, and some of them two or three. I was assured that a year or two before my arrival, Flimnap would have infallibly broke his neck, if one of the King's cushions, that accidentally lay on the ground, had not weakened the force of his fall.

There is likewise another diversion, which is only shown before the Emperor and Empress, and first minister, upon particular occasions. The Emperor lays on the table three fine silken threads of six inches long. One is blue, the other red, and the third green. These threads are proposed as prizes for those persons whom the Emperor hath a mind to distinguish by a peculiar mark of his favor. The ceremony is performed in his Majesty's great chamber of state, where the candidates are to undergo a trial of dexterity very different from the former, and such as I have not observed the least resemblance of in any other country of the Old or the New World. The Emperor holds a stick in his hands, both ends parallel to the horizon, while the candidates advancing one by one, sometimes leap over the stick, sometimes creep under it backward and forward several times, according as the stick is advanced or depressed. Sometimes the Emperor holds one end of the stick, and his first minister the other; sometimes the minister has it entirely to himself. Whoever performs his part with most agility, and holds out the longest in leaping and creeping, is rewarded with the blue-colored silk; the red is given to the next, and the green to the third, which they all wear girt[15] twice round about the middle; and you see few great persons about this court, who are not adorned with one of these girdles. . . .

One morning, about a fortnight after I had obtained my liberty, Reldresal, principal Secretary (as they style him) of Private Affairs, came to my house attended only by one servant. He ordered his coach to wait at a distance, and desired I would give him an hour's audience; which I readily consented to, on account of his quality and personal

11. **rope dancers:** tightrope dancers.
12. **summerset:** somersault.
13. **trencher:** wooden platter usually used for serving food.
14. **packthread:** twine.

15. **girt:** encircled.

Gulliver is measured by the tailors (c. late 19th to early 20th century), illustration by Arthur Rackham.

by a most potent enemy from abroad. As to the first, you are to understand, that for about seventy moons past there have been two struggling parties in this empire, under the names of *Trameck-san* and *Slamecksan,* from the high and low heels on their shoes, by which they distinguish themselves. It is <u>alleged</u> indeed, that the high heels are most agreeable to our ancient constitution: But however this be, his Majesty hath determined to make use of only low heels in the administration of the government, and all offices in the gift of the Crown, as you cannot but observe; and particularly, that his Majesty's Imperial heels are lower at least by a *drurr* than any of his court; (*drurr* is a measure about the fourteenth part of an inch). The animosities between these two parties run so high, that they will neither eat nor drink, nor talk with each other. We compute the *Trameck-san,* or High-Heels, to exceed us in number; but the power is wholly on our side. We apprehend his Imperial Highness, the Heir to the Crown, to have some tendency toward the High-Heels; at least we can plainly discover one of his heels higher than the other, which gives him a hobble in his gait. Now, in the midst of these intestine[16] disquiets, we are threatened with an invasion from the island of Blefuscu, which is the other great empire of the universe, almost as large and powerful as this of his Majesty. For as to what we have heard you affirm, that there are other kingdoms and states in the world inhabited by human creatures as large as yourself, our philosophers are in much doubt, and would rather conjecture that you dropped from the moon, or one of the stars; because it is certain, that an hundred mortals of your bulk would, in a short time, destroy all the fruits and cattle of his Majesty's dominions. Besides, our histories of six thousand moons make no mention of any other regions, than the two great empires of Lilliput and Blefuscu. Which two mighty powers have, as I was going to tell you, been engaged in a most obstinate war for six and thirty moons past. It began upon the following

merits, as well as of the many good offices he had done me during my solicitations at court. I offered to lie down, that he might the more conveniently reach my ear; but he chose rather to let me hold him in my hand during our conversation. He began with compliments on my liberty, said he might pretend to some merit in it; but, however, added, that if it had not been for the present situation of things at court, perhaps I might not have obtained it so soon. "For," said he, "as flourishing a condition as we appear to be in to foreigners, we labor under two mighty evils: a violent faction at home, and the danger of an invasion

16. **intestine:** internal.

- -

WORDS TO OWN

alleged (ə·lejd′) *v.*: declared or asserted, often without proof.

- -

occasion. It is allowed on all hands, that the primitive way of breaking eggs[17] before we eat them, was upon the larger end: But his present Majesty's grandfather, while he was a boy, going to eat an egg, and breaking it according to the ancient practice, happened to cut one of his fingers. Whereupon the Emperor his father published an edict, commanding all his subjects, upon great penalties, to break the smaller end of their eggs. The people so highly resented this law, that our histories tell us there have been six rebellions raised on that account; wherein one Emperor lost his life, and another his crown. These civil commotions were constantly fomented by the monarchs of Blefuscu; and when they were quelled, the exiles always fled for refuge to that empire. It is computed, that eleven thousand persons have, at several times, suffered death, rather than submit to break their eggs at the smaller end. Many hundred large volumes have been published upon this controversy: But the books of the Big-Endians have been long forbidden, and the whole party rendered incapable by law of holding employments. During the course of these troubles, the emperors of Blefuscu

17. **way of breaking eggs:** The English eat a boiled egg by standing it up in an egg cup, cutting off one end with a knife, and scooping out the contents with a spoon.

Lilliput (19th century), illustration by Grandville.

did frequently expostulate by their ambassadors, accusing us of making a schism[18] in religion, by offending against a fundamental doctrine of our great prophet Lustrog, in the fifty-fourth chapter of the Brundrecal (which is their Alcoran).[19] This, however, is thought to be a mere strain upon the text, for the words are these: *That all true believers shall break their eggs at the convenient end;* and which is the convenient end, seems, in my humble opinion, to be left to every man's conscience, or at least in the power of the chief magistrate to determine. Now the Big-Endian exiles have found so much credit in the Emperor of Blefuscu's court, and so much private assistance and encouragement from their party here at home, that a bloody war has been carried on between the two empires for six and thirty moons with various success; during which time we have lost forty capital ships, and a much greater number of smaller vessels, together with thirty thousand of our best seamen and soldiers; and the damage received by the enemy is reckoned to be somewhat greater than ours. However, they have now equipped a numerous fleet, and are just preparing to make a descent upon us; and his Imperial Majesty, placing great confidence in your valor and strength, has commanded me to lay this account of his affairs before you."

I desired the Secretary to present my humble duty to the Emperor, and to let him know, that I thought it would not become me, who was a foreigner, to interfere with parties; but I was ready, with the hazard of my life, to defend his person and state against all invaders.

18. **schism:** division.
19. **Alcoran:** archaic English name for the Koran, Islam's sacred book.

WORDS TO OWN
edict (ē′dikt′) *n.:* official order.
quelled (kweld) *v.:* subdued.

Under the Guise of Lilliput

Swift's contemporaries immediately understood that Swift was doing two things in this part of *Gulliver's Travels.* Under the pretense of describing politics in Lilliput, he was indirectly referring to politicians and political events in his own country. Swift's first readers were quick to identify the actual statesmen lurking behind such made-up names as Reldresal and Flimnap, and they saw parallels between events in Lilliput and events in England.

While it is interesting to know something about the real political background of *Gulliver's Travels,* it is much more important to understand that Swift is **satirizing** certain characteristics to be found in the political struggles of all countries at all times in history. For instance, in the imaginary Lilliput there are two major parties, distinguished by a trivial detail: the height of the heels on the shoes they wear. Similarly, in many actual countries there are also two major parties that struggle for power. Swift wants us to think about what distinguishes such real political parties from each other. Are the issues important or minor?

Later in this section, Gulliver discovers another characteristic that distinguishes the two parties: the way they eat their eggs. The Big-Endians always cut open the big end of the boiled egg, and the Little-Endians always cut open the little end. These parties have had a long and bitter history: One emperor has lost his life, another his throne, and many Lilliputians have had to go live in another country, Blefuscu. All these details suggest that Swift was thinking of specific events in English history, and these events determined what he said about Lilliput. It is even possible to identify the parallels between Swift's fictions and historical facts. Lilliput, for example, represents England; and Blefuscu represents France, where some English Catholics lived in exile.

The Big-Endians are people loyal to Catholicism, England's old religion, and the Little-Endians are those loyal to Anglicanism, England's new religion. The emperor who lost his life can be identified with Charles I; the one who lost his throne is James II.

Any narrative incorporating parallels of this kind is called an **allegory** (see page 451). But again, knowing how to interpret the allegory in a particular way is much less important than understanding the general meaning of the satire, which is directed against follies and excesses wherever they are found.

George III, as the King of Brobdingnag, inspects Napoleon, as Gulliver (c. 1803) by James Gillray.

MAKING MEANINGS

First Thoughts

1. What do you think is the funniest part of Gulliver's adventures in Lilliput? What serious point, if any, do you see beneath the surface of the humor?

Shaping Interpretations

As you answer these questions, refer to your reading notes.

2. The travel books of Swift's time were famous for fantastic lies about exotic places and trivial details about the traveler's daily life there. How does this selection **parody,** or imitate and make fun of, these travel books?

3. Swift also uses the travel book as a medium for **satire.** He expects his readers to find similarities between what happens in Lilliput and what goes on at home. What qualifications are the officials of Lilliput expected to have in order to hold high office? How does Swift use **irony** in his description of the Lilliputian officials?

4. Is there any relationship between the physical size of the Lilliputians and the way Swift wants us to evaluate their behavior? Does their size **symbolize** some other kind of "smallness"? Explain.

5. Compare the way Swift **characterizes** the Lilliputians with the way Chaucer characterizes the pilgrims in the Prologue to *The Canterbury Tales* (page 105). How does each writer **satirize** the moral failings of his characters?

6. How would you describe Swift's **tone**—his attitude toward the Lilliputians? What words or passages support your answer?

Reading Check

a. How large are the Lilliputians? Why doesn't Gulliver seize and harm the Lilliputians who come close to him?

b. What test do the candidates for high office in Lilliput have to undergo? What disaster almost happened to Flimnap?

c. Describe the two evils that threaten Lilliput, according to Reldresal.

d. Explain how the war between Lilliput and Blefuscu began.

7. The institutions for which Swift urges reform here include politics and religion. What does he think of the differences that divide people into factions and sects? What other aspects of Lilliputian (and by implication English) life does Swift suggest are ripe for reform?

8. Because of the bitterness of his satire, some readers have concluded that Swift despaired of true reform and was really a confirmed misanthrope, or hater of humanity. Do you think someone as bitter about life as Swift is has to be a misanthrope? Explain your answer.

Extending the Text

9. The Critical Comment on page 495 explains how Lilliputian politics paralleled British politics of Swift's time. What parallels can you detect between Lilliput and what you know of modern politics, in either this country or some other one?

Gulliver tows the enemy's ships to Lilliput. Illustration from a 19th-century edition of *Gulliver's Travels*.

The Granger Collection, New York.

On his second voyage, Gulliver finds himself marooned in Brobdingnag. Here everything—people, animals, buildings—is twelve times larger than in England or anywhere else in the known world. The situation in Part I is now completely reversed, and Gulliver discovers what it is like to be an insignificant, timid midget among giants. He also learns that nothing is either big or little except by comparison. All sorts of humiliating accidents happen to him: A baby picks him up and tries to suck on his head; a monkey stuffs him with food and carries him up onto a roof; he is almost drowned in a bowl of cream; a farmer exhibits him for money, as though he were a trained flea. Finally he goes to live at court, where he tries to impress the king and queen with his importance, and especially with the importance of England and its civilization, which nobody in Brobdingnag has ever heard of.

Although its inhabitants look like immense and ugly brutes, Brobdingnag is a kind of utopia, a model civilization with an enlightened and benevolent king. Notice how the king treats Gulliver in spite of his opinion of Gulliver's size and civilization. Continue to take notes as you read.

from Part 2: A Voyage to Brobdingnag
Jonathan Swift

It is the custom that every Wednesday (which, as I have before observed, was their Sabbath) the King and Queen, with the royal issue of both sexes, dine together in the apartment of his Majesty, to whom I was now become a favorite; and at these times my little chair and table were placed at his left hand, before one of the salt-cellars.[1] This prince took a pleasure in conversing with me, inquiring into the manners, religion, laws, government, and learning of Europe; wherein I gave him the best account I was able. His apprehension was so clear, and his judgment so exact, that he made very wise reflections and observations upon all I said. But, I confess, that after I had been a little too <u>copious</u> in talking of my own beloved country, of our trade, and wars by sea and land, of our schisms in religion, and parties in the state; the prejudices of his education <u>pre</u><u>vailed</u> so far, that he could not forbear taking me up in his right hand, and stroking me gently with the other, after an hearty fit of laughing, asked me, whether I were a Whig or a Tory.[2] Then turning to his first minister, who waited behind him with a white staff, near as tall as the mainmast of the

Royal Sovereign,[3] he observed how contemptible a thing was human grandeur, which could be mimicked by such diminutive insects as I. "And yet," said he, "I dare engage, those creatures have their titles and distinctions of honor, they contrive little nests and burrows, that they call houses and cities; they make a figure in dress and equipage;[4] they love, they fight, they dispute, they cheat, they betray." And thus he continued on, while my color came and went several times, with indignation to hear our noble country, the mistress of arts and arms, the scourge of France, the arbitress of Europe, the seat of virtue, piety, honor, and truth, the pride and envy of the world, so contemptuously treated.

But as I was not in a condition to resent injuries, so, upon mature thoughts, I began to doubt whether I were injured or no. For, after having

---

3. **Royal Sovereign:** one of the largest British warships of Swift's age. A white staff is the symbol of the office of the British treasurer.
4. **equipage** (ek′wi·pij′): carriage and horses with attendant servants.

- -

WORDS TO OWN
copious (kō′pē·əs) *adj.:* wordy; profuse.
prevailed (prē·vāld′) *v.:* predominated; held sway.

- -

---

1. **saltcellars:** dishes of salt.
2. **Whig . . . Tory:** the two chief political parties of eighteenth-century Great Britain.

Gulliver Exhibited to the Brobdingnag Farmer (19th century) by Richard Redgrave.

been accustomed several months to the sight and converse of this people, and observed every object upon which I cast my eyes, to be of proportionable magnitude, the horror I had first conceived from their bulk and aspect was so far worn off, that if I had then beheld a company of English lords and ladies in their finery and birthday clothes,[5] acting their several parts in the most courtly manner, of strutting, and bowing, and prating;[6] to say the truth, I should have been strongly tempted to laugh as much at them as this King and his grandees[7] did at me. Neither indeed could I forbear smiling at myself, when the Queen used to place me upon her hand toward a looking glass, by which both our persons appeared before me in full view together; and there could be nothing more ridiculous than the comparison; so that I really began to imagine myself dwindled many degrees below my usual size. . . .

I was frequently rallied[8] by the Queen upon account of my fearfulness, and she used to ask me whether the people of my country were as great cowards as myself. The occasion was this: The kingdom is much pestered with flies in summer; and these odious insects, each of them as big as a Dunstable lark, hardly gave me any rest while I sat at dinner, with their continual humming and buzzing about my ears. They would sometimes alight upon my victuals, and leave their loathsome excrement or spawn behind, which to me was very visible, though not to the natives of that country, whose large optics were not so acute as

---

5. birthday clothes: new outfits worn on a royal's birthday.
6. prating: talking pompously.
7. grandees (gran·dēz'): important persons; from *grande*, Spanish and Portuguese for "a nobleman of the highest rank."

8. rallied: teased.

- -

WORDS TO OWN
odious (ō'dē·əs) *adj.*: hateful; offensive.

- -

mine in viewing smaller objects. Sometimes they would fix upon my nose or forehead, where they stung me to the quick, smelling very offensively, and I could easily trace that viscous matter, which our naturalists tell us enables those creatures to walk with their feet upward upon a ceiling. I had much ado to defend myself against these detestable animals, and could not forbear starting when they came on my face. It was the common practice of the dwarf to catch a number of these insects in his hand, as schoolboys do among us, and let them out suddenly under my nose, on purpose to frighten me, and divert the Queen. My remedy was to cut them in pieces with my knife as they flew in the air, wherein my dexterity was much admired. . . .

He [the King] was perfectly astonished with the historical account I gave him of our affairs during the last century, protesting it was only an heap of conspiracies, rebellions, murders, massacres, revolutions, banishments; the very worst effects that avarice, faction, hypocrisy, perfidiousness, cruelty, rage, madness, hatred, envy, lust, malice, and ambition, could produce.

His Majesty, in another audience, was at the pains to recapitulate the sum of all I had spoken; compared the questions he made with the answers I had given; then taking me into his hands, and stroking me gently, delivered himself in these words, which I shall never forget, nor the manner he spoke them in. "My little friend Grildrig,[9] you have made a most admirable panegyric upon your country. You have clearly proved that ignorance, idleness, and vice, are the proper ingredients for qualifying a legislator: that laws are best explained, interpreted, and applied by those whose interest and abilities lie in perverting, confounding, and eluding them. I observe among you some lines of an institution, which in its original might have been tolerable, but these half erased, and the rest wholly blurred and blotted by corruptions. It doth not appear from all you have said, how any one perfection[10] is required toward the procurement of any one station among you; much less that men are ennobled on account of their virtue, that priests are advanced for their piety or learning, soldiers for their conduct or valor, judges for

9. **Grildrig:** the Brobdingnagians' name for Gulliver.
10. **perfection:** virtue.

their integrity, senators for the love of their country, or counselors for their wisdom. As for yourself (continued the King), who have spent the greatest part of your life in traveling, I am well disposed to hope you may hitherto have escaped many vices of your country. But by what I have gathered from your own relation, and the answers I have with much pains wringed and extorted from you, I cannot but conclude the bulk of your natives to be the most pernicious race of little odious vermin that nature ever suffered to crawl upon the surface of the earth."

Gulliver in Brobdingnag (c. late 19th to early 20th century). Original watercolor illustration by Arthur Rackham for *Gulliver's Travels.*

WORDS TO OWN

viscous (vis′kəs) *adj.:* having the form of a sticky fluid.
pernicious (pər·nish′·əs) *adj.:* wicked; extremely harmful.

MAKING MEANINGS

First Thoughts

1. What do you think of the Brobdingnagian royal family? What faults and virtues do you see in them?

Shaping Interpretations

As you answer these questions, be sure to refer to your reading notes.

2. Explain why the king roars with laughter when he asks if Gulliver is a Whig or a Tory.

3. Why does Gulliver begin to think of himself as small?

4. How does Swift **characterize** the king of Brobdingnag? Which actions show the king's personality traits?

5. Where does Swift use **verbal irony** to make his points?

6. What connections can you make between Gulliver's experience with the Brobdingnagian flies and the king's dismissal of humanity as "little odious vermin"?

7. What evidence suggests that Gulliver is learning little from his experiences in Brobdingnag?

8. How would you describe Swift's **tone** as he tells about the Brobdingnags? Find words or passages to support your answer.

Extending the Text

9. Find at least one passage in the Brobdingnag episode that could apply to politics in the United States today.

Reading Check

a. To what form of life does the king first compare Gulliver?

b. In comparison, what do English people think of themselves, according to Gulliver?

c. What feat of dexterity can Gulliver perform that impresses the Brobdingnagians?

d. From Gulliver's defense of England, the king evaluates English officials and institutions. According to the king, what are the qualifications for English legislators?

ELEMENTS OF LITERATURE

Satire: Bitter Laughter

A **satire** is any piece of writing designed to make its readers feel critical—of themselves, of their fellow human beings, of their society. Some satires are intended to make us laugh at human foolishness and weakness; others make us angry and indignant at human vices and crimes. In *The Rape of the Lock* (page 527), Alexander Pope provides many examples of the good-natured, laughable kind of satire. Like Pope's, Swift's satire also provokes laughter, but often laughter of a bitter kind.

While satire is usually directed at humanity in general, or at stereotyped groups of people such as clumsy surgeons or greedy lawyers, it can also be aimed at a particular person. In *Gulliver's Travels,* for instance, Swift satirizes the prime minister Sir Robert Walpole, whom he believed to be corrupt, calling him "Flimnap."

Satirists are dissatisfied with things as they are, and they want to make them better. Instead of giving constructive advice, though, they emphasize what is wrong with the world and its inhabitants. They don't say "Be good!" "Obey the Golden Rule!" "Put others before yourself." Instead, they make fun of vicious, selfish, mean-spirited people in the hope that we will see ourselves in such people and mend our ways. Satirists perform an important function in society when they expose errors and absurdities that we no longer notice because custom and familiarity have blinded us to them.

One of the devices that satirists use to make folly and vice appear ridiculous, and therefore unattractive, is **exaggeration.** We must not expect satirists to be objective, to give both sides of a question, to show the good as well as the bad traits of a character. Instead, satirists are likely to exaggerate by picturing all politicians as corrupt, all members of the clergy as hypocritical, all teachers as pedantic, all young adults as irresponsible. They realize that such generalizations cannot be 100 percent accurate, but for satirical purposes exceptions do not count. Wildly extravagant exaggeration, or **hyperbole,** is conspicuous in popular magazines such as *Mad*—though *Mad*'s satire lacks the moral purposes and subtlety of Swift's and Pope's satire.

The great satirists expect their readers to be alert and intelligent enough to detect the presence of satire even when there is no exaggeration. For instance, Swift once wrote, without any explanation at all, "Last week I saw a woman flayed, and you will hardly believe how much it altered her appearance for the worst." Since to "flay" a person is to peel off the skin (a common form of capital punishment in those days), Swift's remark is a complete **understatement**—the opposite of an exaggeration. By making the statement sound shockingly casual and offhanded, Swift implies that such cruelty is common but that people do not become upset by it and instead pretend to have no concern at all.

Understatement is a form of **irony,** the device of saying one thing and meaning just the opposite. When irony is particularly cruel or cutting, it can come close to **sarcasm.** "Great!" we say sarcastically, when we actually mean "Terrible!" In literature, irony is extended far beyond mere sarcasm. In his *Directions for Servants,* for instance, Swift, under the pretense of telling servants how to behave, actually tells them how to misbehave—and in great detail. Here is how he advises servants to respond to a request for a drink.

Brobdingnag (detail) (c. 1800) drawn by R. Corbould, engraved by C. Warren, from *Cooke's Pocket Edition of Select Novels.*

> When you carry a glass of liquor to any person who hath called for it, do not bob him on the shoulder, or cry, "Sir, or madam, here's the glass!" That would be unmannerly, as if you had a mind to force it down one's throat. But stand at the person's left shoulder and wait his time; and if he strikes it down with his elbow by forgetfulness, that was his fault and not yours.

Ironic advice of this sort is more amusing and much more memorable than straightforward, sincere advice.

A writer who habitually uses irony runs the risk of being misunderstood. As an ironist, Swift earned a reputation for being scandalous, irresponsible, and even irreligious. Yet he claimed he never wrote anything "without a moral view."

Looking at satire. Swift's novel is almost two hundred years old. Look closely at the relevance of his satire to today's world.

1. According to Swift, what is basically wrong with the world and its inhabitants? How do you feel about his stance on morality?

2. Where do you see the techniques of Swiftian satire put to use today? What are some of the specific targets of contemporary satire?

3. Swift's novel is highly visual, and many artists and even political cartoonists have been inspired by Gulliver and his travels. If you like to draw, you might try to illustrate one of Gulliver's adventures. If you see parallels between Swift's satiric book and politics today, draw a cartoon based on an incident or character from *Gulliver's Travels.* (In about 1803, an English cartoonist lampooned Napoleon—whom the English detested—by showing him as the tiny Gulliver being inspected by George III as the king of Brobdingnag. See page 495.)

Before You Read

A MODEST PROPOSAL

Background

This essay, Swift's best and most famous pamphlet, describes the desperate conditions in Ireland and protests the English treatment of the Irish. For three years before Swift published this pamphlet in 1729, the Irish harvests had been so poor that little remained for the farmers, after selling their crops, to pay the rents demanded by their English landlords. Beggars and starving children were everywhere. Money was in short supply. Swift argued that most of the money was shipped off to England, where the landlords lived, and little remained in Ireland to be spent on Irish goods. England's policies kept the Irish poor.

In *A Modest Proposal*, Swift offers an outrageous solution to these problems of human misery—perhaps the most outrageous solution ever offered. But there is nothing outrageous about Swift's manner. In this pamphlet, he assumes the role of a "practical" economic planner, pretending to be objective, full of common sense, even benevolence. It is this difference between its straightforward style and its appalling content that gives the pamphlet its force.

Ultimately, Swift is protesting against a purely statistical view of humanity—a view that would reduce people to breeders and babies to meat. Swift risks appearing as a monster himself in order to expose the monstrous behavior of others.

Reading Skills and Strategies

Recognizing Persuasive Techniques

Swift's essay is perhaps the most famous and most skilled example of **persuasive writing** used for the purpose of **satire**. As you read, take notes, locating examples of the following persuasive techniques: **logical appeals** (supporting a position with evidence, such as facts or statistics); **emotional appeals** (passages that use words that arouse strong feelings); and **ethical appeals** (passages that establish the writer as sincere and qualified to make the remarks). The questions alongside key paragraphs can be used as a guide to your reading.

A Modest Proposal

Jonathan Swift

Oh some of them are too Naked to stand up.

A starving, orphaned Irish child (detail).

FOR PREVENTING THE CHILDREN OF POOR PEOPLE IN IRELAND FROM BEING A BURDEN TO THEIR PARENTS OR COUNTRY, AND FOR MAKING THEM BENEFICIAL TO THE PUBLIC

It is a melancholy object to those, who walk through this great town,[1] or travel in the country, when they see the streets, the roads, and cabin doors, crowded with beggars of the female sex, followed by three, four, or six children, all in rags, and importuning every passenger for an alms.[2] These mothers instead of being able to work for their honest livelihood, are forced to employ all their time in strolling, to beg sustenance for their helpless infants, who, as they grow up either turn thieves for want[3] of work, or leave their

3. **want:** lack; need.

WORDS TO OWN

sustenance (sus′tə·nəns) *n.:* food or money to support life.

1. **town:** Dublin.
2. **importuning . . . alms:** asking passersby for a handout.

dear native country to fight for the Pretender[4] in Spain, or sell themselves to the Barbadoes.[5]

I think it is agreed by all parties, that this prodigious number of children, in the arms, or on the backs, or at the heels of their mothers, and frequently of their fathers, is in the present deplorable state of the kingdom, a very great additional grievance; and therefore whoever could find out a fair, cheap, and easy method of making these children sound and useful members of the commonwealth would deserve so well of the public, as to have his statue set up for a preserver of the nation.

But my intention is very far from being confined to provide only for the children of professed beggars; it is of a much greater extent, and shall take in the whole number of infants at a certain age, who are born of parents in effect as little able to support them, as those who demand our charity in the streets.

> **?** What problem does the narrator propose to solve? In the next paragraph, look for the first statement of his proposal.

As to my own part, having turned my thoughts, for many years, upon this important subject, and maturely weighed the several schemes of other projectors,[6] I have always found them grossly mistaken in their computation. It is true a child, just dropped from its dam,[7] may be supported by her milk, for a solar year[8] with little other nourishment, at most not above the value of two shillings, which the mother may certainly get, or the value in scraps, by her lawful occupation of begging, and it is exactly at one year old that I propose to provide for them, in such a manner, as, instead of being a charge upon their parents, or the parish, or wanting food and raiment[9] for the rest of their lives, they shall, on the contrary, contribute to the feeding and partly to the clothing of many thousands.

There is likewise another great advantage in my scheme, that it will prevent those voluntary abortions, and that horrid practice of women murdering their bastard children, alas! too frequent among us, sacrificing the poor innocent babes, I doubt,[10] more to avoid the expense, than the shame, which would move tears and pity in the most savage and inhuman breast.

The number of souls[11] in Ireland being usually reckoned one million and a half, of these I calculate there may be about two hundred thousand couples whose wives are breeders, from which number I subtract thirty thousand couples, who are able to maintain their own children, although I apprehend there cannot be so many under the present distresses of the kingdom, but this being granted, there will remain an hundred and seventy thousand breeders. I again subtract fifty thousand for those women who miscarry, or whose children die by accident, or disease within the year. There only remain an hundred and twenty thousand children of poor parents annually born: The question therefore is, how this number shall be reared, and provided for, which, as I have already said, under the present situation of affairs, is utterly impossible by all the methods hitherto proposed, for we can neither employ them in handicraft,[12] or agriculture; we neither build houses (I mean in the country) nor cultivate land: They can very seldom pick up a livelihood by stealing until they arrive at six years old, except where they are of towardly parts,[13] although, I confess they learn the rudiments much earlier, during which time, they can however be properly looked upon only as probationers,[14] as I have been informed by a principal gentleman in the county of Cavan,[15] who protested to me, that he never knew above one or two instances under the age of six, even in a part of the kingdom so renowned for the quickest proficiency in that art.[16]

I am assured by our merchants, that a boy or girl, before twelve years old, is no saleable com-

4. the Pretender: James Edward (1688–1766), son of England's last Catholic king, the deposed James II (1633–1701); James Edward made several attempts to gain the English throne.
5. sell . . . Barbadoes: go to the West Indies and work as indentured servants to pay off their passage.
6. projectors: speculators; schemers.
7. dam: mother (ordinarily used only of animals).
8. solar year: from the first day of spring in one year to the last day of winter in the next.
9. raiment (rā′mənt): clothing.

10. doubt: suspect.
11. souls: people.
12. handicraft: manufacturing.
13. of towardly parts: exceptionally advanced or mature for their age.
14. probationers: apprentices.
15. Cavan: inland county in Ireland that is remote from Dublin.
16. that art: stealing.

modity, and even when they come to this age, they will not yield above three pounds, or three pounds and half a crown at most on the exchange, which cannot turn to account[17] either to the parents or the kingdom, the charge of nutriment and rags having been at least four times that value.

I shall now therefore humbly propose my own thoughts, which I hope will not be liable to the least objection.

I have been assured by a very knowing American[18] of my acquaintance in London, that a young healthy child well nursed is at a year old a most delicious, nourishing, and wholesome food, whether stewed, roasted, baked, or boiled, and I make no doubt that it will equally serve in a fricassee,[19] or ragout.[20]

> **?** Here the narrator offers his "modest" proposal. What horrible plan is he actually proposing?

I do therefore humbly offer it to public consideration, that of the hundred and twenty thousand children, already computed, twenty thousand may be reserved for breed, whereof only one-fourth part to be males, which is more than we allow to sheep, black cattle, or swine, and my reason is that these children are seldom the fruits of marriage, a circumstance not much regarded by our savages; therefore one male will be sufficient to serve four females. That the remaining hundred thousand may at a year old be offered in sale to the persons of quality, and fortune, through the kingdom, always advising the mother to let them suck plentifully in the last month, so as to render them plump, and fat for a good table. A child will make two dishes at an entertainment for friends, and when the family dines alone, the fore or hind quarter will make a reasonable dish, and seasoned with a little pepper or salt will be very good boiled on the fourth day, especially in winter.

I have reckoned upon a medium, that a child just born will weigh twelve pounds, and in a solar year if tolerably nursed increaseth to twenty-eight pounds.

I grant this food will be somewhat dear,[21] and therefore very proper for landlords, who, as they have already devoured[22] most of the parents, seem to have the best title to the children.

Infant's flesh will be in season throughout the year, but more plentiful in March, and a little before and after, for we are told by a grave author,[23] an eminent French physician, that fish being a prolific diet, there are more children born in Roman Catholic countries about nine months after Lent, than at any other season, therefore reckoning a year after Lent, the markets will be more glutted than usual, because the number of popish[24] infants, is at least three to one in this kingdom, and therefore it will have one other collateral advantage by lessening the number of papists among us.

> **?** Reread this paragraph carefully. What bias does the narrator reveal?

I have already computed the charge of nursing a beggar's child (in which list I reckon all cottagers,[25] laborers, and four-fifths of the farmers) to be about two shillings per annum,[26] rags included, and I believe no gentleman would repine to give ten shillings for the carcass of a good fat child, which, as I have said will make four dishes of excellent nutritive meat, when he hath only some particular friend, or his own family to dine with him. Thus the squire will learn to be a good landlord, and grow popular among his tenants, the mother will have eight shillings net profit, and be fit for work until she produceth another child.

Those who are more thrifty (as I must confess the times require) may flay[27] the carcass; the skin of which, artificially[28] dressed, will make ad-

21. **dear:** expensive.
22. **devoured:** made poor by charging high rents.
23. **grave author:** François Rabelais (frän·swä′ rab′ə·lā′) (c. 1483–1553), French satirist; his work is comic, not "grave."
24. **popish:** Roman Catholic; a derogatory term.
25. **cottagers:** tenant farmers.
26. **per annum:** Latin for "by the year"; annually.
27. **flay:** remove the skin of.
28. **artificially:** with great artifice; that is, skillfully.

WORDS TO OWN
glutted (glut′id) v.: overfilled.

----

17. **turn to account:** be profitable.
18. **American:** To Swift's readers, this label would suggest a barbaric person.
19. **fricassee** (frik′ə·sē′): stew with a light gravy.
20. **ragout** (ra·gōō′): highly flavored stew.

Images of Ireland (18th century). Hand-colored pastel drawings used for engraving in Mr. and Mrs. S. C. Hail's *Ireland* (1841–1843).

mirable gloves for ladies, and summer boots for fine gentlemen.

As to our city of Dublin, shambles[29] may be appointed for this purpose, in the most convenient parts of it, and butchers we may be assured will not be wanting, although I rather recommend buying the children alive, and dressing them hot from the knife, as we do roasting pigs.

A very worthy person, a true lover of his country, and whose virtues I highly esteem, was lately pleased, in discoursing on this matter, to offer a refinement upon my scheme. He said, that many gentlemen of this kingdom, having of late destroyed their deer, he conceived that the want of venison might be well supplied by the bodies of young lads and maidens, not exceeding fourteen years of age, nor under twelve, so great a number of both sexes in every country being now ready to starve, for want of work and service:[30] and these to be disposed of by their parents if alive, or other-

wise by their nearest relations. But with due <u>deference</u> to so excellent a friend, and so deserving a patriot, I cannot be altogether in his sentiments, for as to the males, my American acquaintance assured me from frequent experience, that their flesh was generally tough and lean, like that of our schoolboys, by continual exercise, and their taste disagreeable, and to fatten them would not answer the charge. Then as to the females, it would, I think with humble submission,[31] be a loss to the public, because they soon would become breeders themselves: And besides it is not improbable that some <u>scrupulous</u> people might be apt to <u>censure</u> such a practice (although in-

31. **with humble submission:** with all due respect to those who hold such opinions.

WORDS TO OWN

deference (def′ər·əns) *n.*: respect.
scrupulous (skroo′pyə·ləs) *adj.*: extremely careful and precise in deciding what is right or wrong.
censure (sen′shər) *v.*: to condemn.

---

29. **shambles:** slaughterhouses.
30. **service:** employment as servants.

deed very unjustly) as a little bordering upon cruelty, which, I confess, hath always been with me the strongest objection against any project, how well soever intended.

? The narrator claims to be sensitive to charges of cruelty. How do you think Swift wants you to feel about the narrator?

But in order to justify my friend, he confessed that this expedient was put into his head by the famous Sallmanaazor,[32] a native of the island Formosa, who came from thence to London, above twenty years ago, and in conversation told my friend, that in his country when any young person happened to be put to death, the executioner sold the carcass to persons of quality, as a prime dainty, and that, in his time, the body of a plump girl of fifteen, who was crucified for an attempt to poison the emperor, was sold to his imperial majesty's prime minister of state, and other great mandarins[33] of the court, in joints[34] from the gibbet,[35] at four hundred crowns. Neither indeed can I deny, that if the same use were made of several plump young girls in this town, who, without one single groat to their fortunes, cannot stir abroad without a chair,[36] and appear at the playhouse, and assemblies in foreign fineries, which they never will pay for; the kingdom would not be the worse.

Some persons of a desponding spirit are in great concern about that vast number of poor people, who are aged, diseased, or maimed, and I have been desired to employ my thoughts what course may be taken, to ease the nation of so grievous an encumbrance. But I am not in the least pain upon that matter, because it is very well known, that they are every day dying, and rotting, by cold, and famine, and filth, and vermin,[37] as fast as can be reasonably expected. And as to the younger laborers they are now in almost as hopeful[38] a condition. They cannot get work, and consequently pine away for want of nourishment, to a degree, that if at any time they are accidentally hired to common labor, they have not strength to perform it, and thus the country and themselves are in a fair way[39] of being soon delivered from the evils to come.

? What other problem does the narrator take up? What is his solution, and how is it similar to his main proposal?

I have too long digressed, and therefore shall return to my subject. I think the advantages by the proposal which I have made are obvious and many as well as of the highest importance.

For first, as I have already observed, it would greatly lessen the number of papists, with whom we are yearly overrun, being the principal breeders of the nation, as well as our most dangerous enemies, and who stay at home on purpose with a design to deliver the kingdom to the Pretender, hoping to take their advantage by the absence of so many good Protestants,[40] who have chosen rather to leave their country, than stay at home, and pay tithes[41] against their conscience, to an idolatrous Episcopal curate.

Secondly, the poorer tenants will have something valuable of their own, which by law may be made liable to distress,[42] and help to pay their landlord's rent, their corn and cattle being already seized, and money a thing unknown.

Thirdly, whereas the maintenance of an hundred thousand children, from two years old, and upwards, cannot be computed at less than ten

---

32. Sallmanaazor: George Psalmanazar (c. 1679–1763), a Frenchman who pretended to be from Formosa, an old Portuguese name for Taiwan; his writings were fraudulent.
33. mandarins (man′də·rinz): officials. The term comes from *mandarim,* the Portuguese word for high-ranking officials in the Chinese empire, with which the Portuguese traded.
34. joints: large cuts of meat, including the bone.
35. gibbet (jib′it): gallows.
36. chair: sedan chair; a covered seat carried by servants.
37. vermin: pests such as lice, fleas, and bedbugs.

38. hopeful: actually, hopeless. Swift is using the word with intentional irony.
39. are in a fair way: have a good chance.
40. good Protestants: that is, in Swift's view, bad Protestants, because they object to the Church of Ireland's bishops and regard them as "idolatrous."
41. tithes (tī*thz*): monetary gifts to the church equivalent to one tenth of each donor's income.
42. liable to distress: That is, the money from the sale of their children may be seized by their landlords.

WORDS TO OWN

expedient (ek·spē′dē·ənt) *n.:* convenient means to an end.

digressed (di·grest′) *v.:* wandered off the subject.

---

shillings apiece per annum, the nation's stock will be thereby increased fifty thousand pounds per annum, besides the profit of a new dish, introduced to the tables of all gentlemen of fortune in the kingdom, who have any refinement in taste, and the money will circulate among ourselves, the goods being entirely of our own growth and manufacture.[43]

Fourthly, the constant breeders, besides the gain of eight shillings sterling per annum, by the sale of their children, will be rid of the charge of maintaining them after the first year.

Fifthly, this food would likewise bring great custom to taverns, where the vintners[44] will certainly be so prudent as to procure the best receipts[45] for dressing it to perfection, and consequently have their houses frequented by all the fine gentlemen, who justly value themselves upon their knowledge in good eating, and a skillful cook, who understands how to oblige his guests will contrive to make it as expensive as they please.

Sixthly, this would be a great inducement to marriage, which all wise nations have either encouraged by rewards, or enforced by laws and penalties. It would increase the care and tenderness of mothers toward their children, when they were sure of a settlement for life to the poor babes, provided in some sort by the public to their annual profit instead of expense, we should soon see an honest emulation[46] among the married women, which of them could bring the fattest child to the market, men would become as fond of their wives, during the time of their pregnancy, as they are now of their mares in foal, their cows in calf, or sows when they are ready to farrow,[47] nor offer to beat or kick them (as is too frequent a practice) for fear of a miscarriage.

Many other advantages might be enumerated. For instance, the addition of some thousand carcasses in our exportation of barreled beef. The propagation of swine's flesh, and improvement in the art of making good bacon, so much wanted among us by the great destruction of pigs, too frequent at our tables, which are no way comparable in taste, or magnificence to a well-grown, fat yearling child, which roasted whole will make a considerable figure at a Lord Mayor's feast, or any other public entertainment. But this, and many others I omit being studious of brevity.

Supposing that one thousand families in this city, would be constant customers for infants' flesh, besides others who might have it at merry meetings, particularly weddings and christenings, I compute that Dublin would take off annually about twenty thousand carcasses, and the rest of the kingdom (where probably they will be sold somewhat cheaper) the remaining eighty thousand.

I can think of no one objection, that will possibly be raised against this proposal, unless it should be urged that the number of people will be thereby much lessened in the kingdom. This I freely own, and it was indeed one principal design in offering it to the world. I desire the reader will observe, that I calculate my remedy for this one individual kingdom of Ireland, and for no other that ever was, is, or, I think, ever can be upon earth. Therefore let no man talk to me of other expedients:[48] *Of taxing our absentees[49] at five shillings a pound; of using neither clothes, nor household furniture, except what is of our own growth and manufacture; of utterly rejecting the materials and instruments that promote foreign luxury; of curing the expensiveness of pride, vanity, idleness, and gaming[50] in our women; of introducing a vein of parsimony,[51]*

> **?** The narrator states the specific advantages of his proposal. Who profits from these "advantages," and who suffers?

---

43. **own growth and manufacture:** home-grown, edible children, not imported ones.
44. **vintners** (vint′nərz): wine merchants.
45. **receipts:** old-fashioned for "recipes."
46. **emulation** (em′yoo·lā′shən): competition.
47. **farrow** (far′ō): to produce piglets.

48. **other expedients:** At one time or another, Swift had advocated all these measures for the relief of Ireland, but they were all ignored by the government. This section was italicized in all editions printed during Swift's lifetime to indicate that Swift made these proposals sincerely rather than ironically.
49. **absentees:** English landowners who refused to live on their Irish property.
50. **gaming:** gambling.
51. **parsimony** (pär′sə·mō′nē): thriftiness; economy.

WORDS TO OWN
procure (prō·kyoor′) *v*.: to obtain; get.
brevity (brev′ə·tē) *n*.: being brief.

---

prudence, and temperance; of learning to love our country, wherein we differ even from Laplanders, and the inhabitants of Topinamboo;[52] of quitting our <u>animosities</u>, and factions,[53] nor act any longer like the Jews, who were murdering one another at the very moment their city[54] was taken; of being a little cautious not to sell our country and consciences for nothing; of teaching landlords to have at least one degree of mercy toward their tenants. Lastly of putting a spirit of honesty, industry, and skill into our shopkeepers, who, if a resolution could now be taken to buy only our native goods, would immediately unite to cheat and exact[55] upon us in the price, the measure, and the goodness, nor could ever yet be brought to make one fair proposal of just dealing, though often and earnestly invited to it.

Therefore I repeat, let no man talk to me of these and the like expedients, till he hath at least a glimpse of hope, that there will ever be some hearty and sincere attempt to put them in practice.

But as to myself, having been wearied out for many years with offering vain, idle, visionary thoughts, and at length utterly despairing of success, I fortunately fell upon this proposal, which as it is wholly new, so it hath something solid and real, of no expense and little trouble, full in our own power, and whereby we can incur no danger in disobliging[56] England. For this kind of commodity will not bear exportation, the flesh being of too tender a consistence, to admit a long continuance in salt, although perhaps I could name a country,[57] which would be glad to eat up our whole nation without it.

After all I am not so violently bent upon my own opinion, as to reject any offer, proposed by wise men, which shall be found equally innocent, cheap, easy, and effectual. But before something of that kind shall be advanced in contradiction to my scheme, and offering a better, I desire the author, or authors will be pleased maturely to consider two points. First, as things now stand, how they will be able to find food and raiment for a hundred thousand useless mouths and backs. And secondly, there being a round million of creatures in human figure, throughout this kingdom, whose whole subsistence[58] put into a common stock would leave them in debt two millions of pounds sterling, adding those who are beggars by profession to the bulk of farmers, cottagers, and laborers, with their wives and children, who are beggars in effect; I desire those politicians, who dislike my overture, and may perhaps be so bold to attempt an answer, that they will first ask the parents of these mortals, whether they would not at this day think it a great happiness to have been sold for food at a year old, in the manner I prescribe, and thereby have avoided such a perpetual scene of misfortunes, as they have since gone through, by the oppression of landlords, the impossibility of paying rent without money or trade, the want of common sustenance, with neither house nor clothes to cover them from inclemencies of weather, and the most inevitable prospect of entailing[59] the like, or great miseries, upon their breed forever.

What two points support the narrator's proposal?

I profess in the sincerity of my heart that I have not the least personal interest in endeavoring to promote this necessary work, having no other motive than the public good of my country, by advancing our trade, providing for infants, relieving the poor, and giving some pleasure to the rich. I have no children, by which I can propose to get a single penny; the youngest being nine years old, and my wife past childbearing.

---

52. **Topinamboo:** Swift is referring to a region of Brazil in which reside various native peoples collectively called the Tupinambá. Here, Swift suggests that if Brazilian peoples and Laplanders can love their seemingly inhospitable lands, the Irish should love Ireland.

53. **factions:** political groups that work against the interests of other such groups or against the main body of government.

54. **their city:** Jerusalem, which the Roman emperor Titus (A.D. 39–81) destroyed in A.D. 70, while Jewish factions fought one another.

55. **exact:** force payment.

56. **disobliging:** offending.

57. **a country:** England.

58. **whole subsistence:** all their possessions.

59. **entailing:** passing on to the next generation.

- -

WORDS TO OWN
animosities (an'ə·mäs'ə·tēz) *n. pl.:* hostilities; violent hatreds or resentments.

- -

Top of the Food Chain

T. Coraghessan Boyle

The thing was, we had a little problem with the insect vector[1] there, and believe me, your tamer stuff, your Malathion and pyrethrum and the rest of the so-called environmentally safe products,[2] didn't begin to make a dent in it, not a dent, I mean it was utterly useless—we might as well have been spraying Chanel No. 5 for all the good it did. And you've got to realize these people were literally covered with insects day and night—and the fact that they hardly wore any clothes just compounded the problem. Picture if you can, gentlemen, a naked little two-year-old boy so black with flies and mosquitoes it looks like he's wearing long johns, or the young mother so racked with the malarial shakes she can't even lift a Diet Coke to her lips—it was pathetic, just pathetic, like something out of the Dark Ages . . . Well, anyway, the decision was made to go with DDT.[3] In the short term. Just to get the situation under control, you understand.

Yes, that's right, Senator, *DDT:* Dichlorodiphenyltrichloroethane.

Yes, I'm well aware of that fact, sir. But just because *we* banned it domestically, under pressure from the bird-watching contingent and the hopheads down at the EPA, it doesn't necessarily follow that the rest of the world—especially the developing world—was about to jump on the bandwagon. And that's the key

Eye of a Fly (1665) by Robert Hooke, from *Micrographia* (The Royal Society, London, 1665).

Rare Books and Manuscripts Division. The New York Public Library. Astor, Lenox and Tilden Foundations.

word here, Senator: developing. You've got to realize this is Borneo we're talking about here, not Port Townsend or Enumclaw. These people don't know from square one about sanitation, disease control, pest eradication. It rains a hundred and twenty inches a year, minimum.[4] They dig up roots in the jungle. They've still got headhunters along the Rajang River, for god's sake.

And please don't forget they *asked* us to come in there, practically begged us—and not only the World Health Organization but the Sultan of Brunei and the government in Sarawak too. We did what we could to accommodate them and reach our objective in the shortest period of time and by the most direct and effective means. We went to the air. Obviously. And no one could have foreseen the consequences, no one, not even if we'd gone

1. **vector:** bearer or carrier of disease.
2. **Malathion** (mal′ə·thī′än′) **and pyrethrum** (pī·reth′rəm) . . . **safe products:** Malathion and pyrethrum are insecticides made from organic substances. Though they are less toxic than synthetic, or human-made, insecticides, their safety is still debated.
3. **DDT:** a synthetic compound first discovered to be an insecticide in 1939. Widely used during World War II, DDT was later found to cause such toxic effects in other animal populations that its use was severely restricted in the United States in 1972.

4. **hundred and twenty inches . . . minimum:** In comparison, the average yearly rainfall in most of the United States is less than half this figure.

out and generated a hundred environmental impact statements—it was just one of those things, a freak occurrence, and there's no defense against that. Not that I know of, anyway . . .

Caterpillars? Yes, Senator, that's correct. That was the first sign: caterpillars.

But let me backtrack a minute here. You see, out in the bush they have these roofs made of thatched palm leaves—you'll see them in the towns too, even in Bintulu or Brunei—and they're really pretty effective, you'd be surprised. A hundred and twenty inches of rain, they've got to figure a way to keep it out of the hut, and for centuries, this was it. Palm leaves. Well, it was about a month after we sprayed for the final time and I'm sitting at my desk in the trailer thinking about the drainage project at

Blue Fly (1665) by Robert Hooke, from *Micrographia* (The Royal Society, London, 1665).

Rare Books and Manuscripts Division. The New York Public Library. Astor, Lenox and Tilden Foundations.

Kuching, enjoying the fact that for the first time in maybe a year I'm not smearing mosquitoes all over the back of my neck, when there's a knock at the door. It's this elderly gentleman, tattooed from head to toe, dressed only in a pair of running shorts—they love those shorts, by the way, the shiny material and the tight machine stitching, the whole country, men and women both, they can't get enough of them. . . . Anyway, he's the headman of the local village and he's very excited, something about the roofs—*atap,* they call them. That's all he can say, *atap, atap,* over and over again.

It's raining, of course. It's always raining. So I shrug into my rain slicker, start up the 4 × 4, and go have a look. Sure enough, all the *atap* roofs are collapsing, not only in his village but

throughout the target area. The people are all huddled there in their running shorts, looking pretty miserable, and one after another the roofs keep falling in, it's bewildering, and gradually I realize the headman's diatribe has begun to feature a new term I was unfamiliar with at the time—the word for caterpillar, as it turns out, in the Iban dialect. But who was to make the connection between three passes with the crop duster and all these staved-in roofs?

Our people finally sorted it out a couple weeks later. The chemical, which, by the way, cut down the number of mosquitoes exponentially, had the unfortunate side effect of killing off this little wasp—I've got the scientific name for it somewhere in my report here, if you're interested—that preyed on a type of caterpillar that in turn ate palm leaves. Well, with the wasps gone, the caterpillars hatched out with nothing to keep them in check and chewed the roofs to pieces, which was unfortunate, we admit it, and we had a real cost overrun on replacing those roofs with tin . . . but the people were happier, I think, in the long run, because, let's face it, no matter how tightly you weave those palm leaves, they're just not going to keep the water out like tin. Of course, nothing's perfect, and we had a lot of complaints about the rain drumming on the panels, people unable to sleep, and what-have-you . . .

Yes, sir, that's correct—the flies were next.

Well, you've got to understand the magnitude of the fly problem in Borneo, there's nothing like it here to compare it with, except maybe a garbage strike in New York. Every minute of every day you've got flies everywhere, up your nose, in your mouth, your ears, your eyes, flies in your rice, your Coke, your Singapore sling, and your gin rickey. It's enough to drive you to distraction, not to mention the diseases these things carry, from dysentery to typhoid to cholera and back round the loop again. And once the mosquito population was down, the flies seemed to breed up to fill in the gap—Borneo wouldn't be Borneo without some damned insect blackening the air.

Of course, this was before our people had tracked down the problem with the caterpillars and the wasps and all of that, and so we figured we'd had a big success with the mosquitoes, why not a series of ground sweeps, mount a fogger in the back of a Suzuki Brat, and sanitize the huts, not to mention the open sewers, which as you know are nothing but a breeding ground for flies, chiggers, and biting insects of every sort. At least it was an error of commission rather than omission. At least we were trying.

I watched the flies go down myself. One day they were so thick in the trailer I couldn't even *find* my paperwork, let alone attempt to get through it, and the next they were collecting on the windows, bumbling around like they were drunk. A day later they were gone. Just like that. From a million flies in the trailer to none . . .

Well, no one could have foreseen that, Senator.

The geckos ate the flies, yes. You're all familiar with geckos, I assume, gentlemen? These are the lizards you've seen during your trips to Hawaii, very colorful, patrolling the houses for roaches and flies, almost like pets, but of course they're wild animals, never lose sight of that, and just about as unsanitary as anything I can think of, except maybe flies.

Yes, well don't forget, sir, we're viewing this with twenty-twenty hindsight, but at the time no one gave a thought to geckos or what they ate—

they were just another fact of life in the tropics. Mosquitoes, lizards, scorpions, leeches—you name it, they've got it. When the flies began piling up on the windowsills like drift, naturally the geckos feasted on them, stuffing themselves till they looked like sausages crawling up the walls. Where before they moved so fast you could never be sure you'd seen them, now they waddled across the floor, laid around in the corners, clung to the air vents like magnets—and even then no one paid much attention to them till they started turning belly-up in the streets. Believe me, we confirmed a lot of things there about the buildup of these products[5] as you move up the food chain and the efficacy—or lack thereof—of certain methods, no doubt about that . . .

The cats? That's where it got sticky, really sticky. You see, nobody really lost any sleep over a pile of dead lizards—though we did tests routinely and the tests confirmed what we'd expected, that is, the product had been concentrated in the geckos because of the number of contaminated flies they consumed. But lizards are one thing and cats are another. These people really have an affection for their cats—no house, no hut, no matter how primitive, is without at least a couple of them. Mangy-looking things, long-legged and scrawny, maybe, not at all the sort of animal you'd see here, but there it was: They loved their cats. Because the cats were functional, you understand—without them, the place would have been swimming in rodents inside of a week.

You're right there, Senator, yes—that's exactly what happened.

You see, the cats had a field day with these feeble geckos—you can imagine, if any of you have ever owned a cat, the kind of joy these animals must have experienced to see their nemesis, this ultra-quick lizard, and it's just barely creeping across the floor like a bug.

5. **these products:** insecticides.

Well, to make a long story short, the cats ate up every dead and dying gecko in the country, from snout to tail, and then the cats began to die . . . which to my mind would have been no great loss if it wasn't for the rats. Suddenly there were rats everywhere—you couldn't drive down the street without running over half-a-dozen of them at a time. They fouled the grain supplies, fell in the wells and died, bit infants as they slept in their cradles. But that wasn't the worst, not by a long shot. No, things really went down the tube after that. Within the month we were getting scattered reports of bubonic plague, and of course we tracked them all down and made sure the people got a round of treatment with antibiotics, but still we lost a few and the rats kept coming . . .

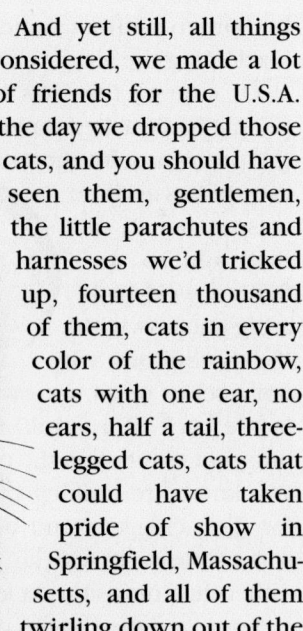

It was my plan, yes. I was brainstorming one night, rats scuttling all over the trailer like something out of a cheap horror film, the villagers in a panic over the threat of the plague and the stream of nonstop hysterical reports from the interior—people were turning black, swelling up and bursting, that sort of thing—well, as I say, I came up with a plan, a stopgap, not perfect, not cheap, but at this juncture, I'm sure you'll agree, something had to be implemented.

We wound up going as far as Australia for some of the cats, cleaning out the SPCA facilities and what-have-you, though we rounded most of them up in Indonesia and Singapore—approximately fourteen thousand in all. And yes, it cost us—cost us upfront purchase money and aircraft fuel and pilots' overtime and all the rest of it—but we really felt there was no alternative. It was like all nature had turned against us.

And yet still, all things considered, we made a lot of friends for the U.S.A. the day we dropped those cats, and you should have seen them, gentlemen, the little parachutes and harnesses we'd tricked up, fourteen thousand of them, cats in every color of the rainbow, cats with one ear, no ears, half a tail, three-legged cats, cats that could have taken pride of show in Springfield, Massachusetts, and all of them twirling down out of the sky like great big oversized snowflakes . . .

It was something. It was really something.

Of course, you've all seen the reports. There were other factors we hadn't counted on, adverse conditions in the paddies and manioc fields[6]—we don't to this day know what predatory species were inadvertently killed off by the initial sprayings, it's just a mystery—but the weevils[7] and whatnot took a pretty heavy toll on the crops that year, and by the time we dropped the cats, well—the people were pretty hungry, and I suppose it was inevitable that we lost a good proportion of them right then and there. But we've got a CARE program going there now and something hit the rat population—we still don't know what, a virus, we think—and the geckos, they tell me, are making a comeback.

So what I'm saying is it could be worse, and to every cloud a silver lining, wouldn't you agree, gentlemen?

6. **paddies and manioc fields:** Paddies, or rice paddies, are small, flooded fields used to grow rice in eastern and southern Asia. Manioc, also called cassava, is a kind of tuber cultivated in tropical areas.
7. **weevils:** snouted beetles extremely destructive to rice and grain crops.

MAKING MEANINGS

First Thoughts

1. Do you think Swift goes too far in *A Modest Proposal*? Why or why not?

Shaping Interpretations

2. Why does the narrator express the hope that his plan "will not be liable to the least objection" just before he introduces it? What is **ironic** in Swift's use of the word *modest* to describe his proposal?

3. How would you state the **purpose** of this essay? Whom or what is Swift trying to reform?

4. Describe the narrator's real meaning when he asserts that England will not mind if Ireland kills and eats its babies. What element of **satire** is evident here?

5. Near the end of the pamphlet, the speaker lists "other expedients" that might help lessen the present distress in Ireland. Some of these options are very constructive. Why, then, does the narrator brush these ideas for reform aside?

6. Find sentences in which the speaker uses **ethical appeals** by describing himself favorably and claiming to possess virtues that— considering the nature of his proposal—he could not possibly have. (Check your reading notes.)

Reading Check

a. Why does the narrator think the food he proposes is "very proper for landlords"?

b. Why does the narrator reject the idea of selling and eating the twelve- to fourteen-year-olds? Why is he unconcerned about old people suffering from sickness, poverty, and neglect?

c. About midway in the pamphlet, the narrator lists the advantages of his proposal. What are the six principal advantages?

d. Describe the one objection that the narrator anticipates to his proposal.

e. Where does Swift tell what his "modest" proposal is? How would you **sum up** his proposal's **main idea**?

---

7. Find places in the proposal where the speaker uses **logical appeals** to support his suggestions. (Be sure to check your reading notes.)

Extending the Text

8. What other human disasters resulting from bureaucratic incompetence around the world could be targets for another "modest proposal"?

READING SKILLS AND STRATEGIES

Interpreting Connotations: Emotional Appeals

Diction, or word choice, is especially important in **persuasive writing.** Swift is particularly skillful in choosing words with strong **connotations**—that is, words loaded with strong feelings, associations, or even judgments. Some of Swift's loaded words follow. (Check your reading notes to see if you spotted more.)

savages	beggars	filth
male and female	rags	idolatrous
popish infants	breeders	carcasses

In each instance, another word or term could have been chosen to create a different, less harsh effect. For example, *male* and *female*—as opposed to *man* and *woman*—make us think of animals, not human beings, which is Swift's intention.

1. Find the places in the text where the words listed above are used. What is the emotional effect of each word choice?

2. What other tamer or more positive words could have been used to create different emotional effects?

CHOICES: Building Your Portfolio

Writer's Notebook

1. Collecting Ideas for a Persuasive Essay

The passion that drove Swift is the right starting point for persuasion. To write a good persuasive essay, you have to *care*. Think about the contemporary issues raised in Extending the Text (pages 496, 500, and 513). If some fire your passion, quickly jot down what you feel about them, and *why*. If none does, find your "hot-button" issue by freewriting about these phrases: *What really makes me angry is _____,* or *If I had the power, I would change _____.* Save your notes for the Writer's Workshop on page 612.

Creative Writing

2. Slumberers Awake

Many characters in literature, like Gulliver, awaken from a deep sleep to find themselves in strange, new circumstances. Rip Van Winkle, for example, wakes to find he's been sleeping for twenty years and that his country is no longer a British colony. The hero of Franz Kafka's *The Metamorphosis* wakes to find he has become a horrible bug. Imagine that overnight some fantastic change happens to you. Write a first-person narrative describing what happened, where and when it happened, and why it happened.

Creative Writing/ Speaking

3. Tell the Tale

With its humorous exaggeration and outlandish plot, *Gulliver's Travels* has some of the characteristics of a **tall tale,** a type of folk literature particularly associated with Mark Twain and the American West. Retell one of Gulliver's adventures in the form of a tall tale, one that cowboys might have told to amuse themselves around a campfire. Make Gulliver an American character.

Comparing Satires

4. Two Satirists

What similarities do you notice between Swift's satire in *A Modest Proposal* and Boyle's satire in the *Connections* story "Top of the Food Chain" (page 509)? In a brief essay, explore how each writer uses satirical devices. At the start of your essay, briefly **summarize** the main points presented in each text.

Persuasive Writing

5. A New Modest Proposal

Attack an evil you see in society today by writing an **ironic** "modest proposal" for its solution—so outrageously horrifying that readers will see at once the tragedy of the situation. Remember: As Swift was, you might be attacked for insensitivity. Your moral outrage must be made clear by gross exaggeration.

Creative Writing

6. Shift the Stance

Swift approached the subjects of corruption in England and poverty in Ireland from the point of view of a reformer. In *A Modest Proposal* he ironically takes the stance of a benevolent humanitarian, something like a modern social worker. Imagine an essay on the Irish problem written by someone with an entirely different **stance,** or position. For example, suppose that the writer is an Irish parent with hungry children or Sir Robert Walpole, lord of the Treasury, or King George II of England. Take a stand other than Swift's, and write an essay expressing your views.

Research/Speaking

7. Artistic Barbs

Research the paintings of William Hogarth (1697–1764), an English artist who, like Swift, was a powerful critic of eighteenth-century English life. Present your findings to your class in an oral report. Show pictures of Hogarth's work if you can.

Reading Skills and Strategies

VOCABULARY: DISTINGUISHING SHADES OF MEANING

Our language is rich and varied, in part because many words communicate various shades of meaning. Even words that have very similar definitions have subtly different meanings, emotional overtones, and associations, including associations with their opposite meanings.

Denotation and connotation. The dictionary definition, or explicit meaning of a word, is called its **denotation.** The denotation of *odious* as it is used in the following quotation from *Gulliver's Travels* is "causing or deserving loathing or disgust."

> I cannot but conclude the bulk of your natives to be the most pernicious race of little **odious** vermin that nature ever suffered to crawl upon the surface of the earth.

However, words can communicate more than ideas; they can also convey attitudes and emotions. These associated attitudes and emotional overtones that are communicated by words are called **connotations.** For example, while both *odious* and *hateful* mean "causing or deserving loathing," most people associate different emotions with each word. *Odious* is associated with a particular, loathsome quality in a thing or person that causes feelings of disgust. On the other hand, *hateful* is associated with a more general unpleasantness of character that causes feelings of strong dislike and aversion.

Synonyms and antonyms. Words that have similar meanings are called **synonyms.** *Odious* and *hateful* are synonyms. Dictionaries usually give one or more synonyms for each word. You can also find synonyms in a **thesaurus,** a dictionary of synonyms.

When choosing a synonym or figuring out the meaning of a word from a synonym, you need to be sure its meaning suits the **context.** For example, *hateful* is a synonym for *odious* when it means "causing or deserving loathing." However, it is not a synonym for *odious* when it means "showing or feeling hate."

1. Everyone at court disliked and avoided the **hateful** young queen.
2. His long illness had made the old king so **hateful** that he no longer loved his own children.

Words that have opposite or almost opposite meanings are called **antonyms.** *Odious* and *lovable* are antonyms. *Attractive* and *appealing* are also antonyms for *odious.* Dictionaries sometimes list antonyms at the end of the entry for a word.

Try It Out

On your own paper, draw a chart like the following one, excluding the example *odious*. In the appropriate column beside each of the other five Words to Own from *Gulliver's Travels,* write the denotation as it is used in the selection, the connotations, a synonym, and an antonym. Use a dictionary and a thesaurus for reference as necessary.

Word to Own	Denotation	Connotations	Synonym	Antonym
odious	causing loathing	loathsome quality, disgust	hateful	lovable
diminutive				
quelled				
copious				
prevailed				
pernicious				

Women Writers of the Restoration and the Eighteenth Century

by C. F. Main

For now that Aphra Behn had done it, girls could go to their parents and say, You need not give me an allowance; I can make money by my pen.

—Virginia Woolf, *from A Room of One's Own*

Living by the Pen

Samuel Johnson once said that a woman who issued her opinions to the public was something like a dog walking on its hind legs. "It is not done well; but you are surprised to find it done at all," he quipped. Had he looked around, Johnson might have been surprised indeed. During his lifetime the number of women writers in England increased enormously. Of course, there had always been many women who wrote letters, kept journals and diaries, and recorded in notebooks their recipes, prayers, poems, and private thoughts. But eighteenth-century women—fortuitously aided by the explosion of the middle class and emergence of a literary marketplace—were increasingly able to have their work published, even able to earn a living by writing. They no longer needed a well-to-do family or patron, as Renaissance women writers had; in this new era, if a woman's work was likely to appeal to readers, a printer was bound to print it.

The variety of these women's writings is astonishing. In the mid-1600s, Katherine Philips—who called herself Orinda, and whom admirers took to calling "the Matchless Orinda"—became England's first famous woman writer. Her rather traditional poems, mostly on the theme of friendship, were addressed to a circle of confidants, mainly but not entirely women, to whom she gave such fancy names as Lucasia, Rosania, Cratander, and Silvander.

Illustration (detail) from an 1803 edition of Ann Radcliffe's Gothic romance *The Mysteries of Udolpho*.

By the late eighteenth century, the Minerva Press was flooding the bookstalls with popular fiction written mostly by women. Scandalous romances and satirical novels, with characters who were often thinly disguised society folk, became a staple. Also popular were the new Gothic novels, in which frightening and apparently supernatural events took place in remote castles. In fact, the best-selling novels of Ann Radcliffe (1764–1823), the most famous writer of eighteenth-century Gothics, are recognizable ancestors of today's horror fiction.

Women also publicly commented—as journalists, advocates, and critics—on the most important and controversial issues of the day. Early feminists like Mary Astell (1666–1731) and Lady Mary Chudleigh (1656–1710) wrote that marriage laws enslaved women, making them little more than their husbands' property. (In contrast, Margaret Cavendish [1623–1674], duchess of Newcastle, took it for granted that marriage was an arrangement ordained by God, and published a huge biography of her husband the duke, whom she presented as a paragon.) Hannah More (1745–1833), an early British voice for the abolition of slavery, produced many widely circulated tracts about the moral education of women and the poor.

Aphra Behn (1640–1689)

Aphra Behn, born Aphra Johnson to working-class parents in Kent, was the first English woman to earn her living by writing. She was a free spirit, the sort of woman who used to be called an adventuress, and she had the luck to write in the era when women were at last permitted to work in the theater as actors, playwrights, and producers. In her lifetime, both she and her writings were very well known, but during the two hundred years after her death, her works and her life came to be regarded as outrageous and were forgotten.

Consequently, at this late date it is impossible to recover many details of her biography. She perhaps spent most of her early years in Guiana, she married a Mr. Behn (usually pronounced "bane") who died in 1666, possibly a casualty of the Great Plague of 1664–1665, and she was a spy for her country during a war against the Dutch. Beyond these bare facts lies much interesting speculation. What is certain is that she left an impressive literary legacy. For nearly ten years in a row, her plays, comedies for the most part, were successively produced in London. In *The Rover* (1677–1681), her best-known play, three young Spanish women, who are curious about sex, encounter three young traveling Englishmen during carnival time in Spain.

Behn also published several collections of translations and poems, as well as a dozen short novels, one of which is her masterpiece *Oroonoko* (1688). Its hero is an African prince, a powerful man with a noble mind and body, who has been tricked into slavery and transported to the island of Surinam.

Aphra Behn.

Behn's genius makes him seem very real to the reader, who is bound to be moved by his suffering.

In the following speech, Oroonoko, who has been renamed Caesar by his slave master, exhorts his fellow slaves to fight the unjust rule of the English.

"And why," said he, "my dear friends and fellow sufferers, should we be slaves to an unknown people? Have they vanquished us nobly in fight? Have they won us in honorable battle? And are we, by the chance of war, become their slaves? This would not anger a noble heart, this would not animate a soldier's soul. No, but we are bought and sold like apes, or monkeys, to be the sport of women, fools, and cowards, and the support of rogues, renegades that have abandoned their own countries for raping, murders, thefts, and villainies. Do you not hear every day how they upbraid each other with infamy of life, below the wildest savages, and shall we render obedience to such a degenerate race, who have no one human virtue left to distinguish them from the vilest creatures? Will you, I say, suffer the lash from such hands?" They all replied with one accord, "No, no, no; Caesar has spoke like a great captain, like a great king."

—Aphra Behn, *from Oroonoko*

Lady Mary Wortley Montagu (1689–1762)

Though she had a more privileged upbringing than Aphra Behn, Lady Mary Wortley Montagu also educated herself, spending much of her childhood buried among the books in her father's vast library. From an early age, she was known as clever and daring. At twenty-three, she eloped on horseback with Edward Wortley Montagu, flouting her family's wish that she marry for money. After a serious bout with smallpox, she championed smallpox inoculations in Britain. Later, she dared to refuse the romantic attentions of her one-time good friend, Alexander Pope, who then tried, unsuccessfully, to destroy her in his satires.

Although she was herself a talented poet, her fame now rests on her letters, which were published in four volumes immediately after her death. They are still a valuable source of information about eighteenth-century life in England, France, and even Turkey, where she lived for a time while her husband was the English ambassador to Constantinople.

In the following passage, taken from a letter written to a friend in 1717, Lady Montagu describes a trip to the women's public baths in the Turkish city of Sofia (now the capital of Bulgaria).

> I was in my traveling habit, which is a riding dress, and certainly appeared very extraordinary to them, yet there was not one of 'em that showed the least surprise or impertinent curiosity, but received me with all the obliging civility possible. I know no European court where the ladies would have behaved themselves in so polite a manner to a stranger. I believe in the whole there were two hundred women and yet none of those disdainful smiles or satiric whispers that never fail in our assemblies when anybody appears that is not dressed exactly in fashion. They repeated over and over to me, "Uzelle, pek uzelle," which is nothing but, "Charming, very charming." The first sofas were covered with cushions and rich carpets, on which sat the ladies, and on the second their slaves behind 'em, but without any distinction of rank by their dress, all being in the state of nature, that is, in plain English, stark naked. . . .
>
> The lady that seemed the most considerable amongst them entreated me to sit by her and would fain have undressed me for the bath. I excused myself with some difficulty, they all being so earnest in persuading me. I was at last forced to open my skirt and show them my stays, which satisfied 'em very well, for I saw they believed I was so locked up in that machine that it was not in my own power to open it, which contrivance they attributed to my husband.
>
> —Lady Mary Wortley Montagu

Montagu spent the last twenty years of her life living alone in a villa in Italy. The letters to her daughter that survive from this period provide a record of Montagu's continuing curiosity about the world; her pride in her granddaughter's scholarly bent, which she encourages her daughter to nourish; and her own deep sense of self-reliance.

Fanny Burney (1752–1840)

Fictionalized letters, as funny and reflective as those of the prolific Lady Montagu, soon found their way into print as epistolary novels, or novels composed of letters.

One of the first and most important epistolary novels is *Evelina* (1778), by Frances "Fanny" Burney, the daughter of well-known musicologist Charles Burney. The heroine of this novel, Burney's first, is a beautiful, intelligent girl who must overcome many obstacles in order to win the man she loves, a good man whose wealth and social position are well beyond her own. Due to a misunderstanding, her father has abandoned her, and most of her other relatives are eccentric and socially awkward.

Frances d'Arblay Burney (1785) by Edward Francis Burney.

By Courtesy of the National Portrait Gallery, London.

But they are also quite funny. Burney had a real gift for comedy, which is a distinguishing feature of the English novel. The plot twists in *Evelina* and the odd behavior of the characters hold the reader's attention right up to the inevitable happy ending.

Burney had a keen eye and ear for the hypocrisy—and humor—of social relations in her day. Her work was praised by such notables as Samuel Johnson and David Garrick, and she was accepted into the Bluestocking Circle, a group of prominent women who shared literary and scholarly interests. Burney was also appointed to a position in the queen's household (which she found dreadfully boring and only escaped when she became quite ill).

This praise and prominence implies Burney had a brilliant education. However, like Behn and Montagu before her, she was largely self-taught. She also had qualms about the propriety of a writing career. At fifteen, thinking that her already voluminous work was inconsequential, Burney made a great bonfire of the pages, including the beginnings of *Caroline Evelyn,* a novel that she later rewrote as *Evelina.* Indeed, Burney was so insecure about her writing that she published *Evelina* anonymously at first; its great success finally encouraged her to put her name on the title page.

In the following passage from her diary, Burney announces the publication of *Evelina* with an endearing mock grandeur.

This year was ushered in by a grand and most important event! At the latter end of January, the literary world was favored with the first publication of the ingenious, learned, and most profound Fanny Burney! I doubt not but this memorable affair will, in future times, mark the period whence chronologers will date the zenith of the polite arts in this island! . . .

My little book, I am told, is now at all the circulating libraries. I have an exceeding odd sensation when I consider that it is now in the power of *any* and *every* body to read what I so carefully hoarded even from my best friends, till this last month or two; and that a work which was so lately lodged, in all privacy, in my bureau, may now be seen by every baker and butcher, cobbler and tinker, throughout the three kingdoms, for the small tribute of threepence.

—Fanny Burney

Yet the thought that she might be identified as *Evelina*'s author (a fact known by few but her sisters Susanna and Charlotte) sends Burney into a panic.

My aunt and Miss Humphries being settled at this time at Brompton, I was going thither with Susan to tea, when Charlotte acquainted me that they were then employed in reading *Evelina* to the invalid, my cousin Richard.

This intelligence gave me the utmost uneasiness—I foresaw a thousand dangers of a discovery—I dreaded the indiscreet warmth of all my confidants. In truth, I was quite sick with apprehension, and was too uncomfortable to go to Brompton, and Susan carried my excuses.

Upon her return, I was somewhat tranquilized, for she assured me that there was not the smallest suspicion of the author, and that they had concluded it to be the work of a *man*!

—Fanny Burney

Despite the assumption of Burney's relatives, and the reading public in general, that most published works were authored by men, eighteenth-century Britain was relatively open to women writers. In fact, for a brief period, women writers were in the ascendancy, and some male writers resorted to using female pseudonyms to get their work into print. Yet this freedom didn't last. By the mid-1800s, when a woman's sphere had again narrowed to home and hearth, women with literary aspirations once more faced enormous obstacles.

Mr. B. Finds Pamela Writing (18th century), illustration by Joseph Highmore from Samuel Richardson's *Pamela.*
Victoria and Albert Museum, London.

Alexander Pope

(1688–1744)

Alexander Pope, the most important poet of the early eighteenth century, was a child prodigy. As a very little boy, he later admitted, he "lisped in numbers." That is, he could speak in meter even before he could pronounce English properly. Such a talented youth would ordinarily be educated at Cambridge or Oxford. But Pope's family was Roman Catholic and therefore prohibited from attending these universities, as well as from voting, from holding public office, and even from practicing their religion.

Pope's father, a retired linen merchant, could afford to educate his son at home, which was perhaps the best place for Pope since his health was very delicate. Early in life he contracted a kind of tuberculosis that stunted his growth and disfigured his body, so that eventually his servants had to lace him into a canvas brace before he could sit upright. Since he continually suffered pains in his head, bones, and joints, it is no wonder he spoke of his life as "this long disease."

In spite of all of this, Pope led a remarkably busy and productive life. When he was sixteen, he began his poetic career, as the Roman poet Virgil did, by writing **pastorals**—poems describing the countryside. When he was twenty-three, he published *An Essay on Criticism,* a poem inspired in part by the Latin poet Horace's *Art of Poetry.* At twenty-four, he published a miniature classical epic, *The Rape of the Lock.* During his thirties he translated into English two enormous Greek epics, Homer's *Iliad* and, with the help of two assistants, Homer's *Odyssey.* In these works, Pope was not at all limited by his classical models, but used them to make works that were fresh and original. For this reason, he is

Alexander Pope and Dog Bounce (detail) (c. 1718) attributed to Jonathan Richardson.
Hagley Hall, Worcestershire, England.

sometimes referred to as a neoclassical (that is, new classical) poet.

Pope's early, brilliant successes inspired envy in lesser writers, who lampooned and ridiculed him. To defend himself he turned to satire, a kind of writing highly congenial to his temperament. The great satires of Pope's maturity include *The Dunciad* (1728, enlarged and revised in 1742), which attacks dull, uninteresting writers of all kinds and shows the forces of stupidity, ignorance, and folly taking over the world, and the *Moral Essays* (1731–1735), which pass judgment on certain immoral men and women as well as on very rich people who lack common sense and good taste. Finally, *An Epistle to Dr. Arbuthnot* (1735) contains both a defense of Pope's career as a writer and attacks on his literary enemies.

As a man Pope was, and still is, both loved and hated. In his lifetime and long after, he had a reputation for cruelty, malice, and ill nature. It now seems clear that he had none of these bad qualities but could appear to have them when provoked—as a caged tiger would have them when poked with a stick. We now realize that he was often goaded into writing satire, but that does not necessarily prove that Pope himself was peevish and mean. On the contrary, Pope had a large circle of friends, men and women, including some of the best writers of the day, who found him good-natured, generous, and brilliant in conversation. His agreeable manners, his large expressive eyes, and his way of dressing elegantly in bright colors charmed his friends. At his beautiful estate on the river Thames below London, he entertained important writers, artists, and political figures of the day. Pope became rich and famous; as for the people who raged against him, most of them are remembered today only because they disliked Alexander Pope.

Before You Read

HEROIC COUPLETS

FROM AN ESSAY ON MAN

Make the Connection

Quotable Wisdom

For the writers of Pope's time, the purpose of poetry was to combine the pleasing with the useful. The clarity, elegance, and compression of Pope's own style ensured that his works would more than fulfill this ideal. With the exception of Shakespeare, Pope is the most widely quoted writer in all of English literature, perhaps because he often wrote in heroic couplets, in which a memorable thought is expressed in a pair of rhyming lines. What sources do we quote from today?

Reading Skills and Strategies

Responding to the Text

As you read Pope, keep your notebook handy. You might record your responses in the form of a double-entry journal: a quote that catches your attention on the left and your response to it on the right.

Pope Quote	My Response

Elements of Literature

Antithesis

Pope habitually expresses himself in antitheses (an·tith′ə·sēz′). An **antithesis** uses parallel structures to present a balanced contrast: "Give me liberty, or give me death." ("Give me liberty, or kill me" fails as an antithesis because it isn't parallel or balanced.) By compressing elements of similarity and difference, antithesis helps to make a statement more forceful and (often) more memorable.

> **A**ntithesis is a contrast of ideas expressed in a grammatically balanced statement.
>
> *For more on Antithesis, see the Handbook of Literary Terms.*

Title page of Pope's *An Essay on Man,* designed by Pope.

ALEXANDER POPE 521

Pope is the greatest master of the **heroic couplet,** so-called because both he and his predecessor John Dryden used this form in their translations of the epic poems of antiquity. Each heroic couplet consists of two rhymed lines of **iambic pentameter.** (For variety, Pope occasionally introduces a **triplet.**) Many express a thought in a complete sentence: Such a couplet is called **closed:**

> Trust not yourself; but your defects to know,
> Make use of every friend—and every foe.

Although this couplet from *An Essay on Criticism* is part of a long and carefully organized explanation, it still makes good sense when it is plucked out of its context and allowed to stand by itself. Yet removing couplets from the poems in which they are embedded is dangerous, because it may lead us to think of the poems as strings of beads that can be easily broken apart. In reality, Pope's couplets are so carefully arranged into verse paragraphs that they are more like the forged links of an iron chain than separable units.

Heroic Couplets

Alexander Pope

1 Music resembles poetry: in each
  Are nameless graces[1] which no methods[2] teach,
  And which a master hand alone can reach.

  —An Essay on Criticism, lines 143–145

2 A little learning is a dangerous thing;
  Drink deep, or taste not the Pierian[3] spring.

  —An Essay on Criticism, lines 215–216

3 Be not the first by whom the new are tried,
  Nor yet the last to lay the old aside.

  —An Essay on Criticism, lines 335–336

4 True ease in writing comes from art, not chance,
  As those move easiest who have learned to dance.

  —An Essay on Criticism, lines 362–363

1. nameless graces: pleasing passages that cannot be explained.
2. methods: instruction books showing how to write poems.
3. Pierian (pī·ir′ē·ən): an allusion to the Muses, Greek goddesses of the arts and literature. The Muses were said to live in a district of Greece called Pieria.

5 Be thou the first true merit to befriend;
His praise is lost, who stays till all commend.

—*An Essay on Criticism*, lines 474–475

6 Good nature and good sense must ever join;
To err is human, to forgive, divine.

—*An Essay on Criticism*, lines 524–525

7 Hope springs eternal in the human breast:
Man never is, but always to be blest.

—*An Essay on Man*, Epistle I, lines 95–96

8 'Tis education forms the common mind,
Just as the twig is bent, the tree's inclined.

—*Moral Essays*, Epistle I, lines 149–150

9 But when to mischief mortals bend their will,
How soon they find fit instruments of ill!

—*The Rape of the Lock*, Canto III, lines 125–126

10 Satire's my weapon, but I'm too discreet
To run amuck, and tilt[4] at all I meet.

—*Imitations of Horace, Satire I*, Book II,
lines 69–70

4. tilt: charge at or thrust a weapon toward an opponent.

*View Across
Greenwich Park
Towards London*
(detail) (18th
century) by
Jean Rigaud.

Roy Miles Gallery,
London.

MAKING MEANINGS

First Thoughts

1. Share the responses to the couplets you recorded in your reading notebook. Do you find the advice in the couplets useful, or does it seem out-of-date? Why?

Shaping Interpretations

2. Tell in which of the couplets Pope does each of the following:
   a. Advocates a mean between two extremes.
   b. Suggests that geniuses are born, not made.
   c. Explains why people are never satisfied with what they have.
   d. Compares writing to putting on clothes.
   e. Shows how important education is for the young.
   f. Advises critics to be generous.
   g. Suggests that good writing results from practice and skill, not luck or accident.

3. Give some examples showing how a little learning can be dangerous (Couplet 2).

4. Read the couplet on true ease in writing, and explain the difference between what is suggested by the words *art* and *chance*.

5. Pope compresses a large amount of meaning into the twenty or so syllables of each of his couplets. Try **paraphrasing,** or expressing in your own words, the idea expressed in any couplet that you find hard to understand. What does Pope gain by compressing his meaning?

6. Pope habitually uses **antithesis** to focus and clarify his meaning. List all the antitheses you can find in these couplets.

Extending the Text

7. Does any couplet particularly connect with life today—in politics, education, or the arts? Explain the connection as you see it.

Challenging the Text

8. Do you take issue with any of these pronouncements? How would you rephrase any of them to get at a different point altogether?

An *Essay on Man* is Pope's long (1,304 lines) philosophical poem, published when he was forty-five. A lifetime of reading, in both English and foreign languages, contributed to its composition. The poem is concerned not only with "man," by which Pope means the whole human race, but with the entire universe as well. It's important to know that the ideas in the poem are not merely the private notions of Pope and his friends, but that they come from many authors, including Plato, Aristotle, St. Thomas Aquinas, Dante, Erasmus, Shakespeare, Bacon, and Milton.

In the following lines from the *Essay*, Pope generalizes about the human race. Pope's "man" is all of us. Do you agree that everyone has the characteristics Pope describes?

from An Essay on Man
Alexander Pope

Know then thyself,° presume not God to scan;°
The proper study of mankind is man.
Placed on this isthmus of a middle state,°
A being darkly wise, and rudely great:
5 With too much knowledge for the skeptic° side,
With too much weakness for the Stoic's pride,°
He hangs between; in doubt to act, or rest;
In doubt to deem himself a god, or beast;
In doubt his mind or body to prefer;
10 Born but to die, and reasoning but to err;
Alike in ignorance, his reason such,
Whether he thinks too little, or too much:
Chaos of thought and passion, all confused;
Still° by himself abused, or disabused;°
15 Created half to rise, and half to fall;
Great lord of all things, yet a prey to all;
Sole judge of truth, in endless error hurled:
The glory, jest, and riddle of the world!

1. Know . . . thyself: a moral precept of Socrates and other ethical philosophers. **scan:** pry into; speculate about.
3. middle state: that is, having the rational intellect of angels and the physical body of beasts.
5. skeptic: The ancient Skeptics doubted that humans can gain accurate knowledge of anything. They emphasized the limitations of human knowledge.
6. Stoic's pride: The ancient Stoics' ideal was a calm acceptance of life and an indifference to both pain and pleasure. Stoics are called proud because they refused to recognize human limitations.
14. still: always; continually. **disabused:** undeceived.

Alexander Pope (18th century). Self-portrait. Oil.

Bryn Mawr College, Bryn Mawr, Pennsylvania.

MAKING MEANINGS

First Thoughts

1. What one word would you use to **summarize** the human condition as Pope describes it?

Shaping Interpretations

2. In almost every sentence of this passage, Pope says something flattering about the human race, only to follow it with something insulting. What characteristics does he think we should be proud of? What characteristics should we be ashamed of?

3. How many **sentences** are in this verse?

4. In what ways do you think human beings could be seen as the "glory" of this world? as its "jest"? as its "riddle"?

5. How does the wording of lines 5–6 and lines 15–16 exhibit **antithesis**? Try **paraphrasing** each of these couplets in your own words.

6. These couplets from the *Essay* are like variations on a single theme, in that each one presents a paradoxical view of humanity. Which couplet do you think is the most interesting and true?

Challenging the Text

7. Discuss your opinion of Pope's opening couplet.

8. **Compare** Pope's view of humanity with the view expressed by William Shakespeare's Hamlet in the following lines: "What a piece of work is a man! how noble in reason! how infinite in faculties! in form and moving how express and admirable! in action how like an angel! in apprehension how like a god! the beauty of the world, the paragon of animals!" (*Hamlet,* Act II, Scene 2). Whose view do you accept?

ELEMENTS OF LITERATURE

Poetic Form and Meter

Heroic couplets. Although heroic couplets follow a rigid metrical pattern, Pope takes pains to keep them from being monotonous. For instance, he varies the location of the main pause within a line, as in this quotation from "Elegy to an Unfortunate Lady" (note the position of the commas).

> Poets themselves must fall, like those they sung;
> Deaf the praised ear, and mute the tuneful tongue;
> Even he, whose soul now melts in mournful lays,
> Shall shortly want the generous tear he pays.

Some lines move fast, and some are slow—as these lines from "Windsor-Forest" show.

> See the bold youth strain up the threatening steep,
> Rush through the thickets, down the valleys sweep,
> Hang o'er their coursers' heads with eager speed,
> And earth rolls back beneath the flying steed.

In the first line of this passage, Pope uses language that imitates the effort of riding a horse uphill; in the second, the speed of riding downhill. For variety, Pope occasionally introduces **triplets**—three rhymed lines instead of two.

Epigrams. Pope had a dog named Bounce, one of whose puppies he gave to his friend Frederick, Prince of Wales, who lived in Kew. Pope had an epigram engraved on the puppy's collar. An **epigram** is a short poem, often satirical, that ends in a witticism or clever turn of thought. To whom do you think the epigram is addressed? (Don't say, "the prince," because surely the prince knows his own dog.)

> **Epigram Engraved on the Collar of a Dog**
> I am his Highness' dog at Kew;
> Pray tell me, sir, whose dog are you?

Read aloud: A Pope performance. Present "Two Minutes of Pope" to the class. Read a selection of couplets aloud to feel the effect of **pauses, rhymes, assonance,** and **alliteration.** Be sure to experiment with alternative readings before you make your presentation.

Make the Connection

A Tempest in a Teapot

If you notice the newspapers and magazines at a supermarket checkout counter, you'll probably agree that ordinary Americans like to read about rich and famous people—those in politics, sports, show business, and society. Many readers find it especially interesting to learn about the trivial problems or petty quarrels of prominent people. *The Rape of the Lock* tells the story of a petty quarrel among the eighteenth-century English nobility. After you've read the first part of the poem, see if you don't agree that some tastes in reading haven't changed very much since Pope's day.

Reading Skills and Strategies

Using Reference Materials

Because Pope's subject is based on a contemporary incident, his poem contains **allusions,** references to people, places, and events that were well known to readers in his day but are probably unfamiliar to you. Sometimes you can understand an allusion by studying its **context.** You can also consult the information under Background on this page and in the side notes, or **glosses,** that accompany the poem.

Elements of Literature

Mock Epic

A poem like *The Rape of the Lock* is called a **mock epic.** The comedy of a mock epic arises from the discrepancy between a subject and its treatment: The subject is trivial, while its treatment is grandiose. In mock epics, fleas become elephants, and cracked teacups become major catastrophes. Pope used the traditional epic devices in a comic way, and his educated contemporaries had the pleasure of recognizing many similarities between *The Rape of the Lock* and serious epics like Homer's *Iliad,* Virgil's *Aeneid, Beowulf,* and Milton's *Paradise Lost.* For instance, the classical epics all have gods and goddesses who intervene in human affairs. Following these models, Pope includes some tiny, airy spirits called sylphs, who try in vain to prevent the "rape" from taking place. Readers would also recognize the epic device of the warning dream: Such a dream comes to Belinda from a supernatural being. Since epics always include battles, Pope includes a card game in his poem as well as a screaming match after Belinda loses her curl. In the complete poem of 794 lines (158 of which appear here), there are many such parallels to serious epics.

> A **mock epic** is a comic narrative poem that parodies the epic by treating a trivial subject in a lofty, grand manner. A mock epic uses dignified language, elaborate figures of speech, and supernatural intervention.
>
> *For more on the Mock Epic, see the Handbook of Literary Terms.*

Background

When Pope wrote about people, he wrote mainly about the rich, perhaps because the general public found it more interesting to read about the rich than about the poor. The chief characters in *The Rape of the Lock* all belong to the leisure classes, and they spend their time amusing themselves rather than working for a living.

The title of Pope's comic masterpiece means "the violent theft of a lock of hair." The poem is based on a real incident. The lock in question belonged to a certain rich and fashionable young lady named Arabella Fermor. The theft in question was committed by a certain rich and fashionable young man named Robert, Lord Petre. When Robert snipped a curl from Arabella's hairdo, he set off a quarrel between the Fermor and the Petre families. Had the two families been less sensible, their row might have escalated into bitter hatred. As it turned out, the feud subsided into laughter—thanks to Alexander Pope.

At the suggestion of a friend of the two families and patron of Pope's, Pope composed *The Rape of the Lock,* changing the name of Arabella to Belinda and calling Robert "the Baron." To make the warring families realize how trivial the "rape" actually was, Pope treated it very, very seriously. He dressed his poem in all the trappings of heroic poetry, as though he were Homer or Virgil writing an epic of the fall of Troy.

- Pope's poem is divided into five sections called **cantos.** Canto I begins like a proper epic, with a statement of the subject and an invocation to the Muse—a female deity who was supposed to inspire poets and other artists. Pope, however, clearly signals his comic intentions in the very first couplet:

> What dire offense from amorous causes springs,
> What mighty contests rise from trivial things,
> I sing—

In Canto II, Belinda and her friends take a boat up the river Thames to a party. All who see her admire the two beautiful curled locks that hang down her back. And despite the small army of sprites (spirits) assigned to protect Belinda's beautiful hair, the Baron resolves to possess these locks.

from The Rape of the Lock
Alexander Pope

Canto III

Close by those meads, forever crowned with flowers,
Where Thames with pride surveys his rising towers,
There stands a structure° of majestic frame,
Which from the neighboring Hampton takes its name.
5 Here Britain's statesmen oft the fall foredoom
Of foreign tyrants, and of nymphs° at home;
Here thou, great Anna!° whom three realms obey,
Dost sometimes counsel take—and sometimes tea.
    Hither the heroes and the nymphs resort,
10 To taste awhile the pleasures of a court;
In various talk th' instructive hours they passed,
Who gave the ball, or paid the visit last;
One speaks the glory of the British queen,
And one describes a charming Indian screen;
15 A third interprets motions, looks, and eyes;
At every word a reputation dies.
Snuff,° or the fan,° supply each pause of chat,
With singing, laughing, ogling, and all that.
    Meanwhile, declining from the noon of day,
20 The sun obliquely shoots his burning ray;
The hungry judges soon the sentence sign,
And wretches hang that jurymen may dine. . . .
Belinda now, whom thirst of fame invites,
Burns to encounter two adventurous knights,
25 At omber° singly to decide their doom;
And swells her breast with conquests yet to come. . . .
The nymph exulting fills with shouts the sky;
The walls, the woods, and long canals reply.
    Oh thoughtless mortals! ever blind to fate,
30 Too soon dejected and too soon elate.

3. structure: Hampton Court, a royal residence on the river Thames, upstream from London.

6. nymphs: young ladies.

7. Anna: Queen Anne (1665–1714), who ruled England, Ireland, and Scotland.

17. snuff: powdered tobacco product sniffed or rubbed on the teeth and gums. **fan:** standard equipment for a lady.

25. omber: a card game for three players, popular in the eighteenth century.

Sudden, these honors shall be snatched away,
And cursed forever this victorious day.
　　For lo! the board with cups and spoons is crowned,
The berries° crackle, and the mill° turns round;
35　On shining altars of Japan° they raise
The silver lamp; the fiery spirits blaze:
From silver spouts the grateful liquors glide,
While China's earth° receives the smoking tide.°
At once they gratify their scent and taste,
40　And frequent cups prolong the rich repast.
Straight hover round the fair her airy band;
Some, as she sipped, the fuming liquor fanned,

34. berries: coffee beans.　**mill:** coffee grinder.
35. altars of Japan: small lacquered tables.

38. China's earth: china cups, made of earthenware.　**smoking tide:** coffee.

Sir Plume Demands the Restoration of the Lock (1854) by C. R. Leslie. Oil.
Private Collection.

Some o'er her lap their careful plumes displayed,
Trembling, and conscious of the rich brocade.
45 Coffee (which makes the politician wise,
And see through all things with his half-shut eyes)
Sent up in vapors to the Baron's brain
New stratagems, the radiant lock to gain.
Ah, cease, rash youth! desist ere 'tis too late,
50 Fear the just gods, and think of Scylla's fate!°
Changed to a bird, and sent to flit in air,
She dearly pays for Nisus' injured hair!
        But when to mischief mortals bend their will,
How soon they find fit instruments of ill!
55 Just then, Clarissa drew with tempting grace
A two-edged weapon from her shining case:
So ladies in romance assist their knight,
Present the spear, and arm him for the fight.
He takes the gift with reverence, and extends
60 The little engine° on his fingers' ends;
This just behind Belinda's neck he spread,
As o'er the fragrant steams she bends her head.
Swift to the lock a thousand sprites repair,
A thousand wings, by turns, blow back the hair;
65 And thrice they twitched the diamond in her ear;
Thrice she looked back, and thrice the foe drew near.
Just in that instant, anxious Ariel° sought
The close recesses of the virgin's thought;
As on the nosegay in her breast reclined,
70 He watched th' ideas rising in her mind,
Sudden he viewed, in spite of all her art,
An earthly lover lurking at her heart.°
Amazed, confused, he found his power expired,
Resigned to fate, and with a sigh retired.
75   The peer now spreads the glittering *forfex*° wide,
T' enclose the lock; now joins it, to divide.
Even then, before the fatal engine closed,
A wretched sylph too fondly interposed;
Fate urged the shears, and cut the sylph in twain,
80 (But airy substance soon unites again).
The meeting points the sacred hair dissever
From the fair head, forever, and forever!
        Then flashed the living lightning from her eyes,
And screams of horror rend th' affrighted skies.
85 Not louder shrieks to pitying Heaven are cast,
When husbands, or when lapdogs breathe their last;
Or when rich china vessels fallen from high,
In glittering dust, and painted fragments lie!
        "Let wreaths of triumph° now my temples twine,"
90 The victor cried, "the glorious prize is mine!
While fish in streams, or birds delight in air,
Or in a coach and six the British fair,

50. Scylla's fate: In Greek mythology, Scylla is turned into a seabird by the gods after she betrays her father Nisus by cutting off his purple lock of hair, on which his life and kingdom depend.

60. engine: instrument.

67. Ariel: chief of the heavenly sprites sent to protect Belinda.

72. earthly lover . . . heart: If in her heart Belinda wants the Baron to succeed, the sprites cannot protect her.

75. *forfex:* Latin for "scissors."

89. wreaths of triumph: like the ones worn by athletic and military heroes in ancient times.

As long as *Atalantis*° shall be read,
Or the small pillow grace a lady's bed,
95 While visits shall be paid on solemn days,
When numerous wax lights in bright order blaze,
While nymphs take treats, or assignations give,
So long my honor, name, and praise shall live!
What time would spare, from steel receives its date,°
100 And monuments, like men, submit to fate!"...

93. Atalantis: *The New Atalantis*
(1709), a fashionable novel by Mrs.
Delarivière Manley (1663–1724),
which thinly disguised some
contemporary scandals.

99. date: destruction.

*In Canto IV, Pope describes an incident that occurs in all
proper epics: a descent into the underworld. Just as Virgil
had Aeneas travel down to Hades, Pope has Umbriel, a
"melancholy sprite," fly down to a dismal, imaginary place
called the Cave of Spleen. (Spleen was the eighteenth century's name for what we call depression; rich, idle people
were particularly subject to spleen in Pope's day.) In the
cave, Umbriel obtains a vial of "soft sobs, melting griefs, and
flowing tears," as well as an immense bag full of "sighs, sobs,
and passions," which somewhat resembles the bag of unfavorable winds in Homer's* Odyssey, *given to Odysseus to
keep tightly closed so his ship won't be blown off course. Umbriel then returns to the earth's surface and empties the contents of the bag and vial over Belinda and her girlfriend,
who is even angrier than Belinda. The canto ends with Belinda lamenting to the Baron:*

> *"O, hadst thou, cruel! been content to seize*
> *Hairs less in sight, or any hairs but these!"*

*The others in Belinda's tea-party audience shed tears of pity,
but the Baron ignores her pleas: "Fate and Jove had stopped
the Baron's ears."*

"Belinda still her downy pillow prest . . ."

Canto V

"To arms, to arms!" the fierce virago° cries,
And swift as lightning to the combat flies.
All side in parties, and begin th' attack;
Fans clap, silks rustle, and tough whalebones° crack;
5 Heroes' and heroines' shouts confus'dly rise,
And bass and treble voices strike the skies.
No common weapons in their hands are found,
Like gods they fight, nor dread a mortal wound.°...
    See, fierce Belinda on the Baron flies,
10 With more than usual lightning in her eyes:
Nor feared the chief th' unequal fight to try,
Who sought no more than on his foe to die.
But this bold lord with manly strength endued,

1. virago: ferocious woman; here,
Belinda's girlfriend, who leads the
attack on the Baron and his friends.

4. whalebones: used to shape and
stiffen women's clothing.

8. like gods . . . mortal wound:
Like gods, who are immortal and
have no fear of physical wounds,
these fighters do not fear the wounds
inflicted by words.

She with one finger and a thumb subdued:
15 Just where the breath of life his nostrils drew,
A charge of snuff the wily virgin threw;
The gnomes direct, to every atom just,
The pungent grains of titillating dust.
Sudden with starting tears each eye o'erflows,
20 And the high dome re-echoes to his nose.
    "Now meet thy fate," incensed Belinda cried,
And drew a deadly bodkin° from her side. . . .
    "Boast not my fall," he cried, "insulting foe!
Thou by some other shalt be laid as low.
25 Nor think, to die dejects my lofty mind:
All that I dread is leaving you behind!
Rather than so, ah, let me still survive,
And burn in Cupid's flames—but burn alive."
    "Restore the lock!" she cries; and all around
30 "Restore the lock!" the vaulted roofs rebound.
Not fierce Othello° in so loud a strain
Roared for the handkerchief that caused his pain.
But see how oft ambitious aims are crossed,
And chiefs contend till all the prize is lost!
35 The lock, obtained with guilt, and kept with pain,
In every place is sought, but sought in vain:
With such a prize no mortal must be blessed,
So Heaven decrees! with Heaven who can contest?
    Some thought it mounted to the lunar sphere,
40 Since all things lost on earth are treasured there.
There heroes' wits are kept in ponderous vases,
And beaux'° in snuffboxes and tweezer cases.
There broken vows and deathbed alms are found,
And lovers' hearts with ends of riband bound. . . .
45   But trust the Muse—she saw it upward rise,
Though marked by none but quick, poetic eyes: . . .
A sudden star, it shot through liquid air,
And drew behind a radiant trail of hair.° . . .
    Then cease, bright nymph! to mourn thy ravished hair,
50 Which adds new glory to the shining sphere!
Not all the tresses that fair head can boast,
Shall draw such envy as the lock you lost.
For, after all the murders° of your eye,
When, after millions slain, yourself shall die;
55 When those fair suns shall set, as set they must,
And all those tresses shall be laid in dust,
This lock, the Muse shall consecrate to fame,
And midst the stars inscribe Belinda's name.

22. bodkin: long, ornamental hair-pin, shaped like a dagger.

31. Othello: Shakespeare's tragic hero Othello gave his wife a handkerchief, which his enemy stole and then used as evidence of the wife's unfaithfulness.

42. beaux': fashionable gentlemen's.

48. trail of hair: the word *comet* derives from a Greek word for "long-haired."

53. murders: Just as Belinda's eyes are said to "eclipse the day" (Canto I, line 14), here they are said to murder the young men who admire her. Both compliments are ancient and trite in love poetry.

The Storm Before the Calm: Baroque Art

The Renaissance did not pass serenely into the order, balance, and cool reason of the neoclassic age. In between—and often coexisting with neoclassicism in England—was the Baroque: a style and culture born of conflict, crisis, and quest.

Colonnades and swirling clouds. What typified the Baroque, a style that developed in seventeenth-century Italy and lasted in Europe and the Americas into the eighteenth century? The **Baroque** was marked by massive colonnaded cathedrals where interior walls seemed alive with sculpture; brightly painted ceilings that tricked the eye into a blue sky of swirling clouds and angels; opera that joined melodic music, elaborate costumes, dance, and melodrama; dramatic religious paintings so naturalistic they shocked; and intimate portraits of common people.

Baroque, a term adopted by later detractors, means "irregular, distorted," but the emphasis of the Baroque was really energy, sensuous appeal, and imaginative synthesis of art forms and ideas. There was, indeed, much to balance: Catholicism and Protestantism, monarchy and democracy, God and science, human genius and human insignificance.

With English restraint. Like the Renaissance, the Baroque Era came later to England than to continental Europe and, tempered by Protestantism, was more restrained. Both **Peter Paul Rubens** (1577–1640) and **Sir Anthony Van Dyck** (1599–1641), two great Baroque artists from Catholic Flanders, painted in England for Charles I. But Van Dyck's elegant, realistic portraits had a greater influence on English portraiture than Rubens's robust, writhing, heroically scaled figures. Later, **William Hogarth** created sensitive portraits of the English middle class, and his satirical series (depicting, for example, a marriage contract) convey a theatrical quality and a sly insistence that appearance is rarely reality.

In architecture, the Baroque shows itself in the restrained but fluid grandeur of the design for St. Paul's Cathedral by **Sir Christopher Wren** (1632–1723) and also in Wren's ambitious, unrealized scheme for rebuilding London after the Great Fire in 1666. Wren's plan was a spatial and aesthetic synthesis of streets, squares, shops, public buildings, and churches, all culminating in St. Paul's.

In Baroque music, elements we take for granted were startlingly new: writing attuned to individual instruments and voices, melody played against a bass line, chordal harmonies, and a solo voice or instrument against an orchestra. While English audiences rejected the flamboyance of Italian and French opera, they acclaimed the composer **Henry Purcell** (1659–1695) and his inventive uses of the new forms—including a brilliant, brief opera, *Dido and Aeneas*.

Baroque art was the natural successor of the High Renaissance. It embraced the complexities, contrasts, and challenges of a new world—and could be neither simple nor still.

Background: Baroque Abbey of Wilhering in Linz, Austria.

MAKING MEANINGS

First Thoughts

1. Who, if anyone, do you think is victorious by the end of the action? Cite examples to support your response.

Shaping Interpretations

2. In the satirical passage that opens Canto III (lines 1–18), what seems to be Pope's **tone**—his attitude toward the queen and her courtiers? Is he scornful or amused? How can you tell?

3. In Canto III, line 86, Pope juxtaposes—that is, places side by side—dying husbands and dying lapdogs. What is the effect of this juxtaposition? Find other juxtapositions in the poem.

4. A mock epic amusingly parodies the style and conventions of the epic. Since Homer, one epic hallmark has been the elaborate **epic simile,** or extended comparison between two unlike things. What comparisons are the basis of the extended similes in Canto III (lines 57–58 and 85–88) and Canto V (lines 31–32)?

5. In the complete poem, Pope frequently makes **satirical** remarks about the world outside the privileged ranks to which Belinda and her friends belong. Two examples of such remarks occur in Canto III, lines 21–22 and lines 45–46. Who or what are Pope's targets in these couplets?

6. The world outside the poem and the world inside it come together in Canto III, lines 7–8. What is the effect of the three words after the dash?

7. Belinda's victory at cards (Canto III, lines 23–28) and her cries of triumph are ironic because her happiness is so momentary; it's about to be shattered by the rape of her lock. **Irony** always involves a discrepancy of some kind. Explain why

> ### Reading Check/ Summary
>
> Get together with two or three classmates, and devise a **story map** that will **summarize the main events** of the poem in **chronological order.** Compare your story outlines in class to see if you all agree on the main events that lead up to and follow the "rape."

Belinda's victory over the Baron (Canto V, lines 13–22) also might be considered ironic.

8. Based on the extracts you have read, how would you state Pope's **theme** in this mock epic?

Extending the Text

9. Do you think any of the satire in Pope's poem could be applied to aspects of contemporary life? If so, how? Cite specific passages from Pope that could serve as satiric commentaries on people's behavior in the late twentieth century.

ELEMENTS OF LITERATURE

Wit: Ne'er So Well Expressed

Pope and his contemporaries admired a quality they called **wit.** Writers and other people who possessed wit were intellectually brilliant. Their ability to detect resemblances enabled them to write in images, similes, metaphors, and other figures of speech. Their language was polished and exact; their manner, cool and controlled.

The opposite of wit was dullness. Pope ridiculed the dull writers of his day, calling them dunces, in a long, brilliant, and insulting poem called the *Dunciad.* The chief dunce of the first version of the *Dunciad* (1728) was Lewis Theobald (pronounced "tibbald"), an editor of Shakespeare whom Pope called "piddling" because he was so concerned with the minute details of Shakespeare's texts. In 1742, when Pope reissued the *Dunciad,* Theobald was replaced as chief dunce by Colley Cibber, an actor and playwright who promoted his own career by publishing an egotistical biography. Theobald and Cibber lacked wit; Pope and such friends of his as Jonathan Swift and John Gay had wit.

Wit, then, meant cleverness. But it also meant something more serious:

> True wit is Nature to advantage dressed:
> What oft was thought, but ne'er so well expressed.

In this couplet from *An Essay on Criticism* (lines 97–98), Pope describes something he calls "true wit." The nearest modern equivalent of true wit is what we think of as great literature, or the classics. According to Pope, these great works express ideas that people have always accepted as true ("what oft was thought"). In great works, these familiar thoughts are not expressed in dull language, but are "to advantage dressed." The term *Nature* in this couplet refers not only to what we now think of as nature—the great outdoors with its birds, beasts, trees, plants, oceans, deserts—but also to human nature and the experiences of human beings.

The couplet on true wit might be summarized as follows: "A great work of literature presents familiar human experiences and perceptions in interesting and distinguished language. A great work reminds us, in an exciting and memorable way, of what we already know about the universe and its inhabitants."

But Pope did not regard wit as the most important quality a person can have:

> A wit's a feather and a chief's a rod;
> An honest man's the noblest work of God.

In this couplet, from Pope's *An Essay on Man* (Epistle IV, lines 247–248), the word *wit* is used as the name of a person, a writer. The writer is compared with a chief (a great leader, such as a general, king, or president) and with an honest man. Of the three, Pope gives first place to the honest man, God's noblest work. In comparison with this virtuous person, a wit is a mere "feather"—a light and flighty decoration—and a great man of action is a mere "rod"—a defender and corrector of society. Pope came to believe that virtue and morality are more important than intellectual brilliance (though he always was inclined to feel that second-rate writing was a kind of immorality, because a bad writer defrauds the reading public). Pope spoke his final words on morality while lying on his deathbed, when he said to the attending priest, "There is nothing that is meritorious but virtue and friendship, and indeed friendship itself is only part of virtue."

Though Pope thought it important to be a wit, he thought it more important to be a virtuous person.

Where is wit? Examine Pope's wit, and think about where wit is found today.

1. Find at least two examples from *The Rape of the Lock* that illustrate wit in the sense of "cleverness."

2. Now find an example of Pope's wit in its deeper sense: the elegant expression of a truth about human nature.

3. How would you define "wit" in today's world? Is there anyone on the contemporary scene whom you admire as an exponent of wit?

Pope's Villa, Twickenham by Samuel Scott.
Ackermann and Johnson Ltd., London.

CHOICES: Building Your Portfolio

Writer's Notebook

1. Collecting Ideas for a Persuasive Essay

Why not, like Pope, use the rich, the famous, and even the trivial to find controversial issues and values to write about in a persuasive essay? Scan TV programs about celebrities, print and TV ads in which celebrities endorse products or causes, and newspaper photos and stories of athletes and stars. Jot down brief descriptions (who, what, and why). Then react imaginatively. Brainstorm *issues*— perhaps of censorship, privacy, morality, sexism, elitism, or wealth. Save your ideas for the Writer's Workshop on page 612.

Analyzing Satire

2. Targeting Pope's Targets

In an essay, identify the targets of Pope's satire in *The Rape of the Lock,* and describe the devices Pope uses to ridicule these targets. To discover Pope's satirical targets, be sure to use the reference sources mentioned on page 526. Consider what Pope says about social role-playing and about the foolishness of human behavior in general.

Comparing Epics

3. From *Beowulf* to Pope

Compare Pope's mock epic with a serious epic: *Beowulf,* or, if you know it well, Homer's *Iliad* or *Odyssey.* Consider these elements of the epic in your discussion: invocations to the Muse, statement of subject, intervention of gods and goddesses, epic battles, a hero or heroine who reflects the values of a particular society, and use of elevated language.

Creative Writing

4. Mocking Modern Life

Write a mock epic about some event in contemporary life that's blown out of proportion: two teenage girls wearing the same dress at a school dance, two teenage boys who show up for a date with the same girl at the same time, a school mascot that gets lost, and so on. Be sure to include these devices: an **invocation to the Muse, intervention by the gods,** an **epic battle,** and a **warning dream.**

Creative Writing

5. Your Mock-Heroic Style

In Canto III of *The Rape of the Lock,* Pope describes making and drinking coffee in rich, elevated, and roundabout language (lines 33–40). This mock-heroic writing style breaks the elementary rule which says that writers must try to use simple, direct language when describing simple activities. As an exercise in mock-heroic writing, write a prose description of a common activity (such as riding a bicycle or cooking and eating a hamburger), using inflated language and rich images.

Speaking / Listening

6. Talking Back to Pope

Which one of Pope's sayings about human nature do you disagree with? Prepare for oral delivery a lighthearted rebuttal of the poet's position, starting with a sentence such as the following: "Resolved: That Alexander Pope erred when he claimed that . . . " Support your rebuttal with specific examples and incidents.

Analyzing Your Reading Process

7. Reading Reflections

Think back over your reading of Pope's poetry, and consult your reading notes. Which of his works did you find easiest to understand, and why? Which was most difficult, and why? How did the heroic couplets affect your reading? **Summarize** your reading experience in a brief essay analyzing the strategies you used to get at Pope's meaning. Conclude your essay by describing your general response to Pope's style.

France

(Map) Europe in 1721.

Voltaire

(1694–1778)

François-Marie Arouet (är·we), better known by his pen name, Voltaire, is remembered chiefly for his lifelong fight against injustice. Throughout his life, he implored his fellow philosophers to "Crush the infamous," by which he meant all things inhumane and oppressive. As a satirist, philosopher, historian, dramatist, and poet, Voltaire continually criticized the wastefulness of war, the intolerance of organized religion, and the plight of the poor.

Voltaire (1833) engraved by James Mollison from an original by Nicolas de Largillière.

Born in Paris to middle-class parents, Voltaire studied law for a time but soon gave it up to become a writer. His early reputation was based on his classical tragedies and his lampoons of the government. Yet Voltaire's celebrity did not prevent his being brutally beaten at the hands of an offended nobleman, imprisoned in the Bastille, and exiled to England in 1726.

In London, Voltaire met Jonathan Swift and Alexander Pope and was deeply influenced by the works of Bacon, Newton, and Locke, which emphasize the experimental method in science. When he returned to Paris, Voltaire wrote philosophical essays and historical studies that reflect this influence—he avoided the abstract in favor of a concrete focus on the way people actually lived and worked according to their beliefs. Many of these writings, collected under the title *Philosophical Letters,* were considered heretical and burned by the French parliament in 1734. Voltaire lived much of his later life near the Swiss border with France. He died during a rare visit to Paris, taken at age eighty-three to see his last play produced. Initially refused a Christian burial, Voltaire's remains were interred in Paris with great ceremony thirteen years later, following the revolution so greatly influenced by his ideas for reform.

(Map) Europe in 1721. Map ©Rand McNally R.L. #98-S-116.

Before You Read

FROM CANDIDE

Background

In the tumultuous social climate of eighteenth-century Europe, writers, scientists, and philosophers questioned the "settled truths" of society as they never had before. Yet direct challenges to authority can be dangerous, in the eighteenth century or in any age. Satire—with its indirect criticism and deflating humor—thus became the weapon of choice for many eighteenth-century thinkers.

Voltaire used the device of the travel book, as Jonathan Swift did in *Gulliver's Travels,* to satirize everything—the Church, the state, and the mindless optimism of some eighteenth-century philosophers. Voltaire's hero Candide is an innocent who has been schooled by the repellent Doctor Pangloss to believe that everything that happens in the world happens for the best. The convictions of sweet-tempered Candide are severely tested in a series of outrageous and hilarious adventures. And, just as Swift's use of the name "Gulliver" may suggest the adjective "gullible," Voltaire's choice of "Candide"—punning on "candor,

King Frederick II Comes to See Voltaire (c. 1750) drawn by Mousiau, engraving by P. Baquoy.

candid"—points to the qualities of childlike honesty, trust, and naiveté.

In the opening chapters of the novel, Voltaire singles out for his wicked satire some of the most important social institutions of eighteenth-century Europe. When Candide presumes to court the Baron's daughter, he is tossed out of the castle in short order. No sooner does he become the hero of the Bulgarians than he is thrown into chains and flogged. (Master of the humorous overstatement, Voltaire has his hero thrashed a ridiculous four thousand times.) Candide's experiences, however funny, reveal that the worlds of both the castle and the army are deeply flawed by snobbery, hypocrisy, and brutality.

Another target for the author's stinging criticism is the complacency of the philosopher Doctor Pangloss, whose name means "all tongue." Throughout the increasingly wretched events of *Candide,* Pangloss blithely mouths the theories of the German philosopher Gottfried Leibniz, who believed that an utterly rational God made a rational world in which everything, including evil, has a place and a purpose. Like Leibniz, Doctor Pangloss's perpetual slogan is "In this best of all possible worlds, . . . all is for the best."

Reading Skills and Strategies

Connecting Text to Current Events

Think about how Voltaire's satire might apply to aspects of today's world. Jot down notes as you read.

from Candide

Voltaire
translated by **Richard Aldington**

Chapter I

How Candide was brought up in a noble castle and how he was expelled from the same

In the castle of Baron Thunder-ten-tronckh in Westphalia[1] there lived a youth, endowed by Nature with the most gentle character. His face was the expression of his soul. His judgment was quite honest and he was extremely simple-minded; and this was the reason, I think, that he was named Candide. Old servants in the house suspected that he was the son of the Baron's sister and a decent honest gentleman of the neighborhood, whom this young lady would never marry because he could only prove seventy-one quarterings,[2] and the rest of his genealogical tree was lost, owing to the injuries of time. The Baron was one of the most powerful lords in Westphalia, for his castle possessed a door and windows. His Great Hall was even decorated with a piece of tapestry. The dogs in his stableyards formed a pack of hounds when necessary; his grooms were his huntsmen; the village curate was his Grand Almoner.[3] They all called him "My Lord," and laughed heartily at his stories. The Baroness weighed about three hundred and fifty pounds, was therefore greatly respected, and did the honors of the house with a dignity which rendered her still more respectable. Her daughter Cunegonde,[4] aged seventeen, was rosy-cheeked, fresh, plump, and tempting. The Baron's son appeared in every respect worthy of his father. The tutor Pangloss[5] was the oracle of the house, and little

Le Baron....voyant ceue caufe & cet effet, chaffa Candide du Château à grands coups de pied dans le derriere;

Candide Chap. 1.er

"The Baron . . . observing this cause and effect, expelled Candide from the castle by kicking him in the backside frequently and hard."

Candide followed his lessons with all the candor of his age and character. Pangloss taught metaphysico-theologo-cosmolonigology.[6] He proved admirably that there is no effect without a cause and that in this best of all possible worlds, My Lord the Baron's castle was the best of castles and his wife the best of all possible Baronesses. "'Tis demonstrated," said he, "that things cannot be otherwise; for, since everything is made for an end, everything is necessarily for the best end. Observe that noses were made to wear spectacles; and so we have spectacles. Legs were visibly instituted to be breeched, and we have breeches.

---

1. **Westphalia** (west·fā′lē·ə): region in western Germany, noted for its excellent ham. In a letter to his niece, Voltaire described Westphalia as "vast, sad, sterile, detestable."

2. **quarterings:** divisions on a coat of arms or family tree. Seventy-one is an absurdly high number, tracing a person's genealogy back over 2,000 years.

3. **Grand Almoner:** member of a noble household responsible for allotting charity to the poor.

4. **Cunegonde** (kyo͞o′nä·gônd′).

5. **Pangloss:** Greek for "all tongue."

6. **metaphysico-theologo-cosmolonigology:** This nonsense term is a satirical poke at the philosopher Leibniz and his followers, especially the embedded syllable *-nig-*, a shortened form of *nigaud*, which is French for "simpleton."

Stones were formed to be quarried and to build castles; and My Lord has a very noble castle; the greatest Baron in the province should have the best house; and as pigs were made to be eaten, we eat pork all the year round; consequently, those who have asserted that all is well talk nonsense; they ought to have said that all is for the best." Candide listened attentively and believed innocently; for he thought Mademoiselle Cunegonde extremely beautiful, although he was never bold enough to tell her so. He decided that after the happiness of being born Baron of Thunderten-tronckh, the second degree of happiness was to be Mademoiselle Cunegonde; the third, to see her every day; and the fourth to listen to Doctor Pangloss, the greatest philosopher of the province and therefore of the whole world. One day when Cunegonde was walking near the castle, in a little wood which was called The Park, she observed Doctor Pangloss in the bushes, giving a lesson in experimental physics to her mother's waiting-maid, a very pretty and docile brunette. Mademoiselle Cunegonde had a great inclination for science and watched breathlessly the reiterated experiments she witnessed; she observed clearly the Doctor's sufficient reason, the effects and the causes, and returned home very much excited, pensive, filled with the desire of learning, reflecting that she might be the sufficient reason of young Candide and that he might be hers. On her way back to the castle she met Candide and blushed; Candide also blushed. She bade him good morning in a hesitating voice; Candide replied without knowing what he was saying. Next day, when they left the table after dinner, Cunegonde and Candide found themselves behind a screen; Cunegonde dropped her handkerchief, Candide picked it up; she innocently held his hand; the young man innocently kissed the young lady's hand with remarkable vivacity, tenderness, and grace; their lips met, their eyes sparkled, their knees trembled, their hands wandered. Baron Thunder-ten-tronckh passed near the screen, and, observing this cause and effect, expelled Candide from the castle by kicking him in the backside frequently and hard. Cunegonde swooned; when she recovered her senses, the Baroness slapped her in the face; and all was in consternation in the noblest and most agreeable of all possible castles.

Chapter II

What happened to Candide among the Bulgarians

Candide, expelled from the earthly paradise, wandered for a long time without knowing where he was going, turning up his eyes to Heaven, gazing back frequently at the noblest of castles which held the most beautiful of young Baronesses; he lay down to sleep supperless between two furrows in the open fields: It snowed heavily in large flakes. The next morning the shivering Candide, penniless, dying of cold and exhaustion, dragged himself toward the neighboring town, which was called Waldberghoff-trarbk-dikdorff. He halted sadly at the door of an inn. Two men dressed in blue noticed him. "Comrade," said one, "there's a well-built young man of the right height."[7] They went up to Candide and very civilly invited him to dinner. "Gentlemen," said Candide with charming modesty, "you do me a great honor, but I have no money to pay my share." "Ah, sir," said one of the men in blue, "persons of your figure and merit never pay anything; are you not five feet five tall?" "Yes, gentlemen," said he, bowing, "that is my height." "Ah, sir, come to table; we will not only pay your expenses, we will never allow a man like you to be short of money; men were only made to help each other." "You are in the right," said Candide, "that is what Doctor Pangloss was always telling me, and I see that everything is for the best." They begged him to accept a few crowns,[8] he took them and wished to give them an IOU, they refused to take it, and all sat down to table. "Do you not love tenderly . . ." "Oh, yes," said he. "I love Mademoiselle Cunegonde tenderly." "No," said one of the gentlemen. "We were asking if you do not tenderly love the King of the Bulgarians." "Not a bit," said he, "for I have never seen him." "What! He is the most charming of kings, and you must drink his health." "Oh, gladly, gentlemen." And he drank. "That is sufficient," he was told. "You are now the support, the aid, the defender, the hero of the Bulgarians, your fortune is made, and your glory assured." They immediately put

7. **height:** Voltaire is making fun of the recruiting practices of the "King of the Bulgarians"—Voltaire's satiric name for King Frederick the Great of Prussia—who chose and organized soldiers according to their height.
8. **crowns:** units of money.

irons on his legs and took him to a regiment. He was made to turn to the right and left, to raise the ramrod and return the ramrod, to take aim, to fire, to march double time, and he was given thirty strokes with a stick; the next day he drilled not quite so badly, and received only twenty strokes; the day after, he only had ten and was looked on as a prodigy by his comrades. Candide was completely mystified and could not make out how he was a hero. One fine spring day he thought he would take a walk, going straight ahead, in the belief that to use his legs as he pleased was a privilege of the human species as well as of animals. He had not gone two leagues[9] when four other heroes, each six feet tall, fell upon him, bound him, and dragged him back to a cell. He was asked by his judges whether he would rather be thrashed thirty-six times by the whole regiment or receive a dozen lead bullets at once in his brain. Although he protested that men's wills are free and that he wanted neither one nor the other, he had to make a choice; by virtue of that gift of God which is called *liberty,* he determined to run the gauntlet[10] thirty-six times and actually did so

9. leagues: A league is a unit of distance equal to about three miles.
10. run the gauntlet: run between two rows of soldiers who strike the victim with clubs or other weapons.

twice. There were two thousand men in the regiment. That made four thousand strokes which laid bare the muscles and nerves from his neck to his backside. As they were about to proceed to a third turn, Candide, utterly exhausted, begged as a favor that they would be so kind as to smash his head; he obtained this favor; they bound his eyes and he was made to kneel down. At that moment the King of the Bulgarians came by and inquired the victim's crime, and as this King was possessed of a vast genius, he perceived from what he learned about Candide that he was a young metaphysician[11] very ignorant in worldly matters, and therefore pardoned him with a clemency which will be praised in all newspapers and all ages. An honest surgeon healed Candide in three weeks with the ointments recommended by Dioscorides.[12] He had already regained a little skin and could walk when the King of the Bulgarians went to war with the King of the Abares.[13]

11. metaphysician (met′ə·fə·zish′ən): philosopher who studies the nature of reality and the origin and structure of the universe.
12. Dioscorides (dī′əs·kôr·ə·dēz′): Greek army physician who wrote a treatise on medicine in the first century A.D. Even in Voltaire's day, Dioscorides' work was out-of-date.
13. Abares (a·bär′): that is, the French, who fought against the "Bulgarians," or Prussians, in the Seven Years' War (1756–1763).

FINDING COMMON GROUND

The disasters that befall the innocent Candide—including expulsion from the Baron's castle and impressment into a foreign army—are presented with such deft wit that readers often laugh out loud. Yet Voltaire's humor never obscures his deeper point, that humanity and social institutions are in need of reform. The need for reform, as well as admonitions couched in satire, may continue to be found in our world.

Thinking back over the story, jot down some brief notes in response to the following questions:

• If a "Candide" were created today, what would he be taught? What attitudes and corruptions in society would a modern Candide face, testing all those platitudes he'd learned about life?

• Are there "Panglosses" in the world today—in education, politics, or religion? Where and why do you still hear people saying things like "It's all for the best"?

• Is *Candide* a **parody** of the popular adventures or romances on today's best-seller lists or in the movies? Why do the kind of romances *Candide* makes fun of continue to appeal to us?

Take a moment to reflect on your responses and the notes you've already made; then, get together with a few classmates for a discussion of *Candide* and its satiric intent. Be sure your agenda includes discussion of whether or not Voltaire's underlying message against intolerance, cruelty, and smugness still has some timely applications in today's world. After your group has finished its discussion, share your findings with the class.

(Opposite) *Astronomy, 1750* by Richard Houston.
Museum of the History of Science, Oxford.

Collection 7

AN APPETITE FOR EXPERIENCE

Pepys   Johnson   Goethe

Defoe   Boswell   Gray

He who neglects to drink of the spring of experience is likely to die of thirst in the desert of ignorance.

—Ling Po (Chinese, 701–762)

Samuel Pepys

(1633–1703)

For nine years—1660 to 1669—Samuel Pepys, whose name is pronounced "peeps," kept a secret diary which, when published long after his death, made him very famous. Pepys was not a writer but an official in the government office that maintained the Royal Navy and provided it with ships and supplies. Although a cousin helped Pepys obtain his first appointment in the Navy Office, it was Pepys's own diligence and skill that accounted for his rapid advancement. He did much to increase the honesty and efficiency of naval supply and maintenance.

Along with his public career, Pepys's private affairs also prospered. Starting humbly in life as the son of a tailor who managed to send him to Cambridge University, Pepys became so rich that when he was forced to retire in 1688 for political reasons, he could live the rest of his life like a gentleman, in leisure, comfort, and elegance.

Pepys had an insatiable appetite for experience, a vast capacity for pleasure, and an immense desire for learning—languages, literature, science, and everything connected with his naval occupation. Small things delighted him. When he heard "a fellow whistle like a bird exceeding well," he resolved to take lessons in bird whistling. Of a new watch he said, "I could not forbear carrying it in my hand and seeing what o'clock it was a hundred times." His house was full of creatures: cats, two dogs, a whistling blackbird, canaries, even for a time an eagle. He owned many books, carpenters' tools, maps and charts, a telescope, and several musical instruments that he could play—a flageolet, a lute, a flute, and a small harpsichord (which he never mastered). He composed a few songs that are still regarded as singable, he was proud of his dancing, and he liked expensive clothes and oil paintings. In everything he sought pleasure, and he usually found it. Whenever his head ached from business or his wife was angry at him for flirting with other women, he took refuge in the theater. He saw so many plays and recorded his impressions of them so accurately that the *Diary* is now regarded as an important document for theater history.

Historians of all kinds find the *Diary* useful because Pepys was a firsthand observer of public events and contemporary life. In 1660, he was one of the Englishmen who went to bring exiled King Charles II back to England. He witnessed joyous occasions like Charles's coronation in 1661 and national disasters like the plague of 1665 and the Great Fire of 1666. These important public happenings he recorded in his *Diary* along with trivial personal ones. For instance, on one occasion he records something that happened at the theater:

> I went to Mr. Crew's house and thence to the theater, where I saw again *The Lost Lady,* which doth now please me better than before. And here, I sitting behind in a dark place, a lady spat backward upon me by a mistake, not seeing me. But after seeing her to be a very pretty lady, I was not troubled at all.

According to the *Diary,* Pepys's life was full of unexpected little events like this one. Reading the *Diary* over Pepys's shoulder, we see the lively panorama of Restoration London—and in many of his observations, we also see ourselves.

Before You Read

FROM THE DIARY OF SAMUEL PEPYS

Make the Connection

Capturing the Moment

Many people kept detailed diaries in the seventeenth century, and a surprisingly large number of these diaries have survived. The pious people we now call Puritans used their diaries to analyze their moral behavior and record their spiritual progress. In contrast, Pepys in his *Diary* pays little attention to the state of his soul, though he almost always mentions going to church on Sunday, often with disparaging comments ("a sorry, silly sermon"). But Pepys was not an introspective person; his *Diary* is interesting because it tells us what he saw and heard and said and did. Many people today keep diaries and journals. What do you think their motives are?

Reading Skills and Strategies

Monitoring Your Reading

Many aspects of Pepys's seventeenth-century usage might give you trouble. Some **archaic words, sentence structures,** and **allusions** will be strange to you. As you read these diary entries, monitor your comprehension. If you are having trouble with archaic words and unfamiliar allusions, the footnotes will help you. If some words still puzzle you, you can refer to the glossary at the back of the book or to a dictionary. Keep notes on your reading process.

Elements of Literature

Diary

Pepys's *Diary* is so detailed, wide-ranging, and frank that it has become a byword for this form of writing. Each page of this vivid chronicle reveals Pepys's curious eye, candid opinions, and clear relish for life in the great city.

A diary is a daily, personal account of feelings, impressions, and events. Unlike journals, which are usually less personal records of events often written with another reader in mind, most diaries are quite intimate and written only for the owner's private reference and pleasure.

For more on the Diary, see the Handbook of Literary Terms.

Background

Pepys's diary was truly a secret one. He wrote it only for his own use and in a kind of shorthand that had recently been invented. He doubly safeguarded the most intimate details of his life by recording them in a private foreign language that appears to mix together Latin, French, and Spanish words. Yet, since he did not destroy the *Diary* at the end of his life but bequeathed it along with his other books to Cambridge University, he must have recognized its value as literature and history. He must, in other words, have imagined people reading it. But not until the 1970s was it possible to read everything in the *Diary* because earlier editors could not bring themselves to transcribe and print the more personal entries. And though it covers only nine years, the *Diary* is immense; in the 1970s and 1980s it was published—along with notes, commentaries, and indices—in eleven fat volumes.

When he began the *Diary,* in 1660, Pepys was twenty-seven, married to twenty-year-old Elizabeth St. Michel, and in the service of Edward Montagu. Until recently, he and his wife had been living in a turret room in Whitehall Palace, without servants or proper facilities for washing and cooking. Nine years later, when he stopped keeping the *Diary* because of eye trouble, Pepys and his family had their own handsome townhouse, one of a complex of buildings that made up the Navy Office. Their household was not much like most modern ones because they had several live-in servants who did most of their work: three housemaids, a waiting woman for Elizabeth, a footboy for Samuel, and a coachman to drive and look after their coach and horses. Although Pepys and his wife had no children, their house was always full of people.

from The Diary of Samuel Pepys

Samuel Pepys

October 13, 1660
A Public Execution, A Private Explosion

To my Lord's[1] in the morning, where I met with Captain Cuttance. But my Lord not being up, I went out to Charing Cross to see Major General Harrison[2] hanged, drawn, and quartered—which was done there—he looking as cheerfully as any man could do in that condition. He was presently cut down and his head and his heart shown to the people, at which there was great shouts of joy. It is said that he said that he was sure to come shortly at the right hand of Christ to judge them that now have judged him. And that his wife doth expect his coming again.[3]

Thus it was my chance to see the King beheaded at Whitehall and to see the first blood shed in revenge for the blood of the King at Charing Cross. From thence to my Lord's and took Captain Cuttance and Mr. Sheply to the Sun tavern and did give them some oysters. After that I went by water home, where I was angry with my wife for her things lying about, and in my passion kicked the little fine basket which I bought her in Holland and broke it, which troubled me after I had done it.

Within all the afternoon, setting up shelves in my study. At night to bed.

April 23, 1661
The Coronation of Charles II

. . . About four in the morning I rose. And got to the Abbey,[4] where I followed Sir J. Denham the surveyor with some company that he was leading in. And with much ado, by the favor of Mr. Cooper his man, did get up into a great scaffold across the north end of the Abbey—where with a great deal of patience I sat from past four till eleven before the King came in. And a pleasure it was to see the Abbey raised in the middle, all covered with red and a throne (that is a chair) and footstool on the top of it. And all the officers of all kinds, so much as the very fiddlers, in red vests.

At last comes in the Dean and Prebends[5] of Westminster with the Bishops (many of them in cloth-of-gold copes[6]); and after them the nobility all in their Parliament robes, which was a most magnificent sight. Then the Duke[7] and the King with a scepter (carried by my Lord of Sandwich) and sword and mond[8] before him, and the crown too.

The King in his robes, bareheaded, which was very fine. And after all had placed themselves—there was a sermon and the service. And then in the choir at the high altar he passed all the ceremonies of the coronation—which, to my very great grief, I and most in the Abbey could not see. The crown being put upon his head, a great shout begun. And he came forth to the throne and there passed more ceremonies: as, taking the oath and having things read to him by the Bishop,[9] and his Lords (who put on their caps as soon as the King put on his crown) and Bishops came and kneeled before him.

And three times the King-at-arms went to the three open places on the scaffold and proclaimed that if anyone could show any reason why Ch. Steward [Charles Stuart] should not be King of England, that now he should come and speak.

And a general pardon also was read by the Lord Chancellor; and medals flung up and down by my

---

1. **my Lord's:** Edward Montagu (1625–1672), earl of Sandwich; he was a cousin of Pepys and his superior at the Naval Office.
2. **Harrison:** Thomas Harrison (1606–1660), one of the people responsible for the execution of King Charles I in 1649.
3. **coming again:** with Christ, on Christ's return to earth.
4. **Abbey:** Westminster Abbey, the church in London where all monarchs of England are crowned and where many of them are buried.

5. **Prebends** (prē′bəndz): prebendaries; clergy who receive a prebend, or salary paid from the church's revenues.
6. **copes:** ceremonial robes.
7. **Duke:** James II (1633–1701), duke of York and the king's brother.
8. **mond:** golden globe and cross; a symbol of royal power.
9. **Bishop:** bishop of London. (The archbishop of Canterbury, who ordinarily would have officiated, was too ill to do so.)

Lord Cornwallis—of silver;[10] but I could not come by any.

But so great a noise, that I could make but little of the music; and indeed, it was lost to everybody. But I had so great a list to piss, that I went out a little while before the King had done all his ceremonies and went round the Abbey to Westminster Hall, all the way within rails, and 10,000 people, with the ground covered with blue cloth —and scaffolds all the way. Into the hall I got—where it was very fine with hangings and scaffolds,

Charles II's entry into London at his restoration, 1660. Engraving.

one upon another, full of brave ladies. And my wife in one little one on the right hand.

Here I stayed walking up and down; and at last, upon one of the side stalls, I stood and saw the King come in with all the persons (but the soldiers) that were yesterday in the cavalcade; and a most pleasant sight it was to see them in their several robes. And the King came in with his crown on and his scepter in his hand—under a canopy borne up by six silver staves, carried by Barons of the Cinque Ports—and little bells at every end.

And after a long time he got up to the farther end, and all set themselves down at their several tables—and that was also a rare sight. And the King's first course carried up by the Knights of the Bath. And many fine ceremonies there was of the heralds leading up people before him and bowing; and my Lord of Albemarles going to the kitchen and eat a bit of the first dish that was to go to the King's table.

But above all was these three Lords, Northumberland and Suffolk and the Duke of Ormond, coming before the courses on horseback and

10. **medals . . . of silver:** coronation badges.

staying so all dinnertime; and at last, to bring up Dymock, the King's Champion, all in armor on horseback, with his speare and target carried before him. And a herald proclaim that if any dare deny Ch. Steward to be lawful King of England, here was a champion that would fight with him; and with those words the champion flings down his gauntlet;[11] and all this he doth three times in his going up toward the King's table. At last, when he is come, the King drinks to him and then sends him the cup, which is of gold; and he drinks it off and then rides back again with the cup in his hand.

I went from table to table to see the Bishops and all others at their dinner, and was infinite pleased with it. And at the Lords' table I met with Wll. Howe and he spoke to my Lord for me and he did give him four rabbits and a pullet; and so I got it, and Mr. Creed[12] and I got Mr. Michell to give us some bread and so we at a stall eat it, as everybody else did what they could get.

I took a great deal of pleasure to go up and down and look upon the ladies—and to hear the music of all sorts; but above all, the twenty-four violins.

About six at night they had dined; and I went up to my wife and there met with a pretty lady

11. **gauntlet:** leather glove covered with metal plates to protect the hand during combat.
12. **Howe . . . Creed:** Pepys's fellow workers in the Navy Office.

LITERATURE AND SCIENCE

Mad for Science

Whether in computers, audio equipment, laser surgery, or virtual reality, dizzying scientific change greets us daily. *New!* shifts to *Obsolete!* at warp speed, so our age seems more scientifically turbulent than any before. Yet today's innovations, in many ways, are a small blip on the screen compared to the scientific revolution taking off in the seventeenth and eighteenth centuries.

From alchemy to method. This new science was a defiant break with the past, with "science" that was really metaphysical philosophy or magical alchemy. Instead, the Enlightenment's "natural philosophy" (physical science) insisted on observation, hypothesis, testing, and mathematical analysis—in short, the scientific method you learn in lab class today.

Geniuses, experiments, and arguments. Dominated by the genius of Isaac Newton (1642–1727), seventeenth-century England was truly ablaze with brilliant scientific minds, avid amateur experimenting, and passionate public quarrels (which Newton's nasty temper inflamed). Robert Boyle (1627–1691) founded modern chemistry. Edmond Halley (1656–1742) accurately predicted a comet's appearance centuries in the future. William Harvey (1578–1657) outlined our blood's circulation. Robert Hooke (1635–1703), a typical encyclopedist, coined the word *cell,* invented a watch spring, built a calculator, and first posed Kepler's planetary-motion laws in mechanical terms.

(Mrs. Frankelyn, a doctor's wife, a friend of Mr. Bowyers) and kissed them both—and by and by took them down to Mr. Bowyers's. And strange it is, to think that these two days have held up fair till now that all is done and the King gone out of the hall; and then it fell a-raining and thundering and lightning as I have not seen it do some years—which people did take great notice of God's blessing of the work of these two days—which is a foolery, to take too much notice of such things. . . .

At Mr. Bowyers's, a great deal of company; some I knew, others I did not. Here we stayed upon the leads[13] and below till it was late, expecting to see the fireworks; but they were not performed tonight. Only, the City had a light like a glory round about it, with bonfires.

At last I went to King Street; and there sent Crockford[14] to my father's and my house to tell them I could not come home tonight, because of the dirt and a coach could not be had.

And so after drinking a pot of ale alone at Mrs. Harper's, I returned to Mr. Bowyers's; and after a little stay more, I took my wife and Mrs. Frankelyn (who I <u>proffered</u> the <u>civility</u> of lying with my wife at Mrs. Hunt's tonight) to Axe Yard. In which, at

14. **Crockford:** apparently a servant.

---

13. **leads:** rooftop; from the sheets of lead used to cover a roof.

WORDS TO OWN
proffered (präf'ərd) *v.:* offered; proposed.
civility (sə·vil'ə·tē) *n.:* courtesy.

Newton (awing even Queen Anne, who knighted him) explained the world's mysteries as never before—partly because he invented a tool to do it: calculus. Among Newton's other stunning achievements were discovering that white light contains all colors, formulating the three laws of motion (every physicist's bedrock), and defining universal gravitation. Newton realized, as no one else had, that gravitational pull accounts both for orbiting planets and for falling apples.

Promoting natural knowledge. But even without Newton's genius, there were so many new ideas and inventions—the vacuum pump, barometer, compound microscope—that a group of Londoners created the "Invisible College," essentially a science club that evolved into the Royal Society of London for the Promotion of Natural Knowledge. While never a government body (its brash motto was *Nullius verba,* "at the dictation of no one"), the Royal Society was chartered by Charles II in 1662. Dedicated both to hands-on experimenting and to publishing journal articles, it was a prototype information highway, giving scientists across Europe new knowledge—faster than ever before.

Newton served as Royal Society president, but so did the nonscientist Samuel Pepys, showing the age's fascination with natural curiosities and cutting-edge thought. While some of the Society's experiments were crackpot and cruel to animals—as satirized by both Joseph Addison and Jonathan Swift—the Society was, and still is centuries later, one of the world's most prestigious and influential scientific groups.

Gunter's scale, globe, dividers, cross staff, sandglass (detail) (all pre-1700). National Maritime Museum, London.

the further end, there was three great bonfires and a great many great gallants,[15] men and women; and they laid hold of us and would have us drink the King's health upon our knee, kneeling upon a fagot;[16] which we all did, they drinking to us one after another—which we thought a strange frolic. But these gallants continued thus a great while, and I wondered to see how the ladies did tipple.

At last I sent my wife and her bedfellow to bed, and Mr. Hunt and I went in with Mr. Thornbury (who did give the company all their wines, he being yeoman of the wine cellar to the King) to his house; and there, with his wife and two of his sisters and some gallant sparks that were there, we drank the King's health and nothing else, till one of the gentlemen fell down stark drunk and there lay spewing. And I went to my Lord's pretty well. But no sooner a-bed with Mr. Sheply but my head begun to turn and I to vomit, and if ever I was foxed it was now—which I cannot say yet, because I fell asleep and sleep till morning—only, when I waked I found myself wet with my spewing. Thus did the day end, with joy everywhere; and blessed be God, I have not heard of any mischance to anybody through it all, but only to Serjeant Glynne,[17] whose horse fell upon him

15. **gallants:** merrymakers.
16. **fagot:** bundle of twigs or sticks used to make a bonfire. The toast of loyalty was often drunk while kneeling.

17. **Serjeant Glynne:** The title is legal rather than military. Sir John Glynne and Sir John Maynard were unpopular because they had been prominent judges during the Commonwealth period.

yesterday and is like to kill him; which people do please themselves with, to see how just God is to punish that rogue at such a time as this—he being now one of the King's Serjeants and rode in the cavalcade with Maynard, to whom people wished the same fortune.

There was also this night, in King Street, [a woman] had her eye put out by a boy's flinging of a firebrand into the coach.

Now after all this, I can say that besides the pleasure of the sight of these glorious things, I may now shut my eyes against any other objects, or for the future [not] trouble myself to see things of state and show, as being sure never to see the like again in this world.

Waked in the morning with my head in a sad taking through the last night's drink, which I am very sorry for. So rise and went out with Mr. Creed to drink our morning draft, which he did give me in chocolate to settle my stomach. And after that to my wife, who lay with Mrs. Frankelyn at the next door to Mrs. Hunt's.

And they were ready, and so I took them up in a coach and carried the lady to Paul's and there set her down; and so my wife and I home—and I to the office.

October 28–29, 1661
Two Ordinary Days

At the office all the morning, and dined[18] at home; and so to Paul's churchyard to Hunt's,[19] and there find my theorbo done. Which pleases me very well, and costs me 26s to the altering—but now he tells me it is as good a lute as any is in England, and is worth well 10£. Hither I sent for Captain Ferrers to me, who comes with a friend of his and they and I to the theater and there saw *Argalus and Parthenia;*[20] where a woman acted Parthenia and came afterward on the stage in man's clothes, and had the best legs that I ever saw; and I was very well pleased with it. Thence to the Ringo alehouse, and thither sent for a belt maker

and bought of him a handsome belt for second mourning,[21] which cost me 24s and is very neat. So home and to bed.

This day I put on my half-cloth black stockings and my new coat of the fashion, which pleases me well; and with my beaver[22] I was (after office was done) ready to go to my Lord Mayor's feast,[23] as we are all invited; but the Sir Wms.[24] were both loath to go because of the crowd, and so none of us went; and I stayed and dined with them, and so home; and in the evening, by consent, we met at the Dolphin, where other company came to us and would have been merry; but their wine was so naught[25] and all other things out of order, that we were not so; but stayed long at night and so home and to bed. My mind not pleased with the spending of this day, because I had proposed a great deal of pleasure to myself this day at Guildhall.

This Lord Mayor, it seems, brings up again the custom[26] of Lord Mayors going the day of their installment to Paul's,[27] and walking round about the cross and offering something at the altar.

July 11, 1664
A Bad Night

. . . Home, weary; and not being very well, I betimes[28] to bed.

And there fell into a most mighty sweat in the night, about eleven o'clock; and there, knowing what money[29] I have in the house and hearing a noise, I begin to sweat worse and worse, till I melted almost to water. I rung, and could not in half an hour make either of the wenches hear me; and this made me fear the more, lest they might be gagged; and then I begin to think that there

---

18. **dined:** Dinner was eaten at midday.
19. **Hunt's:** Hunt, a musical instrument maker, repaired and altered Pepys's theorbo, or lute.
20. *Argalus and Parthenia:* an old play by Henry Glapthorne (c. 1610–c. 1643). In the revival Pepys saw, female actors played the women's roles rather than boy actors, as had been customary.

21. **second mourning:** period of less solemn mourning following the deep mourning Pepys had been observing for his uncle Robert, who had died three months earlier.
22. **beaver:** hat made of beaver fur.
23. **Lord Mayor's feast:** an annual event held at the Guildhall.
24. **Sir Wms.:** Sir William Penn (1621–1670) and Sir William Batten (?–1667), both officials in the Navy Office.
25. **naught:** worthless.
26. **custom:** These ceremonies had not been observed during the Commonwealth period.
27. **Paul's:** St. Paul's Cathedral. A huge cross stood in the square before the cathedral.
28. **betimes:** archaic for "early."
29. **money:** about £1,000—a very large sum.

was some design in a stone being flung at the window over our stairs this evening, by which the thieves meant to try what looking there would [be] after them and know our company. These thoughts and fears I had, and do hence apprehend the fears of all rich men that are covetous and have much money by them. At last Jane[30] rose and then I understand it was only the dog wants a lodging and so made a noise. So to bed, but hardly slept; at last did, and so till morning.

September 2, 1666
The First Day of the Great Fire of London

Lord's Day. Some of our maids sitting up late last night to get things ready against our feast today, Jane called us up, about three in the morning, to tell us of a great fire they saw in the City.[31] So I rose, and slipped on my nightgown and went to her window, and thought it to be on the backside of Mark Lane at the furthest; but being unused to such fires as followed, I thought it far enough off, and so went to bed again and to sleep. About seven rose again to dress myself, and there looked out at the window and saw the fire not so much as it was, and further off. So to my closet[32] to set things to rights after yesterday's cleaning. By and by Jane comes and tells me that she hears that above three hundred houses have been burned down tonight by the fire we saw, and that it was

30. Jane: Jane Birch, the Pepyses' servant.

31. City: London. The Great Fire started in a bakery, raged for four days and four nights, and destroyed some 13,000 residences. It leveled four fifths of the City and left about 100,000 people homeless.
32. closet: private room.

The Great Fire of London (17th century).

The American writer Joan Didion (1934–   ) explains her reasons for keeping a notebook in this excerpt from her collection of essays *Slouching Towards Bethlehem* (1968). While not secret like Pepys's diaries, Didion's notebooks nonetheless serve as a storehouse of her experiences.

On Keeping a Notebook

Joan Didion

. . . So the point of my keeping a notebook has never been, nor is it now, to have an accurate factual record of what I have been doing or thinking. That would be a different impulse entirely, an instinct for reality which I sometimes envy but do not possess. At no point have I ever been able successfully to keep a diary; my approach to daily life ranges from the grossly negligent to the merely absent, and on those few occasions when I have tried dutifully to record a day's events, boredom has so overcome me that the results are mysterious at best. What is this business about "shopping, typing piece, dinner with E, depressed"? Shopping for what? Typing what piece? Who is E? Was this "E" depressed, or was I depressed? Who cares?

In fact I have abandoned altogether that kind of pointless entry; instead I tell what some would call lies. "That's simply not true," the members of my family frequently tell me when they come up against my memory of a shared event. "The party was *not* for you, the spider was *not* a black widow, *it wasn't that way at all.*" Very likely they are right, for not only have I always had trouble distinguishing between what happened and what merely might have happened, but I remain unconvinced that the distinction, for my purposes, matters. The cracked crab that I recall having for lunch the day my father came home from Detroit in 1945 must certainly be embroidery, worked into the day's pattern to lend verisimilitude; I was ten years old and would not now remember the cracked crab. The day's events did not turn on cracked crab. And yet it is precisely that fictitious crab that makes me see the afternoon all over again, a home movie run all too often, the father bearing gifts, the child weeping, an exercise in family love and guilt. Or that is what it was to me. Similarly, perhaps it never did snow that August in Vermont; perhaps there never were flurries in the night wind, and maybe no one else felt the ground hardening and summer already dead even as we pretended to bask in it, but that was how it

increasing and the wind great. So near the fire as we could for smoke; and all over the Thames, with one's face in the wind you were almost burned with a shower of firedrops—this is very true—so as houses were burned by these drops and flakes of fire, three or four, nay five or six houses, one from another. When we could endure no more upon the water, we to a little alehouse on the bankside over against the Three Cranes, and there stayed till it was dark almost and saw the fire grow; and as it grew darker, appeared more and more, and in corners and upon steeples and between churches and houses, as far as we

could see up the hill of the City, in a most horrid malicious bloody flame, not like the fine flame of an ordinary fire. Barbary and her husband away before us. We stayed till, it being darkish, we saw the fire as only one entire arch of fire from this to the other side the bridge, and in a bow up the hill, for an arch of above a mile long. It made me weep to see it. The churches, houses, and all on fire and

---

WORDS TO OWN
malicious (mə·lish′əs) *adj.*: intentionally mischievous or harmful; spiteful.

---

felt to me, and it might as well have snowed, could have snowed, did snow.

How it felt to me: that is getting closer to the truth about a notebook. I sometimes delude myself about why I keep a notebook, imagine that some thrifty virtue derives from preserving everything observed. See enough and write it down, I tell myself, and then some morning when the world seems drained of wonder, some day when I am only going through the motions of doing what I am supposed to do, which is write—on that bankrupt morning I will simply open my notebook and there it will all be, a forgotten account with accumulated interest, paid passage back to the world out there: dialogue overheard in hotels and elevators and at the hatcheck counter in Pavillon (one middle-aged man shows his hat check to another and says, "That's my old football number"); impressions of Bettina Aptheker and Benjamin Sonnenberg and Teddy ("Mr. Acapulco") Stauffer; careful *aperçus* about tennis bums and failed fashion models and Greek shipping heiresses, one of whom taught me a significant lesson (a lesson I could have learned from F. Scott Fitzgerald, but perhaps we all must meet the very rich for ourselves) by asking, when I arrived to interview her in her orchid-filled sitting room on the second day of a paralyzing New York blizzard, whether it was snowing outside.

I imagine, in other words, that the notebook is about other people. But of course it is not. I have no real business with what one stranger said to another at the hatcheck counter in Pavillon; in fact I suspect that the line "That's my old football number" touched not my own imagination at all, but merely some memory of something once read, probably "The Eighty-Yard Run." Nor is my concern with a woman in a dirty crepe de Chine wrapper in a Wilmington bar. My stake is always, of course, in the unmentioned girl in the plaid silk dress. *Remember what it was to be me:* That is always the point. . . .

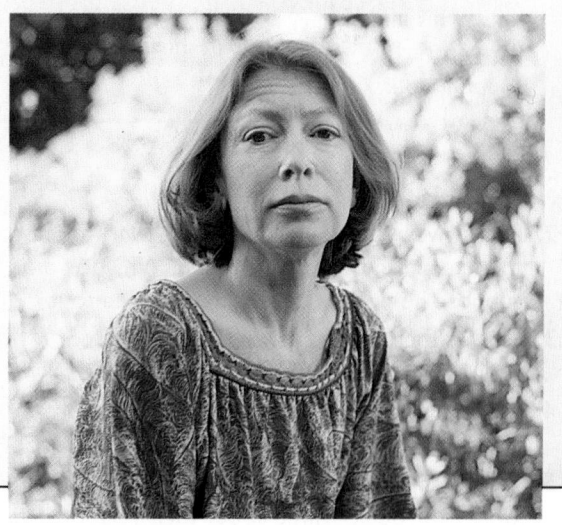

Joan Didion.

flaming at once, and a horrid noise the flames made, and the cracking of houses at their ruin. So home with a sad heart, and there find everybody discoursing and lamenting the fire; and poor Tom Hater came with some few of his goods saved out of his house, which is burned upon Fish Street Hill. I invited him to lie at my house, and did receive his goods: but was deceived in his lying there, the noise coming every moment of the growth of the fire, so as we were forced to begin to pack up our own goods and prepare for their removal. And did by moonshine (it being brave, dry, and moonshine and warm weather) carry much of my goods into the garden, and Mr. Hater and I did remove my money and iron chests into my cellar—as thinking that the safest place. And got my bags of gold into my office ready to carry away, and my chief papers of accounts also there, and my tallies into a box by themselves. So great was our fear, as Sir W. Batten had carts come out of the country to fetch away his goods this night. We did put Mr. Hater, poor man, to bed a little; but

WORDS TO OWN
discoursing (dis·kôrs′in) *v.* used as *adj.*: talking.

he got but very little rest, so much noise being in my house, taking down of goods.

About four o'clock in the morning, my Lady Batten sent me a cart to carry away all my money and plate[42] and best things to Sir W. Rider's at Bednall Green; which I did, riding myself in my nightgown in the cart; and Lord, to see how the streets and the highways are crowded with people, running and riding and getting of carts at any rate to fetch away thing[s]. I find Sir W. Rider tired with being called up all night and receiving things from several friends. His house full of goods—and much of Sir W. Batten and Sir W. Penn's. I am eased at my heart to have my treasure so well secured. Then home with much ado to find a way. Nor any sleep all this night to me nor my poor wife.

42. **plate:** gold- or silver-plated dishes, eating utensils, and the like.

MAKING MEANINGS

First Thoughts

1. Do you think Pepys is totally honest when recording details of his life? Cite entries to support your evaluation.

Reading Check

Trace, day by day, the **major events** covered in these diary entries. You might record the events in the form of a **time line.**

Shaping Interpretations

2. Pepys gives very few details in the *Diary* about the execution that he witnessed. Why do you suppose he doesn't devote much space to it?

3. How is the inauguration of a U.S. president both like and unlike the king's coronation?

4. Of what use would Pepys's account of the Great Fire be as a **primary source** for a later historian?

5. From Pepys's references to his wife, Elizabeth, what can you conclude about their relationship?

Extending the Text

6. How is Pepys's life like or unlike your own? Do you think the values of seventeenth-century life, as Pepys describes them, are similar to or different from those of your own time? Explain.

7. Today, reporting like Pepys's description of the fire would be done by the media. How does Pepys's account compare with reporting today?

8. Which style of keeping a **diary** appeals to you: Pepys's detailed method or Joan Didion's impressionistic approach (described in the ***Connections*** on page 552)? Why?

READING SKILLS AND STRATEGIES

Reading Seventeenth-Century Language

These extracts from Pepys's *Diary* have been modernized for ease of reading. That is, the **archaic spellings** have been brought up to date. For example, in the first entry, the words *abbey, followed, surveyor, chair, footstool,* and *fiddlers* are spelled *abby, fallowed, surveyour, chaire, footstoole,* and *fidlers* by Pepys. **Capitalization** has also been modernized; Pepys tended to capitalize indiscriminately, especially nouns.

1. Here are some other words from these entries (including a surname), spelled as Pepys spelled them. How would each word be spelled today? From these and other **archaic spellings,** what inferences can you make about how some words might have been pronounced in Pepys's day?

bonefyres	turne	alter
musique	themselfs	noyse
frolique	shewe	loaden
tiple	Frankelyn	ruine

2. Look over the diary entries, and find examples of **archaic syntax**—sentence structures that would not be used in formal English today.

3. Find examples of **verb forms** that are different from standard verb forms used today.

Did any other examples of seventeenth-century usage give you difficulty? What strategies did you use to solve your problems? Be sure to check your reading notes.

CHOICES: Building Your Portfolio

Writer's Notebook
1. Collecting Ideas for a Persuasive Essay

Personal records can suggest many controversial issues. Embedded in Pepys's *Diary,* for example, are questions about capital punishment and civil disaster planning. Review these diary entries, and list all the other issues they raise in your mind. Evaluate your list, and jot down notes on issues that you have strong feelings about. Save your notes for the Writer's Workshop on page 612.

Analyzing Character
2. Pepys: What Manner of Man?

Using the *Diary* excerpts as evidence, evaluate Pepys's character: What kind of man does he seem to be—socially, politically, religiously, and personally? Present your conclusions in an essay, using citations from the *Diary* to support your statements. Be sure to open your character study with a thesis statement.

Research/Speaking
3. Find Out More

Pepys's *Diary* is rich in topics for further research. Scan the entries again and find a topic that you would like to know more about—perhaps the public execution of King Charles I in 1649. Using the library and the Internet, prepare material for a brief presentation to the class. You could even work with other students to organize a broad-ranging seminar on seventeenth-century London.

Creative Writing
4. Dear Diary

Write several days' entries for a diary of your own that could serve as a record of the life of an American teenager in the early years of the twenty-first century. As Pepys did, include specific dates, events, and names, or write entries more like those Joan Didion wrote. If you follow Didion, you will write more about what it feels like to live your life.

Creative Writing
5. Opening Up the Diary

More and more writers of fiction are going to historical records, such as diaries and letters, for story ideas. You may have read "The Dog of Pompeii" by Louis Untermeyer, in which the writer imagines what happened to a young boy and his dog when Mount Vesuvius rained fire and ash down on the city of Pompeii in A.D. 79. Take an event from Pepys's *Diary* (perhaps the fire of London) and open it up. In other words, use it as the basis for a story or poem of your own. Put your readers at the scene by including descriptive details—if they are not in the *Diary,* you will have to imagine them.

Leather bucket used in the Great Fire of London (17th century).
London Museum, London.

Daniel Defoe

(1660–1731)

Daniel Foe—he added the aristocratic prefix *De* to his name when he was about thirty-five—attended an excellent academy where he studied history, law, economics, geography, and natural science. Defoe's family were Dissenters, Protestants who did not approve of the Church of England, and so he was barred from attending either Oxford or Cambridge. When he was around twenty, he set himself up as a merchant, trading in haberdashery, brandy, wool, real estate, and eventually civet cats. He married when he was twenty-four. Meanwhile, he began publishing books and pamphlets.

Throughout his long life, Defoe was a very busy person, sometimes successful in business, sometimes bankrupt and hiding from his creditors. He often traveled about the country as a spy, even performing such services for his favorite monarch, King William III. And he constantly wrote and wrote and wrote—altogether over five hundred different works, in prose and verse, including a news pamphlet, *The Review,* which he put out three times a week for over seven years. He touched on every conceivable subject: the choice of a wife, the history of the devil, the manufacture of glass.

Defoe's innumerable writings might be roughly classified into four groups. A large number are concerned with political and religious controversies. His pamphlet *The Shortest Way with the Dissenters* (1702) called for the punishment of the Dissenters—Defoe's own party—and confiscation of their property. When the Church of England party discovered, to their anger, that the pamphlet was ironic, Defoe was arrested, exposed in the pillory three times, and indefinitely jailed. He was released on the condition that he become a spy

Daniel Defoe (detail) (17th century). Engraving.
London Library.

and a writer for the very government that had locked him up because of his satire. A second, didactic group of writings advises people on how to become virtuous as well as rich. A third group is made up of journalistic accounts of sensational events, such as "A True Relation of the Apparition of one Mrs. Veal" (1706), a remarkable ghost story based on the alleged reappearance of a real Mrs. Veal who had died, and *A Journal of the Plague Year* (1722). The fourth group contains Defoe's fiction, including the novels *Robinson Crusoe* (1719) and *Moll Flanders* (1722).

The story of Robinson Crusoe is well known in a general way: A sailor is shipwrecked on a tropical island and for many years manages to lead a more or less civilized life there, without human companionship, until he meets a young native of the island whom he saves from certain death at the hands of "cannibals" and names Friday. This classic book has an almost universal appeal because it portrays a single, strong individual who, all alone, triumphs over his desolate, hostile surroundings.

Many people believe that Defoe modeled Robinson Crusoe on an actual person, a Scottish sailor named Alexander Selkirk, who had written a memoir of his experiences as a castaway. But it was only the *idea* of a marooned man that Defoe used. Though he presents Crusoe's experiences as true autobiography, they are entirely Defoe's own invention; the episodes in the book have nothing to do with Selkirk or with anyone else. It is a tribute to Defoe's skill that many readers have assumed the tale to be true. An irony of literary history becomes apparent when one realizes that, in spite of his voluminous contributions to literature, Defoe is usually remembered as the author of only this one book.

Make the Connection

The Contagion of Fear

The events were grim indeed. When the London plague was at its worst, in August and September of 1665, it may have killed as many as ten thousand people every week—an enormous toll in a city whose total population was less than half a million. During the plague, people who could afford to leave London did so, in large numbers. Wherever they went, to outlying villages and towns, they terrified the local inhabitants, who believed that they could become infected from any city dweller, sick or well. Inside London, if any family member came down with the plague, the whole family was confined by law to its dwelling.

Quarantines of this kind were totally ineffective. Although everybody in those days assumed that the plague could be caught from another person, modern medical research tells us that it is primarily transmitted from rat to rat and from rat to person by fleas. Fleas prefer to bite rats, but when rats become scarce (because they die of plague), the fleas bite people. When the last rat has died of plague, then people stop dying. Since Defoe and his contemporaries did not understand how the plague was communicated, the disease seemed not only horrible, but also mysterious and irrational, as though an angry God were punishing them for their wrongdoings. What contemporary events have confused and frightened people so much that

they began talking about divine punishment?

Elements of Literature

Journal

Defoe was a practical man, and he realized that the materials of history might be a source of profit. Thus, *A Journal of the Plague Year* illustrates the form of the **journal**—but at one remove from an actual eyewitness account. This work is, in effect, a semi-fictional reconstruction of an authentic, contemporaneous record, ingeniously written to make readers feel that the narrator was really an eyewitness to the events—when, in fact, he wasn't.

By blending a nonfiction form with made-up details, Defoe became one of the first writers to fuel a debate that continues into our own time. How far can **journalists** (note the formation of the word from *journal*) go in stretching the literal truth in order to re-create a real event?

> **A journal** is a record of events, kept daily or on a regular basis, by a person who is an eyewitness or a participant. A journal is usually less personal and intimate than a diary.
>
> *For more information on the Journal, see the Handbook of Literary Terms.*

Background

This work, which Defoe published in 1722, pretends to be a firsthand account of an epidemic

of bubonic plague that had ravaged London fifty-seven years before, in 1665, when Defoe was five years old. To tell the story, Defoe invented a narrator called "H. F.," who may be Henry Foe, an uncle of Defoe's who may have lived in London during the epidemic and who may have told Defoe about it. "H. F." is said to be a saddler, one who manufactures, repairs, or sells horses' saddles—in other words, an ordinary citizen.

Altogether, Defoe had four kinds of materials to aid his powerful imagination: his own childhood memories; the reminiscences of his uncle Henry and other older people; city records; and printed matter such as pamphlets, books, and sermons about the plague. He worked these materials into a convincing narrative that seems to be related by somebody who is actually experiencing, from day to day, the grim events that he describes.

Reading Skills and Strategies

Evaluating Sources of Information

As you read Defoe's account of the plague, keep in mind what you have just learned about the sources of his information. Remember that he did not observe firsthand the events he describes. Jot down details that you think make his account believable. Note also any details that seem exaggerated or sensationalized.

from A Journal of the Plague Year
Daniel Defoe

1. The Infection Spreads

Here the opinion of the physicians agreed with my observation afterward, namely, that the danger was spreading insensibly, for the sick could infect none but those that came within reach of the sick person; but that one man who may have really received the infection and knows it not, but goes abroad and about as a sound person, may give the plague to a thousand people, and they to greater numbers in proportion, and neither the person giving the infection or the persons receiving it know anything of it, and perhaps not feel the effects of it for several days after.

For example, many persons in the time of this visitation never perceived that they were infected till they found to their unspeakable surprise, the tokens come out upon them; after which they seldom lived six hours; for those spots they called the tokens were really gangrene spots, or mortified flesh[1] in small knobs as broad as a little silver penny, and hard as a piece of callus or horn; so that, when the disease was come up to that length, there was nothing could follow but certain death; and yet, as I said, they knew nothing of their being infected, nor found themselves so much as out of order, till those <u>mortal</u> marks were upon them. But everybody must allow that they were infected in a high degree before, and must have been so some time, and consequently their breath, their sweat, their very clothes, were contagious for many days before. . . .

2. Dismal Scenes

I had some little obligations, indeed, upon me to go to my brother's house, which was in Coleman Street[2] parish and which he had left to my care, and I went at first every day, but afterward only once or twice a week.

In these walks I had many dismal scenes before my eyes, as particularly of persons falling dead in the streets, terrible shrieks and screechings of women, who, in their agonies, would throw open their chamber windows and cry out in a dismal, surprising manner. It is impossible to describe the variety of postures in which the passions of the poor people would express themselves.

Passing through Tokenhouse Yard, in Lothbury, of a sudden a casement[3] violently opened just over my head, and a woman gave three frightful screeches, and then cried, "Oh! death, death, death!" in a most <u>inimitable</u> tone, and which struck me with horror and a chillness in my very blood. There was nobody to be seen in the whole street, neither did any other window open, for people had no curiosity now in any case, nor could anybody help one another, so I went on to pass into Bell Alley.

Just in Bell Alley, on the right hand of the passage, there was a more terrible cry than that, though it was not so directed out at the window; but the whole family was in a terrible fright, and I could hear women and children run screaming about the rooms like distracted, when a <u>garret</u> window opened and somebody from a window on the other side the alley called and asked, "What is the matter?" upon which, from the first window, it was answered, "Oh Lord, my old master has hanged himself!" The other asked again, "Is he quite dead?" and the first answered, "Ay, ay, quite dead; quite dead and cold!" This person was a merchant and a deputy alderman, and very rich. I care not to mention the name, though I knew his name too, but that would be an hardship to the family, which is now flourishing again.

3. **casement:** hinged window.

----

1. **gangrene . . . flesh:** decay of soft tissues from a blockage of blood flow.
2. **Coleman Street:** This place and other places Defoe names are all within the old City of London, unless otherwise noted.

WORDS TO OWN

mortal (môr′təl) *adj.:* fatal.
inimitable (in·im′i·tə·bəl) *adj.:* difficult or impossible to imitate.
garret (gar′it) *n.:* attic.

Lord, have mercy on London. Woodcut.

But this is but one; it is scarce credible what dreadful cases happened in particular families every day. People in the rage of the distemper, or in the torment of their swellings, which was indeed intolerable, running out of their own government,[4] raving and distracted, and oftentimes laying violent hands upon themselves, throwing themselves out at their windows, shooting themselves, etc.; mothers murdering their own children in their <u>lunacy</u>, some dying of mere grief as a passion, some of mere fright and surprise without any infection at all, others frighted into idiotism and foolish distractions, some into despair and lunacy, others into melancholy madness.

The pain of the swelling was in particular very violent, and to some intolerable; the physicians and surgeons may be said to have tortured many poor creatures even to death. The swellings in some grew hard, and they applied violent drawing

plasters or poultices[5] to break them, and if these did not do they cut and scarified[6] them in a terrible manner. In some those swellings were made hard partly by the force of the distemper and partly by their being too violently drawn, and were so hard that no instrument could cut them, and then they burnt them with caustics,[7] so that many died raving mad with the torment, and some in the very operation. In these distresses, some, for want of help to hold them down in their beds, or to look to them, laid hands upon

4. **out of their own government:** unable to control themselves.

5. **drawing plasters or poultices** (pōl′tis·iz): hot packs used to soften sores and draw infection to the skin's surface.
6. **scarified:** punctured.
7. **caustics:** chemicals that can burn or eat away flesh.

WORDS TO OWN

lunacy (lōō′nə·sē) *n.:* madness. This word is derived from *luna,* Latin for "moon." People once believed that the phases of the moon could affect the human mind.

---

themselves as above. Some broke out into the streets, perhaps naked, and would run directly down to the river if they were not stopped by the watchman or other officers, and plunge themselves into the water wherever they found it.

It often pierced my very soul to hear the groans and cries of those who were thus tormented, but of the two this was counted the most promising particular in the whole infection, for if these swellings could be brought to a head, and to break and run, or, as the surgeons call it, to digest, the patient generally recovered; whereas those who, like the gentlewoman's daughter, were struck with death at the beginning, and had the tokens come out upon them, often went about indifferent easy till a little before they died, and some till the moment they dropped down, as in apoplexies[8] and epilepsies is often the case. Such would be taken suddenly very sick, and would run to a bench or bulk,[9] or any convenient place that offered itself, or to their own houses if possible, as I mentioned before, and there sit down, grow faint, and die. This kind of dying was much the same as it was with those who die of common mortifications,[10] who die swooning, and, as it were, go away in a dream. Such as died thus had very little notice of their being infected at all till the gangrene was spread through their whole body; nor could physicians themselves know certainly how it was with them till they opened their breasts or other parts of their body and saw the tokens.

8. **apoplexies** (ap′ə·plek′sēz): strokes.
9. **bulk:** low stall projecting from a wall or storefront.
10. **mortifications:** early term for gangrene.

3. Escape from Quarantine

I remember one citizen who, having thus broken out of his house in Aldersgate Street or thereabout, went along the road to Islington;[11] he attempted to have gone in at the Angel Inn, and after that the White Horse, two inns known still by the same signs, but was refused; after which he came to the Pied Bull, an inn also still continuing the same sign. He asked them for lodging for one night only, pretending to be going into Lincolnshire,[12] and assuring them of his being very sound and free from the infection, which also at that time had not reached much that way.

They told him they had no lodging that they could spare but one bed up in the garret, and that they could spare that bed for one night, some drovers being expected the next day with cattle; so, if he would accept of that lodging, he might have it, which he did. So a servant was sent up with a candle with him to show him the room. He was very well dressed, and looked like a person not used to lie in a garret; and when he came to the room he fetched a deep sigh, and said to the servant, "I have seldom lain in such a lodging as this." However, the servant assuring him again that they had no better, "Well," says he, "I must make shift; this is a dreadful time; but it is but for one night." So he sat down upon the bedside, and bade the maid, I think it was, fetch him up a pint of warm ale. Accordingly the servant went for the ale, but some hurry in the house, which perhaps

11. **Islington:** suburb north of London.
12. **Lincolnshire:** county on the east coast of England.

Londoners fleeing into the countryside to escape the plague. Woodcut.
The Granger Collection, New York.

employed her other ways, put it out of her head, and she went up no more to him.

The next morning, seeing no appearance of the gentleman, somebody in the house asked the servant that had showed him upstairs what was become of him. She started. "Alas!" says she, "I never thought more of him. He bade me carry him some warm ale, but I forgot." Upon which, not the maid, but some other person was sent up to see after him, who, coming into the room, found him stark dead and almost cold, stretched out across the bed. His clothes were pulled off, his jaw fallen, his eyes open in a most frightful posture, the rug of the bed being grasped hard in one of his hands, so that it was plain he died soon after the maid left him; and 'tis probable, had she gone up with the ale, she had found him dead in a few minutes after he sat down upon the bed. The alarm was great in the house, as anyone may suppose, they having been free from the distemper till that disaster, which, bringing the infection to the house, spread it immediately to other houses round about it. . . .

4. Burial Pits and Dead-Carts

There was a strict order to prevent people coming to those pits, and that was only to prevent infection. But after some time that order was more necessary, for people that were infected and near their end, and delirious also, would run to those pits, wrapped in blankets or rugs, and throw themselves in, and, as they said, bury themselves. . . .

This may serve a little to describe the dreadful condition of that day, though it is impossible to say anything that is able to give a true idea of it to those who did not see it, other than this, that it was indeed very, very, very dreadful, and such as no tongue can express.

I got admittance into the churchyard[13] by being acquainted with the sexton who attended; who, though he did not refuse me at all, yet earnestly persuaded me not to go, telling me very seriously (for he was a good, religious, and sensible man) that it was indeed their business and duty to venture, and to run all hazards, and that in it[14] they might hope to be preserved; but that I had no

apparent call to it but my own curiosity, which, he said, he believed I would not pretend was sufficient to justify my running that hazard. I told him I had been pressed in my mind to go, and that perhaps it might be an instructing sight, that might not be without its uses. "Nay," says the good man, "if you will venture upon that score, name of God go in; for, depend upon it, 'twill be a sermon to you, it may be, the best that ever you heard in your life. 'Tis a speaking sight," says he, "and has a voice with it, and a loud one, to call us all to repentance," and with that he opened the door and said, "Go, if you will."

His discourse had shocked my resolution a little, and I stood wavering for a good while, but just at that interval I saw two links[15] come over from the end of the Minories, and heard the bellman,[16] and then appeared a dead-cart, as they called it, coming over the streets; so I could no longer resist my desire of seeing it, and went in. There was nobody, as I could perceive at first, in the churchyard, or going into it, but the buriers and the fellow that drove the cart, or rather led the horse and cart; but when they came up to the pit they saw a man go to and again, muffled up in a brown cloak, and making motions with his hands under his cloak, as if he was in great agony, and the buriers immediately gathered about him, supposing he was one of those poor delirious or desperate creatures that used to pretend, as I have said, to bury themselves. He said nothing as he walked about, but two or three times groaned very deeply and loud, and sighed as he would break his heart.

When the buriers came up to him they soon found he was neither a person infected and desperate, as I have observed above, or a person distempered in mind, but one oppressed with a dreadful weight of grief indeed, having his wife and several of his children all in the cart that was just come in with him, and he followed in an agony and excess of sorrow. He mourned heartily, as it was easy to see, but with a kind of masculine grief that could not give itself vent by tears; and calmly defying the buriers to let him alone, said he would only see the bodies thrown in and go

---

13. **churchyard:** location of the cemeteries.
14. **in it:** in doing it (going up to the rim of the pits).

15. **links:** torches.
16. **bellman:** bell ringer who accompanied the dead-cart.

away, so they left importuning him. But no sooner was the cart turned round and the bodies shot into the pit promiscuously, which was a surprise to him, for he at least expected they would have been decently laid in, though indeed he was afterward convinced that was impracticable; I say, no sooner did he see the sight but he cried out aloud, unable to contain himself. I could not hear what he said, but he went backward two or three steps and fell down in a swoon. The buriers ran to him and took him up, and in a little while he came to himself, and they led him away to the Pie Tavern over against the end of Houndsditch, where, it seems, the man was known, and where they took care of him. He looked into the pit again as he went away, but the buriers had covered the bodies so immediately with throwing in earth, that though there was light enough, for there were lanterns, and candles in them, placed all night round the sides of the pit, upon heaps of earth, seven or eight, or perhaps more, yet nothing could be seen.

This was a mournful scene indeed, and affected me almost as much as the rest; but the other was awful and full of terror. The cart had in it sixteen or seventeen bodies; some were wrapped up in linen sheets, some in rags, some little other than naked, or so loose that what covering they had fell from them in the shooting out of the cart, and they fell quite naked among the rest; but the matter was not much to them, or the indecency much to any one else, seeing they were all dead, and were to be huddled together into the common grave of mankind, as we may call it, for here was no difference made, but poor and rich went together; there was no other way of burials, neither was it possible there should, for coffins were not to be had for the prodigious numbers that fell in such a calamity as this.

5. A Poor Piper

. . . John Hayward . . . was at that time undersexton of the parish of St. Stephen, Coleman Street. By undersexton was understood at that time gravedigger and bearer of the dead. This man carried, or assisted to carry, all the dead to their graves which were buried in that large parish, and

Plague of London (1665). Woodcut.

who were carried in form;[17] and after that form of burying was stopped, went with the dead-cart and the bell to fetch the dead bodies from the houses where they lay. . . .

It was under this John Hayward's care, and within his bounds, that the story of the piper,[18] with which people have made themselves so merry, happened, and he assured me that it was true. It is said that it was a blind piper; but, as John told me, the fellow was not blind, but an ignorant, weak, poor man, and usually walked his

17. **in form:** according to the customary burial rites.
18. **piper:** bagpiper.

WORDS TO OWN
importuning (im′pôr·tōōn′iŋ) v. used as n.: making repeated demands of.
promiscuously (prə·mis′kyōō·əs·lē) adv.: casually.
prodigious (prō·dij′əs) adj.: huge.

---

rounds about ten o'clock at night and went piping along from door to door, and the people usually took him in at public houses[19] where they knew him, and would give him drink and victuals, and sometimes farthings;[20] and he in return would pipe and sing and talk simply, which diverted the people; and thus he lived. It was but a very bad time for this diversion while things were as I have told, yet the poor fellow went about as usual, but was almost starved; and when anybody asked how he did he would answer, the dead-cart had not taken him yet, but that they had promised to call for him next week.

It happened one night that this poor fellow, whether somebody had given him too much to drink or no—John Hayward said he had not drink in his house, but that they had given him a little more victuals than ordinary at a public house in Coleman Street—and the poor fellow, having not usually had a bellyful for perhaps not a good while, was laid all along upon the top of a bulk or stall, and fast asleep, at a door in the street near London Wall, towards Cripplegate; and that upon the same bulk or stall the people of some house, in the alley of which the house was a corner, hearing a bell which they always rang before the cart came, had laid a body really dead of the plague just by him, thinking, too, that this poor fellow had been a dead body, as the other was, and laid there by some of the neighbors.

Accordingly, when John Hayward with his bell and the cart came along, finding two dead bodies lie upon the stall, they took them up with the instrument they used and threw them into the cart, and all this while the piper slept soundly.

From hence they passed along and took in other dead bodies, till, as honest John Hayward told me, they almost buried him alive in the cart; yet all this while he slept soundly. At length the cart came to the place where the bodies were to be thrown into the ground, which, as I do remember, was at Mount Mill; and as the cart usually stopped some time before they were ready to shoot out the melancholy load they had in it, as soon as the cart stopped the fellow awaked and struggled a little to get his head out from among

the dead bodies, when, raising himself up in the cart, he called out, "Hey! where am I?" This frighted the fellow that attended about the work; but after some pause John Hayward, recovering himself, said, "Lord, bless us! There's somebody in the cart not quite dead!" So another called to him and said, "Who are you?" The fellow answered, "I am the poor piper. Where am I?" "Where are you?" says Hayward. "Why, you are in the dead-cart, and we are going to bury you." "But I an't dead though, am I?" says the piper, which made them laugh a little—though, as John said, they were heartily frighted at first; so they helped the poor fellow down, and he went about his business.

I know the story goes he set up his pipes in the cart and frighted the bearers and others so that they ran away; but John Hayward did not tell the story so, nor say anything of his piping at all; but that he was a poor piper, and that he was carried away as above I am fully satisfied of the truth of. . . .

6. A Violent Cure

I heard of one infected creature who, running out of his bed in his shirt in the anguish and agony of his swellings, of which he had three upon him, got his shoes on and went to put on his coat; but the nurse resisting, and snatching the coat from him, he threw her down, ran over her, ran downstairs and into the street, directly to the Thames in his shirt, the nurse running after him, and calling to the watch to stop him; but the watchman, frighted at the man, and afraid to touch him, let him go on; upon which he ran down to the Stillyard stairs, threw away his shirt, and plunged into the Thames, and, being a good swimmer, swam quite over the river; and the tide being coming in, as they call it (that is, running westward) he reached the land not till he came about the Falcon stairs, where landing, and finding no people there, it being in the night, he ran about the streets there, naked as he was, for a good while, when, it being by that time high water,[21] he takes the river again, and swam back to the Stillyard,

21. **high water:** high tide.

19. **public houses:** taverns.
20. **farthings:** small British coins (no longer in use) worth one quarter of a penny.

landed, ran up the streets again to his own house, knocking at the door, went up the stairs and into his bed again; and that this terrible experiment cured him of the plague, that is to say, that the violent motion of his arms and legs stretched the parts where the swellings he had upon him were, that is to say, under his arms and his groin, and caused them to ripen and break; and that the cold of the water abated the fever in his blood. . . .

7. The Plague Diminishes

. . . The contagion despised all medicine; death raged in every corner; and had it gone on as it did then, a few weeks more would have cleared the town of all, and everything that had a soul. Men everywhere began to despair; every heart failed them for fear; people were made desperate through the anguish of their souls, and the terrors of death sat in the very faces and countenances of the people.

In that very moment when we might very well say, "Vain was the help of man,"—I say, in that very moment it pleased God, with a most agreeable surprise, to cause the fury of it to abate, even of itself; and the malignity declining, as I have said, though infinite numbers were sick, yet fewer died, and the very first weeks' bill[22] decreased 1,843; a vast number indeed!

It is impossible to express the change that appeared in the very countenances of the people that Thursday morning when the weekly bill came out. It might have been perceived in their countenances that a secret surprise and smile of joy sat on everybody's face. They shook one another by the hands in the streets, who would hardly go on the same side of the way with one another before. Where the streets were not too broad they would open their windows and call from one house to another, and ask how they did, and if they had heard the good news that the plague was abated. Some would return, when they said good news, and ask, "What good news?" and when they answered that the plague was abated and the bills decreased almost two thousand, they would cry out, "God be praised!" and would weep aloud for joy, telling them they had heard nothing of it; and such was the joy of the

Title page of *A Collection of All the Bills of Mortality* (1665).

people that it was, as it were, life to them from the grave. I could almost set down as many extravagant things done in the excess of their joy as of their grief; but that would be to lessen the value of it. . . .

8. I'm Alive!

. . . I shall conclude the account of this calamitous year . . . with a coarse but sincere stanza of my own, which I placed at the end of my ordinary memorandums the same year they were written:

> A dreadful plague in London was
>> In the year sixty-five,
> Which swept an hundred thousand souls
>> Away; yet I alive!

H. F.

22. **bill:** count of the dead that was published every week so long as the plague raged.

WORDS TO OWN
abated (ə·bāt′id) *v.:* lessened.
calamitous (kə·lam′ə·təs) *adj.:* bringing great trouble.

MAKING MEANINGS

First Thoughts

1. What did you feel was the strongest **image** in this account of an urban epidemic? Why?

Shaping Interpretations

2. What seems to be the **tone** of the *Journal*—the attitude of the writer toward the events he is recounting? Do you think the tone would have been different if the *Journal* really had been written during the plague?

3. What techniques does Defoe use to make his journal seem authentic?

4. Why does Defoe, or his narrator, say that the manner of burial makes no difference to a dead person? To whom do you think the manner of burial *does* make a difference?

5. Why would the story of the piper be improved if it contained the bit about his playing the pipes while he was in the dead-cart? Why, then, does the narrator refuse to include this bit?

6. Why does H. F. call his little poem "coarse"?

Connecting with the Text

7. How do you think experiencing a plague of this sort would change a person's attitude toward life and death?

Reading Check

a. Where does Defoe let the reader know his *Journal* is being written long after the plague took place? How does he explain this change in form?

b. Who are the four characters whom the narrator features? How does each of their situations differ?

c. What were the symptoms of the disease?

d. What attempts were made to cure people?

Extending the Text

8. What is meant by the expression "morbid curiosity"? Where does this kind of curiosity appear in contemporary life, and how do you account for it?

9. Few words in English have the shock value of *plague*. Can you think of anything in your own world that is described as a plague? How does the plague Defoe describes compare to the "plagues" of today?

Defoe in the Pillory (detail) (17th century), from a chapbook edition of *Jure Divino*.

By permission of the British Library, London.

CHOICES: Building Your Portfolio

Writer's Notebook

1. Collecting Ideas for a Persuasive Essay

Defoe uses officials (the sexton, for example) to make his journal account more convincing—a strategy also important in persuasion. If you are arguing the issue that germ warfare is so dangerous to the survival of human life that all experimentation with biological weapons should cease, support for your opinion may come from an interview with an expert in the field. Make a three-column chart headed *Public Disasters, Issues,* and *Experts.* Then, for each column, brainstorm ideas for persuasive essays (TV and newspaper stories can help). Save your notes for the Writer's Workshop on page 612.

Comparing Journals

2. Charting Pepys and Defoe

In an essay, compare and contrast Defoe's *A Journal of the Plague Year* and Pepys's diary entry about the Great Fire of London (page 549). (Remember that Pepys's *Diary* is a nonfiction account, unlike Defoe's *Journal.*) Gather information

Elements of Comparison	Pepys's Diary	Defoe's Journal
Tone		
Point of view		
Use of details		

for your essay by filling out a chart like the one above. Conclude your essay by deciding how good (or bad) a job Defoe does of imitating a personal journal.

Supporting an Opinion

3. Forgetting or Confronting?

Some people argue that life itself is often very disagreeable—so why should we have to read about dreadful, depressing events in books like Defoe's? Wouldn't it be better just to forget calamities, atrocities, and disasters, and remember only the pleasant things that have happened? How do you feel about this point of view? Using the events in the *Journal* as support, write an essay in which you either defend or attack this position.

Creative Writing

4. You Are There!

Examine several accounts (from newspapers, magazines, or television or radio) of a recent natural disaster. Then, write a narrative of the event as though you were an observer or a participant. Use ei-

ther the format of a newspaper article or that of a TV news documentary. Include the details that will make your story believable: names, dates, places, times, causes, effects, motives, and so on.

Discussion / Evaluating Credibility

5. Do You Believe Him?

Reread the Background material on page 557 that describes Defoe's sources of information. Review also the notes you took while reading the selection. Then, form a group for a round-table discussion of Defoe's sources and how he used them. Consider which of his sources was the most reliable and which the least, and decide how much or how little he may have used each one. Then, discuss the credibility of Defoe's account. Does it stand up most credibly as history, journalism, or fiction? Finally, consider any writer's responsibility in writing a book that claims to be a firsthand account but is not. (Are any such books written today?) At the conclusion of your discussion, present a summation of your group's views.

Joseph Addison and Sir Richard Steele

Wit, morality, and coffeehouse gossip. In the early eighteenth century, London's thriving coffeehouse scene provided politicians, actors, and aristocrats a place to meet, to read newspapers, and to gossip. Coffeehouse conversations reflected the nation's commercial, cultural, and political life to such an extent that they were called "the penny universities" because one could receive a complete education there for the price of a newspaper.

Sir Richard Steele and Joseph Addison's contribution to this intellectual scene was the periodical essay, a forerunner of modern newspapers and magazines. This publication consisted of a single printed sheet, issued at least once a week and usually containing a single piece of writing. Steele and Addison are often paired because of their work on

Joseph Addison (detail) (before 1717) by Sir Godfrey Kneller. Oil on canvas (36″ × 28″).

two enormously popular periodicals, *The Tatler,* which appeared three times a week from April 1709 to January 1711, and *The Spectator,* which appeared daily except Sunday from March 1, 1711, to December 6, 1712. Both publications elevated the periodical essay to an art form.

Two very different talents. Sir Richard Steele (1672–1729), born of English parents in Dublin and orphaned early, was educated in London at a privately endowed school, the Charterhouse. There he met his future collaborator Joseph Addison, a brilliant student who was the son of an English clergyman. Steele followed him to Oxford two years later but left the university before graduating and

Sir Richard Steele (1711) by Sir Godfrey Kneller. Oil on canvas (36″ × 28″).

By Courtesy of the National Portrait Gallery, London.

returned to London, where he became an officer in the Life Guards, the royal escort unit, and a young man about town. After serving in the army at home and abroad, Steele devoted himself to politics, journalism, and managing a theater. He even became a member of Parliament, and for a time edited the *London Gazette,* the government's official newspaper. A warmhearted, jovial, impulsive man, and a devoted husband, Steele was often short of money. Being knighted by George I in 1715 did not make him any richer. In debt and suffering from a stroke, he was thoroughly miserable during the last years of his life.

Joseph Addison (1672–1719) was a different sort of man, with a reputation for being cold and haughty. After receiving bachelor's and master's degrees from Oxford, he wrote poems and dedicated them to various statesmen in hopes of advancing his career in government. Eventually his talents were noticed, and he was elected to Parliament, finally becoming secretary of state. Both Steele and Addison wrote plays, but Steele's, characteristically, were comedies. Addison's most successful play, *Cato*—an immensely successful tragedy first performed in 1713—was a history of Rome that referred to contemporary politics. In politics and literature Addison was successful, but his final years were as troubled as Steele's. Addison quarreled with, and died without being reconciled to, his partner Steele and his good friends Jonathan Swift and Alexander Pope.

A brief but remarkable partnership. Addison and Steele wrote more than nine hundred essays during their partnership; these essays remain the pair's most enduring work. The first issue of *The Tatler* promised current reports from reliable sources. For example, they claimed that new poetry would come straight from Will's Coffeehouse; St. James's Coffeehouse would provide current events; accounts of "gallantry, pleasure, and entertainment" would be obtained from White's Chocolate House. In other words, the paper promised the city's best gossip in a single printed sheet. In the first issue of *The Tatler,* Steele said, "The general purpose of this paper is to expose the false arts of life, to pull off the disguises of cunning, vanity, and affectation, and to recommend a general simplicity in our dress, our discourse, and our behavior." And in issue Number 10 of *The Spectator,* Addison said, "I shall endeavor to enliven morality with wit and temper wit with morality."

Addison and Steele were both ardent Whigs, a political party that supported reforms opposed by the conservative Tories. However, their periodicals practiced moderation when commenting on public affairs. Their essays sought to educate the new reading public of upper-class women and prosperous merchants on matters of taste, style, and politics. In Addison's words, *The Spectator's* goal was to bring "philosophy out of the closets and libraries, schools and colleges, to dwell in clubs and assemblies, at tea tables and in coffeehouses."

One way Addison made philosophy more accessible was by critiquing entertainment. He reviewed popular stage productions, asking why "the

Opening page of *The Tatler,* volume 1 (1709).

ordinary method of making a hero is to clap a huge plume of feathers upon his head." "One would believe," reasons *The Spectator,* "that we thought a great man and a tall man the same thing." The essay urged readers to look beyond scenery and costume and to explore the power of their own imagination:

> A good poet will give the reader a more lively idea of an army or a battle in a description, than if he actually saw them drawn up in squadrons and battalions, or engaged in the confusion of a fight. Our minds should be opened to great conceptions and inflamed with glorious sentiments by what the actor speaks, more than by what he appears. Can all the trappings or equipage of a king or hero give Brutus half that pomp and majesty which he receives from a few lines in Shakespeare?
>
> —from *The Spectator*

Addison and Steele's original combination of satire and sentiment resulted in playful essays such as *The Tatler's* Number 217. This essay comments on marital relations with a clever "translation" of Milton's *Paradise Lost:* In Addison and Steele's version, Adam upbraids Eve by complaining:

> Madam, if my advices had been of any authority with you when that strange desire of gadding possessed you this morning, we had still been happy: But your cursed vanity and opinion of your own conduct . . . has ruined both yourself, and me who trusted you.
>
> —from *The Tatler*

Eve's rebuttal protests:

> Was I to have been always at your side, I might as well have continued there, and been but your rib still: But if I was so weak a creature as you thought me, why did you not interpose your sage authority more absolutely? . . . Had you not been too easy, neither you or I had now transgressed.
>
> —from *The Tatler*

The editors gently, wryly show their readers the folly of domestic strife while advising a moderate path that will avoid "conjugal enmity." Their essays could ridicule bad puns or ponder the nature of true literary "genius." The only constant in their coverage was an intolerance for vanity and excess.

Steele and Addison's collaboration in *The Tatler* and *The Spectator* expanded the genre of the periodical essay with a blend of humor and instruction. In addition, the partnership left a detailed literary record of eighteenth-century society and thought. Their essays are models of insight, wit, and common sense that compel readers of any age.

Stockjobbers Extraordinary (18th century), satirical sketch by Robert Dighton.

Guildhall Library. Corporation of London.

Samuel Johnson

(1709–1784)

Samuel Johnson (detail) (1756) by an unknown artist. Private Collection.

Samuel Johnson was the dominant literary figure in England during the latter part of the eighteenth century. Johnson is famous not for one or two masterpieces, but for a great variety of writings and for three large projects: *A Dictionary of the English Language* (1755); an edition of Shakespeare's plays (1765) with an important critical preface and useful notes; and *The Lives of the Poets* (1779–1781) in ten volumes, a series of biographical-critical introductions. A wise man, a moralist, a talker, an eminent writer and critic, a beloved friend of people rich, poor, young, and old, Johnson became in his own day an English institution. Even today, his personality is vivid because so many of his contemporaries recorded their impressions of him. We think of him as a large, imposing person of untidy appearance and odd mannerisms, very fond of drinking tea and of discoursing with his friends on just about every subject that concerns human beings.

Of course, he was not always like that. Johnson's beginnings were humble and unpromising. The son of an unsuccessful bookseller in the small city of Lichfield, he was a puny, weak infant who suffered from the effects of smallpox and scrofula, an infection of the lymph glands of the neck, which made him blind in one eye and deaf in one ear.

Despite his early weaknesses, Johnson grew into a sturdy youth, gradually exhibiting the qualities that characterized him as an adult: vigor, courage, pride, bossiness, and dedication to learning. He had to leave Oxford after only one year because he lacked money to continue; after that, he was spectacularly unsuccessful as a teacher in a private school. In 1737, Johnson moved to London with his wife, Elizabeth Porter, a widow twenty years his senior, whom he called Tetty and loved passionately.

While Johnson was struggling for recognition as a writer, he became addicted to the city life in London and began to disparage life in the countryside and provincial cities. "There is in London," he once said, "all that life can afford"; and "When a man is tired of London, he is tired of life."

Gradually Johnson's days of poverty and obscurity came to an end. In 1750, a series of essays called *The Rambler* made him famous as "a teacher of moral and religious wisdom," to quote his biographer, James Boswell. Meanwhile, his remarkable *Dictionary* had been published. And in 1762, in recognition of his services to literature, Johnson received a life pension from King George III—an English monarch that most Americans have heard of.

Johnson shared his prosperity with others, for he was always a devout man and his religion required him to be charitable. He also could not stand to be alone, with no one to talk to. He numbered among his intimates the painter Sir Joshua Reynolds, the statesman Edmund Burke, the historian Edward Gibbon, the musicologist Dr. Charles Burney, and his fellow writer Oliver Goldsmith.

Unlike most habitual talkers, Johnson attracted people because he talked so well. He also liked to be asked questions, so that his talk was never a monologue. His words came out in beautifully rounded sentences, just as though he were writing. Many people offered him their hospitality, especially Henry and Hester Thrale, a rich brewer and his wife. After Johnson's death, Mrs. Thrale published her *Anecdotes* about him, in which she said "No man loved laughing better."

Before You Read

FROM A DICTIONARY OF THE ENGLISH LANGUAGE

Background

Johnson's *Dictionary*—the first comprehensive and authoritative one in English—contains about 40,000 words and many, many definitions. The verb *to take,* for instance, has one hundred thirteen different meanings, and *to set,* sixty-six. Most of these definitions Johnson wrote himself; those he took from the word-books of his predecessors he is careful to identify. Before Johnson's time, academies of scholars in France and in Italy had produced large dictionaries of French and Italian, but there was no such academy in England. Therefore, Johnson took on the job himself; England must have its own dictionary, and Johnson was the man to write it!

How did he do it? First, he read an enormous number of literary, religious, philosophical, scientific, and technical books, most of them borrowed from friends. As he read, he marked passages and underlined a key word in each passage; this was the word he intended to define.

Next, his copyists—he had six of them, all Scotsmen except one—copied out the marked passages on slips of paper and filed each slip alphabetically according to the key word. The slips were pasted into eighty large note-books. Finally, using the passages, Johnson wrote definitions of the key words. There were originally about 240,000 passages—too many to be printed. When the *Dictionary* was finally put out in 1755 by a combination of five publishing firms, it contained about 114,000 illustrative passages in two volumes.

Johnson's *Dictionary* was, and is, a prodigious accomplishment. Forty members of the French Academy worked for forty years on the French dictionary; Johnson and his six copyists worked for about nine years on the English one. The *Dictionary* made Johnson's name familiar to every literate person in England and the American Colonies. It was the basis of all subsequent English dictionaries, including those of the American Noah Webster

(1758–1843), who did little else in his lifetime except compile dictionaries that contained thousands of definitions and illustrative quotations taken without acknowledgment from Johnson. Johnson's *Dictionary* was not completely superseded until 1928, when the last of the ten volumes of *A New English Dictionary* was published. This work, revised in twenty volumes, is now called *The Oxford English Dictionary* (*OED*).

Although more comprehensive dictionaries have since been produced, Johnson's *Dictionary* lives on because it reflects its author's interesting character and sense of humor. None of the selections given here is a complete entry; there are no etymologies or origins of the words, no definitions reflecting the various shades of meaning, and few illustrative quotations. For an example of a complete definition, see the entry below for the words *giggle* and *giggler*.

To GI'GGLE. *v. n.* [*gichgelen,* Dutch.] To laugh idly; to titter; to grin with merry levity. It is retained in Scotland.

GI'GGLER. *n. ſ.* [from *giggle.*] A laugher; a titterer; one idly and fooliſhly merry.

  A ſad wiſe valour is the brave complexion,
 That leads the van, and ſwallows up the cities:
  The *giggler* is a milk-maid, whom infection,
 Or the fir'd beacon, frighteth from his ditties.   *Herbert.*
  We ſhew our preſent, joking, *giggling* race;
 True joy conſiſts in gravity and grace.   *Garrick's Epilogue.*

from A Dictionary of the English Language

Samuel Johnson

alligator. The crocodile. This name is chiefly used for the crocodile of America, between which, and that of Africa, naturalists have laid down this difference, that one moves the upper, and the other the lower jaw; but this is now known to be chimerical,[1] the lower jaw being equally moved by both.

to apricate. To bask in the sun.

athletick. Strong of body; vigorous; lusty; robust.

> Science distinguishes a man of honor from one of those *athletick* brutes, whom undeservedly we call heroes.
>
> —Dryden.

autopsy. Ocular demonstration; seeing a thing oneself.

balderdash. Anything jumbled together without judgment; rude mixture; a confused discourse.

bedpresser. A heavy lazy fellow.

> This sanguine coward, this *bedpresser*, this horseback-breaker, this huge hill of flesh.
>
> —Shakespeare, *Henry IV, Part 1.*

to blab. To tell what ought to be kept secret.

board. A piece of wood of more length and breadth than thickness.

to budge. To stir; to move off the place: a low word.

catsup. A kind of pickle, made from mushrooms.

companion. A familiar term of contempt; a fellow.

> I scorn you, scurvy *companion*! What? you poor, base, rascally, cheating, lack-linen mate: Away, you moldy rogue, away.
>
> —Shakespeare, *Henry IV, Part 2.*

cough. A convulsion of the lungs, vellicated by some sharp serosity. It is pronounced *coff*.

dedication. A servile address to a patron.

den. A cavern or hollow running horizontally, or with a small obliquity, underground; distinct from a hole, which runs down perpendicularly.

dull. Not exhilarating; not delightful; as, *to make dictionaries is* dull *work*.

eel. A serpentine, slimy fish that lurks in mud.

essay. A loose sally of the mind; an irregular indigested piece; not a regular and orderly composition.

excise. A hateful tax levied upon commodities, and adjudged not by the common judges of property, but wretches hired by those to whom excise is paid.

favorite. One chosen as a companion by his superior; a mean wretch whose whole business is by any means to please.

fillip. A jerk of the finger let go from the thumb.

frightfully. Disagreeably; not beautifully. A woman's word.

fun. (A low cant[2] word.) Sport; high merriment; frolicsome delight.

gambler. (A cant word, I suppose, for *game* or *gamester*.) A knave whose practice it is to invite the unwary to game and cheat them.

goose. A large waterfowl proverbially noted, I know not why, for foolishness.

gravy. The serous juice that runs from flesh not much dried by the fire.

> They usually boil and roast their meat until it falls almost off from the bones; but we love it half raw, with the blood trickling down from it, delicately terming it the *gravy*, which in truth looks more like an ichorous or raw bloody matter.
>
> —Harvey, *On Consumptions.*

to hiss. To utter a noise like that of a serpent and some other animals. It is remarkable, that this word cannot be pronounced without making the noise which it signifies.

---

1. **chimerical** (kī·mer′i·kəl): fanciful.

2. **cant:** a word Johnson uses to describe language he disapproves of because he perceives it to be of base origins.

immaterial. (1) Incorporeal; void of matter. (2) Unimportant; without weight; impertinent; without relation. This sense has crept into the conversation and writings of barbarians; but ought to be utterly rejected.

jogger. One who moves heavily and dully.

lexicographer. A writer of dictionaries; a harmless drudge, that busies himself in tracing the original, and detailing the signification of words.

to lift. To rob; to plunder.

lingo. Language; tongue; speech. A low cant word.

lunch, luncheon. As much food as one's hand can hold.

merrythought. A forked bone on the body of fowls; so called because boys and girls pull in play at the two sides, the longest part broken off betokening priority of marriage.

mouth. (1) The aperture in the head of any animal at which the food is received. . . . (4) A speaker; a rhetorician; the principal orator. In burlesque language.

> Every coffeehouse has some particular statesman belonging to it, who is the *mouth* of the street where he lives.
>
> —Addison.

mushroom. An upstart; a wretch risen from the dunghill; a director of a company.

network. Anything reticulated or decussated, at equal distances, with interstices between the intersections.

osprey. The sea-eagle, of which it is reported, that when he hovers in the air, all the fish in the water turn up their bellies, and lie still for him to seize which he pleases.

parody. A kind of writing, in which the words of an author or his thoughts are taken, and by a slight change adapted to some new purpose.

pastern. The knee of a horse.

pat. Fit; convenient; exactly suitable either as to time or place. This is a low word, and should not be used but in burlesque writings.

Dr. Samuel Johnson's house, City of London. The house was designed by Johnson in the 18th century.

patron. One who countenances, supports, or protects. Commonly a wretch who supports with insolence, and is paid with flattery.

pension. An allowance made to anyone without an equivalent. In England it is generally understood to mean pay given to a state hireling for treason to his country.

to period. To put an end to. A bad[3] word.

pompous. Splendid; magnificent; grand.

rhinoceros. A vast beast in the East Indies armed with a horn in his front.

river. A land current of water bigger than a brook.

romance. A tale of wild adventures in war and love.

3. **bad:** low; vulgar.

to romp. To play rudely, noisily, and boisterously.

> A stool is the first weapon taken up in a general *romping* or skirmish.
>
> —Swift, *Rules to Servants.*

smoke. The visible effluvium, or sooty exhalation from anything burning.

to sneeze. To emit wind audibly by the nose.

sonnet. A short poem consisting of fourteen lines, of which the rhymes are adjusted by a particular rule. It is not very suitable to the English language, and has not been used by any man of eminence since Milton.

soup. Strong decoction[4] of flesh for the table.

stammel. Of this word I know not the meaning.

suds. A lixivium[5] of soap and water.

tiny. Little; small; puny. A burlesque word.

tittletattle. Idle talk; prattle; empty gabble.

---

4. decoction (dē·käk′shən): extract made by boiling a substance down to its essence.
5. lixivium (liks·iv′ē·əm): mixture; solution.

torpedo. A fish which while alive, if touched even with a long stick, benumbs the hand that so touches it, but when dead is eaten safely.

tory. (A cant term, derived, I suppose, from an Irish word signifying a savage.) One who adheres to the ancient constitution of the state, and the apostolical hierarchy of the Church of England, opposed to a whig.

to traipse. (A low word, I believe, without any etymology.) To walk in a careless or sluttish manner.

tree. A large vegetable rising, with one woody stem, to a considerable height.

unkindly. Unnatural; contrary to nature.

vivacious. Long-lived.

whale. The largest of fish.

whig. The name of a faction.

to worm. To deprive a dog of something, nobody knows what, under his tongue, which is said to prevent him, nobody knows why, from running mad.

zed. The name of the letter *z.*

OATS. *n. ſ.* [aʒen, Saxon.] A grain, which in England is generally given to horſes, but in Scotland ſupports the people.

MAKING MEANINGS

First Thoughts

1. Which definition surprised or interested you the most? Explain your answer.

Shaping Interpretations

2. Which definitions contain what we would regard as errors of fact?

3. What is Johnson's attitude toward slang, which he calls "low words" or "cant"?

4. How does Johnson's personality come through in the voice of the *Dictionary*? Which definitions show the writer's sense of humor? Which show his political bias and religious preferences?

5. Based on your own experiences and the answers you gave to the preceding questions, what inferences can you make about language, especially about the way it changes? Cite examples from the *Dictionary* to support or illustrate your answers.

Connecting with the Text

6. How do these entries compare with entries for the same words in your current dictionary?

Challenging the Text

7. Who, in your opinion, should decide what a word means and how it is pronounced?

Before You Read

LETTER TO LORD CHESTERFIELD

Background

Long before Johnson completed work on his dictionary, he put out a pamphlet titled *Plan of a Dictionary of the English Language* (1747). The pamphlet was dedicated, at his publisher's suggestion, to Philip Dormer Stanhope, fourth earl of Chesterfield—an accomplished, rich, elegant, and learned nobleman. The publisher, Robert Dodsley, wanted Chesterfield's patronage, or financial support, of Johnson's *Dictionary,* a very expensive venture. But nothing came of the attempt to capture the great man's interest. Johnson even called on Chesterfield a few times, but he was denied entrance at least once. He received only a token contribution from Chesterfield: ten pounds.

In 1755, just before the finished dictionary actually appeared, Dodsley again approached Chesterfield, who by this time had probably forgotten all about the *Plan* and its dedication to him. After all, Chesterfield was a very busy and important man. This time he did respond, though not by giving money. Without ever having seen the dictionary, Chesterfield published two letters praising it in a weekly newspaper.

Johnson, not knowing that Dodsley had again approached Chesterfield, read the two generous letters with surprise and indignation. They could easily be

Dr. Johnson in the Anteroom of Lord Chesterfield Waiting for an Audience (1748) by Edward Matthew Ward.

Tate Gallery, London.

misconstrued; the public might conclude that Chesterfield had given what today would be called a "grant" to Johnson. The letters put Johnson in an embarrassing position because he had asserted in the preface to the *Dictionary* that he had received no "patronage of the great." And so he wrote Chesterfield a letter that has since become famous. The letter's language is very formal; how would you describe its **tone**?

Make the Connection

Pride and Protest

Do wealthy and influential people today help struggling writers, artists, and scientists? What do they expect to gain, if anything, from such patronage?

Quickwrite

How would you feel if a wealthy person praised some work you had labored over, but he or she had never responded to your requests for help when you needed it? Jot down some notes on how you might respond.

Letter to Lord Chesterfield

Samuel Johnson

To the Right Honorable the Earl of Chesterfield
February 7, 1755

My Lord:

I have been lately informed by the proprietor of the World,[1] that two papers, in which my Dictionary is recommended to the public, were written by your Lordship. To be so distinguished is an honor which, being very little accustomed to favors from the great, I know not well how to receive, or in what terms to acknowledge.

When, upon some slight encouragement, I first visited your Lordship, I was overpowered, like the rest of mankind, by the enchantment of your address;[2] and could not forbear to wish that I might boast myself le vainqueur du vainqueur de la terre;[3] that I might obtain that regard for which I saw the world contending; but I found my attendance so little encouraged that neither pride nor modesty would suffer me to continue it. When I had once addressed your Lordship in public, I had exhausted all the art of pleasing which a retired and uncourtly scholar can possess. I had done all that I could; and no man is well pleased to have his all neglected, be it ever so little.

Seven years, my Lord, have now passed since I waited in your outward rooms, or was repulsed from your door, during which time I have been pushing on my work through difficulties of which it is useless to complain, and have brought it, at last, to the verge of publication without one act of assistance, one word of encouragement, or one smile of favor. Such treatment I did not expect, for I never had a patron before.

The shepherd in Virgil[4] grew at last acquainted with Love, and found him a native of the rocks.

1. *World:* name of the newspaper in which Chesterfield (1694–1773) published his letters praising Johnson's *Dictionary*.

2. **address:** conversational manner or skill.

3. *le vainqueur . . . terre:* French for "the conqueror of the conqueror of the world." Chesterfield would have recognized that Johnson is quoting a famous line of a poem by the French poet Nicolas Boileau (1636–1711).

4. **the shepherd in Virgil:** In a pastoral poem by the Roman poet Virgil (70–19 B.C.), a shepherd discovers that love is unkind; Johnson similarly discovered that patrons are unkind.

WORDS TO OWN
contending (kən·tend′iŋ) *v.* used as *adj.*: competing; struggling.
repulsed (ri·pulst′) *v.*: driven away.

Is not a patron, my Lord, one who looks with unconcern on a man struggling for life in the water, and, when he has reached ground, <u>encumbers</u> him with help? The notice which you have been pleased to take of my labors, had it been early, had been kind; but it has been delayed till I am indifferent, and cannot enjoy it; till I am solitary,[5] and cannot <u>impart</u> it; till I am known, and do not want[6] it. I hope it is no very <u>cynical asperity</u>[7] not to confess obligations where no benefit has been received, or to be unwilling that the public should consider me as owing that to a patron, which Providence has enabled me to do for myself.

Having carried on my work thus far with so little obligation to any favorer of learning, I shall not be disappointed though I should conclude it, if less be possible, with less; for I have been long wakened from that dream of hope, in which I once boasted myself with so much exultation, my Lord,

Your Lordship's most humble,
most obedient servant,

Sam. Johnson

5. **solitary:** Johnson's wife had been dead for three years.
6. **want:** need.
7. **asperity:** bitterness.

Dr. Johnson, Mrs. Johnson, Mr. Garrick, and others assembled for a play performed by Samuel Richardson (1748) at The Pantiles, Tunbridge Wells. Engraving by Thomas Loggan.

MAKING MEANINGS

First Thoughts

1. If you had been in Johnson's position, what kind of satisfaction would writing this letter have given you?

Shaping Interpretations

2. What, apparently, was Johnson's motive in writing the letter? To set the record straight? To annoy Chesterfield? To rebuke him? To gloat over him?

3. Where in the letter does Johnson use **irony**? How would you describe the letter's **tone**?

4. Johnson refers to himself as an "uncourtly scholar." What traits does such a person typically possess?

5. Chesterfield did not take offense at the letter, but kept it lying on a table in his office where any visitor might read it. Why do you suppose he didn't become angry?

Connecting with the Text

6. Review your Quickwrite notes. What kind of complaint would you make to someone who had failed to help you when you needed it or had praised you for work he or she had once refused to support? Would you write a letter, as Johnson did, or would your protest take another form? Explain your answer.

ELEMENTS OF LITERATURE

Style: A Personal Mark

Like most important writers, Johnson developed an individual style, a way of writing and speaking like

---

Reading Check

a. Johnson says that he had asked the earl for help, but then stopped. Why did he stop?

b. How does Johnson define a patron?

c. To whom does Johnson give credit for his accomplishment?

d. What does Johnson say about hope at the letter's end?

---

nobody else's. Johnson's style is more complicated than the plain, simple style of Swift. Johnson ordinarily wrote long but carefully constructed sentences, like this one from the preface to his *Dictionary*:

> Such is the exuberance of signification which many words have obtained, that it was scarcely possible to collect all their senses; sometimes the meaning of derivatives must be sought in the mother term, and sometimes deficient explanations of the primitive may be supplied in the train of derivation.

This sentence illustrates Johnson's fondness for

1. longish **words of Latin derivation:** *exuberance, signification, derivatives, deficient, explanations.*

2. **parallel structure:** the two clauses beginning *sometimes.*

3. **exact expression:** The words *exuberance of signification* may sound strange, but they say exactly what Johnson means.

Like Sir Francis Bacon in the Renaissance, Johnson could also sum up an idea in a very few words so that it has the sound of an **adage** or **proverb:**

> If you are idle, be not solitary; if you are solitary, be not idle.

Notice how the first part of this sentence is both balanced against and contrasted with the second. Here are two more sentences by Johnson in which the contrasts are held in balance:

> Let me smile with the wise, and feed with the rich.
> Marriage has many pains, but celibacy has no pleasures.

But at times Johnson could be pompous and wordy. Instead of saying "Charity begins at home," he would say, "A man should first relieve those who are nearly connected to him, by whatever tie; and then, if he has anything to spare, may extend his bounty to a wider circle."

And finally, like all great writers, Johnson is a master **inventor of metaphors.** During a conversation about Shakespeare and a forgotten minor writer, for instance, Johnson remarked, "We must not compare the noise made by your teakettle here with the roaring of the ocean."

Analyzing Johnson's style. Look at the *Dictionary* and the "Letter to Lord Chesterfield." Find at least one example of Johnson's use of

1. long, Latin-based words
2. parallel structure and balance in sentences
3. unusual, but exact, expressions
4. concise statements of ideas
5. strong metaphors

CHOICES:
Building Your Portfolio

Writer's Notebook
1. Collecting Ideas for a Persuasive Essay

In his "Letter to Lord Chesterfield," Johnson uses **irony** to protest the unfair treatment he has received at the hands of a powerful person. What behavior of the rich or powerful would you like to protest, perhaps in a letter to the editor? You may want to develop the ideas you discussed in responding to question 6 on page 578. Freewrite ideas on how you might express your protest. Save your work for the Writer's Workshop on page 612.

Analyzing Character
2. The Man Behind the Pen

Study Johnson's definitions and his letter to Lord Chesterfield, and write a long paragraph in which you analyze the character of the man who wrote them. Consider these questions: What are his values? What are his likes and dislikes and biases? Is he proud? Is he capable of laughing at himself? Is he ever modest? Cite details from the *Dictionary* excerpts and the letter to illustrate your points.

Analyzing Tone
3. Killed with Kindness

Johnson's "Letter to Lord Chesterfield" is a masterpiece of the polite put-down. While Johnson's tone appears civilized and restrained, he is slyly savaging Lord Chesterfield. In a short essay, use quotations from the letter to illustrate how Johnson condemns Lord Chesterfield without appearing to utter an angry word.

Creative Writing
4. Imitating Johnson

Make your own dictionary of twenty words. In each entry, first give the part of speech; second, give at least one common definition; last, write a complete sentence that illustrates how the word is used. The only rule for this activity is that you can't look in a dictionary until after your definitions are finished. You might include these in your list of twenty: *apple, door, growl, nose, song, turtle.*

Creative Writing
5. Modernizing the Master

Johnson was a master of both written and oral language, and his "Letter to Lord Chesterfield" illustrates his formal writing style. Use a less formal, more contemporary style to rewrite Johnson's letter, retaining all of his meaning. You may restructure his sentences, but try to make your letter flow smoothly and sound pleasant to the ear.

In Support of Shakespeare

Literature, like certain styles of clothing and music, moves in and out of fashion, and no less a writer than William Shakespeare fell victim to the trend toward neoclassical standards of order and taste. But two key writers of the age, John Dryden and Samuel Johnson, saw beyond contemporary fashion and helped reestablish Shakespeare's reputation with influential critical essays.

Dryden's case for Shakespeare. John Dryden (1631–1700)—poet, dramatist, critic, and translator of foreign works into English—was an all-around "man of letters," perhaps the first Englishman to deserve that title. Samuel Johnson

himself called Dryden "the father of English criticism." Dryden's literary career spanned the last forty years of the seventeenth century, and he cast a long shadow into the eighteenth.

Dryden's lasting reputation is based on his critical writings, and the centerpiece of these is *Of Dramatic Poesy: An Essay* (1668), a work that includes his comments on Shakespeare. (The word *poesy* means "literature.") In order to appreciate Dryden's observations, remember that Shakespeare had been dead only fifty years when Dryden wrote this piece. Shakespeare's plays were not being studied in nearly every English-speaking school, read in translation all over the world, and constantly performed by profes-

David Garrick as Richard III (1745) by William Hogarth.

sionals and amateurs everywhere—as they are today. Shakespeare was then only one of the many dramatists of the preceding age and far from the most popular one. When Dryden praised Shakespeare highly, he was not echoing a commonly held opinion; he was advancing a new idea—that Shakespeare's genius is his ability to represent nature as it really is. (*Nature* here includes human nature as well as the natural universe.) In his trademark lucid prose, Dryden makes the case for Shakespeare in the passage below.

> To begin, then, with Shakespeare: He was the man who, of all modern and perhaps ancient poets, had the largest and most comprehensive soul. All the images of nature were still [always] present to him, and he drew them not laboriously, but luckily; when he describes anything, you more than see it, you feel it too. Those who accuse him to have wanted [lacked] learning give him the greater commendation: He was naturally learned; he needed not the spectacles of books to read nature; he looked inwards, and found her there.
>
> —John Dryden, *from Of Dramatic Poesy: An Essay*

Johnson: defending the Bard. Nearly a century after Dryden argued for Shakespeare's universal appeal, Samuel Johnson published his now-famous *Preface to Shakespeare* in 1765. Following Dryden, Johnson also praises Shakespeare for his ability to render nature truthfully:

> Shakespeare is, above all writers, at least above all modern writers, the poet of nature; the poet that holds up to his readers a faithful mirror of manners and of life. His characters are not modified by . . . the accidents of transient fashions or temporary opinions: They are the genuine progeny of common humanity, such as the world will always supply and observation will always find. His persons act and speak by the influence of those general passions and principles by which all minds are agitated and the whole system of life is continued in motion. In the writings of other poets a character is too often an individual: In those of Shakespeare it is commonly a species.
>
> —Samuel Johnson, *from Preface to Shakespeare*

David Garrick in four of his principal tragic roles: Lear, Macbeth, Richard III, and Hamlet (detail) by an unknown artist.
Victoria and Albert Museum, London.

Convinced of Shakespeare's preeminence as a dramatic poet, Johnson also refutes charges that Shakespeare took too many liberties with the three dramatic unities. These unofficial rules limited dramatists to representing only those events that occur in a single day at a single location, and forbade them to combine elements of tragedy and comedy in a single play. Because he believed so strongly in the value of common sense and experience, Johnson contends that the "unities are not essential to a just drama," and that, especially in Shakespeare's case, "they are always to be sacrificed to the nobler beauties of variety and instruction."

Both Dryden and Johnson left considerable legacies to English literature. Perhaps, though, they are best remembered not just as writers but as eloquent speakers for an entire community of readers.

James Boswell (1740–1795)

Scottish National Portrait Gallery, Edinburgh.

James Boswell (1765) by George Willison. Oil.

James Boswell was a Scotlander, the heir to a large fortune, and eldest son of Lord Auchinleck (pronounced aff-leck), a strait-laced judge who expected his son to settle down in Scotland and carry on the family profession of law. Young Boswell had other plans. While studying law and classics at Glasgow and Edinburgh, he yearned to travel, to write, to visit great cities, to know famous people and become famous himself, to frequent taverns, and to pursue beautiful women. Boswell's father was totally unsympathetic to these desires, but finally, in 1762, he capitulated and allowed his twenty-two-year-old son to escape to London.

There, a year later, Boswell met Samuel Johnson, then age fifty-three and famous for his *Dictionary*. Gradually Boswell discovered a serious purpose for his life: He would become familiar with Johnson, study his character and personality, record his ideas and opinions, and eventually write his biography—one of the greatest biographies in English—*The Life of Samuel Johnson* (1791). Boswell published only two other books: *An Account of Corsica* (1768) and *Journal of a Tour to the Hebrides* (1785).

Johnson advised Boswell not only to read in the literal sense of the word, but also to "read diligently the great book of mankind." This Boswell did, not only in Scotland and England and while studying law in Holland, but also on a leisurely tour of Germany, Switzerland, France, and Italy. Wherever he went, Boswell kept a written record of his own and other people's behavior and conversation. To avoid taking notes in public, he trained his memory to recall the exact details of an event and the exact words of a conversation. These he later wrote down in private. During his lifetime he accumulated an immense number of journals, memoranda to himself, and letters—thousands of pages of personal writing.

Although he used some of this material in his three books, he died with most of it unpublished. For about 125 years, Boswell's papers were stored in such places as an old croquet box and the loft over a stable until—between 1920 and 1949—they were purchased from Boswell's heirs and deposited in the Yale University Library. Now that many of them have been published, we perhaps have available more firsthand written information on Boswell than on any other person, living or dead. The youthful journals, *Boswell's London Journal* and *Boswell on the Grand Tour*, are particularly frank and interesting reading.

"Good Heaven! What is Boswell?" he once asked in a letter to a friend. The journals show that he was a person full of contradictions and contrasts, as all people are to some degree. Eventually he became a family man and followed his father's legal profession in Edinburgh and, later, in London. But after an evening of highly moral conversation, he would prowl for the rest of the night in the more disreputable parts of the city, often behaving in a loud and brash manner. Once, before the beginning of a play, he entertained a theater audience by mooing like a cow. Often he could not restrain himself from "effusions of ludicrous nonsense and intemperate mirth." No wonder to some of his contemporaries he seemed to be an uncouth buffoon. We know better.

Make the Connection

Looking Back

When James Boswell sat down to write his great biography of Johnson in 1785, his subject was already dead. Yet Boswell didn't have to rely on his memory alone. He had a wealth of material to work from: voluminous letters and notes, every scrap of information Johnson's friends could provide, and—most important—his own vivid and detailed journals. Countless other writers have also followed Boswell's method, rereading and transforming their own journal entries into polished pieces of biography, journalism, even fiction.

Quickwrite

Take a few quick notes on a person whose biography you might like to write. The person must be someone you know well and admire very much. Save your notes for further development after you have read Boswell on Johnson.

Elements of Literature

Biography

In his *Life of Samuel Johnson,* Boswell was not only a recorder of facts, but also a master storyteller with an eye for the rich details that make an incident interesting. Boswell brings to life the whole Johnson household: the wretched Dr. Levett, whom Johnson supported; the blind Miss Williams, who made her home with Johnson and who,

when she poured tea, put her finger in the cup to tell when it was full; the black servant Francis Barber, who was Johnson's friend and heir—even the cat Hodge, who loved oysters. Thanks to Boswell, we know of Johnson's deep attachments to women: first to his wife and then, after her death, to others, especially Hester Thrale, who disappointed him so bitterly by marrying a music teacher.

Throughout the biography, we often see Boswell provoking Johnson to speak out on a topic, or manipulating the conversation for dramatic effect, in much the same way a playwright manages the dialogue of his or her characters. Perhaps the most brilliant parts of the *Life* are the civilized conversations it records.

It is precisely this detail—the large number of actual conversations he reports—that sets Boswell's *Life* apart from other biographies. We have more of Johnson's ordinary talk than that of any other person who lived before the invention of tape recorders. Of course, Johnson's talk was never "ordinary"; it was original, forthright, vigorous, astonishing, and well worth preserving.

A **biography** is an account of a person's life written or told by another person.
For more on Biography, see the Handbook of Literary Terms.

Background

To call Boswell a successful biographer is to say that he possessed several literary talents. He was, first of all, an accurate historian. *The Life of Samuel Johnson* was based on a great mass of journals, records, letters, notes, and memoranda, and condensed to produce a reliable account not only of Johnson but of the whole age as well. Johnson had circles of friends from all walks of life, but Boswell emphasized his relations with people whose names are still well known: among many others, the painter Joshua Reynolds, the actor David Garrick, the statesman Edmund Burke, the musicologist Charles Burney, and the novelist and dramatist Oliver Goldsmith. All study of the artistic and intellectual life of the times begins with Boswell's biography.

Boswell also aimed to show his subject "more completely than any man who has ever yet lived." To do so, he had to be a "psychologist" in the popular sense of that word, a person who listens to, understands, and feels deep sympathy for other people. Boswell appreciated Johnson's sudden outbursts of anger, his fits of depression, his morbid fear of madness and death, just as he appreciated Johnson's cheerfulness, cleverness, and fatherly feelings toward himself. What is more important, Boswell's literary talent enabled him to capture in words all the inconsistency and astonishing humanity of Samuel Johnson.

from The Life of Samuel Johnson

James Boswell

Boswell's First Meeting with Johnson, 1763

This is to me a memorable year; for in it I had the happiness to obtain the acquaintance of that extraordinary man whose memoirs I am now writing; an acquaintance which I shall ever esteem as one of the most fortunate circumstances in my life. Though then but two-and-twenty, I had for several years read his works with delight and instruction, and had the highest reverence for their author, which had grown up in my fancy into a kind of mysterious veneration, by figuring to myself a state of solemn elevated abstraction, in which I supposed him to live in the immense metropolis of London. . . .

Mr. Thomas Davies the actor, who then kept a bookseller's shop in Russel Street, Covent Garden, told me that Johnson was very much his friend, and came frequently to his house, where he more than once invited me to meet him; but by some unlucky accident or other he was prevented from coming to us. . . .

At last, on Monday the 16th of May, when I was sitting in Mr. Davies's back parlor, after having drunk tea with him and Mrs. Davies, Johnson unexpectedly came into the shop; and Mr. Davies having perceived him through the glass door in the room in which we were sitting, advancing toward us—he announced his awful[1] approach to me, somewhat in the manner of an actor in the part of Horatio, when he addresses Hamlet on the appearance of his father's ghost, "Look, my Lord, it comes." I found that I had a very perfect idea of Johnson's figure, from the portrait of him painted by Sir Joshua Reynolds soon after he had published his *Dictionary,* in the

Samuel Johnson (18th century) by an unknown artist. From *The Life of Samuel Johnson* by James Boswell.

attitude of sitting in his easy chair in deep meditation, which was the first picture his friend did for him, which Sir Joshua very kindly presented to me, and from which an engraving has been made for this work. Mr. Davies mentioned my name, and respectfully introduced me to him. I was much agitated; and recollecting his prejudice against the Scotch, of which I had heard much, I said to Davies, "Don't tell where I come from."—"From Scotland," cried Davies roguishly. "Mr. Johnson (said I), I do indeed come from Scotland, but I cannot help it." I am willing to flatter myself that I meant this as light pleasantry to soothe and conciliate him, and not as an humiliating abasement at the expense of my country. But however that might be, this speech was somewhat unlucky; for with that quickness of wit for which he was so remarkable, he seized the expression "come from Scotland," which I used in the sense of being of that country, and, as if I had said that I had come away from it, or left it, retorted, "That, Sir, I find, is what a very great many of your countrymen cannot help." This stroke stunned me a good deal; and when we had sat down, I felt myself not a little embarrassed, and apprehensive of what might come next. He then addressed himself to Davies. "What do you think of Garrick?[2] He has refused me an order for the play for Miss Williams, because he knows the house will be full, and that an order would be worth three shillings." Eager to take any opening to get into conversation with him, I ventured to say, "O, Sir, I cannot think Mr. Garrick would grudge such a trifle to you." "Sir (said he, with a stern look), I have known David Garrick longer than you have done: and I know no right you have

---

1. **awful:** producing awe; now more commonly "awesome."

2. **Garrick:** the English actor David Garrick (1717–1779), a former pupil of Johnson.

to talk to me on the subject." Perhaps I deserved this check; for it was rather presumptuous in me, an entire stranger, to express any doubt of the justice of his animadversion[3] upon his old acquaintance and pupil. I now felt myself much mortified, and began to think that the hope which I had long indulged of obtaining his acquaintance was blasted. And, in truth, had not my ardor been uncommonly strong, and my resolution uncommonly persevering, so rough a reception might have deterred me forever from making any further attempts. Fortunately, however, I remained upon the field not wholly discomfited. . . .

I was highly pleased with the extraordinary vigor of his conversation, and regretted that I was drawn away from it by an engagement at another place. I had, for a part of the evening, been left alone with him, and had ventured to make an observation now and then, which he received very civilly; so that I was satisfied that though there was a roughness in his manner, there was no ill nature in his disposition. Davies followed me to the door, and when I complained to him a little of the hard blows which the great man had given me, he kindly took upon him to console me by saying, "Don't be uneasy. I can see he likes you very well."

Boswell's First Visit to Johnson

A few days afterward I called on Davies, and asked him if he thought I might take the liberty of waiting on Mr. Johnson at his Chambers in the Temple.[4] He said I certainly might, and that Mr. Johnson would take it as a compliment. So upon Tuesday the 24th of May, . . . I boldly repaired to Johnson. His Chambers were on the first floor of No. 1, Inner-Temple-lane, and I entered them with an impression given me by the Reverend Dr. Blair,[5] of Edinburgh, who had been introduced to him not long before, and described his having "found the Giant in his den," an expression, which, when I came to be pretty well acquainted with Johnson, I repeated to him, and he was diverted at this picturesque account of himself. . . .

He received me very courteously; but, it must be confessed, that his apartment, and furniture, and morning dress, were sufficiently uncouth. His brown suit of clothes looked very rusty; he had on a little old shriveled unpowdered wig, which was too small for his head; his shirtneck and knees of his breeches were loose; his black worsted stockings ill drawn up; and he had a pair of unbuckled shoes by way of slippers. But all these slovenly particularities were forgotten the moment that he began to talk. Some gentlemen, whom I do not recollect, were sitting with him; and when they went away, I also rose; but he said to me, "Nay, don't go." "Sir (said I), I am afraid that I intrude upon you. It is benevolent to allow me to sit and hear you." He seemed pleased with this compliment, which I sincerely paid him, and answered, "Sir, I am obliged to any man who visits me." I have preserved the following short minute[6] of what passed this day:

"Madness frequently discovers itself merely by unnecessary deviation from the usual modes of the world. My poor friend Smart[7] showed the disturbance of his mind, by falling upon his knees, and saying his prayers in the street, or in any other unusual place. Now although, rationally speaking, it is greater madness not to pray at all, than to pray as Smart did, I am afraid there are so many who do not pray, that their understanding is not called in question."

Concerning this unfortunate poet, Christopher Smart, who was confined in a madhouse, he had, at another time, the following conversation with Dr. Burney:[8] BURNEY. "How does poor Smart do, Sir; is he likely to recover?" JOHNSON. "It seems as if his mind had ceased to struggle with the disease; for he grows fat upon it." BURNEY. "Perhaps, Sir, that may be from want of exercise." JOHNSON. "No, sir; he has partly as much exercise as he used to have, for he digs in the garden. Indeed, before

---

6. **minute:** note; memo.
7. **Smart:** Christopher Smart (1722–1771), a poet.
8. **Dr. Burney:** Charles Burney (1726–1814), a musicologist and father of the novelist Fanny Burney (1752–1840).

---

3. **animadversion** (an'i·məd·vʉr'zhən): critical comment.
4. **Temple:** area in London where lawyers and other professional people lived and worked.
5. **Blair:** Hugh Blair (1718–1800), a Presbyterian clergyman and writer.

WORDS TO OWN
deterred (dē·tʉrd') v.: prevented.
slovenly (sluv'ən·lē) adj.: untidy.

Oliver Goldsmith, James Boswell, and Samuel Johnson (left to right).

his confinement, he used for exercise to walk to the alehouse; but he was *carried* back again. I did not think he ought to be shut up. His infirmities were not <u>noxious</u> to society. He insisted on people praying with him; and I'd as lief[9] pray with Kit Smart as anyone else. Another charge was, that he did not love clean linen; and I have no passion for it." Johnson continued. "Mankind have a great <u>aversion</u> to intellectual labor; but even supposing knowledge to be easily attainable, more people would be content to be ignorant than would take even a little trouble to acquire it." . . .

Boswell Quizzes Johnson

I know not how so whimsical a thought came into my mind, but I asked, "If, Sir, you were shut up in a castle, and a newborn child with you, what would you do?" JOHNSON. "Why, Sir, I should not much like my company." BOSWELL. "But would you take the trouble of rearing it?" He seemed, as may well be supposed, unwilling to pursue the subject: but upon my persevering in my question, replied, "Why yes, Sir, I would; but I must have all conveniences. If I had no garden, I would make a shed on the roof, and take it there for fresh air. I should feed it, and wash it much, and with warm water to please it, not with cold water to give it pain." BOSWELL. "But, Sir, does not heat relax?" JOHNSON. "Sir, you are not to imagine the water is to be very hot. I would not *coddle*[10] the child. No,

9. **lief** (lēf): willingly.
10. **coddle:** cook in hot water. Johnson is having fun with the two distinct meanings of the word, the other being "treat tenderly."

Sir, the hardy method of treating children does no good. I'll take you five children from London, who shall cuff[11] five Highland children. Sir, a man bred in London will carry a burden, or run, or wrestle, as well as a man brought up in the hardiest manner in the country." BOSWELL. "Good living, I suppose, makes the Londoners strong." JOHNSON. "Why, Sir, I don't know that it does. Our chairmen[12] from Ireland, who are as strong men as any, have been brought up upon potatoes. Quantity makes up for quality." BOSWELL. "Would you teach this child that I have furnished you with, anything?" JOHNSON. "No, I should not be apt to teach it." BOSWELL. "Would not you have a pleasure in teaching it?" JOHNSON. "No, Sir, I should *not* have a pleasure in teaching it." BOSWELL. "Have you not a pleasure in teaching men? *There* I have you. You have the same pleasure in teaching men, that I should have in teaching children." JOHNSON. "Why, something about that.". . .

Johnson's Eccentricities

. . . Talking to himself was, indeed, one of his singularities ever since I knew him. I was certain that he was frequently uttering pious ejaculations; for fragments of the Lord's Prayer have been distinctly overheard. His friend Mr. Thomas Davies, of whom Churchill[13] says, "That Davies hath a very pretty wife," when Dr. Johnson muttered "lead us not into temptation," used with waggish and gallant humor to whisper [to] Mrs. Davies, "You, my dear, are the cause of this."

He had another particularity, of which none of his friends ever ventured to ask an explanation. It appeared to me some superstitious habit, which he had contracted early, and from which he had never called upon his reason to disentangle him. This was his anxious care to go out or in at a door or passage by a certain number of steps from a

11. **cuff:** win a fight or a scuffle with.
12. **chairmen:** porters who transported people through the London streets in sedan chairs (covered seats).
13. **Churchill:** Charles Churchill (1731–1764), author of satirical and comic poems.

certain point, or at least so as that either his right or his left foot (I am not certain which) should constantly make the first actual movement when he came close to the door or passage. Thus I conjecture: For I have, upon innumerable occasions, observed him suddenly stop, and then seem to count his steps with a deep earnestness; and when he had neglected or gone wrong in this sort of magical movement, I have seen him go back again, put himself in a proper posture to begin the ceremony, and, having gone through it, break from his abstraction, walk briskly on, and join his companion. A strange instance of something of this nature, even when on horseback, happened when he was in the Isle of Skye.[14] Sir Joshua Reynolds has observed him to go a good way about rather than cross a particular alley in Leicesterfields;[15] but this Sir Joshua imputed to his having had some disagreeable recollection associated with it.

That the most minute singularities which belonged to him, and made very observable parts of his appearance and manner, may not be omitted, it is requisite to mention, that while talking or even musing as he sat in his chair, he commonly held his head to one side toward his right shoulder, and shook it in a tremulous manner, moving his body backward and forward, and rubbing his left knee in the same direction, with the palm of his hand. In the intervals of articulating he made various sounds with his mouth, sometimes as if ruminating, or what is called chewing the cud, sometimes giving a half whistle, sometimes making his tongue play backward from the roof of his mouth, as if clucking like a hen, and sometimes protruding it against his upper gums in front, as if pronouncing quickly under his breath, *too, too, too:* all this accompanied sometimes with a thoughtful look, but more frequently with a smile. Generally when he had concluded a period, in the course of a dispute, by which time he was a good deal exhausted by violence and vociferation, he used to blow out his breath like a whale. This I supposed was a relief to his lungs; and seemed in him to be a contemptuous mode of expression, as if he had made the arguments of his opponent fly like chaff before the wind.

I am fully aware how very obvious an occasion I here give for the sneering jocularity of such as have no relish of an exact likeness; which to render complete, he who draws it must not disdain the slightest strokes. But if witlings[16] should be inclined to attack this account, let them have the <u>candor</u> to quote what I have offered in my defense. . . .

16. **witlings:** people who think they're witty.

WORDS TO OWN
candor (kan′dər) *n.*: honesty.

---

14. **Isle of Skye:** largest of the Inner Hebrides, a group of islands off the west coast of Scotland.
15. **Leicesterfields** (les′tər·fēldz): square in London.

An Early London Coffeehouse (detail) (c. 1705) signed A. S.

British Museum, London.

Johnson's Love of Argument

. . . I mentioned a new gaming club,[17] of which Mr. Beauclerk[18] had given me an account, where the members played to a desperate extent. JOHNSON. "Depend upon it, Sir, this is mere talk. *Who* is ruined by gaming? You will not find six instances in an age. There is a strange rout made about deep play: Whereas you have many more people ruined by adventurous trade,[19] and yet we do not hear such an outcry against it." THRALE. "There may be few people absolutely ruined by deep play; but very many are much hurt in their circumstances by it." JOHNSON. "Yes, Sir, and so are

17. **gaming club:** gambling club.
18. **Beauclerk:** Topham Beauclerk (1739–1780), a fashionable gentleman descended from King Charles II.
19. **trade:** business.

very many by other kinds of expense." I had heard him talk once before in the same manner; and at Oxford he said, "he wished he had learnt to play at cards." The truth, however, is, that he loved to display his ingenuity in argument; and therefore would sometimes in conversation maintain opinions which he was sensible were wrong, but in supporting which, his reasoning and wit would be most conspicuous. He would begin thus: "Why, Sir, as to the good or evil of card playing—" "Now (said Garrick), he is thinking which side he shall take." He appeared to have a pleasure in contradiction, especially when any opinion whatever was delivered with an air of confidence; so that there was hardly any topic, if not one of the great truths of religion and morality, that he might not have been incited to argue, either for or against. . . .

MAKING MEANINGS

First Thoughts

1. Judging from these accounts, what do you think was Johnson's greatest strength as a person? What was his greatest fault?

Shaping Interpretations

2. Before meeting Johnson, Boswell thought that he lived in "a state of solemn elevated abstraction." Explain how the actual experience of meeting and talking with Johnson differed from Boswell's expectations.

3. Do you consider any of Johnson's behavior unconventional? Would others agree with you? Why, do you suppose, didn't Boswell ask

> **Reading Check**
>
> a. How did Boswell feel as he was about to meet Johnson?
>
> b. How was Johnson dressed when Boswell first visited him in his study?
>
> c. What superstitious habit did Johnson have?
>
> d. Describe the peculiar mannerisms Johnson exhibited when he was talking.
>
> e. Why, according to Boswell, did Johnson sometimes express opinions that he did not really believe?

Johnson about his eccentricities or attempt to make him more conventional?

4. By the time of their first meeting, Johnson was already a very famous man. Does Boswell show him as conscious of his own greatness, or is Boswell's picture refreshingly informal on the whole? Discuss your opinions.

5. What defense does Boswell offer for describing Johnson's eccentricities in the *Life*? Do you think the defense is valid?

6. Was Johnson an impolite person, or did he only seem rude? Explain your answer.

7. In this biography, Boswell often mentions himself—his own feelings, impressions, and conclusions about Johnson. Do you think these references contribute significantly to Boswell's work, or should he have been more detached and objective in your view? Explain your answer.

Extending the Text

8. What do we mean when we call someone "eccentric"? How is *eccentricity* different from *insanity*?

9. Do you think Johnson would have been more or less interesting had his behavior been more conventional? Why is eccentricity of behavior important to society? How is eccentricity regarded in our society today?

CHOICES: Building Your Portfolio

Writer's Notebook
1. Collecting Ideas for a Persuasive Essay

Johnson's enjoyment in arguing "either for or against" a position is a good lesson for persuasive writers. To make your position convincing, you must foresee *counterarguments:* opposing points. Which of these subjects in Boswell's remembrance most intrigues you—gambling, childrearing, mental illness, national prejudice? Think of any controversial issue, and state a position you could support ("Our state lottery should be abolished"). Quickly write two possible supporting points. Then disagree with yourself, and write one opposing point. Save your notes for the Writer's Workshop on page 612.

Creative Writing
2. Becoming a Boswell

Refer to your Quick-write notes about a person you might choose as a subject for a biography, and write a two- or three-page **biographical sketch** of that person. Include an account of your first meeting. As Boswell does, record some of your subject's conversations or sayings, and incorporate them into your sketch as dialogue. How will you present yourself?

Analyzing Art
3. Johnson in Pictures

Look carefully at the illustrations of Johnson on pages 584 and 586 and at the one below. What do you see in each illustration? What does each suggest about Johnson's character and activities? Do they echo Boswell's admiring description of Johnson, or are any of them satirical? Write a paragraph in which you analyze these illustrations. If details in the pictures puzzle you, ask questions about them.

Research/History
4. Johnson and His Cronies

Together with a number of his friends, Johnson founded a social group called the Literary Club in 1764. The club met at a tavern called the Turk's Head in the London neighborhood of Soho. Research the membership of the club. See if you can come up with thumbnail biographical sketches as well as pictures of at least three of its famous members besides Boswell, who was elected to membership in 1773.

Samuel Johnson with James Boswell (18th century).

Germany

Johann Wolfgang von Goethe (1749–1832)

Johann Wolfgang von Goethe (gö′tə), born in Frankfurt, Germany, is one of the towering giants in world literature. Goethe had a huge intellectual appetite and was accomplished in several fields. Indeed, when Napoleon, the supreme egotist, met Goethe in 1808, he exclaimed, *"Voilà un homme!"* ("There is a man!"). During his long and prolific career (his published works run to 133 volumes), Goethe made significant contributions to politics, science, and philosophy. As a writer, he is ranked with Shakespeare, Dante, Homer, and Virgil.

Early in Goethe's career he became a leader of the *Sturm und Drang* (Storm and Stress) movement. This movement, which opposed the Enlightenment's emphasis on cool reason and promoted use of the imagination and spontaneous expression, heralded the start of German Romanticism. In 1774, publication of his romantic novel *The Sorrows of Young Werther,* the story of a sensitive young man engaged in an unhappy love affair, gave Goethe international recognition. One year later and for the next decade, he was a cabinet minister at the court of Saxe-Weimar, the cultural center of Germany.

Like many of his characters, Goethe was inspired from youth to old age by a series of love affairs. Bettina von Arnim-Brentano, perhaps the most influential woman in Goethe's life, also loved Ludwig van Beethoven.

Goethe was also an accomplished musician. "I can always work better after I have been listening to music," he wrote. But he was so extremely sensitive to noise that the sound of a barking dog or an orchestra's kettledrums was torture to him.

Goethe in the Countryside (late 18th to early 19th century) by Johann Heinrich Tischbein.

Staedelsches Kunstinstitut, Frankfurt.

(Map) Europe in 1810, at the height of Napoleon's power. Map © Rand McNally R.L. #98-S-116.

Before You Read

FROM FAUST

Background

The selection you are about to read is based on the life of an actual sixteenth-century magician, Georg Faust. Legend has it that this magician sold his soul to the devil in return for comprehensive knowledge about magic. Tales of Faust's exploits circulated widely in the late 1500s. These tales, though crudely narrated and full of clodhopping humor, inspired the English playwright and poet Christopher Marlowe to write his own version, *The Tragical History of Doctor Faustus* (1604). Marlowe invests Faust with a tragic dignity not seen in the earlier folk tales. Centuries later, the German novelist Thomas Mann (1875–1955) created in *Doktor Faustus* a modern composer who sells his soul in exchange for musical genius. The French composer Charles Gounod (1818–1893) also used the legend in his famous opera *Faust.*

Presented as a Romantic hero, Goethe's Faust is unique among all versions of the tragic story. At the end of his long sufferings, this Faust is granted salvation as others are dragged off to Hell.

As this excerpt from Goethe's play opens, Faust is overwhelmed with despair. He feels he doesn't understand the meaning of existence. Scholarship is not enough for him; he wants to *experience* life fully. Distracted from his suicidal thoughts by the sound of church bells, Faust sets out on a walk through the countryside. He is soon soothed by the beauty of spring and concludes that he might be able to accept his own limitations and simply enjoy living. But when he returns to his study, Mephistopheles, a demon, plays the devil's advocate.

Quickwrite

To what lengths would you go to get something that you are passionate about? Write down what you would sacrifice or trade to get what you desire. Then write down your limits—what you would *not* sacrifice or trade for any amount of money or fame.

Faust and Marguerite watched by Mephistopheles.

from Faust, Part I

Johann Wolfgang von Goethe

translated by Louis MacNeice

Mephistopheles.
Stop playing with your grief which battens°
Like a vulture on your life, your mind!
The worst of company would make you feel
That you are a man among mankind.
5   Not that it's really my proposition
To shove you among the common men;
Though I'm not one of the Upper Ten,°
If you would like a coalition
With me for your career through life,
10   I am quite ready to fit in,
I'm yours before you can say knife.
I am your comrade;
If you so crave,
I am your servant, I am your slave.
Faust.
15   And what have I to undertake in return?
Mephistopheles.
Oh it's early days to discuss what that is.
Faust.
No, no, the devil is an egoist
And ready to do nothing gratis°
Which is to benefit a stranger.
20   Tell me your terms and don't prevaricate!
A servant like you in the house is a danger.
Mephistopheles.
I will bind myself to your service in this world,
To be at your beck and never rest nor slack;
When we meet again on the other side,
25   In the same coin you shall pay me back.
Faust.
The other side gives me little trouble;
First batter this present world to rubble,
Then the other may rise—if that's the plan.
This earth is where my springs of joy have started,
30   And this sun shines on me when broken-hearted;
If I can first from them be parted,
Then let happen what will and can!
I wish to hear no more about it—
Whether there too men hate and love
35   Or whether in those spheres too, in the future,
There is a Below or an Above.

1. battens: grows fat.

7. Upper Ten: aristocracy; upper ranks. The phrase is short for "upper ten thousand."

18. gratis (grat′is): for free.

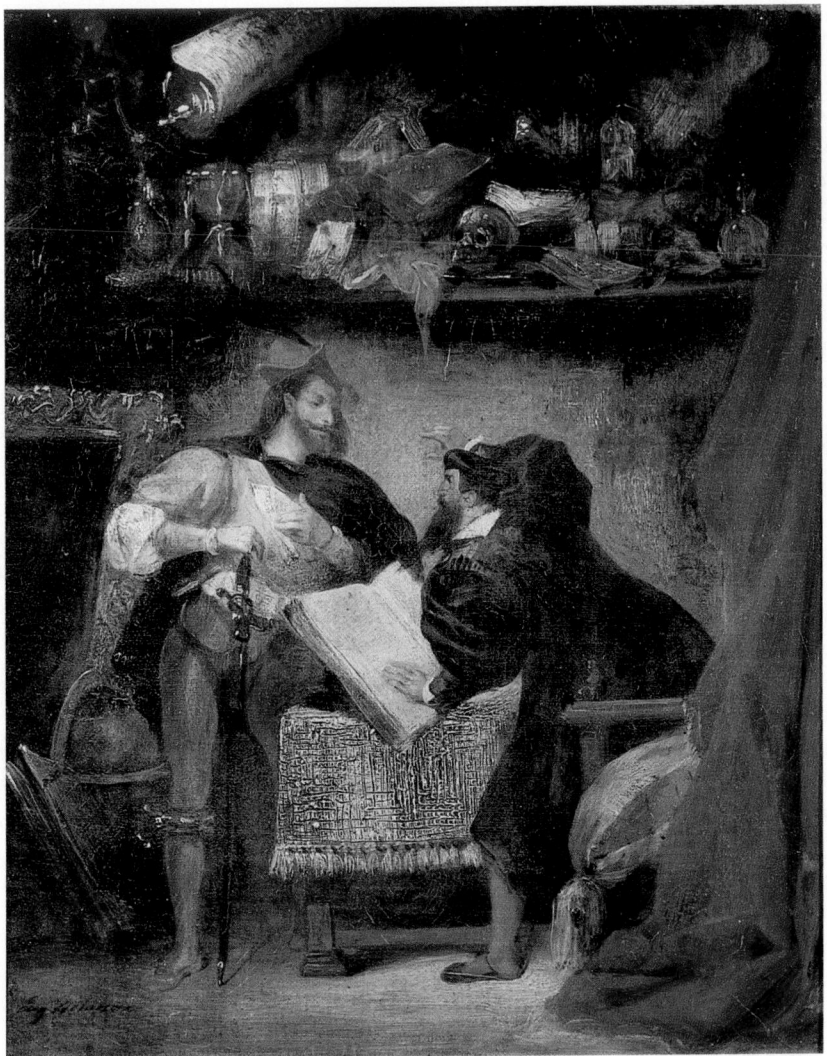

Faust and Mephistopheles
(1826–1827)
by Eugène Delacroix.

Wallace Collection, London.

Mephistopheles.

With such an outlook you can risk it.
Sign on the line! In these next days you will get
Ravishing samples of my arts;
40   I am giving you what never man saw yet.

Faust.

Poor devil, can you give anything ever?
Was a human spirit in its high endeavour
Even once understood by one of your breed?
Have you got food which fails to feed?
45   Or red gold which, never at rest,
Like mercury runs away through the hand?
A game at which one never wins?
A girl who, even when on my breast,
Pledges herself to my neighbour with her eyes?
50   The divine and lovely delight of honour
Which falls like a falling star and dies?

Show me the fruits which, before they are plucked, decay
And the trees which day after day renew their green!

Mephistopheles.

Such a commission° doesn't alarm me,

55   I have such treasures to purvey.
But, my good friend, the time draws on when we
Should be glad to feast at our ease on something good.

Faust.

If ever I stretch myself on a bed of ease,
Then I am finished! Is that understood?

60   If ever your flatteries can coax me
To be pleased with myself, if ever you cast
A spell of pleasure that can hoax me—
Then let *that* day be my last!
That's my wager!

Mephistopheles.

                    Done!

Faust.

                    Let's shake!

65   If ever I say to the passing moment
'Linger a while! Thou art so fair!'
Then you may cast me into fetters,
I will gladly perish then and there!
Then you may set the death-bell tolling,

70   Then from my service you are free,
The clock may stop, its hand may fall,
And that be the end of time for me!

Mephistopheles.

Think what you're saying, we shall not forget it.

Faust.

And you are fully within your rights;

75   I have made no mad or outrageous claim.
If I stay as I am, I am a slave—
Whether yours or another's, it's all the same.

Mephistopheles.

I shall this very day at the College Banquet°
Enter your service with no more ado,

80   But just one point—As a life-and-death insurance
I must trouble you for a line or two.

Faust.

So you, you pedant,° you too like things in writing?
Have you never known a man? Or a man's word? Never?
Is it not enough that my word of mouth

85   Puts all my days in bond for ever?
Does not the world rage on in all its streams
And shall a promise hamper *me*?
Yet this illusion reigns within our hearts
And from it who would be gladly free?

90   Happy the man who can inwardly keep his word;
Whatever the cost, he will not be loath to pay!

54. commission: authorization to perform duties.

Frontispiece of Christopher Marlowe's *Dr. Faustus* (1636).

78. College Banquet: dinner given by a successful candidate for the Ph.D. degree.

82. pedant (ped′′nt): overly precise scholar.

But a parchment, duly inscribed and sealed,
Is a bogey° from which all wince away.
The word dies on the tip of the pen

95 And wax and leather lord it then.
What do you, evil spirit, require?
Bronze, marble, parchment, paper?
Quill or chisel or pencil of slate?
You may choose whichever you desire.

Mephistopheles.

100 How can you so exaggerate
With such a hectic rhetoric?
Any little snippet is quite good—
And you sign it with one little drop of blood.

Faust.

If that is enough and is some use,

105 One may as well pander to your fad.°

Mephistopheles.

Blood is a very special juice.

Faust.

Only do not fear that I shall break this contract.
What I promise is nothing more
Than what all my powers are striving for.

110 I have puffed myself up too much, it is only
Your sort that really fits my case.
The great Earth Spirit has despised me
And Nature shuts the door in my face.
The thread of thought is snapped asunder,

115 I have long loathed knowledge in all its fashions.
In the depths of sensuality
Let us now quench our glowing passions!
And at once make ready every wonder
Of unpenetrated sorcery!

120 Let us cast ourselves into the torrent of time,
Into the whirl of eventfulness,
Where disappointment and success,
Pleasure and pain may chop and change
As chop and change they will and can;

125 It is restless action makes the man.

Mephistopheles.

No limit is fixed for you, no bound;
If you'd like to nibble at everything
Or to seize upon something flying round—
Well, may you have a run for your money!

130 But seize your chance and don't be funny!

Faust.

I've told you, it is no question of happiness.
The most painful joy, enamoured hate, enlivening
Disgust—I devote myself to all excess.
My breast, now cured of its appetite for knowledge,

135 From now is open to all and every smart,

93. bogey: evil spirit.

105. pander to your fad: go along with your frivolous request.

And what is allotted to the whole of mankind
That will I sample in my inmost heart,
Grasping the highest and lowest with my spirit,
Piling men's weal and woe upon my neck,
140   To extend myself to embrace all human selves
And to founder in the end, like them, a wreck.

Mephistopheles.
O believe *me,* who have been chewing
These iron rations many a thousand year,
No human being can digest
145   This stuff, from the cradle to the bier.°
This universe—believe a devil—
Was made for no one but a god!
He exists in eternal light
But *us* he has brought into the darkness
150   While *your* sole portion is day and night.

Faust.
I will all the same!

Mephistopheles.
              That's very nice.
There's only one thing I find wrong;
Time is short, art is long.
You could do with a little artistic advice.
155   Confederate with one of the poets
And let him flog his imagination
To heap all virtues on your head,
A head with such a reputation:
Lion's bravery,
160   Stag's velocity,
Fire of Italy,
Northern tenacity.
Let *him* find out the secret art
Of combining craft with a noble heart
165   And of being in love like a young man,
Hotly, but working to a plan.
Such a person—*I'd* like to meet him;
'Mr. Microcosm'° is how I'd greet him.

Faust.
What am I then if fate must bar
170   My efforts to reach that crown of humanity
After which all my senses strive?

Mephistopheles.
You are in the end . . . what you are.
You can put on full-bottomed wigs° with a million locks,
You can put on stilts instead of your socks,
175   You remain for ever what you are.

Faust.
I feel my endeavours have not been worth a pin
When I raked together the treasures of the human mind,
If at the end I but sit down to find

145. bier (bir): platform on which a coffin or corpse is placed.

168. Mr. Microcosm (mī′krō·kä′zəm): that is, representing the microcosm, or essence, of the world.

173. full-bottomed wigs: wigs that cover the back and shoulders. Popular among men and women in seventeenth-century Europe, such wigs were considered signs of upperclass status.

No new force welling up within.
180 I have not a hair's breadth more of height,
I am no nearer the Infinite.

Mephistopheles.

My very good sir, you look at things
Just in the way that people do;
We must be cleverer than that
185 Or the joys of life will escape from you.
Hell! You have surely hands and feet,
Also a head and you-know-what;
The pleasures I gather on the wing,
Are they less mine? Of course they're not!
190 Suppose I can afford six stallions,
I can add that horse-power to my score
And dash along and be a proper man
As if my legs were twenty-four.
So good-bye to thinking! On your toes!

Mephistopheles
appearing to Faust,
by Alexander Mayer.

195   The world's before us. Quick! Here goes!
       I tell you, a chap who's intellectual
       Is like a beast on a blasted heath
       Driven in circles by a demon
       While a fine green meadow lies round beneath.

Faust.

       How do we start?

Mephistopheles.

200   We just say go—and skip.
       But please get ready for this pleasure trip.

                           [Exit Faust.]

       Only look down on knowledge and reason,
       The highest gifts that men can prize,
       Only allow the spirit of lies
205   To confirm you in magic and illusion,
       And then I have you body and soul.
       Fate has given this man a spirit
       Which is always pressing onwards, beyond control,
       And whose mad striving overleaps
210   All joys of the earth between pole and pole.
       Him shall I drag though the wilds of life
       And through the flats of meaninglessness,
       I shall make him flounder and gape and stick
       And to tease his insatiableness
215   Hang meat and drink in the air before his watering lips;
       In vain he will pray to slake his inner thirst,
       And even had he not sold himself to the devil
       He would be equally accursed.

Faust's covenant with Mephistopheles (detail) by Franz Strassen.

FINDING COMMON GROUND

Working with a small group, discuss plays, movies, novels, or television shows in which a character has wanted—passionately—what he or she could not have. Then, think of people in actual life who have sold out in some way to possess something of great value to them. (Also think about your own Quickwrite entry.) Consider the following questions:

• Do these people have any qualities in common? If so, what are they?

• How do those around these people regard them—fearfully? respectfully? with envy? Why do such people give rise to these responses?

• Can such striving ever have positive effects? Or is it always destructive?

Compare your group's conclusions with those of other groups. What do you agree on? On what issues do you remain divided?

Thomas Gray

(1716–1771)

Thomas Gray is perhaps the best lyric poet of the mid-eighteenth century, an age that is not known for its great lyric poets. The son of a London merchant, he spent nine years at one of the great English "public" schools, Eton College, which is neither public nor a college. (It is the equivalent of a prep school for boys who expect to go to Cambridge or Oxford.) At eighteen, Gray entered Cambridge University, where he lived for the remaining thirty-seven years of his life, reading literature in a variety of languages; studying archaeology, law, history, botany, and zoology; painting landscapes; playing the harpsichord; and growing geraniums in his window boxes. In a quiet, inconspicuous way, he became very learned. These years were interrupted only briefly by a grand tour of France, Switzerland, and Italy with Horace Walpole, a friend from Eton and son of England's prime minister, who paid the expenses.

The great crisis of Gray's life came when Richard West, his best friend from Eton, died of tuberculosis at the age of twenty-four. Gray sought consolation in writing poetry. He was always reluctant to publish his verses; although he carefully and fastidiously revised and rewrote them, they never seemed to him to be quite finished. Moreover, he was painfully shy and, unlike most writers, he really did not want the world's applause. Imagine his distress when his "Elegy Written in a Country Churchyard" made him famous. Gray's other poems—only thirteen of which he published during his lifetime—were also widely admired. Most of them are elegant, gloomy, and artificial: exactly what midcentury taste demanded. Few of these other poems are of much interest today except to historians of English poetry, who find that in several ways Gray anticipated the Romantic Age to come.

Gray led a quiet, frugal, low-key existence. Unlike everybody else in his century, he was never on the back of a horse. Although he was made a professor of history at Cambridge, he never delivered any lectures, which is all that a professor did in those days. He spent his vacations in London, reading in the British Museum (now the British Library), or in the Lake District (a picturesque part of northern England made famous by the poets of the next age), or in Stoke Poges, a village where his mother and aunt lived. There he is buried, beside his mother, in the cemetery that he immortalized in his "Elegy."

Thomas Gray (1747–1748) by John Giles Eccardt. Oil on canvas (15⅞" × 12⅞").

By Courtesy of the National Portrait Gallery, London.

Before You Read

ELEGY WRITTEN IN A COUNTRY CHURCHYARD

Make the Connection

Ordinary People

Have you ever wondered about the hidden lives of ordinary people—or about the dashed hopes that might lie behind the name on a roadside mailbox or a worn tombstone? If fate had been different, could one of those names have been that of a great writer, president of the United States, or maybe the scientist who will discover the cure for cancer? Gray was one of the first writers in English to believe that the lives of ordinary people are suitable subjects for serious poetry.

Haycarting
(18th century)
by George Stubbs.

Board of Trustees of the National Museums and Galleries on Merseyside (Lady Lever Art Gallery, Port Sunlight, England).

Reading Skills and Strategies

Reading Inverted Sentences

Gray wrote his elegy in 1751, so it is not surprising that he uses many **archaic words**—such as *lea* instead of the modern *meadow.* You'll find many of these archaic words defined in the side notes. A greater challenge to the modern reader is Gray's frequent use of **inverted sentence structures.** The normal word order in an English sentence is subject-verb-complement. But to accommodate his meter or rhyme scheme, Gray often inverts, or twists, these sentence elements so that they are out of order. Thus, in line 14, for example, instead of writing "Where the turf heaves" (subject-verb),

Gray writes, "Where heaves the turf" (verb-subject). As you read the poem, look for the subject and verb of each sentence; the more you read, the less awkward the inversions will seem.

Background

Gray had this poem published anonymously in 1751—only because a copy of it had fallen into the hands of an unscrupulous magazine editor who threatened to print it with Gray's name on it. The poem immediately became a great favorite of readers, a position it still maintains because it sounds so beautiful and because what it says about death is so true. Everybody dies: The famous people of the earth are no different from the rest of us in that respect. We all eventually come to the same dusty end. Painfully obvious truths of this kind are called *truisms,* and a poet can be forgiven his truisms only if he utters them memorably. Gray's "Elegy" exemplifies Pope's definition of true wit: "What oft was thought but ne'er so well expressed." Gray wanted this poem printed without any spaces between stanzas "because the sense is in some places continued beyond them." The fact that it is almost never printed in this way perhaps justifies Gray's misgivings about publishers and makes the reading of lines 61–73 a bit more difficult than it should be.

Elegy Written in a Country Churchyard

Thomas Gray

The curfew tolls the knell of parting day,
The lowing herd wind slowly o'er the lea,°　　　　**2. lea:** meadow.
The plowman homeward plods his weary way,
And leaves the world to darkness, and to me.

5　Now fades the glimmering landscape on the sight,
And all the air a solemn stillness holds;
Save where the beetle wheels his droning flight,
And drowsy tinklings lull the distant folds.

Save that from yonder ivy-mantled tower
10　The moping owl does to the moon complain
Of such, as wand'ring near her secret bower,
Molest her ancient solitary reign.

Beneath those rugged elms, that yew tree's shade,
Where heaves the turf in many a mold'ring heap,
15　Each in his narrow cell forever laid,
The rude° forefathers of the hamlet sleep.　　　　**16. rude:** uneducated; unpolished.

The breezy call of incense-breathing morn,
The swallow twitt'ring from the straw-built shed,°　　**18. shed:** nest.
The cock's shrill clarion, or the echoing horn,°　　**19. horn:** hunting horn.
20　No more shall rouse them from their lowly bed.

For them no more the blazing hearth shall burn,
Or busy housewife ply her evening care:
No children run to lisp their sire's return,
Or climb his knees the envied kiss to share.

25　Oft did the harvest to their sickle yield,
Their furrow oft the stubborn glebe° has broke;　　**26. glebe:** soil.
How jocund did they drive their team afield!
How bowed the woods beneath their sturdy stroke!

Let not Ambition mock their useful toil,
30　Their homely joys and destiny obscure;
Nor Grandeur hear with a disdainful smile,
The short and simple annals of the poor.

The boast of heraldry,° the pomp of power,　　　　**33. boast of heraldry:** pride in
And all that beauty, all that wealth e'er gave,　　one's ancestry. Heraldry is the study
35　Awaits alike th' inevitable hour.　　　　　　　　of family coats of arms.
The paths of glory lead but to the grave.

Ode to a Country Churchyard (Gray's Elegy) (1883) by Jasper F. Cropsey. Oil on canvas (13 ½″ × 25 ⅕″).
The Newington-Cropsey Foundation, Hastings-on-Hudson, New York.

Nor you, ye proud, impute to these the fault,
If Mem'ry o'er their tomb no trophies° raise,
Where through the long-drawn aisle and fretted vault°
40 The pealing anthem swells the note of praise.

Can storied urn° or animated° bust
Back to its mansion call the fleeting breath?
Can Honor's voice provoke° the silent dust,
Or Flatt'ry soothe the dull cold ear of Death?

45   Perhaps in this neglected spot is laid
Some heart once pregnant with celestial fire,
Hands that the rod of empire might have swayed,
Or waked to ecstasy the living lyre.

But Knowledge to their eyes her ample page
50 Rich with the spoils of time did ne'er unroll;
Chill Penury° repressed their noble rage,°
And froze the genial current° of the soul.

Full many a gem of purest ray serene,
The dark unfathomed caves of ocean bear:
55 Full many a flower is born to blush unseen,
And waste its sweetness on the desert air.

38. trophies: monuments.
39. fretted vault: elaborately ornamented church ceiling.

41. storied urn: an urn with an inscription on it.   **animated:** lifelike.
43. provoke: evoke; call forth.

51. penury: poverty.   **rage:** emotion; feeling.
52. genial current: warm impulses.

Some village Hampden° that with dauntless breast
The little tyrant of his fields withstood;
Some mute inglorious Milton here may rest,
60 Some Cromwell° guiltless of his country's blood.

Th' applause of list'ning senates to command,
The threats of pain and ruin to despise,
To scatter plenty o'er a smiling land,
And read their hist'ry in a nation's eyes

65   Their lot forbade: nor circumscribed alone
Their growing virtues, but their crimes confined;
Forbade to wade through slaughter to a throne,
And shut the gates of mercy on mankind,

The struggling pangs of conscious° truth to hide,
70 To quench the blushes of ingenuous° shame,
Or heap the shrine of Luxury and Pride
With incense, kindled at the Muse's flame.°

Far from the madding° crowd's ignoble strife,
Their sober wishes never learned to stray;
75 Along the cool sequestered vale of life
They kept the noiseless tenor° of their way.

Yet ev'n these bones from insult to protect
Some frail memorial° still erected nigh,
With uncouth° rhymes and shapeless sculpture decked,
80 Implores the passing tribute of a sigh.

Their name, their years, spelt by th' unlettered muse,°
The place of fame and elegy supply:
And many a holy text around she strews,
That teach the rustic moralist to die.

85   For who to dumb Forgetfulness a prey,
This pleasing anxious being e'er resigned,
Left the warm precincts of the cheerful day,
Nor cast one longing ling'ring look behind?

On some fond breast the parting soul relies,
90 Some pious drops° the closing eye requires;
Ev'n from the tomb the voice of Nature cries,
Ev'n in our ashes live their wonted fires.

For thee,° who mindful of th' unhonored dead
Dost in these lines their artless tale relate;
95 If chance, by lonely Contemplation led,
Some kindred spirit shall inquire thy fate,

57. village Hampden: an obscure person who, with opportunity, might have been famous like John Hampden (1594-1643), an English statesman who defied the king over unjust taxation shortly before the English Civil Wars.
60. Cromwell: Lord Protector Oliver Cromwell, who ruled England from 1653 to 1658.

69. conscious: guiltily aware; conscientious.
70. ingenuous: naively innnocent.

72. incense . . . flame: tributes paid to them by poets.

73. madding: frenzied.

76. tenor: course.

78. frail memorial: modest tombstone, in contrast to the elaborate tombs inside the church.
79. uncouth: unsophisticated; artless.
81. unlettered muse: humble engraver of the tombstone.

90. drops: mourners' tears.

93. thee: Gray himself.

Haply° some hoary-headed swain° may say,
"Oft have we seen him at the peep of dawn
Brushing with hasty steps the dews away
100 To meet the sun upon the upland lawn.

"There at the foot of yonder nodding beech
That wreathes its old fantastic roots so high,
His listless length at noontide would he stretch,
And pore upon the brook that babbles by.

105 "Hard° by yon wood, now smiling as in scorn,
Mutt'ring his wayward fancies he would rove,
Now drooping, woeful wan, like one forlorn,
Or crazed with care, or crossed in hopeless love.

"One morn I missed him on the customed hill,
110 Along the heath, and near his fav'rite tree;
Another came; nor yet beside the rill,°
Nor up the lawn, nor at the wood was he.

"The next with dirges due in sad array
Slow through the churchway path we saw him borne.
115 Approach and read (for thou canst read)° the lay,
Graved on the stone beneath yon aged thorn."°

The Epitaph

Here rests his head upon the lap of Earth
A youth to Fortune and to Fame unknown:
Fair Science frowned not on his humble birth,°
120 And Melancholy marked him for her own.

Large was his bounty, and his soul sincere,
Heaven did a recompense as largely send:
He gave to Mis'ry all he had, a tear:
He gained from Heaven ('twas all he wished) a friend.

125 No farther seek his merits to disclose,
Or draw his frailties from their dread abode,
(There they alike in trembling Hope repose)
The bosom of his Father and his God.

97. haply: perhaps. **hoary-headed swain:** white-haired countryman.

105. hard: close.

111. rill: brook.

115. thou canst read: The "swain" who is speaking is apparently illiterate.
116. thorn: hawthorn bush.

119. fair . . . birth: He was educated—*science* meant learning in general—despite his modest beginnings.

Searching for a Future in the Dusk

In the dusk of a soft summer's eve,
Crushing the cool, prickly lawn,
I lie stretched out
And gaze at the dome sky
like the tip of an enormous egg
Polished to a shiny blue.

I can feel myself soaring
Up, up,
Until I reach out
And touch the thin shell
Of my prison.

The light fades
And my wall drains of color,
Like finger paints in the rain,
Until I can see through it
To the universe beyond;
The purple sea
With a thousand lighthouses
Sprinkling its surface like glitter.

I imagine then,
If I broke the shell,
How far I would tumble
Into my future,
Where I could ride the fireflies
Of possibility
Into the heavens
Of the me to come.

And I wonder,
If I might glance back,
For a moment,
To the shadowing past,
And long
For the prickle of a lawn
At dusk.

—Melynn Minson
Hillcrest High School
Midvale, Utah

MAKING MEANINGS

First Thoughts

1. What did you feel was the strongest **image** in this poem? Why?

Reading Check

a. Where is the speaker, and what time of day is it? What, according to the **images** in stanzas 2 and 3, does he hear?

b. In the fourth through eighth stanzas, the speaker describes the ordinary people in the churchyard. Name the various things they will never again experience.

c. What does the speaker imagine these humble people might have become if they'd had the chance (lines 45–60)? What do the details in lines 53–56 have to do with this idea?

d. What did their "lot," or place in life, forbid the poor people to experience, according to lines 61–72?

e. What does the speaker imagine an old man (the "hoary-headed swain") might say of him one day (lines 98–116)?

Shaping Interpretations

2. The poet **personifies** ambition and grandeur in lines 29 and 31. What does he warn them not to do? What other examples of **personification** can you find in the poem?

3. According to lines 77–92, what evidence on their gravestones shows that humble, ordinary people also wish to be remembered?

4. Many readers of the "Elegy" have assumed that Gray himself is the poet whose epitaph is given in the final lines. Is it necessary to make this assumption to understand the poem? Why does the assumption seem attractive?

5. Suppose that Gray is being autobiographical. What defense does he give of his life? Would *you* be happy with such an epitaph—or would you wish to be remembered differently?

6. From Gray's time almost to the present, many people have thought of poets as possessing the

characteristics described in lines 98–112. Gray established here a **stereotype** that the public long accepted as genuine. Does this stereotype fit any of the poets you have studied so far in this book? (Think particularly of Chaucer, Shakespeare, Donne, Milton, Pope, and Swift.)

7. The poem contains at least two statements that are still frequently quoted:

   a. "The paths of glory lead but to the grave." (line 36)

   b. "Full many a flower is born to blush unseen, And waste its sweetness on the desert air." (lines 55–56)

   How do these lines relate to the poem's **theme**?

8. In one sense, most neoclassical writers thought the purpose of literature was to convey ideas. Most Romantic writers, by contrast, thought the purpose of literature was to convey emotions. Judging by his "Elegy," in which group do you think Gray seems to fit?

Extending the Text

9. What ideas in this old poem still relate to our lives and feelings today? Do you think the student who wrote the poem on page 605 shared any of Gray's feelings?

ELEMENTS OF LITERATURE

The Elegy

The term **elegy** originally referred to a poem written in a particular meter; in Roman literature, elegies are frivolous and sensual. By Gray's time the term *elegy* was applied to longish, serious poems reflecting on death—either death in general or the death of a particular person. Gray ends his "Elegy" with an epitaph—a poem short enough to be inscribed on a particular person's tombstone.

Gray's "Elegy" combines elements from several literary traditions. First of all, it is a **pastoral** elegy. Like Milton's famous elegy *Lycidas,* its setting is outdoors in a beautiful summery landscape. The poet keeps a certain distance from the dirt and bad smells of actual country life. His rural people are not individuals but types: the weary plowman, the busy housewife, the hoary-headed swain. These figures are idealized; oafs and boors do not appear. Rural life in a pastoral is always placid and civilized.

Another element in the "Elegy" is the **Gothic,** which supplies the "moping" owl, the graveyard, and the general gloominess. But unlike most Gothic writers, Gray isn't interested in giving his readers shivers and thrills; he is trying instead to create an atmosphere.

Finally, like many other writers of his time, Gray decorates his poem with polished **generalizations** about life and death: "The paths of glory lead but to the grave." These generalizations give the elegy the solidity of classical architecture.

1. What are five details of **setting** that Gray uses to idealize the **pastoral** landscape in the poem?

2. What are the **Gothic** details that contribute to the atmosphere in lines 13–16?

3. Find at least three additional examples of Gray's use of polished **generalizations**.

READING SKILLS AND STRATEGIES

Analyzing Word Choice and Word Order

Many words in this poem were regarded—until the twentieth century—as particularly "poetic." Examples of such words are *oft* (line 25), *e'er* (line 34), and *ye* (line 37).

1. List three other "poetic" words you find in the elegy. What words would be used in their place today?

2. What effect do such words have on your reading of this poem?

In many of Gray's sentences, the normal word order of English (subject-verb-complement) is violated. Gray writes "The air a solemn stillness holds" instead of "The air holds a solemn stillness."

3. Find other examples of **inverted word order** in the poem. How would you rephrase them so that they conform to normal English word order?

4. Put your reworded sentences back in the poem. What happens to the meter or rhyme?

Perhaps the most difficult lines to sort out syntactically are lines 61–72. The following outline might help to clarify the **syntax** of these lines:

"Their lot forbade" them
    "to command" "the applause of list'ning
        senates"
    "to despise" "the threats of pain and ruin"
    "to scatter plenty o'er a smiling land,
    And read their hist'ry in a nation's eyes."

"Nor" has their lot ever
    "circumscribed alone
    Their growing virtues, but their crimes
        confined."

Their lot also forbade them
    "To hide" "the struggling pangs of conscious
        truth"
    "To quench the blushes of ingenuous shame,
    Or heap the shrine of Luxury and Pride
    With incense, kindled at the Muse's flame."

5. Try now to **paraphrase** lines 61–72 using conventional syntax and as many sentences as you need.

CHOICES: Building Your Portfolio

Writer's Notebook

1. Collecting Ideas for a Persuasive Essay

When Thomas Gray writes "the paths of glory lead but to the grave," you have a clear idea of his stance: Despite fame, one inevitable destination awaits us all. Effective persuasive writing also relies on conveying a clear stance—in a thesis statement giving the writer's position on an issue. Review the controversial issues you've explored in your other Writer's Notebook entries. Which issues grab your interest? Select two issues; then write a thesis statement that conveys your position on each issue. Working with a partner, discuss your thesis statements. How can you make your stance clearer or stronger? Save your work for the Writer's Workshop on page 612.

Comparing Elegies

2. Elegies Across the Centuries

In a brief essay, discuss the similarities and differences between Gray's "Elegy" and another famous elegy, "The Seafarer," on page 56. Consider the elements of **speaker, theme,** and **tone.**

Creative Writing

3. Talking Back to the Poet

Suppose one of the villagers was allowed to speak his or her epitaph. Write out what he or she might say to the poet. You might consider these characters: the busy housewife; the children's sire; the person once full of "celestial fire"; the person who might have ruled an empire; the person who might have "waked" the lyre; the village Hampden; the mute inglorious Milton; the Cromwell; the hoary-headed swain.

Creative Writing

4. Graveyard Meditations

Suppose you were standing in a graveyard today. Write a brief meditation about the experience, including a description of the place, of the imagined lives of the people buried there, and of your feelings about death. Be sure to describe the time of day, the weather, and the sounds you hear. (If you don't want to use yourself as the speaker, make up a speaker.)

Performance

5. Gray Alive!

Prepare the elegy for a group performance. You might want to have a group of male readers, a group of female readers, and several solo parts. Give each reader a copy of the poem so that he or she can take notes on how the assigned lines should be read. Rehearse your performance, and consider asking several student critics to analyze and critique your oral interpretation of the poem.

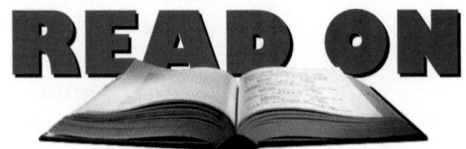

READ ON

Diary of a Castaway

Since its publication in 1719, Daniel Defoe's *Robinson Crusoe* has spawned countless imitations, adaptations, and even a TV sitcom (*Gilligan's Island,* which remains popular decades after its debut in the 1960s). Perhaps the story contained in Crusoe's fictional autobiography has endured because it poses an age-old question: How might *we* react if plucked from our ordinary lives and set on a barren island? Could we face the physical hardships and mental isolation of such an extraordinary new life?

An "Ordinary" Day

As it did in Daniel Defoe's *A Journal of the Plague Year,* the raw material of life serves as a basis for fiction in *One Day in the Life of Ivan Denisovich* (Penguin). Aleksandr Solzhenitsyn took firsthand materials—his own eight years in a Stalinist labor camp—and reworked these personal experiences into a narrative related by an everyman character dubbed Ivan (Russian for John).

Down on the Farm

Like Pope and Swift, George Orwell uses satire to reveal the absurdities of human nature. In his 1945 novel *Animal Farm* (Harcourt Brace), Orwell satirizes the problems of a supposedly equal society. The animals of Manor Farm revolt against their incompetent owner and install the "Seven Commandments of Animalism," which the sheep simply remember as "four legs good, two legs bad." But when the pigs Napoleon and Snowball disagree about the future of the farm, a rivalry for power ensues. (This novel is available in the HRW Library.)

The Mad Monarch

King George III (r. 1760–1820) lost the American Colonies for good, and his mind for a brief spell. His suffering transforms him from a distant, public figure in control of others to a person of flesh and blood, at the mercy of nature and those around him. Nigel Hawthorne stars in *The Madness of King George,* a 1995 film directed by Nicholas Hytner and based on Alan Bennett's play *The Madness of George III.*

A Scientific Star

Scientific activity flourished in the second half of the seventeenth century, with London as an important center. Isaac Newton was the first notable hero of modern science, the man who brought the heavenly bodies down to earth with his theory of gravitation. But did an apple *really* fall on his head? Find out in *Physics: From Newton to the Big Bang* (Franklin Watts), Albert and Eve Stwertka's interesting history of modern physics.

The English Language

Decorum and Order

by **John Algeo**

In the eighteenth century, some English speakers believed that the English language had become as good as it could be. Therefore, they should try to prevent any more changes, which could only lead to the degeneration of the language. It was a foolish opinion, but some people today still hold it. Only, they think that English has reached perfection in *our* time, so any change from the way *we* talk and write will lead to the death of our language.

Change Is Growth

A language does not die or degenerate simply because it changes. A language dies only when nobody speaks it. The oft-predicted death of English is like that of Mark Twain, who read his own obituary in an American newspaper while he was in England. He cabled the newspaper: "The reports of my death are greatly exaggerated." So are reports of the "death" of English.

Throughout its history, English has grown in the number of its speakers and the uses it is put to. Today, English is the most widely distributed language in the world and is used for more purposes—scientific, technical, commercial, and personal—than any other language. Far from being in danger of degenerating or dying, English is among the most vital of all human languages.

Change in language is natural. It is, moreover, a good thing, for without change a language would indeed die. Change in language has many causes. When English speakers first settled North America, they found animals, plants, land formations, and other things for which they had no names. To talk about these unfamiliar things, they had to **adapt old words, coin new words,** or **borrow words from other languages.**

Americans have done all three things. English sailors had used the word *bluff* as an adjective to mean "broad and flat"; Americans adapted it as a noun to mean "cliff," of which they encountered a good many. To name the action of reorganizing an election district for the unfair advantage of one party, Americans coined the word *gerrymander* (from Elbridge *Gerry,* a nineteenth-century governor of Massachusetts, who helped carve out an election district that looked like a *salamander*). In the Southwest, English-speaking cowboys learned from their Spanish-speaking counterparts how to catch horses and cattle with a long rope that had a loop with a slipknot at one end. They borrowed the Spanish name for the rope: *lasso.*

Another cause of change is a natural drift in the way we use language. As each new generation learns English, it introduces little changes. And so over the generations, a language gradually changes, until one day we realize that some very big and important changes have happened over a thousand years, although none of the thirty generations who lived during that time was aware of using language very differently from those who came before or after them.

Change in language, far from being a sign of degeneracy, is the way language adapts to new conditions. It is the way language stays alive. Change is not degeneration; it is growth. All living things must grow

> Change in language, far from being a sign of degeneracy, is the way language adapts to new conditions. It is the way language stays alive.

through change. Languages are no exception.

Stop the Changes!

Some English speakers today are obsessed with the fear that the changes they notice in English mean the language is about to slip into incoherence and to disintegrate, unless we do something about it—and fast. That obsession first became a large-scale concern of English speakers during the eighteenth century.

Jonathan Swift was one of the writers of this period who was concerned about the well-being of English and the dangers he saw it facing. He especially disliked the idea that a language should be "perpetually changing." So Swift wrote *A Proposal for Correcting, Improving, and Ascertaining the English Tongue* (1712), in which he suggested that a group of persons should take the responsibility on themselves of overseeing the language, improving it, unifying it, and above all stabilizing it so that it would stop changing. A number of other countries in Europe had established or were to develop such groups, usually called "academies": Italy, France, and Spain are examples.

The idea of an English Academy never caught on, however. One reason for its failure was the individualism of many English speakers, who were unwilling to let anybody else tell them how they ought to talk. Another reason was the rapid development of English dictionaries, which became "authorities" for English speakers who

were insecure about their own usage and wanted advice about what to say and write.

The Dictionary

The tradition of making English dictionaries reached a high point with Samuel Johnson, who in 1755 published his two-volume *Dictionary of the English Language*. In the United States, Noah Webster produced a dictionary that came to fill the place in U.S. life that Johnson's dictionary filled in Great Britain. Webster wanted to produce a dictionary that would record the English of the United States, not just that of the mother country.

Webster's dictionary was so successful that today many dictionaries use *Webster* in their titles, but none of them preserve anything from old Noah's book. *Webster* in a dictionary's title is no guarantee of anything—it is only an advertising technique to take advantage of the fact that people associate Webster with dictionaries. With dictionaries, you can't always tell a book by its cover.

In the nineteenth century, a group of English scholars began to work on a dictionary to replace Johnson's, which had become very outdated. Their work eventually developed into the greatest dictionary in the world: *The Oxford English Dictionary*. Recently this dictionary has been expanded to twenty volumes and also put into electronic form as a compact disc.

Samuel Johnson composed his dictionary single-handedly and by candlelight. Today, teams

of lexicographers cooperate in producing dictionaries using the latest computer techniques. As the language changes, so do the ways we keep up with it.

Changes Are Happening Today

Jonathan Swift was not able to stop English from changing, however much he wanted to. Nor can anyone else. The nature of language is to change, and we can see change going on around us today.

Pronunciation is constantly changing. Not long ago, many Americans pronounced the words *horse* and *hoarse* or *morning* and *mourning* differently from each other; now most pronounce them alike. Today most Americans still pronounce the words *cot* and *caught* or *pond* and *pawned* differently, but increasingly many of us are pronouncing them alike. In a hundred years or so, it is likely that such pairs will be **homophones** (words that sound the same, but are different in meaning and spelling) for the majority of our fellow citizens. *Forehead* used to be generally pronounced to rhyme with *horrid;* today, it usually rhymes with *more bread*.

The very words we use are also changing. We make up **new words** out of elements already in English, like *to eyeball, feedback,* and *minibike*. We **borrow words from foreign languages,** like *karate* from Japanese, *klutz* from Yiddish, and *macho* from Spanish. Words also change their meaning, or disappear altogether if we stop using them, often because the things they name have changed or disappeared. For example, people used to preserve food by keeping it in a chest with blocks of ice; such a chest was called an *icebox*. When gas and electric refrigerators were invented, some people continued to use the old word for them, thus changing the meaning of *icebox*. But gradually the word has been disappearing; it is rare today and soon will probably drop out of the language altogether.

We also change our **grammar.** For example, the older past tense of the verb *dive* is *dived*. But today we use a new past form, *dove,* invented by analogy with irregular verbs like *drive,* whose past tense is *drove*.

The words we use, the way we use them, and the way we say them are all changing constantly. Often, when a change begins, many people do not like it. It sounds odd, sloppy, or mistaken. And new uses do often begin as mistakes. But whether the new use has been deliberately introduced or has slipped into the language as an error, if many people adopt it, it becomes part of the language— just one more option we have for expressing ourselves. When a change is new or has not yet been widely accepted, we need to be careful about using it, because some people will be so distracted by the way we are talking that they will fail to hear what we are saying.

What Is Good English?

Good English is English that communicates the ideas and effects we want to get across. Bad English is language that does not communicate successfully. Bad English may be ambiguous: "Mike lost his textbook, but somebody found it and put it in his locker." Whose locker did the book go in, Mike's or somebody's? Bad English may actually be clear, but distracting: "Everybody should have his own textbook." Is everybody male? Aren't there any females around? If we say, "Everybody should have their own textbook," someone will object that *everybody* is singular, whereas *their* is plural, so the two don't go together. If we say, "Everybody should have his or her own textbook," someone else will object that the statement sounds too awkward.

Each of the choices above is likely to distract someone who hears or reads it. All of them may interfere with communication, and therefore all of them are, to that extent, bad English. The best English in such cases avoids the problem by rewording the statement: "Everybody should have a textbook" or "All students should have their own textbooks." Good English does not get in the way; it does not call attention to itself and away from the message. Good English communicates just what we want to communicate and nothing else.

Try It Out

1. **Comparing dictionary entries.** Compare the sample entry for the word *giggle* in Johnson's *Dictionary* (page 571) with the entry for that word in a modern dictionary. What kinds of information does the modern dictionary give that Johnson's does not? How do the meanings Johnson gives compare with those in the modern dictionary?

2. **Investigating new words.** The following words and expressions are all relatively new to the English language. How many of them are familiar to you? Which of them are listed in the dictionary you use?

   Catch-22
   ego trip
   laptop
   schlep
   in-line skates
   CD-ROM
   play hardball
   ten-speed

3. **Identifying usage problems.** People disagree about the correct usage of the following words. Do you know what the disagreement is? Look up these words in at least two dictionaries to see what is said about them.

   impact (verb)
   hopefully
   data
   irregardless

Writer's Workshop

**Technology
H E L P**

See Writer's Workshop 2
CD-ROM. *Assignment:
Controversial Issue.*

ASSIGNMENT
Write a persuasive
essay on a controver-
sial issue.

AIM
To persuade; to in-
form and explain.

AUDIENCE
People who disagree
on the issue or are
undecided; readers
of your school or
local newspaper.

PERSUASIVE WRITING

AN ESSAY ON A CONTROVERSIAL ISSUE

Both Jonathan Swift and Alexander Pope were attuned to the **controversial issues** of their day, and they didn't shy away from addressing those issues and trying to win others to their way of thinking. When you care deeply about a controversial issue, it's only natural to take a stand on it and to defend your position against objections. That's the essence of writing a persuasive essay. Persuasive writing will force you to draw on a wide range of writing skills: analyzing causes and effects, comparing and contrasting details, reporting information, and evaluating points for refuting objections to your arguments.

Prewriting

1. **Checking your Writer's Notebook.** By completing the Writer's Notebook activities in Collections 6 and 7, you may have already completed some of the prewriting for a persuasive essay on a controversial issue. Check your entries for usable material, and then proceed with the prewriting activities that follow.

2. **Exploring possible issues.** Today, no less than in Swift's and Pope's time, our society is confronted with controversial social and political issues that responsible people feel compelled to think out for themselves. To find an issue that intrigues you, try the strategies for elaboration that follow.

Strategies for Elaboration: Exploring Issues

- Watch or listen to TV or radio news programs and talk shows. They'll give you ideas about current controversies.

- Look through recent newspapers and magazines, noting the issues raised in articles, editorials, editorial cartoons, and news photos.

- Read through your Writer's Notebooks for entries dealing with issues and controversies.

- Brainstorm with friends, classmates, and family members about possible controversial issues.

- Draw up a series of "Should . . . ?" questions. One example: "Should failing students be allowed to participate in school-sponsored extracurricular activities?"

The history
of the written
word is rich and
Page 1

Once upon a time

3. **Choosing an issue.** After you've explored possible issues, you'll have to select one for your essay. To choose one issue to write about, use these guidelines:

- Do you really care? You'll write more convincingly about an issue that you feel strongly about.

- Is the issue arguable? Make sure the issue is one that reasonable people may disagree on. For instance, you'd have a hard time finding anyone to argue that citizens *shouldn't* vote.

- Is it truly a controversial issue, not merely a matter of taste? You may believe that Broadway musicals are the ultimate American musical form, but you won't convince jazz buffs that jazz is inferior. It's a personal preference.

4. **Taking a stand.** Begin your exploration of the issue by spending a few minutes freewriting about it. Then state your opinion on the issue in one or two sentences. Even if your mind's not completely made up yet, writing a preliminary **thesis statement**—also known as a **proposition** or **position statement**—will guide you as you gather information. Remember that you can always change the wording of your proposition once you've reached a final conclusion.

5. **Targeting your audience.** Even more than other types of writing, persuasive writing is audience-centered. To convince readers that your opinion has merit (even if they don't agree with it), you need to know and understand their views and values. Adopting a formal, serious tone will help you create a favorable impression and make readers inclined to take your ideas seriously, as will approaching them with appeals tailored to their needs and interests.

- **Tap into their feelings. Emotional appeals** stir readers' feelings. Used sparingly, such appeals can help personalize the issue for readers. If you're advocating the use of "signers" to translate sports events for students with hearing disabilities, try to let your audience know how it *feels* to be unable to participate fully in school activities. Words with strong **connotations** (ones with powerful positive *or* negative overtones) can be particularly effective in tapping into people's emotions.

- **Reason with them. Logical appeals** engage your readers' reasoning skills, their ability to think clearly. Readers expect you to offer sound reasons for your position (statements that explain *why* you hold your opinion on the issue) and to back up your reasons with solid evidence, or proof. Appropriate factual evidence may consist of statistics, examples, and anecdotes (brief stories based on personal experience)—all of which can be verified by testing, by drawing on personal observations, or by consulting reliable sources. Expert testimony (statements by recognized authorities on the issue) also qualifies as evidence.

Try It Out

Identify the logical fallacy in each of the following sentences. Then revise the fallacy to make the statement logical.

1. The voting age should be lowered to sixteen because sixteen-year-olds are mature enough to vote.

2. Our school needs a dress code because a dress code is the solution to our problems.

3. Unless the state builds more prisons, the crime rate will continue to rise.

Strategies for Elaboration: Avoiding Fallacies

In listing reasons for your position, take care to avoid these **fallacies,** or mistakes in logic.

- **Hasty generalization**—basing a conclusion on insufficient evidence or overlooking exceptions: *No local merchants will suffer if the proposed chain store is approved.*

- **Attacking the person** (in Latin, *ad hominem,* meaning "to the person"; informally, "name-calling")—attacking people who support the issue: *Hunters just enjoy killing animals.*

- **False authority**—quoting an expert in one field as an authority in an unrelated field: *According to former state Supreme Court Justice Eldon Bates, the state's annual vehicle inspections are a waste of taxpayers' time and money.*

- **Circular reasoning**—offering as a reason a statement that's actually a restatement of an opinion: *The City Council should build more bike paths because our community needs bike paths.*

- **Either-or reasoning**—assuming that an issue has only two possible sides: *Either we abolish the welfare system or we foster perpetual dependence on government handouts.*

- **Non sequitur** (Latin for "It does not follow")—presenting unrelated ideas as though one were the logical consequence of the other: *Our city's rapid population growth demands a higher speed limit.*

- **Earn their trust. Ethical appeals** invoke your readers' sense of fair play, establishing your credibility and character. Demonstrating that you're knowledgeable, reasonable, sincere, and trustworthy helps win respect for you and, in turn, for your ideas.

  One way to establish your trustworthiness is to consider different sides of an issue, to acknowledge the most significant **counterarguments** (opposing points). By **conceding,** or accommodating, opposing points that do have merit, you establish common ground without sacrificing your principles. Then you can concentrate on **refuting,** or providing conclusive evidence against, those counterarguments that you consider invalid.

6. **Coping with counterarguments.** Once you've listed possible reasons in support of your position, get together with a partner or a small group to brainstorm for likely counterarguments. Think about the kinds of evidence that will convince your particular audience to rethink their counterarguments. You may find it helpful to chart the most significant counterarguments and possible refutations for them, as in the following example.

Proposition: The City Council should approve the construction of a sports stadium proposed for the city's south side.

Counterarguments	Refutations
• Taxpayer dollars should not be directed to building this facility.	• Tax revenues generated by the new facility will balance out any expenditures.
• Property taxes will increase city-wide to pay for construction.	• Construction of the new facility will be paid for by a bond issue and by funds from the professional sports teams that will use the facility.
• The new facility will disturb residents in the area.	• Traffic and sound-pollution control measures are a fundamental part of construction plans.

7. **Organizing your material: deduction or induction?** As you begin to organize your material, decide whether you'll present your argument **deductively** (moving from your proposition to your reasons and evidence) or **inductively** (moving from your reasons and evidence to your proposition). These two different approaches can be thought of as a pair of pyramids, one upside-down and the other right-side up.

Communications Handbook HELP

See Taking Notes and Documenting Sources.

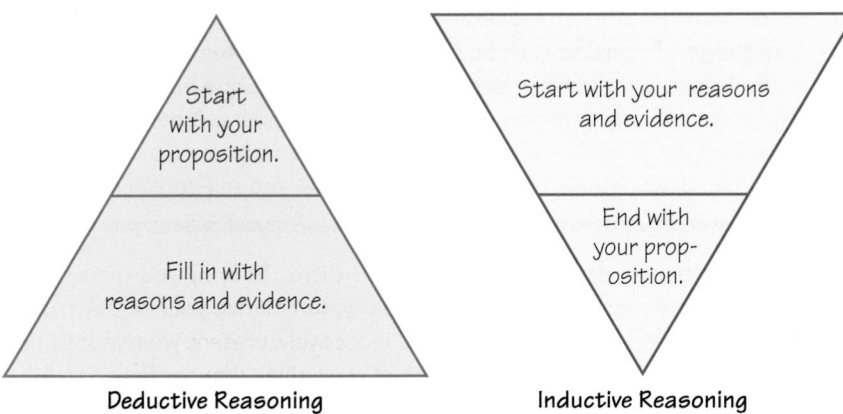

Deductive Reasoning   Inductive Reasoning

Think, too, about how you'll work in the counterarguments you've chosen to concede or refute—before, after, or along with your own argument. Three basic types of organizational patterns can work well for a persuasive essay:

• **Order of importance**—beginning or ending with the appeal likely to have the strongest impact on your audience.

• **Chronological order**—proposing (or attacking) a course of action in the order events occurred or would occur.

Evaluation Criteria

An effective persuasive essay
1. *focuses on a controversial issue*
2. *defines the issue clearly*
3. *provides sufficient background information*
4. *includes a clearly worded position statement*
5. *supports the position with relevant, convincing reasons and evidence*
6. *concedes or refutes counterarguments*
7. *conveys a knowledgeable and sincere tone*
8. *concludes by underscoring the writer's position on the issue*

Language Workshop
H E L P

Parallel structure: page 617.

Communications Handbook
H E L P

See Proofreading.

Revision
S T R A T E G I E S

Is your tone assertive rather than arrogant, reasonable rather than derisive? Working with a partner, circle any words in your draft that seem arrogant or derisive. Then, replace them with words less likely to offend.

• **Logical order**—comparing and contrasting opposing positions and your refutations, either by grouping all objections and following them with all your refutations or by alternating opposing positions and refutations.

Drafting

1. **The introduction: defining the issue.** Before readers can begin to follow your line of reasoning, they need to know precisely what the issue is. Get them involved immediately with a vivid image, a startling statistic, an engaging anecdote, or a rhetorical question (one asked merely for effect). Define the issue clearly, provide any necessary background, and (if you've reasoned deductively) state your proposition succinctly.

2. **The body: developing your argument.** As you present each of your reasons, buttress it with evidence drawn from your investigation of the issue. Emphasize your most compelling reason by devoting the most space to it. In arguing your case and accommodating or refuting counterarguments, remember to keep your tone reasonable and confident.

Strategies for Elaboration: Drafting Persuasively

Focus on the following strategies to develop your persuasive essay:

• **Repetition.** Focus attention on key terms and core ideas by arranging them in parallel structure.

• **Rhythm.** Create a rhythmic flow of sound by using words or syllables with similar vowel or consonant sounds, by varying the length and structure of sentences, and by beginning some sentences with a phrase, a clause, or a one-word modifier instead of the subject.

• **Language.** Formal needn't be forbidding, nor must serious language be stuffy. In fact, using familiar, everyday language is a subtle but effective way of establishing common ground with your readers. A persuasive essay isn't the place for using slang and sentence fragments, but it *is* the place for speaking your mind directly, forcefully, and self-confidently.

3. **The conclusion: driving the message home.** To bring your essay to an effective end, restate your opinion forcefully, summarize your reasons, or issue a call to action. If you've reasoned inductively, present your proposition so that it seems the natural outgrowth of everything that has led up to it.

Evaluating and Revising

As you read your or your partner's draft, evaluate these points:

• Is the issue clearly defined? Is it arguable? Has enough background information been provided?

• Is the proposition clearly stated? Is its placement effective?

• Are the reasons and evidence relevant and convincing?

• Is the tone knowledgeable, reasonable, and appropriate for the issue and the audience?

EFFECTIVE SENTENCES: THE POWER OF PARALLELISM

One way to create a sense of urgency about a persuasive issue is to focus attention on key terms and core ideas by using **parallel structure.**

Parallel structure is the use of matching *forms* for sentence elements that have the same *function.* Pairing adjectives with adjectives, prepositional phrases with prepositional phrases, noun clauses with noun clauses (and so on) emphasizes the relationship between the elements. You can use parallel structure to link coordinate ideas, to compare or contrast ideas, and to link ideas with correlative conjunctions (such as *both . . . and, either . . . or*).

Compare the awkwardness of these examples of faulty parallelism with the clarity of Jonathan Swift's phrasing in *A Modest Proposal*:

FAULTY   **To tax** our absentees at five shillings a pound; **of using** neither clothes, nor household furniture, except what is of our own growth and manufacture. . . . [infinitive paired with prepositional phrase]

PARALLEL   **Of taxing** our absentees at five shillings a pound; **of using** neither clothes, nor household furniture, except what is of our own growth and manufacture. . . . [prepositional phrase paired with prepositional phrase]

—from A Modest Proposal

FAULTY   . . . I rather recommend **buying the children alive,** and **to dress them hot from the knife**. . . . [gerund phrase paired with infinitive phrase]

PARALLEL   . . . I rather recommend **buying the children alive,** and **dressing them hot from the knife**. . . . [gerund phrase paired with gerund phrase]

—from A Modest Proposal

Writer's Workshop Follow-up: Proofreading

Look at the persuasive essay you wrote for the Writer's Workshop on page 612. What key terms or ideas do you want to emphasize? Where could you use parallel structure to stress your ideas? Working with a writing partner, put a check mark next to any sentences where the use of parallel structure would strengthen your essay. Then, revise these sentences to incorporate parallel structures. Also, look for sentences where you have not used parallel structure correctly, and revise these sentences so the grammatical elements are parallel.

**Technology
H E L P**

See Language Workshop CD-ROM. *Key word entry: parallel structure.*

**Language Handbook
H E L P**

See Using Parallel Structure, page 1237.

Try It Out

Correct the faulty parallelism in each of the following sentences.

1. The narrator of *A Modest Proposal* considers his solution fair, cheap, and being easy.

2. He refutes the suggestion of selling and eating twelve- to fourteen-year-olds, arguing that the males' flesh would be too tough and the females to be lost as breeders.

3. His ideas are horrifying, not only because they are vulgar, but also for their cruelty.

Reading for Life

Using Text Organizers

Situation

In this collection you've read about some extraordinary events in seventeenth-century England. Suppose you wanted to find out what was occurring in America at the same time. You might consult a book about American history and make use of the following strategies to **locate** and **categorize information.**

Strategies

Notice how the text is organized.

- Scan the table of contents to get a general idea of the scope of information covered.

- Look at chapter openings and look for overviews that summarize each chapter's content. Summaries may also appear periodically within chapters.

- Notice the structure of the headings. Textbooks often use headings of different sizes to rank information according to major topics and subtopics.

Use headings and the index.

- You can use headings or the index to locate specific information if you don't want to read everything in every chapter. You can also use headings to create an outline or to structure your notes.

Notice graphic features.

- Features may include charts, graphs, time lines, tables, photographs, boxed text, and bulleted or numbered lists.

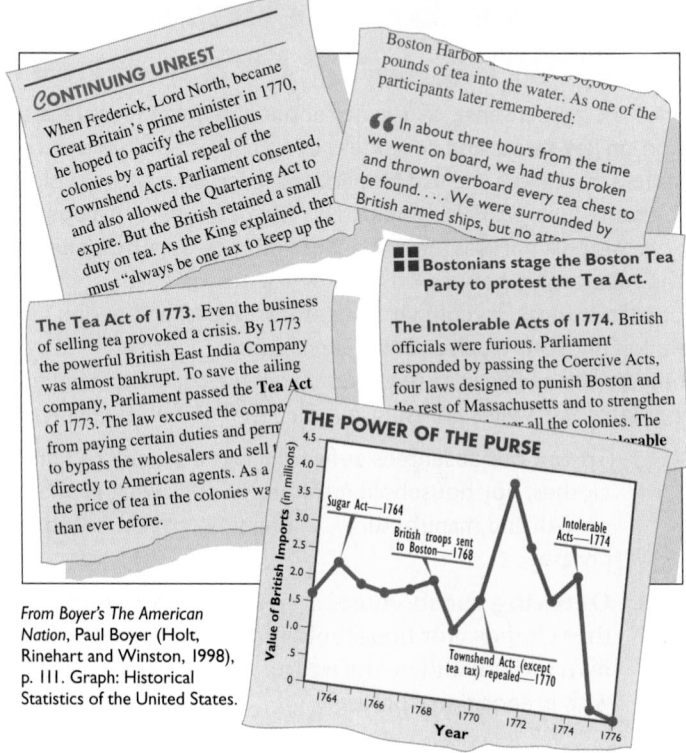

From Boyer's *The American Nation,* Paul Boyer (Holt, Rinehart and Winston, 1998), p. 111. Graph: Historical Statistics of the United States.

Using the Strategies

Answer these questions about the section of a page from the American history textbook that is shown above.

1. Which text heading indicates the start of a major section?

2. Which of the headings indicate subsections?

3. What relationship is illustrated by the graph?

4. Can you find a chapter or section summary?

5. Does the book include first-hand quotations?

Extending the Strategies

- Identify and evaluate the text organizers in one of the collections in this volume of *Elements of Literature.*

- Check the indices in the back of this book to see what information they provide.

- Examine a print or electronic text. Make suggestions on how the text might be reorganized to make it easier to locate information. What additional features would make the text more useful to you?

Learning for Life

Locating Information and Resources

Problem

The poet John Dryden was one of many people put out of work as a result of the political upheavals that took place between 1649 and 1660. What resources exist today for people in your community who lose their jobs through downsizing or layoffs?

Project

Investigate what services are available locally through federal, state, and city or county offices for dislocated workers in need of job-search and placement assistance or retraining. Who is eligible to receive the services, and how does a person go about obtaining them?

Preparation

1. Use brainstorming or clustering to determine what you already know about the topic. Have you seen or heard advertisements about such services? Has anyone you know used one of the services?

2. Plan your strategy for conducting research. What print and nonprint sources will you check? Use the library, but don't overlook such possible sources as the telephone book, the Internet, on-line databases, and the student services offices of the local community college, university, or vocational-technical center.

Procedure

1. As you identify the various services and gather information on them, keep a record of your findings and their sources. If you interview someone, for example, take careful notes, or ask permission to tape-record the interview for later review.

2. Look for ways to personalize the information for your intended audience—those who have lost their jobs through no fault of their own. Facts and figures are important, but an anecdote about someone who found a new job through one of the services might go even further to motivate unemployed workers to use the services available.

Presentation

Use one of the following formats (or another that your teacher approves):

1. **Modern-Day Pamphleteering**

   Design a brochure that details the services available and eligibility requirements and that lists addresses, telephone numbers, and hours of operation. If you have access to desktop publishing software, use it to produce and publish your brochure. Obtain permission to place copies of the brochure where many people will see it—for example, at the public library or at a supermarket, shopping mall, or neighborhood center.

2. **Poster Promotion**

   Design a poster that promotes the services and that motivates people to take advantage of them. Briefly highlight all necessary information (services offered, eligibility requirements, addresses, telephone numbers, and hours of operation), and consider including tear-off strips that people can take with them for later reference. Obtain permission to display the poster at one of the sites suggested.

3. **Going on the Radio**

   Prepare a thirty-second public service announcement (PSA) promoting one of the services for broadcast by a local radio station. To ensure that your PSA is in keeping with the station's format, consider the kind of programming it features (news, sports, music, or a mixture) and the demographics (age, sex, income, and so on) of its intended audience. Ask the station manager to schedule air time for your PSA.

Processing

What is your opinion about the number and variety of services available to dislocated workers? Write a brief reflection for your portfolio.

The Romantic Period
1798–1832

The Curfew (19th century) by
Samuel Palmer.

Agnew and Sons, London.

The Romantic Period

by **Harley Henry**

*The divine arts of imagination: imagination, the real
& eternal world of which this vegetable universe is but
a faint shadow.*

—*William Blake*

Worcester (detail) (19th century) by Sir John Gilbert.
Guildhall Art Gallery, Corporation of London.

During the spring of 1798, two young English poets, aged 27 and 25, sold some of their poems to raise money for a trip to Germany. Each had published books of poetry, but a new joint work was to be anonymous. As Samuel Taylor Coleridge, the younger of the pair, told the printer: "Wordsworth's name is nothing . . . mine *stinks*."

Soon after they left England, their book, *Lyrical Ballads, with a Few Other Poems,* appeared. Among the "few other poems" was Coleridge's long narrative *The Rime of the Ancient Mariner* (page 684) and a last-minute addition, Wordsworth's "Lines Composed a Few Miles Above Tintern Abbey" (page 658). Both of these works are now among the most important poems in English literature.

So began what is now called the "Romantic period" in England. Literary historians have found other momentous events to mark its beginning and end, but we should remember the casual, modest appearance of *Lyrical Ballads* as we consider the Romantic period and the writers associated with it.

The publication of a collection of poems called Lyrical Ballads, a collaboration between William Wordsworth and Samuel Taylor Coleridge, began the Romantic period in England.

Turbulent Times, Bitter Realities

Another way to date the Romantic period is to say that it started with the French Revolution in 1789 and ended with the Parliamentary reforms of 1832 that laid the political foundations for modern Britain. The era was dominated by six poets: Three (William Blake, William Wordsworth, and Samuel Taylor Coleridge) were born before the period began and lived through most or all of it, while three others (the "second generation" of Percy Bysshe Shelley, John Keats, and George Gordon, Lord Byron) began their short careers in the second decade of the new century but died before 1825. It was a turbulent, revolutionary age, one in which England changed from an agricultural society to an industrial nation with a large and restless working class concentrated in the teeming mill towns.

We think about this era in terms of some important historical events. Beginning in America in 1776, an age of revolution swept across

It was the best of times, it was the worst of times, it was the age of wisdom, it was the age of foolishness, it was the epoch of belief, it was the epoch of incredulity, it was the season of Light, it was the season of Darkness, it was the spring of hope, it was the winter of despair, we had everything before us, we had nothing before us, we were all going direct to Heaven, we were all going direct the other way. . . .

—Charles Dickens,
from *A Tale of Two Cities*

Frontispiece of *America: A Prophecy* (1793) by William Blake.

The Romantic Period, 1798–1832

Mary Wollstonecraft critiques female educational restrictions in *A Vindication of the Rights of Woman,* 1792

William Blake publishes *Songs of Innocence,* 1789

Robert Burns publishes *Poems, Chiefly in the Scottish Dialect,* 1786

Maria Edgeworth's *Castle Rackrent,* the first historical novel in English, satirizes absentee landowners in Ireland, 1800

William Wordsworth and **Samuel Taylor Coleridge** publish *Lyrical Ballads,* 1798

Ann Radcliffe's *The Mysteries of Udolpho* popularizes the Gothic novel, 1794

Johann Wolfgang von Goethe publishes Part I of *Faust,* 1808

Charles and Mary Lamb publish *Tales from Shakespeare,* 1807

Jane Austen publishes *Pride and Prejudice,* 1813

Brothers Grimm begin to publish *Grimm's Fairy Tales,* 1812

Charles Dickens born, 1812

Lord Byron publishes first two cantos of *Childe Harold's Pilgrimage,* 1812

1786–1793	1794–1801	1802–1808	1809–1813

Corbis-Bettmann

• Drawing (late 18th century) by Jacques-Louis David of Marie Antoinette, queen of France, being led to execution.

French Revolution begins with storming of Bastille, 1789

King Louis XVI of France beheaded, 1793

France declares war on England, 1793

Thomas Jefferson elected U.S. president, 1800

Napoleon conquers parts of Italy, 1800

Act of Union creates United Kingdom of Great Britain and Ireland, 1801

Workday of pauper children limited to 12 hours in England, 1802

United States purchases Louisiana Territory from France, 1803

Napoleon crowns himself emperor in France, 1804

Egypt gains independence from Ottoman Turks, 1805

Lord Nelson defeats Napoleon's navy at Battle of Trafalgar, 1805

Construction begins on Arc de Triomphe in Paris, 1806

United States bans importation of slaves from Africa, 1808

Simón Bolívar begins series of South American rebellions against Spain, 1810

Venezuela declares independence from Spain, 1811

English artisans called Luddites riot and destroy textile machines, fearing that industrialism threatens their livelihoods, 1811

Napoleon invades Russia, 1812

United States declares war on Great Britain, 1812

Mexico declares its independence from Spain, 1821

• *Napoleon I in Royal Garb* (1806) by Jean Auguste Dominique Ingres. Musée de l'Armée, Paris.

...astille (18th century) by an unknown artist.

...pe, releasing political, economic, and social forces
...ing the next century, some of the most radical c...
...ed in human life.

...n Revolution had lost for England her thirtee...
...economic loss, but it was also a loss of pr...
...more radical revolution in France, which...
...the prison called the Bastille on July 14...
...ercussions. For the ruling classes in F...
...to represent their worst fears: the ...

anointed king by a de...
English conservative...
tion meant the triu...
ples, and they fea...
fever would spr...

But democ...
Wordsworth...
in France. ...
years, the...
view the...
were a...
in Gr...

Natty Bumppo,
om James Fenimore Cooper's
e *Last of the Mohicans*.

ary Shelley, daughter
f Mary Wollstone-
aft, publishes
ankenstein, 1818

Sir Walter Scott
publishes *Ivanho*

oted actor Edmund
ean debuts as Shylock
Shakespeare's *The*
erchant of Venice,
814

John Keats w
his greatest p
between Janu
September,

1814–1818

1819

ritish forces burn
ashington, D.C.,
814

ed British, Dutch,
German forces
at Napoleon at
erloo, 1815

n confederation
to replace Holy
Empire, 1815

One of
fective
prohib
of all
year

Fir
S
A

Storming of the B

western Europ
produced, dur
ever experienc

The America
This was a grea
confidence. The
the storming of
more serious rep
Revolution came

The Executioners, desperate lest th
selves be murdered . . . seize the hap
Louis: six of them desperate, him sir
desperate, struggling there; and bind
to their plank. Abbé Edgeworth
ing, bespeaks him: "Son of Saint Louis
ascend to Heaven" ₒ e Axe clanks
down; a King' ᵣₑ is shorn away.

—T. ᵣₐₛ Carlyle, describing the exec
tion of Louis XVI on January 21, 179

Fin Tragique de Louis XVI (Tragic End of Louis XVI) (18th century) by an unknown artist.

Musée Carnavalet/Photo Bulloz.

was it in that dawn to be alive, / But to be young was very heaven!"

Even Wordsworth became disillusioned, however, when in 1792 the "September massacre" took place in France. Hundreds of French aristocrats—some with only the slightest ties to the regime of King Louis XVI—had their heads severed from their bodies by a grisly new invention, the guillotine.

And that wasn't the end of it. In the midst of the blood and turmoil and calls from France for worldwide revolution, control of the French government changed hands again. Napoleon Bonaparte, an officer in the French army, emerged first as dictator and then, in 1804, as emperor of France. In the end, Napoleon—whose very name today suggests a tyrant—became as ruthless as the executed king himself.

All of these bewildering changes in western Europe made conservatives in England more rigid than ever. England instituted severe repressive measures: They outlawed collective bargaining and kept suspected spies or agitators in prison without a trial. In 1803, England began a long war against Napoleon. English guns first defeated Napoleon's navy at the Battle of Trafalgar and, finally, in 1815, with the help of allies, sent his army packing at Waterloo, Belgium.

The conservatives in England felt they had saved their country from a tyrant and from chaos; the early supporters of the revolution, like Wordsworth, felt betrayed. For them, Waterloo was simply the defeat of one tyrant by another.

London, 1802

Milton! thou shouldst be living at this hour;
England hath need of thee; she is a fen
Of stagnant waters: altar, sword, and pen,
Fireside, the heroic wealth of hall and bower,
Have forfeited their ancient English dower
Of inward happiness. We are selfish men;
Oh! raise us up, return to us again;
And give us manners, virtue, freedom, power.
Thy soul was like a star, and dwelt apart;
Thou hadst a voice whose sound was like the sea;
Pure as the naked heavens, majestic, free,
So didst thou travel on life's common way,
In cheerful godliness; and yet thy heart
The lowliest duties on herself did lay.

—William Wordsworth

Political upheaval in France and the United States touched England as well. Conservative economic and political measures and a lengthy war against Napoleon consolidated the power of the rich.

The Tyranny of Laissez Faire

At the same time, the Industrial Revolution was bringing about other changes in English life. Previously, goods had been made by hand, at home. Now, production switched to factories, where machines worked many times faster than human beings could work by hand. Since factories were in cities, the city populations increased, causing desperate living conditions that would appall even the most hardened social worker today.

In addition, the communal land once shared by small farmers was taken over by individual owners. Some of these rich owners transformed the fields into vast private parks, generously stocked with deer for their own Christmas hunts. Others divided the land neatly into privately held fields. Whatever happened to the land, it was no longer communally owned. This resulted in large numbers of landless people. Just as some unemployed and homeless do today, these landless people migrated to cities in search of work. Or they went on the dole, or welfare.

The economic philosophy that kept all this misery going was a policy called laissez faire (les′ā fer′), "let (people) do (as they please)." According to this policy, economic forces should be allowed to operate freely without government interference. The result of

> Every man, as long as he does not violate the laws of justice, is left perfectly free to pursue his own interest his own way, and to bring both his industry and capital into competition with those of any other man or order of men.
>
> —Adam Smith,
> from The Wealth of Nations

A Surrey Cornfield (19th century) by George Vicat Cole.

laissez faire was that the rich grew richer, and the poor suffered even more. The system, of course, had its most tragic effects on the helpless, especially the children. Small children of the poor were often used like beasts of burden. In the coal pits, for example, very small children were even harnessed to carts for dragging coal, just as if they had been small donkeys.

Frustrated by England's resistance to political and social change that would improve conditions, the Romantic poets turned from the formal, public verse of the eighteenth-century Augustans to a more private, spontaneous, lyric poetry. These lyrics expressed the Romantics' belief that imagination, rather than mere reason, was the best response to the forces of change. Wordsworth spoke of imagination this way:

Bedlam Furnace, Madeley Dale, Shropshire (1803) by Paul Sandby Munn.

Private Collection.

> . . . spiritual love acts not nor can exist
> Without imagination, which, in truth,
> Is but another name for absolute power
> And clearest insight, amplitude of mind,
> And Reason in her most exalted mood.
>
> —*from The Prelude*

The poets of the Romantic period responded to social and economic changes caused by rapid industrialization and to governmental policies that ignored the problems of the poor.

Children pushing a coal cart through a mine shaft (1842).

The Sleeping Princess (19th century) by Sir Edward Burne-Jones.

What Was Romanticism?

Romanticism is characterized by these general features:

- Romanticism turned away from the eighteenth-century emphasis on reason and artifice. Instead, the Romantics embraced imagination and naturalness.

- Romantic-era poets rejected the public, formal, and witty works of the previous century. They preferred poetry that spoke of personal experiences and emotions, often in simple, unadorned language.

- The Romantics each used the lyric as the form best suited to expressions of feeling, self-revelation, and the imagination.

- Wordsworth urged poets to adopt a democratic attitude toward their audiences; though endowed with a special sensibility, the poet was always "a man speaking to men."

- Many Romantics turned to a past or an inner dream world that they felt was more picturesque and magical than the ugly industrial age they lived in.

- Most Romantics believed in individual liberty and sympathized with those who rebelled against tyranny.

- The Romantics thought of nature as transformative; they were fascinated by the ways nature and the human mind "mirrored" the other's creative properties.

What Does "Romantic" Mean?

The word *romantic* comes from the term *romance,* one of the most popular genres of medieval literature. (See page 167.) Later, Romantic writers self-consciously used the elements of romance in an attempt to go back beyond the refinements of neoclassical literature to older types of writing that they saw as more "genuine." The romance genre also allowed writers to explore new, more psychological and mysterious aspects of human experience.

Today, the word *romantic* is often a negative label used to describe sentimental writing, particularly those best-selling paperback "romances" about love—a subject that many people mistakenly think the Romantic poets popularized. As a historical term, however, *romantic* has at least three useful meanings, all of them relevant to the Romantic poets.

First, the term *romantic* signifies a fascination with youth and innocence, with "growing up" by exploring and learning to trust our emotions and our sense of will and identity. Second, the term *romantic* is applied to a stage in the cyclical development of societies: This is the stage when people need to question tradition and authority in order to imagine better—that is, happier, fairer, and healthier—ways to live. *Romantic* in this sense is associated with idealism. (The 1966–1975 period in the United States might be called a romantic era.) And third, in the so-called Romantic period of the first half of the nineteenth century (up to the Civil War in America), Western societies reached the conditions necessary for industrialization. This demanded that people acquire a stronger and stronger awareness of change and that they try to find ways to adapt to it. In this sense, we still live with the legacy of the Romantic period.

> *The term romantic signifies a fascination with youth and innocence, a questioning of authority and tradition for idealistic purposes, and an adaptation to change.*

Poetry, Nature, and the Imagination

Lyrical Ballads did not remain unnoticed or anonymous for long. In 1800, with Coleridge looking over his shoulder, Wordsworth composed a Preface for the expanded collection. In it he declared that he was writing a new kind of poetry that he hoped would be "well adapted to interest mankind permanently. . . ." The subject matter would be different from that of earlier giants of poetry—like Dryden and Pope—who used

Autumn Leaves (20th century) by Daniel Sherrin.

Private Collection.

poetry to satirize, or to persuade the reader with argumentative techniques. For Wordsworth, good poetry was "the spontaneous overflow of powerful feelings." And such poetry should use simple, unadorned language to deal with commonplace subjects for a particular purpose. The form is often a lyric that lends itself to spontaneity, immediacy, a quick burst of emotion, and self-revelation. Furthermore, Wordsworth focused on rural life instead of city life, because in the country "the passions of men are incorporated with the beautiful and permanent forms of Nature." Wordsworth found hope in "certain inherent and indestructible qualities of the human mind, and likewise . . . certain powers in the great and permanent objects that act upon it, which are equally inherent and indestructible." In other words, there is nature, and there are human beings to experience nature.

> Not the poem we have *read,* but that to which we *return,* with the greatest pleasure, possesses the genuine power, and claims the name of *essential poetry.*
>
> —Samuel Taylor Coleridge

A CLOSER LOOK

AN IRRESISTIBLE BAD BOY: THE BYRONIC HERO

"Mad, bad, and dangerous to know."

—Lady Caroline Lamb, speaking of George Gordon, Lord Byron

"A man proud, moody, cynical, with defiance on his brow, and misery in his heart, a scorner of his kind, implacable in revenge, yet capable of deep and strong affection." This model of reckless, wounded manhood described by Thomas Babington Macaulay (1800–1859) became known as the Byronic hero. Both in his life and in his poetry, George Gordon, Lord Byron (1788–1824) gave his name to a type of hero who was devastatingly attractive yet fatally flawed.

Byron's personal charms and poetic talents offset a physical disability (a clubfoot), which embarrassed him terribly, and the complicated romantic entanglements that made him a social outcast. His heroes, whom he often invited his readers to identify with himself, were also passionate yet flawed individualists: intellectually searching, incapable of compromise, forever brooding over some mysterious past sin, painfully yet defiantly alone.

Heroes for an unheroic age. The immense popularity of the Byronic hero and the Romantic-age celebration of his prototypes—Cain, Faust, Prometheus, and Napoleon—wasn't hard to understand. These were rash rebels, hailed or resurrected in reaction to a neoclassical world in which order and restraint ruled the day. Most of these daring figures, whose ambitions were doomed from the start, also embodied the deep pessimism of early nineteenth-century life. The failure of the French Revolution had dampened idealism throughout Europe. And the

Byron, 6th Baron (detail) (1835) by Thomas Phillips.

By Courtesy of the National Portrait Gallery, London.

The Romantics are often called nature poets. This description is misleading if it suggests that their poetry is full of charming scenes of forests, mountains, and streams—like the scenic overlooks on highways or the pictures on travel brochures.

The Romantics prized experiences of the beauty and majesty of nature. They did not think of nature as hostile, but they had a strong sense of its mysterious forces, and they were intrigued by the ways that nature and the human mind act upon each other. In the Preface, Wordsworth says that the poet "considers man and nature as essentially adapted to each other, and the mind of man as naturally a mirror of the fairest and most interesting properties of nature."

Each of the Romantic poets had his own special view of the creative power of the imagination and of the ways in which the human mind is

> I think Poetry should surprise by a fine excess and not by Singularity—it should strike the Reader as a wording of his own highest thoughts, and appear almost a Remembrance.
>
> —John Keats, in a letter written February 27, 1818

labyrinthine restrictions of state, church, and society allowed no suitable outlets for the out-sized energy of creative young men like Byron and his fictional heroes.

Marlon Brando in Laslo Benedek's film *The Wild One* (1954).

The American heirs. The model of a sensitive rebel continues to be an engaging one for popular heroes of recent time: In post–World War II America, for example, as society had settled into a bland conformity, several searching, sensitive malcontents arrested the attention of movie-goers everywhere.

One version of the Byronic bad boy was played by Marlon Brando, who popularized motorcycles, leather jackets, and a sullen demeanor in his 1954 film *The Wild One*. The leader of a motorcycle gang, Brando is asked, "What are you rebelling against?" His response: "What have you got?" The actor James Dean personified youthful rebellion in both his brief film career and his tragically short life. In *Rebel Without a Cause*

(1955), Dean's portrayal of Jim Stark, an alienated character searching for the meaning of manhood, made him a cult hero.

Like all Byronic heroes, these modern characters beckon their admirers to explore personal freedoms and to reject confining conventions. Because this freedom is achieved only by questioning accepted social behavior, these heroes are invariably lonely and misunderstood. And because this freedom often compels them to perform dangerous acts, the lives of these heroes can be much too short. Lord Byron died of a fever at age thirty-six, while fighting for Greek independence. James Dean died in an automobile accident at age twenty-four.

James Dean in Nicholas Ray's film *Rebel Without a Cause* (1955).

adapted to nature. You will notice that the poems usually present imaginative experiences as very powerful or moving. This suggests that, in addition to being a special faculty of the mind, the imagination is also a kind of desire, a motive that drives the mind to learn and to know things it cannot learn by rational and logical thinking. So, although the mind is naturally a "mirror" of nature, as Wordsworth thought, the imagination actually moves the mind in mysterious ways to imitate (without being sacrilegious) the powers of its Maker. The purpose of this imitation is to create new realities in the mind and (as a result) in poetry.

In the Romantic period, poetry was no longer used to make complex arguments in a witty, polished style. Romantic poets used unadorned language to explore the significance of commonplace subjects, the beauty of nature, and the power of the human imagination.

Das Schweigen (Silence) (detail) (1799–1801) by Johann Heinrich Füssli. Oil on canvas (63.5 cm × 51.5 cm).

The Idea of the Poet

In 1802, in order to clarify his remarks about poetry, Wordsworth added to his Preface a long section on the question, *What is a poet?* His answer began: "He is a man speaking to men."

If this seems strange, consider what happens in a good many of the poems in the following collections. There is a person in the poem—we will call him the "speaker" to distinguish him from the poet—who is "speaking to" someone or something else: a young Highland girl, a baby asleep in a cottage, a skylark, even a Greek vase or a season of the year.

Each poem of this type not only asks us to imagine (pretend) that the "speaking" is taking place, but also makes us consider what *kind* of speaking is taking place. Is the speaker praising or confessing or complaining or worshipping or expressing envy? That is, what is the speaker doing by "speaking"?

> I will not Reason & Compare: my business is to Create.
>
> —William Blake

The speaking in lyric poetry is not the Augustan reasoning in verse. It is a more emotional, passionate speaking from the heart. It has been said that we do not *hear* lyric poetry so much as *overhear* it—as if (using our imagination again) we are eavesdropping on a private conversation or on someone talking to himself or herself out loud. The Romantic lyric, then, speaks in what has been called the true voice of feeling or the language of the heart. In writing this way, the Romantics created a kind of poetry that poets today continue to use.

For lyric poetry to be successful, the speaker and the speaking must be convincing. Thus, the poet must create an artful illusion of the voice of the speaker that conveys certain truths or ideas. Though they did not reason in verse like the Neoclassic poets, the Romantics were deeply concerned with the truths of the heart and the imagination—with truth, as Wordsworth said, "carried alive into the heart by passion." Or, as Keats once wrote to a friend, "What the imagination seizes as beauty must be truth whether it existed before or not."

Wordsworth's deceptively simple definition of the poet as "a man speaking to men" was thus a revolutionary concept in a number of ways. If we think of the speaker (not the poet) as an ordinary person, then it is a very democratic definition. Poetry is to be about human experience, about the fundamental relationship between the mind (including the heart and the imagination) and other people and other things. The speaking should be convincing so that it can seem a genuine and sincere account of that experience, no matter how special or extravagant the experience may appear to be.

The speakers in Romantic poetry speak in the language of feelings, or of the heart. This exploration of the emotional experiences of ordinary people was revolutionary.

The Romantic Poet

In saying that the poet is "a man speaking to men," Wordsworth did not mean that the poet is just a man. In the Preface, it is clear that the poet is a special person, "endowed with more lively sensibility, more enthusiasm and tenderness . . . a greater knowledge of human nature, and a more comprehensive soul, than are supposed to be common among mankind." Though the word *supposed* (meaning *thought*) may suggest that Wordsworth thought his fellow citizens had too low an estimate of much of humankind, all of the Romantic poets described the poet in such lofty terms.

> . . . what we have loved,
> Others will love, and we will teach them how;
> Instruct them how the mind of man becomes
> A thousand times more beautiful than the earth
> On which he dwells, above this frame of things
> (Which, 'mid all revolution in the hopes
> And fears of men, doth still remain unchanged)
> In beauty exalted, as it is itself
> Of quality and fabric more divine.
>
> —William Wordsworth,
> *from The Prelude*

A CLOSER LOOK

THE LURE OF THE GOTHIC

Literature of the Romantic period is filled with examples of the eerie and supernatural: Samuel Coleridge's haunted *The Rime of the Ancient Mariner* and Mary Shelley's famously horrible *Frankenstein*. The Romantics' taste for terror grew from a sensibility called "Gothic" that set stories in gloomy medieval castles. The intention of the Gothic? To make readers' blood run cold.

A "little gothick Castel." Much credit for the popularity of the Gothic style must go to a dramatically unorthodox construction project. In 1747, Horace Walpole (1717–1797) began building what he called a "little gothick Castel." A more conventional choice by the son of wealthy, powerful Prime Minister Robert Walpole (1676–1745) would have been a mansion in the popular neoclassical style. Neoclassical architecture—like the White House in the United States—is inspired by ancient Roman and Greek models and emphasizes balance and symmetry. In stark contrast, the Gothic revels in rustic irregularity: quirky battlements (medieval-style fortifications with openings for defenders) or overgrown landscaping. Walpole's home, named Strawberry Hill, was designed to be gloriously imperfect; when its odd, medieval battlements collapsed, the ruin only enhanced its charm and intensified its melancholy atmosphere.

Making monsters. Walpole had constructed a Gothic ruin; in 1764, he filled it with monsters. His novel *The Castle of Otranto* uses ghosts, living statues, and an eerie forest cave to illustrate a royal family's collapse. With this terrifying, imaginative story, Walpole created the first Gothic novel, a genre of horror tales that we recognize today.

The effects of Walpole's creations were far-reaching. The model of his crumbling house and of stories that provoked violent emotions helped begin the Romantic period's love affair with all things Gothic. Contemporary tastes thought that Gothic architecture reflected the wild, unpredictable aspects of nature; its ruins reflected human aspirations and failures. A melancholy painting or a desolate landscape could enhance spiritual awareness. Ann Radcliffe (1764–1823), one of the best-known Gothic novelists, describes this ideal awareness in *The Mysteries of Udolpho* (1794). In twilight gloom, a character finds "that delicious melancholy which no person, who had felt it once, would resign for the gayest pleasures. They awaken our best and purest feelings; disposing us to benevolence, pity, and friendship."

Exploring unseen "evils." The turn from rational enlightenment to Gothic sensationalism indicated

For William Blake, for example, the poet was the bard, an inspired revealer and teacher. The poet, wrote Coleridge, "brings the whole soul of man into activity" by employing "that synthetic and magical power . . . the imagination." Shelley called poets "the unacknowledged legislators of the world." Keats wrote that a poet is a "physician" to all humanity and "pours out a balm upon the world." Nothing, wrote Wordsworth in *The Recluse*,

> . . . can breed such fear and awe
> As fall upon us often when we look
> Into our Minds, into the Mind of Man—
> My haunt, and the main region of my song.

The poet, in sum, is someone human beings cannot do without.

The Romantic poets found a way through the imagination to fulfill the poet's traditional role as "prophet, priest, and king" in a time of change.

more than just a fad for terrifying tales and quirky architecture. The Gothic was one way in which people of the age expressed a sense of helplessness about forces beyond their control: frightening revolutions in Europe and industrialization's unsettling economic changes. The familiar, sensational trappings of the Gothic novel that we know today were less important than its ability to let readers, if only for a moment, share their fears about the age's suffering, injustice, and other unseen "evils."

Two Men Contemplating the Moon (1819) by Caspar David Friedrich.

Staatliche Kunstsammlungen Dresden, Gemäldegalerie Neue Meister.

Europe: A Prophecy: Famine (detail) (1794) by William Blake. Relief etching with white line engraving, watercolor.

Private Collection.

Quickwrite

This introduction to the great Romantic period in English literature is illustrated with pieces of fine art, many of them painted by famous Romantic artists of England and continental Europe. Look over these paintings and take notes on their subjects. (Note their titles.) What exactly does each one make you see? What emotions does each evoke? Do any of the paintings seem mysterious? Which of these paintings or painters might provide material for further research?

(Opposite) *Donati's Comet over Balliol College* (19th century) by William of Oxford (circle of).

The Maas Gallery, London.

Burns
Blake
Wordsworth
Pushkin
Coleridge

The poet's eye, in a fine frenzy rolling,
Doth glance from heaven to earth, from earth to heaven;
And, as imagination bodies forth
The forms of things unknown, the poet's pen
Turns them to shapes, and gives to airy nothing
A local habitation and a name.

—William Shakespeare, *from A Midsummer Night's Dream*

Robert Burns

(1759–1796)

In 1786, a Scottish farmer thrust himself into the Scottish and English literary worlds. The farmer was Robert (Robby) Burns, and the book that catapulted him out of the barnyard was *Poems, Chiefly in the Scottish Dialect.*

Within a year, Burns had left his native Ayrshire (in southwestern Scotland) for the first time and become the toast of Edinburgh. He seized the moment to issue a new edition of his poems (1787) with an Edinburgh publisher. In a new preface to this edition, he proclaimed, "The poetic genius of my country found me . . . at the plow; and threw her inspiring mantle over me. . . . I tuned my wild, artless notes, as she inspired."

Burns was certainly eager to cultivate an audience among the literati of Edinburgh, but he also consciously reinforced his image as an untutored rustic inspired by Scotland itself. He was fully aware that his fame would probably be temporary, and it was. After this auspicious beginning, Burns's stature declined. He actually wrote relatively little poetry afterward. Instead, he devoted himself to collecting, editing, rewriting, and creating over three hundred Scottish folk songs; most of the lyrics he wrote he set to traditional airs. This is the work that established Burns's most enduring reputation. Scottish immigrants to North America and elsewhere took his song collections with them, and they sang Burns's words to remember their homeland. Even now, many people mark the New Year by singing "Auld Lang Syne," one of Burns's lyrics.

Only ten years after his first success, Burns died of heart disease. Though his reputation includes credible legends of heavy drinking, it is clear that poor nutrition and the long-term physical hardships of farming led to his early death.

By the early nineteenth century, Burns was well on the way to becoming the single most important symbol of Scottish literature. Burns was an extraordinary poet in part because

Robert Burns (c. 1792) by Alexander Nasmyth. Oil on canvas (12½″ × 9½″).
By Courtesy of the National Portrait Gallery, London.

Scottish culture, both popular and refined, seems to have spoken through him. He grew up in the folk culture of small isolated Scottish villages and farms, where the few pleasures were all the more precious. Much of what Wordsworth noted as the "presence of human life" in Burns's work comes from his immersion in the lives of ordinary human beings. The pleasure we take from his poetry comes in part from our recognition of things common and enduring in human experience.

At the same time, Burns himself was quite aware of the tradition of Scottish literature, which was undergoing a studied revival in the eighteenth century. Burns had the benefit of some excellent (though short-lived) formal education before he was needed full time for farm labor, and he was well read in English authors. The apparent artlessness of what he wrote and the simple pose he adopted as a humble plowman mask a mastery of literary forms. Burns, in fact, could write perfectly well in the literary English of his time as well as in a range of Scottish, from heavy dialect to a beautiful blending of folk idioms and literary language.

go.hrw.com
LEO 12-8

Before You Read

TO A MOUSE

Make the Connection

The Persistence of the Unforeseen

Here a plowman speaks to a mouse whose nest he has overturned—a seemingly insignificant event. But the speaker also recognizes his own human dilemma in the sudden disruption of the mouse's shelter, carefully constructed against the cruel winter—what the British writer Thomas Hardy was to call "the persistence of the unforeseen."

Elements of Literature

Dialect

Dialect is speech native to a particular geographical area or to a social or political group. People brought up speaking a dialect sometimes know no other kind of speech and need no other to communicate within their community. However, when government transactions, the law, and the business of educated society are conducted in another language, speakers of dialect can be at a disadvantage. This was the case among the rural population of nineteenth-century Scotland, where English was the official language.

> **D**ialect is speech characteristic of a particular region or group.
>
> *For more on Dialect, see the Handbook of Literary Terms.*

Reading Skills and Strategies

Using Context and Glosses

When used as thickly and consistently as Robert Burns uses it here, Scottish dialect sounds like a foreign language. Yet while Burns's poems seem to call for translation, they also contain some easy-to-read passages that will help you understand others that are not easy to grasp. The meanings of some words can be figured out by their sounds or their context in a phrase or line. Others are so deeply rooted in their Scottish origins that you will have to consult the side glosses. When you have finished reading, jot down your reactions to the dialect.

Background

As an educated and well-read man, Burns had the option of using either Scottish dialect or the king's English. Depending on the subject or occasion of a poem, he proceeded to use both. But there is little question that, if it were not for his poems in dialect, he would figure in literary history as no more than a pleasant poet who accepted the genteel conventions of his time and its sentimental distortions of "the simple life."

The difficulties of poems in dialect have caused some people to attempt to translate them into contemporary language. But attempts to render dialect poetry into plain English often fail. This is simply because the logic of a poem is only part of what it means to convey. When sound is divorced from sense, the qualities of rhythm, music, and color are diminished, and meaning becomes prosaic.

To enjoy and relish the music, rhythm, and lilting Scottish dialect of "To a Mouse," listen to it read aloud on audiotape.

Robert Burns's Birthplace (19th century) by George Washington Brownlow.

To a Mouse

Robert Burns

On Turning Her Up in Her Nest,
with the Plow, November, 1785.

    Wee, sleeket,° cowran, tim'rous beastie,
O, what a panic's in thy breastie!
Thou need na start awa sae hasty,
      Wi' bickering brattle!°
5 I wad be laith° to rin an' chase thee,
      Wi' murd'ring pattle!°

    I'm truly sorry man's dominion
Has broken Nature's social union,
An' justifies that ill opinion,
10   Which makes thee startle
At me, thy poor, earth-born companion,
      An' fellow mortal!

    I doubt na, whyles,° but thou may thieve;
What then? poor beastie, thou maun° live!
15 A daimen-icker in a thrave°
      'S a sma request:
I'll get a blessin wi' the lave,°
      An' never miss 't!

    Thy wee-bit housie, too, in ruin!
20 It's silly wa's° the win's are strewin!
An' naething, now, to big° a new ane,
      O' foggage° green!
An' bleak December's winds ensuin,
      Baith snell° an' keen!

1. **sleeket:** sleek.

4. **bickering brattle:** skirmishing, rattling sounds.
5. **laith:** loath; unwilling.
6. **pattle:** plow staff.

13. **whyles:** sometimes.
14. **maun:** must.
15. **daimen-icker in a thrave:** occasional ear of grain out of a bundle.

17. **lave:** remainder.

20. **silly wa's:** feeble walls.
21. **big:** build.
22. **foggage:** moss.

24. **snell:** bitter.

25   Thou saw the fields laid bare an' wast,
     An' weary winter comin fast,
     An' cozie here, beneath the blast,
        Thou thought to dwell,
     Till crash! the cruel coulter° past
30   Out thro' thy cell.

     That wee-bit heap o' leaves an' stibble,
     Has cost thee monie a weary nibble!
     Now thou's turn'd out, for a' thy trouble,
        But° house or hald,°
35 To thole° the winter's sleety dribble,
       An' cranreuch° cauld!

     But Mousie, thou art no thy-lane,°
     In proving foresight may be vain:
     The best laid schemes o' mice an' men
40   Gang aft agley,°
     An' lea'e us nought but grief an' pain,
       For promis'd joy!

     Still, thou art blest, compar'd wi' me!
     The present only toucheth thee:
45 But och! I backward cast my e'e,
       On prospects drear!
     An' forward, tho' I canna see,
       I guess an' fear!

29. coulter: plow blade.

34. but: without. **hald:** land.
35. thole: endure.
36. cranreuch: hoarfrost.

37. no thy-lane: not alone.

40. gang aft agley: go often amiss.

Ploughing (detail) (late 19th or early 20th century) by Aldin Cecil.

MAKING MEANINGS

First Thoughts

1. How would you describe the **speaker's** mood? Do you ever feel the same? When?

Shaping Interpretations

2. Where does the speaker's **tone** change? What does the speaker imply in the last stanza about his own past and his prospects for the future?

3. When you paraphrase the second stanza, what are the meanings of the words *dominion* and *union* here, in your view? What attitude about people and nature does the use of these words imply?

4. What comparisons between the mouse and himself does the speaker make in the last two stanzas?

5. Read aloud some uses of **alliteration** in the poem. Are any of the poem's sound effects comical?

Connecting with the Text

6. How do you feel about the philosophy of the future expressed in lines 39–40 (the best-known lines of the poem)? How does your own experience reflect or contradict these lines? (Do you recognize in these lines the title of a novel by John Steinbeck?)

Extending the Text

7. Burns's use of **dialect** was a great departure from the elegant language of most eighteenth-century poets. What dialects are used in drama, songs, films, and fiction today? How do you feel about the use of dialect for realism?

CHOICES: Building Your Portfolio

Writer's Notebook

1. Collecting Ideas for a Research Paper

You might find an interesting topic for further research in the biography of Burns on page 640. Jot down questions you have about the life of Robert Burns, about his works, or about the political situation of Scotland in the late eighteenth century. Save your notes for the Writer's Workshop on page 773.

Monitoring Your Reading Process

2. Frankly Speaking

Write an essay explaining your response to this poem, including any difficulty you had with the dialect. Be as frank as you want to be, but support your response with specific reasons and quotations from the poem. (Be sure to consult your reading notes.)

Creative Writing

3. Creature Connections

Have another speaker address another creature—fly, cockroach, spider, moth. Imitate Burns, and imagine what the creature is thinking of the encounter. What connection does the speaker see between the creature and himself?

Creative Writing

4. From the Mouse's Mouth

What does the mouse think as her wee bit of leaves and stubble is ruined by the plow? Write the mouse's reply to her fellow mortal. Use dialect if you wish.

By Courtesy of the National
Portrait Gallery, London.

William Blake

(1757–1827)

William Blake (detail) (1807) by
Thomas Phillips. Oil on canvas
(35 ¼″ × 17 ¼″).

William Blake's life is not as "romantic" or "poetic" as the lives of Coleridge, Shelley, and Keats were. By all accounts, he was somewhat happily married to the same woman for much of his life. He never traveled, and he lived outside London for only three years (1800–1803). He began his artistic training at ten, when his father, a London shopkeeper, sent him to one of the best drawing schools. Apprenticed to an engraver at fourteen, Blake worked steadily at his craft as an engraver and as a professional artist throughout a long life, in good times and bad.

During his lifetime, Blake's work received very little attention, and a great deal of his poetry was never published in the sense of being "public." When his work was noticed, readers and viewers too often decided that it, and therefore Blake himself, was weird, confused, or mad. What we really know of Blake—from the enormous energy and variety of his poetry, paintings, drawings, and engravings—is that he was quite simply a great artist in the fullest sense.

A woman at a gathering is said to have asked Blake *where* he had come upon the scene he had just vividly described to her. "*Here,* madam," he said, pointing his finger at his forehead. To paraphrase Blake, if we see with imagination, we see all things in the infinite. But if we see only with reason, we see only ourselves. "I know that this world is a world of imagination & vision," he wrote.

> I see everything I paint in this world, but everybody does not see alike. To the eyes of a miser, a guinea [a coin] is more beautiful than the sun, & a bag worn with the use of money has more beautiful proportions than a vine filled with grapes. . . . But to the eyes of the man of imagination nature is imagination itself. As a man is, so he sees. . . . To me this world is all one continued vision of fancy or imagination.

One of the purposes of Blake's art was to change the way people "see" and thus to open up new worlds to them—"one continued vision" of what had once been ordinary and commonplace, but would become "imagination itself." One of Blake's most famous statements about his art (in the prophetic poem *Jerusalem*) is "I must create a system or be enslaved by another man's." But in creating the "system" for his own works, Blake was also aware that he himself could be trapped by it. The line that follows the one above is "I will not Reason & Compare: my business is to Create."

The history of Blake the poet cannot really be separated from that of Blake the visual artist. Not only did he provide illustrations for most of his poems, but he also printed much of his poetry himself (and sometimes only for himself), using engraving methods he himself had created. According to Blake's nineteenth-century biographer Alexander Gilchrist, "the poet and his wife did everything in making the book [*Songs of Innocence* (1789)]—writing, designing, printing, engraving—everything except manufacturing the paper; the very ink, or color rather, they did make. Never before surely was a man so literally the author of his own book."

A good deal of what Blake wrote other than his poems is cryptic and needs illumination from his art. But one characteristic of the man himself shines through clearly—the optimism sustained by his continuous joy in the "one continued vision" of his art. As one acquaintance described Blake, "He was a man without a mask; his aim single, his path straightforward, and his wants few; so he was free, noble, and happy."

Blake's Poems: Exploring Contraries

William Blake first published the *Songs of Innocence* in 1789. In 1794, these songs and the *Songs of Experience* were issued together in one volume, the title page promising a demonstration of "the two Contrary States of the Human Soul."

Blake conceived the first of these states, "Innocence," as a state of genuine love and naive trust toward all humankind, accompanied by unquestioned belief in Christian doctrine. Though a firm believer in Christianity, Blake thought that its doctrines were being used by the English Church and other institutions as a form of social control: to encourage among the people passive obedience and acceptance of oppression, poverty, and inequality. Recognition of this marks what Blake called the state of "Experience," a profound disillusionment with human nature and society. One entering the state of "Experience" sees cruelty and hypocrisy only too clearly but is unable to imagine a way out. Blake also conceived of a third, higher state of consciousness he called "Organized Innocence," which is expressed in his later works. In this state, one's sense of the divinity of humanity coexists with oppression and injustice, though involving continued recognition of and active opposition to them.

When reading the *Songs of Innocence* and, to a lesser extent, the *Songs of Experience,* it is important to remember that Blake intended them not as simple expressions of religious faith. The poems are demonstrations of viewpoints that are necessarily limited or distorted by each narrator's or speaker's state of consciousness.

The Ghost of Samuel Appearing to Saul (1800) by William Blake. Pen and ink with watercolor over graphite (12 9/16″ × 13 1/2″).

Before You Read
THE TYGER

Make the Connection

More Than Meets the Eye

While almost everyone agrees that "The Tyger" is one of the most powerful of Blake's *Songs of Experience,* there has been much disagreement about the meaning of the poem's central **symbol,** the tiger itself. One possibility is that the tiger represents a strong revolutionary energy that can enlighten and transform society—a positive but dangerous force Blake believed was operating in the French Revolution. The poem's speaker, at any rate, cannot comprehend such a startling energy, and can only wonder whether it is demonic or godlike.

Quickwrite

What will the tiger in Blake's poem mean to you? Spend two minutes freewriting whatever comes into your mind when you think about the word *tiger.*

Background

To William Blake, who saw visions and devoted his life to worshiping God with his poetry and art, the world was filled with symbols. He believed that every object and event on earth had a mystical or spiritual meaning. He gave each symbol a rich assortment of meanings that even his contemporaries could not fully understand.

The Tyger *from* Songs of Experience
William Blake

Tyger! Tyger! burning bright
In the forests of the night,
What immortal hand or eye
Could frame thy fearful symmetry?

5 In what distant deeps or skies
Burnt the fire of thine eyes?
On what wings dare he aspire?
What the hand dare seize the fire?

And what shoulder, and what art,
10 Could twist the sinews of thy heart?
And when thy heart began to beat,
What dread hand? and what dread feet?

What the hammer? what the chain?
In what furnace was thy brain?
15 What the anvil? what dread grasp
Dare its deadly terrors clasp?

When the stars threw down their spears,°
And watered heaven with their tears,
Did he smile his work to see?
20 Did he who made the Lamb make thee?

Tyger! Tyger! burning bright
In the forests of the night,
What immortal hand or eye,
Dare frame thy fearful symmetry?

17. stars . . . spears: a reference to the angels who fell with Satan and threw down their spears after losing the war in heaven.

The Tyger (1793) by William Blake from his book *Songs of Experience.* Hand-colored etching.
Library of Congress, Washington, D.C.

MAKING MEANINGS

First Thoughts

1. Which of the poem's **images** appeals most strongly to you? Why do you think it does?

Shaping Interpretations

2. What question does the poem's **speaker** ask the tiger over and over? What answer is implied?

3. Where in the poem does the speaker wonder if the tiger may have been created by God? What **imagery** tells us that the speaker also suspects that the tiger could be a demonic creation? What images suggest a human creator—like a blacksmith or a goldsmith?

4. What **imagery** suggests that the tiger could be a force of enlightenment? of violence?

5. What do you think is meant by the tiger's "fearful symmetry"? (Picture the tiger's stripes.)

6. The last stanza of the poem virtually repeats the first. In your view, what is the significance of the one word changed in the last stanza?

7. How does the poem testify to the simultaneous attraction to and repulsion from evil?

8. Review your Quickwrite notes. What do you think is the meaning of the poem's central **symbol,** the tiger?

Connecting with the Text

9. If you had to choose your own **symbol** for all the things represented by Blake's tiger, what would your symbol be? Why?

Extending the Text

10. Why do you think this poem has always appealed to children as well as to adults? What qualities might the word *tiger* connote to a young child?

Elohim Creating Adam
(1795–1805) by William Blake.

Tate Gallery, London.

PRIMARY Sources | A LETTER

Charles Lamb (1775–1834), perhaps the most accomplished Romantic essayist, uses a letter to sing his praises of William Blake.

"Blake is a real name..."

To Bernard Barton

Blake is a real name, I assure you, and a most extraordinary man, if he be still living. He is the Robert [William] Blake, whose wild designs accompany a splendid folio edition of the *Night Thoughts,* which you may have seen, in one of which he pictures the parting of soul and body by a solid mass of human form floating off, God knows how, from a lumpish mass (facsimile to itself) left behind on the dying bed. He paints in watercolors marvelous strange pictures, visions of his brain, which he asserts that he has seen. They have great merit. He has *seen* the old Welsh bards on Snowden—he has seen the beautifulest, the strongest, and the ugliest man, left alone from the massacre of the Britons by the Romans, and has painted them from memory (I have

The Agony in the Garden (c. 1799–1800) by William Blake.
Tate Gallery, London.

seen his paintings), and asserts them to be as good as the figures of Raphael and Angelo, but not better, as they had precisely the same retrovisions and prophetic visions with himself. The painters in oil (which he will have it that neither of them practiced) he affirms to have been the ruin of art, and affirms that all the while he was engaged in his water paintings, Titian was disturbing him, Titian the III Genius of Oil Painting. His pictures—one in particular, the Canterbury Pilgrims (far above Stothard's)—have great merit, but hard, dry, yet with grace. He has written a catalogue of them with a most spirited criticism on Chaucer, but mystical and full of vision.

His poems have been sold hitherto only in manuscript. I never read them; but a friend at my desire procured the Sweep Song. There is one to a tiger, which I have heard recited, beginning:

> Tiger, Tiger, burning bright,
> Thro' the desarts of the night,

which is glorious. But, alas! I have not the book; for the man is flown, whither I know not, to Hades or a madhouse—But I must look on him as one of the most extraordinary persons of the age.

—Charles Lamb

Make the Connection

The Balance of Contraries

William Blake's poetry and art reflect his fascination with the Bible and his struggles to find answers to questions that profoundly disturbed him: Why do human beings do evil? Why do evil people sometimes prosper? Why does God allow innocent children to suffer?

One of Blake's early conclusions about the problem of good and evil is his idea that "Without contraries is no progression." "The Lamb" and "The Tyger" reflect what Blake termed "two contrary states of the human soul," both of which are as essential to humanity as joy and sadness, innocence and experience.

Quickwrite

If *tiger* connotes fierceness, mystery, and awe, what qualities does *lamb* suggest? Jot down some words and images that come to mind when you visualize a lamb.

Background

One of the *Songs of Innocence,* this poem has often been read as a statement of Christian faith. However, we know that Blake's other writings show Christ as an active fighter against injustice, not the "meek" and "mild" lamb—a common symbol for Christ—with which this innocent speaker identifies. The speaker's viewpoint is thus an incomplete representation of Blake's beliefs.

The Lamb
from Songs of Innocence
William Blake

Little Lamb, who made thee?
    Dost thou know who made thee?
Gave thee life, and bid thee feed
By the stream and o'er the mead,°
5 Gave thee clothing of delight,
Softest clothing, wooly, bright;
Gave thee such a tender voice,
Making all the vales° rejoice?
    Little Lamb, who made thee?
10   Dost thou know who made thee?

    Little Lamb, I'll tell thee,
    Little Lamb, I'll tell thee:
He° is called by thy name,
For He calls himself a Lamb.
15 He is meek, and he is mild;
He became a little child.
I a child, and thou a lamb,
We are called by his name.
    Little Lamb, God bless thee!
20   Little Lamb, God bless thee!

4. mead: meadow.
8. vales: valleys.
13. He: Christ.

"Auguries of Innocence" by William Blake (transcribed c. 1807) from the Pickering or Ballads Manuscript.

The Pierpont Morgan Library/Art Resource, New York.

MAKING MEANINGS

First Thoughts

1. Look back at your Quickwrite notes. How do your associations with the word *lamb* relate to the associations suggested in this poem?

Shaping Interpretations

2. What did its creator do for the lamb in the first stanza?

3. How does the second stanza respond to the question posed in the first?

4. What do you know about the **speaker** of the poem?

5. How is the lamb both a literal object and a **symbol** in this poem?

6. Christ called himself a lamb because, like the Passover lamb slain to save the people of Israel, he sacrificed himself for the people. What might this imply about the fate of the young **speaker** in this poem?

7. How do you think the voice of the speaker in "The Lamb" is different from the voice of the speaker in "The Tyger"? Why do you think the questions in "The Lamb" get answers?

Connecting with the Text

8. How would you represent innocence? How would you represent experience? Why?

Challenging the Text

9. Blake wrote a two-line poem called "An Answer to the Parson" in which the parson (or preacher) asks, "Why of the sheep do you not learn peace?" The **narrator** replies, "Because I don't want you to shear my fleece." How would the narrator of this poem disagree with the narrator of "The Lamb"?

The Lamb (c. 1789–1794) by William Blake from his book *Songs of Innocence and of Experience*. Relief etching finished in pen and watercolor.

Fitzwilliam Museum, University of Cambridge, Cambridge, England.

Make the Connection

Cold Comfort

In these two poems, one from *Songs of Innocence* and the other from *Songs of Experience,* Blake speaks for the poor children of his day who were forced to do backbreaking labor. In Blake's London, buildings were heated by coal or wood-burning fireplaces, so every house had at least one chimney that had to be cleaned regularly. Poor children were often used to do this dirty work because they could fit easily into the narrow chimney passages. In fact, some poor parents were so desperate that they sold their children to "masters" who managed crews of young sweepers. The work was dangerous, and the children were badly treated by masters concerned only with profits.

Quickwrite

If you could cry out against an evil of our day—and get people to listen—which social problem would you choose?

Background

In the late 1700s, prices increased sharply, and work became scarce. William Blake saw starving people rooting through garbage, homeless families sleeping in doorways, and children begging on the streets or working at backbreaking jobs. Most members of the upper class believed that they deserved their worldly success, and that the poor must be innately evil, deserving the hunger and appalling conditions that they endured.

Blake was said to be mad, not only because he saw visions, but also because his poems cry out against the social problems he saw all around him: the growing division between classes, the wretched working conditions, and child labor. No one should go hungry, he said, in a land as green and wealthy as England.

The Chimney Sweeper
from Songs of Innocence
William Blake

When my mother died I was very young,
And my father sold me while yet my tongue
Could scarcely cry "'weep! 'weep! 'weep! 'weep!"°
So your chimneys I sweep, and in soot I sleep.

5 There's little Tom Dacre, who cried when his head,
That curled like a lamb's back, was shaved: so I said
"Hush, Tom! never mind it, for when your head's bare
You know that the soot cannot spoil your white hair."

And so he was quiet, and that very night,
10 As Tom was a-sleeping, he had such a sight!—
That thousands of sweepers, Dick, Joe, Ned, and Jack,
Were all of them locked up in coffins of black.

And by came an Angel who had a bright key,
And he opened the coffins and set them all free;
15 Then down a green plain leaping, laughing, they run,
And wash in a river, and shine in the Sun.

Then naked and white, all their bags left behind,
They rise upon clouds and sport in the wind;
And the Angel told Tom, if he'd be a good boy,
20 He'd have God for his father, and never want° joy.

And so Tom awoke; and we rose in the dark,
And got with our bags and our brushes to work.
Though the morning was cold, Tom was happy and warm;
So if all do their duty they need not fear harm.

---

3. 'weep . . . 'weep: the child's attempt at the chimney sweepers' cry of "Sweep! Sweep!"
20. want: lack.

Background

Unlike the sweeper in *Songs of Innocence*, this sweeper does not accept oppression and poverty because he believes he will be rewarded in heaven. This little speaker recognizes that the people who pray for him (his parents) are the same ones who sold him into a life of hard labor.

The first three lines are spoken by an adult who finds the child. The rest of the poem is the bitter response of the child.

The Chimney Sweeper
from Songs of Experience
William Blake

A little black thing among the snow
Crying "'weep, 'weep," in notes of woe!
"Where are thy father & mother? say?"
"They are both gone up to the church to pray.

5   "Because I was happy upon the heath,
And smil'd among the winter's snow;
They clothed me in the clothes of death,
And taught me to sing the notes of woe.

"And because I am happy, & dance & sing,
10 They think they have done me no injury,
And are gone to praise God & his Priest & King,
Who make up a heaven of our misery."

MAKING MEANINGS

First Thoughts

1. Did these poems remind you of any tragedies in modern life involving the treatment of young children? (Consult your Quickwrite notes.) Discuss your responses.

Shaping Interpretations

2. What details of the speaker's history do you learn in the first poem? What is his present life like?

3. In the first poem, how does the angel reassure Tom Dacre in his dreams? What **moral lesson** does the speaker in the first poem draw from Tom's dream?

4. How does Tom Dacre's dream contrast with the actual conditions of his daily life?

5. How does the speaker of the first poem feel about his situation? How do you feel about it?

6. In the second poem the young chimney sweeper is asked where his parents are. What is the boy's answer? What do you think are his "clothes of death"?

7. How would you **paraphrase** the last two lines of the second poem?

8. How would you describe the **tone** of the second poem? How does this sweeper's attitude toward his life and his parents contrast with the attitude of the speaker in the first poem?

9. In each poem, what is the emotional effect of the child's mispronunciation of the chimney sweepers' cry?

Extending the Text

10. Do people today sometimes take the attitude expressed by the speaker of the first poem: If you are good, if you do your duty, you need not fear harm? Expand on your responses.

Before You Read

A POISON TREE

Make the Connection

The Fruits of Anger

What happens to anger that is allowed to grow and fester, anger that is nurtured with our own deceit? In this poem, one of

Blake's *Songs of Experience,* the speaker describes what happens when anger is left unresolved. As you read, think about how anger is symbolized in the poem—and about other ways it's portrayed.

Quickwrite

Jot down some notes describing the ways anger can be destructive, not only to the object of the anger, but also to the person feeling it.

A Poison Tree

from **Songs of Experience**

William Blake

I was angry with my friend:
I told my wrath, my wrath did end.
I was angry with my foe:
I told it not, my wrath did grow.

5 And I watered it in fears,
Night and morning with my tears;
And I sunned it with smiles,
And with soft deceitful wiles.°

And it grew both day and night,
10 Till it bore an apple bright;
And my foe beheld it shine,
And he knew that it was mine,

And into my garden stole
When the night had veiled the pole:
15 In the morning glad I see
My foe outstretched beneath the tree.

8. wiles: cunning tricks.

A Poison Tree (1794) by William Blake from his book *Songs of Experience.* Relief etching with watercolor and pen additions.

Private Collection.

MAKING MEANINGS

First Thoughts

1. If you were reading this poem aloud, which part of the last stanza would you emphasize? Why?

Shaping Interpretations

2. What two ways of handling anger are mentioned in the poem? What actually happens to the speaker's foe in the last stanza?

3. What is the "poison tree"?

4. Who are the victims in the poem?

5. How is the speaker both good and evil?

6. What do you see as the **theme** of the poem?

7. What do you make of Blake's allusion to forbidden fruit in the third stanza?

Connecting with the Text

8. Does the poem describe ways in which anger can be destructive that are similar to the ways you wrote about in your Quickwrite notes? Explain your response.

ELEMENTS OF LITERATURE

Parallelism

When words are arranged in balanced, similar structures, they are said to be **parallel.** Blake was especially fond of parallelism, and the use of this device contributes to the childlike simplicity on the surface of his poems. You'll become aware of the rhythmic effects of parallelism if you read Blake's poems aloud.

Much of "The Tyger" consists of questions that start with the word *what.* Sometimes the questions occupy one or two full verses; occasionally, Blake varies them so that one verse is split into two or three questions.

1. What examples of parallelism can you find in "The Lamb"?

2. How does Blake use parallelism in "The Chimney Sweeper" poems?

3. How does "A Poison Tree" use parallelism to link ideas from stanza to stanza?

CHOICES: Building Your Portfolio

Writer's Notebook

1. Collecting Ideas for a Research Paper

Skim Blake's biography, and jot down topics that you would be interested in pursuing, including social conditions in London in the late eighteenth century. Then, review the reproductions of Blake's art. (Be sure to look back through the introduction to the Romantic period.) What questions do you have about his paintings? Save your notes for the Writer's Workshop on page 773.

Comparing/Contrasting Drafts

2. Second-Guessing Blake

In an early draft of "The Tyger," Blake inserted the following lines after the third stanza:

> Could fetch it from the furnace deep
> And in thy horrid ribs dare steep
> In the well of sanguine wee
> In what clay and in what mold
> Were thy eyes of fury rolled

This early version also lacked the fifth stanza of the final version. In a brief essay, compare and contrast the early draft and the final version of "The Tyger," commenting on why you think Blake made the changes he did.

Analyzing Structure and Imagery

3. Below the Surface

In a brief essay, explain how both "The Tyger" and "The Lamb," although they seem to be simple lyrics, are concerned with very profound questions of religion. Comment on the **structure** and **imagery** of the two poems.

Creative Writing

4. Down the Chimney

Based on details in "The Chimney Sweeper," write the opening or closing paragraphs of a prose narrative that tells about the childhood of a chimney sweeper in Blake's London. You may want to write in the first person, as if for an autobiography.

Music

5. To Read By

With a small group, find a piece of classical or popular music that would serve as background for a reading of "A Poison Tree."

Art

6. Be Like Blake

Part of Blake's genius is the illustrations he created for his poems. Be like Blake: Create an illustration for any one of Blake's poems you've read.

William Wordsworth

(1770–1850)

William Wordsworth
(1842) by Benjamin Robert
Haydon. Oil on canvas
(49″ × 39″).

By Courtesy of the National Portrait
Gallery, London.

Surveying Wordsworth's life can be like walking around a large statue, awed by its presence and puzzled by its apparent importance. Sometimes Wordsworth must have felt the same way. As he thought about his early life and re-created it in his autobiographical poem *The Prelude,* Wordsworth said he felt as if he were "two consciousnesses"—one remembering, the other one remembered.

When Wordsworth's mother died in 1778, he and his three brothers were sent to school at Hawkshead in the Lake District. His sister, Dorothy, aged seven, had to live with relatives. When their father died in 1783, the children were placed under the guardianship of two uncles. William managed to get a degree from Cambridge in 1791, but had little interest in the few careers open to him—the main one being the Church—as an educated man with no title, wealth, or head for business. In late 1791, he went to France to learn the language and, as it turned out, discovered the bliss of being young in that time of birth and rebirth known as the French Revolution. Thus began a decade of painful growth, as he searched for and eventually found his vocation as a poet.

After he returned from France in 1792, Wordsworth was sickened by the war between France and England that began in 1793, and he gradually became deeply disillusioned about his hopes for change. Late that year he went on a long walking tour. This experience—and the collapse of his radical hope of perfecting society—drove him back to poetry.

In 1795, his fortunes began to change. He was reunited with his sister, Dorothy, who became a constant companion and inspiration. When he inherited some money from a friend, he and Dorothy took up residence in a rent-free cottage, and the poet Samuel Taylor Coleridge suddenly burst upon their lives. By June 1797, when he and Dorothy moved to a country house four miles from the village where Coleridge lived, Wordsworth had produced a good deal of new poetry, none yet published, including a play and some stark narratives. Coleridge and Wordsworth quickly became powerful influences on each other's work. *Lyrical Ballads* (1798) was the fruit of their friendship and mutual influence. During the following decade, Wordsworth wrote most of his best poetry.

But sometime after 1805, Wordsworth's poetic powers began to decline. By the time he was in his forties, his life was centered on his family; on his duties as a minor government official in the land of his boyhood, the Lake District, where he settled for good in 1799; and on his unflagging diligence as a poet. As his writing lost its energy and his political opinions grew more conservative, he became a kind of literary monument.

By the Victorian era, Wordsworth was the poet laureate (1843), a cartoon image of an old gentleman delighting in daffodils and butterflies while wandering about the Lake District. This image endured in part because the family suppressed the fact that in 1792 Wordsworth had fathered a child in France with a young woman he never married.

The distinguishing quality of Wordsworth's best lyric poetry comes from his simple delight in the nature of experience itself and in the mind's capacity to shape everyday experience into something lasting and poetic. Poetry, he wrote in the preface to *Lyrical Ballads,* is the "spontaneous overflow of powerful feelings"; but, he added, poems of lasting value are produced only by someone who has "thought long and deeply." The marriage of feeling and thought, as Coleridge recognized, made Wordsworth "the best poet of the age."

Make the Connection

Nature's Power

William Wordsworth loved nature in all of its forms, and he believed that nature made him a better person. Loving nature, he writes in this poem, quiets his mind, lightens his mood, guides him to kind acts, and brings him closer to God.

Elements of Literature

Blank Verse

Wordsworth composed poetry in his head while he walked, "his jaws working the whoal time," recalled a country person who observed him. He spoke the words aloud to memorize them and to get the rhythm right. When Wordsworth was a child, under the direction of his father, he had memorized and recited long passages in **blank verse** from the works of Shakespeare and Milton. In "Tintern Abbey," Wordsworth uses for the first time a less formal, "conversational" blank verse that he had learned from Coleridge. The words and phrases he repeats give his poetry the flowing rhythm of natural speech.

> **B**lank verse is poetry written in unrhymed **iambic pentameter.** Each line contains five iambs; each iamb, or metrical foot, is an unstressed syllable followed by a stressed syllable.
>
> *For more on Blank Verse, see the Handbook of Literary Terms.*

Reading Skills and Strategies

Recognizing Patterns of Organization

Before you read this poem aloud, look for the end punctuation and the indents that signal the end of one stanza and the beginning of another. (How many stanzas are in the poem?) Then, as you read, make notes on how Wordsworth used these stanzas to organize his ideas.

Background

"Tintern Abbey" (which refers to the ruined abbey mentioned only in the title) is one of the most important short lyric works in English literature. A major step forward in Wordsworth's writing and a definitive statement of some of the Romantics' ideas, it has inspired and guided many poets since. The ease with which Wordsworth wrote it is therefore even more astonishing.

In July 1798, Wordsworth and his sister, Dorothy, went on a vigorous walking tour in southern Wales. Shortly after leaving the Wye River valley, Wordsworth, by his own account, began to compose this poem about revisiting the valley, concluding it "just as I was entering Bristol in the evening after a ramble of four or five days. . . . Not a line of it was altered, and not any part of it written down till I reached Bristol. It was published almost immediately after."

Wordsworth had previously written two long descriptive poems and a few other descriptive lyrics, but nothing quite like this. He had been hard at work on the narrative ballads that make up *Lyrical Ballads* when he went on his tour. But he had learned something important from two poems by Coleridge, "This Lime-Tree Bower My Prison" and "Frost at Midnight": the use of a flowing blank verse and the easy maneuvering of the meditative poem.

This style was explored and refined in the many poems Coleridge and Wordsworth termed "conversation poems." First perfected by Coleridge, the conversation poem is usually a deeply personal meditation, seemingly spoken to a silent listener or to a loved one who is absent or asleep.

The apparent ease of its composition hides the art of "Tintern Abbey," evident even in the title, which asks us to imagine that these lines were poured out at the time the speaker returned to the Wye Valley after five years' absence. The many days of composition on the way back to Bristol were spent creating a poem in which we seem to hear the easy, immediate utterance of what is going on in the heart and mind of the speaker.

Lines Composed a Few Miles Above Tintern Abbey

On Revisiting the Banks of the Wye During a Tour. July 13, 1798

William Wordsworth

Five years have past; five summers, with the length
Of five long winters! and again I hear
These waters, rolling from their mountain springs
With a soft inland murmur.—Once again
5 Do I behold these steep and lofty cliffs,
That on a wild secluded scene impress
Thoughts of more deep seclusion; and connect
The landscape with the quiet of the sky.
The day is come when I again repose
10 Here, under this dark sycamore, and view
These plots of cottage ground, these orchard tufts,
Which at this season, with their unripe fruits,
Are clad in one green hue, and lose themselves
'Mid groves and copses.° Once again I see
15 These hedgerows,° hardly hedgerows, little lines
Of sportive wood run wild: these pastoral farms,
Green to the very door; and wreaths of smoke
Sent up, in silence, from among the trees!
With some uncertain notice, as might seem
20 Of vagrant dwellers in the houseless woods,
Or of some Hermit's cave, where by his fire
The Hermit sits alone.
               These beauteous forms,
Through a long absence, have not been to me
As is a landscape to a blind man's eye:
25 But oft, in lonely rooms, and 'mid the din
Of towns and cities, I have owed to them
In hours of weariness, sensations sweet,
Felt in the blood, and felt along the heart;
And passing even into my purer mind,
30 With tranquil restoration:—feelings too
Of unremembered pleasure: such, perhaps,
As have no slight or trivial influence
On that best portion of a good man's life,
His little, nameless, unremembered acts
35 Of kindness and of love. Nor less, I trust,
To them I may have owed another gift,
Of aspect more sublime; that blessed mood,
In which the burden of the mystery,

14. copses: areas densely covered with shrubs and small trees.
15. hedgerows: rows of bushes, shrubs, and small trees that serve as fences.

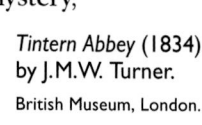

Tintern Abbey (1834)
by J.M.W. Turner.
British Museum, London.

In which the heavy and the weary weight
40 Of all this unintelligible world,
Is lightened:—that serene and blessed mood,
In which the affections° gently lead us on,—
Until, the breath of this corporeal° frame
And even the motion of our human blood
45 Almost suspended, we are laid asleep
In body, and become a living soul:
While with an eye made quiet by the power
Of harmony, and the deep power of joy,
We see into the life of things.
                                    If this
50 Be but a vain belief, yet, oh! how oft—
In darkness and amid the many shapes
Of joyless daylight; when the fretful stir
Unprofitable, and the fever of the world,
Have hung upon the beatings of my heart—
55 How oft, in spirit, have I turned to thee,
O sylvan° Wye! thou wanderer through the woods,
How often has my spirit turned to thee!
    And now, with gleams of half-extinguished thought,
With many recognitions dim and faint,
60 And somewhat of a sad perplexity,
The picture of the mind° revives again:
While here I stand, not only with the sense
Of present pleasure, but with pleasing thoughts
That in this moment there is life and food
65 For future years. And so I dare to hope,
Though changed, no doubt, from what I was when first
I came among these hills; when like a roe°
I bounded o'er the mountains, by the sides
Of the deep rivers, and the lonely streams,
70 Wherever nature led: more like a man
Flying from something that he dreads, than one
Who sought the thing he loved. For nature then
(The coarser pleasures of my boyish days,
And their glad animal movements all gone by)
75 To me was all in all.—I cannot paint
What then I was. The sounding cataract°
Haunted me like a passion: the tall rock,
The mountain, and the deep and gloomy wood,
Their colors and their forms, were then to me
80 An appetite; a feeling and a love,
That had no need of a remoter charm,°
By thought supplied, nor any interest
Unborrowed from the eye.—That time is past,
And all its aching joys are now no more.
85 And all its dizzy raptures. Not for this
Faint° I, nor mourn nor murmur; other gifts

42. **affections:** feelings.
43. **corporeal:** bodily.

56. **sylvan:** associated with the forest or woodlands.

61. **picture of the mind:** primarily the picture in the mind, but also the picture the individual mind has of itself.

67. **roe:** deer.

76. **cataract:** waterfall.

81. **remoter charm:** appeal other than the scene itself.

86. **faint:** become weak; lose heart.

Have followed; for such loss, I would believe,
Abundant recompense.° For I have learned
To look on nature, not as in the hour
90   Of thoughtless youth; but hearing oftentimes
The still, sad music of humanity,
Nor harsh nor grating, though of ample power
To chasten and subdue. And I have felt
A presence that disturbs me with the joy
95   Of elevated thoughts; a sense sublime
Of something far more deeply interfused,
Whose dwelling is the light of setting suns,
And the round ocean and the living air,
And the blue sky, and in the mind of man:
100 A motion and a spirit, that impels
All thinking things, all objects of all thought,
And rolls through all things. Therefore am I still
A lover of the meadows and the woods,
And mountains; and of all that we behold
105 From this green earth; of all the mighty world
Of eye, and ear—both what they half create,
And what perceive; well pleased to recognize
In nature and the language of the sense
The anchor of my purest thoughts, the nurse,
110 The guide, the guardian of my heart, and soul
Of all my moral being.
                              Nor perchance,
If I were not thus taught, should I the more
Suffer° my genial° spirits to decay:
For thou art with me here upon the banks
115 Of this fair river; thou my dearest Friend,°
My dear, dear Friend; and in thy voice I catch
The language of my former heart, and read
My former pleasures in the shooting lights
Of thy wild eyes. Oh! yet a little while
120 May I behold in thee what I was once,
My dear, dear Sister! and this prayer I make,
Knowing that Nature never did betray
The heart that loved her; 'tis her privilege,
Through all the years of this our life, to lead
125 From joy to joy: for she can so inform
The mind that is within us, so impress
With quietness and beauty, and so feed
With lofty thoughts, that neither evil tongues,
Rash judgments, nor the sneers of selfish men,
130 Nor greetings where no kindness is, nor all
The dreary intercourse° of daily life,
Shall e'er prevail against us, or disturb
Our cheerful faith, that all which we behold
Is full of blessings. Therefore let the moon

88. recompense: repayment.

113. suffer: allow.
genial: creative.

115. my dearest Friend: Words-worth's sister Dorothy.

131. intercourse: dealings; social contacts.

(Opposite) *Landscape* (detail) (19th century) by Patrick Nasmy Roy Miles Gallery, London.

135 Shine on thee in thy solitary walk;
And let the misty mountain winds be free
To blow against thee: and, in after years,
When these wild ecstasies shall be matured
Into a sober pleasure; when thy mind
140 Shall be a mansion for all lovely forms,
Thy memory be as a dwelling place
For all sweet sounds and harmonies; oh! then,
If solitude, or fear, or pain, or grief,
Should be thy portion, with what healing thoughts
145 Of tender joy wilt thou remember me,
And these my exhortations!° Nor, perchance—

146. exhortations: strong advice.

If I should be where I no more can hear
Thy voice, nor catch from thy wild eyes these gleams
Of past existence—wilt thou then forget
150 That on the banks of this delightful stream
We stood together; and that I, so long
A worshipper of Nature, hither came
Unwearied in that service: rather say
With warmer love—oh! with far deeper zeal
155 Of holier love. Nor wilt thou then forget
That after many wanderings, many years
Of absence, these steep woods and lofty cliffs,
And this green pastoral° landscape, were to me
More dear, both for themselves and for thy sake!

158. pastoral: relating to herds or flocks, pasture land, and country life.

MAKING MEANINGS

First Thoughts

1. What single **image**, feeling, or idea in this poem do you think you will remember longest? Why?

Shaping Interpretations

2. What do you think is meant by "the burden of the mystery" (line 38)?

3. What three stages of his growing up does the speaker describe (lines 73–111)?

4. What "gifts" (line 86) and "abundant recompense" (line 88) does the speaker believe he has received for his "loss" (line 87)?

5. What do you think the speaker means when he says in lines 88–91 that he has heard "the still, sad music of humanity"?

6. What role does the speaker's sister play in this poem?

7. How is this poem an example of Wordsworth's idea that poetry "takes its origin from emotion recollected in tranquility"?

8. What would you say is Wordsworth's attitude toward his past, his present, and his future?

Reading Check

a. What does the speaker hear and see in the first verse paragraph (lines 1–22)?

b. Why are these "beauteous forms" not, for the speaker, "As is a landscape to a blind man's eye" (line 24)?

c. What has the speaker lost since he first "came among these hills" (line 67)?

d. What does the speaker see in his "dear Sister" that makes him more aware of what he "was once" (line 120)?

e. Scan the **meter** of the poem. Find three examples of **run-on lines** that keep the poem from sounding mechanical and singsong.

---

9. Summarize and comment on the significance of the speaker's conclusion, beginning with line 102. Have you ever had to come to terms with losing part of your past? How did you resign yourself to its loss?

Connecting with the Text

10. Imagine that you were away for five years from a place you loved, just as Wordsworth was away from Tintern Abbey. How do you think you might have changed in that time?

READING SKILLS AND STRATEGIES

Patterns of Organization: Verse Paragraphs

Wordsworth's **blank verse** is best read aloud in the long, rolling movements of his verse paragraphs, or groups of lines that develop a main idea. These verse paragraphs mark five major transitions of thought in "Tintern Abbey." Review your reading notes to see what you wrote about these transitions from one idea to another.

In the first paragraph (lines 1–22), the poet unifies his long clauses by repeating the word *again* in lines 4, 9, and 14. The function of the paragraph is to establish the time interval between the speaker's visits to the Wye (five years) and to describe the scene. In the second paragraph (lines 22–49), Wordsworth makes his thought easier to follow by repeating a phrase ("blessed mood," lines 37 and 41).

Slowly and carefully read aloud another verse paragraph of "Tintern Abbey," observing the punctuation and **run-on lines.** Then, write a few sentences stating whether or not you think that the verse paragraph you have chosen is unified by one **main idea.** If so, state the main idea.

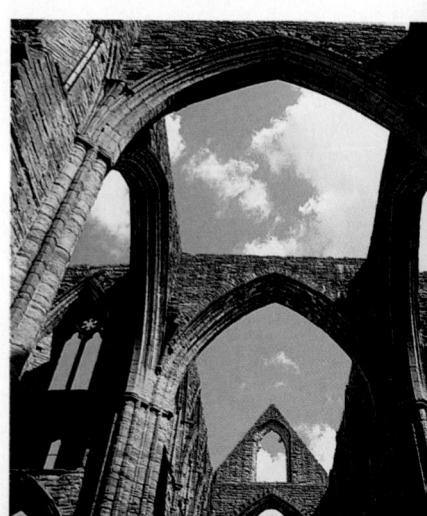

The ruins of Tintern Abbey today.

STRANGE FITS OF PASSION HAVE I KNOWN
SHE DWELT AMONG THE UNTRODDEN WAYS
A SLUMBER DID MY SPIRIT SEAL

Make the Connection

Lucy—Love and Loss

These lyrics, written during Wordsworth's stay in Germany in 1799, are three of five poems called the Lucy poems that were published together in 1800 in the expanded *Lyrical Ballads*. As in other "literary mysteries," where we suspect a hidden connection between the writer's life and his work, there has been much speculation about who Lucy was. "She lived unknown," but because Wordsworth had immortalized her in his poems, Lucy became famous throughout nineteenth-century England as an enduring symbol of the universal experience of love and loss.

Quickwrite

Alfred, Lord Tennyson, who was Wordsworth's contemporary, wrote that it is ". . . better to have loved and lost / Than never to have loved at all." What do you think? Write a brief response to Tennyson's words.

Strange Fits of Passion Have I Known

William Wordsworth

Strange fits of passion have I known:
And I will dare to tell,
But in the Lover's ear alone,
What once to me befell.

5 When she I loved looked every day
Fresh as a rose in June,
I to her cottage bent my way,
Beneath an evening moon.

Upon the moon I fixed my eye,
10 All over the wide lea;°
With quickening pace my horse drew nigh
Those paths so dear to me.

And now we reached the orchard-plot;
And, as we climbed the hill,
15 The sinking moon to Lucy's cot°
Came near, and nearer still.

In one of those sweet dreams I slept,
Kind Nature's gentlest boon!
And all the while my eyes I kept
20 On the descending moon.

My horse moved on; hoof after hoof
He raised, and never stopped:
When down behind the cottage roof,
At once, the bright moon dropped.

25 What fond and wayward thoughts will slide
Into a Lover's head!
"O mercy!" to myself I cried,
"If Lucy should be dead!"

10. lea (lē): meadow.
15. cot: cottage.

She Dwelt Among the Untrodden Ways

William Wordsworth

She dwelt among the untrodden ways
    Beside the springs of Dove,°
A Maid whom there were none to praise
    And very few to love:

5 A violet by a mossy stone
    Half hidden from the eye!
—Fair as a star, when only one
    Is shining in the sky.

She lived unknown, and few could know
10   When Lucy ceased to be;
But she is in her grave, and, oh,
    The difference to me!

2. Dove: river in central England.

When Coleridge read the following poem, he called it an epitaph, which underscores the fact that it is death that the speaker meditates on in each of these "Lucy" poems. Coleridge also thought Wordsworth might have written the poem "in some gloomier moment," when he "fancied the moment when his sister might die."

Manuscript of "Lucy Gray" by William Wordsworth. Though about a girl named Lucy, this poem is not one of the "Lucy" poems.

The Wordsworth Trust, Dove Cottage.

A Slumber Did My Spirit Seal

William Wordsworth

A slumber did my spirit seal;
    I had no human fears:
She seemed a thing that could not feel
    The touch of earthly years.

No motion has she now, no force;
    She neither hears nor sees;
Rolled round in earth's diurnal° course,
    With rocks, and stones, and trees.

7. diurnal (dī·ʉr′nəl): daily.

(Opposite) *Young Girl at Window* (1875) by Winslow Homer. Watercolor on paper mounted on masonite (6¼″ × 4¾″).

From the collection of the New Britain Museum of Art, Connecticut. Harriet Russell Stanley Fund. Photograph by E. Irving Blomstrann.

LITERATURE AND GEOGRAPHY

The "Frightful" Lake District

The novelist Daniel Defoe described the mountainous northwestern corner of his country as "the wildest, most barren and frightful in England." Most of his contemporaries shared his opinion of the Lake District, an area carved by Ice Age glaciers and transformed by volcanoes. The area was set apart even by its place names, which reflect the language of Norsemen who colonized the region: *thwaite* (meadow), *how* (hill), *tarn* (mountain lake), *beck* (stream), and *force* (waterfall). In the late eighteenth century, the haunting beauty of this area began to inspire writers and painters who embraced the Romantic ideal of wild, gothic landscapes. Writers were so drawn to the area's beauty (William Wordsworth wrote thirty-five poems on the Duddon Valley alone) that the literary group including Wordsworth, Samuel Taylor Coleridge, and Robert Southey became known as the Lake Poets.

Situated just below the southern border of Scotland, the Lake District is about thirty miles long and twenty-five miles wide, a small area to contain such geographic diversity. Here sits England's tallest mountain, Scafell Pike, towering over the countryside's lonely moorlands and bracken-covered slopes. The dramatic blue of the Irish Sea, Morecambe Bay, and the district's sixteen lakes contrasts with the intense greens of meadows and forests. Coleridge is credited with popularizing the pastime of "fell walking," which rewards walkers who brave the rocky, barren hills, or "fells," with scenic views of the countryside.

In 1802, Wordsworth's sister Dorothy could enjoy the peacefulness of "the gentle flowing of the stream, the glittering lively lake, [and] green fields without a living creature to be seen on them." Today, ironically, hordes of tourists flock to the region searching for the solitude of England's remotest corner.

Keswick in the Lake District, England.

MAKING MEANINGS

Strange Fits of Passion Have I Known
She Dwelt Among the Untrodden Ways
A Slumber Did My Spirit Seal

First Thoughts

1. Read the poems as if Lucy were the speaker's sister. Then, read them as if she were a young woman he loved romantically. Do you think that the identity of Lucy makes a difference in the way you read the poems?

Shaping Interpretations

2. What has happened to Lucy in each of these poems? What is the speaker feeling in each poem?

3. Whom is the speaker addressing in "Strange Fits of Passion"? What *is* the speaker's strange fit of passion?

4. What is the role of the moon in "Strange Fits of Passion"?

5. What two contrasting **figures of speech** does the speaker use to describe Lucy in "She Dwelt Among the Untrodden Ways"? How could one woman be like both of these things?

6. How would you **paraphrase** the first two lines of "A Slumber Did My Spirit Seal"?

Connecting with the Text

7. Review your Quickwrite notes. Do you think the speaker of any of these poems would agree with what you wrote?

Before You Read

Make the Connection

Clouds of Glory

When we speak of the immortality of the soul, we are usually referring to the idea that the soul lives on after death. In this poem, however, Wordsworth is musing about the state of the soul *before* birth and for a short time after. He remembers how luminous the world appeared to him when he was a young child and how the brightness faded as he grew older. These memories give him a vague sense, or *intimation,* that prior to birth his soul was in a state of bliss and that some of that heavenly joy remained with him through early childhood.

Quickwrite

Do you ever feel that the kind of joy you experienced as a child has changed now that you are grown up? Or do you think you feel joy just as intensely as an adult? Jot down some notes about the special feelings of joy you might have had as a child.

Background

This ode is called Wordsworth's finest short poem (for more on the traditional ode, see page 672; Wordsworth's ode is irregular). Only three of its eleven stanzas are printed here, and the interested student is urged to read the entire poem. Wordsworth says that the poem was inspired by feelings he had as a child—that it was difficult for him to believe that his body would ever die. He used to think that no matter what happened to other people, he would somehow be taken directly up to heaven, as the prophet Elijah was. The sentiments in the ode, suggesting the existence of a prior life, offended some people, and Wordsworth took pains to say that he did not mean to change, or even to challenge, anyone's beliefs. Remember that what you are reading is only a portion of the entire poem. In this part of the ode, Wordsworth traces the origins of joy and how our sense of joy changes as we grow up. These portions of the ode contain some of Wordsworth's most famous lines.

Age of Innocence (1788) by Sir Joshua Reynolds.
Tate Gallery, London.

from Ode

Intimations of Immortality
from Recollections of Early Childhood

William Wordsworth

> *The Child is Father of the Man;*
> *And I could wish my days to be*
> *Bound each to each by natural piety.*

1

There was a time when meadow, grove, and stream,
The earth, and every common sight,
   To me did seem
   Apparelled in celestial light,
5 The glory and the freshness of a dream.
It is not now as it hath been of yore;—
   Turn wheresoe'er I may,
   By night or day,
The things which I have seen I now can see no more.

2

10 The Rainbow comes and goes,
And lovely is the Rose,
The Moon doth with delight
Look round her when the heavens are bare,
Waters on a starry night
15 Are beautiful and fair;
The sunshine is a glorious birth;
But yet I know, where'er I go,
That there hath passed away a glory from the earth.

5

Our birth is but a sleep and a forgetting:
20 The Soul that rises with us, our life's Star,
Hath had elsewhere its setting,
And cometh from afar:
Not in entire forgetfulness,
And not in utter nakedness,
25 But trailing clouds of glory do we come
From God, who is our home:
Heaven lies about us in our infancy!
Shades of the prison-house begin to close
Upon the growing Boy,
30 But He beholds the light, and whence it flows,
He sees it in his joy;
The Youth, who daily farther from the east
Must travel, still is Nature's Priest,
And by the vision splendid
35 Is on his way attended;
At length the Man perceives it die away,
And fade into the light of common day.

MAKING MEANINGS

First Thoughts

1. Do these three stanzas remind you in any way of your own feelings about childhood and adulthood? Check your Quickwrite notes, and compare your responses with those of other readers.

Shaping Interpretations

2. The **epigraph**, or opening quotation, of Wordsworth's poem presents a **paradox**, an apparent contradiction. What can childhood experiences teach us as adults?

3. In stanza 1, what did the speaker once have but has now lost? What does the image "apparelled in celestial light" make you see?

4. According to stanza 2, how does the speaker feel now when he looks on nature?

5. What **mood**, or feeling, do the first two stanzas create for you? (Pay particular attention to the closing lines of each stanza.)

6. In stanza 5, how does the speaker see "birth" as "a sleep and a forgetting"? What does he say we forget after we are born?

7. How does stanza 5 go on to describe infancy, boyhood, and adulthood?

Challenging the Text

8. In these stanzas, Wordsworth offers his explanation for the intense joys of childhood that later disappear. How do you feel about his conclusions? What arguments could you present to challenge the poet's explanations for these emotional shifts from childhood to maturity?

9. Wordsworth describes growing up as "shades of the prison-house begin[ning] to close." Can you think of actual life experiences that either support or challenge that view? Explain your responses to Wordsworth's views.

10. Wordsworth had a happy childhood. How about someone who had an unhappy childhood—would Wordsworth's ideas hold up for that person? Explain.

Make the Connection

The Effect of Imagination

Wordsworth chose to spend most of his time in the English countryside, especially in the beautiful Lake District where, he believed, Nature had made him a poet. First published in 1807, this sonnet shows that Wordsworth, the nature lover, could be moved not only by mountains and water-falls, but also by the majesty of a sleeping city, in this case London. But this is clearly a different London from the one where Blake's chimney sweeper lived and from the one known as the "great wen [boil]" that shocked many of Wordsworth's contemporaries because of its filth and poverty. It is London seen from a distance, and by a man happily journeying to see his daughter in France. Here, London's filth and poverty are disguised and transfigured by the poet's imagination.

Quickwrite

What are your impressions of a city at the start of the day? Freewrite on your ideas about a wakening cityscape.

Elements of Literature

Personification

Wordsworth breathes life into his sonnet by using **personification,** a kind of metaphor in which a nonhuman thing is talked about as if it were human. Look for details that personify the city, the sun, the river, even the houses of London.

Composed upon Westminster Bridge
September 3, 1802

William Wordsworth

Earth has not anything to show more fair:
Dull would he be of soul who could pass by
A sight so touching in its majesty:
This City now doth, like a garment, wear
5 The beauty of the morning; silent, bare,
Ships, towers, domes, theaters, and temples lie
Open unto the fields, and to the sky;
All bright and glittering in the smokeless air.
Never did sun more beautifully steep
10 In his first splendor, valley, rock, or hill;
Ne'er saw I, never felt, a calm so deep!
The river glideth at his own sweet will:
Dear God! the very houses seem asleep;
And all that mighty heart is lying still!

Westminster Bridge, London (detail)
(late 19th or early 20th century)
by Louis H. Grimshaw.

MAKING MEANINGS

First Thoughts

1. What feature of the city described in the poem appeals to you most? Does any detail in the poem surprise you? Why? Compare your responses with another reader's.

Shaping Interpretations

2. What details and features of the city are noticed by the speaker?

3. What details **personify** the city?

4. What **paradox,** or seeming contradiction, do you find in the poem's last line?

5. What quality or characteristic of the scene seems to move the speaker most deeply?

Connecting with the Text

6. Compare the city that you know best, either from personal experience or from reading, with the London described in this poem. Be sure to check your Quickwrite notes.

Mosaic of Tritons, Nereids, and sea-antelope (1st century) from Ostia, Italy.
Museo Ostiense, Ostia, Italy.

The Wave (19th century) by Gustave Courbet.

Before You Read

THE WORLD IS TOO MUCH WITH US

Make the Connection

Out of Tune

The "world" is usually thought of as the world of material objects—the world of money and status symbols, the world of power, competition, and ambition. In seeking out the pleasures of this material world, what could a person lose?

Quickwrite

Do you ever feel "out of tune" with the world you live in? Freewrite for a few minutes about times when you have felt that modern life was taking you away from something you cherished or toward something you felt was wrong.

Background

Wordsworth wrote this sonnet in 1807 at a time when he realized that his imaginative powers were beginning to fail. Although he continued to compose new works and to edit *The Prelude,* a long poem published after his death, he knew he was no longer responding to nature with the youthful passion that had inspired his earlier poems.

This sonnet also counterattacks the ferocious criticism that Wordsworth was receiving from conservative reviewers, especially Francis Jeffrey in the *Edinburgh Review.* Jeffrey accused Wordsworth of using unpoetic language, but, even more, of conspiring against society, brooding needlessly over problems "instead of contemplating the wonders and pleasures which civilization has created for mankind." A critic considered Wordsworth an enemy of progress because of his "idle discontent with the existing institutions of society" and his yearning for an earlier, less civilized time when people lived in harmony with nature.

The World Is Too Much with Us

William Wordsworth

The world is too much with us; late and soon,
Getting and spending, we lay waste our powers:
Little we see in Nature that is ours;
We have given our hearts away, a sordid boon!°
5   This Sea that bares her bosom to the moon;
The winds that will be howling at all hours,
And are upgathered now like sleeping flowers;
For this, for everything, we are out of tune;
It moves us not.—Great God! I'd rather be
10 A Pagan suckled in a creed outworn;
So might I, standing on this pleasant lea,°
Have glimpses that would make me less forlorn;
Have sight of Proteus° rising from the sea;
Or hear old Triton° blow his wreathèd horn.

4. sordid boon: foul gift. That is, the act of giving our hearts away is shameful.

11. lea: meadow.
13. Proteus (prō′tē·əs): in Greek mythology, a sea god who can change shape at will.
14. Triton (trī′tən): in Greek mythology, a sea god who controls the waves by blowing a conch shell. (See the mosaic on page 670.)

Russia

Alexander Pushkin (19th century) by W. Troponin.

Alexander Pushkin

(1799–1837)

The Russians revere, re-read, and quote Pushkin as the English do Shakespeare. A master of verse, drama, and fiction, Pushkin is usually called the father of modern Russian literature. Even in his early works, influenced in style by the Russian Romantics and French neoclassicists, he focused on Russian settings and folk tales. As his genius matured, he developed a new realism in characterization and a vigorous, simple, and natural language unlike any in Russian literature. Born into an old aristocratic (though not wealthy) family in Moscow, Pushkin had an African great-grandfather—Abram Hannibal, a general under Peter the Great—whose ancestry he cherished.

Through both his father's extensive library and his beloved nurse's old tales, Pushkin steeped himself in imaginative literature. He gained fame early and took a government post, but his radical political verse and wild living resulted in years of exile from St. Petersburg—and the beginning of his masterwork, *Eugene Onegin,* a verse novel. Pushkin, like one of his own Romantic characters, was fatally wounded in a duel over his wife's honor, fought under circumstances that remain partly mysterious today. While his wife was a great flirt, the evidence against her came in anonymous letters that some thought were motivated by a political vendetta against Pushkin.

(Map) Europe in 1815, after the Treaty of Vienna.

Map ©Rand McNally R.L. #98-S-116.

Before You Read

I HAVE VISITED AGAIN

Background

Though Alexander Pushkin was only in his mid-thirties when he wrote this poem, he had already led a tumultuous, often disappointing, yet brilliant life in nineteenth-century Russia. Like Wordsworth revisiting Tintern Abbey, Pushkin is returning to a dearly remembered place: his ancestral home near Pskov. Some dark memories hover too, however, for his previous visit was enforced—a two-year exile from St. Petersburg because of his revolutionary sympathies. Partly because Pushkin was a literary hero, Czar Nicholas I ended the exile—but not the close surveillance and censorship of Pushkin. As Pushkin writes this poem, he is again a "free" man working in the government in St. Petersburg, but now he hates court social life (which his young wife loves). He wants only to live in the country and write, but his repeated requests to leave have been denied.

Quickwrite

Project yourself ten years into the future, living in another place. What one setting from your life now, or from your childhood, would you be drawn to revisit? Describe it briefly, and explain why it has meaning for you.

An Autumn Lane (detail) (late 19th or early 20th century) by Edward Wilkins Waite.

By Courtesy of Burlington Paintings, London.

I Have Visited Again

Alexander Pushkin

translated by **D. M. Thomas**

> . . . I have visited again
> That corner of the earth where I spent two
> Unnoticed, exiled years. Ten years have passed
> Since then, and many things have changed for me,
> 5 And I have changed too, obedient to life's law—
> But now that I am here again, the past
> Has flown out eagerly to embrace me, claim me,
> And it seems that only yesterday I wandered
> Within these groves.
>
> 10   Here is the cottage, sadly
> Declined now, where I lived with my poor old nurse.
> She is no more. No more behind the wall
> Do I hear her heavy footsteps as she moved
> Slowly, painstakingly about her tasks.
>
> 15   Here are the wooded slopes where often I
> Sat motionless, and looked down at the lake,
> Recalling other shores and other waves . . .
> It gleams between golden cornfields and green meadows,
> A wide expanse; across its fathomless waters
> 20 A fisherman passes, dragging an ancient net.

Birch Trees by Arkhip Kuindzhi.
Tretyakov Gallery, Moscow.

Along the shelving banks, hamlets are scattered
—Behind them the mill, so crooked it can scarcely
Make its sails turn in the wind . . .

                              On the bounds
25 Of my ancestral acres, at the spot
    Where a road, scarred by many rainfalls, climbs
    The hill, three pine trees stand—one by itself,
    The others close together. When I rode
    On horseback past them in the moonlit night,
30 The friendly rustling murmur of their crowns
    Would welcome me. Now, I have ridden out
    Upon that road, and seen those trees again.
    They have remained the same, make the same murmur—
    But round their aging roots, where all before
35 Was barren, naked, a thicket of young pines
    Has sprouted; like green children round the shadows
    Of the two neighboring pines. But in the distance
    Their solitary comrade stands, morose,
    Like some old bachelor, and round its roots
40 All is barren as before.

                              I greet you, young
    And unknown tribe of pine trees! I'll not see
    Your mighty upward thrust of years to come
    When you will overtop these friends of mine
45 And shield their ancient summits from the gaze
    Of passersby. But may my grandson hear
    Your welcome murmur when, returning home
    From lively company, and filled with gay
    And pleasant thoughts, he passes you in the night,
50 And thinks perhaps of me . . .

FINDING COMMON GROUND

Only one speaker appears in Pushkin's poem, but the lovely landscape he describes becomes practically a second character. The narrator greets new pine trees, recalls past encounters with wooded hills, and imagines his own grandchild engaging in the same conversations with nature. Working with a small group and referring to your Quickwrite notes, respond to Pushkin's description of his particular "corner of the earth." Here are some ideas you might focus on.

• Can an urban landscape evoke the kinds of feelings that Pushkin describes? Why or why not?

• In the Romantic period, many writers looked to nature to explain complex feelings about themselves or their culture. With a group of classmates, review the responses to nature in Percy Bysshe Shelley's "Ode to the West Wind" (page 734), John Keats's "Ode to a Nightingale" (page 755), or William Wordsworth's "Tintern Abbey" (page 658). How does Pushkin's relationship with nature compare with these?

Samuel Taylor Coleridge

(1772–1834)

Samuel Taylor Coleridge (1792)
by Peter Vandyke. Oil on canvas
(21½" × 17½").

He was "the most wonderful man that I have ever known," said Wordsworth. The two poems that follow are only sketches in comparison with the full portrait of Coleridge, a man who was unquestionably a genius.

The youngest child of a village parson, Coleridge began his classical education at home. When he arrived at Cambridge University in 1792, he already had a reputation for insatiable curiosity and wide reading in "out-of-the-way" books.

He left the university in 1794 without a degree but with a commitment to a utopian colony in America. The experiment never materialized, but Coleridge gave radical lectures and married one of the prospective utopians. In 1796, he moved to a village in Somerset, with one book of poetry published but no prospects of a career. The next twenty months, which ended when he and Wordsworth went to Germany to study, were a time of miracles. In 1798, Lyrical Ballads was published, and by then English Romanticism had begun.

Wordsworth and Coleridge became catalysts for each other, and the friendship helped Coleridge write most of his best poems. But convinced that Wordsworth was "the best poet of the age," the poet in Coleridge hid in the giant's shadow. After the year in Germany, Wordsworth returned in late 1799 to his native Lake District. Coleridge abandoned his own roots and followed (as he told a friend) "a great, a true poet, I am only a kind of metaphysician."

Despite this characteristic modesty, Coleridge was, if only in brief periods, a "true poet" and, moreover, a profound philosopher. The middle period of his life, from 1800 to 1818, produced great achievements, most notably his lectures on Shakespeare and the Biographia Literaria, a work on philosophy and criticism. These writings laid the foundations of twentieth-century literary theory.

But for Coleridge this period was also a time of pain and despair, memorialized in "Dejection: An Ode" (1802) and played out in the collapse of his marriage, his increasing addiction to opium (prescribed for painful attacks of arthritis), and his inability to discipline his wonderful mind.

By 1816, Coleridge had put himself under the care of a kindly physician, Dr. James Gillman. Despite the effect he had on others, Coleridge himself was lonely. The loneliness came from a lifelong need for affection and support—a need that made the isolation of the writer's life often unbearable for him. His addiction to laudanum (a mixture of alcohol and opium), which began before he was thirty, was not controlled until his residence with the Gillmans.

Living at a time when common pains are easily relieved by aspirin, we may find it difficult to imagine the need for a painkiller like laudanum, which was commonly used in Coleridge's time—even given to infants. Little was known then about withdrawal symptoms. Coleridge's addiction was made worse by the laudanum he took to relieve the discomforts he suffered when he tried to stop using the drug. Although scholars disagree about the destructive effect of opium on his achievements, there is no question that he was badly addicted.

Coleridge was truly magnanimous, generous of his intellect and spirit and devoted to the good of his fellow human beings. The full portrait of Coleridge, however, is too great for anyone to master. Anyone, that is, except someone like Coleridge himself.

go.hrw.com
LE0 12-8

Before You Read

KUBLA KHAN

Make the Connection

Dream World

The poem you are about to read may challenge the limits of your imagination. Fantastical and strange, it is like a vivid yet incomprehensible dream. Coleridge, in fact, suggested that the poem came to him in a dream. And like a dream, the poem contains allusions to the deepest human desires—for pleasure, order, beauty, awe, even chaos and war. It also holds within it the moment when—upon awaking—the vividness and logic of the dream are suddenly, perhaps forever, lost to the dreamer. As you read, think about how dreams work and how the poem may imitate or reproduce that process.

Reading Skills and Strategies

Responding to the Text

Take notes as someone reads this poem aloud to you or as you listen to it on an audiotape. After the reading is over, describe at least one image that remains vividly in your mind. Jot down at least one question you'd like to ask the poet.

Background

An enchanting poem, "Kubla Khan" has a lyrical tone and manner that resemble a meditative ode. Full of mystery and dread, "Kubla Khan" was composed at about the same time (late 1797 or early 1798) as *The Rime of the Ancient Mariner.*

"Kubla Khan" has always intrigued readers, including Byron, who, after reading it in manuscript, apparently prevailed on Coleridge to publish it in 1816. At the time, Coleridge added a prose introduction that offered a rational account of the poem's origins. He claimed it was written in a reverie brought on by opium taken after he read a provocative passage in a seventeenth-century travel book. Coleridge contended that he woke from his dream and was interrupted by a visitor while composing the poem. Only a fragment of his original vision could be reproduced, he claimed.

Kubla Khan (1216–1294) was the grandson of Genghis Khan and was the Mongol conqueror of China.

Kublai Khan (Yüan Dynasty, China).

Kubla Khan

Samuel Taylor Coleridge

In Xanadu did Kubla Khan
A stately pleasure-dome decree:
Where Alph,° the sacred river, ran
Through caverns measureless to man
5   Down to a sunless sea.
So twice five miles of fertile ground
With walls and towers were girdled round:
And there were gardens bright with sinuous rills,°
Where blossomed many an incense-bearing tree;
10 And here were forests ancient as the hills,
Enfolding sunny spots of greenery.

But oh! that deep romantic chasm which slanted
Down the green hill athwart a cedarn cover!°
A savage place! as holy and enchanted
15 As e'er beneath a waning moon was haunted
By woman wailing for her demon-lover!

3. Alph: probably a reference to the Greek river Alpheus, which flows into the Ionian Sea, and whose waters are fabled to rise up again in Sicily.

8. sinuous (sin′yoo·əs) **rills:** winding streams.

13. athwart a cedarn cover: crossing diagonally under a covering growth of cedar trees.

Palace of Kublai Khan at Peking (14th century).
Miniature from the *Livre des Merveilles*. Ms. Fr. 2810, fol. 37.
© cliché Bibliothèque Nationale de France, Paris.

And from this chasm, with ceaseless turmoil seething,
As if this earth in fast thick pants were breathing,
A mighty fountain momently° was forced:

20 Amid whose swift half-intermitted burst
Huge fragments vaulted like rebounding hail,
Or chaffy grain beneath the thresher's flail:°
And 'mid these dancing rocks at once and ever
It flung up momently the sacred river.

25 Five miles meandering with a mazy° motion
Through wood and dale the sacred river ran,
Then reached the caverns measureless to man,
And sank in tumult to a lifeless ocean:
And 'mid this tumult Kubla heard from far

30 Ancestral voices prophesying war!
   The shadow of the dome of pleasure
   Floated midway on the waves;
   Where was heard the mingled measure°
   From the fountain and the caves.

35 It was a miracle of rare device,
A sunny pleasure-dome with caves of ice!

   A damsel with a dulcimer°
   In a vision once I saw:
   It was an Abyssinian° maid,
40   And on her dulcimer she played,
   Singing of Mount Abora.°
   Could I revive within me
   Her symphony and song,
   To such a deep delight 'twould win me,

45 That with music loud and long,
I would build that dome in air,
That sunny dome! those caves of ice!
And all who heard should see them there,
And all should cry, Beware! Beware!

50 His flashing eyes, his floating hair!
Weave a circle round him thrice,
And close your eyes with holy dread,
For he on honeydew hath fed,
And drunk the milk of Paradise.

19. momently: at each moment.

22. thresher's flail: heavy, whiplike tool used to thresh, or beat, grain in order to separate the kernels from their chaff, or husks.
25. mazy: like a maze; having many turns.

33. measure: rhythmic sound.

37. dulcimer: musical instrument that is often played by striking the strings with small hammers.
39. Abyssinian: Ethiopian. Ethiopia is in northeast Africa.
41. Mount Abora: probably a reference to John Milton's (1608-1674) *Paradise Lost,* in which Mount Amara, in Ethiopia, is a mythical, earthly paradise.

Dorothy Wordsworth, William Wordsworth's sister, wrote this letter to Mary Hutchinson, the woman who would later become William's wife. Coleridge, by the way, returned Dorothy's admiration.

Dorothy Wordsworth Describes Coleridge

Racedown, June, 1797

. . . You had a great loss in not seeing Coleridge. He is a wonderful man. His conversation teems with soul, mind, and spirit. Then he is so benevolent, so good tempered and cheerful, and, like William, interests himself so much about every little trifle. At first I thought him very plain, that is, for about three minutes: he is pale and thin, has a wide mouth, thick lips, and not very good teeth, longish loose-growing half-curling rough black hair. But if you hear him speak for five minutes you think no more of them. His eye is large and full, not dark but gray, such an eye as would receive from a heavy soul the dullest expression; but it speaks every emotion of his animated mind; it has more of the "poet's eye in a fine frenzy rolling" than I ever witnessed. He has fine dark eyebrows, and an overhanging forehead. . . .

MAKING MEANINGS

First Thoughts

1. What **image** in the poem do you remember most vividly? (Check your reading notes.)

Shaping Interpretations

2. Why is the "deep romantic chasm" of line 12 called a "savage place"? What ominous note is introduced in the second stanza?

3. What does the speaker see in a vision in the third stanza? How does the speaker imagine himself in this stanza?

4. Describe the **rhyme scheme** and **meter** of the poem. What examples of **alliteration** add to the poem's music?

5. Who is the **speaker** of the poem? Compare him with Kubla Khan. Why is the "damsel with a dulcimer" important to the speaker?

6. How could the speaker "build that dome in air"? What do you think the dome **symbolizes**?

7. Where does the poet use contrasting **images**? In your view, does he offer any synthesis of these images in the concluding stanza?

8. Many ancient cultures regarded poets as seers who had a special relationship with the gods and thus were to be treated with special reverence. How may Coleridge be alluding to such beliefs in the closing lines of the last stanza?

Challenging the Text

9. Does the poem seem to you to bear out Coleridge's own description of it as a fragment? Or do you think that these lines were all the poet really intended to write? Why?

Before You Read

THE RIME OF THE ANCIENT MARINER

Make the Connection

Crime and Confession

Have you ever done something on impulse, knowing even while you were doing it that you would regret it forever? The Ancient Mariner's strange tale turns on just such an action. And the dreadful consequences of his impulsive deed are as hypnotizing to us as they are to the Mariner's spellbound listener. As you read, try to chart your responses to the Mariner's story. When do you feel sympathy for the Mariner—or sorrow or horror or fear? When do you feel his story is true, and when is it hopelessly distorted by his own guilt?

Quickwrite

Jot down a few ideas about what confession means to you. What purpose does confession have for the teller and the listener? Is a listener even necessary? Why do you think the act of confession plays such an important part in law and religion?

Elements of Literature

The Literary Ballad

Coleridge's **literary ballad** imitates the traditional **folk ballad** in both subject matter and form. Like the old folk ballads, his sensational narrative blends real with supernatural events. Coleridge was a skilled poet, and to avoid monotony, he often varies his **meter** and **rhyme scheme.**

He also uses sophisticated sound devices like **internal rhyme** ("The guests are *met,* the feast is *set*") and **assonance** ("'Tis sweeter far to *me*"). To give his ballad an archaic sound, he uses language that was even old-fashioned in his own time.

> **A literary ballad, a** songlike poem that tells a story, is written in imitation of the folk ballad, which springs from a genuine oral tradition.
>
> *For more on the Literary Ballad, see the Handbook of Literary Terms.*

Background

Coleridge wrote *The Rime of the Ancient Mariner* as part of the collaboration with Wordsworth in 1797–1798 that culminated in *Lyrical Ballads.* Twenty years later, in the *Biographia Literaria,* Coleridge recalled that he and Wordsworth had made a poetic division of labor based on their interest in the two powers of poetry: (1) to represent ordinary events and objects in an unfamiliar way so as to make them fresh and interesting and (2) to make believable the unfamiliar and strange.

Coleridge's task was to write about "persons and characters supernatural, or at least romantic; yet so far as to transfer from our inward nature a human interest and semblance of truth sufficient to procure for these shadows of imagination that willing suspension of disbelief for the moment, which constitutes poetic faith." "With this view," he said, "I wrote the *Ancient Mariner.*" The poem was the first item in the 1798 edition of *Lyrical Ballads.* But partly because of Wordsworth's discomfort with the incongruity between it and the rest of the poems in the volume, Coleridge modernized many of the deliberately old-fashioned words he had used. The marginal notes were added in 1817 and need to be viewed as "modern" and rational comments on the Mariner's tale.

Coleridge's poem no doubt reflects his avid reading of travelers' accounts of strange lands. It was apparently Wordsworth who suggested the use of the albatross. It is helpful in reading this hypnotic narrative to keep in mind three things. First, there is no explanation for the killing of the albatross. The results of the act, rather than the act itself, are important. Second, the moral of the story, pronounced by the Mariner at the end, is, as Coleridge later observed, too much and too little; that is, it is too obtrusive and yet not adequate. Finally, the poem must be seen in the light of Coleridge's own more settled religious convictions, which contrast with the spiritual despair of the Mariner:

> Alone on a wide wide sea:
> So lonely 'twas, that God himself
> Scarce seemed there to be.

SAMUEL TAYLOR COLERIDGE **683**

The Rime of the Ancient Mariner

Samuel Taylor Coleridge

Argument

How a Ship having passed the Line was driven by storms to the cold Country toward the South Pole; and how from thence she made her course to the tropical Latitude of the Great Pacific Ocean; and of the strange things that befell; and in what manner the Ancient Mariner came back to his own Country.

"It is an ancient Mariner, / And he stoppeth one of three."

Part I

It is an ancient Mariner,
And he stoppeth one of three.
"By thy long gray beard and glittering eye,
Now wherefore stopp'st thou me?

5   The Bridegroom's doors are opened wide,
And I am next of kin;
The guests are met, the feast is set:
May'st hear the merry din."

He holds him with his skinny hand,
10 "There was a ship," quoth he.
"Hold off! unhand me, gray-beard loon!"
Eftsoons° his hand dropt he.

He holds him with his glittering eye—
The Wedding Guest stood still,
15 And listens like a three years' child:
The Mariner hath his will.

The Wedding Guest sat on a stone:
He cannot choose but hear;
And thus spake on that ancient man,
20 The bright-eyed Mariner.

"The ship was cheered, the harbor cleared,
Merrily did we drop
Below the kirk,° below the hill,
Below the lighthouse top.

25 The Sun came up upon the left,
Out of the sea came he!
And he shone bright, and on the right
Went down into the sea.

Higher and higher every day,
30 Till over the mast at noon°—"
The Wedding Guest here beat his breast,
For he heard the loud bassoon.

The bride hath paced into the hall,
Red as a rose is she;
35 Nodding their heads before her goes
The merry minstrelsy.°

The Wedding Guest he beat his breast,
Yet he cannot choose but hear;
And thus spake on that ancient man,
40 The bright-eyed Mariner.

*An ancient Mariner meeteth three
Gallants bidden to a wedding feast,
and detaineth one.*

12. eftsoons: archaic for "at once."

*The Wedding Guest is spellbound
by the eye of the old seafaring man,
and constrained to hear his tale.*

23. kirk: church.

*The Mariner tells how the ship
sailed southward with a good wind
and fair weather, till it reached the
Line.*

30. over . . . noon: The ship has
reached the equator, here called the
Line.

*The Wedding Guest heareth the
bridal music; but the Mariner
continueth his tale.*

36. minstrelsy (minˊstrəl·sē):
group of musicians.

"And now the STORM-BLAST came, and he
Was tyrannous and strong:
He struck with his o'ertaking wings,
And chased us south along.

The ship driven by a storm toward the South Pole.

45 With sloping masts and dipping prow,
As who° pursued with yell and blow
Still° treads the shadow of his foe,
And forward bends his head,
The ship drove fast, loud roared the blast,
50 And southward aye° we fled.

46. who: one.
47. still: archaic for "always."

50. aye: archaic for "continually."

And now there came both mist and snow,
And it grew wondrous cold:
And ice, mast-high, came floating by,
As green as emerald.

55 And through the drifts° the snowy cliffs°
Did send a dismal sheen:
Nor shapes of men nor beasts we ken°—
The ice was all between.

The land of ice, and of fearful sounds where no living thing was to be seen.
55. drifts: windblown snow and fog.
cliffs: icebergs.
57. ken: archaic for "saw."

The ice was here, the ice was there,
60 The ice was all around:
It cracked and growled, and roared and howled,
Like noises in a swound!°

62. swound: swoon.

At length did cross an Albatross,
Thorough the fog it came;
65 As if it had been a Christian soul,
We hailed it in God's name.

Till a great seabird, called the Albatross, came through the snow fog, and was received with great joy and hospitality.

It ate the food it ne'er had eat,
And round and round it flew.
The ice did split with a thunder fit;
70 The helmsman steered us through!

And a good south wind sprung up behind;
The Albatross did follow,
And every day, for food or play,
Came to the mariners' hello!

And lo! the Albatross proveth a bird of good omen, and followeth the ship as it returned northward through fog and floating ice.

75 In mist or cloud, on mast or shroud,°
It perched for vespers° nine;
Whiles all the night, through fog-smoke white,
Glimmered the white Moonshine."

75. shroud: support rope that stretches from the top of the mast to the side of the ship.
76. vespers: evenings; also, evening prayers.

"God save thee, ancient Mariner!
80 From the fiends, that plague thee thus!—
Why look'st thou so?"—With my crossbow
I shot the ALBATROSS.

The ancient Mariner inhospitably killeth the pious bird of good omen.

Part II

The Sun now rose upon the right:
Out of the sea came he,
85 Still hid in mist, and on the left
Went down into the sea.

And the good south wind still blew behind,
But no sweet bird did follow,
Nor any day for food or play
90 Came to the mariners' hello!

And I had done a hellish thing,
And it would work 'em woe:
For all averred,° I had killed the bird
That made the breeze to blow.
95 Ah wretch! said they, the bird to slay,
That made the breeze to blow!

His shipmates cry out against the ancient Mariner for killing the bird of good luck.
93. averred (ə·vʉrd'): asserted; claimed.

Nor dim nor red, like God's own head,
The glorious Sun uprist:°
Then all averred, I had killed the bird
100 That brought the fog and mist.
'Twas right, said they, such birds to slay,
That bring the fog and mist.

But when the fog cleared off, they justify the same, and thus make themselves accomplices in the crime.
98. uprist: archaic for "rose."

The fair breeze blew, the white foam flew,
The furrow° followed free;
105 We were the first that ever burst
Into that silent sea.

The fair breeze continues; the ship enters the Pacific Ocean, and sails northward, even till it reaches the Line.
104. furrow: ship's wake.

Down dropt the breeze, the sails dropt down,
'Twas sad as sad could be;
And we did speak only to break
110 The silence of the sea!

The ship hath been suddenly becalmed.

All in a hot and copper sky,
The bloody Sun, at noon,
Right up above the mast did stand,
No bigger than the Moon.

115 Day after day, day after day,
We stuck, nor breath nor motion;
As idle as a painted ship
Upon a painted ocean.

Water, water, everywhere,
120 And all the boards did shrink;
Water, water, everywhere,
Nor any drop to drink.

The very deep did rot: O Christ!
That ever this should be!
125 Yea, slimy things did crawl with legs
Upon the slimy sea.

About, about, in reel and rout°
The death-fires° danced at night;
The water, like a witch's oils,
130 Burnt green, and blue and white.

And some in dreams assured were
Of the Spirit that plagued us so;
Nine fathom deep he had followed us
From the land of mist and snow.

135 And every tongue, through utter drought,
Was withered at the root;
We could not speak, no more than if
We had been choked with soot.

Ah! welladay!° what evil looks
140 Had I from old and young!
Instead of the cross, the Albatross
About my neck was hung.

*And the Albatross begins to
be avenged.*

*A Spirit had followed them; one
of the invisible inhabitants of this
planet, neither departed souls nor
angels; concerning whom the
learned Jew, Josephus, and the
Platonic Constantinopolitan,
Michael Psellus, may be consulted.
They are very numerous, and there
is no climate or element without
one or more.*
127. reel and rout: violent,
whirling movement.
128. death-fires: a firelike,
luminous glow that is said to be
seen over dead bodies.

*The shipmates, in their sore distress,
would fain throw the whole guilt
on the ancient Mariner: in sign
whereof they hang the dead seabird
round his neck.*
139. welladay: archaic for "alas," an
exclamation of sorrow.

Part III

There passed a weary time. Each throat
Was parched, and glazed each eye.
145 A weary time! a weary time!
How glazed each weary eye,
When looking westward, I beheld
A something in the sky.

At first it seemed a little speck,
150 And then it seemed a mist;
It moved and moved, and took at last
A certain shape, I wist.°

A speck, a mist, a shape, I wist!
And still it neared and neared:
155 As if it dodged a water sprite,
It plunged and tacked and veered.°

*The ancient Mariner beholdeth a
sign in the element afar off.*

152. wist: archaic for "knew."

156. tacked and veered: turned
toward and then away from the wind.

With throats unslaked,° with black lips baked,
We could not laugh nor wail;
Through utter drought all dumb we stood!
160 I bit my arm, I sucked the blood,
And cried, A sail! a sail!

With throats unslaked, with black lips baked,
Agape° they heard me call:
Gramercy!° they for joy did grin,
165 And all at once their breath drew in,
As they were drinking all.

See! see! (I cried) she tacks no more!
Hither to work us weal;°
Without a breeze, without a tide,
170 She steadies with upright keel!

The western wave was all aflame.
The day was well-nigh done!
Almost upon the western wave
Rested the broad bright Sun;
175 When that strange shape drove suddenly
Betwixt us and the Sun.

"Through utter drought all dumb
we stood!"

*At its nearer approach, it seemeth
him to be a ship; and at a dear
ransom, he freeth his speech from
the bonds of thirst.*
157. unslaked: unrelieved of thirst.

163. agape: with mouths wide open
in wonder or fear.
A flash of joy.
164. gramercy (grə·mʉr′sē): from
Middle French *grand merci,* an exclamation of great thanks.

*And horror follows. For can it be a
ship that comes onward without
wind or tide?*
168. work us weal: do us good.

And straight the Sun was flecked with bars,
(Heaven's Mother send us grace!)
As if through a dungeon grate he peered
180 With broad and burning face.

Alas! (thought I, and my heart beat loud)
How fast she nears and nears!
Are those *her* sails that glance in the Sun,
Like restless gossameres?°

185 Are those *her* ribs through which the Sun
Did peer, as through a grate?
And is that Woman all her crew?
Is that a DEATH? and are there two?
Is DEATH that woman's mate?

190 *Her* lips were red, *her* looks were free,
Her locks were yellow as gold:
Her skin was as white as leprosy,
The Nightmare LIFE-IN-DEATH was she,
Who thicks man's blood with cold.

195 The naked hulk alongside came,
And the twain were casting dice;
"The game is done! I've won! I've won!"
Quoth she, and whistles thrice.

The Sun's rim dips; the stars rush out:
200 At one stride comes the dark;
With far-heard whisper, o'er the sea,
Off shot the specter bark.°

We listened and looked sideways up!
Fear at my heart, as at a cup,
205 My lifeblood seemed to sip!
The stars were dim, and thick the night,
The steersman's face by his lamp gleamed white;
From the sails the dew did drip—
Till clomb° above the eastern bar
210 The hornèd° Moon, with one bright star
Within the nether tip.°

One after one, by the star-dogged Moon,
Too quick for groan or sigh,
Each turned his face with a ghastly pang,
215 And cursed me with his eye.

Four times fifty living men,
(And I heard nor sigh nor groan)
With heavy thump, a lifeless lump,
They dropped down one by one.

It seemeth him but the skeleton of a ship.

And its ribs are seen as bars on the face of the setting Sun.

184. gossameres: filmy cobwebs.

The Specter Woman and her Death-mate, and no other onboard the skeleton ship.

Like vessel, like crew!

Death and Life-in-Death have diced for the ship's crew, and she (the latter) winneth the ancient Mariner.

No twilight within the courts of the Sun.

202. specter bark: ghost ship.

At the rising of the Moon,

209. clomb (klōm): archaic for "climbed."
210. hornèd: crescent.
210–211. star . . . tip: A star dogging, or following, the moon is believed by sailors to be an evil omen.
One after another,

His shipmates drop down dead.

220 The souls did from their bodies fly,—
They fled to bliss or woe!
And every soul, it passed me by,
Like the whizz of my crossbow!

But Life-in-Death begins her work on the ancient Mariner.

Part IV

"I fear thee, ancient Mariner!
225 I fear thy skinny hand!
And thou art long, and lank, and brown,
As is the ribbed sea sand.

The Wedding Guest feareth that a Spirit is talking to him;

I fear thee and thy glittering eye,
And thy skinny hand, so brown."—
230 Fear not, fear not, thou Wedding Guest!
This body dropt not down.

Alone, alone, all, all alone,
Alone on a wide wide sea!
And never a saint took pity on
235 My soul in agony.

But the ancient Mariner assureth him of his bodily life, and proceedeth to relate his horrible penance.

The many men, so beautiful!
And they all dead did lie:
And a thousand thousand slimy things
Lived on; and so did I.

He despiseth the creatures of the calm,

240 I looked upon the rotting sea,
And drew my eyes away;
I looked upon the rotting deck,
And there the dead men lay.

And envieth that they should live, and so many lie dead.

I looked to heaven, and tried to pray;
245 But or° ever a prayer had gusht,
A wicked whisper came, and made
My heart as dry as dust.

245. or: before.

I closed my lids, and kept them close,
And the balls like pulses beat;
250 For the sky and the sea, and the sea and the sky
Lay like a load on my weary eye,
And the dead were at my feet.

The cold sweat melted from their limbs,
Nor rot nor reek did they:
255 The look with which they looked on me
Had never passed away.

But the curse liveth for him in the eye of the dead men.

An orphan's curse would drag to hell
A spirit from on high;
But oh! more horrible than that
260 Is the curse in a dead man's eye!
Seven days, seven nights, I saw that curse,
And yet I could not die.

The moving Moon went up the sky,
And nowhere did abide:
265 Softly she was going up,
And a star or two beside—

Her beams bemocked the sultry main,°
Like April hoarfrost° spread;
But where the ship's huge shadow lay,
270 The charmèd water burnt alway°
A still and awful red.

267. main: archaic for "open sea."
268. hoarfrost: crystalline deposits
from freezing dew; frost.

270. alway: archaic for "always."

Beyond the shadow of the ship,
I watched the water snakes:
They moved in tracks of shining white,
275 And when they reared, the elfish light
Fell off in hoary° flakes.

*By the light of the Moon he behold-
eth God's creatures of the great
calm.*

276. hoary: white or gray.

Within the shadow of the ship
I watched their rich attire:
Blue, glossy green, and velvet black,
280 They coiled and swam; and every track
Was a flash of golden fire.

O happy living things! no tongue
Their beauty might declare:
A spring of love gushed from my heart,
285 And I blessed them unaware:
Sure my kind saint took pity on me,
And I blessed them unaware.

Their beauty and their happiness.

He blesseth them in his heart.

The selfsame moment I could pray;
And from my neck so free
290 The Albatross fell off, and sank
Like lead into the sea.

The spell begins to break.

Part V

Oh sleep! it is a gentle thing,
Beloved from pole to pole!
To Mary Queen the praise be given!
295 She sent the gentle sleep from Heaven,
That slid into my soul.

The silly° buckets on the deck,
That had so long remained,
I dreamt that they were filled with dew;
300 And when I awoke, it rained.

My lips were wet, my throat was cold,
My garments all were dank;
Sure I had drunken in my dreams,
And still my body drank.

305 I moved, and could not feel my limbs:
I was so light—almost
I thought that I had died in sleep,
And was a blessèd ghost.

And soon I heard a roaring wind:
310 It did not come anear;
But with its sound it shook the sails,
That were so thin and sere.°

The upper air burst into life!
And a hundred fire flags sheen,
315 To and fro they were hurried about!
And to and fro, and in and out,
The wan stars danced between.°

And the coming wind did roar more loud,
And the sails did sigh like sedge;°
320 And the rain poured down from one black cloud;
The Moon was at its edge.

The thick black cloud was cleft,° and still
The Moon was at its side:
Like waters shot from some high crag,
325 The lightning fell with never a jag,
A river steep and wide.

"I dreamt that they were filled with dew;
And when I awoke, it rained."

The loud wind never reached the ship,
Yet now the ship moved on!
Beneath the lightning and the Moon
330 The dead men gave a groan.

They groaned, they stirred, they all uprose,
Nor spake, nor moved their eyes;
It had been strange, even in a dream,
To have seen those dead men rise.

335 The helmsman steered, the ship moved on;
Yet never a breeze up-blew;
The mariners all 'gan work the ropes,
Where they were wont° to do;
They raised their limbs like lifeless tools—
340 We were a ghastly crew.

The body of my brother's son
Stood by me, knee to knee:
The body and I pulled at one rope,
But he said nought to me.

345 "I fear thee, ancient Mariner!"
Be calm, thou Wedding Guest!
'Twas not those souls that fled in pain,
Which to their corses° came again,
But a troop of spirits blest:

350 For when it dawned—they dropt their arms,
And clustered round the mast;
Sweet sounds rose slowly through their mouths,
And from their bodies passed.

Around, around, flew each sweet sound,
355 Then darted to the Sun;
Slowly the sounds came back again,
Now mixed, now one by one.

Sometimes a-dropping from the sky
I heard the skylark sing;
360 Sometimes all little birds that are,
How they seemed to fill the sea and air
With their sweet jargoning!°

And now 'twas like all instruments,
Now like a lonely flute;
365 And now it is an angel's song,
That makes the heavens be mute.

The bodies of the ship's crew are inspired and the ship moves on.

338. **wont** (wänt): accustomed.

But not by the souls of the men, nor by demons of earth or middle air; but by a blessed troop of angelic spirits, sent down by the invocation of the guardian saint.
348. **corses:** archaic for "corpses."

362. **jargoning:** archaic for "twittering."

It ceased; yet still the sails made on
A pleasant noise till noon,
A noise like of a hidden brook
370 In the leafy month of June,
That to the sleeping woods all night
Singeth a quiet tune.

Till noon we quietly sailed on,
Yet never a breeze did breathe:
375 Slowly and smoothly went the ship,
Moved onward from beneath.

Under the keel nine fathom deep,
From the land of mist and snow,
The spirit slid: and it was he
380 That made the ship to go.
The sails at noon left off their tune,
And the ship stood still also.

*The lonesome Spirit from the South
Pole carries on the ship as far as the
Line, in obedience to the angelic
troop, but still requireth vengeance.*

The Sun, right up above the mast,
Had fixed her° to the ocean:
385 But in a minute she 'gan stir,
With a short uneasy motion—
Backwards and forwards half her length
With a short uneasy motion.

384. fixed her: seemed to hold the
ship motionless.

Then like a pawing horse let go,
390 She made a sudden bound:
It flung the blood into my head,
And I fell down in a swound.

How long in that same fit I lay,
I have not to declare;
395 But ere my living life returned,
I heard and in my soul discerned
Two voices in the air.

*The Polar Spirit's fellow demons, the
invisible inhabitants of the element,
take part in his wrong; and two of
them relate, one to the other, that
penance long and heavy for the
ancient Mariner hath been accorded
to the Polar Spirit, who returneth
southward.*

"Is it he?" quoth one, "Is this the man?
By him who died on cross,
400 With his cruel bow he laid full low
The harmless Albatross.

The spirit who bideth by himself
In the land of mist and snow,
He loved the bird that loved the man
405 Who shot him with his bow."

The other was a softer voice,
As soft as honeydew:
Quoth he, "The man hath penance done,
And penance more will do."

Part VI

FIRST VOICE

410 "But tell me, tell me! speak again,
Thy soft response renewing—
What makes that ship drive on so fast?
What is the ocean doing?"

SECOND VOICE

"Still as a slave before his lord,
415 The ocean hath no blast;°
His great bright eye most silently
Up to the Moon is cast—

If he may know which way to go;
For she guides him smooth or grim.
420 See, brother, see! how graciously
She looketh down on him."

FIRST VOICE

"But why drives on that ship so fast,
Without or wave or wind?"°

SECOND VOICE

"The air is cut away before,
425 And closes from behind.

Fly, brother, fly! more high, more high!
Or we shall be belated:
For slow and slow that ship will go,
When the Mariner's trance is abated."°

430 I woke, and we were sailing on
As in a gentle weather:
'Twas night, calm night, the Moon was high;
The dead men stood together.

All stood together on the deck,
435 For a charnel dungeon° fitter:
All fixed on me their stony eyes,
That in the Moon did glitter.

The pang, the curse, with which they died,
Had never passed away:
440 I could not draw my eyes from theirs,
Nor turn them up to pray.

415. blast: wind.

The Mariner hath been cast into a trance; for the angelic power causeth the vessel to drive northward faster than human life could endure.
423. without . . . wind: with neither wave nor wind.

429. abated: lessened.

The supernatural motion is retarded; the Mariner awakes, and his penance begins anew.

435. charnel (chär′nəl) **dungeon:** burial vault.

And now this spell was snapt: once more
I viewed the ocean green,
And looked far forth, yet little saw
445 Of what had else° been seen—

Like one, that on a lonesome road
Doth walk in fear and dread,
And having once turned round walks on,
And turns no more his head;
450 Because he knows, a frightful fiend
Doth close behind him tread.

But soon there breathed a wind on me,
Nor sound nor motion made:
Its path was not upon the sea,
455 In ripple or in shade.

It raised my hair, it fanned my cheek
Like a meadow gale of spring—
It mingled strangely with my fears,
Yet it felt like a welcoming.

460 Swiftly, swiftly flew the ship,
Yet she sailed softly too:
Sweetly, sweetly blew the breeze—
On me alone it blew.

Oh! dream of joy! is this indeed
465 The lighthouse top I see?
Is this the hill? is this the kirk?
Is this mine own countree?

We drifted o'er the harbor bar,
And I with sobs did pray—
470 O let me be awake, my God!
Or let me sleep alway.

The harbor bay was clear as glass,
So smoothly it was strewn!°
And on the bay the moonlight lay,
475 And the shadow of the Moon.

The rock shone bright, the kirk no less,
That stands above the rock:
The moonlight steeped in silentness
The steady weathercock.°

445. had else: would have otherwise.

"And on the bay the moonlight lay,
And the shadow of the Moon."

*And the ancient Mariner beholdeth
his native country.*

473. strewn: stretched out; calmed.

479. weathercock: rooster-shaped
weather vane.

480 And the bay was white with silent light,
Till rising from the same,
Full many shapes, that shadows were,
In crimson colors came.

A little distance from the prow
485 Those crimson shadows were:
I turned my eyes upon the deck—
Oh, Christ! what saw I there!

Each corse lay flat, lifeless and flat,
And, by the holy rood!°
490 A man all light, a seraph man,°
On every corse there stood.

This seraph band, each waved his hand:
It was a heavenly sight!
They stood as signals to the land,
495 Each one a lovely light;

This seraph band, each waved his hand,
No voice did they impart—
No voice; but oh! the silence sank
Like music on my heart.

500 But soon I heard the dash of oars,
I heard the Pilot's cheer;
My head was turned perforce away
And I saw a boat appear.

The Pilot and the Pilot's boy,
505 I heard them coming fast:
Dear Lord in Heaven! it was a joy
The dead men could not blast.

The angelic spirits leave the dead bodies,

And appear in their own forms of light.

489. rood: crucifix.
490. seraph man: angel of the highest rank.

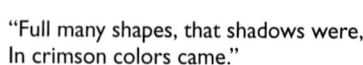

"Full many shapes, that shadows were,
In crimson colors came."

I saw a third—I heard his voice:
It is the Hermit good!
510 He singeth loud his godly hymns
That he makes in the wood.
He'll shrieve° my soul, he'll wash away
The Albatross's blood.

Part VII

This Hermit good lives in that wood
515 Which slopes down to the sea.
How loudly his sweet voice he rears!
He loves to talk with marineres
That come from a far countree.

He kneels at morn, and noon, and eve—
520 He hath a cushion plump:
It is the moss that wholly hides
The rotted old oak stump.

The skiff boat° neared: I heard them talk,
"Why, this is strange, I trow!°
525 Where are those lights so many and fair,
That signal made but now?"

"Strange, by my faith!" the Hermit said—
"And they answered not our cheer!
The planks looked warped! and see those sails,
530 How thin they are and sere!
I never saw aught° like to them,
Unless perchance it were

Brown skeletons of leaves that lag°
My forest brook along;
535 When the ivy tod° is heavy with snow,
And the owlet whoops to the wolf below,
That eats the she-wolf's young."

"Dear Lord! it hath a fiendish look—
(The Pilot made reply)
540 I am afeared"—"Push on, push on!"
Said the Hermit cheerily.

The boat came closer to the ship,
But I nor spake nor stirred;
The boat came close beneath the ship,
545 And straight° a sound was heard.

512. shrieve (shrēv): archaic for "after hearing confession, release from guilt."

The Hermit of the Wood,

523. skiff boat: rowboat.
524. trow: archaic for "believe."

Approacheth the ship with wonder.

531. aught: anything.

533. lag: drift; move more slowly than the current.

535. ivy tod: clump of ivy.

545. straight: straightaway; at once.

Under the water it rumbled on,
Still louder and more dread:
It reached the ship, it split the bay;
The ship went down like lead.

550 Stunned by that loud and dreadful sound,
Which sky and ocean smote,°
Like one that hath been seven days drowned
My body lay afloat;
But swift as dreams, myself I found
555 Within the Pilot's boat.

Upon the whirl, where sank the ship,
The boat spun round and round;
And all was still, save that the hill
Was telling of the sound.

560 I moved my lips—the Pilot shrieked
And fell down in a fit;
The holy Hermit raised his eyes,
And prayed where he did sit.

I took the oars: the Pilot's boy,
565 Who now doth crazy go,
Laughed loud and long, and all the while
His eyes went to and fro.
"Ha! ha!" quoth he, "full plain I see,
The Devil knows how to row."

570 And now, all in my own countree,
I stood on the firm land!
The Hermit stepped forth from the boat,
And scarcely he could stand.

The ship suddenly sinketh.

The ancient Mariner is saved in the Pilot's boat.
551. smote: struck.

"It reached the ship, it split the bay;
The ship went down like lead."

"O shrieve me, shrieve me, holy man!"
575 The Hermit crossed° his brow.
"Say quick," quoth he, "I bid thee say—
What manner of man art thou?"

Forthwith° this frame of mine was wrenched
With a woeful agony,
580 Which forced me to begin my tale;
And then it left me free.

Since then, at an uncertain hour,
That agony returns:
And till my ghastly tale is told,
585 This heart within me burns.

The ancient Mariner earnestly en-treateth the Hermit to shrieve him; and the penance of life falls on him.

575. crossed: made the sign of the cross.

578. forthwith: at once.

And ever and anon throughout his future life an agony constraineth him to travel from land to land;

"Upon the whirl, where sank the ship,
The boat spun round and round."

"'Ha! ha!' quoth he, 'full plain I see,
The Devil knows how to row.'"

I pass, like night, from land to land;
I have strange power of speech;
That moment that his face I see,
I know the man that must hear me:
590 To him my tale I teach.

What loud uproar bursts from that door!
The wedding guests are there:
But in the garden bower the bride
And bridemaids singing are:
595 And hark the little vesper bell,
Which biddeth me to prayer!

O Wedding Guest! this soul hath been
Alone on a wide wide sea:
So lonely 'twas, that God himself
600 Scarce seemed there to be.

O sweeter than the marriage feast,
'Tis sweeter far to me,
To walk together to the kirk
With a goodly company!—

605 To walk together to the kirk,
And all together pray,
While each to his great Father bends,
Old men, and babes, and loving friends
And youths and maidens gay!

610 Farewell, farewell! but this I tell
To thee, thou Wedding Guest!
He prayeth well, who loveth well
Both man and bird and beast.

He prayeth best, who loveth best
615 All things both great and small;
For the dear God who loveth us,
He made and loveth all.

The Mariner, whose eye is bright,
Whose beard with age is hoar,
620 Is gone: and now the Wedding Guest
Turned from the bridegroom's door.

He went like one that hath been stunned,
And is of sense forlorn:°
A sadder and a wiser man,
625 He rose the morrow morn.

"The Mariner, whose eye is bright,
Whose beard with age is hoar,
Is gone."

*And to teach, by his own example,
love and reverence to all things that
God made and loveth.*

623. forlorn: deprived.

Joseph Cottle was a close friend of the poet and the first publisher of *Lyrical Ballads*.

Coleridge Describes His Addiction

To JOSEPH COTTLE

April 26, 1814

You have poured oil in the raw and festering wound of an old friend's conscience, Cottle! but it is *oil of vitriol*! I but barely glanced at the middle of the first page of your letter, and have seen no more of it—not from resentment, God forbid! but from the state of my bodily and mental sufferings, that scarcely permitted human fortitude to let in a new visitor of affliction.

The object of my present reply is to state the case just as it is—first, that for ten years the anguish of my spirit has been indescribable, the sense of my danger staring, but the conscience of my GUILT worse, far worse than all! I have prayed with drops of agony on my brow, trembling not only before the justice of my Maker, but even before the mercy of my Redeemer. "I gave thee so many talents. What hast thou done with them?" Secondly, overwhelmed as I am with the sense of my direful infirmity, I have never attempted to disguise or conceal the cause. On the contrary, not only to friends have I stated the whole case with tears, and the very bitterness of shame; but in two instances, I have warned young men, mere acquaintances, who had spoken of having taken laudanum, of the direful consequences, by an ample exposition of its tremendous effects on myself.

Thirdly, though before God I cannot lift up my eyelids, and only do not despair of his mercy, because to despair would be adding crime to crime, yet to my fellow men I may say, that I was seduced into the ACCURSED habit ignorantly. I had been almost bedridden for many months with swelling in the knees. In a medical journal I unhappily met with an account of a cure performed in a similar case, or what appeared to me so, by rubbing in of laudanum, at the same time taking a given dose internally. It acted like a charm, like a miracle! I recovered the use of my limbs, of my appetite, of my spirits, and this continued for near a fortnight. At length, the unusual stimulus subsided, the complaint returned—the supposed remedy was recurred to—but I cannot go through the dreary history. Suffice it to say, that effects were produced, which acted on me by terror and cowardice of PAIN and sudden death, not (so help me God!) by any temptation of pleasure, or expectation, or desire of exciting pleasurable sensations. On the very contrary, Mrs. Morgan and her sister will bear witness so far, as to say that the longer I abstained, the higher my spirits were, the keener my enjoyments—till the moment, the direful moment arrived, when my pulse began to fluctuate, my heart to palpitate, and such a dreadful falling abroad, as it were, of my whole frame, such intolerable restlessness and incipient bewilderment, that in the last of my several attempts to abandon the dire poison, I exclaimed in agony, what I now repeat in seriousness and solemnity, "I am too poor to hazard this!" Had I but a few hundred pounds, but £200, half to send to Mrs. Coleridge, and half to place myself in a private madhouse, where I could procure nothing but what a physician thought proper, and where a medical attendant could be constantly with me for two or three months (in less than that time, life or death would be determined) then there might be hope. Now there is none! O God! how willing would I place myself under Dr. Fox in his establishment; for my case is a species of madness, only that it is a derangement, an utter impotence of the volition, and not of the intellectual faculties. You bid me rouse myself: go, bid a man paralytic in both arms to rub them briskly together, and that will cure him. "Alas," he would reply, "that I cannot move my arms is my complaint and my misery."

Your affectionate, but most afflicted,

S. T. Coleridge

In this passage from his classic travel book, the writer Bruce Chatwin (1940–1989) tells a chilling story. Before this extract opens, Chatwin has said: "Albatrosses and penguins are the last birds I'd want to murder." He had been describing the penguin colony in Patagonia, on the south coast of Argentina. Now he flashes back to 1593.

from In Patagonia

Bruce Chatwin

On October 30, 1593, the ship *Desire,* of 120 tons, limping home to England, dropped anchor in the river at Port Desire, this being her fourth visit since Thomas Cavendish named the place in her, his flagship's, honor, seven years before.

The captain was now John Davis, a Devon man, the most skilled navigator of his generation. Behind him were three Arctic voyages in search of the Northwest Passage. Before him were two books of seamanship and six fatal cuts of a Japanese pirate's sword.

Davis had sailed on Cavendish's Second Voyage "intended for the South Sea." The fleet left Plymouth on August 26, 1591, the Captain-General in the galleon *Leicester;* the other ships were the *Roebuck,* the *Desire,* the *Daintie,* and the *Black Pinnace.* . . .

Cavendish was puffed up with early success, hating his officers and crew. On the coast of Brazil, he stopped to sack the town of Santos. A gale scattered the ships off the Patagonian coast, but they met up, as arranged, at Port Desire.

The fleet entered the Magellan Strait with the southern winter already begun. A sailor's frostbitten nose fell off when he blew it. Beyond Cape Froward, they ran into northwesterly gales and sheltered in a tight cove with the wind howling over their mastheads. Reluctantly, Cavendish agreed to revictual in Brazil and return the following spring.

On the night of May 20, off Port Desire, the Captain-General changed tack without warning. At dawn, the *Desire* and the *Black Pinnace* were alone on the sea. Davis made for port, thinking his commander would join him as before, but Cavendish set course for Brazil and thence to St. Helena. One day he lay down in his cabin and died, perhaps of apoplexy, cursing Davis for desertion: "This villain that hath been the death of me."

Davis disliked the man but was no traitor. The worst of the winter over, he went south again to look for the Captain-General. Gales blew the two ships in among some undiscovered islands, now known as the Falklands.

This time, they passed the Strait and out into the Pacific. In a storm off Cape Pilar, the *Desire* lost the *Pinnace,* which went down with all hands. Davis was alone at the helm, praying for a speedy end, when the sun broke through the clouds. He took bearings, fixed his position, and so regained the calmer water of the Strait.

He sailed back to Port Desire, the crew scurvied and mutinous and lice lying in their flesh, "clusters of lice as big as peason, yea, and some as big as beans." He repaired the ship as best he could. The men lived off eggs, gulls, baby seals, scurvy grass, and the fish called *pejerrey.* On this diet they were restored to health.

Ten miles down the coast, there was an island, the original Penguin Island, where the sailors clubbed twenty thousand birds to death. They had no natural enemies and were unafraid of their murderers. John Davis ordered the penguins dried and salted and stowed fourteen thousand in the hold. . . .

As they came up to the Equator, the penguins took their revenge. In them bred a "loathsome worme" about an inch long. The worms ate everything, iron only excepted—clothes, bedding, boots, hats, leather lashings, and live human flesh. The worms gnawed through the ship's side and threatened to sink her. The more worms the men killed, the more they multiplied.

Around the Tropic of Cancer, the crew came down with scurvy. Their ankles swelled and their chests, and their parts swelled so horribly that "they could neither stand nor lie nor go."

The Captain could scarcely speak for sorrow. Again he prayed for a speedy end. He asked the men to be patient; to give thanks to God and accept his chastisement. But the men were raging mad, and the ship howled with the groans and curses of the dying. Only Davis and a ship's boy were in health, of the seventy-six who left Plymouth. By the end there were five men who could move and work the ship.

And so, lost and wandering on the sea, with topsails and spritsails torn, the rotten hulk drifted, rather than sailed, into the harbor of Berehaven on Bantry Bay on June 11, 1593. The smell disgusted the people of that quiet fishing village. . . .

"The Southern Voyage of John Davis" appeared in Hakluyt's edition of 1600. Two centuries passed and another Devon man, Samuel Taylor Coleridge, set down the 625 controversial lines of *The Ancient Mariner,* with its hammering repetitions and story of crime, wandering, and expiation.

John Davis and the Mariner have these in common: a voyage to the Black South, the murder of a bird or birds, the nemesis which follows, the drift through the tropics, the rotting ship, the curses of dying men. Lines 236–239 are particularly resonant of the Elizabethan voyage:

The many men, so beautiful!
And they all dead did lie:
And a thousand thousand slimy things
Lived on; and so did I.

In *The Road to Xanadu,* the American scholar John Livingston Lowes traced the Mariner's victim to a "disconsolate Black Albitross" shot by one Hatley, the mate of Captain George Shelvocke's privateer in the eighteenth century. Wordsworth had a copy of this voyage and showed it to Coleridge when the two men tried to write the poem together. . . .

Lowes demonstrated how the voyages in Hakluyt and Purchas fueled Coleridge's imagination. "The mighty great roaring of ice" that John Davis witnessed on an earlier voyage off Greenland reappears in line 61: "It cracked and growled, and roared and howled." But he did not, apparently, consider the likelihood that Davis's voyage to the Strait gave Coleridge the backbone for his poem.

Engraving (1875) by Gustave Doré for Coleridge's *The Rime of the Ancient Mariner.*

MAKING MEANINGS

First Thoughts

1. Do you think that this poem tells us something significant about human conduct? Why or why not? If so, would it apply to most people?

Shaping Interpretations

2. Where in the poem is the wedding mentioned? How does this context for the ballad affect your response to it?

3. Describe in detail the changing states of the Mariner in Part IV. Given the circumstances, are these changes believable?

4. After he shoots the albatross, the Mariner experiences both shame and guilt. What is the difference between these two emotions? Where in the poem does he experience each emotion?

5. What is the Mariner's "penance" (line 408)? What penance does he have left to do? Does it seem fair to you that he should have to do any sort of penance? Why? (Refer to your Quickwrite notes for ideas.)

Reading Check

a. Who is presented as the **narrator** of the ballad? To whom is he telling his story? In a **time line,** summarize the main events of the Mariner's story.

b. According to Part II, what consequences follow the Mariner's killing of the albatross?

c. Who are the occupants of the strange ship that appears in Part III? What results from their appearance?

d. In Part IV, why is the Mariner unable to pray? What happens that enables him to pray?

e. At the end of the ballad, how does the Mariner describe his current life? What lesson does he draw for the Wedding Guest from this tale?

---

6. Explain in your own terms the Mariner's **moral** (lines 612–617). Does the story indicate that he ought to have added something to his moral conclusion? Explain.

7. Why is the Wedding Guest sadder but wiser after hearing the Mariner's tale? What other figures in Coleridge's poems in this collection are also listening to a speaker?

8. What do you think of Coleridge's side notes to the poem? Do you think reading them alters the meaning of the poem? Should they be consulted in a careful reading of the poem? Why or why not?

9. This ballad is famous for its use of vivid **figurative language** and memorable sound devices. What do you think are several especially effective examples of **simile, metaphor, personification, alliteration, assonance,** and **internal rhyme**?

10. For the most part, the form of the poem is the regular **ballad stanza.** Occasionally, however, Coleridge varies the **meter** of the lines and the length of the stanzas. Read aloud several examples of such variations.

11. What differences do you notice between Coleridge's tale of the Ancient Mariner and the story described in Bruce Chatwin's *In Patagonia*? (See *Connections* on page 704.)

Extending the Text

12. There was a time in American history when almost every schoolchild could recite parts of *The Rime of the Ancient Mariner*. Find some stanzas that strike you as particularly quotable. What situations in contemporary life could you apply the lines to?

Challenging the Text

13. Coleridge once said that he would have preferred to write *The Rime of the Ancient Mariner* as a work of "pure imagination." He believed that it had "too much" of a moral, and that the moral was stated too openly. Do you agree or disagree with Coleridge about the message in his poem? Why?

READING SKILLS AND STRATEGIES

Reading Archaic Words

To give his ballad an antique flavor, Coleridge used many words that were **archaic,** or out of date, even at the time of his writing.

1. Here is a list of some of the archaic words in the poem. Note what each one means, and then substitute a modern **synonym** in the poem for each one. How does the flavor of the ballad change?

   a. *eftsoons* (line 12)

   b. *uprist* (line 98)

   c. *wist* (line 152)

   d. *Gramercy* (line 164)

   e. *clomb* (line 209)

   f. *wont* (line 338)

   g. *corses* (line 348)

   h. *rood* (line 489)

   i. *shrieve* (line 512)

   j. *trow* (line 524)

2. Are any forms of those words still in use today? Which ones?

3. Sometimes the archaic meaning of a word gives us a clue to the history of a word in current use. Look at the use of the word *jargoning* in line 362. What does the word *jargon* mean today? How is contemporary jargon like a bird twittering? (Check the etymology of the word in a dictionary.)

"With my crossbow / I shot the ALBATROSS."

CHOICES: Building Your Portfolio

Writer's Notebook

1. Collecting Ideas for a Research Paper

The writer Bruce Chatwin did research to see if a real incident might have been the source of Coleridge's story of crime and punishment. (See *Connections* on page 704.) Chatwin's article or Coleridge's ballad might have raised some interesting questions in your mind that could be the subject of a research paper. Review the poem and the article, and jot down topics that you would like to know more about. You might start with expeditions to Patagonia or with John Davis's expedition of 1593. Save your notes.

WORK IN PROGRESS

Analyzing a Theme

2. Imagination Probing

There is general agreement that one of the major themes of "Kubla Khan" concerns the power of imagination. In a brief essay, analyze how Coleridge develops this theme in the poem. What symbolic hints does he provide about the powers, dangers, and limits of the human imagination? At the end of your essay, explain your own views of Coleridge's theme.

Analyzing the Melodies of Language

3. Sound and Sense

Listen to "The Rime of the Ancient Mariner" on an audiotape, or read it aloud yourself. Take notes on the sound effects: **meter, rhyme, alliteration,** and **assonance.** In an essay, analyze the effects of sound on the meaning of the poem. How does Coleridge use sound effects to create a mood and to evoke feelings? Cite specific lines from the poem to illustrate your points.

Analyzing the Plot

4. Asking Why

Like the old ballads, this strange story of the Ancient Mariner leaves some questions unanswered. For example, how could the Mariner tell that the Wedding Guest was a fit audience for this tale? Why did the Mariner shoot the albatross? How can the Mariner's punishment be regarded as fitting his crime? In a brief essay, analyze these or other questions that you think are unsatisfactorily resolved by the ballad.

Interpreting Symbolism

5. A Symbolizing Tale

An **allegory** is a prose or verse tale in which the characters, actions, and settings are **symbolic;** that is, they have both a literal and a figurative meaning. Could Coleridge's ballad be regarded as an allegory? If so, what do the various elements in the ballad symbolize? How may the tale as a whole be interpreted on an allegorical level? In a brief essay, explain your answers.

Creative Writing

6. Finishing Out the Khan

Suppose that we take Coleridge at his word and assume that "Kubla Khan" is really an unfinished fragment. Basing your idea on the existing lines, write a summary in prose of how the poem might be completed. Specify what you imagine the story line might be.

Creative Writing

7. Finding Peace

The Ancient Mariner has much in common with other legendary figures, such as the Flying Dutchman, who are condemned to wander the world in a quest for atonement or redemption. Imagine that the Mariner ultimately finds peace. Describe in a brief narrative how this might occur.

Art

8. Dreaming, Drawing, Remembering

Suppose that Coleridge kept a dream journal, and that he drew pictures in it to remind him of what he had seen in the dream that resulted in "Kubla Khan." Sketch three or four drawings that he might have used to help him recall the images he saw in his dream.

THE QUEST FOR BEAUTY

Byron   Keats

Shelley   Li Po

Tu Fu

**A thing of beauty is a joy forever:
Its loveliness increases; it will never
Pass into nothingness.
—John Keats,** *from Endymion*

Night (detail) (late
19th or early 20th
century) by Edward
Robert Hughes.

Before You Read

THE DESTRUCTION OF SENNACHERIB

Make the Connection

Old Tales of Miracles

The Romantics loved old stories, old ballads, tales of heroism and fantasy—like this Biblical story of the miraculous deliverance of the Israelites from the Assyrian army. Watch for the images that romanticize the conflict—that glorify the victor and demonize the enemy. Can you think of ways in which people demonize their enemies today?

Reading Skills and Strategies

Dialogue with the Text

Be sure to read this poem aloud. After the first stanza, jot down a few notes about the picture Byron is creating. Then, as you continue to read, make notes on how the picture changes.

Elements of Literature

Anapestic Rhythm

Byron skillfully uses the bouncy **anapestic rhythm** (ˇ ˇ ´), which was quite popular in the nineteenth century but has seldom been used by serious poets since.

Background

In both Kings and Chronicles, the Bible tells the story of the attempt of the Assyrian king Sennacherib (sə·nak′ər·ib) to capture and enslave Jerusalem. With his mighty army about to descend on the city, "the Angel of Death"—in the form of a sudden pestilence or plague—killed man and beast alike, yet spared the king. In the Biblical account, Sennacherib's failure so disgraced "Ashur" (Assyria) that his own sons murdered him on his return. This poem and "She Walks in Beauty" are from a collection called *Hebrew Melodies,* lyrics that were to be set to music.

Cavalryman Fording a Stream.
Fragment of a wall relief (8th–7th century B.C.) from the palace of Sennacherib at Nineveh, Assyria.

The Metropolitan Museum of Art, New York. Gift of John D. Rockefeller, Jr., 1932. Photograph ©1981 The Metropolitan Museum of Art.

The Destruction of Sennacherib

George Gordon, Lord Byron

The Assyrian came down like the wolf on the fold,
And his cohorts were gleaming in purple and gold;
And the sheen of their spears was like stars on the sea,
When the blue wave rolls nightly on deep Galilee.°

5 Like the leaves of the forest when summer is green,
That host° with their banners at sunset were seen:
Like the leaves of the forest when autumn hath blown,
That host on the morrow lay withered and strown.

For the Angel of Death spread his wings on the blast,
10 And breathed in the face of the foe as he passed;
And the eyes of the sleepers waxed deadly and chill,
And their hearts but once heaved, and forever grew still!

And there lay the steed with his nostril all wide,
But through it there rolled not the breath of his pride;
15 And the foam of his gasping lay white on the turf,
And cold as the spray of the rock-beating surf.

And there lay the rider distorted and pale,
With the dew on his brow, and the rust on his mail:°
And the tents were all silent, the banners alone,
20 The lances unlifted, the trumpet unblown.

And the widows of Ashur are loud in their wail,
And the idols are broke in the temple of Baal;°
And the might of the Gentile,° unsmote° by the sword,
Hath melted like snow in the glance of the Lord!

4. Galilee: Sea of Galilee, a lake north of Jerusalem.

6. host: the army; also, a great number.

18. mail: kind of body armor made of linked metal rings.

22. Baal (bā′əl): the Assyrian god.
23. Gentile: Sennacherib and the Assyrians (non-Israelites).
unsmote: not destroyed.

MAKING MEANINGS

First Thoughts

1. What do you think killed the Assyrians?

Shaping Interpretations

2. What are the Assyrians doing in the first stanza, and what has happened in the second? What **similes** describe the changing scenes? (Look at your reading notes for ideas.)

3. How is death **personified** in stanza 3?

4. What **images** and **similes** in the last three stanzas help you see the aftermath of the defeat?

5. Read aloud to hear the poem's **meter.** How does it help reinforce the poem's action? How do you think this meter would suit a modern battle poem?

6. Who is the hero of this battle?

Challenging the Text

7. Do you think Byron demonizes the Assyrians in this poem? Explain.

8. Read the poem aloud again and listen to the **couplets.** How do you feel about Byron's use of rhyme?

Before You Read

FROM DON JUAN

Make the Connection

Chasing a Dream

The legendary Don Juan (in Spanish, hwän) is a notorious seducer of women, the greatest lover in history, a man whose passion for women drove him from one affair to another—with narrow escapes in between. But Byron's Don Juan (jōō′ən) is different from other versions. His hero is an innocent who becomes involved in many amorous adventures simply because he is, like Byron, so handsome and irresistible. However, the narrator (also like Byron) is not innocent, and that makes for lively satire. As women chase the innocent beauty of Don Juan around the world, the narrator shows us another fruitless quest: for pure beauty and love in a hypocritical world.

Reading Skills and Strategies

Dialogue with the Text

Some things in this excerpt are sure to catch you off guard. Label a column in your notebook "Surprises." Every time Byron or his lively speaker catches you with something unexpected—a joke, a change of tone, a funny rhyme, an odd detail, a "modern" idea—make a quick note, with line numbers.

Elements of Literature

Ottava Rima

The eight-line stanza form of *Don Juan* is based on the Italian ottava rima (ō·tä′və rē′mə). While Byron adheres strictly to the demands of the form, his **tone** is loosely conversational, colloquial, and continually punctuated by digressions. One of the poem's charms is that it moves at a pace appropriate to the narrator's quick shifts of attention. He is confident that the reader will stay with him when, every now and then, he slows down and dawdles over something he sees from the corner of his eye.

> **O**ttava rima, in its English form, is eight lines of iambic pentameter, rhyming *abababcc*.
>
> *For more on Ottava Rima, see the Handbook of Literary Terms.*

Background

Don Juan is the longest satirical poem in English literature. Left unfinished at Byron's death, it comprises sixteen long divisions (cantos) and part of a seventeenth. The form the poem would take came to Byron late in his comparatively brief life. But once Byron mastered it, he found it accommodated everything he wanted to say about the world he knew. The result was a poem of enormous popularity and scandalous interest, since Byron's own erotic exploits lay behind it. In contrast with the solemn lyricism of his contemporaries, Byron hearkened back to poets like Alexander Pope, with their penchant for wit as both social grace and weapon against folly. This extract comes from the early part of *Don Juan,* where the hero finds himself shipwrecked on a Greek island. Haidee, the daughter of a pirate, falls in love with Don Juan. To enjoy the fun, read the poem aloud.

Sunset on the Yorkshire Coast (c. 1885) by Richard Weatherill.

Chris Beetles Ltd., London.

from Don Juan, Canto II

George Gordon, Lord Byron

It was a wild and breaker-beaten coast,
    With cliffs above, and a broad sandy shore,
Guarded by shoals and rocks as by an host,°
    With here and there a creek, whose aspect wore
5 A better welcome to the tempest tost;°
    And rarely ceased the haughty billow's roar,
Save on the dead long summer days, which make
The outstretched ocean glitter like a lake.

· · · · · · · · · · · · · · · ·

The coast—I think it was the coast that I
10   Was just describing—Yes, it *was* the coast—
Lay at this period quiet as the sky,
    The sands untumbled, the blue waves untost,
And all was stillness, save the seabird's cry,
    And dolphin's leap, and little billow crost
15 By some low rock or shelf, that made it fret
Against the boundary it scarcely wet.

And forth they° wandered, her sire being gone,
    As I have said, upon an expedition;
And mother, brother, guardian, she had none,
20   Save Zoe, who, although with due precision
She waited on her lady with the sun,
    Thought daily service was her only mission,
Bringing warm water, wreathing her long tresses,
And asking now and then for castoff dresses.

25 It was the cooling hour, just when the rounded
    Red sun sinks down behind the azure° hill,
Which then seems as if the whole earth it bounded,
    Circling all nature, hushed, and dim, and still,
With the far mountain crescent half surrounded
30   On one side, and the deep sea calm and chill
Upon the other, and the rosy sky,
With one star sparkling through it like an eye.

And thus they wandered forth, and hand in hand,
    Over the shining pebbles and the shells,
35 Glided along the smooth and hardened sand,
    And in the worn and wild receptacles
Worked by the storms, yet worked as it were planned,
    In hollow halls, with sparry° roofs and cells,
They turned to rest; and, each clasped by an arm,
40 Yielded to the deep twilight's purple charm.

3. host: army.

5. tempest tost: storm tossed.

17. they: Haidee and Don Juan.

26. azure: sky-blue.

38. sparry: made of shiny rock.

They looked up to the sky, whose floating glow
    Spread like a rosy ocean, vast and bright;
They gazed upon the glittering sea below,
    Whence the broad moon rose circling into sight;
45 They heard the wave's splash, and the wind so low,
    And saw each other's dark eyes darting light
Into each other—and, beholding this,
Their lips drew near, and clung into a kiss;

A long, long kiss, a kiss of youth and love,
50   And beauty, all concentrating like rays
Into one focus, kindled from above;
    Such kisses as belong to early days,
Where heart, and soul, and sense, in concert° move,   **53. in concert:** together.
    And the blood's lava, and the pulse a blaze,
55 Each kiss a heart quake—for a kiss's strength,
I think, it must be reckoned by its length.

By length I mean duration; theirs endured
    Heaven knows how long—no doubt they never reckoned;
And if they had, they could not have secured
60   The sum of their sensations to a second:
They had not spoken; but they felt allured,
    As if their souls and lips each other beckoned,
Which, being joined, like swarming bees they clung—
Their hearts the flowers from whence the honey sprung.

65 They were alone, but not alone as they
    Who shut in chambers think it loneliness;
The silent ocean, and the starlight bay,
    The twilight glow, which momently° grew less,   **68. momently:** at each moment.
The voiceless sands, and dropping° caves, that lay   **69. dropping:** dripping.
70   Around them, made them to each other press,
As if there were no life beneath the sky
Save theirs, and that their life could never die.

They feared no eyes nor ears on that lone beach,
    They felt no terrors from the night, they were
75 All in all to each other: Though their speech
    Was broken words, they *thought* a language there—
And all the burning tongues the passions teach
    Found in one sigh the best interpreter
Of nature's oracle°—first love—that all   **79. oracle:** revelation.
80 Which Eve has left her daughters since her fall.

Haidee spoke not of scruples, asked no vows,
    Nor offered any; she had never heard
Of plight° and promises to be a spouse,   **83. plight:** promise of marriage.
    Or perils by a loving maid incurred;
85 She was all which pure ignorance allows,
    And flew to her young mate like a young bird;
And, never having dreamt of falsehood, she
Had not one word to say of constancy.

Night and Sleep (1888)
by Simeon Solomon.
Pencil and chalk (349 mm × 286 mm).

Birmingham Museums & Art Gallery,
Birmingham, England.

She loved, and was beloved—she adored,
90   And she was worshipped; after nature's fashion,
Their intense souls, into each other poured,
    If souls could die, had perished in that passion,—
But by degrees their senses were restored,
    Again to be o'ercome, again to dash on;
95 And, beating 'gainst *his* bosom, Haidee's heart
Felt as if never more to beat apart.

Alas! they were so young, so beautiful,
    So lonely, loving, helpless, and the hour
Was that in which the heart is always full,
100   And, having o'er itself no further power,
Prompts deeds eternity can not annul,°
    But pays off moments in an endless shower
Of hellfire—all prepared for people giving
Pleasure or pain to one another living.

105 Alas! for Juan and Haidee! they were
    So loving and so lovely—till then never,
Excepting our first parents, such a pair
    Had run the risk of being damned forever;
And Haidee, being devout as well as fair,

101. annul: cancel.

110   Had, doubtless, heard about the Stygian river,°
And hell and purgatory—but forgot
Just in the very crisis she should not.

. . . .

And when those deep and burning moments passed,
    And Juan sunk to sleep within her arms,
115 She slept not, but all tenderly, though fast,°
    Sustained his head upon her bosom's charms;
And now and then her eye to heaven is cast,
    And then on the pale cheek her breast now warms,
Pillowed on her o'erflowing heart, which pants
120 With all it granted, and with all it grants.

An infant when it gazes on a light,
    A child the moment when it drains the breast,
A devotee when soars the Host° in sight,
    An Arab with a stranger for a guest,
125 A sailor when the prize has struck in fight,°
    A miser filling his most hoarded chest,
Feel rapture; but not such true joy are reaping
As they who watch o'er what they love while sleeping.

110. Stygian river: the river Styx. In Greek mythology, the Styx encircles Hades (hā′dēz′), the underworld.

115. fast: firmly.

123. Host: the Eucharistic wafer that is lifted up during the Anglican or Catholic Mass. Devout church members believe it is the Body of Christ.
125. prize . . . fight: captured enemy ship that has lowered its flag in surrender.

Miranda (1878)
by Sir Frank Dicksee.
The Maas Gallery, London.

For there it lies so tranquil, so beloved,
130   All that it hath of life with us is living;
So gentle, stirless, helpless, and unmoved,
    And all unconscious of the joy 'tis giving;
All it hath felt, inflicted, passed, and proved,
    Hushed into depths beyond the watcher's diving;
135 There lies the thing we love with all its errors
And all its charms, like death without its terrors.

The lady watched her lover—and that hour
    Of Love's, and Night's, and Ocean's solitude,
O'erflowed her soul with their united power;
140   Amidst the barren sand and rocks so rude°
She and her wave-worn love had made their bower,°
    Where nought upon their passion could intrude,
And all the stars that crowded the blue space
Saw nothing happier than her glowing face.

145 Alas! the love of women! it is known
    To be a lovely and a fearful thing;
For all of theirs upon that die° is thrown,
    And if 'tis lost, life hath no more to bring
To them but mockeries of the past alone,
150   And their revenge is as the tiger's spring,
Deadly, and quick, and crushing; yet, as real
Torture is theirs, what they inflict they feel.

They are right; for man, to man so oft unjust,
    Is always so to women; one sole bond
155 Awaits them, treachery is all their trust;°
    Taught to conceal, their bursting hearts despond°
Over their idol, till some wealthier lust
    Buys them in marriage—and what rests beyond?
A thankless husband, next a faithless lover,
160 Then dressing, nursing, praying, and all's over.

Some take a lover, some take drams° or prayers,
    Some mind their household, others dissipation,°
Some run away, and but exchange their cares,
    Losing the advantage of a virtuous station;
165 Few changes e'er can better their affairs,
    Theirs being an unnatural situation,
From the dull palace to the dirty hovel:°
Some play the devil, and then write a novel.

Haidee was Nature's bride, and knew not this;
170   Haidee was Passion's child, born where the sun
Showers triple light, and scorches even the kiss
    Of his gazelle-eyed daughters; she was one
Made but to love, to feel that she was his
    Who was her chosen: What was said or done
175 Elsewhere was nothing—She had nought to fear,
Hope, care, nor love beyond, her heart beat *here.*

140. rude: rough.
141. bower: rustic dwelling place.

147. die: one of a pair of dice.

155. treachery . . . trust: Treachery is the only thing women can count on getting from men.
156. despond: despair.

161. drams: shots of liquor.
162. dissipation: riotous, wild living.

167. hovel: open shed or hut; miserable dwelling.

And oh! that quickening of the heart, that beat!
How much it costs us! yet each rising throb
Is in its cause as its effect so sweet,
180　That Wisdom, ever on the watch to rob
Joy of its alchemy,° and to repeat
Fine truths, even Conscience, too, has a tough job
To make us understand each good old maxim,
So good—I wonder Castlereagh° don't tax 'em.

185　And now 'twas done—on the lone shore were plighted
Their hearts; the stars, their nuptial torches, shed
Beauty upon the beautiful they lighted:
Ocean their witness, and the cave their bed,
By their own feelings hallowed° and united,
190　Their priest was Solitude, and they were wed:
And they were happy, for to their young eyes
Each was an angel, and earth paradise.

181. alchemy (al′kə·mē): chemistry (here, miraculous power to change things).

184. Castlereagh: British foreign secretary from 1812 to 1822, much disliked by radicals, including Byron and Shelley.

189. hallowed: made holy.

MAKING MEANINGS

First Thoughts

1. Though Byron insisted it was a moral poem, *Don Juan* was the focus of scandalous interest when it was published. How would readers today respond to the supposed "scandalous" passages?

Shaping Interpretations

2. What do you think the speaker

Reading Check

a. What is the **setting**?
b. Who is Haidee's only companion (besides Don Juan), and why?
c. In what ways is Haidee, lines 81–88, described as totally innocent? Why doesn't she ask her lover for a vow of constancy?
d. According to lines 145–168, what do women do when they lose love? Why?
e. Describe the nuptials that Haidee and Juan celebrate in lines 185–190.

means by linking Haidee with "pure ignorance" (line 85)?

3. In what way could this story be analogous to the story of Adam and Eve (page 416)? Where does Byron suggest the association directly?

4. Find at least three exaggerated **figures of speech,** and discuss Byron's intended effects.

5. Where does Byron use the final couplet in the **ottava rima** for comic effect?

6. What is the speaker's **tone** when he describes Don Juan and Haidee falling in love?

7. If *Don Juan* is in part witty **satire,** who or what are Byron's targets? Where do you find some barbs directed at the whole Romantic tradition, as exemplified by Wordsworth and Coleridge?

Connecting with the Text

8. Discuss your reading notes in class. What was your favorite or biggest "surprise" in the poem?

9. What do you think of Byron's attitude toward women?

Make the Connection

The Journey Out—and In

A quest may have a goal, but if the journey is long enough, the traveler may discover that in the quest itself lies the prize. What is explored, all alone on a journey, is the lonely self. That may be true even when the pilgrim, like Byron's Childe Harold, cuts a spirited path through exotic lands. And it is especially true when the pilgrim is alone in vast, glorious, but heartless nature.

Quickwrite

Briefly freewrite about your strongest memory or mental image of the ocean. How do you feel about the sea?

Background

This long poem—which made Byron suddenly famous—appeared in sections (cantos) from 1812 to 1818. It is a thinly disguised autobiographical account of Byron's own journeys. Its pilgrim, Childe Harold, became the prototype for the moody, dashingly handsome character type who would eventually be dubbed the "Byronic hero." (In medieval times, *child* likely meant a young noble awaiting knighthood; Byron uses it as a title, like Lord or Sir, for a youth of "gentle" birth.) In this excerpt from the final canto, the speaker addresses the ocean. The last two verses are Byron's personal conclusion to the whole poem. By this time, Byron said, he had ceased trying to separate himself from the figure of Childe Harold.

The Wanderer over the Sea of Clouds (1818) by Caspar David Friedrich.

Hamburger Kunsthalle, Hamburg, Germany.

from Childe Harold's Pilgrimage, Canto IV

George Gordon, Lord Byron

1

There is a pleasure in the pathless woods,
There is a rapture on the lonely shore,
There is society, where none intrudes,
By the deep sea, and music in its roar:
5   I love not man the less, but Nature more,
From these our interviews, in which I steal°
From all I may be, or have been before,
To mingle with the Universe, and feel
What I can ne'er express, yet cannot all conceal.

6. steal: remove myself.

2

10   Roll on, thou deep and dark blue Ocean—roll!
Ten thousand fleets sweep over thee in vain;
Man marks the earth with ruin—his control
Stops with the shore; upon the watery plain
The wrecks are all thy deed, nor doth remain
15   A shadow of man's ravage, save his own,
When, for a moment, like a drop of rain,
He sinks into thy depths with bubbling groan,
Without a grave, unknelled,° uncoffined, and unknown.

18. unknelled (un·neld′): without the traditional ringing of a church bell to announce his death.

3

And I have loved thee, Ocean! and my joy
20   Of youthful sports was on thy breast to be
Borne, like thy bubbles, onward: From a boy
I wantoned° with thy breakers—they to me
Were a delight; and if the freshening° sea
Made them a terror—'twas a pleasing fear,
25   For I was as it were a child of thee,
And trusted to thy billows far and near,
And laid my hand upon thy mane—as I do here.

22. wantoned: frolicked; played happily.
23. freshening: becoming rough as the wind comes up.

4

My task is done, my song hath ceased, my theme
Has died into an echo; it is fit
30   The spell should break of this protracted dream.
The torch shall be extinguished which hath lit
My midnight lamp—and what is writ, is writ;
Would it were worthier! but I am not now

That which I have been—and my visions flit
35 Less palpably° before me—and the glow
Which in my spirit dwelt is fluttering, faint, and low.

35. palpably: clearly.

5

Farewell! a word that must be, and hath been—
A sound which makes us linger;—yet—farewell!
Ye! who have traced the Pilgrim to the scene
40 Which is his last, if in your memories dwell
A thought which once was his, if on ye swell
A single recollection, not in vain
He wore his sandal shoon and scallop shell;°
Farewell! with *him* alone may rest the pain,
45 If such there were—with *you,* the moral of his strain.°

43. sandal shoon . . . shell: *Shoon* is archaic for "shoes." Sandals and a scallop shell worn on a hat were traditional emblems of pilgrims. The scallop shell is a symbol of St. James, whose shrine in Spain was a great attraction to pilgrims.
45. strain: passage of poetry or song.

Wreckers off the Brittany Coast (1911) by Georges P. C. Maroniez.
Bonhams, London.

The poet John Keats had died of tuberculosis in Rome on February 23, 1821. Here is Byron's rather self-centered response to the news. (He thinks bad critical reviews hastened Keats's death.) The child mentioned in the first sentence is Allegra, the daughter Byron had with Claire Clairmont, Mary Shelley's stepsister. Allegra would not live long.

Byron Writes to Shelley

Ravenna, April 26, 1821

The child continues doing well, and the accounts are regular and favorable. It is gratifying to me that you and Mrs. Shelley do not disapprove of the step which I have taken, which is merely temporary.

I am very sorry to hear what you say of Keats—is it *actually* true? I did not think criticism had been so killing. Though I differ from you essentially in your estimate of his performances, I so much abhor all unnecessary pain, that I would rather he had been seated on the highest peak of Parnassus than have perished in such a manner. Poor fellow! though with such inordinate self-love he would probably have not been very happy. I read the review of *Endymion* in the *Quarterly.* It was severe— but surely not so severe as many reviews in that and other journals upon others.

. . . I have published a pamphlet on the Pope controversy, which you will not like. Had I known Keats was dead—or that he was alive and so sensitive—I should have omitted some remarks upon his poetry, to which I was provoked by his *attack* upon *Pope,* and my disapprobation of *his own* style of writing.

You want me to undertake a great poem—I have not the inclination nor the power. As I grow older, the indifference—*not* to life, for we love it by instinct—but to stimuli of life, increases. Besides, this late failure of the Italians has latterly disappointed me for many reasons—some public, some personal. My respects to Mrs. S.

Yours ever,
B.

P. S.—Could not you and I contrive to meet this summer? Could not you take a run here *alone*?

Byron Among the Ancient Ruins (early 19th century). Steel engraving.

The Granger Collection, New York.

MAKING MEANINGS

First Thoughts

1. Think about your Quickwrite notes. How do your memories and feelings about the sea compare with the speaker's?

Shaping Interpretations

2. In stanza 2, what does the speaker say man does to earth? What can man do to the sea—or the sea do to him?

3. In stanza 3, what **figure of speech** describes the sea as a horse?

4. What single aspect of the ocean does the speaker repeatedly emphasize?

5. In spite of the ocean's destructive aspects, the speaker professes that he loves it passionately. What does this tell you about his personality?

6. What link does the speaker imply between the pilgrim and himself in the final two stanzas?

7. From this brief excerpt, what would you guess the pilgrim was searching for?

Extending the Text

8. How can the fierce identification and rapture experienced by this speaker in the presence of nature be felt today? Which of the poem's lines strike you as being particularly **ironic,** from the vantage point of this century? Why?

CHOICES: Building Your Portfolio

Writer's Notebook

1. Collecting Ideas for a Research Paper

Byron's visit to the Shelleys in Switzerland resulted in a famous novel, *Frankenstein,* written by Shelley's young wife. Several topics for research might be found in the life of Mary Wollstonecraft Shelley (see page 728). Byron's letter about Keats's death might also inspire research (see page 724). Research begins with questions. What questions are raised by the information on Mary Shelley or by Byron's letter? Save your notes for the Writer's Workshop on page 773.

Another Point of View

2. Answering Byron

Write a response to one of Byron's poems from another point of view. You might speak as the dark beauty, the Assyrian, Haidee, or even the ocean. Try to answer in rhyme.

Comparing Poems

3. Wit Across Centuries

In an essay, compare Byron's *Don Juan* and Alexander Pope's *The Rape of the Lock* (page 527). Consider each work's narrative and at least two of these elements: **verse form, tone, satirical targets,** and use of **irony.**

Analyzing Verse Form

4. From Spenser to Byron

Byron's verse form in *Childe Harold's Pilgrimage* is the **Spenserian stanza** (page 221). Describe the technical requirements of the form, and discuss how Byron uses it.

Creative Writing

5. Don Juan Lives On

Using Byron's hints in the selection, write a brief sequel, in poetry or prose, about Don Juan and Haidee's future. How will he treat her, and she him? You might also include some satirical jabs at popular romance novels that top the best-seller lists today.

Creative Writing

6. Speaking to Nature

In stanzas 2 and 3 of *Childe Harold,* the speaker uses an **apostrophe** (see page 738) to address the sea. Write a prose apostrophe, or address, to some element of nature— sea, wind, fire, snow, rain. Use stanzas 2 and 3 as a model.

Women Writers in the Romantic Period

Critics and historians may continue to quibble over the dates and definitions of Romanticism, but all agree that the period 1798–1832 in England was characterized by profound social change and unprecedented literary productivity. These phenomena altered the position that women occupied in society and brought about new opportunities and new problems for women writers. As the major male Romantic writers (the so-called Big Six) solidified their claim to poetry as the genre that represented the highest literary achievement, women writers turned to the novel. Two of these writers, Mary Shelley and Jane Austen, can be said to be Romantics; however, their social position as women writers prevented them from simply adopting their male contemporaries' philosophies and literary styles.

Mary Wollstonecraft (late 18th century) by John Opie.

Romantic writers embraced certain elements of Enlightenment philosophy; for example, they applauded Enlightenment philosophers' idealism and faith in the perfectibility of human beings. However, these writers deplored the insistence on reason over emotion, and an emphasis on science that discounted the spiritual and supernatural. As a result, male writers increasingly incorporated qualities associated with women—such as extreme emotional sensitivity—into their own work. Inspired by Mary Wollstonecraft's *A Vindication of the Rights of Woman* (1792), literary women, on the other hand, countered the prevailing Romantic trends by writing books that portrayed women as rational as well as sensitive creatures, possessing both sense *and* sensibility, to borrow the title of one of Jane Austen's novels.

As encouraging as Wollstonecraft's *Vindication* must have been to some women of the day, it produced quite the opposite reaction in most male, and many female, members of society: The novelist Horace Walpole (1717–1797) called her "a hyena in petticoats." The resulting backlash, which had been simmering since the publication of *Vindication* in 1792, reached full boil when William Godwin published *Memoirs of the Author of a "A Vindication of the Rights of Woman"* (1798), a tribute to his late wife that scandalized the public with its accounts of her illicit love affairs. In this climate, women who challenged the conventional views of marriage and women's roles were ridiculed. Those who spoke their minds in print risked being publicly renounced and having their work rejected by publishers.

Jane Austen (1775–1817)

Jane Austen was already practicing her craft when Mary Shelley was born. The daughter of an Anglican minister, Austen grew up in a respectable family with social status but little money. What few resources they had were spread thin among two

Tate Gallery, London.

Jane Austen (late 18th or early 19th century). Engraving.

New York Public Library. Miriam and Ira D. Wallach Division of Art, Prints, and Photographs. Astor, Lenox and Tilden Foundations.

daughters and five sons, with the largest expenses being devoted, as was common practice, to the formal education of the boys. Jane and her sister received an education typical for girls of the gentry: two years at a boarding school and lessons at home in the female accomplishments of drawing, music, and needlework. Jane also must have made good use of her father's library.

In an era when being known as a lady novelist was often more a stigma than an honor, it is not surprising that Austen published all her novels anonymously, despite the fact that critics generally agreed her stories would not harm young female readers' moral development. Careful readers, however, could see Austen's subtle but fierce satire of the social and educational status quo. Austen's novels about the social habits, marriage conventions, and manners of the English gentry quietly insist that women are rational creatures, much the same assertion that brought so much scorn upon the writer of *A Vindication of the Rights of Woman.* Furthermore, Austen's exquisitely rendered descriptions of her characters are often cloaked in an irony detectable only to those sympathetic to her critique of society's constraints on women. The opening sentences of her most famous novel, *Pride and Prejudice,* illustrate her trademark irony and humor:

It is a truth universally acknowledged that a single man in possession of a good fortune must be in want of a wife.

However little known the feelings or views of such a man may be on his first entering a neighborhood, this truth is so well fixed in the minds of the surrounding families that he is considered as the rightful property of some one or other of their daughters.

"My dear Mr. Bennet," said his lady to him one day, "have you heard that Netherfield Park is let at last?"

Mr. Bennet replied that he had not.

"But it is," returned she; "for Mrs. Long has just been here, and she told me all about it."

Mr. Bennet made no answer.

"Do not you want to know who has taken it?" cried his wife impatiently.

"*You* want to tell me, and I have no objection to hearing it."

This was invitation enough.

"Why, my dear, you must know, Mrs. Long says that Netherfield is taken by a young man of large fortune from the north of England. . . ."

"Is he married or single?"

"Oh! single, my dear, to be sure! A single man of large fortune . . . What a fine thing for our girls!"

"How so? how can it affect them?"

"My dear Mr. Bennet," replied his wife, "how can you be so tiresome! You must know that I am thinking of his marrying one of them."

"Is that his design in settling here?"

"Design! nonsense, how can you talk so! But it is very likely that he *may* fall in love with one of them, and therefore you must visit him as soon as he comes."

—Jane Austen, *from Pride and Prejudice*

The Austen family remained so protective of their daughter's reputation (and presumably their own as well) that when Jane Austen died at the age of forty-one, the headstone made for her grave made no mention of the six novels that, to this day, have never been out of print. Instead, it praised "the benevolence of her heart, the sweetness of her temper, and the extraordinary endowments of her mind."

Mary Wollstonecraft Shelley (1797–1851)

Mary Wollstonecraft Shelley, child of two of the most influential writers of the period, grew up in an unconventional and intellectual household frequented by leading artists and writers of the day. Her famous mother had died a few days after giving birth, and William Godwin remarried a woman who was everything Mary Wollstonecraft was not: dull and conventional. Because her stepmother tried to force her into domesticity, the young girl escaped by reading in her father's library and engaging in stimulating adult conversation with the artists and intellectuals who considered themselves students of William Godwin's philosophy. One of these guests was a brilliant young poet named Percy Bysshe Shelley, with whom Mary went on to share a brief eight years of passion, intellectual partnership, adventure, and tragedy.

In 1814, a teenage Mary Wollstonecraft Godwin eloped with Shelley (who was married at the time), and in 1816 she married him after the death of his legal wife. The couple endured the deaths of three of their four children, and in 1822, Shelley drowned in a boating accident in Italy. Mary Shelley never remarried, and when she died at age fifty-three she was survived by her son, Percy Florence Shelley, and by a literary legacy of six novels, volumes of essays, poems, travel narratives, and a comprehensive journal. Whatever her other accomplishments, however, the reputation of Mary Shelley is forever linked to her first novel, *Frankenstein,* which she began when she was just nineteen.

Mary Shelley (1840) by Richard Rothwell.
Oil on canvas (29″ × 24″).

By Courtesy of the National Portrait Gallery, London.

The Author's Introduction to the 1831 edition explains the origins of this most famous book. The Shelleys spent the summer of 1816 at Lake Geneva with Mary Shelley's stepsister Claire and Lord Byron. Since the weather had been cold and rainy, the group decided that for amusement and an exercise in composition, each one of them would make up a ghost story. Frustrated during the daylight hours by her lack of inspiration, Mary Shelley was visited in her dreams by a vision that would become the subject of the most enduring horror story in English literature.

> I saw—with shut eyes, but acute mental vision—I saw the pale student of unhallowed arts kneeling beside the thing he had put together. I saw the hideous phantasm of a man stretched out, and then, on the working of some powerful engine, show signs of life and stir with an uneasy, half-vital motion. . . . He would hope that, left to itself, the slight spark of life which he had communicated would fade, that this thing which had received such imperfect animation would subside into dead matter, and he might sleep in the belief that the silence of the grave would quench forever the transient existence of the hideous corpse which he had looked upon as the cradle of life. He sleeps; but he is awakened; he opens his eyes; behold, the horrid thing stands at his bedside, opening his curtains and looking on him with yellow, watery, but speculative eyes.
>
> —Mary Wollstonecraft Shelley, *from Frankenstein*

With the story of Victor Frankenstein's monstrous, motherless creation, Mary Shelley could examine her own fears of motherhood and her own orphaned condition; in addition, she could vent an anger and violence considered especially unfeminine in her day.

For today's readers, poetry dominates the literary landscape of the Romantic period; however, novelists such as Mary Shelley and Jane Austen remind us of women's participation in a flourishing genre. In the fantasies of Gothic novels, in the privacy of letters and journals, or in very public and forceful essays, women writers recorded their perspectives on the events of a turbulent age.

Percy Bysshe Shelley
(1792–1822)

When young Percy Shelley arrived at Oxford in 1810, his father introduced him to that bookish town's most important bookseller: "My son here," he said, "has a literary turn; he's already an author . . . do pray indulge him in his printing freaks." By spring, one of those "freaks"—an unsigned pamphlet on atheism—got Percy expelled and started a lifelong quarrel with his father. It was the first of many upheavals in the short, ill-fated life of an "author" who followed his "literary turn" wherever it led. In his own time, though, Shelley was better known for his shocking domestic life and opinions than for his impressive body of writing.

Shelley was convinced that human thought and expression had the power to change life for the better. Neither the upheavals of his personal life nor the strenuous reaching of his imagination toward a cosmic vision ever subverted his energies or optimism.

At nineteen, already estranged from his family, Shelley embarked on a career of courting the unconventional. To "rescue" her from a tyrannical father, he eloped with sixteen-year-old Harriet Westbrook, a classmate of his sisters'. Three years later he abandoned Harriet and ran away with seventeen-year-old Mary Godwin, the daughter of two of the most important radicals of the 1790s, Mary Wollstonecraft and William Godwin. Godwin was a rationalist who had once been Percy's intellectual idol. Percy's alliance with Mary also involved responsibility for Mary's fifteen-year-old stepsister, Jane Clairmont (she soon changed

Shelley Composing
Prometheus Unbound
(detail) (1845) by
Joseph Severn.

Keats-Shelley Memorial
House, Rome.

her name to Claire), who accompanied the pair on their elopement to Switzerland. Claire's brief affair with Byron brought Shelley and Byron together in Switzerland in 1816 in one of the age's most important literary relationships.

Shortly after their return to England after a second trip to Switzerland, Mary's older half sister, Fanny, committed suicide. Then Harriet, only twenty-one, drowned herself in a pond in London's Hyde Park. Percy was now free to wed Mary, but was denied custody of his two children with Harriet.

Shelley and Mary now fled their debts and notoriety in England and returned to the Continent. The next four years were Shelley's most productive, with one inspired work following another. The year 1821 saw the publication of his great elegy on the death of Keats, *Adonais.*

In 1822, when he was not yet even thirty, Shelley and a companion, Edward Williams, drowned when their sailing boat, the *Ariel,* sank in a storm off the northwestern coast of Italy. Almost two weeks later, Shelley's body washed ashore, a copy of Sophocles in one pocket and of Keats in the other. The body was burned in a pyre on the beach while friends (including Byron) stood by, and Shelley's ashes were buried in the Protestant cemetery in Rome. The epitaph on Shelley's gravestone, composed by his friend and fellow poet Leigh Hunt, read *Cor Cordium,* Latin for "heart of hearts."

Shelley's literary career, though obscured by the soap-opera character of his life, is all the more remarkable because of it. His literary productivity was, with but a few slow periods, unceasing. As his father recognized, Shelley was certainly an "author."

It is said that the Italian sailors who encountered Shelley's boat in the storm on July 8, 1822, offered in vain to take Shelley and Williams on board. When this offer was refused, the sailors pleaded with the Englishmen to furl their sails lest they be lost. As Williams tried to do so, Shelley seized his arm and stopped him. We must certainly regret Shelley's untimely death, but at the same time, we can't help but wonder at his power to capture, and be captured by, the great dark forces that so fascinated him.

Before You Read
OZYMANDIAS

Make the Connection
The Test of Time

All human beings, and all human beauty, must perish. But can't our works survive us? We leave, but isn't what we leave behind proof that our passage matters? Like the poets of another restless age, the Renaissance, the Romantic poets posed these questions.

Reading Skills and Strategies

Identifying Speakers

As you read the poem, think about who is speaking to you. Be aware of clues in the text that indicate a change in speaker. Jot down notes on who the speakers are and when their speeches start and stop.

Background

Shelley wrote relatively few sonnets, and this is certainly one of his best. It is all the more interesting because it was written as part of a friendly and informal poetry competition with Keats in 1817. Their poetic topic was Egypt: Some extraordinary fragments from the empires of several Egyptian kings named Ramses had recently been put on display at the British Museum in London. Ozymandias is the Greek name for Ramses II (ruled c. 1290–1224 B.C.), who left monuments all over Egypt, including the temples of Karnak and Luxor. This Ramses is thought to be the pharaoh who contended with Moses at the time of the Hebrews' exodus from Egypt.

Ozymandias

Percy Bysshe Shelley

I met a traveler from an antique land
Who said: Two vast and trunkless legs° of stone
Stand in the desert . . . Near them, on the sand,
Half sunk, a shattered visage° lies, whose frown,
5 And wrinkled lip, and sneer of cold command,
Tell that its sculptor well those passions read
Which yet survive, stamped on these lifeless things,
The hand that mocked them, and the heart° that fed:
And on the pedestal these words appear:
10 "My name is Ozymandias, king of kings:
Look on my works, ye Mighty, and despair!"
Nothing beside remains. Round the decay
Of that colossal wreck, boundless and bare
The lone and level sands stretch far away.

2. trunkless legs: that is, the legs without the rest of the body.

4. visage: face.

8. hand . . . heart: the hand of the sculptor who, with his art, derided the passions to which Ozymandias gave himself wholeheartedly.

Fallen colossus, Ramesseum, Thebes, Egypt. Photograph (1857) by Francis Frith.

Private Collection.

MAKING MEANINGS

First Thoughts

1. What do you think are the passions that the sculptor captured in Ozymandias's "visage"?

Shaping Interpretations

2. Even in the brief space of a sonnet, Shelley suggests a number of narrative frames. How many **speakers** do you hear in this poem? (Be sure to check your reading notes.)

3. **Irony** is a discrepancy between expectations and reality. Explain the fundamental irony in the sonnet.

4. Discuss what you think is the speaker's **message** about pride—and whom you think the message is for.

Extending the Text

5. Could this poem apply to any contemporary figures who wield political power? Explain.

Manuscript pages from "Ozymandias" by Percy Bysshe Shelley. MS. Shelley e. 4, fol. 85 recto and verso.

The Bodleian Library, Oxford.

A Glimpse of an Antique Land

In 1807, the poet Robert Southey complained about a new British fad. "Everything now must be Egyptian," he said. "The ladies wear crocodile ornaments and you sit on a sphinx in a room hung round with mummies." General Napoleon Bonaparte, later emperor of France, started this craze when he invaded Egypt in 1798. Bonaparte's campaign was unusual because his troops were accompanied by a small army of geographers, astronomers, geologists, meteorologists, and artists. The general wanted information about his new territory, and scholars' pictures and reports on Egyptian culture fascinated Western audiences. In England, the people who decorated their homes in Egyptian style wanted more information on the vanished culture of ancient Egypt, with its immense wealth and knowledge. The carefully preserved bodies of ancient pharaohs, a religion that stressed a belief in the afterlife, the tales of fantastic temples buried in desert sand—all these fed Romantic appetites for the occult, the exotic, and the mysterious.

Poster (19th century) advertising Professor Pepper at Egyptian Hall.

The Hulton Deutsch Collection.

Looking for loot. When Napoleon returned to France, he took his wife, Josephine, seven small antiquities. That tiny collection began a plundering of Egypt's art that eventually filled museums around the world. Soon collectors were producing a steady stream of antiquities: immense appendages—arms, feet, heads—that had been broken from larger statues; elaborate stone tombs called sarcophagi; and tapered pillars, called obelisks, that represented the holy rays of the sun and guarded the tombs of kings. These, in turn, were incorporated into the Romantic imagination as they were painted by artists and described by poets—for example, the "two vast and trunkless legs of stone" in Percy Bysshe Shelley's "Ozymandias."

Art collecting or grave robbing? One of the best-known collectors was the Italian adventurer Giovanni Battista Belzoni (1778–1823). Many of his findings were sold to the British Museum. In 1815, he described a bust of Ramses II as lying on the sand "apparently smiling at me, at the thought of being taken to England." The success of collectors like Belzoni, however, ensures that today many Egyptian treasures can be seen only in museums in London, Paris, and New York. Before the discovery of King Tutankhamen's tomb in 1922, explorers were thought to be the rightful owners of Egypt's historical artifacts. In the controversy surrounding that excavation, a member of the British Parliament questioned the fairness of this policy when he asked the prime minister "if he has received any request from Egyptian citizens for permission to ransack the tombs of British kings and queens in Westminster Abbey." Governments and archaeologists now have a heightened awareness of the importance of a nation's treasures, and removing such important artifacts would be impossible today. King Tut's body remains in its grave, and most of the magnificent artifacts from his tomb are housed in the Egyptian Museum, in Cairo.

Edfu Temple, Egypt.

Make the Connection

Swept Away

The faces of nature range from pacifying to terrifying, all of which the Romantics explored. Yet what so often attracted them in nature was the aspect philosophers call the sublime: the wildness, immensity, terror, and awesome grandeur of natural phenomena like the Alps or violent storms. To grasp nature's power suddenly—whether just by seeing Niagara Falls or by living through a hurricane—is,

while terrible, also exhilarating, even transporting. When you read this poem, consider why people find such power (and fear) thrilling. Why would Shelley shout to the wind, "Be thou me . . . !"?

Quickwrite

Have you ever experienced the sublime aspect of nature? When? Freewrite for a few minutes, describing the scene and your emotions.

Background

This major lyric, written in late October 1819, was provoked by Shelley's watching an oncoming storm near Florence, Italy, where he was living. It marks, in his creative life, a temporary note of exaltation after a period of intense grief over the death of his three-year-old son, William. The ode demands to be read aloud.

Ode to the West Wind

Percy Bysshe Shelley

I

O wild West Wind, thou breath of Autumn's being,
Thou, from whose unseen presence the leaves dead
Are driven, like ghosts from an enchanter fleeing,

Yellow, and black, and pale, and hectic° red,
5 Pestilence-stricken multitudes: O thou,
Who chariotest to their dark wintry bed

The winged seeds, where they lie cold and low,
Each like a corpse within its grave, until
Thine azure° sister of the Spring shall blow

10 Her clarion° o'er the dreaming earth, and fill
(Driving sweet buds like flocks to feed in air)
With living hues and odors plain and hill:

Wild Spirit, which art moving everywhere;
Destroyer and preserver; hear, oh, hear!

4. hectic: relating to the feverish flush caused by wasting diseases such as tuberculosis.

9. azure: sky-blue.

10. clarion: type of trumpet.

(Opposite) *The Bard* (1817) by John Martin.

Laing Art Gallery, Newcastle-upon-Tyne, England (Tyne & Wear Museums).

II

15 Thou on whose stream, mid the steep sky's commotion,
Loose clouds like earth's decaying leaves are shed,
Shook from the tangled boughs of Heaven and Ocean,

Angels of rain and lightning: there are spread
On the blue surface of thine aery° surge,
20 Like the bright hair uplifted from the head

Of some fierce Maenad,° even from the dim verge
Of the horizon to the zenith's height,
The locks of the approaching storm. Thou dirge°

Of the dying year, to which this closing night
25 Will be the dome of a vast sepulcher,
Vaulted with all thy congregated might

Of vapors, from whose solid atmosphere
Black rain, and fire, and hail will burst: oh, hear!

19. aery: archaic for "airy"; unsubstantial; seen only in the mind.

21. Maenad (mē′nad′): in Greek mythology, a woman who performs frenzied dances in the worship of Dionysus, the Greek god of wine and crops.

23. dirge: slow, solemn poem or song that expresses grief or mourning.

III

Thou who didst waken from his summer dreams
30 The blue Mediterranean, where he lay,
Lulled by the coil of his crystalline streams,

Beside a pumice° isle in Baiae's bay,°
And saw in sleep old palaces and towers
Quivering within the wave's intenser day,

35 All overgrown with azure moss and flowers
So sweet, the sense faints picturing them! Thou
For whose path the Atlantic's level powers

Cleave° themselves into chasms, while far below
The sea-blooms and the oozy woods which wear
40 The sapless foliage of the ocean, know

Thy voice, and suddenly grow gray with fear,
And tremble and despoil° themselves: oh, hear!

32. pumice: light, porous volcanic stone. **isle . . . bay:** in the Bay of Naples where pumice is found. These islands were once summer resorts for Roman nobility and, in Shelley's time, were notable for their ruins of ancient villas and monumental baths.

38. cleave: divide.

42. despoil: strip.

IV

If I were a dead leaf thou mightest bear;
If I were a swift cloud to fly with thee;
45 A wave to pant beneath thy power, and share

The impulse of thy strength, only less free
Than thou, O uncontrollable! If even
I were as in my boyhood, and could be

The comrade of thy wanderings over Heaven,
50 As then, when to outstrip thy skiey° speed
Scarce seemed a vision; I would ne'er have striven

50. skiey: like the sky; also, coming from the sky.

As thus with thee in prayer in my sore need.
Oh, lift me as a wave, a leaf, a cloud!
I fall upon the thorns of life! I bleed!

55 A heavy weight of hours has chained and bowed
One too like thee: tameless, and swift, and proud.

V

Make me thy lyre,° even as the forest is:
What if my leaves are falling like its own!
The tumult of thy mighty harmonies

60 Will take from both a deep, autumnal tone,
Sweet though in sadness. Be thou, Spirit fierce,
My spirit! Be thou me, impetuous° one!

Drive my dead thoughts over the universe
Like withered leaves to quicken a new birth!
65 And, by the incantation of this verse,

Scatter, as from an unextinguished hearth°
Ashes and sparks, my words among mankind!
Be through my lips to unawakened earth

The trumpet of a prophecy! O, Wind,
70 If Winter comes, can Spring be far behind?

57. lyre: the Aeolian (ē·ō′lē·ən) harp, a stringed instrument that emits sound when the wind blows across its strings.

62. impetuous: forceful; rushing.

66. unextinguished hearth: from "A Defense of Poetry": "The mind in creation is as a fading coal, which some invisible influence, like an inconstant wind, awakens to transitory brightness. . . ."

Critical Comment

Shelley and the Ode

This ode is both an expression of Shelley's sense of purpose as a public poet, and a personal meditation on the role. In what a biographer calls a moment of both "triumph and defiance," Shelley copied a Greek phrase from the dramatist Euripides in his notebook after finishing the poem: "By virtuous power, I, a mortal, vanquish thee, a mighty god."

A genuine **ode** in its overall style and arrangement, the form of this poem is special. It consists of five sonnets in **terza rima,** with each section ending, as a Shakespearean **sonnet** does, with a couplet. Each group of three lines picks up the rhyme of the second line of the preceding three lines.

Shelley's admirers have been a little embarrassed by the exaggerated self-dramatization of "I fall upon the thorns of life! I bleed!" (line 54). But the poem is full of such heightened effects. They are consistent with the manner of the ode, with its large scale—the earth, the air, and the sea—with its imagery, and with the situation of the speaker, who is striving in "sore need" in prayer with a higher power.

"Ode to the West Wind" expresses Shelley's fascination with power and with those forces—both destroyers and preservers—that inspire the same powers within the poet.

MAKING MEANINGS

First Thoughts

1. Which lines of this poem do you think are most important or have the most beautiful sounds?

Shaping Interpretations

2. What is the central **image** of each of the first three sections?

3. How are sections IV and V different in approach and emphasis from the first three?

4. How can the wind be both "destroyer and preserver" (line 14)? Cite lines to support your ideas.

5. Why do you think the speaker identifies with the wind so intensely?

6. How do you explain the **paradox** that words are like "ashes and sparks" (line 67)?

7. What do you think lines 68–70 mean?

8. What lines of this ode can you connect with the grief of a parent who has just seen a child die? What comfort does the parent find?

Connecting with the Text

9. What aspect of nature would you choose to represent the sublime? Refer to your Quickwrite notes for ideas.

Challenging the Text

10. To some, this ode argues that poetry is created only when the poet is inspired by an outside, greater force. Explain whether you agree.

ELEMENTS OF LITERATURE

Apostrophe: Throwing Words to the Wind

An **apostrophe** is a figure of speech in which a writer directly addresses a person (usually absent), a personified inanimate object, or an abstract idea. Shelley's opening invocation "O wild West Wind" is an apostrophe, with the device recurring repeatedly. In fact, this poem, like several of Shelley's might be called an **extended apostrophe.**

Perhaps the origins of the apostrophe lie in the repeated invocations of prayer, when the faithful call upon God to hear them. Indeed, not only is the apostrophe a favorite Romantic device, but many Romantic poems are also titled or described as "hymns."

Analyzing apostrophe. The apostrophe also has an interesting relation to Romantic "empathy," or deep sympathy or identification with a person or object. Shelley, for example, closes "Ode to the West Wind" with an ecstatic prayer to *be* or *become* what he apostrophizes. In what lines of "Ode to the West Wind" does Shelley directly address the wind? (How many direct addresses can you find?)

Terza Rima and the Sonnet

In "Ode to the West Wind," Shelley adapts a rhyme scheme called **terza rima** to the sonnet form. Terza rima consists of sequences of three lines of interlocking rhyme. As a technician, Shelley adjusts sound to sense in passages of chiming, onomatopoeic beauty; as a thinker, he dramatizes cycles of death and rebirth.

Analyzing the ode's structure. Take Shelley's great ode apart to see how it works.

1. Identify Shelley's **rhyme scheme** in each fourteen-line section. Are the schemes all the same?

2. Each section is also a **sonnet.** Review sonnet forms (pages 219 and 223), and tell how Shelley has adapted them. Explain whether Shelley's sonnets have **turns.**

Working in groups, prepare each section of the ode for choral reading. When you prepare your scripts, be sure to note passages that use **onomatopoeia** and **alliteration.**

Make the Connection

Sky-Drunk, Earthbound

The singing bird is a favorite romantic comparison or *analogue* for the poet: The human singer yearns to capture the ethereal beauty of the bird's song but feels, as Shelley does here, that a human being can never produce pure song. (See also John Keats's "Ode to a Nightingale," page 755.)

While the Romantic poets loved nature, they were not interested in making exact and detailed observations of natural phenomena. To them, nature often represented a higher realm of being, harmony, and even divinity. Shelley composed this poem in June 1820 at his summer residence on the northwestern coast of Italy.

Reading Skills and Strategies

Hearing the Music

Be sure to listen to this poem read aloud. As you listen, follow the text and note the lines that help you imagine the skylark's song.

Elements of Literature

Symbol

Shelley's skylark is used in the poem as a **symbol**—it is a skylark, but at the same time, it stands for something much larger than itself. As you read, think about what the skylark symbolizes to the poet, and then consider how appropriate the comparison is. The lark is a small bird resembling a sparrow. It seldom lights in trees or shrubs but soars high above the ground, singing. Often the skylark soars so high it cannot be seen—only its song can be heard. There are no skylarks in the United States.

The Skylark (c. 1792–1797) by Thomas Bewick.

Iain Bain Collection, Hertfordshire, England.

To a Skylark

Percy Bysshe Shelley

> Hail to thee, blithe° Spirit!
>   Bird thou never wert,
> That from Heaven, or near it,
>   Pourest thy full heart
> 5 In profuse° strains of unpremeditated° art.
>
>   Higher still and higher
>   From the earth thou springest
>   Like a cloud of fire;
>   The blue deep thou wingest,
> 10 And singing still dost soar, and soaring ever singest.
>
>   In the golden lightning
>   Of the sunken sun,
>   O'er which clouds are bright'ning,
>   Thou dost float and run;
> 15 Like an unbodied joy whose race is just begun.

1. blithe: joyful; carefree.

5. profuse: abundant. **unpremeditated:** unplanned; done without forethought.

The pale purple even°

   Melts around thy flight;

Like a star of Heaven,

   In the broad daylight

20 Thou art unseen, but yet I hear thy shrill delight,

   Keen as are the arrows

    Of that silver sphere,°

Whose intense lamp narrows

    In the white dawn clear

25 Until we hardly see—we feel that it is there.

   All the earth and air

    With thy voice is loud,

As, when night is bare,

    From one lonely cloud

30 The moon rains out her beams, and Heaven is overflowed.

   What thou art we know not;

    What is most like thee?

From rainbow clouds there flow not

    Drops so bright to see

35 As from thy presence showers a rain of melody.

   Like a Poet hidden

    In the light of thought,

Singing hymns unbidden,

    Till the world is wrought

40 To sympathy with hopes and fears it heeded not:

   Like a high-born maiden

    In a palace-tower,

Soothing her love-laden

    Soul in secret hour

45 With music sweet as love, which overflows her bower:°

   Like a glow-worm golden

    In a dell° of dew,

Scattering unbeholden

    Its aereal hue

50 Among the flowers and grass, which screen it from the view!

   Like a rose embowered°

    In its own green leaves,

By warm winds deflowered,

    Till the scent it gives

55 Makes faint with too much sweet those heavy-winged thieves:

   Sound of vernal° showers

    On the twinkling grass,

Rain-awakened flowers,

    All that ever was

60 Joyous, and clear, and fresh, thy music doth surpass:

16. even: archaic for "evening."

22. silver sphere: "a star of Heaven" (line 18).

45. bower: archaic for "boudoir," a woman's bedroom, dressing room, or private sitting room.
47. dell: small valley.

51. embowered: enclosed; sheltered.

56. vernal: occurring in the spring.

Teach us, Sprite or Bird,
　　What sweet thoughts are thine:
I have never heard
　　Praise of love or wine
65 That panted forth a flood of rapture so divine.

Chorus Hymeneal,°
　　Or triumphal chant,
Matched with thine would be all
　　But an empty vaunt,°
70 A thing wherein we feel there is some hidden want.

What objects are the fountains
　　Of thy happy strain?°
What fields, or waves, or mountains?
　　What shapes of sky or plain?
75 What love of thine own kind? what ignorance of pain?

With thy clear keen joyance°
　　Languor° cannot be:
Shadow of annoyance
　　Never came near thee:
80 Thou lovest—but ne'er knew love's sad satiety.°

Waking or asleep,
　　Thou of death must deem
Things more true and deep
　　Than we mortals dream,
85 Or how could thy notes flow in such a crystal stream?

We look before and after,
　　And pine for what is not:
Our sincerest laughter
　　With some pain is fraught;
90 Our sweetest songs are those that tell of saddest thought.

Yet if we could scorn
　　Hate, and pride, and fear;
If we were things born
　　Not to shed a tear,
95 I know not how thy joy we ever should come near.

Better than all measures
　　Of delightful sound,
Better than all treasures
　　That in books are found,
100 Thy skill to poet were, thou scorner of the ground!

Teach me half the gladness
　　That thy brain must know,
Such harmonious madness
　　From my lips would flow
105 The world should listen then—as I am listening now.

66. chorus Hymeneal: wedding song. *Hymeneal* is derived from Hymen, the Greek god of marriage.

69. vaunt: boast.

72. strain: melody.

76. joyance: archaic for "rejoicing."
77. languor: indifference; lack of spirit or interest.

80. satiety: feeling of weariness due to overfulfillment of appetite or desire.

Nature's Glory (c. 1860s) by John Wainwright.
Courtesy Christopher Cole, Beaconsfield, England.

MAKING MEANINGS

First Thoughts

1. What, in your opinion, does the speaker most envy about a skylark?

Shaping Interpretations

2. What questions does the speaker ask the bird, and what does he ask the bird to teach him?

3. As you listened to the poem read aloud, which words helped you to imagine (and hear) the skylark's song? What one word would you use to sum up the bird's special music? (Refer to your reading notes.)

4. How are the four **similes** in lines 36–55 related, and what do you think they show about the skylark and about the speaker?

5. What, according to lines 91–95, would be necessary for "harmonious madness" to flow from the speaker of the poem?

6. In your opinion, what does this skylark **symbolize** to the speaker? What lines support your interpretation?

7. What passages in the poem seem to reflect the Romantics' esteem for spontaneity in poetry?

8. How do you interpret these phrases: "unbodied joy" (line 15), "ignorance of pain" (line 75), "ne'er knew love's sad satiety" (line 80), "scorner of the ground" (line 100), "harmonious madness" (line 103)?

Connecting with the Text

9. Lines 86–90 are among the most quoted in English poetry. Do you see these lines reflected in your life? If so, how?

Challenging the Text

10. Even one of the greatest lyrics in the English language can be challenged! Look closely at what Shelley says to the skylark. What might a scientist say to Shelley's request to "Teach us . . . What sweet thoughts are thine"? Do you feel that in some ways the songs of humans are more transporting than the song of the skylark? (How are they different?) Discuss your challenges to the text.

CHOICES: Building Your Portfolio

Writer's Notebook

1. Collecting Ideas for a Research Paper

Suppose you wanted to do a research paper on how people today feel about nature. One way to gather information is to give ten people copies of "Ode to the West Wind" and "To a Skylark," along with a questionnaire that explores their attitudes toward nature. Work with a partner to develop the survey questions, and write up a summary of the responses. Keep your notes for the Writer's Workshop on page 773.

Responding to Language Melodies

2. Turning Words into Music

Shelley's poetry is marked by sound effects (**alliteration, onomatopoeia, assonance, and rhyme**) that create a musical quality. In a brief essay, cite outstanding examples of these sound effects in "Ode to the West Wind" and "To a Skylark." Conclude your essay with a statement of your response to Shelley's style.

Comparing and Contrasting Sonnets

3. Shelley's Renaissance Ancestors

Compare and contrast the **structure, subject, theme,** and **tone** of "Ozymandias" with those of any Renaissance sonnet you read in Collection 3.

Creative Writing

4. I Bleed! I Swoon! I Parody!

The Romantics, like all great writers, have been objects of parody. **Parody** is an amusing imitation of a work's style or subject matter. Try your hand at a parody of one of Shelley's great poems. You might get a start by using one of Shelley's first lines. If you're artistic, try a cartoon sequence parodying one of the poems.

WORLD LITERATURE

Tu Fu

(712–770)

In a poem, Tu Fu (dōō fōō) wrote, "I shall not die in peace until I have found words that will startle the readers." At once an unequaled innovator and a master of exacting *lü-shih* (lyōō'shi), or "regulated verse," Tu Fu indeed changed Chinese poetry forever. Unlike earlier poets, he did not restrict a poem to a single subject, setting, or mood; he mixed private and public concerns; and he wrote honestly—even bitterly and blackly—about current events. Yet he could see humor even in his own poverty, and his striking images show how nature nourished him. Tu Fu's difficult life began when he failed the imperial writing exams. Thereafter, he took minor government positions (he

Portrait of Tu Fu (Ch'ing dynasty). Rubbing from a Chinese carving, from *Travels of a Chinese Poet* by Florence Ayscough (London: Jonathan Cape, 1934).

New York Public Library, General Research Division. Foundations. Photographer: Robert Rubic.

eventually passed a special exam), constantly moving throughout China to support a large family he cherished.

In 759, he bravely left official service without any financial support. Though Tu Fu barely eked out a living from patrons, he wrote nearly 80 percent of his elegant, objective poetry in his last years. Along with his friend Li Po (page 766), Tu Fu was one of the most brilliant poets of the High T'ang. During Tu Fu's life, his reputation never matched Li Po's, but now Tu Fu is often called China's greatest poet.

(Above) Map of Mongolia showing Japan and China (c. 1680) by Frederick de Wit.

Before You Read

JADE FLOWER PALACE

Background

Two intense quests informed Tu Fu's troubled life: to write poetry and to obtain a high government position. The combination could have been glorious, for Tu Fu lived during the eighth century, part of China's T'ang era: a peak of cultural and artistic achievement. Although Tu Fu showed great brilliance, in 736 (at twenty-four) he failed the imperial examinations and lost all chance at an exalted office. For a Confucian who saw service to the emperor as life's greatest good, the blow cut deeply. An even sharper and sadder blow—but one that produced great poetry—was Tu Fu's disillusionment with imperial wisdom and power. In a 755 rebellion that Tu Fu witnessed, 36 million of China's 53 million people were killed or driven from their homes. His own son died of starvation. During this period, Tu Fu wrote "Jade Flower Palace."

Quickwrite

"Who can say what the years will bring?" Write your thoughts on Tu Fu's question.

A Keepsake from the Cloud Gallery (1750). Chinese. ADD Ms. 22689.

By permission of the British Library, London.

Jade Flower Palace

Tu Fu

translated by **Kenneth Rexroth**

The stream swirls. The wind moans in
The pines. Gray rats scurry over
Broken tiles. What prince, long ago,
Built this palace, standing in
5 Ruins beside the cliffs? There are
Green ghost fires in the black rooms.
The shattered pavements are all
Washed away. Ten thousand organ
Pipes whistle and roar. The storm
10 Scatters the red autumn leaves.
His dancing girls are yellow dust.
Their painted cheeks have crumbled
Away. His gold chariots
And courtiers are gone. Only
15 A stone horse is left of his
Glory. I sit on the grass and
Start a poem, but the pathos of
It overcomes me. The future
Slips imperceptibly away.
20 Who can say what the years will bring?

FINDING COMMON GROUND

The similarities between this poem and Shelley's "Ozymandias" (page 731) are striking. Like these eighth- and eighteenth-century observers, you can also ponder the ruins of power.

• With one or more classmates, compare your Quickwrite notes on the passing of time.

• Working with a partner or small group, explore the differences and similarities between "Jade Flower Palace" and "Ozymandias."

• To write a poem on the same theme today, what physical site would you choose? (It might be an abandoned site, not necessarily a destroyed one.) What objects would you focus on? Work with a partner or a small group to write a poem on Tu Fu's theme.

John Keats

(1795–1821)

It is surprising that Keats became a poet at all, and surely a wonder that, when he died at the age of twenty-five, he had accomplished enough to become one of our major poets.

John Keats by Charles Armitage Brown.

By courtesy of the National Portrait Gallery, London.

John Keats's short life was plagued with troubles, and he lacked most of the advantages a poet often needs to get started. His father, who ran a London livery stable, died when Keats was eight. His mother died of tuberculosis when he was fourteen, leaving the family finances tied up and inaccessible to the Keats children. After four years in a school where his literary interests were encouraged, he was apprenticed at the age of fifteen to learn medicine. Keats saw something of his own country as a young man, but his only foreign travel was a desperate trip to Italy when he was dying, enduring what he called a "posthumous existence." He had friends and supporters who recognized his poetic genius, but he never enjoyed a close collaborative relationship with another poet. A man of small stature (he was barely over five feet tall), he lived in close acquaintance with death and the fragile nature of human life.

In 1816, not yet twenty-one, Keats completed his medical studies at Guy's Hospital in London. Before he could be legally licensed as a surgeon, he made the momentous decision to become a poet. Some harsh reviews of his first book of poetry (1817) stung him and added to the periodic doubts that made his dedication to poetry sometimes seem an awful burden. Now much of Keats's time was spent nursing his brother Tom, who was dying of tuberculosis.

After Tom's death in December 1818, Keats had a little more than two years to make what he could of his determination to lead a "literary life." Great passages and nearly perfect poems poured from him in that miraculous time. Already in failing health, he never knew the greatness of his achievements, which might have given him at least the consolation of literary success. He had also fallen in love—her name was Fanny Brawne—but his poor health and money problems kept him from marrying. "I am three and twenty," he wrote despairingly in March 1819, "with little knowledge and middling intellect. It is true that in the height of enthusiasm I have been cheated into some fine passages, but that is not the thing."

In the next six months, he wrote some of his most glorious poems. Yet, he lamented in a November letter to his brother George (who had immigrated to Kentucky in 1817), "Nothing could have in all circumstances fallen out worse for me than the last year has done, or could be more damping to my poetical talent." Three months later he coughed up blood. His medical training and the nursing of Tom made the truth obvious: "That drop of blood is my death warrant." His only chance, a slim one, was to live in a warmer climate.

After declining an invitation from the Shelleys to join them in Pisa, Italy, Keats and his friend Joseph Severn, an artist, settled in Rome in late 1820. There Keats died in February 1821 and was buried in the Protestant cemetery—that "camp of death," as Shelley called it in *Adonais,* his powerful elegy for Keats.

The stark sadness of Keats's life heightens our awareness of the qualities of his poems—not bleak, subdued, or heavy with resignation, but rich in sensuous detail and exciting representations of intense emotional experiences, full of courageous hope for what the imagination can seize and enjoy in life. Above all, they show us what Keats was able to wrest from his troubled life by singlemindedly working at the art of poetry.

Before You Read

ON FIRST LOOKING INTO CHAPMAN'S HOMER

Make the Connection

The Wonder of Words

For all the Romantics, poetry was the true adventure. Imagination opened whole worlds; the best poetry opened thrilling vistas of absolute newness—as Keats says here.

Reading Skills and Strategies

Reading Inverted Syntax

Keats, like many other poets of his time, often inverts the syntax of his sentences to meet the demands of meter and rhyme. The word order of a traditional English sentence is subject-verb-complement. If you have trouble with Keats's syntax, look for the subject and verb of each sentence.

Elements of Literature

The Sonnet

Sonnets usually have two parts, no matter what the stanzaic structure is. The first part may present a problem, question, or idea that the second part resolves, answers, or emphasizes. The **turn** begins the second part. Keats wrote this sonnet in the Italian form, using an eight-line octave and a six-line sestet. Keats's next sonnet, "When I Have Fears" (page 748), marks a change to the Shakespearean form. (See pages 219 and 223.)

Background

In 1816—just before his twenty-first birthday—Keats wrote this poem, his first mature work, in a few hours. Keats once said that "if poetry comes not as naturally as the leaves to a tree, it had better not come at all."

This poem was connected with an exciting literary experience. Keats's favorite teacher, Charles Cowden Clarke, had invited him to spend an evening reading a translation of Homer's *Iliad* by George Chapman, a contemporary of Shakespeare. They stayed up all night. Keats went home at dawn and by ten that morning sent Clarke this sonnet.

The Chariot of Apollo (late 19th or early 20th century) by Odilon Redon.
Louvre, Paris.

go.hrw.com
LEO 12-9

On First Looking into Chapman's Homer

John Keats

Much have I traveled in the realms of gold,
    And many goodly states and kingdoms seen;
    Round many western islands have I been
Which bards in fealty to Apollo° hold.
5 Oft of one wide expanse had I been told
    That deep-browed Homer ruled as his demesne;°
    Yet did I never breathe its pure serene°
Till I heard Chapman speak out loud and bold:
Then felt I like some watcher of the skies
10   When a new planet swims into his ken;°
Or like stout Cortez° when with eagle eyes
    He stared at the Pacific—and all his men
Looked at each other with a wild surmise—
    Silent, upon a peak in Darien.

4. bards in fealty to Apollo: poets in loyal service (as feudal tenants to their lord) to Apollo, the Greek god of poetry.
6. demesne (di·mān'): domain.
7. serene: archaic for "clear air."
10. ken: range of vision.
11. Cortez: sixteenth-century Spanish explorer. In this now famous mistake, Keats confuses Cortez with Balboa, another Spanish explorer. Balboa was actually the first European to see the eastern shore of the Pacific Ocean from the heights of Darien in Panama.

MAKING MEANINGS

First Thoughts

1. Which **image** from the poem can you still see?

Shaping Interpretations

2. Paraphrase this poem line by line, reordering Keats's inverted syntax. Do any lines still give you difficulty?

3. How would you sum up each of the two parts of this **sonnet**?

4. What does the speaker say he had already experienced before he read Homer? How does he say he felt on reading Homer?

5. What could "realms of gold" (line 1) be?

6. Look at the two famous **similes** in lines 9–14. What is Keats telling you about how he felt on reading Homer? By implication, what is he comparing the experience of reading poetry to?

Extending the Text

7. Keats could not have dreamed of film, computers, and virtual reality. What do you think of their powers, as compared with those of poetry?

Manuscript of "On First Looking into Chapman's Homer" by John Keats.

Before You Read

WHEN I HAVE FEARS

Make the Connection

The End in Sight

An intense creative mission may be both a blessing and a burden: It focuses life but increases time's pressure. In Keats's case, the fears he expressed in this poem are even more poignant because we know that his death at age twenty-five confirmed them. His aspirations to both love and fame were frustrated. John Keats did "cease to be" within three years of writing this sonnet.

Quickwrite

If you knew your time on earth was short, what would you most regret not being able to do or experience? Jot down your thoughts.

Background

By 1820, shortly before he died, Keats had published his new poems in "one of the richest volumes in the history of English poetry." He also hoped to nurture his "little dramatic skill" by writing a few more narrative poems to "nerve me up to the writing of a few fine plays—my greatest ambition." He longed to follow Shakespeare into "the fierce dispute/Betwixt damnation and impassioned clay."

Our tragedy is that he could not. Our wonder must be that none of the great poets who came before him—Chaucer, Spenser, Shakespeare, Milton, Pope, or Wordsworth—would be found in this book if they had died at twenty-five.

When I Have Fears

John Keats

When I have fears that I may cease to be
 Before my pen has gleaned my teeming brain,
Before high-pilèd books, in charact'ry,°
 Hold like rich garners the full-ripened grain;
5 When I behold, upon the night's starred face,
 Huge cloudy symbols of a high romance,
And think that I may never live to trace
 Their shadows, with the magic hand of chance;
And when I feel, fair creature of an hour,
10 That I shall never look upon thee more,
Never have relish in the fairy° power
 Of unreflecting love!—then on the shore
Of the wide world I stand alone, and think
Till Love and Fame to nothingness do sink.

3. **charact'ry:** the characters of the alphabet.
11. **fairy:** supernatural; unearthly.

The Poet's Theme (19th century) by John Callcott Horsley.

Keats's Last Letter

Rome, 30 November 1820

My dear Brown,

'Tis the most difficult thing in the world to me to write a letter. My stomach continues so bad, that I feel it worse on opening any book, yet I am much better than I was in quarantine. Then I am afraid to encounter the pro-ing and con-ing of anything interesting to me in England. I have an habitual feeling of my real life having passed, and that I am leading a posthumous existence. God knows how it would have been—but it appears to me—however, I will not speak of that subject. I must have been at Bedhampton nearly at the time you were writing to me from Chichester—how unfortunate—and to pass on the river too! There was my star predominant! I cannot answer anything in your letter, which followed me from Naples to Rome, because I am afraid to look it over again. I am so weak (in mind) that I cannot bear the sight of any handwriting of a friend I love so much as I do you. Yet I ride the little horse, and, at my worst, even in quarantine, summoned up more puns, in a sort of desperation, in one week than in any year of my life. There is one thought enough to kill me; I have been well, healthy, alert, etc., walking with her, and now—the knowledge of contrast, feeling for light and shade, all that information (primitive sense) necessary for a poem, are great enemies to the recovery of the stomach. There, you rogue, I put you to the torture; but you must bring your philosophy to bear, as I do mine, really, or how should I be able to live? Dr. Clark is very attentive to me; he says, there is very little the matter with my lungs, but my stomach, he says, is very bad. I am well disappointed in hearing good news from George [Keats's brother], for it runs in my head we shall all die young. I have not written to Reynolds yet, which he must think very neglectful; being anxious to send him a good account of my health, I have delayed it from week to week. If I recover, I will do all in my power to correct the mistakes made during sickness; and if I should not, all my faults shall be forgiven. Severn is very well, though he leads so dull a life with me. Remember me to all friends, and tell Haslam I should not have left London without taking leave of him, but from being so low in body and mind. Write to George as soon you receive this, and tell him how I am, as far as you can guess; and also a note to my sister—who walks about my imagination like a ghost—she is so like Tom. I can scarcely bid you goodbye, even in a letter. I always made an awkward bow.

God bless you!
John Keats

MAKING MEANINGS

First Thoughts

1. How do the feelings you recorded in your Quickwrite notes compare with the ones Keats expresses in this poem?

Shaping Interpretations

2. What **simile** describes the books the speaker hopes to write?

3. Whom does the speaker address, and what line tells you?

4. Where is this sonnet's **turn**?

5. Describe the speaker's **tone**. Do you think it is constant or does it change? Explain.

Connecting with the Text

6. What do you think the last line means? How does it make you feel about the speaker and what is soon to happen to him?

Before You Read

LA BELLE DAME SANS MERCI

Make the Connection

Under Beauty's Spell

The figure of woman as temptress—irresistibly beautiful, but emotionally cold—is ancient. Indifferent to the fate of those who come under her spell, she vanishes as swiftly and mysteriously as she arrives, leaving her victim spiritless, deprived of his manhood—and forever obsessed with the unobtainable. Let your reading of this poem move on two levels: How does the woman so captivate the speaker? What is it about the tale that so captivates Keats, the Romantic poet?

Reading Skills and Strategies

Recognizing Common Motifs

Before you read, jot down examples of beautiful, heartless women from books, movies, television, folk tales, or any other source. Why are these women able to bend men to their will?

Elements of Literature

Ballad

Like many of Wordsworth's ballads, this songlike **ballad** has a seemingly direct simplicity. Like Coleridge's story of the ancient

Mariner, it re-creates the medieval ballad's air of mystery and enchantment. The poem looks back to older literature, but the story it tells is still heard in today's folk music repertoire.

Background

"La Belle Dame sans Merci" (The Beautiful Woman Without Pity) repeats the title of a poem by the fifteenth-century French poet Alain Chartier. Keats, who was fascinated with the self-destroying experiences of intense passion, wrote his poem in the spring of 1819.

La Belle Dame sans Merci (late 19th or early 20th century) by Sir Frank Dicksee.

La Belle Dame sans Merci

John Keats

O, what can ail thee, knight-at-arms,
 Alone and palely loitering?
The sedge° has withered from the lake,
 And no birds sing.

5 O, what can ail thee, knight-at-arms,
 So haggard and so woebegone?
The squirrel's granary° is full,
 And the harvest's done.

I see a lily on thy brow,
10 With anguish moist and fever dew,
And on thy cheeks a fading rose
 Fast withereth too.

I met a lady in the meads,°
 Full beautiful—a fairy's child,
15 Her hair was long, her foot was light,
 And her eyes were wild.

I made a garland for her head,
 And bracelets too, and fragrant zone;°
She looked at me as she did love,
20 And made sweet moan.

I set her on my pacing steed,
 And nothing else saw all day long,
For sidelong would she bend and sing
 A fairy's song.

25 She found me roots of relish sweet,
 And honey wild, and manna dew,°
And sure in language strange she said
 "I love thee true."

She took me to her elfin grot,°
30 And there she wept and sighed full sore,
And there I shut her wild wild eyes
 With kisses four.

And there she lulled me asleep,
 And there I dreamed—Ah! woe betide!
35 The latest° dream I ever dreamed
 On the cold hill side.

I saw pale kings and princes too,
 Pale warriors, death-pale were they all;
They cried, "La Belle Dame sans Merci
40 Hath thee in thrall!"°

3. sedge: reedy plants.

7. granary: place for storing grain.

13. meads: archaic for "meadow-lands."

18. zone: archaic for "belt" or "girdle."

26. manna dew: the sweet juice exuded by the European ash tree and by certain other plants. Also, in Exodus 16:13–36, manna is the food God miraculously provides for the Israelites.
29. grot: archaic for "cave" or "grotto."

35. latest: archaic for "last."

40. in thrall: archaic for "enslaved."

I saw their starved lips in the gloam,°
    With horrid warning gaped wide,
And I awoke, and found me here,
    On the cold hill's side.

45 And this is why I sojourn° here,
    Alone and palely loitering,
Though the sedge is withered from the lake,
    And no birds sing.

41. gloam: archaic for "twilight."

45. sojourn: visit.

La Belle Dame Sans Merci (1926)
by Frank Cadogan Cowper.
Private Collection/Bridgeman.

A Poem Within a Poem

Once I was pensive, very pensive
watching a mysterious, melancholic poet
writing a poem

All that he was writing
was just a poem within a poem:

A dark night of bitterness,
the song of a bird,
the solitude of the Aurora,
the smell of a rose
make a poem within a poem

Take this poem to a poet
who remembers a beloved who does not come—
Take it to a disconsolate poet who wants to reach Diana
Take it to a singer who wants the moon to fall in love
To a man who feels the sadness of being alone
To Neruda who once wrote the sad verses of the night
To the passionate poet
who writes what comes from his heart.

—Arnulfo J. López
James Madison High School
Vienna, Virginia

MAKING MEANINGS

First Thoughts

1. What to you is the most important word in the descriptions of the woman, and why?

Shaping Interpretations

2. Who are the poem's two **speakers,** and where does one stop speaking and the other begin?
3. How do the poem's **images** help you visualize the knight and the time of year?
4. How do you interpret the dream in stanza 10?

5. Where does Keats vary each stanza's **meter,** and what is the effect of the rhythmic change?

Extending the Text

6. How does the poem above relate to the poems by Keats and the other Romantic poets?
7. How does Keats's literary **ballad** compare with the old folk ballads on pages 91–95?
8. Compare Keats's La Belle Dame with the seducers you listed in your reading notes. Why do you think this character type is so prevalent across cultures? Is it fair to women? What is the comparable male type?

And haply the Queen-Moon is on her throne,
    Clustered around by all her starry Fays;°
      But here there is no light,
  Save what from heaven is with the breezes blown
40   Through verdurous° glooms and winding mossy ways.

37. Fays: fairies.

40. verdurous (vʉr′jər·əs): full of green foliage.

Forge Valley, Scarborough (19th century) by John Atkinson Grimshaw.

5

I cannot see what flowers are at my feet,
    Nor what soft incense hangs upon the boughs,
But, in embalmèd° darkness, guess each sweet
    Wherewith the seasonable month endows
45 The grass, the thicket, and the fruit tree wild;
    White hawthorn, and the pastoral eglantine;°
        Fast fading violets covered up in leaves;
            And mid-May's eldest child,
    The coming° musk rose, full of dewy wine,
50   The murmurous haunt of flies on summer eves.

43. embalmèd: perfumed.

46. eglantine (eg′lən·tīn′): kind of rose.

49. coming: soon to bloom.

6

Darkling° I listen; and, for many a time
    I have been half in love with easeful Death,
Called him soft names in many a musèd rhyme,
    To take into the air my quiet breath;
55 Now more than ever seems it rich to die,
    To cease upon the midnight with no pain,
        While thou art pouring forth thy soul abroad
            In such an ecstasy!
    Still wouldst thou sing, and I have ears in vain—
60   To thy high requiem° become a sod.°

51. darkling: archaic for "in the dark."

60. requiem (rek′wē·əm): Mass or song for the dead. **sod:** piece of topsoil held together by the matted roots of living grasses.

7

Thou wast not born for death, immortal Bird!
    No hungry generations tread thee down;
The voice I hear this passing night was heard
    In ancient days by emperor and clown:
65 Perhaps the selfsame song that found a path
    Through the sad heart of Ruth,° when, sick for home,
        She stood in tears amid the alien corn;°
            The same that ofttimes hath
    Charmed magic casements,° opening on the foam
70   Of perilous seas, in fairy lands forlorn.

66. Ruth: in the Bible, a young widow who left her own people to go with her mother-in-law to a strange land.
67. corn: British generic term for grain.
69. casements: windows. Images of open windows intrigued Keats.

8

Forlorn! the very word is like a bell
    To toll me back from thee to my sole self!
Adieu! the fancy° cannot cheat so well
    As she is famed to do, deceiving elf.
75 Adieu! adieu! thy plaintive° anthem fades
    Past the near meadows, over the still stream,
        Up the hillside; and now 'tis buried deep
            In the next valley glades:
    Was it a vision, or a waking dream?
80   Fled is that music:—Do I wake or sleep?

73. fancy: imagination.

75. plaintive: sad; mournful.

The American poet E. E. Cummings (1894–1962) uses his unique style to praise both nature's mystery and its capacity to elude our scientific probings.

O sweet spontaneous

E. E. Cummings

O sweet spontaneous
earth how often have
the
doting

5   fingers of
prurient philosophers pinched
and
poked

thee
10 ,has the naughty thumb
of science prodded
thy

    beauty   .how
often have religions taken
15 thee upon their scraggy knees
squeezing and

buffeting thee that thou mightest conceive
gods
     (but
20 true

to the incomparable
couch of death thy
rhythmic
lover

25   thou answerest

them only with

        spring)

La Primavera (1883) by Walter Crane.
Oil on canvas (15″ × 36″).
Roy Miles Gallery, London.

Dialogue with the Soul

Keats's completed poem is not "about" or "on" the nightingale but, as the title tells us, "to" the nightingale. The speaker seems, as the poem opens, to have already passed beyond the limit of ordinary experience and become "too" happy in the experience conveyed in the nightingale's song. The poem consists of a series of propositions, each containing its own rejection as to how the speaker might imitate the "ease" of the song he hears—wine, poetry, even death are considered. Each time, the speaker in his humanness is drawn back to his "sole self," to a preference for poetry as a celebration, not of "summer" but of human life as a process of soul making.

MAKING MEANINGS

First Thoughts

1. When you finish Keats's poem, what **image** is strongest in your mind?

Shaping Interpretations

2. Describe the **setting** of the poem—its time and place.

3. Why do you think the speaker wants to capture the nightingale's "ease," and why is he "too happy in [its] happiness" (stanza 1)?

4. Describe the changing desires and ideas that the speaker passes through in stanzas 2–3, 4–5, and 6–7. How does he resolve each one?

5. What differences are emphasized between the realm (or experience) of the nightingale and that of the speaker?

6. What do you think the speaker realizes by the end of the poem?

7. Review your reading notes, and explain whether you feel the speaker's **mood** is more, or less, exalted at the poem's end than at its beginning.

Connecting with the Text

8. How would you answer the speaker's final question? Explain your response.

Extending the Text

9. How would you compare Keats's response to nature with Cummings's "O sweet spontaneous" (see *Connections* on page 758)?

10. Can you think of any experience a person today might have that compares with Keats's— say, a city person? Explain your response.

ELEMENTS OF LITERATURE

Imagery: Poets' Conjurings

This poem is famous for its lush imagery. Several of its images, in fact, have been used by other writers as titles. (The American novelist F. Scott Fitzgerald called one of his tragic love stories *Tender Is the Night.*)

1. What concrete **images** in the poem conjure up quite different historical or mythological periods?

2. In the poetic device called **synaesthesia,** one sense experience (such as smell) is described in terms of another (such as touch): "soft incense" (line 42). Find other examples of **synaesthesia** in Keats's ode.

3. If you were going to illustrate this poem, which images would you focus on?

JOHN KEATS 759

Before You Read
ODE ON A GRECIAN URN

Make the Connection

Unheard Melodies

This poem is a work of art about the contemplation of a work of art—a Grecian urn, or jar. That means the ode is both concrete (descriptive) and contemplative (philosophical). It moves from rich images to abstract ideas about art versus life, permanence versus change, and body versus spirit.

Reading Skills and Strategies

Constructing Images

Stop after reading stanzas 1–3 aloud and then after stanza 4, and describe the urn's pictures as you see them. Make sketches if you like.

Background

Antique Greek vases are usually black with reddish painting, often depicting mythological subjects. Many vases show gods, goddesses, heroes, and mortals entangled in adventures. Traditionally, urns have been used for planting or burial. No one knows exactly what urn Keats had in mind when he wrote this ode. Probably it is an imaginative combination of several vases he had seen, including two in the British Museum. The vase Keats describes has a series of scenes going around it, something like the one on page 762.

Youth singing and playing the kithara, attributed to the Berlin Painter. Terra-cotta amphora (c. 490), said to be from Nola.

The Metropolitan Museum of Art, New York. Fletcher Fund, 1956. (56.171.38). Photograph ©1989 The Metropolitan Museum of Art.

Ode on a Grecian Urn

John Keats

1

Thou still unravished bride of quietness,
    Thou foster child of silence and slow time,
Sylvan° historian, who canst thus express
    A flowery tale more sweetly than our rhyme:
5 What leaf-fringed legend haunts about thy shape
    Of deities or mortals, or of both,
        In Tempe or the dales of Arcady?°
        What men or gods are these? What maidens loath?°
What mad pursuit? What struggle to escape?
10   What pipes and timbrels?° What wild ecstasy?

3. sylvan: of the forest. (The urn is decorated with a rural scene.)

7. Tempe (tem′pē) . . . **Arcady** (är′kə·dē): valleys in ancient Greece; ideal types of rural beauty.
8. loath: reluctant.
10. timbrels: tambourines.

2

Heard melodies are sweet, but those unheard
    Are sweeter; therefore, ye soft pipes, play on;
Not to the sensual ear, but, more endeared,
    Pipe to the spirit ditties° of no tone:
15 Fair youth, beneath the trees, thou canst not leave
    Thy song, nor ever can those trees be bare;
        Bold Lover, never, never canst thou kiss,
Though winning near the goal—yet, do not grieve;
        She cannot fade, though thou hast not thy bliss,
20   Forever wilt thou love, and she be fair!

14. ditties: short, simple songs.

3

Ah, happy, happy boughs! that cannot shed
    Your leaves, nor ever bid the Spring adieu;°
And, happy melodist, unwearied,
    Forever piping songs forever new;
25 More happy love! more happy, happy love!
    Forever warm and still to be enjoyed,
        Forever panting, and forever young;
All breathing human passion far above,
    That leaves a heart high-sorrowful and cloyed,°
30   A burning forehead, and a parching tongue.

22. adieu (à·dyö′): French for "goodbye."

29. cloyed (kloid): satiated; wearied with excess.

4

Who are these coming to the sacrifice?
    To what green altar, O mysterious priest,
Lead'st thou that heifer lowing° at the skies,
    And all her silken flanks° with garlands dressed?

33. lowing: mooing.
34. flanks: sides between the ribs and the hips.

35   What little town by river or seashore,
          Or mountain-built with peaceful citadel,°
              Is emptied of this folk, this pious morn?
          And, little town, thy streets forevermore
              Will silent be; and not a soul to tell
40   Why thou art desolate, can e'er return.

5

          O Attic° shape! Fair attitude!° with brede°
              Of marble men and maidens overwrought,°
          With forest branches and the trodden weed;
              Thou, silent form, dost tease us out of thought
45   As doth eternity: Cold Pastoral!°
              When old age shall this generation waste,
                  Thou shalt remain, in midst of other woe
              Than ours, a friend to man, to whom thou say'st,
          "Beauty is truth, truth beauty,"—that is all
50   Ye know on earth, and all ye need to know.

Attic vase painting showing
transport of amphoras.
Louvre, Paris.

The Arc of Experience

This poem depicts a beautiful curve of emotion and engagement that begins and ends with detachment. At its center, it abandons all restraints, including those of art itself, to live in that world which is "happy" and "forever." By itself, the third stanza seems "overwrought" (a word used in the more detached fifth stanza)— so much so that we feel that all controls have been lost. But this is precisely the nature of the speaker's experience. Bit by bit, a miniature world of human passions comes alive, only to remind us that it is as dead as the clay on which it is represented. Keats has shown us that in the midst of change, art seems to provide the only truth. Yet this is a truth that depends not on sensory experience, but on the human imagination.

MAKING MEANINGS

First Thoughts

1. What passages in this poem do you think are most important, and why?

Shaping Interpretations

2. Discuss your understanding of the three **metaphors** for the urn in lines 1–3.

3. Describe the details and actions "frozen" on the vase. Be sure to refer to your reading notes.

4. How do you interpret lines 28–30?

5. Why do you think "unheard" melodies (line 11) are "sweeter" to the speaker? How would you relate this idea to Romanticism?

6. If the urn could "tease us out of thought" (line 44), what state would we be in, and would it be better than thinking? Explain.

7. What do lines 46–50 mean to you?

8. According to stanza 5, what will happen to the urn when the speaker is dead? What message does the urn give to people?

Challenging the Text

9. Some critics complain that stanza 3 is badly written because Keats used "happy" and "forever" too many times. How would you respond to this criticism? Explain.

10. A famous textual difficulty surrounds the poem's last two lines. Based on the manuscript, some scholars enclose the entire couplet within quotation marks. Explain how this could change the meaning. (Would the sentiments expressed in the couplet be the urn's or the poet's?)

CHOICES: Building Your Portfolio

Writer's Notebook

1. Collecting Ideas for a Research Paper

These poems by Keats and the tragic details of his life could provide you with many subjects for further research. You might want to focus on the plague of tuberculosis; on Keats's stay in Rome, in a small house near the Spanish Steps that is a museum today; on Keats's family and what happened to his brothers and sister; on Fanny Brawne, of whom Keats wrote, "I can bear to die—I cannot bear to leave her." You might start your research with W. Jackson Bate's biography *John Keats*.

Analyzing Text Structure

2. Taking a Turn

Choose one of Keats's **sonnets** (pages 747 and 748), and show how it follows the structure of the Shakespearean sonnet. Be sure to identify where the shift in focus or attention, the **turn,** occurs.

Comparing Odes

3. Poets on Poets

Both Keats's "Ode to a Nightingale" and Shelley's "Ode to the West Wind" (page 734) are concerned, at least partially, with the subject of poetic inspiration. In a brief essay, write a comparison of these two odes. Focus on how each poem treats the subject.

Comparing and Contrasting Text Elements

4. Poets on Birds

Like Keats, Shelley addresses a poem to a bird—a skylark. In an essay, compare and contrast Shelley's "To a Skylark" (page 739) with Keats's "Ode to a Nightingale." Consider **subject, symbolism** of the bird, **theme,** and **tone.**

Analyzing Text Structure

5. Life for Art's Sake

Many of Keats's odes portray the speaker in a state of tension or ambiguity that is explored and then tentatively resolved. In a brief essay, trace this structure in "Ode on a Grecian Urn." What positive and negative aspects of human art are explored in this ode?

Art

6. "La Belle Dame" Illustrated

Illustrate "La Belle Dame sans Merci" in the form of a cartoon. First, block out the plot of the story. Then, decide whether you will include dialogue in cartoon bubbles or use quotations from the poem as captions for the frames of your cartoon.

Creative Writing

7. If You Have Fears . . .

From your perspective— nearly two hundred years after this sonnet was written— write a personal letter to the speaker of "When I Have Fears," and respond to his fears.

Creative Writing

8. The Knight Talks Back

Are you satisfied with the knight's explanation of his problem in "La Belle Dame sans Merci"? Create your own explanation of what "ails" the knight in Keats's poem.

Creative Writing

9. Copying Keats

Select a painting in this book, and, like Keats in "Ode on a Grecian Urn," directly address it. In a paragraph, tell what is happening in the painting, pose questions about what will never happen, and describe your feelings.

Music

10. Being a Balladeer

Try to improvise a musical setting for "La Belle Dame sans Merci." Write a melody for the poem, and perform your song.

Reading Skills and Strategies

VOCABULARY: HOMONYMS, HOMOPHONES, AND HOMOGRAPHS

Some words cause reading, spelling, and pronunciation problems because they either are spelled *or* sound like other words or they are spelled *and* sound like other words. These homonymous words have different origins and different meanings. Therefore, they have separate entries in the dictionary. As a group, homonymous words are sometimes simply called homonyms. However, this may seem somewhat confusing because one of the three specific classes of words in this group is also called homonyms. The other two kinds are classified as homophones and homographs.

Homonyms. Two or more individual words that have the same spelling and the same pronunciation are called **homonyms.** Notice how Wordsworth uses the word *roe* in the following excerpt.

> when like a **roe**
> I bounded o'er the mountains, by the sides
> Of the deep rivers, and the lonely streams,
> Wherever nature led. . . .

> —William Wordsworth, *from*
> "Tintern Abbey"

Roe, as Wordsworth uses it, means "deer." However, *roe,* meaning "eggs of a fish," has the same pronunciation as well as the same spelling. Thus, *roe* and *roe* are homonyms.

Homophones. You are probably most familiar with this category. **Homophones** are two or more words that sound alike but have different spellings, such as *soar* and *sore.* In the following passages, *soar* means "to fly upward"; *sore* means "extreme."

> The blue deep thou wingest,
> And singing still dost **soar,** and soaring ever singest.

> —Percy Bysshe Shelley, *from* "To a Skylark"

> I would ne'er have striven
> As thus with thee in prayer in my **sore** need.

> —Percy Bysshe Shelley, *from* "Ode to the West Wind"

Homographs. Two or more words that have the same spelling but are pronounced differently are homographs. In the following lines, Shelley uses the word *desert* (dez′ərt), meaning "arid geographical region."

> I met a traveler from an antique land
> Who said: Two vast and trunkless legs of stone
> Stand in the **desert** . . .

> —Percy Bysshe Shelley, *from* "Ozymandias"

The meaning of the word *desert* (dez′ərt), as Shelley uses it, may be the one you most often associate with the word's spelling. However, *desert* (di·zʉrt′) means "deserved punishment or reward." For example, a criminal who receives punishment is said to receive his just *deserts* (di·zʉrts′). A second homograph for *desert* (dez′ərt) is the verb *desert* (di·zʉrt′), which has the same etymology as the noun *desert* but means "to abandon" or "forsake."

Classification	Homonymous Word	Meaning
Homonyms	host	an army
	host	one who entertains a guest
	host	the Eucharist wafer
Homophones	holy	sacred
	wholly	completely
Homographs	wind (wind)	air movement
	wind (wīnd)	to coil

Try It Out

Using a dictionary. Find a homonym, homophone, or homograph for each of the words listed below. Remember that the words you look up will be separate dictionary entries. On your own paper, write each word, and indicate whether it is a homonym, homophone, or homograph. Then, use each homonym, homophone, or homograph in a sentence.

1. slay **2.** bark **3.** fair **4.** bow **5.** bare

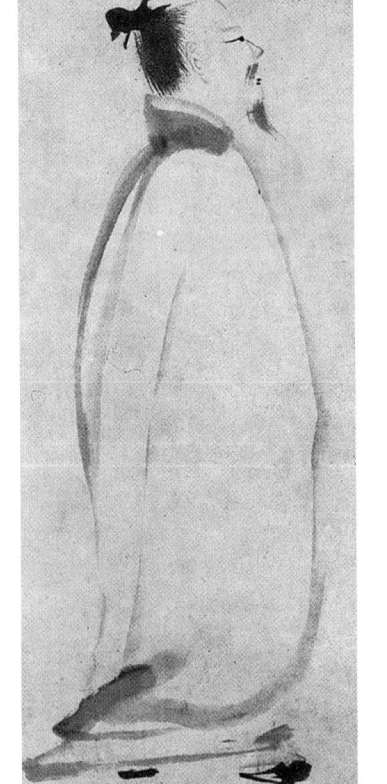

Li Po

(701–762)

A wandering, pleasure-loving poet, Li Po (lē bō) embodies for many the creative spirit of the T'ang dynasty (618–906) at its peak. Unlike the age's other great poet, Tu Fu (page 743), Li Po had no desire for government service or advancement. Reared in a wealthy family in Szechwan province, he chose life as a hermit-poet, drifting where his spirit took him. Walking, writing, marrying (four times), and socializing with poets, peasants, and leaders, Li Po became famous and was eventually invited to the emperor's court. With his unconventional be-havior, he was dismissed after only three years.

While an excellent poetic technician, Li Po favored looser folk forms, which he adapted for his original, bold, and sometimes ecstatic language. In a legend appropriate to a nature mystic, Li Po suppos-edly drowned while trying to embrace the moon's reflection in water. In fact, he may have died from mercury poisoning. Like other Taoists, he took alchemical potions believed to guarantee immortality.

Li Po Chanting in Stroll (southern Sung dynasty, 13th century) by Liang Kai.
Tokyo National Museum.

(Map) Mongolia showing Japan and China (c. 1680) by Frederick de Wit.

QUESTION AND ANSWER AMONG THE MOUNTAINS
WORD-PATTERN
TO TAN-CH'IU

Background

Li Po believed in the Taoist philosophy and religion, in which nature—spontaneous, creative, uncomplicated by will—shows life's essence. The conventional human world, on the other hand, debased and deformed by ambition and materialism, is not true reality. Li Po was a social man who had many friends, but for spiritual and poetic renewal, he retreated reclusively to nature.

Quickwrite

Would your ideal life include frequent solitary retreats into nature? Why or why not?

Fragment of Chinese wallpaper (18th century).

Victoria and Albert Museum, London.

Question and Answer Among the Mountains

Li Po

translated by **Robert Kotewall** *and* **Norman L. Smith**

You ask me why I dwell in the green mountain;
I smile and make no reply for my heart is free of care.
As the peach-blossom flows down stream and is gone into
    the unknown,
I have a world apart that is not among men.

Word-Pattern

Li Po

translated by **Florence Ayscough** *and* **Amy Lowell**

The Autumn wind is fresh and clear;
The Autumn moon is bright.
Fallen leaves whirl together and scatter.
The jackdaws, who have gone to roost, are startled again.
We are thinking of each other, but when shall we see each other?
Now, tonight, I suffer, because of my passion.

To Tan-Ch'iu

Li Po

translated by **Arthur Waley**

My friend is lodging high in the Eastern Range,
Dearly loving the beauty of valleys and hills.
At green Spring he lies in the empty woods,
And is still asleep when the sun shines on high.
A pine-tree wind dusts his sleeves and coat;
A pebbly stream cleans his heart and ears.
I envy you, who far from strife and talk
Are high-propped on a pillow of blue cloud.

The Emperor Ming Huang Traveling in Shu (T'ang dynasty, A.D. 618–906) by an unknown artist.

Collection of the National Palace Museum, Taiwan, Republic of China.

FINDING COMMON GROUND

These terse poems may seem very different from those of the English Romantics. And yet, in Li Po's poems, the same profound communion with nature is present. Their subject is not just nature, but what nature means to human life.

- How does nature affect you? In a small group, try to pinpoint a significant personal experience (not necessarily dramatic or earth-shattering) linked to a natural setting.

- Now, focus on Li Po's poems with these questions:

What do you think the last line of "Question and Answer Among the Mountains" means? What does the image in the third line suggest to you? Try changing any sensory word in "Word-Pattern" to another, and notice the effect. What is changed or lost? Which images in "To Tan-Ch'iu" evoke the qualities of remoteness, pleasure, and peace?

- If you were planning a poetry anthology, which of Li Po's poems would you pair with Keats's "Ode to a Nightingale"? Why? Discuss in your group the similarities and differences you see in the two poets. Which one do most readers prefer?

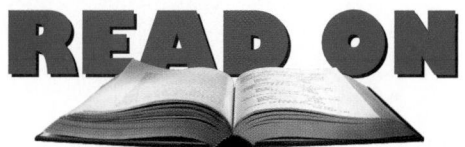

Revolutionary Fever

The revolution that occurred in France at the end of the eighteenth century had enormous repercussions on the other side of the English Channel. *A Tale of Two Cities,* one of Charles Dickens's most popular (and shortest) novels, examines the period that "was the spring of hope" as well as "the winter of despair." (This novel is available in the HRW Library.)

Share in the Terror

Mary Shelley said of *Frankenstein* (Penguin) that she wanted to write a story that "would speak to the mysterious fears of our nature and awaken thrilling horror." She succeeded, writing what many consider to be the first science fiction novel as well as a vivid version of the Romantic mythology of the self. The 1931 film, which made Boris Karloff a star, is the best of the film versions.

The Evil That Men Do

In his classic novel *The Strange Case of Dr. Jekyll and Mr. Hyde,* Robert Louis Stevenson advances the genre Mary Shelley began. When his experiments succeed and the utterly evil Mr. Hyde emerges, Dr. Jekyll's problems begin— and multiply. (Also available on videotape in several classic versions.)

Tinkering with Nature

Like the Romantic poets, Annie Dillard turns to nature for inspiration and re-flection. In *Pilgrim at Tinker Creek* (Harper's Magazine Press), her collection of essays, Dillard muses about her past, her present, and her environment while describing the interplay among the plants and animals of Virginia's Tinker Creek. For Dillard, life at the creek reflects "the intricacy of beauty, the pressure of fecundity, the elusiveness of the free, and the flawed nature of perfection."

Love and Marriage

Originally published in 1813, Jane Austen's novel *Pride and Prejudice* (Norton) is about five husband-hunting sisters in nineteenth-century England and the delicate tangles of love and courtship they ensnare themselves in. What struck people then, and strikes us now, is Austen's ability to make commonplace people and events interesting. The superficially trivial content is deceptive; it masks a deeper irony that exposes the manners and mores of the period. (This novel is available in the HRW Library.)

The English Language

Variety in Language

*by **John Algeo***

William Wordsworth wrote a preface to *Lyrical Ballads,* in which he talked about the kind of poetry he and Samuel Taylor Coleridge tried to produce, especially about its subjects and its language. He said that their subject matter was to be "incidents and situations from common life" and that their language was to be that "really used" by ordinary people. One aspect of the Romantic movement was its fascination with common, especially rural, life and customs; with earthiness; and with simple people and their language.

The study of dialect was encouraged by a Romantic conviction that the simple country life was better than the complex city life. As a result, we often think of dialect as a form of language spoken by uneducated rural people. But, in fact, it is far more than that.

What Are Dialects?

We have seen that language has many ways of saying the same thing. How we talk depends partly on where we come from, what ethnic or social group we belong to, whether we are male or female, what education we have had, and how old we are. Such kinds of variation are called **dialects.** Dialects are the various forms in which a language exists, not some peculiar or quaint versions of it.

A language is like ice cream; it comes in various flavors. If you want ice cream, you ask for chocolate, vanilla, butter pecan, peppermint, or a lot of other flavors. But it would make no sense to say, "I just want plain ice cream—none of those flavors, just the real stuff." Ice cream only comes in flavors; apart from its flavors, no ice cream exists. In the same way, a language only comes in dialects; apart from its dialects, no language exists.

Many of us think that the way we talk is real English, whereas the way others talk is some odd dialect. However, we all talk dialects, none intrinsically odder (or better) than any of the others.

How Odd That You Should Say That

Dialects differ among themselves in the words that are used, the way words are pronounced, and the way words are put together.

> Many of us think that the way we talk is real English, whereas the way others talk is some odd dialect. However, we all talk dialects, none intrinsically odder (or better) than any of the others.

Vocabulary. Depending on where you come from, a *porch* may be a *gallery, piazza, stoop,* or *veranda.* A *dragonfly* may be a *darning needle, mosquito hawk, snake doctor,* or *snake feeder.* *Pancakes* may be *batter cakes, flannel cakes, fritters,* or *hot cakes.*

In most parts of the United States, *rubber band* is the term for an elastic loop that holds things together; but if you are from the Minneapolis–St. Paul area, you may call it a *rubber binder. Soft drink* is what most of us call a flavored carbonated beverage; it may also be *soda, pop,* or *soda pop;* an old-fashioned term is *phosphate.* If you are from New England, you may call it *tonic,* which means something more specific (quinine water) in the rest of the country.

Pronunciation. Most Americans pronounce *fog, hog,* and *log* as "fawg," "hawg," and "lawg," with the same vowel they use in *law, paw,* and *raw.* But they use a different vowel sound in *lock, pot,* and *top.* In parts of New York and the north central states, however, *fog, hog,* and *log* have the same vowel as *lock, pot,* and *top,* whereas *law, paw,* and

go.hrw.com
LE0 12-English Language

raw have a different sound. In eastern New England and in western Pennsylvania and some places to the west, including most of the Far West, all of those words may be pronounced with the same vowel (either an "aw"-like or an "ah"-like sound).

Those who come from the southern United States tend to pronounce *greasy* as "greazy," whereas those from the northern states tend to make it sound like "greassy." TV ads for dishwasher detergents generally use the northern pronunciation, which seems to be gaining ground. Some people, having heard both pronunciations, use them both, but may develop special meanings for the two ways of saying the word. They may think that "greassy" means literally "coated with grease," while using "greazy" as a metaphor meaning "untrustworthy, disagreeable." In this way, two pronunciations of the same word may eventually turn into different words, as happened long ago with *shade* and *shadow, of* and *off,* and *flour* and *flower.*

Regional usage. Prepositions are especially subject to dialect variation. Whether you are sick *to, at, in,* or *on* your stomach depends mainly on where you learned to talk. So also does how you tell time—whether you say a quarter *of, till,* or *to* the hour. In most of the United States, people stand *in line,* but in New York City, they stand *on line.* Most Americans, when they are not away, are *at home,* but some are *to home.*

For a long time, English has had a problem with the second person pronoun *you.* We make one word do double duty—for both the singular and the plural, for talking to one person and for talking to many. Some dialects, however, have tried to

"A host? You call that a host! Why, back in the States . . ."

distinguish between the singular and plural forms. In certain parts of the North, especially in cities, some people say *youse* or *yuzz* for the plural; in the Appalachian Mountain region, some people say *you'uns.* But neither of those forms has ever made much headway in educated use. Throughout the South, however, the plural form *y'all* is widely used by the best-educated speakers, only, however, when referring to more than one person. Another new plural form that is gaining ground, especially in informal speech, is *you guys.*

American Regional Dialects

The first English settlers in America brought with them the dialects that they spoke in the British Isles. As soon as they settled into their new country, however, they began to develop new dialects.

Today, regional dialect boundaries are clearest along the eastern coast of the United States, where English speakers first settled. There are three main dialect areas: Northern, Midland, and Southern.

Nowadays, some of the traditional differences among these regions are disappearing as our life styles change and become more uniform. What used to be called a *skillet* in the South and a *spider* in parts of the North is now almost everywhere a *frying pan* or a *frypan.* When horses pulled wagons, the horizontal wooden bar by which the wagon was attached to the animals' harness was called a *singletree* or *swingletree* in the South and a *whippletree* or *whiffletree* in the North. But now the object is foreign to the experience of most of us, so we have no name whatever for it.

New dialect terms, however, will doubtless come into existence. For example, we might expect dialect variation in the terms we use for limited-access highways, for the rest areas along them, and for the center

ROTHCO

Cartoon by Mike Williams. © Punch. Courtesy Rothco.

barrier that divides the two directions of traffic. In addition, there will be varied terms for a small neighborhood store that is open early and late hours, or for an informal kind of open shoe that has a strap between the big toe and the other toes. Such objects have many names.

American Ethnic Dialects

Another important kind of dialect is ethnic speech. People who share a common cultural heritage tend to talk alike. Almost every immigrant group has its own ethnic dialect. Among the larger are Yiddish English, spoken by many Jews; Hispanic English of several kinds, spoken by Latinos, Cuban Americans, and Puerto Ricans; and black English, a mixture of African influences, Southern dialect, and features that developed in the African American community.

Among the features of black English (which are, however, by no means found in the speech of all African Americans) are the following: In pronunciation, final clusters of consonants are simplified, usually by dropping all except the first consonant: *most* becomes "mose," and *find* becomes "fine." *Nice* and *mine* become something like "nahs" and "mahn." The article *a* is used instead of *an* before words beginning with a vowel: *a orange, a apple.* These features are typical of the Southern dialect too.

Other features, although often found in Southern speech, are much more common in black English. The ending *–s* is frequently omitted from verbs, possessive nouns, and plural nouns that have a number before them: "He work hard," "my brother car," "four ticket." The verb *be* is either omitted altogether or used in the unchanged form of *be,* rather than *am, is, are.* These two uses, however, mean different things: "She here" means "She is here right now," while "She be here" means "She is usually or regularly here."

Black English also has distinctive words, some of which have become a part of general English vocabulary: *chigger* (sand flea), *goober* (Southern and Midland for peanut), *gumbo, jazz, juke (box), nitty-gritty,* and *zombie.* Other uses are known outside the black-English-speaking community as slang, such as *bad* pronounced with a long, drawn-out vowel ("baaaad"), meaning "very good."

As new influences come to bear on the life and language of the nation, new dialects are likely to arise. Language changes continually, but in different ways among different groups—and that is why dialects exist.

Try It Out

1. **Connecting to your experience.** Which of the following groups contains words that seem most familiar to you?

   a. pail, quarter of, angleworm, mud wasp, fuss-budget, brook

   b. bucket, quarter till, fishing worm, mud dauber, fuss-button, run

   c. bucket, quarter to, wiggler, dirt dauber, fuss-box, branch

   The first group is of predominantly Northern words, the second of Midland words, and the third of Southern words. Name at least two other words that are part of your regional dialect, and then locate their equivalents in at least one other regional dialect. (Classmates or neighbors from different parts of the country might be good resources.)

2. **Using the dictionary.** Here are some terms with special meanings in dialect use. Look up these words in the *Dictionary of American Regional English* (or some other dialect dictionary) to find out where they are used and what they mean.

acknowledge the corn	bayou
	bismarck
Adam's off-ox	blinky
all in	chill bumps

3. **Connecting past and present.** The Romantics were concerned with change in life and society. Some of them were also concerned with varieties of dialects. How are these two concerns connected? How could these concerns also be important in contemporary life?

BUILDING YOUR PORTFOLIO

Writer's Workshop

The history
of the written
word is rich an

Page 1

EXPOSITORY WRITING
THE RESEARCH PAPER

Much of the writing you encounter every day—in the magazines and newspapers you read, the textbooks you study, and the Web sites you browse—has an informative purpose. **Expository** (or informative) **writing** is also the kind of writing you will be asked to do most often in your school and working life. When you write a research paper, your goal is to inform, and your task is to collect, organize, and present information that will expand your readers' knowledge and understanding of your topic.

Prewriting

1. **Find a topic.** Whether you choose the topic yourself or a teacher or editor assigns a general subject area, you should begin by brainstorming to find topics that interest you. Make a list of potential topics. Your Writer's Notebook jottings from Collections 8 and 9 may already contain ideas for topics. Highlight a few of the strongest possibilities. Decide which topic most intrigues you, and be sure it will also appeal to your readers. For example, you may want to find out more about Lord Byron's scandalous life. You may want to learn about the nationalist revolutions that the Romantic poets championed or the scourge of the nineteenth century—tuberculosis.

2. **Narrow your topic, and freewrite about it.** In most cases, the first topic you come up with will be too broad to handle effectively in a research paper. Your next step, then, will be to narrow the focus—from Lord Byron's reputation, for example, to the specific reasons why he left England in 1816.

    Once you have narrowed your topic, freewrite what you already know about it, and then generate questions you want to answer.

3. **Be sure the topic can be researched.** The questions you decide to explore should be ones you can find answers to in available research sources. You will need at least five or six good sources of information, either **print sources,** such as books or magazine articles that you find in a library, or **nonprint sources,** such as Web sites or personal interviews.

4. **Anticipate your audience's needs.** Before you start to write, think about the people who will read your paper. To anticipate your audience's needs, ask yourself the following questions:

    • What will my readers already know about the topic?

    • What more will they need to know to understand the topic?

    • What will they be curious about? What will interest them the most?

Technology HELP

See Writer's Workshop 2 CD-ROM. *Assignment: Informative Report.*

ASSIGNMENT
Write a research paper on a topic of interest to you and your readers.

AIM
To gather, organize, and present ideas for the purpose of informing readers.

AUDIENCE
Your teacher, classmates, or others interested in learning more about your topic.

Try It Out
With a partner or a small group, review the introduction to "The Romantic Period" (pages 622–638). On the basis of that introduction, brainstorm a list of topics that you might like to research and write about.

Strategies for Evaluating Sources

To decide which of your sources are most useful, apply the four Rs:

1. How **relevant** to your topic is the information in the source?
2. How **reliable** are the facts found in the source?
3. How **recent** is the source?
4. How **representative** of different sides of the issue is the source?

Guidelines for Doing Research

- Start with a list of major topics and questions to look up.
- Write down definitions of key terms you discover as you do your research. You may need to define some of these terms in your paper.
- To ensure the accuracy of all quotations, copy the words exactly. Also keep a precise record of the source so that you can double-check the quote and document it correctly.

5. **Research your topic.** Though general reference books will help you get an overview of your topic, specialized reference books, such as biographical dictionaries and encyclopedias on particular subjects, will provide more detailed information. Check a library catalog for books on your topic, and consider whether sources such as the *Readers' Guide to Periodical Literature,* indices to major newspapers, and an Internet search engine might direct you to useful information. You might also contact experts at a government office, museum, or historical society.

As you do your research, be aware of the need to strike a balance between primary and secondary sources. A **primary source** is original, firsthand information: letters, journal entries, autobiographies, historical documents such as marriage records. A **secondary source** is information about or derived from primary sources: critical writings, reviews, encyclopedia entries, biographies. Secondary sources are usually readily available, but you should not, if possible, rely on them exclusively. Be sure to evaluate all sources for accuracy. Take notes on index cards or in a computer file.

6. **State your controlling idea.** Reread your notes, and summarize your **controlling idea,** or **thesis,** in a brief statement. In a research paper, the controlling idea is an objective statement of your main concern; it defines the boundaries of your topic and the approach you are taking. Here are two thesis statements:

- Lord Byron was less a typical Romantic figure in his poetry than in his life; he defied contemporary social conventions, but he was conservative in his literary expressions.
- The American poet Walt Whitman echoed the values of the Romantics, including their emphasis on lyricism, self-expression, and individual freedom.

7. **Organize.** Present your information in a logical sequence. You can create a framework for organizing a research paper by using one of these methods:

- **Order of importance.** Go from your most important point to your least important, or vice versa.
- **Chronological.** Organize your events in time order.
- **Block comparison and contrast.** Examine several aspects of one subject; then, examine the same aspects in the same order for a second subject, and so on.
- **Point-by-point comparison and contrast.** Examine one aspect for the first subject; then, examine the same aspect for the second subject, and so on.
- **Cause and effect.** Organize your details according to their causal relationships.

8. **Outline.** List the major aspects of your topic as main headings, using an order that reflects your approach to the subject. Your preliminary outline may change during the drafting and revising processes. For now, consider making separate piles of index cards—or printouts of the notes in your computer file—to represent your major headings. Within each pile, cluster information under subheadings. Look for holes—aspects that haven't been fully explored and relevant questions that haven't been answered. Do additional research to fill in the holes.

Drafting

1. **Begin forcefully.** The introductory paragraph of a research paper has two purposes: to define the topic clearly and to get the reader interested. Try to accomplish both purposes in one stroke by defining your topic in an engaging way. You might begin with one of the following: a surprising fact or statistic that has a bearing on your thesis, a quotation from an expert, a question that highlights different views of the subject. Describing a scene or narrating an anecdote is another effective way to open a research paper.

2. **Develop your points.** Follow your outline. Check off each item as you cover it to be sure you don't omit essential information. As you write your draft, however, you may find yourself reworking the outline as you revise your understanding of what is important about your topic.

3. **Define your terms.** Define the terms that your readers might not understand. Do not define terms they already know. For example, if you were writing an article for historians on the Greek fight for independence from Turkey in the nineteenth century, you would not have to define *nationalism,* but you would have to do so if you were writing a paper on the same topic for a general audience.

4. **Support your points.** Back up generalizations with specific details. If space permits, use anecdotes. Try to use concrete words rather than abstract ones. Use facts and figures to demonstrate the validity of your statements, and provide all necessary background information.

5. **Use quotations for forcefulness.** The exact words from expert sources can add interest and authority to a research paper, but you should avoid overusing direct quotations. In general, use quotations when they are strong. Otherwise, **summarize** or **paraphrase**—but be sure to use your own words and sentence structure. In other words, don't **plagiarize**—don't pass off another writer's words or ideas as if they were yours.

6. **Maintain an authoritative stance.** When you write, keep your tone consistent and confident, to assure your audience that you know your subject. Use language that is more or less formal, depending upon your audience. Most research papers assigned in class should be written in the third person and in relatively formal language, with a serious and objective tone.

7. **Wrap it up neatly.** The ending of a research paper usually restates the main point or points in a different way. It might also put the subject in a larger context or suggest related topics that could be explored further.

Model Outline

Title: Tuberculosis in the Nineteenth Century

Thesis statement: In the nineteenth century, tuberculosis was a widespread and deadly disease that could be neither cured nor prevented.

I. Causes of disease
   A. Medical understanding
   B. Popular understanding
II. Course of disease
   A. Symptoms
   B. Treatments
      1. Rest cure
      2. Change of climate
   C. Mortality
III. Failure to prevent contagion
   A. Inadequate quarantine
   B. Poor ventilation

Language Handbook
H E L P

See Quotation Marks, page 1247.

**Communications
Handbook
H E L P**

See Research Strategies; Evaluating the Credibility of Sources; Model Research Paper.

**Revision
S T R A T E G I E S**

Clear transitions guide your reader from subtopic to subtopic, from idea to idea. If you are dealing with the development of a subject over time, transitions such as first, then, next, last, *and* finally *will be important. For discussions of cause and effect, consider transitions such as* therefore, thus, so, *and* because.

Evaluation Criteria

A good research paper
1. *contains an identifiable controlling idea, or thesis, which is clearly stated early in the report*
2. *tailors the tone and level of the language to the audience*
3. *presents facts objectively*
4. *supports the points adequately*
5. *documents all sources correctly*
6. *conveys a consistent, authoritative tone*

Documenting Sources: Parenthetical Citations and Works Cited

It is crucial, when writing a research paper, to decide which information you need to *document* (cite the source for). Use these guidelines to determine which pieces of information need documentation:

• In general, don't document information that is readily available in several reference books, such as the basic facts of Byron's life.

• Document unusual, little-known facts or facts and statistics that your readers might question.

• Document all direct quotations and paraphrases.

• Document theories or opinions that are not your own.

• Document any data from surveys, experiments, or research studies.

When you document a source, you provide the information in two places: a parenthetical citation within the body of the paper and the works cited list at the end of the paper.

Parenthetical citations appear in parentheses immediately after material from a particular source. In most cases, all you need to cite is the author's last name and a page number. For example, here's a parenthetical citation for a report on Byron:

> According to one critic, the "main pleasure of reading Byron is the contact with a singular personality" (West, 111).

That parenthetical citation shows that the writer has used a quotation from a work by West. Here's how the entry for the same source will look in the **works cited** list:

> West, Paul. Byron and the Spoiler's Art. New York: Lumen Books, 1992.

The works cited list contains full bibliographic information on all the works cited in the paper so that readers can locate the sources. For more complete information on documenting sources, consult the *MLA Handbook for Writers of Research Papers,* fourth edition.

Evaluating and Revising

Exchange papers with a partner, and discuss these questions:

• Do you need more or stronger evidence to support your thesis statement?

• Have you presented your ideas in a logical sequence?

• Have you punctuated direct quotations correctly?

• Have you documented your sources clearly and completely?

Language Workshop

The history
of the written
word is rich and

Page 1

ASPECTS OF A WRITER'S STYLE

The Romantic poets drew upon the expressive power of ordinary speech and rejoiced in the uniqueness of each writer's **voice**. As a result, the **style** of Romantic poetry differs from that of eighteenth-century poetry. Style and voice are closely related elements of poetry. Two other elements that contribute to the overall effect of a work are **tone** and **diction**. These four elements come together like the threads of a fabric, each woven into the others. Technically, they can be defined in this way:

- **Style** is the way a writer uses and adapts language to express ideas. Writers adapt their language to the situation much as people adapt their dress to the occasion: formal for formal occasions, casual for casual occasions—and a whole range of choices in between. Style is a matter of making choices about sentence structure, punctuation, and diction.

- **Voice** is the unique sound and rhythm of the writer's language—the writer's personal way of communicating. In other words, the writer sounds like himself or herself, no matter what the situation, just as the writer would be recognizable in formal wear or in jogging clothes.

- **Tone** is the attitude the writer takes toward his or her subject. A writer's voice is capable of more than one tone. For instance, a writer may sound both angry and sarcastic or both sad and sentimental.

- **Diction,** the writer's choice of words, is an element of style and helps to establish both voice and tone.

Sentences that are formal in style can become informal with a few changes.

EXAMPLE   Earth has not anything to show more fair . . .
—William Wordsworth, *from* "Composed upon Westminster Bridge"

Nothing on earth is more beautiful.

Tone can be changed by substituting synonyms with different connotations.

EXAMPLE   It is an ancient Mariner. . . .
—Samuel Taylor Coleridge, *from The Rime of the Ancient Mariner*

It is a doddering old sailor.

Writer's Workshop Follow-Up: Revision

Reread the research paper you wrote for the Writer's Workshop on page 773. Is your overall style relatively formal? Do you communicate a serious and objective attitude? Is your tone consistently authoritative? Examine your diction. For words that seem imprecise, substitute more exact words. For words loaded with emotional connotations, substitute synonyms that convey a more balanced stance.

Try It Out

Rank the words in each group below, identifying them as most formal, formal, somewhat formal, or least formal. Then discuss your choices with some classmates.

1. rationalization, excuse, alibi, cop-out

2. hit, strike, percuss, wallop

3. knowledge, erudition, know-how, learning

4. soil, earth, dirt, alluvium

Reading for Life

Evaluating Credibility of Sources

Situation

The human-made monster! It's now a fixture in literature, movies, and television, but it began with Mary Wollstonecraft Shelley's novel *Frankenstein.* You're curious to know how a nineteen-year-old woman of the Romantic era could have invented such a fantastic and original story. To learn about the author's life, you've gathered some sources; now you want to evaluate their **credibility,** or reliability.

Strategies

For information on a well-known figure, look for primary sources.

- Primary sources include letters, journals, diaries, and autobiographies written by the subject and his or her contemporaries.

Select secondary sources on your subject (books and articles by experts).

- Check the writer's credentials. Is he or she knowledgeable on the subject? For example, has the writer written other works on the same or a related topic?

- Evaluate the writer's motivation. Is it to inform, persuade, or entertain? How might the purpose affect the presentation?

- Be alert to any ideological bias that might interfere with the writer's objectivity.

- Evaluate the publisher. Does

it publish reputable, highly regarded works, such as scholarly journals or academic books?

- Check the publication dates. Recent sources may be more comprehensive and more accurate, but older sources may provide important historical details.

Evaluate electronic and video sources carefully.

- Government (*gov*) and non-profit (*org*) Web sites are more often reliable than commercial (*com*) sites.

- Documentaries are more reliable than true stories that have been fictionalized.

Sources

1. Mary Wollstonecraft Shelley, <u>The Letters of Mary Wollstonecraft Shelley</u>, ed. Betty T. Bennett. 3 vols. Baltimore: Johns Hopkins University Press, 1988.
2. Muriel Spark, <u>Mary Shelley: A Biography</u>. New York: New American Library, 1987.
3. Mary Wollstonecraft Shelley, <u>Mary Shelley's Journal</u>, ed. Frederick L. Jones. Norman: University of Oklahoma Press, 1947.
4. Linda Badley, "Frankenstein's Progeny," in <u>Film, Horror, and the Body Fantastic</u>. Greenwich, Conn.: Greenwood Press, 1995.
5. Arthur Penn Patterson, "A Frankenstein FAQ [Frequently Asked Question]: Question 7," <u>Watershed Online</u>, August 1, 1998. <http://www.watershed.winniped.mb.ca/MS7.html>.
6. "The Mary Shelley Page," <u>San Antonio College LitWeb</u>, March 9, 1998. <http://www.accd.edu/sac/english/bailey/mshelley/htm>.
7. James Whale, director, <u>Frankenstein</u>, starring Boris Karloff, Colin Clive, Mae Clarke, and John Boles. Universal Pictures, 1931.

Using the Strategies

1. Which sources listed in the box above would you eliminate without investigating further? Why?

2. What two primary sources would you select?

3. Which secondary source would you choose?

4. Which seems to be the most promising Internet site? Why?

Extending the Strategies

- Compile a list of credible sources of information on the life and works of one of your favorite writers.

- Compare a film version of a novel with the novel itself.

Learning for Life

Researching
Labor and Population Trends

Problem

During the Romantic period, as the Industrial Revolution progressed, cities often grew up around factories. How is the current change from an industrial to a service- and information-based economy affecting the places where people live and work?

Project

Research current and projected population trends in the United States. What factors account for the growth of some areas and the decline of others? Where will people work in the future?

Preparation

1. Working with a partner or a small group, use brainstorming or the *5W-How?* questions (*Who? What? When? Where? Why? How?*) to develop questions to guide your research.

2. Exchange ideas about the kinds of information that will help you answer your research questions and about possible sources, including the Internet and government publications.

Procedure

1. One way to gain an overview of your topic is to read several newspaper or magazine articles written for a general audience. (Check a library's indices to newspapers, essays, and articles.) Such articles may mention other sources as well as authors who are experts in the field.

2. Two good secondary sources for data on population distribution are *The World Almanac and Book of Facts* and the *Statistical Abstract of the United States*. The Census Bureau also issues numerous publications, such as *Current Population Reports* (available on microfiche in some libraries).

3. As you review the facts, opinions, and theories you find, draw your own conclusions about the relationship between the nation's transformation to a service- and information-based economy, the distribution of the population, and changes in the places where people work.

Presentation

Use one of the following formats (or another that your teacher approves):

1. **Communicating Graphically**

   Communicate your findings in a graphic display combining two or more types of illustrations, such as maps, charts, and graphs. Include only essential information, so that the finished product will be legible and uncluttered, and use color, patterns, or both to make the display accurate and attractive. Ask one of your high school's American history or economics teachers to field-test the display with his or her students at a suitable point in the course.

2. **Persuading**

   Write an editorial summarizing your findings and expressing your views on why students should use the information in planning their careers. Persuade your readers to take your ideas seriously by using a formal tone and by tailoring your appeals to their needs and interests. Submit your editorial to the school newspaper or to a local newspaper.

3. **Speaking Out**

   Prepare a speech explaining what your research suggests about your community's future. Since your investigation focused on national trends, you'll need to extrapolate from your findings—that is, to speculate on the basis of what you discovered. Present your speech to a meeting of a civic or professional group, such as the Rotary Club or the American Business Women's Association.

Processing

Did this activity make you rethink your career plans? Did it change your ideas about where you're likely to live and work in the future? Write a brief reflection for your portfolio.

The Victorian Period
1832-1901

The Railway Station
(detail) (19th century)
by William Powell Frith.

The Victorian Period

by **Donald Gray**

So many worlds, so much to do,
So little done, such things to be . . .

—*Alfred, Lord Tennyson*

(Inset) P⦚
lid depict
ing Cryst⦚
Palace,
Dale Hal
Longpor⦚
Stafford-
shire
(1851), b
T. J. and
J. Mayer.

Fitzwilliam
Museum,
University
Cambridge

Transept of the Crystal Palace
by G. Hawkins (19th century). Published by Day
and Son and Ackerman and Co.

Stapleton Collection, London.

Many Victorians thought of themselves as living in a time of great change. They were right. But the changes during Queen Victoria's long reign (1837–1901) occurred in a period of relative political and social stability, and many were the result of conditions that began before Victoria and most of her subjects were born.

Peace and Economic Growth: Britannia Rules

After Napoleon's defeat at Waterloo in 1815, Britain was not involved in a major European war until World War I began in 1914. The empire that had begun in the seventeenth and eighteenth centuries with British interests in India and North America grew steadily, until by 1900, Victoria was queen-empress of more than two hundred million people living outside Great Britain.

At the same time, the Industrial Revolution of the eighteenth century greatly expanded. It moved through booms and depressions, but over the course of the century it steadily created new towns, new goods, new wealth, and new jobs for tens of thousands of people climbing through the complicated levels of the middle class. These social and economic changes were expressed in gradual political reforms. Piece by piece, middle-class and ultimately working-class politicians and voters achieved political power while leaving the monarchy and aristocracy in place.

The Victorian era was a time of relative peace and economic growth. The British Empire grew steadily, the Industrial Revolution expanded, and political power was extended to the middle and working classes.

Cotton handkerchief probably produced for Queen Victoria's Golden Jubilee in 1887 (PC86).
Museum of London.

The Idea of Progress: "An Acre in Middlesex"

The English historian Thomas Babington Macaulay eloquently voiced the middle-class Victorian attitude toward government, history, and civilization. For Macaulay, history meant progress, and progress largely meant material improvement that could be seen and touched, counted and measured. "An acre in Middlesex is better than a principality in Utopia," he once

> The history of England is emphatically the history of progress.
> —Thomas Babington Macaulay

The Victorian Period, 1832–1901

LITERARY EVENTS

Elizabeth Barrett and **Robert Browning** elope; during their courtship, she writes poems included in *Sonnets from the Portuguese,* 1846

William Wordsworth becomes poet laureate, 1843

Nikolai Gogol draws attention to the plight of Russian serfs with his comic epic *Dead Souls,* 1842

Margaret Fuller helps found *The Dial,* a U.S. Transcendentalist journal that publishes Henry David Thoreau and Ralph Waldo Emerson, 1840

Edgar Allan Poe publishes "The Fall of the House of Usher," 1839

Charles Dickens publishes *Oliver Twist* in periodical form, 1837–1838

Charles Darwin publishes *On the Origin of Species by Means of Natural Selection,* 1859

Mary Ann Evans publishes stories in *Blackwood's Magazine,* using her pen name, George Eliot, 1857

Sojourner Truth delivers her "Ain't I a Woman?" speech in Akron, Ohio, 1852

Nathaniel Hawthorne publishes *The Scarlet Letter,* 1850

Alfred, Lord Tennyson becomes poet laureate, 1850

Karl Marx and Friedrich Engels publish *The Communist Manifesto,* 1848

Charlotte Brontë publishes *Jane Eyre;* Emily Brontë publishes *Wuthering Heights,* 1847

1832–1846

1847–1859

CULTURAL/HISTORICAL EVENTS

First Reform Bill extends vote to men who own property worth £10 or more annually, 1832

Mexican army defeats Texans at the Alamo, 1836

Victoria becomes queen of the United Kingdom of Great Britain and Ireland, 1837

Reforms included in Custody Act allow divorced women legal access to their children, 1839

First of what China terms "unequal treaties" makes Hong Kong a British colony, 1842

Potato famine begins in Ireland; close to one million people die from starvation or famine-related diseases; massive emigration begins, 1845

Ten Hours Act limits the number of hours that women and children can work in factories, 1847

Seneca Falls, New York, women's rights convention is led by Elizabeth Cady Stanton and Lucretia Mott, 1848

Social and political revolutions in France, Germany, and the Austrian Empire mostly fail, 1848

Japan opens trade to West, 1854

Change in laws allows Lionel de Rothschild to become first Jewish member of Parliament, 1858

Medical Act closes loophole that briefly allowed women to become physicians in Great Britain, 1858

• Imperial State Crown (1837) made for Victoria's coronation.

• Front page of *The Lily* (August 1852).

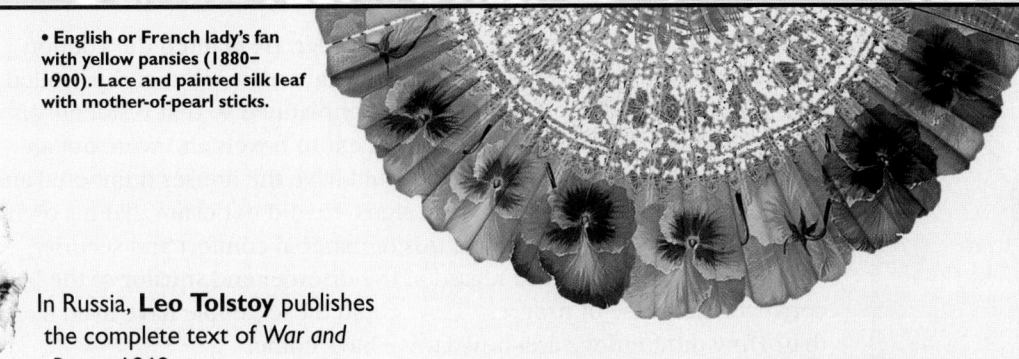

• Charles Darwin.

• English or French lady's fan with yellow pansies (1880–1900). Lace and painted silk leaf with mother-of-pearl sticks.

In Russia, **Leo Tolstoy** publishes the complete text of *War and Peace,* 1869

Louisa May Alcott publishes *Little Women,* 1868–1869

Lewis Carroll publishes *Alice's Adventures in Wonderland,* 1865

In France, Victor Hugo publishes *Les Misérables,* 1862

L. Frank Baum publishes *The Wonderful Wizard of Oz,* 1900

Arthur Conan Doyle introduces the world to Sherlock Holmes with *A Study in Scarlet,* 1887

Mark Twain's *Adventures of Huckleberry Finn* appears, 1884

Olive Schreiner describes South African life in *The Story of an African Farm,* a novel introducing the independent "New Woman," 1883

1860–1869

1870–1901

U.S. Civil War begins, 1861

Russian serfs are emancipated, 1861

Abraham Lincoln's Emancipation Proclamation declares slavery illegal in Confederate territories, 1863

Last Japanese shogun resigns; power returns to emperor, 1867

Second Reform Act gives vote to most male industrial workers, doubling the number of voters, 1867

Britain ends eighty-year practice of sending convicts to Australia, 1868

Debtors' prisons are abolished in England, 1869

Suez Canal opens, 1869

Mohandas K. Gandhi born in India, 1869

Zulu War against British in South Africa begins, 1879

Thomas Edison invents an incandescent lamp, 1879

Married Women's Property Act allows wives possession of property held before and after marriage, 1882

Indian National Congress is formed; begins agitating for Indian self-rule, 1885

Emmeline Pankhurst forms Women's Franchise League, arguing for British women's suffrage, 1889

More than 140 Sioux villagers are killed by U.S. soldiers at Wounded Knee Creek, South Dakota, 1890

Home Rule Bill (to create an Irish Parliament) defeated by British Parliament for second time, 1893

French scientists Pierre and Marie Curie discover radium, 1898

Queen Victoria dies, 1901

wrote. Macaulay admired cleanliness and order. He wanted the London streets free of garbage, drained and paved, lighted at night, and patrolled by a sober police force. He wanted the city planned so that residents of respectable neighborhoods did not live next to hovels and were not annoyed by beggars and peddlers. He would have the houses numbered and a population literate enough to read signs. He did not claim that his own time had entirely met these standards of material comfort and security, but his cool, almost amazed regard of the disorder and squalor of the past conveyed his sense of progress: How could those people have lived like that? How different we are; how far we have come.

Many Victorians regretted or disputed Macaulay's confident tone and materialistic standards. But in his satisfaction with the improvements that empire had brought to England, his views were typical of those of his contemporaries.

Middle-class Victorians prided themselves on their material advances and on their ability to solve social problems.

The "Hungry Forties"

Whatever its advances, the first decade of Victoria's reign was troubled—the period came to be known as the "Hungry Forties." Victoria came to the throne in the first year of a depression that by 1842 had put a million and a half unemployed workers and their families (in a population of sixteen million in England and Wales) on some form of poor relief. Government commissions investigating working conditions learned of children mangled when they fell asleep at machines at the end of a twelve-hour working day. They discovered young girls and boys hauling sledges of coal through narrow mine tunnels, working shifts so long that in winter they saw the sun only on Sundays.

The years of the Famine [in Ireland], of the bad life and of the hunger, arrived and broke the spirit and strength of the community. People simply wanted to survive. Their spirit of comradeship was lost. It didn't matter what ties or relations you had; you considered that person to be your friend who gave you food to put in your mouth. Recreation and leisure ceased. Poetry, music, and dancing died. These things were lost and completely forgotten. When life improved in other ways, these pursuits never returned as they had been. The famine killed everything.

The old people said that in the summer of 1846 the potato blight struck for the first time. People went to sleep at night with the potato fields looking green and healthy; when they got up the next day, every stem in the fields was ruined by the disease. . . .

They [the starving people] used to stay inside in their cabins, not able to walk, so weak were they with hunger. They would go out in the fields on all fours and eat their fill of grass and weeds and then they'd be able to walk home. Mothers lay in their beds with the children beside them and they were so weak they were not able to get up. They used to lie there until one after another they died of hunger.

—Maire ni Grianna, *from Memories of the Famine*

London Street Scene (1835) by J. O. Parry.

In Ireland, the potato blight (1845–1849) caused a famine that killed perhaps a million people and forced two million others—more than 25 percent of Ireland's population—to emigrate. Some went to English cities, where they lived ten or twelve to a room in slums that had two toilets for every 250 people.

The rapid growth of cities often made them filthy and disorderly. Nearly two million people lived in London during the 1840s, and commercial and industrial cities such as Manchester and Liverpool expanded rapidly. In Manchester in the 1840s, 40 percent of the streets were still unpaved. The Thames River in London was polluted by sewage, industrial waste, and the drainage from graveyards where bodies were buried in layers six or eight deep. In the 1850s, Parliament sometimes had to adjourn from its new riverside building because of the stench from the Thames.

From the butchers' and greengrocers' shops the gaslights flared and flickered, wild and ghastly, over haggard groups of slipshod dirty women, bargaining for scraps of stale meat and frostbitten vegetables, wrangling about short weight and bad quality. Fish stalls and fruit stalls lined the edge of the greasy pavement, sending up odors as foul as the language of sellers and buyers. Blood and sewer water crawled from under doors and out of spouts, and reeked down the gutters among offal, animal and vegetable, in every stage of putrefaction.

—Charles Kingsley

Serious problems surfaced during the early years of Victoria's reign: economic depression, widespread unemployment, famine in Ireland, and deplorable living and working conditions brought on by rapid urbanization and a lack of measures safeguarding young workers.

AN AGE IN NEED OF HEROINES: REFORM IN VICTORIAN BRITAIN

Be good, sweet maid, and let who will be clever;
Do noble things, not dream them, all day long.

—Charles Kingsley

Great Britain was the world's first industrialized nation, and its smoky cities illustrated the dangers of "progress": Unsanitary housing and rampant disease were unremarkably common. There were legal remedies for abuses, but Victorian social reform was not only a parliamentary process. It was also a passionate struggle to change public opinion through hard work and education.

"Do noble things." Following the Reverend Charles Kingsley's urging to "Do noble things, not dream them," many women approached social reform as a moral and religious duty. The social worker Octavia Hill (1838–1912) believed that adequate housing could "make individual life noble, homes happy, and family life good," and she became an authority on housing reform. She was also a conservationist, founding the National Trust to protect historic buildings and scenic spots from industrial development. Because of Hill's efforts, the public can visit sites such as the Runnymede meadow. Thanks to the National Trust, it looks much as it did when King John accepted the Magna Carta there in 1215.

Spoiling the "brutes." Perhaps the best-known Victorian reformer is Florence Nightingale (1820–1910), who transformed the public's perception of modern nursing during the Crimean War. Two unlikely inventions—the camera and the war correspondent—made her career possible. Newspaper reports revealed that bureaucratic bungling had cost thousands of lives in the army's hospitals in Scutari, Turkey. Public indignation gave Nightingale the unprecedented opportunity to become an army nurse. In Turkey, she saw scores of wounded soldiers dying from diseases caused by poor hygiene, lack of medical supplies, and sheer neglect. The ordinary British soldier was thought to be, in the words of the duke of Wellington, "the scum of the earth." When Nightingale asked medical authorities for clean bedding or warm clothing, she was told: "You will spoil the brutes."

Nightingale believed British soldiers were "murdered" by incompetence, and she vowed to avenge them. With gritty tenacity, she became an authority on public health, observing that sanitation could save lives. Queen Victoria read her meticulous reports and said, "I wish we had her at the War Office." Nightingale's efforts fundamentally changed hospital management and made nursing a respected career.

The Movement for Reform: Food, Factories, and Optimism

Violence broke out at massive political rallies called in the 1840s to protest government policies that kept the price of bread and other food high and deprived most working men (and all women) of the vote and representation in Parliament. In 1848, a year of revolution in Europe, nervous British politicians got the army ready and armed the staffs of museums and government offices when working-class political reformers organized what they called a "monster rally" in London to petition Parliament and the queen.

Still, most middle-class Victorians believed that things were better than in the past and that they were going to be better yet in the future. Their opinion was in part founded on a steady improvement throughout the Victorian era in the material condition of people in all social classes. The

Florence Nightingale tending the wounded during the Crimean War (19th century).

"We make no compromise." Reformers such as Nightingale and Hill devoted themselves to aiding the victims of Victorian "progress," agitating for better conditions and for improved educational opportunities. In the name of charity, they often stepped outside the bounds of "ladylike" behavior. Josephine Butler (1828–1906) exposed the exploitation of women and girls, working to repeal acts that deprived poor women of their constitutional rights.

In the name of reform, she declared that "we make no compromise; and we are ready to meet all the powers of earth and hell combined."

These reformers redefined the idea of "women's work"; in the process, they set public policies that curbed many abuses and saved countless lives. As we enter the twenty-first century, we continue to benefit from their efforts to improve the Victorian quality of life.

price of food dropped after midcentury, largely because of trade with other countries and the growing empire. Diet improved as meat, fruit, and margarine (a Victorian invention) began to appear regularly in working-class households. Factories and railroads made postage, newspapers, clothing, furniture, travel, and other goods and services cheap.

A series of political reforms gave the vote to almost all adult males by the last decades of the century. In 1832, the First Reform Bill extended the vote to all men who owned property worth ten pounds or more in yearly rent. Continued pressure led to the Second

> The principle which regulates the existing social relations between the two sexes—the legal subordination of one sex to the other—is wrong in itself, and now one of the chief hindrances to human improvement.
>
> —John Stuart Mill,
> *from The Subjection of Women*

Reform Act in 1867, which gave the right to vote to most working-class men except for agricultural workers. Decades of agitation by Victorian women for suffrage succeeded only in the next century. Strengthened by their domestic contributions during the Great War, women age thirty and over won the vote in 1918. Universal adult suffrage in 1928 extended the vote to women at age twenty-one.

A series of Factory Acts limited child labor and reduced the usual working day to ten hours, with a half-holiday on Saturday. State-supported schools were established in 1870, made compulsory in 1880, and made

A CLOSER LOOK

THE PRE-RAPHAELITE BROTHERHOOD: CHALLENGING ARTISTIC AUTHORITY

The Times called it "plainly revolting." The *Literary Gazette* found it "a nameless atrocity." Charles Dickens thought its central character "a hideous, wry-necked, blubbering, red-haired boy in a nightgown." The painting that elicited such scathing abuse was *Christ in the House of His Parents* (1850) by John Everett Millais (1829–1896). Millais shocked the art world with his innovative techniques and the treatment of his subject—he portrayed the Holy Family as ordinary people in a shavings-strewn carpentry shop.

Millais belonged to the Pre-Raphaelite Brotherhood (PRB), a group that embraced the ordinary while rejecting "conventionalities and feeble reminiscences from the Old Masters." Dissatisfied with Victorian complacency, a group of seven young men modeled their work after medieval painters— those *before* the Renaissance painter Raphael—that they believed had a more natural vision. Founded in 1848, the PRB never shared a unifying style or principle. But they were united in their sense, as the artist Sir Edward Burne-Jones (1833–1898) said, that "the time is out of joint."

Christ in the House of His Parents (1850) by Sir John Everett Millais.

Tate Gallery, London.

free in 1891. In the 1840s, 40 percent of the couples getting married could not write their names on their marriage certificates. By 1900, using that simple definition of literacy, more than 90 percent of the population was literate.

As the nineteenth century progressed, living conditions gradually improved. Food and other commodities became more readily available, most adult males won the right to vote, laws regulated the use of child labor, and compulsory education brought about widespread literacy.

Proserpine (1874) by Dante Gabriel Rossetti.

Tate Gallery, London.

Artistic "treason." The PRB is widely known for Dante Gabriel Rossetti's sensuous portraits. A favorite model was Jane Morris, and her long neck and abundant, wavy hair in works such as *Proserpine* (1874) are a PRB trademark.

To members of the Royal Academy of Art, however, PRB members were artistic outlaws. Their shading techniques violated the academy's guidelines that one "principal light" should focus a painting's main elements. Their minute rendering of details seemed busy and bewildering, "a strange disorder of the mind or the eyes." PRB member William Holman Hunt (1827–1910) prided himself on botanical and geologic accuracy, laboring over his paintings' individual rocks and flowers. "Our talk is the deepest treason against our betters," Hunt said.

Art and cultural values. The PRB disbanded in 1853, but it attracted followers, drawn by the PRB's medieval models, who had turned away from industrial Britain's materialism. The art critic John Ruskin (1819–1900) asserted that art and artists suffered from mechanization: He argued that the way art was produced could shape a culture's values.

The artist William Morris (1834–1896) applied these theories in a decorating firm that revived traditional methods of producing furniture, tapestries, and stained glass. His Kelmscott Press crafted fine books with the painstaking detail of hand-printed engravings and hand-sewn bindings. Morris, Ruskin, and former PRB members taught artisans these skills

and principles at the Working Men's College, an educational experiment begun in London in 1854.

Modern viewers delight in the PRB's exuberant excess of elaborate designs and glorious medieval trappings. Yet the Pre-Raphaelites' work also made a social statement. The tensions of the Industrial Revolution bonded the Brotherhood, and their rebellious movement raised difficult questions about the place of art and artists in a rapidly changing society.

The Drawing Room (late 19th or early 20th century) by Paul Gustav Fischer.

Decorum and Authority

Many Victorians thought of themselves as progressing morally and intellectually, as well as materially. In fact, the powerful, mostly middle-class obsession with gentility or decorum has made *prudery* almost a synonym for *Victorianism.* Book publishers and magazine editors deleted or altered words and episodes that might, in the phrase of the day, bring a blush to the cheek of a young person. In art and popular fiction, sex, birth, and death were softened by sentimental conventions into tender courtships, joyous motherhoods, and deathbed scenes in which old people became saints and babies became angels. In the real world, people were arrested for distributing information about sexually transmitted diseases. Victorian society regarded seduced or adulterous women (but not their male partners) as "fallen" and pushed them to the margins of respectability.

Victorian decorum also supported powerful ideas about authority. Many Victorians were uneasy about giving strong authority to a central government (although it is revealing of the fundamental decorum of British society that its version of the 1848 European revolutions was a meeting to petition Parliament). In Victorian private lives, however, the autocratic father of middle-class households is a vivid figure in both fact (Elizabeth Barrett Browning's father, for example) and fiction.

I still cling fondly to the hope that some system of female instruction will be discovered, by which the young women of England may be sent from school to the homes of their parents, habituated to be on the watch for every opportunity of doing good to others; making it the first and the last inquiry of every day, "What can I do to make my parents, my brothers, or my sisters, more happy? . . . I hope to pursue the plan to which I have been accustomed, of seeking my own happiness only in the happiness of others."

—Sarah Stickney Ellis, essayist who argued that women's education should cultivate "the heart," not the mind

Women in particular were subject to male authority. Middle-class women especially were expected to marry and make their homes a comfortable refuge for their husbands from the male domains of business, politics, and the professions. Women who did not marry had few occupations open to them. Working-class women could find jobs as servants in affluent households, while unmarried middle-class ladies could become governesses or teachers. Many middle-class women remained unmarried because men often postponed marriage until they achieved financial security. The problem of these unmarried, "redundant women," as they were called, was painful, although in literature, especially literature written by men, the figure of the middle-aged maiden was often played for comedy.

The excesses, cruelties, and hypocrisies of all these repressions were obvious to many Victorians. But the codes and barriers of decorum changed slowly because they were part of the ideology of progress. Prudery and social order were intended to control the licentiousness that Victorians associated with the political revolutions of the eighteenth century and the social corruption of the regency of George IV (1811–1820).

> When the views advanced by me in this volume . . . are generally admitted, we can dimly foresee that there will be a considerable revolution in natural history.
>
> —Charles Darwin, *from On the Origin of Species*

The Victorian emphasis on decorum grew from the conviction that life would be improved if it steadily became more refined, more rationally organized, better policed, and therefore safer.

Intellectual Progress: The March of Mind

The intellectual advances of the Victorian period were dramatically evident to those living in it. Humans began to understand the earth, its creatures, and its natural laws. Geologists worked out the history written in rocks and fossils. Based on countless

Applicants for Admission to a Casual Ward (1874) by Luke Fildes. Oil on canvas.

Royal Holloway and Bedford New College, University of London.

observations, Charles Darwin and other biologists theorized about the evolution of species. The industrialization of England depended on and supported science and technology, especially chemistry (in the iron and textile industries) and engineering.

Those who made and used scientific and technological knowledge had a confidence of their own. Thomas Huxley, a variously accomplished scientist who wrote and lectured frequently on the necessity of scientific education, imagined science as an exhilarating, high-stakes chess game with the physical universe.

> The chessboard is the world, the pieces are the phenomena of the universe, the rules of the game are what we call the laws of Nature. The player on the other side is hidden from us. We know that his play is always fair, just, and patient. But also we know, to our cost, that he never overlooks a mistake, or makes the smallest allowance for ignorance. To the man who plays well, the highest stakes are paid, with that sort of overflowing generosity with which the strong shows delight in strength. And one who plays ill is checkmated—without haste, but without remorse.
>
> —Thomas Huxley, *from A Liberal Education*

Huxley resembles those confident Victorians who built railways and sewers, organized markets and schools, and pushed through electoral reforms and laws regulating the conditions of work. These reformers believed that the world offered a challenging set of problems that could be understood by human intelligence and solved by science, government, and other human institutions. Huxley made the game exciting by warning that humans could lose. But so long as the game is played in the material world, Huxley and others like him saw no reason that they would not win.

Charles Dickens (1859) by William Powell Frith.
Victoria and Albert Museum, London.

Advances in science and technology convinced nineteenth-century intellectuals and reformers that human efforts could overcome all material problems.

Questions and Doubts

The Victorian period, and especially its literature, was filled with voices asking questions and raising doubts. Speaking for many of their contemporaries, and speaking to others they thought shallow and complacent, Victorian writers asked whether material comfort fully satisfied human needs and wishes. They questioned the cost of exploiting the earth and human beings to achieve such comfort. They protested or mocked codes of decorum and authority.

In the first half of the period, some writers complained that materialist ideas of reality completely overlooked the spirit or soul that made life beautiful and just. Later in the century, writers like Thomas Hardy and A. E. Housman thought that Macaulay's and Huxley's ideas of history and nature presupposed a coherence and generosity that did not really exist.

Literature in Victorian culture often reassured its readers that, rightly perceived, the universe made sense. But some writers unsettled their readers by telling them that they were not rightly perceiving the universe, or by asking them to consider whether human life and the natural world made as much sense as they had once hoped.

Charles Dickens, the most popular and most important figure in Victorian literature, is a case in point. The son of a debt-ridden clerk, Dickens lived out one of the favorite myths of the age: Through his own enormous talents and energy, he rose from poverty to become a wealthy and famous man. His was a peculiarly Victorian success, made possible by the increasing affluence and literacy, which gave him a large reading public, and by improved printing and distribution, which made book publishing a big business.

The conventional happy endings of Dickens's novels satisfied his readers', and probably his own, conviction that things usually work out well for decent people. But from the beginning of his career in the 1830s to the publication of his last complete novel in 1865, many of Dickens's most memorable scenes showed decent people

> There is no law of history any more than of a kaleidoscope.
>
> —John Ruskin

Who Were the Victorians?

Here are some of the social and material changes that marked the long reign of Queen Victoria.

- Industrialism made England the workshop of the world, with a mechanized factory system and extensive railways.
- Much of the British population moved from rural areas to rapidly growing cities.
- Expanded educational opportunities increased literacy; flourishing lending libraries and cheap periodicals created a mass reading public.
- Continued advances in science and technology gave Victorians hope that all social problems—disease, poverty, even immorality—could be resolved by the march of "progress."
- The human cost of industrialization was heavy: abuses of child labor, unsafe conditions in factories, and widespread disease from contaminated air and water.
- By the end of the century, the disruption and materialism of the era made people question changes brought on by rapid industrialization and reevaluate their definitions of progress.

neglected, abused, and exploited. The hungry Oliver Twist asks for more gruel in the workhouse; the crippled Tiny Tim in *A Christmas Carol* cheerfully hobbles toward his possible early death; and David Copperfield is beaten and exiled by the cold, dark Mr. Murdstone.

In his later novels, Dickens also created characters and scenes to show that even the winners in the competition for material gain had reason to be as desperate and unhappy as the losers. In *Our Mutual Friend,* his last novel, he describes a dinner party at the home of a family called the Veneerings, a name that emphasizes the family's superficial qualities. They are "bran-new people in a bran-new house in a bran-new quarter of London":

> The great looking-glass above the sideboard reflects the table and the company. Reflects the new Veneering crest, in gold and eke in silver, frosted and also thawed, a camel of all work. The Herald's College found out a Crusading ancestor for Veneering who bore a camel on his shield (or might have done it if he had thought of it), and a caravan of camels take charge of the fruits and flowers and candles, and kneel down to be loaded with the salt. Reflects Veneering; forty, wavy-haired, dark, tending to corpulence, sly, mysterious, filmy. . . . Reflects Mrs. Veneering; fair, aquiline-nosed and fingered, not so much light hair as she might have, gorgeous in raiment and jewels. . . . Reflects Podsnap; prosperously feeding, two little light-colored wiry wings, one on either side of his else bald head, looking as like his hairbrushes as his hair. . . . Reflects Mrs. Podsnap; . . . quantity of bone, neck, and nostrils like a rocking horse, hard

Many Happy Returns of the Day (19th century) by William Powell Frith.

features, majestic headdress in which Podsnap has hung golden offerings. . . . Reflects . . . mature young gentleman; with too much nose in his face, too much ginger in his whiskers, too much sparkle in his studs, his eyes, his buttons, his talk, and his teeth.

—Charles Dickens, *from Our Mutual Friend*

Attacks like Dickens's on the hollowness, glitter, superficiality, and excesses of Victorian affluence were common in Victorian literature, for example, in Robert Browning's portrayal of the murderously possessive duke in "My Last Duchess." Dickens also raised questions about the costs of progress in his descriptions of the huddle and waste of cities and the smoke and fire of industrial landscapes. In 1871, the art historian and social critic John Ruskin noted a new phenomenon that we call smog; he called it the plague wind, or "the storm-cloud of the nineteenth century," and concluded, chillingly, ". . . [M]ere smoke would not blow to and fro in that wild way. It looks more to me as if it were made of dead men's souls."

> **Lady Bracknell.** . . . I do not approve of anything that tampers with natural ignorance. Ignorance is like a delicate exotic fruit; touch it and the bloom is gone. The whole theory of modern education is radically unsound. Fortunately in England, at any rate, education produces no effect whatsoever. If it did, it would prove a serious danger to the upper classes, and probably lead to acts of violence in Grosvenor Square.
>
> —Oscar Wilde, *from The Importance of Being Earnest*

The materialism, secularism, vulgarity, and sheer waste that accompanied Victorian progress led some writers to wonder if their culture was really advancing by any measure.

From Trust to Skepticism and Denial

Trust in a transcendental power was characteristic of the early Victorian writers. They were the immediate heirs of the Romantic idea of a finite natural world surrounded by and interfused with an infinite, ideal transcendental reality. The highest purpose of a poet, of any writer, was to make readers aware of the connection between earth and heaven, body and soul, material and ideal. Fundamentally, as Thomas Carlyle wrote in his essay "The Hero as Poet," reality is spiritual, a divine idea. "All Appearances, from the starry sky to the grass of the field, but especially the Appearance of Man and his work, is but *vesture,* the embodiment that renders it [the divine idea] possible." The poet penetrates to the divine idea and makes it palpable in language and story to those of lesser power and vision. "That is always his message; he is to reveal that to us— that sacred mystery which he more than others lives ever present with."

> If we had a keen vision of all that is ordinary in human life, it would be like hearing the grass grow or the squirrel's heart beat, and we should die of that roar which is the other side of silence.
>
> —George Eliot, *from Middlemarch*

With some exceptions—Gerard Manley Hopkins is one and Christina Rossetti another—writers younger than Alfred Tennyson and Ruskin found it increasingly difficult to believe in an infinite power and order that made sense of material and human existence. Some simply thought it unnecessary. Algernon Charles Swinburne and Rudyard Kipling, in their different ways, celebrated a relation between humans and the natural world that could be joyous and even redemptive.

> Yes! in the sea of life enisled,
> With echoing straits between us thrown,
> Dotting the shoreless watery wild,
> We mortal millions live *alone.*
>
> —Matthew Arnold, *from*
> "To Marguerite—Continued"

Other writers at midcentury, sometimes reacting to explanations of the world that excluded the spiritual, were saddened by what seemed to them to be the withdrawal of the divine from the world. The dominant note of much mid-Victorian writing was struck by Matthew Arnold in his poem "Dover Beach": "The Sea of Faith," Arnold wrote, had ebbed. There was no certainty; or if there was, what was certain was that existence was not governed by a benevolent intelligence that cared for its creatures.

By the end of the century, this skepticism and denial had become pervasive in the works of Hardy, Housman, and others. Early- and mid-Victorian novelists such as Dickens and George Eliot had dramatized a human ideal achieved through sympathy and unselfishness. They made sad or frightening examples of people like the Murdstones in *David Copperfield* and Godfrey Cass in *Silas Marner*—all hard surface and no

A CLOSER LOOK

VICTORIAN DRAMA: FROM RELIEF TO REALISM

Interior of Drury Lane Theater, 1808 (19th century) by Thomas Rowlandson and A. Pugin.

Guildhall Library, Corporation of London.

Though Queen Victoria, who came to the throne in 1837, loved the theater, it was she who once remarked, "We are not amused." And certainly the theater of the early part of her reign provided little to amuse anyone. Comedy must have license to explore, to expose, to look under the bed, and to ridicule, but Victoria's England was marked by prudery, good taste, repression of natural feelings, high-mindedness, and official censorship.

Irreverent ridicule. The operettas that William S. Gilbert wrote to Arthur Sullivan's music, beginning with *Trial by Jury* (1875), provided some delightful comic relief. Though today we think of these operettas (such as *The Pirates of Penzance* and *H.M.S. Pinafore*) merely as charming, tuneful, witty entertainments, in their period they irreverently ridiculed the law, the navy, the world of aesthetes, and the aristocracy.

soul. Their heroes and heroines learned to find happiness in nurturing marriages and in small communities of family and friends. But there were few such marriages and communities in the fiction and poetry of Hardy and Housman. These late-Victorian writers told stories of lovers and friends bereft and betrayed by unfaithfulness, war, and the other troubles that humans add to the natural troubles of mortal life.

> *Over the century, the trust in a transcendental power inherited from the Romantics eroded, giving way to uncertainty and spiritual doubt. Late-Victorian writers turned to a pessimistic exploration of the human struggle against indifferent natural forces.*

Revealing Reality, Creating Coherence

Victorian writers had purposes as various as the ideas of reality they believed in. Some writers wanted to scare or shame readers into effective moral and political actions that they optimistically believed were possible. Some wanted to show readers what it is like to live in a pleasurable moment of intense feeling like that caught in a lyric or in the interesting perspectives of a character in a dramatic monologue or novel. Victorian literature entertained, informed, warned, and reassured.

Program cover for October 17, 1881, Savoy Theatre production of *Patience* by Sir W. S. Gilbert and Sir Arthur Sullivan.

Intrinsic to Gilbert and Sullivan operettas was a world-turned-on-its-head view of life that would influence both Oscar Wilde and Bernard Shaw. In Gilbert and Sullivan, "Things are seldom what they seem. / Skim milk masquerades as cream."

Moving toward realism. Coming into the era of Oscar Wilde and Bernard Shaw, drama was moving toward realism, which has been the dominant dramatic mode for the last hundred years. In England and in Europe, fiction writers were dealing with the social realities of the time—Charles Dickens among others in England, Émile Zola in France. From Scandinavia came the revolutionary voices of Henrik Ibsen in plays such as *An Enemy of the People* (1882) and of August Strindberg in *Miss Julie* (1888).

While some playwrights were assimilating new points of view and style, the theaters were also undergoing changes to accommodate the new plays. For years, London had been dominated by two huge

theaters, Covent Garden and Drury Lane, each seating well over three thousand people—large theaters not congenial to intimate realistic drama.

In the early part of the nineteenth century, new, smaller theaters were built. The forestage, or apron, was removed, and gaslight (and soon electricity) took the place of candles once used to illuminate the stage. These changes cleared the way for the staging of smaller-scale realistic dramas, which an audience might view as though through an invisible "fourth wall," allowing the audience to eavesdrop on the action. In smaller theaters, on such a stage with new lighting, playwrights could now achieve an illusion of reality.

Even the playfulness of Lewis Carroll and Oscar Wilde shows the two most important and consistent purposes or effects of Victorian literature. The first was to make readers hope, or wonder if, reality was really like that—really as whole and satisfying as in Tennyson's *In Memoriam,* as briskly coherent as in a poem by Browning or an essay by Macaulay. The second principal purpose or effect was to demonstrate that, however bleak and chaotic reality seemed to be, the writer and reader could make a pleasing order in it. Even when a story or poem said that the world was ugly or made no sense, the story or the poem could seem beautiful and make sense to its audience. In every successful act of writing and reading literature, one more satisfyingly coherent thing in the world is created or discovered.

Finally, it is important to remember that these purposes and effects happened first to readers who were living Victorian lives. Victorian literature did not exist above or outside the comfortable and often confident lives of its readers. Many of the people who read Dickens settled down with his books after dining in rooms as garishly decorated as the Veneerings'. Most of the young men and women who thrilled to Dante Gabriel Rossetti's sensualism and to Housman's tender gloom probably moved on to make proper and modestly happy marriages and to find worthy occupations. People who were making a lot of money listened to Carlyle and Ruskin telling them that they were foolish and damned. People who were disturbed by how much money was being made listened to Macaulay reminding them that a century or so before they might not have been able to afford, or even to read, his book.

> **Lord Darlington.** . . . we are all in the gutter, but some of us are looking at the stars.
>
> —Oscar Wilde, *from Lady Windermere's Fan*

Victorian literature needs to be read not just as a comment on the complexity of its culture, but also as an important part of that culture. Its writers sent their words to work in the world to alter, to reinforce, to challenge, to enlarge, or to temper the ideas and feelings with which their contemporaries managed their lives.

Victorian writing reflects the dangers and benefits of rapid industrialization, while encouraging readers to examine closely their own understanding of the era's progress.

Quickwrite What do you think of the Victorian idea of progress? Do you agree that tangible improvements in material comfort and security constitute human progress? Or do you think there's more to it than that? Why? Jot down your thoughts about what progress means to you. If you'd like to, ask a classmate to respond to your written ideas.

(Opposite) *The Daydream* (19th century) by Dante Gabriel Rossetti.
Victoria and Albert Museum, London.

LOVE AND LOSS

Tennyson

Browning

Barrett Browning

Hopkins

I cannot say what loves have come and gone;
I only know that summer sang in me
A little while, that in me sings no more.

—Edna St. Vincent Millay (American, 1892 –1950),
from "What Lips My Lips Have Kissed"

Alfred, Lord Tennyson

(1809–1892)

When Alfred Tennyson learned that Lord Byron had died while helping Greek nationalist rebels, he went to the woods and carved on a piece of sandstone, "Byron is dead." Tennyson was fourteen years old. He felt sure that he would be a poet, and he was already practicing the dramatic gestures of the Romantic poets he admired.

Tennyson's father was a clergyman of good family but little money, who encouraged young Alfred's interest in poetry. At Cambridge University Alfred joined a group of young intellectuals, called the Apostles, who believed that their friend was destined to become the greatest poet of their generation.

In 1831, when his father died, lack of funds forced Tennyson to leave Cambridge, and he entered a troubled period. In 1832, he published his first significant book of poems, which some reviewers derided for its melancholy themes and weak imitations of Keats's language. The next year Tennyson was devastated by the death of his closest friend, Arthur Henry Hallam. He became engaged to marry in 1836, but the marriage was postponed for fourteen years because of his uncertain financial prospects. In 1843, his family invested in a woodcarving machine and lost what little remained of their money.

During this difficult period, when both his physical and mental health suffered, Tennyson apparently never considered any career but poetry. He polished his style to develop the melodious line and rich imagery of poems like "The Lady of Shalott." Tennyson published almost nothing in his "ten years' silence" from 1832 to 1842, but the friends to whom he read his poems remained convinced of his promise.

Gradually, Tennyson began to make his way. The two-volume *Poems* (1842) was favorably reviewed, and in 1845 the government granted him an annual pension of two hundred pounds. In 1850, he published *In Memoriam,* an elegy to

Caricature of Alfred, Lord Tennyson (1872) by Frederick Waddy.

Hallam that was immediately successful. It tells the story of his own recovery of faith in the immortality of the soul and of the harmony of creation—despite the new, unsettling discoveries of science and his deep sense of the unfairness of Hallam's death. That year, he was named poet laureate (after Wordsworth's death), and he finally married. Now Tennyson settled into the long, successful career that had been expected of him, and for the rest of his life he was considered the greatest living English poet.

In the forty years before his death in 1892, Tennyson published nearly a dozen volumes of poems. These include *The Idylls of the King,* which makes the rise, fall, and possible return of King Arthur into a kind of parable about the moral qualities of good political leaders and of their betrayal by the rest of us. His books sold like best-selling novels and made him rich. In 1884, he was made a peer of the realm and became Alfred, Lord Tennyson.

Tennyson never lost the melancholy and sense of chaos that friends and reviewers found in his early poems. He was immensely popular with his contemporaries because he spoke in a beautiful, measured language of their sense of the precariousness and sadness of life. And he also assured his readers that his own experience of sadness and disorder had taught him that everything was part of a benevolent plan in which eventually all losses would be made good.

Before You Read

TEARS, IDLE TEARS

Make the Connection

Shadows of the Past

Remembering the past: Do you find it sad or satisfying to look backward? You're probably thinking, "Obviously, that depends on what's being remembered—happy or sad times." But is that the only view? Is there a way in which memory itself—the very *fact* of the past—always shadows life in the present?

Quickwrite

How can tears be "idle"—can you cry without knowing why? Write a quick response.

Background

This poem is the most famous of eleven lyric songs that are interspersed in *The Princess,* a long narrative poem about women's education and emancipation. Tennyson wrote the lyric while visiting Tintern Abbey in the autumn, the same site Wordsworth contemplated in his famous meditation (page 658).

Disappointed Love (1821) by Francis Danby.

By Courtesy of The Board of Trustees of the Victoria and Albert Museum, London.

Tears, Idle Tears

Alfred, Lord Tennyson

Tears, idle tears, I know not what they mean,
Tears from the depth of some divine despair
Rise in the heart, and gather to the eyes,
In looking on the happy autumn fields,
5 And thinking of the days that are no more.

Fresh as the first beam glittering on a sail,
That brings our friends up from the underworld,
Sad as the last which reddens over one
That sinks with all we love below the verge;
10 So sad, so fresh, the days that are no more.

Ah, sad and strange as in dark summer dawns
The earliest pipe of half-awakened birds
To dying ears, when unto dying eyes
The casement slowly grows a glimmering square;
15 So sad, so strange, the days that are no more.

Dear as remembered kisses after death,
And sweet as those by hopeless fancy feigned
On lips that are for others; deep as love,
Deep as first love, and wild with all regret;
20 O Death in Life, the days that are no more!

The Offer (1866) by Thomas Faed.

MAKING MEANINGS

First Thoughts

1. After reading this poem, would you change what you wrote about "idle tears" in your Quickwrite notes? Why or why not?

Shaping Interpretations

2. What is the scene of each stanza of "Tears, Idle Tears"? Why do you think Tennyson orders the stanzas as he does?

3. Do you think the poem's sequence of images creates an increasingly dark **tone**? Explain.

4. What do you think the "divine despair" is in line 2? Could you relate it to Adam and Eve's fall in Genesis (page 416)—would that story explain the speaker's existential sadness? Explain.

5. Stanzas 2–4 present a series of comparisons that attempt to make concrete the abstract memory of "the days that are no more." What are these comparisons?

Connecting with the Text

6. Does the contradiction in the phrase "Death in Life" (line 20) make sense to you? Explain. What is your response to this line?

Make the Connection

Lessons Large and Small

The poet, the scientist, and the religious believer don't necessarily have conflicting ideas about the phrase *mysteries of nature*. Yet to some nineteenth-century artists and believers, modern science's scrutiny of nature was a threat—a fearful one. Would a microscope reveal the secrets of matter, but at the expense of our traditional concepts of beauty and faith?

Part of Tennyson's immense popularity was that he addressed these philosophical issues and, for many, offered ways of resolving them.

Reading Skills and Strategies

Dialogue with the Text

Stop after reading each poem, and jot down the quality of nature that you think each poem evokes.

Elements of Literature

Tercet

Although Tennyson called "The Eagle" a fragment, its verse form and organization give it a feeling of completeness. Each stanza is a **tercet:** three lines with one rhyme. The eagle and the world are at rest in the first stanza and are moving in the second.

The Eagle: A Fragment

Alfred, Lord Tennyson

He clasps the crag with crooked hands;
Close to the sun in lonely lands,
Ringed with the azure world, he stands.

The wrinkled sea beneath him crawls;
He watches from his mountain walls,
And like a thunderbolt he falls.

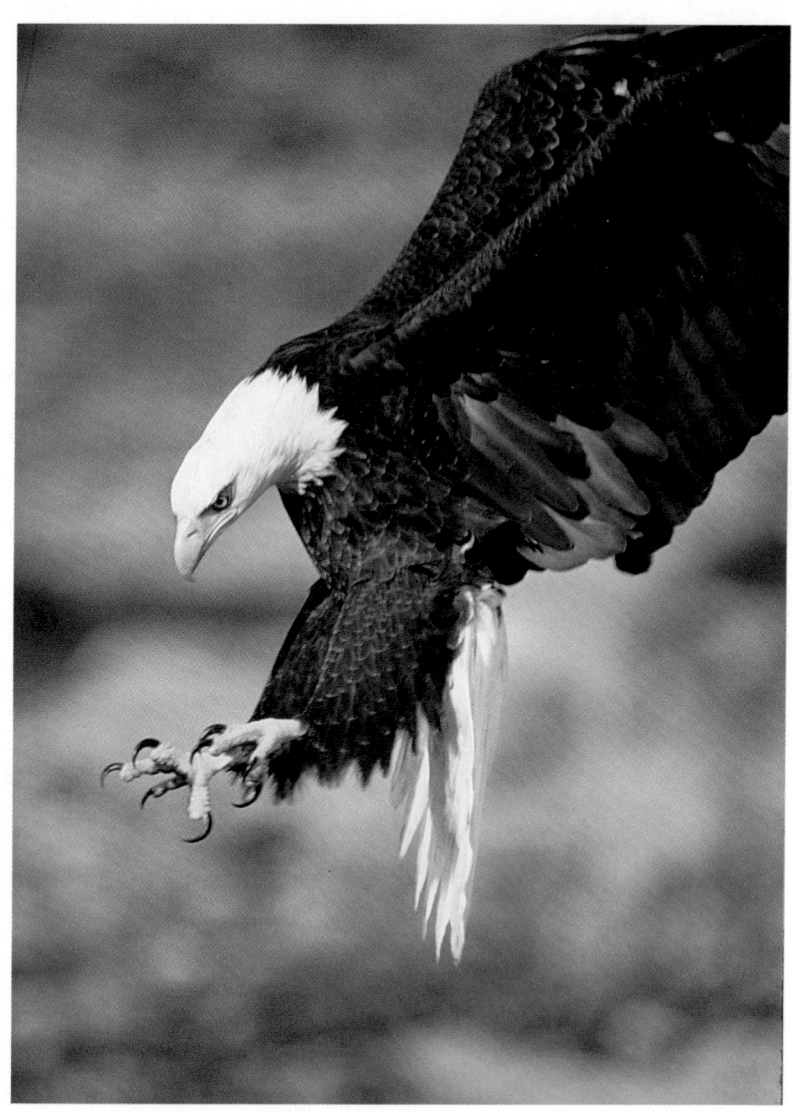

Flower in the Cranied Wall

Alfred, Lord Tennyson

Flower in the crannied wall,
I pluck you out of the crannies,
I hold you here, root and all, in my hand,
Little flower—but *if* I could understand
What you are, root and all, and all in all,
I should know what God and man is.

MAKING MEANINGS

The Eagle: A Fragment
Flower in the Cranied Wall

First Thoughts

1. What contrasting qualities of nature do you think Tennyson captures in these lyrics? (Check your reading notes.)

Shaping Interpretations

2. How does Tennyson use the **tercet** form to describe what is happening in "The Eagle"?

3. How could the sea, in "The Eagle," be "wrinkled"? What is suggested about the eagle's power in the last **simile**?

4. What do you think "all in all" (line 5) means in "Flower in the Crannied Wall"? What does the speaker seek to learn from the flower?

5. Suppose the eagle and the flower are used as **symbols.** What would you say they symbolize to Tennyson?

Challenging the Text

6. Do you agree with what Tennyson says a flower could tell us? How would a scientist regard the same flower?

Lord Tennyson (1903) by George Frederick Watts. The statue stands outside Lincoln Cathedral in Lincolnshire, England.

Before You Read
THE LADY OF SHALOTT

Make the Connection
Shattering Glass

One of the main symbols in this dreamlike ballad is a mirror that the Lady uses with her weaving. Watch for how the mirror with its reflected images is in opposition to the "real" world. This is only one opposition, or tension, in the world of the Lady of Shalott, of whom Tennyson said: "The newborn love for something, for someone in the wide world from which she had been so long secluded, takes her out of the region of shadows into that of realities."

Reading Skills and Strategies

Noting Text Structures

As you read, be alert to **oppositions**—in setting, actions, or imagery—and record the first example you notice. Then, when Sir Lancelot appears in Part III, jot down at least one other contrast that he introduces.

Elements of Literature
Word Music

Be sure to read this poem aloud to hear the famous music of Tennyson's language. That music is created by the expert use of **meter** and by the dazzling use of **rhymes, alliteration,** and **assonance.** For many years schoolchildren in both England and the United States could recite the mysterious story of the Lady of Shalott from memory. You might try it.

The Lady of Shalott (1888) by John William Waterhouse.

Tate Gallery, London.

The Lady of Shalott

Alfred, Lord Tennyson

Part I

On either side the river lie
Long fields of barley and of rye,
That clothe the wold° and meet the sky;
And through the field the road runs by
5   To many-towered Camelot;°
And up and down the people go,
Gazing where the lilies blow°
Round an island there below,
      The island of Shalott.

10 Willows whiten,° aspens quiver,
Little breezes dusk and shiver
Through the wave that runs forever
By the island in the river
      Flowing down to Camelot.
15 Four gray walls, and four gray towers,
Overlook a space of flowers,
And the silent isle imbowers°
      The Lady of Shalott.

By the margin, willow-veiled,
20 Slide the heavy barges trailed
By slow horses; and unhailed
The shallop° flitteth silken-sailed
      Skimming down to Camelot:
But who hath seen her wave her hand?
25 Or at the casement seen her stand?
Or is she known in all the land,
      The Lady of Shalott?

Only reapers, reaping early
In among the bearded barley,
30 Hear a song that echoes cheerly°
From the river winding clearly,
      Down to towered Camelot;
And by the moon the reaper weary,
Piling sheaves in uplands airy,
35 Listening, whispers "'Tis the fairy
      Lady of Shalott."

3. wold: rolling plain.

5. Camelot: legendary city, site of King Arthur's court and Round Table.

7. blow: blossom.

10. whiten: show the white undersides of their leaves when blown by the wind.

17. imbowers: shelters with trees, gardens, and flowers.

22. shallop: small, open boat.

30. cheerly: archaic for "cheerily."

The Lady of Shalott (c. 1886–1905)
by William Holman Hunt. Oil.

©Manchester City Art Galleries, England.

Part II

There she weaves by night and day
A magic web with colors gay.
She has heard a whisper say,
40 A curse is on her if she stay
      To look down to Camelot.
She knows not what the curse may be,
And so she weaveth steadily,
And little other care hath she,
45   The Lady of Shalott.

And moving through a mirror clear°
That hangs before her all the year,
Shadows of the world appear.
There she sees the highway near
50   Winding down to Camelot;
There the river eddy whirls,
And there the surly village churls,°
And the red cloaks of market girls,
      Pass onward from Shalott.

46. mirror clear: Weavers worked on the back of the tapestry so that they could easily knot their yarns. To see the front of their designs, weavers looked in a mirror that reflected the front of the tapestry.

52. churls: peasants; country folk.

55 Sometimes a troop of damsels glad,
An abbot on an ambling pad,°
Sometimes a curly shepherd lad,
Or long-haired page in crimson clad,
     Goes by to towered Camelot;
60 And sometimes through the mirror blue
The knights come riding two and two:
She hath no loyal knight and true,
     The Lady of Shalott.

But in her web she still delights
65 To weave the mirror's magic sights,
For often through the silent nights
A funeral, with plumes and lights
     And music, went to Camelot;
Or when the moon was overhead,
70 Came two young lovers lately wed:
"I am half sick of shadows," said
     The Lady of Shalott.

Part III

A bowshot from her bower eaves,
He rode between the barley sheaves,
75 The sun came dazzling through the leaves,
And flamed upon the brazen greaves°
     Of bold Sir Lancelot.
A red-cross knight° forever kneeled
To a lady in his shield,
80 That sparkled on the yellow field,
     Beside remote Shalott.

The gemmy° bridle glittered free,
Like to some branch of stars we see
Hung in the golden Galaxy.°
85 The bridle bells rang merrily
     As he rode down to Camelot;
And from his blazoned baldric° slung
A mighty silver bugle hung,
And as he rode his armor rung,
90   Beside remote Shalott.

All in the blue unclouded weather
Thick-jeweled shone the saddle leather,
The helmet and the helmet feather
Burned like one burning flame together,
95   As he rode down to Camelot;
As often through the purple night,
Below the starry clusters bright,
Some bearded meteor, trailing light,
     Moves over still Shalott.

56. pad: easy-gaited horse.

76. greaves: armor for the lower legs.

78. red-cross knight: The red cross is the emblem of St. George, England's patron saint.

82. gemmy: set with jewels.

84. Galaxy: Milky Way.

87. blazoned baldric: richly decorated sash worn across the chest diagonally.

100 His broad clear brow in sunlight glowed;
On burnished° hooves his war horse trode;
From underneath his helmet flowed
His coal-black curls as on he rode,
  As he rode down to Camelot.
105 From the bank and from the river
He flashed into the crystal mirror,
"Tirra lirra," by the river
  Sang Sir Lancelot.

She left the web, she left the loom,
110 She made three paces through the room,
She saw the waterlily bloom,
She saw the helmet and the plume,
  She looked down to Camelot.
Out flew the web and floated wide;
115 The mirror cracked from side to side;
"The curse is come upon me," cried
  The Lady of Shalott.

Part IV

In the stormy east wind straining,
The pale yellow woods were waning,
120 The broad stream in his banks complaining,
Heavily the low sky raining
  Over towered Camelot;
Down she came and found a boat
Beneath a willow left afloat,
125 And round about the prow° she wrote
  The Lady of Shalott.

And down the river's dim expanse
Like some bold seër° in a trance,
Seeing all his own mischance—
130 With a glassy countenance
  Did she look to Camelot.
And at the closing of the day
She loosed the chain, and down she lay;
The broad stream bore her far away,
135   The Lady of Shalott.

Lying, robed in snowy white
That loosely flew to left and right—
The leaves upon her falling light—
Through the noises of the night
140   She floated down to Camelot;
And as the boat head wound along
The willowy hills and fields among,
They heard her singing her last song,
  The Lady of Shalott.

101. burnished: polished.

125. prow: front part of a boat.

128. seër: prophet.

145 Heard a carol, mournful, holy,
    Chanted loudly, chanted lowly,
    Till her blood was frozen slowly,
    And her eyes were darkened wholly,
        Turned to towered Camelot.
150 For ere she reached upon the tide
    The first house by the waterside,
    Singing in her song she died,
        The Lady of Shalott.

    Under tower and balcony,
155 By garden wall and gallery,
    A gleaming shape she floated by,
    Dead-pale between the houses high,
        Silent into Camelot.
    Out upon the wharfs they came,
160 Knight and burgher,° lord and dame,
    And round the prow they read her name,
        The Lady of Shalott.

    Who is this? and what is here?
    And in the lighted palace near
165 Died the sound of royal cheer;
    And they crossed themselves for fear,
        All the knights at Camelot:
    But Lancelot mused a little space;
    He said, "She has a lovely face;
170 God in his mercy lend her grace,
        The Lady of Shalott."

160. burgher: townsperson.

The Lady of Shalott
(19th century) by John
William Waterhouse.

Escaping a World of Shadows

Readers may differ in regard to the meaning or moral of the simple story this richly ornamented and carefully wrought poem tells. As you learned before you read the poem, no one should disregard the clue offered by Tennyson himself: "The newborn love for something," he said of the Lady of Shalott, "for someone in the wide world from which she had been so long secluded, takes her out of the region of shadows into that of realities." He is referring particularly to the last lines of Part II when, having watched a young bride and groom in the moonlight, the Lady declares that she is "half sick of shadows."

Like the weaving that perpetually occupies the heroine—"A magic web with colors gay"—the narrative moves from scene to scene with a tapestried grace that quietly captures the romantic heart of the Age of Chivalry. The Lady is appropriately beautiful, wan, sequestered, and mysterious. Sir Lancelot, panoplied to the hilt with every object in the book of heraldry, is less a man than a vision of a man. And Camelot itself, "many-towered," exists like a little city afloat in time.

The "mirror clear" in line 46 is crucial both to the poem's narrative line and to its meaning. In the custom of weavers, the Lady has placed this mirror in a spot facing the loom from which she is able to see at a glance how her work is going. But, for the purposes of the story, the more important function of the mirror is to allow the Lady glimpses or "shadows" of the world in which she takes no part.

MAKING MEANINGS

First Thoughts

1. What do you think the Lady's "curse" is? Why do you think so?

Shaping Interpretations

2. Summarize the main events in the **plot** of this narrative poem. What moment marks its **climax**?

3. Scan the poem to find its metrical form. What is its **rhyme scheme**? What examples of **alliteration** and **assonance** help create the haunting music?

4. Point out **images** of dazzling light associated with Sir Lancelot in Part III. Find **contrasting images** associated with the Lady. What do you think is the meaning of this contrast? (Refer to your reading notes.)

5. Explain why lines 66–72 could **foreshadow** Lancelot's arrival and the Lady's actions in the second half of the poem. What yearning do you think the Lady expresses when she exclaims, "I am half sick of shadows" (line 71)?

6. How does Tennyson **contrast** the Lady's life with the lives of the villagers and court in Camelot? Do you think that Tennyson indicates a preference for any of these ways of life?

7. This poem was written during Tennyson's ten years of silence. Can you see any connection between the poem and his own life? Explain.

Challenging the Text

8. Think of the "magic web" the Lady weaves and the conditions under which she creates her art. What commentary do you think Tennyson is making on the role and life of an artist? How do you feel about his ideas? When would artistic seclusion be necessary, and when might it be undesirable?

Before You Read

FROM IN MEMORIAM A.H.H.

Make the Connection

Surviving Grief

Why? That is often the first question an early or terrible death wrings from us. Tragic loss can make life seem arbitrary or ruthless; grief can even cause us to question our personal beliefs.

Quickwrite

Think of someone (perhaps a public figure) you admire who has died. What questions and feelings did that death raise for you?

Background

In Memoriam (Latin for "in memory of") is Tennyson's elegy for Arthur Henry Hallam, his closest friend at Cambridge and his sister's fiancé. Hallam, who died of a sudden brain seizure, was thought to be an extraordinarily promising young man, and his death shook the poet deeply.

Tennyson struggled to survive not only his grief but also the religious doubt that Hallam's death bred. In the 131 separate lyrics of his elegy, which was written over seventeen years, Tennyson asks and gradually answers profound questions about life and death, religion and science, and the immortality of the soul.

Autumn Morning (19th century) by John Atkinson Grimshaw.

from In Memoriam A.H.H.

Alfred, Lord Tennyson

55

The wish, that of the living whole
    No life may fail beyond the grave,
    Derives it not from what we have
The likest God within the soul?

5 Are God and Nature then at strife,
    That Nature lends such evil dreams?
    So careful of the type° she seems,
So careless of the single life,

That I, considering everywhere
10   Her secret meaning in her deeds,
    And finding that of fifty seeds
She often brings but one to bear,

I falter where I firmly trod,
    And falling with my weight of cares
15   Upon the great world's altar stairs
That slope through darkness up to God,

I stretch lame hands of faith, and grope,
    And gather dust and chaff, and call
    To what I feel is Lord of all,
20 And faintly trust the larger hope.°

56

"So careful of the type?" but no.
    From scarpèd° cliff and quarried stone
    She° cries, "A thousand types are gone;
I care for nothing, all shall go.

5 "Thou makest thine appeal to me:
    I bring to life, I bring to death;
    The spirit does but mean the breath:
I know no more." And he, shall he,

Man, her last work, who seemed so fair,
10   Such splendid purpose in his eyes,
    Who rolled the psalm to wintry skies,
Who built him fanes° of fruitless prayer,

Who trusted God was love indeed
    And love Creation's final law—
15   Though Nature, red in tooth and claw°
With ravine, shrieked against his creed—

7. type: species.

20. larger hope: Tennyson explains this phrase in his *Memoirs:* "that the whole human race would through, perhaps, ages of suffering, be at length purified and saved."

2. scarpèd: eroded to a steep slope.
3. She: Nature.

12. fanes: temples.

15. red . . . claw: The phrase refers to the view of all life as a ruthless struggle for survival.

The Victorian Reputation: The Queen and the Poet Laureate

Queen Victoria's reign (1837–1901) is often associated with prudery and acts of repression such as rejecting the works of bawdy Aphra Behn or, as in Thomas Bowdler's *Family Shakespeare,* censoring the exuberance of the Elizabethan bard. If, today, we imagine that Victorians were moralistic and restrained, the idea results in part from two nineteenth-century voices famous for their inconsolable yet dignified grief: Queen Victoria and Alfred, Lord Tennyson.

Grieving poet, grief-stricken queen. *In Memoriam A.H.H.* is Tennyson's tribute to Arthur Henry Hallam, the Cambridge soul mate who helped Tennyson find his poetic voice. Hallam died from a brain seizure at age twenty-two, and much of Tennyson's best poetry—"Ulysses," *Morte d'Arthur,* "Tears, Idle Tears"—indicates that Tennyson never recovered from the loss. One critic called *In Memoriam* "the solace and delight of every house where poetry is loved." England's queen put that solace to the test.

Queen Victoria's love of Prince Albert was legendary. Her private journal describes her 1840 wedding day as "bliss beyond belief" as she basked in her husband's "excessive love and affection." What is less well known is the frankness of Victoria's passion, which belies her reputation for stuffiness. "It is quite a pleasure to look at Albert when he gallops and valses [waltzes]," the queen wrote in 1839.

Who loved, who suffered countless ills,
   Who battled for the True, the Just,
   Be blown about the desert dust,
20 Or sealed within the iron hills?°

No more? A monster then, a dream,
   A discord. Dragons of the prime,
   That tare° each other in their slime,
Were mellow music matched with him.

25 O life as futile, then, as frail!
   O for thy° voice to soothe and bless!
   What hope of answer, or redress?
Behind the veil, behind the veil.°

20. sealed . . . hills: preserved like fossils in rock.

23. tare: archaic for "tore."

26. thy: Hallam's.

28. veil: the veil of death.

"He does it so beautifully, and holds himself so well with that beautiful figure of his." Victoria was inconsolable when the prince consort died of typhoid in 1861.

Poetic comfort. Victoria took comfort from *In Memoriam;* even the descriptions of Hallam's blue eyes reminded her of Albert. Because of this poem, the queen interrupted her mourning to entertain the poet laureate. Tennyson recalled that the solemn widow compared herself to "Mariana," the poem's heroine, who weeps for an absent lover. She greeted him, saying, "I am like your Mariana now." Tennyson dedicated the 1862 edition of *Idylls of the King* to Prince Albert, offering a public consolation to his widow: "Break not, O woman's-heart, but still endure; / Break not, for thou art royal, but endure."

Setting a new standard. Victoria formally mourned her husband for forty years—until her death in 1901. At Windsor Castle, she ordered that Albert's clothes continue to be laid out each night and that his basin be filled with water each morning. If the queen's grief was extreme, it also was dignified, and dignity was a quality that the British monarchy sorely lacked before Victoria's reign. Her "wicked uncles" had given the House of Hanover a reputation for rakish carousing, and in her widowhood, Victoria continued the task, begun with Albert, of restoring popularity and respectability to a badly tarnished crown. Her sense of duty won her subjects' heartfelt admiration, and the poet who shared her grief comforted her by saying, "The love of all thy people comfort thee, / Till God's love set thee at his side again!"

95

By night we lingered on the lawn,
    For underfoot the herb was dry;
    And genial warmth; and o'er the sky
The silvery haze of summer drawn;

5 And calm that let the tapers° burn
    Unwavering: Not a cricket chirred;
    The brook alone far off was heard,
and on the board the fluttering urn.°

And bats went round in fragrant skies,
10   And wheeled or lit the filmy shapes°
    That haunt the dusk, with ermine capes
And woolly breasts and beaded eyes;

Design for printed linen (detail) (1893) by Charles Francis Annesley Voysey, printed by G. O. and J. Baker.

Victoria and Albert Museum, London.

5. tapers: candles.

8. fluttering urn: teapot or coffee urn heated by a candle.

10. filmy shapes: moths.

While now we sang old songs that pealed
   From knoll to knoll, where, couched at ease,
15   The white kine° glimmered, and the trees
Laid their dark arms about the field.

But when those others, one by one,
   Withdrew themselves from me and night,
   And in the house light after light
20 Went out, and I was all alone,

A hunger seized my heart; I read
   Of that glad year which once had been,
   In those fallen leaves which kept their green,
The noble letters of the dead.

25 And strangely on the silence broke
   The silent-speaking words, and strange
   Was love's dumb cry defying change
To test his worth; and strangely spoke

The faith, the vigor, bold to dwell
30   On doubts that drive the coward back,
   And keen through wordy snares to track
Suggestion to her inmost cell.

So word by word, and line by line,
   The dead man touched me from the past,
35   And all at once it seemed at last
The living soul° was flashed on mine,

And mine in this was wound, and whirled
   About empyreal° heights of thought,
   And came on that which is, and caught
40 The deep pulsations of the world,

Aeonian° music measuring out
   The steps of Time—the shocks of Chance—
   The blows of Death. At length my trance
Was canceled, stricken through with doubt.

45 Vague words! but ah, how hard to frame
   In matter-molded forms of speech,
   Or even for intellect to reach
Through memory that which I became;

Till now the doubtful dusk revealed
50   The knolls once more where, couched at ease,
   The white kine glimmered, and the trees
Laid their dark arms about the field;

And sucked from out the distant gloom
   A breeze began to tremble o'er
55   The large leaves of the sycamore,
And fluctuate all the still perfume,

15. kine: archaic for "cattle."

36. the living soul: Originally, the phrase read "his living soul." Tennyson said he changed it because he wanted the soul to be not Hallam's but the soul of "the Deity, maybe."
38. empyreal (em·pir′ē·əl): heavenly.

41. aeonian (ē·ō′nē·ən): eternal.

And gathering freshlier overhead
    Rocked the full-foliaged elms, and swung
    The heavy-folded rose, and flung
60 The lilies to and fro, and said,

"The dawn, the dawn," and died away;
    And East and West, without a breath,
    Mixed their dim lights, like life and death,
To broaden into boundless day.

View on the Coast of Cornwall (detail)
(19th century) by Frank Goodwin.
Maidstone Museum and Art Gallery,
Kent, England.

130

Thy° voice is on the rolling air;
  I hear thee where the waters run;
  Thou standest in the rising sun,
And in the setting thou art fair.

5 What art thou then? I cannot guess;
  But though I seem in star and flower
  To feel thee some diffusive power,
I do not therefore love thee less.

  My love involves the love before;
10   My love is vaster passion now;
  Though mixed with God and Nature thou,
I seem to love thee more and more.

  Far off thou art, but ever nigh;
  I have thee still, and I rejoice;
15   I prosper, circled with thy voice;
I shall not lose thee though I die.

1. Thy: Hallam's.

MAKING MEANINGS

First Thoughts

1. What word or phrase would you use to describe the speaker's final emotional state? Why?

Shaping Interpretations

2. In Lyric 55, why does the speaker envision the possibility that God and Nature may be "at strife" (line 5)? What complaint does the speaker voice against Nature in this poem?

3. How does Nature answer this complaint in Lyric 56?

4. Describe the **setting** at the beginning of Lyric 95. How does this setting contrast with the setting at the end of the poem?

5. What is the difference between the aspects of Nature described in Lyrics 55 and 56 and those in Lyric 130?

6. Lyric 95 moves from a local scene to "empyreal heights of thought" to the original scene. How is this movement related to the speaker's mood in Lyrics 55 and 56 as well as in Lyric 130?

7. Describe the **rhyme scheme** of these lyrics. How do the poem's short lines and stanzas and the rhyme scheme affect you as the reader?

8. Did Tennyson address the issues you raised in your Quickwrite notes? Were any of his questions, worries, or doubts surprising to you? Why or why not?

Challenging the Text

9. This poem was popular because it satisfied readers who believed poetry should deal with serious subjects, such as grieving. Do you agree or disagree with such expectations for poetry? What do you think are the proper functions of poetry?

Before You Read
ULYSSES

Make the Connection

Acting Your Age

An old adage says that youth is wasted on the young—that only older people have the experience and perspective to appreciate the joys of youthful health and exuberance. Stereotypes of "proper" activities for older adults may not take into account the skills and talents honed in a lifetime of living. Tennyson's adventure-seeking Ulysses may appear to be pursuing a young man's dream, but how can he abandon the passions of a lifetime merely because of his age?

Quickwrite

Some famous singers, dancers, and athletes continue their careers long after their skills have peaked. What (besides money) do you think motivates them, and would you do the same in their place?

Background

Ulysses (*Odysseus* in Greek) is one of the Greek leaders who fought in the ten-year-long Trojan War. Homer's epic poem *The Odyssey* tells of his equally long journey home from Troy to Ithaca. In Tennyson's poem, Ulysses, an old king, is at home with his wife and son, Telemachus (tə·lem'ə·kəs). After a tumultuous life of both marvels and horrors, the old king might finally rest—either thankfully or regretfully. But here Ulysses wants to leave home again for a final journey. He knows lost youth cannot be regained, but he seeks something else.

Tennyson said of this poem, "'Ulysses' was written soon after Arthur Hallam's death, and gave my feeling about the need of going forward, and braving the struggle of life perhaps more simply than anything in *In Memoriam*."

Ulysses Deriding Polyphemus (19th century) by J.M.W. Turner.

ALFRED, LORD TENNYSON 821

Ulysses

Alfred, Lord Tennyson

It little profits that an idle king,
By this still hearth, among these barren crags,
Matched with an aged wife, I mete and dole°
Unequal laws unto a savage race,
5 That hoard, and sleep, and feed, and know not me.
I cannot rest from travel; I will drink
Life to the lees.° All times I have enjoyed
Greatly, have suffered greatly, both with those
That loved me, and alone; on shore, and when
10 Through scudding drifts the rainy Hyades°
Vexed the dim sea. I am become a name;
For always roaming with a hungry heart
Much have I seen and known,—cities of men
And manners, climates, councils, governments,
15 Myself not least, but honored of them all,—
And drunk delight of battle with my peers,
Far on the ringing plains of windy Troy.
I am a part of all that I have met;
Yet all experience is an arch wherethrough
20 Gleams that untraveled world whose margin fades
Forever and forever when I move.
How dull it is to pause, to make an end,
To rust unburnished, not to shine in use!
As though to breathe were life! Life piled on life
25 Were all too little, and of one to me
Little remains; but every hour is saved
From that eternal silence, something more,
A bringer of new things; and vile it were
For some three suns to store and hoard myself,
30 And this gray spirit yearning in desire
To follow knowledge like a sinking star,
Beyond the utmost bound of human thought.
    This is my son, mine own Telemachus,
To whom I leave the scepter and the isle,°—
35 Well-loved of me, discerning to fulfill
This labor, by slow prudence to make mild
A rugged people, and through soft degrees
Subdue them to the useful and the good.
Most blameless is he, centered in the sphere
40 Of common duties, decent not to fail
In offices of tenderness, and pay
Meet° adoration to my household gods,
When I am gone. He works his work, I mine.

3. mete and dole: measure and give out.

7. lees: dregs or sediment.

10. Hyades (hī′ə·dēz′): stars that were thought to indicate rainy weather.

34. isle: Ithaca, Ulysses' island kingdom off the west coast of Greece.

42. meet: proper.

There lies the port; the vessel puffs her sail;
45 There gloom the dark, broad seas. My mariners,
Souls that have toiled, and wrought, and thought with me,—
That ever with a frolic welcome took
The thunder and the sunshine, and opposed
Free hearts, free foreheads,—you and I are old;
50 Old age hath yet his honor and his toil.
Death closes all; but something ere the end,
Some work of noble note, may yet be done,
Not unbecoming men that strove with Gods.
The lights begin to twinkle from the rocks;
55 The long day wanes; the slow moon climbs; the deep
Moans round with many voices. Come, my friends,
'Tis not too late to seek a newer world.
Push off, and sitting well in order smite
The sounding furrows;° for my purpose holds
60 To sail beyond the sunset, and the baths
Of all the western stars, until I die.
It may be that the gulfs will wash us down;
It may be we shall touch the Happy Isles,°
And see the great Achilles,° whom we knew.
65 Though much is taken, much abides; and though
We are not now that strength which in old days
Moved earth and heaven, that which we are, we are,—
One equal temper of heroic hearts,
Made weak by time and fate, but strong in will
70 To strive, to seek, to find, and not to yield.

59. smite . . . furrows: row against the waves.

63. Happy Isles: in Greek mythology, Elysium (ē·liz′ē·əm), where dead heroes lived for eternity.
64. Achilles (ə·kil′ēz′): Greek warrior and leader in the Trojan War.

MAKING MEANINGS

First Thoughts

1. "Ulysses" is about a brave, or foolish, response to the securities and comforts of an orderly life very like that of middle-class mid-Victorian England. What do you think of Ulysses' decision? (Refer to your Quickwrite notes.)

Shaping Interpretations

2. How does Ulysses **contrast** his past and present lives? From this comparison, what conclusions can you draw about his values?

3. In lines 19–21, what does Ulysses claim about "all experience"?

4. Whom does Ulysses address in the second half of the poem? In the concluding lines of the poem, what qualities does he say that he shares with his mariners?

5. Where does Tennyson emphasize Ulysses' great endurance and insatiable curiosity? How would you **characterize** Ulysses?

6. Find Ulysses' references to his wife and son, and tell what you think his words reveal about his underlying feelings toward them. Then, explain whether you accept Ulysses' point of view.

7. What do you think Ulysses is determined not to "yield" to (line 70)?

Connecting with the Text

8. What lines in this poem do you think would encourage someone who needed to go forward despite the temptation to give up the struggle?

Challenging the Text

9. Ulysses knows that his journey is like pursuing the horizon. Do you think he is foolish for setting out on a journey he cannot complete? Explain.

Make the Connection
Riding the Tide

In the last forty years of his life, Tennyson lived in the country like an affluent gentleman. Occasionally, he went to London to walk about in his black cloak and broad-brimmed hat and meet with distinguished writers, scientists, churchmen, politicians, and sometimes the queen. Tourists hung around his country house on the Isle of Wight and climbed trees to get a glimpse of him. People sent him mountains of poetry; he once estimated that he had received a verse for every three minutes of his life. How would you expect such a person to face death?

Quickwrite

What do you predict the images of harbor, bar (sandbar), and sea in this poem will stand for?

Background

Tennyson wrote this poem in 1889, at the age of eighty, while crossing the channel that separates England from the Isle of Wight. Before his death in 1892, he directed that the poem be printed at the end of all editions of his collected verse.

Crossing the Bar

Alfred, Lord Tennyson

Sunset and evening star,
    And one clear call for me!
And may there be no moaning of the bar,
    When I put out to sea,

5 But such a tide as moving seems asleep,
    Too full for sound and foam,
When that° which drew from out the boundless deep
    Turns again home.

Twilight and evening bell,
10   And after that the dark!
And may there be no sadness of farewell,
    When I embark;

For though from out our bourne° of Time and Place
    The flood may bear me far,
15 I hope to see my Pilot face to face
    When I have crossed the bar.

7. that: the soul.
13. bourne (bōrn): archaic for "boundary."

Sunset on Wet Sand (1845) by J.M.W. Turner. Watercolor over pencil.

The Whitworth Art Gallery, University of Manchester, England.

MAKING MEANINGS

First Thoughts

1. Do you find this poem personally comforting, or do you feel some other emotion? Explain.

Shaping Interpretations

2. Explain how Tennyson **extends** his **metaphor** of life as a voyage. How close did you come in your Quickwrite notes to predicting what those three images would stand for?

3. Who might the "Pilot" be in line 15?

4. Paraphrase each of the speaker's wishes and hopes, and explain what you think they show about the feelings of an older person. Is the speaker accepting, afraid, or both?

5. What mental image does Tennyson's poem create for you? Describe it.

CHOICES: Building Your Portfolio

Writer's Notebook

1. Collecting Ideas for an Evaluation

Suppose you're a critic assigned to review one of Tennyson's poems. Your review can be high praise, harsh criticism, or some judgment in between. Which poem could you sink your teeth into? State whether you'll give the poem a positive or negative evaluation, and write the quality or element of the poem that influences your initial reaction. Save your work for the Writer's Workshop on page 899.

Responding to a Generalization

2. An Overview

Tennyson's poems are about how to respond to the losses and disorders of love, death, old age, the passing of leaders, and challenges to old standards of political and moral authority.

In an essay, respond to this generalization about Tennyson's poems. Take your evidence from the poems in this collection.

Evaluating a Revision

3. New Ending, New Meaning

When Tennyson published the first version of "The Lady of Shalott" in 1832, the last stanza ended thus:

> *"The web was woven curiously*
> *The charm is broken utterly*
> *Draw near and fear not—this is I,*
> *   The Lady of Shalott."*

In an essay, compare this scenario to what occurs in the last stanza on page 812. What do you think of Tennyson's revision? Which ending do you think is more moving? Explain.

Comparing and Contrasting Heroes

4. Ulysses Across Time

Research the plot of Homer's *Odyssey*, and read portions of the epic, especially from Books 8, 13, and 19. In an essay, compare and contrast Homer's and Tennyson's hero figures. At the end of your essay, draw conclusions about what Tennyson's alterations to Homer's text reveal about Tennyson and his times.

Creative Writing

5. Man to Man

Write Telemachus's reply (poetry or prose) to his father's speech in "Ulysses." How does Telemachus feel about his father's leaving him and his mother for more adventures?

Literature and Film

6. Visualizing the Enchantment

"The Lady of Shalott" is vividly descriptive. Sketch a storyboard of shot-by-shot illustrations for a filmed version of the story. Show Tennyson's sparse dialogue (including the "whispers" of the curse) in captions.

The Enduring Arthurian Legend

Chivalry rediscovered. Blame King George IV, who remodeled Windsor Castle with the feudal embellishments of arms and chivalric heraldry. Or perhaps blame the immensely popular Sir Walter Scott, whose novels were packed full of jousting tournaments and knights errant. With the help of these influential figures and many more, the ideals of King Arthur's royal city, Camelot, flourished in the nineteenth century. The model of chivalry had seemed barbarous in the elegant, classical eighteenth century; however, as scholars looked back on English history, they rediscovered fascinating rituals and antiquities. Historians republished medieval ballads, printed illustrations of medieval architecture, and, in the process, piqued public interest in the Middle Ages. Tennyson's "The Lady of Shalott" (page 808) is just one example of the nineteenth century's medieval mania, which reintroduced images of "many-towered Camelot" into popular culture.

Hope, honor, and nobility. Chivalry's message was, in part, one of hope. Kenelm Henry Digby's 1844 manual on chivalry asserts that "the noble fellowship of the Round Table cannot be broken forever; but fresh aspirants will again appear to . . . keep ahead of the degraded world." In describing the renewal of "noble fellowship," Digby provides a Victorian interpretation of an enduring English legend. The myth of King Arthur combines Christian morals with ancient pagan fertility rites to form a fascinating story of romance, magic, and betrayal. Key to an understanding of the Round Table and its code of chivalry is the work of Sir Thomas Malory (see page 169).

Tennyson made the story of Arthur into a kind of parable about the ideal political leader. Here is how Tennyson describes Arthur as he faces death. The king is mortally wounded. Sir Bedivere, who knows Arthur will die, remains with him.

Then loudly cried the bold Sir Bedivere,
"Ah! My Lord Arthur, whither shall I go?
Where shall I hide my forehead and my eyes?
For now I see the true old times are dead,
When every morning brought a noble chance,
And every chance brought out a noble knight.
Such times have been not since the light
    that led
The holy Elders with the gift of myrrh.
But now the whole Round Table is dissolved
Which was an image of the mighty world;
And I, the last, go forth companionless,
And the days darken round me, and the
    years,
Among new men, strange faces, other minds."
    And slowly answered Arthur from the
    barge:
"The old order changeth, yielding place
    to new,
And God fulfills Himself in many ways,
Lest one good custom should corrupt the
    world.
Comfort thyself: what comfort is in me?
I have lived my life, and that which I
    have done
May He within Himself make pure! but thou,
If thou shouldst never see my face again,
Pray for my soul. More things are wrought
    by prayer
Than this world dreams of. . . . "

—Alfred, Lord Tennyson,
from Morte d'Arthur

La Mort d'Arthur (1860) by Jones Archer. Oil on millboard (17″ × 20″).

According to Tennyson, the mission of the knights is to "live pure, speak true, right wrong, [and] follow the king." Sir Lancelot becomes the ideal of chivalrous behavior. Sir Ector describes Lancelot as "the courteoust knight that ever bore shield! And . . . the kindest man that ever struck with sword."

Beguiling contradictions. The story of Camelot is a bundle of contradictions. Lancelot, the perfect flower of knighthood, betrays his king by falling in love with Queen Guinevere. The revelation of their affair plunges the court into a war in which Arthur is killed. Arthur encourages his knights to undertake religious quests, yet he himself is not without sin: His illegitimate son seals his own downfall. The darker side of chivalry, it seems, is bound up inextricably with compelling ideals of bravery and honesty. The novelist John Steinbeck describes how these contradictions captured his attention the moment he read the tales of Camelot. "In that scene were all

the vices that ever were—and courage and sadness and frustration, but particularly gallantry. . . . I was not frightened to find that there were evil knights, as well as noble ones. . . . Children are violent and cruel—and good—and I was all of these—and all of these were in the secret book."

In an age of industrial change, Victorians were drawn to images of simple feudal loyalties. They romanticized an age when disputes could be settled by the king's champion, a knight on horseback who threw down his gauntlet to anyone challenging royal authority. Similarly, modern readers are drawn to the magic of Camelot, nostalgically hoping for goodness and nobility to succeed in the face of overwhelming odds. Or, as the youthful King Arthur is taught in T. H. White's *The Once and Future King* (1958), "right" *can* prevail over "might." Malory tells us that "King Arthur is not dead" but "shall come again, and he shall win the Holy Cross." For five hundred years, readers have believed.

Robert Browning

(1812–1889)

Robert Browning wrote of his first published book, a long poem about the spiritual development of a poet, that it was part of a "foolish plan." He intended, he said, to write in many forms and under different names. Browning eventually gave up this idea, but he held on to his ambition of dazzling the world with his range and variety.

Browning's education allowed him to indulge his wide-ranging interests in music, art, the history of medicine, drama, literature, entomology, and other oddly assorted topics. Browning attended boarding school briefly but was mainly educated at home in a London suburb by tutors and by his omnivorous reading in his banker father's extensive library. As a teenager, Browning was brilliant, undisciplined, and determined to be a poet like his idol, Percy Bysshe Shelley. After a term at the University of London, he published (at his family's expense) several poems, plays, and pamphlets, but not until he began writing the short dramatic monologues of the 1840s—poems like "My Last Duchess" and "Porphyria's Lover"—did Browning find his proper form. While Browning struggled to gain recognition for his writing, he lived comfortably at home, supported by his parents, until he married at thirty-four.

In 1845, Browning wrote to Elizabeth Barrett, already an established poet: "I do . . . love these books with all my heart—and I love you too." Barrett was then a semi-invalid in her father's London house, where she submitted to his sternly protective care. Four months after the two poets began their correspondence, they met and fell in love. They secretly married in 1846, and a week later eloped to Italy. Mr. Barrett estranged himself from his famous daughter for the rest of his life.

Browning's happy marriage confirmed his belief that only by acting boldly can one wrest

Robert Browning (1858) by Michele Gordigiani. Oil on canvas (29″ × 23″).

By Courtesy of the National Portrait Gallery, London.

what is good from an imperfect world. "I was ever a fighter," he wrote in "Prospice." He liked to see himself in strenuous but joyous contests with difficulties. In his dramatic poems, he also liked to emphasize the error, weakness, and even the viciousness of his characters. His standing as a poet grew slowly in the 1840s and 1850s, for readers did not know how to react to speakers like the Duke in "My Last Duchess" and the lover in "Porphyria's Lover," who act boldly but for selfish and perverse motives. It was also hard for readers used to Tennyson's melodic lyrics to hear the music in Browning's quick, rough sounds.

Browning lived in Italy until Elizabeth's death in 1861, when he returned to England with their twelve-year-old son. During the 1860s, his fame began to grow. His first immediate success came with *The Ring and the Book* (1868–1869), a long poem spoken by characters involved in a seventeenth-century murder in Rome. Gradually, readers understood that by asking them to figure out and judge wicked men like the Duke in "My Last Duchess," Browning was really challenging them to discover what is virtuous and healthy, when love nourishes, and when and why it kills. Browning believed that human beings must act by a moral standard, just as he believed that those who love constantly and act bravely will be rewarded.

During the 1880s, admirers all over England and the United States founded Browning Societies and met to read and discuss his work and philosophy. By the time of his death in 1889, Browning had won a place next to Tennyson as the other great Victorian poet. Like Tennyson, he was read as a kind of sage who assured his contemporaries that "This world's no blot for us, / Nor blank; it means intensely, and means good" ("Fra Lippo Lippi").

Before You Read

MY LAST DUCHESS

Make the Connection

Portrait of a Marriage

The speaker in this poem is a powerful nobleman of Renaissance Italy. The poem opens with the speaker describing a painting of a woman whom he calls his "last Duchess." By the poem's end the speaker has suggested an entire relationship. Yet we get the feeling that he does not realize just how much he has revealed.

Reading Skills and Strategies

Drawing Inferences from Textual Clues

As you read, jot down the names of the three characters that Browning introduces, starting with the speaker. Next to each name, write down details from the poem that give clues to that person's **character, situation,** and **motives.** After several readings, try to reconstruct the relationships among the characters and the motives for their actions by drawing **inferences,** or logical conclusions, from the clues you have recorded. Of course, another basis for your inferences will be your own experience with people.

Elements of Literature

Dramatic Monologue

"My Last Duchess" is one of Browning's earliest and most popular **dramatic monologues,** poems in which a speaker who is not the poet addresses a listener who does not speak. Instead of telling us directly what the speaker and the other characters are like, Browning allows the speaker to indirectly reveal himself, the other characters, and the situation by dropping clues that we must piece together.

Background

Browning identified his speaker as the Duke of Ferrara, who married three times. In the poem the Duke is negotiating to marry the daughter of a Count. He is addressing the Count's representative.

A Lady with a Gold Chain and Earrings (1861) by Robert Braithwaite Martineau. Oil on panel (14″ × 10″).

© Manchester City Art Galleries, England.

My Last Duchess

Robert Browning

That's my last Duchess painted on the wall,
Looking as if she were alive. I call
That piece a wonder, now; Frà Pandolf's° hands
Worked busily a day, and there she stands.
5 Will 't please you sit and look at her? I said
"Frà Pandolf" by design, for never read
Strangers like you that pictured countenance,
The depth and passion of its earnest glance,
But to myself they turned (since none puts by
10 the curtain I have drawn for you, but I)
And seemed as they would ask me, if they durst,
How such a glance came there; so, not the first
Are you to turn and ask thus. Sir, 'twas not
Her husband's presence only, called that spot
15 Of joy into the Duchess' cheek; perhaps
Frà Pandolf chanced to say, "Her mantle° laps
Over my lady's wrist too much," or, "Paint
Must never hope to reproduce the faint
Half flush that dies along her throat." Such stuff
20 Was courtesy, she thought, and cause enough
For calling up that spot of joy. She had
A heart—how shall I say?—too soon made glad,
Too easily impressed; she liked whate'er
She looked on, and her looks went everywhere.
25 Sir, 'twas all one! My favor° at her breast,
The dropping of the daylight in the West,

3. Frà Pandolf's: Brother Pandolf, a fictitious painter and monk.

16. mantle: cloak.

25. favor: gift; token of love.

Man with Glove (16th century) by Titian (Tiziano Vecellio).
Louvre, Paris.

The bough of cherries some officious fool
Broke in the orchard for her, the white mule
She rode with round the terrace—all and each
30 Would draw from her alike the approving speech,
Or blush, at least. She thanked men—good! but thanked
Somehow—I know not how—as if she ranked
My gift of a nine-hundred-years-old name
With anybody's gift. Who'd stoop to blame
35 This sort of trifling? Even had you skill
In speech—(which I have not)—to make your will
Quite clear to such an one, and say, "Just this
Or that in you disgusts me; here you miss,
Or there exceed the mark"—and if she let
40 Herself be lessoned so, nor plainly set
Her wits to yours, forsooth,° and made excuse,
—E'en then would be some stooping; and I choose
Never to stoop. Oh sir, she smiled, no doubt,
Whene'er I passed her; but who passed without
45 Much the same smile? This grew; I gave commands;
Then all smiles stopped together. There she stands
As if alive. Will 't please you rise? We'll meet
The company below, then. I repeat,
The Count your master's known munificence
50 Is ample warrant° that no just pretense
Of mine for dowry will be disallowed;
Though his fair daughter's self, as I avowed
At starting, is my object. Nay, we'll go
Together down, sir. Notice Neptune,° though,
55 Taming a seahorse, thought a rarity,
Which Claus of Innsbruck° cast in bronze for me!

41. forsooth: archaic for "in truth."

50. warrant: guarantee.

54. Neptune: in Roman mythology, god of the sea.
56. Claus of Innsbruck: an imaginary sculptor.

MAKING MEANINGS

First Thoughts

1. What do you think happened to the Duchess?

Shaping Interpretations

2. According to the Duke, what happened to his last Duchess?

3. In a graphic form, identify the **characters** in this poem, their **relationships,** and their **motives.** (Refer to your reading notes.)

4. What impression of himself do you think the Duke intends to create by his remarks to the Count's emissary? Why would he choose to present himself in this way?

5. What do you think of the Duke's description of his last Duchess? Do you question his assessments? Why or why not?

6. Describe the poem's **rhyme** and **meter.** Read aloud two passages that strike you as examples of natural, colloquial speech.

Extending the Text

7. Can you imagine the events implied in this poem taking place today? Explain.

8. Many people like to read autobiographical details into literature. How does the marriage in this poem compare with the Brownings' own marriage? (See "Scenes from a Modern Marriage," the *Connections* on page 832.)

Scenes from a Modern Marriage

BY JULIA MARKUS

The letter that began the most famous courtship of the 19th century opened, "I love your verses with all my heart, dear Miss Barrett." The writer, Robert Browning, a thirty-three-year-old poet respected in literary circles, was writing to a woman six years his senior, an invalid and a poet of national and international fame. Elizabeth Barrett had not long before recognized his own genius in a poem, "Lady Geraldine's Courtship," likening his poetic heart to a pomegranate "blood-tinctured" with "a veined humanity."

Cloistered in the airless bed-sitting room she never left, Elizabeth Barrett was a famous yet mysterious poet. Little could Robert know that her household on Wimpole Street was one of enforced celibacy. Her father, scion of Jamaican wealth, forbade any of his nine adult children, male or female, to marry; all were still living at home. Elizabeth's allowing Robert to visit for the first time was in its own way a dangerous act, a rebellion.

The courtship that followed—daily letters for more than twenty months, secret weekly visits while Papa Barrett was at work—is one of the most romantic and obsessively documented love stories in our tradition.

They met 150 years ago, but their successful marriage has something to say to us today as we race toward the millennium wondering if we have learned anything at all about the art of love.

Not that any marriage is easy. Robert was disturbed by his wife's lifelong use of morphine, which she believed kept her alive, and he was skeptical of her attraction to spiritualism and furious at some of the mediums she befriended. Elizabeth also suffered four miscarriages, giving birth at the age of forty-three to one healthy son. But the birth of Pen Browning came on the day Robert's mother died in England, and his despondency drew him away from his son.

Desperate to help, Elizabeth told Robert she had once secretly written poems about him, during the courtship. She hesitantly handed him the *Sonnets from the Portuguese* as if to say, Look how love led me from despair; can I now lead you from it? "How I see the gesture, and hear the tones," he remembered years after her death, "and, for the matter of that, see the window at which I was standing, with the tall mimosa in front, and the little church court to the right."

The careers of these two poets were on different levels, which could have led to the kind of troubled celebrity marriage we read about today in the tabloids. Though they both wrote their best poetry during their marriage, Robert Browning's greatest collection, "Men and Women"—still in print—was hacked to death by the critics and sold fewer than two hundred copies. This failure added to his money worries—and, since the interest on her money supported them through most of their marriage, to his grave discomfort.

She in the meantime had written a daring novel in verse, "Aurora Leigh," which exposed the abuses against women in Victorian society and suggested, among other things, that what a female artist needed was not a husband but enough money for a garret of her own.

Elizabeth defied conventions only to find her book a best-seller that quickly went through five editions and was read and discussed everywhere. Yet while he was bitter about the critics who destroyed his hopes of critical and commercial success, "golden-hearted" Robert was thrilled by her success. He could talk of nothing else, and he always considered her the superior artist. To her sister Arabel she wrote, when people "write & talk of the 'jealousy' of authors & husbands, let them look at him!"

If this all seems too good to be true, let it be known the couple quarreled. They had very different ideas about child rearing, for one thing. Elizabeth, coming from a home in which her father's "thunder" dictated obedience and having been a child prodigy, wished for her son happy, carefree, unstructured days. Robert, who was doted on by his parents, wanted Pen to take his piano lessons seriously and learn to count. She kept Pen in long curls and velvet frocks; he wanted him to look like a real boy.

But both believed that arguments were important to the marriage. "You know I do think for myself (if the thought is right or wrong) and I do speak the truth (as I am capable of apprehending it) to my husband always," Elizabeth wrote to Arabel. "What you used to call 'our quarreling' is an element of our loving one another, & a very important element too."

—from The New York Times, February 14, 1995

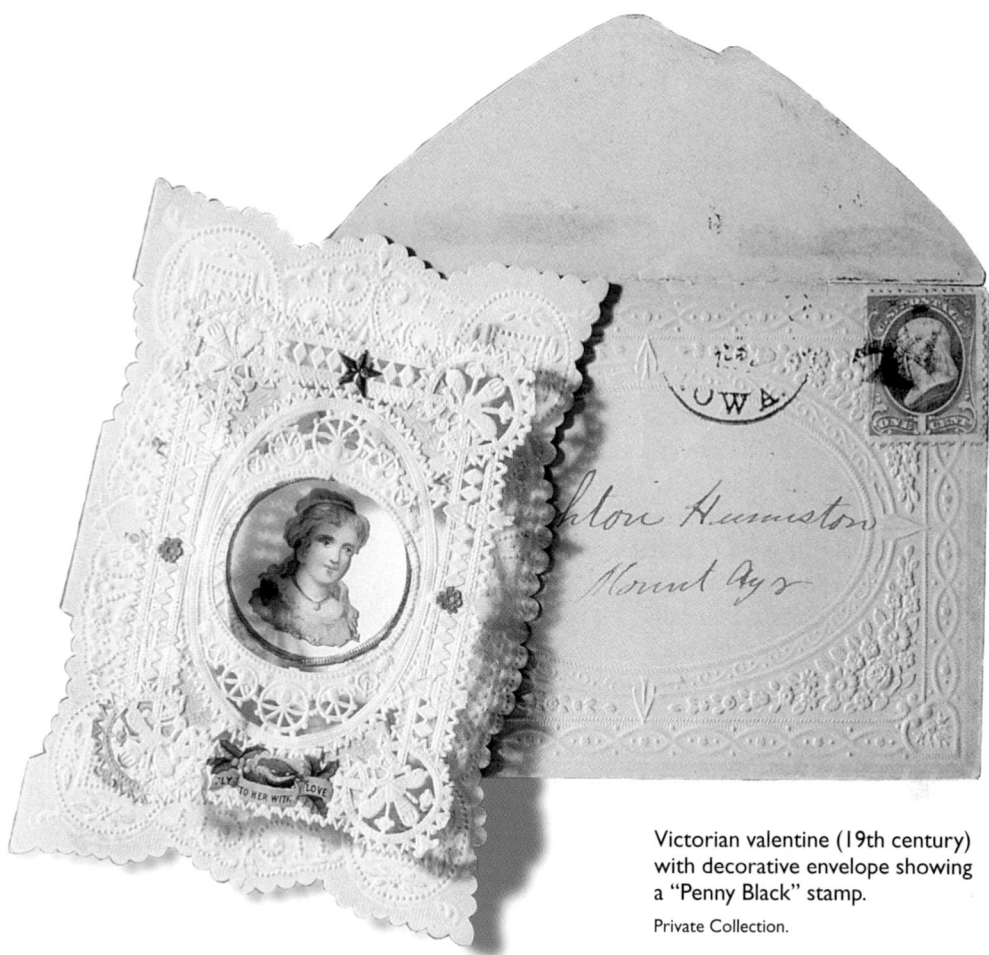

Victorian valentine (19th century) with decorative envelope showing a "Penny Black" stamp.

Private Collection.

Before You Read

PORPHYRIA'S LOVER

Make the Connection

Mad for Love

Readers might expect a poem titled "Porphyria's Lover" to be a romance. The speaker in the poem is a man whose character and identity we can deduce only by what he says. However, one thing is clear: He is a man of intense emotion. Impressed by his direct speech and unruffled manner, we then shudder at what we learn late in the poem. Yet we continue to hear the man out—fascinated, however uneasy—and are eventually led to ask, "Is he lovesick or genuinely disturbed?"

Quickwrite

Someone has said that the opposite of love is not hate but control. Think about some examples from history or fiction. What is your reaction to this idea?

Background

Like his American contemporary Edgar Allan Poe, Browning had a taste for morbid psychology; he once accused his wife, Elizabeth Barrett Browning, of lacking "a scientific interest in evil." In poems such as "Porphyria's Lover," he pursues that interest, exploring the complexity of human motivations. Browning is different from other nineteenth-century authors. This psychological poet seems more modern to us than his Victorian contemporaries.

Porphyria's Lover

Robert Browning

The rain set early in tonight,
    The sullen wind was soon awake,
It tore the elm tops down for spite,
    And did its worst to vex the lake:
5   I listened with heart fit to break.
When glided in Porphyria; straight
    She shut the cold out and the storm,
And kneeled and made the cheerless grate
    Blaze up, and all the cottage warm;
10   Which done, she rose, and from her form
Withdrew the dripping cloak and shawl,
    And laid her soiled gloves by, untied
Her hat and let the damp hair fall,
    And, last, she sat down by my side
15   And called me. When no voice replied,
She put my arm about her waist,
    And made her smooth white shoulder bare,
And all her yellow hair displaced,
    And, stooping, made my cheek lie there,
20   And spread, o'er all, her yellow hair,
Murmuring how she loved me—she
    Too weak, for all her heart's endeavor,
To set its struggling passion free
    From pride, and vainer ties dissever,°
25   And give herself to me forever.
But passion sometimes would prevail,
    Nor could tonight's gay feast restrain
A sudden thought of one so pale
    For love of her, and all in vain:
30   So, she was come through wind and rain.
Be sure I looked up at her eyes
    Happy and proud; at last I knew
Porphyria worshipped me: Surprise
    Made my heart swell, and still it grew
35   While I debated what to do.
That moment she was mine, mine, fair,
    Perfectly pure and good: I found
A thing to do, and all her hair
    In one long yellow string I wound
40   Three times her little throat around,
And strangled her. No pain felt she;
    I am quite sure she felt no pain.
As a shut bud that holds a bee,
    I warily oped° her lids; again
45   Laughed the blue eyes without a stain.

24. dissever: separate.

44. oped: archaic for "opened."

And I untightened next the tress
　　About her neck; her cheek once more
Blushed bright beneath my burning kiss:
　　I propped her head up as before,
50　　Only, this time my shoulder bore
Her head, which droops upon it still;
　　The smiling rosy little head,
So glad it has its utmost will,
　　That all it scorned at once is fled,
55　　And I, its love, am gained instead!
Porphyria's love: She guessed not how
　　Her darling one wish would be heard.
And thus we sit together now,
　　And all night long we have not stirred,
60　　And yet God has not said a word!

April Love (1856)
by Arthur Hughes.
Tate Gallery, London.

MAKING MEANINGS

First Thoughts

1. What, to you, is the most disturbing passage in the poem? Why?

Shaping Interpretations

2. What are the speaker's different moods in the poem?

3. What reasons does the speaker give for strangling Porphyria? Do any of his reasons relate to the ideas in your Quickwrite notes?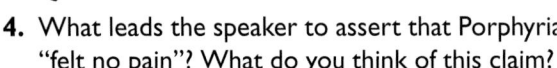

4. What leads the speaker to assert that Porphyria "felt no pain"? What do you think of this claim?

5. Browning first published this poem, with another, under the general title *Madhouse Cells*. How does a knowledge of that **setting** affect your response to and interpretation of the poem? Where did you think the poem was set before you knew about Browning's original title?

6. "And yet God has not said a word!" Why do you think the speaker expects God to say something? What does the line tell you about the speaker's **character** and his awareness of what he has done?

Connecting with the Text

7. If you were serving on a jury for a trial of Porphyria's lover, would you find him not guilty by reason of insanity? Why or why not?

Extending the Text

8. From this poem, what do you think Browning's views might be on the legal plea not guilty by reason of insanity? What details in the poem make you think so?

CHOICES: Building Your Portfolio

Writer's Notebook

1. Collecting Ideas for an Evaluation

An evaluation doesn't depend on personal taste. Your dislike of westerns, for instance, doesn't mean there are *no* good westerns. In evaluation, you use criteria, or standards of judgment, specific to the type of work, whether westerns or dramatic monologues. Use the Before You Read information (pages 829 and 833) and the Making Meanings questions (pages 831 and 836) to list criteria for a strong dramatic poem—for example, realistic dialogue. Save your work for the Writer's Workshop on page 899.

Comparing Themes

2. Love Stories?

In a brief essay, compare the themes of "My Last Duchess" and "Porphyria's Lover." Which poem do you consider the more effective monologue? Cite reasons to support your opinion.

Creative Writing

3. The Duchess Talks Back

Write a **dramatic monologue,** in prose, using the voice of the wife in "My Last Duchess." Base your monologue on an imaginary incident, and take into account the personality portraits of both the Duchess and the Duke in Browning's poem.

Improvisational Theater

4. Prelude to a Crime

Working with other students, imaginatively reconstruct the relationship between Porphyria and her lover before Porphyria's last visit. Look for clues in the poem that help you set up the speaker's state of mind and the time, place, and basic circumstances of a next-to-last meeting. Improvise the scene for the class.

Elizabeth Barrett Browning

(1806–1861)

Elizabeth Barrett Browning was one of the most famous poets of her day—more successful during her lifetime than her husband, Robert Browning. She is remembered today for her *Sonnets from the Portuguese,* of which "How Do I Love Thee?" is the best known.

During her lifetime, Barrett Browning was well known as an audacious, versatile poet who frequently wrote on intellectual, religious, and political matters. As a girl, she studied Greek, Latin, French, Italian, history, and philosophy—an uncommon education for a woman in nineteenth-century England. She published long narratives, a novel in verse, translations of Greek plays, and poems that dealt with the abolition of slavery, the exploitation of children in factories, religious belief, and Italian nationalism.

Through the first half of her busy literary career, Elizabeth Barrett was a semi-invalid. Her illnesses have been variously diagnosed, but it is certain that their effect was enlarged by the sometimes bullying protectiveness of her father and perhaps by the drugs routinely prescribed in those days for a "nervous collapse." She wrote to Robert Browning during their

Elizabeth Barrett Browning (1858) by Michele Gordigiani. Oil on canvas (73.7 cm × 58.4 cm).

By Courtesy of the National Portrait Gallery, London.

courtship, "Papa says sometimes when he comes into this room unexpectedly and convicts me of having dry toast for dinner, . . . that obstinacy and dry toast have brought me to my present condition, and if I *pleased* to have porter and beefsteaks instead, I should be as well as ever I was, in a month!"

In 1845, she met Robert Browning, and the next year they married secretly and eloped to the Continent. Her father never forgave her for the marriage (he had forbidden all his children to marry), nor did he ever see her again. Barrett Browning flourished in Italy and bore a son when she was forty-three years old: her own "young Florentine" with "brave blue English eyes."

The Browning Readers
(late 19th or early 20th century)
by Sir William Rothenstein.

Bradford Galleries and Museums, London.

Before You Read

SONNET 43

Make the Connection

Love Without Limits

This poem expresses an ardent, joyful love—a truly transforming love. And yet, it is not a blind, infatuated love. Amid the fervor, you may find hints that love must weather more than joy.

Quickwrite

Expressions of love are often exaggerated. Robert Burns wrote a love poem in which the speaker vows to love until the seas go dry. Think of some exaggerations you could use to say "I love you."

Elements of Literature

Petrarchan Sonnet

All forty-four poems in *Sonnets from the Portuguese* are written in traditional **Petrarchan,** or Italian, **sonnet** form: an octave (eight lines) and sestet (six lines) in iambic pentameter, rhyming *abbaabba cdcdcd.* Sonnet 43 does not have the usual **turn,** or break in thought, at the sestet. Rather, the poem is broken into short units of thought.

Background

Barrett Browning wrote her sonnets before her marriage, but did not show them to her husband until three years later. Reluctant to publish the poems because they were so autobiographical, she deliberately gave them a title that suggested that they were a translation into English from an original Portuguese source.

Sonnet 43

Elizabeth Barrett Browning

How do I love thee? Let me count the ways.
I love thee to the depth and breadth and height
My soul can reach, when feeling out of sight
For the ends of Being and ideal Grace.
5 I love thee to the level of everyday's
Most quiet need, by sun and candlelight.
I love thee freely, as men strive for Right;
I love thee purely, as they turn from Praise.
I love thee with the passion put to use
10 In my old griefs, and with my childhood's faith.
I love thee with a love I seemed to lose
With my lost saints°—I love thee with the breath,
Smiles, tears, of all my life!—and, if God choose,
I shall but love thee better after death.

12. lost saints: childhood faith.

Love Among the Ruins (1894) by Sir Edward Burne-Jones.
Wightwick Manor/National Trust Photographic Library, London.

Tu B'shvat
(A Jewish holiday that celebrates trees)

When I turn to look for you
the door swings back and forth
chilling the air
and smoke wavers in the empty doorway.
I become a tree
capable of nothing
but to stand here
and watch you go
hoping one of my branches
will snag
on your mulberry silk skirt
and bring you back.

—Michelle Dorrien
Clarkstown High School North
New City, New York

MAKING MEANINGS

First Thoughts

1. If someone sent Sonnet 43 to you, how would you feel?

Shaping Interpretations

2. How many distinct ways does the speaker say that she loves her beloved?

3. What do you think the poem expresses about the speaker's religious faith?

4. How are the pauses in the last three lines different in **rhythm** from those in the rest of the poem? What do you think is the effect of this change in rhythm?

Challenging the Text

5. In your opinion, has Barrett Browning described all of the important aspects and emotions of love? Explain your response. (Refer to your Quickwrite notes for ideas.)

CHOICES:
Building Your Portfolio

Writer's Notebook
1. Collecting Ideas for an Evaluation

In an evaluation of a literary work, you can find evidence for your position by comparing the work to another of the same type. What do you think is the best love sonnet you've read in this book? (There are many examples in the lyrics of the Renaissance poets, including William Shakespeare on pages 225–229.) Reread that other poem and Sonnet 43, and then create a dialectical journal entry comparing the two. On the left, write a positive statement about the earlier poem; on the right, freewrite a response about Sonnet 43. Save your work for the Writer's Workshop on page 899.

Creative Writing
2. Counting the Ways

Write a short love poem that answers the question: How do I love you? You might even try to write your poem in **sonnet** form. Before you begin, examine the ways that Barrett Browning and the student writer of "Tu B'shvat" (left column) use **metaphor** in their love poems.

Oral Performance
3. How Do You Say Love?

Select some other love poems from this book, and present an hour of "love talk." You might be able to arrange your poems as a series of statements and responses. Which poems should be spoken by men? Which by women? If you are interested in adding a modern woman's voice, read Edna St. Vincent Millay's "What Lips My Lips Have Kissed" (lines from the poem are quoted on page 801). Don't forget the love poem by E. E. Cummings on page 213.

Gerard Manley Hopkins

(1844–1889)

Hopkins was the eldest son of highly educated parents who were devoted to the Church of England. His father, British consul-general of the Hawaiian Islands, sent the young Hopkins to Highgate, a London boarding school, where he won a poetry prize and later a scholarship to study classics at Oxford University. Hopkins intended to prepare himself for the Anglican ministry, but after much soul-searching, he converted to Roman Catholicism in 1866—a radical and shocking thing to do at the time.

In 1868, when he entered the Jesuit order, Hopkins burned almost all his poetry (a few poems remain) and "resolved to write no more, as not belonging to my profession, unless it were by the wish of my superiors." He wrote no poetry for seven years, but in 1875, he was asked to write an ode in memory of five Franciscan nuns who had drowned at sea. He sent "The Wreck of the *Deutschland*" to a Jesuit periodical, whose editors "dared not print it."

Hopkins, an unusually conscientious man, was ordained as a Jesuit priest in 1877 and devoted himself to the immediate demands of the priesthood. He served in parishes in poor sections of English and Scottish cities, writing sermons and ministering to the sick. As a teacher of classics at a Jesuit seminary and later as a professor of Greek at the Roman Catholic university in Dublin, Hopkins worked hard at lecturing, grading papers, and planning a series of scholarly papers. In 1889, at the age of forty-four, he died of typhoid fever in Dublin.

Hopkins published one of his poems in 1863, the year he entered college, but after that only a few insignificant poems appeared during his lifetime. He composed a small but very powerful body of poetry that he sent to his friends with careful instructions about how to understand them. In his letters, he elaborated on his ideas about using the stock of native English words for the diction of his verse. Hopkins's poems are also characterized by what he called **sprung rhythm,** and by **assonance, alliteration,** and **internal rhyme.** Robert Bridges, a friend and fellow poet, published the first edition of Hopkins's poems after his death.

Hopkins attempted in his sprung rhythm to imitate the sound of natural speech. He explained: "It consists in scanning by accents or stresses alone, . . . so that a foot may be but one strong syllable or it may be many light and one strong." In conventional metrics, a foot consists of a prescribed number of stressed and unstressed syllables (an *iamb,* for example, is an unstressed syllable followed by a stressed syllable). Sprung rhythm is not concerned with using only one kind of foot in a poem; in Hopkins's poems, a line may consist of many kinds of feet: iambs, trochees, dactyls, spondees, and so on.

For a while, literary critics regarded Hopkins as a twentieth-century poet—rather than a Victorian poet—because of his strongly individual language, compression of meaning, unconventional forms, and singular sound. But Hopkins is unmistakably rooted in the nineteenth century. In his almost ecstatic love of nature, his passionate conviction of a transcendental power, and his striving for individuality, Hopkins resembled the Romantic poets. In the "terrible sonnets" of his last four years, Hopkins expressed the doubts and spiritual anguish of many late-nineteenth-century writers.

Gerard Manley Hopkins (1880). Photograph by Forshaw and Coles.

By Courtesy of the National Portrait Gallery, London.

Before You Read

SPRING AND FALL

Make the Connection

A Change of Seasons

Human life is often compared to the year's seasons, and in that metaphor, youth is springtime. In this deceptively simple lyric, Hopkins combines autumn, a child, and an adult speaker for a layered, poignant effect. From the girl's sorrow and sense of loss over falling leaves, the speaker moves to a much deeper grief.

Reading Skills and Strategies

Recognizing Multiple-Meaning Words

When you first read the poem aloud, be alert to words that could have more than one meaning. Then, read it again silently, jotting down multiple-meaning words and their line numbers in one column and their meanings in the other. Remember: A single word can function as more than one part of speech. For example, *spring* can be a noun naming a season or a water flow *and* a verb describing a movement upward or forward. It is a word's **context,** or placement in the text, that gives it its meaning.

Elements of Literature

Assonance

Assonance is the repetition of similar vowel sounds followed by different consonants in words that appear near one another. *Hate* and *pale* create assonance. *Hate* and *fate* are exact rhymes. Read "Spring and Fall" aloud to hear its unusual music.

Autumn Leaves (1856) by Sir John Everett Millais.
Oil on canvas (41 $1/16$″ × 57 $1/16$″).
© Manchester City Art Galleries, England.

Spring and Fall:
To a Young Child

Gerard Manley Hopkins

Márgarét, áre you gríeving
Over Goldengrove unleaving?°
Leáves, líke the things of man, you
With your fresh thoughts care for, can you?
5 Áh! ás the heart grows older
It will come to such sights colder
By and by, nor spare a sigh
Though worlds of wanwood° leafmeal° lie;
And yet you *will* weep and know why.
10 Now no matter, child, the name:
Sórrow's spríngs áre the same.
Nor° mouth had, no nor mind, expressed
What heart heard of, ghost° guessed:
It ís the blight man was born for,
15 It is Margaret you mourn for.

2. Goldengrove unleaving: grove of trees whose autumn leaves are falling.

8. wanwood: pale wood. **leafmeal:** reduced to decaying leaves (a pun on "piecemeal").

12. nor: neither.
13. ghost: spirit.

MAKING MEANINGS

First Thoughts

1. What questions do you have after reading this poem twice?

Shaping Interpretations

2. What is Margaret grieving for at the opening? Whom does the speaker say she is really grieving for?

3. What does the speaker predict about Margaret's feelings when her "heart grows older"?

4. What do you think the speaker means by saying "sorrow's springs are the same" (line 11)? Think back to the account of Adam and Eve in Genesis (page 416), and explain the "blight man was born for" (line 14).

5. How does the speaker's attitude toward Margaret and her grief shift in the course of the poem? How would you interpret the poem's last line?

6. Read the poem aloud. Identify at least four examples of **alliteration** and **assonance**.

7. Discuss the multiple meanings of *spring, fall,* and *leaves* in the poem. (Refer to your reading notes.)

Extending the Text

8. How does the source of grief in this poem compare with the "divine despair" in Tennyson's "Tears, Idle Tears" (page 804)?

Make the Connection

In Praise of Imperfection

This poem, perhaps not surprising from a poet as unconventional as Hopkins, is his song of praise to God for all things that are *pied*: covered with different-colored spots. As you read, think of the poem as being like a psalm—a praise song.

Quickwrite

What examples of spotted things do you think Hopkins will offer? Give two guesses, and tell why you do or don't find them beautiful.

Elements of Literature

Imagery

Imagery is language that appeals to the senses. In this poem, Hopkins's images follow one another with the instantaneous clarity of a movie's quick cuts. Most of his images are visual, but a few tap other senses, too.

Pied Beauty

Gerard Manley Hopkins

Glory be to God for dappled things—
 For skies of couple-color as a brinded° cow;
  For rose-moles all in stipple° upon trout that swim;
Fresh-firecoal chestnut-falls;° finches' wings;
5 Landscape plotted and pieced°—fold, fallow, and plow;
  And áll trádes, their gear and tackle and trim.
All things counter, original, spare, strange;
 Whatever is fickle, freckled (who knows how?)
  With swift, slow; sweet, sour; adazzle, dim;
10 He fathers-forth° whose beauty is past change:
    Praise him.

2. **brinded:** archaic for "brindled"; streaked with a darker color.
3. **stipple:** random dots or spots.
4. **fresh-firecoal chestnut-falls:** freshly roasted chestnuts.
5. **pieced:** parceled into fields.
10. **fathers-forth:** creates.

Evening Shadows (late 19th or early 20th century) by Viggo Christien Frederik Wilhelm Pedersen.

MAKING MEANINGS

First Thoughts

1. How would you describe the speaker's emotional state, and did this poem make you share it?

Shaping Interpretations

2. What specific examples of pied beauty does the poet mention in lines 2–6?

3. What do you think the poet means by saying "all things counter" (line 7)?

4. How does the poet combine **alliteration** with **antithesis** (opposites) in line 9?

5. According to the last two lines, why does the poet offer glory and praise to God?

6. In line 10, what contrast does the poet suggest between the beauty of the physical world and the beauty of God the creator?

7. How does the **rhythm** of the last line make it especially effective?

Extending the Text

8. How is this poem, like Psalm 23 (page 422), a "praise song"?

Manuscript of "In the Valley of the Elwy" by Gerard Manley Hopkins.

CHOICES:
Building Your Portfolio

Writer's Notebook

1. Collecting Ideas for an Evaluation

A highly original and unconventional text is always a challenge to evaluate. Is the newness a breakthrough we should learn to admire, or is it merely odd (as it first seems)? In Hopkins's case, what is your judgment? Review both poems and find three examples of inverted word order, of unusual compounds, and of invented words. For each example, write what you feel is Hopkins's intended effect and your judgment of its success. Save your work for the Writer's Workshop on page 899.

Paraphrasing a Poem

2. Literal Meanings

Rewrite "Spring and Fall" in a prose paraphrase, using normal syntax and changing figurative language. Be sure to include all the poem's major ideas in your paraphrase.

Creative Writing

3. Another Look at Loveliness

Hopkins catalogs a number of "dappled" things whose beauty he celebrates. Starting from your Quickwrite notes, make your own list of things that are "original, spare, strange" in Hopkins's sense.

Research/Special Vocabulary

4. Pied Lexicon

Hopkins's poem contains a number of unusual words, such as "brinded" and "stipple." The poet also coins some compound words, such as "couple-color" and "fresh-firecoal." Use a dictionary to help you define at least six unusual terms from the poem. If illustrations will help, provide them.

(Opposite) *The Astrologer* (detail) (19th century) by Sir Edward Burne-Jones.

Agnew and Sons, London.

Arnold
Hardy
Housman
Kipling
Tolstoy

Wandering between two worlds, one dead,
The other powerless to be born . . .

—Matthew Arnold, *from Stanzas
from the Grande Chartreuse*

Matthew Arnold

(1822–1888)

Portrait of Matthew Arnold (1880) by George Frederic Watts.

By Courtesy of the National Portrait Gallery, London.

Unlike the other major Victorian poets, Matthew Arnold achieved fame as both a poet and a critic. He is as famous today for his essays of literary and social criticism as he is for his poetry. His poems stand with the achievements of Tennyson and Browning, their quiet tones and carefully shaped figures of speech expressing his reflections on what Victorian society was like, what it would become, and what it had cost.

Arnold had difficulty in his youth living up to the expectations of his famous father, Dr. Thomas Arnold, one of the leading thinkers of the Victorian era and headmaster of Rugby School. An uneven student at Rugby, Arnold nevertheless won a scholarship to Oxford University in 1841. Although he was less than enthusiastic as a student, he seemed to thoroughly enjoy playing the role of a dandy. His performance at Oxford was a failure by Rugby standards, and he graduated without knowing clearly what he wanted to do. In 1847, he became private secretary to Lord Lansdowne, head of the Council of Education.

Arnold had won prizes for his poetry at both Rugby and Oxford. In 1849, he published his first book of poetry, *The Strayed Reveller,* to mixed reviews. Two more volumes of poetry followed in 1852 and 1853, and as a result Arnold was elected an Oxford professor of poetry in 1857.

After his marriage in 1851, Arnold became a government inspector of schools for poor children, a job he held for thirty-five years. His work was exhausting, requiring him to travel all over England and write daily reports. Though he continued to write poetry in his free time, he found it increasingly difficult. In 1853, he told a friend, "I am past thirty, and three parts iced over—and my pen, it seems to me, is even stiffer and more cramped than my feeling."

After 1860, Arnold almost completely stopped writing poetry and began a second career as a critic. His travels and his work had given him firsthand knowledge of pressing social problems, and he became an energetic essayist and lecturer on literary, political, social, and religious questions. *Essays in Criticism,* his first work on literary topics, was published in 1865; a second series appeared after his death in 1888. During the 1870s, Arnold's essays addressed religion and education. In *Culture and Anarchy* (1869) and in his essays on literature and religion, Arnold urged his readers to acquire a knowledge of history and to study "the best that has been thought and known in the world"—the Greeks, Dante, and Shakespeare—in order to judge ideas and personal conduct. Without the steadying influence of what he called culture, Arnold warned, the nineteenth century's technological and political changes would accelerate into a grossly materialistic democracy. He feared also an intellectual anarchy in which every opinion was seen to be as good as any other.

All through his life, Arnold was capable of knowing both the excitement of trying to change the temper of his age and the loneliness of not being comfortable in his own time. Lionel Trilling, the twentieth-century literary critic, writes that as both poet and critic, Arnold remains fresh and relevant for modern readers: "As a poet he reaches us not more powerfully but, we sometimes feel, more intimately than any other. As a critic he provided us with the essential terms for our debate in matters of taste and judgment."

Before You Read

DOVER BEACH

Make the Connection

On a Darkling Plain

Where do people look for answers in times of crisis? Do they look to science? to religion? to government? Enormous problems may seem to call for sweeping solutions. Instead of thinking big, however, what if we thought *small*? Arnold reminds people that they also can look to personal relationships to find the hope, love, and integrity that can make sense of the world.

Quickwrite

What do you think people cling to in troubled times? Write down a short list of people, places, or things you value the most when times are tough.

Elements of Literature

Mood

Arnold creates a **mood** that shifts at certain points in the poem like the ebb and flow of the tide he describes. **Mood** is the feeling, or **atmosphere,** in a work created by the writer's choice of descriptive details, images, and sounds.

Background

Arnold's first draft of "Dover Beach" dates from 1851, when he and his wife spent a night at Dover during their honeymoon trip on the English coast.

At the Gallery (late 19th or early 20th century) by Paul Gustav Fischer.

Dover Beach

Matthew Arnold

The sea is calm tonight.
The tide is full, the moon lies fair
Upon the straits°—on the French coast the light
Gleams and is gone; the cliffs of England stand,
5 Glimmering and vast, out in the tranquil bay.
Come to the window, sweet is the night air!
Only, from the long line of spray
Where the sea meets the moon-blanched land,
Listen! you hear the grating roar
10 Of pebbles which the waves draw back, and fling,
At their return, up the high strand,°
Begin, and cease, and then again begin,
With tremulous cadence slow, and bring
The eternal note of sadness in.

15 Sophocles° long ago
Heard it on the Aegean,° and it brought
Into his mind the turbid ebb and flow
Of human misery; we
Find also in the sound a thought,
20 Hearing it by this distant northern sea.

The Sea of Faith
Was once, too, at the full, and round earth's shore
Lay like the folds of a bright girdle° furled.
But now I only hear
25 Its melancholy, long, withdrawing roar,
Retreating, to the breath
Of the night wind, down the vast edges drear
And naked shingles° of the world.

Ah, love, let us be true
30 To one another! for the world, which seems
To lie before us like a land of dreams,
So various, so beautiful, so new,
Hath really neither joy, nor love, nor light,
Nor certitude, nor peace, nor help for pain;
35 And we are here as on a darkling plain
Swept with confused alarms of struggle and flight,
Where ignorant armies clash by night.

3. straits: Strait of Dover, a body of water separating southeastern England and northwestern France.

11. strand: shore.

15. Sophocles (säf′ə·klēz′) (c. 496–406 B.C.): one of the principal writers of ancient Greek tragedies.
16. Aegean (ē·jē′ən): sea between Greece and Turkey.

23. girdle: belt.

28. shingles: beaches covered with pebbles.

Pegwell Bay, Kent—A Recollection of October 5, 1858 (1859–1860) by William Dyce.
Tate Gallery, London.

Critical Comment

Love Is Itself a Faith

More than any other poem written in the nineteenth century, "Dover Beach" continues to echo through the consciousness of every generation of the twentieth century. To say why involves matters of both technique and meaning.

Compared with the characteristic product of the Romantic or Victorian poets, "Dover Beach" is low-keyed. The speaker's tone is largely that of quiet conversation in which iambs and anapests are congenially mixed. For all its conversational tone, however, the poem is remarkably ambitious in its claim to render a universal condition.

Unlike his predecessors and contemporaries, Arnold neither reaches for the sublime nor dwells on the sentimental in this poem. Instead, he writes a love poem that, incidentally, expresses the crisis of conscience brought about by the dwindling of religion—"the Sea of Faith"—and the rise of science. Science has transformed human life through industrialism and through the mass warfare that scientific inventions made possible. Against these bewildering developments, Arnold poses the notion that love is itself a faith to cling to and, by implication, that individual integrity and a humanistic vision broad enough to include the tragic conclusions of Sophocles are the only defenses against a world moving toward anarchy.

MAKING MEANINGS

First Thoughts

1. Which lines of the poem do you respond to most strongly? Why?

Shaping Interpretations

2. What is the **setting** of the first stanza? Who is the speaker, and whom is he addressing?

3. What **mood** do the first six lines evoke for you? What details in these lines create that mood?

4. What **images** in the second half of the first stanza begin to change this mood?

5. Where does the poem begin to move from a personal experience to a timeless and universal theme? What does the speaker imagine Sophocles also heard long ago?

6. Explain the **figures of speech** used to describe faith in lines 21–23. What do you think has happened to the speaker's faith, according to lines 24–28?

7. What does the speaker urge in the last stanza, and why? How does the speaker's resolution compare with the comforting things you cited in your Quickwrite entry?

Extending the Text

8. What is the speaker's view of his world as it is presented in the last stanza? Do you think this view is relevant to today's world? (Do "ignorant armies" still "clash by night"?) Explain why or why not.

9. Certainly the world had progressed when Arnold wrote his poem in the mid-1800s, but industrialization and scientific advances had also brought problems. (This is the "paradox of progress.") How is progress a paradox for us today—that is, how has progress both helped us and hurt or confused us?

CHOICES: Building Your Portfolio

Writer's Notebook

1. Collecting Ideas for an Evaluation

In evaluating a poem, one of the things you will most likely focus on is **meaning.** The reader of any poem asks: What is the poet telling me, and how do I feel about that "message"? Ask yourself these questions about "Dover Beach." Save your notes about the poem's meaning and your response to it for the Writer's Workshop on page 899.

Analyzing Imagery

2. A Changing Picture of the World

Arnold starts his poem with a moonlit sea and ends with a dark plain. Write a brief essay focusing on the **contrasting imagery** in "Dover Beach." Discuss the importance of these contrasts in developing the universal **theme** of the poem.

Creative Writing

3. Newlywed Dialogue

Working with another student, write the **dialogue** between newlywed Arnold and his wife, Fanny Lucy (Arnold called her Flu), that might have inspired this poem. Be sure to express the feelings of both characters.

Matthew Arnold (1871), published in Vanity Fair.

Reading Skills and Strategies

VOCABULARY: CONTEXT AND FIGURATIVE LANGUAGE

You can sometimes figure out the meaning of a new word—or a familiar word used in a new way—by using **context clues.** These are hints that are found in the surrounding words, phrases, and sentences.

Similes and **metaphors** often provide excellent context clues. In a **simile,** words such as *like, as, than,* or *resemble* are used to compare one thing to another, as in "an inquisitive child is like a blossoming flower." In a **metaphor,** one thing is referred to as if it were something else, either directly, as in "an inquisitive child is a blossoming flower," or indirectly, as in "an inquisitive child grows and blossoms."

Because each of the two equivalent parts of the comparison describes the other, each part provides clues to the meanings of words in the other part. For example, if you read "an inquisitive child is like a blossoming flower" and do not know what *inquisitive* means, you can probably at least figure out that it is a desirable and pleasant quality because you know that in the equivalent part of the comparison the word *blossoming* signifies a desirable and pleasant quality.

Simile. In Robert Browning's poem "Porphyria's Lover" (page 834), the lover uses a simile to describe how he opens Porphyria's eyes after strangling her to death.

> As a shut bud that holds a bee,
>   I warily oped her lids.

In this simile, the word *as* is used to compare the two similar actions. The lover warily opens the dead woman's eyes, as he would open a bud that holds a bee. The following diagram shows the almost equivalent relationship of the two parts.

| open a bud that holds a bee | as ≈ | warily open the dead woman's eyes |

If *warily* is an unfamiliar word, knowing that it describes an action similar to opening a bud that holds a bee gives you a clue. You might guess that it means "cautiously."

Metaphor. In the following passage from "Ulysses" by Alfred, Lord Tennyson (page 822), Ulysses, who had been a warrior and world traveler, uses a metaphor that equates his "pause"—his current retirement—to an unused sword.

> How dull it is to pause, to make an end,
> To rust unburnished, not to shine in use!

This metaphor includes what might be an unfamiliar word—*unburnished.* However, like many metaphors, this one is rich with context clues. It contains three clues. First, the metaphoric comparison implies that an inactive warrior is an unburnished sword. The following diagram shows the equivalent relationship of the two parts.

| inactive warrior | = | unburnished sword |

The equivalent descriptive word for *unburnished,* then, is *inactive,* meaning "idle, retired, dull, sluggish." Second, the sword is rusting, and third, it does not "shine in use." From these clues, you may not yet know that *unburnished* means "unpolished," but you can probably guess that it does have something to do with a neglected condition in which the blade is not brilliantly shiny.

Try It Out

On your own paper, identify the first of the two figures of speech in the following passage from "Dover Beach" by Matthew Arnold as either a metaphor or a simile. Then, draw two boxes as in the preceding diagrams. For a metaphor, use = (equals) between the two boxes; for a simile, use ≈ (almost equals). Write one of the things being compared in each box. Repeat this procedure for the second figure of speech. Finally, write your guess at the meaning of the italicized word, *furled.* Check your guess in a dictionary.

> The Sea of Faith
> Was once, too, at the full, and round earth's shore
> Lay like the folds of a bright girdle *furled.*

Thomas Hardy

(1840–1928)

Thomas Hardy was one of the principal novelists of late-Victorian Britain, but he began and ended his literary career as a poet. The oldest of four children, Hardy was born in a small village in Dorsetshire in southwestern England, the setting (under its ancient name of Wessex) of many of his novels and poems. His father was a stonemason and carpenter who loved music and taught Hardy to play the violin. Hardy went

Thomas Hardy (1894).

to the village school until he was sixteen, when he became an apprentice to an architect. He read widely on his own for the next six years, "reading the *Iliad,* the *Aeneid,* or the Greek Testament from six to eight in the morning, would work at Gothic architecture all day, and then in the evening rush off with his fiddle under his arm . . . to play country dances, reels, and hornpipes at an agriculturist's wedding." In 1862, Hardy began working as an architect in London, writing poems and stories in his free time. He tried unsuccessfully to publish his poems, but by the time he returned to Dorset in 1867 as an architect specializing in church restoration, he had started to publish fiction.

Hardy's fourth novel, *Far from the Madding Crowd* (1874), was enough of a popular success to enable him to stop working as an architect. During the next twenty years, he published ten novels and three collections of stories. The plots and themes of Hardy's fiction, like those of his poetry, express his belief in a world governed by chance and natural laws that are not hostile, but simply indifferent, to what humans want and deserve. Chance gives us pain when we try for gladness or glory; sometimes in his novels the entire course of lives is determined

by coincidence. Hardy liked to play the big scenes of his novels against the backdrop of powerful natural forces that take no account of human life, such as the vast heath of *The Return of the Native* (1878). To chance and the indifference of nature, humans add the folly of war, the cruelty of ingratitude and neglect, and the irrationality of laws and customs that frustrate talent and desire. Finally, the central characters' own weaknesses—Henshard in *The Mayor of Casterbridge* (1886), Jude in *Jude the Obscure* (1895), even Tess in *Tess of the D'Urbervilles* (1891)—make them vulnerable to the destructive powers of nature and society.

The bleakness, pessimism, and irony of Hardy's novels disturbed many of his readers. In 1892, after reading an unfavorable review of *Tess of the D'Urbervilles,* he wrote, "Well, if this sort of thing continues no more novel-writing for me. A man must be a fool to deliberately stand up to be shot at." In 1895, when *Jude the Obscure* was severely denounced by readers and critics (some called it "Jude the Obscene"), Hardy decided to have his say thereafter in poetry: "Perhaps I can express more fully in verse ideas and emotions which run counter to the inert crystallized opinion—hard as a rock—which the vast body of men have vested interests in supporting."

He began collecting old, new, and revised poems in a series of volumes. He published the first in 1898 and was putting together an eighth collection thirty years later, the year of his death. "My poetry was revolutionary," he wrote, "in the sense that I meant to avoid the jeweled line." Twentieth-century critics have praised Hardy's poems for their simple, compressed forms and their sad, ironic tone.

Make the Connection

Difficult Transitions

A stark winter scene can suggest physical and emotional desolation. Yet the gloom of winter is followed by springtime renewal. Gloomy though it may appear at the time, the midwinter death of an old year marks the birth of a new one, and with it the hope for a new beginning.

Quickwrite

Why, in your opinion, do people have such strong feelings about the last day of the year or the last day of the century? Do you share those feelings? Write down your responses.

Background

Hardy wrote this poem on December 31, 1900, the last day of both the year and the century. As night falls, the speaker in the poem hears a thrush (a bird) singing joyfully. His thrush, like the century, is worn out and diminished—but still singing.

The Darkling Thrush

Thomas Hardy

I leant upon a coppice° gate
    When Frost was specter-gray,
And Winter's dregs made desolate
    The weakening eye of day.
5 The tangled bine-stems° scored the sky
    Like strings of broken lyres,
And all mankind that haunted nigh
    Had sought their household fires.

The land's sharp features seemed to be
10   The Century's corpse outleant,°
His crypt the cloudy canopy,
    The wind his death-lament.
The ancient pulse of germ° and birth
    Was shrunken hard and dry,
15 And every spirit upon earth
    Seemed fervorless as I.

At once a voice arose among
    The bleak twigs overhead
In a fullhearted evensong
20   Of joy illimited;
An aged thrush, frail, gaunt, and small,
    In blast-beruffled plume,
Had chosen thus to fling his soul
    Upon the growing gloom.

25 So little cause for carolings
    Of such ecstatic sound
Was written on terrestrial things
    Afar or nigh around,
That I could think there trembled through
30   His happy good-night air
Some blessed Hope, whereof he knew
    And I was unaware.

1. **coppice:** thicket of small trees or shrubs.
5. **bine-stems:** climbing plants.
10. **outleant:** leaning out. Here, the word refers to leaning out of the crypt.
13. **germ:** seed or bud.

MAKING MEANINGS

First Thoughts

1. Compare the speaker's feelings about the end of the century with what you described in your Quickwrite. What feelings, if any, do you and the speaker share?

Shaping Interpretations

2. What details in the first stanza establish the **setting** for the poem? Describe what you see.

3. At what point in the poem is the thrush introduced? How does the bird first come to the attention of the speaker?

4. Does the speaker's **mood** change significantly in the course of the poem? If so, how?

5. What does the speaker say about the thrush's "air," or song, in the last stanza?

6. What do you think is the significance of the word *darkling* in the title? Do you think the thrush's song seems hopeful or hopeless? Explain.

Connecting with the Text

7. Has something in nature ever given you hope or cheered you? If so, describe your experience.

Extending the Texts

8. Both Arnold (page 846) and Hardy wrote their poems many years ago—well before two global wars shattered the world. Do you think the poems are prophetic—do they **foreshadow** what was to come in the twentieth century in a particular way? Explain.

Winter Work (late 19th or early 20th century) by Sir George Clausen.

Make the Connection

Wake-up Call

In an age of almost miraculous technological advances, humanity sometimes stops to ask itself: When will we be too advanced, or too civilized, or too sane to wage war? Hardy's poem brings a different perspective to that question. He imagines what the dead would say if they were awakened by violence in the land of the living.

Quickwrite

If they could speak, what do you think the dead would say to the living? Briefly write down your ideas.

Background

The subject of "Channel Firing" is the testing of guns at sea and on the shores of the English Channel. Hardy wrote this poem in April 1914, when a naval rivalry was growing between Great Britain and Germany. Four months later, World War I began.

The word *chancel* (line 3) refers to the part of a church nearest the altar; a *glebe* (line 9) is a plot of land attached to a church or its rectory. In the poem's last stanza, the sound of guns reaches three sites famous in British history: Alfred's Tower, near Stourton, which honors King Alfred's defeat of the Danes in 879; Camelot, the legendary site of King Arthur's court; and Stonehenge, the prehistoric arrangement of huge stones on the Salisbury Plain (see page 2).

Channel Firing

Thomas Hardy

That night your great guns, unawares,
Shook all our coffins as we lay,
And broke the chancel window-squares,
We thought it was the Judgment Day

5 And sat upright. While drearisome
Arose the howl of wakened hounds:
The mouse let fall the altar-crumb,
The worms drew back into the mounds,

The glebe cow drooled. Till God called, "No;
10 It's gunnery practice out at sea
Just as before you went below;
The world is as it used to be:

"All nations striving strong to make
Red war yet redder. Mad as hatters
15 They do no more for Christés sake
Than you who are helpless in such matters.

"That this is not the judgment hour
For some of them's a blessed thing,
For if it were they'd have to scour
20 Hell's floor for so much threatening. . . .

"Ha, ha. It will be warmer when
I blow the trumpet (if indeed
I ever do; for you are men,
And rest eternal sorely need)."

25 So down we lay again. "I wonder,
Will the world ever saner be,"
Said one, "than when He sent us under
In our indifferent century!"

And many a skeleton shook his head.
30 "Instead of preaching forty year,"
My neighbor Parson Thirdly said,
"I wish I had stuck to pipes and beer."

Again the guns disturbed the hour,
Roaring their readiness to avenge,
35 As far inland as Stourton Tower,
And Camelot, and starlit Stonehenge.

L'Enfer (Hell) (detail) (early 20th century) by Georges Paul Leroux.

MAKING MEANINGS

First Thoughts

1. Does any detail in the poem surprise or even shock you? Explain why or why not. (Be sure to check your Quickwrite notes.)

Shaping Interpretations

2. What do you know about the **speakers** in the poem? To whom are the speakers talking? (To whom does "your" in line 1 refer?)

3. What do you make of God's irritation at those who fire the guns?

4. Point out at least three examples of **irony** in the poem.

5. What does God say about Judgment Day in the fifth stanza?

6. What do you think this poem says about war? Explain whether you agree or disagree with the **theme** of the poem.

Challenging the Text

7. In his own time, Hardy was criticized for his deliberate use of "unpoetic" **diction** (such as "drooled" in line 9 and "mad as hatters" in line 14). What is your response to Hardy's critics? Would the poem have a different effect if the speakers used perfect "king's English"?

Make the Connection

Do You Miss Me?

It's comforting to know that people miss us when we're gone. What if we could come back from the dead and find out how *much* they miss us? We all have expectations of how loved ones would respond to our absence, but we might be surprised at what they say about us when we're not around.

Quickwrite

Write a few sentences explaining what you think this poem is about, based on its title.

Elements of Literature

Anticlimax

The power of this poem in part depends on Hardy's use of **anticlimax,** the surprising occurrence of something trivial when something significant is expected. In this poem, Hardy challenges our conventional beliefs about death and grieving by creating a **narrator,** or speaker, who has only limited information about her situation—she therefore receives some very unexpected answers to her repeated question.

Ah, Are You Digging on My Grave?

Thomas Hardy

"Ah, are you digging on my grave,
    My loved one?—planting rue?"°
—"No: Yesterday he went to wed
One of the brightest wealth has bred.
5 'It cannot hurt her now,' he said,
    'That I should not be true.'"

"Then who is digging on my grave?
    My nearest dearest kin?"
—"Ah, no: They sit and think, 'What use!
10 What good will planting flowers produce?
No tendance of her mound can loose
    Her spirit from Death's gin.'"°

"But some one digs upon my grave?
    My enemy?—prodding sly?"
15 —"Nay: When she heard you had passed the Gate
That shuts on all flesh soon or late,
She thought you no more worth her hate,
    And cares not where you lie."

"Then, who is digging on my grave?
20   Say—since I have not guessed!"
—"O it is I, my mistress dear,
Your little dog, who still lives near,
And much I hope my movements here
    Have not disturbed your rest?"

25 "Ah, yes! *You* dig upon my grave . . .
    Why flashed it not on me
That one true heart was left behind!
What feeling do we ever find
To equal among human kind
30   A dog's fidelity!"

"Mistress, I dug upon your grave
    To bury a bone, in case
I should be hungry near this spot
When passing on my daily trot.
35 I am sorry, but I quite forgot
    It was your resting place."

2. **rue:** yellow-flowered herb associated with grief.
12. **gin:** trap.

MAKING MEANINGS

First Thoughts

1. After reading this poem, tell how you think Hardy feels about sentimental attitudes toward death. How close did you come in your Quickwrite notes to predicting what the poem would be about?

Shaping Interpretations

2. In the first three stanzas, what information about the dead woman's life do you get from her guesses and from the dog's answers?

3. In the last stanza, how does the dog's answer combine animal traits with qualities we consider human?

4. **Anticlimax** is the deflating effect we feel when our lofty expectations are let down. How does Hardy employ the device of anticlimax in each of the first three stanzas?

5. How would you describe the **tone** of this poem?

Challenging the Text

6. In **irony of situation,** there is a sharp discrepancy between what is expected and what actually happens. Do you think that Hardy's use of irony is effective in this poem? Why or why not?

CHOICES: Building Your Portfolio

Writer's Notebook

1. Collecting Ideas for an Evaluation

On page 856, questions 6 and 7 ask you to evaluate the elements of **theme** and **diction** in "Channel Firing." Whatever your evaluations were, you need concrete evidence from the poem to support them in an essay. Cite two quotations from the poem to support each of your responses to questions 6 and 7. Save your notes for the Writer's Workshop on page 899.

Comparing Poems

2. Bird Sightings

In a brief essay, compare "The Darkling Thrush" with any poem in this book in which the poet uses the conventional Romantic **images** of bird and song—for example, Keats's "Ode to a Nightingale" (page 755) or Shelley's "To a Skylark" (page 739).

Creative Writing

3. Passages and Reflections

Imagine that you are in a creative mood on the final evening of the year or the century. Write a short essay or poem summing up your view of the past and your hopes or fears for the future.

Persuasive Writing

4. What's Your Opinion?

Hardy's "Channel Firing" indirectly makes a point about war through the use of an imaginary dialogue. Write a persuasive editorial that directly expresses your ideas about war.

Creative Writing

5. The Rest of the Story

Write a short biography of the woman who speaks in "Ah, Are You Digging on My Grave?"

Oral Interpretation

6. Acting the Part

In a small group, present a dramatic reading of "Channel Firing" or "Ah, Are You Digging on My Grave?" Decide who will speak each line, and rehearse your interpretation. Include music, costumes, and sound effects to make your presentation more dramatic. Ask your listeners to evaluate your interpretations of the poems.

Victorian Novelists

I am neither a man nor a woman but an author.

—Charlotte Brontë, 1849

Victorian tastes seem remarkable today for the excesses of abundant hoop skirts and living rooms crowded with knickknacks. Literary fashions of the period were no different.

Magnificent Storytelling, Huge Books

The most remarkable product of Victorian literature was the novel—hefty volumes regularly published in three-volume editions called three-deckers. The lucrative phenomenon of magazine serialization encouraged authors to write long texts sometimes criticized as "loose, baggy monsters"; in this wealth of pages, however, novelists of the period perfected the art of storytelling. Victoria's reign produced notable poetry, but the period is best known for the passion, scope, and originality of its novels.

A nineteenth-century audience recognized categories of novels including historical fiction, suspenseful detective stories, and "Newgate" or criminal novels with tales taken directly from prison records. Novels became a medium for instruction and were considered a legitimate way to learn history and etiquette. Writers also could address the social problems caused by the nineteenth century's rapid industrialization. For example, Charles Dickens lampoons the abuses of the court system in *Bleak House* (1852–1853) and exposes the horrors of workhouses in *Oliver Twist* (1837–1838). These books reached an increasingly large audience through lending libraries, periodicals, and affordable "cheap editions," ensuring a diverse Victorian readership that included a growing middle class and increasing numbers of female readers.

"Lady Novelists"

In the nineteenth century, the novel was a relatively new genre that was still developing its own traditions. The originality of this format, combined with the increase in literacy and the explosion of nineteenth-century publishing, presented large numbers of average, middle-class women with unprecedented opportunities to showcase their talents. Women no longer had to have exceptional wealth or education in order to write, and, though their work was often slighted by the literary men of the period, female novelists were no longer in danger of being branded "outrageous" or "unladylike" merely because they wrote. The success of "lady novelists" is reflected in the American writer Nathaniel Hawthorne's complaint about "the d——d mob of scribbling women" whom he saw as competition. William Thackeray, a well-known novelist, could grumble at the success of Frances Trollope's *The Vicar of Wrexhill* (1837) by saying that the author "had much better remained at home, pudding making or stocking mending." The complaints of such established writers only confirm the success of female novelists. Prohibited from entering many lucrative professions, the "lady novelists" produced profitable books that often addressed the difficulties faced by talented, literary women.

George Eliot (1819–1880)

The author Mary Ann Evans adopted the pen name George Eliot to keep her identity secret at a time when serious literature by women could receive biased criticism—like Thackeray's. Known for her ability to capture rural village life in novels such as *Silas Marner* (1861), Eliot created talented heroines limited by circumstance and social propriety. For example, the young protagonist of *The Mill on the Floss* (1860) tires of her troublesome long hair and asks for her brother Tom's aid. In the process, Maggie Tulliver calls our attention to the Victorians' emphasis on "proper" feminine appearance.

George Eliot (1849), age 30. Engraving by G. J. Stodart from a painting by M. D'Albert-Durand.

Tom followed Maggie upstairs into her mother's room, and saw her go at once to a drawer, from which she took out a large pair of scissors.

"What are they for, Maggie?" said Tom, feeling his curiosity awakened.

Maggie answered by seizing her front locks and cutting them straight across the middle of her forehead.

"Oh, my buttons, Maggie, you'll catch it!" exclaimed Tom; "you'd better not cut any more off."

Snip! went the great scissors again while Tom was speaking; and he couldn't help feeling it was rather good fun: Maggie would look so queer. . . .

Maggie felt an unexpected pang. She had thought beforehand chiefly of her own deliverance from her teasing hair and teasing remarks about it, and something also of the triumph she should have over her mother and her aunts by this very decided course of action: she didn't want her hair to look pretty—that was out of the question—she only wanted people to think her a clever little girl, and not to find fault with her.

—George Eliot, *from The Mill on the Floss*

Eliot's novels show that a clever little girl's problems only increase when she grows into a clever young woman. Unlike Dickens, who provides his audience with miraculous happy endings, George Eliot looks unflinchingly at heroines whose intelligence and talent have no place in their culture. Her perspective indicates the limitations of Victorian progress and prosperity.

The Sisters Brontë: Charlotte (1816–1855) and Emily (1818–1848)

The Brontë sisters offer a striking example of the novel's success because they produced two of the most perpetually popular novels, *Jane Eyre* and *Wuthering Heights,* while living in the same Yorkshire household. The daughters of a minister, Charlotte and Emily determined that they could support themselves as novelists, and they wrote passionately of the isolated moor country they loved. Like George Eliot, they adopted men's names, Currer Bell and Ellis Bell, in the hopes of receiving fair, unbiased responses to their work. Describing the sisters, the writer Virginia Woolf said, "There is in them some untamed ferocity perpetually at war with the accepted order of things which makes them desire to create instantly rather than to observe patiently."

We can see this "ferocity" in Emily's *Wuthering Heights* (1847), a disturbing love story that draws on the Gothic themes of the Romantic poets she loved. Brontë attributes to her characters Catherine Earnshaw and Heathcliff a love that transcends even death, with Cathy haunting her soul mate from the grave. Heathcliff recalls these events from the day of her funeral:

"Being alone, and conscious two yards of loose earth was the sole barrier between us, I said to myself—

"'I'll have her in my arms again! If she be cold, I'll think it is this north wind that chills *me;* and if she be motionless, it is sleep.'

"I got a spade from the toolhouse, and began to delve with all my might—it scraped the coffin; I fell to work with my hands, the wood commenced crackling about the screws, I was on the point of attaining my object, when it seemed that I heard a sigh from some one above, close at the edge of the grave, and bending down.—'If I can only get this off,' I muttered, 'I wish they may shovel in the earth over us both!' and I wrenched at it more desperately still. There was another sigh, close at my ear. I appeared to feel the warm breath of it displacing the sleet-laden wind. I knew no living thing in flesh and blood was by—but as certainly as you perceive the approach to some substantial body in the dark, though it cannot be discerned, so certainly I felt that Cathy was there, not under me, but on the earth. . . ."

—Emily Brontë, *from Wuthering Heights*

Emily's novel shocked Victorian audiences by bringing Gothic evil, violence, and horror into a seemingly safe domestic setting. Charlotte's *Jane Eyre* (1847) was no less shocking in its rejection of

The Brontë Sisters (1834) by Patrick Branwell Brontë.

By Courtesy of the National Portrait Gallery, London.

docile, sentimental heroines. The popular novelist Margaret Oliphant wrote in 1855, "Ten years ago we professed an orthodox system of novel making. Our lovers were humble and devoted, when suddenly, without warning, *Jane Eyre* stole upon the scene." Charlotte constructs a love story containing a scandalous secret marriage and a madwoman hidden in the attic of a country mansion. Just as daring, though, is the independence of Jane Eyre, the self-possessed governess who refuses to accept the limitations of her social station or her sex:

Nobody knows how many rebellions besides political rebellions ferment in the masses of life which people earth. Women are supposed to be very calm generally: but women feel just as men feel; they need exercise for their faculties, and a field for their efforts as much as their brothers do; they suffer from too rigid a restraint, too absolute a stagnation, precisely as men would suffer; and it is narrow-minded in their more privileged fellow creatures to say that they ought to confine themselves to making puddings and knitting stockings, to playing on the piano and embroidering bags. It is thoughtless to condemn them, or laugh at them, if they seek to do more or learn more than custom has pronounced necessary for their sex.

—Charlotte Brontë, *from Jane Eyre*

Three-Deckers and Victorian Values

Novels offered Victorian audiences opportunities to discuss, explore, and explain the rapid changes in the nineteenth-century social fabric. Female authors often described the friction between the period's social constraints and their own need for autonomy. Many modern authors reject the idea that stories can—or should—convey lessons in morality, just as they reject the notion that simple remedies exist for difficult social problems. Yet in Victoria's reign, with its proud, growing empire, Britons could still harbor bright hopes for social and scientific progress. The novels of the era could capture audiences with three-deckers that examined conflicts in fascinating detail; their hope, whether stated or not, was that solutions could be found.

A. E. Housman

(1859–1936)

Housman said that he was careful not to think of poetry while he was shaving, for "if a line of poetry strays into my memory, my skin bristles so that the razor ceases to act." For Housman, poetry was all feeling. The feelings produced physical effects (shivers along the spine, tears, the sensation of being pierced by a spear) that came from what Housman said was the source of his own poems, "the pit of the stomach."

Housman's poetry is more restrained than his comments suggest. His poems evoke a narrow range of subdued feelings that are controlled by simple, tight verse forms and clear language and syntax. Although he uses simple words, his diction is precise and carefully polished: Each word is the right word in the right place.

Alfred Edward Housman was born in Worcestershire in western England, the oldest of seven children. He was close to his mother, who died on his twelfth birthday. His father, a lawyer, allowed his practice, money, and talent to dwindle away in despondency and drink. At sixteen, Housman won a scholarship to Oxford, where he prepared for a career as a scholar and teacher of classical literature. But he attended classes irregularly, preferring to study on his own, and failed his final examinations.

In 1882, Housman entered the civil service as a clerk in the patent office, determined to prove himself as a classical scholar despite his failure at Oxford. For the next ten years, he set himself a rigorous program: writing and publishing papers on Greek and Latin literature while working as a patent clerk. In 1892, his series of scholarly papers won him an appointment as professor of Latin at London University. He stayed until 1911, when he moved to Cambridge University as professor of Latin and fellow at Trinity College. Housman spent the rest of his life as a

Alfred Edward Housman (1926) by Francis Dodd. Pencil drawing (14¾" × 10¾").
By Courtesy of the National Portrait Gallery, London.

formal and rather aloof teacher, a reserved participant in the small world of his college, and an authority in the yet smaller world of classical scholarship.

During his lifetime, Housman published only two books of poems containing a little more than one hundred poems. His first collection, *A Shropshire Lad* (1896), became popular because its graceful recollection of youthful pleasures and their transience fit a late-century mood of disillusionment in a world that has "much good, but much less good than ill." In "Terence, This Is Stupid Stuff," Housman acknowledged that his poems could be dismissed as self-indulgent bellyaching. The test of poetry, he believed, is not what is said but how it is said. In the refined elegance of his poems, he expressed his pessimistic vision of a cold, empty world. Unlike the major Romantic and Victorian poets who preceded him, Housman saw no hope of improvement or change, but only the possibility of enduring and making bearable the painful conditions of human existence.

go.hrw.com
LE0 12-11

Before You Read

WHEN I WAS ONE-AND-TWENTY

Make the Connection

Advice to the Lovelorn

Thousands of poems have been written about the experience of falling in love, and not all of the stories end happily. The tale told in "When I Was One-and-Twenty" is an ancient one, and the young speaker isn't the first to be disillusioned.

Quickwrite

What is "first love" like? How do people feel about love as they grow older? Jot down your thoughts about these questions.

Background

The tone of Housman's poetry is often nostalgic and bittersweet. This brief lyric from *A Shropshire Lad* is a good example. In fact, its lesson may have come from events in the poet's own life. At age twenty-two, Housman fell in love and was rejected. He became severely depressed and failed his Oxford examinations.

When I Was One-and-Twenty

A. E. Housman

When I was one-and-twenty
   I heard a wise man say,
"Give crowns and pounds and guineas°
   But not your heart away;
5 Give pearls away and rubies
   But keep your fancy free."
But I was one-and-twenty,
   No use to talk to me.

When I was one-and-twenty
10   I heard him say again,
"The heart out of the bosom
   Was never given in vain;
'Tis paid with sighs a plenty
   And sold for endless rue."°
15 And I am two-and-twenty,
   And oh, 'tis true, 'tis true.

3. crowns and pounds and guineas: units of money in Great Britain.

14. rue: sorrow; regret.

The Sonnet (1839)
by William Mulready.

Victoria and Albert
Museum, London.

MAKING MEANINGS

First Thoughts

1. Did the speaker's story move you? Why or why not?

Shaping Interpretations

2. How much time has passed between the first and second stanzas? In your opinion, what has the speaker learned in this time?

3. What is the effect of Housman's use of **repetition** in the last line of the poem? What other kinds of repetition do you find in the poem?

4. What do you think is the poem's **theme,** or message? Do you think Housman is being serious or humorous in his attitude toward falling in love?

Connecting with the Text

5. If the wise man advised you that it is better to give away money than to give away your heart, what would you say in reply? Refer to your Quickwrite notes, and explain your response.

Make the Connection

The Prime of Life

The strong, healthy athletes who earn fame and fortune seem to live charmed lives. But what happens when the cheering stops? When an athlete dies in the prime of life and at the peak of fame, faithful supporters discover a very sobering truth: Even these special young men and women are not invincible.

Quickwrite

At what age do you think you might be in the prime of your life—in top physical and mental condition? Jot down your thoughts about when you expect to achieve your peak and what you hope to be doing at that time.

Background

In 1896, Housman himself paid to have the first edition of *A Shropshire Lad* published. He scarcely made a profit from his book of sixty-three verses, which often tell stories in the voice of a young soldier or farm boy. However, Housman lived to see his poems become enormously popular during World War I. Soldiers saw themselves in the homesick lad from Shropshire and heard in his voice the echo of their own melancholy.

To an Athlete Dying Young

A. E. Housman

The time you won your town the race
We chaired you through the marketplace;
Man and boy stood cheering by,
And home we brought you shoulder-high.

5 Today, the road all runners come,
Shoulder-high we bring you home,
And set you at your threshold down,
Townsman of a stiller town.

Smart lad, to slip betimes° away
10 From fields where glory does not stay
And early though the laurel° grows
It withers quicker than the rose.

Eyes the shady night has shut
Cannot see the record cut,
15 And silence sounds no worse than cheers
After earth has stopped the ears:

Now you will not swell the rout
Of lads that wore their honors out,
Runners whom renown outran
20 And the name died before the man.

So set, before its echoes fade,
The fleet foot on the sill of shade,
And hold to the low lintel° up
The still-defended challenge cup.

25 And round that early-laureled head
Will flock to gaze the strengthless dead,
And find unwithered on its curls
The garland briefer than a girl's.

9. **betimes:** archaic for "early."
11. **laurel:** classical symbol of victory. Victorious Greek and Roman athletes were crowned with laurel wreaths.
23. **lintel:** top of a doorframe.

Young man, from *Penelope and Her Suitors* (detail) (1912) by John William Waterhouse.

City of Aberdeen Art Gallery and Museums Collection, Scotland.

MAKING MEANINGS

First Thoughts

1. How would you react to this poem if it were written about you or a close friend?

Shaping Interpretations

2. What parallel events are described in the first and second stanzas? What is the significance of repeating "shoulder-high"?

3. In line 9, why does the speaker call the athlete "smart"? Do you think the speaker means what he says in lines 9–20? Explain.

4. What scene do you see in the last two stanzas of the poem? (Where is the athlete now?)

5. The speaker suggests that it's best to die at one's peak, before glory begins to fade. After thinking about your Quickwrite entry, describe your response to this idea.

Challenging the Text

6. Housman's poem movingly describes a young athlete's death. If he had written a similar poem about an aging athlete, could the poem be as powerful? Explain your answer.

By Unfrequented Ways (late 19th or early 20th century) by William Henry Gore.

Make the Connection

Remember Me?

When friends tell you they missed you while you were away, it confirms that you're an important part of their lives. But how long should loyalty—and love—last?

Quickwrite

Imagine you have moved away from your friends. What kinds of questions would you ask them after a long absence? Briefly record your response.

Elements of Literature

Literary Ballads

Housman once claimed that his inspiration came from "Shake-speare's songs, [and] the Scottish Border ballads." To describe the country life of a "Shropshire lad," Housman borrows from the simple style of traditional folk ballads, featuring a question-and-answer format in a conversation. In **literary ballads,** such as this one by Housman, poets adapt the structure and spirit of tradi-tional ballads to modern uses. Hardy also used the structure of the old ballads, as in his poems told in the form of dialogues (pages 855 and 857).

Is My Team Ploughing

A. E. Housman

"Is my team ploughing,
    That I was used to drive
And hear the harness jingle
    When I was man alive?"

5 Ay, the horses trample,
    The harness jingles now;
No change though you lie under
    The land you used to plough.

"Is football playing
10   Along the river shore,
With lads to chase the leather,
    Now I stand up no more?"

Ay, the ball is flying,
    The lads play heart and soul;
15 The goal stands up, the keeper
    Stands up to keep the goal.

"Is my girl happy,
    That I thought hard to leave,
And has she tired of weeping
20   As she lies down at eve?"

Ay, she lies down lightly,
    She lies not down to weep:
Your girl is well contented.
    Be still, my lad, and sleep.

25 "Is my friend hearty,
    Now I am thin and pine,
And has he found to sleep in
    A better bed than mine?"

Yes, lad, I lie easy,
30   I lie as lads would choose;
I cheer a dead man's sweetheart,
    Never ask me whose.

Housman's poems somberly explore death. In the following excerpt, Daniel Pool explains the rituals the Victorians developed to respond to death.

Death and Other Grave Matters

Daniel Pool

Death—early death—was no stranger to the nineteenth-century English family, and perhaps that is why they loved to weep over the lingering demises of Dickens's small heroes and heroines. Certainly, they made a big production out of it in every other respect.

In some rural communities the ritual began even before one died, with the ringing of a "passing bell" in the parish church to signal that a member of the community lay on his or her deathbed. Characteristically, the bell tolled six times to indicate the passing of a woman, nine (the famous "nine tailors") to indicate the passing of a man, followed by a peal for each year of the dying person's life.

When a person died, a large funeral was held with everyone dressed in black (unless the deceased were a child or a young, unmarried girl, when the costume was white); mourners received black gloves and black scarfs. . . .

In most communities, funerals were an important social event, and propriety and due regard for the family's social standing necessitated that they be done right. . . . Characteristically, the undertaker would provide professional mourners, or "mutes," dressed in black to stand about and lend dignity to the affair. "There's an expression of melancholy in his face, my dear," says Mr. Sowerberry, the undertaker, to his wife when he takes on Oliver Twist as an apprentice, "which is very interesting. He would make a delightful mute, my love . . . I don't mean a regular mute to attend grown-up people, my dear, but only for children's practice. It would be very new to have a mute in proportion." When the body was actually brought to the gravesite for burial, there was often an additional tolling of the bells—the death knell—to let the parish know of the final laying to rest of the deceased. . . .

The departed were always to be mourned for specifically prescribed periods of time, which, in practice, affected mostly the clothes the survivors were permitted to wear and whether they could have fun or not. Men had it easy; they needed only to wear black armbands, a custom adopted from the military in the early years of the century. Women, however, were supposed to dress all in black. "My dear Celia," says Lady Catherine Chettam of Dorothea Casaubon [in George Eliot's novel *Middlemarch*] after her husband's death, "a widow must wear mourning at least a year." This meant an all-black wardrobe (the so-called widow's weeds), frequently of bombazine, a material especially favored because it did not gleam in light, and no jewelry or ornaments except for beads made of jet, a kind of coal. . . . A widow was expected to mourn her husband for two years, but she could moderate her funereal clothing a bit after a while to "half mourning," which consisted of pinstripe black. Parents and children were to be mourned for a year, a brother, sister, or grandparent for six months, an uncle or aunt for three months, and a first cousin got six weeks. (In-laws were mourned too, but for lesser periods of time.) Some women remained in their mourning garb for the rest of their lives. . . .

Of course, the lead in this fashionable mourning was set in part by the queen. After the death of her beloved Albert in 1861 until her own death in 1901, portraits generally show Victoria in the somber black and white attire suitable for honoring the memory of a late departed.

—from What Jane Austen Ate and Charles Dickens Knew

MAKING MEANINGS

First Thoughts

1. Why do you think the speaker has been forgotten so quickly? Is this cruel, or is it just realistic?

Shaping Interpretations

2. Housman's dialogue format doesn't explain the speakers' identities. Who are the two **speakers**?

3. What significance do you find in the order of the four questions asked in the poem? How do these questions compare with the ones you asked in your Quickwrite entry?

4. How would you describe the speaker's attitude in the last stanza? Was he a true friend to his dead companion? Why or why not?

Extending the Text

5. Why do you think people write poetry about death and practice rituals like the ones Daniel Pool describes in "Death and Other Grave Matters" (see *Connections* on page 868)? What are some of the ways we deal with death today?

CHOICES: Building Your Portfolio

Writer's Notebook

1. Collecting Ideas for an Evaluation

Housman's "Is My Team Ploughing" and Hardy's "Ah, Are You Digging on My Grave?" (page 857) have many similarities. Reread both poems now, and decide quickly which you think is more effective. Then make a chart comparing specific elements in the two poems (you *may* change your judgment). You could focus on such elements as theme, imagery, emotional content, and music. Save your notes for the Writer's Workshop on page 899.

Comparing Poems
2. Heartaches

In a brief essay, compare Housman's treatment of death and loss in these three poems. What is his attitude toward suffering and pain? Do you think he is a pessimist?

Comparing Poems Across the Centuries
3. Renaissance Versus Victorian Poetry

Collection 3, "Love, Death, and Time," opens on page 213. In an essay, compare and contrast the **tones** and **messages** of Housman's poems with the tones and messages of any three poems from that collection (if you wish, include the poem by the American poet E. E. Cummings that opens the collection).

Creative Writing
4. To an Athlete Today

Write a tribute to an athlete you admire. Write in either prose or poetry, and address your tribute directly to the athlete. You might open with Housman's words: "The time you . . ."

Creative Writing
5. In Your Own Voice

Imagine that you are the speaker, the Shropshire lad, in all three poems by Housman. (In "Is My Team Ploughing," assume that you are the speaker who answers.) Write three diary entries that tell about the events suggested in each poem.

Music and Literature
6. Housman's Soundtrack

Find a musical background for one of Housman's poems. Tape a dramatic reading of the poem with the music you selected for presentation, or present it live.

Rudyard Kipling

(1865–1936)

Rudyard Kipling was born in Bombay, India, where his father was a professor at the University of Bombay. Since it was customary for English citizens living in India (Anglo-Indians) to send their children home for their education, the six-year-old Kipling and his sister were left in the care of foster parents in England. Kipling recalled some of the unhappiness and rebelliousness of his school years in a novel called *Stalky & Co.* (1899).

At seventeen, Kipling returned to India to work as a journalist on a newspaper in Lahore. He quickly became popular for his stories, sketches, and poems that were published in newspapers and then collected in cheap editions sold at Indian railroad stations. His books were distributed in England as well, preparing the way for his return to England as a writer in 1889. *Barrack-Room Ballads* (1892), his first collection of poems published in England, went into three editions in its first year, and fifty more editions over the next thirty years. By the end of Queen Victoria's reign, Kipling had become the most popular British poet since Tennyson, and the most popular prose writer since Dickens. Kipling's popularity and public influence

Rudyard Kipling (1899) by Philip Burne-Jones.
Oil on canvas (29½″ × 24½″).

By Courtesy of the National Portrait Gallery, London.

can be attributed in part to his strong endorsement of the British Empire.

But Kipling's ideas about "empire" were not simple. He was fascinated by the contrast and conflict of European civilization with the ancient cultures of the places into which it intruded. This conflict is the theme of many of his Indian stories, beginning with *Plain Tales from the Hills* (1888) and continuing in *Kim* (1901), his novel about a British boy submerged in the mystery of India. Kipling did not always see European culture as superior (though he nearly always presented it as such), and he knew that empires do fall. He urged readers not to trust in guns to justify their dominion over large parts of the earth. The purpose of the British Empire, he argued, was not to make the imperial nation rich, but rather to extend British efficiency, decency, and comfort throughout the world. Today, however, many readers—even as they admire Kipling's craft—view his argument as a rationalization of the often brutal practices of British imperialism.

In 1907, Kipling became the first British writer to win the Nobel Prize in literature.

HRW · go.hrw.com · *LEO 12-11*

Before You Read
THE MARK OF THE BEAST

Make the Connection

When Cultures Collide

As a member of the English ruling class in colonial India, Kipling was a witness to the conflicts that inevitably occur when two cultures are brought into contact by force. Although the battle lines between imperial Britain and colonial India seem clearly drawn in this story, the identity of the victor (if there is one) is less obvious. Indeed, what is most unsettling about Kipling's story may be the questions he poses, which go well beyond the specifics of this strange tale.

Reading Skills and Strategies

Identifying Conflicts and Resolutions

As you read, fill in the first column of a chart like the one below. Write down the names of individuals, groups, and ideas that come into conflict in the story. After you have completed the story, review the conflicts and decide if there is a clear-cut victor. If you think there is, write that name in the second column. If not, write *unclear*.

Conflict	Victor?

The first conflict on your chart should be the one suggested by the proverb that opens the story.

Elements of Literature

Allusion

An **allusion** is an indirect or passing reference to a person, event, place, quotation, or work of art the reader might be expected to know. Through allusion, a reader's knowledge can supply enriching details and relevance, without the writer's explicitly providing them.

Background

Kipling's writing reveals both a respect for the religions of India and a thorough knowledge of the Christian Bible. The title of this story is an allusion to the final book of the New Testament, the prophetic and mystical Book of Revelation. According to Chapter 13 of that book, great evil will take over the world at some unknown time. A beast somewhat like a leopard will rule that evil world, and all the beast's followers will be branded with his mark. Like the Book of Revelation, Kipling's story is more symbolic and suggestive than literal and realistic.

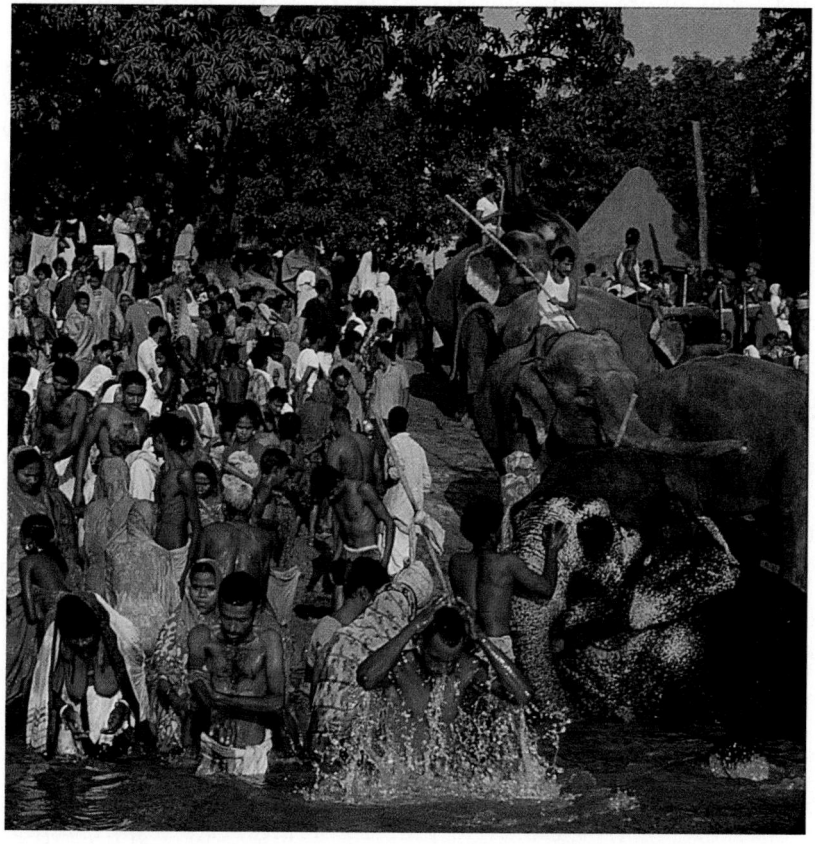

Elephants and pilgrims,
Sonepur Fair in Binhar, India (1988).

The Mark of the Beast

Rudyard Kipling

Your Gods and my Gods—do you or I know
which are the stronger?

—*Indian Proverb*

East of Suez, some hold, the direct control of
Providence ceases; Man being there handed
over to the power of the Gods and Devils of Asia,
and the Church of England Providence only exercising an occasional and modified supervision in
the case of Englishmen.

This theory accounts for some of the more unnecessary horrors of life in India; it may be
stretched to explain my story.

My friend Strickland of the Police, who knows
as much of natives of India as is good for any man,
can bear witness to the facts of the case. Dumoise, our doctor, also saw what Strickland and I
saw. The inference which he drew from the evidence was entirely incorrect. He is dead now; he
died in a rather curious manner, which has been
elsewhere described.

When Fleete came to India he owned a little
money and some land in the Himalayas, near a
place called Dharmsala. Both properties had been
left him by an uncle, and he came out to finance
them. He was a big, heavy, genial, and inoffensive
man. His knowledge of natives was, of course,
limited, and he complained of the difficulties of
the language.

He rode in from his place in the hills to spend
New Year in the station, and he stayed with Strickland. On New Year's Eve there was a big dinner
at the club, and the night was excusably wet.[1]
When men foregather from the uttermost ends of
the Empire they have a right to be riotous. The
Frontier had sent down a contingent o' Catch-'em-
Alive-O's[2] who had not seen twenty white faces
for a year, and were used to ride fifteen miles to
dinner at the next Fort at the risk of a Khyberee[3]
bullet where their drinks should lie. They profited
by their new security, for they tried to play pool
with a curled-up hedgehog found in the garden,
and one of them carried the marker round the
room in his teeth. Half a dozen planters had come
in from the south and were talking "horse" to the
Biggest Liar in Asia, who was trying to cap all their
stories at once. Everybody was there, and there
was a general closing up of ranks and taking stock
of our losses in dead or disabled that had fallen
during the past year. It was a very wet night, and
I remember that we sang "Auld Lang Syne" with
our feet in the Polo Championship Cup, and our
heads among the stars, and swore that we were
all dear friends. Then some of us went away and
annexed Burma, and some tried to open up the
Sudan and were opened up by Fuzzies[4] in that
cruel scrub outside Suakim,[5] and some found stars
and medals, and some were married, which was
bad, and some did other things which were worse,
and the others of us stayed in our chains and
strove to make money on insufficient experiences.

Fleete began the night with sherry and bitters,
drank champagne steadily up to dessert, then raw,
rasping Capri with all the strength of whiskey,
took benedictine with his coffee, four or five
whiskeys and sodas to improve his pool strokes,
beer and bones[6] at half-past two, winding up with
old brandy. Consequently, when he came out, at
half-past three in the morning, into fourteen degrees of frost, he was very angry with his horse
for coughing, and tried to leapfrog into the saddle. The horse broke away and went to his stables;

---

2. Catch-'em-Alive-O's: men who were forced into service as soldiers.
3. Khyberee: reference to the people of Khyber (kī′bər),
a region now part of Pakistan and Afghanistan.
4. Fuzzies: Sudanese natives. British soldiers gave them
this name because of their long, frizzy hair. In the poem
"Fuzzy-Wuzzy" (1890), Kipling calls the Sudanese soldier
"a first-class fightin' man."
5. Suakim: Suakin (swä′kən), Sudan; city on the Red Sea.
6. bones: dice.

WORDS TO OWN
genial (jēn′yəl) *adj.:* mild-mannered; friendly.

---

1. the night was excusably wet: In other words, they
drank a lot.

Shrine to the Monkey-god in Chamundi Hill Temple, Mysore, India.

so Strickland and I formed a Guard of Dishonor to take Fleete home.

Our road lay through the bazaar, close to a little temple of Hanuman, the Monkey-god, who is a leading divinity worthy of respect. All gods have good points, just as have all priests. Personally, I attach much importance to Hanuman, and am kind to his people—the great gray apes of the hills. One never knows when one may want a friend.

There was a light in the temple, and as we passed we could hear voices of men chanting hymns. In a native temple the priests rise at all hours of the night to do honor to their god. Before we would stop him, Fleete dashed up the steps, patted two priests on the back, and was gravely grinding the ashes of his cigar butt in to the forehead of the red stone image of Hanuman. Strickland tried to drag him out, but he sat down and said solemnly:

"Shee that? Mark of the B—beasht! *I* made it. Ishn't it fine?"

In half a minute the temple was alive and noisy, and Strickland, who knew what came of polluting gods, said that things might occur. He, by virtue of his official position, long residence in the country, and weakness for going among the natives, was known to the priests and he felt unhappy. Fleete sat on the ground and refused to move. He said that "good old Hanuman" made a very soft pillow.

Then, without any warning, a Silver Man came out of a recess behind the image of the god. He was perfectly naked in that bitter, bitter cold, and his body shone like frosted silver, for he was what the Bible calls "a leper as white as snow." Also he had no face, because he was a leper of some years' standing, and his disease was heavy upon him. We two stooped to haul Fleete up, and the temple was filling and filling with folk who seemed to spring from the earth, when the Silver Man ran in under our arms, making a noise exactly like the mewing of an otter, caught Fleete round the body and dropped his head on Fleete's breast before we could wrench him away. Then he retired to a corner and sat mewing while the crowd blocked all the doors.

The priests were very angry until the Silver Man touched Fleete. That nuzzling seemed to sober them.

At the end of a few minutes' silence one of the priests came to Strickland and said, in perfect English, "Take your friend away. He has done with Hanuman but Hanuman has not done with him." The crowd gave room and we carried Fleete into the road.

Strickland was very angry. He said that we might all three have been knifed, and that Fleete should thank his stars that he had escaped without injury.

Fleete thanked no one. He said that he wanted to go to bed. He was gorgeously drunk.

We moved on, Strickland silent and wrathful, until Fleete was taken with violent shivering fits and sweating. He said that the smells of the bazaar were overpowering, and he wondered why

---

WORDS TO OWN
divinity (də·vin′ə·tē) *n.:* god; sacred being.
recess (rē′ses) *n.:* indentation.

---

slaughterhouses were permitted so near English residences. "Can't you smell the blood?" said Fleete.

We put him to bed at last, just as the dawn was breaking, and Strickland invited me to have another whiskey and soda. While we were drinking he talked of the trouble in the temple, and admitted that it baffled him completely. Strickland hates being mystified by natives, because his business in life is to overmatch them with their own weapons. He has not yet succeeded in doing this, but in fifteen or twenty years he will have made some small progress.

"They should have mauled us," he said, "instead of mewing at us. I wonder what they meant. I don't like it one little bit."

I said that the Managing Committee of the temple would in all probability bring a criminal action against us for insulting their religion. There was a section of the Indian Penal Code which exactly met Fleete's offense. Strickland said he only hoped and prayed that they would do this. Before I left I looked into Fleete's room, and saw him lying on his right side, scratching his left breast. Then I went to bed cold, depressed, and unhappy, at seven o'clock in the morning.

At one o'clock I rode over to Strickland's house to inquire after Fleete's head. I imagined that it would be a sore one. Fleete was breakfasting and seemed unwell. His temper was gone, for he was abusing the cook for not supplying him with an underdone chop. A man who can eat raw meat after a wet night is a curiosity. I told Fleete this and he laughed.

"You breed queer mosquitoes in these parts," he said. "I've been bitten to pieces, but only in one place."

"Let's have a look at the bite," said Strickland. "It may have gone down since this morning."

While the chops were being cooked, Fleete opened his shirt and showed us, just over his left breast, a mark, the perfect double of the black rosettes—the five or six irregular blotches arranged in a circle—on a leopard's hide. Strickland looked and said, "It was only pink this morning. It's grown black now."

Fleete ran to a glass.

"By Jove!" he said, "this is nasty. What is it?"

We could not answer. Here the chops came in, all red and juicy, and Fleete bolted three in a most offensive manner. He ate on his right grinders only, and threw his head over his right shoulder as he snapped the meat. When he had finished, it struck him that he had been behaving strangely, for he said apologetically, "I don't think I ever felt so hungry in my life. I've bolted like an ostrich."

After breakfast Strickland said to me, "Don't go. Stay here, and stay for the night."

Seeing that my house was not three miles from Strickland's, this request was absurd. But Strickland insisted, and was going to say something, when Fleete interrupted him by declaring in a shamefaced way that he felt hungry again. Strickland sent a man to my house to fetch over my bedding and a horse, and we three went down to Strickland's stables to pass the hours until it was time to go out for a ride. The man who has a weakness for horses never wearies of inspecting them; and when two men are killing time in this way they gather knowledge and lies the one from the other.

There were five horses in the stables, and I shall never forget the scene as we tried to look them over. They seemed to have gone mad. They reared and screamed and nearly tore up their pickets;[7] they sweated and shivered and lathered and were distraught with fear. Strickland's horses used to know him as well as his dogs; which made the matter more curious. We left the stable for fear of the brutes throwing themselves in their panic. Then Strickland turned back and called me. The horses were still frightened, but they let us "gentle" and make much of them, and put their heads in our bosoms.

"They aren't afraid of *us*," said Strickland. "D'you know, I'd give three months' pay if *Outrage* here could talk."

But *Outrage* was dumb, and could only cuddle up to his master and blow out his nostrils, as is the custom of horses when they wish to explain things but can't. Fleete came up when we were in the stalls, and as soon as the horses saw him, their

---

7. **pickets:** hitching posts.

WORDS TO OWN
distraught (di·strôt′) *adj.*: agitated.

---

fright broke out afresh. It was all that we could do to escape from the place unkicked. Strickland said, "They don't seem to love you, Fleete."

"Nonsense," said Fleete; "my mare will follow me like a dog." He went to her; she was in a loose box;[8] but as he slipped the bars she plunged, knocked him down, and broke away into the garden. I laughed, but Strickland was not amused. He took his moustache in both fists and pulled at it till it nearly came out. Fleete, instead of going off to chase his property, yawned, saying that he felt sleepy. He went to the house to lie down, which was a foolish way of spending New Year's Day.

Strickland sat with me in the stables and asked if I had noticed anything peculiar in Fleete's manner. I said that he ate his food like a beast; but that this might have been the result of living alone in the hills out of the reach of society as refined and elevating as ours for instance. Strickland was not amused. I do not think that he listened to me, for his next sentence referred to the mark on Fleete's breast, and I said that it might have been caused by blister flies, or that it was possibly a birthmark newly born and now visible for the first time. We both agreed that it was unpleasant to look at, and Strickland found occasion to say that I was a fool.

"I can't tell you what I think now," said he, "because you would call me a madman; but you must stay with me for the next few days, if you can. I want you to watch Fleete, but don't tell me what you think till I have made up my mind."

"But I am dining out tonight," I said.

"So am I," said Strickland, "and so is Fleete. At least if he doesn't change his mind."

We walked about the garden smoking, but saying nothing—because we were friends, and talking spoils good tobacco—till our pipes were out. Then we went to wake up Fleete. He was wide awake and fidgeting about his room.

"I say, I want some more chops," he said. "Can I get them?"

We laughed and said, "Go and change. The ponies will be round in a minute."

"All right," said Fleete. "I'll go when I get the chops—underdone ones, mind."

He seemed to be quite in earnest. It was four o'clock, and we had had breakfast at one; still, for a long time, he demanded those underdone chops. Then he changed into riding clothes and went out into the veranda. His pony—the mare had not been caught—would not let him come near. All three horses were unmanageable—mad with fear—and finally Fleete said that he would stay at home and get something to eat. Strickland and I rode out wondering. As we passed the Temple of Hanuman the Silver Man came out and mewed at us.

"He is not one of the regular priests of the temple," said Strickland. "I think I should peculiarly like to lay my hands on him."

There was no spring in our gallop on the racecourse that evening. The horses were stale, and moved as though they had been ridden out.

"The fright after breakfast has been too much for them," said Strickland.

That was the only remark he made through the remainder of the ride. Once or twice, I think, he swore to himself; but that did not count.

We came back in the dark at seven o'clock, and saw that there was no lights in the bungalow. "Careless ruffians my servants are!" said Strickland.

My horse reared at something on the carriage drive, and Fleete stood up under its nose.

"What are you doing, groveling about the garden?" said Strickland.

But both horses bolted and nearly threw us. We dismounted by the stables and returned to Fleete, who was on his hands and knees under the orange bushes.

"What the devil's wrong with you?" said Strickland.

"Nothing, nothing in the world," said Fleete, speaking very quickly and thickly. "I've been gardening—botanizing, you know. The smell of the earth is delightful. I think I'm going for a walk—a long walk—all night."

Then I saw that there was something excessively out of order somewhere, and I said to Strickland, "I am not dining out."

8. **loose box:** stall in which the horse is free to move about.

WORDS TO OWN

ruffians (ruf′ē·ənz) n. pl.: hoodlums; lawless persons.
groveling (gräv′əl·iŋ) v.: crawling with the face close to the ground.

The Age of Empire

A breakfast table during the time of Queen Victoria's reign held many of the same items that we expect to find today: Indian tea, Kenyan coffee (more popular in the United States and Germany), perhaps Brazilian cocoa—all sweetened with Caribbean sugar.

Victorians were keenly aware that traders circled the globe to provide their morning beverages. Their knowledge came in part from writers such as Rudyard Kipling and Olive Schreiner (1855–1920), who so carefully documented the experience of Europeans abroad. (Schreiner wrote of South Africa.) Kipling's descriptions of the British presence in India capture the controversies of a period known as the Age of Empire. The nineteenth century provided European scholars with opportunities to study ancient civilizations, but the emphasis on indigenous peoples was eclipsed by the lucrative market for raw tropical materials: rubber, oil, cotton. The relationship between Europe and its colonies is summarized by the remark of an administrator, who observed in 1862 that "the traffic with half-civilized peoples has risks of its own, which are generally compensated by more than ordinary profits."

European powers were in such keen competition for colonies that, between 1876 and 1914, more than a quarter of the globe's land surface was distributed as colonies among a half-dozen countries. In Victoria's reign, the British prided themselves on the fact that the sun never set on their far-flung empire.

"Bless you!" said Strickland. "Here, Fleete, get up. You'll catch fever there. Come in to dinner and let's have the lamps lit. We'll dine at home."

Fleete stood up unwillingly, and said, "No lamps—no lamps. It's much nicer here. Let's dine outside and have some more chops—lots of 'em and underdone—bloody ones with gristle."

Now a December evening in Northern India is bitterly cold, and Fleete's suggestion was that of a maniac.

"Come in," said Strickland sternly. "Come in at once."

Fleete came, and when the lamps were brought, we saw that he was literally plastered with dirt from head to foot. He must have been rolling in the garden. He shrank from the light and went to his room. His eyes were horrible to look at. There was a green light behind them, not in them, if you understand, and the man's lower lip hung down.

Strickland said, "There is going to be trouble—big trouble—tonight. Don't you change your riding things."

We waited and waited for Fleete's reappearance, and ordered dinner in the meantime. We could hear him moving about his own room, but there was no light there. Presently from the room came the long-drawn howl of a wolf.

People write and talk lightly of blood running cold and hair standing up, and things of that kind. Both sensations are too horrible to be <u>trifled</u> with.

WORDS TO OWN
trifled (trī′fəld) v.: mocked; treated lightly.

The postcolonial legacy. As trading spread, it changed irrevocably the cultures of the colonial peoples. Ancient customs were seen as primitive, and Western models became the standards for language, education, and religion. Europeans were confident in their technological and cultural superiority; indeed, a governor of Africa's Cape Colony could tell a group of native chiefs in 1836 that British "customs and institutions are the wonder of the world." To achieve the rewards of "civilization," inhabitants of tropical climates were fitted with heavy wool clothing, taught to prepare hearty English mutton dishes, and encouraged to enjoy the game of cricket.

Colonial empires and their international markets reaped profits for industrialized nations until this heyday ended with World War I. Most former colonies now have won independence, but these independent countries are still struggling with a past that encouraged them to abandon or to diminish their native heritage. The novelist Chinua Achebe (1930–   ) describes a clash of cultures in *Things Fall Apart* (1959) when a district commissioner imposes British law on a group of Nigerian people. When the commissioner asks to settle a dispute, a tribesman says, "We cannot leave the matter in his hands because he does not understand our customs, just as we do not understand his. We say he is foolish because he does not know our ways, and perhaps he says we are foolish because we do not know his." The unexpected legacy of empire has been a redefinition of "civilized" behavior, a renewed appreciation of native customs, and an ongoing dialogue about the foolishness of judging cultures too quickly.

Silk handkerchief commemorating the coronation of Queen Victoria in 1837. (C245).

Museum of London.

My heart stopped as though a knife had been driven through it, and Strickland turned as white as the tablecloth.

The howl was repeated, and was answered by another howl far across the fields.

That set the gilded roof on the horror. Strickland dashed into Fleete's room. I followed, and we saw Fleete getting out of the window. He made beast noises in the back of his throat. He could not answer us when we shouted at him. He spat.

I don't quite remember what followed, but I think that Strickland must have stunned him with the long bootjack,[9] or else I should never have been able to sit on his chest. Fleete could not speak, he could only snarl, and his snarls were those of a wolf, not of a man. The human spirit must have been giving way all day and have died out with the twilight. We were dealing with a beast that had once been Fleete.

The affair was beyond any human and rational experience. I tried to say "hydrophobia,"[10] but the word wouldn't come, because I knew that I was lying.

We bound this beast with leather thongs of the punkah[11] rope, and tied its thumbs and big toes together, and gagged it with a shoehorn, which makes a very efficient gag if you know how to

9. bootjack: device for pulling off boots, often made of cast iron.

10. hydrophobia: rabies. One of the effects of rabies is an inability to swallow water.
11. punkah (puŋ′kə): swinging fan suspended from the ceiling. It is operated by pulling an attached cord or rope.

arrange it. Then we carried it into the dining room, and sent a man to Dumoise, the doctor, telling him to come over at once. After we had dispatched the messenger and were drawing breath, Strickland said, "It's no good. This isn't any doctor's work." I, also, knew that he spoke the truth.

The beast's head was free, and it threw it about from side to side. Anyone entering the room would have believed that we were curing a wolf's pelt. That was the most loathsome accessory of all.

Strickland sat with his chin in the heel of his fist, watching the beast as it wriggled on the ground, but saying nothing. The shirt had been torn open in the scuffle and showed the black rosette mark on the left breast. It stood out like a blister.

In the silence of the watching we heard something without mewing like a she-otter. We both rose to our feet, and, I answer for myself, not Strickland, felt sick—actually and physically sick. We told each other, as did the men in *Pinafore*,[12] that it was the cat.

Dumoise arrived, and I never saw a little man so unprofessionally shocked. He said that it was a heart-rending case of hydrophobia, and that nothing could be done. At least any palliative measures would only prolong the agony. The beast was foaming at the mouth. Fleete, as we told Dumoise, had been bitten by dogs once or twice. Any man who keeps half a dozen terriers must expect a nip now and again. Dumoise could offer no help. He could only certify that Fleete was dying of hydrophobia. The beast was then howling, for it had managed to spit out the shoehorn. Dumoise said that he would be ready to certify to the cause of death, and that the end was certain. He was a good little man, and he offered to remain with us; but Strickland refused the kindness. He did not wish to poison Dumoise's New Year. He would only ask him not to give the real cause of Fleete's death to the public.

So Dumoise left, deeply agitated; and as soon as the noise of the cart wheels had died away, Strickland told me, in a whisper, his suspicions. They were so wildly improbable that he dared not say them out aloud; and I, who entertained all Strickland's beliefs, was so ashamed of owning to them that I pretended to disbelieve.

"Even if the Silver Man had bewitched Fleete for polluting the image of Hanuman, the punishment could not have fallen so quickly."

As I was whispering this the cry outside the house rose again, and the beast fell into a fresh paroxysm of struggling till we were afraid that the thongs that held it would give way.

"Watch!" said Strickland. "If this happens six times I shall take the law into my own hands. I order you to help me."

He went into his room and came out in a few minutes with the barrels of an old shotgun, a piece of fishing line, some thick cord, and his heavy wooden bedstead. I reported that the convulsions had followed the cry by two seconds in each case, and the beast seemed perceptibly weaker.

Strickland muttered, "But he can't take away the life! He can't take away the life!"

I said, though I knew that I was arguing against myself, "It may be a cat. It must be a cat. If the Silver Man is responsible, why does he dare to come here?"

Strickland arranged the wood on the hearth, put the gun barrels into the glow of the fire, spread the twine on the table, and broke a walking stick in two. There was one yard of fishing line, gut lapped with wire, such as is used for *mahseer*[13] fishing, and he tied the two ends together in a loop.

Then he said, "How can we catch him? He must be taken alive and unhurt."

I said that we must trust in Providence, and go out softly with polo sticks into the shrubbery at the front of the house. The man or animal that made the cry was evidently moving round the house as regularly as a night watchman. We could wait in the bushes till he came by and knock him over.

Strickland accepted this suggestion, and we slipped out from a bathroom window into the front veranda and then across the carriage drive into the bushes.

12. *Pinafore:* *H.M.S. Pinafore* (1878), a comic operetta by W. S. Gilbert and Arthur Sullivan. Lovers in the play attempt to elope. When they are discovered, the cast sings, "Why, what was that? . . . It was—it was the cat!"

13. mahseer (mä′sir): large Indian freshwater fish of the carp family.

In the moonlight we could see the leper coming round the corner of the house. He was perfectly naked, and from time to time he mewed and stopped to dance with his shadow. It was an unattractive sight, and thinking of poor Fleete, brought to such degradation by so foul a creature, I put away all my doubts and resolved to help Strickland from the heated gun barrels to the loop of twine—from the loins to the head and back again—with all tortures that might be needful.

The leper halted in the front porch for a moment and we jumped out on him with the sticks. He was wonderfully strong, and we were afraid that he might escape or be fatally injured before we caught him. We had an idea that lepers were frail creatures, but this proved to be incorrect. Strickland knocked his legs from under him and I put my foot on his neck. He mewed hideously, and even through my riding boots I could feel that his flesh was not the flesh of a clean man.

He struck at us with his hand- and feet-stumps. We looped the lash of a dog-whip round him under the armpits, and dragged him backward into the hall and so into the dining room where the beast lay. There we tied him with trunk straps. He made no attempt to escape, but mewed.

When we confronted him with the beast the scene was beyond description. The beast doubled backward into a bow as though he had been poisoned with strychnine, and moaned in the most pitiable fashion. Several other things happened also, but they cannot be put down here.

"I think I was right," said Strickland. "Now we will ask him to cure this case."

But the leper only mewed. Strickland wrapped a towel round his hand and took the gun barrels out of the fire. I put the half of the broken walking stick through the loop of fishing line and buckled the leper comfortably to Strickland's

English officer attended by his Indian servant (1870s).
Albumen print by Willoughby Wallace Hooper and George Western.
By permission of the British Library, London.

bedstead. I understood then how men and women and little children can endure to see a witch burnt alive; for the beast was moaning on the floor, and though the Silver Man had no face, you could see horrible feelings passing through the slab that took its place, exactly as waves of heat play across red-hot iron—gun barrels, for instance.

Strickland shaded his eyes with his hands for a moment and we got to work. This part is not to be printed.

The dawn was beginning to break when the leper spoke. His mewings had not been satisfactory up to that point. The beast had fainted from exhaustion and the house was very still. We unstrapped the leper and told him to take away the evil spirit. He crawled to the beast and laid his hand upon the left breast. That was all. Then he fell face down and whined, drawing in his breath as he did so.

We watched the face of the beast, and saw the soul of Fleete coming back into the eyes. Then a sweat broke out on the forehead and the eyes—they were human eyes—closed. We waited for an hour, but Fleete still slept. We carried him to his room and bade the leper go, giving him the bed-stead, and the sheet on the bedstead to cover his nakedness, the gloves and the towels with which we had touched him, and the whip that had been hooked round his body. He put the sheet about him and went out into the early morning without speaking or mewing.

Strickland wiped his face and sat down. A night gong, far away in the city, made seven o'clock.

"Exactly four-and-twenty hours!" said Strickland. "And I've done enough to ensure my dismissal from the service, besides permanent quarters in a lunatic asylum. Do you believe that we are awake?"

The red-hot gun barrel had fallen on the floor and was singeing the carpet. The smell was entirely real.

That morning at eleven we two together went to wake up Fleete. We looked and saw that the black leopard rosette on his chest had disappeared. He was very drowsy and tired, but as soon as he saw us, he said, "Oh! Confound you fellows. Happy New Year to you. Never mix your liquors. I'm nearly dead."

"Thanks for your kindness, but you're over time," said Strickland. "Today is the morning of the second. You've slept the clock round with a vengeance."

The door opened, and little Dumoise put his head in. He had come on foot, and fancied that we were laying out Fleete.

"I've brought a nurse," said Dumoise. "I suppose that she can come in for . . . what is necessary."

"By all means," said Fleete cheerily, sitting up in bed. "Bring on your nurses."

Dumoise was dumb. Strickland led him out and explained that there must have been a mistake in the diagnosis. Dumoise remained dumb and left the house hastily. He considered that his professional reputation had been injured, and was inclined to make a personal matter of the recovery. Strickland went out too. When he came back, he said that he had been to call on the Temple of Hanuman to offer redress for the pollution of the god, and had been solemnly assured that no white man had ever touched the idol, and that he was an incarnation of all the virtues laboring under a delusion. "What do you think?" said Strickland.

I said, "'There are more things . . .'"[14]

But Strickland hates that quotation. He says that I have worn it threadbare.

One other curious thing happened which frightened me as much as anything in all the night's work. When Fleete was dressed he came into the dining room and sniffed. He had a quaint trick of moving his nose when he sniffed. "Horrid doggy smell, here," said he. "You should really keep those terriers of yours in better order. Try sulfur, Strick."

But Strickland did not answer. He caught hold of the back of a chair, and, without warning, went into an amazing fit of hysterics. It is terrible to see a strong man overtaken with hysteria. Then it struck me that we had fought for Fleete's soul with the Silver Man in that room, and had disgraced ourselves as Englishmen forever, and I laughed and gasped and gurgled just as shamefully as Strickland, while Fleete thought that we had both gone mad. We never told him what we had done.

Some years later, when Strickland had married and was a churchgoing member of society for his wife's sake, we reviewed the incident dispassionately, and Strickland suggested that I should put it before the public.

I cannot myself see that this step is likely to clear up the mystery; because, in the first place, no one will believe a rather unpleasant story, and, in the second, it is well known to every right-minded man that the gods of the heathen are stone and brass, and any attempt to deal with them otherwise is justly condemned.

---

14. "There are more things": a reference to William Shakespeare's *Hamlet*, Act I, scene 5, lines 166–167: "There are more things in heaven and earth, Horatio, than are dreamt of in your philosophy."

WORDS TO OWN
redress (rē′dres′) *n.*: compensation for wrong.
delusion (di·lōō′zhən) *n.*: false belief.
dispassionately (dis·pash′ə·nət·lē) *adv.*: without emotion; impartially.

MAKING MEANINGS

First Thoughts

1. Is Kipling's story as scary as other werewolf stories or movies you know? Why or why not?

> **Reading Check**
>
> Working with others, map the **main conflict, important events,** points of keen **suspense, climax,** and **outcome** of the story.

Shaping Interpretations

2. Complete the chart that you filled out as you read the story. How many **conflicts**—external and internal—did you find? Which conflicts resulted from cultural misunderstandings?

3. What about the victors in these conflicts? Were some conflicts left unresolved? Be sure to compare your answers in class.

4. Compare the **characterizations** of Fleete, Strickland, and the narrator. How does **point of view** affect what you know about each character?

5. Who or what is the Silver Man? What details in the story support your interpretation?

6. What does this story reveal about the British presence in India?

7. What **allusions** to the Book of Revelation in the Bible are made in this story? Consider these allusions, and tell what you think the story's **theme** is.

8. Do you think the events of this story illustrate the "paradox of progress"? Explain why or why not.

Challenging the Text

9. Do you think this story has something important to say to us today despite—or even because of—its racist elements? Cite details from the story to support your answer.

10. Critics have called this story "nasty," "poisonous," and even "sadistic." Explain why you agree or disagree with these assessments.

CHOICES:
Building Your Portfolio

Writer's Notebook
1. Collecting Ideas for an Evaluation

How do you rate Kipling's story? Is it a well-told, suspenseful horror story? Is it a racist story? Are its characters stereotypes? Is it offensive or problematic in other respects? Make three general statements evaluating Kipling's story. Then list at least two details from the text to support each evaluation. Keep your notes for the Writer's Workshop on page 899.

Creative Writing
2. A Silver Man Sequel

The Silver Man survives, and the temple priests deny the whole incident. Use these facts to create a story outline for "The Mark of the Beast II."

Research / Speaking
3. The Evolution of a Myth

Werewolfism, or lycanthropy, is an ancient, enduring myth, but its significance can change. In Kipling's 1890 story and in the 1985 American film *Teen Wolf,* the werewolves have different characteristics. Prepare a multimedia report about werewolf stories in different periods and cultures, showing both the universal and specific social concerns they reflect.

Historical Research
4. The Jewel in the Crown

India was part of the British Empire until 1947; Victoria referred to it as the jewel in her crown. Explore the Anglo-Indian connection by researching the kind of life a British civil servant like Kipling might have lived in late-nineteenth-century India. As a contrast, describe the way of life of most Indians. Present your findings in an informal report.

Russia

Portrait of Leo Tolstoy (1873)
by Ivan Nikolayevich Kramskoy.

Leo Tolstoy

(1828–1910)

Ironically, Tolstoy, whose story provides a surprising answer to the title question, was born into wealthy, landed aristocracy. Count Leo Niko-layevich Tolstoy was orphaned at nine; at age nineteen, he took possession of a huge rural estate. There he wrote *War and Peace* and *Anna Karenina,* masterpieces of realistic fiction that capped his already immense reputation.

But by age fifty, Tolstoy had reached a moral and spiritual crisis. Aspiring to be holy and to do good, he found his best models in Russia's self-suffi-cient Christian peasants. His writings became fervent at-tacks on the government, church, and private ownership (because he felt all three oper-ated by threat of force). In-stead, Tolstoy celebrated com-munal, utopian ideals of pure love and honest labor.

Because he was already a famous writer, educational reformer, and war hero, the repressive Russian government left him alone as pilgrims worldwide journeyed to his home. Tolstoy tried to live the simple life he preached, but he was a man with many children and a wife who did not share his extreme views. With much bitter quarreling, she obtained Tolstoy's substantial royalties to support the family. Finally, as an old man of eighty-two, Tolstoy decided to lead a poor, reclusive life. He fled his home in secret, at night, with his doctor and youngest daughter. At a tiny, remote railroad sta-tion, the fugitives got off the train, and Tolstoy, ill with a high fever, was taken to the stationmaster's house. There, amid a mob scene of reporters and family who had eventually tracked him down, Tolstoy died of pneumonia.

(Map) Europe in 1914. Map © Rand McNally #98-S-116.

Background

You will have no trouble seeing why this story is included under the theme "The Paradox of Progress." Very early, one character proclaims, "Loss and gain are brothers twain." Yet the historical setting makes the paradox much deeper. The nineteenth-century Russia that Leo Tolstoy is describing had just abandoned feudalism—a way of life dead in England since the Middle Ages.

Until Czar Alexander II ordered an emancipation in 1861, Russian peasants, called serfs, were virtual slaves of landowners and aristocrats: They could be bought or sold, and they owned no property. When Tolstoy wrote this story, serfs had had twenty-five years of freedom and rights. No one, certainly not the reformer Tolstoy, would wish to see them in bondage again. Yet in this parable he could wonder—with sharp humor—whether the peasants' progress had brought losses they would regret.

Quickwrite

Answer these questions as honestly as you can. First, if you could have everything you wanted, how much property (a home and land) would you wish for? Second, how much property do you think you really need?

How Much Land Does a Man Need?

Leo Tolstoy
translated by **Louise** *and* **Aylmer Maude**

An elder sister came to visit her younger sister in the country. The elder was married to a tradesman in town, the younger to a peasant in the village. As the sisters sat over their tea talking, the elder began to boast of the advantages of town life: saying how comfortably they lived there, how well they dressed, what fine clothes her children wore, what good things they ate and drank, and how she went to the theater, promenades, and entertainments.

The younger sister was piqued, and in turn disparaged the life of a tradesman, and stood up for that of a peasant.

"I would not change my way of life for yours," said she. "We may live roughly, but at least we are free from anxiety. You live in better style than we do, but though you often earn more than you need, you are very likely to lose all you have. You know the proverb, 'Loss and gain are brothers twain.' It often happens that people who are wealthy one day are begging their bread the next. Our way is safer. Though a peasant's life is not a fat one, it is a long one. We shall never grow rich, but we shall always have enough to eat."

The elder sister said sneeringly:

"Enough? Yes, if you like to share with the pigs and the calves! What do you know of elegance or manners! However much your goodman may slave, you will die as you are living—on a dung heap—and your children the same."

"Well, what of that?" replied the younger. "Of course our work is rough and coarse. But, on the other hand, it is sure, and we need not bow to anyone. But you, in your towns, are surrounded by temptations; today all may be right, but tomorrow the Evil One may tempt your husband with cards, wine, or women, and all will go to ruin. Don't such things happen often enough?"

Pahom, the master of the house, was lying on the top of the stove[1] and he listened to the women's chatter.

"It is perfectly true," thought he. "Busy as we are from childhood tilling mother earth, we peasants have no time to let any nonsense settle in our heads. Our only trouble is that we haven't land enough. If I had plenty of land, I shouldn't fear the Devil himself!"

The women finished their tea, chatted a while about dress, and then cleared away the tea things and lay down to sleep.

But the Devil had been sitting behind the stove, and had heard all that was said. He was pleased that the peasant's wife had led her husband into boasting, and that he had said that if he had plenty of land he would not fear the Devil himself.

"All right," thought the Devil. "We will have a tussle. I'll give you land enough; and by means of that land I will get you into my power."

Close to the village there lived a lady, a small landowner who had an estate of about three hundred acres. She had always lived on good terms with the peasants until she engaged as her steward an old soldier, who took to burdening the people with fines. However careful Pahom tried to be, it happened again and again that now a horse of his got among the lady's oats, now a cow strayed into her garden, now his calves found their way into her meadows—and he always had to pay a fine.

Pahom paid up, but grumbled and, going home in a temper, was rough with his family. All through that summer, Pahom had much trouble because of this steward, and he was even glad when winter came and the cattle had to be stabled. Though he grudged the fodder when they could no longer graze on the pastureland, at least he was free from anxiety about them.

In the winter the news got about that the lady was going to sell her land and that the keeper of

the inn on the high road was bargaining for it. When the peasants heard this they were very much alarmed.

"Well," thought they, "if the innkeeper gets the land, he will worry us with fines worse than the lady's steward. We all depend on that estate."

So the peasants went on behalf of their Commune,[2] and asked the lady not to sell the land to the innkeeper, offering her a better price for it themselves. The lady agreed to let them have it. Then the peasants tried to arrange for the Commune to buy the whole estate, so that it might be held by them all in common. They met twice to discuss it, but could not settle the matter; the Evil One sowed discord among them and they could not agree. So they decided to buy the land individually, each according to his means; and the lady agreed to this plan as she had to the other.

Presently Pahom heard that a neighbor of his was buying fifty acres, and that the lady had consented to accept one half in cash and to wait a year for the other half. Pahom felt envious.

"Look at that," thought he, "the land is all being sold, and I shall get none of it." So he spoke to his wife.

"Other people are buying," said he, "and we must also buy twenty acres or so. Life is becoming impossible. That steward is simply crushing us with his fines."

So they put their heads together and considered how they could manage to buy it. They had one hundred rubles laid by. They sold a colt and one half of their bees, hired out one of their sons as a laborer, and took his wages in advance; borrowed the rest from a brother-in-law, and so scraped together half the purchase money.

Having done this, Pahom chose out a farm of forty acres, some of it wooded, and went to the lady to bargain for it. They came to an agreement, and he shook hands with her upon it and paid her a deposit in advance. Then they went to town and signed the deeds, he paying half the price down, and undertaking to pay the remainder within two years.

So now Pahom had land of his own. He borrowed seed, and sowed it on the land he had bought. The harvest was a good one, and within a year he had managed to pay off his debts both

---

1. **lying . . . stove:** Pahom's house is lacking in luxury if the family's oven, made of brick or tile, is used as an item of furniture.

2. **Commune:** village council.

to the lady and to his brother-in-law. So he became a landowner, plowing and sowing his own land, making hay on his own land, cutting his own trees, and feeding his cattle on his own pasture. When he went out to plow his fields, or to look at his growing corn,[3] or at his grass

3. **corn:** any plants producing grain, such as wheat, rye, or oats.

meadows, his heart would fill with joy. The grass that grew and the flowers that bloomed there seemed to him unlike any that grew elsewhere. Formerly, when he had passed by that land, it had appeared the same as any other land, but now it seemed quite different.

So Pahom was well contented, and everything would have been right if the neighboring peasants would only not have trespassed on his cornfields

The Gleaners (1885–1886) by Isidore Verheyden. Oil on canvas (92 cm × 69 cm).

Collection Crédit Communal, Brussels, Belgium.

and meadows. He appealed to them most civilly, but they still went on: Now the Communal herdsmen would let the village cows stray into his meadows, then horses from the night pasture would get among his corn. Pahom turned them out again and again, and forgave their owners, and for a long time he forbore to prosecute anyone. But at last he lost patience and complained to the District Court. He knew it was the peasants' want of land, and no evil intent on their part, that caused the trouble, but he thought:

"I cannot go on overlooking it or they will destroy all I have. They must be taught a lesson."

So he had them up, gave them one lesson, and then another, and two or three of the peasants were fined. After a time Pahom's neighbors began to bear him a grudge for this, and would now and then let their cattle on to his land on purpose. One peasant even got into Pahom's wood at night and cut down five young lime trees[4] for their bark. Pahom passing through the wood one day noticed something white. He came nearer and saw the stripped trunks lying on the ground, and close by stood the stumps where the trees had been. Pahom was furious.

"If he had only cut one here and there it would have been bad enough," thought Pahom, "but the rascal has actually cut down a whole clump. If I could only find out who did this, I would pay him out."

He racked his brain as to who it could be. Finally he decided: "It must be Simon—no one else could have done it." So he went to Simon's homestead to have a look round, but he found nothing, and only had an angry scene. However, he now felt more certain than ever that Simon had done it, and he lodged a complaint. Simon was summoned. The case was tried, and retried, and at the end of it all Simon was acquitted, there being no evidence against him. Pahom felt still more aggrieved, and let his anger loose upon the Elder and the Judges.

"You let thieves grease your palms," said he. "If you were honest folk yourselves you would not let a thief go free."

So Pahom quarreled with the Judges and with his neighbors. Threats to burn his building began to be uttered. So though Pahom had more land, his place in the Commune was much worse than before.

About this time a rumor got about that many people were moving to new parts.

"There's no need for me to leave my land," thought Pahom. "But some of the others might leave our village and then there would be more room for us. I would take over their land myself and make my estate a bit bigger. I could then live more at ease. As it is, I am still too cramped to be comfortable."

One day Pahom was sitting at home when a peasant, passing through the village, happened to call in. He was allowed to stay the night, and supper was given him. Pahom had a talk with this peasant and asked him where he came from. The stranger answered that he came from beyond the Volga,[5] where he had been working. One word led to another, and the man went on to say that many people were settling in those parts. He told how some people from his village had settled there. They had joined the Commune, and had had twenty-five acres per man granted them. The land was so good, he said, that the rye sown on it grew as high as a horse, and so thick that five cuts of a sickle made a sheaf. One peasant, he said, had brought nothing with him but his bare hands, and now he had six horses and two cows of his own.

Pahom's heart kindled with desire. He thought:

"Why should I suffer in this narrow hole, if one can live so well elsewhere? I will sell my land and my homestead here, and with the money I will start afresh over there and get everything new. In this crowded place one is always having trouble. But I must first go and find out all about it myself."

Toward summer he got ready and started. He went down the Volga on a steamer to Samara,[6] then walked another three hundred miles on foot, and at last reached the place. It was just as the stranger had said. The peasants had plenty of land: Every man had twenty-five acres of Communal land given him for his use, and anyone who had money could buy, besides, at a ruble an acre as much good freehold land as he wanted.

---

4. **lime trees:** linden trees.

5. **Volga:** river in western Russia flowing into the Caspian Sea.
6. **Samara** (su·mä′rə): city on the Volga River in southwestern Russia.

Having found out all he wished to know, Pahom returned home as autumn came on, and began selling off his belongings. He sold his land at a profit, sold his homestead and all his cattle, and withdrew from membership in the Commune. He only waited till the spring, and then started with his family for the new settlement.

As soon as Pahom and his family reached their new abode, he applied for admission into the Commune of a large village. He stood treat to the Elders[7] and obtained the necessary documents. Five shares of Communal land were given him for his own and his sons' use: that is to say—125 acres (not all together, but in different fields) besides the use of the Communal pasture. Pahom put up the buildings he needed, and bought cattle. Of the Communal land alone he had three times as much as at his former home, and the land was good corn land. He was ten times better off than he had been. He had plenty of arable land and pasturage, and could keep as many head of cattle as he liked.

At first, in the bustle of building and settling down, Pahom was pleased with it all, but when he got used to it he began to think that even here he had not enough land. The first year, he sowed wheat on his share of the Communal land and had a good crop. He wanted to go on sowing wheat, but had not enough Communal land for the purpose, and what he had already used was not available; for in those parts wheat is only sown on virgin soil or on fallow land. It is sown for one or two years, and then the land lies fallow till it is again overgrown with prairie grass. There were many who wanted such land and there was not enough for all; so that people quarreled about it. Those who were better off wanted it for growing wheat, and those who were poor wanted it to let to dealers, so that they might raise money to pay their taxes. Pahom wanted to sow more wheat, so he rented land from a dealer for a year. He sowed much wheat and had a fine crop, but the land was too far from the village—the wheat had to be carted more than ten miles. After a time Pahom noticed that some peasant dealers were living on separate farms and were growing wealthy; and he thought:

"If I were to buy some freehold land and have a homestead on it, it would be a different thing altogether. Then it would all be nice and compact."

The question of buying freehold land recurred to him again and again.

He went on in the same way for three years, renting land and sowing wheat. The seasons turned out well and the crops were good, so that he began to lay money by. He might have gone on living contentedly, but he grew tired of having to rent other people's land every year, and having to scramble for it. Wherever there was good land to be had, the peasants would rush for it and it was taken up at once, so that unless you were sharp about it you got none. It happened in the third year that he and a dealer together rented a piece of pastureland from some peasants; and they had already plowed it up, when there was some dispute and the peasants went to law about it, and things fell out so that the labor was all lost.

"If it were my own land," thought Pahom, "I should be independent, and there would not be all this unpleasantness."

So Pahom began looking out for land which he could buy; and he came across a peasant who had bought thirteen hundred acres, but having got into difficulties was willing to sell again cheap. Pahom bargained and haggled with him, and at last they settled the price at 1,500 rubles,[8] part in cash and part to be paid later. They had all but clinched the matter when a passing dealer happened to stop at Pahom's one day to get a feed for his horses. He drank tea with Pahom and they had a talk. The dealer said that he was just returning from the land of the Bashkirs,[9] far away, where he had bought thirteen thousand acres of land, all for 1,000 rubles. Pahom questioned him further, and the tradesman said:

"All one need do is to make friends with the chiefs. I gave away about one hundred rubles' worth of silk robes and carpets, besides a case of tea, and I gave wine to those who would drink it; and I got the land for less than a penny an acre." And he showed Pahom the title deeds, saying:

"The land lies near a river, and the whole prairie is virgin soil."

Road in the Woods (detail) (late 19th century) by Fiodor Vasilyev.

Pahom plied him with questions, and the tradesman said:

"There is more land there than you could cover if you walked a year, and it all belongs to the Bashkirs. They are as simple as sheep, and land can be got almost for nothing."

"There now," thought Pahom, "with my one thousand rubles, why should I get only thirteen hundred acres, and saddle myself with a debt besides? If I take it out there, I can get more than ten times as much for the money."

Pahom inquired how to get to the place, and as

On and on they went until they had gone more than three hundred miles, and on the seventh day they came to a place where the Bashkirs had pitched their tents. It was all just as the tradesman had said. The people lived on the steppes, by a river, in felt-covered tents. They neither tilled the ground, nor ate bread. Their cattle and horses grazed in herds on the steppe. The colts were tethered behind the tents, and the mares were driven to them twice a day. The mares were milked, and from the milk kumiss[10] was made. It was the women who prepared kumiss, and they also made cheese. As far as the men were concerned, drinking kumiss and tea, eating mutton, and playing on their pipes, was all they cared about. They were all stout and merry, and all the summer long they never thought of doing any work. They were quite ignorant, and knew no Russian, but were good natured enough.

As soon as they saw Pahom, they came out of their tents and gathered round their visitor. An interpreter was found, and Pahom told them he had come about some land. The Bashkirs seemed very glad; they took Pahom and led him into one of the best tents, where they made him sit on some down cushions placed on a carpet, while they sat round him. They gave him some tea and kumiss, and had a sheep killed, and gave him mutton to eat. Pahom took presents out of his cart and distributed them among the Bashkirs, and divided the tea amongst them. The Bashkirs were delighted. They talked a great deal among themselves, and then told the interpreter to translate.

"They wish to tell you," said the interpreter, "that they like you, and that it is our custom to do all we can to please a guest and to repay him for his gifts. You have given us presents, now tell us which of the things we possess please you best, that we may present them to you."

"What pleases me best here," answered Pahom, "is your land. Our land is crowded and the soil is exhausted; but you have plenty of land and it is good land. I never saw the like of it."

The interpreter translated. The Bashkirs talked among themselves for a while. Pahom could not understand what they were saying, but saw that they were much amused and that they shouted and

soon as the tradesman had left him, he prepared to go there himself. He left his wife to look after the homestead, and started on his journey taking his man with him. They stopped at a town on their way and bought a case of tea, some wine, and other presents, as the tradesman had advised.

10. **kumiss** (kōō′mis): fermented drink made from mare's milk.

laughed. Then they were silent and looked at Pahom while the interpreter said:

"They wish me to tell you that in return for your presents they will gladly give you as much land as you want. You have only to point it out with your hand and it is yours."

The Bashkirs talked again for a while and began to dispute. Pahom asked what they were disputing about, and the interpreter told him that some of them thought they ought to ask their chief about the land and not act in his absence, while others thought there was no need to wait for his return.

While the Bashkirs were disputing, a man in a large fox-fur cap appeared on the scene. They all became silent and rose to their feet. The interpreter said, "This is our chief himself."

Pahom immediately fetched the best dressing gown and five pounds of tea, and offered these to the chief. The chief accepted them, and seated himself in the place of honor. The Bashkirs at once began telling him something. The chief listened for a while, then made a sign with his head for them to be silent, and addressing himself to Pahom, said in Russian:

"Well, let it be so. Choose whatever piece of land you like; we have plenty of it."

"How can I take as much as I like?" thought Pahom. "I must get a deed to make it secure, or else they may say, 'It is yours,' and afterward may take it away again."

"Thank you for your kind words," he said aloud. "You have much land, and I only want a little. But I should like to be sure which bit is mine. Could it not be measured and made over to me? Life and death are in God's hands. You good people give it to me, but your children might wish to take it away again."

"You are quite right," said the chief. "We will make it over to you."

"I heard that a dealer had been here," continued Pahom, "and that you gave him a little land, too, and signed title deeds to that effect. I should like to have it done in the same way."

The chief understood.

"Yes," replied he, "that can be done quite easily. We have a scribe, and we will go to town with you and have the deed properly sealed."

"And what will be the price?" asked Pahom.

"Our price is always the same: one thousand rubles a day."

Pahom did not understand.

"A day? What measure is that? How many acres would that be?"

"We do not know how to reckon it out," said the chief. "We sell it by the day. As much as you can go round on your feet in a day is yours, and the price is one thousand rubles a day."

Pahom was surprised.

"But in a day you can get round a large tract of land," he said.

The chief laughed.

"It will all be yours!" said he. "But there is one condition: If you don't return on the same day to the spot whence you started, your money is lost."

"But how am I to mark the way that I have gone?"

"Why, we shall go to any spot you like, and stay there. You must start from that spot and make your round, taking a spade with you. Wherever you think necessary, make a mark. At every turning, dig a hole and pile up the turf; then afterward we will go round with a plow from hole to hole. You may make as large a circuit as you please, but before the sun sets you must return to the place you started from. All the land you cover will be yours."

Pahom was delighted. It was decided to start early next morning. They talked a while, and after drinking some more kumiss and eating some more mutton, they had tea again, and then the night came on. They gave Pahom a featherbed to sleep on, and the Bashkirs dispersed for the night, promising to assemble the next morning at daybreak and ride out before sunrise to the appointed spot.

Pahom lay on the featherbed, but could not sleep. He kept thinking about the land.

"What a large tract I will mark off!" thought he. "I can easily do thirty-five miles in a day. The days are long now, and within a circuit of thirty-five miles what a lot of land there will be! I will sell the poorer land, or let it to peasants, but I'll pick out the best and farm it. I will buy two ox teams, and hire two more laborers. About a hundred and fifty acres shall be plow land, and I will pasture cattle on the rest."

Pahom lay awake all night, and dozed off only just before dawn. Hardly were his eyes closed when he had a dream. He thought he was lying in that same tent and heard somebody chuckling outside. He wondered who it could be, and rose and went out, and he saw the Bashkir chief sitting in front of the tent holding his sides and rolling about with laughter. Going nearer to the chief, Pahom asked: "What are you laughing at?" But he saw that it was no longer the chief, but the dealer who had recently stopped at his house and had told him about the land. Just as Pahom was going to ask, "Have you been here long?" he saw that it was not the dealer, but the peasant who had come up from the Volga, long ago, to Pahom's old home. Then he saw that it was not the peasant either, but the Devil himself with hoofs and horns, sitting there and chuckling, and before him lay a man barefoot, prostrate on the ground, with only trousers and a shirt on. And Pahom dreamt that he looked more attentively to see what sort of a man it was that was lying there, and he saw that the man was dead, and that it was himself! He awoke horror-struck.

"What things one does dream," thought he.

Looking round he saw through the open door that the dawn was breaking.

"It's time to wake them up," thought he. "We ought to be starting."

He got up, roused his man (who was sleeping in his cart), bade him harness, and went to call the Bashkirs.

"It's time to go to the steppe to measure the land," he said.

The Bashkirs rose and assembled, and the chief came too. Then they began drinking kumiss again, and offered Pahom some tea, but he would not wait.

The Rainbow by Arkhip Kuindzhi (1842–1910).

"If we are to go, let us go. It is high time," said he.

The Bashkirs got ready and they all started: some mounted on horses, and some in carts. Pahom drove in his own small cart with his servant and took a spade with him. When they reached the steppe, the morning red was beginning to kindle. They ascended a hillock (called by the Bashkirs a *shikhan*) and dismounting from their carts and their horses, gathered in one spot. The chief came up to Pahom and stretching out his arm toward the plain:

"See," said he, "all this, as far as your eye can reach, is ours. You may have any part of it you like."

Pahom's eyes glistened: It was all virgin soil, as flat as the palm of your hand, as black as the seed of a poppy, and in the hollows different kinds of grasses grew breast high.

The chief took off his fox-fur cap, placed it on the ground, and said:

"This will be the mark. Start from here, and return here again. All the land you go round shall be yours."

Pahom took out his money and put it on the cap. Then he took off his outer coat, remaining in his sleeveless undercoat. He unfastened his girdle and tied it tight below his stomach, put a little bag of bread into the breast of his coat, and tying a flask of water to his girdle, he drew up the tops of his boots, took the spade from his man, and stood ready to start. He considered for some moments which way he had better go—it was tempting everywhere.

"No matter," he concluded, "I will go toward the rising sun."

He turned his face to the east, stretched himself, and waited for the sun to appear above the rim.

"I must lose no time," he thought, "and it is easier walking while it is still cool."

The sun's rays had hardly flashed above the horizon, before Pahom, carrying the spade over his shoulder, went down into the steppe.

Pahom started walking neither slowly nor quickly. After having gone a thousand yards he stopped, dug a hole, and placed pieces of turf one on another to make it more visible. Then he went on; and now that he had walked off his stiffness he quickened his pace. After a while he dug another hole.

Pahom looked back. The hillock could be distinctly seen in the sunlight, with the people on it,

and the glittering tires of the cart wheels. At a rough guess Pahom concluded that he had walked three miles. It was growing warmer; he took off his undercoat, flung it across his shoulder, and went on again. It had grown quite warm now; he looked at the sun, it was time to think of breakfast.

"The first shift is done, but there are four in a day, and it is too soon yet to turn. But I will just take off my boots," said he to himself.

He sat down, took off his boots, stuck them into his girdle, and went on. It was easy walking now.

"I will go on for another three miles," thought he, "and then turn to the left. This spot is so fine, that it would be a pity to lose it. The further one goes, the better the land seems."

He went straight on for a while, and when he looked round, the hillock was scarcely visible and the people on it looked like black ants, and he could just see something glistening there in the sun.

"Ah," thought Pahom, "I have gone far enough in this direction, it is time to turn. Besides I am in a regular sweat, and very thirsty."

He stopped, dug a large hole, and heaped up pieces of turf. Next he untied his flask, had a drink, and then turned sharply to the left. He went on and on; the grass was high, and it was very hot.

Pahom began to grow tired: He looked at the sun and saw that it was noon.

"Well," he thought, "I must have a rest."

He sat down, and ate some bread and drank some water; but he did not lie down, thinking that if he did he might fall asleep. After sitting a little while, he went on again. At first he walked easily: The food had strengthened him; but it had become terribly hot and he felt sleepy, still he went on, thinking: "An hour to suffer, a lifetime to live."

He went a long way in this direction also, and was about to turn to the left again, when he perceived a damp hollow: "It would be a pity to leave that out," he thought. "Flax would do well there." So he went on past the hollow, and dug a hole on the other side of it before he turned the corner. Pahom looked toward the hillock. The heat made the air hazy: It seemed to be quivering, and through the haze the people on the hillock could scarcely be seen.

"Ah!" thought Pahom, "I have made the sides too long; I must make this one shorter." And he went

The Sower (1888) by Vincent van Gogh.

along the third side, stepping faster. He looked at the sun: It was nearly halfway to the horizon, and he had not yet done two miles of the third side of the square. He was still ten miles from the goal.

"No," he thought, "though it will make my land lopsided, I must hurry back in a straight line now. I might go too far, and as it is I have a great deal of land."

So Pahom hurriedly dug a hole, and turned straight toward the hillock.

Pahom went straight toward the hillock, but he now walked with difficulty. He was done up with the heat, his bare feet were cut and bruised, and his legs began to fail. He longed to rest, but it was impossible if he meant to get back before sunset. The sun waits for no man, and it was sinking lower and lower.

"Oh dear," he thought, "if only I have not blun-dered trying for too much! What if I am too late?"

He looked toward the hillock and at the sun. He was still far from his goal, and the sun was already near the rim.

Pahom walked on and on; it was very hard walking but he went quicker and quicker. He pressed on, but was still far from the place. He began running, threw away his coat, his boots, his flask, and his cap, and kept only the spade which he used as a support.

"What shall I do," he thought again. "I have grasped too much and ruined the whole affair. I can't get there before the sun sets."

And this fear made him still more breathless. Pahom went on running, his soaking shirt and trousers stuck to him, and his mouth was parched. His breast was working like a blacksmith's bellows, his heart was beating like a hammer, and his legs were giving way as if they did not belong to him. Pahom was seized with terror lest he should die of the strain.

Though afraid of death, he could not stop. "After having run all that way they will call me a fool if I stop now," thought he. And he ran on and on, and drew near and heard the Bashkirs yelling and shouting to him, and their cries inflamed his heart still more. He gathered his last strength and ran on.

The sun was close to the rim, and cloaked in mist looked large, and red as blood. Now, yes now, it was about to set! The sun was quite low, but he was also quite near his aim. Pahom could already see the people on the hillock waving their arms to hurry him up. He could see the fox-fur cap on the ground and the money on it, and the chief sitting on the ground holding his sides. And Pahom remembered his dream.

"There is plenty of land," thought he, "but will God let me live on it? I have lost my life, I have lost my life! I shall never reach that spot!"

Pahom looked at the sun, which had reached the earth: One side of it had already disappeared. With all his remaining strength he rushed on, bending his body forward so that his legs could hardly follow fast enough to keep him from falling. Just as he reached the hillock it suddenly grew dark. He looked up— the sun had already set! He gave a cry: "All my labor has been in vain," thought he, and was about to stop, but he heard the Bashkirs still shouting, and remembered that though to him, from below, the sun seemed to have set, they on the hillock could still see it. He took a long breath and ran up the hillock. It was still light there. He reached the top and saw the cap. Before it sat the chief laughing and holding his sides. Again Pahom remembered his dream, and he uttered a cry: His legs gave way beneath him, he fell forward and reached the cap with his hands.

"Ah, that's a fine fellow!" exclaimed the chief. "He has gained much land!"

Pahom's servant came running up and tried to raise him, but he saw that blood was flowing from his mouth. Pahom was dead!

The Bashkirs clicked their tongues to show their pity.

His servant picked up the spade and dug a grave long enough for Pahom to lie in, and buried him in it. Six feet from his head to his heels was all he needed.

FINDING COMMON GROUND

Tolstoy's story of a Russian farmer's land acquisition illustrates the perils of greed. In describing his disillusionment with private land ownership, Tolstoy provides today's readers with a parable about the "progress" of materialism. In small groups, talk about the contrast the story presents between the attitude of the Russians of Tolstoy's day and that of the traditional peoples, who are said to be "simple as sheep." Be sure to check your Quickwrite notes as you discuss the story.

• Find examples in the text that reveal the Bashkir culture's attitudes about property and values. How would you compare them with the beliefs of your own culture?

• The nomadic Bashkirs come into contact with outsiders who buy their land for a token sum. How is this clash of cultures similar to or different from the one depicted in Kipling's "The Mark of the Beast" (page 872)?

• You have seen British writers questioning the benefits of nineteenth-century industrialization and modernization. Does this questioning change in a Russian setting? In what ways does Tolstoy share or extend the debate about progress?

• Pahom's dreams of wealth are mocked in the story's ironic last line. Think of the stark contrast between what he wanted and "all he needed." What parallels do you find with our culture today? How and why do people's wants differ from their actual needs?

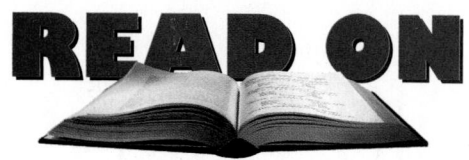

Dark Shadows

Although there have been numerous movie (and stage) versions in the twentieth century, Bram Stoker's *Dracula* (Putnam) is rooted firmly in the Victorian psyche. Written in 1897, this Gothic masterpiece is not only a supreme story of horror and suspense, but also a reflection of the dark underside of an extremely moralistic age. The progressive values of high Victorian culture are pitted against—and ultimately triumph over—the deep-rooted desires and dreads of the subconscious.

Romantic Rebellion

"If there's one thing Papa will never, *never* permit, it's a marriage in the family." Rudolf Besier's play *The Barretts of Wimpole Street* (Little, Brown) is based on the relationship between Elizabeth Barrett and Robert Browning, which developed under less than auspicious circumstances: Elizabeth's father forbade any of his nine adult children to marry. But in spite of Mr. Barrett's extraordinary attitude, his whole house is literally seething with romance and rebellion.

A Peek at Victorian Private Lives

Welcome to nineteenth-century England! In *What Jane Austen Ate and Charles Dickens Knew* (Simon and Schuster), Daniel Pool gives new life to the daily life of the last century. Both the nitty-gritty details (How did they keep clean?) and the posh etiquette (How did one address a duke?) of the time are covered. Find out what the Victorians ate, what they wore, how they traveled, and whom they married.

Found in a Handbag

Much of the satire in Oscar Wilde's play *The Importance of Being Earnest* (Penguin) is targeted at the British class system. Wilde openly flouted Victorian ideas of respectability and presented his own philosophy as an alternative. The seemingly contradictory logic of the play is part of this philosophy: "The truth is rarely pure and never simple." The play is also available as a film, made in England in 1952, with Michael Redgrave. (This title is available in the HRW Library.)

Pastoral Problems

Thomas Hardy's *Far from the Madding Crowd* (Oxford University Press) is about one very beautiful woman and the profound effect she has on three very different men. Opening on a note of almost lighthearted comedy, the novel gradually evolves into a starker tale of thoughtlessness, abandonment, death, and derangement. The 1967 British film version of the novel, with Julie Christie, Peter Finch, and Alan Bates, is available on videotape.

The English Language

One Language—Many Nations

by John Algeo

Although the spread of English outside the British Isles began in the early seventeenth century, it was during the Victorian Age that English became a world language. Primarily because of the influence of the British Empire, English became either the first or an important second language in the British Isles, the United States, and Canada, as well as in Jamaica, Trinidad and Tobago, Australia, New Zealand, Malaysia, Myanmar, India, Sri Lanka, Pakistan, Israel, Ghana, Sierra Leone, Nigeria, Sudan, Kenya, Tanzania, Malawi, Zambia, Zimbabwe, Swaziland, and South Africa. American expansion, although modest by comparison, extended English to the Philippines, Liberia, and a few other places.

English as an International Language

English first spread around the world as a result of political and commercial activities, empire building, and colonization. In addition, scientific and technological advances, movies and television programs, popular music, and fashions of clothing have all served to reinforce the prestige of English as an international language. Today, English is used more widely and for more purposes as a second language than any other human tongue.

To take only one example: English is the language of international aviation. If a Swedish pilot is landing an airplane in Greece, he or she uses English to converse with the controller on the ground. Having a single language for international aviation is obviously sensible. It would not do for a pilot who spoke only Swedish to ask for landing instructions from ground controllers who spoke only Greek. A common language is needed as a safety measure for international flights, and English was chosen because of the prominence of English-speaking people in making and flying airplanes. It is for such reasons that English has become the most widely used international language.

Dialects of English

Today, there are dialects of English all over the world. Each place where it is spoken has its own variety of the language, and old countries like England or large ones like the United States have many regional dialects. However, standard English—the English found in books, magazines, and large newspapers—is relatively uniform. That uniformity also helps to make English useful as an international language. Differences exist, to be sure, but they are minor fluctuations in what is obviously a single language.

Each country in which English is the main language of communication has its own national standard that differs in small, but recognizable, ways from the standards of other English-speaking lands. Among these national standards are those of Australia, Canada, the United Kingdom (England, Scotland, Wales, and Northern Ireland), Jamaica, New Zealand, the Republic of Ireland, and the United States.

Two Close Cousins: British and American English

The two most important national standards are those of the United Kingdom and of the United States: British and American English. The differences between them can be illustrated by a few expressions:

American	British
baby stroller	push-chair
baked potato	jacket potato
barrette	hair slide
coffee with cream	coffee white
daylight saving time	summer time

divided highway	dual carriage way
hood (of a car)	bonnet
Main Street	High Street
pharmacist	dispensing chemist
public restroom	convenience
savings and loan association	building society
subway	underground or tube
traffic circle	roundabout
trunk (of a car)	boot
wastepaper basket	bin
Watch your step.	Mind your step.
whole-wheat bread	brown bread
yield (highway sign)	give way

Entrance to the underground station at Piccadilly Circus, London.

The differences tend to occur especially in technical areas like automotive terms, in domestic matters like food names, and in specialized commercial terms like names for kinds of businesses. The specialized terminologies of American and British English differ considerably, but the words of the ordinary language—the everyday nouns and most verbs, adverbs, adjectives, and connecting words like prepositions and conjunctions—are very much alike in the two national standards.

Each national standard also has words for which there is no exact equivalent in the other. For example, in England a *bap* is a soft roll that may be used to make a sandwich; a *crumpet* is a kind of muffin; a *gateau* is a kind of cake; *chips* are French fries; a *free house* is a *pub* or bar where more than one brand of beer is sold; and a *purveyor* is a company that sells or deals in some product.

Each country has influenced the language of the other. In America, people who drive British cars may begin to use British automotive terms because they appear in the cars' operating manuals. The expression "Not to worry" is a Briticism that has become popular here. On the other hand, American expressions like "nitty-gritty" turn up in England, as do many technical terms.

Strange combinations of the two national standards sometimes emerge. American clothing, food, and television programs are very popular in England. A store in the Chelsea area of London announces itself as the "Texas Lone Star Saloon, Purveyors of the Best Chili, Tacos, Nachos." Everything about the store's sign is pure American— except the word *purveyors*, which is as British as crumpets and chips.

Pronunciation, Spelling, and Grammar

British and American English obviously differ in pronunciation. The British pronounce words like *bath, class,* and *can't* with the vowel sound of *father,* rather than with the vowel sound of *cat.* Like people from eastern New England, New York City, and the coastal South, but unlike most other Americans, the British drop *r* sounds unless they have a vowel after them, so that *poppa* and *popper* sound alike. American English tends to have more stresses on its words than does British English; so we pronounce *secretary* as sek'rə·ter'ē, whereas the British say it as sek'rə·trē. Perhaps the most striking difference between the two national standards, however, is in intonation, the "tune" of the sentence. To British ears, American speech sounds flat and dull—it has a more uniform, lower pitch and minimizes the difference between high and low notes. To

American ears, British speech sounds fluting, high-pitched, quavering, and slightly hysterical—British speech has a more varied, higher pitch and exaggerates the difference between high and low notes.

Spelling also differs slightly in the two countries. British English uses -our in words like colour and honour, where American English uses -or. British uses -re in words like centre and metre, where American uses -er. British doubles the l at the end of unstressed syllables before adding a suffix beginning with a vowel in words like travelling, for which American usage typically keeps a single l, traveling. There are also a few miscellaneous differences: British pyjamas versus American pajamas. The differences are all trivial, although the British often insist that American books published in England be reset using British spelling. Americans seldom notice the difference.

Grammatical differences between the two forms of English are also few and unimportant. The British sometimes omit the definite article where we would use it: "in hospital" (British) versus "in the hospital" (American). They use a plural verb with some collective nouns (the word government and names of sports teams) for which we use a singular verb: "The government have decided . . ." "Nebraska are winning the bowl game." They treat have as a special verb that does not require an auxiliary in questions: "Have you the answer?" versus "Do you have the answer?" The British use only the past participle got, whereas we use both got and gotten, in different ways: "I've got it" versus American "I've got it" (meaning "I have it") and "I've gotten it" (meaning "I've obtained it"). Other British and American grammatical differences are equally minor.

Actually, the differences between British and American English have often been exaggerated, as they were by Oscar Wilde, who said that the English "have really everything in common with America nowadays, except, of course, language." In fact, not only these two countries, but all the nations of the English-speaking world share a common linguistic heritage that goes back to the Anglo-Saxons and, before them, to Proto-Indo-European tribes that wandered from Asia across Europe. Today, despite the linguistic differences that divide us—the small distinctions of grammar, spelling, and pronunciation, and the greater but still not insuperable ones of terminology—English is a unified language. The core of English—our basic words and how we use them—is one.

> Oscar Wilde said that the English "have really everything in common with America nowadays, except, of course, language."

Try It Out

1. Comparing vocabularies. What are the American counterparts of the British English terms listed below? (Look up the British words in a dictionary.)

accumulator	queue
banger	rates
flog	scoff
lift	toffee-nosed
nous	wellies

2. Rewriting British English. The following sentences in British English have grammatical constructions that differ from American usage. Rewrite each sentence as you would say it.

   a. What had you in mind to do this afternoon?

   b. She says she tried to ring us, but she can't have done.

   c. It looks like being a close vote.

   d. After long discussions, they agreed the plan.

   e. I carry two pencils in case one goes missing.

3. Comparing spellings. The following words are spelled in the British fashion. Write the American spellings.

ageing	labour
analyse	marvelled
centre	

4. Investigating word origins. The following words come from several different national varieties of English. Use a dictionary to see what they mean and where they originated.

boomerang	trek
boondocks	walkabout
thug	

Writer's Workshop

The history
of the written
word is rich an

Page 1

PERSUASIVE WRITING

AN EVALUATION

"I love it!" "I hate it!" "It's boring." "It's great!" Every day of our lives we make a range of judgments. Some are based on personal preference or whim, but others are careful, reasoned evaluations. Many Victorian writers considered it a *duty* to evaluate the changes taking place around them: Hardy, Arnold, and Dickens each made judgments, carefully measuring the benefits of industrial growth against the misery of the working-class English. Often our own judgments concern smaller things than what makes an ideal society, but they are still vital—our lives would be chaos if we failed to evaluate the opportunities and choices available to us, from jobs to political candidates. Evaluation, or judging something against a definite standard, is one of the most basic forms of writing—and thinking.

Prewriting

1. **Checking your Writer's Notebook.** By doing the Writer's Notebook activities in Collections 10 and 11, you may already have done some of the prewriting necessary for an evaluation. Look back through your entries for usable ideas, and then proceed with the prewriting activities that follow.

2. **Exploring the possibilities: art or life?** What will you evaluate? Because you've studied literature for several years, you're probably prepared to make some judgments about poetry, drama, or fiction—perhaps one of the selections you've recently read. Other possible subjects related to literature and the arts include movies, television shows, music, and dance or theater performances. You should also consider subjects from the real world: candidates for local or national office, sports equipment, or ideas about the formation of black holes in space. For a few minutes, freewrite a list of things that pique your interest or that you remember well—stories, shows, theories you've read or heard about, consumer goods. Then circle the one or two that you have strong feelings about. (It doesn't matter whether these feelings are positive or negative. The important thing is that you choose something to write about that prompts strong feelings in you.)

3. **How do I judge thee?** With a firm subject to evaluate, you can now determine the criteria for your evaluation. **Criteria** are the characteristics a particular thing must have to be judged an excellent example of its type or kind—that is, an excellent lyric poem, mystery story, sports car, action movie, economic theory, or some other thing. You need to look beyond your subject to the particular type, or genre, it belongs to. For example, if you're going to evaluate a poem, is the poem a narrative or a lyric? Ask

Technology HELP

See Writer's Workshop 2 CD-ROM. *Assignment: Evaluation.*

ASSIGNMENT
Write an evaluation, based on appropriate criteria and supported by reasons and evidence.

AIM
To persuade your readers to accept your informed judgment.

AUDIENCE
Your classmates or a specialized audience within your school—a literary society, a film club, or the student council, for example.

yourself: *What makes this a lyric poem?* or *What makes this a narrative poem?* You can't evaluate a narrative and a lyric poem with the same criteria any more than you can evaluate a four-wheel-drive utility vehicle and a luxury car with the same criteria.

4. **Making a judgment, backing it up.** Establishing criteria is an important step in evaluating something, but it's just one step on the way. You also have to measure your subject against the criteria you've developed, *and* you have to convince your audience that the judgments you develop are sound. To be convincing, you need to supply reasons and evidence for your judgments. **Reasons** tell why a judgment should be accepted; **evidence** provides proof for each reason: quotations, examples, facts, details, or expert opinions. Generating reasons and evidence will build a convincing argument—the informed judgment that makes your evaluation worth reading (and accepting).

One way to develop your case is to create a three-column chart. In the first column, list each of your criteria for judging your subject, starting with your most important criterion. In the second column, list each **reason** for judging your particular subject successful or unsuccessful, worthy or unworthy. In the third column, supply specific **evidence** for the judgments you've made in the second column. The following chart lists criteria, reasons, and evidence for evaluating *Sense and Sensibility,* a 1995 film adaptation of Jane Austen's 1811 novel.

Try It Out

What criteria would you apply to evaluate the following subjects?

1. An extraordinary person (a politician, an artist, an athlete, or some other noteworthy figure)
2. A local restaurant
3. A new way of doing things (such as a medical advancement or a governmental policy)
4. A product (such as a car or a brand of cereal)
5. A magazine or newspaper

Model

Criteria	Reasons	Evidence
Well-developed characters	Characters complex enough to seem real; flaws and strengths both shown.	Sisters reveal different facets with family, with suitors, and alone; Elinor's humor tempers her moral highhandedness.
Theme	Without preaching, story reveals a truth about the real world.	By end, Marianne realizes what Elinor already knows—that ordinary pleasures of real love outweigh any grand passion.

This writer draws evidence from the movie itself. Other kinds of evidence often used in evaluations include

- personal anecdotes (your own experiences with the subject, particularly those your readers might have shared)
- illustrations (quotations, descriptive details, paraphrases)
- statistics (for example, published data indicating that the car you're evaluating gets 35 miles per gallon while similar ones get 25)
- testimony (what others, especially those with personal experience or authoritative knowledge, have said about your topic)

5. **Whittling away.** Winnow your list down to the most compelling criteria, reasons, and evidence you have. The less convincing material you've thought about can be eliminated or briefly described in your essay. If you think your audience will expect you to deal with aspects of your subject for which you don't have a strong case, think about how you will discuss them without weakening your overall argument.

   This involves analyzing your **audience.** Are they beginners or experts? The members of your school's film club will probably have more knowledge about filmmaking than a general audience, so you'll want to address some fine points of direction and cinematography in a movie review. If your subject is personal computers, and you're writing for your classmates, think about how you will explain your technical points.

6. **Shaping your argument.** The points you make in your evaluation should be arranged in some logical order. You may decide to proceed from most obvious to least obvious, from most general to most complicated, from least important to most important, or the reverse. Whatever pattern you choose, your readers should be able to easily follow your argument. At this point, try to outline your evaluation, at least in rough form.

Communications Handbook H E L P

See Taking Notes and Documenting Sources; Proofreading.

Strategies for Elaboration: Avoiding Pitfalls

As you evaluate and refine your points and shape your argument, make sure you've avoided the following pitfalls:

- **Avoid using criteria based merely on personal tastes.** Make sure that your praise for a television show doesn't rely on the fact that the main character reminds you of your nice neighbor Hank.

- **Avoid using irrelevant criteria.** Are your criteria appropriately connected to the subject of your essay? Don't fault a certain model bicycle because you don't like the salesperson's shoes.

- **Avoid making hasty generalizations.** Don't praise something because you have overvalued a certain part of it. A play is not worthy of praise just because you've always liked the leading actor's work; a novel is not good just because the novelist's other novels are considered classics.

- **Avoid making one-sided comparisons.** No one will believe you if you claim your subject is absolute perfection (or thoroughly horrible) when compared with other things like it. To appear thoughtful and convincing, you must mention weaknesses in the things you praise and strengths in the things you criticize.

- **Avoid including straw-man arguments.** If there are closer comparisons to be made, don't compare the subject of your essay with something clearly inferior (or clearly superior). Your audience will suspect you have unfairly rigged your argument in favor of your judgment. (A straw man is something easily knocked down or dismissed.)

- **Don't avoid accepting the burden of proof.** Make sure that you can supply concrete evidence for all the judgments you make in your essay. It's up to you to show why your judgment is sound.

An effective evaluation
1. *orients the reader to the subject being evaluated*
2. *includes a clear statement of the writer's judgment*
3. *includes criteria that are appropriate, clear, and, if necessary, explained by the writer*
4. *includes relevant, convincing, and logically ordered reasons for the writer's judgment*
5. *includes sufficient evidence to support each reason*
6. *has a tone that is authoritative, consistent throughout, and appropriate for the intended audience*
7. *has an engaging beginning and an ending that restates the judgment in a satisfying way*

Revision
S T R A T E G I E S

Consider your readers one last time. Do you need to explain anything more clearly? Or have you overexplained anything they probably know already? Working with a writing partner, mark any explanations that need further clarification or some that need cutting. Revise, and then consult with your writing partner again to discuss your revisions.

Language Workshop
H E L P

Sentence style: page 903.

Drafting

1. **Reflecting on purpose and audience: the message and the messenger.** Before you begin drafting, think again about what you want your readers to believe after they read your evaluation. Who are your readers? Will they need extensive description or definitions of unfamiliar terms before you move into the meat of your evaluation?

   Your **tone** should be authoritative and convincing but engaging. It should also be consistent throughout your essay. Think about what kind of tone will suit your subject *and* your audience: formal or casual, serious or humorous?

2. **The introduction: finding a hook.** How will you capture your readers' attention right from the start? You might begin with an anecdote, a startling image, or a quote from an authority. Or you could just throw down the gauntlet and begin by announcing your judgment (of course, you'll still need to justify it later on). You've already thought quite a bit about your readers, so you know how much knowledge they have about your subject and whether you'll need to begin with a thorough description before moving into your evaluation.

3. **The body: building your case.** Your judgment of your subject is the controlling idea, or thesis, of your evaluation. Now you must construct the case to support your judgment, brick by brick. Before you begin writing, consult the outline you formulated in prewriting. Do you still think the order of reasons and evidence you established is the most effective? If not, reorder them. (And remember that even this order isn't engraved in stone—often a different or more logical pattern will emerge as you're writing.) Make sure that each reason for your judgment is adequately reinforced with evidence, and explain any criteria you think your readers will question or mistrust. Also, try to achieve balance, giving proper emphasis to description, reasons, and evidence without overexplaining or scrimping on any of them.

4. **The ending: driving it home.** Here's your chance to leave your readers thoroughly convinced that your evaluation is solid. You might end with a summary of the reasons you've presented or a restatement of your judgment, or you might refer to the beginning of the essay. In any event, leave your readers with something memorable—some ideas to turn over in their minds. (Any essay that just ends leaves readers feeling as though they were engaged in conversation with someone who abruptly walked away.)

Evaluating and Revising

1. **Peer review.** One of the most helpful ways to respond to someone else's writing is to ask questions. As you read, pause where you have a question, and write it either in the margin or on a separate sheet of paper. Then discuss your questions with the writer of the evaluation.

2. **Self-evaluation.** Using your peer reviewer's comments as a map, go through your essay again. Address any concerns about your criteria and evidence first. Put a check mark next to each criterion; then underscore the evidence that supports it. If your reviewer has raised any counterarguments to your case, think about how to defuse them. Finally, check to see if you should vary your sentence style.

Language Workshop

The history
of the written
word is rich and

Page 1

SENTENCE STYLE: WAYS OF STRENGTHENING MEANING

Most writers tend to have an identifiable general style that distinguishes their writing. For example, Matthew Arnold's poetic style differs from that of Gerard Manley Hopkins. **Style** is the way a writer uses language to express ideas and adapts language to suit the occasion. Style involves both the kinds of words a writer chooses (or **diction,** which you studied in the Language Workshop on page 777) and the way that writer joins those words to form sentences. In all good writing, the **sentence style** reflects the substance, or content, of the work. The beginning of Charles Dickens's *A Tale of Two Cities* contains one famous example of meaning reinforced by style. Notice how the use of **parallelism** contributes to the paradoxical nature of the passage—each statement is weighed against another, and both appear to be true:

> It was the best of times, it was the worst of times, it was the age of wisdom, it was the age of foolishness, it was the epoch of belief, it was the epoch of incredulity, it was the season of Light, it was the season of Darkness, it was the spring of hope, it was the winter of despair. . . .
> —Charles Dickens, *from A Tale of Two Cities*

Strategies for Analyzing Sentence Style

The following questions are useful in analyzing a writer's style. When answering each question, make notes about how each characteristic affects the meaning and overall impact of the writing.

- Are the sentences long, short, or varied?
- Are the sentences primarily declarative, interrogative, or imperative?
- Are the sentences simple, compound, complex, compound-complex, or varied in structure?
- Are the sentences primarily in the active or passive voice?
- Do the sentences follow the normal word order of English, or is the syntax inverted or varied in some way?
- Do the sentences use stylistic devices such as repetition or parallelism?

Writer's Workshop Follow-Up: Revision

Look back at the evaluation you wrote for the Writer's Workshop on page 899. Use the questions given above to analyze the sentence style of your evaluation. Working with a writing partner, identify at least three sentences you can revise to reinforce their meaning; then, share your revisions with your partner.

Technology HELP

See Language Workshop CD-ROM. *Key word entry: sentence style.*

Language Handbook HELP

See Sentence Style, page 1236.

Try It Out

How does Kipling's style affect the impact of the passage below? Rewrite the passage in other styles: Is the impact changed?

Everybody was there, and there was a general closing up of ranks and taking stock of our losses in dead or disabled that had fallen during the past year. It was a very wet night, and I remember that we sang "Auld Lang Syne" with our feet in the Polo Championship Cup, and our heads among the stars, and swore that we were all dear friends.

—*from* "The Mark of the Beast"

Reading for Life

Reading a Historical Map

Situation

You've read about the British Empire during the Victorian era and you're curious about how far it extended into Asia. While browsing in a bookstore, you find a book on British history in which there's a map of the empire in the East. To interpret the map, you can apply these map-reading strategies.

Strategies

Identify the category of map you're reading. The two principal categories into which maps fall are political maps and special-purpose maps.

- Political maps show political units, such as states and nations. They often use different colors to show different countries. A historical map shows political boundaries at a certain time in history.

- Among the numerous kinds of special, or thematic, maps are road maps, aviation maps, navigational maps, geologic maps, and maps that show the amount of rainfall, the distribution of populations and crops, or agricultural and industrial areas.

Know how to use special map features. Most maps include one or more of the following:

- a compass rose, indicating directions on the earth's surface
- lines of longitude and latitude
- a distance scale

British Empire in the East, 1897

British possessions

British spheres of influence

- a grid with labeled coordinates to help readers locate places on the map
- a map key, or legend, identifying special symbols

Using the Strategies

Answer these questions, using the map above.

1. Which countries were British possessions?

2. Which countries or parts of countries were within the sphere of British influence?

3. If Queen Victoria had traveled by land from Bombay to Delhi to Calcutta and then to Madras and back to Bombay, approximately how many miles would she have traveled?

4. Which British-controlled city between India and the Dutch East Indies is likely to have been an important trading center?

Extending the Strategies

- Compare a contemporary map of Central Asia with the historical map above. What inferences can you make about political changes that took place in the twentieth century?

- Plan an expedition to one of Great Britain's former colonies. Use an appropriate map to develop your itinerary.

- Use the Internet to obtain current information on one of the countries on the map.

Learning for Life

Evaluating a Community

Problem

Progress in the form of rapid growth made some cities in Victorian England practically unlivable. How has progress affected communities today? What makes a good community?

Project

Identify the qualities you consider essential to a livable community. Are job opportunities an absolute necessity? What about size, location, climate, and quality of life? How has progress affected these qualities in communities in your area?

Preparation

1. Use brainstorming or free-writing to generate an initial list of qualities essential to a livable community.
2. With a group, examine the ways progress has changed your target community.

Procedure

1. From the group's master list, select the three or four qualities you consider most important, keeping in mind that this winnowing process will involve a series of trade-offs—for example, would you be willing to give up recreational facilities for more industry and thus more jobs? Then, rank the items in order of their importance to you.

2. Gather evidence—facts, statistics, examples, or anecdotes—to support each of your essential qualities.
3. Examine your list of the ways progress has affected your target community. Divide your list into positive effects and negative effects. Try to think of ways each negative effect could be corrected. Be sure to cite situations that might block the correction of the negative effects.

Presentation

Use one of the following formats (or another that your teacher approves):

1. **Agreeing to Disagree**
   With a classmate whose list of essential qualities differs significantly from yours, plan a debate. First, agree on two or three judges for the debate. Next, develop a proposition in the form of an evaluation—for example: *Resolved,* That job opportunities are more important in a community than recreational facilities. Finally, decide which one of you will take the affirmative position. After you've each prepared a debate brief, stage the debate in front of judges.

2. **Down to Scale**
   Design and build a scale model of a community that incorporates your choice of essential qualities. Before you begin construction, think about how you'll allocate space for residential, commercial, and industrial areas and how you'll lay out the streets. Display your model at the public library along with comment cards for viewers' responses.

3. **Appealing to Residents**
   If your investigation of the effects of progress on your target community has generated broad interest, prepare a report that includes your suggestions for changes. In your report, be sure to take into account the reasons why change may be difficult. Give convincing reasons why your recommendations should be considered. Your report should include a list of the qualities you think are essential to a livable community. You might ask the editor of your local newspaper to publish your report.

Processing

Did doing this activity change your feelings about your community? Why? Write a reflection for your portfolio.

Landscape from a Dream (1936–1938) by Paul Nash. Oil on canvas (26¾″ x 40″).
Tate Gallery, London, Great Britain.

The Twentieth Century

The Twentieth Century

by John Leggett

. . . England will still be England, an everlasting animal stretching into the future and the past, and, like all living things, having the power to change out of recognition and yet remain the same.

—George Orwell

The Tube Train (c. 1934) by Cyril E. Power.

© British Museum, London.

A View of Fleet Street (20th century) by Christian Snijders.

W hat a story of change, of the erosion of a proud, complacent, well-ordered society, is told by the early years of the twentieth century in Great Britain!

If we had lived in the era of Victoria, which ended with the great queen's death in 1901, or during the nine-year reign of her son Edward VII, we would have believed that Britain, with its moral and economic dominance of the world, would sail on majestically forever. But of course that is the misconception of every stable age and society—that life will go on just as it always has.

Even during this long, fairly stable period in Great Britain, though, profound changes were taking place, both externally and internally. Although the British imperial policy remained much the same throughout the Victorian era, several major colonies—Australia, South Africa, and New Zealand—gained their independence in the first decade of the twentieth century. Internally, Britain was experiencing social reforms that were to have far-reaching consequences. The rise in literacy, the growing power and influence of the Labour party, the widespread interest in socialist ideology—all were to dramatically change Great Britain and the world.

Political and social events during the early twentieth century would alter Great Britain's preeminent position as a world power and would dramatically change its society.

The Arrival (1923–1924) by Christopher R. W. Nevinson.
Tate Gallery, London.

The Twentieth Century

• Sir Winston Churchill.

LITERARY EVENTS

Swedish writer Selma Lagerlöf is first woman awarded the Nobel Prize in literature, 1909

Dublin's Abbey Theatre founded by **W. B. Yeats** and Lady Gregory to produce plays by and about the Irish, 1904

Joseph Conrad's *Heart of Darkness* published, 1902

James Joyce publishes *A Portrait of the Artist as a Young Man,* 1916

Czech writer Franz Kafka's *The Metamorphosis* published, 1915

G. B. Shaw's *Pygmalion* first produced; **D. H. Lawrence**'s *Sons and Lovers* published, 1913

African American writer Langston Hughes publishes first book of verse, *The Weary Blues,* 1926

E. M. Forster's *A Passage to India* published, 1924

W. B. Yeats receives the Nobel Prize in literature, 1923

Publication of **Joyce**'s *Ulysses* and **T. S. Eliot**'s *The Waste Land,* 1922

Spanish writer Federico García Lorca's play *Blood Wedding* produced, 1933

W. H. Auden's *Poems* published; Noel Coward's play *Private Lives* produced, 1930

Virginia Woolf publishes *To the Lighthouse,* 1927

1900–1910	1911–1916	1917–1926	1927–1939

CULTURAL/HISTORICAL EVENTS

Queen Victoria dies and is succeeded by her son Edward VII, 1901

Sigmund Freud visits U.S. to lecture on psychoanalysis, 1909

South Africa gains independence from Britain; Union of South Africa formed; racial segregation becomes governing rule, 1910

In New York City, the Armory Show introduces postimpressionism and cubism in art; in Paris, the first performance of Stravinsky's *Rite of Spring* causes a riot among bewildered spectators, 1913

World War I begins after the assassination of Archduke Francis Ferdinand, 1914

Albert Einstein announces his general theory of relativity, 1915

Easter Rebellion in Dublin; uprising's leaders executed by British, 1916

U.S. enters the war in Europe; Russian Revolution begins, 1917

World War I ends with nearly 10 million dead; voting rights in England extended to women over 30, 1918

Ireland is divided by treaty, with six northern counties remaining part of United Kingdom; civil war begins in Ireland, 1922

U.S. stock market crashes, triggering worldwide depression, 1929

Adolf Hitler appointed chancellor of Germany; Germans build first concentration camp, at Dachau, 1933

In Russia, Stalinist purges force over 10 million people into labor camps, 1934–1938

Spanish Civil War fought, 1936–1939

Pablo Picasso paints *Guernica,* protesting German firebombing of the Spanish city, 1937

Germany invades Poland; World War II begins, 1939

N 69. BRITISH MINISTRY OF FOOD
HOTEL MAJESTIC, PARIS. B N° 03013

• Food coupon issued by the Ministry of Food during World War I.

• Formerly unemployed men go to work selling apples.

• *Guernica* (1937) by Pablo Picasso. Museo Nacional Centro de Arte Reina Sofia, Madrid. On permanent loan from the Museo del Prado, Madrid.

Irish writer **Seamus Heaney** receives Nobel Prize in literature, 1995

Japanese writer Kenzaburo Oe awarded Nobel Prize in literature, 1994

Winston Churchill receives Nobel Prize in literature; Samuel Beckett's play *Waiting for Godot* first produced in Paris, 1953

Colombian writer Gabriel García Márquez publishes *One Hundred Years of Solitude,* 1967

St. Lucian writer **Derek Walcott** publishes *Omeros,* a long poem inspired by Homer's *Odyssey,* 1990

George Orwell's *Animal Farm* published; Chilean poet Gabriela Mistral awarded Nobel Prize in literature, 1945

Nigerian writer **Chinua Achebe**'s *Things Fall Apart* published, 1958

Egyptian writer **Naguib Mahfouz** awarded Nobel Prize in literature, 1988

1940–1954 | 1955–1974 | 1975–2000

In the Battle of Britain, British Royal Air Force prevents German invasion of England, 1940

Martin Luther King, Jr., leads boycott of buses in Montgomery, Alabama, 1955

• The Beatles (1964).

U.S. declares war on Italy, Germany, and Japan, 1941

Nigeria wins independence from Britain, 1960

Germany surrenders; U.S. drops atom bombs over Hiroshima and Nagasaki, ending World War II, 1945

British singing group the Beatles revolutionizes popular music, 1960s

Fall of Saigon marks end of Vietnam War, 1975

Nuclear disaster at Chernobyl plant in Ukraine, 1986

Development of ENIAC at the University of Pennsylvania marks first generation of modern computers, 1946

Apollo 11 astronauts are first men to walk on the moon, as 600 million people watch live telecast, 1969

Berlin Wall is dismantled; Chinese army cracks down on pro-democracy students in Tiananmen Square, 1989

India gains independence from Britain, 1947; Mohandas Gandhi assassinated, 1948

Soviet Union is dissolved, 1991

Nelson Mandela elected president of South Africa, 1994

UN partitions Palestine, 1947; State of Israel created, 1948

Britain returns Hong Kong to China, 1997

Twenty-six of thirty-two counties in Ireland achieve full status as an independent republic, 1949

Peace plan for Northern Ireland signed and ratified by referendum, 1998

• Mushroom cloud (August 9, 1945) from the atomic bomb dropped on Nagasaki, Japan, during World War II.

• Astronaut Edwin E. Aldrin, Jr., lunar module pilot (1969).

Darwin, Marx, and Freud: Undermining Victorian Ideas

Many of the social and intellectual changes that were taking place in the early years of the twentieth century had their roots in the nineteenth-century work of three men: Charles Darwin (1809–1882), Karl Marx (1818–1883), and Sigmund Freud (1856–1939).

Darwin's *Origin of Species* (1859) sets forth a theory of the evolution of animal species based on natural selection—those species that successfully adapt to their environments survive and reproduce; those that do not become extinct. This theory, which seems to contradict the Biblical account of the special creation of each species, fueled a debate that has continued from Victorian times to the present. So-called social Darwinism, the notion that in society, as in nature, only the fittest should survive and flourish, was a nasty extension of Darwin's scientific theories—although Darwin had nothing to do with its formulation. "Social Darwinism" was used to justify unrestricted competition, rigid class distinctions, indifference to social problems, and even doctrines of racial superiority.

In *Das Kapital* (1867), Karl Marx, a German philosopher and political economist who spent the last thirty years of his life in London, advocates the abolition of private property. Marx traces economic injustices to the capitalist system of ownership and argues that workers should own the means of production. His theories of social and economic justice revolutionized political thought and eventually led to sweeping changes in many governments and economic systems, including those of Britain.

The psychological theories of Sigmund Freud, a doctor in Vienna, were equally revolutionary and far-reaching in their effects. In *The Interpretation of Dreams* (1900) and later works, Freud finds the motives for human behavior not in our rational, conscious minds but in the irrational and sexually driven realm of the unconscious, which is manifest mainly in our dreams. Conservative Victorians were outraged by Freud's claims that sexual drives influenced their behavior, but artists and writers found the notion of the unconscious and its mysterious, illogical workings fascinating.

> The proletarians have nothing to lose but their chains. They have a world to win. Working men of all countries, unite!
>
> —Karl Marx and Friedrich Engels

> The poets and philosophers before me discovered the unconscious; what I discovered was the scientific method by which the unconscious can be studied.
>
> —Sigmund Freud

Portrait of Charles Darwin (1840) by George Richmond.

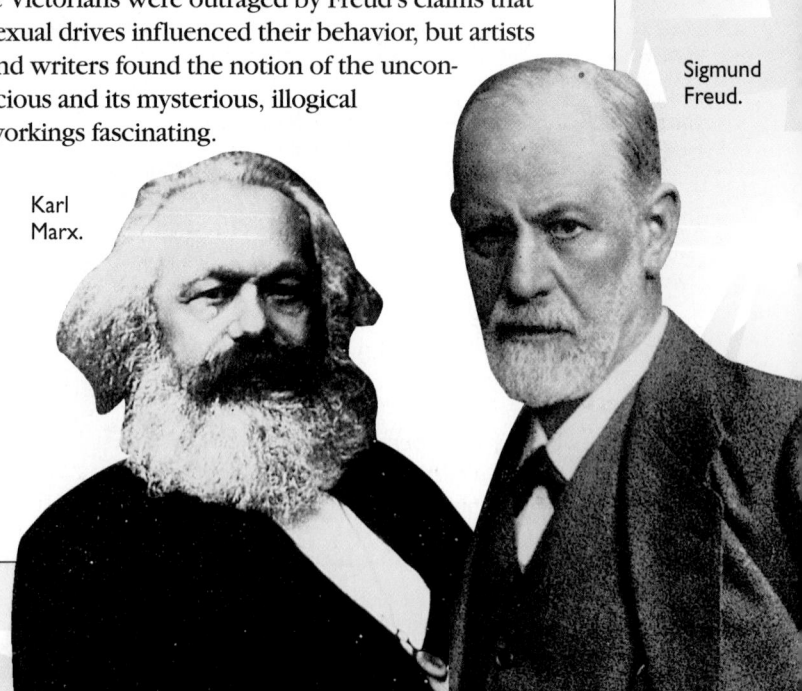

Karl Marx.

Sigmund Freud.

The work of these thinkers helped to undermine the political, religious, and psychological assumptions that had served as the foundation of British society and the British Empire for generations. With the calamity of the Great War and the events that followed, that foundation was largely swept away.

The writings of Charles Darwin, Karl Marx, and Sigmund Freud caused people to question many of the social, religious, and economic beliefs of the Victorian period.

The Great War: "A War to End All Wars"

The truly great disaster of the first half of the century was the breakdown of the European balance of power. In 1914, Britain, France, and Russia, bound by treaties, were locked in opposition to Germany and Austria-Hungary. The confrontation plunged the whole of Europe into World War I, or what was known as the Great War.

The Victorian writer Rudyard Kipling celebrated the British character as essentially patriotic, and he was right. When war broke out, a young Englishman felt that to be called on to defend his nation was likely to be the most exalted experience of his life. For centuries, in all sorts of wars and skirmishes, the ordinary youth of England had donned smart uniforms and marched off to faraway battlefields, just as they might go off to a sports event. On the battlefield, they would perform heroic acts, and for the most part they would return to be honored at home and to add their tales to the romantic lore of their regiments.

When Britain declared war on Germany in 1914, young Britons crowded to the recruiting stations to enlist. Six months later, hordes of them lay slaughtered in the miserable, rain-soaked, vermin-infested trenches of France. Sixty thousand young British men were killed or wounded on the first day of the Battle of the Somme alone. Three hundred thousand were killed, wounded, or frozen to death at the Battle of Ypres. The generals would not stop the terrible—and in the end futile—carnage, and over the

Return to the Front, 1917 by Richard Jack. York City Art Gallery, York, England.

> You are ordered abroad as a soldier of the king to help our French comrades against the invasion of a common enemy. . . . Do your duty bravely. Fear God. Honor the king.
>
> —Lord Kitchener to the British Expeditionary Force, 1914

> To be in the trenches was to experience an unreal, unforgettable enclosure and constraint, as well as a sense of being unoriented and lost. One saw two things only: the walls of an unlocalized, undifferentiated earth and the sky above. . . . It was the sight of the sky, almost alone, that had the power to persuade a man that he was not already lost in a common grave.
>
> —Paul Fussell

course of four years an entire generation of young Englishmen was fed to the insatiable furnace of the war.

With the armistice in 1918, a new cynicism arose. The old values of national honor and glory had endorsed a war whose results were gradually recognized as a weakened economy, a tottering colonial empire, and a loss of life equal to that caused by many plagues. Out of disillusionment came a pessimism about the state and the individual's relation to society. A new realism swept in, an antidote to the "romantic nonsense" of the past and in particular to the propaganda machine that had led a whole people into war.

After the Great War, in which nearly one million British soldiers died, many people in Great Britain developed a cynical attitude toward government and such values as national honor and glory.

A CLOSER LOOK

ROYAL TRADITION AND SCANDAL

In its thousand-year history, England's monarchy has seen turbulent times. The fates of Henry VIII's wives (divorced, beheaded, died, divorced, beheaded, survived) provide a notorious example. Britons pride themselves on their love of ritual and tradition, but their liege lords often appear to be awkward anachronisms. When the extravagant and hugely unpopular George IV died in 1830, the London *Times* reflected, "There never was an individual less regretted by his fellow creatures."

The House of Windsor. As the British monarchy enters the twenty-first century, the House of Windsor rules a kingdom in transition from its colonial past. Today, the crown's functions are mostly ceremonial. Royals serve at official functions and

charitable affairs, and the family's joking reference to itself as "the firm" indicates they take their business seriously.

Yet, with the business of ceremony comes the pressure of public scrutiny.

The royal family with Princess Diana in 1992.

Experimentation in the Arts: Shocking in Form and Content

The decade before the war had seen the beginnings of a transformation in all the arts, especially on the Continent. In Paris, Henri Matisse and other new painters exhibiting in 1905 were called *les fauves* (the wild beasts) by critics for their bold, new use of line and color. Pablo Picasso's first cubist painting, *Les Demoiselles d'Avignon,* was finished in 1907, the same year that John Millington Synge's play *The Playboy of the Western World* caused a riot at its première at Dublin's Abbey Theatre. (The audience was outraged by the suggestion that the Irish would make a hero out of a boy who claimed to have murdered his father.) In 1913, Igor Stravinsky's revolutionary music for the ballet *The Rite of Spring,* which was marked by strong, primitive (read "sexual") rhythms and dissonant harmonies, caused a riot at its première in Paris. The year after that, James Joyce's *Dubliners,* containing stories written up to a decade before, finally found an Irish publisher brave enough to publish it. All these works challenged traditional values of beauty and order and opened new avenues of expression.

> Never trust the artist. Trust the tale.
> —D. H. Lawrence

Queen Elizabeth II called 1992 the *annus horribilis,* or "horrible year," because during that time two of her children separated from their spouses and several were caught in scandals highly publicized by the British tabloids. The year also saw another disaster: Ancient Windsor Castle caught fire, and the public balked at paying for the restoration of Elizabeth's family home. Responding to public opinion, Queen Elizabeth instituted a number of reforms. In 1992, she voluntarily agreed to pay income taxes on her fortune and to publish an annual accounting of spending on royal palaces.

In 1997, however, the royal family faced an even greater challenge when the much loved Princess Diana, the former wife of Prince Charles, was killed in a car accident. When the queen and the prince were slow to respond publicly to the tragedy, they were bitterly criticized by the public for their apparent coldness and formality. For many, Diana had represented the warmth and humanity that the royal family lacked. The queen once again responded to what her people wanted, however, and arranged a funeral for Diana of such great dignity that many British subjects reembraced the House of Windsor.

Institution or anachronism? Still, the larger question remains: What is the monarchy's role in postcolonial Britain? Prince Philip, the queen's husband, has said that if "people feel it has no further part to play, then for goodness' sake let's end the thing on amicable terms without having a row about it." Ending the monarchy might be economical, but such a pragmatic solution would end a thousand years of tradition. The monarchy has endured not only because it provides historical continuity, but also because it captures the public imagination and, in an unromantic age, feeds the public appetite for pageantry and for a need to escape.

The Sadness of the King (1952) by Henri Matisse. Gouache cutout pasted on canvas (292 cm × 386 cm).

Musée Nationale d'Art Moderne, Paris. © 1997 Succession H. Matisse, Paris / Artists Rights Society (ARS), New York.

The twentieth century's vision of the future might well be summed up in the final line of Joseph Conrad's *Heart of Darkness* (1902): "The offing was barred by a black bank of clouds, and the tranquil waterway leading to the uttermost ends of the earth flowed somber under an overcast sky—seemed to lead into the heart of an immense darkness."

The novelists that followed Conrad were moving from a concern with society to a focus on introspection. Virginia Woolf even rejected traditional chronological order in storytelling. Experimenting with novelistic structure and with a shifting point of view, Woolf probed the human mind with the delicacy of a surgeon, examining all its shifts of moods and impressions.

In his novels, D. H. Lawrence was expressing his own strong resentment against British society, with its class system, industrialism, militarism, and prudery. Lawrence shocked the British with his glorification of the senses and his heated descriptions of relations between the sexes. His novel *Lady Chatterley's Lover* (1928), about an affair between an upper-class woman and her gamekeeper, is explicitly sexual, and its full publication was banned in England until 1960.

Most influential of all was the Irish poet and novelist James Joyce, whose novel *Ulysses* appeared to a storm of controversy in 1922. *Ulysses,* based on Homer's *Odyssey,* narrates the events of a single day in the

Les Demoiselles d'Avignon. Paris (June–July 1907), by Pablo Picasso. Oil on canvas 8′ × 7′8″ (243.9 x 233.7 cm).

The Museum of Modern Art, New York. Acquired through the Lillie P. Bliss Bequest. Photograph © 2000 The Museum of Modern Art, New York. © 2000 Estate of Pablo Picasso / Artists Rights Society (ARS), New York.

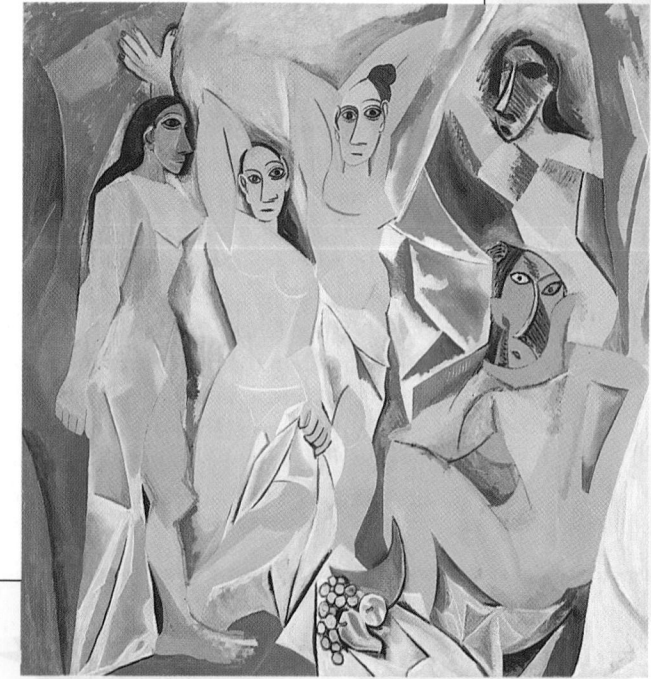

> Signatures of all things I am here to read, sea-spawn and seawrack, the nearing tide, that rusty boot. Snotgreen, bluesilver, rust: coloured signs.
>
> —James Joyce, *from Ulysses*

lives of a Jewish Dubliner named Leopold Bloom and a young man named Stephen Dedalus, as they unwittingly recapitulate the actions of Homer's Odysseus and his son Telemachus. Joyce drew, in a wholly revolutionary way, on myth and symbol, on Freudian explorations of sexuality, and on new conceptions of time and the workings of human consciousness.

Joseph Conrad, James Joyce, Virginia Woolf, and D. H. Lawrence experimented with form and content to challenge the conventions and limits of the novel.

The Rise of Dictatorships: Origins of World War II

The Great War, which had been called a war to end all wars, ironically led to another war. The League of Nations, the idealistic dream of U.S. president Woodrow Wilson, had no sooner been created than it was abandoned by a newly isolationist U.S. government. A worldwide economic depression that began in 1929 fostered the rise of dictators in Germany, Italy, and Russia.

In Italy and Germany, the form of totalitarianism that developed was fascism, a type of government that relies on the rule of a single dictator whose power is absolute and backed by force. Benito Mussolini, who came to power in Italy in 1922, held control through brutality and manipulation. Adolf Hitler and the Nazi party capitalized on Germany's economic woes to convince many Germans that their problems were caused by Jews, Communists, and immigrants.

> You cannot make a revolution with silk gloves.
>
> —attributed to Joseph Stalin

Russia's totalitarian government, based on the political theories of the economist Karl Marx, was Communist. Its founder, Nikolai Lenin, had sought in the 1920s to create a society without a class system, one in which the state would distribute the country's wealth equally among the people. But, in reality, the new government became as repressive as the rule of the czars had been. After Lenin's death in 1924, Joseph Stalin took power. In 1941, he became premier and continued to rule with an iron fist. Under Stalin's rule, as many as 15 million people were sent to the gulag, or system of forced-labor and detention camps.

The following ideas and events distinguished the twentieth century:

- Radically new thinking in science, psychology, and economics challenged many treasured convictions of the Victorian period.
- With the huge British losses suffered in the Great War, conventional patriotism and romantic notions of bravery were swept away.
- Disillusioned by the war, British and European artists radically experimented with, even rejected, traditional notions of beauty and order.
- After a worldwide economic depression, Fascist dictatorships arose in Spain, Germany, and Italy, along with an equally brutal Communist regime in Russia.
- By the end of World War II, the Nazis had murdered 6 million Jews in what is now known as the Holocaust. Between 35 and 60 million people perished in World War II.
- Its postwar economy in shambles, Britain could not hold on to the territories that had constituted its empire; one after another, most of Britain's colonies won their independence.
- Since the 1960s, many extraordinary writers in English have come from Britain's former colonies.

Two Apprehensive Shelterers (1942) by Henry Moore.

By 1939, the Nazis were sweeping through Europe with their motorized army and crack air force. Hitler's plan for the systematic destruction of the Jews and other minorities, scapegoats on whom he blamed Germany's economic woes, resulted in the deaths of millions of innocent men, women, and children—including the 6 million Jews who were killed in the Holocaust. Only twenty years after the "war to end all wars," Europe had again plunged into a bloody, brutal conflict. In 1940, Germany defeated France and then prepared to invade Britain by launching devastating air attacks against London and other cities. Prime Minister Winston Churchill declared: "We shall go on to the end." The British *did* persevere, but only after the Soviet Union and the United States entered the war did Germany's defeat become inevitable. In Japan, the war ended in the ultimate horror. On August 6, 1945, the entire city of Hiroshima was wiped out by a single atomic bomb dropped from an American plane. Small wonder, then, that much of the literature following the Second World War was dark and pessimistic.

> We shall not flag or fail. We shall go on to the end, we shall fight in France, we shall fight on the seas and oceans, we shall fight with growing confidence and growing strength in the air, we shall defend our island, whatever the cost may be, we shall fight on the beaches, we shall fight on the landing grounds, we shall fight in the fields and in the streets, we shall fight in the hills; we shall never surrender.
>
> —Sir Winston Churchill, June 4, 1940

The worldwide depression of the 1930s gave rise to dictatorships in Europe and led to the horrors of World War II.

Britain After World War II: The Sun Sets on the Empire

After the war ended in Europe, Winston Churchill and his Conservative party were defeated by the Labour party, and Britain was transformed into a welfare state. The government assumed responsibility for providing medical care and other basic benefits for its citizens. While recovering from the war and rebuilding its own economy, Great Britain could not hold on to its many colonies. Most of them, including India, the "jewel in the crown," became independent nations, and the sun now sank nightly over the British Empire.

In the spring of 1998, an end to thirty years of violent conflict over the status of the six British-controlled counties of Northern Ireland seemed near at hand. After years of fighting in the streets of Ulster and a bombing campaign by the Irish Republican Army (IRA) that at times extended into England, representatives of the Catholics and Protestants of Northern Ireland and the prime ministers of Great Britain and Ireland hammered out a promising formula for peace. An amazing 71 percent of the population of Northern Ireland and 94 percent of the population of the republic of Ireland voted yes in a referendum on the historic agreement on May 24, 1998.

> Little do town dwellers know how the semistarved masses of India are slowly sinking to lifelessness. Little do they know that their miserable comfort represents the brokerage they get for the work they do for the foreign exploiter, that the profits and the brokerage are sucked from the masses. Little do they realize that the government established by law in British India is carried on for this exploitation of the masses. No sophistry, no jugglery in figures can explain away the evidence that the skeletons in many villages present to the naked eye. I have no doubt whatsoever that both England and the town dwellers of India will have to answer, if there is a God above, for this crime against humanity which is perhaps unequaled in history.
>
> —Mohandas K. Gandhi, 1922

After World War II, most of Great Britain's colonies became independent, and Britain's role in world affairs decreased.

British Writing Today: A Remarkable Diversity

Two of the most conspicuous literary figures in England before World War II were the poets W. H. Auden and Stephen Spender (see "Twentieth-Century British Poetry," pages 932–934). They shared a common intellectual background and a left-wing, antifascist political point of view. But after the war, a group of younger novelists and playwrights emerged who disliked the values of the Auden group. These writers, who became known as the Angry Young Men, criticized the pretensions of intellectuals and the bland lives of the newly prosperous middle class. One of the major works of the period was Kingsley Amis's novel *Lucky Jim* (1953), a scathing satire of British university life.

The period since the 1960s has been marked by great diversity, though it is still satire that the British excel at. Landmark novels published in Britain from the 1960s on include the sharp and witty novels of Muriel Spark (*The Prime of Miss Jean Brodie,* 1961), the moral and linguistic experiments of Anthony Burgess (*A Clockwork Orange,* 1963), the feminist novels of Margaret Drabble (*Gates of Ivory,* 1991), and the exuberant novels of Dubliner Roddy Doyle (*Paddy Clarke Ha Ha Ha,* 1993).

DRY, DELICIOUS PARODY

Humor is practically the only thing about which the English are utterly serious.

—Malcolm Muggeridge

In "London Homesick Blues," the unamused American songwriter Gary P. Nunn offers to "substantiate the rumor that the English sense of humor is drier than the Texas sand." British humor is a source of national pride, although uncomprehending foreigners may not get the joke. Their comedy is notable for its ability to parody the national reputation for stiff-upper-lip reserve. For example, the novelist Sir P. G. Wodehouse mocks the notoriously poor traveling skills of British tourists, describing his character's "look of furtive shame, the shifty hangdog look which announces that an Englishman is about to talk French."

"Fabulous" silliness. British comedy revels in the ridiculous, and the television series *Absolutely Fabulous* brought that absurdity to its spoof of the fashion industry. American audiences clamored to see the ruthless fashion sitcom, even acquiring bootleg tapes of *AbFab* when no American network would buy the series.

Bubble: I've booked every model in the world. . . .
Edina: I know, darling, but what about the party?
Bubble: That is all completely under control. We've moved Stonehenge to a tent in Hyde Park.
Edina: Did you get permission for that, darling?
Bubble: They were very happy for us to use it, as long as it's back for the summer solstice. They realize how important the fashion industry is to this country.

When they recognized the program's devoted American followers, television officials aired *AbFab* in the United States. Yet, despite its success, one American public television official explained that his station does not buy British comedies because "most . . . are quite silly."

Pythons and dead parrots. The comedy troupe Monty Python's Flying Circus made silliness its specialty. In a scene well known to Python followers, a customer complains to a pet-shop proprietor that he has been sold a dead parrot. As the store owner ignores the obvious

An important development in the years since the war is the growing eminence of writers from Britain's former dependencies. One result of Great Britain's empire was the spread of English around the world. We are now seeing the effects of that linguistic dominance, with works written in English from the Caribbean (V. S. Naipaul, Derek Walcott), Africa (Doris Lessing, Wole Soyinka, Nadine Gordimer, Chinua Achebe, Ben Okri), and India (R. K. Narayan, Ruth Prawer Jhabvala, Salman Rushdie, Anita Desai).

Contemporary British literature is marked by great diversity, though satire is still a dominant mode.

World Literature: Writing from Afar Near at Hand

Though our world isn't really a global village, innovations in technology and transportation have linked us in ways our ancestors couldn't have imagined. Ideas travel as fast as myriad channels can carry them, and one writer may profoundly influence another living continents away. Today, evidence, the exasperated customer finds increasingly imaginative ways to describe the dead bird.

> It's not pining. It's passed on. This parrot is no more. It has ceased to be. It's expired and gone to meet its maker. This is a late parrot. It's a stiff. Bereft of life, it rests in peace. If you hadn't nailed it to its perch, it would be pushing up the daisies. It's rung down the curtain and joined the choir invisible. This is an ex-parrot.

The Pythons began their career by horrifying audiences with their bawdy, outrageous performances. Yet the parrot speech became so celebrated that the former prime minister Margaret Thatcher mentioned it in a political speech—which just goes to show that British humor is an acquired taste.

A scene from *Monty Python's The Meaning of Life* (1983), with John Cleese, Terry Jones, and Eric Idle.

Globe Photos.

when important British, Asian, European, or Latin American authors write in their native languages, enterprising publishers have the work promptly translated for eager book buyers around the world. Thus, readers of English can go to bookstores or libraries and find translations of works by Naguib Mahfouz (Egyptian), Julio Cortázar (Argentine), Pablo Neruda (Chilean), Aleksandr Solzhenitsyn (Russian), and hundreds of others.

> All paths lead to the same goal: to convey to others what we are. And we must pass through solitude and difficulty, isolation and silence, in order to reach forth to the enchanted place where we can dance our clumsy dance and sing our sorrowful song.
>
> —Pablo Neruda, on receiving the Nobel Prize in literature, 1971

Political concerns appear more often in current world literature than they have appeared in past British literature. The Nobel Prize–winner Aleksandr Solzhenitsyn, for example, has written much about human suffering and loss of freedom under the totalitarian government of the Soviet Union. Literally hundreds of writers from former British colonies explore the problems of personal identity and the effects of cultural domination and racism.

Tea Time
(20th century)
by Penelope
Beaton.

Photograph
by kind permission
of Waterman Fine
Art Ltd., St. James,
London.

And many writers in developing nations, to whom the niceties of Western living are foreign, document their raw struggle for existence. Such a variety of writing can only broaden and deepen our understanding of the human condition. As Solzhenitsyn said in his Nobel Prize acceptance speech, "The only substitute for what we ourselves have not experienced is art and literature. They have the marvelous capacity of transmitting from one nation to another—despite differences in language, customs, and social structure—practical experience, the harsh national experience of many decades never tasted by the other nation."

Twentieth-century technology has made an extraordinary amount of world literature available to readers around the world.

Quickwrite Throughout the first half of this century, writers and artists responded to the general disillusionment of the times. Many works portrayed a civilization in ruins, traditional beliefs and morals challenged. What do you think the artistic expression of our day—from television to painting, music to comic books—reveals about our own society? List a few examples; then jot down some ideas about how our art and entertainment reflect where we are today.

The title of this poem refers to a prophecy that Jesus will return to earth one day and usher in an era of peace. The First Coming was the birth of Jesus in Bethlehem two thousand years ago. The theme is introduced in the first two lines: A falconer is unable to control his hawk as it spirals out of control. This poem was written after the horrors of World War I. Yeats asks: Have we, like the falconer, lost control of the means to halt our descent into chaos?

The Second Coming

Turning and turning in the widening gyre
The falcon cannot hear the falconer;
Things fall apart; the center cannot hold;
Mere anarchy is loosed upon the world,
The blood-dimmed tide is loosed, and everywhere
The ceremony of innocence is drowned;
The best lack all conviction, while the worst
Are full of passionate intensity.

Surely some revelation is at hand;
Surely the Second Coming is at hand.
The Second Coming! Hardly are those words out
When a vast image out of Spiritus Mundi
Troubles my sight: somewhere in sands of the desert
A shape with lion body and the head of a man,
A gaze blank and pitiless as the sun,
Is moving its slow thighs, while all about it
Reel shadows of the indignant desert birds.
The darkness drops again; but now I know
That twenty centuries of stony sleep
Were vexed to nightmare by a rocking cradle,
And what rough beast, its hour come round at last,
Slouches towards Bethlehem to be born?

—William Butler Yeats

Before You Read

THE REAR-GUARD
DULCE ET DECORUM EST

Make the Connection

No Man's Land

In war, *no man's land* is the few hundred yards that separate one army's lines from another's. But for the group of writers who became known as the Trench Poets, war itself became a no man's land: a dehumanizing, horrific experience that made a mockery of civilization. Each of the Trench Poets either died in the muddy trenches of World War I (as Wilfred Owen did) or survived as a bitter but articulate ghost trapped by memories from which there was no escape (see page 932).

Quickwrite

During World War I, it was poetry that first brought home war's full brutality to many English people. Today people who have never been in battle see vivid images of war in movies and newspapers or on TV.

What is your most vivid mental image of war's horror? Recall impressions you've absorbed from film, photographs, the nightly news, what veterans have told you, literary works, or other sources. Close your eyes, think "war," and then record, in words, what you saw in your mind.

Elements of Literature

The Oxymoron

Have you ever had a bittersweet moment, a moment when you felt happy and sad at the same time? The word *bittersweet* is an example of an **oxymoron,** a figure of speech that combines apparently contradictory ideas to create a strong emphasis. Other oxymorons common in ordinary speech are *cold comfort, honest thief,* and *tough love.* In literature, "darkness visible" is a famous example from Milton. The Trench Poets found oxymorons useful in describing the unimaginable slaughter of trench warfare.

> **A**n **oxymoron** is a figure of speech that combines apparently contradictory ideas.
>
> *For more on Oxymorons, see the Handbook of Literary Terms.*

The Menin Road, 1919 by Paul Nash.

Siegfried Sassoon

(1886–1967)

Siegfried Sassoon was born into that high level of English society at which lifelong privilege is sustained by income from landed estates and assured inheritances. Educated at Cambridge University, and under no pressure to adopt a profession, he lived the life of a country gentleman until the outbreak of World War I. Along with the pursuit of leisure—which he would later write about in a famous book called *Memoirs of a Fox-Hunting Man* (1928)—Sassoon also wrote poetry. He had sufficient skill to win a place in the anthologies of the Georgian movement, in which the value of all things English was celebrated—from scones and honey at teatime to the bells of Winchester Cathedral.

The war would change all that. For Sassoon, it would also lead to a career entirely at odds with his earlier expectations. Enlisting in the army as a patriot and an idealist determined to put an end to "Teutonic barbarism," he distinguished himself as an officer and was awarded a prestigious medal for bravery under fire. But, within two years of his enlistment, Sassoon's attitude toward the war underwent a change amounting to a total reversal of his earlier commitment. His new attitude was expressed in stark, almost savage poems detailing the brutality and debasement of trench warfare. The publication of these bitter testaments sent a shock wave of doubt through the minds of

Siegfried Sassoon (1915). Photograph by Beresford.

the English (among them, Winston Churchill, then minister of munitions, whose secretary, Edward Marsh, was the leader of the comforting Georgian poets and their most outspoken publicist).

Dissatisfied even with the depth of response his poems evoked, Sassoon wrote to the war department to protest a war he now believed was "being deliberately prolonged by those who have the power to end it." In a statement handed to his commanding officer, which Sassoon himself regarded as "an act of willful defiance," he spelled out his disillusionment: "I believe that this war, upon which I entered as a war of defense and liberation, has now become a war of aggression and conquest."

Expecting court-martial, and entirely prepared to sacrifice himself for his own cause, Sassoon was thwarted by the unsolicited and unwanted kindness of some of his friends, notably the poet Robert Graves, who shunted him toward a medical board of examiners. Diagnosed as shellshocked, Sassoon was committed to a military hospital in Scotland. There he met fellow patient Wilfred Owen, and the two began one of the most famous and mutually beneficial relationships in modern literature.

Disgust controlled by irony gives Sassoon's war poems their indelible imprint; the poems stand by themselves in an otherwise pedestrian career marked by one great parenthesis—the Great War itself.

In the battlefield trenches of World War I, enlisted men lived for weeks, sometimes years, in interconnected underground caverns infested by rats, with no drainage, poor ventilation, and only occasional dim shafts of natural light. In this poem, the "he" who recalls a grisly trench episode is the officer-poet, Siegfried Sassoon himself.

The Rear-Guard

Siegfried Sassoon

(Hindenburg Line,° April 1917.)

Groping along the tunnel, step by step,
He winked his prying torch° with patching glare
From side to side, and sniffed the unwholesome air.

Tins, boxes, bottles, shapes too vague to know,
5   A mirror smashed, the mattress from a bed;
And he, exploring fifty feet below
The rosy gloom of battle overhead.

Tripping, he grabbed the wall; saw someone lie
Humped at his feet, half-hidden by a rug,
10   And stooped to give the sleeper's arm a tug.
"I'm looking for headquarters." No reply.
"God blast your neck!" (For days he'd had no sleep.)

"Get up and guide me through this stinking place."
Savage, he kicked a soft, unanswering heap,
15   And flashed his beam across the livid face
Terribly glaring up, whose eyes yet wore
Agony dying hard ten days before;
And fists of fingers clutched a blackening wound.

Alone he staggered on until he found
20   Dawn's ghost that filtered down a shafted stair
To the dazed, muttering creatures underground
Who hear the boom of shells in muffled sound.
At last, with sweat of horror in his hair,
He climbed through darkness to the twilight air,
25   Unloading hell behind him step by step.

Hindenburg Line: German defensive barricade running across northern France. It was made of massive barbed-wire entanglements and deep trenches.
2. torch: flashlight.

Oppy Wood, 1917 by John Northcote Nash.

MAKING MEANINGS

First Thoughts

1. What did you feel when you finished this poem? What do you think the poet *wanted* you to feel?

Shaping Interpretations

2. Why is the man in the tunnel, and what happens there? How is the man's behavior simultaneously brutal and pathetic?

3. Where does **onomatopoeia** help you hear the sounds in the tunnel? What **oxymoron** does the poet use to describe the battle overhead?

4. The poet uses many strong present and past participles, such as *groping, prying, smashed,* and *humped.* What do these words help you *see*?

5. Explain the **irony** of what the speaker says in line 13.

6. How do you interpret the phrase "unloading hell" in line 25?

Connecting with the Text

7. How do the images in "The Rear-Guard" compare with your own mental pictures of war? (Recall what you recorded in your Quickwrite notes on page 924.) Are visual depictions of war more or less powerful than verbal descriptions—like the ones in Sassoon's poem?

Wilfred Owen
(1893–1918)

Wilfred Owen.

Wilfred Owen is one of the most poignant figures in modern literature. "The Poetry is in the pity," he said, and this famous remark could serve as his epitaph. Within the few adult years granted to him, Owen pursued a course of development that went from strength to strength. His interest in experimental techniques led him to master the use of half rhyme; this would become his most easily recognizable poetic signature. He also had a gift for lyricism that was bitterly tempered by "the truth untold, / The pity of war, the pity war distilled." The result was a series of elegies and metrical statements as terse and stark as those carved on tombstones.

Like an apprentice determined to master his art, Owen immersed himself in the long history of English poetry. He chose for his model and mentor the poet John Keats, whose astonishing life's work ended with his death at twenty-five (about the same age Shakespeare was when he began to write his plays). As a tutor in France for two years, Owen studied the French poets who were producing the tradition-shattering art that would become known as modernist. But all these literary influences were to become secondary to the devastating impact of a war Owen witnessed firsthand.

World War I broke out when Owen was twenty-one; he joined the British army, and the course of his life was determined. His progress in poetry was not made in the arcades of an ancient university or in the pastoral retreats where his literary forerunners were privileged to pursue their careers. His progress took place in the muddy purgatory of trench warfare and in the twilight existence of military hospitals.

In one of those hospitals, Craiglockhart, in Edinburgh, the young Owen met Siegfried Sassoon, a fellow officer and poet who had already distinguished himself for bravery in battle. Ironically, Sassoon was also the author of some of the most biting antiwar verses ever written. Temperamentally, the two men were far apart. Owen was an idealistic youth thwarted by circumstance; Sassoon was an aristocrat appalled by the wartime complacency of his own class. Even so, they became friends and artistic colleagues at once. After Owen's death, Sassoon became the first important British writer to herald the younger man's genius and to call attention to what he had accomplished under the most appalling conditions. By that time, events had told the sad story.

In 1918, Owen was listed among those killed in action—a mere seven days before the war ended with a joyous ringing of bells and dancing in the streets.

go.hrw.com
LEO 12-12

This poem's title is taken from the Latin statement *Dulce et decorum est pro patria mori,* meaning "It is sweet and honorable to die for one's country." The statement originally appeared in an ode by the ancient Roman poet Horace and has been used for centuries as a morale builder—and an epitaph—for soldiers. Here the motto is given a bitter twist by a soldier-poet who cannot reconcile the thought it expresses with the reality he has experienced.

After the introduction of poison gas as a battlefield weapon during World War I, every man in the trenches was equipped with a gas mask: lifesaving armor, if donned in time. This poem describes the horrible consequences of not getting the mask on promptly.

Dulce et Decorum Est

Wilfred Owen

Bent double, like old beggars under sacks,
Knock-kneed, coughing like hags, we cursed through sludge,
Till on the haunting flares we turned our backs
And toward our distant rest began to trudge.
5 Men marched asleep. Many had lost their boots
But limped on, blood-shod. All went lame; all blind;
Drunk with fatigue; deaf even to the hoots
Of tired, outstripped Five-Nines° that dropped behind.

Gas! GAS! Quick, boys!—An ecstasy of fumbling,
10 Fitting the clumsy helmets just in time;
But someone still was yelling out and stumbling
And flound'ring like a man in fire or lime . . .
Dim, through the misty panes and thick green light,
As under a green sea, I saw him drowning.

15 In all my dreams, before my helpless sight,
He plunges at me, guttering, choking, drowning.

If in some smothering dreams you too could pace
Behind the wagon that we flung him in,
And watch the white eyes writhing in his face,
20 His hanging face, like a devil's sick of sin;
If you could hear, at every jolt, the blood
Come gargling from the froth-corrupted lungs,
Obscene as cancer, bitter as the cud
Of vile, incurable sores on innocent tongues,—
25 My friend, you would not tell with such high zest
To children ardent for some desperate glory,
The old Lie: *Dulce et decorum est*
Pro patria mori.

8. Five-Nines: gas shells measuring 5.9 inches each.

Paths of Glory, 1917 by Christopher R. W. Nevinson.

MAKING MEANINGS

First Thoughts

1. Do you think a poem like this has any relevance to wars as they are fought today? Why or why not?

Shaping Interpretations

2. What are the "misty panes" in line 13 through which the speaker glimpses the dying man?

3. What **oxymorons** can you find in the poem's second and last stanzas? Why is a figure of speech that expresses contradiction appropriate for the speaker's purposes?

4. What is the poem's **rhyme scheme**? Can you find any **half rhymes**?

5. Who is the "you" addressed in the final stanza?

6. Explain the **similes** in lines 23–24. How do they relate to the **theme** of the poem?

7. How would you describe the speaker's **tone**? How does it compare to the tone of today's war stories or war movies? (Cite some examples in your answer.)

Extending the Text

8. In recent years, the U.S. Army has recruited with the slogan "Be all that you can be," referring to educational and job opportunities in the military. Compare this slogan with the one mentioned in the poem. Which emotion or value does each slogan appeal to?

CHOICES: Building Your Portfolio

Writer's Notebook

1. Collecting Ideas for an Informative Report

Reading can give you ideas for informative reports. Think about the biographies of the two Trench Poets and what the poems themselves suggest about their experiences of World War I. Brainstorm for a few minutes, and jot down topics suggested by the poems that you might want to learn more about. It's possible that you might focus on details in the lives of the two young poets themselves. (Both are subjects of a 1997 film called *Regeneration,* based on an acclaimed trilogy about World War I by Pat Barker.) Save your notes for the Writer's Workshop on page 1053.

Comparing/Contrasting Poems

2. Side-by-Side Poems

In an essay, compare and contrast the **imagery, structure,** and **sound devices** of "The Rear-Guard" and "Dulce et Decorum Est."

Evaluating a Poet's Stance

3. It's Your Turn

In the last lines of his poem, Owen refers to an honorable death for one's country as "the old Lie." Do you agree that patriotism's high-minded idealism is a lie? Or is Owen perhaps stacking the deck by including so many gruesome battle details? Or do you think the poem presents a valid but insoluble conflict? In a brief essay, relate Owen's poem to your own concept of patriotism.

Comparing/Contrasting Poems

4. Another View

In an essay, point out the similarities and differences between Owen's "Dulce et Decorum Est" and the poem below by Rupert Brooke. (Brooke served in World War I but did not experience trench warfare; he died of blood poisoning en route to Europe.) Consider how each poet uses at least three of these elements:

imagery, theme and sentiments about war, **tone, sound devices,** and **figurative language.**

Viewing and Representing

5. Through the Artists' Eyes

Review the art used to illustrate the introduction to "The Twentieth Century" (pages 906–922) and these poems by the Trench Poets. In an essay, analyze one of the pieces of art. First, describe what you see in the painting, and then analyze how the painting's elements work together to create an overall effect (consider such elements as **"story," color, light, form, tone**). You might also want to consider the work's **title.** Conclude your essay by describing your response to the work.

The Soldier

If I should die, think only this of me;
   That there's some corner of a foreign field
That is forever England. There shall be
   In that rich earth a richer dust concealed;
A dust whom England bore, shaped, made aware,
   Gave, once, her flowers to love, her ways to roam,
A body of England's breathing English air,
   Washed by the rivers, blest by suns of home.

And think, this heart, all evil shed away,
   A pulse in the eternal mind, no less
   Gives somewhere back the thoughts by England given;
Her sights and sounds; dreams happy as her day;
   And laughter, learnt of friends; and gentleness,
   In hearts at peace, under an English heaven.

—Rupert Brooke (1887–1915)

Twentieth-Century British Poetry

by **John Malcolm Brinnin**

British poets in the early twentieth century were not experimenters. They did not make the daring adaptations that their American cousins were quick to try out. Instead, the main concern of British poets in the twentieth century has been to express themselves in very conventional forms—even when they are responding to the most violent of experiences.

The Trench Poets: Poetry and Pity

You will see this use of traditional forms in a group of poets who wrote about the first great war of our war-torn century: the Trench Poets. What these poets wrote was categorized as "war poetry." Yet the poets themselves hoped their works would stand as testaments beyond the usual reach of poetic art—and as warnings.

As **Wilfred Owen** wrote, "The Poetry is in the pity," meaning that the shame of war overwhelms every attempt to make sense of it, in verse or by any other means. Intimately acquainted with miseries and horrors inconceivable to civilians, the Trench Poets stripped war of its glory. They positioned themselves against the Romantic rhetoric of their immediate predecessor, **Rupert Brooke** (himself a casualty of the Great War), who put into rhyme the expected patriotic response.

In contrast, the Trench Poets dwelt on the degradation of body and soul caused by trench warfare, and the humiliation that the trenches represented. In their view, the war that began as an assertion of righteousness and a test of national will became an exercise in slaughter. To them, the war demeaned the very idea of civilization and turned history itself into a "no man's land"—the few hundred yards of dead terrain that divided German trenches from British trenches, a terrain that bore

all the features of hell. Killed in action, or crippled, blinded, gassed, and shellshocked, the Trench Poets, dead and alive, spoke to and for the youth of generations to come.

The two poets among them who most clearly showed signs of genius were the young soldiers Wilfred Owen and **Isaac Rosenberg.** On April 1, 1918, Rosenberg was killed in action. Owen, whose poems later formed the libretto for Benjamin Britten's *War Requiem,* met the same fate six months later.

The English Group: A Political Agenda

One of the most exciting developments of the early 1930s was the emergence of four poets popularly known in America as "the English Group." The group consisted of the British writers **W. H. Auden** (page 1091) and **Stephen Spender** and the Irish-born writers **Cecil Day-Lewis** and **Louis MacNeice.** The audience for these poets was a generation that blamed the failure of capitalism for the devastation of World War I. This failure, they felt, was made even more apparent in the social unrest of the 1920s and in the economic collapse of 1929 that led to the Great Depression. The English Group's audience was also the generation that began to look toward socialism as an alternative to Great Britain's capitalist class system, and to the unequal distribution of wealth that perpetuated that system.

The most important concern in these poets' political thinking, however, was the rise of fascism. Fascism was the dictatorial, militaristic system that swept Germany, Italy, and Spain—it would eventually unite the democracies of the world in opposition to it and lead to World War II.

Without quite being aware of the fact, poetry, like everything else, was becoming politicized:

The qualities which distinguished us from the writers of the previous decade lay not in ourselves, but in the events to which we reacted. These were unemployment, economic crisis, . . . fascism, approaching war. . . . The older writers were reacting . . . to the exhaustion and hopelessness of a Europe in which the old regimes were falling to pieces. We were a "new generation," but it took me some time to appreciate the meaning of this phrase . . . that we had begun . . . in circumstances strikingly different from those of our immediate predecessors and that a consciousness of this was shown in our writing. . . . We were the 1930s.

—Stephen Spender, *from World Within World*

Already entrenched in Italy and Germany, fascism threatened to spread to Spain when General Francisco Franco overthrew the elected Spanish Republican government in 1936. Franco's move was supported by Benito Mussolini, dictator of Italy, and Adolf Hitler. More than any other event of the decade, the Fascist threat to Spanish democracy unified the artists and intellectuals of a generation. The Spanish Civil War became *their* war. Some, unwilling to remain bystanders, enlisted as volunteers in the Republican Army and were counted among its casualties. As in World War I, some of the most brilliant poets of an era were silenced by the Spanish Civil War before they could fulfill their promise.

Dylan Thomas: A Return to Romanticism

When Auden, whose poetry surpassed that of others in the English Group, became an American citizen and established residence in New York City, it was the opinion of at least one critic that British poetry was "up the creek," but not "without a paddle." The paddle that he thought might rescue British poetry was **Dylan Thomas** (page 1032). This young man from Wales effectively ended one phase of poetic history and set the stage for another.

Never a part of any group, Thomas established his own poetic goals as a very young man. On the evidence of the remarkable notebooks he left behind, he pursued these goals throughout the brief course of his adult life. Yet, in the minds of critics who are more comfortable with poetry when it comes as the product of a "school" or a movement than from an individual of genius, Thomas was associated with certain writers more or less his own age. As time would tell, these other writers were more gifted as theorists than as poets.

Ambitious and bold, they called themselves "the New Apocalypse." In their opinion, it was time to halt the tendency of British poets to be concerned with politics and psychology—a concern that had turned poetry into a form of intellectual debate. They wanted a return to poetry as incandescent language—the language of the great English Romantics. They wanted to render individual experience in sacramental imagery—such as that found in the Psalms and in the high rhetoric of the King James Bible, in the visionary world of William Blake, and in the compacted wordplay and religious wit of Gerard Manley Hopkins. The young poets also admired the dream imagery of the subconscious, which had been dredged up and used by the spectacular new painters who called themselves surrealists.

These poets of the New Apocalypse believed that a new wave of Romanticism was about to break, bringing with it a heightening of verbal music and a delight in language for its own sake. They believed that this kind of poetry had been curbed by other kinds of poetry that emulated public speech and demanded clarity, logic, and a message. True to

Expansion of the Lyric (1913) by Leonardo Dudreville.
Richard Miller Collection, New York.

the name they chose, they saw themselves as apocalyptic: They regarded poems not as arguments or conclusions but as revelations, not as commentaries upon experience but, literally, as re-creations of experience still in the process of becoming intelligible.

The poets of the New Apocalypse got their message across, but they did not have the talent to give it substance. As they faded from the scene, Dylan Thomas alone was left to carry on their ideas. His famous career brought a new dimension to British poetry, reminding readers that poetry could be both as sensually exciting as music and as philosophically profound as Greek tragedy.

The Contemporary Scene

But Dylan Thomas died at the age of thirty-nine, and British poetry again entered a conservative and technically unadventurous phase. Then, out of this fallow period, two exceptional poetic personalities arose. Each in his own way showed that individual talent can make a mark and still have nothing to do with groups or movements. Each poet also rejected the nineteenth-century belief that—like sermons or editorials—poetry should be morally uplifting, or, at least, addressed to public issues.

These two poets were **Ted Hughes** (page 960), who was poet laureate of England, and **Philip Larkin** (1922–1985). Philip Larkin was the most widely admired poet in the generation succeeding that of Dylan Thomas. In their quiet, low-keyed way, his poems reflect all the great themes of contemporary experience. In his handling of these themes, Larkin keeps to an intimately human scale, in which the balance lies somewhere between disgust and disdain on the one hand, and heartbreak and despairing humor on the other.

The Mower

The mower stalled, twice; kneeling, I found
A hedgehog jammed up against the blades,
Killed. It had been in the long grass.

I had seen it before, and even fed it, once.
Now I had mauled its unobtrusive world
Unmendably. Burial was no help:

Next morning I got up and it did not.
The first day after a death, the new absence
Is always the same; we should be careful

Of each other, we should be kind
While there is still time.

—Philip Larkin

Today, British poetry is closer to its twentieth-century beginnings than it has been for many years. British poetry was never modern in the energetically experimental ways that produced the extraordinary succession of American poets that includes Ezra Pound, T. S. Eliot, Hart Crane, Wallace Stevens, William Carlos Williams, Elizabeth Bishop, Robert Lowell, and James Merrill. But now that the age of poetic schools, movements, and other kinds of labeled association seems to have run its course, certain older British poets who followed no program but their own have begun to shine more brightly than ever. Chief among these are Thomas Hardy and D. H. Lawrence. As it comes full circle, British poetry may have surrendered some of its vitality, but none of its character. The individual voice is still the one to listen for, and the measure of English poets today is still the degree to which they make our common language sound like their own.

Diurnal Rhythm (20th century) by Maurice Cockrill.

Richard Miller Collection, New York.

WORLD LITERATURE

Spain

Drawing of Federico García Lorca,
by Gregorio Prieto.

Federico García Lorca

(1898–1936)

In 1936, Spain was in the grip of a civil war. Republicans and Fascist-oriented Nationalists were locked in a bloody struggle for control of the government. On the night of July 19, 1936, in Granada, Nationalist fighters seized a popular young writer named Federico García Lorca, took him to a graveyard, forced him to dig his own grave, and then shot him. The world was outraged—Lorca was not political. It's possible that the Nationalists had felt threatened by the poet's work, which was at once deeply rooted in Spain and very modern.

Lorca was born on a prosperous farm just outside of Granada, in Andalusia, that sunny part of Spain where Moorish and Gypsy elements have mixed with a conservative Catholic culture. In 1919, he went to Madrid to study. Immensely handsome, charming, and intelligent,

Lorca mingled easily with avant-garde artists there, including the surrealist painter Salvador Dali. But when Lorca began writing poetry and dramas of his own, he turned to the folklore and Gypsy music of Andalusia for inspiration.

Lorca wrote a series of dark tragedies, including *Bodas de sangre (Blood Wedding),* still produced on American stages today, about a bride who runs away on her wedding day with the man she secretly loves and who is murdered by her husband. *La casa de Bernarda Alba (The House of Bernarda Alba),* like a Greek tragedy, traces the workings of malignant fate in a family trapped by stifling tradition from which there is no escape but death. Lorca's most famous poem, lamenting the fatal goring of his friend, a bullfighter, is also one of the great elegies in all literature. *Llanto por Ignacio Sánchez Mejías (Lament for Ignacio Sánchez Mejías)* seemed also to prophesy the young writer's own violent death.

(Map) ©Rand McNally.

Before You Read

THE GUITAR

Background

Music and song were essential to Lorca. Even before his feet could reach the pedals, he was composing songs at the piano. He seemed to breathe the native music of Andalusia, what is called *cante jondo,* or "deep song." This dirgelike music is believed to have come with the Gypsies from India. In Spain it melded with Iberian and Moorish elements to form a wailing, almost obsessive rhythm that is hauntingly primitive and extraordinarily expressive. Best known abroad in its derivative form, flamenco, *cante jondo* is the wellspring of Lorca's intense, dramatic, and richly musical poetry. His themes, emotions, and images echo those ancient songs, which he compared to "the trilling of birds, the crowing of the rooster, and the natural music of forest and fountain."

Since no translation, no matter how accomplished, can ever completely capture Lorca's Andalusian sounds, it is important to hear his poetry in the original Spanish.

Quickwrite

Can you remember a time when the sound of music moved you deeply? What did you feel? What did the music remind you of?

The Old Guitarist (1903) by Pablo Picasso. Oil on panel (122.9 cm × 82.6 cm).

La guitarra

Federico García Lorca

Empieza el llanto
de la guitarra.
Se rompen las copas
de la madrugada.
5 Empieza el llanto
de la guitarra.
Es inútil callarla.
Es imposible
callarla.
10 Llora monótona
como llora el agua,
como llora el viento
sobre la nevada.

Es imposible
15 callarla.
Llora por cosas
lejanas.
Arena del Sur caliente
que pide camelias blancas.
20 Llora flecha sin blanco,
la tarde sin mañana,
y el primer pájaro muerto
sobre la rama.
¡Oh guitarra!
25 Corazón malherido
por cinco espadas.

The Guitar

Federico García Lorca
translated by **Robert Bly**

The crying of the guitar
starts.
The goblets
of the dawn break.
5 The crying of the guitar
starts.
No use to stop it.
It is impossible
to stop it.
10 It cries repeating itself
as the water cries,
as the wind cries
over the snow.
It is impossible
15 to stop it.
It is crying for things
far off.
The warm sand of the South
that asks for white camellias.
20 For the arrow with nothing to hit,
the evening with no dawn coming,
and the first bird of all dead
on the branch.
Guitar!
25 Heart wounded, gravely,
by five swords.

The Guitar

Federico García Lorca
translated by **Elizabeth du Gué Trapier**

Now begins the cry
Of the guitar,
Breaking the vaults
Of dawn.
5 Now begins the cry
Of the guitar.
Useless
To still it.
Impossible
10 To still it.
It weeps monotonously
As weeps the water,
As weeps the wind
Over snow.
15 Impossible
To still it.
It weeps
For distant things,
Warm southern sands
20 Desiring white camellias.
It mourns the arrow without a target,
The evening without morning.
And the first bird dead
Upon a branch.
25 O guitar!
A wounded heart,
Wounded by five swords.

FINDING COMMON GROUND

Extending themes across cultures. First, in a group, discuss the poem's meaning. Be sure to consider how the poem relates to the theme of this collection, "The Center Cannot Hold." Do any of the images remind you of images in the poem that opens the collection, "The Second Coming" (page 923)?

Evaluating oral presentations and performances. Next, assign different readers in your group to prepare the poems—the Spanish version and each English translation—for performance. Before you evaluate the performances, work together to draw up **criteria** that you think should characterize an effective performance. After the performances, analyze the readings in a group discussion, and evaluate their effectiveness.

Evaluating translations. With your group, discuss the translations of the poem. Before you open your discussion, agree on the **criteria** you look for in an effective translation of a poem into another language.

Translating the poem. If you or anyone else in your group is fluent in Spanish, try a new translation of "La guitarra."

T. S. Eliot: The Voice of an Age

by John Malcolm Brinnin

Unlike poets whose long, outstanding careers eventually turn them into cultural monuments, T. S. Eliot was a monument who later became known as a man. Internationally famous at an early age, he was the product of an aristocratic New England family. The Eliots valued privacy and regarded self-exploitation and public exposure—even fame itself—as a form of vulgarity. Consequently, millions of readers knew T. S. Eliot less as a real personality than as a presence. Eliot was remote, austere, and self-possessed, a man whose sparse output was nevertheless the most celebrated and influential poetry written in English over a span of three decades.

T. S. Eliot was born in 1888 in St. Louis, Missouri, where his grandfather had established Washington University. In spite of this geographical displacement, the Eliots remained New Englanders. They could trace their ancestry back to the first Puritan settlements in North America. Young Tom Eliot was educated at Harvard College, after which he did graduate studies at the Sorbonne in Paris. Like many other young American writers of his generation, he found life abroad so stimulating that he decided not to return home. Settling in London before World War I, he worked in a bank, married an Englishwoman, and became an editor and a publisher. He made his expatriation complete by becoming a British citizen in 1927. In 1948, he was awarded the Nobel Prize. Not long before his death in 1965, on one of his several visits to the United States, so many people wanted to see and hear Eliot read his poetry that a football stadium had to be taken over to hold the audience.

Eliot had a vast influence as a poet. His techniques, along with those of his friend and fellow American, Ezra Pound, became the hallmarks of modern poetry. For over thirty years, in classrooms and in critical studies, his was *the* voice that expressed the dislocation and despair of the twentieth century. Eliot's world-weariness, his grave, restrained, and impersonal cadences, so much like the voices he heard in New England pulpits, were widely imitated and instantly recognized. Eliot dominated English literature in a way not seen since the days of Dr. Johnson.

Eliot's critical studies were also far-reaching. He argued against the commonly held view that

T. S. Eliot (1907) during his first year at Harvard, age 19.

By permission of the Houghton Library, Harvard University, Cambridge, Massachusetts.

go.hrw.com

LE0 12-12

poets were romantics who had superior powers of observation and expression. Eliot regarded poets as craftspeople who used traditional literary materials not for personal revelations but for the creation of better-made poems. The poet, according to these theories, was like those anonymous master artisans who made individual contributions to the great medieval cathedrals but who remained personally unknown. Like these humble artisans, the poet was just part of the background. What is important is the poem (or the cathedral), not the worker who made it. This point of view deplored the notion that a search through the poet's life would give clues to the meaning of the work. The work, all-important, stood apart from its creator. Submitting to Eliot's instruction, poets, students, and critics for generations studied a poem not for its messages or meaning, but for its method and structure—for its architecture.

In 1950, when I was director of New York's Poetry Center, Eliot made a visit to the United States. I recalled the event in a book called *Sextet:*

"This late in his life (he was sixty-one) Eliot had given less than a handful of readings in the United States and had read only once before in New York. The response to our announcement of the event suggested that many people thought his reading at the Poetry Center might well be his last. On the morning after we had named his date in *The New York Times,* fifteen or twenty requests were made for every seat available. Pursued and badgered to use my influence to produce tickets, I found that people who'd never read a sonnet since the seventh grade were suddenly lovers of poetry whose devotion I was implored not to dismiss."

A Vision of the Street

In music, *preludes* are brief works, usually free in form, that introduce larger and more formal compositions. When Eliot chose a musical title, he no doubt meant to suggest that these short poems introduced the mood and method of longer works written in the same period.

The images in "Preludes" are all drawn from city life. Horse-drawn carriages had not yet been replaced by automobiles, nor gas lamps by electricity, but nevertheless the dehumanizing aspects of a growing metropolis like Eliot's Boston were already sadly in evidence. Eliot saw multitudes of workers

every day moving to and fro like debris washed in and out by the tides. He saw massive slums that blocked out forever the gentle rural landscapes of a preindustrial age.

"Preludes" are the observations of a wanderer through city streets. The speaker attempts to come to some conclusion about the meaning of the life around him, yet he finally gives up. Still, in the process, he gives us "a vision of the street," a scene for which he feels compassion but which, finally, he considers beyond redemption. Eliot wrote these poems when he was in his twenties. How many images suggest life as a wasteland? How do these descriptions of city life relate to urban landscapes today? (Note: In line 2, "steaks" refers to cheap cuts of meat.)

Preludes

T. S. Eliot

I

The winter evening settles down
With smell of steaks in passageways.
Six o'clock.
The burnt-out ends of smoky days.
5 And now a gusty shower wraps
The grimy scraps
Of withered leaves about your feet
And newspapers from vacant lots;
The showers beat
10 On broken blinds and chimney-pots,
And at the corner of the street
A lonely cab-horse steams and stamps.
And then the lighting of the lamps.

II

The morning comes to consciousness
15 Of faint stale smells of beer
From the sawdust-trampled street
With all its muddy feet that press
To early coffee-stands.
With the other masquerades
20 That time resumes,
One thinks of all the hands
That are raising dingy shades
In a thousand furnished rooms.

III

You tossed a blanket from the bed,
25 You lay upon your back, and waited;
You dozed, and watched the night revealing
The thousand sordid images
Of which your soul was constituted;
They flickered against the ceiling.
30 And when all the world came back
And the light crept up between the shutters
And you heard the sparrows in the gutters,
You had such a vision of the street
As the street hardly understands;
35 Sitting along the bed's edge, where
You curled the papers from your hair,
Or clasped the yellow soles of feet
In the palms of both soiled hands.

IV

His soul stretched tight across the skies
40 That fade behind a city block,
Or trampled by insistent feet
At four and five and six o'clock;
And short square fingers stuffing pipes,
And evening newspapers, and eyes
45 Assured of certain certainties,
The conscience of a blackened street
Impatient to assume the world.

I am moved by fancies that are curled
Around these images, and cling:
50 The notion of some infinitely gentle
Infinitely suffering thing.

Wipe your hand across your mouth, and
laugh;
The worlds revolve like ancient women
Gathering fuel in vacant lots.

City Square
(*La Place*) (1948)
by Alberto Giacometti.
Bronze
(8½″ × 25⅜″ × 17¼″)
(21.6 × 64.5 × 43.8 cm).

The Museum of Modern Art,
New York. Purchase.
Photograph © 2000
The Museum of Modern Art,
New York.
© 1997 Artists Rights Society
(ARS), New York, ADAGP,
Paris.

A Lament for the Weary

There are many references to religion in Eliot's poem "The Hollow Men," which follows. You may, for instance, recognize on sight a line from the Lord's Prayer (see lines 77 and 91–94). But Eliot's main concern here is not to affirm his Christianity, but to give us a picture of a world of godless despair, a world without religion or the promise of salvation.

Taken from Joseph Conrad's famous story *Heart of Darkness,* the first line after the title is significant in two ways. First, it calls attention to the story of a man named Kurtz, who journeys to the center of Africa and falls into degradation. Kurtz is redeemed by self-awareness, only to find that this painful knowledge is not liberating but useless. Second, the line strikes the note of futility heard throughout the poem.

The next line—"A penny for the Old Guy"—refers to one of the most notorious incidents in British history, the Gunpowder Plot. On November 5, 1605, a band of conspirators made plans to kill King James I by planting barrels of gunpowder in the underground vaults of Parliament. The man chosen to light the fuse that would result in a fatal explosion was a soldier named Guy Fawkes. But before the plot could be carried out, the conspirators were discovered. Guy Fawkes was arrested and, in the cruel custom of the day, first hanged, then drawn and quartered.

To commemorate this grisly event, every year on November 5, huge bonfires are set all over England. When these fires are lit, straw-filled effigies of Fawkes—the "stuffed men" of the poem—that look like scarecrows go up in flames, lighting up the skies. Children join in the fun by becoming beggars who ask passersby to give them "a penny for the guy."

The last four lines of this poem are among the most famous in modern poetry. What is the difference between ending with a "bang" and ending with only a "whimper"?

The Hollow Men

T. S. Eliot

Mistah Kurtz—he dead.

A penny for the Old Guy

I

We are the hollow men
We are the stuffed men
Leaning together
Headpiece filled with straw. Alas!
5 Our dried voices, when
We whisper together
Are quiet and meaningless
As wind in dry grass
Or rats' feet over broken glass
10 In our dry cellar.

    Shape without form, shade without color,
Paralyzed force, gesture without motion;

    Those who have crossed
With direct eyes, to death's other Kingdom°
15 Remember us—if at all—not as lost
Violent souls, but only
As the hollow men
The stuffed men.

II

Eyes I dare not meet in dreams
20 In death's dream kingdom
These do not appear:
There, the eyes are
Sunlight on a broken column
There, is a tree swinging
25 And voices are
In the wind's singing
More distant and more solemn
Than a fading star.

Let me be no nearer
30 In death's dream kingdom
Let me also wear
Such deliberate disguises
Rat's coat, crowskin, crossed staves°
In a field
35 Behaving as the wind behaves
No nearer—

    Not that final meeting
In the twilight kingdom

III

This is the dead land
40 This is cactus land
Here the stone images
Are raised, here they receive
The supplication of a dead man's hand
Under the twinkle of a fading star.

45   Is it like this
In death's other kingdom
Waking alone
At the hour when we are
Trembling with tenderness
50 Lips that would kiss
Form prayers to broken stone.

IV

The eyes are not here
There are no eyes here
In this valley of dying stars
55 In this hollow valley
This broken jaw of our lost kingdoms

13–14. Those . . . Kingdom: Those with "direct eyes" have crossed from the hollow men's haunts into Paradise. The allusion is to Dante's *Paradiso*.

33. staves: rods or staffs; "crossed staves / in a field" form a scarecrow.

In this last of meeting places
We grope together
And avoid speech
60 Gathered on this beach of the tumid river°

Sightless, unless
The eyes reappear
As the perpetual star
Multifoliate rose°
65 Of death's twilight kingdom
The hope only
Of empty men.

V

Here we go round the prickly pear°
Prickly pear prickly pear
70 *Here we go round the prickly pear*
At five o'clock in the morning.

Between the idea
And the reality
Between the motion
75 And the act°
Falls the Shadow
                    For Thine is the Kingdom°

Between the conception
And the creation
80 Between the emotion
And the response
Falls the Shadow
                         Life is very long

Between the desire
85 And the spasm
Between the potency
And the existence
Between the essence
And the descent
90 Falls the Shadow
                    For Thine is the Kingdom

For Thine is
Life is
For Thine is the

95 *This is the way the world ends*
This is the way the world ends
This is the way the world ends
Not with a bang but a whimper.

---

60. tumid river: Hell's swollen river, the Acheron (ak′ər·än′), in Dante's *Inferno.* The damned must cross this river to enter the land of the dead.
64. multifoliate rose: Dante describes Paradise as a rose of many leaves (*Paradiso,* Canto 32).
68. prickly pear: cactus.
74–75. Between . . . act: a reference to Shakespeare's *Julius Caesar:* "Between the acting of a dreadful thing / And the first motion, all the interim is / Like a phantasma or a hideous dream" (Act II, Scene1, lines 63–65).
77. For . . . Kingdom: closing lines of the Lord's Prayer: "For thine is the kingdom, and the power, and the glory, forever and ever."

Russia

Anna Akhmatova (1889–1966)

Anna Akhmatova grew up near St. Petersburg, the capital of Russia before the 1917 revolution that led to a Communist takeover of the government. As a young writer just before the revolution, she was one of the founders of a literary movement called *acmeism* (ak′mē·iz′əm), which rejected ambivalent symbols in poetry and strove instead to present clearly etched ideas. (Just as Yeats is almost synonymous with Ireland, Akhmatova is regarded as a major Russian lyric poet.)

After the revolution, however, Akhmatova's poetry did not find a sympathetic ear with the new Communist regime. The official outlook was that art should exist in the service of the state and should treat themes that were politically and socially "useful." Akhmatova's first husband, the poet Nikolai Gumilev, was executed as a counterrevolutionary in 1921, and Akhmatova herself was forbidden to publish. As the terrifying years of Joseph Stalin's dictatorship wore on, she saw more and more of her friends arrested and her own son imprisoned. Throughout this period, however, she continued to write and to serve as mentor for a younger generation of Russian poets.

After Stalin's death in 1953, the works of many Russian writers were again publicly accepted. Akhmatova was finally able to enjoy a brief period of official recognition in the last years of her life. Boris Pasternak, a Russian novelist and poet who was himself threatened with banishment, paid tribute to Akhmatova in these words: "Your work throbs high with our remembered past."

Anna Akhmatova.

(Map) ©Rand McNally R. L. #98-S-116.

Before You Read
LOT'S WIFE

Background

Besides its significance as a religious document, the Bible has served over the centuries as a source of literary inspiration for countless writers. In "Lot's Wife," the speaker focuses on a Biblical incident recounted in Genesis 19. Angered by the wickedness of the city of Sodom, God sends angels to punish the inhabitants. When the angels arrive in disguise as men, only Lot treats them hospitably. Lot's reward is a warning of the city's wholesale destruction. He is told to flee Sodom with his family and not to look back under any conditions. As Lot's family

escapes, however, his wife disobeys the angels' command and turns her head to gaze upon the city. She is immediately turned into a pillar of salt.

For the twentieth-century Russian poet Anna Akhmatova, this ancient story assumed a poignant, almost painful relevance. She lived under a totalitarian regime that dictated the terms under which artists and writers could work. Yet, when Akhmatova had an opportunity to flee oppression in her homeland, she remained. In the following poem, Akhmatova views the story of Lot's wife, an ancient, unwilling exile, from the perspective of a modern woman

who was sorely tempted by the lure of exile but who resisted.

Reading Skills and Strategies

Drawing on Personal Experience

As you read, jot down notes on how you might feel if you came under intense pressure to leave your homeland because life there had become intolerable. Would you regard such a departure as an act of desertion, or as a wise investment in the future? After you have thought about your own reactions, try to gauge the degree of sympathy with which the speaker regards Lot's wife.

Lot's Wife

Anna Akhmatova

translated by **Richard Wilbur**

The just man followed then his angel guide
Where he strode on the black highway, hulking and bright;
But a wild grief in his wife's bosom cried,
Look back, it is not too late for a last sight

5 *Of the red towers of your native Sodom, the square*
Where once you sang, the gardens you shall mourn,
And the tall house with empty windows where
You loved your husband and your babes were born.

She turned, and looking on the bitter view
10 Her eyes were welded shut by mortal pain;
Into transparent salt her body grew,
And her quick feet were rooted in the plain.

Who would waste tears upon her? Is she not
The least of our losses, this unhappy wife?
15 Yet in my heart she will not be forgot
Who, for a single glance, gave up her life.

Woman with a Rake (late 19th or early 20th century) by Kasimir Malevich.

Tretyakov Gallery, Moscow.

FINDING COMMON GROUND

Meet in small groups to discuss this poem. Your first task will be to formulate the questions you'd like to focus on. In your discussions, be sure to consider your reading notes and how your responses to exile compare with those of the speaker. Also, be sure to

address how Akhmatova imaginatively used this Biblical story to stand for something else. Assign a recorder for your group. At the completion of your discussion, have the recorder report to the class at large on your responses to the poem.

As a class, try to agree on at least three responses to the poem—in other words, try to find some common ground.

Graham Greene
(1904–1991)

Graham Greene (1957).

For his serious idealistic novels dealing with contemporary moral dilemmas and for his light "entertainments" and thrillers, Graham Greene has won a rare combination of popular and critical admiration. His intention in his writing was always to tell the truth, which he saw as a primary duty of the artist, and, as you will see, Greene often wrote about life's losers—at least those whom we conventionally think of as losers.

Henry Graham Greene was born to a comfortable family in Berkhamsted, Hertfordshire. His father was the headmaster of Berkhamsted School, which Greene attended as a child. For reasons that are not clear, as Greene grew into adolescence, he became increasingly depressed and unhappy at school, which he described as his first impression of hell. After he tried to run away, he was sent to London to undergo psychoanalysis. He would later recall those six months in London as among the happiest of his life.

While he was still at Berkhamsted, Greene had a story published by a local newspaper, and he recalled feeling a sense of true literary triumph "for the first and last time." The experience convinced him to become a professional writer. He attended Oxford University, wrote a novel that failed to find a publisher, and published a book of poems in 1925, the year he graduated. As an apprenticeship, he went to work as a reporter for the Nottingham *Journal*.

In 1926, Greene became engaged to a Roman Catholic woman, Vivien Dayrell-Browning, and agreed to take instruction in her faith. Although he had been a confirmed atheist, he became convinced of "the probable existence of something we call God." His Catholic faith would turn out to be an important factor in his writing.

Greene took a job with the London *Times* and worked there until his first novel, *The Man Within,* was published in 1929. His next books were adventure stories, but they received little attention. Greene began to come into his own with the thriller *Stamboul Train* (1932; also published under the title *Orient Express*). This story of a train journey to Istanbul was the first of Greene's works that were made into movies.

Greene brought his religious concerns into his fiction with the novel *Brighton Rock* (1938), in which he explored the nature of good and evil and the inexplicable workings of divine grace. Pursuing the theme further in *The Power and the Glory* (1940), Greene revealed an unorthodox kind of Catholicism in which naturally sinful men and women, living in a fallen world, are often given a last-minute chance at redemption. As one critic notes, Greene's characters live "on the border between love and hate, good and evil, heaven and hell."

During World War II, Greene worked for the British Foreign Office, and afterward he became a director for a publishing house. During the 1950s, he was a celebrated foreign correspondent assigned to Malaysia, Indochina, Africa, and Cuba. His experiences as a journalist were reflected in novels such as *The Quiet American* (1955), which prophetically dealt with the implications of American involvement in Vietnam.

Greene's novels came out steadily, among them *The Heart of the Matter* (1948), *The End of the Affair* (1951), and *A Burnt-Out Case* (1961). Many of his books have been made into films, including *The Third Man* (1950) and *Our Man in Havana* (1958). He also published several plays, as well as a number of travel books describing his journeys.

In the first volume of his autobiography, *A Sort of Life* (1971), Greene revealed his motives for writing fiction as "a desire to reduce the chaos of experience to some sort of order, and a hungry curiosity. We cannot love others, so the theologians teach, unless in some degree we can love ourselves, and curiosity too begins at home."

Make the Connection

The Rage to Destroy

This story is set in 1954, nine years after the end of World War II. During the war, the city of London had been regularly "blitzed" by German planes dropping firebombs, which destroyed many buildings in the city. Years after the war, the people of London still walked along bomb-blasted streets. More troubling than this physical destruction, though, was what many people saw as the moral destruction of society, the collapse of goodness and hope, especially among gangs of young people. Before you read, think about your own knowledge of or experience with vandalism. What motivates some people to want to destroy beautiful things?

Reading Skills and Strategies

Inferring Motives

Each section of this story gives you a bit more insight into the enigmatic main character, T. After each section, jot down how you see him, and note details of his words and actions that you find revealing. What needs or conflicts do you think motivate him to act as he does?

Elements of Literature

Setting

At one point in this story, the word *beautiful* appears several times. As readers, we are struck by the word's incongruity. We recognize, as do certain characters in the story, that the word somehow doesn't belong here. Until this scene and in all the scenes that follow, we are immersed in the seediness of Greene's **setting.** Greene's characteristic use of coarse imagery and language has created a drab world full of shabby violence.

The Destructors

Graham Greene

1

It was on the eve of August Bank Holiday that the latest recruit became the leader of the Wormsley Common gang. No one was surprised except Mike, but Mike at the age of nine was surprised by everything. "If you don't shut your mouth," somebody once said to him, "you'll get a frog down it." After that Mike had kept his teeth tightly clamped except when the surprise was too great.

The new recruit had been with the gang since the beginning of the summer holidays, and there were possibilities about his brooding silence that all recognized. He never wasted a word even to tell his name until that was required of him by the rules. When he said "Trevor" it was a statement of fact, not as it would have been with the others a statement of shame or defiance. Nor did anyone laugh except Mike, who finding himself without support and meeting the dark gaze of the newcomer opened his mouth and was quiet again. There was every reason why T., as he was afterward referred to, should have been an object of mockery—there was his name (and they substituted the initial because otherwise they had no excuse not to laugh at it), the fact that his father, a former architect and present clerk, had "come down in the world" and that his mother considered herself better than the neighbors. What but an odd quality of danger, of the unpredictable, established him in the gang without any <u>ignoble</u> ceremony of initiation?

WORDS TO OWN
ignoble (ig·nō′bəl) *adj.*: shameful; degrading.

Juvenile Counsel: Boys on a Doorstep (20th century) by Henry Lamb.

The gang met every morning in an <u>impromptu</u> car-park, the site of the last bomb of the first blitz. The leader, who was known as Blackie, claimed to have heard it fall, and no one was precise enough in his dates to point out that he would have been one year old and fast asleep on the down platform of Wormsley Common Underground Station. On one side of the car-park leaned the first occupied house, number 3, of the shattered Northwood Terrace—literally leaned, for it had suffered from the blast of the bomb and the side walls were supported on wooden struts. A smaller bomb and some incendiaries had fallen beyond, so that the house stuck up like a jagged tooth and carried on the further wall relics of its neighbor, a dado,[1] the remains of a fireplace. T., whose words were almost confined to voting "Yes" or "No" to the plan of operations proposed each day by Blackie, once startled the whole gang by saying broodingly, "Wren[2] built that house, father says."

"Who's Wren?"

"The man who built St. Paul's."[3]

"Who cares?" Blackie said. "It's only Old Misery's."

Old Misery—whose real name was Thomas—had once been a builder and decorator. He lived alone in the crippled house, doing for himself: Once a week you could see him coming back across the common with bread and vegetables, and once as the boys played in the car-park he put his head over the smashed wall of his garden and looked at them.

2. Wren: Sir Christopher Wren (1632–1723), a celebrated English architect.
3. St. Paul's: cathedral in London.

1. dado (dā′dō): wood paneling along the lower part of the walls of a room.

WORDS TO OWN
impromptu (im·prämp′too′) *adj.*: unplanned.

"Been to the loo,"[4] one of the boys said, for it was common knowledge that since the bombs fell something had gone wrong with the pipes of the house and Old Misery was too mean to spend money on the property. He could do the redecorating himself at cost price, but he had never learned plumbing. The loo was a wooden shed at the bottom of the narrow garden with a star-shaped hole in the door: It had escaped the blast which had smashed the house next door and sucked out the window frames of number 3.

The next time the gang became aware of Mr. Thomas was more surprising. Blackie, Mike, and a thin yellow boy, who for some reason was called by his surname Summers, met him on the common coming back from the market. Mr. Thomas stopped them. He said glumly, "You belong to the lot that play in the car-park?"

Mike was about to answer when Blackie stopped him. As the leader he had responsibilities. "Suppose we are?" he said ambiguously.

"I got some chocolates," Mr. Thomas said. "Don't like 'em myself. Here you are. Not enough to go round, I don't suppose. There never is," he added with somber conviction. He handed over three packets of Smarties.

The gang were puzzled and perturbed by this action and tried to explain it away. "Bet someone dropped them and he picked 'em up," somebody suggested.

"Pinched 'em and then got in a bleeding funk," another thought aloud.

"It's a bribe," Summers said. "He wants us to stop bouncing balls on his wall."

"We'll show him we don't take bribes," Blackie said, and they sacrificed the whole morning to the game of bouncing that only Mike was young enough to enjoy. There was no sign from Mr. Thomas.

Next day T. astonished them all. He was late at the rendezvous, and the voting for that day's exploit took place without him. At Blackie's suggestion the gang was to disperse in pairs, take buses at random, and see how many free rides could be snatched from unwary conductors (the operation was to be carried out in pairs to avoid cheating).

They were drawing lots for their companions when T. arrived.

"Where you been, T.?" Blackie asked. "You can't vote now. You know the rules."

"I've been *there*," T. said. He looked at the ground, as though he had thoughts to hide.

"Where?"

"At Old Misery's." Mike's mouth opened and then hurriedly closed again with a click. He had remembered the frog.

"At Old Misery's?" Blackie said. There was nothing in the rules against it, but he had a sensation that T. was treading on dangerous ground. He asked hopefully, "Did you break in?"

"No. I rang the bell."

"And what did you say?"

"I said I wanted to see his house."

"What did he do?"

"He showed it me."

"Pinch anything?"

"No."

"What did you do it for then?"

The gang had gathered round: It was as though an impromptu court were about to form and to try some case of deviation. T. said, "It's a beautiful house," and still watching the ground, meeting no one's eyes, he licked his lips first one way, then the other.

"What do you mean, a beautiful house?" Blackie asked with scorn.

"It's got a staircase two hundred years old like a corkscrew. Nothing holds it up."

"What do you mean, nothing holds it up. Does it float?"

"It's to do with opposite forces, Old Misery said."

"What else?"

"There's paneling."

"Like in the Blue Boar?"

"Two hundred years old."

"Is Old Misery two hundred years old?"

Mike laughed suddenly and then was quiet again. The meeting was in a serious mood. For the first time since T. had strolled into the car-park on the first day of the holidays his position was in danger. It only needed a single use of his real name and the gang would be at his heels.

---

4. **loo:** British slang for "bathroom." *Loo* comes from the French word *lieux,* short for *les lieux d'aisances* (lā lyŏ de·zäns'), which means "places of convenience."

"What did you do it for?" Blackie asked. He was just, he had no jealousy, he was anxious to retain T. in the gang if he could. It was the word "beautiful" that worried him—that belonged to a class world that you could still see parodied at the Wormsley Common Empire by a man wearing a top hat and a monocle, with a haw-haw accent. He was tempted to say, "My dear Trevor, old chap," and unleash his hell hounds. "If you'd broken in," he said sadly—that indeed would have been an exploit worthy of the gang.

"This was better," T. said. "I found out things." He continued to stare at his feet, not meeting anybody's eye, as though he were absorbed in some dream he was unwilling—or ashamed—to share.

"What things?"

"Old Misery's going to be away all tomorrow and Bank Holiday."

Blackie said with relief, "You mean we could break in?"

"And pinch things?" somebody asked.

Blackie said, "Nobody's going to pinch things. Breaking in—that's good enough, isn't it? We don't want any court stuff."

"I don't want to pinch anything," T. said. "I've got a better idea."

"What is it?"

T. raised his eyes, as gray and disturbed as the drab August day. "We'll pull it down," he said. "We'll destroy it."

Blackie gave a single hoot of laughter and then, like Mike, fell quiet, daunted by the serious implacable gaze. "What'd the police be doing all the time?" he said.

"They'd never know. We'd do it from inside. I've found a way in." He said with a sort of intensity, "We'd be like worms, don't you see, in an apple. When we came out again there'd be nothing there, no staircase, no panels, nothing but just walls, and then we'd make the walls fall down—somehow."

"We'd go to jug," Blackie said.

"Who's to prove? And anyway we wouldn't have pinched anything." He added without the smallest flicker of glee, "There wouldn't be anything to pinch after we'd finished."

"I've never heard of going to prison for breaking things," Summers said.

"There wouldn't be time," Blackie said. "I've seen housebreakers at work."

"There are twelve of us," T. said. "We'd organize."

"None of us know how—"

"I know," T. said. He looked across at Blackie. "Have you got a better plan?"

"Today," Mike said tactlessly, "we're pinching free rides—"

"Free rides," T. said. "You can stand down, Blackie, if you'd rather. . . ."

"The gang's got to vote."

"Put it up then."

Blackie said uneasily, "It's proposed that tomorrow and Monday we destroy Old Misery's house."

"Here, here," said a fat boy called Joe.

"Who's in favor?"

T. said, "It's carried."

"How do we start?" Summers asked.

"He'll tell you," Blackie said. It was the end of his leadership. He went away to the back of the car-park and began to kick a stone, dribbling it this way and that. There was only one old Morris[5] in the park, for few cars were left there except lorries:[6] Without an attendant there was no safety. He took a flying kick at the car and scraped a little paint off the rear mudguard. Beyond, paying no more attention to him than to a stranger, the gang had gathered round T.; Blackie was dimly aware of the fickleness of favor. He thought of going home, of never returning, of letting them all discover the hollowness of T.'s leadership, but suppose after all what T. proposed was possible—nothing like it had ever been done before. The fame of the Wormsley Common car-park gang would surely reach around London. There would be headlines in the papers. Even the grown-up gangs who ran the betting at the all-in wrestling and the barrow-boys[7] would hear with respect of how Old Misery's house had been destroyed. Driven by the pure,

---

5. **Morris:** car made by the Morris firm, a British automaker.
6. **lorries:** British for "trucks."
7. **barrow-boys:** boys who sold fruit or vegetables from a barrow, or cart.

WORDS TO OWN

implacable (im·plā′kə·bəl) *adj.:* inflexible; relentless; obstinate.

---

simple, and <u>altruistic</u> ambition of fame for the gang, Blackie came back to where T. stood in the shadow of Misery's wall.

T. was giving his orders with decision: It was as though this plan had been with him all his life, pondered through the seasons, now in his fifteenth year crystallized with the pain of puberty. "You," he said to Mike, "bring some big nails, the biggest you can find, and a hammer. Anyone else who can better bring a hammer and a screwdriver. We'll need plenty of them. Chisels too. We can't have too many chisels. Can anybody bring a saw?"

"I can," Mike said.

"Not a child's saw," T. said. "A real saw."

Blackie realized he had raised his hand like any ordinary member of the gang.

"Right, you bring one, Blackie. But now there's a difficulty. We want a hacksaw."

"What's a hacksaw?" someone asked.

"You can get 'em at Woolworth's," Summers said.

The fat boy called Joe said gloomily, "I knew it would end in a collection."

"I'll get one myself," T. said. "I don't want your money. But I can't buy a sledgehammer."

Blackie said, "They are working on number fifteen. I know where they'll leave their stuff for Bank Holiday."

"Then that's all," T. said. "We meet here at nine sharp."

"I've got to go to church," Mike said.

"Come over the wall and whistle. We'll let you in."

2

On Sunday morning all were punctual except Blackie, even Mike. Mike had had a stroke of luck. His mother felt ill, his father was tired after Saturday night, and he was told to go to church alone with many warnings of what would happen if he strayed. Blackie had had difficulty in smuggling out the saw, and then in finding the sledgehammer at the back of number 15. He approached the house from a lane at the rear of the garden, for fear of the policeman's beat along the main road. The tired evergreens kept off a stormy sun: Another wet Bank Holiday was being prepared over the Atlantic, beginning in swirls of dust under the trees. Blackie climbed the wall into Misery's garden.

There was no sign of anybody anywhere. The loo stood like a tomb in a neglected graveyard. The curtains were drawn. The house slept. Blackie lumbered nearer with the saw and the sledgehammer. Perhaps after all nobody had turned up: The plan had been a wild invention: They had woken wiser. But when he came close to the back door he could hear a confusion of sound, hardly louder than a hive in swarm: a clickety-clack, a bang bang bang, a scraping, a creaking, a sudden painful crack. He thought, It's true, and whistled.

They opened the back door to him and he came in. He had at once the impression of organization, very different from the old happy-go-lucky ways under his leadership. For a while he wandered up and down stairs looking for T. Nobody addressed him: He had a sense of great urgency, and already he could begin to see the plan. The interior of the house was being carefully demolished without touching the outer walls. Summers with hammer and chisel was ripping out the skirting-boards[8] in the ground floor dining room: He had already smashed the panels of the door. In the same room Joe was heaving up the parquet[9] blocks, exposing the soft wood floorboards over the cellar. Coils of wire came out of the damaged skirting and Mike sat happily on the floor, clipping the wires.

On the curved stairs two of the gang were working hard with an inadequate child's saw on the banisters—when they saw Blackie's big saw they signaled for it wordlessly. When he next saw them a quarter of the banisters had been dropped into the hall. He found T. at last in the bathroom—he sat moodily in the least cared-for room in the house, listening to the sounds coming up from below.

"You've really done it," Blackie said with awe. "What's going to happen?"

---

8. **skirting-boards:** baseboards; boards placed along the base of the walls of a room.
9. **parquet** (pär·kā′): fancy wood floor made of boards arranged in geometric patterns.

WORDS TO OWN

altruistic (al′trōō·is′tik) *adj.:* unselfish.

"We've only just begun," T. said. He looked at the sledgehammer and gave his instructions. "You stay here and break the bath and the washbasin. Don't bother about the pipes. They come later."

Mike appeared at the door. "I've finished the wire, T.," he said.

"Good. You've just got to go wandering round now. The kitchen's in the basement. Smash all the china and glass and bottles you can lay hold of. Don't turn on the taps—we don't want a flood—yet. Then go into all the rooms and turn out drawers. If they are locked get one of the others to break them open. Tear up any papers you find and smash all the ornaments. Better take a carving knife with you from the kitchen. The bedroom's opposite here. Open the pillows and tear up the sheets. That's enough for the moment. And you, Blackie, when you've finished in here crack the plaster in the passage up with your sledgehammer."

"What are you going to do?" Blackie asked.

"I'm looking for something special," T. said.

It was nearly lunchtime before Blackie had finished and went in search of T. Chaos had advanced. The kitchen was a shambles of broken glass and china. The dining room was stripped of parquet, the skirting was up, the door had been taken off its hinges, and the destroyers had moved up a floor. Streaks of light came in through the closed shutters where they worked with the seriousness of creators—and destruction after all is a form of creation. A kind of imagination had seen this house as it had now become.

Mike said, "I've got to go home for dinner."

"Who else?" T. asked, but all the others on one excuse or another had brought provisions with them.

They squatted in the ruins of the room and swapped unwanted sandwiches. Half an hour for lunch and they were at work again. By the time Mike returned, they were on the top floor, and by six the superficial damage was completed. The doors were all off, all the skirtings raised, the furniture pillaged and ripped and smashed—no one could have slept in the house except on a bed of broken plaster. T. gave his orders—eight o'clock next morning—and to escape notice they climbed singly over the garden wall, into the car-park. Only Blackie and T. were left; the light had nearly gone, and when they touched a switch, nothing worked—Mike had done his job thoroughly.

"Did you find anything special?" Blackie asked.

T. nodded. "Come over here," he said, "and look." Out of both pockets he drew bundles of pound notes. "Old Misery's savings," he said. "Mike ripped out the mattress, but he missed them."

"What are you going to do? Share them?"

"We aren't thieves," T. said. "Nobody's going to steal anything from this house. I kept these for you and me—a celebration." He knelt down on the floor and counted them out—there were seventy in all. "We'll burn them," he said, "one by one," and taking it in turns they held a note upward and lit the top corner, so that the flame burnt slowly toward their fingers. The gray ash floated above them and fell on their heads like age. "I'd like to see Old Misery's face when we are through," T. said.

"You hate him a lot?" Blackie asked.

"Of course I don't hate him," T. said. "There'd be no fun if I hated him." The last burning note illuminated his brooding face. "All this hate and love," he said, "it's soft, it's hooey. There's only things, Blackie," and he looked round the room crowded with the unfamiliar shadows of half things, broken things, former things. "I'll race you home, Blackie," he said.

3

Next morning the serious destruction started. Two were missing—Mike and another boy, whose parents were off to Southend and Brighton in spite of the slow warm drops that had begun to fall and the rumble of thunder in the estuary like the first guns of the old blitz. "We've got to hurry," T. said.

Summers was restive. "Haven't we done enough?" he said. "I've been given a bob for slot machines. This is like work."

"We've hardly started," T. said. "Why, there's all the floors left, and the stairs. We haven't taken

---

WORDS TO OWN
shambles (sham′bəlz) *n*.: scene of great disorder. Derived from *schamel*, a Middle English name for a bench used to display raw meat for sale, the word came to mean a butcher shop or slaughterhouse and, by extension, any great mess.
restive (res′tiv) *adj*.: impatient; nervous.

---

out a single window. You voted like the others. We are going to *destroy* this house. There won't be anything left when we've finished."

They began again on the first floor picking up the top floorboards next the outer wall, leaving the joists exposed. Then they sawed through the joists and retreated into the hall, as what was left of the floor heeled and sank. They had learned with practice, and the second floor collapsed more easily. By the evening an odd <u>exhilaration</u> seized them as they looked down the <u>great hollow of the house</u>. They ran risks and made mistakes: When they thought of the windows it was too late to reach them. "Cor,"[10] Joe said, and dropped a penny down into the dry rubble-filled well. It cracked and span among the broken glass.

"Why did we start this?" Summers asked with astonishment; T. was already on the ground, digging at the rubble, clearing a space along the outer wall. "Turn on the taps," he said. "It's too dark for anyone to see now, and in the morning it won't matter." The water overtook them on the stairs and fell through the floorless rooms.

It was then they heard Mike's whistle at the back. "Something's wrong," Blackie said. They could hear his urgent breathing as they unlocked the door.

"The bogies?"[11] Summers asked.

"Old Misery," Mike said. "He's on his way." He put his head between his knees and retched. "Ran all the way," he said with pride.

"But why?" T. said. "He told me. . . ." He protested with the fury of the child he had never been, "It isn't fair."

"He was down at Southend," Mike said, "and he was on the train coming back. Said it was too cold and wet." He paused and gazed at the water. "My, you've had a storm here. Is the roof leaking?"

"How long will he be?"

"Five minutes. I gave Ma the slip and ran."

"We better clear," Summers said. "We've done enough, anyway."

"Oh, no, we haven't. Anybody could do this—" "This" was the shattered hollowed house with nothing left but the walls. Yet walls could be pre-served. <u>Façades</u> were valuable. They could build inside again more beautifully than before. This could again be a home. He said angrily, "We've got to finish. Don't move. Let me think."

"There's no time," a boy said.

"There's got to be a way," T. said. "We couldn't have got thus far . . ."

"We've done a lot," Blackie said.

"No. No, we haven't. Somebody watch the front."

"We can't do any more."

"He may come in at the back."

"Watch the back too." T. began to plead. "Just give me a minute and I'll fix it. I swear I'll fix it." But his authority had gone with his ambiguity. He was only one of the gang. "Please," he said.

"Please," Summers mimicked him, and then suddenly struck home with the fatal name. "Run along home, Trevor."

T. stood with his back to the rubble like a boxer knocked groggy against the ropes. He had no words as his dreams shook and slid. Then Blackie acted before the gang had time to laugh, pushing Summers backward. "I'll watch the front, T.," he said, and cautiously he opened the shutters of the hall. The gray wet common stretched ahead, and the lamps gleamed in the puddles. "Someone's coming, T. No, it's not him. What's your plan, T.?"

"Tell Mike to go out to the loo and hide close beside it. When he hears me whistle he's got to count ten and start to shout."

"Shout what?"

"Oh, 'Help,' anything."

"You hear, Mike," Blackie said. He was the leader again. He took a quick look between the shutters. "He's coming, T."

"Quick, Mike. The loo. Stay here, Blackie, all of you till I yell."

"Where are you going, T.?"

"Don't worry. I'll see to this. I said I would, didn't I?"

---

10. **cor:** British exclamation of strong surprise or irritation. *Cor* is from *Gor*, or *Gord*, an earlier regional dialect pronunciation of "God."
11. **bogies** (bō′gēz): slang for "police."

WORDS TO OWN
exhilaration (eg·zil′ə·rā′shən) *n.:* excitement; high spirits.
façades (fə·sädz′) *n. pl.:* fronts of buildings.

Old Misery came limping off the common. He had mud on his shoes and he stopped to scrape them on the pavement's edge. He didn't want to soil his house, which stood jagged and dark between the bomb sites, saved so narrowly, as he believed, from destruction. Even the fanlight had been left unbroken by the bomb's blast. Somewhere somebody whistled. Old Misery looked sharply round. He didn't trust whistles. A child was shouting: It seemed to come from his own garden. Then a boy ran into the road from the car-park. "Mr. Thomas," he called, "Mr. Thomas."

"What is it?"

"I'm terribly sorry, Mr. Thomas. One of us got taken short, and we thought you wouldn't mind, and now he can't get out."

"What do you mean, boy?"

"He's got stuck in your loo."

"He'd no business—Haven't I seen you before?"

"You showed me your house."

"So I did. So I did. That doesn't give you the right to—"

"Do hurry, Mr. Thomas. He'll suffocate."

"Nonsense. He can't suffocate. Wait till I put my bag in."

"I'll carry your bag."

"Oh, no, you don't. I carry my own."

"This way, Mr. Thomas."

"I can't get in the garden that way. I've got to go through the house."

"But you *can* get in the garden this way, Mr. Thomas. We often do."

"You often do?" He followed the boy with a scandalized fascination. "When? What right . . ."

"Do you see . . . ? The wall's low."

"I'm not going to climb walls into my own garden. It's absurd."

"This is how we do it. One foot here, one foot there, and over." The boy's face peered down, an arm shot out, and Mr. Thomas found his bag taken and deposited on the other side of the wall.

"Give me back my bag," Mr. Thomas said. From the loo a boy yelled and yelled. "I'll call the police."

"Your bag's all right, Mr. Thomas. Look. One foot there. On your right. Now just above. To your left." Mr. Thomas climbed over his own garden wall. "Here's your bag, Mr. Thomas."

"I'll have the wall built up," Mr. Thomas said. "I'll not have you boys coming over here, using my loo." He stumbled on the path, but the boy caught his elbow and supported him. "Thank you, thank you, my boy," he murmured automatically. Somebody shouted again through the dark. "I'm coming, I'm coming," Mr. Thomas called. He said to the boy beside him, "I'm not unreasonable. Been a boy myself. As long as things are done regular. I don't mind you playing round the place Saturday mornings. Sometimes I like company. Only it's got to be regular. One of you asks leave and I say Yes. Sometimes I'll say No. Won't feel like it. And you come in at the front door and out at the back. No garden walls."

"Do get him out, Mr. Thomas."

"He won't come to any harm in my loo," Mr. Thomas said, stumbling slowly down the garden. "Oh, my rheumatics," he said. "Always get 'em on Bank Holiday. I've got to go careful. There's loose stones here. Give me your hand. Do you know what my horoscope said yesterday? 'Abstain from any dealings in first half of week. Danger of serious crash.' That might be on this path," Mr. Thomas said. "They speak in parables and double meanings." He paused at the door of the loo. "What's the matter in there?" he called. There was no reply.

"Perhaps he's fainted," the boy said.

"Not in my loo. Here, you, come out," Mr. Thomas said, and giving a great jerk at the door he nearly fell on his back when it swung easily open. A hand first supported him and then pushed him hard. His head hit the opposite wall and he sat heavily down. His bag hit his feet. A hand whipped the key out of the lock and the door slammed. "Let me out," he called, and heard the key turn in the lock. "A serious crash," he thought, and felt dithery and confused and old.

A voice spoke to him softly through the star-shaped hole in the door. "Don't worry, Mr. Thomas," it said, "we won't hurt you, not if you stay quiet."

Mr. Thomas put his head between his hands and pondered. He had noticed that there was only one lorry in the car-park, and he felt certain that the driver would not come for it before the morn-

---

WORDS TO OWN

abstain (ab·stān′) v.: refrain from; hold oneself back from.

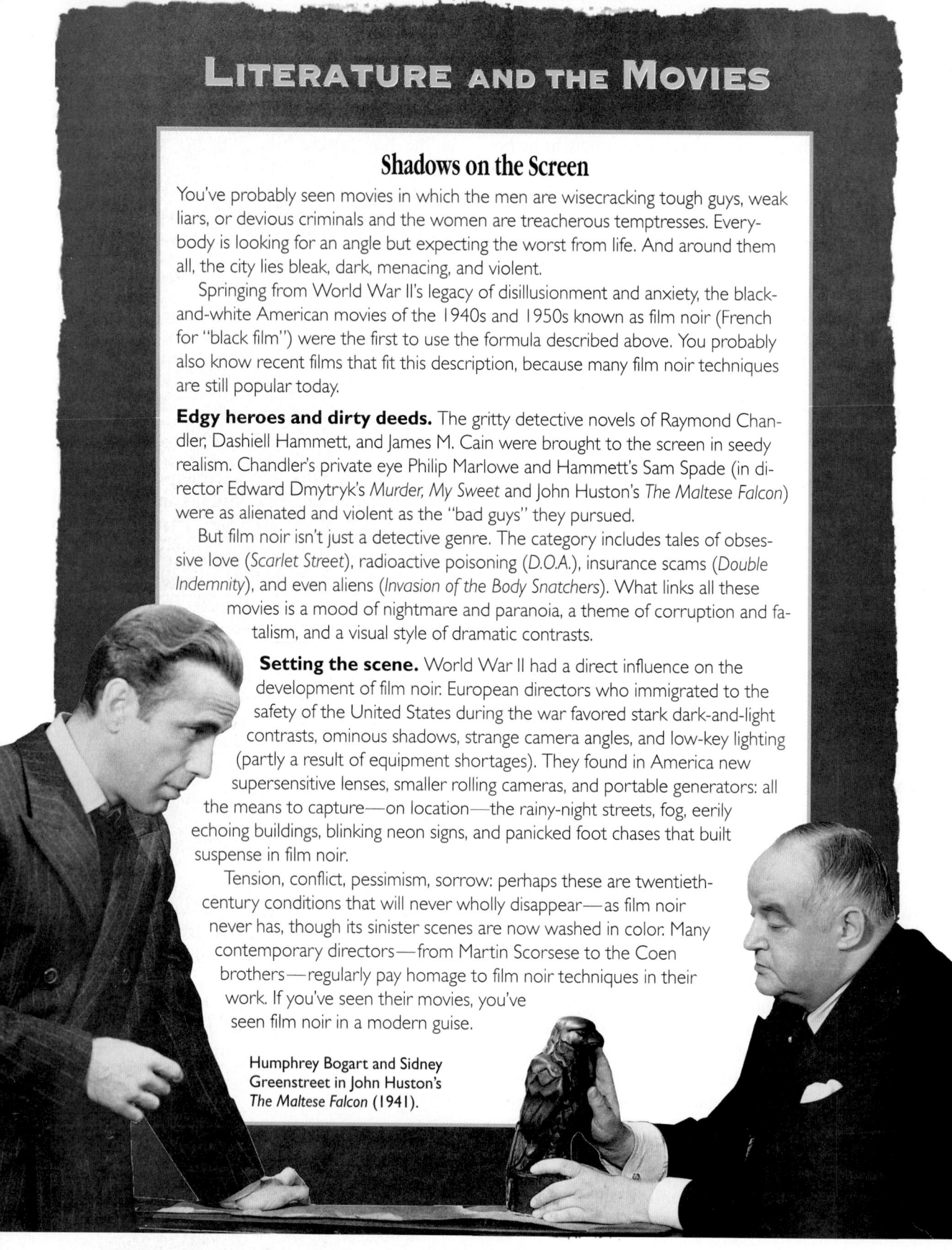

LITERATURE AND THE MOVIES

Shadows on the Screen

You've probably seen movies in which the men are wisecracking tough guys, weak liars, or devious criminals and the women are treacherous temptresses. Everybody is looking for an angle but expecting the worst from life. And around them all, the city lies bleak, dark, menacing, and violent.

Springing from World War II's legacy of disillusionment and anxiety, the black-and-white American movies of the 1940s and 1950s known as film noir (French for "black film") were the first to use the formula described above. You probably also know recent films that fit this description, because many film noir techniques are still popular today.

Edgy heroes and dirty deeds. The gritty detective novels of Raymond Chandler, Dashiell Hammett, and James M. Cain were brought to the screen in seedy realism. Chandler's private eye Philip Marlowe and Hammett's Sam Spade (in director Edward Dmytryk's *Murder, My Sweet* and John Huston's *The Maltese Falcon*) were as alienated and violent as the "bad guys" they pursued.

But film noir isn't just a detective genre. The category includes tales of obsessive love (*Scarlet Street*), radioactive poisoning (*D.O.A.*), insurance scams (*Double Indemnity*), and even aliens (*Invasion of the Body Snatchers*). What links all these movies is a mood of nightmare and paranoia, a theme of corruption and fatalism, and a visual style of dramatic contrasts.

Setting the scene. World War II had a direct influence on the development of film noir. European directors who immigrated to the safety of the United States during the war favored stark dark-and-light contrasts, ominous shadows, strange camera angles, and low-key lighting (partly a result of equipment shortages). They found in America new supersensitive lenses, smaller rolling cameras, and portable generators: all the means to capture—on location—the rainy-night streets, fog, eerily echoing buildings, blinking neon signs, and panicked foot chases that built suspense in film noir.

Tension, conflict, pessimism, sorrow: perhaps these are twentieth-century conditions that will never wholly disappear—as film noir never has, though its sinister scenes are now washed in color. Many contemporary directors—from Martin Scorsese to the Coen brothers—regularly pay homage to film noir techniques in their work. If you've seen their movies, you've seen film noir in a modern guise.

Humphrey Bogart and Sidney Greenstreet in John Huston's *The Maltese Falcon* (1941).

ing. Nobody could hear him from the road in front, and the lane at the back was seldom used. Anyone who passed there would be hurrying home and would not pause for what they would certainly take to be drunken cries. And if he did call "Help," who, on a lonely Bank Holiday evening, would have the courage to investigate? Mr. Thomas sat on the loo and pondered with the wisdom of age.

After a while it seemed to him that there were sounds in the silence—they were faint and came from the direction of his house. He stood up and peered through the ventilation-hole—between the cracks in one of the shutters he saw a light, not the light of a lamp, but the wavering light that a candle might give. Then he thought he heard the sound of hammering and scraping and chipping. He thought of burglars—perhaps they had employed the boy as a scout, but why should burglars engage in what sounded more and more like a stealthy form of carpentry? Mr. Thomas let out an experimental yell, but nobody answered. The noise could not even have reached his enemies.

4

Mike had gone home to bed, but the rest stayed. The question of leadership no longer concerned the gang. With nails, chisels, screwdrivers, anything that was sharp and penetrating they moved around the inner walls worrying at the mortar between the bricks. They started too high, and it was Blackie who hit on the damp course[12] and realized the work could be halved if they weakened the joints immediately above. It was a long, tiring, unamusing job, but at last it was finished. The gutted house stood there balanced on a few inches of mortar between the damp course and the bricks.

There remained the most dangerous task of all, out in the open at the edge of the bomb site. Summers was sent to watch the road for passers by, and Mr. Thomas, sitting on the loo, heard clearly now the sound of sawing. It no longer came from his house, and that a little reassured him. He felt less concerned. Perhaps the other noises too had no significance.

12. **damp course:** layer of waterproof material placed between two layers of brick in a house's foundation to keep moisture from rising up through the walls.

A voice spoke to him through the hole. "Mr. Thomas."

"Let me out," Mr. Thomas said sternly.

"Here's a blanket," the voice said, and a long gray sausage was worked through the hole and fell in swathes over Mr. Thomas's head.

"There's nothing personal," the voice said. "We want you to be comfortable tonight."

"Tonight," Mr. Thomas repeated incredulously.

"Catch," the voice said. "Penny buns—we've buttered them, and sausage-rolls. We don't want you to starve, Mr. Thomas."

Mr. Thomas pleaded desperately. "A joke's a joke, boy. Let me out and I won't say a thing. I've got rheumatics. I got to sleep comfortable."

"You wouldn't be comfortable, not in your house, you wouldn't. Not now."

"What do you mean, boy?" but the footsteps receded. There was only the silence of night: no sound of sawing. Mr. Thomas tried one more yell, but he was daunted and rebuked by the silence—a long way off an owl hooted and made away again on its muffled flight through the soundless world.

At seven next morning the driver came to fetch his lorry. He climbed into the seat and tried to start the engine. He was vaguely aware of a voice shouting, but it didn't concern him. At last the engine responded and he backed the lorry until it touched the great wooden shore[13] that supported Mr. Thomas's house. That way he could drive right out and down the street without reversing. The lorry moved forward, was momentarily checked as though something were pulling it from behind, and then went on to the sound of a long rumbling crash. The driver was astonished to see bricks bouncing ahead of him, while stones hit the roof of his cab. He put on his brakes. When he climbed out the whole landscape had suddenly altered. There was no house beside the car-park, only a hill of rubble. He went round and examined the back of his car for damage, and found a rope tied there that was still twisted at the other end round part of a wooden strut.

The driver again became aware of somebody shouting. It came from the wooden erection which was the nearest thing to a house in that desolation of broken brick. The driver climbed the smashed wall and unlocked the door. Mr. Thomas came out of the loo. He was wearing a

13. **shore:** beam

After the Blitz, 7th September 1940 by Lawrence Stephen Lowry.

gray blanket to which flakes of pastry adhered. He gave a sobbing cry. "My house," he said. "Where's my house?"

"Search me," the driver said. His eye lit on the remains of a bath and what had once been a dresser and he began to laugh. There wasn't anything left anywhere.

"How dare you laugh," Mr. Thomas said. "It was my house. My house."

"I'm sorry," the driver said, making heroic efforts, but when he remembered the sudden check to his lorry, the crash of bricks falling, he became convulsed again. One moment the house had stood there with such dignity between the bomb sites like a man in a top hat, and then, bang, crash, there wasn't anything left—not anything. He said, "I'm sorry. I can't help it, Mr. Thomas. There's nothing personal, but you got to admit it's funny."

MAKING MEANINGS

First Thoughts

1. What acts of vandalism and destruction in our culture does this story remind you of?

Shaping Interpretations

2. T.'s **motives** for destroying Old Misery's house are important. What motives can you *eliminate* based on how the boys treat Old Misery and on what they do with the money?

3. What *are* T.'s motives? Support your answer with details from the story. (Your reading notes will help.)

4. How are these elements of the story **ironic**: (a) T.'s special talents, (b) T.'s father's former profession, (c) the history of the house, (d) Old Misery's horoscope?

5. A gang is a social group with a shared set of values. What are this gang's values, and where do you think they spring from?

6. What **images** are used to describe the setting of the Wormsley Common car-park and its surroundings? How does the **setting** contribute to the story's emotional **atmosphere**?

7. Consider the following excerpt from the story:

   ". . . they worked with the seriousness of creators—and destruction after all is a form of creation. A kind of imagination had seen this house as it had now become."

   Do you think it expresses the story's **theme**? Explain.

8. When Blackie asks T. whether he hates Mr. Thomas, T. answers, "Of course I don't. . . . There'd be no fun if I hated him." How would you explain T.'s answer? Do you think children are capable of this kind of cruelty? Explain.

Reading Check

a. Who is the gang's leader at first? Who takes over? Why?

b. What is T.'s family background?

c. Why is Mr. Thomas's house valuable?

d. Describe how the house is destroyed.

CHOICES: Building Your Portfolio

Writer's Notebook

1. Collecting Ideas for an Informative Report

Even though "The Destructors" takes place half a century ago in London, the problem it examines is a timeless one. Explore what you know about the prevalence of random violence and vandalism in your own community, using the *5W-How?* questions (*Who? What? When? Where? Why? How?*). Then jot down your ideas about what library and community resources you might use to gather additional details for an informative paper. Save your work for the Writer's Workshop on page 1053.

Interpreting Imagery

2. Rotten to the Core?

Images of hollowness—of rotting from within—pervade the story. In the first part of an essay, cite these **images,** and discuss how they apply to the house, to Wormsley Common, and even to the story's characters. In the second part of the essay, discuss the ways "The Destructors" connects with images in W. B. Yeats's "The Second Coming" (page 923) and in T. S. Eliot's "The Hollow Men" (page 942).

Evaluating Oral Persuasion

3. The Destructor Trial

Is T. a vicious criminal who should be punished or a disturbed victim of society who deserves understanding? Prepare speeches to persuade people to accept your position on what should happen to T. (You might assume the roles of defense and prosecuting attorneys.) Your audience (the jury?) should analyze and evaluate your persuasive arguments and your performance. To review the techniques of persuasion, see pages 612–616. Before the speeches are presented, be sure the presenters and the evaluators agree on the criteria that should be used to analyze and evaluate oral persuasion.

Ted Hughes

(1930–1998)

Ted Hughes (1959).
© Rollie McKenna.

Ted Hughes, who often used violent nature imagery to symbolize the human condition, has been called "a twentieth-century Aesop whose fables lack an explicit moral." Hughes was born in West Yorkshire, where his father was a carpenter. After serving two years in the Royal Air Force, he studied archaeology and anthropology at Cambridge. In 1956, he married the brilliant young American poet Sylvia Plath. In 1963, after the couple had been separated for a short time, Plath, ill and depressed, took her own life in an unheated flat during one of the worst winters in London history.

An intensely private person, Hughes maintained an almost complete silence about his relationship with Sylvia Plath and the accusations that he somehow (because he had separated from her) was responsible for her death. That silence was broken in 1998 with the publication of a collection of poems called *Birthday Letters*. One of those poems is reprinted on page 962. (Also see Background on that page.)

The titles of Hughes's other books of poetry reveal his recurring subjects: *The Hawk in the Rain* (1957), *Animal Poems* (1967), *A Few Crows* (1970), *Cave Birds* (1975), and *Wolfwatching* (1991). Although Hughes writes of nature, he has nothing in common with the Romantics, who saw in nature a reflection of divine providence and primeval innocence. In Hughes's poems, nature represents the darkest impulses of the human heart; violence is not only an accepted fact of life, but also the impulse that links all creatures on earth. In 1984, Hughes was named poet laureate of England.

Before You Read

HAWK ROOSTING

Make the Connection

Deadly Instincts

Is violence really part of the natural order of things in the world? And what about the human capacity for murder and war? Is it *natural,* too, or a *distortion* of a natural force? This poem—or rather its unusual speaker, a hawk—makes us face these troubling questions.

The single-minded feathered killing machine of this poem presents us with a shocking truth:

There are forces in nature that destroy without remorse or rationalization.

Quickwrite

Quickly write down whatever comes to mind when you hear the word *hawk:* characteristics, images, behavior, your emotional response.

Elements of Literature

Personification

We're so accustomed to discussing our pets' "personalities"— a haughty cat, a mischievous puppy—that we don't think of these descriptions as a form of **personification,** but in reality they are. When Ted Hughes tries to imagine what it's like to be a hawk, he gives the creature characteristics akin to human consciousness, desire, and will. His entire poem is a personification.

Hawk Roosting

Ted Hughes

I sit in the top of the wood, my eyes closed.
Inaction, no falsifying dream
Between my hooked head and hooked feet:
Or in sleep rehearse perfect kills and eat.

5 The convenience of the high trees!
The air's buoyancy and the sun's ray
Are of advantage to me;
And the earth's face upward for my inspection.

My feet are locked upon the rough bark.
10 It took the whole of Creation
To produce my foot, my each feather:
Now I hold Creation in my foot

Or fly up, and revolve it all slowly—
I kill where I please because it is all mine.
15 There is no sophistry° in my body:
My manners are tearing off heads—

The allotment of death.
For the one path of my flight is direct
Through the bones of the living.
20 No arguments assert my right:

The sun is behind me.
Nothing has changed since I began.
My eye has permitted no change.
I am going to keep things like this.

15. sophistry: clever but unsound
reasoning.

Before You Read

CHAUCER

Background

In the many years since Sylvia Plath's suicide, controversy about her relationship with Ted Hughes and the extent of his responsibility for her death has swirled around Hughes. He maintained absolute silence on the subject, however, until the release in 1998 of *Birthday Letters*. In this collection of poems, all but two of which are addressed directly to Plath on the occasion of what would have been her sixty-fifth birthday, Hughes gives an intimate account of their relationship and the forces that, in his view, led to her poetry and to her death.

In this poem, Hughes speaks to a woman (we assume she is the young Sylvia) who is passionately reciting from Chaucer's *Canterbury Tales* in an English field in spring. The couple met in England when Plath arrived to study literature on a Fulbright grant.

Quickwrite

Imagine yourself in a field in the country on a sunny day in April with someone you love. How would you be feeling? Would you want to shout out to the world any snatch of poetry or song? Take some notes.

Chaucer

Ted Hughes

"Whan that Aprille with his shoures soote
The droghte of March hath perced to the roote..."
At the top of your voice, where you swayed on the top of a stile,°
Your arms raised—somewhat for balance, somewhat
5   To hold the reins of the straining attention
Of your imagined audience—you declaimed Chaucer
To a field of cows. And the Spring sky had done it
With its flying laundry, and the new emerald
Of the thorns, the hawthorn, the blackthorn,
10 And one of those bumpers of champagne
You snatched unpredictably from pure spirit.
Your voice went over the fields towards Grantchester.
It must have sounded lost. But the cows
Watched, then approached: they appreciated Chaucer.
15 You went on and on. Here were reasons
To recite Chaucer. Then came the Wyf of Bath,
Your favorite character in all literature.
You were rapt. And the cows were enthralled.
They shoved and jostled shoulders, making a ring,
20 To gaze into your face, with occasional snorts
Of exclamation, renewed their astounded attention,
Ears angling to catch every inflection,
Keeping their awed six feet of reverence
Away from you. You just could not believe it.
25 And you could not stop. What would happen
If you were to stop? Would they attack you,
Scared by the shock of silence, or wanting more—?
So you had to go on. You went on—
And twenty cows stayed with you hypnotized.
30 How did you stop? I can't remember
You stopping. I imagine they reeled away—
Rolling eyes, as if driven from their fodder.
I imagine I shooed them away. But
Your sostenuto° rendering of Chaucer
35 Was already perpetual. What followed
Found my attention too full
And had to go back into oblivion.

3. **stile:** steps over a wall or fence.
34. **sostenuto** (sôs′te nōō′tô): at a slower but sustained tempo. *Sostenuto* is a musical direction.

MAKING MEANINGS

Hawk Roosting

First Thoughts

1. How did you react to the hawk's philosophy?

Shaping Interpretations

2. What human qualities does the poet give the hawk in this **personification**? How do these qualities compare with your Quickwrite associations?

3. What does the hawk mean by saying it holds Creation in its foot? How is this different from the idea that God has "the whole world in His hands"?

4. How would you **paraphrase** lines 16–20?

5. What two meanings can you propose for the line "The sun is behind me"?

6. How is the hawk like some people?

Chaucer

First Thoughts

1. What do you see when you read this poem?

Shaping Interpretations

2. How did the cows respond to the recitation of Chaucer? Is the speaker's response like that of the cows? Explain.

3. Chaucer's great poem opens in the spring. What **images** of spring can you find in this poem?

4. In line 35, the speaker says that the woman's rendering of Chaucer was "already perpetual." What could he be suggesting about Sylvia Plath's poetry?

5. In the tragic story of Plath and Hughes, the "center could not hold." Does it surprise you that such joy could turn into pain? Explain.

6. How would you **paraphrase,** or restate in your own words, the poem's final sentence? (Is there agreement on what it means?)

Connecting with the Text

7. Do the feelings in this poem connect in any way to the ones you wrote about in your Quickwrite notes?

Writer's Notebook

1. Collecting Ideas for an Informative Report

Hughes's aim in "Hawk Roosting" is neither to inform nor to explain, yet he manages to distill a great deal of information about hawks into these few lines. To explore how you might approach the same subject in an informative paper, reread the poem slowly, jotting down questions it raises about the hawk's physiology and place in the food chain. Save your work for the Writer's Workshop on page 1053.

Analyzing Theme

2. What's It All About?

In a paragraph, state and discuss what you take to be the main **theme** of "Hawk Roosting" or "Chaucer." In a second paragraph, present your response to the theme.

Comparing Views of Nature

3. Birds of a Feather?

In a brief essay, compare the view of nature expressed in "Hawk Roosting"—and Hughes's bird itself—with those of Shelley's "To a Skylark" (page 739) and Keats's "Ode to a Nightingale" (page 755). Be sure to discuss how the poems differ and how they are alike.

Comparing and Contrasting Poems

4. Be My Love

Compare "Chaucer" with one of the robust love poems of the Renaissance (see pages 214–266) or with any other love poem in this book. In your essay, focus on one or two elements in the poems that are either very similar or very different—perhaps **themes, images, tones, sounds.** At the end of your essay, describe your response to each love poem.

Russia

Aleksandr Solzhenitsyn

(1918–   )

If to Aleksandr Solzhenitsyn (sōl'zhə·nēt'sin) his Soviet homeland was the burning log of "The Bonfire and the Ants," you could say he was swept from the fire in 1974. That's when he was arrested and exiled—for writing *The Gulag Archipelago,* a factual account of Soviet labor camps. Yet twenty years later, in May 1994, his apparently unquenchable love for his country drew him back to live again, as a free citizen, in Moscow.

Solzhenitsyn's troubled relationship with his homeland began much earlier. After becoming a decorated front-line officer in World War II, he was suddenly arrested in 1945 and served eight years in prison and labor camps for criticizing the premier, Joseph Stalin, in a letter to a friend.

(Map) ©Rand McNally R. L. #98-S-116.

Later, under the anti-Stalinist premier Nikita Khrushchev, Solzhenitsyn was able to publish his famous prison novel, *One Day in the Life of Ivan Denisovich* (1962). But during the 1960s and 1970s, the Soviet government continually harassed him, attempting to silence his criticisms of political realities. On winning the Nobel Prize in 1970, Solzhenitsyn did not travel to Sweden for the ceremonies because he feared the Soviet regime would bar his return.

In 1974, the Soviet government revoked Solzhenitsyn's citizenship. Solzhenitsyn was deported and, for most of his twenty-year exile, lived quietly and wrote prolifically in Cavendish, Vermont. Now on Russian soil again, he is a world-famous symbol of both the former Soviet Union's repression and the ongoing search for a renewed Russia.

Aleksandr Solzhenitsyn (1994).

Before You Read

FREEDOM TO BREATHE
THE BONFIRE AND THE ANTS

Quickwrite

Take a minute to brainstorm images of the place that you think of as home. Don't stop with your physical dwelling, though. Include the neighborhood, the section of the city or countryside, the whole city or county—whatever gives you a sense of the place and the people that are your own.

Once you've done your brainstorming, consider how you feel about home. Are you dying to get away, or do you hope you never have to leave?

Whatever your answer, your feelings would probably be different, or sharper, if you were forced out of your homeland and exiled to a faraway place. They would almost certainly be affected if danger suddenly loomed—perhaps gunfire or a raging flood—and common sense said, "Leave *now!*"

The two prose poems you are about to read were written by a Russian who had to contemplate his homeland from a prison cell and, later, from a twenty-year exile. Keeping in mind the powerful emotions and images that make up your idea of "home," jot down notes on how you might feel if you were suddenly forced to leave it.

Freedom to Breathe

Aleksandr Solzhenitsyn

translated by **Michael Glenny**

A shower fell in the night and now dark clouds drift across the sky, occasionally sprinkling a fine film of rain.

I stand under an apple tree in blossom and I breathe. Not only the apple tree but the grass round it glistens with moisture; words cannot describe the sweet fragrance that pervades the air. I inhale as deeply as I can, and the aroma invades my whole being; I breathe with my eyes open, I breathe with my eyes closed—I cannot say which gives me the greater pleasure.

This, I believe, is the single most precious freedom that prison takes away from us: the freedom to breathe freely, as I now can. No food on earth, no wine, not even a woman's kiss is sweeter to me than this air steeped in the fragrance of flowers, of moisture and freshness.

No matter that this is only a tiny garden, hemmed in by five-story houses like cages in a zoo. I cease to hear the motorcycles backfiring, radios whining, the burble of loudspeakers. As long as there is fresh air to breathe under an apple tree after a shower, we may survive a little longer.

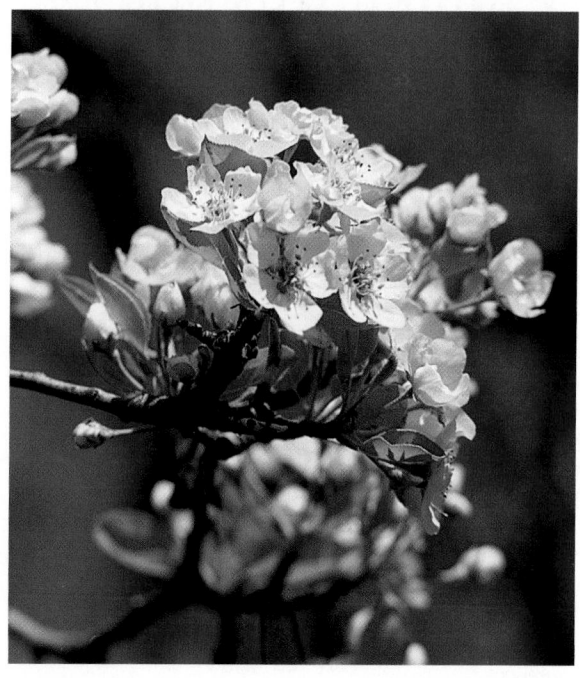

The Bonfire and the Ants

Aleksandr Solzhenitsyn

translated by **Michael Glenny**

I threw a rotten log onto the fire without noticing that it was alive with ants.

The log began to crackle, the ants came tumbling out and scurried around in desperation. They ran along the top and writhed as they were scorched by the flames. I gripped the log and rolled it to one side. Many of the ants then managed to escape onto the sand or the pine needles.

But, strangely enough, they did not run away from the fire.

They had no sooner overcome their terror than they turned, circled, and some kind of force drew them back to their forsaken homeland. There were many who climbed back onto the burning log, ran about on it, and perished there.

FINDING COMMON GROUND

Reading these two thought sketches isn't really like following an arrow-straight path. For a while, you may have *thought* you understood the speaker every step of the way, but by the end, he probably managed to surprise you with a sudden twist of thought. What was your reading experience like? Did it resemble other people's? Discuss with classmates how and why, in each sketch, your perceptions of the prose poem changed as you read further.

Once you've absorbed Solzhenitsyn's surprises, though, here's the question: What do these writings mean to *you*? In the Quickwrite on page 965, you were invited to think of your own home and how you might respond to being exiled from it—a fertile field for discussion. Another way of "finding common ground," of connecting with Solzhenitsyn or any other writer, is by digging into the differences

between your perspective and the writer's—just as a discussion of differences can sometimes bring friends into a closer relationship with one another. You aren't necessarily expected to understand or agree with everything a writer says.

For each prose poem, challenge or query Solzhenitsyn on some point, whether an idea, an experience, an image, or something else. Here are examples of two challenges:

- Isn't it possible to have "fresh air to breathe" and not be free?

- Isn't an **allegory,** or symbolic story, that equates people with ants already manipulating readers? Would all humans drawn back to a homeland just "run about" and perish pointlessly?

Vietnam

Nguyen Thi Vinh

(1924–   )

Nguyen Thi Vinh (nōō′yin tī vin′), while never a soldier, drew on her own experience for "Thoughts of Hanoi." Born in North Vietnam, she fled south to Saigon, the capital of newly created South Vietnam, in the 1950s to escape Communist rule. She quickly gained acclaim as a fiction writer with *Two Sisters* (1953), beginning a distinguished and successful literary career.

Her work constantly probed the pain, loss, and dislocation of a civil war that transformed friends into foes. When the Communists gained control of all of Vietnam in 1975, Nguyen stayed, despite the danger that made millions in the south flee.

Finally, however, in 1983, she followed others in her family to Norway. Her exile seems particularly wrenching since Nguyen's ancestors, for centuries, were members of one of Vietnam's two ruling families.

(Map) ©Rand McNally R. L. #98-S-116.

Make the Connection

If you've ever been caught up in a feud, or observed one from the sidelines, you know how senseless the consequences can sometimes be. Often entire communities are divided—sometimes for generations—over a simple misunderstanding or a perceived slight.

Other feuds, of course, aren't trivial. They start over important and painful issues, and people are drawn into dangerous conflicts with those they love. That is what happens in the poem you are about to read. The "feud" is the devastating civil war between North and South Vietnam, which lasted from 1957 to 1975. The speaker, a southern soldier who grew up in the north, is addressing his "brother." His longing for his old way of life and the people from his past is heartfelt. The stakes are the ultimate: life itself.

Quickwrite

Make a list of some of the civil wars that have torn countries and peoples apart in the past fifty years or so. What caused each conflict? How could "friends" become "foes"? Have any of these wars been resolved?

Thoughts of Hanoi

Nguyen Thi Vinh

translated by **Nguyen Ngoc Bich**

The night is deep and chill
as in early autumn. Pitchblack,
it thickens after each lightning flash.
I dream of Hanoi:
5 Co-ngu° Road   5. Co-ngu (kō′nōō′).
ten years of separation
the way back sliced by a frontier of hatred.
I want to bury the past
to burn the future
10 still I yearn
still I fear
those endless nights
waiting for dawn.

Brother,
15 how is Hang Dao° now?   15. **Hang Dao**
How is Ngoc Son° temple?   (häng′ dou′).
Do the trains still run   16. **Ngoc Son**
each day from Hanoi   (nōk′ sōn′).
to the neighboring towns?
20 To Bac-ninh,° Cam-giang,° Yen-bai,°   20. **Bac-ninh**
the small villages, islands   (bäk′nin′),
of brown thatch in a lush green sea?   **Cam-giang**
                                (käm′gyäng′),
                              Yen-bai (yen′bī′):
The girls   towns near Hanoi.
    bright eyes
25   ruddy cheeks
    four-piece dresses
      raven-bill scarves°   27. **raven-bill**
    sowing harvesting   **scarves:** head
      spinning weaving   scarves folded into
30 all year round,   straight-edged
the boys   triangular forms,
    ploughing   like the bill or beak
      transplanting   of a raven.
    in the fields
35   in their shops
    running across   39. **alternating**
      the meadow at evening   **songs:** songs sung in
    to fly kites   rounds, with singers
      and sing alternating songs.°   beginning at stag-
                                gered intervals.

40 Stainless blue sky,
    jubilant voices of children
stumbling through the alphabet,
    village graybeards strolling to the temple,
grandmothers basking in twilight sun,
45   chewing betel leaves°
while the children run—

Brother,
how is all that now?
Or is it obsolete?
50 Are you like me,
reliving the past,
imagining the future?
Do you count me as a friend
or am I the enemy in your eyes?
55 Brother, I am afraid
that one day I'll be with the March-North Army°
meeting you on your way to the South.
I might be the one to shoot you then
or you me
60 but please
not with hatred.

For don't you remember how it was,
you and I in school together,
plotting our lives together?
65 Those roots go deep!

Brother, we are men,
conscious of more
than material needs.
How can this happen to us
70 my friend
my foe?

45. betel (bēt′'l) **leaves:** leaves of the betel pepper. These and the nuts of the betel palm are mild stimulants, often chewed like chewing gum in Southeast Asia.

56. March-North Army: that is, the South Vietnamese army marching into North Vietnam.

FINDING COMMON GROUND

With a small group of classmates, discuss the subject of civil war in the past fifty years or so. Use this poem and the human dimension it provides as a springboard for your discussion. Be sure to establish an agenda: Decide what questions you wish to discuss. (Refer to the Quickwrite notes you took before reading the poem.) At the conclusion of your group meeting, write a summation of your discussion, highlighting the topics you talked about and the group's responses to those topics.

After you have completed writing your discussion reports, meet together as a class and exchange views. Can you, as a class, find common ground in your responses?

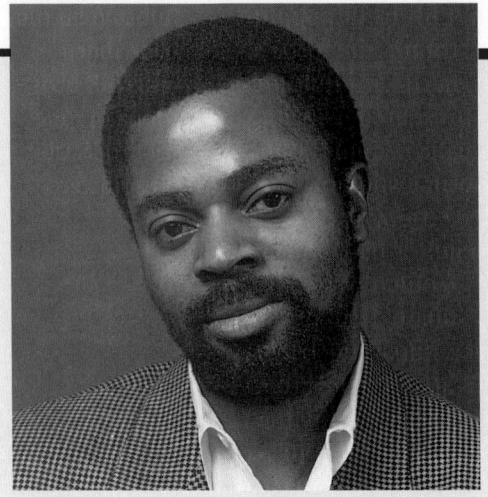

Ben Okri

(1959–)

Ben Okri grew up in the delta area of southern Nigeria. Although he later moved to London, his stories are set in Nigeria. Okri seems especially haunted by remembrances of the Nigerian Civil War (1967–1970), often called the Biafran War. This war began when the Ibo (ē′bō) people tried to secede from Nigeria and form their own state, called the Republic of Biafra. Thousands of people were killed in the civil war that ensued, and many more died of starvation. In fact, the very word *Biafra* today suggests images of swollen-bellied children holding up bowls and begging for food. The image of the starving child in Okri's story is

Ben Okri.

a stark reminder of the horror of this war.

Okri first gained recognition in England with the publication of two novels, *Flowers and Shadows* (1980) and *The Landscapes Within* (1981), and a collection of short stories, *Incidents at the Shrine* (1986). The short story that follows, "In the Shadow of War," is from *Stars of the New Curfew* (1988), Okri's first book to be published in the United States.

Okri's awards include the Commonwealth Writers' Prize for Africa and the *Paris Review* Aga Khan Prize for fiction. His 1991 novel, *The Famished Road,* received England's Booker Prize. *Songs of Enchantment,* a sequel to *The Famished Road,* appeared in 1993 and *Astonishing the Gods,* in 1995.

Before You Read

IN THE SHADOW OF WAR

Make the Connection

Siege Mentality

The United States has not known war on its own soil since 1865. But in some parts of the world, a state of war is almost constant, especially in places where ethnic and religious strife runs high.

Reading Skills and Strategies

Analyzing the Time Frame

This story is set in a village in the heart of Nigeria during the Nigerian Civil War (1967–1970). We are not given this information in

the story itself, however, because the story is told through the eyes of a child who would neither know nor understand these details. What we are given instead is a vivid picture of what the child, Omovo, sees and hears immediately around him. As you read, keep a two-column chart. In the first column, jot down details about his surroundings that Omovo gives. In the second column, note the conclusions that you draw from these details. Then, decide if it is necessary to know anything more than the story tells you about its historical context.

Elements of Literature

Point of View

Ben Okri was only eight years old when the Nigerian Civil War broke out, so it's not surprising that his main character, Omovo, is a child. Okri uses the **limited third-person point of view** to tell the story from Omovo's perspective.

War is a frightening, confusing time for children. Are the soldiers in this story good or evil? Is the veiled woman supernatural or mortal? Because Omovo's understanding is limited, the point of view deepens these enigmas.

In the Shadow of War

Ben Okri

That afternoon three soldiers came to the village. They scattered the goats and chickens. They went to the palm-frond bar and ordered a calabash[1] of palm wine. They drank amidst the flies.

Omovo watched them from the window as he waited for his father to go out. They both listened to the radio. His father had bought the old Grundig[2] cheaply from a family that had to escape the city when the war broke out. He had covered the radio with a white cloth and made it look like a household fetish.[3] They listened to the news of bombings and air raids in the interior of the country. His father combed his hair, parted it carefully, and slapped some after-shave on his unshaven face. Then he struggled into the shabby coat that he had long outgrown.

Omovo stared out of the window, irritated with his father. At that hour, for the past seven days, a strange woman with a black veil over her head had been going past the house. She went up the village paths, crossed the Express road, and disappeared into the forest. Omovo waited for her to appear.

The main news was over. The radio announcer said an eclipse of the moon was expected that night. Omovo's father wiped the sweat off his face with his palm and said, with some bitterness:

"As if an eclipse will stop this war."

"What is an eclipse?" Omovo asked.

"That's when the world goes dark and strange things happen."

"Like what?"

His father lit a cigarette.

"The dead start to walk about and sing. So don't stay out late, eh."

Omovo nodded.

"Heclipses hate children. They eat them."

Omovo didn't believe him. His father smiled, gave Omovo his ten kobo[4] allowance, and said:

"Turn off the radio. It's bad for a child to listen to news of war."

Omovo turned if off. His father poured a libation[5] at the doorway and then prayed to his ancestors. When he had finished he picked up his briefcase and strutted out briskly. Omovo watched him as he threaded his way up the path to the bus stop at the main road. When a danfo bus[6] came, and his father went with it, Omovo turned the radio back on. He sat on the windowsill and waited for the woman. The last time he saw her she had glided past with agitated flutters of her yellow smock. The children stopped what they were doing and stared at her. They had said that she had no shadow. They had said that her feet never touched the ground. As she went past, the children began to throw things at her. She didn't flinch, didn't quicken her pace, and didn't look back.

The heat was stupefying. Noises dimmed and lost their edges. The villagers stumbled about their various tasks as if they were sleepwalking. The three soldiers drank palm wine and played draughts[7] beneath the sun's oppressive glare. Omovo noticed that whenever children went past the bar the soldiers called them, talked to them, and gave them some money. Omovo ran down the stairs and slowly walked past the bar. The soldiers stared at him. On his way back one of them called him.

"What's your name?" he asked.

Omovo hesitated, smiled mischievously, and said:

"Heclipse."

The soldier laughed, spraying Omovo's face with spit. He had a face crowded with veins. His companions seemed uninterested. They swiped flies and concentrated on their game. Their guns

---

1. **calabash** (kal′ə·bash′): cup made from a calabash, a type of gourd.
2. **Grundig:** German brand of radio.
3. **fetish** (fet′ish): object believed to have magical powers.
4. **kobo** (käb′ō): Nigerian monetary unit.

5. **libation** (lī·bā′shən): liquid poured onto the ground as a sacrifice to the gods.
6. **danfo bus:** small bus. In the region surrounding Lagos, *danfo* means "in disrepair."
7. **draughts** (drafts): British game of checkers.

WORDS TO OWN

stupefying (stoo′pə·fī′iŋ) *v.* used as *adj.*: dulling the mind and senses; bringing on a state of lethargy.
oppressive (ə·pres′iv) *adj.*: hard to bear.

At Obudu Cattle Ranch on Sonkwala Mountain, Nigeria (May 1989).

were on the table. Omovo noticed that they had numbers on them. The man said:

"Did your father give you that name because you have big lips?"

His companions looked at Omovo and laughed. Omovo nodded.

"You are a good boy," the man said. He paused. Then he asked, in a different voice:

"Have you seen that woman who covers her face with a black cloth?"

"No."

The man gave Omovo ten kobo and said:

"She is a spy. She helps our enemies. If you see her, come and tell us at once, you hear?"

Omovo refused the money and went back upstairs. He repositioned himself on the windowsill. The soldiers occasionally looked at him. The heat got to him and soon he fell asleep in a sitting position. The cocks, crowing dispiritedly, woke him up. He could feel the afternoon softening into evening. The soldiers dozed in the bar. The hourly news came on. Omovo listened without comprehension to the day's casualties. The announcer <u>succumbed</u> to the stupor, yawned, apologized, and gave further details of the fighting.

Omovo looked up and saw that the woman had already gone past. The men had left the bar. He saw them weaving between the eaves of the thatch houses, stumbling through the heat-mists.

The woman was further up the path. Omovo ran downstairs and followed the men. One of them had taken off his uniform top. The soldier behind had buttocks so big they had begun to split his pants. Omovo followed them across the Express road. When they got into the forest the men stopped following the woman, and took a different route. They seemed to know what they were doing. Omovo hurried to keep the woman in view.

He followed her through the dense vegetation. She wore faded wrappers and a gray shawl, with the black veil covering her face. She had a red basket on her head. He completely forgot to determine if she had a shadow, or whether her feet touched the ground.

He passed unfinished estates, with their flaking, <u>ostentatious</u> signboards and their collapsing fences. He passed an empty cement factory: Blocks lay crumbled in heaps and the workers' sheds were deserted. He passed a baobab[8] tree,

---

8. baobab (bā′ō·bab′): thick-trunked African tree; often called "upside-down tree" because its branches look like roots.

WORDS TO OWN

succumbed (sə·kumd′) v.: yielded; gave way to.
ostentatious (äs′tən·tā′shəs) adj.: showy.

under which was the intact skeleton of a large animal. A snake dropped from a branch and slithered through the undergrowth. In the distance, over the cliff edge, he heard loud music and people singing war slogans above the noise.

He followed the woman till they came to a rough camp on the plain below. Shadowy figures moved about in the half-light of the cave. The woman went to them. The figures surrounded her and touched her and led her into the cave. He heard their weary voices thanking her. When the woman reappeared she was without the basket. Children with kwashiorkor[9] stomachs and women wearing rags led her halfway up the hill. Then, reluctantly, touching her as if they might not see her again, they went back.

He followed her till they came to a muddied river. She moved as if an invisible force were trying to blow her away. Omovo saw capsized canoes and trailing, waterlogged clothes on the dark water. He saw floating items of sacrifice: loaves of bread in polythene[10] wrappings, gourds of food, Coca-Cola cans. When he looked at the canoes again they had changed into the shapes of swollen dead animals. He saw outdated currencies on the riverbank. He noticed the terrible smell in the air. Then he heard the sound of heavy breathing from behind him, then someone coughing and spitting. He recognized the voice of one of the soldiers urging the others to move faster. Omovo crouched in the shadow of a tree. The soldiers strode past. Not long afterward he heard a scream. The men had caught up with the woman. They crowded round her.

"Where are the others?" shouted one of them.

The woman was silent.

"You dis witch! You want to die, eh? Where are they?"

She stayed silent. Her head was bowed. One of the soldiers coughed and spat toward the river.

"Talk! Talk!" he said, slapping her.

The fat soldier tore off her veil and threw it to the ground. She bent down to pick it up and stopped in the attitude of kneeling, her head still bowed. Her head was bald, and disfigured with a deep corrugation.[11] There was a livid gash along the side of her face. The bare-chested soldier pushed her. She fell on her face and lay still. The lights changed over the forest and for the first time Omovo saw that the dead animals on the river were in fact the corpses of grown men. Their bodies were tangled with riverweed and their eyes were bloated. Before he could react, he heard another scream. The woman was getting up, with the veil in her hand. She turned to the fat soldier, drew herself to her fullest height, and spat in his face. Waving the veil in the air, she began to howl dementedly. The two other soldiers backed away. The fat soldier wiped his face and lifted the gun to the level of her stomach. A moment before Omovo heard the shot a violent beating of wings just above him scared him from his hiding place. He ran through the forest screaming. The soldiers tramped after him. He ran through a mist which seemed to have risen from the rocks. As he ran he saw an owl staring at him from a canopy of leaves. He tripped over the roots of a tree and blacked out when his head hit the ground.

When he woke up it was very dark. He waved his fingers in front of his face and saw nothing. Mistaking the darkness for blindness he screamed, thrashed around, and ran into a door. When he recovered from his shock he heard voices outside and the radio crackling on about the war. He found his way to the balcony, full of wonder that his sight had returned. But when he got there he was surprised to find his father sitting on the sunken cane chair, drinking palm wine with the three soldiers. Omovo rushed to his father and pointed frantically at the three men.

"You must thank them," his father said. "They brought you back from the forest."

Omovo, overcome with delirium, began to tell his father what he had seen. But his father, smiling apologetically at the soldiers, picked up his son and carried him off to bed.

---

9. **kwashiorkor** (kwä′shē·ôr′kôr′): severe disease of young children, caused by deficiency of protein and calories and marked by stunted growth and a protruding belly.
10. **polythene** (päl′i·thēn′): term used in most English-speaking countries other than the United States for *polyethylene* (päl′ē·eth′ə·lēn′), a synthetic substance used to make tough, lightweight plastics, films, and the like.

11. **corrugation** (kôr′ə·gā′shən): groove or furrow.

- -

WORDS TO OWN
dementedly (dē·ment′id·lē) *adv.*: madly; wildly.

- -

The letter below was written on April 7, 1992, shortly after full-scale war erupted in the former Yugoslavia over land claimed by several ethnic groups. Sent from Zagreb, the historical capital of Croatia, Drakulíc's letter provides a poignant and personal history of the conflict in her homeland. She had thought, however hopefully, that her daughter might be able to live free of the past, outside the shadow of war.

Zagreb: A Letter to My Daughter

Slavenka Drakulíc

My dear R,

This morning I went to your empty room. Its tidiness was so strange: your usually unmade bed now covered with a blue quilt, a spotless desk, a chair without your T-shirts hanging from it, a carpet free of your scattered shoes. I miss you, I miss your voice, the notes that you left on the table when you came in late at night and that I read with my first morning coffee.

Today marks nine months since you left the country. I knew that you would go eventually, that you'd leave me, this house, your room where your childhood toys and books sit side by side with your evening dresses and makeup. That thought comforts me. *Living on her own will make her stronger, she will see the world, it is good for a young person to live abroad, and Vienna is only six hours away:* I keep repeating this to myself like some kind of mantra. Except that I know you didn't intend to leave so soon and so abruptly, didn't expect to leave me and your room, your university, and, more important, your friends here. You left so many things unfinished. You left because of the war.

It began on June 26, 1991, when the Yugoslav Federal Army attacked Slovenia. I was in London at that time, glued to a TV screen and a telephone. We both cried. "What do I do, Mama?" you asked on that first day of the war, but I didn't know how to advise you. What does one say to one's child when war begins? I didn't want you to panic after the army attacked Slovenia—even though it is only a hundred miles from Zagreb. One part of me could not believe that it was a real war because a real war could not happen—it would be too stupid, too absurd—here in Europe. But there was another part of me that knew it was real and knew there was no turning back.

One afternoon while I was still in London—I remember with great clarity that it was Tuesday, July 2—we were speaking on the telephone, and in the middle of our conversation you started screaming, "Mama, they're shooting next door!" I could hear the shots in the garden next to ours; I could visualize its high wall covered with roses and bunches of grapes hanging from the vine, the way the sun shone through its leaves at that particular moment of the late afternoon. And I could see you standing there, by the window overlooking it, lost and pale, trembling. You dropped the receiver, and then I heard your voice, half-cry and half-whimper, a voice I did not recognize. I don't think I have ever experienced such helplessness. I can hear it now, every sound that entered the receiver on that day, the distant hum of radio news in the background, the tram that passed by outside, and the sudden silence that followed it. Then the frightened yet soft voice of your boyfriend, Andrej, trying to calm you down. *Hush, it's nothing, it's nothing, just a drunken soldier,* he said, but it was too late, because at that moment the war began for both of us.

Recent events here have led me to think about your father, sitting in Toronto. We married when I was eighteen and he was nineteen. He was from a Serbian family and I was from a Croatian one, but that didn't mean anything to us then. World War II had long been over by the time we were born, and people of my generation were trying to escape the war's shadow, to forget and just live our lives. Your father and I never discussed our family's different nationalities. Not because it was forbidden but because it felt unimportant. Perhaps our attitude was a consequence of the repression of the Communist regime, of the brainwashing of our education system, the plan to create an artificial "Yugoslav" nation. All I know is that we were interested not in the past, in who killed whom and why, but in our own lives.

The tragedy and the paradox of this situation now is that you will have to decide to take his side or mine, to become Serb or Croat. In this war there is no middle ground. You as a Croat or a Serb become responsible for what all other Croats or Serbs do. You are reduced to a single nationality—almost sentenced to it, since nationality in a war brings a danger of getting killed just because of it. You are now in a situation where you are forced to choose, to identify with something that has always been irrelevant to you, a total abstraction. "I am from Zagreb," you used to say, and perhaps it is the only right answer—to be a citizen. But not now. Not here.

—*from Harper's Magazine*

Horror and Scream by Dinko, age 12, from Pozega, from *I DREAM OF PEACE: Images of War by Children of Former Yugoslavia.* Preface by Maurice Sendak.

MAKING MEANINGS

First Thoughts

1. At what point in Okri's story were you most worried about what might happen to Omovo?

Shaping Interpretations

Reading Check

a. What does Omovo's father say might happen during an eclipse of the moon?

b. What do the children believe about the veiled woman? What happens to her?

2. What are Omovo's feelings toward the soldiers? toward the woman?

3. Why do you think Omovo's father tells him about the eclipse? How does the boy react?

4. What is the soldier's **motive** for offering Omovo money? Why does Omovo refuse it?

5. Why do you think Omovo follows the soldiers who are following the veiled woman?

6. The story's **limited third-person point of view** means that we see the action and setting through a child's eyes. How do you interpret details that Omovo sees on the riverbank—such as the unfinished estates, the empty factory, the skeleton, the outdated currencies? (Be sure to check your reading notes.)

7. What do you think the woman brings to the people in the cave? What clues are provided?

8. At the end of the story, Omovo wakes up to find his father drinking with the soldiers. When Omovo tries to tell his father what happened, his father smiles "apologetically" at the soldiers. How do you think Omovo feels toward his father at this point? Explain.

9. How do you explain the transformations Omovo observes (canoes to dead animals to dead men)? Is he frightened? delirious? Or is there some other explanation?

10. Both Okri's story and "Zagreb: A Letter to My Daughter" (see *Connections* on page 974) concern war, but they are told from different points of view. How are the two narratives alike? How are they different?

CHOICES: Building Your Portfolio

Writer's Notebook

1. Collecting Ideas for an Informative Report

Unless you're already familiar with the Ibo people's customs and culture, reading "In the Shadow of War" probably made you curious about them. What questions come to mind as you reflect on the story and think about the Nigerian Civil War or the current situation in Nigeria? (See Okri's biography on page 970.) Jot down your thoughts, and save your notes for the Writer's Workshop on page 1053.

Analyzing a Symbol

2. Tuned In

The radio plays a **symbolic** role in Okri's story. Find all the references to the radio, and then write a short essay explaining its significance. Here are some questions to get you started: Why is the brand name of the radio (a trivial detail) given? What is significant about the radio's resembling a fetish? What does Omovo listen to on the radio? What is the difference between hearing a disembodied voice on a radio and actually seeing an event?

Comparing Literary Works

3. Holding the Center

In an essay discuss the connections between the famous poem that opens this collection (W. B. Yeats's "The Second Coming") and the two prose selections here: Ben Okri's story and Slavenka Drakulíc's letter to her daughter (see *Connections* on page 974). Find specific details and images from the Yeats poem that relate to images and details in Okri's story and in the mother's letter. You might also discuss in your essay the child's painting on page 975.

THE TRANSFORMING IMAGINATION

Yeats
Joyce
Lawrence
Bowen
Cortázar
Thomas
Naipaul
Atwood

I f one is lucky, a solitary
fantasy can totally
transform one million
realities.

—Maya Angelou, *from*
The Heart of a Woman
(American, 1928–   )

William Butler Yeats

(1865–1939)

Generally regarded as the twentieth century's greatest poet writing in English, William Butler Yeats (rhymes with *crates*) was born in Dublin, Ireland, the son of a well-known portrait painter. He came on to the literary scene when the Pre-Raphaelite movement of the mid-nineteenth century was reviving as a result of new influences from the Continent.

The revival, called Art Nouveau in the world of painting, emphasized the mysterious and unfathomable—especially those recesses of the mind just then being scrutinized by the great pioneers in psychology, Sigmund Freud and Carl Jung. Particularly in poetry, the revival recommended evocation above statement, symbols above facts, and musical measures above common speech. It was within this atmosphere that the young Yeats established a reputation as a lyricist of great delicacy and as a versifier of old tales drawn from Irish folklore and mythology. In a collection of his early poems, *The Wanderings of Oisin and Other Poems* (1889), Yeats was a romantic dreamer, evoking the mythic and heroic past of Ireland. At this stage of his career, he was a pioneer of the Celtic Revival, determined to make the Irish conscious of their heroic past.

Yeats came abruptly into a new phase in 1914 when, heeding the advice of the American poet Ezra Pound, he set out to create a stark, chiseled, and eloquently resonant kind of poetry. That same year, he published a volume aptly titled *Responsibilities*. The man who had once seen himself as the prophet-priest of Ireland's national destiny was now grappling with his own personal realities. For years, Yeats had idolized and yearned for Maud Gonne, the beautiful Irish political activist who rejected his hand and instead chose another, more politically radical suitor. Finally, Yeats accepted that rejection and in 1917, at fifty-two, married Georgie Hyde-Lees, an Englishwoman who would remain his "delight and comfort" for the next twenty-two years.

With his private life settled, Yeats then cultivated a public role. From 1922 to 1928, he served as a senator of the newly formed Irish Free State. He also toured the United States, giving ritualized readings of the poems for which, in 1923, he was awarded the Nobel Prize in literature.

As a poet, Yeats may be said to have carved out of English a language distinctly his own. Monumentally spare and unadorned, "cold and passionate as the dawn" in Yeats's own words, it confirms the basic definition of poetry as "heightened speech."

Yeats was also a dramatist, and in this role he helped his friend Lady Gregory establish Dublin's Abbey Theatre as a monument to Irish culture and high literary standards. As a playwright, he dealt in poetic drama, allegories, and other nonrealistic approaches, often making adaptations of the ceremonial choreography of the Japanese Nō theater. Although Yeats's dramas are more theatrical than dramatic, they continue to be produced by small theater groups. Some audiences may agree with Yeats himself, who felt that some of his most memorable poems are embedded, like gems, in the scripts of his plays.

Yeats dramatized himself in the grand manner, which was entirely in keeping with his accomplishments and aristocratic pretensions. Nearly ten years after his death and burial in the south of France, his body was disinterred and returned to Ireland, like that of a primitive king, with full ceremony and military pomp, on the deck of a battleship.

THE LAKE ISLE OF INNISFREE

Make the Connection

A Place of Peace

Our imagination can transport us from our busy lives to the calm of a peaceful retreat.

Quickwrite

What is your own vision of a peaceful retreat from everyday, routine life? Briefly describe your ideas, or draw a sketch of an ideal place of peace.

Elements of Literature

Verbal Music

As a young man, Yeats inherited much of the vocabulary and poetic posturing of his nineteenth-century predecessors. Phrases in the poem like "veils of the morning" and "midnight's all a glimmer" come from this old-fashioned vocabulary, and Innisfree itself represents all the impossibly idyllic, great good places that weary Victorians "on the roadway, or on the pavements gray" yearned for. Nevertheless, Yeats's lyrical skills, especially his haunting use of **assonance** (the repetition of similar vowel sounds), have created a poem whose verbal music has echoed in readers' memories for over a hundred years.

Background

Innisfree is a real island in Sligo, the beautiful county in the west of Ireland where Yeats spent many summers as a child, visiting his grandparents. Yeats once said that the poem came to him when he was in London on a dreary day. He passed a store display that used dripping water in a fountain, and he thought at once of the lake island of his childhood. Yeats's father had once read Thoreau's *Walden* to him. The bean rows and cabin in this poem are straight from Thoreau's account of his life in Walden Woods in Massachusetts.

The Lake Isle of Innisfree

William Butler Yeats

I will arise and go now, and go to Innisfree,
And a small cabin build there, of clay and wattles° made:
Nine bean-rows will I have there, a hive for the honey-bee,
And live alone in the bee-loud glade.

5 And I shall have some peace there, for peace comes dropping slow,
Dropping from the veils of the morning to where the cricket sings;
There midnight's all a glimmer, and noon a purple glow,
And evening full of the linnet's° wings.

I will arise and go now, for always night and day
10 I hear lake water lapping with low sounds by the shore;
While I stand on the roadway, or on the pavements gray,
I hear it in the deep heart's core.

2. **wattles:** interwoven twigs or branches.
8. **linnet's:** A linnet is a European songbird.

Lakeside Cottages (c. 1929) by Paul Henry. Oil on canvas (16″ × 24″).

Hugh Lane Municipal Gallery of Modern Art, Dublin.

MAKING MEANINGS

First Thoughts

1. How does the place of peace you sketched in your Quickwrite notes compare with Yeats's "lake isle"?

Shaping Interpretations

2. In the first stanza, what does the speaker say he will do?

3. What sounds does the speaker describe in the poem?

4. What does the speaker compare peace to?

5. How do the surroundings of the lake island contrast with the speaker's actual location?

6. Why do you think the speaker cannot find peace in the city setting?

Connecting with the Text

7. How might the memory of a place like Innisfree affect you if you found yourself in dreary surroundings?

Challenging the Text

8. How would you describe the **tone** of this poem? Do you think it could be called a Romantic poem? Explain why or why not.

ELEMENTS OF LITERATURE

Assonance and Alliteration

The music of this poem comes in part from Yeats's use of **assonance,** the repetition of similar vowel sounds in nearby words. The poem is also notable for a famous line (line 10) of **alliteration**—the repetition of consonant sounds in nearby words.

1. What vowel sounds dominate the first stanza?

2. What vowel sounds are emphasized by the rhyming words?

3. In line 10, what repeated consonant sounds echo the sound of lake water?

4. How would you describe the total effect of the vowel sounds in the poem? (How would the poem have been different if the poet had used more hard consonants, like *k, d,* or *p*?)

Make the Connection

The speakers of Yeats's early poems are like the lovers in nineteenth-century romantic poetry: The beloved they search for is usually not of this world. As a young writer, Yeats was captivated by the old Celtic fantasies he heard in western Ireland. Here is what he writes in *The Celtic Twilight*: "It is far easier to be sensible in cities than in many country places I could tell you of. When one walks on those gray roads at evening by the scented elder bushes of the white cottages, watching the faint mountains gathering the clouds upon their heads, one all too readily discovers beyond the thin cobweb veil of the sense, those creatures, the goblins, hurrying from the white square stone door to the north, or from the Heart Lake in the south."

Yeats said that Aengus, the speaker of this poem, is the master of love in Celtic stories.

Quickwrite

What stories, including those told in film, present romantic love as a passionate encounter that ends quickly and is forever remembered and longed for? Jot down what you think of this scenario.

The Song of Wandering Aengus

William Butler Yeats

I went out to the hazel wood,
Because a fire was in my head,
And cut and peeled a hazel wand,
And hooked a berry to a thread;
5 And when white moths were on the wing,
And moth-like stars were flickering out,
I dropped the berry in a stream
And caught a little silver trout.

When I had laid it on the floor
10 I went to blow the fire aflame,
But something rustled on the floor,
And some one called me by my name:
It had become a glimmering girl
With apple blossom in her hair
15 Who called me by my name and ran
And faded through the brightening air.

Though I am old with wandering
Through hollow lands and hilly lands,
I will find out where she has gone,
20 And kiss her lips and take her hands;
And walk among long dappled grass,
And pluck till time and times are done
The silver apples of the moon,
The golden apples of the sun.

MAKING MEANINGS

First Thoughts

1. What do you think of the romantic notion behind this poem?

Shaping Interpretations

2. Could the poem be read **symbolically** as a quest for beauty, especially the poet's search for beauty in his art? Use details in the poem to justify your response.

3. This poem makes an intensely visual impression. What **images** does the poet make you see? (Look especially at the use of color.)

4. How does the story of Aengus and his "glimmering girl" compare with Keats's romantic poem "La Belle Dame sans Merci" (page 751)?

Make the Connection

Time Marches On

Yeats first saw the scene described in this poem when he was thirty-two. He wrote the poem at the age of fifty-one. How might the passing of time transform an experience?

Quickwrite

Think of a familiar scene you have returned to over the years. Describe how time has affected your responses to the scene.

Elements of Literature

Symbol

Yeats's swans can be regarded as **symbols,** but what do they represent? As you read the poem, keep in mind that symbols, by their very nature, are open-ended: Their meanings are various and open to interpretation.

Background

Yeats's good friend and fellow writer Lady Gregory lived on an estate known as Coole Park in Ireland's County Galway. When Yeats first visited there in 1897, he was in love with Maud Gonne, the beautiful activist for Irish independence, who was more interested in politics than in marriage. This poem, written in 1916, recalls Yeats's first view of the swans; now, nineteen years later, he realizes that "All's changed."

The swans are "wild," or migratory. Like the poet, they return annually to familiar places. Yeats knew that swans were monogamous, that "lover by lover" they continued to live in a state of mated bliss denied to him. But the larger meanings of the poem lie in the relation between memory, time, loss, and the inflexible patterns of natural life represented by the swans.

The Wild Swans at Coole

William Butler Yeats

The trees are in their autumn beauty,
The woodland paths are dry,
Under the October twilight the water
Mirrors a still sky;
5　Upon the brimming water among the stones
Are nine-and-fifty swans.

The nineteenth autumn has come upon me
Since I first made my count;
I saw, before I had well finished,
10　All suddenly mount
And scatter wheeling in great broken rings
Upon their clamorous wings.

I have looked upon those brilliant creatures,
And now my heart is sore.
15　All's changed since I, hearing at twilight,
The first time on this shore,
The bell-beat of their wings above my head,
Trod with a lighter tread.

Unwearied still, lover by lover,
20　They paddle in the cold
Companionable streams or climb the air;
Their hearts have not grown old;
Passion or conquest, wander where they will,
Attend upon them still.

25　But now they drift on the still water,
Mysterious, beautiful;
Among what rushes will they build,
By what lake's edge or pool
Delight men's eyes when I awake some day
30　To find they have flown away?

MAKING MEANINGS

First Thoughts

1. What do you think is the most important word or passage in this poem? Be sure to compare your responses with those of other readers.

Shaping Interpretations

2. How is the speaker feeling as he gazes at the swans? How did he feel nineteen years earlier when he heard the beating of their wings?

3. The second, third, and fourth stanzas offer hints about the personal experience that underlies the poem. What are these hints? Why do you think the speaker's heart is "sore" (line 14)?

4. **Paraphrase,** or state in your own words, the question the speaker asks in the last stanza.

5. What qualities of the swans do you think the speaker envies? Why? What might the swans **symbolize** to the speaker?

6. How are the time of year and the time of day in this poem appropriate to its **mood**?

7. The word *awake* in the next-to-last line is mysterious at first reading. Do you think it signifies that the poem has all been a dream? Or could it mean something else? How might this word offer a clue to the **theme** of the poem?

8. How could this poem be said to be in the **elegiac** mode? How does the poem relate in **theme, tone,** and **imagery** to any of the other famous elegies in this book?

Connecting with the Text

9. Review your Quickwrite notes about how time and experience affected your response to a familiar place. How are your changed responses similar to the speaker's? How are they different?

CHOICES:
Building Your Portfolio

Writer's Notebook

1. Collecting Ideas for an Informative Report

Many scholars believe that the 1916 Easter Rebellion in Ireland against the British might not have happened without the reawakening of Irish cultural identity that Yeats and his circle spearheaded. Develop a series of questions on the Celtic Revival and on Yeats's impact on Irish nationalism. Save your notes for the Writer's Workshop on page 1053.

Analyzing the Author's Stance

2. Time and Tide

Some critics consider Yeats the first modern poet. Others see him as continuing in the Romantic tradition of Shelley and Keats. On the basis of the poems you have read, including "The Second Coming," on page 923, analyze in a brief essay Yeats's attitude toward the past and toward modern life as he experienced it. Consider also his expectations for the future.

Comparing Poems

3. Birds of a Feather

In a brief essay, compare the **themes, imagery,** and **progression of thought** in "The Wild Swans at Coole" with those of Keats's "Ode to a Nightingale" (page 755).

Creative Writing

4. Your Own "Bee-Loud Glade"

The first line of "The Lake Isle of Innisfree" is often quoted. Write your own poem or paragraph beginning with the words "I will arise and go now." Then, go on to describe your own ideal place of peace. (You may want to refer to the Quickwrite notes you made for page 979.)

James Joyce
(1882–1941)

James Joyce (1934) by Jacques-Émile Blanche.
Courtesy of the National Gallery of Ireland, Dublin.

James Joyce's masterpiece, *Ulysses* (1922), has probably had a greater effect on twentieth-century fiction than any other work of our times. Yet while he lived, Joyce was known largely as the author of what was thought a nearly unintelligible and scandalous book. Based on Homer's *Odyssey*, Joyce's *Ulysses* describes the events of a single day in Dublin, the city where Joyce grew up. And just as Homer's epic interpreted the world of the ancient Greeks, so does Joyce's epic mirror and interpret for us our own lives in the twentieth century.

Joyce was born in Rathgar, Ireland, a Dublin suburb. One of ten children of an improvident tax collector, he was educated at a series of Roman Catholic schools, but by the time he entered University College, Dublin, he had lost his faith. After graduating, he went to Paris and existed frugally by giving English lessons and writing book reviews.

In 1903, Joyce returned home to be at his dying mother's bedside. Afterward he lived briefly in a Martello Tower (a former military fortification) on the coast near Dublin, a site that has now become Ireland's James Joyce Museum. There he began an autobiographical novel, *Stephen Hero,* and also wrote some of the stories later published in *Dubliners* (1914).

In June 1904, Joyce met and fell in love with a Galway girl named Nora Barnacle. The date of their first walk, June 16, 1904, was later immortalized as Bloomsday, the date on which the action of *Ulysses* takes place. When Joyce's debts mounted, he persuaded Nora to leave Ireland with him; Joyce was never to live in Ireland again.

The penniless couple settled first in the Italian city of Trieste, where their two children, George and Lucia, were born. Joyce's book of poems, *Chamber Music,* was published in 1907 but brought him no royalties. His luck began to turn after 1914, when the influential American poet Ezra Pound reviewed *Dubliners* favorably and persuaded a British magazine to serialize *A Portrait of the Artist as a Young Man,* Joyce's rewritten version of *Stephen Hero.*

When Italy entered World War I in 1915, the Joyces left Trieste for Zurich, where Joyce worked on the early chapters of *Ulysses.* Because of sizable gifts from anonymous patrons, Joyce's financial troubles had begun to ease, but his physical problems increased. Between 1917 and 1930, he endured twenty-five operations for glaucoma and cataracts. Sometimes he was totally blind, yet he continued work on *Ulysses,* which appeared in magazine installments from 1918 through 1920, when it was suppressed.

The completed *Ulysses* did not easily find its way into print. Indeed, British printers found it so scandalous that they refused to set it in type. Finally, in 1922, Sylvia Beach, the American owner of a bookstore in Paris called Shakespeare & Co., agreed to put out an edition of one thousand copies. Many of the reviews were favorable, but the book was banned in both Britain and the United States. Not until 1934, after a famous court case, was *Ulysses* published in America. A British edition soon followed, and the book's fame spread rapidly worldwide.

Meanwhile, Joyce had completed a new novel, *Finnegans Wake,* about a Dublin barkeep named Earwicker. This complex experimental work finally was published in 1939 to inconclusive reviews. Some critics took it as a bad joke, others as madness, and Joyce, who considered it his masterpiece, grew morose over the dismal response. The Joyces, who had been living in Paris, returned to Zurich in 1940, when France fell to Nazi Germany. There Joyce became increasingly ill, his eye troubles complicated by a duodenal ulcer. He died on January 13, 1941, one month short of his fifty-ninth birthday.

Before You Read
ARABY

Make the Connection

When Dreams Meet Reality

Have you ever taken on a task that seemed vital to your happiness—or hoped, fervently, that a childhood dream would come true? Perhaps you can remember just wishing to accomplish something grand, to win the admiration and praise of others.

Reading Skills and Strategies

Using a Graphic Organizer

In "Araby," the main character has a vivid imagination that sometimes causes him to misconstrue the realities of his life. As you read the story, look for differences between the way he imagines things to be and the way they really are. List these discrepancies in a two-column comparison-contrast chart like the one below.

Imagination	Reality

Elements of Literature

Epiphany

Joyce called the moments of revelation that occur in his stories "epiphanies." Here is an excerpt from *Stephen Hero,* an early draft of Joyce's semiautobiographical novel *A Portrait of the Artist as a Young Man,* in which his hero explains what he means by *epiphany:*

A young lady was standing on the steps of one of those brown brick houses which seem the very incarnation of Irish paralysis. A young gentleman was leaning on the rusty railings of the area. Stephen as he passed on his quest heard the following fragment of colloquy out of which he received an impression keen enough to afflict his sensitiveness very severely.

The Young Lady—(drawling discreetly) . . . O, yes . . . I was . . . at the . . . cha . . . pel . . .

The Young Gentleman—(inaudibly) . . . I . . . (again inaudibly) . . . I . . .

The Young Lady—(softly) . . . O . . . but you're . . . ve . . . ry . . . wick . . . ed . . .

This triviality made him think of collecting many such moments together in a book of epiphanies. By an epiphany he meant a sudden spiritual manifestation, whether in the vulgarity of speech or of gesture or in a memorable phase of the mind itself. He believed that it was for the man of letters to record these epiphanies with extreme care, seeing that they themselves are the most delicate and evanescent of moments.   —James Joyce

In fiction, an **epiphany** is a moment of sudden insight or revelation experienced by a character.

For more on Epiphany, see the Handbook of Literary Terms.

Background

On May 14, 1894, a five-day charity bazaar came to the city of Dublin. The bazaar was called Araby, a reference to Arabia, where bazaars—markets with long rows of stalls or shops—are common. For the children of Dublin, Arabia seemed a mysterious, exotic place, very different from the dark, all-too-real streets of the dreary city in which they lived.

The house in this story is based on one in which Joyce and his family actually lived. It stood on the same "blind," or dead-end, street as the Christian Brothers' School Joyce attended. When the Joyce children moved to this musky, dark house, they missed the open fields and woods of their former home.

Araby

James Joyce

North Richmond Street, being blind, was a quiet street except at the hour when the Christian Brothers' School set the boys free. An uninhabited house of two stories stood at the blind end, detached from its neighbors in a square ground. The other houses of the street, conscious of decent lives within them, gazed at one another with brown imperturbable faces.

The former tenant of our house, a priest, had died in the back drawing-room. Air, musty from having been long enclosed, hung in all the rooms, and the waste room behind the kitchen was littered with old useless papers. Among these I found a few paper-covered books, the pages of which were curled and damp: *The Abbot,* by Walter Scott, *The Devout Communicant,* and *The Memoirs of Vidocq.*[1] I liked the last best because its leaves were yellow. The wild garden behind the house contained a central apple-tree and a few straggling bushes under one of which I found the late tenant's rusty bicycle-pump. He had been a very charitable priest; in his will he had left all his money to institutions and the furniture of his house to his sister.

When the short days of winter came dusk fell before we had well eaten our dinners. When we met in the street the houses had grown somber. The space of sky above us was the color of ever-changing violet and toward it the lamps of the street lifted their feeble lanterns. The cold air stung us and we played till our bodies glowed. Our shouts echoed in the silent street. The career[2] of our play brought us through the dark muddy lanes behind the houses where we ran the gauntlet of the rough tribes from the cottages, to the back doors of the dark dripping gardens where odors arose from the ashpits, to the dark odorous stables where a coachman smoothed and combed the horse or shook music from the buckled harness. When we returned to the street light from the kitchen windows had filled the areas. If my uncle was seen turning the corner we hid in the shadow until we had seen him safely housed. Or if Mangan's sister came out on the doorstep to call her brother in to his tea we watched her from our shadow peer up and down the street. We waited to see whether she would remain or go in and, if she remained, we left our shadow and walked up to Mangan's steps resignedly. She was waiting for us, her figure defined by the light from the half-opened door. Her brother always teased her before he obeyed and I stood by the railings looking at her. Her dress swung as she moved her body and the soft rope of her hair tossed from side to side.

Every morning I lay on the floor in the front parlor watching her door. The blind was pulled down to within an inch of the sash so that I could not be seen. When she came out on the doorstep my heart leaped. I ran to the hall, seized my books, and followed her. I kept her brown figure always in my eye and, when we came near the point at which our ways diverged, I quickened my pace and passed her. This happened morning after morning. I had never spoken to her, except for a few casual words, and yet her name was like a summons to all my foolish blood.

Her image accompanied me even in places the most hostile to romance. On Saturday evenings when my aunt went marketing I had to go to carry

---

1. *The Abbott . . . Vidocq* (vē·duk′): in order, a historical romance about Mary, Queen of Scots, by Sir Walter Scott; an 1813 religious manual written by a Franciscan friar; and the memoirs (though not actually written by François Vidocq) of a French criminal who later became a detective.
2. **career:** course; path.

WORDS TO OWN
imperturbable (im′pər·tur′bə·bəl) *adj.:* calm; impassive.
somber (säm′bər) *adj.:* gloomy.
gauntlet (gônt′lit) *n.:* series of challenges. Derived from *gatlopp,* Swedish for "running down a lane," the term originally referred to a form of military punishment in which a wrongdoer had to run between two rows of soldiers who struck him as he passed.
diverged (dī·vurjd′) *v.:* branched off; separated.

Summer Night's Dream (The Voice) (1893) by Edvard Munch.

some of the parcels. We walked through the flaring streets, jostled by drunken men and bargaining women, amid the curses of laborers, the shrill litanies[3] of shop-boys who stood on guard by the barrels of pigs' cheeks, the nasal chanting of street-singers, who sang a *come-all-you* about O'Donovan Rossa,[4] or a ballad about the troubles in our native land. These noises converged in a single sensation of life for me: I imagined that I bore my chalice[5] safely through a throng of foes. Her name sprang to my lips at moments in strange prayers and praises which I myself did not understand. My eyes were often full of tears (I could not tell why) and at times a flood from my heart seemed to pour itself out into my bosom. I thought little of the future. I did not know whether I would ever speak to her or not or, if I spoke to her, how I could tell her of my confused adoration. But my body was like a harp and her words and gestures were like fingers running upon the wires.

One evening I went into the back drawing-room in which the priest had died. It was a dark rainy evening and there was no sound in the house. Through one of the broken panes I heard

3. litanies: repeated sales cries. Literally, a litany is a prayer composed of a series of specific invocations and responses.

4. *come-all-you* . . . Rossa: A come-all-you (kum·al′yə) is a type of Irish ballad that usually begins "Come all you [young lovers, rebels, Irishmen, and so on]." O'Donovan Rossa was Jeremiah O'Donovan (1831–1915) from County Cork. He was active in Ireland's struggle against British rule in the mid–nineteenth century.

5. chalice (chal′is): cup; specifically, the cup used for Holy Communion wine. Joyce's use of the term evokes the image of a young man on a sacred mission.

Bloom's mind moves by association from the tea label to the Far East to the picture he saw of a man who, he realizes, wasn't in the Far East but in the Near East, on the Dead Sea. This makes him think of the principles behind floating and falling, which reminds him of his school days and of a teacher who cracked his knuckles. Bloom's mind, as this passage demonstrates, contains a mix of personal memories, sensations, and half-remembered bits of information.

Joyce worked on his last novel, *Finnegans Wake*, for seventeen years, from 1922 to 1939. When it appeared, some critics claimed that it announced the death of the novel as a literary form. In the book, the author has completely disappeared, and the consciousness is that of a dreamer. Finnegan is a bricklayer's helper who falls from a ladder and dies on the first page of the novel.

The experiments of others. Joyce's experiments with stream of consciousness were soon adopted by Virginia Woolf (see page 1122). (Woolf detested *Ulysses*, however, which she called illiterate and underbred.) Woolf's novel *Mrs. Dalloway*, published three years after *Ulysses* in 1925, focuses on the memories, dreams, and feelings of a central character in the course of just one day in London. Like Joyce, Woolf aimed at compressing time so that she could present an entire way of life through the detailed examination of a tiny part of it.

As the book opens, Mrs. Dalloway is on her way to buy flowers for a party she will give that evening:

James Joyce (1902) in Paris, age 20.

> Mrs. Dalloway said she would buy the flowers herself. For Lucy had her work cut out for her. The doors would be taken off their hinges; Rumpelmayer's men were coming. And then, thought Clarissa Dalloway, what a morning— fresh as if issued to children on a beach.
>
> —Virginia Woolf, *from Mrs. Dalloway*

Stream of consciousness, as this passage shows, can place unusual demands on the reader. For example, we have to infer from the context that Lucy is one of the household servants, that the doors will be removed for the party, and that Mrs. Dalloway is leaving her house to go shopping on a glorious summer's morning in London.

The narrative method that Joyce and Woolf pioneered has grown so popular that we no longer regard it as unusual. Among its practitioners have been some of the greatest twentieth-century novelists in world literature, including William Faulkner (United States) and Samuel Beckett (Ireland). Its influence has extended even into film, into the technique of *montage*, in which images shown in rapid succession suggest a train of thought.

D. H. Lawrence
(1885–1930)

David Herbert Lawrence was born in the English Midlands, the frailest child of a coal miner and a former schoolteacher. An able scholar, he too chose to become a teacher, for he resented the physical and spiritual ugliness that the mines had engendered in the Midlands.

While he was teaching, Lawrence began publishing poems and stories in magazines. In 1912, a year after publishing his first novel, Lawrence called on his former professor, Ernest Weekley, and became enchanted with Weekley's German-born wife, Frieda. Within weeks, Frieda Weekley had left her husband and three children and fled with Lawrence to Germany. For the next two years, the couple traveled through Austria and Italy. During this short time, Lawrence finished his novel *Sons and Lovers* (1913) and began work on two others, *The Rainbow* (1915) and *Women in Love* (1920).

Reviews of *Sons and Lovers* were cautiously favorable, but the moral controversy over Lawrence's work (a debate that continued for decades) was already heating up. While in Italy, Lawrence began to see industrialized England as corrosive and oppressive and the Victorian world he had known as overcivilized and prudish. He embraced a belief in "blood knowledge," in putting one's animal self in balance with one's intellect. Returning to England in 1914, he announced that "the source of all life and knowledge is in man and woman, and the source of all living is in the interchange and the meeting and mingling of these two." When a privately printed edition of Lawrence's novel *Women in Love* was published in 1920, one London critic judged it "a loathsome study of sex depravity leading youth to unspeakable disaster."

Around this time, a wealthy American writer, Mabel Dodge Luhan, who deeply admired Lawrence's work, invited him to come to Taos, New Mexico. Lawrence found New Mexico gorgeous, but he had his doubts about Americans, calling them "a host of people who must all have a sense of inferiority complex somewhere, striving to make good over everybody else." Meanwhile, in New York, those Lawrence called "the vice people" had been trying to suppress publication of *Women in Love*. Lawrence rejoiced to learn that a magistrate had declared that his novels were not obscene. On the contrary, he found they made a "distinct contribution to the literature of the present day."

By now, however, Lawrence was growing inured to the invective his work provoked on each publication day. But then he learned that he had incurable tuberculosis. Knowing he had only a few years remaining, Lawrence left the United States and returned to Italy. He now wrote continually, producing *Lady Chatterley's Lover* (1928), the work for which he is best remembered. The novel draws on his favorite theme—that of the sleeping beauty, the sexual awakening of a woman. The book drew new waves of anger from the censors. U.S. customs officers seized copies as they arrived on the docks, and the novel was banned in Britain. Ironically, as a result of this tremendous publicity, all of Lawrence's work, including his poetry, was in demand.

Giving in at last to doctors' advice, Lawrence retreated in early 1930 to a sanitarium in southern France, where he wrote every day until the end of his life. On March 2, 1930, with Frieda at his bedside, Lawrence died. He is buried at Taos.

D. H. Lawrence.

Before You Read

THE ROCKING-HORSE WINNER

Make the Connection

The Root of All Evil

The old saying that "the love of money is the root of all evil" dates back to the Bible. Over the centuries, immeasurable evil—hatred, war, murder—has sprung from the lust for riches. Even on the most personal level—wife to husband, parent to child, friend to friend—the craving for wealth can have devastating effects.

Quickwrite

Jot down some associations about money that come to your mind—and what people will do to get it.

Elements of Literature

Symbol

Beginning with the title, the image of a child's rocking horse dominates this story. The horse is associated with every important development in the plot. As this story's tragedy unfolds, the horse seems to take on more than its literal meaning as a child's toy. It is slowly transformed into a **symbol,** richly suggestive of themes and meanings for the story as a whole.

Background

Lawrence saw men and women as torn between the promptings of their instincts (which he saw as natural and therefore good) and the demanding voices of their upbringing and education (which he saw as destructive). As you read "The Rocking-Horse Winner," which is told like a modern fable, notice which voices permeate the house and what effects these voices have on the characters.

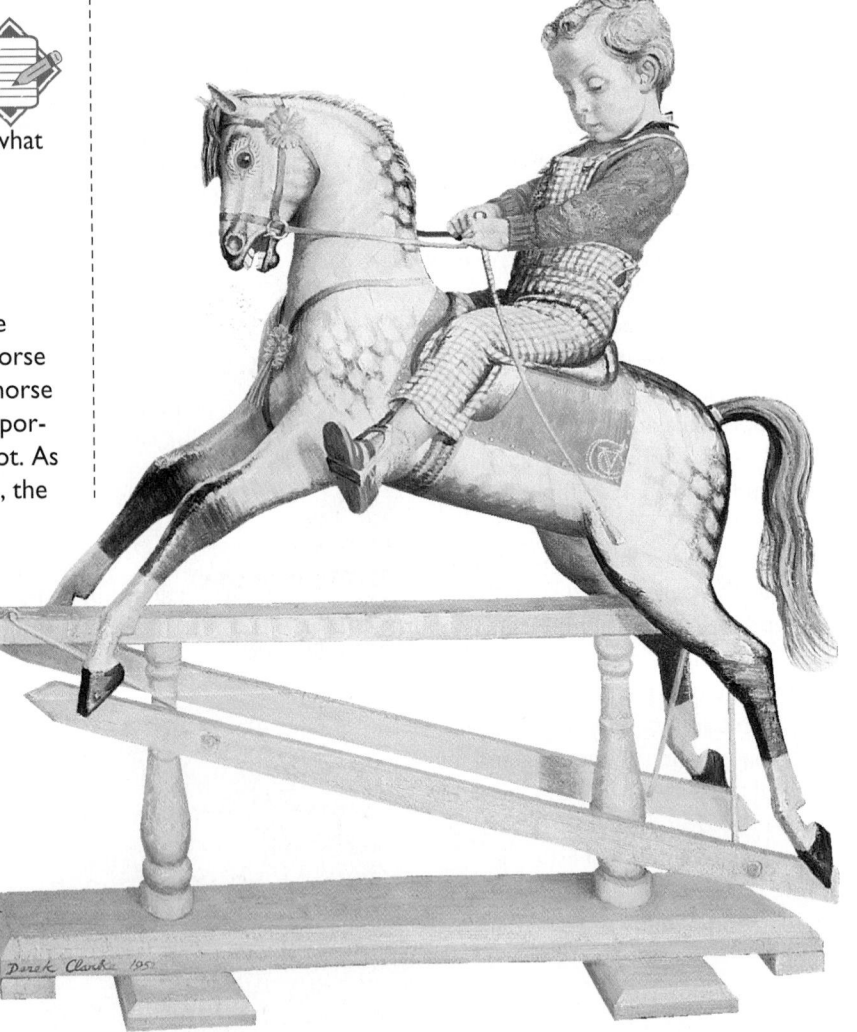

Ride a Cock Horse (detail) (c. 1952) by Derek H. Clarke.

John Noott Galleries, Broadway, Worcester, England.

The Rocking-Horse Winner

D. H. Lawrence

There was a woman who was beautiful, who started with all the advantages, yet she had no luck. She married for love, and the love turned to dust. She had bonny children, yet she felt they had been thrust upon her, and she could not love them. They looked at her coldly, as if they were finding fault with her. And hurriedly she felt she must cover up some fault in herself. Yet what it was that she must cover up she never knew. Nevertheless, when her children were present, she always felt the center of her heart go hard. This troubled her, and in her manner she was all the more gentle and anxious for her children, as if she loved them very much. Only she herself knew that at the center of her heart was a hard little place that could not feel love, no, not for anybody. Everybody else said of her: "She is such a good mother. She adores her children." Only she herself, and her children themselves, knew it was not so. They read it in each other's eyes.

There were a boy and two little girls. They lived in a pleasant house, with a garden, and they had discreet servants, and felt themselves superior to anyone in the neighborhood.

Although they lived in style, they felt always an anxiety in the house. There was never enough money. The mother had a small income,[1] and the father had a small income, but not nearly enough for the social position which they had to keep up. The father went into town to some office. But though he had good prospects, these prospects never materialized. There was always the grinding sense of the shortage of money, though the style was always kept up.

At last the mother said: "I will see if *I* can't make something." But she did not know where to begin. She racked her brains, and tried this thing and the other, but could not find anything successful. The failure made deep lines come into her face. Her children were growing up, they would have to go to school. There must be more money, there must be more money. The father, who was always very handsome and expensive in his tastes, seemed as if he never *would* be able to do anything worth doing. And the mother, who had a great belief in herself, did not succeed any better, and her tastes were just as expensive.

And so the house came to be haunted by the unspoken phrase: *There must be more money! There must be more money!* The children could hear it all the time, though nobody said it aloud. They heard it at Christmas, when the expensive and splendid toys filled the nursery. Behind the shining modern rocking horse, behind the smart doll's house, a voice would start whispering: "There *must* be more money! There *must* be more money!" And the children would stop playing, to listen for a moment. They would look into each other's eyes, to see if they had all heard. And each one saw in the eyes of the other two that they too had heard. "There *must* be more money! There *must* be more money!"

It came whispering from the springs of the still-swaying rocking horse, and even the horse, bending his wooden, champing head, heard it. The big doll, sitting so pink and smirking in her new pram,[2] could hear it quite plainly, and seemed to be smirking all the more self-consciously because of it. The foolish puppy, too, that took the place of the teddy bear, he was looking so extraordinarily foolish for no other reason but that he heard the secret whisper all over the house: "There *must* be more money!"

Yet nobody ever said it aloud. The whisper was everywhere, and therefore no one spoke it. Just as no one ever says: "We are breathing!" in spite of the fact that breath is coming and going all the time.

"Mother," said the boy Paul one day, "why don't we keep a car of our own? Why do we always use uncle's, or else a taxi?"

"Because we're the poor members of the family," said the mother.

"But why *are* we, mother?"

"Well—I suppose," she said slowly and bitterly, "it's because your father has no luck."

---

1. **income:** money from an inheritance or investments—not a salary.

2. **pram:** chiefly British for "baby carriage." The word is short for *perambulator*.

The boy was silent for some time.

"Is luck money, mother?" he asked, rather timidly.

"No, Paul. Not quite. It's what causes you to have money."

"Oh!" said Paul vaguely. "I thought when Uncle Oscar said *filthy lucker,* it meant money."

"*Filthy lucre*[3] does mean money," said the mother. "But it's lucre, not luck."

"Oh!" said the boy. "Then what *is* luck, mother?"

"It's what causes you to have money. If you're lucky you have money. That's why it's better to be born lucky than rich. If you're rich, you may lose your money. But if you're lucky, you will always get more money."

"Oh! Will you? And is father not lucky?"

"Very unlucky, I should say," she said bitterly.

The boy watched her with unsure eyes.

"Why?" he asked.

"I don't know. Nobody ever knows why one person is lucky and another unlucky."

"Don't they? Nobody at all? Does *nobody* know?"

"Perhaps God. But He never tells."

"He ought to, then. And aren't you lucky either, mother?"

"I can't be, if I married an unlucky husband."

"But by yourself, aren't you?"

"I used to think I was, before I married. Now I think I am very unlucky indeed."

"Why?"

"Well—never mind! Perhaps I'm not really," she said.

The child looked at her to see if she meant it. But he saw, by the lines of her mouth, that she was only trying to hide something from him.

"Well, anyhow," he said stoutly, "I'm a lucky person."

"Why?" said his mother, with a sudden laugh.

He stared at her. He didn't even know why he had said it.

"God told me," he asserted, brazening it out.[4]

"I hope He did, dear!" she said, again with a laugh, but rather bitter.

"He did, mother!"

"Excellent!" said the mother, using one of her husband's exclamations.

The boy saw she did not believe him; or rather, that she paid no attention to his assertion. This angered him somewhere, and made him want to compel her attention.

He went off by himself, vaguely, in a childish way, seeking for the clue to "luck." Absorbed, taking no heed of other people, he went about with a sort of stealth, seeking inwardly for luck. He wanted luck, he wanted it, he wanted it. When the two girls were playing dolls in the nursery, he would sit on his big rocking horse, charging madly into space, with a frenzy that made the little girls peer at him uneasily. Wildly the horse careered,[5] the waving dark hair of the boy tossed, his eyes had a strange glare in them. The little girls dared not speak to him.

When he had ridden to the end of his mad little journey, he climbed down and stood in front of his rocking horse, staring fixedly into its lowered face. Its red mouth was slightly open, its big eye was wide and glassy-bright.

"Now!" he would silently command the snorting steed. "Now, take me to where there is luck! Now take me!"

And he would slash the horse on the neck with the little whip he had asked Uncle Oscar for. He *knew* the horse could take him to where there was luck, if only he forced it. So he would mount again and start on his furious ride, hoping at last to get there. He knew he could get there.

"You'll break your horse, Paul!" said the nurse.

"He's always riding like that! I wish he'd leave off!" said his elder sister Joan.

But he only glared down on them in silence. Nurse gave him up. She could make nothing of him. Anyhow, he was growing beyond her.

One day his mother and his Uncle Oscar came in when he was on one of his furious rides. He did not speak to them.

"Hallo, you young jockey! Riding a winner?" said his uncle.

"Aren't you growing too big for a rocking

5. careered: rushed.

WORDS TO OWN
asserted (ə·surt'id) v.: declared.

----

3. filthy lucre (lōō'kər): riches (a derogatory usage).

4. brazening it out: acting boldly.

horse? You're not a very little boy any longer, you know," said his mother.

But Paul only gave a blue glare from his big, rather close-set eyes. He would speak to nobody when he was in full tilt. His mother watched him with an anxious expression on her face.

At last he suddenly stopped forcing his horse into the mechanical gallop and slid down.

"Well, I got there!" he announced fiercely, his blue eyes still flaring, and his sturdy long legs straddling apart.

"Where did you get to?" asked his mother.

"Where I wanted to go," he flared back at her.

"That's right, son!" said Uncle Oscar. "Don't you stop till you get there. What's the horse's name?"

"He doesn't have a name," said the boy.

"Gets on without all right?" asked the uncle.

"Well, he has different names. He was called Sansovino last week."

"Sansovino, eh? Won the Ascot.[6] How did you know this name?"

"He always talks about horse races with Bassett," said Joan.

The uncle was delighted to find that his small nephew was posted with all the racing news. Bassett, the young gardener, who had been wounded in the left foot in the war and had got his present job through Oscar Cresswell, whose batman[7] he had been, was a perfect blade of the "turf."[8] He lived in the racing events, and the small boy lived with him.

Oscar Cresswell got it all from Bassett.

"Master Paul comes and asks me, so I can't do more than tell him, sir," said Bassett, his face terribly serious, as if he were speaking of religious matters.

"And does he ever put anything on a horse he fancies?"

"Well—I don't want to give him away—he's a young sport, a fine sport, sir. Would you mind asking him himself? He sort of takes a pleasure in it, and perhaps he'd feel I was giving him away, sir, if you don't mind."

Bassett was serious as a church.

---

6. **Ascot:** famous horse race held annually at Ascot Heath in England. Several traditional British races are mentioned in the story.
7. **batman:** an officer's personal attendant.
8. **blade of the "turf":** stylish young racing fan.

The uncle went back to his nephew and took him off for a ride in the car.

"Say, Paul, old man, do you ever put anything on a horse?" the uncle asked.

The boy watched the handsome man closely.

"Why, do you think I oughtn't to?" he parried.

"Not a bit of it! I thought perhaps you might give me a tip for the Lincoln."

The car sped on into the country, going down to Uncle Oscar's place in Hampshire.

"Honor bright?" said the nephew.

"Honor bright, son!" said the uncle.

"Well, then, Daffodil."

"Daffodil! I doubt it, sonny. What about Mirza?"

"I only know the winner," said the boy. "That's Daffodil."

"Daffodil, eh?"

There was a pause. Daffodil was an obscure horse comparatively.

"Uncle!"

"Yes, son?"

"You won't let it go any further, will you? I promised Bassett."

"Bassett be damned, old man! What's he got to do with it?"

"We're partners. We've been partners from the first. Uncle, he lent me my first five shillings, which I lost. I promised him, honor bright, it was only between me and him; only you gave me that ten-shilling note I started winning with, so I thought you were lucky. You won't let it go any further, will you?"

The boy gazed at his uncle from those big, hot, blue eyes, set rather close together. The uncle stirred and laughed uneasily.

"Right you are, son! I'll keep your tip private. Daffodil, eh? How much are you putting on him?"

"All except twenty pounds," said the boy. "I keep that in reserve."

The uncle thought it a good joke.

"You keep twenty pounds in reserve, do you, you young romancer?[9] What are you betting, then?"

---

9. **romancer:** imaginative storyteller.

- -

WORDS TO OWN

parried (par′ēd) v.: replied evasively.
obscure (əb·skyoor′) adj.: little-known.
comparatively (kəm·par′ə·tiv′lē) adv.: relatively; in comparison to others.

- -

The Merry-Go-Round (20th century) by Mark Gertler.

Tate Gallery, London.

"I'm betting three hundred," said the boy gravely. "But it's between you and me, Uncle Oscar! Honor bright?"

The uncle burst into a roar of laughter.

"It's between you and me all right, you young Nat Gould,"[10] he said, laughing. "But where's your three hundred?"

"Bassett keeps it for me. We're partners."

"You are, are you! And what is Bassett putting on Daffodil?"

10. **Nat Gould:** famous British authority on racing.

"He won't go quite as high as I do, I expect. Perhaps he'll go a hundred and fifty."

"What, pennies?" laughed the uncle.

"Pounds," said the child, with a surprised look at his uncle. "Bassett keeps a bigger reserve than I do."

Between wonder and amusement Uncle Oscar was silent. He pursued the matter no further, but he determined to take his nephew with him to the Lincoln races.

"Now, son," he said, "I'm putting twenty on Mirza, and I'll put five on for you on any horse you fancy. What's your pick?"

"Daffodil, uncle."

"No, not the fiver on Daffodil!"

"I should if it was my own fiver," said the child.

"Good! Good! Right you are! A fiver for me and a fiver for you on Daffodil."

The child had never been to a race meeting before, and his eyes were blue fire. He pursed his mouth tight and watched. A Frenchman just in front had put his money on Lancelot. Wild with excitement, he flayed his arms up and down, yelling *"Lancelot! Lancelot!"* in his French accent.

Daffodil came in first, Lancelot second, Mirza third. The child, flushed and with eyes blazing, was curiously serene. His uncle brought him four five-pound notes, four to one.

"What am I to do with these?" he cried, waving them before the boy's eyes.

"I suppose we'll talk to Bassett," said the boy. "I expect I have fifteen hundred now; and twenty in reserve; and this twenty."

His uncle studied him for some moments.

"Look here, son!" he said. "You're not serious about Bassett and that fifteen hundred, are you?"

"Yes, I am. But it's between you and me, uncle. Honor bright?"

"Honor bright all right, son! But I must talk to Bassett."

"If you'd like to be a partner, uncle, with Bassett and me, we could all be partners. Only, you'd have to promise, honor bright, uncle, not to let it go beyond us three. Bassett and I are lucky, and you must be lucky, because it was your ten shillings I started winning with. . . ."

Uncle Oscar took both Bassett and Paul into Richmond Park for an afternoon, and there they talked.

"It's like this, you see, sir," Bassett said. "Master Paul would get me talking about racing events, spinning yarns, you know, sir. And he was always keen on knowing if I'd made or if I'd lost. It's about a year since, now, that I put five shillings on Blush of Dawn for him: And we lost. Then the luck turned, with that ten shillings he had from you: That we put on Singhalese. And since that time, it's been pretty steady, all things considering. What do you say, Master Paul?"

"We're all right when we're sure," said Paul. "It's when we're not quite sure that we go down."

"Oh, but we're careful then," said Bassett.

"But when are you *sure*?" smiled Uncle Oscar.

"It's Master Paul, sir," said Bassett in a secret, religious voice. "It's as if he had it from heaven. Like Daffodil, now, for the Lincoln. That was as sure as eggs."

"Did you put anything on Daffodil?" asked Oscar Cresswell.

"Yes, sir. I made my bit."

"And my nephew?"

Bassett was obstinately silent, looking at Paul.

"I made twelve hundred, didn't I, Bassett? I told uncle I was putting three hundred on Daffodil."

"That's right," said Bassett, nodding.

"But where's the money?" asked the uncle.

"I keep it safe locked up, sir. Master Paul he can have it any minute he likes to ask for it."

"What, fifteen hundred pounds?"

"And twenty! And *forty*, that is, with the twenty he made on the course."

"It's amazing!" said the uncle.

"If Master Paul offers you to be partners, sir, I would, if I were you: if you'll excuse me," said Bassett.

Oscar Cresswell thought about it.

"I'll see the money," he said.

They drove home again, and sure enough, Bassett came round to the garden house with fifteen hundred pounds in notes. The twenty pounds reserve was left with Joe Glee, in the Turf Commission[11] deposit.

"You see, it's all right, uncle, when I'm *sure*! Then we go strong, for all we're worth. Don't we, Bassett?"

"We do that, Master Paul."

"And when are you sure?" said the uncle, laughing.

"Oh, well, sometimes I'm *absolutely* sure, like about Daffodil," said the boy; "and sometimes I have an idea; and sometimes I haven't even an idea, have I, Bassett? Then we're careful, because we mostly go down."

"You do, do you! And when you're sure, like about Daffodil, what makes you sure, sonny?"

"Oh, well, I don't know," said the boy uneasily. "I'm sure, you know, uncle; that's all."

---

11. **Turf Commission:** committee of the Jockey Club, the chief governing body for horse racing. This committee operates a bank in which bettors can deposit money for future bets.

"It's as if he had it from heaven, sir." Bassett reiterated.

"I should say so!" said the uncle.

But he became a partner. And when the Leger was coming on Paul was "sure" about Lively Spark, which was a quite inconsiderable horse. The boy insisted on putting a thousand on the horse, Bassett went for five hundred, and Oscar Cresswell two hundred. Lively Spark came in first, and the betting had been ten to one against him. Paul had made ten thousand.

"You see," he said, "I was absolutely sure of him."

Even Oscar Cresswell had cleared two thousand.

"Look here, son," he said, "this sort of thing makes me nervous."

"It needn't, uncle! Perhaps I shan't be sure again for a long time."

"But what are you going to do with your money?" asked the uncle.

"Of course," said the boy, "I started it for mother. She said she had no luck, because father is unlucky, so I thought if *I* was lucky, it might stop whispering."

"What might stop whispering?"

"Our house. I *hate* our house for whispering."

"What does it whisper?"

"Why—why"—the boy fidgeted—"why, I don't know. But it's always short of money, you know, uncle."

"I know it, son, I know it."

"You know people send mother writs,[12] don't you, uncle?"

"I'm afraid I do," said the uncle.

"And then the house whispers, like people laughing at you behind your back. It's awful, that is! I thought if I was lucky——"

"You might stop it," added the uncle.

The boy watched him with big blue eyes, that had an uncanny cold fire in them, and he said never a word.

"Well, then!" said the uncle. "What are we doing?"

"I shouldn't like mother to know I was lucky," said the boy.

"Why not, son?"

"She'd stop me."

"I don't think she would."

"Oh!"—and the boy writhed in an odd way—"I *don't* want her to know, uncle."

"All right, son! We'll manage it without her knowing."

They managed it very easily. Paul, at the other's suggestion, handed over five thousand pounds to his uncle, who deposited it with the family lawyer, who was then to inform Paul's mother that a relative had put five thousand pounds into his hands, which sum was to be paid out a thousand pounds at a time, on the mother's birthday, for the next five years.

"So she'll have a birthday present of a thousand pounds for five successive years," said Uncle Oscar. "I hope it won't make it all the harder for her later."

Paul's mother had her birthday in November. The house had been "whispering" worse than ever lately, and, even in spite of his luck, Paul could not bear up against it. He was very anxious to see the effect of the birthday letter, telling his mother about the thousand pounds.

When there were no visitors, Paul now took his meals with his parents, as he was beyond the nursery control. His mother went into town nearly every day. She had discovered that she had an odd knack of sketching furs and dress materials, so she worked secretly in the studio of a friend who was the chief "artist" for the leading drapers.[13] She drew the figures of ladies in furs and ladies in silk and sequins for the newspaper advertisements. This young woman artist earned several thousand pounds a year, but Paul's mother only made several hundreds, and she was again dissatisfied. She so wanted to be first in something, and she did not succeed, even in making sketches for drapery advertisements.

She was down to breakfast on the morning of her birthday. Paul watched her face as she read her letters. He knew the lawyer's letter. As his mother read it, her face hardened and became more expressionless. Then a cold, determined

13. **drapers:** dealers in cloth and dry goods.

---

12. **writs:** legal papers; here, those demanding payment.

WORDS TO OWN
reiterated (rē·it′ə·rāt′id) *v.:* repeated.
uncanny (un·kan′ē) *adj.:* strange; eerie; weird.

---

look came on her mouth. She hid the letter under the pile of others, and said not a word about it.

"Didn't you have anything nice in the post for your birthday, mother?" said Paul.

"Quite moderately nice," she said, her voice cold and absent.

She went away to town without saying more.

But in the afternoon Uncle Oscar appeared. He said Paul's mother had had a long interview with the lawyer, asking if the whole five thousand could not be advanced at once, as she was in debt.

"What do you think, uncle?" said the boy.

"I leave it to you, son."

"Oh, let her have it, then! We can get some more with the other," said the boy.

"A bird in the hand is worth two in the bush, laddie!" said Uncle Oscar.

"But I'm sure to *know* for the Grand National; or the Lincolnshire; or else the Derby. I'm sure to know for *one* of them," said Paul.

So Uncle Oscar signed the agreement, and Paul's mother touched the whole five thousand. Then something very curious happened. The voices in the house suddenly went mad, like a chorus of frogs on a spring evening. There were certain new furnishings, and Paul had a tutor. He was *really* going to Eton,[14] his father's school, in the following autumn. There were flowers in the winter, and a blossoming of the luxury Paul's mother had been used to. And yet the voices in the house, behind the sprays of mimosa and almond blossom, and from under the piles of iridescent cushions, simply trilled and screamed in a sort of ecstasy: "There *must* be more money! Oh-h-h; there *must* be more money. Oh, now, now-w! Now-w-w—there *must* be more money!—more than ever! More than ever!"

It frightened Paul terribly. He studied away at his Latin and Greek with his tutor. But his intense hours were spent with Bassett. The Grand National had gone by: He had not "known," and had lost a hundred pounds. Summer was at hand. He was in agony for the Lincoln. But even for the Lincoln he didn't "know," and he lost fifty pounds. He became wild-eyed and strange, as if something were going to explode in him.

14. **Eton:** Eton College, a private prep school for boys, near London.

"Let it alone, son! Don't you bother about it!" urged Uncle Oscar. But it was as if the boy couldn't really hear what his uncle was saying.

"I've got to know for the Derby! I've got to know for the Derby!" the child reiterated, his big blue eyes blazing with a sort of madness.

His mother noticed how overwrought he was.

"You'd better go to the seaside. Wouldn't you like to go now to the seaside, instead of waiting? I think you'd better," she said, looking down at him anxiously, her heart curiously heavy because of him.

But the child lifted his uncanny blue eyes.

"I couldn't possibly go before the Derby, mother!" he said. "I couldn't possibly!"

"Why not?" she said, her voice becoming heavy when she was opposed. "Why not? You can still go from the seaside to see the Derby with your Uncle Oscar, if that's what you wish. No need for you to wait here. Besides, I think you care too much about these races. It's a bad sign. My family has been a gambling family, and you won't know till you grow up how much damage it has done. But it has done damage. I shall have to send Bassett away, and ask Uncle Oscar not to talk racing to you, unless you promise to be reasonable about it: Go away to the seaside and forget it. You're all nerves!"

"I'll do what you like, mother, so long as you don't send me away till after the Derby," the boy said.

"Send you away from where? Just from this house?"

"Yes," he said, gazing at her.

"Why, you curious child, what makes you care about this house so much, suddenly? I never knew you loved it."

He gazed at her without speaking. He had a secret within a secret, something he had not divulged, even to Bassett or to his Uncle Oscar.

But his mother, after standing undecided and a little bit sullen for some moments, said:

"Very well, then! Don't go to the seaside till after the Derby, if you don't wish it. But promise

WORDS TO OWN
iridescent (ir′i·des′ənt) *adj.*: showing rainbowlike colors.
overwrought (ō′vər·rôt′) *adj.*: overly excited.

me you won't let your nerves go to pieces. Promise you won't think so much about horse racing and *events,* as you call them!"

"Oh no," said the boy casually, "I won't think much about them, mother. You needn't worry. I wouldn't worry, mother, if I were you."

"If you were me and I were you," said his mother, "I wonder what we *should* do!"

"But you know you needn't worry, mother, don't you?" the boy repeated.

"I should be awfully glad to know it," she said wearily.

"Oh, well, you *can,* you know. I mean, you *ought* to know you needn't worry," he insisted.

"Ought I? Then I'll see about it," she said.

Paul's secret of secrets was his wooden horse, that which had no name. Since he was emancipated from a nurse and a nursery-governess, he had had his rocking horse removed to his own bedroom at the top of the house.

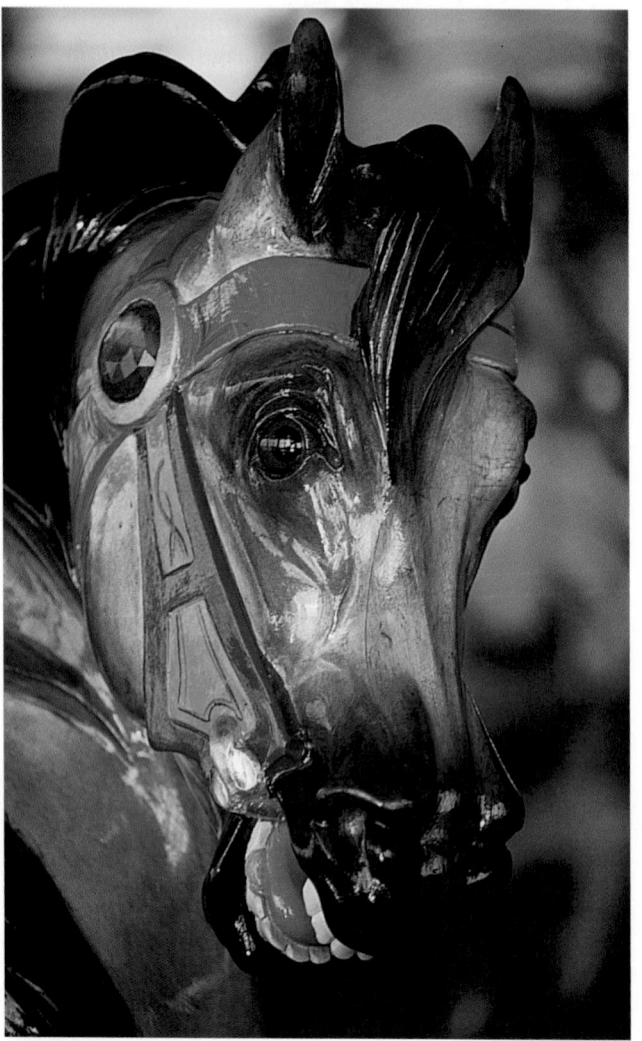

"Surely you're too big for a rocking horse!" his mother had remonstrated.

"Well, you see, mother, till I can have a *real* horse, I like to have *some* sort of animal about," had been his quaint answer.

"Do you feel he keeps you company?" she laughed.

"Oh yes! He's very good, he always keeps me company, when I'm there," said Paul.

So the horse, rather shabby, stood in an arrested prance in the boy's bedroom.

The Derby was drawing near, and the boy grew more and more tense. He hardly heard what was spoken to him, he was very frail, and his eyes were really uncanny. His mother had sudden strange seizures of uneasiness about him. Sometimes, for half an hour, she would feel a sudden anxiety about him that was almost anguish. She wanted to rush to him at once, and know he was safe.

Two nights before the Derby, she was at a big party in town, when one of her rushes of anxiety about her boy, her firstborn, gripped her heart till she could hardly speak. She fought with the feeling, might and main, for she believed in common sense. But it was too strong. She had to leave the dance and go downstairs to telephone to the country. The children's nursery-governess was terribly surprised and startled at being rung up in the night.

"Are the children all right, Miss Wilmot?"

"Oh yes, they are quite all right."

"Master Paul? Is he all right?"

"He went to bed as right as a trivet. Shall I run up and look at him?"

"No," said Paul's mother reluctantly. "No! Don't trouble. It's all right. Don't sit up. We shall be home fairly soon." She did not want her son's privacy intruded upon.

"Very good," said the governess.

It was about one o'clock when Paul's mother and father drove up to their house. All was still. Paul's mother went to her room and slipped off

---

WORDS TO OWN
remonstrated (ri·män′strāt′id) *v.:* protested.
arrested (ə·rest′id) *v.* used as *adj.:* checked or halted in motion.

her white fur cloak. She had told her maid not to wait up for her. She heard her husband downstairs, mixing a whiskey and soda.

And then, because of the strange anxiety at her heart, she stole upstairs to her son's room. Noiselessly she went along the upper corridor. Was there a faint noise? What was it?

She stood, with arrested muscles, outside his door, listening. There was a strange, heavy, and yet not loud noise. Her heart stood still. It was a soundless noise, yet rushing and powerful. Something huge, in violent, hushed motion. What was it? What in God's name was it? She ought to know. She felt that she knew the noise. She knew what it was.

Yet she could not place it. She couldn't say what it was. And on and on it went, like a madness.

Softly, frozen with anxiety and fear, she turned the door handle.

The room was dark. Yet in the space near the window, she heard and saw something plunging to and fro. She gazed in fear and amazement.

Then suddenly she switched on the light, and saw her son, in his green pajamas, madly surging on the rocking horse. The blaze of light suddenly lit him up, as he urged the wooden horse, and lit her up, as she stood, blonde, in her dress of pale green and crystal, in the doorway.

"Paul!" she cried. "Whatever are you doing?"

"It's Malabar!" he screamed in a powerful, strange voice. "It's Malabar!"

His eyes blazed at her for one strange and senseless second, as he ceased urging his wooden horse. Then he fell with a crash to the ground, and she, all her tormented motherhood flooding upon her, rushed to gather him up.

But he was unconscious, and unconscious he remained, with some brain fever. He talked and tossed, and his mother sat stonily by his side.

"Malabar! It's Malabar! Bassett, Bassett, I *know*! It's Malabar!"

So the child cried, trying to get up and urge the rocking horse that gave him his inspiration.

"What does he mean by Malabar?" asked the heart-frozen mother.

"I don't know," said the father stonily.

"What does he mean by Malabar?" she asked her brother Oscar.

"It's one of the horses running for the Derby," was the answer.

And, in spite of himself, Oscar Cresswell spoke to Bassett, and himself put a thousand on Malabar: at fourteen to one.

The third day of the illness was critical: They were waiting for a change. The boy, with his rather long, curly hair, was tossing ceaselessly on the pillow. He neither slept nor regained consciousness, and his eyes were like blue stones. His mother sat, feeling her heart had gone, turned actually into a stone.

In the evening, Oscar Cresswell did not come, but Bassett sent a message, saying could he come up for one moment, just one moment? Paul's mother was very angry at the intrusion, but on second thoughts she agreed. The boy was the same. Perhaps Bassett might bring him to consciousness.

The gardener, a shortish fellow with a little brown moustache and sharp little brown eyes, tiptoed into the room, touched his imaginary cap to Paul's mother, and stole to the bedside, staring with glittering, smallish eyes at the tossing, dying child.

"Master Paul!" he whispered. "Master Paul! Malabar came in first all right, a clean win. I did as you told me. You've made over seventy thousand pounds, you have; you've got over eighty thousand. Malabar came in all right, Master Paul."

"Malabar! Malabar! Did I say Malabar, mother? Did I say Malabar? Do you think I'm lucky, mother? I knew Malabar, didn't I? Over eighty thousand pounds! I call that lucky, don't you, mother? Over eighty thousand pounds! I knew, didn't I know I knew? Malabar came in all right. If I ride my horse till I'm sure, then I tell you, Bassett, you can go as high as you like. Did you go for all you were worth, Bassett?"

"I went a thousand on it, Master Paul."

"I never told you, mother, that if I can ride my horse, and *get there,* then I'm absolutely sure—oh, absolutely! Mother, did I ever tell you? I *am* lucky!"

"No, you never did," said his mother.

But the boy died in the night.

And even as he lay dead, his mother heard her brother's voice saying to her: "My God, Hester, you're eighty-odd thousand to the good, and a poor devil of a son to the bad. But, poor devil, poor devil, he's best gone out of a life where he rides his rocking horse to find a winner."

D. H. Lawrence on Money

A theme that runs through nearly all Lawrence's works is the celebration of life—the human energy and force that express the joy of existence. Opposing this natural energy is materialism, which Lawrence believed misdirects our energies and warps the soul.

Rolf Gardiner, one of Lawrence's first admirers, managed a large farm in Dorset. In 1926, Lawrence wrote to Gardiner: "And don't be too ernest—earnest—how does one spell it?—nor overburdened by a mission: neither too self-willed. One must be simple and direct, and a bit free from oneself above all."

In another letter to Gardiner, Lawrence makes a rare, brief mention of the evils of materialism.

> Villa Mirenda, Scandicci
> Florence
> 18 Dec., 1927

Dear Rolf Gardiner,

. . . If I were talking to the young, I should say only one thing to them: Don't you live just to make money, either for yourself or for anybody else. Don't look on yourself as a wage slave. Try to find out what life itself is, and live. Repudiate the money idea.

And then I'd teach 'em, if I could, to dance and sing together. The togetherness is important.

But they must first overthrow in themselves the money-fear and money-lust. . . .

MAKING MEANINGS

First Thoughts

1. What did you think of the mother's treatment of her son? of her outlook on life generally?

Shaping Interpretations

2. How do you explain the ever louder voices in the house? In your opinion, why do only Paul and his sisters hear and react to the voices?

3. How would you describe what has happened to Paul by the end of the story?

4. What might the rocking horse **symbolize**?

Reading Check

a. The opening, written in the style of a fairy tale, tells of a woman who "had no luck." How had she been unlucky? What else does the writer tell directly about the mother's **character**?

b. How does Paul's mother define *luck* when Paul asks her what it means? What is Paul's confusion about the word *luck*?

c. What step does Paul take to ease his mother's anxiety over the family's debts? How does she react when she learns of her birthday surprise?

d. Who is Bassett? Why does he keep Paul's secret?

e. Does Paul solve his mother's problem? Why or why not?

5. State the **theme** of the story, using the words *love* and *money*.

6. How would you describe the **tone** of the story?

Connecting with the Text

7. Review your Quickwrite notes. Can you think of any current examples of tragedy resulting from an obsession with wealth?

Challenging the Text

8. In what ways is the story's ending a distortion of the usual fairy-tale ending? What do you think of Lawrence's decision to end it as he did?

Before You Read
SNAKE

Make the Connection
Lords of Life
Are we the rulers of the natural world, or does nature in some way rule us? D. H. Lawrence, who was intensely interested in this question, came down on the side of nature. He believed that we are connected to nature through our instincts and that we are misguided by a social education that teaches us to rely on our intellect and distrust our senses. Thus, it is not surprising that when Lawrence writes about a snake, his vision is far from the conventional literary one that sees the snake as loathsome and evil.

Quickwrite

Write down what you see, hear, and feel when you imagine a snake.

Background
The water trough in the first line was part of the garden fountain at a house where Lawrence lived in the early 1920s. The house was in the outskirts of the Sicilian town of Taormina, not far from the snowcapped and ever-smoking Mount Etna, one of the world's active volcanoes. This **setting** is important in that "the burning bowels of the earth" (line 20) is not just a figurative description but also a literal one. It is from this "infernal region" that the snake emerges, recalling the Genesis account (page 416) of the garden of Eden.

Bacchus on Mt. Vesuvius. Fresco from the Casa del Centenario, Pompeii, 1st century A.D.).

Museo Archeologico Nazionale, Naples, Italy.

Snake

D. H. Lawrence

A snake came to my water trough
On a hot, hot day, and I in pajamas for the heat,
To drink there.

In the deep, strange-scented shade of the great dark carob tree
5 I came down the steps with my pitcher
And must wait, must stand and wait, for there he was at the
    trough before me.

He reached down from a fissure° in the earth-wall in the gloom
And trailed his yellow-brown slackness soft-bellied down, over
    the edge of the stone trough
And rested his throat upon the stone bottom,
And where the water had dripped from the tap, in a small
10 clearness,
He sipped with his straight mouth,
Softly drank through his straight gums, into his slack long body,
Silently.

Someone was before me at my water trough,
15 And I, like a second-comer, waiting.

He lifted his head from his drinking, as cattle do,
And looked at me vaguely, as drinking cattle do,
And flickered his two-forked tongue from his lips, and mused a
    moment,
And stooped and drank a little more,
Being earth-brown, earth-golden from the burning bowels of
20 the earth
On the day of Sicilian July, with Etna smoking.

7. fissure: (fish′ər): long, narrow, deep cleft or crack.

D. H. LAWRENCE 1007

The voice of my education said to me
He must be killed,
For in Sicily the black black snakes are innocent, the gold are
    venomous.

25 And voices in me said, If you were a man
You would take a stick and break him now, and finish him off.

But I must confess how I liked him,
How glad I was he had come like a guest in quiet, to drink at
    my water trough
And depart peaceful, pacified, and thankless
30 Into the burning bowels of this earth.

Was it cowardice, that I dared not kill him?
Was it perversity, that I longed to talk to him?
Was it humility, to feel so honored?
I felt so honored.

35 And yet those voices:
If you were not afraid, you would kill him!

And truly I was afraid, I was most afraid,
But even so, honored still more
That he should seek my hospitality
40 From out the dark door of the secret earth.

He drank enough
And lifted his head, dreamily, as one who has drunken,
And flickered his tongue like a forked night on the air, so
    black,
Seeming to lick his lips,
45 And looked around like a god, unseeing, into the air,
And slowly turned his head,
And slowly, very slowly, as if thrice adream
Proceeded to draw his slow length curving round
And climb again the broken bank of my wall-face.

50 And as he put his head into that dreadful hole,
And as he slowly drew up, snake-easing his shoulders, and
    entered further,
A sort of horror, a sort of protest against his withdrawing into
    that horrid black hole,
Deliberately going into the blackness, and slowly drawing
    himself after,
Overcame me now his back was turned.

55 I looked around, I put down my pitcher,
I picked up a clumsy log
And threw it at the water trough with a clatter.

I think it did not hit him;
But suddenly that part of him that was left behind convulsed in
    undignified haste,

Mt. Etna erupting, from *Campi—Phlegraei:
Observations on the Volcanos* (1776–1779)
by Sir William Hamilton. Plates etched and
hand-colored by Petro Fabris.

60 Writhed like lightning, and was gone
Into the black hole, the earth-lipped fissure in the wall-front
At which, in the intense still noon, I stared with fascination.

And immediately I regretted it.
I thought how paltry, how vulgar, what a mean act!
I despised myself and the voices of my accursed human
65   education.

And I thought of the albatross,°
And I wished he would come back, my snake.

For he seemed to me again like a king,
Like a king in exile, uncrowned in the underworld,
70 Now due to be crowned again.

And so, I missed my chance with one of the lords
Of life.
And I have something to expiate:°
A pettiness.

66. albatross (al′bə·trôs′): allusion to large seabird used as a symbol of guilt in the poem *The Rime of the Ancient Mariner* by Samuel Taylor Coleridge (see page 684).

73. expiate (eks′pē·āt′): atone, or make amends, for.

MAKING MEANINGS

First Thoughts

1. How did you respond to the speaker's feelings for the snake? How do your responses compare with the responses you recorded in your Quickwrite notes and with other readers' responses?

Shaping Interpretations

2. Describe the **setting** of the poem. What details help you see, hear, and feel what the speaker is experiencing?

3. Find the lines that describe the forces in **conflict** within the speaker's mind.

4. Why do you think the speaker refers to himself as "a second-comer" in line 15? How does he see himself in relationship to the snake?

5. List all the **similes** and **metaphors** used to describe the snake. What do these comparisons reveal about the speaker's attitude toward the snake?

6. Why does the speaker throw a log at the snake? Why does he immediately regret his action?

7. In line 66, the speaker connects the snake with the albatross, the central **symbol** in Coleridge's *The Rime of the Ancient Mariner* (page 684). How does Lawrence's experience connect with the ancient Mariner's story?

8. What do you think Lawrence's snake **symbolizes**?

9. What is the effect of the speaker's referring to "my snake" in line 67? How does this detail add to the speaker's sense of transgression, or wrongdoing, at the end of the poem?

10. Where in this poem can you find **allusions** to Pluto (or Hades), the king of the underworld in Greek mythology? Where can you spot allusions to the serpent in the Book of Genesis (see page 416)?

Extending the Text

11. Can you think of occasions when the voices of our "human education" might make us do something that would later cause shame or regret?

12. What solution does the poem suggest to the conflict between nature and culture, or "human education"? How do you feel about the poem's message?

CHOICES: Building Your Portfolio

Writer's Notebook

1. Collecting Ideas for an Informative Report

In linking Paul's illness to his emotional state, Lawrence draws on his knowledge of a subject that has lured writers and thinkers for centuries: the mind-body connection. Brainstorm to develop a set of questions you could use to investigate the current status of research on the role of the emotions in health and illness. Save your work for the Writer's Workshop on page 1053.

Supporting a Thesis

2. Keeping Up with the Joneses

The mother's extravagance results partly from social pressure—the need to keep up appearances. Find evidence in the story to support this statement, and write a brief essay presenting what you find.

Exploring a Theme

3. A Sense of Sin

In the Genesis account of the temptation of Adam and Eve (page 416), in Coleridge's *The Rime of the Ancient Mariner* (page 684), and in Lawrence's "Snake," there is a sense that a sacred prohibition has been violated. In a brief essay, explore the ways in which this **theme** of transgression is handled in the three works. Be sure to identify the violation and its results.

Creative Writing

4. Inside His Mind

Review the information on stream of consciousness as a narrative form (pages 993–994), and write a sketch in which you reveal the workings of Paul's mind as he rides his rocking horse to that tragic victory. What is he sensing? What associations come to his mind?

Creative Writing

5. Close Encounters

Write a free-verse poem in which you describe an encounter you had with an animal. Before you begin, think about whether the encounter taught you anything about nature. As Lawrence does, use **sensory images** and **figures of speech** to make the scene come alive.

Playwriting / Performance

6. Staging the Mysterious

Working with a partner or a small group, outline notes for how you would prepare a portion of Lawrence's story for the stage. How would you set the scene? What kinds of lighting and music would you use? How would you communicate the more intangible or mysterious aspects of the story, like what really happens to Paul as he rides? Then get together with other groups in your class to compare notes. If you feel you have some good ideas, try giving a live performance. (Be sure to read the discussion of the film version of the story, on page 1015.)

Reading Skills and Strategies

VOCABULARY: FORMATION OF NEW WORDS

Much as your vocabulary is constantly growing and changing as you learn, the English language is constantly growing and changing to accommodate what is new and different. There are at least four ways in which new words are commonly formed. Established words are joined to form new words, called **compounds** or **blends.** Words are shortened in a process called **shortening.** And when established words are used in new ways and assume new grammatical functions, they are said to undergo a **functional shift.**

Compounds. Speakers create **compounds** to describe or name something new with words that already exist. *Briefcase,* for example, is a compound formed to name the piece of luggage designed to encase legal documents, called briefs.

Blends. Like compounds, **blends** come from two or more established words. However, blends partially omit or slightly alter at least one of the established words in the process. Consequently, blends are sometimes more difficult to recognize and analyze than compounds. Would you have guessed that the common word *alone* is a blend of *all* and *one*?

Shortenings. Established words are sometimes abbreviated for the sake of convenience. The resulting new words are called **shortenings.** If the length of a frequently used word is cumbersome, you might give the word a "nickword" of sorts, just as you might give someone you know well a nickname. For instance, the more you talk about telephones, the more inclined you might be to call them *phones.*

Acronyms and back-formations are two specific kinds of shortenings. An **acronym,** the most extreme shortening, is a word formed from the first letter or letters of the words in a name or phrase. *Scuba* is an acronym for s(elf)-c(ontained) u(nderwater) b(reathing) a(pparatus).

A **back-formation** is a shortening that results when a syllable or syllables, usually affixes, are removed from a word. Affixes are usually added on, not taken away—thus the name back-formation. The word *photo,* for example, is a back-formation from *photograph.*

Functional shifts. Established words can assume new grammatical functions and meanings, resulting in **functional shifts.** For example, the noun *telephone* very quickly gave rise to a new verb, *to telephone,* meaning "to speak to by telephone."

New Word Forms		
Form	Example	Analysis
compound	sweatshop	sweat + shop, to depict an unhealthy workplace
blend	smog	sm(oke) + (f)og, to describe fog polluted by smoke
shortening	flu	shortening of *influenza* by removing syllables
acronym	radar	abbreviation of ra(dio), d(etection), a(nd) r(anging)
back-formation	sulk	removal of y affix from adjective *sulky* to form noun meaning "a state of sullen aloofness"
functional shift	spoon (v.)	Noun for a utensil shifted to serve as a transitive verb, as in "to spoon soup into a bowl."

Try It Out

Speculate about how each of the following words was formed. Then, based on the way you think each one was formed, identify it as one of the following: compound, blend, shortening, back-formation, or result of a functional shift. Confirm or correct your guesses by finding each word in a dictionary.

bosun • overwrought • taxi • curio • parry

Film as Literature: More Than Meets the Eye

by **William V. Costanzo**

The Anglo-Saxons who assembled in great wooden halls to hear the *Beowulf* bard recite his epic poem of monsters and heroic feats lived in a land of menacing forests and incessant warfare. We can picture the bard singing his tale to the strumming of a harp while his listeners huddled round, delighted to be part of the evening's entertainment, protected from the mournful wind, enthralled by the exploits of their epic hero, their dragon slayer. Nearly thirteen hundred years later, we live in a different world. The dazzling variety of modern life reflected in the windows of our shopping malls and in the images of music videos would have baffled the Anglo-Saxons or even the Victorians. Yet the basic human need for stories has never been stronger than it is today. We still enjoy listening to stories. Our bookstores teem with works of fiction. But for the past one hundred years, we have been turning with increasing relish to a new form of storytelling: the movies.

Audience wearing 3-D electronic headsets.

Enlarging the House of Fiction

Statistics tell us that Americans now spend more time watching movies—in theaters, on television, and on VCRs—than they do reading books. Does this mean that movies are replacing literature? Or does it mean that movies are enlarging the house of fiction, building new rooms out of earlier literary forms, just as the sonnet grew from a tradition of love songs and the novel grew out of such forms as the novella and the pastoral romance. If films can be understood and appreciated as literature, then some attention to film literacy—our ability to view, interpret, analyze, evaluate, and communicate with movies—can enrich our understanding and appreciation of good films.

Seeing film as literature helps us to trace important continuities in the stream of stories that has flowed from the lips of bards, the pens of novelists, and the cameras of our film directors. For example, a comparative look at heroes and their adversaries—from Beowulf and Macbeth to Frankenstein and Forrest Gump—might reveal common themes about humanity: what it means to be human or to feel alienated from human society. A comparative look at the characters of Shakespeare, the Brontës, and Jerry Seinfeld might show a gradual decline in the stature of our heroes and heroines, from nobility to common citizens and antiheroes. By focusing this way on **content,** what literature is about, we can take a measure of our personal values and cultural beliefs.

We can also focus on **craft,** how different types of literature communicate their meanings. In Britain, storytelling began as a spoken art and evolved into a written literary tradition. New tools for shaping messages developed with each new literary form. The *Beowulf* poet was a master of rhythm, alliteration, and the other tools of epic poetry. Dickens mastered dialogue, description, and other elements of written fiction to tell his stories in the form of novels. The craft of cinema borrows from these previous forms yet offers something new. Like other narrative artists, filmmakers give us stories with strong characters and settings depicted from particular points of view. But the filmmaker's toolbox includes cameras, actors, microphones, and lights. With such instruments of sight and sound, filmmakers coax their characters and settings to life.

Elements of Fiction, Elements of Film

Character, setting, plot, mood, symbol, theme, point of view: these elements are found in nearly every work of fiction, on the page or screen. Writers shape these elements with words. Filmmakers use actors and technology as well, moving through distinct stages of development.

Typically, a film begins with an idea. The idea for a story may be sketched out in a brief synopsis or in a longer treatment, which may contain some scenes, character development, and dialogue. Later, the complete story may be fleshed out in a screenplay or in a shooting script, a shot-by-shot blueprint for the film. This is the development stage of film production.

The next stage, preproduction, consists of preparations for the shooting. Here the elements of character, setting, and symbol begin to take on physical forms. The actors are cast; the locations are selected; the sets and props are built.

Production, the third stage, is led by the director, whose job is to turn the shooting script into a film. Particular attention is given to mood and point of view. For every shot, the camera must be placed to show the action from a particular vantage point. For example, a close-up might emphasize a revealing gesture or some symbolic detail. Every shot must also be lighted. Bright illumination (high-key lighting) might create a cheerful mood; dim light and contrasting shadows (low-key lighting) might communicate tension and suspense. Meanwhile, a sound crew works the microphones, recording dialogue and sound effects.

Other hands join in during the postproduction stage. The editor assembles each day's film into a continuous sequence, trimming here, inserting

Production shot from Terry Gilliam's film *The Adventures of Baron Munchausen* (1989).

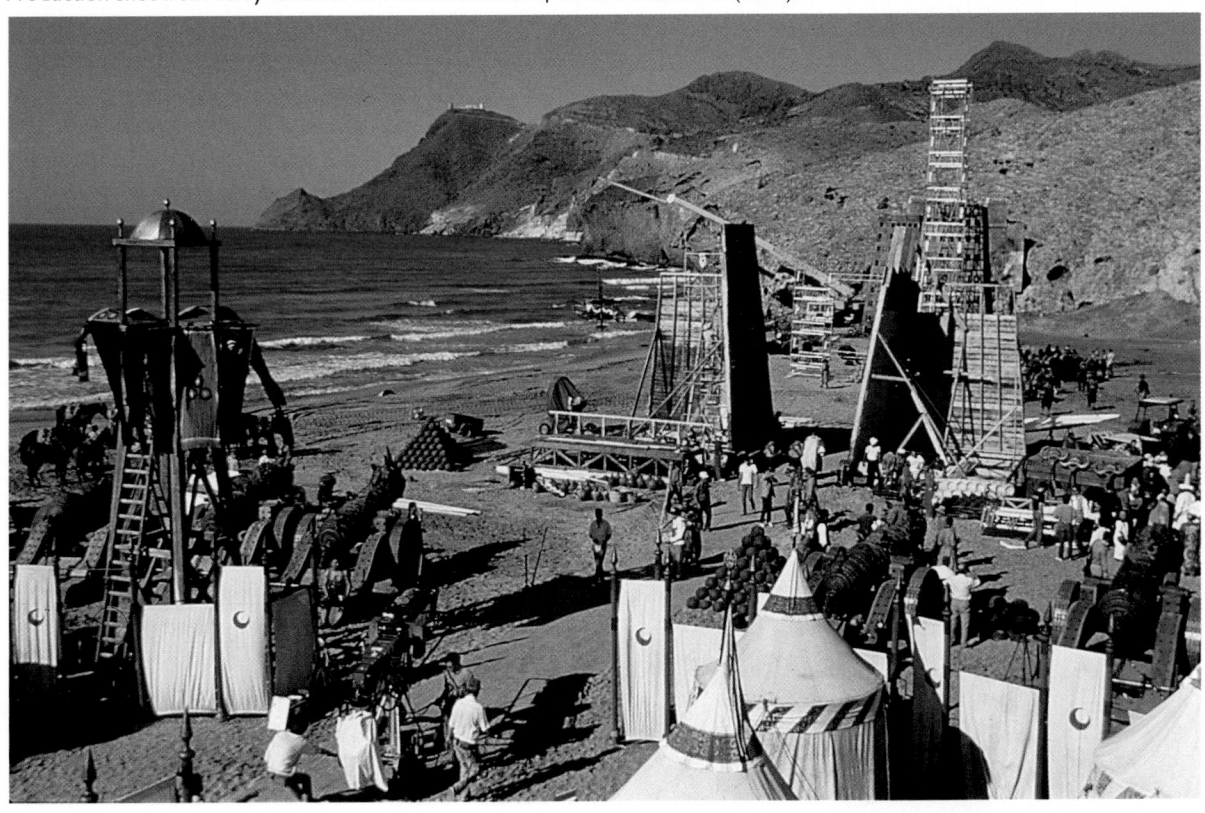

there, until a final cut is approved by the director. A sound lab may add music, sound effects, dialogue, and perhaps a voice-over narration. An optical lab may contribute special effects. By the time the film is ready for release, the original idea has gone through many transformations. Creative artists, technicians, and business interests have all shaped the final outcome. Unlike most written works, few movies have a single author.

The Art of Adaptation

Nearly all the heroes of great literature have appeared in movies. From Sir Gawain and Macbeth to Gulliver and Robinson Crusoe, from Jane Eyre and David Copperfield to Stephen Dedalus and Orlando, the leading figures of British fiction and their imagined worlds have been adapted for the screen. Why so many adaptations? Some reasons are economic. A published book offers a ready-made plot and a receptive audience; it takes less work to develop the story or publicity. But the appeal of adaptations lies in something deeper. The stories that have endured as classics speak to us across broad boundaries of time and space. We like to

Poster from James Whale's film version of *Frankenstein* (1931).

A scene from Michael Anderson's film version of *1984*.

have them told again in a familiar medium. But what happens when a book is translated into the language of film?

A good way to explore the differences between film and written fiction is to compare a book to its film version. When you read a book like George Orwell's *1984* or Mary Shelley's *Frankenstein* before or after you see the film version, you notice differences in your experience. Some differences are a matter of content. For example, the 1931 film adaptation of *Frankenstein* eliminates the seagoing narrator and simplifies the plot as a struggle between the monster and its victims. Other differences lie in the medium itself, the particular methods by which films appeal to our emotions and imagination. Shelley's description provokes our visual imagination but leaves more room for us to picture the monster than do Boris Karloff's makeup and performance. Shelley's nineteenth-century prose is a steady, rational vehicle for ideas that seem to be eclipsed by the frightening faces, places, and special effects on the screen.

Every film adaptation is a performance, an interpretation of the text. Just as an orchestra can translate a sheet of music into the vibrant sounds of a recorded symphony, the creators of a film cooperate to transform the written work into a performance, an experience that will be seen and heard in countless movie theaters. Of course, every reading of a novel or short story is an interpretation, too. When we read, we cast the characters in our imagination. We construct sets and create the sound effects on a kind of mental movie screen. That's why we're often disappointed when we see a film adapted from a book we like. It's also why a movie sometimes limits our experience of reading; if we see the movie first, its images keep getting in the way. Yet a faithful adaptation can be rewarding in its own right.

"The Rocking-Horse Winner": A Case in Point

Consider "The Rocking-Horse Winner" (page 997). D. H. Lawrence's story opens like a fable. "There was a woman who was beautiful, who started with all the advantages, yet she had no luck." If you were filming the story, how would you capture its fairy-tale quality? How would you communicate the abstract concept that the woman had no luck? The story's narrator goes on to say that "she felt she must cover up some fault in herself. Yet what it was that she must cover up she never knew." Without a narrator, how would your film convey this insight into her character? You might invent a scene to reveal the woman's feelings. You might direct the actor to behave a certain way. Yet how can you know if your audience will interpret her performance as intended? How can you even know that the audience will think she's beautiful?

Already, your efforts to adapt the story have come up against some basic differences between written language and the visual language of film. First, abstract concepts like beauty and luck are easier to specify in words. How do you show luck on the screen without showing someone who is lucky? Second, writers can make precise statements through narration while filmmakers generally depend on the viewer's interpretation of images and sounds. How long would it take for a film to show that a character doesn't know what she feels she must cover up? Such a complex thought might require a whole scene, drawing on the resources of acting, camera work, lighting, and music to capture its complexities. On the other hand, a single shot of the woman's home at Christmas might convey in an instant what a writer couldn't describe in a thousand words.

Beyond these questions of setting, character, and theme is the question of genre. What kind of story is it? A moral fable? A supernatural tale? A psychological study of a dysfunctional family? How do other stories—or films—of this kind create the right mood for their genre? How, for example, would you shoot the frenzied rocking-horse scenes? How would you handle the voices in the house that whisper "There *must* be more money"?

"The Rocking-Horse Winner" was adapted in 1949 by Anthony Pelissier, a British film director. Pelissier expands Lawrence's story to a ninety-minute film. He develops some characters, like the father and the nurse, and invents other characters, including a repugnant pawnbroker and an insolent bailiff. Uncle Oscar becomes a middle-aged gentleman, reproachful to his sister but kindly to her son. Pelissier also adds some scenes. Paul first meets Bassett in the gardener's shed. This provides an opportunity to reveal some background information through dialogue. Paul gets the rocking horse on Christmas Day, an occasion for displaying the

A scene from Anthony Pelissier's film version of *The Rocking Horse Winner* (1949).

material values of the household. A scene in which Paul's mother puts her children to sleep is set against a scene between the children and the nurse, both scenes working together to reveal the mother's haughtiness and the limits of her maternal love. If you have an opportunity to view the film, compare it to the story as you saw it in your mind. Notice what is missing, what is added, what is different. Pay particular attention to the movie's ending, which continues beyond Uncle Oscar's final words. How might the changes be explained? How faithful is the movie to the letter and the spirit of Lawrence's story? Is the film a valid work of literature in its own terms?

Evaluating Film as Literature

To answer the last question, consider your evaluative criteria. What do you look for in a film? Do you like action, drama, or romance? Your preference for a particular genre, like mysteries or science fiction, might be a good place to begin a self-study, but try to probe deeper. Why are some romantic movies more appealing than others? What makes an action film successful? In other words, focus on the craft of film as well as on the content. Most of us like a good story well told. We respond to characters that draw us into their lives. We enjoy the intensity of a strong scene or the working out of a provocative idea. This absorption in the elements of fiction makes us responsive viewers, sensitive to artistic merit. But we can also look beyond the immediate screen experience to the many hands that shaped the film, to the technical and artistic choices made by scriptwriters, actors, editors, and camera operators. In this way, we also become critical viewers, able to understand the reasons for our response.

This does not mean that moviegoing ought to be an exercise in cataloging camera angles. We need to ask what makes a scene significant for us. We need to explore our own sense of the film, our emotional and intellectual engagement, and we need to take into account other films and other viewers.

Finally, we should consider the experience of watching films as members of an audience. The sense of community that we feel in a theater is quite different from the experience of reading alone. In this respect, our multiplex cinema has much in common with the Anglo-Saxon hall. The next time that you watch those flickering images on the movie screen, think back to the origins of British literature. Remember the Anglo-Saxons gathering together, focusing their collective imagination on a flickering fire while the voices and visions of *Beowulf* emanated from their bard. Today, as then, the stories that come to us through literature connect us to others and to our humanity. Whether we hear them, read them, or watch them on a movie screen, these stories belong to a great tradition that reminds us where we're from, who we are, and what we might become.

GUIDELINES FOR EVALUATING FILMS

General Responses

1. How does the film make you feel? What does it make you think about?
2. Which scenes engage you most or least? Why?
3. What keeps you interested throughout the film?
4. What other films or literary works does the film remind you of?
5. How does the director use the elements of fiction: plot, character development, setting, theme, mood, symbol, point of view, and suspense?

Elements of Film

1. **Acting.** Are the performances believable? Are they overstated? understated?
2. **Camera work.** How does the camera frame events? When does it move, shift angles, or otherwise change our focus of attention?
3. **Lighting and set design.** Consider the location chosen for each scene. Is the set realistic and believable? How was the place made to look as if it belonged to a certain era? How does the lighting or use of color contribute to the atmosphere?
4. **Sound.** What kind of music sets the mood? Are any sound effects especially significant? Does the film use the voice of an unseen narrator to tell part of the story?
5. **Editing.** How are separate shots combined into a continuous sequence? How often does the camera cut, fade, or dissolve to a new view of events?

Hugh Grant and Emma Thompson in Ang Lee's film version of *Sense and Sensibility* (1995).

Elizabeth Bowen
(1899–1973)

Elizabeth Bowen was born in Dublin, Ireland, and spent her early years in Ireland's County Cork, on her family's splendid country estate, Bowen's Court. As Bowen later wrote, her family strove "to live as though living gave them no trouble." An only child, Bowen was looked after by a governess, taken to the Anglican church on Sundays, and taught to dance, wear gloves, and pay attention to manners. On her mother's orders, she was not taught to read until she was seven. When Bowen's father, a lawyer, was confined to a mental hospital, Elizabeth was not allowed to dwell on it. By her twelfth year, her father had recovered, but her mother had contracted fatal cancer. ("Good news," her mother is reported to have remarked, with her characteristic optimism. "Now I'm going to see what Heaven's like.") Elizabeth was not allowed to attend her mother's funeral or to mourn her.

Bowen's fiction clearly bears the stamp of her early years. Much of her writing is concerned with the processes of growing up, of losing innocence, of coming to terms with reality. Her main characters are often wealthy, sensitive, and well-mannered women; yet her novels also reveal a sense of insecurity, a feeling that life cannot be trusted, that existence is a struggle. Dislocation is a major theme, as is the brittleness of romance.

At seventeen, after attending a boarding school in England, Bowen moved to London to write stories. There she attended readings at the Poetry Bookshop, where she made the first of the literary friendships that were to become the fabric of her life. Among these literary friends were Rose Macaulay, Edith Sitwell, Ezra Pound, and Aldous Huxley.

In 1923, Bowen published her first collection of stories, *Encounters,* to little notice. She also married Alan Cameron, a teacher. For most of

Elizabeth Bowen.
Photograph by Robin Adler.

the next ten years, the couple lived in the university town of Oxford, where Cameron taught and his wife wrote industriously. Her first novel, *The Hotel,* was published in 1927. Thereafter, she produced story collections regularly and wrote nearly a novel a year.

In 1935, the couple moved back to London, where Bowen won acclaim for her novel *The Death of the Heart* (1938) and became a notable hostess of the literary world. During World War II, with its nightly air raids on London, Bowen was a dedicated air-raid warden, but she also went right on giving parties.

Once, while entertaining guests on her balcony, she took no notice of the magnesium flares, but when she had gathered everyone inside, she said, in a typical understatement, "I feel I should apologize for the noise." During the same period, she was writing the stories published in 1945 in *The Demon Lover,* a collection she called a "diary" of her reactions to the war. She described the stories as "flying particles of something enormous and inchoate." *The Heat of the Day* (1949), perhaps Bowen's finest novel, is a classic love story also set in wartime London.

After the war, Bowen and her husband returned to Bowen's Court but had barely begun this new, serene era when Cameron died of a heart attack. Predictably, Bowen became more active than ever. She traveled to Europe, visited her American publishers in New York, and lectured at Princeton, Vassar, Bryn Mawr, and the University of Wisconsin. All the while, she wrote steadily.

Although Bowen had been irrepressibly healthy all her life, a persistent cough proved to be a symptom of lung cancer. She died in 1973 and is buried in an Irish churchyard.

Before You Read
THE DEMON LOVER

Make the Connection
Did I Scare You?

Ghost stories can be mesmerizing—even when they're scaring us to death. And part of why we're so drawn to them is that they make us think about which events are real and which are happening only in our imagination, or in the imagination of a character. See how well you can figure out what's real and what's not in this story. Is it a ghost story at all?

Reading Skills and Strategies

Modifying Your Predictions

Think about the title of this story. Then, freewrite for a few minutes, predicting what you think the story will be about. As you read, **modify,** or change, your predictions based on what happens in the story. Note the details that lead you to modify a prediction. You may find yourself changing your predictions several times as you learn more about the characters and the situation.

Elements of Literature
Flashback

A **flashback** is a scene in a narrative or dramatic work that interrupts the present action to tell what happened at an earlier time. "The Demon Lover" uses a **flashback** to provide important background information about the main character, Mrs. Drover. To recognize where the flashback begins, look for the sudden appearance of a verb in the past

perfect tense (that is, preceded by the helping verb *had*).

Background

"The Demon Lover" has been compared to the movies of the director Alfred Hitchcock, a master of style, mood, and suspense. An amusing Hitchcock trademark is his appearance as a walk-on character somewhere in each of his films. Generations of moviegoers have delighted in trying to discover Hitchcock's fleeting but very recognizable presence. In a similarly unobtrusive way, Bowen is present in her work for those who recognize her. As you read "The Demon Lover," watch for a few descriptive words or emotional remarks that suddenly remind you of something you read in her biography.

"The Demon Lover" takes place in London in the early 1940s during World War II, when frequent German air raids over the city drove many Londoners to find temporary lodgings in the country. In the story, Mrs. Drover visits her "shut-up house," which is being looked after by a caretaker.

Cat on a Pile of Blankets
(1985) by Edward Bawden.
The Fine Art Society, London.

The Demon Lover

Elizabeth Bowen

Toward the end of her day in London Mrs. Drover went round to her shut-up house to look for several things she wanted to take away. Some belonged to herself, some to her family, who were by now used to their country life. It was late August; it had been a steamy, showery day: At the moment the trees down the pavement glittered in an escape of humid yellow afternoon sun. Against the next batch of clouds, already piling up ink-dark, broken chimneys and parapets[1] stood out. In her once familiar street, as in any unused channel, an unfamiliar queerness had silted up; a cat wove itself in and out of railings, but no human eye watched Mrs. Drover's return. Shifting some parcels under her arm, she slowly forced round her latchkey in an unwilling lock, then gave the door, which had warped, a push with her knee. Dead air came out to meet her as she went in.

The staircase window having been boarded up, no light came down into the hall. But one door, she could just see, stood ajar, so she went quickly through into the room and unshuttered the big window in there. Now the prosaic woman, looking about her, was more perplexed than she knew by everything that she saw, by traces of her long former habit of life—the yellow smoke stain up the white marble mantelpiece, the ring left by a vase on the top of the escritoire;[2] the bruise in the wallpaper where, on the door being thrown open widely, the china handle had always hit the wall. The piano, having gone away to be stored, had left what looked like claw marks on its part of the parquet.[3] Though not much dust had seeped in, each object wore a film of another kind; and, the only ventilation being the chimney, the whole drawing room smelled of the cold hearth. Mrs. Drover put down her parcels on the escritoire and left the room to proceed upstairs; the things she wanted were in a bedroom chest.

She had been anxious to see how the house was—the part-time caretaker she shared with some neighbors was away this week on his holiday, known to be not yet back. At the best of times he did not look in often, and she was never sure that she trusted him. There were some cracks in the structure, left by the last bombing, on which she was anxious to keep an eye. Not that one could do anything—

A shaft of refracted daylight now lay across the hall. She stopped dead and stared at the hall table—on this lay a letter addressed to her.

She thought first—then the caretaker *must* be back. All the same, who, seeing the house shuttered, would have dropped a letter in at the box? It was not a circular, it was not a bill. And the post office redirected, to the address in the country, everything for her that came through the post. The caretaker (even if he *were* back) did not know she was due in London today—her call here had been planned to be a surprise—so his negligence in the manner of this letter, leaving it to wait in the dusk and the dust, annoyed her. Annoyed, she picked up the letter, which bore no stamp. But it cannot be important, or they would know . . . She took the letter rapidly upstairs with her, without a stop to look at the writing till she reached what had been her bedroom, where she let in light. The room looked over the garden and other gardens: The sun had gone in; as the clouds sharpened and lowered, the trees and rank lawns seemed already to smoke with dark. Her reluctance to look again at the letter came from the fact that she felt intruded upon—and by someone contemptuous of her ways. However, in the tenseness preceding the fall of rain she read it: It was a few lines.

> Dear Kathleen: You will not have forgotten that today is our anniversary, and the day we said. The years have gone by at once slowly and fast. In view of the fact that nothing has changed, I shall rely upon you to keep your promise. I was sorry to see you leave London, but was satisfied

---

WORDS TO OWN

prosaic (prō·zā′ik) *adj.*: ordinary; dull.
refracted (ri·frakt′id) *v.* used as *adj.*: bent by its passage from one medium to another.

---

1. **parapets** (par′ə·pets′): low walls around rooftops.
2. **escritoire** (es′kri·twär′): writing table.
3. **parquet** (pär·kā′): wood floor made of boards arranged in geometric patterns.

that you would be back in time. You may expect me, therefore, at the hour arranged. Until then . . .   K.

Mrs. Drover looked for the date: It was today's. She dropped the letter onto the bedsprings, then picked it up to see the writing again—her lips, beneath the remains of lipstick, beginning to go white. She felt so much the change in her own face that she went to the mirror, polished a clear patch in it, and looked at once urgently and stealthily in. She was confronted by a woman of forty-four, with eyes starting out under a hat brim that had been rather carelessly pulled down. She had not put on any more powder since she left the shop where she ate her solitary tea.[4] The pearls her husband had given her on their marriage hung loose round her now rather thinner throat, slipping in the V of the pink wool jumper her sister knitted last autumn as they sat round the fire. Mrs. Drover's most normal expression was one of controlled worry, but of <u>assent</u>. Since the birth of the third of her little boys, attended by a quite serious illness, she had had an <u>intermittent</u> muscular flicker to the left of her mouth, but in spite of this she could always sustain a manner that was at once energetic and calm.

Turning from her own face as <u>precipitately</u> as she had gone to meet it, she went to the chest where the things were, unlocked it, threw up the lid, and knelt to search. But as rain began to come crashing down she could not keep from looking over her shoulder at the stripped bed on which the letter lay. Behind the blanket of rain the clock of the church that still stood struck six—with rapidly heightening apprehension she counted each of the slow strokes. "The hour arranged . . . My God," she said, "*what* hour? How should I . . . ? After twenty-five years . . . "

The young girl talking to the soldier in the garden had not ever completely seen his face. It was dark; they were saying goodbye under a tree. Now and then—for it felt, from not seeing him at this intense moment, as though she had never seen him at all—she verified his presence for these few moments longer by putting out a hand, which he each time pressed, without very much kindness, and painfully, on to one of the breast buttons of

4. **tea:** in Britain, a light, late-afternoon meal, served with tea.

his uniform. That cut of the button on the palm of her hand was, principally, what she was to carry away. This was so near the end of a leave from France that she could only wish him already gone. It was August 1916. Being not kissed, being drawn away from and looked at intimidated Kathleen till she imagined spectral glitters in the place of his eyes. Turning away and looking back up the lawn she saw, through branches of trees, the drawing-room window alight: She caught a breath for the moment when she could go running back there into the safe arms of her mother and sister, and cry: "What shall I do, what shall I do? He has gone."

Hearing her catch her breath, her fiancé said, without feeling: "Cold?"

"You're going away such a long way."

"Not so far as you think."

"I don't understand?"

"You don't have to," he said. "You will. You know what we said."

"But that was—suppose you—I mean, suppose."

"I shall be with you," he said, "sooner or later. You won't forget that. You need do nothing but wait."

Only a little more than a minute later she was free to run up the silent lawn. Looking in through the window at her mother and sister, who did not for the moment perceive her, she already felt that unnatural promise drive down between her and the rest of all humankind. No other way of having given herself could have made her feel so apart, lost and forsworn.[5] She could not have plighted a more sinister troth.[6]

Kathleen behaved well when, some months later, her fiancé was reported missing, presumed killed. Her family not only supported her but were able to praise her courage without <u>stint</u> because

5. **forsworn** (fôr·swôrn'): having lied under oath; perjured.
6. **plighted . . . troth:** made a more sinister promise of marriage.

- -

WORDS TO OWN

assent (ə·sent') *n.*: acceptance.
intermittent (in'tər·mit''nt) *adj.*: starting and
   stopping at intervals; periodic.
precipitately (pri·sip'ə·tit'lē) *adv.*: suddenly.
stint *n.*: limitation.

- -

they could not regret, as a husband for her, the man they knew almost nothing about. They hoped she would, in a year or two, console herself—and had it been only a question of consolation things might have gone much straighter ahead. But her trouble, behind just a little grief, was a complete dislocation from everything. She did not reject other lovers, for these failed to appear: For years she failed to attract men—and with the approach of her thirties she became natural enough to share her family's anxiousness on this score. She began to put herself out,[7] to wonder; and at thirty-two she was very greatly relieved to find herself being courted by William Drover. She married him, and the two of them settled down in this quiet, arboreal[8] part of Kensington: In this house the years piled up, her children were born, and they all lived till they were driven out by the bombs of the next war. Her movements as Mrs. Drover were circumscribed, and she dismissed any idea that they were still watched.

As things were—dead or living the letter writer sent her only a threat. Unable, for some minutes, to go on kneeling with her back exposed to the empty room, Mrs. Drover rose from the chest to sit on an upright chair whose back was firmly against the wall. The desuetude[9] of her former bedroom, her married London home's whole air of being a cracked cup from which memory, with its reassuring power, had either evaporated or leaked away, made a crisis—and at just this crisis the letter writer had, knowledgeably, struck. The hollowness of the house this evening canceled years on years of voices, habits, and steps. Through the shut windows she only heard rain fall on the roofs around. To rally herself, she said she was in a mood—and for two or three seconds shutting her eyes, told herself that she had imagined the letter. But she opened them—there it lay on the bed.

On the supernatural side of the letter's entrance she was not permitting her mind to dwell. Who, in London, knew she meant to call at the house today? Evidently, however, this had been known. The caretaker, *had* he come back, had had no cause to expect her: He would have taken the letter in his pocket, to forward it, at his own time, through the post. There was no other sign that the caretaker had been in—but, if not? Letters dropped in at doors of deserted houses do not fly or walk to tables in halls. They do not sit on the dust of empty tables with the air of certainty that they will be found. There is needed some human hand—but nobody but the caretaker had a key. Under circumstances she did not care to consider, a house can be entered without a key. It was possible that she was not alone now. She might be being waited for, downstairs. Waited for—until when? Until "the hour arranged." At least that was not six o'clock: Six has struck.

She rose from the chair and went over and locked the door.

The thing was, to get out. To fly? No, not that: She had to catch her train. As a woman whose <u>utter</u> dependability was the keystone of her family life she was not willing to return to the country, to her husband, her little boys, and her sister, without the objects she had come up to fetch. Resuming work at the chest she set about making up a number of parcels in a rapid, fumbling-decisive way. These, with her shopping parcels, would be too much to carry; these meant a taxi—at the thought of the taxi her heart went up and her normal breathing resumed. I will ring up the taxi now; the taxi cannot come too soon: I shall hear the taxi out there running its engine, till I walk calmly down to it through the hall. I'll ring up—But no: the telephone is cut off . . . She tugged at a knot she had tied wrong.

The idea of flight . . . He was never kind to me, not really. I don't remember him kind at all. Mother said he never considered me. He was set on me, that was what it was—not love. Not love, not meaning a person well. What did he do, to make me promise like that? I can't remember—But she found that she could.

She remembered with such dreadful acuteness that the twenty-five years since then dissolved like smoke and she instinctively looked for the weal[10] left by the button on the palm of her hand. She

10. **weal** (wēl): lump; welt.

7. **put herself out:** vex or distress herself.
8. **arboreal** (är·bôr′ē·əl): full of trees.
9. **desuetude** (des′wi·tōod′): disuse.

Words to Own
utter *adj.*: total.

Rainy Weather (late 19th or early 20th century) by Vilhelm Hammershoi.

remembered not only all that he said and did but the complete suspension of *her* existence during that August week. I was not myself—they all told me so at the time. She remembered—but with one white burning blank as where acid has dropped on a photograph: *Under no conditions* could she remember his face.

So, wherever he may be waiting, I shall not know him. You have no time to run from a face you do not expect.

The thing was to get to the taxi before any clock struck what could be the hour. She would slip down the street and round the side of the square to where the square gave on the main road. She would return in the taxi, safe, to her own door, and bring the solid driver into the house with her to pick up the parcels from room to room. The idea of the taxi driver made her decisive, bold: She unlocked her door, went to the top of the staircase, and listened down.

She heard nothing—but while she was hearing nothing the *passé*[11] air of the staircase was disturbed by a draft that traveled up to her face. It <u>emanated</u> from the basement: Down there a door or window was being opened by someone who chose this moment to leave the house.

The rain had stopped; the pavements steamily shone as Mrs. Drover let herself out by inches

---

11. **passé** (pä·sā′): no longer fresh; rather old.

WORDS TO OWN
emanated (em′ə·nāt′id) *v.*: flowed; came forth.

---

from her own front door into the empty street. The unoccupied houses opposite continued to meet her look with their damaged stare. Making toward the thoroughfare and the taxi, she tried not to keep looking behind. Indeed, the silence was so intense—one of those creeks of London silence exaggerated this summer by the damage of war—that no tread could have gained on hers unheard. Where her street debouched[12] on the square where people went on living, she grew conscious of, and checked, her unnatural pace. Across the open end of the square two buses <u>impassively</u> passed each other: Women, a perambulator,[13] cyclists, a man wheeling a barrow signalized, once again, the ordinary flow of life. At the square's most populous corner should be—and was—the short taxi rank. This evening, only one taxi—but this, although it presented its blank rump, appeared already to be alertly waiting for her. Indeed, without looking round the driver started his engine as she panted up from behind and put her hand on the door. As she did so, the clock struck seven. The taxi faced the main road: To make the trip back to her house it would have to turn—she had settled back on the seat and the taxi *had* turned before she, surprised by its knowing movement, recollected that she had not "said where." She leaned forward to scratch at the glass panel that divided the driver's head from her own.

The driver braked to what was almost a stop, turned round, and slid the glass panel back: The jolt of this flung Mrs. Drover forward till her face was almost into the glass. Through the <u>aperture</u> driver and passenger, not six inches between them, remained for an eternity eye to eye. Mrs. Drover's mouth hung open for some seconds before she could issue her first scream. After that she continued to scream freely and to beat with her gloved hands on the glass all round as the taxi, accelerating without mercy, made off with her into the hinterland of deserted streets.

---

12. **debouched** (dē·bōōshd′): came out; emerged.
13. **perambulator** (pər·am′byōō·lāt′ər): chiefly British for "baby carriage." The word is often shortened to *pram*.

- -

WORDS TO OWN
impassively (im·pas′iv·lē) *adv.*: calmly; indifferently.
aperture (ap′ər·chər) *n.*: opening.

- -

MAKING MEANINGS

First Thoughts

1. Did you feel emotionally involved in Mrs. Drover's story? Why or why not?

Reading Check

Using the following schema, create a story map for "The Demon Lover."

| Basic situation |
| Conflict |
| Characters |
| Event |
| Event |
| Event, etc. |
| Climax |
| Resolution |

Shaping Interpretations

2. In some stories, descriptions of the **setting** provide much more than the physical background—they also create a particular **mood.** List the **images** in the story's first paragraph that help create a strong mood of foreboding.

3. Why has the Drover family left their London home? Cite two places in the text that make the reason clear. For what purpose has Mrs. Drover returned?

4. What details in the lovers' last meeting **foreshadow** a sinister, threatening reunion? What does Mrs. Drover tell us about her fiancé that explains why she is terrified of him?

5. The use of an **omniscient narrator** allows Bowen to give readers information about Mrs. Drover's psychological makeup that Mrs. Drover herself is not consciously aware of. Identify several such passages in the text.

6. **Dramatic irony** occurs when the audience is aware of something that a character does not know. What is the central dramatic irony of the story?

7. Contributing to the story's richness and depth is the interplay between present and past. Think about the **flashback** that tells what happened earlier in Mrs. Drover's life. Do you think the abrupt shift into the past is effective or merely confusing? Why?

8. The two world wars bracket this story like bookends. During each war, Mrs. Drover experiences dislocation and confusion. During each war, the demon lover is part of her life. Yet he doesn't appear during the intervening twenty-five years. Use these strands of the story (war, Mrs. Drover's inner turmoil, and the lover's appearances) in a statement of the story's **theme.**

Challenging the Text

9. One possible interpretation of the story is that Mrs. Drover's experience is a hallucination: Her powers of imagination have combined with the pressures of wartime life to transform everyday reality into a waking nightmare. Another way of looking at the story is to consider it an out-and-out ghost story. Which interpretation do you favor, or do you have another? Support your interpretation with evidence from the text.

CHOICES: Building Your Portfolio

Writer's Notebook

1. Collecting Ideas for an Informative Report

The setting of Bowen's story is critical to the plot: It is wartime London, when German bombing raids were terrifying the populace, destroying neighborhoods and landmarks with an unnerving randomness. Reread the opening of the story, and review Bowen's biography. Jot down some topics about wartime London that you might be interested in researching. The air raids and their psychological effects might be one topic. Another might be the deportation of children from London (some came to the United States). Save your notes for the Writer's Workshop on page 1053.

Comparing Texts

2. The Same Old Song?

"The Demon Lover" is also one title of the following famous ballad. In an essay, compare the ballad to Bowen's story. Before you write, gather the material for your comparison by filling out a chart like the one below. (Consider also the prediction you made in your reading notes based on the story's title.)

Elements	Bowen Story	Ballad
Characters		
Plot		
Mood		
Theme		

Conclude your essay by indicating whether or not you believe the story is based in any way on the old song.

The Demon Lover

"O where have you been, my long, long love,
  This long seven years and mair?"
"O I'm come to seek my former vows
  Ye granted me before."

"O hold your tongue of your former vows,
  For they will breed sad strife;
O hold your tongue of your former vows,
  For I am become a wife."

He turned him right and round about,
  And the tear blinded his ee:
"I wad never hae trodden on Irish ground,
  If it had not been for thee.

I might have had a king's daughter,
  Far, far beyond the sea;
I might have had a king's daughter,
  Had it not been for love o thee."

"If ye might have had a king's daughter,
  Yer sel ye had to blame;
Ye might have taken the king's daughter,
  For ye kend that I was nane.

"If I was to leave my husband dear,
    And my two babes also,
O what have you to take me to,
    If with you I should go?"

"I hae seven ships upon the sea—
    The eighth brought me to land—
With four-and-twenty bold mariners,
    And music on every hand."

She has taken up her two little babes,
    Kissed them baith cheek and chin:
"O fair ye weel, my ain two babes,
    For I'll never see you again."

She set her foot upon the ship,
    No mariners could she behold;
But the sails were o the taffetie,
    And the masts o the beaten gold.

She had not sailed a league, a league,
    A league but barely three,
When dismal grew his countenance,
    And drumlie grew his ee.

They had not sailed a league, a league,
    A league but barely three,
Until she espied his cloven foot,
    And she wept right bitterlie.

"O hold your tongue of your weeping," says he,
    "Of your weeping now let me be;
I will shew you how lilies grow
    On the banks of Italy."

"O what hills are yon, yon pleasant hills,
    That the sun shines sweetly on?"
"O yon are the hills of heaven," he said,
    "Where you will never win."

"O whaten mountain is yon?" she said,
    "All so dreary wi frost and snow?"
"O yon is the mountain of hell," he cried,
    "Where you and I will go."

He strack the tap-mast wi his hand,
    The foremast wi his knee,
And he brake that gallant ship in twain,
    And sank her in the sea.

3. No Prince Charming

At no time in the story are we given a description of the demon lover's face. At the end of the story, however, when Mrs. Drover is finally within six inches of his face, she begins to scream. Describe what you imagine Mrs. Drover sees. You might also do a drawing or painting of him.

4. The Silver Screen

Suppose that you are the producer-director of a movie version of "The Demon Lover." You have to consider these tasks:

a. Casting both the younger and the older Mrs. Drover, her lover, and the minor characters of the family

b. Creating scenery, lighting, and background music to establish atmosphere

c. Creating suspense by such means as the chiming of the clock

d. Telling your screenwriters how you would expand parts of the story for a feature-length film

Write a proposal outlining your ideas on how you would convert the story into a film. Will you film the story as a horror tale or as a psychological study of love? (You may wish to consult the essay "Film as Literature," on page 1012.)

5. Lovers—Romantic and Demonic

In an essay, compare Bowen's story with these other accounts of encounters with a romantic or demonic lover: Keats's "La Belle Dame sans Merci" (page 751) and Yeats's "The Song of Wandering Aengus" (page 981). In your essay, consider **plot, characters, theme,** and **mood.**

Julio Cortázar.

Argentina

Julio Cortázar

(1914–1984)

Julio Cortázar (kho͞ol'yō kôr·tä'sär) believed that fantasy and reality, the rational and the irrational, exist on intersecting planes. In part, this philosophy surely stemmed from the fact that Cortázar himself had a foot in two very different worlds—Latin America and Europe. He was born in Brussels to Argentine parents, but his family returned to Argentina when he was five years old. After attending the University of Buenos Aires, he first taught high school and then taught French literature at a university. In 1946, he was briefly jailed for his opposition to Juan Perón's military dictatorship of Argentina and was forced to give up his academic career. At about this time, his first short story, "House Taken Over," was published, the first in a long and prolific career. Cortázar worked for a short time as a literary translator in Buenos Aires (fittingly, he translated the stories of Edgar Allan Poe into Spanish) before he moved to Paris to work as a translator for the United Nations. He continued in this post until his death in 1984.

Cortázar's works are always playful and experimental. In 1963, his masterpiece, *Rayuela* (translated into English as *Hopscotch*), was published to great acclaim. Named for a child's game, this dizzying and demanding novel includes instructions for the different ways it can be read. Although Cortázar traveled widely and was granted French citizenship in 1981, he always thought of himself as Argentine.

(Map) ©Rand McNally R. L. #98-S-116.

Background

Fantastical occurrences are often the stuff of sleep. Surreal images and irrational happenings flood our dreams, yet during the day, our lives seem ordered, routine, rational. What happens when these two worlds overlap or intersect—when we can't distinguish between them?

In "Axolotl," as in all literature of the fantastic, the impossible and the possible, fantasy and reality are set in opposition. The author often introduces some surrealistic element or extraordinary event into an otherwise entirely realistic environment, and the two become so intertwined that neither character nor reader can separate them.

In Julio Cortázar's fantastical short stories—among the best of the genre—daily life is often mysteriously subverted by unknown forces. This "invasion by the imaginary," as Cortázar called it, creates a tension that both exhilarates and disturbs.

The creatures shown on pages 1029 and 1030 are not from a sci-fi movie. They are real axolotls.

Reading Skills and Strategies

Monitoring Your Reading
As you read the story, keep track of when you yourself are unsure about what is *really* happening.

Axolotl

Julio Cortázar
translated by **Paul Blackburn**

There was a time when I thought a great deal about the axolotls. I went to see them in the aquarium at the Jardin des Plantes[1] and stayed for hours watching them, observing their immobility, their faint movements. Now I am an axolotl.

I got to them by chance one spring morning when Paris was spreading its peacock tail after a wintry Lent. I was heading down the boulevard Port-Royal, then I took Saint-Marcel and L'Hôpital and saw green among all that gray and remembered the lions. I was friend of the lions and panthers, but had never gone into the dark, humid building that was the aquarium. I left my bike against the gratings and went to look at the tulips. The lions were sad and ugly and my panther was asleep. I decided on the aquarium, looked obliquely at banal fish until, unexpectedly, I hit it off with the axolotls. I stayed watching them for an hour and left, unable to think of anything else.

In the library at Sainte-Geneviève, I consulted a dictionary and learned that axolotls are the larval stage (provided with gills) of a species of salamander of the genus *Ambystoma*. That they were Mexican I knew already by looking at them and their little pink Aztec faces and the placard at the top of the tank. I read that specimens of them had been found in Africa capable of living on dry land during the periods of drought, and continuing their life under water when the rainy season came. I found their Spanish name, *ajolote,* and the mention that they were edible, and that their oil was used (no longer used, it said) like cod-liver oil.

I didn't care to look up any of the specialized works, but the next day I went back to the Jardin des Plantes. I began to go every morning, morning and afternoon some days. The aquarium

1. **Jardin des Plantes** (zhär·da*n'* dā plä*n*t): Paris botanical garden, part of the French National Museum of Natural History. The name literally means "garden of plants" in French.

guard smiled perplexedly taking my ticket. I would lean up against the iron bar in front of the tanks and set to watching them. There's nothing strange in this, because after the first minute I knew that we were linked, that something infinitely lost and distant kept pulling us together. It had been enough to detain me that first morning in front of the sheet of glass where some bubbles rose through the water. The axolotls huddled on the wretched narrow (only I can know how narrow and wretched) floor of moss and stone in the tank. There were nine specimens, and the majority pressed their heads against the glass, looking with their eyes of gold at whoever came near them. Disconcerted, almost ashamed, I felt it a lewdness to be peering at these silent and immobile figures heaped at the bottom of the tank. Mentally I isolated one, situated on the right and somewhat apart from the others, to study it better. I saw a rosy little body, translucent (I thought of those Chinese figurines of milky glass), looking like a small lizard about six inches long, ending in a fish's tail of extraordinary delicacy, the most sensitive part of our body. Along the back ran a transparent fin which joined with the tail, but what obsessed me was the feet, of the slenderest nicety, ending in tiny fingers with minutely human nails. And then I discovered its eyes, its face. Inexpressive features, with no other trait save the eyes, two orifices, like brooches, wholly of transparent gold, lacking any life but looking, letting themselves be penetrated by my look, which seemed to travel past the golden level and lose itself in a diaphanous[2] interior mystery. A very slender black halo ringed the eye and etched it onto the pink flesh, onto the rosy stone of the head, vaguely triangular, but with curved and irregular sides which gave it a total likeness to a statuette corroded by time. The mouth was masked by the triangular plane of the face, its considerable size would be guessed only in profile; in front a delicate crevice barely slit the lifeless stone. On both sides of the head where the ears should have been, there grew three tiny sprigs red as coral, a vegetal outgrowth, the gills, I suppose. And they were the only thing quick about it; every ten or fifteen seconds the sprigs pricked up stiffly and

again subsided. Once in a while a foot would barely move, I saw the diminutive toes poise mildly on the moss. It's that we don't enjoy moving a lot, and the tank is so cramped—we barely move in any direction and we're hitting one of the others with our tail or our head—difficulties arise, fights, tiredness. The time feels like it's less if we stay quietly.

It was their quietness that made me lean toward them fascinated the first time I saw the axolotls. Obscurely I seemed to understand their secret will, to abolish space and time with an indifferent immobility. I knew better later; the gill contraction, the tentative reckoning of the delicate feet on the stones, the abrupt swimming (some of them swim with a simple undulation[3] of the body) proved to me that they were capable of escaping that mineral lethargy in which they spent whole hours. Above all else, their eyes obsessed me. In the standing tanks on either side of them, different fishes showed me the simple stupidity of their handsome eyes so similar to our own. The eyes of the axolotls spoke to me of the presence of a different life, of another way of seeing. Glueing my face to the glass (the guard would cough fussily once in a while), I tried to see better those diminutive golden points, that entrance to the infinitely slow and remote world of these rosy creatures. It was useless to tap with one finger on the glass directly in front of their faces; they never gave the least reaction. The golden eyes continued burning with their soft, terrible light; they continued looking at me from an unfathomable depth which made me dizzy.

And nevertheless they were close. I knew it before this, before being an axolotl. I learned it the day I came near them for the first time. The anthropomorphic[4] features of a monkey reveal the reverse of what most people believe, the distance that is traveled from them to us. The absolute lack of similarity between axolotls and human beings proved to me that my recognition was valid, that I was not propping myself up with easy analogies. Only the little hands . . . But an eft,[5] the common newt, has such hands also, and

2. **diaphanous:** transparent.

3. **undulation:** wavelike movement.
4. **anthropomorphic:** having human shape or characteristics; humanlike.
5. **eft:** archaic for "newt," kind of amphibious salamander.

we are not at all alike. I think it was the axolotls' heads, that triangular pink shape with the tiny eyes of gold. That looked and knew. That laid the claim. They were not *animals*.

It would seem easy, almost obvious, to fall into mythology. I began seeing in the axolotls a metamorphosis which did not succeed in revoking a mysterious humanity. I imagined them aware, slaves of their bodies, condemned infinitely to the silence of the abyss, to a hopeless meditation. Their blind gaze, the diminutive gold disc without expression and nonetheless terribly shining, went through me like a message: "Save us, save us." I caught myself mumbling words of advice, conveying childish hopes. They continued to look at me, immobile; from time to time the rosy branches of the gills stiffened. In that instant I felt a muted pain; perhaps they were seeing me, attracting my strength to penetrate into the impenetrable thing of their lives. They were not human beings, but I had found in no animal such a profound relation with myself. The axolotls were like witnesses of something, and at times like horrible judges. I felt ignoble in front of them; there was such a terrifying purity in those transparent eyes. They were larvas, but larva means disguise and also phantom. Behind those Aztec faces, without expression but of an implacable cruelty, what semblance was awaiting its hour?

I was afraid of them. I think that had it not been for feeling the proximity of other visitors and the guard, I would not have been bold enough to remain alone with them. "You eat them alive with your eyes, hey," the guard said, laughing; he likely thought I was a little cracked. What he didn't notice was that it was they devouring me slowly with their eyes, in a cannibalism of gold. At any distance from the aquarium, I had only to think of them, it was as though I were

the tank each morning, the recognition was greater. They were suffering, every fiber of my body reached toward that stifled pain, that stiff torment at the bottom of the tank. They were lying in wait for something, a remote dominion destroyed, an age of liberty when the world had been that of the axolotls. Not possible that such a terrible expression which was attaining the overthrow of that forced blankness on their stone faces should carry any message other than

being affected from a distance. It got to the point that I was going every day, and at night I thought of them immobile in the darkness, slowly putting a hand out which immediately encountered another. Perhaps their eyes could see in the dead of night, and for them the day continued indefinitely. The eyes of axolotls have no lids.

I know now that there was nothing strange, that that had to occur. Leaning over in front of

one of pain, proof of that eternal sentence, of that liquid hell they were undergoing. Hopelessly, I wanted to prove to myself that my own sensibility was projecting a nonexistent consciousness upon the axolotls. They and I knew. So there was nothing strange in what happened. My face was pressed against the glass of the aquarium, my eyes were attempting once more to penetrate the mystery of those eyes of gold without iris, without pupil. I saw from very close up the face of an axolotl immobile next to the glass. No transition and no surprise, I saw my face against the glass, I saw it on the outside of the tank, I saw it on the other side of the glass. Then my face drew back and I understood.

Only one thing was strange: to go on thinking as usual, to know. To realize that was, for the first moment, like the horror of a man buried alive awaking to his fate. Outside, my face came close to the glass again, I saw my mouth, the lips compressed with the effort of understanding the axolotls. I was an axolotl and now I knew instantly that no understanding was possible. He was outside the aquarium, his thinking was a thinking outside the tank. Recognizing him, being him himself, I was an axolotl and in my world. The horror began—I learned in the same moment—of believing myself prisoner in the body of an axolotl, metamorphosed into him with my human mind intact, buried alive in an axolotl, condemned to move lucidly among unconscious creatures. But that stopped when a foot just grazed my face, when I moved just a little to one side and saw an axolotl next to me who was looking at me, and understood that he knew also, no communication possible, but very clearly. Or I was also in him, or all of us were thinking humanlike, incapable of expression, limited to the golden splendor of our eyes looking at the face of the man pressed against the aquarium.

He returned many times, but he comes less often now. Weeks pass without his showing up. I saw him yesterday, he looked at me for a long time and left briskly. It seemed to me that he was not so much interested in us any more, that he was coming out of habit. Since the only thing I do is think, I could think about him a lot. It occurs to me that at the beginning we continued to communicate, that he felt more than ever one with the mystery which was claiming him. But the bridges were broken between him and me, because what was his obsession is now an axolotl, alien to his human life. I think that at the beginning I was capable of returning to him in a certain way—ah, only in a certain way—and of keeping awake his desire to know us better. I am an axolotl for good now, and if I think like a man it's only because every axolotl thinks like a man inside his rosy stone semblance. I believe that all this succeeded in communicating something to him in those first days, when I was still he. And in this final solitude to which he no longer comes, I console myself by thinking that perhaps he is going to write a story about us, that, believing he's making up a story, he's going to write all this about axolotls.

FINDING COMMON GROUND

When we first hear the narrator of "Axolotl" speak, he has already undergone his fantastic transformation. "Now I am an axolotl," he confides to the reader in one of the very first sentences of the story. He seems to accept fully this extraordinary event and wishes to convince us that it really did occur, that it could occur, that its occurrence was *logical.* The narrator wishes to make the impossible—a psychological identification so complete that it becomes a physical transformation—appear as rational as a trip to the zoo.

In a group, discuss this strange short story. It might be helpful, given the suggestiveness of the story, to have it read aloud once before your discussions begin. The notes and questions you take as you read or listen to the story can form the basis for your discussion.

The first task of your discussion group is to set an agenda for your conversation. Be sure you cover these elements in your discussion: **point of view, conflict,** and **theme,** as well as connections to your own life and connections to other selections in this collection.

When your discussions are completed, report to the class. In your report, include questions you could not answer or could not agree on answers to.

Dylan Thomas

(1914–1953)

Born in Swansea, Wales, Dylan Thomas was a prodigy—a poet who wrote some of his most famous works before he was twenty. By that time, he had also sketched out themes, ideas, and angles of perspective for poems that he drew on for the rest of his life. Largely self-educated, he chose the rough-and-tumble life of a newspaper reporter over the comparative serenity of a university education. His recognition by the leading poets and literary critics of Britain and the United States came early, and with it came international fame. Neither was enough to prevent him from having to live on the edge of poverty until his death.

The only son of parents who lived by a code of "good appearances" among their neighbors, Thomas as a child was continually torn between a deep-seated wish to live up to the expectations of his schoolmaster father and an equally strong impulse to please his doting mother. At the same time, he rejected both parents' pretensions to gentility. This conflict was later intensified by a strangely childish self-indulgence that continually defeated his attempts to be a devoted husband to his wife, Caitlin, and a loving father to their three children. The temporary solace he found in alcohol led to that "insult to the brain" that caused his early and sudden death, in St. Vincent's Hospital in New York City. At the time, Thomas was making his fourth visit to the United States and preparing to collaborate on an opera with the composer Igor Stravinsky.

A man of magical presence, with an endless flow of wit and a transparent hunger for affection, Thomas charmed both his British and his American contemporaries. When he first came to America in 1950, he was regarded as the most charismatic British visitor since Oscar Wilde in 1885. His first reading tour of American colleges and universities was followed by ever more extensive trips, in which he crisscrossed

Portrait of Dylan Thomas by Augustus John.

National Museum of Wales, Cardiff.

the continent from Florida to British Columbia. Beyond their response to his personal magnetism, those who attended Thomas's oral readings heard something new in modern poetry—a kind of expression combining the oratorical *hywl,* or chanting eloquence, of the Welsh chapel service with the theatrical delivery of the Victorian actors who once thrilled American audiences with thunderous recitations from Shakespeare and Marlowe. Thomas's poems are a mixture of intricate complication and preacherlike eloquence, of sonorous solemnity combined with a playful use of language apparent even in his most serious works.

In his last years, Thomas found that the concentration needed to write poetry was more and more difficult to achieve. Consequently, he turned to less demanding forms of expression and produced two works that became familiar around the world: *Under Milk Wood* (1954), which he called a "play for voices," and his lyrical memoir *A Child's Christmas in Wales* (1955), now a holiday classic.

Celebrated by critics, sought after by American lecture agencies, and idolized almost like a rock star, Thomas died at the height of a fame he could neither accept nor enjoy. "Once I was lost and proud," he told a reporter from *The New York Times;* "now I'm found and humble. I prefer that other."

go.hrw.com
LEO 12–13

Before You Read
FERN HILL

Make the Connection
Memories of Childhood

Childhood is often remembered as a time of carefree innocence. Therefore, most of us have some memory of an idyllic moment from childhood, when the world was a glorious place and everything seemed just right.

Quickwrite

Sketch one happy childhood memory of your own. Then, list three adjectives besides *happy* that describe your emotions as you recall this experience.

Elements of Literature
Lyric Poetry

Lyric poetry focuses on expressing emotions or thoughts rather than on telling a story. In the lyric poem "Fern Hill," Dylan Thomas uses a full range of **sound effects** and **figures of speech** to convey vivid memories of a young boy's enchanted life in the Welsh countryside. Although the speaker's memories are colored by reflection and experience, it is the exuberance of his feelings, above all, that claims our attention.

Background

As a child, Thomas spent his summers among relatives who worked on a farm that, in his poem, he calls Fern Hill. Set in an apple orchard, the farmhouse is of the whitewashed stucco typical of Wales and has a number of outlying barns for livestock and hay storage. Not far from the sea, Fern Hill looks down upon enormous tidal flats in an ever-changing seascape that provides a bountiful habitat for thousands of water birds.

"Fern Hill" is a memory of childhood joy, a vision of an earthly paradise as well as the playground of a boy for whom every day is an enchanted adventure. Yet, typical of Thomas, joy is never unadulterated or unshadowed. At the end of this extended song of praise, "time" holds him not, as we might expect, "green and growing," but "green and dying." Here we have a variation on one of Thomas's persistent themes—the lurking presence of death in life, of the worm in the seed.

Dylan Thomas and his family.

© Rollie McKenna.

Fern Hill

Dylan Thomas

Now as I was young and easy under the apple boughs
About the lilting house and happy as the grass was green,
    The night above the dingle° starry,
       Time let me hail and climb
5   Golden in the heydays of his eyes,
And honored among wagons I was prince of the apple towns
And once below a time I lordly had the trees and leaves
       Trail with daisies and barley
    Down the rivers of the windfall light.

10 And as I was green and carefree, famous among the barns
About the happy yard and singing as the farm was home,
    In the sun that is young once only,
       Time let me play and be
    Golden in the mercy of his means,
15 And green and golden I was huntsman and herdsman, the calves
Sang to my horn, the foxes on the hills barked clear and cold,
      And the sabbath rang slowly
    In the pebbles of the holy streams.

All the sun long it was running, it was lovely, the hay
20 Fields high as the house, the tunes from the chimneys, it was air
    And playing, lovely and watery
      And fire green as grass.
    And nightly under the simple stars
As I rode to sleep the owls were bearing the farm away,
25 All the moon long I heard, blessed among stables, the nightjars°
    Flying with the ricks,° and the horses
      Flashing into the dark.

And then to awake, and the farm, like a wanderer white
With the dew, come back, the cock on his shoulder: it was all
30   Shining, it was Adam and maiden,
      The sky gathered again
    And the sun grew round that very day.
So it must have been after the birth of the simple light
In the first, spinning place, the spellbound horses walking warm
35   Out of the whinnying green stable
      On to the fields of praise.

3. dingle: little wooded valley, nestled between steep hills.

25. nightjars: common, gray-brown nocturnal birds, named for their jarring cries.
26. ricks: haystacks.

And honored among foxes and pheasants by the gay house
Under the new made clouds and happy as the heart was long,
   In the sun born over and over,
40   I ran my heedless ways,
   My wishes raced through the house high hay
And nothing I cared, at my sky blue trades, that time allows
In all his tuneful turning so few and such morning songs
   Before the children green and golden
45   Follow him out of grace,

Nothing I cared, in the lamb white days, that time would take me
Up to the swallow thronged loft by the shadow of my hand,
   In the moon that is always rising,
     Nor that riding to sleep
50   I should hear him fly with the high fields
And wake to the farm forever fled from the childless land.
Oh as I was young and easy in the mercy of his means,
    Time held me green and dying
   Though I sang in my chains like the sea.

Dylan Thomas's youngest child,
Colm, four years old (1953).

Make the Connection

For Whom the Poet Writes

Do you think poets have an image of their audience in mind when they write? Or do they write mostly for themselves and other poets? Perhaps each poet works differently, and we would have to speak to each one to get an answer to our question. Dylan Thomas describes his audience in this poem.

Quickwrite

What ideas and feelings come to mind when you hear the word *sullen*? Track your association on a cluster diagram like the one below.

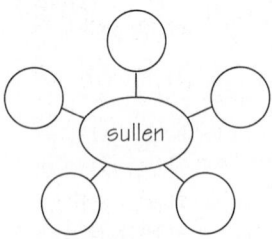

After you read the poem, look back at your diagram to see if any of your ideas and feelings match the meaning suggested in this poem.

In my craft or sullen art

Dylan Thomas

In my craft or sullen art
Exercised in the still night
When only the moon rages
And the lovers lie abed
5 With all their griefs in their arms,
I labor by singing light
Not for ambition or bread
Or the strut and trade of charms
On the ivory stages
10 But for the common wages
Of their most secret heart.

Not for the proud man apart
From the raging moon I write
On these spindrift° pages
15 Nor for the towering dead
With their nightingales and psalms
But for the lovers, their arms
Round the griefs of the ages,
Who pay no praise or wages
20 Nor heed my craft or art.

14. spindrift (spin'drift'): literally, spray blown from a rough sea or surf.

Thomas's writing shack, Laugharne, Wales.
©Rollie McKenna.

MAKING MEANINGS

Fern Hill

First Thoughts

1. Is the experience described in "Fern Hill" universal? Explain your response. (You may want to refer to your Quickwrite notes.)

Shaping Interpretations

2. What details tell how the speaker felt when he was "young and easy"?

3. What lines in the poem seem to refer to the Biblical account of paradise?

4. In what specific ways was the speaker's childhood like the life Adam and Eve led in the Biblical garden of Eden? In what ways is the boy's "waking" in the last stanza like the "waking" of Adam and Eve as they left the garden?

5. Where is time **personified** in the poem? Describe the different kinds of intentions that time seems to have regarding the boy.

6. How would you explain the **paradox,** or seeming contradiction, in the next-to-last line of the poem?

7. Read this entire **lyric poem** aloud, or listen to a recording of it, and try to hear the many elements that produce its music. Where does Thomas use **alliteration** and **onomatopoeia** to provide the sound effects?

Connecting with the Text

8. Which lines in "Fern Hill" could apply to all our lives?

Challenging the Text

9. Years after this poem was published, Thomas told a friend that one line continued to bother him because it was "bloody bad." The friend asked what line it was. "I ran my heedless ways," said Thomas, and he winced. Why do you think Thomas felt so strongly about a line that most people accept and even quote as part of his most celebrated poem? How do you feel about the line?

In my craft or sullen art

First Thoughts

1. Does the last line surprise you? Why, or why not?

Shaping Interpretations

2. *Sullen* means "sad" or "gloomy" today, but an older sense of the word is "solitary." (Its root is *solus,* which is Latin for "alone.") How might this explain why the speaker calls his art sullen? (What ideas and feelings did you associate with the word *sullen* in your Quickwrite?)

3. Describe the picture you see of the poet at work.

4. The speaker says that he writes "for the lovers, their arms / Round the griefs of the ages." What kind of people do you think he is describing? What might some of their griefs be?

5. For whom or for what is the poet *not* writing?

6. The speaker says that his readers "pay" him "no praise or wages / Nor heed my craft or sullen art." Why, then, does he write for them? (Lines 10–11 may give you a clue.)

7. Think about the word *spindrift* (line 14). Could this word suggest that the poet thinks his art might not last? Why, or why not?

Connecting with the Text

8. Do you feel that you are one of the people for whom the poet-speaker is writing? Give reasons for your answer.

ELEMENTS OF LITERATURE

Wordplay

Even at his most somber, Thomas continually indulges in wordplay—sometimes turning a **cliché** upside down, sometimes making chilling or amusing **puns,** sometimes using modifiers in surprising ways, often giving a twist of emphasis and new luster to an old saying.

How many instances of wordplay can you identify in "Fern Hill" and in "In my craft or sullen art"?

Before You Read

DO NOT GO GENTLE INTO THAT GOOD NIGHT

Make the Connection

Challenging Death

Death may conquer every living thing in the end, but the instinct for survival remains remarkably strong. In contemporary literature, as in the *Gilgamesh* epic of four thousand years ago (page 53), heroes often battle against death's inevitability. Literature also records the frequent, fierce refusal of the living to accept a loved one's death. Suppose you knew someone who was facing death. How would you advise that person to behave? What attitude would you want that person to have?

Quickwrite

How would you personify death? Would you compare it to a grim reaper? an impartial judge? Would you picture it as a fearsome, skeletal figure? Jot down some images for death.

Elements of Literature

Elegy

The typical **elegy** is a poem that mourns a death that has already occurred. This poem is an elegy that speaks to a dying man, urging him not to surrender but to meet death in a spirit of challenge. As he often did in his poetry, here Thomas gives his own twist to a familiar subject. The poem may invite charges of irreverence, but its lyrical solemnity, not its argument, is what reverberates in the reader's mind.

Only two end-rhyme sounds occur in the poem, but both are blended into iambic pentameter with such skill that the many repetitions of similar sounds become a somber and delicate music. The use of *gentle* instead of the adverb *gently* may seem ungrammatical. But when we read the line as "Do not go, gentle, into that good night," as Thomas insisted, we gain the additional meaning of all that is gentle, including the gentle man who was Thomas's father.

Study for Portrait V (after life mask of William Blake) (1956) by Francis Bacon.

A memorial to Dylan Thomas at the edge of a small pond, Cwmdonkin Park, Swansea, Wales.

© Rollie McKenna.

Do Not Go Gentle into That Good Night

Dylan Thomas

Do not go gentle into that good night,
Old age should burn and rave at close of day;
Rage, rage against the dying of the light.

Though wise men at their end know dark is right,
5 Because their words had forked no lightning they
Do not go gentle into that good night.

Good men, the last wave by, crying how bright
Their frail deeds might have danced in a green bay,
Rage, rage against the dying of the light.

10 Wild men who caught and sang the sun in flight,
And learn, too late, they grieved it on its way,
Do not go gentle into that good night.

Grave men, near death, who see with blinding sight
Blind eyes could blaze like meteors and be gay,
15 Rage, rage against the dying of the light.

And you, my father, there on the sad height,
Curse, bless, me now with your fierce tears, I pray.
Do not go gentle into that good night.
Rage, rage against the dying of the light.

MAKING MEANINGS

First Thoughts

1. What feelings does the poet reveal about his father's death? Are they at all contradictory?

Shaping Interpretations

2. What four types of people are described in stanzas 2–5? How do all these people respond to the dying of the light?

3. What does the speaker pray for at the end?

4. What is the "good night"? What **pun** on the phrase do you catch?

5. Given Thomas's feelings about the "good night," do you see anything contradictory in his use of the word *good*? Explain your answer.

6. Identify at least three **metaphors** in the poem. How do the ideas you recorded in your Quickwrite notes compare with the images that Thomas uses?

7. Why would any son beg his father to "Curse, bless, me now with your fierce tears"? What might this strange request indicate about the relationship between this father and son?

Challenging the Text

8. Soon after this poem was finished, Thomas sent it to Princess Caetani in Rome, hoping she might publish it in her literary magazine. In an accompanying letter, he wrote: "The only person I can't show the little enclosed poem to is, of course, my father, who doesn't know he's dying." Given the fact that the poem became one of the most famous elegies of the century, do you think Thomas's reluctance was justified? What would you have done in his situation?

ELEMENTS OF LITERATURE

The Villanelle

Thomas has written his poem in an old form called a **villanelle,** invented by French poets. At first this term, which means "rural" or "countrylike," was limited to light, lyric poems about the countryside. Today, villanelles are written on many topics and, as Thomas's illustrates, do not require a light **tone.**

The villanelle is a complex form. The trick is to make it sound spontaneous and fresh, yet still adhere to its strict limits:

• It should have nineteen lines divided into five three-line stanzas (tercets) and a concluding four-line stanza (quatrain).

• It can use only two end-rhyme sounds in this rhyme scheme: *aba aba aba aba aba abaa.*

• It should repeat line 1 in lines 6, 12, and 18, and it should repeat line 3 in lines 9, 15, and 19.

1. How faithfully has Thomas followed the rules for a villanelle?

2. The repeated lines in a villanelle must be significant. Has Thomas repeated ideas important to his poem? Explain your answer.

CHOICES: Building Your Portfolio

Writer's Notebook
1. Collecting Ideas for an Informative Report
You might be interested enough in Dylan Thomas's work to do research on the poet's tempestuous life. To start with, you might prepare a bibliography of books about Thomas that would give you the information you are interested in. Save your work for the Writer's Workshop on page 1053.

Identifying a Theme
2. What's It All About?
In a brief essay, state the **theme** of "Fern Hill" or "In my craft or sullen art," and cite the details from the poem that support that theme. At the conclusion of your report, tell how you respond to Thomas's handling of this theme.

Creative Writing
3. The Way Things Were
Narrate a joyful episode from your own childhood. In some of your sentences, try to imitate the lyrical style of "Fern Hill." Open with the words "Now as I was young and easy . . ."

Creative Writing
4. Feedback
Write a response to "Do Not Go Gentle into That Good Night," using the voice of a very old person who is facing death. Your response might be a poem, an essay, or a letter.

Creative Writing
5. The Audience Answers
As a reader of Dylan Thomas's poetry, write a response to his claim in "In my craft or sullen art" that his audience does not "praise" him or even "heed" his craft or art. Tell the poet in a letter or poem how you feel about his poetry.

V. S. Naipaul

(1932–   )

When V. S. (Vidiadhar Surajprasad) Naipaul was born, his homeland, the Caribbean island of Trinidad, was still under the colonial rule of Britain. Like many Asian Indians, Naipaul's family had immigrated to Trinidad in the nineteenth century to work as indentured servants on the sugar plantations. With their Asian background and Hindu religion, the Naipauls felt themselves to be members of a transplanted society. As a result, from his earliest days, Naipaul felt a degree of rootlessness. He also felt—on the small island—a sense of the world as a kind of prison.

Fortunately, he was an outstanding student. Scholastic honors won him a place at Trinidad's Queen's Royal College and provided him a chance to leave the island. Granted a scholarship to England's prestigious Oxford University, Naipaul was one of only a few dark-skinned students at a university famous for educating England's privileged white upper classes.

Naipaul's father had pursued a faltering career as an island journalist, and this background inspired Naipaul to become a writer. Leaving Oxford in 1954, with no desire to return to Trinidad's narrow possibilities, he sought his identity in writing. He worked part time for the British Broadcasting Corporation (BBC) and tried his hand at writing fiction about the island life he had fled. His first short stories, which later became *Miguel Street,* went begging until he was able to publish his two earlier novels set in Trinidad, *The Mystic Masseur* (1957) and *The Suffrage of Elvira* (1958).

Naipaul's first masterpiece, *A House for Mr. Biswas,* came along in 1961. The novel, which some critics compared to Dickens's comic satires, tells about a poor, ineffectual Trinidadian (much like Naipaul's father) who finds stability by marrying into an influential family. Deprived of independence, Mr. Biswas's rebellion takes shape in the desperate quest for a house of his own. The novel reveals Naipaul's special gifts as a storyteller: his unique, ironic voice; his clear vision of so-called Third World people; and his understanding of life's essentials. The book established him as a major novelist throughout the world of letters.

Naipaul's search for roots has sent him traveling, first back to the West Indies and then to Africa, the Middle East, and India itself, as he pursues the meaning of his own mixed heritage. These voyages and inquiries have led Naipaul to produce more than twenty books, both fiction and nonfiction, including *A Bend in the River* (a 1979 novel set in Africa), *India: A Million Mutinies Now* (a 1991 travel book about his return to India), and *A Way in the World* (a 1994 autobiographical novel about a writer's journey toward self-understanding). All of Naipaul's works have been acclaimed for their clear and bitter yet compassionate insights into the human struggle for identity and survival.

Naipaul has won virtually all the major British literary prizes available to a prose writer and is a perennial nominee for the Nobel Prize in literature.

V. S. Naipaul (1981).

Before You Read
B. WORDSWORTH

Make the Connection

A Touch of the Poet

How would you describe a poet? Would you know one if you met him or her in the street? In the story you are about to read, a young boy's encounter with a poet transforms his world into "a most exciting place." Would you agree that part of a poet's function is to suggest new angles of vision for the rest of us? Do poets really help "transform" the world?

Quickwrite

Jot down four or five qualities that you associate with poets. Then, as you read, see how your image of a poet corresponds with that of the poet in the story.

Elements of Literature

Setting

The story's **setting** is the back streets of Port-of-Spain, the capital of Trinidad, the Caribbean island where Naipaul lived as a child. As you read, notice how Naipaul uses **imagery** and **dialogue,** as well as factual details, to bring this setting to life.

Background

A story about the magical world of childhood innocence, "B. Wordsworth" brims with all the surprise and joy that children feel when they glimpse a road to the future opening before their eyes. The humor of the story, of which there is plenty, springs from the contrast between the young narrator's view of things and his mother's more cynical view. Whereas Ma sees a funny old geezer at the back gate, the boy sees a poet, a man who lives for beauty, for mango trees, for the stars of heaven, and for ice cream. He sees a man with a wildly romantic and tragic history, someone who can feel for all the creatures of the world. What an opening of a boy's narrow horizon!

The poet in the story is a black Trinidadian who calls himself B. Wordsworth. Before you read, review what you know of another Wordsworth, the one with the first initial W. You might reread page 656 of this book.

Laventille (1984), Port-of-Spain, Trinidad.

B. Wordsworth

V. S. Naipaul

Three beggars called punctually every day at the hospitable houses in Miguel Street. At about ten an Indian came in his dhoti[1] and white jacket, and we poured a tin of rice into the sack he carried on his back. At twelve an old woman smoking a clay pipe came and she got a cent. At two a blind man led by a boy called for his penny.

Sometimes we had a rogue.[2] One day a man called and said he was hungry. We gave him a meal. He asked for a cigarette and wouldn't go until we had lit it for him. That man never came again.

The strangest caller came one afternoon at about four o'clock. I had come back from school and was in my home clothes. The man said to me, "Sonny, may I come inside your yard?"

He was a small man and he was tidily dressed. He wore a hat, a white shirt, and black trousers.

I asked, "What you want?"

He said, "I want to watch your bees."

We had four small gru-gru palm trees[3] and they were full of uninvited bees.

I ran up the steps and shouted, "Ma, it have a man outside here. He say he want to watch the bees."

My mother came out, looked at the man, and asked in an unfriendly way, "What you want?"

The man said, "I want to watch your bees."

His English was so good, it didn't sound natural, and I could see my mother was worried.

She said to me, "Stay here and watch him while he watch the bees."

The man said, "Thank you, Madam. You have done a good deed today."

He spoke very slowly and very correctly as though every word was costing him money.

We watched the bees, this man and I, for about an hour, squatting near the palm trees.

The man said, "I like watching bees. Sonny, do you like watching bees?"

1. **dhoti** (dō′tē): loincloth worn by many Hindu men.
2. **rogue** (rōg): archaic for "wandering beggar."
3. **gru-gru** (grōō′grōō′) **palm trees:** spiny-trunked West Indian palm trees.

I said, "I ain't have the time."

He shook his head sadly. He said, "That's what I do, I just watch. I can watch ants for days. Have you ever watched ants? And scorpions, and centipedes, and *congorees*[4]—have you watched those?"

I shook my head.

I said, "What you does do, mister?"

He got up and said, "I am a poet."

I said, "A good poet?"

He said, "The greatest in the world."

"What your name, mister?"

"B. Wordsworth."

"B for Bill?"

"Black. Black Wordsworth. White Wordsworth was my brother. We share one heart. I can watch a small flower like the morning glory and cry."

I said, "Why you does cry?"

"Why, boy? Why? You will know when you grow up. You're a poet, too, you know. And when you're a poet you can cry for everything."

I couldn't laugh.

He said, "You like your mother?"

"When she not beating me."

He pulled out a printed sheet from his hip pocket and said, "On this paper is the greatest poem about mothers and I'm going to sell it to you at a bargain price. For four cents."

I went inside and I said, "Ma, you want to buy a poetry for four cents?"

My mother said, "Tell that blasted man to haul his tail away from my yard, you hear."

I said to B. Wordsworth, "My mother say she ain't have four cents."

B. Wordsworth said, "It is the poet's tragedy."

And he put the paper back in his pocket. He didn't seem to mind.

I said, "Is a funny way to go round selling poetry like that. Only calypsonians[5] do that sort of thing. A lot of people does buy?"

He said, "No one has yet bought a single copy."

"But why you does keep on going round, then?"

4. *congorees* (kän′gə·rēz′): conger eels; long, scaleless eels found in the warm waters of the West Indies.
5. **calypsonians** (kə·lip′so′nē·ənz): West Indian folk musicians who traditionally perform satirical, syncopated songs that are improvised, or composed on the spot. *Calypso* possibly comes from *kaiso*, a Trinidadian dialect word meaning "town crier."

He said, "In this way I watch many things, and I always hope to meet poets."

I said, "You really think I is a poet?"

"You're as good as me," he said.

And when B. Wordsworth left, I prayed I would see him again.

About a week later, coming back from school one afternoon, I met him at the corner of Miguel Street.

He said, "I have been waiting for you for a long time."

I said, "You sell any poetry yet?"

He shook his head.

He said, "In my yard I have the best mango tree in Port-of-Spain.[6] And now the mangoes are ripe and red and very sweet and juicy. I have waited here for you to tell you this and to invite you to come and eat some of my mangoes."

He lived in Alberto Street in a one-roomed hut placed right in the center of the lot. The yard seemed all green. There was the big mango tree. There was a coconut tree and there was a plum tree. The place looked wild, as though it wasn't in the city at all. You couldn't see all the big concrete houses in the street.

He was right. The mangoes were sweet and juicy. I ate about six, and the yellow mango juice ran down my arms to my elbows and down my mouth to my chin and my shirt was stained.

My mother said when I got home, "Where you was? You think you is a man now and could go all over the place? Go cut a whip for me."

She beat me rather badly, and I ran out of the house swearing that I would never come back. I went to B. Wordsworth's house. I was so angry, my nose was bleeding.

B. Wordsworth said, "Stop crying, and we will go for a walk."

I stopped crying, but I was breathing short. We went for a walk. We walked down St. Clair Avenue to the Savannah[7] and we walked to the racecourse.

B. Wordsworth said, "Now, let us lie on the grass and look up at the sky, and I want you to think how far those stars are from us."

6. **Port-of-Spain:** seaport on the island of Trinidad; capital of Trinidad and Tobago.
7. **Savannah** (sə·van′ə): two-hundred-acre park in the center of Port-of-Spain. The racecourse is located there.

I did as he told me, and I saw what he meant. I felt like nothing, and at the same time I had never felt so big and great in all my life. I forgot all my anger and all my tears and all the blows.

When I said I was better, he began telling me the names of the stars, and I particularly remembered the constellation of Orion the Hunter,[8] though I don't really know why. I can spot Orion even today, but I have forgotten the rest.

Then a light was flashed into our faces, and we saw a policeman. We got up from the grass.

The policeman said, "What you doing here?"

B. Wordsworth said, "I have been asking myself the same question for forty years."

We became friends, B. Wordsworth and I. He told me, "You must never tell anybody about me and about the mango tree and the coconut tree and the plum tree. You must keep that a secret. If you tell anybody, I will know, because I am a poet."

I gave him my word and I kept it.

I liked his little room. It had no more furniture than George's front room,[9] but it looked cleaner and healthier. But it also looked lonely.

One day I asked him. "Mister Wordsworth, why you does keep all this bush in your yard? Ain't it does make the place damp?"

He said, "Listen, and I will tell you a story. Once upon a time a boy and girl met each other and they fell in love. They loved each other so much they got married. They were both poets. He loved words. She loved grass and flowers and trees. They lived happily in a single room, and then one day, the girl poet said to the boy poet, 'We are going to have another poet in the family.' But this poet was never born, because the girl died, and the young poet died with her, inside her. And the girl's husband was very sad, and he said he would

8. **Orion** (ō·rī′ən) **the Hunter:** constellation named for a hunter in Greek and Roman mythology whom Diana—the goddess of the moon and of hunting—loves but accidentally kills.
9. **George's front room:** George is a character in another story in Naipaul's book *Miguel Street*.

- -

WORDS TO OWN

constellation (kän′stə·lā′shən) *n.*: group of stars, usually named after the object, animal, or mythological being its outline, or configuration, suggests.

- -

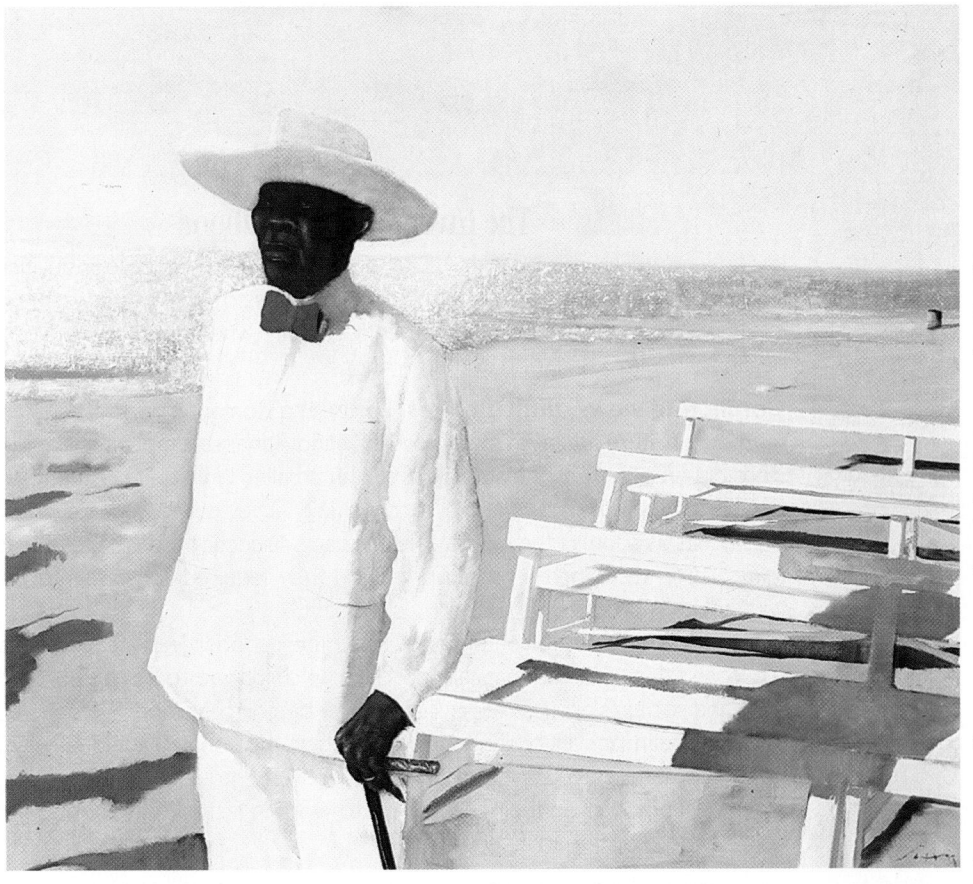

The Trial (1986) by Julio Larraz. Oil on canvas.

never touch a thing in the girl's garden. And so the garden remained, and grew high and wild."

I looked at B. Wordsworth, and as he told me this lovely story, he seemed to grow older. I understood his story.

We went for long walks together. We went to the Botanical Gardens and the Rock Gardens. We climbed Chancellor Hill in the late afternoon and watched the darkness fall on Port-of-Spain, and watched the lights go on in the city and on the ships in the harbor.

He did everything as though he were doing it for the first time in his life. He did everything as though he were doing some church rite.

He would say to me, "Now, how about having some ice cream?"

And when I said, yes, he would grow very serious and say, "Now, which café shall we patronize?" As though it were a very important thing. He would think for some time about it, and finally say, "I think I will go and negotiate the purchase with that shop."

The world became a most exciting place.

One day, when I was in his yard, he said to me, "I have a great secret which I am now going to tell you."

I said, "It really secret?"

"At the moment, yes."

I looked at him, and he looked at me. He said, "This is just between you and me, remember. I am writing a poem."

"Oh." I was disappointed.

He said, "But this is a different sort of poem. This is the greatest poem in the world."

I whistled.

He said, "I have been working on it for more than five years now. I will finish it in about twenty-two years from now, that is, if I keep on writing at the present rate."

WORDS TO OWN

botanical (bə·tan′i·kəl) *adj.:* of plants or plant life; connected to the science of botany, which is the study of plants, their structure, growth, and so on.

rite *n.:* formal ceremony.

patronize (pā′trən·īz′) *v.:* be a customer of.

LITERATURE AND SOCIETY

The Invention of Childhood

In our century, we often think of childhood as a time free of responsibilities and full of imaginative adventure. But this wasn't always so. Childhood wasn't seen as a special period until the early nineteenth century, when poets and philosophers began to idealize childhood in their writings.

Conflicting views, difficult lives. Before the Romantic period, children were seen as miniature adults. In many medieval and Renaissance paintings, children were drawn exactly as the adults were, only smaller. Until quite recently, children also lived mostly as part of an adult community: They conversed, ate, and worked with adults as soon as they were able to. If any distinction was made, it was merely that children were slightly more primitive—they required constant interaction with adults in order to be properly "civilized."

In the late eighteenth century, the French philosopher Jean Jacques Rousseau challenged this belief, dramatically proclaiming childhood to be the purest human state and society's process of "civilization" to be corrosive and corrupt. Yet upper-class European families continued to mold their children in traditional ways, and lower-class families, often reliant on every family member's contribution to the communal pot, packed their children off to work in factories as soon as they could hold a broom or thread a needle.

"You does write a lot, then?"

He said, "Not any more. I just write one line a month. But I make sure it is a good line."

I asked, "What was last month's good line?"

He looked up at the sky, and said, "*The past is deep.*"

I said, "It is a beautiful line."

B. Wordsworth said, "I hope to <u>distill</u> the experiences of a whole month into that single line of poetry. So, in twenty-two years, I shall have written a poem that will sing to all humanity."

I was filled with wonder.

Our walks continued. We walked along the sea wall at Docksite one day, and I said, "Mr. Wordsworth, if I drop this pin in the water, you think it will float?"

He said, "This is a strange world. Drop your pin, and let us see what will happen."

The pin sank.

I said, "How is the poem this month?"

But he never told me any other line. He merely said, "Oh, it comes, you know. It comes."

Or we would sit on the sea wall and watch the liners come into the harbor.

But of the greatest poem in the world I heard no more.

I felt he was growing older.

"How you does live, Mr. Wordsworth?" I asked him one day.

He said, "You mean how I get money?"

When I nodded, he laughed in a crooked way.

WORDS TO OWN
distill (di·stil′) v.: to draw out the essence of.

Children's lives became slightly more free only as the European middle class grew and child labor laws were introduced. Still, it took some time before this new view of children—as special creatures to be nurtured and protected—took root in people's minds.

The influence of psychology, the embrace of art. The change in attitude about childhood mostly took place in the twentieth century. As psychology revolutionized the way people thought about themselves and the world, it also transformed the way society viewed children. For the first time, childhood (and its imaginative play) was seen as the foundation for a healthy, productive life.

After two bruising world wars, artists and writers also turned to childhood as a symbol of innocence. In his *Remembrance of Things Past* (1913–1927), the French writer Marcel Proust treated childhood memories as sustenance for trying and unhappy times. James Joyce and Virginia Woolf often portrayed events through a child's eye to distinguish a childlike wonder from a disappointing reality.

For many other artists, childhood also came to symbolize creativity itself. Artistic movements like surrealism sought to retrieve a childhood energy then thought absent in the world. After decades of war and cultural exhaustion, many believed an appreciation of childlike qualities—imagination, curiosity, faith—was the only way a wounded civilization might heal itself.

He said, "I sing calypsos in the calypso season."

"And that last you the rest of the year?"

"It is enough."

"But you will be the richest man in the world when you write the greatest poem?"

He didn't reply.

One day when I went to see him in his little house, I found him lying on his little bed. He looked so old and so weak, that I found myself wanting to cry.

He said, "The poem is not going well."

He wasn't looking at me. He was looking through the window at the coconut tree, and he was speaking as though I wasn't there. He said, "When I was twenty I felt the power within myself." Then, almost in front of my eyes, I could see his face growing older and more tired. He said, "But that—that was a long time ago."

And then—I felt it so keenly, it was as though I had been slapped by my mother. I could see it clearly on his face. It was there for everyone to see. Death on the shrinking face.

He looked at me, and saw my tears and sat up.

He said, "Come." I went and sat on his knees.

He looked into my eyes, and he said, "Oh, you can see it, too. I always knew you had the poet's eye."

He didn't even look sad, and that made me burst out crying loudly.

He pulled me to his thin chest, and said, "Do you want me to tell you a funny story?" and he smiled encouragingly at me.

But I couldn't reply.

He said, "When I have finished this story, I want you to promise that you will go away and never come back to see me. Do you promise?"

I nodded.

He said, "Good. Well, listen. That story I told you about the boy poet and the girl poet, do you remember that? That wasn't true. It was something I just made up. All this talk about poetry and the greatest poem in the world, that wasn't true, either. Isn't that the funniest thing you have heard?"

But his voice broke.

I left the house, and ran home crying, like a poet, for everything I saw.

I walked along Alberto Street a year later, but I could find no sign of the poet's house. It hadn't vanished, just like that. It had been pulled down, and a big, two-storied building had taken its place. The mango tree and the plum tree and the coconut tree had all been cut down, and there was brick and concrete everywhere.

It was just as though B. Wordsworth had never existed.

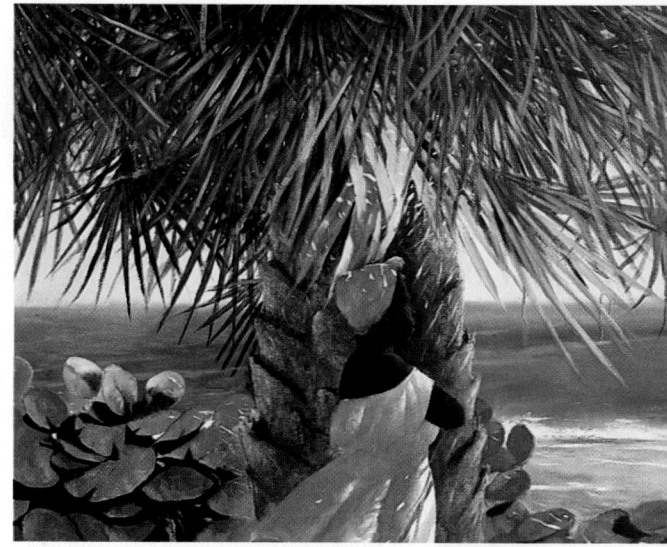

Papiamento (1987) by Julio Larraz. Oil on canvas.
© Julio Larraz, Private Collection, Courtesy Nohra Haime Gallery, New York City.

MAKING MEANINGS

First Thoughts

1. How did this story make you feel about B. Wordsworth? How do you account for your reaction?

Shaping Interpretations

2. What does the boy learn from B. Wordsworth?

3. Do you think B. Wordsworth's tragic love story is true? If it is true, why would he deny it?

4. Consider what B. Wordsworth says to the policeman who asks, "What you doing here?" What deeper significance do you see in his reply? (Is this what poets also seek to know?)

Reading Check

With two other students, devise a story map that shows all the important events in **chronological order**. Who is B. Wordsworth? How does he explain his connection with W. Wordsworth, the great nineteenth-century Romantic poet?

5. Find some of B. Wordsworth's statements about poetry, and then consider the story's **theme**. What might Naipaul want to express about the nature of poetry?

6. What specific pictures of the **setting** are most vivid in your mind? If you were going to illustrate the story, what **images** would you concentrate on?

7. If we think of the narrator in the story as the author's recollection of himself at that age, what does the story suggest about the influences that made Naipaul a writer? What does it suggest about his view of the poet's position and role in society?

Connecting with the Text

8. Review your Quickwrite notes about poets. Then, find passages in the story that contrast the mother's no-nonsense ways with the poetic vision of B. Wordsworth. Do you find these two types of people in your own world? Explain.

READING SKILLS AND STRATEGIES

Analyzing the Vernacular

The speech recorded in this story sounds unusual to people who live outside Trinidad. What Naipaul has captured is the **vernacular,** or everyday speech, of people who live on the island. The Trinidad vernacular is a creole form of English, which means it incorporates **idioms, pronunciations,** and **grammatical constructions** of the island's African, Spanish, Asian Indian, and other settlers.

1. Find three conversations in the Trinidad vernacular in this story, and read them aloud to hear their special rhythm.

2. Try to make a generalization describing how this Trinidad vernacular uses verb forms.

CHOICES:
Building Your Portfolio

Writer's Notebook
1. Collecting Ideas for an Informative Report

One kind of informative report traces a character's development throughout a story. What changes does the boy undergo from the beginning to the end of "B. Wordsworth"? Make a list of the changes, and list evidence from the story to support your ideas. What thesis statement, or controlling idea, could you write to express what you've determined about the boy's development? Save your work for the Writer's Workshop on page 1053.

Expository Writing
2. Seeing Things Differently

Near the end of the story, the poet pays the boy the highest of compliments, saying "I always knew you had the poet's eye." In a brief essay, explain what you think the poet's eye sees. How is poetic vision different from an everyday perspective, both in the story and in your own world?

Analyzing a Character
3. Heart of a Poet

Write a brief essay in which you analyze the **character** of B. Wordsworth. What is he like? Why does he call himself B. Wordsworth? Before you write, gather your details by skimming the story and filling in a chart like the following:

Methods of Characterization	Details	What They Reveal
Actions		
Speech		
Responses of others		
Appearance		
Writer's direct evaluations		

Creative Writing
4. People Portraits

Naipaul has immortalized an unusual character by describing him in words. Think of someone you have known who is unusual in some way, and write a character sketch of that person. Describe his or her home, appearance, job, personality, and actions. Be sure you show how you feel about your subject.

Social Studies / Music
5. Day-o

Find out more about calypso—its origins, developments, and influence. Present your findings in an oral report accompanied by recorded (or live) music.

Margaret Atwood
(1939–   )

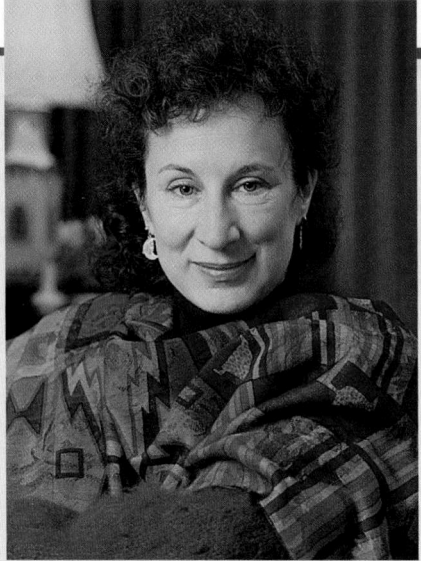

Margaret Atwood (1989).

One of Canada's foremost writers and critics, Margaret Atwood was born in Ottawa and now lives in Toronto. Her often bizarre short stories have frequently appeared in *The New Yorker* and have been collected in *Dancing Girls* (1977) and *Blue-beard's Egg* (1983). Her many novels often feature unusual heroines, like the daughter of the wilderness in *Surfacing* (1972) and the high-waywoman in *The Robber Bride* (1993). Atwood also frequently explores the problems of living in an increasingly technological—and often alien—environment. Her 1986 novel *The Handmaid's Tale* is a nightmarish vision of a future dictatorship in which women are used chiefly for breeding purposes. *Alias Grace* (1996) is a disturbing, mysteri-ous novel based on a notorious nineteenth-century Canadian murder case, in which a young Irish maid, Grace Marks, was accused and convicted of murdering her employer and his mistress. The book grew out of Atwood's research into women and their roles in Canada's early history.

Atwood's father was an expert on insects, and as a child, Atwood spent a good part of each year with her parents in the wilderness. Consequently, she developed a keen eye for nature, as her poem "Mushrooms" demonstrates. In speaking about her poems, Atwood once said, "I don't think of poetry as a 'rational' activity but as an aural one. My poems usually begin with words or phrases which appeal more because of their sound than their meaning, and the movement and phrasing of a poem are very important to me."

Before You Read
MUSHROOMS

Make the Connection
The Cycle of Life
A curious property of the imagination is its power to expand upon the most ordinary subjects. The growth and decay of a common plant, for example, can trigger reflections about the arc of human life or the vast, seemingly unending cycle of birth and death in nature.

Quickwrite
What do you associate with mushrooms? Before you read this poem, jot down a few notes.

Elements of Literature
Free Verse
You will notice striking imagery and hear sound effects in Atwood's poem, but you will not hear the regular repetition of stressed and unstressed syllables we call **meter.** That is because "Mushrooms" is written in **free verse,** poetry that does not use regular meter or a fixed rhyme scheme. To create music, free-verse poems use devices like internal rhyme, alliteration, assonance, and onomatopoeia. **Rhythm** is created by the use of irregular line lengths and repeated grammatical structures.

go.hrw.com
LE0 12-13

Mushrooms

Margaret Atwood

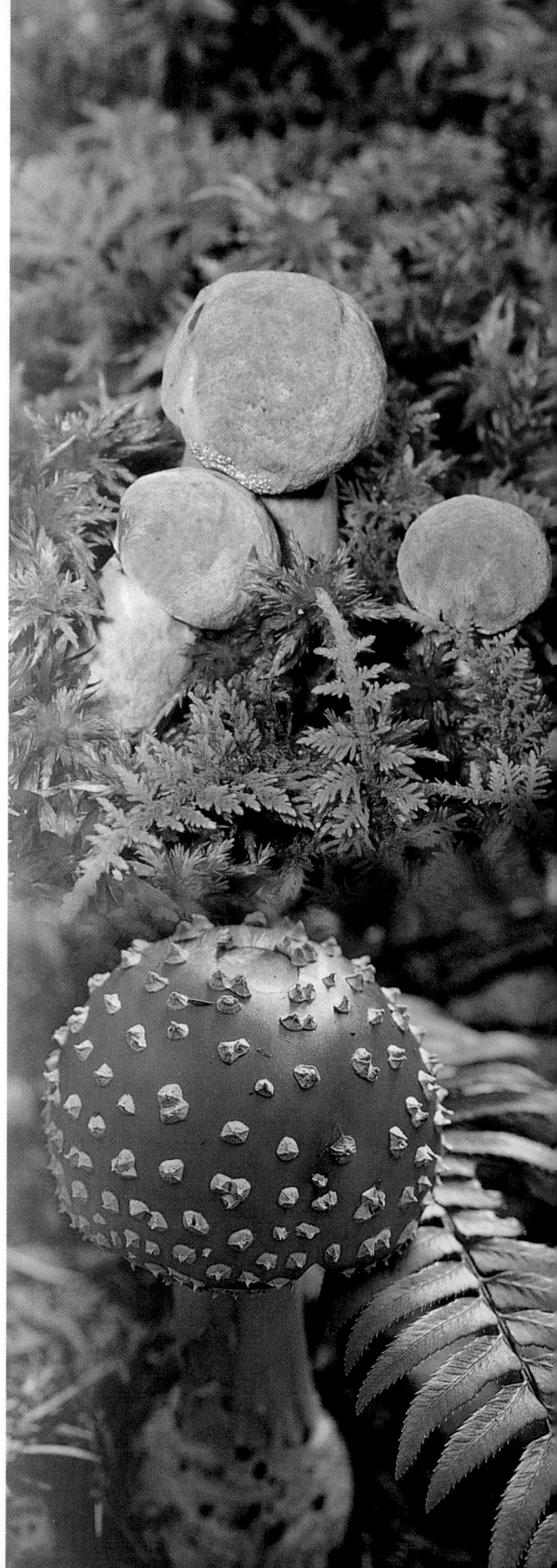

i

In this moist season,
mist on the lake and thunder
afternoons in the distance

they ooze up through the earth
5 during the night,
like bubbles, like tiny
bright red balloons
filling with water;
a sound below sound, the thumbs of rubber
10 gloves turned softly inside out.

In the mornings, there is the leaf mold
starred with nipples,
with cool white fishgills,
leathery purple brains,
15 fist-sized suns dulled to the color of embers,
poisonous moons, pale yellow.

ii

Where do they come from?

For each thunderstorm that travels
overhead there's another storm
20 that moves parallel in the ground.
Struck lightning is where they meet.

Underfoot there's a cloud of rootlets,
shed hairs or a bundle of loose threads
blown slowly through the midsoil.
25 These are their flowers, these fingers
reaching through darkness to the sky,
these eyeblinks
that burst and powder the air with spores.

iii

They feed in shade, on halfleaves
30 as they return to water,
on slowly melting logs,
deadwood. They glow
in the dark sometimes. They taste
of rotten meat or cloves
35 or cooking steak or bruised
lips or new snow.

iv

It isn't only
for food I hunt them
but for the hunt and because
40 they smell of death and the waxy
skins of the newborn,
flesh into earth into flesh.

Here is the handful
of shadow I have brought back to you:
45 this decay, this hope, this mouthful of dirt, this poetry.

MAKING MEANINGS

First Thoughts

1. What do you feel is the poem's strongest **image**? Why?

Shaping Interpretations

2. Read the poem aloud. What uses of **assonance** and **alliteration** help create its music? Where do repeated grammatical structures help create a **rhythm**?

3. In lines 6–10, what repeated consonant suggests the sound of the fingers of rubber gloves turning inside out?

4. "Leaf mold" can be defined as "soil enriched by decayed leaves" or "mold that grows on leaves." Which definition applies in line 11?

5. In lines 6–16, the poet describes various kinds of mushrooms, some against the background of leaf mold. Which mushrooms in the photographs on pages 1051 and 1052 would you match up with Atwood's descriptions? After you review your Quickwrite notes, think up a **metaphor** of your own for each of the photographs.

6. What biological process does line 42 refer to?

7. What senses does the poem appeal to? Quote examples from the poem.

8. Explain the poem's last four lines. How could mushrooms suggest decay, hope, mouthfuls of dirt, and poetry?

Challenging the Text

9. Explain the poem's **extended metaphor** in your own words. In your view, how effective is it?

CHOICES:
Building Your Portfolio

Writer's Notebook
1. Collecting Ideas for an Informative Report

Atwood's clinical and unsentimental poem certainly shows that she knows a great deal about mushrooms. Brainstorm to develop a list of subjects from the natural world— animal, vegetable, or mineral—that you want to know more about. Save your notes for use in the Writer's Workshop on page 1053.

Creative Writing
2. Poetry of the Everyday

Choose a simple subject from nature such as butterflies, lions, sand, or worms. What sounds do you associate with your subject? List words that have these sounds and also have some meaning associated with your subject. Then, use these words in a four- or five-line **free verse** poem about your subject. Try to include sensory images.

BUILDING YOUR PORTFOLIO

Writer's Workshop

The history
of the written
word is rich and

Page 1

EXPOSITORY WRITING

AN INFORMATIVE REPORT

In "Araby," James Joyce uses his extraordinary imagination to transform his native city into a fictional setting. Yet Joyce's writing was also firmly grounded in his comprehensive knowledge of Dublin. In this Writer's Workshop you'll write an informative report about something *you* know well. In the process, you'll use skills fundamental to other types of writing as you collect, synthesize, and organize information.

Technology HELP

See Writer's Workshop 2 CD-ROM. *Assignment: Informative Report.*

ASSIGNMENT
Write a factual report sharing information on a subject.

AIM
To inform your readers.

AUDIENCE
Your classmates or other people interested in your subject.

Prewriting

1. **Checking your Writer's Notebook.** By doing the Writer's Notebook activities in Collections 12 and 13, you've already begun the prewriting for an informative report. Check through your entries for usable material and ideas; then proceed with the prewriting activities that follow.

   WORK IN PROGRESS

2. **Searching for subjects.** Nearly any subject can lend itself to an informative report, as long as you can answer yes to the following four questions:

   • Does it interest you?

   • Do you know something about it already?

   • Will it interest your particular audience (in this case, your classmates)?

   • Can you put together enough information to write about the subject clearly and accurately?

   Begin your search by taking five to ten minutes to brainstorm for possible subjects that meet these four requirements. Here's the list one writer came up with:

Model

> volunteering at the animal shelter
> stream of consciousness—Joyce, Woolf, Faulkner, others?
> Rolling Stones retrospective
> plots of soap operas
> talk shows today
> stepfamilies
> computer-animated cartoons
> Walt Disney

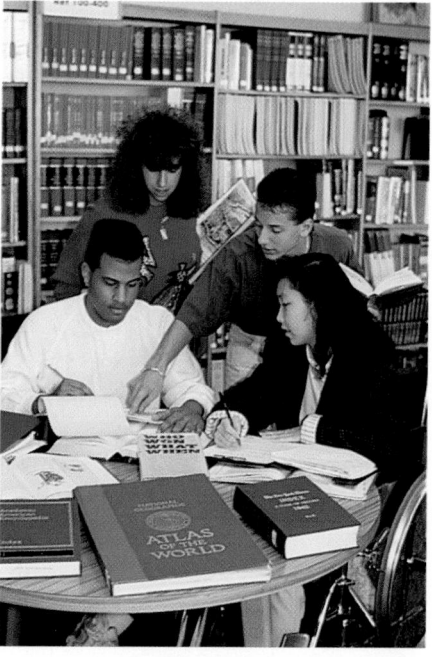

3. **Choosing a subject.** Look at the subjects you've listed, and circle the two or three that most appeal to you. Then write a few sentences telling how you might approach each subject. If some of your subjects are broad ones, such as "music," analyze them (break them down into parts or aspects) to determine how to make them more manageable for a short report. In analyzing music, for example, you might come up with "jazz," "alternative rock," or "reggae." Also, check to see whether any of your subjects suggest a comparison-contrast approach. If you jotted down "stream of consciousness—Joyce, Woolf, Faulkner, others?" for example, you might decide to compare and contrast Joyce's and Woolf's use of the technique.

In choosing a subject, keep in mind that your purpose is to inform—not to describe, persuade, evaluate, or speculate about causes and effects. Check to make sure that the subject you select is one you can approach in an objective, impartial way.

4. **Exploring what you know.** To find out what you already know about your subject, you might simply list facts and examples in the order they occur to you. (Using the *5W-How?* questions—*Who? What? When? Where? Why?* and *How?*—can help you brainstorm.) Or you might create a cluster diagram like this one:

Try It Out

For each of the following broad subjects, suggest three or more subjects suitable for an informative report.

1. contemporary writers
2. part-time jobs
3. home computers

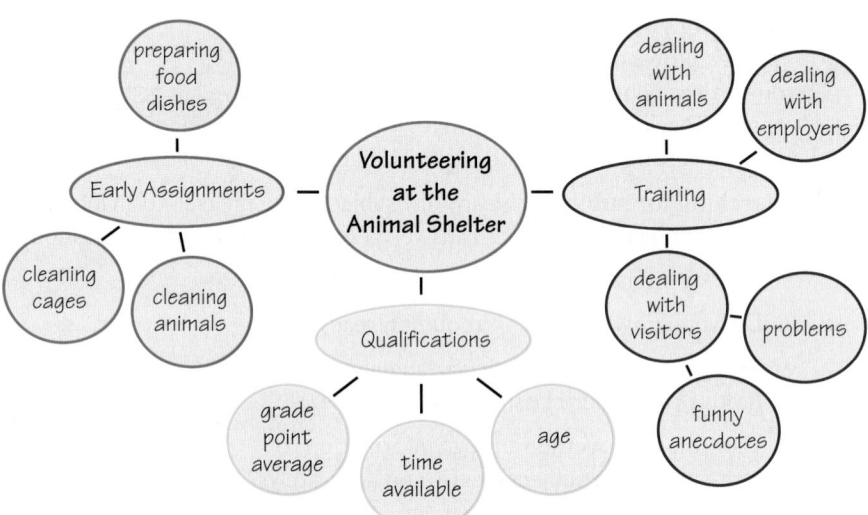

5. **Analyzing your audience.** Before you go on, stop to think about the audience you plan to share the information with. Jot down answers to these questions:

- What do they already know about the subject?
- What might they like to learn about the subject?
- What background information will they need?
- What terms will I need to define or explain?

Analyzing your audience in this way will help you settle on an appropriate tone for your report, one that makes you sound knowledgeable and authoritative rather than pompous and pretentious. It will also help you decide whether you already have enough information or whether you need more.

6. **Gathering information.** Specific, interesting details are what make the difference between a so-so report and a spirited one. If you find that you need more information—facts and statistics, examples, sensory details, or perhaps an anecdote or two—to fulfill your purpose and to intrigue your audience, now is the time to track it down.

Communications Handbook
H E L P

See Research Strategies.

Strategies for Elaboration: Crediting Sources

Although you're not writing a formal research paper for this Writer's Workshop, you do need to acknowledge your sources when you use someone else's words or ideas. Otherwise, you'll be committing plagiarism. Use these guidelines to help you decide when to give credit to your sources.

Information you must credit:

- quotations, unless they're widely known, such as Patrick Henry's "Give me liberty or give me death."
- one-of-a-kind or little-known facts, such as data from scientific studies, surveys, and polls
- any original theory, opinion, or conclusion, even if you summarize or paraphrase it

Information you needn't credit:

- facts from standard reference works or multiple sources, such as the birth and death dates of James Joyce
- general information, such as the fact that a well-balanced diet is essential for sound nutrition

7. **Developing your thesis.** Look over the material you've gathered, and write one or two sentences stating the main idea you want your readers to take away from your report. The **thesis,** or **controlling idea,** should identify the subject and the focus of your report and suggest your purpose. Since it will point the way for your readers, make it as clear and specific as you can; but remember that you can always revise it later, if you need to.

8. **Organizing your support.** Clearly presenting the information you've gathered to support your thesis is essential for your readers. The wording of your thesis may suggest a natural order for your supporting material. For example, if your thesis focuses on three significant events in Dylan Thomas's childhood, you might group details about each of the events together and present them in **order of importance.** For a thesis that compares two part-time jobs, you could use the **block method,** presenting first the features of one job and then those of the other. Or you could use the **point-by-point method,** discussing one feature at a time, first for one job and then for the other. For a thesis focusing on change over time, such as one on computer advances in animation, you could use **chronological order.** Experiment until you find the arrangement that best suits your thesis and illustrates the relationships between your ideas.

Language Workshop
H E L P

*Effective sentences: page
1057.*

■ *Evaluation Criteria*

*An effective informative
report*
1. *clearly identifies the
   subject and the writer's
   thesis, or controlling
   idea, about the subject*
2. *supports the thesis and
   the writer's key points
   with relevant facts, examples, and other details*
3. *organizes the information so that the writer's
   ideas are easy to follow*
4. *includes enough direct
   references and transi-
   tional expressions to
   enable readers to follow
   the writer's ideas*
5. *establishes and main-
   tains an objective,
   authoritative tone*
6. *concludes by refocusing
   on the writer's thesis*

Revision
S T R A T E G I E S

*Are the ideas within and
between your paragraphs
clearly connected? If not,
add direct references or
transitional expressions.*

Drafting

1. **The introduction: inviting them in.** Draw your readers in by grabbing
   their attention so that they'll want to read on to learn more. In setting the
   tone, try to sound objective, authoritative, and genuinely interested in sharing information about your subject. Be sure to include a thesis statement
   that identifies both your subject and your main idea about it.

2. **The body: escorting them through.** Devote a paragraph or two to each
   of your key points, including enough details to help readers understand and
   remember each point. Try to pace the details in such a way that readers
   aren't left feeling either overwhelmed or shortchanged. Where possible, use
   vivid images that will help them picture the information. Introduce sentence
   variety to keep your readers interested.

Strategies for Elaboration: Keeping Your Ideas Clear

You don't want your readers to misunderstand the gist of your report.
To help keep your ideas clear, incorporate definitions and connections
between ideas.

Definitions. If you use a term or concept that probably isn't familiar to
your readers, include a brief definition. First identify the large group or
class to which it belongs (A *plié* is "a ballet movement . . ."). Then identify
features that distinguish the term or concept from all others in its class
(". . . in which the back is held straight and the knees are bent outward").

Connections. In addition to arranging your ideas so that they're easy to
follow, you can connect ideas within and between paragraphs with **direct
references** and **transitional expressions.** Direct references refer to,
repeat, or provide a synonym for a word or phrase used earlier. Transitional expressions show *how* ideas are connected. Since different transitional expressions indicate different relationships—time, space, or
comparison/contrast, for example—choose such expressions carefully.

3. **The conclusion: showing them out.** In your conclusion, refocus on the
   main idea in your introduction, giving readers a sense that you've taken
   them where you said you would and that their time has been well spent.

Evaluating and Revising

As you evaluate and revise your report, make the changes *you* think will best
help you share information on your subject. As you evaluate your paper,
underline each point you've included to support your thesis. Then put a check
mark next to the facts, examples, or other details you've included to explain
each point. If supporting details are missing, add information to strengthen
your points.

Language Workshop

EFFECTIVE SENTENCES: THE VALUE OF VARIETY

When you're reporting on a subject that truly interests you, the last thing you want to do is bore your readers with monotonous writing. Varying the length and word order of your sentences can help you create lively, energetic paragraphs that encourage readers to keep reading. Here are two techniques:

1. **Intersperse an occasional short sentence among longer ones.** Imaginative writers know the value of this technique, too, as Margaret Atwood's poem "Mushrooms" (page 1051) illustrates. Atwood devotes a total of seventy-six words to the two sentences that make up the first section of the poem. As the second section begins, the pace abruptly shifts: "Where do they come from?"

2. **Vary the subject-first order** that is normal in English sentences. By beginning some sentences with an introductory element—an appositive, a single-word modifier, or a phrase or clause modifier—you can not only add emphasis but also clarify the logical connections between sentences. Notice how D. H. Lawrence uses this technique:

> He went off by himself, vaguely, in a childish way, seeking for the clue to "luck." **Absorbed, taking no heed of other people,** he went about with a sort of stealth, seeking inwardly for luck. He wanted luck, he wanted it, he wanted it. **When the two girls were playing dolls in the nursery,** he would sit on his big rocking horse, charging madly into space, with a frenzy that made the little girls peer at him uneasily. **Wildly** the horse careered, the waving dark hair of the boy tossed, his eyes had a strange glare in them. The little girls dared not speak to him.
>
> —*from* "The Rocking-Horse Winner"

By using the different introductory elements indicated in boldface type, Lawrence sets up a fast pace in the paragraph, in which the rhythm of the sentence structures mirrors the action of the story. He makes us want to keep reading.

Writer's Workshop Follow-Up: Revision

Look back at the informative report you wrote for the Writer's Workshop on page 1053. Select one paragraph in the body to focus on. Underline the subject of each sentence in this paragraph. Do you ever depart from normal word order by not placing the subject first in each sentence? What sentences could you revise to introduce some sentence variety? Are there any places in the paragraph where a short sentence would create unexpected interest for the reader? Then look at the other paragraphs in your informative paper to see where else you might make revisions to improve sentence variety.

Technology HELP

See Language Workshop CD-ROM. *Key word entry: sentence style.*

Language Handbook HELP

See Revising for Variety, page 1238.

Try It Out

Revise the following paragraph, varying the length and word order of some of the sentences.

James Joyce's stream-of-consciousness technique is one of the most notable features of his later works. Joyce used the technique in his autobiographical novel *A Portrait of the Artist as a Young Man* (1916). It reveals the thought processes of Stephen Dedalus.

Reading for Life

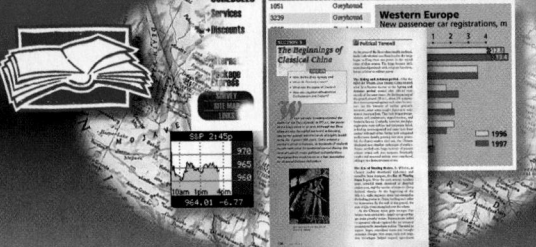

Reading a Persuasive Speech

Situation

The text on the right is an excerpt from one of the most effective speeches of the twentieth century. It was delivered by President Franklin Delano Roosevelt at his first inauguration, in 1933, at a time when the nation and a good part of the world were in the midst of a crippling economic depression.

Here are strategies you can apply to reading this speech and any other political speech.

from Franklin D. Roosevelt's First Inaugural Address, 1933

This is preeminently the time to speak the truth, the whole truth, frankly and boldly. Nor need we shrink from honestly facing conditions in our country today. This great nation will endure as it has endured, will revive, and will prosper. So, first of all, let me assert my firm belief that the only thing we have to fear is fear itself—nameless, unreasoning, unjustified terror which paralyzes needed efforts to convert retreat into advance. In every dark hour of our national life, a leadership of frankness and vigor has met with that understanding and support of the people themselves, which is essential to victory. I am convinced that you will again give that support to leadership in these critical days. . . .

Restoration [of confidence] calls, however, not for changes in ethics alone. This nation asks for action, and action now.

Our greatest primary task is to put people to work. This is no unsolvable problem if we face it wisely and courageously.

Strategies

Recognize the speaker's subject, main idea, and point of view.

- Does the speaker present a clear position on the issue? Is he or she a knowledgeable and believable source on the subject?

Recognize and evaluate rhetorical techniques.

- These techniques include defining terms, giving examples, using analogies, showing cause-and-effect relationships, comparing and contrasting, and appealing to emotions. Does the speaker use techniques to influence you, to persuade you to accept a political position? Does the speaker present several points of view? Or is the speech slanted toward only one position?

Recognize the tone.

- Does the speaker address the audience with respect? with condescension? Is the tone serious? cynical? humorous?

Evaluate the speaker's choice of words.

- Is the vocabulary appropriate to the audience and the purpose? Are any loaded words used to support a position or make a point?

Using the Strategies

Answer these questions about Roosevelt's first inaugural address.

1. What is FDR's subject?
2. How does he engage the audience's attention in the first sentence? What word gives the sentence special appeal?
3. What is his **point of view** toward the subject and toward the audience? What specific words and ideas illustrate his position?
4. How would you characterize the **tone** of the speech? What examples support your judgment?
5. As a **call to action,** do you think the speech achieves FDR's purpose? What actions might the audience have taken?

Extending the Strategies

- Identify an issue in your community, and prepare a persuasive speech designed to rouse people to action.
- Listen, read, and analyze effective speeches by politicians, community leaders, or national and world leaders. Identify reasons why each speech succeeds or fails to persuade or motivate.

OURSELVES AMONG OTHERS

Mansfield

Dinesen

Smith

O'Connor

Auden

Camus

Desai

Heaney

We live, as we dream—alone.

—Joseph Conrad,
from Heart of Darkness

*Nocturne in Blue and Gold,
Old Battersea Bridge*
(c. 1872–1875)
by James Abbott McNeill
Whistler.

Tate Gallery, London

Katherine Mansfield

(1888–1923)

Katherine Mansfield.

Katherine Mansfield was born Kathleen Mansfield Beauchamp in Wellington, New Zealand, the third child of an ambitious merchant. As a child she was aware of the rugged beauty of her island home, but she shared her mother's distaste for being "out here," oceans away from England, the source of their culture.

At home she was "difficult" and prone to nightmares, a lonely, resentful child who saw her father as an adversary. At school she was moody and had few friends. She had her father's head for figures and could memorize verse at sight, yet she was a slovenly scholar.

When Mansfield was fifteen, the Beauchamp family sailed for England to enroll their daughters in Queen's College in London. Mansfield was delighted with every aspect of her new life, and when she was summoned home to New Zealand in 1906, she closeted herself in her room and grieved for lost London.

In 1908, when she was nineteen, Mansfield's family permitted her to return to London alone. But with only the meager allowance her father granted her, Mansfield was painfully poor and frequently sick. Her first literary encouragement came in 1910, when A. R. Orage, editor of the progressive journal *The New Age,* accepted several of her stories. These stories, which showed the strong influence of the Russian writer Anton Chekhov, were collected in a volume called *In a German Pension* (1911).

About the same time, an Oxford undergraduate named John Middleton Murry accepted a story and some of her poems for his new literary magazine, *Rhythm,* and the two began a long and stormy relationship. Eventually, they married and became publishing partners. The couple became close friends with D. H. Lawrence and his wife, Frieda; the friendship soured, however, and Lawrence later ridiculed Mansfield and Murry by using them as models for a couple in a destructive relationship in his novel *Women in Love* (1920).

When Mansfield's younger brother Leslie died in World War I, she was overcome with grief. When she at last emerged from this cloud, she vowed to write about New Zealand from then on as "a sacred debt . . . because my brother and I were born there." She called it a "debt of love. . . . I shall tell everything, even of how the laundry basket squeaked."

As her stories were published, Mansfield became recognized as a supremely gifted writer and an innovator of the short story. Up to this time, the short story had been seen as merely a finger exercise for the novel. People expected stories to have strong, chronological plots. Mansfield's stories downplayed attention to plot and action; instead, she tried to illuminate moments of significance.

Despite her growing success, Mansfield's personal life continued to be troubled. In 1917, she learned that she had tuberculosis. She and Murry were married the following spring, but three weeks later they separated. As Mansfield's health worsened, her characteristic verve gave way to loneliness, anger, and fear of death. But as she entered the final year of her life, she was reconciled to her illness. She renewed her relationship with Murry and showed a new compassion in her writing. In the brief time left to her, she also wrote some of her finest stories, many with New Zealand backgrounds, which are collected in *The Garden Party and Other Stories* (1922) and *The Dove's Nest and Other Stories* (1923).

A belief that some miracle might save her led Mansfield to an institute run by a healer named George Gurdjieff in France. The treatment did not work. There, with Murry at her side, she died in January 1923.

Before You Read
THE DOLL'S HOUSE

Make the Connection
Better Than You

Wherever people come together in groups, there is almost always competition for status, or high position. Some people will inevitably try to prove that they are superior to other people in the group, or that their group is superior to other groups.

Quickwrite

What gives one "superior" status in our society? Is status always dependent on material wealth?

In what environments do you think competition for status is especially fierce? Jot down your thoughts about competition.

Elements of Literature
Symbol

As you read, think about what this doll's house and its little lamp represent in a world where wealth and social position are important, in a society that mocks the ideal of compassion for the less fortunate.

> A **symbol** is an object, an animal, a place, or a person used in fiction to stand for itself and for something broader than itself. The meanings of symbols are often elusive, and readers frequently disagree on their exact significance.
>
> *For more on Symbol, see the Handbook of Literary Terms.*

Background

This story is set early in the twentieth century in a small village in New Zealand. At that time, New Zealand was still a British colony, and the British colonists had brought England's rigid class system with them to New Zealand. In this system, people's status in society was automatically determined by their family background. People with inherited wealth and privilege did not ordinarily associate with the poor or even with those who earn what we consider a middle-class income. In New Zealand, however, because of the shortage of schools, wealthy children attended school with children of different social classes.

Miss Miles's Dollhouse
(c. 1890).

Bethnal Green Museum of Childhood. Courtesy of the Trustees of the Victoria and Albert Museum, London.

The Doll's House

Katherine Mansfield

When dear old Mrs. Hay went back to town after staying with the Burnells, she sent the children a doll's house. It was so big that the carter[1] and Pat carried it into the courtyard, and there it stayed, propped up on two wooden boxes beside the feed-room door. No harm could come of it; it was summer. And perhaps the smell of paint would have gone off by the time it had to be taken in. For, really, the smell of paint coming from that doll's house ("Sweet of old Mrs. Hay, of course; most sweet and generous!")—but the smell of paint was quite enough to make anyone seriously ill, in Aunt Beryl's opinion. Even before the sacking was taken off. And when it was . . .

There stood the doll's house, a dark, oily, spinach green, picked out with bright yellow. Its two solid little chimneys, glued onto the roof, were painted red and white, and the door, gleaming with yellow varnish, was like a little slab of toffee. Four windows, real windows, were divided into panes by a broad streak of green. There was actually a tiny porch, too, painted yellow, with big lumps of congealed paint hanging along the edge.

But perfect, perfect little house! Who could possibly mind the smell? It was part of the joy, part of the newness.

"Open it quickly, someone!"

The hook at the side was stuck fast. Pat pried it open with his penknife, and the whole housefront swung back, and—there you were, gazing at one and the same moment into the drawing room and dining room, the kitchen and two bedrooms. That is the way for a house to open! Why don't all houses open like that? How much more exciting than peering through the slit of a door into a mean little hall with a hatstand and two umbrellas! That is—isn't it?—what you long to know about a house when you put your hand on the knocker. Perhaps it is the way God opens houses at dead of night when He is taking a quiet turn with an angel . . .

"O-oh!" The Burnell children sounded as though they were in despair. It was too marvelous; it was too much for them. They had never seen anything like it in their lives. All the rooms were papered. There were pictures on the walls, painted on the paper, with gold frames complete. Red carpet covered all the floors except the kitchen; red plush chairs in the drawing room, green in the dining room; tables, beds with real bedclothes, a cradle, a stove, a dresser with tiny plates, and one big jug. But what Kezia liked more than anything, what she liked frightfully, was the lamp. It stood in the middle of the dining-room table, an exquisite little amber lamp with a white globe. It was even filled all ready for lighting, though, of course, you couldn't light it. But there was something inside that looked like oil, and that moved when you shook it.

The father and mother dolls, who sprawled very stiff as though they had fainted in the drawing room, and their two little children asleep upstairs, were really too big for the doll's house. They didn't look as though they belonged. But the lamp was perfect. It seemed to smile at Kezia, to say, "I live here." The lamp was real.

The Burnell children could hardly walk to school fast enough the next morning. They burned to tell everybody, to describe, to—well—to boast about their doll's house before the school bell rang.

"I'm to tell," said Isabel, "because I'm the eldest. And you two can join in after. But I'm to tell first."

There was nothing to answer. Isabel was bossy, but she was always right, and Lottie and Kezia knew too well the powers that went with being eldest. They brushed through the thick buttercups at the road edge and said nothing.

"And I'm to choose who's to come and see it first. Mother said I might."

For it had been arranged that while the doll's house stood in the courtyard they might ask the

---

1. **carter:** delivery person.

WORDS TO OWN
congealed (kən·jēld′) v. used as adj.: thickened.

girls at school, two at a time, to come and look. Not to stay to tea, of course, or to come traipsing through the house. But just to stand quietly in the courtyard while Isabel pointed out the beauties, and Lottie and Kezia looked pleased . . .

But hurry as they might, by the time they had reached the tarred palings[2] of the boys' playground the bell had begun to jangle. They only just had time to whip off their hats and fall into line before the roll was called. Never mind. Isabel tried to make up for it by looking very important and mysterious and by whispering behind her hand to the girls near her, "Got something to tell you at playtime."

Playtime came and Isabel was surrounded. The girls of her class nearly fought to put their arms round her, to walk away with her, to beam flatteringly, to be her special friend. She held quite a court under the huge pine trees at the side of the playground. Nudging, giggling together, the little girls pressed up close. And the only two who stayed outside the ring were the two who were always outside, the little Kelveys. They knew better than to come anywhere near the Burnells.

For the fact was, the school the Burnell children went to was not at all the kind of place their parents would have chosen if there had been any choice. But there was none. It was the only school for miles. And the consequence was all the children in the neighborhood, the Judge's little girls, the doctor's daughters, the storekeeper's children, the milkman's, were forced to mix together. Not to speak of there being an equal number of rude, rough little boys as well. But the line had to be drawn somewhere. It was drawn at the Kelveys. Many of the children, including the Burnells, were not allowed even to speak to them. They walked past the Kelveys with their heads in the air, and as they set the fashion in all matters of behavior, the Kelveys were shunned by everybody. Even the teacher had a special voice for them, and a special smile for the other children when Lil Kelvey came up to her desk with a bunch of dreadfully common-looking flowers.

They were the daughters of a spry, hardworking little washerwoman, who went about from house to house by the day. This was awful enough. But where was Mr. Kelvey? Nobody knew for certain. But everybody said he was in prison. So they were the daughters of a washerwoman and a jailbird. Very nice company for other people's children! And they looked it. Why Mrs. Kelvey made them so conspicuous was hard to understand. The truth was they were dressed in "bits" given to her by the people for whom she worked. Lil, for instance, who was a stout, plain child, with big freckles, came to school in a dress made from a green art-serge[3] tablecloth of the Burnells', with red plush sleeves from the Logans' curtains. Her hat, perched on top of her high forehead, was a grown-up woman's hat, once the property of Miss Lecky, the postmistress. It was turned up at the back and trimmed with a large scarlet quill. What a little guy[4] she looked! It was impossible not to laugh. And her little sister, our Else, wore a long white dress, rather like a nightgown, and a pair of little boy's boots. But whatever our Else wore she would have looked strange. She was a tiny wishbone of a child, with cropped hair and enormous solemn eyes—a little white owl. Nobody had ever seen her smile; she scarcely ever spoke. She went through life holding on to Lil, with a piece of Lil's skirt screwed up in her hand. Where Lil went our Else followed. In the playground, on the road going to and from school, there was Lil marching in front and our Else holding on behind. Only when she wanted anything, or when she was out of breath, our Else gave Lil a tug, a twitch, and Lil stopped and turned round. The Kelveys never failed to understand each other.

Now they hovered at the edge; you couldn't stop them listening. When the little girls turned round and sneered, Lil, as usual, gave her silly, shamefaced smile, but our Else only looked.

---

2. **palings** (pāl′iŋz): fence stakes.

3. **art-serge** (ärt·sʉrj): type of woven wool fabric.
4. **guy:** British for "an odd-looking person." The word comes from the name of Guy Fawkes, an English conspirator executed for taking part in the 1605 Gunpowder Plot to bomb the king and the houses of Parliament. In England, handmade likenesses of Guy Fawkes are burned annually on November 5—Guy Fawkes Day.

- -

WORDS TO OWN

traipsing (trāps′iŋ) v. used as adj.: colloquial for "wandering."
conspicuous (kən·spik′yo͞o·əs) adj.: attracting attention by being unusual.

- -

And Isabel's voice, so very proud, went on telling. The carpet made a great sensation, but so did the beds with real bedclothes, and the stove with an oven door.

When she finished Kezia broke in. "You've forgotten the lamp, Isabel."

"Oh, yes," said Isabel, "and there's a teeny little lamp, all made of yellow glass, with a white globe that stands on the dining-room table. You couldn't tell it from a real one."

"The lamp's best of all," cried Kezia. She thought Isabel wasn't making half enough of the little lamp. But nobody paid any attention. Isabel was choosing the two who were to come back with them that afternoon and see it. She chose Emmie Cole and Lena Logan. But when the others knew they were all to have a chance, they couldn't be nice enough to Isabel. One by one they put their arms round Isabel's waist and walked her off. They had something to whisper to her, a secret. "Isabel's *my* friend."

Only the little Kelveys moved away forgotten; there was nothing more for them to hear.

Days passed, and as more children saw the doll's house, the fame of it spread. It became the one subject, the rage. The one question was, "Have you seen Burnells' doll's house? Oh, ain't it lovely!" "Haven't you seen it? Oh, I say!"

Even the dinner hour was given up to talking about it. The little girls sat under the pines eating their thick mutton sandwiches and big slabs of johnny cake spread with butter. While always, as near as they could get, sat the Kelveys, our Else holding on to Lil, listening too, while they chewed their jam sandwiches out of a newspaper soaked with large red blobs . . .

"Mother," said Kezia, "can't I ask the Kelveys just once?"

"Certainly not, Kezia."

"But why not?"

"Run away, Kezia; you know quite well why not."

At last everybody had seen it except them. On that day the subject rather <u>flagged</u>. It was the dinner hour. The children stood together under the pine trees, and suddenly, as they looked at the Kelveys eating out of their paper, always by themselves, always listening, they wanted to be horrid to them. Emmie Cole started the whisper.

"Lil Kelvey's going to be a servant when she grows up."

"O-oh, how awful!" said Isabel Burnell, and she made eyes at Emmie.

Emmie swallowed in a very meaning way and nodded to Isabel as she'd seen her mother do on those occasions.

"It's true—it's true—it's true," she said.

Then Lena Logan's little eyes snapped. "Shall I ask her?" she whispered.

"Bet you don't," said Jessie May.

"Pooh, I'm not frightened," said Lena. Suddenly she gave a little squeal and danced in front of the other girls. "Watch! Watch me! Watch me now!" said Lena. And sliding, gliding, dragging one foot, giggling behind her hand, Lena went over to the Kelveys.

Lil looked up from her dinner. She wrapped the rest quickly away. Our Else stopped chewing. What was coming now?

"Is it true you're going to be a servant when you grow up, Lil Kelvey?" shrilled Lena.

Dead silence. But instead of answering, Lil only gave her silly, shamefaced smile. She didn't seem to mind the question at all. What a sell[5] for Lena! The girls began to <u>titter</u>.

Lena couldn't stand that. She put her hands on her hips; she shot forward. "Yah, yer father's in prison!" she hissed, spitefully.

This was such a marvelous thing to have said that the little girls rushed away in a body, deeply, deeply excited, wild with joy. Someone found a long rope, and they began skipping. And never did they skip so high, run in and out so fast, or do such daring things as on that morning.

In the afternoon Pat called for the Burnell children with the buggy and they drove home. There were visitors. Isabel and Lottie, who liked visitors, went upstairs to change their pinafores.[6] But Kezia thieved out at the back. Nobody was about; she began to swing on the big white gates of the courtyard. Presently, looking along the road, she

---

5. **sell:** slang for "trick."
6. **pinafores** (pin′ə·fôrz′): sleeveless, apronlike garments that young girls wear over dresses.

WORDS TO OWN
flagged (flagd) v.: declined; lost strength or interest.
titter (tit′ər) v.: to giggle.

---

saw two little dots. They grew bigger, they were coming toward her. Now she could see that one was in front and one close behind. Now she could see that they were the Kelveys. Kezia stopped swinging. She slipped off the gate as if she was going to run away. Then she hesitated. The Kelveys came nearer, and beside them walked their shadows, very long, stretching right across the road with their heads in the buttercups. Kezia clambered back on the gate; she had made up her mind; she swung out.

"Hullo," she said to the passing Kelveys.

They were so astounded that they stopped. Lil gave her silly smile. Our Else stared.

"You can come and see our doll's house if you want to," said Kezia, and she dragged one toe on the ground. But at that Lil turned red and shook her head quickly.

"Why not?" asked Kezia.

Lil gasped, then she said, "Your ma told our ma you wasn't to speak to us."

"Oh, well," said Kezia. She didn't know what to reply. "It doesn't matter. You can come and see our doll's house all the same. Come on. Nobody's looking."

But Lil shook her head still harder.

"Don't you want to?" asked Kezia.

Suddenly there was a twitch, a tug at Lil's skirt. She turned round. Our Else was looking at her with big, imploring eyes; she was frowning; she wanted to go. For a moment Lil looked at our Else very doubtfully. But then our Else twitched her skirt again. She started forward. Kezia led the way. Like two little stray cats they followed across the courtyard to where the doll's house stood.

"There it is," said Kezia.

There was a pause. Lil breathed loudly, almost snorted; our Else was still as a stone.

"I'll open it for you," said Kezia kindly. She undid the hook and they looked inside.

"There's the drawing room and the dining room, and that's the—"

"Kezia!"

Oh, what a start they gave!

"Kezia!"

It was Aunt Beryl's voice. They turned round.

At the back door stood Aunt Beryl, staring as if she couldn't believe what she saw.

"How dare you ask the little Kelveys into the courtyard?" said her cold, furious voice. "You know as well as I do, you're not allowed to talk to them. Run away, children, run away at once. And don't come back again," said Aunt Beryl. And she stepped into the yard and shooed them out as if they were chickens.

"Off you go immediately!" she called, cold and proud.

They did not need telling twice. Burning with shame, shrinking together, Lil huddling along like her mother, our Else dazed, somehow they crossed the big courtyard and squeezed through the white gate.

"Wicked, disobedient little girl!" said Aunt Beryl bitterly to Kezia, and she slammed the doll's house to.

The afternoon had been awful. A letter had come from Willie Brent, a terrifying, threatening letter, saying if she did not meet him that evening in Pulman's Bush, he'd come to the front door and ask the reason why! But now that she had frightened those little rats of Kelveys and given Kezia a good scolding, her heart felt lighter. That ghastly pressure was gone. She went back to the house humming.

When the Kelveys were well out of sight of Burnells', they sat down to rest on a big red drainpipe by the side of the road. Lil's cheeks were still burning; she took off the hat with the quill and held it on her knee. Dreamily they looked over the hay paddocks,[7] past the creek, to the group of wattles[8] where Logan's cows stood waiting to be milked. What were their thoughts?

Presently our Else nudged up close to her sister. But now she had forgotten the cross lady. She put out a finger and stroked her sister's quill; she smiled her rare smile.

"I seen the little lamp," she said, softly.

Then both were silent once more.

---

7. **paddocks** (pad′əks): fenced pieces of land.
8. **wattles** (wät′′lz): acacia trees.

PRIMARY Sources   **LETTERS AND JOURNALS**

The following extracts are from *The Letters and Journals of Katherine Mansfield: A Selection.* The first is a journal entry dated May 30, 1917; the second is a letter to her painter friend Richard Murry.

Katherine Mansfield: On Being a Writer

May 30   To be alive and to be a "writer" is enough. Sitting at my table just now I saw one person turning to another, smiling, putting out his hand—speaking. And suddenly I clenched my fist and brought it down on the table and called out—There is *nothing* like it!

            20 June 1921
. . . About the old masters. What I feel about them (all of them—writers too, of course) is the more one *lives* with them the better it is for one's work. It's almost a case of living *into* one's ideal world—the world that one desires to express. Do you know what I mean? For this reason I find that if I stick to men like Chaucer and Shakespeare and Marlowe and even Tolstoy, I keep much nearer what I want to do than if I confuse things with reading a lot of lesser men. I'd like to make the old masters my *daily* bread—in the sense in which it's used in the Lord's Prayer, really—to make them a kind of essential nourishment. All the rest is—well—it comes *after*. . . .

In this poem, written by the former U.S. poet laureate Rita Dove (1952–), the speaker gazes at a childhood photograph. Do her memories remind you of the events in "The Doll's House"?

Sisters

Rita Dove

for Robin Dove Waynesboro

Environment No. V (1969) by Eldzier Cortor.
Etching/intaglio (27″ × 35″).
Courtesy of the artist.

This is the one we called
Bird of the Dead, Double Bird
Who Feeds on Carrion. Dark
with a red organdy dress
5 for her third birthday,
she cried and cried,
snap-eyed imp whose brow sprouted horns
whenever she screwed up her face.

"Buzzard!" we shrieked
10 and when that was forbidden:
"Schmawk Schmawk Bird!"° after the local radio
personality. Several beatings later
the first literary effort appeared, a story
called "Blank the Buzzard,"
15 for which I claimed the First Amendment.
It was confiscated and shredded.

11. Schmawk Schmawk Bird: cartoonlike
voice created by a radio disc jockey in Dove's
childhood hometown of Akron, Ohio.

I can't believe she's taller
than me now, that my smile
lines sag where her Indian cheekbones soar.
20 This is my home, my knothole
we're posing in front of. The palm tree
throws a boa° across our shoulders.
Light seals the cracks.

22. boa (bō′ə): long, fluffy scarf made of feathers or other soft material. Here, the shadow created by the palm tree looks like a boa.

MAKING MEANINGS

First Thoughts

1. Which character in "The Doll's House" do you identify with most? Why?

Shaping Interpretations

2. Why does Isabel invite friends to see the doll's house? Why does Kezia invite Lil and Else to see it?

3. Describe the relationship between Lil and Else. Is it significant that Else speaks the last line of dialogue in the story?

4. What do you think the doll's house **symbolizes** in the story? What does the little lamp symbolize to Kezia? What does it symbolize to Else as she says at the end, "I seen the little lamp"?

5. How would you state this story's **theme**—what does it reveal to you about cruelty, about status and families and outsiders? Be sure to compare your statements of theme in class.

6. How do you feel about the extraordinary meanness shown by Lil and Else's classmates? How do you account for it?

Connecting with the Text

7. How does the relationship between Lil and Else compare with that of the sisters in "Sisters" (see *Connections* on page 1067)? Do you think this kind of sibling rivalry is common? What causes it?

Extending the Text

8. Look back at your Quickwrite notes about status. What similarities, if any, exist between your world and the world of the story?

Reading Check

a. With a partner, review the description of the doll's house. What do the furniture and the dolls themselves look like?

b. Also, review the descriptions of the characters in the story. Who among them appears comfortable, or to truly "belong," in the world?

ELEMENTS OF LITERATURE

The Modern Short Story

People have been telling stories since the first campfire, but the short story as a separate form is really an invention of the nineteenth century. A number of factors probably contributed to the rise of the short story at roughly the same time in France, Germany, and the United States. Growing literacy, the consequent popularity of magazines, and the form's flexibility and appeal to a wide variety of writers were doubtless responsible for its success.

The American critic and writer Edgar Allan Poe created the most influential theoretical foundations for the short story in his 1842 review of Nathaniel Hawthorne's *Twice-Told Tales.* In this essay, Poe claimed that the story should be considered superior to the novel because, since a story could be read in one sitting, it could have a more unified aesthetic effect on the reader. To Poe, a unified effect was the most important literary goal. "A skillful artist," he wrote, "having conceived a certain *single effect* . . . then combines such events . . . as may best serve him in establishing this preconceived effect. . . . [T]here should be no word written of which the tendency, direct or indirect, is not to the one pre-established design." The effect that Poe aimed for in most of his stories was shock or horror.

The stories of other nineteenth-century writers frequently involved people in extreme states—physical, emotional, or both. It was not unusual for characters to go mad or die at the end. Such grand events satisfied both writers' and readers' need for **closure,** or the feeling that one has reached a satisfactory conclusion. Some writers, such as Guy de Maupassant in France and O. Henry in the United States, provided this closure through the use of a surprising twist, or **trick ending.**

Realism, a literary movement that developed in the latter part of the nineteenth century, served to decrease some of the excesses of earlier writers. The realists strove to portray life as it really is, not as we might wish or fear it to be. Some realists, such as the Russian Anton Chekhov, often wrote stories that had no strong beginning or end, but merely portrayed the events of daily life. These **slice-of-life** stories provided readers with snapshots of life in a variety of places and social classes. The American Henry James wrote stories that faithfully depicted not only settings and ways of life, but also his characters' perceptions and motivations. This **psychological realism** also had a great effect on the modern short story.

Some writers today still agree with Poe that effect is the most important aspect of a story. However, the modern story more often aims not at a sensory effect *on* the reader but at *revelation to* the reader—the revelation of some essential truth implicit in the story. The main character of the story may remain ignorant of this truth even at the end, and **dramatic irony,** the result of the reader's knowing more than the character does, is a common element in modern fiction. Though readers may clearly see dramatic irony in "The Doll's House," the story doesn't at first appear to have the unity of form that Poe espoused. But closer examination reveals a coherence of language, theme, and imagery, in this case all related to the central symbol of the doll's house.

In a general sense, we can say three things about the modern short story:

1. It is more likely to be concerned with nuances of character than with the construction of a fast-paced plot.

2. It is more apt to imply important facts and psychological truths than to state them directly.

3. It is more apt to move toward a revelation of truth than toward an effect.

What would Poe think about the development of the modern short story? Some twentieth-century story elements might puzzle him, but he would certainly recognize the continuation of his own interest in coherence and care for detail.

Katherine Mansfield once wrote of another short story, "it seems to me there mustn't be one single word out of place, or one word that could be taken out." With that statement, Poe would heartily agree.

Analyzing a modern short story. With some classmates, choose a story from a recent periodical. Then, collaborate in writing a critique of the story for the entire class. As part of the critique, consider to what extent the story demonstrates the characteristics of the modern short story listed above.

CHOICES:
Building Your Portfolio

Writer's Notebook
1. Collecting Ideas for a Problem-Solution Essay

As in "The Doll's House," peer pressure often keeps people (of all ages) from befriending those outside their own cliques. Working with a partner or a small group, brainstorm to explore how widespread the problem is at your school and what could be done to ease its negative effects. Save your notes for use in the Writer's Workshop on page 1179.

Evaluating Point of View
2. Know-It-All Narrator

As you read "The Doll's House," you enter the minds of several characters. In an essay of at least three paragraphs, tell whether you think the author's **omniscient point of view** adds to the power of the story or makes the narrative confusing. Support your opinion with specific passages.

Creative Writing
3. "The Doll's House" Revisited

In a group, collaborate in writing the opening paragraphs of a new, updated story based on "The Doll's House." Decide together what might be different in the story if it were to take place in a contemporary setting.

Listening and Speaking
4. "The Doll's House" Dramatized

Prepare a group reading of "The Doll's House." First, determine how many readers are needed. Then, prepare a script and be sure each reader has his or her own copy. Practice various ways of interpreting the characters' feelings and various ways of delivering the lines. Before the final reading, rehearse before a small group, and ask for an evaluation of your performance.

Denmark

Isak Dinesen.

Isak Dinesen

(1885–1962)

Isak Dinesen (the pen name of Baroness Karen Blixen-Finecke) led a series of lives, any one of which might be considered adventurous for a woman of her time. She first inherited a love of adventure and storytelling from her father, a dashing Danish aristocrat, and a sense of duty, obligation, and guilt from her mother, the daughter of a bourgeois merchant. As a young woman, she wrote stories and studied painting. Then, at the age of twenty-nine, she embarked on a new life. She defiantly married her cousin and moved to what is now Kenya, where the couple set up and operated a coffee plantation. Her husband, who was blatantly unfaithful to Dinesen, infected her with syphilis, a progressive disease from which she suffered for the rest of her life. In 1921 the couple divorced, and Dinesen ran the six-thousand-acre plantation by herself for another ten years. A collapse in coffee prices and her failing health forced Dinesen to return to Denmark in 1931.

Starting over with no money, Dinesen began revising stories she had drafted in her beloved Africa. Her first collection, *Seven Gothic Tales,* was published in 1934. Her best-known work, *Out of Africa,* an account of her life in Kenya, appeared in 1937 and established her as a major literary presence. Even in her seventies, although she was often so ill she had to dictate to a secretary, Dinesen continued to earn her living by writing.

(Map) ©Rand McNally R. L. #98-S-116.

Before You Read

THE RING

Background

To her contemporaries, Isak Dinesen often seemed old-fashioned, for most of her stories are set between 1770 and 1870 and have the atmosphere of an era long past. During this time period, Dinesen's native Denmark was controlled by a few wealthy, aristocratic landowners. The wealthy often had little sympathy for the poor, who sometimes became outlaws, stealing fish or game on a landowner's property to feed themselves and their families. If they were caught, they risked being put to death.

"The Ring" was published in a collection of stories titled *Anecdotes of Destiny*. And to a large extent, all of Dinesen's stories are just what that title suggests. Each focuses on a turning point in human life, a moment when some important truth is revealed and a particular life is changed forever.

Reading Skills and Strategies

Dialogue with the Text

The rich young couple in "The Ring" seem at first to have a perfect relationship. As you read, jot down any indications that the young wife is heading toward a critical turning point, a moment when her life will be altered forever.

The Ring

Isak Dinesen

On a summer morning a hundred and fifty years ago a young Danish squire and his wife went out for a walk on their land. They had been married a week. It had not been easy for them to get married, for the wife's family was higher in rank and wealthier than the husband's. But the two young people, now twenty-four and nineteen years old, had been set on their purpose for ten years; in the end her haughty parents had had to give in to them.

They were wonderfully happy. The stolen meetings and secret, tearful love letters were now things of the past. To God and man they were one; they could walk arm in arm in broad daylight and drive in the same carriage, and they would walk and drive so till the end of their days. Their distant paradise had descended to earth and had proved, surprisingly, to be filled with the things of everyday life: with jesting and railleries,[1] with breakfasts and suppers, with dogs, haymaking, and sheep. Sigismund, the young husband, had promised himself that from now there should be no stone in his bride's path, nor should any shadow fall across it. Lovisa, the wife, felt that now, every day and for the first time in her young life, she moved and breathed in perfect freedom because she could never have any secret from her husband.

To Lovisa—whom her husband called Lise[2]—the rustic atmosphere of her new life was a matter of wonder and delight. Her husband's fear that the existence he could offer her might not be good enough for her filled her heart with laughter. It was not a long time since she had played with dolls; as now she dressed her own hair, looked over her linen press, and arranged her flowers, she again lived through an enchanting and cherished experience: One was doing everything gravely and solicitously, and all the time one knew one was playing.

It was a lovely July morning. Little woolly clouds drifted high up in the sky, the air was full

---

1. **railleries** (rāl′ər·ēz): good-natured ridicule; teasing acts or remarks.

2. **Lise** (lē′zə).

Forest Palace (1918) by Jóhannes S. Kjarval (102 cm × 110 cm).

of sweet scents. Lise had on a white muslin frock and a large Italian straw hat. She and her husband took a path through the park; it wound on across the meadows, between small groves and groups of trees, to the sheep field. Sigismund was going to show his wife his sheep. For this reason she had not brought her small white dog, Bijou,[3] with her, for he would yap at the lambs and frighten them, or he would annoy the sheepdogs. Sigismund prided himself on his sheep; he had studied sheep breeding in Mecklenburg[4] and England,

and had brought back with him Cotswold rams[5] by which to improve his Danish stock. While they walked he explained to Lise the great possibilities and difficulties of the plan.

She thought: "How clever he is, what a lot of things he knows!" and at the same time: "What an absurd person he is, with his sheep! What a baby he is! I am a hundred years older than he."

But when they arrived at the sheepfold the old sheepmaster Mathias met them with the sad news that one of the English lambs was dead and two

3. Bijou (bē′zhoo′): French for "jewel."
4. Mecklenburg: agricultural district in northeastern Germany.

5. Cotswold rams: the males of a kind of sheep with very long hair, originally from the Cotswold Hills of south-western England.

were sick. Lise saw that her husband was grieved by the tidings; while he questioned Mathias on the matter she kept silent and only gently pressed his arm. A couple of boys were sent off to fetch the sick lambs, while the master and servant went into the details of the case. It took some time.

Lise began to gaze about her and to think of other things. Twice her own thoughts made her blush deeply and happily, like a red rose, then slowly her blush died away, and the two men were still talking about sheep. A little while after, their conversation caught her attention. It had turned to a sheep thief.

This thief during the last months had broken into the sheepfolds of the neighborhood like a wolf, had killed and dragged away his prey like a wolf, and like a wolf had left no trace after him. Three nights ago the shepherd and his son on an estate ten miles away had caught him in the act. The thief had killed the man and knocked the boy senseless, and had managed to escape. There were men sent out to all sides to catch him, but nobody had seen him.

Lise wanted to hear more about the horrible event, and for her benefit old Mathias went through it once more. There had been a long fight in the sheephouse, in many places the earthen floor was soaked with blood. In the fight the thief's left arm was broken; all the same, he had climbed a tall fence with a lamb on his back. Mathias added that he would like to string up the murderer with these two hands of his, and Lise nodded her head at him gravely in approval. She remembered Red Ridinghood's wolf, and felt a pleasant little thrill running down her spine.

Sigismund had his own lambs in his mind, but he was too happy in himself to wish anything in the universe ill. After a minute he said: "Poor devil."

Lise said: "How can you pity such a terrible man? Indeed Grandmamma was right when she said that you were a revolutionary and a danger to society!" The thought of Grandmamma, and of the tears of past days, again turned her mind away from the gruesome tale she had just heard.

The boys brought the sick lambs and the men began to examine them carefully, lifting them up and trying to set them on their legs; they squeezed them here and there and made the little creatures whimper. Lise shrank from the show and her husband noticed her distress.

"You go home, my darling," he said, "this will take some time. But just walk ahead slowly, and I shall catch up with you."

So she was turned away by an impatient husband to whom his sheep meant more than his wife. If any experience could be sweeter than to be dragged out by him to look at those same sheep, it would be this. She dropped her large summer hat with its blue ribbons on the grass and told him to carry it back for her, for she wanted to feel the summer air on her forehead and in her hair. She walked on very slowly, as he had told her to do, for she wished to obey him in everything. As she walked she felt a great new happiness in being altogether alone, even without Bijou. She could not remember that she had ever before in all her life been altogether alone. The landscape around her was still, as if full of promise, and it was hers. Even the swallows cruising in the air were hers, for they belonged to him,[6] and he was hers.

She followed the curving edge of the grove and after a minute or two found that she was out of sight to the men by the sheephouse. What could now, she wondered, be sweeter than to walk along the path in the long flowering meadow grass, slowly, slowly, and to let her husband overtake her there? It would be sweeter still, she reflected, to steal into the grove and to be gone, to have vanished from the surface of the earth from him when, tired of the sheep and longing for her company, he should turn the bend of the path to catch up with her.

An idea struck her; she stood still to think it over.

A few days ago her husband had gone for a ride and she had not wanted to go with him, but had strolled about with Bijou in order to explore her domain. Bijou then, gamboling, had led her straight into the grove. As she had followed him, gently forcing her way into the shrubbery, she had suddenly come upon a glade in the midst of it, a narrow space like a small alcove with hangings of thick green and golden brocade, big enough to hold two or three people in it. She had felt at that moment that she had come into the very heart of her new home. If today she could find the spot

6. **him:** that is, Sigismund. In Denmark at the time of the story, birds and other wild animals on an estate were the owner's property.

again she would stand perfectly still there, hidden from all the world. Sigismund would look for her in all directions; he would be unable to understand what had become of her and for a minute, for a short minute—or, perhaps, if she was firm and cruel enough, for five—he would realize what a void, what an unendurably sad and horrible place the universe would be when she was no longer in it. She gravely scrutinized the grove to find the right entrance to her hiding place, then went in.

She took great care to make no noise at all, therefore advanced exceedingly slowly. When a twig caught the flounces of her ample skirt she loosened it softly from the muslin, so as not to crack it. Once a branch took hold of one of her long golden curls; she stood still, with her arms lifted, to free it. A little way into the grove the soil became moist; her light steps no longer made any sound upon it. With one hand she held her small handkerchief to her lips, as if to emphasize the secretness of her course. She found the spot she sought and bent down to divide the foliage and make a door to her sylvan closet. At this the hem of her dress caught her foot and she stopped to loosen it. As she rose she looked into the face of a man who was already in the shelter.

He stood up erect, two steps off. He must have watched her as she made her way straight toward him.

She took him in in one single glance. His face was bruised and scratched, his hands and wrists stained with dark filth. He was dressed in rags, barefooted, with tatters wound round his naked ankles. His arms hung down to his sides, his right hand clasped the hilt of a knife. He was about her own age. The man and the woman looked at each other.

This meeting in the wood from beginning to end passed without a word; what happened could only be rendered by pantomime. To the two actors in the pantomime it was timeless; according to a clock it lasted four minutes.

She had never in her life been exposed to danger. It did not occur to her to sum up her position, or to work out the length of time it would take to call her husband or Mathias, whom at this moment she could hear shouting to his dogs. She beheld the man before her as she would have beheld a forest ghost: the apparition itself, not the

sequels of it, changes the world to the human who faces it.

Although she did not take her eyes off the face before her, she sensed that the alcove had been turned into a covert.[7] On the ground a couple of sacks formed a couch; there were some gnawed bones by it. A fire must have been made here in the night, for there were cinders strewn on the forest floor.

After a while she realized that he was observing her just as she was observing him. He was no longer just run to earth and crouching for a spring, but he was wondering, trying to know. At that she seemed to see herself with the eyes of the wild animal at bay in his dark hiding place: her silently approaching white figure, which might mean death.

He moved his right arm till it hung down straight before him between his legs. Without lifting the hand he bent the wrist and slowly raised the point of the knife till it pointed at her throat. The gesture was mad, unbelievable. He did not smile as he made it, but his nostrils distended, the corners of his mouth quivered a little. Then slowly he put the knife back in the sheath by his belt.

She had no object of value about her, only the wedding ring which her husband had set on her finger in church, a week ago. She drew it off, and in this movement dropped her handkerchief. She reached out her hand with the ring toward him. She did not bargain for her life. She was fearless by nature, and the horror with which he inspired her was not fear of what he might do to her. She commanded him, she besought him to vanish as he had come, to take a dreadful figure out of her life, so that it should never have been there. In the dumb movement her young form had the grave authoritativeness of a priestess conjuring down some monstrous being by a sacred sign.

He slowly reached out his hand to hers, his finger touched hers, and her hand was steady at the touch. But he did not take the ring. As she let it go it dropped to the ground as her handkerchief had done.

For a second the eyes of both followed it. It rolled a few inches toward him and stopped be-

7. **covert** (kō′vərt): hiding place; shelter.

fore his bare foot. In a hardly perceivable movement he kicked it away and again looked into her face. They remained like that, she knew not how long, but she felt that during that time something happened, things were changed.

He bent down and picked up her handkerchief. All the time gazing at her, he again drew his knife and wrapped the tiny bit of cambric round the blade. This was difficult for him to do because his left arm was broken. While he did it his face under the dirt and suntan slowly grew whiter till it was almost phosphorescent. Fumbling with both hands, he once more stuck the knife into the sheath. Either the sheath was too big and had never fitted the knife, or the blade was much worn—it went in. For two or three more seconds his gaze rested on her face; then he lifted his own

face a little, the strange radiance still upon it, and closed his eyes.

The movement was definitive and unconditional. In this one motion he did what she had begged him to do: He vanished and was gone. She was free.

She took a step backward, the immovable, blind face before her, then bent as she had done to enter the hiding place, and glided away as noiselessly as she had come. Once outside the grove she stood still and looked round for the meadow path, found it, and began to walk home.

Her husband had not yet rounded the edge of the grove. Now he saw her and helloed to her gaily; he came up quickly and joined her.

The path here was so narrow that he kept half behind her and did not touch her. He began to

Svartbekken (1909) by Henrik Sørensen. (120 cm × 110.5 cm).

Bergen Kommunes Kunstsamlinger, Norway.

explain to her what had been the matter with the lambs. She walked a step before him and thought: All is over.

After a while he noticed her silence, came up beside her to look at her face, and asked, "What is the matter?"

She searched her mind for something to say, and at last said: "I have lost my ring."

"What ring?" he asked her.

She answered, "My wedding ring."

As she heard her own voice pronounce the words, she conceived their meaning.

Her wedding ring. "With this ring"—dropped by one and kicked away by another—"with this ring I thee wed." With this lost ring she had wedded herself to something. To what? To poverty, persecution, total loneliness. To the sorrows and the sinfulness of this earth. "And what therefore God has joined together let man not put asunder."

"I will find you another ring," her husband said. "You and I are the same as we were on our wedding day; it will do as well. We are husband and wife today too, as much as yesterday, I suppose."

Her face was so still that he did not know if she had heard what he said. It touched him that she should take the loss of his ring so to heart. He took her hand and kissed it. It was cold, not quite the same hand as he had last kissed. He stopped to make her stop with him.

"Do you remember where you had the ring on last?" he asked.

"No," she answered.

"Have you any idea," he asked, "where you may have lost it?"

"No," she answered. "I have no idea at all."

FINDING COMMON GROUND

The couple in the story seem, at first, to live in a kind of fairy-tale paradise far from the concerns of unfortunates who might have to steal for food. All too soon, however, the troubles of the wider world intrude on their personal happiness.

Think about your own response to Lise's experience with the stranger. (Be sure to check your reading notes.) Get together with a small group to talk about the story. Here are some questions you might consider, though you also might want to set your own agendas:

• Why doesn't the stranger accept Lise's ring? Why doesn't he try to hurt her?

• Why doesn't Lise tell her husband about her experience with the stranger?

• How has Lise changed by the end of the story? How has her relationship with her husband changed?

• Be sure to comment on the relevance of the story to your life today. When your group has finished its discussion, assign one member to report to the class. Then see if, as a class, you can sum up your responses to the story—including your disagreements as well as any consensus you may reach.

Stevie Smith
(1902–1971)

She was christened Florence Margaret Smith but got the nickname "Stevie" because she was short, like the British jockey Steve Donohue. She grew up in a suburb of London, abandoned by her father and raised by her mother and an aunt. Smith lived with her aunt for sixty-six years, until "Auntie Lion" died in 1968 at the age of ninety-six.

After finishing school, Smith worked as a secretary for a magazine publisher. She remained there for thirty years and began to publish poetry and fiction while in her early thirties. Her first publication, *Novel on Yellow Paper* (1936), is a playful monologue spoken by a character very much like Smith herself.

Smith's other early publications—mostly novels—also reflect her offbeat outlook and writing style. But it is in her poems that she fully displays her cleverness. The light side of her poetry often reflects a darker side as well, making her verse seriocomic (partly serious, partly humorous). Her poems often deal with death, loneliness, or despair, but Smith is never self-pitying. Her humor adds sparkle, allowing her to distance herself from her subject. Smith herself best summed up her paradoxical views when she claimed that she was "straightforward, but not simple." The poet Robert Lowell described her poetic "voice" as "cheerfully gruesome," and the poet-humorist Ogden Nash admired her "songs of deadly innocence."

Stevie Smith (1954).

Before You Read
NOT WAVING BUT DROWNING

Make the Connection

Life's Misunderstandings

Everyone has misunderstandings. In fact, we misread each other's signals about nearly everything—from the most trivial to the most important things in life. We say one thing. People think we mean something else. We act a certain way for one reason. People think our action is motivated by something entirely different. The results of our misunderstandings can sometimes be tragic, as in this poem.

Quickwrite

Freewrite for a few minutes as you focus on Smith's **title:** What do you predict it means?

Background

Stevie Smith published ten volumes of verse, but, with the exception of this one poem, most of her poetry is unknown to American readers. Why this poem should have become more famous than all of her other poems is a question best answered by readers like you.

Here's what the poet reveals about her state of mind when she wrote the poem:

"I often try to pull myself together, having been well brought up in the stiff-upper-lip school of thought and not knowing whether other people find Death as merry as I do. But it's a tightrope business, this pulling oneself together, and can give rise to misunderstandings which may prove fatal, as in the poem I wrote about a poor fellow who got drowned. His friends thought he was waving to them but really he was asking for help."

Not Waving but Drowning

Stevie Smith

Nobody heard him, the dead man,
But still he lay moaning:
I was much further out than you thought
And not waving but drowning.

5　Poor chap, he always loved larking°
And now he's dead
It must have been too cold for him his heart gave way,
They said.

Oh, no no no, it was too cold always
10　(Still the dead one lay moaning)
I was much too far out all my life
And not waving but drowning.

5. larking: playing; having a good time.

Blue and Silver—Chopping Channel
(c. 1890) by James Abbott McNeill Whistler.

Courtesy of the Freer Gallery of Art, Smithsonian
Institution, Washington, D.C.

The Truths About Poetry

Here are some of the truths about poetry. She is an Angel, very strong. It is not poetry but the poet who has a feminine ending, not the Muse who is weak, but the poet. She makes a strong communication. Poetry is like a strong explosion in the sky. She makes a mushroom shape of terror and drops to the ground with a strong infection. Also she is a strong way out. The human creature is alone in his carapace. Poetry is a strong way out. . . .

Poetry does not like to be up-to-date, she refuses to be neat. ("Anglo-Saxon," wrote Gavin Bone, "is a good language to write poetry in because it is impossible to be neat.") All the poems Poetry writes may be called "Heaven, a Detail," or "Hell, a Detail." (She only writes about heaven and hell.) . . .

All Poetry has to do is to make a strong communication. All the poet has to do is to listen. The poet is not an important fellow. There will always be another poet.

—Stevie Smith, *from Me Again*

MAKING MEANINGS

First Thoughts

1. What does the **title** of the poem mean to you? (How do your ideas after reading the poem compare with your Quickwrite notes?)

Shaping Interpretations

2. How many different voices do you hear speaking in the poem?

3. What does the speaker mean by "it was too cold always" and "I was much too far out all my life"?

4. It seems bizarre that a dead man is talking. What might "dead" signify in the poem, besides its literal meaning? How is the dead man misunderstood or ignored?

Extending the Text

5. How could this poem be a summing up of one's whole life, or of the human condition in general?

Challenging the Text

6. Stevie Smith once said that good writing had to be "sad, true, economical, and funny." Does her poem meet these criteria? Do you agree with Smith's prescription for good writing?

CHOICES:
Building Your Portfolio

Writer's Notebook

1. Collecting Ideas for a Problem-Solution Essay

Many people are "drowning" and in need of help. What obligation does society have to people in trouble, people who need a helping hand? Freewrite your ideas on this issue—focus on identifying the problems and listing possible solutions. You might want to jot down your response to the words of Joseph Conrad that open this collection (page 1059). Save your notes for the Writer's Workshop on page 1179.

Exploring a Metaphor

2. Sinking or Swimming

In an essay, explain how the sea is often used, in literature and in ordinary conversation, as a metaphor for life and death. What comparisons do we often make between living and swimming, floating, sinking, diving, or drowning?

Frank O'Connor

(1903–1966)

Frank O'Connor.

Frank O'Connor was born Michael Francis O'Donovan in Cork City, Ireland. He was the only child of a bitterly poor couple whose battling shadowed his life.

O'Connor read endlessly, first boys' magazines and then, finding his way to the library, books of all kinds. Ironically, he particularly enjoyed stories of English schoolboys, and while he knew there would never be money for any such formal education in his own life, he imagined its privileges and yearned to be an educated man.

The reality of his own schooling was not half so appealing. O'Connor attended the Christian Brothers' school in Cork but in the end gave up on school, feeling it was a place where he would always be "useless, frightened, or hurt." But he had no intention of abandoning his dream of an education. At fourteen, he took a series of clerk's jobs that gave him money to buy the books he needed to educate himself.

In 1916, the long-standing hostility between England and Ireland flared into open rebellion, and O'Connor was caught up in the new patriotism. He read Irish history with new fervor and, along with other young Irishmen, thought of heroism. "I was improvising an education I could not afford," he said later, "and the country was improvising a revolution it could not afford." After England had brought up its artillery and "blown the center of Dublin flat . . . the country had to content itself with a make-believe revolution and I had to content myself with a make-believe education and the curious thing is that it was the make-believe that succeeded."

Truce with England came in 1921, when O'Connor was just short of eighteen, but its terms were unacceptable to a large number of Irish people. The treaty was immediately followed by a civil war in which O'Connor took the Republican side (the side that favored severing all ties to England and establishing an Irish republic). Throughout the next two years, he was active in the war, and while on a mission in the spring of 1923, he was arrested and imprisoned.

When at last he was released, he went on to educate himself further and to take part in the Irish literary revival, a movement that tried to restore the Irish language (it had been nearly wiped out by the English) and to create a purely Irish literature. For his pen name, he chose his beloved mother's maiden name.

O'Connor began writing stories, and in 1935, with his friend the poet W. B. Yeats, he became a director of the Abbey Theatre in Dublin. The theater was the heart of the Irish revival, which also involved Lady Gregory, Sean O'Casey, Seán O'Faoláin, and Liam O'Flaherty.

In his writing, O'Connor sought to capture the essence of Irish lyrical speech. His stories are all set in Ireland because "I know to a syllable how everything in Ireland can be said." O'Connor became a richly productive literary figure, bringing forth volumes of poetry, stories, a novel, an autobiography, plays, criticism, and translations. He was a regular contributor to such American magazines as *The New Yorker, The Atlantic Monthly,* and *Esquire.* Speaking of his mastery of the short-story form, Yeats said, "O'Connor is doing for Ireland what Chekhov did for Russia."

O'Connor came to the United States in 1952. In his later years, he taught at Harvard, Northwestern, and Stanford. For a poor boy with very little formal education, he had done quite well.

go.hrw.com
HRW
LE0 12-14

Before You Read

MY OEDIPUS COMPLEX

Make the Connection

Three's a Crowd

Have you ever heard the saying "Two's company; three's a crowd"? The saying reflects a basic human truth: Triangles often mean trouble in human relationships.

Many of us encounter our first troublesome triangle very early in life: If we're a first or an only child, we may compete with one parent for the attention of the other parent. In bigger families or families with a single parent, we may compete with a brother or sister to see who can capture a parent's attention. Among our childhood friends, alliances often shift daily.

Even later, with those we love deeply, a certain possessiveness may grip us when a third person enters the scene. Why do we have such a desire for the sole attentions of another? Are these feelings inevitable?

Quickwrite

Have you ever ob-served a young child competing with a father or mother for the attention of the other parent? Have you noticed any comical aspects of this earliest of all triangles in our lives? How about so-called sibling rivalry—what have you observed about brothers' and sisters' competing for the love and attention of the parents?

Elements of Literature

Dramatic Irony

The narrator of this story is a little boy competing with his father for his mother's love. In his innocence, the child assumes that he will marry his mother when he grows up. We, the readers, know, of course, that this will never happen. The child's lack of understanding of his parents' relationship fills the story with hilarious examples of **dramatic irony**.

> **D**ramatic irony occurs when the reader knows something important that a character does not know.
>
> *For more on Irony, see the Handbook of Literary Terms.*

Background

In Greek mythology, King Oedipus (ed′i·pəs) of Thebes, unaware of his true parentage, kills his father and marries his mother. The term *Oedipus complex* was first used in 1899 by the Austrian "father of psychoanalysis," Sigmund Freud, to describe the unconscious desire of a child for the exclusive love of the parent of the opposite sex. This desire results in rivalry with the parent of the same sex. In psychoanalytic theory, the Oedipus complex is a stage in normal human development, lasting from about age three to age five or six, and ending when the child identifies with the parent of the same sex.

My Oedipus Complex

Frank O'Connor

Father was in the army all through the war—the first war,[1] I mean—so, up to the age of five, I never saw much of him, and what I saw did not worry me. Sometimes I woke and there was a big figure in khaki peering down at me in the candlelight. Sometimes in the early morning I heard the slamming of the front door and the clatter of nailed boots[2] down the cobbles of the lane. These were Father's entrances and exits. Like Santa Claus he came and went mysteriously.

In fact, I rather liked his visits, though it was an uncomfortable squeeze between Mother and him when I got into the big bed in the early morning. He smoked, which gave him a pleasant musty smell, and shaved, an operation of astounding interest. Each time he left a trail of souvenirs—model tanks and Gurkha[3] knives with handles made of bullet cases, and German helmets and cap badges and button sticks,[4] and all sorts of military equipment—carefully stowed away in a long box on top of the wardrobe, in case they ever came in handy. There was a bit of the magpie[5] about Father; he expected everything to come in handy. When his back was turned, Mother let me get a chair and rummage through his treasures. She didn't seem to think so highly of them as he did.

The war was the most peaceful period of my life. The window of my attic faced southeast. My mother had curtained it, but that had small effect. I always woke with the first light and, with all the responsibilities of the previous day melted, feeling myself rather like the sun, ready to illumine and rejoice. Life never seemed so simple and clear and full of possibilities as then. I put my feet out from under the clothes[6]—I called them Mrs. Left and Mrs. Right—and invented dramatic situations for them in which they discussed the problems of the day. At least Mrs. Right did; she was very demonstrative, but I hadn't the same control of Mrs. Left, so she mostly contented herself with nodding agreement.

They discussed what Mother and I should do during the day, what Santa Claus should give a fellow for Christmas, and what steps should be taken to brighten the home. There was that little matter of the baby, for instance. Mother and I could never agree about that. Ours was the only house in the terrace[7] without a new baby, and Mother said we couldn't afford one till Father came back from the war because they cost seventeen and six.[8] That showed how simple she was. The Geneys up the road had a baby, and everyone knew they couldn't afford seventeen and six. It was probably a cheap baby, and Mother wanted something really good, but I felt she was too exclusive. The Geneys' baby would have done us fine.

Having settled my plans for the day, I got up, put a chair under the attic window, and lifted the frame high enough to stick out my head. The window overlooked the front gardens of the terrace behind ours, and beyond these it looked over a deep valley to the tall, red-brick houses terraced up the opposite hillside, which were all still in shadow, while those at our side of the valley were all lit up, though with long strange shadows that made them seem unfamiliar; rigid and painted.

After that I went into Mother's room and climbed into the big bed. She woke and I began to tell her of my schemes. By this time, though I never seem to have noticed it, I was petrified[9] in my nightshirt, and I thawed as I talked until, the last frost melted, I fell asleep beside her and woke again only when I heard her below in the kitchen, making the breakfast.

After breakfast we went into town; heard Mass at St. Augustine's and said a prayer for Father, and did the shopping. If the afternoon was fine we either went for a walk in the country or a visit to

---

1. **first war:** World War I (1914-1918).
2. **nailed boots:** boots with short, broad-headed nails on the soles to prevent slipping and wear; also called hobnail boots.
3. **Gurkha** (goor′kä′): people of the mountains of Nepal, many of whom served in the British army.
4. **button sticks:** slotted strips of metal or wood that fit over a row of buttons on a military tunic, allowing the buttons to be polished without soiling the cloth.
5. **magpie:** type of bird that picks up all kinds of unlikely materials to build its nest.

6. **clothes:** bedclothes.
7. **terrace:** row of houses.
8. **seventeen and six:** seventeen shillings and sixpence.
9. **petrified** (pe′tri·fĭd′): rigid from the cold.

Mother's great friend in the convent, Mother St. Dominic. Mother had them all praying for Father, and every night, going to bed, I asked God to send him back safe from the war to us. Little, indeed, did I know what I was praying for!

One morning, I got into the big bed, and there, sure enough, was Father in his usual Santa Claus manner, but later, instead of uniform, he put on his best blue suit, and Mother was as pleased as anything. I saw nothing to be pleased about, because, out of uniform, Father was altogether less interesting, but she only beamed, and explained that our prayers had been answered, and off we went to Mass to thank God for having brought Father safely home.

The irony of it! That very day when he came in to dinner he took off his boots and put on his slippers, donned the dirty old cap he wore about the house to save him from colds, crossed his legs, and began to talk gravely to Mother, who looked anxious. Naturally, I disliked her looking anxious, because it destroyed her good looks, so I interrupted him.

"Just a moment, Larry!" she said gently.

This was only what she said when we had boring visitors, so I attached no importance to it and went on talking.

"Do be quiet, Larry!" she said impatiently. "Don't you hear me talking to Daddy?"

This was the first time I had heard those <u>ominous</u> words, "talking to Daddy," and I couldn't help feeling that if this was how God answered prayers, he couldn't listen to them very attentively.

"Why are you talking to Daddy?" I asked with as great a show of indifference as I could muster.

"Because Daddy and I have business to discuss. Now, don't interrupt again!"

In the afternoon, at Mother's request, Father took me for a walk. This time we went into town instead of out the country, and I thought at first, in my usual optimistic way, that it might be an improvement. It was nothing of the sort. Father and I had quite different notions of a walk in town. He had no proper interest in trams,[10] ships, and horses, and the only thing that seemed to divert him was talking to fellows as old as himself. When I wanted to stop he simply went on, dragging me behind him by the hand; when he wanted to stop

10. **trams:** streetcars.

I had no alternative but to do the same. I noticed that it seemed to be a sign that he wanted to stop for a long time whenever he leaned against a wall. The second time I saw him do it I got wild. He seemed to be settling himself forever. I pulled him by the coat and trousers, but, unlike Mother who, if you were too persistent, got into a wax[11] and said: "Larry, if you don't behave yourself, I'll give you a good slap," Father had an extraordinary capacity for amiable inattention. I sized him up and wondered would I cry, but he seemed to be too remote to be annoyed even by that. Really, it was like going for a walk with a mountain! He either ignored the wrenching and pummeling[12] entirely, or else glanced down with a grin of amusement from his peak. I had never met anyone so absorbed in himself as he seemed.

At teatime, "talking to Daddy" began again, complicated this time by the fact that he had an evening paper, and every few minutes he put it down and told Mother something new out of it. I felt this was foul play. Man for man, I was prepared to compete with him any time for Mother's attention, but when he had it all made up for him by other people it left me no chance. Several times I tried to change the subject without success.

"You must be quiet while Daddy is reading, Larry," Mother said impatiently.

It was clear that she either genuinely liked talking to Father better than talking to me, or else that he had some terrible hold on her which made her afraid to admit the truth.

"Mummy," I said that night when she was tucking me up, "do you think if I prayed hard God would send Daddy back to the war?"

She seemed to think about that for a moment.

"No, dear," she said with a smile. "I don't think he would."

"Why wouldn't he, Mummy?"

"Because there isn't a war any longer, dear."

"But, Mummy, couldn't God make another war, if He liked?"

11. **got into a wax:** became upset.
12. **pummeling** (pum′əl·iŋ): hitting repeatedly with the fists.

WORDS TO OWN
ominous (äm′ə·nəs) adj.: threatening.

"He wouldn't like to, dear. It's not God who makes wars, but bad people."

"Oh!" I said.

I was disappointed about that. I began to think that God wasn't quite what he was cracked up to be.

Next morning I woke at my usual hour, feeling like a bottle of champagne. I put out my feet and invented a long conversation in which Mrs. Right talked of the trouble she had with her own father till she put him in the Home. I didn't quite know what the Home was but it sounded the right place for Father. Then I got my chair and stuck my head out of the attic window. Dawn was just breaking, with a guilty air that made me feel I had caught it in the act. My head bursting with stories and schemes, I stumbled in next door, and in the half-darkness scrambled into the big bed. There was no room at Mother's side so I had to get between her and Father. For the time being I had forgotten about him, and for several minutes I sat bolt upright, racking my brains to know what I could do with him. He was taking up more than his fair share of the bed, and I couldn't get comfortable, so I gave him several kicks that made him grunt and stretch. He made room all right, though. Mother waked and felt for me. I settled back comfortably in the warmth of the bed with my thumb in my mouth.

"Mummy!" I hummed, loudly and contentedly.

"Sssh! dear," she whispered. "Don't wake Daddy!"

This was a new development, which threatened to be even more serious than "talking to Daddy." Life without my early-morning conferences was unthinkable.

"Why?" I asked severely.

"Because poor Daddy is tired."

This seemed to me a quite inadequate reason, and I was sickened by the sentimentality of her "poor Daddy." I never liked that sort of gush; it always struck me as insincere.

"Oh!" I said lightly. Then in my most <u>winning</u> tone: "Do you know where I want to go with you today, Mummy?"

"No, dear," she sighed.

"I want to go down the Glen and fish for thornybacks with my new net, and then I want to go out to the Fox and Hounds, and—"

"Don't-wake-Daddy!" she hissed angrily, clapping her hand across my mouth.

But it was too late. He was awake, or nearly so. He grunted and reached for the matches. Then he stared <u>incredulously</u> at his watch.

"Like a cup of tea, dear?" asked Mother in a meek, hushed voice I had never heard her use before. It sounded almost as though she were afraid.

"Tea?" he exclaimed indignantly. "Do you know what the time is?"

"And after that I want to go up the Rathcooney Road," I said loudly, afraid I'd forget something in all those interruptions.

"Go to sleep at once, Larry!" she said sharply.

I began to snivel. I couldn't concentrate, the way that pair went on, and smothering my early-morning schemes was like burying a family from the cradle.

Father said nothing, but lit his pipe and sucked it, looking out into the shadows without minding Mother or me. I knew he was mad. Every time I made a remark Mother hushed me irritably. I was mortified. I felt it wasn't fair; there was even something sinister in it. Every time I had pointed out to her the waste of making two beds when we could both sleep in one, she had told me it was healthier like that, and now here was this man, this stranger, sleeping with her without the least regard for her health!

He got up early and made tea, but though he brought Mother a cup he brought none for me.

"Mummy," I shouted, "I want a cup of tea, too."

"Yes, dear," she said patiently. "You can drink from Mummy's saucer."

That settled it. Either Father or I would have to leave the house. I didn't want to drink from Mother's saucer; I wanted to be treated as an equal in my own home, so, just to spite her, I drank it all and left none for her. She took that quietly, too.

But that night when she was putting me to bed she said gently:

"Larry, I want you to promise me something."

"What is it?" I asked.

"Not to come in and disturb poor Daddy in the morning. Promise?"

WORDS TO OWN

winning (win′iŋ) *adj.*: charming.

incredulously (in·krej′oo·ləs·lē) *adv.*: disbelievingly.

"Poor Daddy" again! I was becoming suspicious of everything involving that quite impossible man.

"Why?" I asked.

"Because poor Daddy is worried and tired and he doesn't sleep well."

"Why doesn't he, Mummy?"

"Well, you know, don't you, that while he was at the war Mummy got the pennies from the Post Office?"

"From Miss MacCarthy?"

"That's right. But now, you see, Miss MacCarthy hasn't any more pennies, so Daddy must go out and find us some. You know what would happen if he couldn't?"

"No," I said, "tell us."

"Well, I think we might have to go out and beg for them like the poor old woman on Fridays. We wouldn't like that, would we?"

"No," I agreed. "We wouldn't."

"So you'll promise not to come in and wake him?"

"Promise."

Mind you, I meant that. I knew pennies were a serious matter, and I was all against having to go out and beg like the old woman on Fridays. Mother laid out all my toys in a complete ring round the bed so that, whatever way I got out, I was bound to fall over one of them.

When I woke I remembered my promise all right. I got up and sat on the floor and played—for hours, it seemed to me. Then I got my chair and looked out the attic window for more hours. I wished it was time for Father to wake; I wished someone would make me a cup of tea. I didn't feel in the least like the sun; instead, I was bored and so very, very cold! I simply longed for the warmth and depth of the big featherbed.

At last I could stand it no longer. I went into the next room. As there was still no room at Mother's side I climbed over her and she woke with a start.

"Larry," she whispered, gripping my arm very tightly, "what did you promise?"

"But I did, Mummy," I wailed, caught in the very act. "I was quiet for ever so long."

"Oh, dear, and you're perished!"[13] she said sadly, feeling me all over. "Now, if I let you stay will you promise not to talk?"

13. **perished:** frozen.

"But I want to talk, Mummy," I wailed.

"That has nothing to do with it," she said with a firmness that was new to me. "Daddy wants to sleep. Now, do you understand that?"

I understood it only too well. I wanted to talk, he wanted to sleep—whose house was it, anyway?

"Mummy," I said with equal firmness, "I think it would be healthier for Daddy to sleep in his own bed."

That seemed to stagger her, because she said nothing for a while.

"Now, once for all," she went on, "you're to be perfectly quiet or go back to your own bed. Which is it to be?"

The injustice of it got me down. I had convicted her out of her own mouth of inconsistency and unreasonableness, and she hadn't even attempted to reply. Full of spite, I gave Father a kick, which she didn't notice but which made him grunt and open his eyes in alarm.

"What time is it?" he asked in a panic-stricken voice, not looking at Mother but at the door, as if he saw someone there.

"It's early yet," she replied soothingly. "It's only the child. Go to sleep again. . . . Now, Larry," she added, getting out of bed, "you've wakened Daddy and you must go back."

This time, for all her quiet air, I knew she meant it, and knew that my principal rights and privileges were as good as lost unless I asserted them at once. As she lifted me, I gave a screech, enough to wake the dead, not to mind Father. He groaned.

"That damn child! Doesn't he ever sleep?"

"It's only a habit, dear," she said quietly, though I could see she was vexed.

"Well, it's time he got out of it," shouted Father, beginning to heave in the bed. He suddenly gathered all the bedclothes about him, turned to the wall, and then looked back over his shoulder with nothing showing only two small, spiteful, dark eyes. The man looked very wicked.

To open the bedroom door, Mother had to let me down, and I broke free and dashed for the farthest corner, screeching. Father sat bolt upright in bed.

"Shut up, you little puppy!" he said in a choking voice.

I was so astonished that I stopped screeching.

Mysterious Dreams and Secret Wishes

Frank O'Connor probably didn't read about the "Oedipus complex" in Sigmund Freud's twenty-four-volume collected works. This Freudian theory, and countless others, had already become a permanent part of twentieth-century culture by the time O'Connor wrote his story. Even today, Freud's work lives on in the very words we use to talk about the mind. You may have heard terms like "Freudian slip" or "wish fulfillment." But do you know where they come from?

Tell me what you're thinking. After early training as a physician, Sigmund Freud (1856–1939) became a leader in the new study of the mind. Cartoons of Freud often portray him as a bearded old man, scribbling away in a notebook while his patient lies on a comfortable couch and talks a blue streak. In fact, this was exactly the way Freud worked with his patients in Vienna: He thought that emotional problems were caused by memories his patients could not consciously remember, and he required his patients to "free associate," or speak their thoughts as randomly as they appeared in the mind. Freud believed such free as-sociation would lead back to an original traumatic experience, the discovery of which would cause the illness to dissolve.

Freud was also the first to propose that our deepest desires and fears lie buried in our unconscious, or "id." For Freud, the *id* (Latin for "it") represents our

---

Never, never had anyone spoken to me in that tone before. I looked at him incredulously and saw his face convulsed with rage. It was only then that I fully realized how God had codded[14] me, listening to my prayers for the safe return of this monster.

"Shut up, you!" I bawled, beside myself.

"What's that you said?" shouted Father, making a wild leap out of the bed.

"Mick, Mick!" cried Mother. "Don't you see the child isn't used to you?"

"I see he's better fed than taught," snarled Father, waving his arms wildly. "He wants his bottom smacked."

14. **codded:** British slang for "tricked."

All his previous shouting was as nothing to these obscene words referring to my person. They really made my blood boil.

"Smack your own!" I screamed hysterically. "Smack your own! Shut up! Shut up!"

At this he lost his patience and let fly at me. He did it with the lack of conviction you'd expect of a man under Mother's horrified eyes, and it ended up as a mere tap, but the sheer indignity of being struck at all by a stranger, a total stranger who had cajoled his way back from the war into our big

---

WORDS TO OWN
cajoled (kə·jōld′) *v.*: coaxed with flattery.

infant selves, the part of us which seeks gratification of every desire—or "wish fulfillment." The *ego* corresponds to a more adult self, and the *superego* is an internalized parental voice, an inner censor that reminds us what is morally right. In Freud's view, the three parts of the mind work together, or in conflict, with every human action.

Buried truths and slips of the tongue. Some of Freud's most influential ideas appeared in *The Interpretation of Dreams,* published in 1900. Here, Freud holds that dreams, rich with strange objects and illogical events, can be decoded to reveal unconscious wishes, fears, and memories. He also thought that common mistakes in everyday speech are connected to unconscious thoughts that somehow slip past the watchful superego (hence the "Freudian slip"). At dinner, for example, when we wish to comment on anything but a friend's ridiculous purple hat, we might say "Please pass the purple," and immediately draw attention to what we most wanted to avoid.

Recent critics have suggested that Freud, who originally wanted to be a novelist, forced his patients' histories into tidy packages, with convenient beginnings and endings, thus making them more like fiction than actual life. Nevertheless, Freud's ideas have given us invaluable concepts—and a lasting vocabulary—with which to contemplate ourselves and others.

bed as a result of my innocent <u>intercession</u>, made me completely dotty.[15] I shrieked and shrieked, and danced in my bare feet, and Father, looking awkward and hairy in nothing but a short gray army shirt, glared down at me like a mountain out for murder. I think it must have been then that I realized he was jealous too. And there stood Mother in her nightdress, looking as if her heart was broken between us. I hoped she felt as she looked. It seemed to me that she deserved it all.

From that morning out my life was a hell. Father and I were enemies, open and avowed. We conducted a series of skirmishes against one another, he trying to steal my time with Mother and

I his. When she was sitting on my bed, telling me a story, he took to looking for some pair of old boots which he alleged he had left behind him at the beginning of the war. While he talked to Mother I played loudly with my toys to show my total lack of concern. He created a terrible scene one evening when he came in from work and found me at his box, playing with his regimental badges, Gurkha knives, and button sticks. Mother got up and took the box from me.

15. **dotty:** crazy.

WORDS TO OWN
intercession (inʹtər·seshʹən) *n.:* pleading on behalf of another.

"You mustn't play with Daddy's toys unless he lets you, Larry," she said severely. "Daddy doesn't play with yours."

For some reason Father looked at her as if she had struck him and then turned away with a scowl.

"Those are not toys," he growled, taking down the box again to see had I lifted[16] anything. "Some of those curios are very rare and valuable."

But as time went on I saw more and more how he managed to <u>alienate</u> Mother and me. What made it worse was that I couldn't grasp his method or see what attraction he had for Mother. In every possible way he was less winning than I. He had a common accent and made noises at his tea. I thought for a while that it might be the newspapers she was interested in, so I made up bits of news of my own to read to her. Then I thought it might be the smoking, which I personally thought attractive, and took his pipes and went round the house dribbling into them till he caught me. I even made noises at my tea, but Mother only told me I was disgusting. It all seemed to hinge round that unhealthy habit of sleeping together, so I made a point of dropping into their bedroom and nosing round, talking to myself, so that they wouldn't know I was watching them, but they were never up to anything that I could see. In the end it beat me. It seemed to depend on being grown-up and giving people rings, and I realized I'd have to wait.

But at the same time I wanted him to see that I was only waiting, not giving up the fight. One evening when he was being particularly <u>obnoxious</u>, chattering away well above my head, I let him have it.

"Mummy," I said, "do you know what I'm going to do when I grow up?"

"No, dear," she replied. "What?"

"I'm going to marry you," I said quietly.

Father gave a great <u>guffaw</u> out of him, but he didn't take me in. I knew it must only be pretense. And Mother, in spite of everything, was pleased. I felt she was probably relieved to know that one day Father's hold on her would be broken.

"Won't that be nice?" she said with a smile.

16. **lifted:** British slang for "stolen."

"It'll be very nice," I said confidently. "Because we're going to have lots and lots of babies."

"That's right, dear," she said placidly. "I think we'll have one soon, and then you'll have plenty of company."

I was no end pleased about that because it showed that in spite of the way she gave in to Father she still considered my wishes. Besides, it would put the Geneys in their place.

It didn't turn out like that, though. To begin with, she was very <u>preoccupied</u>—I supposed about where she would get the seventeen and six—and though Father took to staying out late in the evenings it did me no particular good. She stopped taking me for walks, became as touchy as blazes, and smacked me for nothing at all. Sometimes I wished I'd never mentioned the confounded baby—I seemed to have a genius for bringing calamity on myself.

And calamity it was! Sonny arrived in the most appalling hullabaloo—even that much he couldn't do without a fuss—and from the first moment I disliked him. He was a difficult child—so far as I was concerned he was always difficult—and demanded far too much attention. Mother was simply silly about him, and couldn't see when he was only showing off. As company he was worse than useless. He slept all day, and I had to go round the house on tiptoe to avoid waking him. It wasn't any longer a question of not waking Father. The slogan now was "Don't-wake-Sonny!" I couldn't understand why the child wouldn't sleep at the proper time, so whenever Mother's back was turned I woke him. Sometimes to keep him awake I pinched him as well. Mother caught me at it one day and gave me a most unmerciful flaking.[17]

One evening, when Father was coming in from work, I was playing trains in the front garden. I let

17. **flaking:** spanking.

- -

WORDS TO OWN

alienate (āl′ē·ən·āt′) v.: to drive apart.

obnoxious (əb·näk′shəs) adj.: offensive.

guffaw (gu·fô′) n.: loud laugh. "Guffaw" is an echoic word—one that imitates the sound it stands for.

preoccupied (prē·äk′yo͞o·pīd′) adj.: absorbed in one's own thoughts.

- -

on not to notice him; instead, I pretended to be talking to myself, and said in a loud voice: "If another bloody baby comes into this house, I'm going out."

Father stopped dead and looked at me over his shoulder.

"What's that you said?" he asked sternly.

"I was only talking to myself," I replied, trying to conceal my panic. "It's private."

He turned and went in without a word. Mind you, I intended it as a solemn warning, but its effect was quite different. Father started being quite nice to me. I could understand that, of course. Mother was quite sickening about Sonny. Even at mealtimes she'd get up and gawk at him in the cradle with an idiotic smile, and tell Father to do the same. He was always polite about it, but he looked so puzzled you could see he didn't know what she was talking about. He complained of the way Sonny cried at night, but she only got cross and said that Sonny never cried except when there was something up with him—which was a flaming lie, because Sonny never had anything up with him, and only cried for attention. It was really painful to see how simpleminded she was. Father wasn't attractive, but he had a fine intelligence. He saw through Sonny, and now he knew that I saw through him as well.

One night I woke with a start. There was someone beside me in the bed. For one wild moment I felt sure it must be Mother, having come to her senses and left Father for good, but then I heard Sonny in convulsions in the next room, and Mother saying: "There! There! There!" and I knew it wasn't she. It was Father. He was lying beside me, wide awake, breathing hard and apparently as mad as hell.

After a while it came to me what he was mad about. It was his turn now. After turning me out of the big bed, he had been turned out himself. Mother had no consideration now for anyone but that poisonous pup, Sonny. I couldn't help feeling sorry for Father. I had been through it all myself, and even at that age I was <u>magnanimous</u>. I began to stroke him down and say: "There! There!" He wasn't exactly responsive.

"Aren't you asleep either?" he snarled.

"Ah, come on and put your arm around us, can't you?" I said, and he did, in a sort of way. Gingerly, I suppose, is how you'd describe it. He was very bony but better than nothing.

At Christmas he went out of his way to buy me a really nice model railway.

MAKING MEANINGS

First Thoughts

1. Which of Larry's opinions or misunderstandings did you find most comical? Share your favorite passages with other readers.

> ### Reading Check
>
> Larry describes the war, ironically, as the most peaceful part of his life. Outline the details of Larry's peaceful morning ritual during the war. How does his life change when his father comes home?

Shaping Interpretations

2. At one point in the story, Larry realizes that he and his father are conducting "a series of skirmishes against one another, he trying to steal my time with Mother and I his." What details justify Larry's conclusion that his father is really jealous of him?

3. What event finally resolves the **conflict** between Larry and his father?

4. What is the **dramatic irony** in Larry's remarks about the cost of a baby? Find and explain one additional example of dramatic irony in Larry's comments about sharing his mother with his father.

5. At the end of the story, how can you tell that Larry's Oedipal stage is over? But what new problem has arisen in the household?

6. The plot of a **comedy** often involves a young person who is in love, who has to fight people who block his (or her) love, and who ultimately triumphs. How does O'Connor use this typical comic plot?

7. How would you state the **theme** of this story?

Extending the Text

8. How does O'Connor's story compare with Joyce's "Araby" (page 986) in **plot, theme,** and **tone**?

9. Do you think O'Connor is having some fun with psychoanalytic theory in this story, or is there a serious situation beneath the comic surface? Explain your opinion.

CHOICES: Building Your Portfolio

Writer's Notebook

1. Collecting Ideas for a Problem-Solution Essay

O'Connor takes a comical view of his young narrator's conflicts, but the problems of childhood can be serious. Read the comment by O'Connor below, taken from his autobiography *An Only Child* (1961), in which he talks about his father. Then, consider the conflicts young Larry has to struggle with, and take notes on how those struggles could have serious consequences in real life. How can children be helped to adapt to family problems that they are too young to understand? Save your notes for the Writer's Workshop on page 1179.

> ...the house would be a horror. Only when he had money for drink would we have peace for an hour.... When I was old enough to go to school, I would come back at three o'clock and scout around to make sure that he was not at home.... When I talked of him to Mother, I always called him "he" or "him," carefully eschewing the name of "Father," which would have seemed like profanation to me.
>
> —Frank O'Connor,
> *from An Only Child*

Creative Writing

2. That Was Then

Refer to your Quickwrite notes. Have you ever observed a child struggling for the attention of a parent or coping with sibling rivalry? Using O'Connor's story as a model, write an account of a humorous incident from childhood—your own or someone else's. You will have to decide who will narrate your story, a child or an adult.

W. H. Auden
(1907–1973)

Wystan Hugh Auden gave a name to his times—"the Age of Anxiety"—and he lived to see the day when his influence was so broad and deep that, as far as poetry was concerned, that same era could have been called "the Age of Auden."

Auden was born in York, a city in northern England near the city of Leeds. He was the son of a physician and a nurse who encouraged his early interest in science and engineering. But in his adolescence, Auden discovered poetry, and he studied, with an analytical eye, all its forms, from Chaucer onward. By the time he entered Oxford, he was as much a teacher as he was a student, and he quickly gathered about himself other young poets, who accepted him as their leader.

Auden as a poet was difficult to classify, and he remains so to this day. By the time they have been recognized and acclaimed, most of the outstanding poets of any generation have produced individual works by which, rightly or wrongly, they will be identified. Sometimes these poems are masterpieces; sometimes they are rather run-of-the-mill poems which, for one reason or another, have caught the popular imagination. To this pattern, Auden is an exception. In spite of their virtuosity, uniform excellence, and formal variety, Auden's poems— lyrics, oratorios, ballads—tend to cohere as a body of work rather than to distinguish themselves as easily separable entities. For this reason, Auden is often regarded less as the author of certain individual poems than as the creator of a climate in which all things Audenesque thrive in an atmosphere uniquely his own.

Auden put his indelible stamp on the poetry of the 1930s, establishing his preeminence among the brilliant group of poets that included Stephen Spender, Louis MacNeice, and Cecil Day-Lewis. Auden caused his British compatriots shock and dismay when, in the critical year of 1939, as Hitler's divisions were about to

W. H. Auden (1950s).

©Rollie McKenna

march into Poland and initiate World War II, he decided to make his home in the United States. Auden had come to feel that, as the rise of fascism made war in Europe inevitable, his chances of enjoying creative freedom and of making a livelihood were available only in America. From 1939 to 1942, he taught at the University of Michigan and various other American universities. In 1946, he became a U.S. citizen.

For the next ten years, Auden lived mostly in New York City and California. He spent his summers in Kirchstetten, Austria, in a house he bought in 1957 with profits from his extensive reading tours—the first, and last, home of his own. This retreat, not far from Vienna, provided him with much-needed privacy and the opportunity to experience firsthand the culture of central Europe.

In England, Auden's emigration to the United States was, at the time, widely regarded as a defection, if not an outright betrayal. But the British eventually welcomed him back— first by electing him professor of poetry at Oxford, and later by making it possible for him to live on the campus of Christ Church College as a guest of the university whenever he returned to England.

Before You Read

MUSÉE DES BEAUX ARTS
THE UNKNOWN CITIZEN

Make the Connection

The Value of the Individual
Every generation sees imperfections and injustices in the way things are. For Auden, during what he termed the Age of Anxiety, people had grown indifferent to human suffering, and society no longer treasured the individual. This indifference to the plight of others and disregard for the value of individuality were, to Auden, the symptoms of a society in need of reform.

Quickwrite

To what extent do you think individuality and compassion are valued or disregarded today? Jot down some thoughts and examples.

Elements of Literature

Diction
Auden's poems combine eloquent and elegant poetic language with down-to-earth **colloquial** words and **technical** terms, the jargon of trades and professions. Notice how he uses contrasting diction in these poems not only to surprise you but also to relate his language to his ideas.

> **D**iction is a writer's or speaker's choice of words.
>
> *For more on Diction, see the Handbook of Literary Terms.*

The Fall of Icarus (16th century) by Pieter Bruegel the Elder.

Musées Royaux des Beaux-Arts, Brussels, Belgium.

The source and inspiration for this poem are found in the famous painting by Pieter Bruegel showing Icarus drowning, permanently on display in the Musée des Beaux Arts (myoo·zā' dā bō zȧr'), or Fine Arts Museum, in Brussels, Belgium. The painting depicts a dramatic moment in the Greek legend of Daedalus and his son, Icarus. According to the legend, the two were imprisoned on the island of Crete. In order to escape, Daedalus constructed wings of feathers and wax. Together they managed to take off from the island, but Icarus flew so high that the sun's heat melted the wax in his wings, causing him to fall into the sea and drown.

According to one critic, the painting represents "the greatest conception of indifference" in the history of art. The indifference, whether it is the artist's attitude or merely a strategy of technique, lies in its unexpected focus. The painting's center of interest is not Icarus, but a peasant plowing a field. He is handsomely dressed—in medieval rather than in Greek costume—and the furrows he tills are richly realistic. In the lower right-hand corner of the painting, almost as an afterthought, Icarus is seen splashing into the water not far from a passing ship.

Study the painting, and find the figure of the boy falling into the sea. Then, read the poem to see how Auden interprets the painting. Has he confirmed in words what the painter expressed with pigment?

Musée des Beaux Arts

W. H. Auden

About suffering they were never wrong,
The Old Masters: how well they understood
Its human position; how it takes place
While someone else is eating or opening a window or just walking dully along;
5 How, when the aged are reverently, passionately waiting
For the miraculous birth, there always must be
Children who did not specially want it to happen, skating
On a pond at the edge of the wood:
They never forgot
10 That even the dreadful martyrdom must run its course
Anyhow in a corner, some untidy spot
Where the dogs go on with their doggy life and the torturer's horse
Scratches its innocent behind on a tree.

In Bruegel's *Icarus,* for instance: how everything turns away
15 Quite leisurely from the disaster; the plowman may
Have heard the splash, the forsaken cry,
But for him it was not an important failure; the sun shone
As it had to on the white legs disappearing into the green
Water; and the expensive delicate ship that must have seen
20 Something amazing, a boy falling out of the sky,
Had somewhere to get to and sailed calmly on.

W. H. Auden's handwritten manuscript for "Musée des Beaux Arts."

Library of Congress, Washington, D.C.

MAKING MEANINGS

First Thoughts

1. Does this poem remind you of any times when the world seemed oblivious to individual suffering? Explain.

Shaping Interpretations

2. Who are the "Old Masters" (line 2)? What examples does the speaker provide to show how the Old Masters understood suffering? (Do you think Auden is right about this?)

3. Lines 5–13 describe two other paintings by Bruegel. What do you think are the events that Bruegel portrays? How do these paintings resemble *The Fall of Icarus*?

4. What example of his theory about suffering does the speaker offer in lines 14–21?

5. What contrast in **diction** can you see between expressions like "dreadful martyrdom" and "anyhow in a corner"? Find another example of contrasting diction.

6. What do you think is the overall **theme** of the poem? Which lines in the poem do you think are most important?

Connecting with the Text

7. Do you agree with the speaker that, in general, people are indifferent to the suffering they see around them? Why or why not? Look back at your Quickwrite notes as you answer.

One of the persistent themes of twentieth-century literature is the anonymity of the individual in an ever more bureaucratic world. Here, Auden uses diction that mimics the jargon and technical language of officialdom in a report that covers everything except the fact that "the unknown citizen" had a heart and a soul.

The Unknown Citizen

W. H. Auden

(To JS/07/M/378
This Marble Monument Is Erected by the State)

He was found by the Bureau of Statistics to be
One against whom there was no official complaint,
And all the reports on his conduct agree
That, in the modern sense of an old-fashioned word, he was a saint,
5   For in everything he did he served the Greater Community.
Except for the War till the day he retired
He worked in a factory and never got fired,
But satisfied his employers, Fudge Motors Inc.
Yet he wasn't a scab° or odd in his views,
10   For his Union reports that he paid his dues,
(Our report on his Union shows it was sound)
And our Social Psychology workers found
That he was popular with his mates and liked a drink.
The Press are convinced that he bought a paper every day
15   And that his reactions to advertisements were normal in every way.
Policies taken out in his name prove that he was fully insured,
And his Health-card shows he was once in hospital but left it cured.
Both Producers Research and High-Grade Living declare
He was fully sensible to the advantages of the Installment Plan
20   And had everything necessary to the Modern Man,
A phonograph, a radio, a car, and a frigidaire.
Our researchers into Public Opinion are content
That he held the proper opinions for the time of year;
When there was peace, he was for peace; when there was war, he went.
25   He was married and added five children to the population,
Which our Eugenist° says was the right number for a parent of his generation,
And our teachers report that he never interfered with their education.
Was he free? Was he happy? The question is absurd:
Had anything been wrong, we should certainly have heard.

9. scab: slang term for a worker who refuses to join a union.
26. eugenist (yoo'jə·nist): specialist in controlling the population in order to effect an ideal gene pool.

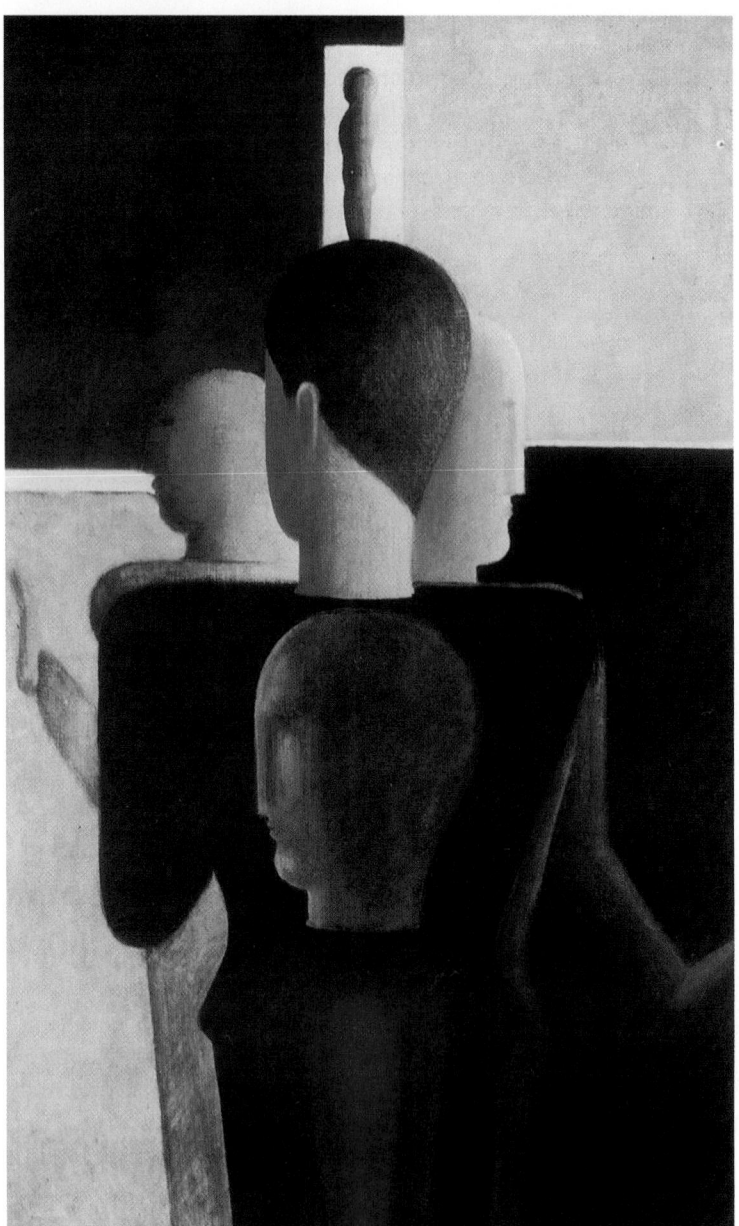

Concentric Group (1925)
by Oskar Schlemmer.
Oil on canvas.

© 2000 The Oskar Schlemmer
Family Estate and Archive, courtesy
Photo Archive C. Raman Schlemmer,
28824 Oggebbio, Italy.

MAKING MEANINGS

First Thoughts

1. Do you think this poem gives a true picture of our society today? Which details do or do not ring true? (Refer to your Quickwrite notes.)

Shaping Interpretations

2. What did the unknown citizen do for a living? What facts are reported on his conduct, and what agencies and groups contribute to this report?

3. Who do you think is the **speaker** of the poem? Although the poet does not directly state his opinions in this poem, they clearly emerge from the speaker's **tone.** How would you describe this tone?

4. Who do you think might have asked the questions in line 28?

5. What do you make of the inscription under the title? What other "monuments" are you reminded of?

6. What would you say is the message, or **theme,** of the poem? How do you feel about Auden's message?

7. Find examples of impersonal, bureaucratic diction in the poem. Do you read or hear **technical vocabulary** and **jargon** like this today? If so, where?

8. The poem seems to depict the "unknown citizen" as a colorless stereotype. Did you, however, sympathize with the citizen? Explain your response to him.

Extending the Text

9. Auden's message about modern life is quite pessimistic. What sources of optimism do you find in modern life? Your Quickwrite notes may give you some ideas.

Challenging the Text

10. Could this poem have been written in any other time of history but the twentieth century? Why or why not?

CHOICES:
Building Your Portfolio

Writer's Notebook
1. Collecting Ideas for a Problem-Solution Essay

As Auden's poems make clear, apathy and an impersonal bureaucracy can seriously affect not only the individual but also society as a whole. Is apathy or a mindless bureaucracy that ignores individual differences a serious problem in your school or community or in society as a whole? Get together with several other students to discuss this question and to explore the causes and effects of the problem. Take notes on your group's comments, and save them for possible use in the Writer's Workshop on page 1179.

Comparing Texts Across Cultures
2. Back to the Source

Read a translation or summary of Ovid's version of the myth of Daedalus and Icarus in Book 8 of the *Metamorphoses*. Then, in a brief essay, relate the myth to Auden's treatment of it in "Musée des Beaux Arts."

Interpreting a Painting
3. What Did Bruegel Mean?

Study the reproduction of Bruegel's *Icarus* on page 1092. In a paragraph, describe as precisely as you can what you see happening in the painting. Do you think Auden has correctly interpreted Bruegel's intent?

Analyzing Satire
4. Right on Target?

In a brief essay, analyze the targets and the methods of Auden's satire in "The Unknown Citizen." Does Auden manage to combine satire and sympathy? Explain your answer.

Creative Writing
5. Inspired by Art

Imitate Auden and write a poem, a brief essay, or a short story inspired by a painting or a piece of music. You might find a subject in a painting in this book.

Creative Writing
6. A Few Kind Words

Imagine that you are a good friend of the deceased citizen. Write your friend's obituary from this new point of view.

Creative Writing
7. Today's Unknown Citizen

Write your own epitaph for an unknown high school student, athlete, parent, or worker. Use the questions "Was he or she free? Was he or she happy?" as the focus of your account.

Contemporary British Drama

by **Robert Anderson**

It is difficult to know which of the playwrights of the twentieth century will stand the test of time—mostly because we are still too close to it. Plays are volatile creations, often written out of present concerns and emotions to reach an audience in the present. In a changing world with changing fashions, there is no way of knowing how people will respond to plays in the future. The highly regarded play of one generation is often viewed with contempt by the next generation: "How could they have thought that was a great play?"

Yet we can say with certainty that the twentieth century saw sweeping changes in both the content and the form of plays. Censorship of the stage in England ended in 1968, and since then there is virtually nothing that playwrights have not written about or cannot write about.

While the broadening of subject matter is a significant advance, some playwrights have been less interested in new subject matter than in new ways to get our attention—to shock us into recognizing old and new truths. These playwrights have followed various paths. Some have broken up the usual linear structure of a story—a beginning, a middle, and an end arranged in that order. In their plays they jump backward and forward in time,

Scene from a 1976 production of Samuel Beckett's *Waiting for Godot* at the Brooklyn Academy of Music, New York City.

hither and yon in space. Some, like the German playwright Bertolt Brecht, do not want to engage our sympathy for any character, but force us to keep our distance. Brecht called this "the alienation effect." Others, like the Irish playwright Samuel Beckett, ignore the usual ingredients of drama—character, conflict, development, and progression to a climax—and present us instead with a static situation.

Playwrights who depart from the familiar conventions of playwriting take a great risk; they are like performers on a high wire without the safety net of a story. They had better be star performers every time out, or there will be a disaster. If they deny their audiences the pleasure of narrative ("Tell me a story!"), they have to keep them fascinated by other means.

Theater of the Absurd: Samuel Beckett

Though Samuel Beckett (1906–1989) was born in Ireland, he lived most of his life in France and wrote many of his plays in French, which he then translated into English. Whether or not he can be considered a British playwright, his *Waiting for Godot* (1953) is a modern classic, and his work is a prime example of what is known as the Theater of the Absurd.

Deriving to some degree from James Joyce and surrealism, the Theater of the Absurd is an almost complete departure from the traditional theater of the preceding four hundred years. The Theater of the Absurd, first of all, represents an attitude toward life expressed in part by the French writer Albert Camus:

> A world that can be explained even with bad reasons is a familiar world. But, on the other hand, in a universe suddenly divested of illusions and lights, man feels an alien, a stranger. . . . This divorce between man and his life . . . is properly the feeling of absurdity.
>
> —Albert Camus, *from* "An Absurd Reasoning"

The Absurdists do not want to tell us a story with characters arguing about the emptiness of life. They want instead to *present* us with this emptiness, this absurdity, moment by moment, so that we can experience it. There is usually no progression, no development in an Absurdist play. As we shall see in Beckett's *Waiting for Godot,* the "action" is waiting. The French title for Beckett's play is *En Attendant Godot,* literally, "While Waiting for Godot." The play is about the "while." Since the Absurdists' view is that the world is irrational, unmotivated, without cause and effect, they convey this idea not only as "the message" of the play but also in the fragmented, irrational method of the playwriting. *Waiting for Godot* was first produced in Paris in 1953 and in London in 1955. Two tramps, Vladimir and Estragon, are on a stage, bare except for a tree.

Estragon. Charming spot. *(He turns, advances to the front, halts facing auditorium.)* Inspiring prospects. *(He turns to Vladimir.)* Let's go.

Vladimir. We can't.

Estragon. Why not?

Vladimir. We're waiting for Godot.

Estragon *(despairingly).* Ah! *(Pause.)* You're sure it was here?

Vladimir. What?

Estragon. That we were to wait.

Vladimir. He said by the tree. *(They look at the tree.)* Do you see any others?

Estragon. What is it?

Vladimir. I don't know. A willow.

Estragon. Where are the leaves?

Vladimir. It must be dead.

Estragon. No more weeping.

Vladimir. Or perhaps it's not the season.

Estragon. Looks to me more like a bush.

Vladimir. A shrub.

Estragon. A bush.

Vladimir. A ———. What are you insinuating? That we've come to the wrong place?

Estragon. He should be here.

Vladimir. He didn't say for sure he'd come.

Estragon. And if he doesn't come?

Vladimir. We'll come back tomorrow.

Estragon. And then the day after tomorrow.

Vladimir. Possibly.

Estragon. And so on.

Vladimir. The point is———

Estragon. Until he comes.

Vladimir. You're merciless.

Estragon. We came here yesterday.

Scene from a June 1984 production of Samuel Beckett's *Endgame* at the Cherry Lane Theater, New York.

Vladimir. Ah no, there you're mistaken.

Estragon. What did we do yesterday?

Vladimir. What did we do yesterday?

Estragon. Yes.

Vladimir. Why . . . *(Angrily.)* Nothing is certain when you're about.

Estragon. In my opinion we were here.

Vladimir *(looking around)*. You recognize the place?

Estragon. I didn't say that.

Vladimir. Well?

Estragon. That makes no difference.

Vladimir. All the same . . . that tree . . . *(turning toward auditorium)* that bog.

Estragon. You're sure it was this evening?

Vladimir. What?

Estragon. That we were to wait.

Vladimir. He said Saturday. *(Pause.)* I think.

Estragon. You think.

Vladimir. I must have made a note of it. *(He fumbles in his pockets, bursting with miscellaneous rubbish.)*

Estragon *(very insidious)*. But what Saturday? And is it Saturday? Is it not rather Sunday? *(Pause.)* Or Monday? *(Pause.)* Or Friday?

Vladimir *(looking wildly about him as though the date was inscribed in the landscape)*. It's not possible!

Estragon. Or Thursday?

Vladimir. What'll we do?

Estragon. If he came yesterday and we weren't here you may be sure he won't come again today.

Vladimir. But you say we were here yesterday.

Estragon. I may be mistaken. *(Pause.)* Let's stop talking for a minute. Do you mind?

Vladimir *(feebly)*. All right.

—Samuel Beckett, *from* Waiting for Godot

Thus ends one of the series of "riffs" that make up the play. After a few moments' pause, the characters will start up again, terrified by the silence and the momentary view of nothingness.

Many people find the work of the Absurdists (Beckett, Eugène Ionesco, Jean Genêt, and Edward Albee) maddening. They say, "That's not a play!" just as some years ago, steeped in representational painting, some said of abstract expressionism,

"That's not art!" Our expectations of what a play or a picture should be are deeply rooted in us, planted and nurtured by years of exposure to only certain kinds of dramatic experience or certain kinds of painting experience. The best we can do when faced with the strange is to try to remain open to the new, to let it try to educate us and broaden our appreciation, rather than to reject it because it is strange and new.

Who is Godot? When someone asked Beckett this question, he answered that if he had known, he would have revealed it in the play. Possibly Godot is best explained by Tennessee Williams when he has Tom say in *The Glass Menagerie* that the Gentleman Caller is "the long delayed but always expected something that we live for."

Beckett's tramps, like Laurel and Hardy in the old movies, bicker in scene after scene, sometimes sounding like husband and wife in a standard domestic **farce,** or low comedy. They seem to be derived in part from the end men who passed jokes and wisecracks back and forth in vaudeville and music halls. They also resemble the comedian and straight man in the comedy teams of movies, radio, and television. Though Beckett discarded all the ideas of progression and dramatic development, he employs a number of the appealing theatrical tricks of slapstick and vaudeville. There are pratfalls, difficulty getting shoes on and off, trousers falling down, futile efforts at suicide. The tramps are joined by a bizarre pair, Pozzo and Lucky, one a master, the other a slave on the end of a rope—a vivid theatrical picture.

Toward the end of Act I, a boy arrives from Godot to say he will not arrive today, but "surely tomorrow." Act II is almost a repetition of Act I, except that when Pozzo and Lucky enter, Pozzo is blind and Lucky is dumb. The boy again arrives at the end of the act to say that Godot will not arrive today, but tomorrow, "without fail."

Beckett regarded habit as "the lightning conductor" of our existence—in other words, the small habitual activities that keep us busy every day, all day, prevent us from being hit with the truth, which (as Beckett sees it) is loneliness, nothingness.

Regarding language, the Absurdist movement is antiliterary. The Absurdists believe that language has broken down and can no longer convey meaning. When asked why, then, he used words, Beckett replied that words are all we have to work with. Actually, although Beckett turned his back on naturalism (the exact, detailed duplication of real life), he was a naturalist in his dialogue and sometimes even achieved a kind of poetry by his fidelity to real speech.

The nature of Beckett's work almost demands that it be performed in small, intimate theaters,

Scene from a 1979 production of Samuel Beckett's *Happy Days* at the Beckett Theater, New York.

where every flutter of an eye can register. Beckett's plays are done in such theaters all over the world, and he is the "master," the point of reference for many of the experimenters now working in the theater. He was awarded the Nobel Prize in literature in 1969.

The Plays of Harold Pinter

Harold Pinter (1930–   ), an avowed disciple of Beckett and probably the most influential of the new English playwrights, is on the fringe of the Absurdist Theater. While Beckett deals with often grotesque characters in bizarre settings (the two tramps in *Waiting for Godot,* two old people in ash-cans in *Endgame,* a woman buried in sand up to her neck in *Happy Days*), Pinter most often presents us with more or less real settings and identifiable characters speaking everyday language. The whole, however, is stylized in a manner that is now called Pinteresque.

With Pinter, we are not in a storytelling theater. To summarize what happens in these plays is as meaningless as trying to describe an abstract expressionist painting. Pinter's is a drama of ambiguities, implications, and contradictions. A critic reviewing a Pinter play might start by saying, "This is a play about a man who did or did not meet a woman a year ago in a restaurant." It is a world where the real is menacing, the pregnant pauses (all carefully indicated by Pinter) are full of terror, and the banal speech is full of mystery.

In a traditional play, we watch the gradual unfolding of a character, as though we were watching an onion being peeled, until the psychological center of the person is exposed. In Pinter's plays, we are not dealing with the complex psychology of character. Pinter's people are often without pasts—or they have self-contradicting pasts. Though Pinter avoids the conventional dramatic principles of progression and development, he starts from arresting situations, and he sustains mystery and suspense.

But it is Pinter's dialogue that is the hallmark of his art. He has taken the chitchat of everyday speech and stylized it to the point where it becomes a kind of poetry. The following revue sketch titled *That's All* was first presented on BBC Radio in 1964. This is the entire text.

That's All

Mrs. A. I always put the kettle on about that time.

Mrs. B. Yes. (*Pause.*)

Mrs. A. Then she comes round.

Mrs. B. Yes. (*Pause.*)

Mrs. A. Only on Thursdays.

Mrs. B. Yes. (*Pause.*)

Mrs. A. On Wednesdays I used to put it on. When she used to come round. Then she changed it to Thursdays.

Mrs. B. Oh yes.

Mrs. A. After she moved. When she used to live round the corner, then she always came in on Wednesdays, but then when she moved she used to come down to the butcher's on Thursdays. She couldn't find a butcher up there.

Mrs. B. No.

Mrs. A. Anyway, she decided she'd stick to her own butcher. Well, I thought, if she can't find a butcher, that's the best thing.

Mrs. B. Yes. (*Pause.*)

Mrs. A. So she started to come down on Thursdays. I didn't know she was coming down on Thursdays until one day I met her in the butcher.

Mrs. B. Oh yes.

Mrs. A. It wasn't my day for the butcher. I don't go to the butcher on Thursday.

Mrs. B. No, I know. (*Pause.*)

Mrs. A. I go on Friday.

Mrs. B. Yes. (*Pause.*)

Mrs. A. That's where I see you.

Mrs. B. Yes. (*Pause.*)

Mrs. A. You're always in there on Fridays.

Mrs. B. Oh yes. (*Pause.*)

Mrs. A. But I happened to go in for a bit of meat, it turned out to be a Thursday. I wasn't going in for my usual weekly on Friday. I just slipped in, the day before.

Mrs. B. Yes.

Mrs. A. That was the first time I found out she couldn't find a butcher up there, so she decided to come back here, once a week, to her own butcher.

Mrs. B. Yes.

Mrs. A. She came on Thursday so she'd be able

to get meat for the weekend. Lasted her till Monday, then from Monday to Thursday they'd have fish. She can always buy cold meat, if they want a change.

Mrs. B. Oh yes. *(Pause.)*

Mrs. A. So I told her to come in when she came down after she'd been to the butcher's and I'd put a kettle on. So she did. *(Pause.)*

Mrs. B. Yes. *(Pause.)*

Mrs. A. It was funny because she always used to come in Wednesdays. *(Pause.)* Still, it made a break. *(Long pause.)*

Mrs. B. She doesn't come in no more, does she? *(Pause.)*

Mrs. A. She comes in. She doesn't come in so much, but she comes in. *(Pause.)*

Mrs. B. I thought she didn't come in. *(Pause.)*

Mrs. A. She comes in. *(Pause.)* She just doesn't come in so much. That's all.

—Harold Pinter

It is, of course, questionable how many situations, characters, or subjects can be dealt with in the Pinter manner. It would seem to be limiting. But over the last thirty years, he has written such notable full-length plays as *The Caretaker* (1960), *The Homecoming* (1965), *Old Times* (1971), and *Betrayal* (1978); and a series of highly effective short plays, including *The Dumb Waiter* (1960), *The Collection* (1961), *Landscape* (1968), *Silence* (1969), and *Moonlight* (1993). He has also adapted for motion pictures novels such as *The French Lieutenant's Woman* and *The Last Tycoon.*

British Theater Today

Beckett and Pinter are only two among the diverse lot of contemporary British playwrights. Many others—including John Osborne, Athol Fugard, Tom Stoppard, and Caryl Churchill—have written in a wide range of styles and forms, all more or less influenced by Beckett and Bertolt Brecht. Yesterday's avant-garde has become today's mainstream, and perhaps the avant-garde of tomorrow will be a return to some form of the conventional well-made play.

Americans have always considered London a great theater town, and it still is. Though seasons may vary in quality, in almost any year one may see productions from the rich dramatic literature of the country, past and present. The major British playwrights from Shakespeare to Shaw to Pinter form a galaxy to make Americans envious. Though the contemporary English theater may lack such tragic American masterworks as Eugene O'Neill's *Long Day's Journey into Night,* Arthur Miller's *Death of a Salesman,* and Tennessee Williams's *A Streetcar Named Desire,* we have nothing to match, as yet, the brilliance of Beckett or Pinter. But, as they say in baseball, "Wait until next year."

Poster for a 1995 production of Tom Stoppard's *Arcadia* in New York.
Art by James McMullan.

Algeria/France

Albert Camus

(1913–1960)

For many people, Albert Camus (ka·moo′) was the very embodiment of the existential philosopher, a writer who asked questions about the foundations of our existence. Camus and his friends were associated with the Left Bank of Paris, where, in its smoky cafes, they argued about the meaning of human life. To Camus and other existentialists, we are uninvited guests in a meaningless universe.

Albert Camus was born in Algeria, at a time when Algeria was a colony of France. Raised in extreme poverty, he became one of the most influential writers of the twentieth century.

When Camus was less than a year old, his father died of wounds suffered in World War I. His illiterate mother earned their living by cleaning houses. It is not surprising, therefore, that Camus viewed working-class people as

Albert Camus (1959).

individuals worthy of honor for their patient, silent labor, so like the toils of Sisyphus.

One of Camus's teachers noticed his potential for learning and helped him pursue his education, first through high school and then through the University of Algiers, where Camus studied philosophy. When he was seventeen, an attack of tuberculosis ended Camus's dream of a sports career, and by 1935, he had turned to writing and the theater. In 1940, after writing a group of newspaper articles about injustices in Algeria, Camus was asked to leave, and he emigrated to Paris.

During World War II, Camus served as editor of *Combat,* an underground newspaper of the Resistance movement that courageously opposed the German occupation of France. In his plays, novels, and essays—of which the most famous is his 1946 novel *The Stranger*—he spoke out fearlessly against all forms of exploitation, cruelty, aggression, and hypocritical morality. Often ill and close to death, Camus kept writing and working in behalf of humanitarian causes throughout his life. In 1957, he was awarded the Nobel Prize in literature. Three years later, at the age of forty-six, he was killed in a car accident. A draft of Camus's unfinished autobiographical novel, *The First Man,* was found in the wreckage of his car. The book was not published until 1994.

(Map) ©Rand McNally R. L. #98-S-116.

Before You Read
THE MYTH OF SISYPHUS

Background

Imagine that the year is 1942. Germany has invaded and is now occupying your country. Bombs are falling on cities all over Europe. Already millions of innocent people have been killed. You are desperately ill with tuberculosis. As everything that you thought was important in the world crashes around you, how would you react? Albert Camus chose to write "The Myth of Sisyphus," an essay that affirms life, no matter how meaningless or difficult it may be.

Camus based his essay on the Greek myth of Sisyphus, a clever but arrogant human who loved life and dared to defy the gods. After his death, Sisyphus even man-

aged to escape from Pluto's dark underworld kingdom and return to life, a crime that deeply offended Zeus, king of the gods. To punish Sisyphus, Zeus condemned him to roll a huge rock eternally up a steep hill. As soon as Sisyphus reached the top of the hill, he had to stand by and watch while the rock rolled back downhill. Then he had to return to the bottom of the hill and roll the rock to the top again, and again, and again.

To Camus, the absurdity of Sisyphus's task symbolizes human existence. Camus's essay is often considered one of the important documents of **existentialism,** a philosophical and literary move-

ment that holds that individuals must struggle to create their own meaning and morality in the absence of any absolute values. Many existentialists focus on a belief that the universe is indifferent to human suffering. However, Camus was an optimist. By becoming conscious of his terrible destiny, Camus's Sisyphus—and all of humanity—rises above it. For Camus, people achieve a kind of victory when they accept the meaninglessness of life with dignity, and even with joy.

Reading Skills and Strategies

Dialogue with the Text

As you read this challenging essay, make a note of any ideas in it that you find interesting, puzzling, or open to debate.

The Idleness of Sisyphus (1981) by Sandro Chia. Oil on canvas, in two parts, overall 10′ 2″ × 12′ 8¼″ (307 x 386.7 cm); top panel: 6′ 9″ × 12′ 8¼″ (205.5 x 386.7 cm); bottom panel: 41″ × 12′ 1¼″ (104.5 x 386.7 cm).

The Myth of Sisyphus

Albert Camus

translated by **Justin O'Brien**

The gods had condemned Sisyphus to ceaselessly rolling a rock to the top of a mountain, whence the stone would fall back of its own weight. They had thought with some reason that there is no more dreadful punishment than futile and hopeless labor.

If one believes Homer, Sisyphus was the wisest and most prudent of mortals. According to another tradition, however, he was disposed to practice the profession of highwayman. I see no contradiction in this. Opinions differ as to the reasons why he became the futile laborer of the underworld. To begin with, he is accused of a certain levity[1] in regard to the gods. He stole their secrets. Aegina, the daughter of Aesopus, was carried off by Jupiter. The father was shocked by that disappearance and complained to Sisyphus. He, who knew of the abduction, offered to tell about it on condition that Aesopus would give water to the citadel of Corinth.[2] To the celestial thunderbolts he preferred the benediction of water. He was punished for this in the underworld. Homer tells us also that Sisyphus had put Death in chains. Pluto could not endure the sight of his deserted, silent empire. He dispatched the god of war, who liberated Death from the hands of her conqueror.

It is said also that Sisyphus, being near to death, rashly wanted to test his wife's love. He ordered her to cast his unburied body into the middle of the public square. Sisyphus woke up in the underworld. And there, annoyed by an obedience so contrary to human love, he obtained from Pluto permission to return to earth in order to chastise his wife. But when he had seen again the face of this world, enjoyed water and sun, warm stones and the sea, he no longer wanted to go back to the infernal darkness. Recalls, signs of anger, warnings were of no avail. Many years more he lived facing the curve of the gulf, the sparkling sea, and the smiles of earth. A decree of the gods was necessary. Mercury came and seized the impudent man by the collar and, snatching him from his joys, led him forcibly back to the underworld, where his rock was ready for him.

You have already grasped that Sisyphus is the absurd hero. He *is,* as much through his passions as through his torture. His scorn of the gods, his hatred of death, and his passion for life won him that unspeakable penalty in which the whole being is exerted toward accomplishing nothing. This is the price that must be paid for the passions of this earth. Nothing is told us about Sisyphus in the underworld. Myths are made for the imagination to breathe life into them. As for this myth, one sees merely the whole effort of a body straining to raise the huge stone, to roll it and push it up a slope a hundred times over; one sees the face screwed up, the cheek tight against the stone, the shoulder bracing the clay-covered mass, the foot wedging it, the fresh start with arms outstretched, the wholly human security of two earth-clotted hands. At the very end of his long effort measured by skyless space and time without depth, the purpose is achieved. Then Sisyphus watches the stone rush down in a few moments toward that lower world whence he will have to push it up again toward the summit. He goes back down to the plain.

It is during that return, that pause, that Sisyphus interests me. A face that toils so close to stones is already stone itself! I see that man going back down with a heavy yet measured step toward the torment of which he will never know the end. That hour like a breathing space which returns as surely as his suffering, that is the hour of consciousness. At each of those moments when he leaves the heights and gradually sinks toward the lairs of the gods, he is superior to his fate. He is stronger than his rock.

If this myth is tragic, that is because its hero is conscious. Where would his torture be, indeed, if

---

1. levity (lev′i·tē): disrespectful lightness or frivolity.
2. Corinth (kôr′inth): ancient city in Greece.

at every step the hope of succeeding upheld him? The workman of today works every day in his life at the same tasks, and this fate is no less absurd. But it is tragic only at the rare moments when it becomes conscious. Sisyphus, proletarian[3] of the gods, powerless and rebellious, knows the whole extent of his wretched condition: It is what he thinks of during his descent. The lucidity that was to constitute his torture at the same time crowns his victory. There is no fate that cannot be surmounted by scorn.

If the descent is thus sometimes performed in sorrow, it can also take place in joy. This word is not too much. Again I fancy Sisyphus returning toward his rock, and the sorrow was in the beginning. When the images of earth cling too tightly to memory, when the call of happiness becomes too insistent, it happens that melancholy rises in man's heart: This is the rock's victory, this is the rock itself. The boundless grief is too heavy to bear. These are our nights of Gethsemane.[4] But crushing truths perish from being acknowledged. Thus, Oedipus[5] at the outset obeys fate without knowing it. But from the moment he knows, his tragedy begins. Yet at the same moment, blind and desperate, he realizes that the only bond linking him to the world is the cool hand of a girl. Then a tremendous remark rings out: "Despite so many ordeals, my advanced age and the nobility of my soul make me conclude that all is well." Sophocles' Oedipus, like Dostoevsky's Kirilov,[6] thus gives the recipe for the absurd victory. Ancient wisdom confirms modern heroism.

One does not discover the absurd without being tempted to write a manual of happiness. "What! by such narrow ways—?" There is but one world, however. Happiness and the absurd are two sons of the same earth. They are inseparable. It would be a mistake to say that happiness necessarily springs from the absurd discovery. It happens as well that the feeling of the absurd springs from happiness. "I conclude that all is well," says Oedipus, and that remark is sacred. It echoes in the wild and limited universe of man. It teaches that all is not, has not been, exhausted. It drives out of this world a god who had come into it with dissatisfaction and a preference for futile sufferings. It makes of fate a human matter, which must be settled among men.

All Sisyphus' silent joy is contained therein. His fate belongs to him. His rock is his thing. Likewise, the absurd man, when he contemplates his torment, silences all the idols. In the universe suddenly restored to its silence, the myriad wondering little voices of the earth rise up. Unconscious, secret calls, invitations from all the faces, they are the necessary reverse and price of victory. There is no sun without shadow, and it is essential to know the night. The absurd man says yes and his effort will henceforth be unceasing. If there is a personal fate, there is no higher destiny, or at least there is but one which he concludes is inevitable and despicable. For the rest, he knows himself to be the master of his days. At that subtle moment when man glances backward over his life, Sisyphus returning toward his rock, in that slight pivoting he contemplates that series of unrelated actions which becomes his fate, created by him, combined under his memory's eye, and soon sealed by his death. Thus, convinced of the wholly human origin of all that is human, a blind man eager to see who knows that the night has no end, he is still on the go. The rock is still rolling.

I leave Sisyphus at the foot of the mountain! One always finds one's burden again. But Sisyphus teaches the higher fidelity that negates the gods and raises rocks. He too concludes that all is well. This universe henceforth without a master seems to him neither sterile nor futile. Each atom of that stone, each mineral flake of that night-filled mountain, in itself forms a world. The struggle itself toward the heights is enough to fill a man's heart. One must imagine Sisyphus happy.

3. **proletarian** (prō′lə·ter′ē·ən): member of the working class.
4. **Gethsemane** (geth·sem′ə·nē): garden east of Jerusalem where Jesus Christ suffered intensely as he contemplated his possible death.
5. **Oedipus** (ed′i·pəs): character in Greek mythology who unknowingly kills his father and marries his mother. In *Oedipus at Colonus,* the last of three plays written by the Greek dramatist Sophocles (496–406 B.C.) about this tragic hero, Oedipus has blinded himself and is led by the hand by his daughter Antigone.
6. **Kirilov** (kē·rē′luf): character in Dostoevsky's 1872 novel *The Possessed.*

The Castle of the Pyrenees
(1959) by René Magritte.

Israel Museum, Jerusalem
© 1997 C. Hersovici, Brussels /
Artists Rights Society (ARS),
New York.

FINDING COMMON GROUND

You can probably recognize in Camus's writing the voice of a man who wanted human labor and art to serve human needs. Perhaps you can also recognize the voice of someone with a lifelong commitment to the unfortunate of the world. Can you also hear that Camus was a man who faced hopelessness and despair in his own life, yet reacted to setbacks with renewed vigor and hope?

Explore your responses to Camus's essay (check your reading notes) and to his philosophy in one or more of these ways:

- According to Camus, "the workman of today works every day in his life at the same tasks, and this fate is no less absurd" than the tasks Sisyphus carries out. Imagine yourself as one of the workers Camus had in mind. Discuss the ways in which Camus's philosophy might help you face your life with hope and joy.

- A **myth** is an imaginative narrative, usually involving gods or other supernatural beings, that often explains something about the world or human beings. Myths reflect the beliefs and values of the society that produces them. Camus found meaning in the myth of Sisyphus. W. H. Auden (page 1091) was moved by the myth of Icarus, and Frank O'Connor (page 1080) was inspired by a modern interpretation of the ancient myth of Oedipus. In a group, make a list of myths from Greek and other cultures. Discuss connections between these myths and your own lives.

- Camus's writing has been called epigrammatic. That means he writes in **epigrams,** brief statements packed with meaning. Find one sentence in "The Myth of Sisyphus" that has particular meaning for you, and find a way to share it with the class. (For instance, use it on a poster.)

Anita Desai
(1937–   )

Born in Mussoorie, India, Anita Desai has been writing since the age of seven "as instinctively as I breathe." Desai's father was Bengali and her mother German, and Desai grew up hearing Hindi, English, and German spoken at home. However, it was in English that Desai learned to read and write. Educated at the University of Delhi, Desai began publishing in 1963.

Desai's fiction explores the struggles of contemporary Indian characters as they respond to cultural and social change. She sees her work as an attempt to discover "the truth that is nine-tenths of the iceberg that lies submerged beneath the one-tenth visible portion we call

Anita Desai.

Reality." To evoke this "truth," Desai uses rich, sensual language and intense imagery. Because of her sensuous style and rich use of image and symbol, Desai has been referred to as an "imagist-novelist."

Desai's novels often focus on the emotional and spiritual lives of wives, older women, or sisters who take responsibility for others but are unable to create satisfactory lives for themselves. Her novels include *Cry, the Peacock* (1963), *In Custody* (1984), and *Baumgartner's Bombay* (1988).

Writing in *The New Republic,* Anthony Thwaite describes Desai "as such a consummate artist that she [is able to suggest], beyond the confines of the plot and the machinations of her characters, the immensities that lie beyond them—the immensities of India."

Before You Read
GAMES AT TWILIGHT

Make the Connection
Childhood Business
Work may be the business of adults, but play is often considered the "business" of little children. For it is through play that children do the hard work of learning many of life's important lessons. They learn about rules and strategies, strength and weakness. They learn that life is not always fair.

Elements of Literature
Imagery
Desai's vibrant **imagery** captures the smells, textures, shouts, and colors of a sizzling summer afternoon in India. From the beginning of the story, when

the children burst out the door, to its end at twilight, Desai enables you to experience the world through the eyes and ears of her characters.

Imagery is the use of language to evoke sensory impressions. Images are chiefly visual, but they can also appeal to the senses of smell, hearing, taste, and touch.

For more on Imagery, see the Handbook of Literary Terms.

Reading Skills and Strategies

Analyzing Evocative Words
As you read, jot down words and phrases that help you imagine the scene and share the characters' experiences. When you have finished reading, discuss the impression created by these words.

Background
This story is set not long after India's independence from Britain, in 1947. During the long British rule in India, many upper-class Indian families adopted Western values and behaviors, including games like the one played in the story.

go.hrw.com
LEO 12-14

Games at Twilight

Anita Desai

It was still too hot to play outdoors. They had had their tea, they had been washed and had their hair brushed, and after the long day of confinement in the house that was not cool but at least a protection from the sun, the children strained to get out. Their faces were red and bloated with the effort, but their mother would not open the door, everything was still curtained and shuttered in a way that stifled the children, made them feel that their lungs were stuffed with cotton wool and their noses with dust and if they didn't burst out into the light and see the sun and feel the air, they would choke.

"Please, ma, please," they begged. "We'll play in the veranda and porch—we won't go a step out of the porch."

"You will, I know you will, and then——"

"No—we won't, we won't," they wailed so horrendously that she actually let down the bolt of the front door so that they burst out like seeds from a crackling, overripe pod into the veranda, with such wild, <u>maniacal</u> yells that she retreated to her bath and the shower of talcum powder and the fresh sari that were to help her face the summer evening.

They faced the afternoon. It was too hot. Too bright. The white walls of the veranda glared <u>stridently</u> in the sun. The bougainvillea[1] hung about it, purple and magenta, in livid balloons. The garden outside was like a tray made of beaten brass, flattened out on the red gravel and the stony soil in all shades of metal—aluminum, tin, copper, and brass. No life stirred at this arid time of day—the birds still drooped, like dead fruit, in the papery tents of the trees; some squirrels lay limp on the wet earth under the garden tap. The outdoor dog lay stretched as if dead on the veranda mat, his paws and ears and tail all reaching out like dying travelers in search of water. He rolled his eyes at the children—two white marbles rolling in the purple sockets, begging for sympathy—and at-

tempted to lift his tail in a wag but could not. It only twitched and lay still.

Then, perhaps roused by the shrieks of the children, a band of parrots suddenly fell out of the eucalyptus tree, tumbled frantically in the still, sizzling air, then sorted themselves out into battle formation and streaked away across the white sky.

The children, too, felt released. They too began tumbling, shoving, pushing against each other, frantic to start. Start what? Start their business. The business of the children's day which is—play.

"Let's play hide-and-seek."

"Who'll be It?"

"You be It."

"Why should I? You be——"

"You're the eldest——"

"That doesn't mean——"

The shoves became harder. Some kicked out. The motherly Mira intervened. She pulled the boys roughly apart. There was a tearing sound of cloth, but it was lost in the heavy panting and angry grumbling, and no one paid attention to the small sleeve hanging loosely off a shoulder.

"Make a circle, make a circle!" she shouted, firmly pulling and pushing till a kind of vague circle was formed. "Now clap!" she roared, and, clapping, they all chanted in melancholy unison: "Dip, dip, dip—my blue ship——" and every now and then one or the other saw he was safe by the way his hands fell at the crucial moment—palm on palm, or back of hand on palm—and dropped out of the circle with a yell and a jump of relief and jubilation.

Raghu was It. He started to protest, to cry "You cheated—Mira cheated—Anu cheated——" but it was too late, the others had all already streaked away. There was no one to hear when he called out, "Only in the veranda—the porch—Ma said— Ma *said* to stay in the porch!" No one had

---

1. **bougainvillea** (bōō′gən·vil′ē·ə): woody, tropical vine with showy, purplish leaves.

If All the World Were Paper and All the Waters Ink (1962) by Jess.

The Fine Arts Museums of San Francisco, California. Courtesy of the Odyssia Gallery, New York.

stopped to listen, all he saw were their brown legs flashing through the dusty shrubs, scrambling up brick walls, leaping over compost heaps and hedges, and then the porch stood empty in the purple shade of the bougainvillea, and the garden was as empty as before; even the limp squirrels had whisked away, leaving everything gleaming, brassy, and bare.

Only small Manu suddenly reappeared, as if he had dropped out of an invisible cloud or from a bird's claws, and stood for a moment in the center of the yellow lawn, chewing his finger and near to tears as he heard Raghu shouting, with his head pressed against the veranda wall, "Eighty-three, eighty-five, eighty-nine, ninety . . ." and then made

off in a panic, half of him wanting to fly north, the other half counseling south. Raghu turned just in time to see the flash of his white shorts and the uncertain skittering of his red sandals, and charged after him with such a bloodcurdling yell that Manu stumbled over the hosepipe, fell into its rubber coils, and lay there weeping, "I won't be It—you have to find them all—all—All!"

"I know I have to, idiot," Raghu said, <u>superciliously</u> kicking him with his toe. "You're dead,"

ANITA DESAI **1141**

he said with satisfaction, licking the beads of perspiration off his upper lip, and then stalked off in search of worthier prey, whistling spiritedly so that the hiders should hear and tremble.

Ravi heard the whistling and picked his nose in a panic, trying to find comfort by burrowing the finger deep—deep into that soft tunnel. He felt himself too exposed, sitting on an upturned flowerpot behind the garage. Where could he burrow? He could run around the garage if he heard Raghu come—around and around and around—but he hadn't much faith in his short legs when matched against Raghu's long, hefty, hairy footballer legs. Ravi had a frightening glimpse of them as Raghu combed the hedge of crotons and hibiscus, trampling delicate ferns underfoot as he did so. Ravi looked about him desperately, swallowing a small ball of snot in his fear.

The garage was locked with a great heavy lock to which the driver had the key in his room, hanging from a nail on the wall under his workshirt. Ravi had peeped in and seen him still sprawling on his string cot in his vest and striped underpants, the hair on his chest and the hair in his nose shaking with the vibrations of his phlegm-obstructed snores. Ravi had wished he were tall enough, big enough to reach the key on the nail, but it was impossible, beyond his reach for years to come. He had sidled away and sat dejectedly on the flowerpot. That at least was cut to his own size.

But next to the garage was another shed with a big green door. Also locked. No one even knew who had the key to the lock. That shed wasn't opened more than once a year, when Ma turned out all the old broken bits of furniture and rolls of matting and leaking buckets, and the white anthills were broken and swept away and Flit sprayed into the spider webs and rat holes so that the whole operation was like the looting of a poor, ruined, and conquered city. The green leaves of the door sagged. They were nearly off their rusty hinges. The hinges were large and made a small gap between the door and the walls—only just large enough for rats, dogs, and, possibly, Ravi to slip through.

Ravi had never cared to enter such a dark and depressing mortuary of defunct household goods seething with such unspeakable and alarming animal life but, as Raghu's whistling grew angrier and sharper and his crashing and storming in the hedge wilder, Ravi suddenly slipped off the flowerpot and through the crack and was gone. He chuckled aloud with astonishment at his own temerity so that Raghu came out of the hedge, stood silent with his hands on his hips, listening, and finally shouted, "I heard you! I'm coming! *Got* you——" and came charging round the garage only to find the upturned flowerpot, the yellow dust, the crawling of white ants in a mud hill against the closed shed door—nothing. Snarling, he bent to pick up a stick and went off, whacking it against the garage and shed walls as if to beat out his prey.

Ravi shook, then shivered with delight, with self-congratulation. Also with fear. It was dark, spooky in the shed. It had a muffled smell, as of graves. Ravi had once got locked into the linen cupboard and sat there weeping for half an hour before he

Two young girls, Rajasthan, India.

was rescued. But at least that had been a familiar place, and even smelled pleasantly of starch, laundry, and, reassuringly, of his mother. But the shed smelled of rats, anthills, dust, and spider webs. Also of less definable, less recognizable horrors. And it was dark. Except for the white-hot cracks along the door, there was no light. The roof was very low. Although Ravi was small, he felt as if he could reach up and touch it with his fingertips. But he didn't stretch. He hunched himself into a ball so as not to bump into anything, touch or feel anything. What might there not be to touch him and feel him as he stood there, trying to see in the dark? Something cold, or slimy—like a snake. Snakes! He leapt up as Raghu whacked the wall with his stick—then, quickly realizing what it was, felt almost relieved to hear Raghu, hear his stick. It made him feel protected.

But Raghu soon moved away. There wasn't a sound once his footsteps had gone around the garage and disappeared. Ravi stood frozen inside the shed. Then he shivered all over. Something had tickled the back of his neck. It took him a while to pick up the courage to lift his hand and explore. It was an insect—perhaps a spider—exploring *him*. He squashed it and wondered how many more creatures were watching him, waiting to reach out and touch him, the stranger.

There was nothing now. After standing in that position—his hand still on his neck, feeling the wet splodge of the squashed spider gradually dry—for minutes, hours, his legs began to tremble with the effort, the inaction. By now he could see enough in the dark to make out the large solid shapes of old wardrobes, broken buckets, and bedsteads piled on top of each other around him. He recognized an old bathtub—patches of enamel glimmered at him, and at last he lowered himself onto its edge.

He contemplated slipping out of the shed and into the fray. He wondered if it would not be better to be captured by Raghu and be returned to the milling crowd as long as he could be in the sun, the light, the free spaces of the garden, and the familiarity of his brothers, sisters, and cousins. It would be evening soon. Their games would become legitimate. The parents would sit out on the lawn on cane basket chairs and watch them as they tore around the garden or gathered in knots to share a loot of mulberries or black, teeth-splitting *jamun*[2] from the garden trees. The gardener would fix the hosepipe to the water tap, and water would fall lavishly through the air to the ground, soaking the dry yellow grass and the red gravel and arousing the sweet, the <u>intoxicating</u> scent of water on dry earth—that loveliest scent in the world. Ravi sniffed for a whiff of it. He half-rose from the bathtub, then heard the despairing scream of one of the girls as Raghu bore down upon her. There was the sound of a crash, and of rolling about in the bushes, the shrubs, then screams and accusing sobs of "I touched the den——" "You did not——" "I did——" "You liar, you did *not*" and then a fading away and silence again.

Ravi sat back on the harsh edge of the tub, deciding to hold out a bit longer. What fun if they were all found and caught—he alone left unconquered! He had never known that sensation. Nothing more wonderful had ever happened to him than being taken out by an uncle and bought a whole slab of chocolate all to himself, or being flung into the soda man's pony cart and driven up to the gate by the friendly driver with the red beard and pointed ears. To defeat Raghu—that hirsute,[3] hoarse-voiced football champion—and to be the winner in a circle of older, bigger, luckier children—that would be thrilling beyond imagination. He hugged his knees together and smiled to himself almost shyly at the thought of so much victory, such laurels.

There he sat smiling, knocking his heels against the bathtub, now and then getting up and going to the door to put his ear to the broad crack and listening for sounds of the game, the pursuer and the pursued, and then returning to his seat with the <u>dogged</u> determination of the true winner, a breaker of records, a champion.

---

2. *jamun* (jä·mən): plumlike fruit.
3. hirsute (hʉr′so͞ot′): hairy; shaggy.

WORDS TO OWN
intoxicating (in·täks′i·kāt′iŋ) *v.* used as *adj.*: causing wild excitement or happiness, often to a point beyond self-control; heady.
dogged (dôg′id) *adj.*: persistent; stubborn.

It grew darker in the shed as the light at the door grew softer, fuzzier, turned to a kind of crumbling yellow pollen that turned to yellow fur, blue fur, gray fur. Evening. Twilight. The sound of water gushing, falling. The scent of earth receiving water, slaking its thirst in great gulps and releasing that green scent of freshness, coolness. Through the crack Ravi saw the long purple shadows of the shed and the garage lying still across the yard. Beyond that, the white walls of the house. The bougainvillea had lost its lividity, hung in dark bundles that quaked and twittered and seethed with masses of homing sparrows. The lawn was shut off from his view. Could he hear the children's voices? It seemed to him that he could. It seemed to him that he could hear them chanting, singing, laughing. But what about the game? What had happened? Could it be over? How could it when he was still not found?

It then occurred to him that he could have slipped out long ago, dashed across the yard to the veranda, and touched the "den." It was necessary to do that to win. He had forgotten. He had only remembered the part of hiding and trying to elude the seeker. He had done that so successfully, his success had occupied him so wholly, that he had quite forgotten that success had to be clinched by that final dash to victory and the ringing cry of "Den!"

With a whimper he burst through the crack, fell on his knees, got up, and stumbled on stiff, benumbed legs across the shadowy yard, crying heartily by the time he reached the veranda so that when he flung himself at the white pillar and bawled, "Den! Den! Den!" his voice broke with rage and pity at the disgrace of it all, and he felt himself flooded with tears and misery.

Out on the lawn, the children stopped chanting. They all turned to stare at him in amazement. Their faces were pale and triangular in the dusk. The trees and bushes around them stood inky and sepulchral, spilling long shadows across them. They stared, wondering at his reappearance, his passion, his wild animal howling. Their mother rose from her basket chair and came toward him, worried, annoyed, saying, "Stop it, stop it, Ravi. Don't be a baby. Have you hurt yourself?" Seeing him attended to, the children went back to clasping their hands and chanting, "The grass is green, the rose is red. . . ."

But Ravi would not let them. He tore himself out of his mother's grasp and pounded across the lawn into their midst, charging at them with his head lowered so that they scattered in surprise. "I won, I won, I won," he bawled, shaking his head so that the big tears flew. "Raghu didn't find me. I won, I won——"

It took them a minute to grasp what he was saying, even who he was. They had quite forgotten him. Raghu had found all the others long ago. There had been a fight about who was to be It next. It had been so fierce that their mother had emerged from her bath and made them change to another game. Then they had played another and another. Broken mulberries from the tree and eaten them. Helped the driver wash the car when their father returned from work. Helped the gardener water the beds till he roared at them and swore he would complain to their parents. The parents had come out, taken up their positions on the cane chairs. They had begun to play again, sing and chant. All this time no one had remembered Ravi. Having disappeared from the scene, he had disappeared from their minds. Clean.

"Don't be a fool," Raghu said roughly, pushing him aside, and even Mira said, "Stop howling, Ravi. If you want to play, you can stand at the end of the line," and she put him there very firmly.

The game proceeded. Two pairs of arms reached up and met in an arc. The children trooped under it again and again in a <u>lugubrious</u> circle, ducking their heads and <u>intoning</u>

"The grass is green,
The rose is red;
Remember me
When I am dead, dead, dead, dead . . ."

And the arc of thin arms trembled in the twilight, and the heads were bowed so sadly, and their feet tramped to that melancholy refrain so mournfully, so helplessly, that Ravi could not bear it. He would not follow them, he would not be

---

WORDS TO OWN

lugubrious (lə·gōō′brē·əs) *adj.:* very solemn or mournful, especially in a way that seems exaggerated or ridiculous.

intoning (in·tōn′iŋ) *v.* used as *adj.:* chanting.

---

included in this funereal game. He had wanted victory and triumph—not a funeral. But he had been forgotten, left out, and he would not join them now. The <u>ignominy</u> of being forgotten— how could he face it? He felt his heart go heavy and ache inside him unbearably. He lay down full length on the damp grass, crushing his face into it, no longer crying, silenced by a terrible sense of his insignificance.

Lesson of the Bamboo Crates

It's a soppy, rainy day. As I leave the subway station, I see a woman with one hand holding on to her daughter and the other hand grasping a big sack. This scene reminds me of another woman, miles away, in China.

She was my classmate Dai's mother. She only showed up in school on rainy days in the same worn, out-of-style clothes. Always, she brought a big bag of rice to pay for Dai's boarding expenses.

"Village people," we, the mean ones, thought. When she and Dai stood together, with the same self-styled chopped haircut, we couldn't stop laughing.

One summer, I was assigned to a family in a nearby village to learn farming skills to get summer activity credits. Imagine my surprise to discover that Dai lived next door. My host told me that Dai had lost her father when she was a baby, and that her mother worked for a factory. All day she stood under the sun breaking bricks into little pieces. And when it rained, she worked from her home twining bamboo into crates.

I was such a city girl. Early in the summer, I twisted my ankle trying to work in the fields. I worried, "How will I earn my summer credits?" Just when I was about to give up, Dai's mom offered to teach me how to make bamboo crates. It was not easy. After many hours, I was still clumsy at it. I started feeling uncomfortable for keeping Dai's mother up way past her bedtime, but she was always patient.

"Don't rush," she said. "It takes time. There is plenty of laundry for me to wash while you are practicing."

The "sha-sha-sha" sounds of the wash started, and somehow, I couldn't concentrate. I raised my head and suddenly saw her as though for the first time. Under the light of the moon, I saw a pair of deep eyes, full of light, and the wrinkles that years had marked on her face.

"Did Dai ever tell you about some of the mean kids in school?" I asked. "Did she tell you I was one of them?"

"Yes. She did."

"Then why do you help me—an almost stranger and a mean kid?"

"I told her that those mean children are just immature. They don't know anything about life. When Dai's father died, people in the village helped us out. And I know how much their help meant to us. So now whenever I can help someone, I do. I help you because I don't like to see anyone give up. There aren't all that many next times."

She smiled. I nodded my head silently and smiled back.

I gained ten credits that summer, and I left the bamboo crate to her as a gift. When I returned to school, I never joined the mean kids again.

—Christy Ma
Seward Park High School
New York, New York

MAKING MEANINGS

First Thoughts

1. How much empathy for Ravi did you feel at the end of the story? Did his experience remind you of any of your childhood experiences?

> **Reading Check**
>
> Create a story map that outlines the important events in the story in **chronological order**—the order in which they happen.

Shaping Interpretations

2. What specific **words** and **images** in this story are most vivid to you? (Look over your reading notes.) If you had to draw one picture to illustrate the story, what would you draw?

3. Which **images** suggest loss and death to you? How do these images make you feel?

4. Why is everyone so surprised to see Ravi when he finally comes out of his hiding place?

5. What kind of game are the children playing at twilight?

6. What has Ravi discovered by the end of the story? Find a passage of the text that supports your answer.

7. How would you state the **theme** of this story—what revelation about human life does it make to you? As you think about the theme, think also about how the story's **title** reinforces its theme. (Think of the layers of meanings you can give to the word *games*.) Be sure to compare your statements of theme in class: Are there differences?

8. How do Ravi's experiences in the shed contribute to the **mood** of the story?

Extending the Text

9. Are the children in this story (and childhood itself) more realistically portrayed than the children in television situation comedies, or less so? Give examples to support your view.

CHOICES:
Building Your Portfolio

Writer's Notebook

1. Collecting Ideas for a Problem-Solution Essay

Suppose you were designing a course of study in literature for seniors in high school. What problems do you see in the ways such courses are presently taught? What solutions would you propose for those problems? Take notes now on your thoughts on these issues. Base your ideas in part on your experience with the selections in this textbook. One thing you might consider is the kinds of literature you think seniors should be reading and the themes you think they should focus on. Save your notes for possible use in the Writer's Workshop on page 1179.

Comparing and Contrasting Stories

2. Comparing Childhoods

Here are three unusual stories about childhood: "The Doll's House" (page 1062), "My Oedipus Complex" (page 1082), and "Games at Twilight." In an essay, compare and contrast two of these stories. Focus on the **discoveries** made by the children in each story, the **theme** of each story, and the writer's **tone**. Remember that in a comparison-and-contrast essay, you are looking for similarities and differences.

Creative Writing

3. The Cost of Cruelty

The student essay on page 1115 deals with the theme "Ourselves Among Others." Write a short narrative of your own about a person (adult or child) who comes face-to-face with his or her own cruelty or unkindness.

Seamus Heaney

(1939–)

Portrait of Seamus Heaney (1973) by Edward McGuire. Oil on canvas (56″ × 44″).

Seamus Heaney was born to Roman Catholic parents in largely Protestant Northern Ireland. His boyhood on a farm in County Derry contributed profoundly to his identity as a poet. But Heaney never promoted himself as a rustic or regarded his work as an expression of regionalism. He earned his education as a scholarship student, first at a Catholic preparatory school and then at Queen's University in Belfast where, still in his midtwenties, he was appointed lecturer in English.

Instead of leading him away from his roots in Irish soil, Heaney's studies—particularly those having to do with the history and psychology of myth—opened for him a way of seeing anew not only the misty grandeur of his native landscape, but also the figures in it who, unknowingly, unite the past with the present. Heaney is an acute observer of rural life and of life lived on the industrial margins of cities, and he deals with both without romanticizing them.

Regarded by Robert Lowell as "the best Irish poet since William Butler Yeats," Heaney now occupies the chair at Harvard left vacant by Lowell's death in 1977. In 1995, commended for his works "of lyrical beauty and ethical depth, which exalt everyday miracles and the living past," Heaney was awarded the Nobel Prize in literature. He divides his time between Cambridge, Massachusetts, and a home in the republic of Ireland.

Before You Read

DIGGING
THE GRAUBALLE MAN

Make the Connection

Out of the Earth

Both of these poems, in their different ways, are about *digging*.

In 1969, Heaney read *The Bog People* by the archaeologist P. V. Glob, about the discovery in Denmark of the remarkably well-preserved bodies of several Iron Age men. One of those bog men was dug up near the village of Grauballe in Jutland in 1952. Heaney was particularly struck by the amazing photographs of those two-thousand-year-old humans who had been preserved in the boggy earth by a chemical process that resembles tanning. Here Heaney found a rich symbol of the earth's power to preserve the past. But Grauballe man, whose throat was slit in a ritual sacrifice, was also a reminder of the darker continuities in human experience—and of the earth's role as a tomb as well as a cradle.

Quickwrite

What do you associate with the word *digging*? Take a few minutes to make a list of your associations.

Elements of Literature

Metaphors and Similes

Up until the last line of "Digging," you may not realize that the poem contains an **extended metaphor,** a comparison between the father's work and the poet's that resonates throughout the poem.

In "The Grauballe Man," Heaney also uses a series of comparisons (**similes** and **metaphors**) to describe the extraordinary appearance of the bog man and the meaning the magnificent body has for the poet.

Digging

Seamus Heaney

Between my finger and my thumb
The squat pen rests; snug as a gun.

Under my window, a clean rasping sound
When the spade sinks into gravelly ground:
5 My father, digging. I look down

Till his straining rump among the flowerbeds
Bends low, comes up twenty years away
Stooping in rhythm through potato drills°
Where he was digging.

10 The coarse boot nestled on the lug,° the shaft
Against the inside knee was levered firmly.
He rooted out tall tops, buried the bright edge deep
To scatter new potatoes that we picked
Loving their cool hardness in our hands.

15 By God, the old man could handle a spade.
Just like his old man.

My grandfather cut more turf in a day
Than any other man on Toner's bog.
Once I carried him milk in a bottle
20 Corked sloppily with paper. He straightened up
To drink it, then fell to right away
Nicking and slicing neatly, heaving sods
Over his shoulder, going down and down
For the good turf. Digging.

25 The cold smell of potato mould, the squelch and slap
Of soggy peat, the curt cuts of an edge
Through living roots awaken in my head.
But I've no spade to follow men like them.

Between my finger and my thumb
30 The squat pen rests.
I'll dig with it.

8. **drills:** furrows or rows of planted
seeds.
10. **lug:** earlike prong or projection
by which a spade is supported.

The Grauballe Man

Seamus Heaney

As if he had been poured
in tar, he lies
on a pillow of turf
and seems to weep

5   the black river of himself.
The grain of his wrists
is like bog oak,
the ball of his heel

like a basalt° egg.
10 His instep has shrunk
cold as a swan's foot
or a wet swamp root.

His hips are the ridge
and purse of a mussel,
15 his spine an eel arrested
under a glisten of mud.

The head lifts,
the chin is a visor
raised above the vent
20 of his slashed throat

that has tanned and toughened.
The cured wound
opens inwards to a dark
elderberry place.

25 Who will say "corpse"
to his vivid cast?
Who will say "body"
to his opaque repose?

And his rusted hair,
30 a mat unlikely
as a fetus's.
I first saw his twisted face

in a photograph,
a head and shoulder
35 out of the peat,
bruised like a forceps baby,

but now he lies
perfected in my memory,
down to the red horn
40 of his nails,

hung in the scales
with beauty and atrocity:
with the Dying Gaul°
too strictly compassed

45 on his shield,
with the actual weight
of each hooded victim,
slashed and dumped.

9. **basalt:** dark volcanic rock.
43. **Dying Gaul:** famous third-century
B.C. statue of an Iron Age Celtic warrior
dying on his shield.

MAKING MEANINGS

Digging
The Grauballe Man

First Thoughts

1. What word or passage from each poem most vividly communicates to you what the speaker sees, hears, smells, or feels?

Shaping Interpretations

2. Describe what the speaker of "Digging" sees from his window.

3. Why do you think the father comes up "twenty *years*" away in line 7 of "Digging"? (What word did you expect to find there?)

4. What different things does the speaker compare his pen to in "Digging"? What significance can you find in these comparisons, particularly the one in the last stanza?

5. Explain the **extended metaphor** in "Digging." What kind of digging does the speaker intend to do?

6. List all the **similes** and **metaphors** the speaker uses to describe the Grauballe man. How do some of these comparisons make you feel about the man and his dark fate?

7. Why do you think Heaney dares anyone to call the man a "corpse" or "body" (lines 25–28)?

8. Why do you think the speaker uses **images** from the animal, vegetable, and mineral worlds in describing the Grauballe man?

9. Think about what the Grauballe man might **symbolize** for Heaney. What connections and contradictions in human experience might he represent? (Pay attention especially to lines 41–42.)

Connecting with the Text

10. What associations did you make with the word *digging*? How does the activity of digging link both these poems?

CHOICES:
Building Your Portfolio

Writer's Notebook

1. Collecting Ideas for a Problem-Solution Essay

When the Grauballe man was discovered in Denmark, some of the local people were skeptical of the scientists' extraordinary claim that he was nearly two thousand years old. The locals did not know whether to trust the outside "experts" and feared they were the victims of a hoax. They preferred a more homely and less alarming explanation: The body was that of a local man named Red Christian, who, according to witnesses still living at the time, had gotten drunk and drowned in a bog seventy years earlier. With a small group, discuss other instances of mistrust or misunderstanding of scientists by ordinary people. What are some possible solutions to this problem? Take notes on your discussion, and save them for the Writer's Workshop on page 1179.

Creative Writing

2. Do Your Own Digging

Seamus Heaney once wrote that in "Digging" he truly found his own voice: "Finding a voice means that you can get your own feeling into your own words and that your words have the feel of you about them." Beginning with the last three lines of Heaney's poem "Digging," write your own poem, being careful to do your "digging" with words that suit your own voice. You might want to begin by recalling something about your parents, grandparents, or other older family members.

CLASHES OF CULTURE

As the traveler who has once been from home is wiser than he who has never left his own doorstep, so a knowledge of one other culture should sharpen our ability to scrutinize more steadily, to appreciate more lovingly, our own.

—Margaret Mead, *from Coming of Age in Samoa* (American, 1901–1978)

Woolf   Gordimer

Mahfouz   Walcott

Orwell   Achebe

Lessing   Soyinka

Virginia Woolf

(1882–1941)

Virginia Woolf was born in Victorian London to the scholar and literary critic Sir Leslie Stephen and his artistic wife, Julia. In her youth, Woolf enjoyed all the advantages of a financially comfortable and intellectually challenging environment. Too frail to attend school regularly, she was privately tutored and given the luxury of her father's extensive library.

After her father's death in 1904, Virginia, her sister, Vanessa, and their two brothers moved to the area of London known as Bloomsbury. Soon they and their friends began to meet in what came to be called the Bloomsbury Group, an intellectual circle whose other prominent members included the writer E. M. Forster, the artist Duncan Grant, and the economist John Maynard Keynes. One member of the group was Leonard Woolf, a journalist and economist, whom Virginia married in 1912.

An informal gathering with the highest cultural standards, the Bloomsbury Group helped provide the right environment for Virginia Woolf's sensitive, experimental fiction. Only after her death, when her diaries were published, was it clear how powerful the emotional effect of her friends' praise or criticism had been on her.

Woolf had been writing since she was fourteen and reviewing books since her early twenties, but it was not until she was thirty-three, in 1915, that her first novel, *The Voyage Out,* was published. The publication of *Jacob's Room*

Virginia Woolf.

(1922) and *Mrs. Dalloway* (1925) established her position as one of the foremost writers of her time. With these novels—and with subsequent novels such as *To the Lighthouse* (1927) and *The Waves* (1931)—Woolf pursued an experimental vision that emphasized personal impressions over external events and focused on the experience of life as it was being lived.

Like James Joyce, Woolf used the technique of stream of consciousness, although her version of it was somewhat different from his. For example, while *Mrs. Dalloway,* like Joyce's *Ulysses,* takes place on a single day, it covers, through the thoughts of its characters, an entire lifetime. Woolf was a great admirer of Joyce's *Portrait of the Artist as a Young Man,* but she considered *Ulysses* an "illiterate, underbred book." Still, she worried that "what I am doing is probably being better done by Mr. Joyce."

Woolf also wrote a great many reviews and essays, a number of them focusing on women authors who she felt had been neglected or exploring female writers in general. In 1917, she and her husband established the Hogarth Press, which published many of the most important writers—both male and female—of the day.

Troubled by sudden deaths and mental illness in her family, Woolf throughout her life suffered from bouts of depression and anxiety. These deepened with the German bombing raids over England in World War II, and in March 1941, she took her own life.

go.hrw.com
LEO 12-15

Before You Read

SHAKESPEARE'S SISTER

Make the Connection

Gender and Genius

Gender is perhaps the most basic difference between human beings in every culture. Beyond the biological differences are the social and cultural realities: the everyday concerns that men and women have and the work they are or are not able to accomplish. Virginia Woolf scrutinized those realities in her 1929 essay collection *A Room of One's Own,* from which the following selection is taken. Focusing on the creation of great literature, Woolf went back to Shakespeare's day and drew firm conclusions about the lack of equal opportunity for women through the ages.

Reading Skills and Strategies

Evaluating a Persuasive Message

After you read this essay, write Woolf's **main idea** across the top of a sheet of paper. Underneath it, list the arguments she makes to support her thesis. Next to each argument, indicate whether it appeals mainly to your intellect or to your emotions.

Background

A Room of One's Own is considered a pioneering work of feminist criticism, a field that did not even exist in 1929 but has since blossomed. Aims of feminist criticism include exposing sexist attitudes in or toward literature, reinterpreting earlier works from a feminist perspective, uncovering neglected women writers, and analyzing how gender affects a writer's subjects, themes, and even style. Some early feminists believed that "female language" is different from male language—richer in emotion, for example, and freer in patterns of meaning. Today, many feminists are exploring how cultural and economic forces help to shape the identities of women *and* men.

Virginia Woolf laid the foundation for much of this thinking. She was truly ahead of her time in insisting that social conditions can determine writing, that male literary language may not truly express women's experiences, and that the imagination can transcend gender.

Virginia Woolf in a Deck Chair (20th century) by Vanessa Bell.

Shakespeare's Sister
from A Room of One's Own

Virginia Woolf

Here am I asking why women did not write poetry in the Elizabethan age, and I am not sure how they were educated; whether they were taught to write; whether they had sitting rooms to themselves; how many women had children before they were twenty-one; what, in short, they did from eight in the morning till eight at night. They had no money evidently; according to Professor Trevelyan[1] they were married whether they liked it or not before they were out of the nursery, at fifteen or sixteen very likely. It would have been extremely odd, even upon this showing, had one of them suddenly written the plays of Shakespeare, I concluded, and I thought of that old gentleman, who is dead now, but was a bishop, I think, who declared that it was impossible for any woman, past, present, or to come, to have the genius of Shakespeare. He wrote to the papers about it. He also told a lady who applied to him for information that cats do not as a matter of fact go to heaven, though they have, he added, souls of a sort. How much thinking those old gentlemen used to save one! How the borders of ignorance shrank back at their approach! Cats do not go to heaven. Women cannot write the plays of Shakespeare.

Be that as it may, I could not help thinking, as I looked at the works of Shakespeare on the shelf, that the bishop was right at least in this; it would have been impossible, completely and entirely, for any woman to have written the plays of Shakespeare in the age of Shakespeare. Let me imagine, since facts are so hard to come by, what would have happened had Shakespeare had a wonderfully gifted sister, called Judith, let us say. Shakespeare himself went, very probably—his mother was an heiress—to the grammar school, where he may have learnt Latin—Ovid, Virgil, and Horace—and the elements of grammar and logic. He was, it

is well known, a wild boy who poached rabbits, perhaps shot a deer, and had, rather sooner than he should have done, to marry a woman in the neighborhood, who bore him a child rather quicker than was right. That escapade sent him to seek his fortune in London. He had, it seemed, a taste for the theater; he began by holding horses at the stage door. Very soon he got work in the theater, became a successful actor, and lived at the hub of the universe, meeting everybody, knowing everybody, practicing his art on the boards, exercising his wits in the streets, and even getting access to the palace of the queen. Meanwhile his extraordinarily gifted sister, let us suppose, remained at home. She was as adventurous, as imaginative, as agog to see the world as he was. But she was not sent to school. She had no chance of learning grammar and logic, let alone of reading Horace and Virgil. She picked up a book now and then, one of her brother's perhaps, and read a few pages. But then her parents came in and told her to mend the stockings or mind the stew and not moon about with books and papers. They would have spoken sharply but kindly, for they were substantial people who knew the conditions of life for a woman and loved their daughter—indeed, more likely than not she was the apple of her father's eye. Perhaps she scribbled some pages up in an apple loft on the sly, but was careful to hide them or set fire to them. Soon, however, before she was out of her teens, she was to be betrothed to the son of a neighboring wool stapler.[2] She cried out that marriage was hateful to her, and for that she was severely beaten by her father. Then he ceased to scold her. He begged her instead not to hurt him, not to shame him in this matter of her marriage. He would give her a chain of beads or a fine petticoat, he said; and there were tears in his eyes. How could she disobey him? How could she break his heart? The force of her own gift alone drove her to it. She made up a small parcel of her belongings, let herself down by a rope one summer's night, and took the road to London. She was not seventeen. The birds that sang in the hedge were not more musical than she was. She had the quickest fancy, a gift like her brother's, for the tune of words. Like him, she had

---

1. **Professor Trevelyan:** G. M. Trevelyan, author of *The History of England* (1926).

2. **wool stapler:** dealer in wool, a product sorted according to its fiber, or "staple."

a taste for the theater. She stood at the stage door; she wanted to act, she said. Men laughed in her face. The manager—a fat, loose-lipped man—guffawed. He bellowed something about poodles dancing and women acting—no woman, he said, could possibly be an actress. He hinted—you can imagine what. She could get no training in her craft. Could she even seek her dinner in a tavern or roam the streets at midnight? Yet her genius was for fiction and lusted to feed abundantly upon the lives of men and women and the study of their ways. At last—for she was very young, oddly like Shakespeare the poet in her face, with the same gray eyes and rounded brows—at last Nick Greene the actor-manager took pity on her; she found herself with child by that gentleman and so—who shall measure the heat and violence of the poet's heart when caught and tangled in a woman's body?—killed herself one winter's night and lies buried at some crossroads where the omnibuses now stop outside the Elephant and Castle.[3]

That, more or less, is how the story would run, I think, if a woman in Shakespeare's day had had Shakespeare's genius. But for my part, I agree with the deceased bishop, if such he was—it is unthinkable that any woman in Shakespeare's day should have had Shakespeare's genius. For genius like Shakespeare's is not born among laboring, uneducated, servile people. It was not born in England among the Saxons and the Britons. It is not born today among the working classes. How, then, could it have been born among women whose work began, according to Professor Trevelyan, almost before they were out of the nursery, who were forced to it by their parents and held to it by all the power of law and custom? Yet genius of a sort must have existed among women as it must have existed among the working classes. Now and again an Emily Brontë or a Robert Burns blazes out and proves its presence. But certainly it never got itself onto paper. When, however, one reads of a witch being ducked, of a woman possessed by devils, of a wise woman selling herbs, or even of a very remarkable man who had a mother, then I think we are on the track of a

lost novelist, a suppressed poet, of some mute and inglorious[4] Jane Austen, some Emily Brontë who dashed her brains out on the moor or mopped and mowed about the highways crazed with the torture that her gift had put her to. Indeed, I would venture to guess that Anon, who wrote so many poems without signing them, was often a woman. It was a woman Edward Fitzgerald,[5] I think, suggested who made the ballads and the folk songs, crooning them to her children, beguiling her spinning with them, or the length of the winter's night.

This may be true or it may be false—who can say?—but what is true in it, so it seemed to me, reviewing the story of Shakespeare's sister as I had made it, is that any woman born with a great gift in the sixteenth century would certainly have gone crazed, shot herself, or ended her days in some lonely cottage outside the village, half witch, half wizard, feared and mocked at. For it needs little skill in psychology to be sure that a highly gifted girl who had tried to use her gift for poetry would have been so thwarted and hindered by other people, so tortured and pulled asunder by her own contrary instincts, that she must have lost her health and sanity to a certainty. No girl could have walked to London and stood at a stage door and forced her way into the presence of actor-managers without doing herself a violence and suffering an anguish which may have been irrational—for chastity may be a fetish invented by certain societies for unknown reasons—but were nonetheless inevitable. Chastity had then, it has even now, a religious importance in a woman's life, and has so wrapped itself round with nerves and instincts that to cut it free and bring it to the light of day demands courage of the rarest. To have lived a free life in London in the sixteenth century would have meant for a woman who was poet and playwright a nervous stress

4. **mute and inglorious:** allusion to line 59 of "Elegy Written in a Country Churchyard" (page 601).
5. **Edward Fitzgerald** (1809-1883): English translator and poet.

WORDS TO OWN
servile (sur′vil) *adj.:* like or characteristic of a slave; humbly submissive or yielding.

---

3. **buried . . . Elephant and Castle:** Suicides were commonly buried at crossroads. The Elephant and Castle is a pub set at a busy crossroads in south London.

and dilemma which might well have killed her. Had she survived, whatever she had written would have been twisted and deformed, issuing from a strained and morbid imagination. And undoubtedly, I thought, looking at the shelf where there are no plays by women, her work would have gone unsigned. That refuge she would have sought certainly. It was the relic of the sense of chastity that dictated anonymity to women even so late as the nineteenth century. Currer Bell, George Eliot, George Sand,[6] all the victims of inner strife as their writings prove, sought ineffectively to veil themselves by using the name of a man. Thus they did homage to the convention, which if not implanted by the other sex was liberally encouraged by them (the chief glory of a woman is not to be talked of, said Pericles,[7] himself a much-talked-of man), that publicity in women is detestable. Anonymity runs in their blood. The desire to be veiled still possesses them. They are not even now as concerned about the health of their fame as men are, and, speaking generally, will pass a tombstone or a signpost without feeling an irresistible desire to cut their names on it, as Alf, Bert, or Chas. must do in obedience to their instinct, which murmurs if it sees a fine woman go by, or even a dog, *Ce chien est à moi*.[8] And, of course, it may not be a dog, I thought, remembering Parliament Square, the Sieges Allee,[9] and other avenues; it may be a piece of land or a man with curly black hair. It is one of the great advantages of being a woman that one can pass even a very fine negress without wishing to make an Englishwoman of her.

That woman, then, who was born with a gift of poetry in the sixteenth century, was an unhappy woman, a woman at strife against herself. All the conditions of her life, all her own instincts, were hostile to the state of mind which is needed to set free whatever is in the brain. But what is the state of mind that is most <u>propitious</u> to the act of creation, I asked. Can one come by any notion of the state that furthers and makes possible that strange activity? Here I opened the volume containing the Tragedies of Shakespeare. What was Shakespeare's state of mind, for instance, when he wrote *Lear* and *Antony and Cleopatra*? It was certainly the state of mind most favorable to poetry that there has ever existed. But Shakespeare himself said nothing about it. We only know casually and by chance that he "never blotted a line." Nothing indeed was ever said by the artist himself about his state of mind until the eighteenth century perhaps. Rousseau[10] perhaps began it. At any rate, by the nineteenth century self-consciousness had developed so far that it was the habit for men of letters to describe their minds in confessions and autobiographies. Their lives also were written, and their letters were printed after their deaths. Thus, though we do not know what Shakespeare went through when he wrote *Lear*, we do know what Carlyle went through when he wrote *The French Revolution*; what Flaubert went through when he wrote *Madame Bovary*; what Keats was going through when he tried to write poetry against the coming of death and the indifference of the world.

And one gathers from this enormous modern literature of confession and self-analysis that to write a work of genius is almost always a feat of prodigious difficulty. Everything is against the likelihood that it will come from the writer's mind whole and entire. Generally material circumstances are against it. Dogs will bark; people will interrupt; money must be made; health will break down. Further, accentuating all these difficulties and making them harder to bear is the world's <u>notorious</u> indifference. It does not ask people to

---

6. Currer Bell, George Eliot, George Sand: male pseudonyms for the female writers Charlotte Brontë, Mary Ann Evans, and Amantine-Aurore-Lucile Dupin.

7. Pericles (c. 495–429 B.C.): Athenian legislator and general.

8. *Ce chien est à moi* (sə shē·en′ āt ä mwä): French for "This dog is mine."

9. Sieges Allee (zē′gəs ä·lā′): busy thoroughfare in Berlin. The name—more commonly written as one word "Siegesallee"—is German for "Avenue of Victory."

10. Rousseau: Jean-Jacques Rousseau (1712–1778), French author whose candid, autobiographical *Confessions* began a vogue in literature for confessional accounts.

- -

WORDS TO OWN

propitious (prō·pish′əs) *adj.*: favorable.

notorious (nō·tôr′ē·əs) *adj.*: widely but unfavorably known; famous.

- -

write poems and novels and histories; it does not need them. It does not care whether Flaubert finds the right word or whether Carlyle scrupulously verifies this or that fact. Naturally, it will not pay for what it does not want. And so the writer, Keats, Flaubert, Carlyle, suffers, especially in the creative years of youth, every form of distraction and discouragement. A curse, a cry of agony, rises from those books of analysis and confession. "Mighty poets in their misery dead"[11]—that is the burden of their song. If anything comes through in spite of all this, it is a miracle, and probably no book is born entire and uncrippled as it was conceived.

But for women, I thought, looking at the empty shelves, these difficulties were infinitely more <u>formidable</u>. In the first place, to have a room of her own, let alone a quiet room or a soundproof room, was out of the question, unless her parents were exceptionally rich or very noble, even up to the beginning of the nineteenth century. Since her pin money,[12] which depended on the goodwill of her father, was only enough to keep her clothed, she was debarred from such <u>alleviations</u> as came even to Keats or Tennyson or Carlyle, all poor men, from a walking tour, a little journey to France, from the separate lodging which, even if it were miserable enough, sheltered them from the claims and tyrannies of their families. Such material difficulties were formidable; but much worse were the immaterial. The indifference of the world which Keats and Flaubert and other men of genius have found so hard to bear was in her case not indifference but hostility. The world did not say to her as it said to them, Write if you choose; it makes no difference to me. The world said with a guffaw, Write? What's the good of your writing?

A Corner of the Artist's Room, Paris (late 19th or early 20th century) by Gwen John.

Sheffield City Art Galleries, England.

WORDS TO OWN

formidable (fôr′mə·də·bəl) *adj.:* difficult to handle or overcome.

alleviations (ə·lē′vē·ā′shənz) *n. pl.:* things that lighten, relieve, or make easier to bear.

---

11. **Mighty poets . . . dead:** line from William Wordsworth's poem "Resolution and Independence."
12. **pin money:** small allowance given for personal expenses.

LITERATURE
AND
POLITICS

Suffragists with sandwich boards in London (c. 1910).

Votes for Women!

In December 1913, during an opera about Joan of Arc staged especially for the British royal family, three elegantly dressed women stood and addressed the king with a megaphone. The crowd was thrown into a panic as the women likened their struggle for the vote to Joan of Arc's fifteenth-century fight for liberty. When the police finally removed them, other women, hidden in the balcony, showered the audience with suffragist pamphlets. The king, of course, did not respond. But the dramatic protest joined the suffragists to Joan and other brave forerunners, just as Virginia Woolf's portrait of Shakespeare's fictional sister drew on the past to spur change in her own time.

The vote—a right not granted to British women over the age of thirty until 1918, and not granted to women over twenty-one until 1928—was the key to meaningful change for women in Woolf's day. Woolf herself was among thousands of women who joined suffrage organizations during the first decade of the century. Although she could have written articles for publications such as *The Suffragette* or *Votes for Women,* she instead lent her support in more humble ways: She sat on the platform at public meetings and folded countless mailings (she later recalled spending "hours writing names like Cowgill on envelopes"). Yet Woolf was a pacifist, and her views against the use of physical force prevented her wholehearted involvement in the increasingly combative woman suffrage movement of the early 1900s.

A new phase in an old fight. Universal suffrage was not a new idea. Women and men had campaigned for it since the mid-1800s; in fact, the philosopher John Stuart Mill had brought a suffrage bill before the British Parliament in 1866. But the fight entered a new phase in 1904, when the ardent suffragist Christabel Pankhurst strode off to the Manchester Free Trade Hall to challenge Winston Churchill on the subject of voting rights for women. Churchill refused to acknowledge Pankhurst's demands, and she was howled down by the crowd, but she counted it as her first "militant" step.

Afterward, members of the Women's Social and Political Union, which Pankhurst and her mother, Emmeline, had founded in 1903, were emboldened to take other steps: They held rallies and marches, staged suffrage plays at public meetings, broke the windows of government buildings, and interrupted Parliament by shouting "Votes for women!" from their enclosed seats in the "Ladies' Gallery." (Later, several women chained themselves to the metal grille that separated this gallery from the main chamber.) From 1906 to 1914, more than a thousand suffragists were arrested and carted off to jail. Held in tiny cells, and prohibited from speaking to one another, these women still found other ways to protest, mostly through hunger strikes. In answer, the government force-fed the protesters until the procedure permanently damaged many women's health. Thereafter, in what came to be called "Cat and Mouse" licenses, hunger strikers were released from prison only until they regained their strength, then were rearrested.

Success at last. The sight of "respectable" women getting roughed up by hostile crowds and held for months in prison did alter public opinion: Many came to realize how badly women wanted the right to full citizenship. Yet protests continued without results until the beginning of World War I, when the Pankhursts and others abruptly turned their interests to the war effort. Ironically, many historians now think that women's work during the war, mostly as they filled the absent soldiers' jobs, was the turning point in the suffrage movement. When the war was over, most Britishers felt that women shouldn't—indeed couldn't—be deprived of the vote any longer.

MAKING MEANINGS

First Thoughts

1. How did Judith's story make you feel about women's lives, past and present?

Shaping Interpretations

2. Woolf uses an invented **biography** in this essay. Why do you think she uses such a device? Is her biography of Judith Shakespeare convincing to you? Cite reasons for your answer.

3. In her essay, Woolf says that for women "Anonymity runs in their blood." According to Woolf, why do women shy away from the limelight? What do you think of her reasons?

4. Woolf focuses on the unhappy psychological state of a gifted female writer in the age of Shakespeare. How would you state the **main idea** of her essay? Do you agree with Woolf's thesis? Why or why not? (Review the notes you took while reading.)

5. Where do you detect a tone of contemptuous **irony** in Woolf's essay? How would you read these passages aloud to convey Woolf's **tone**?

Extending the Text

6. In her essay, Woolf concludes that to write great literature, a woman *must* have money and a private place. Do you think this is still true today—for anyone, male *or* female? Explain your response.

Challenging the Text

7. Did Woolf make any **generalizations** in this essay that you think are unsupported by historical or contemporary evidence? Explain your response.

Reading Check

a. What happens to "Judith Shakespeare" when she goes to London?

b. According to Woolf, what general conditions make works of genius difficult to produce? What special conditions do women face?

CHOICES:
Building Your Portfolio

Writer's Notebook

1. Collecting Ideas for a Problem-Solution Essay

One way to identify a possible topic for a problem-solution essay is to focus on the local aspects of a far-reaching societal problem, such as the lack of equal opportunity for women that Woolf discusses in "Shakespeare's Sister." Spend a few minutes brainstorming or clustering to discover inequalities you perceive in the opportunities your school or community offers males and females of your age. Save your notes for the Writer's Workshop on page 1179.

Evaluating an Argument

2. The Gender Gap

Woolf's essay contains many ideas, both explicit and implicit, about gender roles. In an essay, (a) discuss how Woolf depicts men and women, (b) analyze how the characterizations work in her argument, and (c) evaluate her ideas. (Your reading notes may help you.)

Creative Writing

3. Reimagining Judith's Life

In Judith's story, where was her famous brother? What if Queen Elizabeth had heard of Judith's ambitions or her famous brother had recognized them? Rewrite Judith's life so that it *does not* end in tragedy.

Creative Writing

4. Another Mute Milton

Imagine a person of today or from the past who, if circumstances had been different, might have been a great writer, painter, or political leader. Write an imaginary life of that intensely creative but thwarted person.

Naguib Mahfouz

(1911–   )

Egypt

Naguib Mahfouz (nä′gēb′ mä′fo͞oz), often heralded as Egypt's finest writer, grew up in a middle-class family similar to the family he traces in his acclaimed *Cairo Trilogy*. Mahfouz began sending stories to magazines when he was a philosophy student at Cairo University. When he first got paid for a story, he is reputed to have exclaimed, in disbelief, "One gets paid for them as well!"

Naguib Mahfouz.

For most of his life, Mahfouz worked as a civil servant for the Egyptian government, first in the Ministry of Religious Affairs, later in the Arts Administration, and still later as head of the State Cinema Organization. He has written more than forty novels and short-story collections, several plays, and many film scripts. Almost all his writing is set in Cairo. "Like their author," writes the translator Denys Johnson-Davies, "his stories never travel abroad, not even to the Egyptian countryside." Most of his novels are set in an area known as Khan al-Khalili, which is filled with mosques, restaurants, shops, and colorful people.

Despite their limited settings, Mahfouz's works are read widely throughout the Middle East and are considered highly influential. The subjects of his writings are the repression of women, social injustice, and the superficial values of modern life. Ironically, some of his books were banned in Arab countries, including Egypt, especially after he expressed support for the 1979 peace treaty between Egypt and Israel. Nevertheless, in Egypt and throughout the world, he is widely regarded as the outstanding writer of contemporary Arabic literature. In 1988, Mahfouz won the Nobel Prize in literature.

(Map) ©Rand McNally R. L. #98-S-116.

Before You Read
THE CAIRO ROOFTOP

Background

Picture a world in which a girl marries at thirteen and from then on lives within the walls of her husband's home, unseen and unknown to those beyond the family circle. Her knowledge of the world outside is confined to what she can see from a rooftop.

Naguib Mahfouz introduces you to a woman who leads just such a confined life in "The Cairo Rooftop," a chapter from his novel *Palace Walk. Palace Walk* is one of three volumes in Mahfouz's *Cairo Trilogy,* which he wrote in Arabic and published in the mid-1950s. Because of translation delays, the trilogy was almost unknown outside the Middle East until 1988, when Mahfouz won the Nobel Prize in literature.

The English translation of the *Cairo Trilogy* opens the world of modern Egypt to Western readers. Spanning the years 1917 to 1952, the trilogy follows three generations of a middle-class Muslim family before, during, and after the 1919 uprising that led Britain to declare Egypt a sovereign state. The personal struggles within the family reflect not only Egypt's political history but also its increasing interest in education and science, the gradual emancipation of women, and the transformation of traditional attitudes toward Western life.

Palace Walk, the first book in the trilogy, chronicles the period from 1917 to 1919, two of the five years during which Egypt was a British protectorate. The main character in "The Cairo Rooftop" is Amina, who has been married to Ahmad, the family patriarch, since she was thirteen. Amina is totally, but willingly, dominated by her husband at a time when a virtuous woman of Islam rarely steps outside her husband's home, and never shows her face to a man who is not a close relative. There are five younger people in the family: Yasin, the twenty-one-year-old son of Ahmad's first wife; two other sons, Fahmy and Kamal; and two daughters, Khadija and Aisha.

Ahmad's family lives in a two-story house on Palace Walk, a street in Cairo that centuries ago connected two palaces. The street name that is the book's title can also be translated as "between two palaces" and refers not only to the street but also to the two political situations that frame the book and to the change from traditional to more modern ways that frames the family's experiences.

The map on page 1131 reflects the story's time frame: This is not the Middle East today.

Quickwrite

Start with what you know. Spend two or three minutes jotting down what you know about Egyptian history in the twentieth century.

Cairo rooftops.

The Cairo Rooftop *from* Palace Walk

Naguib Mahfouz

translated by **William Maynard Hutchins** *and* **Olive E. Kenny**

When they had finished breakfast, the mother said, "Aisha, you do the laundry today and Khadija will clean the house. Afterward meet me in the oven room."

Amina divided the work between them right after breakfast. They were content to be ruled by her, and Aisha would not question her assignment. Khadija would take the trouble to make a few comments, either to show her worth or to start a quarrel. Thus she said, "I'll let you clean the house if you think washing the clothes is too much. But if you make a fuss over the washing so you can stay in the bathroom till all the work in the kitchen is finished, that's an excuse that can be rejected in advance."

Aisha ignored her remark and went off to the bath humming. Khadija commented sarcastically, "Lucky for you that sound reverberates in the bathroom like a phonograph speaker. So sing and let the neighbors hear it."

Their mother left the room and went through the hall to the stairs. She climbed to the roof to make her morning rounds there before descending to the oven room. The bickering between her daughters was nothing new to her. Over the course of time it had turned into a customary way of life when the father was not at home and no one could think of anything pleasant to say. She had tried to stop it by using entreaty, humor, and tenderness. That was the only type of discipline she employed with her children. It fit her nature, which could not stand anything stronger. She lacked the firmness that rearing children occasionally requires. Perhaps she would have liked to be firm but was not able to. Perhaps she had attempted to be firm but had been overcome by her emotions and weakness. It seemed she could not bear for the ties between her and her children to be anything but love and affection. She let the father or his shadow, which dominated the children from afar, straighten them out and lay down the law. Thus their silly quarrel did not weaken her admiration for her two girls or her satisfaction with them. Even Aisha, who was insanely fond of singing and standing in front of the mirror, her laziness notwithstanding, was no less skillful and organized than Khadija.

Amina would have been justified in allowing herself long periods of relaxation, but she was prevented by a natural tendency that was almost a disease. She insisted on supervising everything in the house, no matter how small. When the girls finished their work, she would go around energetically inspecting the rooms, living areas, and halls, with a broom in one hand and a feather duster in the other. She searched the corners, walls, curtains, and all the furnishings to eliminate an overlooked speck of dust, finding as much pleasure and satisfaction in that as in removing a speck from her eye. She was by nature such a perfectionist that she examined the clothes about to be laundered. If she discovered a piece of clothing that was unusually dirty, she would not spare the owner a gentle reminder of his duty, whether it was Kamal, who was going on ten, or Yasin, who had two clear and contradictory approaches to caring for himself. He was excessively fastidious about his external appearance—his suit, fez, shirt, necktie, and shoes—but shockingly neglectful of his underwear.

Naturally this comprehensive concern of hers did not exclude the roof and the pigeons and chickens that inhabited it. In fact, the time she spent on the roof was filled with love and delight from the opportunities it presented for work, not to mention the joys of play and merriment she found there. No wonder, for the roof was a new world she had discovered. The big house had known nothing of it until she joined the family. She had created it afresh through the force of her spirit, back when the house retained the appearance it had always had since being built ages before. It was her idea to have these cages with the cooing pigeons put on some of the high walls. She had arranged these wooden chicken coops where the hens clucked as they foraged for food. How much joy she got from scattering grain for them or putting the water container on the ground as the hens raced for it, preceded by their rooster. Their beaks fell on the grain quickly and

regularly, like sewing-machine needles, leaving little indentations in the dust like the pockmarks from a drizzle. How good she felt when she saw them gazing at her with clear little eyes, inquisitive and questioning, while they cackled and clucked with a shared affection that filled her heart with tenderness.

She loved the chickens and pigeons as she loved all of God's creatures. She made little noises to them, thinking they understood and responded. Her imagination had bestowed conscious, intelligent life on all animals and occasionally even on inanimate objects. She was quite certain that these beings praised her Lord and were in contact, by various means, with the spirit world. Her world with its earth and sky, animals and plants, was a living, intelligent one. Its merits were not confined

Street scene in Cairo.

to the blessing of life. It found its completion in worship. It was not strange, then, that, relying on one excuse or another, she prolonged the lives of the roosters and hens. One hen was full of life, another a good layer. This rooster woke her in the morning with his crowing. Perhaps if it had been left entirely to her, she would never have consented to put her knife to their throats. If circumstances did force her to slaughter one, she selected a chicken or pigeon with a feeling close to anguish. She would give it a drink, seek God's mercy for it, invoke God's name, ask forgiveness, and then slaughter it. Her consolation was that she was exercising a right that God the Benefactor had granted to all those who serve Him.

The most amazing aspect of the roof was the southern half overlooking al-Nahhasin Street.[1] There in years past she had planted a special garden. There was not another one like it in the whole neighborhood on any of the other roofs, which were usually covered with chicken droppings. She had first begun with a small number of pots of carnations and roses. They had increased year by year and were arranged in rows parallel to the sides of the walls. They grew splendidly, and she had the idea of putting a trellis over the top. She got a carpenter to install it. Then she planted both jasmine and hyacinth bean vines. She attached them to the trellis and around the posts. They grew tall and spread out until the area was transformed into an arbor garden with a green sky from which jasmine flowed down. An enchanting, sweet fragrance was diffused throughout.

This roof, with its inhabitants of chickens and pigeons and its arbor garden, was her beautiful, beloved world and her favorite place for relaxation out of the whole universe, about which she knew nothing. As usual at this hour, she set about caring for it. She swept it, watered the plants, fed the chickens and pigeons. Then for a long time, with smiling lips and dreamy eyes, she enjoyed the scene surrounding her. She went to the end of the garden and stood behind the interwoven, coiling vines, to gaze out through the openings at the limitless space around her.

She was awed by the minarets[2] which shot up, making a profound impression on her. Some were near enough for her to see their lamps and crescent distinctly, like those of Qala'un and Barquq. Others appeared to her as complete wholes, lacking details, like the minarets of the mosques of al-Husayn, al-Ghuri, and al-Azhar. Still other minarets were at the far horizon and seemed phantoms, like those of the Citadel and Rifa'i mosques. She turned her face toward them with devotion, fascination, thanksgiving, and hope. Her spirit soared over their tops, as close as possible to the heavens. Then her eyes would fix on the minaret of the mosque of al-Husayn, the dearest one to her because of her love for its namesake.[3] She looked at it affectionately, and her yearnings mingled with the sorrow that pervaded her every time she remembered she was not allowed to visit the son of the Prophet of God's daughter, even though she lived only minutes away from his shrine.

She sighed audibly and that broke the spell. She began to amuse herself by looking at the roofs and streets. The yearnings would not leave her. She turned her back on the wall. Looking at the unknown had overwhelmed her: both what is unknown to most people, the invisible spirit world, and the unknown with respect to her in particular, Cairo, even the adjacent neighborhood, from which voices reached her. What could this world of which she saw nothing but the minarets and roofs be like? A quarter of a century had passed while she was confined to this house, leaving it only on infrequent occasions to visit her mother in al-Khurunfush. Her husband escorted her on each visit in a carriage, because he could not bear for anyone to see his wife, either alone or accompanied by him.

She was neither resentful nor discontented, quite the opposite. All the same, when she peeked through the openings between the jasmine and the hyacinth bean vines, off into space, at the minarets and rooftops, her delicate lips would rise in a tender, dreamy smile. Where

---

1. **al-Nahhasin Street:** a main street in the Bayn al-Qasrayn, or Palace Walk, section of Cairo. This street is also called Coppersmiths Street for the artisans who line its sidewalks.

2. **minarets:** mosque towers. Minarets are often used by special criers to announce daily calls to worship.
3. **mosque . . . namesake:** mosque named for Husayn (626–680), a Shiite Muslim hero and grandson of the prophet Mohammed. A climactic moment in the novel comes when, against the wishes of her husband, Amina sneaks out to visit this mosque.

might the law school be where Fahmy was sitting at this moment? Where was the Khalil Agha School, which Kamal assured her was only a minute's trip from the mosque of al-Husayn? Before leaving the roof, she spread her hands out in prayer and called on her Lord: "God, I ask you to watch over my husband and children, my mother and Yasin, and all the people: Muslims and Christians, even the English, my Lord, but drive them from our land as a favor to Fahmy, who does not like them."[4]

4. **Fahmy . . . them:** Amina's son Fahmy, an Egyptian nationalist, fervently hopes for the end of English colonial rule.

FINDING COMMON GROUND

Review your Quickwrite notes, and think about what you would like to know about modern Egyptian history. Then, get together with others to discuss how you will respond to "The Cairo Rooftop." Discuss questions of your own, or try one of these questions or activities.

- How do you think this selection relates to the collection theme, "Clashes of Culture"?

- Is geography—and timing—everything? Suppose you had been born in Egypt or in China or anywhere else except the United States. Suppose you had been born in the early 1900s. What might your life have been like?

- Find out about dating and marriage customs or about educational and work opportunities for women in any country except yours. Take notes, and either give a talk to the class or hold a panel discussion with others who chose different countries.

- In many places in the world even today, the birth of a daughter causes less joy than the birth of a son. What do you think might be some reasons for this attitude?

Mosque of Sultan Barkut, Cairo.

George Orwell

(1903–1950)

George Orwell was born Eric Blair in Bengal, India, where his British father was a member of the Indian civil service. A few years afterward, his family returned to England. A lonely child, Orwell spent a good deal of time making up stories and poems. He later wrote that from an early age he knew he was going to be a writer.

After graduating from Eton, Orwell joined the Indian Imperial Police, serving in Burma from 1922 to 1927, when he resigned to devote more time to writing. Returning to Europe, he taught and took part-time, ill-paying jobs in France and England. His first book, *Down and Out in Paris and London* (1933), was based on these experiences. He based his next novel, *Burmese Days* (1934), on his life in Burma.

Although he published journalistic pieces under his real name, with his earliest books he began to publish as George Orwell, and he continued to do so until his death. After publishing three novels, Orwell was asked to write a study of conditions among industrial workers in northern England for the socialist Left Book Club. This became *The Road to Wigan Pier* (1937), a moving portrait of the difficult lives of working-class people.

Deeply disturbed by the rise of fascism in the 1930s, Orwell fought against the Fascists in the Spanish Civil War and published a book based on these experiences—*Homage to Catalonia* (1938). "The Spanish war," he wrote, "turned the scale and thereafter I knew where I stood. Every line of serious work that I have written since 1936 has been written, directly or indirectly, *against* totalitarianism and *for* democratic socialism."

His two most famous novels, *Animal Farm* (1945) and *1984* (1949), illustrate this point. *Animal Farm* is a political allegory that points out the dangers of totalitarianism, whether practiced by the left or the right. And *1984* has given us an entire vocabulary for the excesses of totalitarian regimes, including such terms as *newspeak* and *double-think*. In this book, Orwell stresses the connections between language, thought, and power, dramatizing in fiction the ideas he earlier explored in his famous essay *Politics and the English Language* (1946)—especially the idea that corrupt language can be used to promote political oppression.

George Orwell making a radio broadcast for the BBC.

Before You Read
SHOOTING AN ELEPHANT

Make the Connection

An Enemy Within

Wherever there were British colonies, there were British people who went to these colonies to live and to govern. No matter how long these people lived overseas, they generally remained outsiders, an alien minority holding power over a resentful people. As a police officer in British-controlled Burma in the 1920s, George Orwell did not just symbolize foreign rule—he was its agent. His awareness of being an enemy within another culture kindled enormous conflicts inside him. Just who was *his* enemy? Look for the answer that comes to him, elephant rifle in hand, in the upcoming essay.

Quickwrite

Have you ever witnessed a situation where group pressure forces someone to act in a way he or she might not really want to act? How can one's personality or individuality be taken away as a result of pressure from a crowd or any larger group? Jot down your thoughts on this issue of group pressure versus individuality.

Elements of Literature

Irony

The dominant literary mode in the twentieth century is irony (see page 991). Orwell's essay uses several strategies to evoke a sense of irony. He uses **verbal irony**—saying one thing and meaning something else, often something just the opposite. He also uses **situational irony**—in which something happens that is completely different from what we expect, or from what we think is appropriate. Irony cuts deeply into our feelings, perhaps because we sense that life itself is deeply and pervasively ironic.

> **I**rony is a discrepancy between expectations and reality or between appearances and reality. There are three types of irony: verbal irony, situational irony, and dramatic irony.
>
> *For more on Irony, see page 991 and the Handbook of Literary Terms.*

Background

This essay is set in Burma, a country in Southeast Asia. After a series of wars with Great Britain during the 1800s, Burma finally came under British control in the 1880s. Although allowed some self-rule in 1937, Burma became fully independent only in 1948, after a period of Japanese occupation during World War II. In 1989, the government changed the country's official name to the Union of Myanmar.

House used by British officers or planters. Chapra, India.

Shooting an Elephant

George Orwell

In Moulmein, in Lower Burma, I was hated by large numbers of people—the only time in my life that I have been important enough for this to happen to me. I was subdivisional police officer of the town, and in an aimless, petty kind of way anti-European feeling was very bitter. No one had the guts to raise a riot, but if a European woman went through the bazaars alone somebody would probably spit betel juice over her dress. As a police officer I was an obvious target and was baited whenever it seemed safe to do so. When a nimble Burman tripped me up on the football field and the referee (another Burman) looked the other way, the crowd yelled with hideous laughter. This happened more than once. In the end the sneering yellow faces of young men that met me everywhere, the insults hooted after me when I was at a safe distance, got badly on my nerves. The young Buddhist priests were the worst of all. There were several thousands of them in the town and none of them seemed to have anything to do except stand on street corners and jeer at Europeans.

All this was perplexing and upsetting. For at that time I had already made up my mind that imperialism was an evil thing and the sooner I chucked up my job and got out of it the better. Theoretically—and secretly, of course—I was all for the Burmese and all against their oppressors, the British. As for the job I was doing, I hated it more bitterly than I can perhaps make clear. In a job like that you see the dirty work of Empire at close quarters. The wretched prisoners huddling in the stinking cages of the lockups, the gray, cowed faces of the long-term convicts, the scarred buttocks of the men who had been flogged with bamboos—all these oppressed me with an intolerable sense of guilt. But I could get nothing into perspective. I was young and ill-educated and I had had to think out my problems in the utter silence that is imposed on every Englishman in the East. I did not even know that the British Empire is dying, still less did I know that it is a great deal better than the younger empires that are going to supplant it. All I knew was that I was stuck between my hatred of the empire I served and my rage against the evil-spirited little beasts who tried to make my job impossible. With one part of my mind I thought of the British Raj[1] as an unbreakable tyranny, as something clamped down, *in saecula saeculorum,*[2] upon the will of prostrate peoples; with another part I thought that the greatest joy in the world would be to drive a bayonet into a Buddhist priest's guts. Feelings like these are the normal by-products of imperialism; ask any Anglo-Indian official, if you can catch him off duty.

One day something happened which in a roundabout way was enlightening. It was a tiny incident in itself, but it gave me a better glimpse than I had had before of the real nature of imperialism—the real motives for which despotic governments act. Early one morning the subinspector at a police station the other end of the town rang me up on the phone and said that an elephant was ravaging the bazaar. Would I please come and do something about it? I did not know what I could do, but I wanted to see what was happening and I got on to a pony and started out. I took my rifle, an old .44 Winchester and much too small to kill an elephant, but I thought the noise might be useful *in terrorem.*[3] Various Burmans stopped me on the way and told me about the elephant's doings. It was not, of course, a wild elephant, but a tame one which had gone "must."[4] It had been chained up, as tame elephants always are when their attack of "must" is due, but on the previous night it had

1. **Raj** (räj): rule over India. The word is derived from *rajya,* Hindi for "kingdom."
2. *in saecula saeculorum* (in sē'kōō·lə sē'kōō·lôr'əm): Latin for "forever and ever" (literally, "into ages of ages").
3. *in terrorem* (in ter·ôr'əm): Latin for "for terror." In other words, the gun might serve to frighten the elephant.
4. **must:** state of frenzy in animals. The word comes from *mast,* Hindi for "intoxicated."

- -

WORDS TO OWN
supplant (sə·plant') v.: to replace; displace.

- -

broken its chain and escaped. Its mahout,[5] the only person who could manage it when it was in that state, had set out in pursuit, but had taken the wrong direction and was now twelve hours' journey away, and in the morning the elephant had suddenly reappeared in the town. The Burmese population had no weapons and were quite helpless against it. It had already destroyed somebody's bamboo hut, killed a cow, and raided some fruit stalls and devoured the stock; also it had met the municipal rubbish van and, when the driver jumped out and took to his heels, had turned the van over and inflicted violences upon it.

The Burmese subinspector and some Indian constables were waiting for me in the quarter where the elephant had been seen. It was a very poor quarter, a labyrinth of squalid bamboo huts, thatched with palm leaf, winding all over a steep hillside. I remember that it was a cloudy, stuffy morning at the beginning of the rains. We began questioning the people as to where the elephant had gone and, as usual, failed to get any definite information. That is invariably the case in the East; a story always sounds clear enough at a distance, but the nearer you get to the scene of events the vaguer it becomes. Some of the people said that the elephant had gone in one direction, some said that he had gone in another, some professed not even to have heard of any elephant. I had almost made up my mind that the whole story was a pack of lies, when we heard yells a little distance away. There was a loud, scandalized cry of "Go away, child! Go away this instant!" and an old woman with a switch in her hand came round the corner of the hut, violently shooing away a crowd of naked children. Some more women followed, clicking their tongues and exclaiming; evidently there was something that the children ought not to have seen. I rounded the hut and saw a man's dead body sprawling in the mud. He was an Indian, a black Dravidian coolie,[6] almost naked, and he could not have been dead many minutes. The

people said that the elephant had come suddenly upon him round the corner of the hut, caught him with its trunk, put its foot on his back, and ground him into the earth. This was the rainy season and the ground was soft, and his face had scored a trench a foot deep and a couple of yards long. He was lying on his belly with arms crucified and head sharply twisted to one side. His face was coated with mud, the eyes wide open, the teeth bared and grinning with an expression of unendurable agony. (Never tell me, by the way, that the dead look peaceful. Most of the corpses I have seen looked devilish.) The friction of the great beast's foot had stripped the skin from his back as neatly as one skins a rabbit. As soon as I saw the dead man I sent an orderly to a friend's house nearby to borrow an elephant rifle. I had already sent back the pony, not wanting it to go mad with fright and throw me if it smelled the elephant.

The orderly came back in a few minutes with a rifle and five cartridges, and meanwhile some Burmans had arrived and told us that the elephant was in the paddy fields below, only a few hundred yards away. As I started forward practically the whole population of the quarter flocked out of the houses and followed me. They had seen the rifle and were all shouting excitedly that I was going to shoot the elephant. They had not shown much interest in the elephant when he was merely ravaging their homes, but it was different now that he was going to be shot. It was a bit of fun to them, as it would be to an English crowd; besides they wanted the meat. It made me vaguely uneasy. I had no intention of shooting the elephant—I had merely sent for the rifle to defend myself if necessary—and it is always unnerving to have a crowd following you. I marched down the hill, looking and feeling a fool, with the rifle over my shoulder and an ever-growing army of people jostling at my heels. At the bottom, when you got away from the huts, there was a metaled[7] road and beyond that a miry waste of

---

5. **mahout** (mə·hout′): elephant keeper. The word derives from *mahaut,* Hindi for "great in measure" and, thus, "important officer."

6. **Dravidian** (drə·vid′ē·ən) **coolie:** *Dravidian* denotes any of several intermixed races living chiefly in southern India and northern Sri Lanka. A coolie is an unskilled laborer. The word is derived from *quli,* Hindi for "hired servant," and has become offensive.

7. **metaled:** paved with cinders, stones, or the like.

WORDS TO OWN

labyrinth (lab′ə·rinth′) *n.:* maze; complex or confusing arrangement.

squalid (skwäl′id) *adj.:* foul or unclean; wretched.

---

paddy fields a thousand yards across, not yet plowed but soggy from the first rains and dotted with coarse grass. The elephant was standing eight yards from the road, his left side toward us. He took not the slightest notice of the crowd's approach. He was tearing up bunches of grass, beating them against his knees to clean them, and stuffing them into his mouth.

I had halted on the road. As soon as I saw the elephant I knew with perfect certainty that I ought not to shoot him. It is a serious matter to shoot a working elephant—it is comparable to destroying a huge and costly piece of machinery—and obviously one ought not to do it if it can possibly be avoided. And at that distance, peacefully eating, the elephant looked no more dangerous than a cow. I thought then and I think now that his attack of "must" was already passing off; in which case he would merely wander harmlessly about until the mahout came back and caught him. Moreover, I did not in the least want to shoot him. I decided that I would watch him for a little while to make sure that he did not turn savage again, and then go home.

But at that moment I glanced round at the crowd that had followed me. It was an immense crowd, two thousand at the least and growing every minute. It blocked the road for a long distance on either side. I looked at the sea of yellow faces above the garish clothes—faces all happy and excited over this bit of fun, all certain that the elephant was going to be shot. They were watching me as they would watch a conjurer about to perform a trick. They did not like me, but with the magical rifle in my hands I was momentarily worth watching. And suddenly I realized that I should have to shoot the elephant after all. The people expected it of me and I had got to do it; I could feel their two thousand wills pressing me forward, irresistibly. And it was at this moment, as I stood there with the rifle in my hands, that I first grasped the hollowness, the futility of the white man's dominion in the East. Here was I, the white man with his gun, standing in front of the unarmed native crowd—seemingly the leading actor of the piece; but in reality I was only an absurd puppet pushed to and fro by the will of those yellow faces behind. I perceived in this moment that when the white man turns tyrant it is his own freedom that he destroys. He becomes a

sort of hollow, posing dummy, the conventionalized figure of a sahib.[8] For it is the condition of his rule that he shall spend his life in trying to impress the "natives," and so in every crisis he has got to do what the "natives" expect of him. He wears a mask, and his face grows to fit it. I had got to shoot the elephant. I had committed myself to doing it when I sent for the rifle. A sahib has got to act like a sahib; he has got to appear resolute, to know his own mind and do definite things. To come all that way, rifle in hand, with two thousand people marching at my heels, and then to trail feebly away, having done nothing—no, that was impossible. The crowd would laugh at me. And my whole life, every white man's life in the East, was one long struggle not to be laughed at.

But I did not want to shoot the elephant. I watched him beating his bunch of grass against his knees, with that preoccupied grandmotherly air that elephants have. It seemed to me that it would be murder to shoot him. At that age I was not squeamish about killing animals, but I had never shot an elephant and never wanted to. (Somehow it always seems worse to kill a *large* animal.) Besides, there was the beast's owner to be considered. Alive, the elephant was worth at least a hundred pounds; dead, he would only be worth the value of his tusks, five pounds, possibly. But I had got to act quickly. I turned to some experienced-looking Burmans who had been there when we arrived, and asked them how the elephant had been behaving. They all said the same thing: He took no notice of you if you left him alone, but he might charge if you went too close to him.

It was perfectly clear to me what I ought to do. I ought to walk up to within, say, twenty-five yards of the elephant and test his behavior. If he charged, I could shoot; if he took no notice of me, it would be safe to leave him until the mahout came back. But also I knew that I was going to do no such thing. I was a poor shot with a rifle and the ground was soft mud into which one would sink at every step. If the elephant charged and I missed him, I should have about as much chance as a toad under a steamroller. But even then I was not thinking particularly of my own skin, only of the watchful yellow faces behind. For at that

---

8. sahib (sä′ib′): master; sir. In colonial India, the title was used as a sign of respect for a European gentleman.

Jumbo Elephant #2 (1988) by William Hawkins. Enamel and collage on masonite (48″ × 57″).

Ricco/Maresca Gallery, New York.

moment, with the crowd watching me, I was not afraid in the ordinary sense, as I would have been if I had been alone. A white man mustn't be frightened in front of "natives"; and so, in general, he isn't frightened. The sole thought in my mind was that if anything went wrong those two thousand Burmans would see me pursued, caught, trampled on, and reduced to a grinning corpse like that Indian up the hill. And if that happened it was quite probable that some of them would laugh. That would never do. There was only one alternative. I shoved the cartridges into the magazine and lay down on the road to get a better aim.

The crowd grew very still, and a deep, low, happy sigh, as of people who see the theater curtain go up at last, breathed from innumerable throats. They were going to have their bit of fun after all. The rifle was a beautiful German thing with cross-hair sights. I did not then know that in shooting an elephant one would shoot to cut an imaginary bar running from earhole to earhole. I ought, therefore, as the elephant was sideways on, to have aimed straight at his earhole; actually I aimed several inches in front of this, thinking the brain would be further forward.

When I pulled the trigger I did not hear the bang or feel the kick—one never does when a shot goes home—but I heard the devilish roar of glee that went up from the crowd. In that instant, in too short a time, one would have thought, even for the bullet to get there, a mysterious, terrible

change had come over the elephant. He neither stirred nor fell, but every line of his body had altered. He looked suddenly stricken, shrunken, immensely old, as though the frightful impact of the bullet had paralyzed him without knocking him down. At last, after what seemed a long time—it might have been five seconds, I dare say—he sagged flabbily to his knees. His mouth slobbered. An enormous senility seemed to have settled upon him. One could have imagined him thousands of years old. I fired again into the same spot. At the second shot he did not collapse but climbed with desperate slowness to his feet and stood weakly upright, with legs sagging and head drooping. I fired a third time. That was the shot that did for him. You could see the agony of it jolt his whole body and knock the last remnant of strength from his legs. But in falling he seemed for a moment to rise, for as his hind legs collapsed beneath him he seemed to tower upward like a huge rock toppling, his trunk reaching skyward like a tree. He trumpeted, for the first and only time. And then down he came, his belly toward me, with a crash that seemed to shake the ground even where I lay.

I got up. The Burmans were already racing past me across the mud. It was obvious that the elephant would never rise again, but he was not

WORDS TO OWN

senility (si·nil′ə·tē) *n*.: state of deterioration that sometimes accompanies old age.

dead. He was breathing very rhythmically with long rattling gasps, his great mound of a side painfully rising and falling. His mouth was wide open—I could see far down into caverns of pale pink throat. I waited a long time for him to die, but his breathing did not weaken. Finally I fired my two remaining shots into the spot where I thought his heart must be. The thick blood welled out of him like red velvet, but still he did not die. His body did not even jerk when the shots hit him, the tortured breathing continued without a pause. He was dying, very slowly and in great agony, but in some world remote from me where not even a bullet could damage him further. I felt that I had got to put an end to that dreadful noise. It seemed dreadful to see the great beast lying there, powerless to move and yet powerless to die, and not even to be able to finish him. I sent back for my small rifle and poured shot after shot into his heart and down his throat. They seemed to make no impression. The tortured gasps continued as steadily as the ticking of a clock.

In the end I could not stand it any longer and went away. I heard later that it took him half an hour to die. Burmans were bringing dahs[9] and baskets even before I left, and I was told they had stripped his body almost to the bones by the afternoon.

Afterward, of course, there were endless discussions about the shooting of the elephant. The owner was furious, but he was only an Indian and could do nothing. Besides, legally I had done the right thing, for a mad elephant has to be killed, like a mad dog, if its owner fails to control it. Among the Europeans opinion was divided. The older men said I was right, the younger men said it was a damn shame to shoot an elephant for killing a coolie, because an elephant was worth more than any damn Coringhee[10] coolie. And afterward I was very glad that the coolie had been killed; it put me legally in the right and it gave me a sufficient <u>pretext</u> for shooting the elephant. I often wondered whether any of the others grasped that I had done it solely to avoid looking a fool.

9. **dahs** (däz): large carving knives.
10. **Coringhee** (kôr·ing′ē): port in southeastern India.

WORDS TO OWN
pretext (prē′tekst′) *n.*: excuse.

MAKING MEANINGS

First Thoughts

1. What do you think of Orwell's decision to shoot the elephant?

Shaping Interpretations

2. What seems to be Orwell's attitude toward the Burmese? Do you think he embodies an imperialist perspective? Use details from the story to support your answer.

3. Explain in your own words the meaning of Orwell's **ironic** insight: Tyrants destroy their own freedom. Then, identify three other ironies contained in this essay.

4. What do you think this essay reveals about the real nature of imperialism?

5. There are two Orwells in this essay: the one acting and the one looking back. Discuss the differences between the two observers, using examples from the text. How does the older Orwell feel about the younger one?

Reading Check

a. What problem is Orwell asked to solve?

b. About how big is the crowd following Orwell, and why does he say they have come along?

c. When Orwell finds the elephant, what are two reasons he gives for not shooting it?

d. How does the animal react when shot?

Connecting with the Text

6. The essay is filled with remarkable physical descriptions. Which description did you find most compelling? How did it make you feel?

Extending the Text

7. In what ways are Orwell's experiences like and unlike those of a contemporary police officer or of a soldier on a peacekeeping mission?

CHOICES:
Building Your Portfolio

Writer's Notebook

1. Collecting Ideas for a Problem-Solution Essay

Pressure to conform is experienced by everyone who lives within a social group. Refer to your Quickwrite notes, and develop your ideas on group pressure. Think of specific occasions in your school or community when you or someone else experienced pressure to conform to group values or behavior. What happened, whom did it happen to, and why did it happen? Save your notes for possible use in the Writer's Workshop on page 1179.

Explaining a Response

2. A Significant Passage

Review the essay, and find one passage that you think is especially important, or controversial, or even upsetting. Write a brief essay in which you cite the passage and explain why you have chosen it. In your essay, be sure to describe your response to the passage and tell whether you think it connects to any situation in society as you know it today.

Interpreting a Symbol

3. Elephant Meanings

The elephant has tremendous importance in this essay. Could it **symbolize** the British Empire? Orwell himself? something else? Write an essay that presents your interpretation of the elephant's symbolic meaning. Cite details from the text to support your interpretation.

Creative Writing

4. Shooting "Shooting an Elephant"

Imagine that you are turning "Shooting an Elephant" into a short film. Create a storyboard, showing the scenes you'd include in your film. For which scenes would you add dialogue to move the film along? Which scene will mark the climax of your film?

Reading Skills

VOCABULARY: ANALYZING WORD ANALOGIES

An **analogy** is a similarity or likeness between two things that are unlike in other ways. When you state an analogy, you compare two things to show their likeness. A **word analogy** is a formally written statement that compares two pairs of words. The pairs of words are alike in that the relationship between the two words in the first pair is the same as the relationship between the two words in the second pair.

Standardized tests frequently include analogy questions, which measure your mastery of vocabulary and your ability to perceive relationships and patterns between words. Practice with analogies will help you develop the logical abilities to identify these relationships and patterns.

Reading word analogies. Although unlike in other ways, *cool* and *chilly* have a synonymous relationship to each other, just as *sad* and *unhappy* have. The following example shows how a word analogy using these words is written:

COOL : CHILLY :: sad : unhappy.

The colon (:) stands for the phrase "is related to." The double colon (::) between the two pairs of words stands for the phrase "in the same way that." Here are two ways to read the analogy:

- COOL [is related to] CHILLY
  [in the same way that]
  sad [is related to] *unhappy.*

- COOL is to CHILLY as *sad* is to *unhappy.*

Understanding word analogy problems.
The word analogy items you will find in exercises and on tests will be one of the following two kinds:

- One pair of words is given, and you must select a second pair with the same relationship.

- One pair of words and one word from the second pair are given, and you must select the word that completes the second pair.

In both kinds of problems, the parts of speech and relative order of the words in each pair must match.

and Strategies

Identifying relationships. The chart on the right will help you identify some of the relationships that are frequently expressed in word analogies. Other possible relationships between words might include whole and part, function, action to object, action to performer, degree, and time sequence.

Solving word analogies. On standardized tests, analogy questions are usually presented in the two formats discussed on page 1144. You can use the following three steps to solve an analogy question:

- Analyze the first pair of words to identify the relationship between them.
- State the analogy in sentence or question form.
- Identify the best available choice to complete the analogy.

Try It Out

For each item, write, on your own paper, the type of relationship the words in the complete pair have to each other. Then, write the word from the following list that appropriately completes each word analogy. (An example is provided.)

conspicuous	obnoxious	senility
guffaw	pretext	squalid
labyrinth	propitious	temerity
magnanimous		

Relationship	Analogy
location	CLOUD : SKY :: student : school
1. _____	DUMP : _____ :: system : organized
2. _____	SOB : _____ :: grin : frown
3. _____	_____ : FORGETFULNESS :: exercise : fitness
4. _____	THOUGHTFUL : CONSIDERATE :: _____ : offensive
5. _____	PATH : _____ :: piece : puzzle

Word Analogies		
Relationship	Example	Explanation
Antonym	SOILED : CLEAN :: careless : careful	Soiled is the opposite of clean, just as careless is the opposite of careful.
Synonym	COOL : CHILLY :: sad : unhappy	Cool and chilly are similar in meaning, as are sad and unhappy.
Cause and Effect	TRAGEDY : SADNESS :: comedy : happiness	Tragedy generally causes sadness, just as comedy generally causes happiness.
Characteristic Quality	OCEAN : LARGE :: pond : small	Oceans are characteristically large, just as ponds are characteristically small.
Part and Whole	CHAPTER : BOOK :: fender : car	A chapter is a part of a book, just as a fender is a part of a car.
Location	FISH : SEA :: moose : forest	A fish can be found in the sea, just as a moose can be found in a forest.
Classification	TANGO : DANCE :: neon : gas	The tango is classified as a kind of dance, just as neon is classified as a kind of gas.

Doris Lessing

(1919–   )

Doris Lessing was born in Persia (now Iran) to British parents who had fled England to escape its narrowness and provincialism. When she was five, her father gave up his job running a bank, and the family moved to a three-thousand-acre farm in Southern Rhodesia (now Zimbabwe). The farm employed some thirty to fifty black African laborers, each of whom earned the equivalent of about $1.50 a month and who lived in mud huts with no sanitation.

In Africa, Lessing's mother was homesick for England and often ill, while her father grew increasingly eccentric. Lessing describes her own childhood as "hellishly lonely"; the nearest neighbor was miles away. Only as an adult did she appreciate that her solitude had fostered a fine education, since the lack of company allowed her to spend her time slowly reading the classics of European and American fiction.

At fourteen, Lessing left school and went to work in Salisbury, the capital of Rhodesia, first as a nursemaid and then as a stenographer and telephone operator. The city had a white population of about ten thousand, and a larger black population that Lessing discovered "didn't count." When her first marriage collapsed, she entered radical politics. At twenty-six, she married a second time, but that marriage also ended in divorce.

"I can't remember a time when I didn't want to come to England," she later recalled. In 1949, she left Africa for England with her two-year-old son and the manuscript of her first novel,

Doris Lessing (1984).

The Grass Is Singing (1950). Tracing a complex relationship between a white farmer's wife and her black servant, the book commanded attention as one of the earliest novels about Africa's racial problems.

The short stories collected in Lessing's *African Stories* (1964) also take place in the Africa of her childhood. Also semiautobiographical is Lessing's quintet of novels, *Children of Violence* (1952–1969), which tells the story of the aptly named Martha Quest, who like her creator spent her childhood in Africa and her mature life in postwar Britain. The narrative continues to an apocalyptic ending in an unnamed city in the year 2000.

Lessing's most widely read and discussed book is probably *The Golden Notebook* (1962), an ambitious, complexly structured work that combines fiction, parody, and factual reporting to explore Lessing's concerns with politics, mental illness, and the problems of women in modern life. Another well-known book, *Briefing for a Descent into Hell* (1971), introduces readers to what Lessing calls "inner-space fiction," in which an individual mental breakdown is related to a wider social breakdown. In contrast, Lessing's five-volume series *Canopus in Argos: Archives* (1979–1983) is a sequence of fantasies set in outer space. However, one reviewer remarked that the series shows less of a relationship to typical space-travel science fiction than it does to the Book of Revelation in the Bible.

Among Lessing's more recent novels are *The Good Terrorist* (1985), about a group of young radicals in contemporary London, and *The Fifth Child* (1988), about the effects a "demon child" has on his family and society. She also continues to write nonfiction works on subjects ranging from political correctness to the 1980s war in Afghanistan. In 1994, she published *Under My Skin,* the first volume of her autobiography.

In all of Lessing's work, there is evidence of the responsibility she feels as a writer to be "an instrument of change." "It is not merely a question of preventing evil," she says, "but of strengthening a vision of a good which may defeat the evil."

Before You Read

NO WITCHCRAFT FOR SALE

Make the Connection

The Power to Heal

The upcoming story asks troubling, complex questions about cultural conflict. Some of its cultural clashes are obvious, some are bridged by the unifying force of deep affection, and some remain mysterious—for the people involved, and perhaps for us. Do you think that some cultural differences cannot be bridged no matter how much goodwill the parties bring to their encounter? Or do you think that with effort, people truly *can* understand one another's beliefs and aspirations? See whether "No Witchcraft for Sale"—which really is not about witchcraft at all—clarifies, confuses, or changes your ideas.

Quickwrite

Think of someone you know or know about who comes from a culture or background very different from your own. What do you think that person would find difficult or impossible to understand about your culture? What is mysterious to you about that person's culture? Write down your ideas.

Elements of Literature

Theme

A story may have many threads. A wide assortment of ideas may be conveyed through characters' attitudes, through conflicts and their outcomes, through symbols, and even through a title. Yet despite the variety of ideas a reader may glean from a story, one dominant, central idea, or **theme,** will unify the work.

> **T**heme is a central idea or insight embodied in a work of literature.
>
> *For more on Theme, see the Handbook of Literary Terms.*

Background

This tale from Doris Lessing's *African Stories* takes place in Southern Rhodesia at a time when that southern African country was still under British rule. The Farquars in the story are part of the British ruling class; their servants are black Africans. In her preface to *African Stories,* Lessing writes: "If people had been prepared to listen, two decades earlier, to the small, but shrill-enough, voices crying out for the world's attention, perhaps the present suffering in South Africa and Southern Rhodesia could have been prevented. Britain, who is responsible, became conscious of her responsibility too late; and now the tragedy must play itself slowly out." In the 1960s, when Lessing wrote these words, Southern Rhodesia was an independent nation under minority rule by whites. Attempts by black African leaders to gain a voice in government were vigorously opposed by the white leadership. After much fighting between black nationalists and government troops, Southern Rhodesia emerged as the republic of Zimbabwe under the leadership of a black African, Robert Mugabe (moo·gäb′ē), in 1980.

No Witchcraft for Sale

Doris Lessing

The Farquars had been childless for years when little Teddy was born; and they were touched by the pleasure of their servants, who brought presents of fowls and eggs and flowers to the homestead when they came to rejoice over the baby, exclaiming with delight over his downy golden head and his blue eyes. They congratulated Mrs. Farquar as if she had achieved a very great thing, and she felt that she had—her smile for the lingering, admiring natives was warm and grateful.

Later, when Teddy had his first haircut, Gideon the cook picked up the soft gold tufts from the ground, and held them <u>reverently</u> in his hand. Then he smiled at the little boy and said: "Little Yellow Head." That became the native name for the child. Gideon and Teddy were great friends from the first. When Gideon had finished his work, he would lift Teddy on his shoulders to the shade of a big tree,

and play with him there, forming curious little toys from twigs and leaves and grass, or shaping animals from wetted soil. When Teddy learned to walk it was often Gideon who crouched before him, clucking encouragement, finally catching him when he fell, tossing him up in the air till they both became breathless with laughter. Mrs. Farquar was fond of the old cook because of his love for her child.

There was no second baby; and one day Gideon said: "Ah, missus, missus, the Lord above sent this one; Little Yellow Head is the most good thing we have in our house." Because of that "we" Mrs. Farquar felt a warm impulse toward her cook; and at the end of the month she raised his wages. He had been with her now for several years; he was one of the few natives who had his wife and children in the compound and never wanted to go home to his kraal,[1] which was some hundreds of miles away. Sometimes a small piccanin[2] who had been born the same time as Teddy, could be seen peering from the edge of the bush, staring in awe at the little white boy with his miraculous fair hair and Northern blue eyes. The two little children would gaze at each other with a wide, interested gaze, and once Teddy put out his hand curiously to touch the black child's cheeks and hair.

Gideon, who was watching, shook his head wonderingly, and said: "Ah, missus, these are both children, and one will grow up to be a baas,[3] and one will be a servant"; and Mrs. Farquar smiled and said sadly, "Yes, Gideon, I was thinking the same."

1. **kraal** (kräl): South African village.
2. **piccanin** (pik′ə·nin): black African child. Derived from *pequeno* (pā·kā′noo), Portuguese for "small," the term is often considered offensive.
3. **baas** (bäs): Afrikaans for "master." Afrikaans, a language developed from seventeenth-century Dutch, is spoken in South Africa.

WORDS TO OWN
reverently (rev′ər·ənt·lē) *adv.:* with deep respect, love, or awe, as for something sacred.

She sighed. "It is God's will," said Gideon, who was a mission boy.[4] The Farquars were very religious people; and this shared feeling about God bound servant and masters even closer together.

Teddy was about six years old when he was given a scooter, and discovered the intoxications of speed. All day he would fly around the homestead, in and out of flowerbeds, scattering squawking chickens and irritated dogs, finishing with a wide dizzying arc into the kitchen door. There he would cry: "Gideon, look at me!" And Gideon would laugh and say: "Very clever, Little Yellow Head." Gideon's youngest son, who was now a herdsboy, came especially up from the compound to see the scooter. He was afraid to come near it, but Teddy showed off in front of him. "Piccanin," shouted Teddy, "get out of my way!" And he raced in circles around the black child until he was frightened, and fled back to the bush.

"Why did you frighten him?" asked Gideon, gravely reproachful.

Teddy said defiantly: "He's only a black boy," and laughed. Then, when Gideon turned away from him without speaking, his face fell. Very soon he slipped into the house and found an orange and brought it to Gideon, saying: "This is for you." He could not bring himself to say he was sorry; but he could not bear to lose Gideon's affection either. Gideon took the orange unwillingly and sighed. "Soon you will be going away to school, Little Yellow Head," he said wonderingly, "and then you will be grown up." He shook his head gently and said, "And that is how our lives go." He seemed to be putting a distance between himself and Teddy, not because of resentment, but in the way a person accepts something inevitable. The baby had lain in his arms and smiled up into his face: The tiny boy had swung from his shoulders and played with him by the hour. Now Gideon would not let his flesh touch the flesh of the white child. He was kind, but there was a grave formality in his voice that made Teddy pout and sulk away. Also, it made him into a man: With Gideon he was polite, and carried himself formally, and if he came into the kitchen to ask for something, it was in the way a white man uses toward a servant, expecting to be obeyed.

4. **mission boy:** one educated by Christian missionaries.

But on the day that Teddy came staggering into the kitchen with his fists to his eyes, shrieking with pain, Gideon dropped the pot full of hot soup that he was holding, rushed to the child, and forced aside his fingers. "A snake!" he exclaimed. Teddy had been on his scooter, and had come to a rest with his foot on the side of a big tub of plants. A tree snake, hanging by its tail from the roof, had spat full into his eyes. Mrs. Farquar came running when she heard the commotion. "He'll go blind," she sobbed, holding Teddy close against her. "Gideon, he'll go blind!" Already the eyes, with perhaps half an hour's sight left in them, were swollen up to the size of fists: Teddy's small white face was distorted by great purple oozing protuberances.[5] Gideon said: "Wait a minute, missus, I'll get some medicine." He ran off into the bush.

Mrs. Farquar lifted the child into the house and bathed his eyes with permanganate.[6] She had scarcely heard Gideon's words; but when she saw that her remedies had no effect at all, and remembered how she had seen natives with no sight in their eyes, because of the spitting of a snake, she began to look for the return of her cook, remembering what she heard of the efficacy of native herbs. She stood by the window, holding the

5. **protuberances** (prō·tōō′bər·əns·iz): swellings; bulges.
6. **permanganate** (pər·maŋ′gə·nāt′): dark purple chemical compound used as a disinfectant.

WORDS TO OWN

reproachful (ri·prōch′fəl) *adj.:* full of or expressing blame.

---

terrified, sobbing little boy in her arms, and peered helplessly into the bush. It was not more than a few minutes before she saw Gideon come bounding back, and in his hand he held a plant.

"Do not be afraid, missus," said Gideon, "this will cure Little Yellow Head's eyes." He stripped the leaves from the plant, leaving a small white fleshy root. Without even washing it, he put the root in his mouth, chewed it vigorously, and then held the spittle there while he took the child forcibly from Mrs. Farquar. He gripped Teddy down between his knees, and pressed the balls of his thumbs into the swollen eyes, so that the child screamed and Mrs. Farquar cried out in protest: "Gideon, Gideon!" But Gideon took no notice. He knelt over the writhing child, pushing back the puffy lids till chinks of eyeball showed, and then he spat hard, again and again, into first one eye, and then the other. He finally lifted Teddy gently into his mother's arms, and said: "His eyes will get better." But Mrs. Farquar was weeping with terror, and she could hardly thank him: It was impossible to believe that Teddy could keep his sight. In a couple of hours the swellings were gone: The eyes were inflamed and tender but Teddy could see. Mr. and Mrs. Farquar went to Gideon in the kitchen and thanked him over and over again. They felt helpless because of their gratitude: It seemed they could do nothing to express it. They gave Gideon presents for his wife and children, and a big increase in wages, but these things could not pay for Teddy's now completely cured eyes. Mrs. Farquar said: "Gideon, God chose you as an instrument for His goodness," and Gideon said: "Yes, missus, God is very good."

Now, when such a thing happens on a farm, it cannot be long before everyone hears of it. Mr. and Mrs. Farquar told their neighbors and the story was discussed from one end of the district to the other. The bush is full of secrets. No one can live in Africa, or at least on the veld,[7] without learning very soon that there is an ancient wisdom of leaf and soil and season—and, too, perhaps most important of all, of the darker tracts of the human mind—which is the black man's heritage. Up and down the district people were

telling anecdotes, reminding each other of things that had happened to them.

"But I saw it myself, I tell you. It was a puff-adder bite. The kaffir's[8] arm was swollen to the elbow, like a great shiny black bladder. He was groggy after a half a minute. He was dying. Then suddenly a kaffir walked out of the bush with his hands full of green stuff. He smeared something on the place, and next day my boy was back at work, and all you could see was two small punctures in the skin."

This was the kind of tale they told. And, as always, with a certain amount of exasperation, because while all of them knew that in the bush of Africa are waiting valuable drugs locked in bark, in simple-looking leaves, in roots, it was impossible to ever get the truth about them from the natives themselves.

The story eventually reached town; and perhaps it was at a sundowner party,[9] or some such function, that a doctor, who happened to be there, challenged it. "Nonsense," he said. "These things get exaggerated in the telling. We are always checking up on this kind of story, and we draw a blank every time."

Anyway, one morning there arrived a strange car at the homestead, and out stepped one of the workers from the laboratory in town, with cases full of test tubes and chemicals.

Mr. and Mrs. Farquar were flustered and pleased and flattered. They asked the scientist to lunch, and they told the story all over again, for the hundredth time. Little Teddy was there too, his blue eyes sparkling with health, to prove the truth of it. The scientist explained how humanity might benefit if this new drug could be offered for sale; and the Farquars were even more pleased: They were kind, simple people, who liked to think of something good coming about because of them. But when the scientist began talking of the money that might result, their manner showed discomfort. Their feelings over the miracle (that was how they thought of it) were so strong and deep and religious, that it was distasteful to them

---

7. veld: in South Africa, open country with very few bushes or trees; grassland. *Veld,* also spelled *veldt,* is Afrikaans for "field."

8. kaffir's (kaf′ərz): *Kaffir* is a contemptuous term for a black African, derived from *kāfir,* Arabic for "infidel."
9. sundowner party: British colloquial term for "cocktail party." The term derives from the British custom of gathering for drinks at sunset.

to think of money. The scientist, seeing their faces, went back to his first point, which was the advancement of humanity. He was perhaps a trifle perfunctory: It was not the first time he had come salting the tail of a fabulous bush secret.[10]

Eventually, when the meal was over, the Farquars called Gideon into their living room and explained to him that this baas, here, was a Big Doctor from the Big City, and he had come all that way to see Gideon. At this Gideon seemed afraid; he did not understand; and Mrs. Farquar explained quickly that it was because of the wonderful thing he had done with Teddy's eyes that the Big Baas had come.

Gideon looked from Mrs. Farquar to Mr. Farquar, and then at the little boy, who was showing great importance because of the occasion. At last he said grudgingly: "The Big Baas want to know what medicine I used?" He spoke incredulously, as if he could not believe his old friends could so betray him. Mr. Farquar began explaining how a useful medicine could be made out of the root, and how it could be put on sale, and how thousands of people, black and white, up and down the continent of Africa, could be saved by the medicine when that spitting snake filled their eyes with poison. Gideon listened, his eyes bent on the ground, the skin of his forehead puckering in discomfort. When Mr. Farquar had finished he did not reply. The scientist, who all this time had been leaning back in a big chair, sipping his coffee and smiling with skeptical good humor, chipped in and explained all over again, in different words, about the making of drugs and the progress of science. Also, he offered Gideon a present.

There was silence after this further explanation, and then Gideon remarked indifferently that he could not remember the root. His face was sullen and hostile, even when he looked at the Farquars, whom he usually treated like old friends. They were beginning to feel annoyed; and this feeling annulled the guilt that had been sprung into life by Gideon's accusing manner. They were beginning to feel that he was unreasonable. But it was at that moment that they all realized he would never give in. The magical drug would remain where it was, unknown and useless except for the tiny scattering of Africans who had the knowledge, natives who might be digging a ditch for the municipality in a ragged shirt and a pair of patched shorts, but who were still born to healing, hereditary healers, being the nephews or sons of the old witch doctors whose ugly masks and bits of bone and all the uncouth properties of magic were the outward signs of real power and wisdom.

The Farquars might tread on that plant fifty times a day as they passed from house to garden, from cow kraal to mealie[11] field, but they would never know it.

But they went on persuading and arguing, with all the force of their exasperation; and Gideon continued to say that he could not remember, or that there was no such root, or that it was the wrong season of the year, or that it wasn't the root itself, but the spit from his mouth that had cured Teddy's eyes. He said all these things one after another, and seemed not to care they were contradictory. He was rude and stubborn. The Farquars could hardly recognize their gentle, lovable old servant in this ignorant, perversely obstinate African, standing there in front of them with lowered eyes, his hands twitching his cook's apron, repeating over and over whichever one of the stupid refusals that first entered his head.

And suddenly he appeared to give in. He lifted his head, gave a long, blank angry look at the circle of whites, who seemed to him like a circle of yelping dogs pressing around him, and said: "I will show you the root."

They walked single file away from the homestead down a kaffir path. It was a blazing December afternoon, with the sky full of hot rain clouds. Everything was hot: The sun was like a bronze tray whirling overhead, there was a heat shimmer over the fields, the soil was scorching underfoot, the dusty wind blew gritty and thick and warm in

11. **mealie:** corn.

10. **salting . . . bush secret:** An allusion to the ironic advice given to children about how to catch a bird: by putting salt on its tail. In other words, the scientist knows his search may be futile.

WORDS TO OWN
perfunctory (pər·fuŋk′tə·rē) *adj.*: halfhearted; indifferent.
annulled (ə·nuld′) *v.*: did away with; canceled.
perversely (pər·vʉrs′lē) *adv.*: disagreeably; contrarily.

their faces. It was a terrible day, fit only for reclining on a veranda with iced drinks, which is where they would normally have been at that hour.

From time to time, remembering that on the day of the snake it had taken ten minutes to find the root, someone asked: "Is it much further, Gideon?" And Gideon would answer over his shoulder, with angry politeness: "I'm looking for the root, baas." And indeed, he would frequently bend sideways and trail his hand among the grasses with a gesture that was insulting in its perfunctoriness. He walked them through the bush along unknown paths for two hours, in that melting destroying heat, so that the sweat trickled coldly down them and their heads ached. They were all quite silent: the Farquars because they were angry, the scientist because he was being proved right again; there was no such plant. His was a tactful silence.

At last, six miles from the house, Gideon suddenly decided they had had enough; or perhaps his anger evaporated at that moment. He picked up, without an attempt at looking anything but casual, a handful of blue flowers from the grass, flowers that had been growing plentifully all down the paths they had come.

He handed them to the scientist without looking at him, and marched off by himself on the way home, leaving them to follow him if they chose.

When they got back to the house, the scientist went to the kitchen to thank Gideon: He was being very polite, even though there was an amused look in his eyes. Gideon was not there. Throwing the flowers casually into the back of his car, the eminent visitor departed on his way back to his laboratory.

Gideon was back in his kitchen in time to prepare dinner, but he was sulking. He spoke to Mr. Farquar like an unwilling servant. It was days before they liked each other again.

The Farquars made inquiries about the root from their laborers. Sometimes they were answered with distrustful stares. Sometimes the natives said: "We do not know. We have never heard of the root." One, the cattle boy, who had been with them a long time, and had grown to trust them a little, said: "Ask your boy in the kitchen. Now, there's a doctor for you. He's the son of a famous medicine man who used to be in these parts, and there's nothing he cannot cure." Then he added politely: "Of course, he's not as good as

the white man's doctor, we know that, but he's good for us."

After some time, when the soreness had gone from between the Farquars and Gideon, they began to joke: "When are you going to show us the snake root, Gideon?" And he would laugh and shake his head, saying, a little uncomfortably: "But I did show you, missus, have you forgotten?"

Much later, Teddy, as a schoolboy, would come into the kitchen and say: "You old rascal, Gideon! Do you remember that time you tricked us all by making us walk miles all over the veld for nothing? It was so far my father had to carry me!"

And Gideon would double up with polite laughter. After much laughing, he would suddenly straighten himself up, wipe his old eyes, and look sadly at Teddy, who was grinning mischievously at him across the kitchen: "Ah, Little Yellow Head, how you have grown! Soon you will be grown up with a farm of your own. . . ."

MAKING MEANINGS

First Thoughts

1. What did you focus on most intently as you read the story—what word, phrase, image, or idea? Explain.

Shaping Interpretations

2. Mrs. Farquar and Gideon share a sense of sadness about the reality of their children's future lives. What is the reality that gives these two characters, and this whole story, a feeling of sadness?

> **Reading Check**
>
> a. Describe Gideon and Teddy's relationship at the story's start. What incident signals a change in their relationship?
>
> b. What crisis sets the **plot** in motion?
>
> c. What does Gideon do for Teddy?
>
> d. Cite sentences showing that the Farquars do not really understand Gideon and his response to the doctor's request.
>
> e. How does Teddy's relationship with Gideon change as he grows up?

3. Does the narrator's presentation of the Farquars as people of goodwill seem **ironic** or straight-forward? How did you respond to them?

4. What implicit criticism can you detect in the fact that while Teddy is riding a scooter, Gideon's son of the same age is a herdboy?

5. Why do you think Gideon refuses to share his wisdom with the Farquars? How do you feel about his refusal?

6. In what ways is this story about a clash of cultures? Reread Gideon's comment at the end of the story. What does it reveal about his understanding of the relationship between white European and black African cultures?

7. How would you state the **theme** of this story?

Connecting with the Text

8. Look back at your Quickwrite notes. How does the story affect your own notions about cultural differences?

9. Describe how you feel about the "Big Doctor." Did you find yourself identifying most with him, Gideon, or the Farquars? Explain your responses.

CHOICES:
Building Your Portfolio

Writer's Notebook

1. Collecting Ideas for a Problem-Solution Essay

In this story, Lessing explores how different cultural values can lead to problems of misunderstanding and mistrust. What problems do you suppose you'd encounter if you were placed in a different culture? (You may want to expand on the Quickwrite notes you began on page 1147.) Freewrite for a few minutes about what you think you'd have to grapple with. Save your notes for the Writer's Workshop on page 1179.

Analyzing Conflict
2. Between Two Worlds

The conflict in the story between the scientist and the Farquars on the one hand and Gideon on the other comes about because Gideon does not wish to share his knowledge. The conflict is not between right and wrong, good and evil, or enlightened and unenlightened viewpoints. Rather, it is over cultural differences. In an essay, discuss the similarities in and differences between the Farquars' and the scientist's point of view and Gideon's. Use details from the story to back up your opinions.

Evaluating Point of View
3. Angle of Vision

In a brief essay, discuss the effects of the narrator's point of view. Also, consider how the story might be different if it were narrated by Gideon or by the adult Teddy Farquar. Cite passages to support your analysis.

Comparing Texts
4. Paradox or Progress?

In an essay, compare and contrast Lessing's story with Kipling's "The Mark of the Beast" (page 872). Consider **point of view, theme,** and **characters.** For help in writing a comparison-contrast essay, see the Writer's Workshop on page 185.

Science and Medicine / Research
5. Ancient Cures, Modern Proofs

Research and report orally on folk medicines and other traditional cures. (You may concentrate on a single culture if you wish or research remedies that are found in several cultures.) What sorts of studies have been done to determine their effects? Do these studies confirm or disprove a belief in the effectiveness of folk medicines and traditional cures?

Nadine Gordimer

(1923–   )

Nadine Gordimer was born in Springs, a small town located thirty miles from Johannesburg, on the gold-mining ridge that has brought South Africa much of its wealth. Her father was a Jewish jeweler who had emigrated from Lithuania as a teenager; her mother was a native of England. Gordimer grew up in a middle-class colonial society that imitated European conventions and values. She has said that she spent much of her childhood reading because she found that atmosphere extremely dull.

Gordimer began writing at the age of nine when, as a sickly child, she was taken out of school for a time. At fifteen she published her first story in a Johannesburg weekly. When her first internationally published short-story collection, *The Soft Voice of the Serpent,* appeared in 1952, critics hailed Gordimer as a strong new voice who could draw fresh, authentic perceptions of African life. Her first novel, *The Lying Days,* appeared the following year to favorable reviews. Since then, she has continued to win praise and honors, and, in 1991, she won the Nobel Prize in literature.

Gordimer is known for her ability to show, as one critic said, "the infinite variety of human character, the rich and surprising drama inherent in human personality and in the clash of personality." She has been compared to Virginia Woolf for her talent in capturing the revealing moments in people's lives, what the critic Robert F. Haugh called "the illuminating moment, the quick perceptive glance of the author which sparkles like a gem."

Although she deals with universal themes and a variety of settings, much of Gordimer's writing concerns the troubles that her own

Nadine Gordimer.

nation has experienced. She has observed that "white culture imported from Europe never had a chance in the South African context. . . . All it did was to harm black culture. . . . In the process we suffered more than they." Commenting on Gordimer's writing about the effects of apartheid, the enforced separation of races, on South Africa, one critic called her "one of the very few links between white and black in South Africa. She is a bearer of culture in a barbaric society. And she is a luminous symbol of at least one white person's understanding of the black man's burden."

Perhaps Gordimer's greatest achievement is her ability to treat South Africa's problems from a literary rather than a political perspective. "Here I live in a society which is fundamentally out of joint. One can't but be politically concerned," she has said, but she disclaims a political allegiance. "I don't understand politics except in terms of what politics does to influence lives," she once observed. "What interests me is the infinite variety of effects apartheid has on men and women."

Among her best-known works are *A Guest of Honor* (1970) and *July's People* (1981), the latter set in an unnamed future when the whites in South Africa become the servants of the blacks.

Although Gordimer is respected around the world, she was a thorn in the side of her own country's government when apartheid was still in effect, and three of her novels were banned in South Africa. Nevertheless, she has always considered herself "an intensely loyal South African. I care deeply for my country. If I didn't, I wouldn't still be there."

Before You Read
ONCE UPON A TIME

Make the Connection
Walls and Barriers
Isolation is one way to keep conflict at bay. Opposing parties cannot clash if they do not meet, or so the reasoning goes. The remedy has certainly been tried repeatedly throughout history and all over the world. Reservations, compounds, borders—these are all isolating walls, literal or figurative, that keep some people away from others. Even on the household level, we have today's "security systems," a phrase to keep in mind as you read Gordimer's "Once upon a Time." Does a security system do its job? Is it worth its price? Is it protecting life—or maintaining a fantasy of safety?

Quickwrite
When you think of a wall, what do you picture? What does your wall keep in and keep out? Record your ideas.

Elements of Literature
Parody
"Once upon a Time" is a **parody,** or imitation, of a fairy tale. Though parodies are often written for amusement, they also may make serious points. As you read Gordimer's story, consider why she chose to imitate a fairy tale.

> **P**arody is the imitation of a work of literature, art, or music for amusement or instruction.
>
> *For more on Parody, see the Handbook of Literary Terms.*

Background
Until recently, South Africa, Nadine Gordimer's native land, practiced a policy called *apartheid,* the legal segregation of the races. Not only did black South Africans and other non-whites experience economic and political discrimination, but they were also forced to live in remote areas or in all-black "townships" bordering white cities. They could not leave these areas or enter white cities without "passbooks" that identified them by name, residency, and race.

Decades of rebellions, riots, and strikes left thousands of blacks dead and most of their leaders jailed. Finally, in 1991, the white government headed by F. W. de Klerk—under both internal and international pressure—repealed the apartheid laws. Three years later, the first all-race election swept the black South African Nelson Mandela, a former political prisoner and leader of the African National Congress, into office as president.

Blue at Noon (1955) by Adolph Gottlieb. Oil on canvas.

Collection Walker Art Center, Minneapolis. Gift of the T. B. Walker Foundation, 1963. Adolph and Esther Gottlieb Foundation/Licensed by VAGA, New York, N.Y.

Once upon a Time

Nadine Gordimer

Someone has written to ask me to contribute to an anthology of stories for children. I reply that I don't write children's stories; and he writes back that at a recent congress/book fair/seminar a certain novelist said every writer ought to write at least one story for children. I think of sending a postcard saying I don't accept that I "ought" to write anything.

And then last night I woke up—or rather was wakened without knowing what had roused me.

A voice in the echo chamber of the subconscious?

A sound.

A creaking of the kind made by the weight carried by one foot after another along a wooden floor. I listened. I felt the apertures of my ears distend with concentration. Again: the creaking. I was waiting for it; waiting to hear if it indicated that feet were moving from room to room, coming up the passage—to my door. I have no burglar bars, no gun under the pillow, but I have the same fears as people who do take these precautions, and my windowpanes are thin as rime,[1] could shatter like a wineglass. A woman was murdered (how do they put it) in broad daylight in a house two blocks away, last year, and the fierce dogs who guarded an old widower and his collection of antique clocks were strangled before he was knifed by a casual laborer he had dismissed without pay.

I was staring at the door, making it out in my mind rather than seeing it, in the dark. I lay quite still—a victim already—but the arrhythmia[2] of my heart was fleeing, knocking this way and that against its body-cage. How finely tuned the senses are, just out of rest, sleep! I could never listen intently as that in the distractions of the day; I was reading every faintest sound, identifying and classifying its possible threat.

But I learned that I was to be neither threatened nor spared. There was no human weight pressing on the boards, the creaking was a buck-

ling, an epicenter[3] of stress. I was in it. The house that surrounds me while I sleep is built on undermined ground; far beneath my bed, the floor, the house's foundations, the stopes[4] and passages of gold mines have hollowed the rock, and when some face trembles, detaches, and falls, three thousand feet below, the whole house shifts slightly, bringing uneasy strain to the balance and counterbalance of brick, cement, wood, and glass that hold it as a structure around me. The misbeats of my heart tailed off like the last muffled flourishes on one of the wooden xylophones made by the Chopi and Tsonga[5] migrant miners who might have been down there, under me in the earth at that moment. The stope where the fall was could have been disused, dripping water from its ruptured veins; or men might now be interred there in the most profound of tombs.

I couldn't find a position in which my mind would let go of my body—release me to sleep again. So I began to tell myself a story; a bedtime story.

In a house, in a suburb, in a city, there were a man and his wife who loved each other very much and were living happily ever after. They had a little boy, and they loved him very much. They had a cat and a dog that the little boy loved very much. They had a car and a caravan trailer for holidays, and a swimming pool which was fenced so that the little boy and his playmates would not fall in and drown. They had a housemaid who was absolutely trustworthy and an itinerant gardener who was highly recommended by the neighbors. For when they began to live happily ever after they were

---

3. **epicenter:** central point.
4. **stopes:** excavations.
5. **Chopi** (chō′pē) **and Tsonga** (tsäŋ′gä): Bantu-speaking peoples of Mozambique in southeastern Africa. Tsonga is often spelled *Thonga*.

WORDS TO OWN

distend (di·stend′) *v.*: expand; stretch out; swell.
itinerant (ī·tin′ər·ənt) *adj.*: traveling.

---

1. **rime:** frost.
2. **arrhythmia** (ə·ri*th*′mē·ə): irregular beating.

warned, by that wise old witch, the husband's mother, not to take on anyone off the street. They were inscribed[6] in a medical benefit society, their pet dog was licensed, they were insured against fire, flood damage, and theft, and subscribed to the local Neighborhood Watch, which supplied them with a plaque for their gates lettered YOU HAVE BEEN WARNED over the silhouette of a would-be intruder. He was masked; it could not be said if he was black or white, and therefore proved the property owner was no racist.

It was not possible to insure the house, the swimming pool, or the car against riot damage. There were riots, but these were outside the city, where people of another color were quartered. These people were not allowed into the suburb except as reliable housemaids and gardeners, so there was nothing to fear, the husband told the wife. Yet she was afraid that some day such people might come up the street and tear off the plaque YOU HAVE BEEN WARNED and open the gates and stream in. . . . Nonsense, my dear, said the husband, there are police and soldiers and tear gas and guns to keep them away. But to please her—for he loved her very much and buses were being burned, cars stoned, and school-children shot by the police in those quarters out of sight and hearing of the suburb—he had electronically controlled gates fitted. Anyone who pulled off the sign YOU HAVE BEEN WARNED and tried to open the gates would have to announce his intentions by pressing a button and speaking into a receiver relayed to the house. The little boy was fascinated by the device and used it as a walkie-talkie in cops and robbers play with his small friends.

The riots were suppressed, but there were many burglaries in the suburb and somebody's trusted housemaid was tied up and shut in a cupboard by thieves while she was in charge of her employers' house. The trusted housemaid of the man and wife and little boy was so upset by this misfortune befalling a friend left, as she herself often was, with responsibility for the possessions of the man and his wife and the little boy that she implored her employers to have burglar bars attached to the doors and windows of the house, and an alarm system installed. The wife

6. **inscribed:** enrolled.

said, She is right, let us take heed of her advice. So from every window and door in the house where they were living happily ever after they now saw the trees and sky through bars, and when the little boy's pet cat tried to climb in by the fanlight[7] to keep him company in his little bed at night, as it customarily had done, it set off the alarm keening[8] through the house.

The alarm was often answered—it seemed—by other burglar alarms, in other houses, that had been triggered by pet cats or nibbling mice. The alarms called to one another across the gardens in shrills and bleats and wails that everyone soon became accustomed to, so that the din roused the inhabitants of the suburb no more than the croak of frogs and musical grating of cicadas'[9] legs. Under cover of the electronic harpies'[10] discourse intruders sawed the iron bars and broke into homes, taking away hi-fi equipment, television sets, cassette players, cameras and radios, jewelry and clothing, and sometimes were hungry enough to devour everything in the refrigerator or paused audaciously to drink the whiskey in the cabinets or patio bars. Insurance companies paid no compensation for single malt, a loss made keener by the property owner's knowledge that the thieves wouldn't even have been able to appreciate what it was they were drinking.

Then the time came when many of the people who were not trusted housemaids and gardeners hung about the suburb because they were unemployed. Some importuned for a job: weeding or painting a roof; anything, *baas*,[11] madam. But the man and his wife remembered the warning about taking on anyone off the street. Some drank liquor and fouled the street with discarded bottles. Some

7. **fanlight:** semicircular window over a door or a larger window.
8. **keening:** wailing.
9. **cicadas'** (si·kā′dəz): Cicadas are large, flylike insects.
10. **harpies':** Harpies are shrewish or grasping people. The word comes from the mythological Harpies, hideous winged monsters that have the head and trunk of a woman and the tail, legs, and talons of a bird.
11. **baas** (bäs): Afrikaans for "master." Afrikaans, a language developed from seventeenth-century Dutch, is spoken in South Africa.

WORDS TO OWN
audaciously (ô·dā′shəs·lē) *adv.:* boldly.

----

begged, waiting for the man or his wife to drive the car out of the electronically operated gates. They sat about with their feet in the gutters, under the jacaranda[12] trees that made a green tunnel of the street—for it was a beautiful suburb, spoiled only by their presence—and sometimes they fell asleep lying right before the gates in the midday sun. The wife could never see anyone go hungry. She sent the trusted housemaid out with bread and tea, but the trusted housemaid said

12. **jacaranda** (jak'ə·ran'də): tropical American trees with large clusters of blue or lavender flowers.

Untitled (1982) by Jannis Kounellis.
Feather River travertine,
cast plaster, and steel.

Collection Walker Art Center, Minneapolis.
Walker Special Purchase Fund, 1987.

these were loafers and *tsotsis,*[13] who would come and tie her up and shut her in a cupboard. The husband said, She's right. Take heed of her advice. You only encourage them with your bread and tea. They are looking for their chance. . . . And he brought the little boy's tricycle from the garden into the house every night, because if the house was surely secure, once locked and with the alarm set, someone might still be able to climb over the wall or the electronically closed gates into the garden.

You are right, said the wife, then the wall should be higher. And the wise old witch, the husband's mother, paid for the extra bricks as her Christmas present to her son and his wife—the little boy got a Space Man outfit and a book of fairy tales.

But every week there were more reports of intrusion: in broad daylight and the dead of night, in the early hours of the morning, and even in the lovely summer twilight—a certain family was at dinner while the bedrooms were being ransacked upstairs. The man and his wife, talking of the latest armed robbery in the suburb, were distracted by the sight of the little boy's pet cat effortlessly arriving over the seven-foot wall, descending first with a rapid bracing of extended forepaws down on the sheer vertical surface, and then a graceful launch, landing with swishing tail within the property. The whitewashed wall was marked with the cat's comings and goings; and on the street side of the wall there were larger red-earth smudges that could have been made by the kind of broken running shoes, seen on the feet of unemployed loiterers, that had no innocent destination.

When the man and wife and little boy took the pet dog for its walk round the neighborhood streets they no longer paused to admire this show of roses or that perfect lawn; these were hidden behind an array of different varieties of security fences, walls, and devices. The man, wife, little boy, and dog passed a remarkable choice: There was the low-cost option of pieces of broken glass embedded in cement along the top of walls, there were iron grilles ending in lance points, there

13. *tsotsis* (tsät'sis): colloquial expression for flashily dressed street thugs.

were attempts at reconciling the aesthetics of prison architecture with the Spanish Villa style (spikes painted pink) and with the plastic urns of neoclassical façades (twelve-inch pikes finned like zigzags of lightning and painted pure white). Some walls had a small board affixed, giving the name and telephone number of the firm responsible for the installation of the devices. While the little boy and the pet dog raced ahead, the husband and wife found themselves comparing the possible effectiveness of each style against its appearance; and after several weeks when they paused before this barricade or that without needing to speak, both came out with the conclusion that only one was worth considering. It was the ugliest but the most honest in its suggestion of the pure concentration-camp style, no frills, all evident efficacy. Placed the length of walls, it consisted of a continuous coil of stiff and shining metal serrated into jagged blades, so that there would be no way of climbing over it and no way through its tunnel without getting entangled in its fangs. There would be no way out, only a struggle getting bloodier and bloodier, a deeper and sharper hooking and tearing of flesh. The wife shuddered to look at it. You're right, said the husband, anyone would think twice. . . . And they took heed of the advice on a small board fixed to the wall: Consult DRAGON'S TEETH The People For Total Security.

Next day a gang of workmen came and stretched the razor-bladed coils all round the walls of the house where the husband and wife and little boy and pet dog and cat were living happily ever after. The sunlight flashed and slashed, off the serrations, the cornice of razor thorns encircled the home, shining. The husband said, Never mind. It will weather. The wife said, You're wrong. They guarantee it's rustproof. And she waited until the little boy had run off to play before she said, I hope the cat will take heed. . . . The husband said, Don't worry, my dear, cats always look before they leap. And it was true that from that day on the cat slept in the little boy's bed and kept to the garden, never risking a try at breaching security.

One evening, the mother read the little boy to sleep with a fairy story from the book the wise old witch had given him at Christmas. Next day he pretended to be the Prince who braves the terrible thicket of thorns to enter the palace and kiss the Sleeping Beauty back to life: He dragged a ladder to the wall, the shining coiled tunnel was just wide enough for his little body to creep in, and with the first fixing of its razor teeth in his knees and hands and head he screamed and struggled deeper into its tangle. The trusted housemaid and the itinerant gardener, whose "day" it was, came running, the first to see and to scream with him, and the itinerant gardener tore his hands trying to get at the little boy. Then the man and his wife burst wildly into the garden and for some reason (the cat, probably) the alarm set up wailing against the screams while the bleeding mass of the little boy was hacked out of the security coil with saws, wire cutters, choppers, and they carried it—the man, the wife, the hysterical trusted housemaid, and the weeping gardener—into the house.

Le Ciel Rouge (*The Red Sky*) (1952) by Nicolas de Staël. Oil on canvas.

Collection Walker Art Center, Minneapolis.
Gift of the T. B. Walker Foundation, 1954.
©1997 Artists Rights Society (ARS), New York/ADAGP, Paris.

- -

Words to Own

aesthetics (es·thet′iks) *n*.: principles of beauty.
serrated (sə·rāt′id) *v*. used as *adj*.: having jagged, saw-like notches along the edge.

- -

MAKING MEANINGS

First Thoughts

1. What were your feelings when you read the grisly end of this story?

Shaping Interpretations

Reading Check

Outline the course of this story through the four improvements to home security that the family makes. What is each improvement, what occasions it, and how well does it work?

2. Which passages in the story obviously have humorous intent? Did you find them funny? Overall, what is Gordimer's **tone**?

3. Point out elements of the fairy-tale genre that are used by Gordimer. (For example, the setting is not specified and the characters are not named.) How would you describe the effect of Gordimer's **parody**?

4. Why do you think Gordimer uses a nonfictional opening? How do you interpret the opening after reading the story?

5. How can the wall in the story be seen as a **symbol**?

6. Fairy tales often contain **moral** lessons. What are some of the morals of fairy tales you've read? What, in contrast, is the moral of "Once upon a Time"?

Connecting with the Text

7. In your opinion, are the husband and wife racists who cause their own tragedy? Explain your answer.

8. Look back at your Quickwrite notes. How does "Once upon a Time" support or change your picture of a wall?

Extending the Text

9. Think about ads for home protection systems. What messages do they give visually and verbally? What emotions do they play on?

Challenging the Text

10. Do you think this story is too brutal or violent? Compare and discuss your responses in class.

CHOICES: Building Your Portfolio

Writer's Notebook

1. Collecting Ideas for a Problem-Solution Essay

As Gordimer's story suggests, the fear of crime can have as powerful an impact as the experience of crime itself. In fact, polls in this country often reveal that people's perceptions of the crime rate usually exceed the actual rate. Yet crime is a very real problem. In a small group, brainstorm about what some of the causes of crime are and how they might be eliminated. Evaluate your proposed solutions by filling in a three-column chart headed "Possible Solutions," "Advantages," and "Disadvantages." Save your notes for the Writer's Workshop on page 1179.

Comparing Texts

2. The Great Divide

Both Gordimer's tale and George Orwell's "Shooting an Elephant" (page 1139) carry messages about cultural clashes. Compare the two works, focusing on **themes, genres, styles,** and **tone.**

Creative Writing

3. Not So Happily Ever After

Use "Once upon a Time" as a model to write your own fairy tale about a clash of cultures. Include in it some kind of wall or boundary.

Research / Speaking

4. Other Walls, Other Bridges

Investigate the current state of affairs in South Africa, or in another part of the world beset by long-standing divisions between groups of people. What separates people in this area, and what efforts are being taken to bring them together? Prepare a brief oral report, and present it to your classmates.

Derek Walcott

(1930–   )

Derek Walcott was born and raised on St. Lucia, an island in the West Indies noted for its green valleys, vast banana plantations, and sleeping volcano. St. Lucia was a colony of Britain when Walcott was a boy, and its official language remains English.

The son of a schoolteacher father and a mother who was headmistress of the island's Methodist Infant School, Walcott was introduced to the classics of English literature at an early age and showed great promise in the use of language. As he grew older, he also enjoyed the peculiar brand of "Englishness" that belonged to even the most far-flung colonies of the British Empire. Yet, in spite of these skills and interests, no one ever dreamed that a boy from a tiny tropical island would one day be regarded as one of the leading English-language poets of his day or be awarded the 1992 Nobel Prize in literature.

A scholarship student at the University of the West Indies in Jamaica, Walcott stayed on after graduation to teach comparative literature. He then embarked on an independent career that took him to the island of Trinidad, where he lived for many years. Walcott has spent a good deal of time in the United States, where the scope of his activities has included not only writing poetry but also writing plays and teaching classes in creative writing at Harvard and Boston Universities. Among his best-known works are *Dream on Monkey Mountain and Other Plays* (1970), the long narrative poems *Another Life* (1973) and *Omeros* (1990), and the lyric collections *Sea Grapes* (1976) and *Midsummer* (1984).

Walcott's characteristic language is elegant, gracefully formal, and filled with the resourcefulness that comes only from a well-trained talent. Yet he has also tried, particularly in his plays, to capture the native rhythms, the diction, and the dialect variations of the speech of the islands he knows.

In his Nobel lecture, Walcott used a strong metaphor to describe how a poet must reject language imposed from outside the self:

> Tonally, the individual voice is a dialect; it shapes its own accent, its own vocabulary and melody in defiance of an imperial concept of language, the language of Ozymandias [see page 731], libraries and dictionaries, law courts and critics, and churches, universities, political dogma, the diction of institutions. Poetry is an island that breaks away from the main.

Derek Walcott.

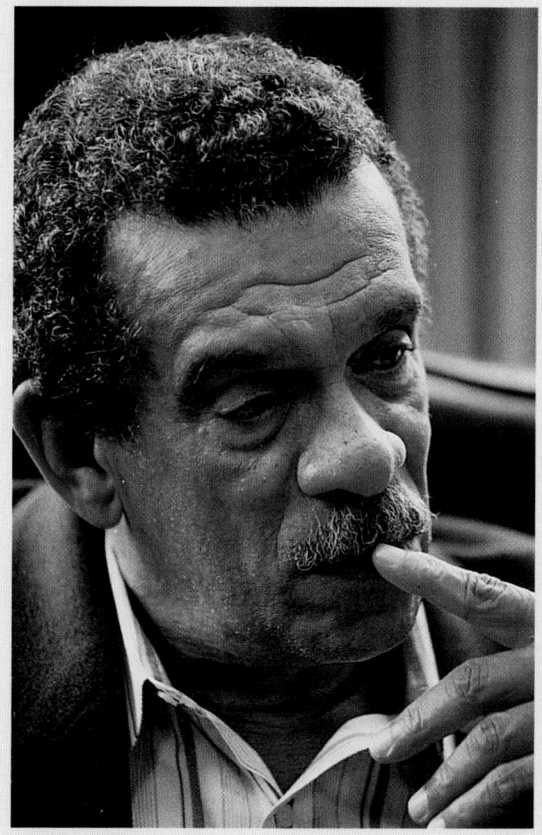

Before You Read

THE VIRGINS

Make the Connection

Give and Take

Helping developing countries to strengthen their economies by sending international aid seems to be, and often is, a positive act. If poorer countries ask and richer countries give, isn't the result progress? Isn't this a co-operation of cultures, not a clash? That depends, Derek Walcott might say, on what is given—and on what is taken away.

Quickwrite

Throughout the developing world, many people yearn for the benefits of "the American dream." But just what is the American dream? And is achieving this "dream" always a sign of "progress"? Record your responses to these questions.

Background

"The Virgins," or Virgin Islands, form an island chain in the West Indies. The U.S. Virgin Islands, an American possession since 1917,

has a republican government whose governor and other political leaders are elected by island residents. In this poem, Walcott describes Frederiksted, one of the old port cities on the U.S. Virgin Island of St. Croix (sānt krȯi). Frederiksted is now a free port where tourists can purchase goods without paying custom duties. The economy of St. Croix, once based on sugar cane, is now dependent on tourism. As you read, keep in mind that *virgin* refers to the Virgin Islands, but that it can also mean "unspoiled or untouched," as in *virgin forest*.

Tourists at the Nassau Bazaar, the Bahamas.

The Virgins

Derek Walcott

Down the dead streets of sun-stoned Frederiksted,
the first free port to die for tourism,
strolling at funeral pace, I am reminded
of life not lost to the American dream;
5 but my small-islander's simplicities
can't better our new empire's civilized
exchange of cameras, watches, perfumes, brandies
for the good life, so cheaply underpriced
that only the crime rate is on the rise
10 in streets blighted with sun, stone arches
and plazas blown dry by the hysteria
of rumor. A condominium drowns
in vacancy; its bargains are dusted,
but only a jeweled housefly drones
15 over the bargains. The roulettes spin
rustily to the wind—the vigorous trade
that every morning would begin afresh
by revving up green water round the pierhead
heading for where the banks of silver thresh.

MAKING MEANINGS

First Thoughts

1. Did you find yourself sympathizing with or questioning the speaker's viewpoint? Explain.

Shaping Interpretations

2. What is the tourist reminded of as he strolls the streets of Frederiksted?

3. How does Walcott **ironically** represent the "good life" of "the American dream"? How does his picture compare with your Quickwrite notes?

4. How do you explain line 2? What other **images** in the poem suggest decay and emptiness?

5. What positive images suggest the island "simplicities" that once existed in Frederiksted?

6. Sum up what you think Walcott is saying about the changes he sees. Who or what is responsible for the changes? Are the changes for the better or for the worse?

Extending the Text

7. Have places within the United States fallen victim to "the American dream" in ways similar to Walcott's description of Frederiksted? Explain your answer, and discuss your reactions.

Frederiksted, St. Croix, Virgin Islands.

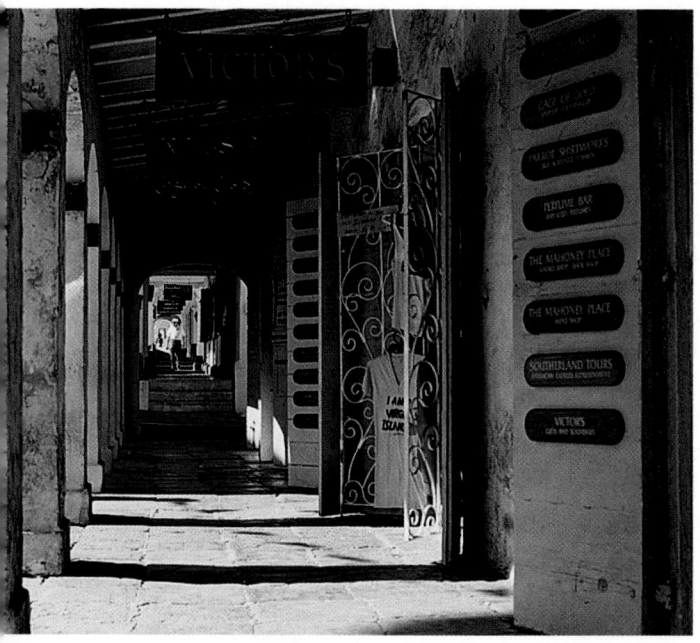

CHOICES:
Building Your Portfolio

Writer's Notebook

1. Collecting Ideas for a Problem-Solution Essay

In his poem, Walcott explores what happens when outside forces impose change on a way of life. Your response to question 7 under Extending the Text could be the starting point for an investigation into the causes and effects of a similar problem in your community. Use the *5W-How?* questions (*Who? What? When? Where? Why? How?*) to find out what you already know about the problem. Save your notes for the Writer's Workshop on page 1179.

Supporting a Thesis

2. Double Meanings

The scholar Laurence Perrine feels that Walcott's poems "are sharpened by his skillful use of irony and of words and phrases of double meanings." Support this statement in an essay, citing words and passages from the poem. Be sure to consider the title.

Creative Writing

3. My Own Islands

Imagine the other people who exist in this lyric's landscape, even if they are not mentioned: tourists, shopkeepers, fishers, and so on. Choose one, and write a lyric about Frederiksted in which he or she is the speaker.

Panel Discussion

4. What *Is* the American Dream?

Hold a panel discussion with some classmates about your own perceptions of "the American dream." What does each panel member see as ideal? What forces shape the dream you each hold? Do you feel pressure to conform to someone else's notion of what's ideal?

Chinua Achebe

(1930–)

Chinua Achebe.

Nigerian author Chinua Achebe (chin'wä' ä·chā'bā) planned to study medicine, but literature and his country's nationalist movement forever changed his plans. As a student, he came to realize the destructive effects of colonialism and dedicated himself to redefining Africa, to telling Africans' true story, including their achievements and failures. In his words, the European idea that "Africa was the Primordial Void, was sheer humbug; . . . Africa had a history, a religion, a civilization."

His novels, beginning with the celebrated *Things Fall Apart* (1958), focus on the changes in Nigerian life that occurred in the twentieth century. The novels trace life in Nigeria— sometimes presented as a fictionalized nation— from the arrival of early English missionaries, through years of colonial rule, to a post-independence era rife with corruption and political turmoil. Achebe believes that "Africa's meeting with Europe must be accounted a terrible disaster in this matter of human understanding and respect," yet his African characters are not idealized. They are held responsible for their private decisions and for solving the problems that threaten their nation's future.

Achebe is himself an Ibo, born in the eastern Nigerian town of Ogidi, where his father, a Christian convert, taught at the mission school. He has chosen to write in English, which he began to learn at age eight, in order to reach a wide audience.

During Nigeria's civil war of the late 1960s, Achebe worked for the cause of the secessionist Biafrans. Since then he has concentrated on teaching, and on encouraging and publishing promising young authors. Through his many works of fiction, nonfiction, and poetry, he has been a catalyst for an entire younger generation of African writers.

Before You Read

MARRIAGE IS A PRIVATE AFFAIR

Make the Connection

Coming Together

Like the United States, many nations are conglomerations of diverse peoples. And when people of diverse backgrounds come together, conflicts tend to arise. People may focus on differences in customs, religion, and ethnic heritage and fail to notice all the things they have in common. Yet, age-old distinctions often become less significant as people expand their horizons. They travel, they read, they watch, they listen. They go beyond "their kind."

Quickwrite

If your parents or guardians were to choose a perfect spouse for you, what kind of person would they choose? What qualities will *you* consider important in a partner? Jot down similarities and differences between your generation's attitudes toward love and marriage and those of the generation before you.

Background

The African nation of Nigeria has more than 250 ethnic groups. These groups have different languages and frequently differ in religion, customs, and traditions. The Ibo and Ibibio both live in southeastern Nigeria but traditionally did not intermarry. In Achebe's story, a young Ibo man and an Ibibio woman have moved from their native regions to Lagos, a large and modern city in southwestern Nigeria.

go.hrw.com

LE0 12-15

Marriage Is a Private Affair

Chinua Achebe

"Have you written to your dad yet?" asked Nene[1] one afternoon as she sat with Nnaemeka[2] in her room at 16 Kasanga Street, Lagos.[3]

"No. I've been thinking about it. I think it's better to tell him when I get home on leave!"

"But why? Your leave is such a long way off yet—six whole weeks. He should be let into our happiness now."

Nnaemeka was silent for a while, and then began very slowly as if he groped for his words: "I wish I were sure it would be happiness to him."

"Of course it must," replied Nene, a little surprised. "Why shouldn't it?"

"You have lived in Lagos all your life, and you know very little about people in remote parts of the country."

"That's what you always say. But I don't believe anybody will be so unlike other people that they will be unhappy when their sons are engaged to marry."

"Yes. They are most unhappy if the engagement is not arranged by them. In our case it's worse—you are not even an Ibo."[4]

This was said so seriously and so bluntly that Nene could not find speech immediately. In the <u>cosmopolitan</u> atmosphere of the city it had always seemed to her something of a joke that a person's tribe could determine whom he married.

At last she said, "You don't really mean that he will object to your marrying me simply on that account? I had always thought you Ibos were kindly disposed to other people."

"So we are. But when it comes to marriage, well, it's not quite so simple. And this," he added, "is not peculiar to the Ibos. If your father were alive and lived in the heart of Ibibio-land[5] he would be exactly like my father."

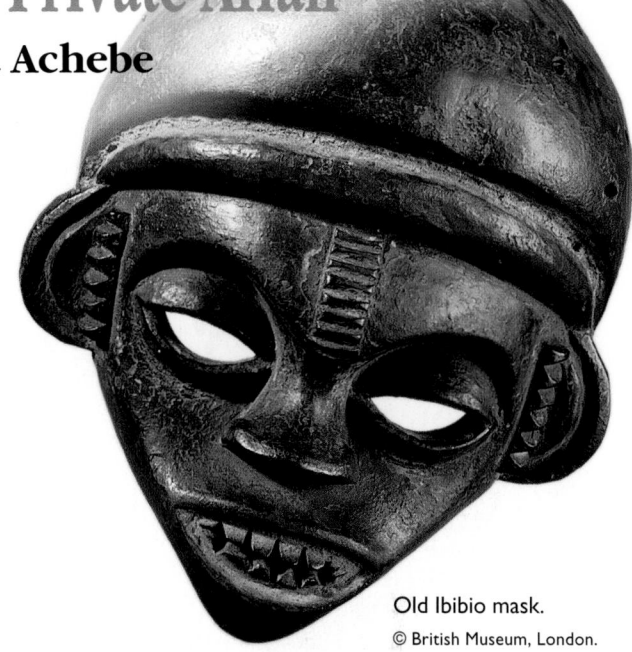

Old Ibibio mask.
© British Museum, London.

"I don't know. But anyway, as your father is so fond of you, I'm sure he will forgive you soon enough. Come on then, be a good boy and send him a nice lovely letter . . ."

"It would not be wise to break the news to him by writing. A letter will bring it upon him with a shock. I'm quite sure about that."

"All right, honey, suit yourself. You know your father."

As Nnaemeka walked home that evening he turned over in his mind different ways of overcoming his father's opposition, especially now that he had gone and found a girl for him. He had thought of showing his letter to Nene but decided on second thoughts not to, at least for the moment. He read it again when he got home and couldn't help smiling to himself. He remembered Ugoye[6] quite well, an Amazon[7] of a girl who used

1. **Nene** (nā′nā).
2. **Nnaemeka** (′n·nä·ā·mä′kə).
3. **Lagos** (lā′gōs′): former capital of Nigeria.
4. **Ibo** (ē′bō′): member of an African ethnic group living chiefly in southeastern Nigeria.
5. **Ibibio-land** (ib′ə·bē′o′land): area of southeastern Nigeria that is the traditional homeland of the Ibibio, another African ethnic group.

6. **Ugoye** (oo·gō′yā).
7. **Amazon:** tall, strong, aggressive woman. The term is taken from the name for the Amazons, a race of female warriors in Greek mythology.

- -
WORDS TO OWN
cosmopolitan (käz′mə·päl′ə·tən) *adj.*: representative of many parts of the world; not constrained by provincial habits or prejudices.
- -

Wood mask. Ibo, Nigeria (37 cm).
© British Museum, London.

to beat up all the boys, himself included, on the way to the stream, a complete dunce at school.

I have found a girl who will suit you admirably—Ugoye Nweke,[8] *the eldest daughter of our neighbor, Jacob Nweke. She has a proper Christian upbringing. When she stopped schooling some years ago her father (a man of sound judgment) sent her to live in the house of a pastor where she has received all the training a wife could need. Her Sunday school teacher has told me that she reads her Bible very fluently. I hope we shall begin negotiations when you come home in December.*

On the second evening of his return from Lagos, Nnaemeka sat with his father under a cassia tree. This was the old man's retreat where he went to read his Bible when the parching December sun had set and a fresh, reviving wind blew on the leaves.

"Father," began Nnaemeka suddenly, "I have come to ask for forgiveness."

"Forgiveness? For what, my son?" he asked in amazement.

8. **Nweke** (ʼn·wāʹkā).

"It's about this marriage question."

"Which marriage question?"

"I can't—we must—I mean it is impossible for me to marry Nweke's daughter."

"Impossible? Why?" asked his father.

"I don't love her."

"Nobody said you did. Why should you?" he asked.

"Marriage today is different . . ."

"Look here, my son," interrupted his father, "nothing is different. What one looks for in a wife are a good character and a Christian background."

Nnaemeka saw there was no hope along the present line of argument.

"Moreover," he said, "I am engaged to marry another girl who has all of Ugoye's good qualities, and who . . ."

His father did not believe his ears. "What did you say?" he asked slowly and <u>disconcertingly</u>.

"She is a good Christian," his son went on, "and a teacher in a girls' school in Lagos."

"Teacher, did you say? If you consider that a qualification for a good wife I should like to point out to you, Emeka, that no Christian woman should teach. St. Paul in his letter to the Corinthians[9] says that women should keep silence." He rose slowly from his seat and paced forward and backward. This was his pet subject, and he condemned <u>vehemently</u> those church leaders who encouraged women to teach in their schools. After he had spent his emotion on a long homily he at last came back to his son's engagement, in a seemingly milder tone.

"Whose daughter is she, anyway?"

"She is Nene Atang."

"What!" All the mildness was gone again. "Did you say Neneataga, what does that mean?"

"Nene Atang from Calabar.[10] She is the only girl I can marry." This was a very rash reply and Nnaemeka expected the storm to burst. But it did

9. **St. Paul . . . Corinthians:** reference to a passage in the Bible's New Testament (1 Corinthians 14:34).
10. **Calabar:** seaport city in southeastern Nigeria.

WORDS TO OWN

disconcertingly (dis·kən·sʉrtʼiŋ·lē) *adv.*: in a manner that embarrasses, confuses, or flusters.

vehemently (vēʹə·mənt·lē) *adv.*: passionately; strongly.

------

not. His father merely walked away into his room. This was most unexpected and perplexed Nnaemeka. His father's silence was infinitely more menacing than a flood of threatening speech. That night the old man did not eat.

When he sent for Nnaemeka a day later he applied all possible ways of dissuasion. But the young man's heart was hardened, and his father eventually gave him up as lost.

"I owe it to you, my son, as a duty to show you what is right and what is wrong. Whoever put this idea into your head might as well have cut your throat. It is Satan's work." He waved his son away.

"You will change your mind, Father, when you know Nene."

"I shall never see her," was the reply. From that night the father scarcely spoke to his son. He did not, however, cease hoping that he would realize how serious was the danger he was heading for. Day and night he put him in his prayers.

Nnaemeka, for his own part, was very deeply affected by his father's grief. But he kept hoping that it would pass away. If it had occurred to him that never in the history of his people had a man married a woman who spoke a different tongue, he might have been less optimistic. "It has never been heard," was the verdict of an old man speaking a few weeks later. In that short sentence he spoke for all of his people. This man had come with others to commiserate with Okeke[11] when news went round about his son's behavior. By that time the son had gone back to Lagos.

"It has never been heard," said the old man again with a sad shake of his head.

"What did Our Lord say?" asked another gentleman. "Sons shall rise against their Fathers; it is there in the Holy Book."

"It is the beginning of the end," said another.

The discussion thus tending to become theological, Madubogwu, a highly practical man, brought it down once more to the ordinary level.

"Have you thought of consulting a native doctor about your son?" he asked Nnaemeka's father.

"He isn't sick," was the reply.

"What is he then? The boy's mind is diseased and only a good herbalist can bring him back to his right senses. The medicine he requires is *Amalile,* the same that women apply with success

11. **Okeke** (ō·kā′kā).

to recapture their husbands' straying affection."

"Madubogwu is right," said another gentleman. "This thing calls for medicine."

"I shall not call in a native doctor." Nnaemeka's father was known to be obstinately ahead of his more superstitious neighbors in these matters. "I will not be another Mrs. Ochuba. If my son wants to kill himself let him do it with his own hands. It is not for me to help him."

"But it was her fault," said Madubogwu. "She ought to have gone to an honest herbalist. She was a clever woman, nevertheless."

"She was a wicked murderess," said Jonathan, who rarely argued with his neighbors because, he often said, they were incapable of reasoning. "The medicine was prepared for her husband, it was his name they called in its preparation, and I am sure it would have been perfectly beneficial to him. It was wicked to put it into the herbalist's food, and say you were only trying it out."

Six months later, Nnaemeka was showing his young wife a short letter from his father:

It amazes me that you could be so unfeeling as to send me your wedding picture. I would have sent it back. But on further thought I decided just to cut off your wife and send it back to you because I have nothing to do with her. How I wish that I had nothing to do with you either.

When Nene read through this letter and looked at the mutilated picture her eyes filled with tears, and she began to sob.

"Don't cry, my darling," said her husband. "He is essentially good-natured and will one day look more kindly on our marriage." But years passed and that one day did not come.

For eight years, Okeke would have nothing to do with his son, Nnaemeka. Only three times (when Nnaemeka asked to come home and spend his leave) did he write to him.

"I can't have you in my house," he replied on one occasion. "It can be of no interest to me

Ikenga headdress.
Wood and
feathers (76.1 cm).

UCLA Fowler Museum
of Cultural History,
Los Angeles. Gift of
Wellcome Trust.

where or how you spend your leave—or your life, for that matter."

The prejudice against Nnaemeka's marriage was not confined to his little village. In Lagos, especially among his people who worked there, it showed itself in a different way. Their women, when they met at their village meeting, were not hostile to Nene. Rather, they paid her such excessive deference as to make her feel she was not one of them. But as time went on, Nene gradually broke through some of this prejudice and even began to make friends among them. Slowly and grudgingly they began to admit that she kept her home much better than most of them.

The story eventually got to the little village in the heart of the Ibo country that Nnaemeka and his young wife were a most happy couple. But his father was one of the few people in the village who knew nothing about this. He always displayed so much temper whenever his son's name

was mentioned that everyone avoided it in his presence. By a tremendous effort of will he had succeeded in pushing his son to the back of his mind. The strain had nearly killed him but he had <u>persevered</u>, and won.

Then one day he received a letter from Nene, and in spite of himself he began to glance through it perfunctorily until all of a sudden the expression on his face changed and he began to read more carefully.

> . . . *Our two sons, from the day they learnt that they have a grandfather, have insisted on being taken to him. I find it impossible to tell them that you will not see them. I implore you to allow Nnaemeka to bring them home for a short time during his leave next month. I shall remain here in Lagos . . .*

The old man at once felt the resolution he had built up over so many years falling in. He was telling himself that he must not give in. He tried to steel his heart against all emotional appeals. It was a reenactment of that other struggle. He leaned against a window and looked out. The sky was overcast with heavy black clouds and a high wind began to blow, filling the air with dust and dry leaves. It was one of those rare occasions when even Nature takes a hand in a human fight. Very soon it began to rain, the first rain in the year. It came down in large sharp drops and was accompanied by the lightning and thunder which mark a change of season. Okeke was trying hard not to think of his two grandsons. But he knew he was now fighting a losing battle. He tried to hum a favorite hymn but the pattering of large raindrops on the roof broke up the tune. His mind immediately returned to the children. How could he shut his door against them? By a curious mental process he imagined them standing, sad and forsaken, under the harsh angry weather—shut out from his house.

That night he hardly slept, from remorse—and a vague fear that he might die without making it up to them.

WORDS TO OWN

persevered (pʉr′sə·vird′) v.: continued in a course of action despite difficulty or opposition; persisted.

This is an excerpt from Chinua Achebe's address to the graduating class of Bates College in Lewiston, Maine, on May 27, 1996.

Diversity Is Reality

The world is big. Some people are unable to comprehend that simple fact. They want the world on their own terms, its peoples just like them and their friends, its places like the manicured little patch on which they live. But this is a foolish and blind wish. Diversity is not an abnormality but the very reality of our planet.

The human world manifests the same reality and will not seek our permission to celebrate itself in the magnificence of its endless varieties. Civility is a sensible attribute in this kind of world we have; narrowness of heart and mind is not.

Connections
A POEM

As you read the following poem by the poet Maurice Kenny (1929–   ), a member of the Mohawk people, who once lived in Brooklyn, New York, think back to the conflict between the father and son in "Marriage Is a Private Affair." How will Nnaemeka's own sons in that story relate to their grandfather's cultural legacy?

Going Home

Maurice Kenny

The book lay unread in my lap
snow gathered at the window
from Brooklyn it was a long ride
the Greyhound followed the plow
5 from Syracuse to Watertown
to country cheese and maples
tired rivers and closed paper mills
home to gossipy aunts . . .
their dandelions and pregnant cats . . .
10 home to cedars and fields of boulders
cold graves under willow and pine
home from Brooklyn to the reservation
that was not home
to songs I could not sing
15 to dances I could not dance
from Brooklyn bars and ghetto rats
to steaming horses stomping frozen
     earth
barns and privies lost in blizzards
home to a Nation, Mohawk
20 to faces I did not know
and hands which did not recognize me
to names and doors
my father shut

MAKING MEANINGS

First Thoughts

1. How would you compare the attitudes you described in your Quickwrite notes with the attitudes between generations in this story?

Shaping Interpretations

2. What is the **irony** of the story's title?

3. This story bursts with **conflicts** among people and ideas. What are at least two of these conflicts? Does the story resolve them? If so, how?

4. How would you describe Okeke's **character**? Use details from the story to support your answer.

5. What do you think happened to the herbalist, and why would Achebe include that anecdote?

6. What might the rain at the end of the story **symbolize**?

7. The story's subject is a marriage that occurs against a parent's wishes, but what is the story's **theme**?

8. Both Achebe's story and the poem "Going Home" (see *Connections* on page 1169) are about generational and cultural conflict, but they differ in narrative **point of view.** From whose point of view is each told? How does the point of view shape your response to each work?

Extending the Text

9. You hear much talk today about "traditional values" and about the "multicultural society." What are some contemporary examples of clashes in values, and how would you relate them to this story's plot and theme?

Reading Check

a. What are Okeke's objections to his son's marriage and choice of wife?

b. How much time passes from the marriage to the story's end? During that time, how does Okeke act toward his son?

c. How are Nnaemeka and his father different?

d. Why does Nene send a letter to Nnaemeka's father?

CHOICES:
Building Your Portfolio

Writer's Notebook

1. Collecting Ideas for a Problem-Solution Essay

Personal problems such as Okeke's disapproval of his son's choice of a wife aren't suitable for a problem-solution essay, but their underlying causes—in this case, attitudes weighted by centuries of tradition—may be. Brainstorm to develop a list of intergenerational problems you're familiar with, and then work with a partner to analyze their underlying causes. Save your notes for the Writer's Workshop on page 1179.

Interpreting an Ending

2. Final Analysis

In an essay, present and support your interpretation of what happens at the story's end. Be sure to examine the nature **imagery.** Include your personal response to the way the story ends.

Evaluating an Opinion

3. A Failure of Imagination

In an interview, Chinua Achebe made this comment about poverty in Nigeria and elsewhere: "If we really could project into the skin of the beggar under the bridge in Lagos, we would immediately start doing something to bring about a just society. It is that lack of imagination which . . . is at the root of cruelty." Do you agree with Achebe, or would you explain the persistence of poverty differently? Organize a debate to discuss the issue.

Creative Writing

4. And Then What?

Working with a partner, continue the story. One of you, alone, will write a scene showing what Okeke does next; then the other will take up the action in a second scene. Be true to Achebe's characterizations.

Wole Soyinka

(1934–   )

Wole Soyinka celebrates at UNESCO in Paris after winning the 1986 Nobel Prize in literature.

A voice of modern Africa, Wole Soyinka in 1986 became the first African to win the Nobel Prize in literature. Soyinka's favorite African deity is Ogun, god of both war and creative fire—a fitting muse for a multitalented writer and performer whose plays, songs, novels, and poetry combine political activism, universal themes, and African traditions.

Born Akinwande Oluwole Soyinka in a village in western Nigeria, Soyinka was the son of the principal of a Christian school and a teacher. His parents both supported European-style education, but his father also retained strong ties to his heritage as a member of the Yoruba tribe. Soyinka grew up respecting both traditions; his 1981 autobiography, *Aké: The Years of Childhood,* tells of his later struggle with this duality.

After attending University College at Ibadan, Nigeria, Soyinka studied English literature in England at the University of Leeds. In London in the late 1950s, he wrote plays and poetry for theater and radio. During this period of African nationalism and pressure for independence, Soyinka's themes were racism, injustice, tyranny, and corruption, all treated with satiric wit. Also concerned with the collision of ancient traditions and modern realities, he peppered his plays with vivid Yoruba masquerade ritual.

Soyinka felt brutal despotism firsthand during Nigeria's civil war of the late 1960s, when he was imprisoned for two years for the "crime" of meeting with secessionist leaders such as the writer Chinua Achebe. He describes these experiences in *The Man Died: Prison Notes,* published in 1972. Since then he has continued to record and dramatize, with both passion and humor, the struggle and spirit of modern-day Africa and Africans.

Before You Read

TELEPHONE CONVERSATION

Make the Connection

Subtle Discriminations

The following poem, written during Soyinka's college career in Britain in the late 1950s, records one of his own experiences with discrimination at a time when millions of people from former British colonies were arriving in England in search of economic and intellectual opportunity. As you read the poem, think about how Soyinka communicates this experience—is it presented as painful, or as humorously absurd?

Is Soyinka's criticism straightforward or indirect?

Quickwrite

Think about the ways, both thoughtless and intentional, in which people practice discrimination. Then jot down some examples. How can those who are discriminated against make others mindful of what they've suffered?

Background

Soyinka's poem presents ideas primarily through a **dialogue.** The first speaker is talking from one of the red public telephone booths that were common in London years ago. To use such a phone, a person had to push one button to speak and another to listen. The first speaker is a well-educated black African and the second, a British woman who has property to rent. Soyinka's poem doesn't just describe their exchange; it re-creates it.

go.hrw.com
LEO 12-15

Telephone Conversation

Wole Soyinka

The price seemed reasonable, location
Indifferent. The landlady swore she lived
Off premises. Nothing remained
But self-confession. "Madam," I warned,
5   "I hate a wasted journey—I am African."
Silence. Silenced transmission of
Pressurized good-breeding. Voice, when it came,
Lipstick coated, long gold-rolled
Cigarette-holder pipped. Caught I was, foully.

10   "HOW DARK?" . . . I had not misheard . . . "ARE YOU LIGHT
OR VERY DARK?" Button B. Button A. Stench
Of rancid breath of public hide-and-speak.
Red booth. Red pillar-box.° Red double-tiered
Omnibus° squelching tar. It *was* real! Shamed
15   By ill-mannered silence, surrender
Pushed dumbfoundment to beg simplification.
Considerate she was, varying the emphasis—

"ARE YOU DARK? OR VERY LIGHT?" Revelation came.
"You mean—like plain or milk chocolate?"
20   Her assent was clinical, crushing in its light
Impersonality. Rapidly, wavelength adjusted,
I chose. "West African sepia"—and as an afterthought,
"Down in my passport." Silence for spectroscopic
Flight of fancy,° till truthfulness clanged her accent
25   Hard on the mouthpiece. "WHAT'S THAT?" conceding,
"DON'T KNOW WHAT THAT IS." "Like brunette."

"THAT'S DARK, ISN'T IT?" "Not altogether.
Facially, I am brunette, but madam, you should see
The rest of me. Palm of my hand, soles of my feet
30   Are a peroxide blonde. Friction, caused—
Foolishly, madam—by sitting down, has turned
My bottom raven black—One moment madam!"—sensing
Her receiver rearing on the thunderclap
About my ears—"Madam," I pleaded, "wouldn't you rather
35   See for yourself?"

13. pillar-box: chiefly British for "mailbox."
14. double-tiered / omnibus: bus with two decks, or tiers.

24. spectroscopic (spek′trō·skäp′ik) **. . . fancy:** wide range, or spectrum, of ideas.

MAKING MEANINGS

First Thoughts

1. This poem dramatizes a battle. Who do you think finally wins, and why?

Shaping Interpretations

2. Paraphrase what happens in this poem, and then state what you feel is the poem's **theme**.

3. What does their **dialogue** reveal about these two **characters**?

4. This poem is full of colors—and not just of skin. What colors do you see in the poem? What does Soyinka want to communicate through these **images** of color?

5. What **irony** do you find in lines 23–26? What irony do you find in the description of the woman as well-bred?

6. What do you think of the speaker's final question?

Connecting with the Text

7. Since the speaker was prepared for prejudice, why do you think the woman's question disturbs him so much?

8. If you faced this kind of discrimination, how would you react to it?

Challenging the Text

9. Review your Quickwrite notes, and then think about whether Soyinka's poem is an effective way of making others aware of prejudice. Is it more, or less, effective than other ways? How so? Explain.

Nigerian bronze head, thought to be an Ife king (13th century).
British Museum, London.

CHOICES:
Building Your Portfolio

Writer's Notebook
1. Collecting Ideas for a Problem-Solution Essay

Newcomers to this country who encounter incidents of racial prejudice like the one Soyinka relates in "Telephone Conversation" may not realize that housing discrimination is illegal. What solutions could you pose for this problem? Working with a small group, discuss ways your class could work with existing community groups to educate newcomers about their housing rights. Save your notes for the Writer's Workshop on page 1179.

Analyzing Character
2. An Unpleasant Character

What kind of person is the landlady in Soyinka's poem? In an essay, analyze the character of Soyinka's landlady. What do you learn about her from the speaker's assumptions, judgments, and tone, and from the woman's own words? Cite specific details from the poem to support your analysis.

Law/Speaking
3. Home Sweet Home

Should laws restrict where a person can live? What about zoning laws that prohibit trailers in suburban neighborhoods? or laws that ban group homes in single-family developments? Research such laws in your community, and present an oral report, opening the issue for debate with your classmates.

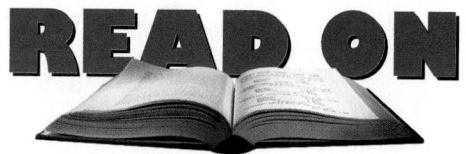

READ ON

A Plea for Peace

Vera Brittain, born in England in 1893, grew up in an age of rich materialism and romantic idealism. But World War I suddenly and violently ended this time of comfortable isolation. After losing her fiancé and brother and serving as a volunteer nurse in France, she realized that "the world was mad and we were all victims." In her autobiography, *Testament of Youth* (Penguin), she explores how the war affected her and her generation and writes of her subsequent work for world peace.

In Black and White

Kaffir Boy (Macmillan) was one of the first accounts of growing up black in twentieth-century South Africa. When Mark Mathabane (mä·tä′bä·nä) published this autobiography in America in 1986, it became an international best-seller but was banned in his own country. Mathabane's exploration of South Africa's apartheid system, which has now been dismantled, shows the damage that ignorance of and contempt for other cultures can cause.

A Prophetic Voice

Brave New World (HarperCollins) was first published in 1932, but Aldous Huxley's satirical fantasy of the future has remained surprisingly contemporary. In the world-state portrayed in the novel, a supposedly scientific caste system determines social status, and individual freedom is forbidden. But Bernard Marx, a character whose social conditioning has gone wrong, disturbs all this.

An Angry Young Man

Alan Sillitoe was one of a group of young writers who emerged in the 1950s and 1960s and who were dubbed Angry Young Men. Their main themes were rebellion and isolation; they confronted society's mores and institutions head-on. Sillitoe's long short story *The Loneliness of the Long Distance Runner* (Penguin), about a young man in reform school, is among the best of the genre. (Director Tony Richardson's film of the story, available on videotape, was a key British film of the 1960s.)

Peaceful Protest

Mohandas K. Gandhi (1869–1948), also called Mahatma Gandhi, was a leader of the Indian nationalist movement against British rule. His doctrine of non-violence advocated vigorous protest against social and political evils but did not sanction violence as a means to achieve change. The epic movie *Gandhi* (1982), a sweeping account of his life and times, is filmmaking at its best. Available on videotape, the film is directed by Richard Attenborough and features Ben Kingsley, Candice Bergen, John Gielgud, and Martin Sheen.

The English Language

English Today and Tomorrow

by John Algeo

In the twentieth century, English spread all over the world. It developed from a language spoken by a few wandering Germanic tribes to a world language used for more purposes than any other human tongue. Because its uses have continued to grow, it has continued to change. We can see change going on in English right now—especially in its vocabulary.

Tracking New Words: Where They Come From

We are constantly in need of new words—to talk about new things or to talk about old things in new ways. We borrow new words from other languages, or we make them up by combining, shortening, blending, or shifting the use of old words.

Some words echo not other words but the sounds of things in the world around us. For example, the word *vroom* began as an imitation of how a car or motorcycle engine sounds when it is being raced. Then it was used as a verb referring to how a vehicle operates at very high speed: "The car vroomed around the corner and disappeared."

Sacking Other Languages for Words: Loanwords

French is the modern language from which we have borrowed most. French loanwords include *chief, choice, honor, machine, menu, picnic, police, prairie, restaurant, soup,* and a great many other familiar words, as well as more obvious loans such as *chauffeur, crepe, etiquette, rapport,* and *souvenir.* From Spanish we have taken *canyon, lasso, patio, ranch, rodeo,* and, more recently, *macho;* from Portuguese, *flamingo, molasses, pagoda,* and others. From Italian we get musical terms, including *duet, soprano,* and *trombone,* and a variety of other words, such as *balloon, bandit, carnival, studio, umbrella,* and *volcano.*

Dutch has given us sailing terms such as *deck, dock,* and *yacht,* as well as *boss, dollar, knapsack, pickle, Santa Claus,* and *skate.* From German we have borrowed *frankfurter, hamburger, kindergarten, nickel,* and *pretzel.*

From more distantly related languages we have borrowed *banjo* (African, probably Bantu), *boomerang* (native Australian),

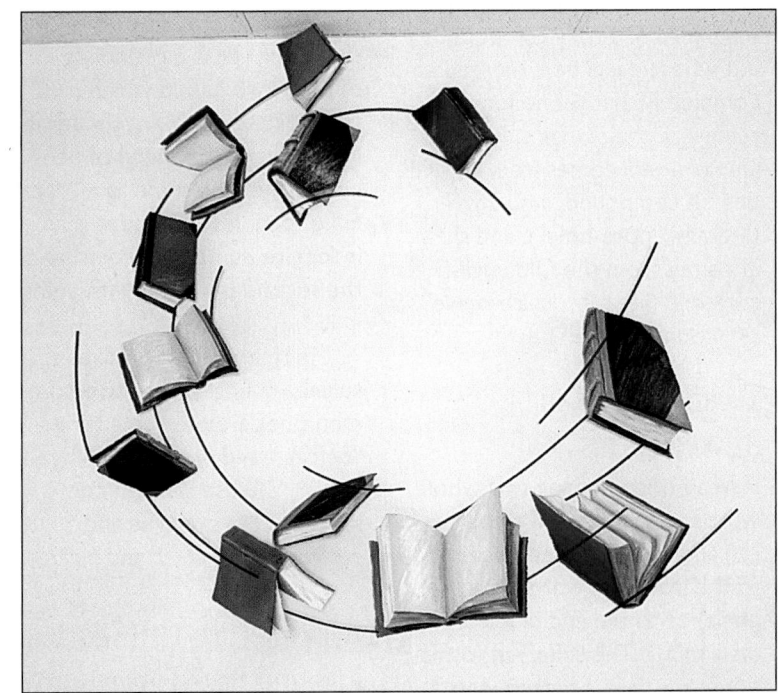

Incident in the Library (1983) by Julian Opie.
Oil paint on steel, wall installation (10 ft × 10 ft).
Photo courtesy Hal Bromm Gallery, New York.

ketchup (Malay), *coffee* (Turkish, from Arabic), *mammoth* (Russian), *pal* (Romany), *pecan* (various Algonquian dialects), *shawl* (Persian), *shampoo* (Hindi), *soy* (Japanese), *tattoo* (Tahitian), *tea* (Chinese), *tom-tom* (Hindi), and *ukulele* (Hawaiian).

English is much richer for all these words we have borrowed from other languages.

Stacking Words Together: Compounds

We often make new words by joining existing words into a *compound*. A compound may mean something different from the literal sense of its parts. Thus, a *blackboard* is not necessarily black; it is often green instead.

Compounds have always been a favorite type of word formation in English. In Modern English, we have some words that were originally compounds but whose parts have merged so completely that we no longer recognize their origins. For example, *nostril* comes from an Old English compound, *nosu-thyrel* (literally, "nose-hole"), and *sheriff* comes from the Old English *scirgerefa* (literally, "shire-reeve" or "county official").

Tacking Parts On: Affixed Forms

Instead of combining two whole words to make a new one, we can add a word element (an *affix*) to the front of a word (as a *prefix*) or to the end of a word (as a *suffix*). The suffix *–ist* forms nouns meaning a person who believes in something or who has a particular profession. A *royalist*

Q3 (1994) by Mark Wallinger. Acrylic on canvas (218.5 cm × 218.5 cm).

Private Collection. © The Artist, Courtesy Anthony Reynolds Gallery, London.

follows royalty, a *lobbyist* lobbies, and a *flat-earthist* believes that the earth is really flat as a pancake, despite what astronomers and geologists may say.

Some suffixes were originally independent words that dwindled into mere affixes. For instance, the suffix *–ful* is a dwindling of the word *full,* to which it is still close, though not the same, in meaning. A "handful of pennies" is not the same as a "hand full of pennies." The first is an indefinite number of coins, and the second is a hand with coins in it.

There are fewer prefixes than suffixes in English, but two common ones are *pre–*, meaning "before," and *post–*, meaning "after." We use them in combinations like *pregame* and *postgame* or *preteen* and *postteen.*

Hacking Parts Off: Shortenings and Back-Formations

We can also make new words by removing part of a word to shorten it. This process is quite common, probably because we don't like to use more energy than we have to in saying long words if short ones will do. *Gymnasium* is shortened to *gym; telephone* becomes *phone.*

Some shortenings are more complicated. The label *hazardous material* indicates that a container has dangerous chemicals or radioactive matter inside it. But the label is too long—a warning ought to be short and snappy. So both words in the expression are clipped, to produce *HAZMAT,* a short, easy to say, and (provided you know what it means) clear expression. When a phrase is shortened to the first parts of each of its words, the result is an *acronym* (from two Greek forms meaning "tip-name," that is, a name formed from the tips of other words).

The most extreme kind of acronym includes only the first letter of each original word. It may be said by pronouncing the names of the letters, like *CB* (citizens' band) or *RV* (recreational vehicle), or by pronouncing it as a word, like *ZIP* (zone improvement plan) *Code.*

A special kind of shortening occurs when an affix is taken off. Typewriters are more than a hundred years old now. When they first came into use, the word *typewriter* meant either the machine or the person who operated it. Then someone decided that a typewriter is for typewriting, and so the verb *to typewrite* was formed by taking off the suffix *–er.* Such words are called *back-formations* because the sequence of their formation is the reverse of the usual order of adding affixes.

A similar example is *to burgle,* which is what a burglar does. A difference between *burgle* and *typewrite,* however, is that while *typewrite* was shortened from *typewriter* very quickly (within twelve years after the longer word was introduced to English), *burgle* took a lot of time, more than three hundred years, to work its way out of *burglar.* And some people still don't like it.

Packing Words Together: Blends

A *blend* is a word that is made by combining two or more words while omitting part of at least one of them. Familiar examples are *brunch* (*breakfast* plus *lunch*) and *smog* (*smoke* plus *fog*). In Lewis Carroll's *Through the Looking-Glass,* Humpty Dumpty called such terms *portmanteau words.* A portmanteau is a suitcase with two sides that are folded together to make a single case. Humpty Dumpty said that in a portmanteau word, "There are two meanings packed up into one word."

An example of a technical blend is *shuttle craft,* from *space shuttle* plus *spacecraft.* A feminist example is *herstory* (meaning "history of women," or "history told from a woman's point of view"), from *her* plus *history.*

A special kind of blending is *folk etymology.* We sometimes take an unfamiliar word, especially a word borrowed from another language, and change its form by associating it with familiar English words. For example, we borrowed the Dutch word *koolsla* (which means "cabbage salad") as *coleslaw;* but then some people associated the first part of the word with the English word *cold* and came up with *cold slaw,* which makes sense because slaw is generally served cold.

Ramen Four Five Six (20th century) by Gregory B. Larson.
Private Collection.

Racking Up New Meanings: Shifted Words

Perhaps the most frequent way to make a new word is to use an old word in a new way. Today, *censure* means "to judge unfavorably" or "to condemn"; in Shakespeare's day, it meant simply "to judge or form an opinion." Shifts of meaning are going on all the time. *Bulletin board* can now be used for a computer service that provides information, instead of just for a board on which notices are posted.

A different kind of shift occurs when a word changes its part of speech. For example, we use the noun *hand* as a verb in "Hand me that book, please," the verb *sing* as a noun in "We are having a community sing," the adjective *tough* as a noun in "the young toughs," the noun *fun* as an adjective in "a really fun evening," the adverb *up* as a verb in "They upped the price," and so on. Such functional shifts are an easy and common way of making new words in Modern English.

Tomorrow's English

English is changing today even as we use it. Indeed, it is changing *because* we use it. Each change, however small, makes the language somewhat different from the English of yesterday. As the changes accumulate, little by little, day by day, they eventually make the language very different from what it was. But that is nothing to fear. Languages grow, as they must to live. By the way we speak English today and by the changes we introduce into it, we are creating the English of tomorrow.

Over the years, English speakers have written some of the greatest literature known to humanity, literature that is read all over the world by people of diverse cultures. In the future, English will doubtless continue to be a medium for the expression of our common fears, hopes, aspirations, and exaltations.

> English belongs to all those all over the world who speak and write it, who read its literature, and who treasure it.

The English language, like English literature, is something we can take pride in. This language and this literature do not belong to one nation or to one people only, but are shared by many. English belongs to all those all over the world who speak and write it, who read its literature, and who treasure it.

Try It Out

1. **Finding word origins.** The following words illustrate various ways in which words are made. Look them up in a dictionary that gives etymologies, and describe their origins.

blizzard	kitty-cornered
escalate	lengthwise
gas	motel
hiccup	pep
jeep	scarecrow

2. **Inferring etymologies.** Words change their meanings over time, but some words keep evidence of their earlier meanings. Try to guess from their forms the earlier meanings of the following words.

   Then, look up their etymologies to see whether your guesses are correct.

bonfire	cupboard	doff
business	disease	

3. **Using a dictionary.** Look in a recent newspaper or magazine for words that are completely new to you. Find at least five such words, and on a sheet of paper, copy the sentences in which the words are used. Underline the unfamiliar words. Then, look up the words in a college or unabridged dictionary. If you find them, read their etymologies to find out where they come from. If you do not find them, do you think they may be new words or old but rare words?

4. **Locating sources of information.** Several dictionaries and periodicals list new words. Locate one of the following collections of new words in a library.

   - *The Oxford Dictionary of New Words,* eds. Elizabeth Knowles and Julia Elliot

   - *The Third Barnhart Dictionary of New English*

   - "Among the New Words" (a regular article in the magazine *American Speech*)

   - <u>American Heritage Dictionary</u>, WordStar, 1993 (an electronic dictionary that includes new words)

   Make a list of five new words from any of these sources. Tell what each word means.

A Conversation (1913–1916) by Vanessa Bell.

Writer's Workshop

The history
of the written
word is rich and

Page 1

PERSUASIVE WRITING

A PROBLEM-SOLUTION ESSAY

Reading the selections in Collections 14 and 15 has shown you how twentieth-century writers used both fiction and nonfiction to explore social problems. By now, you've peered into the lives of an alienated bureaucrat, children shunned by their peers, and families and compatriots locked in conflict. Although many of these selections only hint at solutions, the clear-eyed portrayal of human problems, combined with the search for practical answers, is an important form of writing. Problem-solution essays, or proposals that call for definite action, are written every day—by scientists investigating solar energy, by citizens concerned about crime, by newspaper columnists proposing changes in the economy, and by politicians seeking office. In this Writer's Workshop, you'll write your own problem-solution essay, carefully analyzing a problem and proposing one or more specific solutions to it.

Prewriting

1. **Checking your Writer's Notebook.** By doing the Writer's Notebook activities throughout Collections 14 and 15, you may have already done some of the prewriting necessary for a problem-solution essay. Look back at your entries, and decide if you'd like to develop any of the ideas or problems you find there. Then proceed with the prewriting steps that follow.

2. **Identifying suitable problems.** Since you'll be presenting your findings to an audience, steer clear of strictly personal problems such as family squabbles or romantic entanglements. Instead, consider problems that significantly affect a number of people. For example, a family dispute over your plans to attend an unsupervised graduation party is too personal for a problem-solution essay. But the lack of an alternative to such private parties in your community would affect many seniors and their families. Another approach is to focus on the local aspects of a national or international problem. Instead of tackling "homelessness in the United States," for example, you might investigate the causes and effects of a local homeless shelter's policy of turning people back out onto the streets each morning.

   To identify suitable problems, try freewriting about problems you've noticed in your school, neighborhood, or city. You can also find ideas by reading newspaper and magazine articles, listening to radio and TV news and talk shows, and attending public meetings.

3. **Investigating a problem.** Once you start exploring the problem you've chosen, you may find that you need more information to understand it

Technology HELP

See Writer's Workshop 2 CD-ROM. *Assignment: Controversial Issue.*

ASSIGNMENT

Write an essay that explores a problem and proposes one or more solutions to it.

AIM

To persuade; to explore; to explain.

AUDIENCE

People who share (or can be led to share) your interest in solving the problem.

fully. First, though, determine precisely what you *do* know about it by brainstorming or clustering or by asking yourself the *5W-How?* questions (*Who? What? When? Where? Why?* and *How?*). Then move outward, using a variety of sources to gather information: Read, listen, observe, and question others to discover their views. For example, if you're exploring the problem of flooding in your neighborhood, you might begin by jotting down an account of your own experiences and then reading newspaper articles on the causes and effects of the problem. You might also interview your neighbors and local officials, such as the county's director of stormwater engineering.

Try It Out

For each of the following problems, suggest at least three potential sources of information.

1. a lack of affordable housing in a community
2. pollution in a local lake
3. vandalism at a school
4. a town's lack of employment opportunities
5. low reading scores

Strategies for Elaboration: Scrutinizing Your Subject

Looking at a problem from different points of view can help you understand it more fully. Try using these questions to analyze the problem you're investigating.

- What is the problem? How widespread is it?
- What is the history of the problem? What caused the problem? What effects has the problem had, and on whom?
- How is the problem like other problems? How is it different from them? What are the major parts of the problem?
- How serious is the problem? Why?

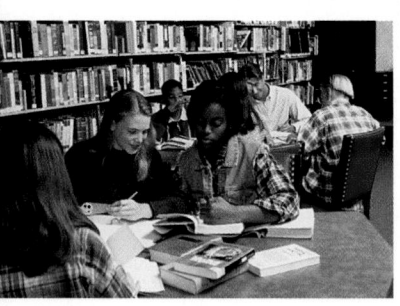

4. **Exploring possible solutions.** Now your focus shifts from the problem to ways to solve it. To avoid duplicating other people's efforts, begin by finding out as much as you can about past and current attempts to solve the problem. Then use freewriting, brainstorming, or clustering to devise your own creative solution(s).

Strategies for Elaboration: Reflecting on Solutions

Use these questions to explore other people's solutions and then your own ideas for solving the problem.

Other People's Ideas
- What solutions have already been tried?
- How well have those solutions worked?
- Why haven't they worked better?
- What solutions are now being considered?

Your Ideas
- Could some of the problem's causes be eliminated? If so, how?
- What could be done to ease or eliminate the effects of the problem?
- Does one part of the problem seem especially difficult to solve? Why?
- Which part of the problem seems easiest to solve? Why?
- What is the most promising solution (or part of the solution) you can think of?

One student used two of the questions on page 1180 as prompts for a focused freewrite on the problem of traffic accidents on graduation night. Here are the ideas that resulted:

Model

Could some of the causes of traffic accidents on graduation night be eliminated? How? One cause of traffic accidents on graduation night is unsafe driving by students who have been drinking at unsupervised private parties. We could eliminate this cause by having a party at the Civic Center supervised by teachers and parents. But where would the money come from, and would students attend the party? Maybe local businesses would be willing to donate food, music, decorations, and door prizes in exchange for publicity. The donations would defray the cost of putting on the party and might also entice people to come to the party.

What is the most promising part of the solution you can think of? Maybe the Parent-Teacher Organization could hire buses to transport students to and from the party — maybe the school board would even allow school buses to be used. A student committee could decorate the buses with streamers and balloons.

5. **Evaluating alternative solutions.** A perfect solution to your problem may not exist. Usually, though, some solutions are clearly better than others, and in most cases, one solution can be shown to be the best choice. Use these questions to evaluate possible solutions and to identify the best solution to your problem.

- What are the advantages and disadvantages of each solution?

- Which solution is the most practical?

- Does one solution have a comparative advantage? In other words, which solution will do the most good for the most people?

Sometimes, two solutions may seem equally good—or none may seem feasible. In such cases, resist the urge to declare the problem unsolvable. Instead, search for a compromise. If your school doesn't have enough guidance counselors, for example, don't assume that students either have to do without career planning or have to pay an outside career-counseling service. A compromise solution might be for one of the guidance counselors to sponsor a student group offering peer counseling.

In other cases, the problem may have more than one cause or may affect more than one group. Such situations may call for a variety of solutions. For example, if neighborhood residents object to the traffic and noise a new teen center will generate, one solution—having a new access road built—is not enough. You also need a solution for the noise.

Making a chart like the one on page 1182 can help you analyze and evaluate alternative solutions. The writer is trying to discover solutions to the following problem: Not all students have home computers, which provide instant access to information needed for doing homework.

Possible Solutions	Advantages	Disadvantages
Abolish homework	Eliminates inequity in grading; makes students' lives less stressful.	Removes valuable assessment tool; removes opportunity to apply research skills independently.
Keep school open two hours longer each weekday.	Gives students who need it access to computers in a familiar place; computers already budgeted for.	The school's budget can't cover additional costs for teachers' salaries, utilities, and school bus drivers' wages.
Establish next branch of county library at the school.	Opens services to all city residents, not just students; staff and equipment costs already budgeted for; saves cost of building a new facility.	County commissioners would have to be convinced of neighborhood support; residents of other parts of town might object.

Practicality

Keeping school open longer hours isn't practical—the school just doesn't have the money.

Comparative Advantage

Establishing the next branch of the county library at the school will do the most good for the most people and will make the best use of available money, staff, and facilities.

6. **Steps to success.** Once you've settled on a practical, workable solution—the end—turn your attention to the specific steps needed to make it a reality—the means. Focus on these questions:

- What needs to be done?
- How will it be done?
- In what order will it be done?

For example, establishing the next branch of the county library at your school might involve the following steps:

- Develop support for the idea in your school zone by visiting or distributing literature to neighborhood residents.
- Ask the newspaper to send a reporter to speak with students and residents about the need for and benefits of the proposal.
- Contact your local county commissioner to arrange to have the proposal included on the commission's agenda.
- Recruit students and other area residents to attend the commission meeting at which you will present the proposal and explain its benefits.

7. **Analyzing your audience, setting your tone.** As in persuasive writing, audience considerations are central to a problem-solution essay. Here, your purpose is twofold: to *explain* the problem and possible solutions and to *prove* that the problem is serious and your solution is the best one. Use the questions in the following chart to plan your approach.

Questions	Analysis	Approach
What does the audience already know about the problem?	very little	Provide detailed background information.
	a little	Include some background details.
	a lot	Remind them of their stake in solving the problem.
What solutions might the audience favor?	the one you are proposing	Lead them from agreement to action.
	one you have rejected	Explain in detail the comparative advantage of your solution.
What kind of objections might the audience have to your solution?	major ones	Devote extra space to countering their objections and to explaining the benefits your solution offers.
	minor ones	Emphasize that your solution offers the greatest good for the greatest number of people.

In setting your tone, use objective language to demonstrate that your proposal isn't simply self-serving. Avoid emotionally charged words and, to keep from coming across as a know-it-all, qualify your recommendations: Use words such as *could, might,* and *perhaps* rather than *should, must,* and *unquestionably.* Using first-person pronouns can be especially effective in a problem-solution essay—*I, my, mine,* and *me* to recount your own experiences; *we* and *our* to describe the problem; and *ours* and *us* to underscore common concerns.

8. **Providing support.** Vague generalities and sweeping statements won't persuade readers to accept your analysis of the problem and its possible solutions or to accept your proposed solution as the best solution. Readers will expect you to provide sound reasons and specific evidence—facts, examples, and statistics. Compare the effectiveness of these two statements:

VAGUE   Sixteen-year-old drivers are a lot more dangerous than older teen drivers.

**Language Handbook
H E L P**

See Personal Pronouns, page 1227.

Nationwide, according to the Insurance Institute for Highway Safety, sixteen-year-old drivers are involved in more than twice as many fatal crashes as seventeen-, eighteen-, and nineteen-year-old drivers.

Drafting

1. **The introduction: engage them.** Especially if your readers aren't aware of the problem or aren't convinced of its relevance to their lives, it's important to grab their attention immediately. Try beginning with an unusual fact, a stirring scenario, or a personal anecdote. Then define the problem explicitly, using descriptive terms that will help readers visualize the situation.

2. **The body: enlighten them.** As you explain the problem's seriousness, remember to support your reasons with facts, examples, and statistics. In discussing the alternative solutions you have rejected, clarify their specific disadvantages, again using solid evidence to back up your reasons. Then present your own solution, pointing out its comparative advantages and outlining the steps needed to implement it.

Strategies for Elaboration: Putting It All Together

- **Distributing emphasis.** The amount of space you devote to explaining the problem and its seriousness, describing your proposed solution, discussing rejected solutions, and countering possible objections to your solution will depend on your readers' concerns. If they're well aware of the problem, for example, you may spend more time discussing your solution. A very complex problem may call for a greater emphasis on its causes and effects than on your proposed solution.

- **Crediting your sources.** Your teacher may ask you to credit your sources formally, using parenthetical citations and a list of works cited. If not, you may credit your sources informally by weaving them into the sentences in which you refer to them, as in the "precise" example under "Providing Support," above.

---

3. **The conclusion: energize them.** To bring your essay to a compelling close, restate your proposed solution. Consider ending with a clear call to action—specific steps readers can take to help make your solution a reality.

Evaluating and Revising

Self-evaluation. Take a hard look at the solution you've proposed in your essay. Circle the solution, and number the necessary steps to achieve it that you've discussed. Next, underline each counterargument you've addressed. If you find few items to circle, number, or underline, you know what to focus on when you revise. Also, review your classmate's responses, looking especially for comments that will help you make your paper clearer and more persuasive. Then, revise your essay, making any necessary changes.

Page 1

The history
of the written
word is rich and

Language Workshop

EFFECTIVE SENTENCES: RELATIONSHIPS BETWEEN IDEAS

A common problem in writing comes about when several clauses are strung together with only the word *and*. You can make your writing more precise by using subordinating conjunctions instead of *and*, when appropriate. A *subordinating conjunction* is a word that clarifies the relationships between ideas by indicating **time** (*after, as, before, until, when*), **cause** (*because, since, unless*), **purpose** (*so that*), or **condition** (*although, if, though*).

Here are some sentences that string together a series of ideas with the word *and*. Note that the relationships between the ideas are not too clear.

UNCLEAR Without even washing it, he put the root in his mouth, chewed it vigorously, and then held the spittle there, **and** he took the child forcibly from Mrs. Farquar.

He spoke incredulously, **and** he could not believe his old friends could so betray him.

Here is how Doris Lessing combined the same ideas using subordination. Notice that now the relationships between ideas are more precisely stated.

CLEAR Without even washing it, he put the root in his mouth, chewed it vigorously, and then held the spittle there **while** he took the child forcibly from Mrs. Farquar.

—*from "No Witchcraft for Sale"*

He spoke incredulously, **as if** he could not believe his old friends could so betray him.

—*from "No Witchcraft for Sale"*

Usually, there are several ways to indicate subordination. Here are two edited versions of the second sentence above:

He spoke incredulously **because** he could not believe his old friends could so betray him.

Because he could not believe his old friends could so betray him, he spoke incredulously.

Writer's Workshop Follow-Up: Revision

Review the essay you wrote for the Writer's Workshop on page 1179. Focus on one paragraph in the body of your essay to see where you can combine sentences to make relationships clearer; then study the other paragraphs. Share your changes with a writing partner.

Technology HELP

See Language Workshop CD-ROM. *Key word entry: subordinate clause.*

Language Handbook HELP

See Clauses, page 1232; Combining by Subordinating Ideas, page 1239; Commas, page 1245.

Try It Out

Combine the sentences below, using subordinating conjunctions to clarify relationships.

1. Gideon was a cook for the Farquar family. He would often play with their son, Teddy.

2. Gideon knew which plant had healing powers. He refused to identify it for the Farquars and he withheld his secret information.

Reading for Life

Reading a Business Memorandum or Electronic Mail

Situation

Imagine you're working as a summer intern for an American company in Indonesia. During your first few days, you receive a memorandum (often shortened to *memo*) on the subject of respect for your co-workers' culture.

Strategies

Understand the purpose of a memorandum.

- A printed or electronic (e-mail) business memo is a method of sharing information among workers. Memos deal with issues such as workplace procedures and policies, records of meetings, and the status of projects.

Recognize the format of a memo.

- Print and electronic memos have these features: A heading indicates the date, the name of the person or department issuing the memo, the people to whom the memo is sent, and the subject of the memo. The heading is followed by the body of the memo. Either in the heading or below the body, there may be a list of names or initials following the abbreviation *cc*. This list refers to the people to whom copies of the memo are sent.

Read the memo.

- If there are abbreviations or special terms you don't

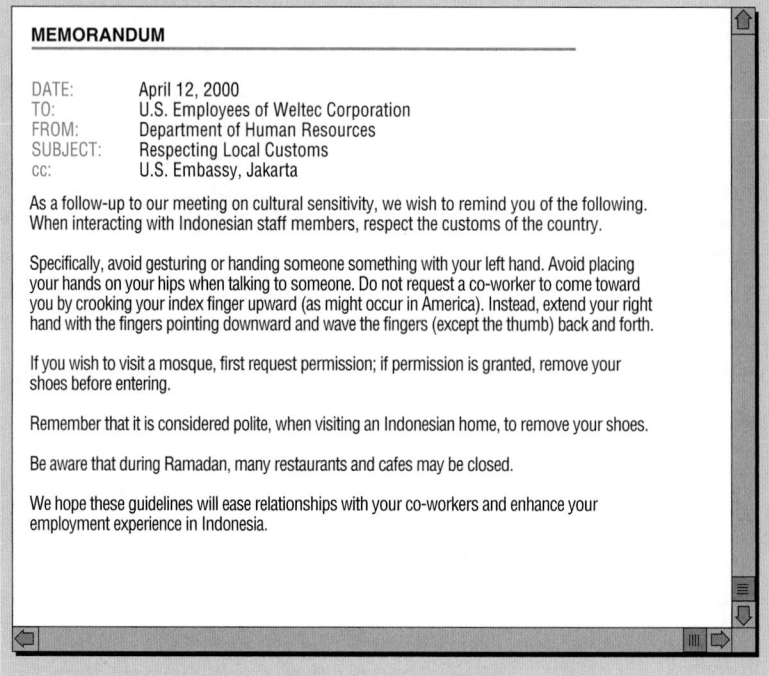

MEMORANDUM

DATE: April 12, 2000
TO: U.S. Employees of Weltec Corporation
FROM: Department of Human Resources
SUBJECT: Respecting Local Customs
cc: U.S. Embassy, Jakarta

As a follow-up to our meeting on cultural sensitivity, we wish to remind you of the following. When interacting with Indonesian staff members, respect the customs of the country.

Specifically, avoid gesturing or handing someone something with your left hand. Avoid placing your hands on your hips when talking to someone. Do not request a co-worker to come toward you by crooking your index finger upward (as might occur in America). Instead, extend your right hand with the fingers pointing downward and wave the fingers (except the thumb) back and forth.

If you wish to visit a mosque, first request permission; if permission is granted, remove your shoes before entering.

Remember that it is considered polite, when visiting an Indonesian home, to remove your shoes.

Be aware that during Ramadan, many restaurants and cafes may be closed.

We hope these guidelines will ease relationships with your co-workers and enhance your employment experience in Indonesia.

recognize, ask someone to explain them to you.

- Take appropriate action. You may be expected to make changes in your behavior or your work routine.

- Determine whether the memo requires a written response.

Using the Strategies

Answer these questions about the memo above.

1. What is the purpose of this memo? What part of the memo tells you this succinctly?

2. Who receives a copy of the memo? Why might a copy be sent?

3. Can you think of any other individuals who might have been sent copies of this memo? Why?

4. What if any action is called for by this memo?

5. Does this memo require a written response?

6. Do you need to keep this memo?

Extending the Strategies

- Write a memorandum to your classmates on an issue of classroom procedure that is important to you.

- Ask someone you know to show you a business memo he or she has received.

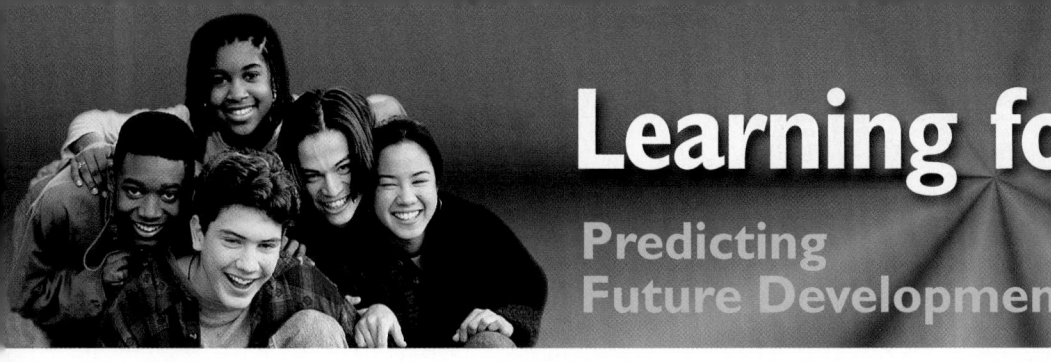

Learning for Life

Predicting Future Developments

Problem

Many of the profound changes that occurred in the twentieth century grew out of Victorian-era developments. How might developments in the latter half of the twentieth century affect life in the twenty-first century?

Project

Predict how one twentieth-century development—social, cultural, or techno-logical—may affect life in the next one hundred years. Will it change the pace and pattern of daily life? Will it alter the way people view themselves and the world around them?

Preparation

1. With a partner or a small group, brainstorm to generate a list of twentieth-century events, situations, and trends. To get started, you might focus on such categories as art, literature, computers, education, politics, medicine, and so on. Or you might begin with people: Who were the leading inventors, entre-preneurs, authors, artists, and scientists of the late twentieth century?

2. Choose the topic that interests you most, and freewrite to explore what you already know about it and what you think its long-range conse-quences may be.

Procedure

1. Using library and community resources, explore your topic through the eyes of others who share your interest. Look for facts, statistics, ex-amples, anecdotes, and ex-pert opinions that will answer as many of the *5W-How?* questions (*Who? What? When? Where? Why? How?*) as apply. Be sure to investigate what the experts called futur-ists suggest about future de-velopments. You can cite the experts' views and give data to support your position.

2. Stimulate your imagination by asking, and answering, a series of *What if?* questions—for example, What if cities ban all cars in the future? Your an-swers needn't (in fact, can't) be provable, but they should be plausible.

Presentation

Use one of the following formats (or another that your teacher approves):

1. Be a Television Star

Get together with two or three classmates who've cho-sen different topics to plan a talk show on your predictions for the future. Ask another student to serve as the show's host, and stage the show live (or ask a friend to videotape it for repeated showings) for your school's

American history classes during their unit on the twentieth century.

2. Display with Style

Design a triptych (a three-panel composition) illustrating your predictions for the fu-ture. Your triptych may be two- or three-dimensional, and you may choose the ma-terials, medium (or media), and style. Give your finished work a title, and display it in the school cafeteria.

3. Future Fiction

Write a short story, set in the late twenty-first century, in which you depict the con-sequences you foresee. Whether your story is fantas-tic or realistic, be sure to in-clude in your story plan a basic conflict and a satisfying means of resolving it. With other students who have chosen this option, tape-record your story. Listen to one another's tapes, and share your responses to your stories. Then, add the tapes to your media center's books-on-tape collection.

Processing

Did this activity make you more (or less) optimistic about the fu-ture? Did it make you curious about what life will be like even further into the future? Write a brief reflection for your portfolio.

RESOURCE CENTER

HANDBOOK OF LITERARY TERMS

ALEXANDRINE **A line of poetry made up of six iambs**—that is, a line written in iambic hexameter. The following alexandrine is from Percy Bysshe Shelley's "To a Skylark" (Collection 9):

> Our sweetest songs are those that tell of saddest thought.

See page 221.

ALLEGORY **A story in which the characters, settings, and events stand for abstract or moral concepts.** Allegories thus have two meanings: a literal meaning and a symbolic meaning. Allegories were a popular literary form during the Middle Ages. Later, Edmund Spenser's *The Faerie Queene* (Collection 3) elaborately fused moral and political allegory: Spenser's Redcrosse Knight stands both for St. George, the patron saint of England, and for the more abstract idea of holiness. The best-known English allegory is John Bunyan's *The Pilgrim's Progress* (Collection 5), which recounts the adventures of a character named Christian. The hero's journey to the Celestial City brings him up against many trials that stand for the pitfalls facing the Christian traveling through this world toward the spiritual world.

See pages 221, 451, 495.

ALLITERATION **The repetition of consonant sounds in words that are close to one another.** Alliteration occurs most often at the beginning of words, as in "<u>r</u>ough and <u>r</u>eady." But consonants within words sometimes alliterate, as in "<u>b</u>aby <u>b</u>lue." The echoes that alliteration creates can increase a poem's rhythmic and musical effects and make its lines especially memorable. In this line from Alfred, Lord Tennyson's "The Eagle: A Fragment" (Collection 10), the alliteration of harsh *k* sounds reinforces the stark image of the bird:

> He clasps the crag with crooked hands

Alliteration is an essential feature of Anglo-Saxon poetry; in most lines, two or three of the four stressed syllables alliterate.

See pages 49, 807, 980.

ALLUSION **A reference to a statement, person, place, event, or thing that is known from literature, history, religion, mythology, politics, sports, science, or popular culture.** For example, the concluding lines of Wilfred Owen's poem "Dulce et Decorum Est" (Collection 12) are *"Dulce et decorum est / Pro patria mori"* ("It is sweet and proper to die for one's country"). These lines allude to a line from an ode by the Latin poet Horace. The title of William Faulkner's *The Sound and the Fury* is an allusion to a line from Shakespeare's *Macbeth* (Collection 4). The cartoon above alludes to William Butler Yeats's poem "The Second Coming" (Collection 12).

See pages 414, 871, 941.

ANALOGY **A comparison of two things to show that they are alike in certain respects.** Writers often make analogies to show how something unfamiliar is like

"Basil, do you think the center is going to hold?"

Drawing by Booth; © 1984 The New Yorker Magazine, Inc.

something well known or widely experienced. For example, people often draw an analogy between creating a work of art and giving birth to a child.

See page 1144.

ANTAGONIST **The character or force that opposes or blocks the protagonist, or main character, in a narrative.** Usually the antagonist is human, like Sir Mordred, the villainous rebel who destroys the Round Table in Sir Thomas Malory's *Le Morte Darthur* (Collection 2) or the schoolgirls who mercilessly taunt the Kelvey sisters in Katherine Mansfield's "The Doll's House" (Collection 14). Sometimes the antagonist is supernatural, like Satan, who opposes God in John Milton's *Paradise Lost* (Collection 5).

ANTICLIMAX *See* Climax.

ANTITHESIS **A contrast of ideas expressed in a grammatically balanced statement.** In the following line from Canto III of *The Rape of the Lock* (Collection 6), Alexander Pope balances noun against noun and verb against verb:

> And wretches hang that jurymen may dine.

See pages 521, 844.

APHORISM **A concise, sometimes witty saying that expresses a principle, truth, or observation about life.** Alexander Pope's poetry contains some of the most famous aphorisms in the English language, as in this example from *An Essay on Criticism* (Collection 6):

> To err is human, to forgive, divine.

APOSTROPHE **A figure of speech in which a speaker directly addresses an absent or dead person, an abstract quality, or something nonhuman as if it were present and capable of responding.** Apostrophe was a popular device with the Romantic poets: Wordsworth, for example, apostrophizes the river Wye in his "Tintern Abbey" (Collection 8). Among the second-generation Romantics, Shelley apostrophized the west wind and a skylark;

Byron apostrophized the ocean; and Keats apostrophized a nightingale and a Greek urn (all in Collection 9).

See pages 672, 738.

ASIDE **Private words that a character in a play speaks to the audience or to another character and that are not supposed to be overheard by others on-stage.** Stage directions usually tell when a speech is an aside. For example, in Act I, Scene 3, of Shakespeare's *Macbeth* (Collection 4), Macbeth makes numerous asides to the audience as he ruminates about the possibility of becoming king.

See page 383.

ASSONANCE **The repetition of similar vowel sounds followed by different consonant sounds in words that are close together.** Assonance differs from **exact rhyme** in that it does not repeat the consonant sound following the vowel. The words *face* and *base* rhyme, while the words *face* and *fade* are assonant. Like alliteration, assonance can create musical and rhythmic effects. In this line from Alfred, Lord Tennyson's "The Lotos-Eaters," the repetition of long *o* sounds is **onomatopoetic:**

All day the wind breathes low with mellower tone

See pages 683, 807, 841, 979, 980.

ATMOSPHERE **The mood or feeling in a literary work.** Atmosphere is usually created through descriptive details and evocative language. For example, Ben Okri sets the mood of his short story "In the Shadow of War" (Collection 12) with a dreamlike description of the war-torn forest around Lagos, Nigeria.

See page 847.

AUTOBIOGRAPHY **A written account of the author's own life.** Unlike **diaries, journals,** and letters, autobiographies are unified narratives usually prepared for a public audience. Also unlike memoirs, which often focus on famous events and people, autobiographies are usually quite introspective. George Orwell's "Shooting an Elephant" (Collection 15) is a well-known autobiographical essay.

See also Diary, Journal.

BALLAD **A song or songlike poem that tells a story.** Most ballads have a regular pattern of **rhythm** and **rhyme,** and they use simple language with a great deal of repetition. Ballads generally have a **refrain**—lines or words that are repeated at regular intervals. And they usually tell sensational stories of tragedy, adventure, betrayal, revenge, and jealousy. **Folk ballads** are composed by anonymous singers and are passed down orally from generation to generation before they are written down (often in several different versions). "Lord Randall" (Collection 2) is an example of a folk ballad. **Literary ballads,** on the other hand, are composed and written down by known poets, usually in the style of folk ballads. John Keats's "La Belle Dame sans Merci" (Collection 9) is a famous literary ballad.

The typical **ballad stanza** is a quatrain with the rhyme scheme *abcb.* The first and third lines have four stressed syllables, and the second and fourth lines have three. The number of unstressed syllables in each line may vary, but often the meter is primarily **iambic.**

See pages 90, 93, 96, 683, 750, 867.

BIOGRAPHY **An account of a person's life written by another person.** *The Life of Samuel Johnson* by James Boswell (Collection 7) is one of the most famous biographies ever written. Virginia Woolf's account of Shakespeare's sister in *A Room of One's Own* (Collection 15) is an invented biography.

See page 583.

BLANK VERSE **Poetry written in unrhymed iambic pentameter.** "Blank" means the poetry is unrhymed. "Iambic pentameter" means that each line contains five iambs, or metrical **feet,** each consisting of an unstressed syllable followed by a stressed syllable (˘ '). Blank verse is the most important metrical form used in English dramatic and epic poetry. It is the verse line used in Shakespeare's plays and John Milton's *Paradise Lost* (Collection 5). One of the reasons blank verse has been so popular, even among modern poets, is that it combines the naturalness of unrhymed verse with the structure of metrical verse. Except for **free verse,** it is the poetic form that sounds the most like natural speech. It also lends itself easily to slight variations within the basic pattern. Like most of the English Romantic poets, William Wordsworth made extensive use of blank verse, as in these lines from *The Prelude:*

Oh! yet a few short years of useful life,
And all will be complete, thy race be run,
Thy monument of glory will be raised.

See pages 318, 385, 438, 450, 657, 662, 672.

CADENCE **The natural rise and fall of the voice.** Poets who write in **free verse** often try to imitate the cadences of spoken language.

See also Rhythm.

CAESURA **A pause or break within a line of poetry, usually indicated by the natural rhythm of the language.** A midline, or **medial,** caesura is a characteristic of Anglo-Saxon poetry; it divides the four-beat line in half. Later poets use the caesura less predictably, as in the following lines from Wilfred Owen's "Dulce et Decorum Est" (Collection 12). Here, the caesuras are indicated by the symbol ‖.

Bent double, ‖ like old beggars under sacks,
Knock-kneed, ‖ coughing like hags, ‖ we cursed through sludge

See pages 49, 216.

CANTO **A subdivision in a long poem, corresponding to a chapter in a book.** Poems divided into cantos include Dante's *The Divine Comedy* (Collection 4), Pope's *The Rape of the Lock* (Collection 6), and Byron's *Don Juan* and

Childe Harold's Pilgrimage (both in Collection 9). Not all major subdivisions of long poems are called cantos: Milton's *Paradise Lost* (Collection 5) is divided into books, and Coleridge's *The Rime of the Ancient Mariner* (Collection 8), into parts.

The word *canto* comes from a Latin word for song and originally designated a section of a narrative poem that a minstrel could sing in one session.

See page 527.

CARPE DIEM **A Latin phrase that literally means "seize the day"—that is, "make the most of present opportunities."** The *carpe diem* theme is quite common in sixteenth- and seventeenth-century English poetry, as in this famous line from Robert Herrick's "To the Virgins, to Make Much of Time": "Gather ye rosebuds while ye may." The theme is also forcefully expressed in Andrew Marvell's "To His Coy Mistress" (both in Collection 3).

See pages 231, 239.

CHARACTER **An individual in a story or play.** A character always has human traits, even if the character is an animal, like the March Hare in Lewis Carroll's *Alice's Adventures in Wonderland;* or a god, as in the Greek and Roman myths; or a monster, as in *Beowulf* (Collection 1). A character may also be a godlike human, like Superman. But most characters are ordinary human beings, like Geoffrey Chaucer's colorful pilgrims in *The Canterbury Tales* (Collection 2), the eccentrics and paupers in Charles Dickens's novels, and the disillusioned boy in James Joyce's "Araby" (Collection 13).

The process by which the writer reveals the personality of a character is called **characterization.** A writer can reveal a character in the following ways:

1. By telling us directly what the character is like: humble, ambitious, impetuous, easily manipulated, and so on
2. By describing how the character looks and dresses
3. By letting us hear the character speak
4. By revealing the character's private thoughts and feelings
5. By revealing the character's effect on other people— showing how other characters feel or behave toward the character
6. By showing the character's actions

The first method of revealing a character is called **direct characterization.** When a writer uses this method, we do not have to figure out what a character's personality is like— the writer tells us directly. The other five methods of revealing a character are known as **indirect characterization.** When a writer uses these methods, we have to exercise our own judgment, putting clues together to figure out what a character is like—just as we do in real life when we are getting to know someone.

Characters can be classified as static or dynamic. A **static character** is one who does not change much in the course of a story. A **dynamic character,** on the other hand, changes in some important way as a result of the story's action. Characters can also be classified as flat or round. **Flat characters** have only one or two personality traits. They are one-dimensional—they can be summed up by a single phrase. In contrast, **round characters** have more dimensions to their personalities—they are complex, solid, and multifaceted, like real people.

See pages 103, 384, 1069.

CLASSICISM **A movement in art, literature, and music that advocates imitating the principles manifested in the art and literature of ancient ("classical") Greece and Rome.** Classicism emphasizes reason, clarity, balance, harmony, restraint, order, and universal themes. Classicism is often placed in direct opposition to **Romanticism,** with its emphasis on unrestrained emotions and personal themes. However, this opposition should be approached with caution, as it is sometimes exaggerated for effect.

See also Neoclassicism, Romanticism.

CLICHÉ **An expression that was fresh and apt when first coined but is now so overused that it has become hackneyed and stale.** "Busy as a bee" and "fresh as a daisy" are two examples. Clichés are often likened to **dead metaphors**—figures of speech ("leg of a chair," "mouth of a river") whose power to surprise has now been completely lost.

See page 1037.

CLIMAX **The point of greatest emotional intensity or suspense in a plot.** The climax usually marks the moment when the conflict is decided, one way or another. In Shakespeare's plays, the climax usually occurs in the last act, just before the final scene. Following the climax, the story is **resolved,** or closed.

Some critics talk of more than one climactic moment in a long work (though usually the greatest climax still occurs near the end of the plot). In drama, one such climactic moment is called the **turning point,** or **crisis.** In Shakespeare's plays, this moment usually occurs in the third act. The turning point is the pivotal moment when the hero's fortunes begin to decline or improve. All the action leading up to this turning point is **rising action,** and all the action following it is **falling action.** The turning point in *Macbeth* (Collection 4) occurs during the banquet scene in Act III, Scene 4, when Macbeth sees Banquo's ghost. From that point onward, it is downhill for Macbeth—everything goes wrong, culminating in the play's climax in Act V, Scene 8. It is at this point that we finally learn for certain that Macbeth will be defeated. The witches' prophecies are borne out: Birnam Wood does come to Dunsinane, and Macduff, "not born of woman," faces Macbeth. This confrontation is the climax of the play. After this point, the play moves rapidly toward its resolution, with Malcolm, Duncan's legitimate heir, assuming the throne.

In contrast, when something trivial or comical occurs at the point in a narrative when one expects something important or serious, the accompanying deflation is called an **anticlimax.** Thomas Hardy's poem "Ah, Are You Digging on My Grave?" (Collection 11) contains such an anticlimactic moment.

See pages 351, 388, 857.
See also Plot.

COMEDY **In general, a story that ends happily.** The hero of a comedy is usually an ordinary character who overcomes a series of obstacles that block what he or she wants. Often a comedy pits two young people who wish to marry against parental blocking figures who want to prevent the marriage. The wedding that concludes these comedies suggests the formation of a new society and a renewal of life. Comedy is distinct from **tragedy,** in which a great person comes to an unhappy or disastrous end, often through some lapse in judgment or character flaw. Comedies are often, but not always, intended to make us laugh. Two famous comedies are Oscar Wilde's play *The Importance of Being Earnest* and George Bernard Shaw's *Pygmalion.* Frank O'Connor's "My Oedipus Complex" (Collection 14) is a comedic short story.

See pages 283, 300, 393, 526, 798.
See also Farce, Tragedy.

CONCEIT **A fanciful and elaborate figure of speech that makes a surprising connection between two seemingly dissimilar things.** Although a conceit may be a brief metaphor, it usually forms the framework of an entire poem. One of the most important kinds of conceits is the **metaphysical conceit,** so called because it was widely used by the seventeenth-century metaphysical poets. This type of conceit is especially startling, complex, and ingenious. Two famous examples are John Donne's comparison of separated lovers to the legs of a compass in "A Valediction: Forbidding Mourning" (Collection 3) and George Herbert's comparison of belief in God to a pulley in "The Pulley."

See pages 220, 229, 247, 457.

CONFLICT **A struggle or clash between opposing characters, forces, or emotions.** In an **external conflict,** a character struggles against some outside force: another character, society as a whole, or some natural force. An **internal conflict,** on the other hand, is a struggle between opposing needs, desires, or emotions within a single character. Many works, especially longer ones, contain both internal and external conflicts. For example, in Shakespeare's *Macbeth* (Collection 4), Macbeth undergoes an internal conflict between his excessive ambition and his obsessive guilt. He also experiences various external conflicts with characters who attempt to block his ambition. In Doris Lessing's "No Witchcraft for Sale" (Collection 15), the conflict between Gideon and the scientist illustrates larger cultural conflicts.

See also Plot.

CONNOTATIONS **All the meanings, associations, or emotions that a word suggests.** For example, an expensive restaurant might prefer to advertise its "delicious cuisine" rather than its "delicious cooking." *Cuisine* and *cooking* have the same literal meaning—"prepared food." But *cuisine* has connotations of elegance and sophistication, while *cooking* does not. The same restaurant would certainly not describe its food as "great grub."

Notice the difference between the following pairs of words: *young/immature, ambitious/cutthroat, uninhibited/shameless, lenient/lax.* We might describe ourselves using the first word but someone else using the second. The English philosopher Bertrand Russell once gave a classic example of the different connotations of words: "I am firm. You are obstinate. He is a pigheaded fool."

See pages 513, 515, 650.
See also Denotation.

CONSONANCE **The repetition of final consonant sounds after different vowel sounds.** The words *east* and *west, dig* and *dog, turn* and *torn,* and Shakespeare's famous *"struts* and *frets"* (from *Macbeth,* in Collection 4) are examples of consonance. The term is also used sometimes to refer to repeated consonant sounds in the middle of words, as in *solemn stillness.* (Consonance, when loosely defined, can be a form of **alliteration.** Strictly speaking, however, alliteration is the repetition of initial consonant sounds.) Like **assonance,** consonance is one form of **approximate rhyme.**

See also Alliteration, Assonance.

COUPLET **Two consecutive lines of poetry that rhyme.** The couplet has been widely used since the Middle Ages, especially to provide a sense of closure. A couplet that presents a completed thought is called a **closed couplet.** Shakespeare used closed couplets to end his sonnets, as in this example from Sonnet 18 (Collection 3):

> So long as men can breathe or eyes can see,
> So long lives this, and this gives life to thee.

A couplet written in **iambic pentameter** is called a **heroic couplet.** Although the heroic couplet has been used in English literature since Chaucer, it was perfected during the eighteenth century. Here is an example from Pope's *Essay on Man:*

> ˘ ́ ˘ ́ ˘ ́ ˘ ́ ˘ ́
> Two principles in human nature reign;
> ˘ ́ ˘ ́ ˘ ́ ˘ ́ ˘ ́
> Self-love, to urge, and Reason, to restrain.

See pages 149, 522.

DENOTATION **The literal, dictionary definition of a word.** Ironically, the definitions Samuel Johnson provides in his famous *A Dictionary of the English Language* (Collection 7) are rarely denotative.

See page 515.
See also Connotations.

DENOUEMENT See Plot.

DEUS EX MACHINA **Any artificial or contrived device used at the end of a plot to resolve or untangle the complications.** The term is Latin, meaning "god from a machine." The phrase refers to a device used in ancient Greek and Roman drama: At the conclusion of the play, a god would be lowered onto the stage by a mechanical device so that he could save the hero and end the story happily. The term now refers to any device that resolves a plot in a forced or ridiculously implausible way: An orphan finds that he has inherited a fortune just as he is being packed off to the poorhouse; a hero is saved because the villain has forgotten to load his gun. Oscar Wilde's *The Importance of Being Earnest* and Charles Dickens's *Oliver Twist* both contain examples of *deus ex machina.*

See page 283.

DIALECT **A way of speaking that is characteristic of a particular region or group of people.** A dialect may have a distinct vocabulary, pronunciation system, and grammar. In the Middle Ages, when Latin was the "literary" language of Europe, writers such as Geoffrey Chaucer (Collection 2) began writing for middle-class audiences in their own regional languages, or what are now interchangeably called dialects or **vernaculars.** Today one dialect usually becomes accepted as the standard for a country or culture. In the United States, the dialect used in formal writing and spoken by most TV and radio announcers is known as standard English.

Writers often use other dialects, however, to establish character or to create local color. For example, Robert Burns (Collection 8) wrote his poetry in Scottish dialect, and V. S. Naipaul (Collection 13) has used the dialect spoken by Trinidad's Asian Indian population in many of his works. The East London cockney dialect, and the lower-class background it betrays, are at the very heart of George Bernard Shaw's famous play *Pygmalion* (1913). In this excerpt from the play, Henry Higgins, with his friend Colonel Pickering in attendance, begins to instruct the young flower girl Eliza Doolittle in how to speak "proper" English:

> **Higgins.** Say your alphabet.
>
> **Liza.** I know my alphabet. Do you think I know nothing? I dont need to be taught like a child.
>
> **Higgins** (*thundering*). Say your alphabet.
>
> **Pickering.** Say it, Miss Doolittle. You will understand presently. Do what he tells you; and let him teach you in his own way.
>
> **Liza.** Oh well, if you put it like that—Ahyee, bəyee, cəyee, dəyee——
>
> **Higgins** (*with the roar of a wounded lion*). Stop. Listen to this, Pickering. . . . (*To* Eliza) Say A, B, C, D.
>
> **Liza** (*almost in tears*). But I'm saying it. Ahyee, Bəee, Cə-ee——

See pages 98, 641, 770, 896, 1049.

DIALOGUE **Conversation between two or more people.** Writers use dialogue to advance the action of a plot, to present an interplay of ideas and personalities, and to reveal the background, occupation, or social level of the characters through **tone** and **dialect.**

See pages 1102, 1171.

DIARY **A day-by-day record of events and thoughts kept by an individual.** A diary is usually an intimate **autobiographical** chronicle that is not intended for publication, although diarists sometimes have a reader in mind. The diary of Samuel Pepys (Collection 7) is a famous diary in English. Diaries of such modern writers as Virginia Woolf (Collection 15) have also been published.

See page 543.
See also Autobiography, Journal.

DICTION **A writer's or speaker's choice of words.** Speakers and writers use different types of words depending on the audience they're addressing, the subject they're dis-

cussing, and the effect they're trying to produce. For example, slang that would be suitable in a casual conversation with a friend ("He's a total nerd") would be unsuitable in a political debate. Similarly, the language that a nutritionist would use to describe a meal would be different from the language that a restaurant reviewer or a novelist would use.

Diction is an essential element of a writer's **style.** A writer's diction can be simple or flowery (*shop/boutique*), modern or old-fashioned (*pharmacy/apothecary*), general or specific (*sandwich/grilled cheese on rye*). Notice that the **connotations** of words (rather than their strict, literal meanings, or **denotations**) are an important aspect of diction.

See pages 513, 1092.

DISSONANCE **A harsh, discordant combination of sounds.** The opposite of **euphony,** a pleasant, harmonious combination of sounds, dissonance is usually created by the repetition of harsh consonant sounds. Dissonance is often used in poetry to communicate energy. The following lines from Gerard Manley Hopkins's "The Windhover" are dissonant:

> shéer plód makes plough down sillion
> Shine, and blue-bleak embers, ah my dear,
> Fall, gall themselves, and gash gold-vermilion.

Also called **cacophony,** dissonance is often used as a poetic device by John Donne (Collection 3) and Robert Browning (Collection 10).

DRAMATIC MONOLOGUE **A poem in which a character addresses one or more listeners who remain silent or whose replies are not revealed.** The occasion is usually a critical one in the speaker's life. Tennyson's "Ulysses" and Browning's "My Last Duchess" and "Porphyria's Lover" (all in Collection 10) are famous dramatic monologues.

See page 829.

ELEGY **A poem that mourns the death of a person or laments something lost.** Elegies may lament the passing of life and beauty, or they may be meditations on the nature of death. A type of **lyric,** an elegy is usually formal in language and structure and solemn or even melancholy in tone. Much of English poetry is elegiac, from the Anglo-Saxon lyric "The Seafarer" (Collection 1) to John Milton's "Lycidas," Thomas Gray's somber "Elegy Written in a Country Churchyard" (Collection 7), and the great elegy of the Victorian era, Alfred, Lord Tennyson's *In Memoriam A.H.H.* (Collection 10).

See pages 55, 435, 481, 606, 814, 1038.

END-STOPPED LINE **A line of poetry in which the meter and the meaning conclude with the end of the line.** Often the end-of-line pause is marked with punctuation, though it need not be. These lines from Alexander Pope's *An Essay on Man* (Collection 6) are end-stopped:

> Know then thyself, presume not God to scan;
> The proper study of mankind is man.

See also Run-on Line.

EPIC **A long narrative poem that relates the great deeds of a larger-than-life hero who embodies the values of a particular society.** Most epics include elements of myth, legend, folklore, and history. Their tone is serious and their language grand. Most **epic heroes** undertake quests to achieve something of tremendous value to themselves or their society. Homer's *Odyssey* and *Iliad* and Virgil's *Aeneid* are the best-known epics in the Western tradition. The two most important English epics are the Anglo-Saxon poem *Beowulf* (Collection 1) and John Milton's *Paradise Lost* (Collection 5).

See pages 18, 20, 221, 393, 438, 526.

EPIGRAM   A brief, clever, and usually memorable statement. Alexander Pope's writings are **epigrammatic** in style. Here is an example from his *Essay on Criticism:*

We think our fathers fools, so wise we grow,
Our wiser sons, no doubt, will think us so.

See pages 257, 525, 1108.

EPIPHANY   In a literary work, a moment of sudden insight or revelation that a character experiences. The word comes from the Greek and can be translated as "manifestation" or "showing forth." The term has religious meanings that have been transferred to literature by many modern writers. James Joyce first gave the word its literary meaning in an early draft of *A Portrait of the Artist as a Young Man.* In Joyce's story "Araby" (Collection 13), the narrator experiences an epiphany at the end of the story when he recognizes the cheap vulgarity of the bazaar and the emptiness of his dream.

See pages 985, 992.

EPITAPH   An inscription on a tombstone or a commemorative poem written about a person who has died. Epitaphs range from the solemn to the farcical. Ben Jonson's poem "On My First Son" (Collection 3) contains a famously poignant epitaph. The following epitaph, Robert Burns's "On William Graham of Mossknowe," is a more comic example:

"Stop Thief!" Dame Nature call'd to Death,
As Willie drew his latest breath:
"How shall I make a fool again?
My choicest model thou hast ta'en."

EPITHET   An adjective or other descriptive phrase that is regularly used to characterize a person, place, or thing. Phrases such as "Peter the Great," "Richard the Lion-Hearted," and "America the Beautiful" are epithets. Homer created so many descriptive epithets in his *Iliad* and *Odyssey* that his name has been permanently associated with a type of epithet. The **Homeric epithet** consists of a compound adjective that is regularly used to modify a particular noun. Famous examples are "the wine-dark sea," "the gray-eyed goddess Athena," and the "rosy-fingered dawn."

See also Kenning.

ESSAY   A short piece of nonfiction prose that examines a single subject from a limited point of view. There are two major types of essays. **Informal essays** (also called **personal essays**) generally reveal a great deal about the personalities and feelings of their authors. They tend to be conversational, sometimes even humorous, in tone, and they are usually highly subjective. **Formal essays** (also called **traditional essays**) are usually serious and impersonal in tone. Because they are written to inform or persuade, they are expected to be factual, logical, and tightly organized.

In English literature, the essay began with Sir Francis Bacon, who published his extremely formal *Essays* (Collection 5) in 1597. The English informal essay was pioneered by Joseph Addison and Sir Richard Steele (both in Collection 7) in the early eighteenth century. Notable twentieth-century English essayists include Virginia Woolf and George Orwell (both in Collection 15).

See pages 404, 567, 1123, 1138.

EXAGGERATION   See Hyperbole.

FABLE   A very brief story in prose or verse that teaches a moral, or a practical lesson about life. The characters in most fables are animals that behave and speak like humans. Some of the most popular fables are those attributed to Aesop, who was supposed to have been a slave in ancient Greece. Several of the pilgrims' tales in Geoffrey Chaucer's *The Canterbury Tales* (Collection 2) also contain fables.

See also Parable.

FALLING ACTION   See Climax.

FARCE   A type of comedy in which ridiculous and often stereotyped characters are involved in far-fetched, silly situations. The humor in farce is based on crude physical action, slapstick, and clowning. Characters may slip on banana peels, get pies thrown in their faces, and knock one another on the head with ladders. The movies featuring Abbott and Costello, Laurel and Hardy, and the Marx brothers are all examples of farces.

The word *farce* comes from a Latin word for "stuffing," and in fact farces were originally used to fill in the waiting time between the acts of a serious play. Even in tragedies, farcical elements are often included to provide **comic relief,** or a break from the pervading tension. Shakespeare frequently lets his "common" characters engage in farcical actions.

See pages 283, 332, 1101.

FIGURATIVE LANGUAGE   Language that intentionally departs from the normal construction or meaning of words in order to create a certain effect or to make an analogy between two seemingly dissimilar things. Figurative language includes all **figures of speech.**

See page 389.

FIGURE OF SPEECH   A word or phrase that describes one thing in terms of another and is not meant to be understood on a literal level. Figures of speech always involve some sort of imaginative comparison between seemingly unlike things.

Some 250 different types of figures of speech have been identified, but the most common are the **simile** ("My love is like a red, red rose"), the **metaphor** ("The Lord is my shepherd"), and **personification** ("Death, be not proud").

See also Hyperbole, Metaphor, Metonymy, Oxymoron, Personification, Simile, Symbol.

FLASHBACK   A scene in a movie, play, short story, novel, or narrative poem that interrupts the present action of the plot to "flash backward" and tell what happened at an earlier time. "The Demon Lover" by

Elizabeth Bowen (Collection 13) includes a flashback that describes Mrs. Drover's farewell to her fiancé twenty-five years before the main action of the story takes place.

See page 1018.

FOIL   A character who sets off another character by strong contrast. This contrast emphasizes the differences between two characters, bringing out the distinctive qualities in each. In *Macbeth* (Collection 4), Banquo is a foil to Macbeth. Though the witches prophesy similar fame for both Macbeth and Banquo, only Macbeth's appetite for power is excited by the prediction; Banquo remains loyal to the king.

FORESHADOWING   The use of clues to hint at what is going to happen later in the plot. Foreshadowing arouses the reader's curiosity and builds up **suspense.** In *Macbeth* (Collection 4), the witches' prophecies foreshadow Macbeth's tragic end. Foreshadowing also occurs in Elizabeth Bowen's "The Demon Lover" (Collection 13) when Mrs. Drover imagines "spectral glitters in the place of" her fiancé's eyes, and when we learn that she made an "unnatural promise" to him—that she "could not have plighted a more sinister troth."

See pages 333, 813.
See also Suspense.

FRAME STORY   An introductory narrative within which one or more of the characters proceed to tell a story. Perhaps the best-known example of stories contained in a frame story is the Persian collection called *The Thousand and One Nights.* In English literature, Geoffrey Chaucer's *The Canterbury Tales* (Collection 2) uses a frame story involving a group of people on a pilgrimage; within the narrative frame, each of the pilgrims then tells his or her own story. Giovanni Boccaccio's *Decameron* (Collection 2) contains another notable example of the frame-story device.

See pages 99, 103, 153.

FREE VERSE   Poetry that has no regular meter or rhyme scheme. Free verse usually relies instead on the natural **rhythms** of ordinary speech. Poets writing in free verse may use **alliteration, internal rhyme, onomatopoeia,** and other musical devices to achieve their effects. They may also place great emphasis on **imagery.** Matthew Arnold's "Dover Beach" (Collection 11) is an early example of free verse, and T. S. Eliot's poems, including "The Hollow Men" (Collection 12), are especially fine and famous examples. Much of today's poetry is written in free verse: Margaret Atwood's "Mushrooms" (Collection 13) is one contemporary example.

See page 1050.

GOTHIC   A term used to describe literary works that contain primitive, medieval, wild, mysterious, or natural elements. Such elements were frowned upon by eighteenth-century neoclassicists but hailed by the Romantic writers of the following era. The **Gothic novel,** a genre popular in the late eighteenth and early nineteenth centuries, is chiefly characterized by gloomy settings and an atmosphere of terror and mystery. Mary Wollstonecraft Shelley's *Frankenstein* is one of the most widely known Gothic novels.

See pages 516, 606, 636, 728.

HYPERBOLE   A figure of speech that uses exaggeration to express strong emotion or create a comic effect. While hyperbole (also known as **overstatement**) does not express the *literal* truth, it is often used in the service of truth to capture a sense of intensity or to emphasize the essential nature of something. For instance, if you claim that it was 250 degrees in the shade, you are using hyperbole to express the truth that it was miserably hot.

See pages 245, 500.

IAMBIC PENTAMETER   A line of poetry made up of five iambs. An **iamb** is a metrical foot, or unit of measure, consisting of an unstressed syllable followed by a stressed syllable (˘ ´). The word *suggest,* for example, is made up of one iamb. *Pentameter* derives from the Greek words *penta* (five) and *meter* (measure). Here are two lines from John Keats's "Ode to a Nightingale" (Collection 9) that are written in iambic pentameter:

> Forlorn! the very word is like a bell
>> To toll me back from thee to my sole self!

Iambic pentameter is by far the most common verse line in English poetry. Shakespeare's sonnets and plays, for example, are written primarily in this meter. Many modern poets, such as W. H. Auden (Collection 14), have continued to use iambic pentameter. Other than **free verse,** it is the poetic meter that sounds the most like natural speech.

See pages 99, 216, 318, 450.
See also Blank Verse.

IMAGERY   Language that appeals to the senses. Most images are visual—that is, they appeal to the sense of sight. But imagery can also appeal to the senses of hearing, touch, taste, or smell. While imagery is an element in all types of writing, it is especially important in poetry, as in these lines from John Keats's "Sleep and Poetry":

> What is more gentle than a wind in summer?
> What is more soothing than the pretty hummer
> That stays one moment in an open flower,
> And buzzes cheerily from bower to bower?
> What is more tranquil than a musk-rose blowing
> In a green island, far from all men's knowing?

See pages 127, 384, 389, 415, 759, 843, 1109.

INCREMENTAL REPETITION   A device widely used in ballads whereby a line or lines are repeated with slight variations from stanza to stanza. Each repetition advances the plot of the narrative. Incremental repetition is used in the folk ballad "Lord Randall" (Collection 2).

See page 96.

IN MEDIAS RES   The technique of starting a story in the middle and then using a flashback to tell what happened earlier. *In medias res* is Latin for "in the middle of things." Traditional epics begin *in medias res.* For example, John Milton's *Paradise Lost* (Collection 5) opens with Satan and his cohorts in Hell, after the war in Heaven and their fall, events that are recounted later in a flashback.

INTERIOR MONOLOGUE See Stream of Consciousness.

IRONY **A contrast or discrepancy between expectation and reality—between what is said and what is really meant, between what is expected and what really happens, or between what appears to be true and what really is true.**

    Verbal irony occurs when a writer or speaker says one thing but really means something quite different—often the opposite of what he or she has said. If you tell your friend that you "just love being kept waiting in the rain," you are using verbal irony. A classic example of verbal irony is Jonathan Swift's suggestion in *A Modest Proposal* (Collection 6) that the Irish solve their poverty and overpopulation problems by selling their babies as food to their English landlords.

    Situational irony occurs when what actually happens is the opposite of what is expected or appropriate. In James Joyce's story "Araby" (Collection 13), the boy hears about a bazaar called Araby and imagines that it will be a splendid, exotic place. Yet when he arrives, he finds that in reality Araby is cheap and commonplace.

    Dramatic irony occurs when the audience or the reader knows something important that a character in a play or story does not know. Forceful dramatic irony occurs at several points in Shakespeare's *Macbeth* (Collection 4). One example is in Act II, Scene 4: Macduff suspects that Duncan has been murdered by his own sons, but the audience knows that Macbeth is the murderer. Dramatic irony is also a powerful device in William Blake's "The Chimney Sweeper" from *Songs of Innocence* (Collection 8). The speaker is a child who believes what he has been told—that "if all do their duty they need not fear harm." But the reader, who is not so innocent, realizes that this is not so.

See pages 129, 487, 501, 991, 1069, 1081, 1138.

JOURNAL **A day-by-day record of events and personal impressions kept by an individual.** A journal is somewhat less intimate than a **diary** and more strictly chronological than an **autobiography,** which can jump back and forth in time in order to tell a coherent story or emphasize a particular theme. The term *journal* is also applied to periodicals that contain news or matters of current interest. In *A Journal of the Plague Year* (Collection 7), Daniel Defoe created a fictional journal.

See pages 557, 582, 583.
See *also* Autobiography, Diary.

KENNING **In Anglo-Saxon poetry, a metaphorical phrase or compound word used to name a person, place, thing, or event indirectly.** *Beowulf* (Collection 1) includes the kennings "whale-road" for the sea and "shepherd of evil" for Grendel.

See page 49.
See *also* Epithet.

LITERARY BALLAD See Ballad.

LYRIC POETRY **Poetry that focuses on expressing emotions or thoughts, rather than on telling a story.** Most lyrics are short, and they usually imply rather than directly state a single strong emotion. The term *lyric* comes from the Greek. In ancient Greece, lyric poems were recited to the accompaniment of a stringed instrument called the lyre. Today, poets still try to make their lyrics melodious, but they rely only on the musical effects they can create with words (such as **rhyme, rhythm, alliteration,** and **onomatopoeia**). Alexander Pushkin's "I Have Visited Again," William Wordsworth's "Tintern Abbey" (both in Collection 8), and Matthew Arnold's "Dover Beach" (Collection 11) are all lyric poems.

See pages 629, 631, 672, 1033.

METAPHOR **A figure of speech that makes a comparison between two seemingly unlike things without using a connective word *like, as, than,* or *resembles*.** You are using a metaphor if you say you're "at the end of your rope" or describe two political candidates as "running neck and neck."

    Some metaphors are **directly** stated, like Percy Bysshe Shelley's comparison "My soul is an enchanted boat." (If he had written, "My soul is *like* an enchanted boat," he would have been using a **simile.**) Other metaphors are **implied,** like John Suckling's line "Time shall molt away his wings." The words *molt* and *wings* imply a comparison between time and a bird shedding its feathers.

    An **extended metaphor** is a metaphor that is extended, or developed, over several lines of writing or even throughout an entire poem. In the following stanza, from "My Beloved Is Mine and I Am His" by Francis Quarles, the speaker develops a comparison between two lovers and two separate streams that flow into the same river. (The title and last line allude to the Biblical Song of Songs.)

    Even like two little bank-dividing brooks,
        That wash the pebbles with their wanton
            streams,
    And having ranged and searched a thousand
            nooks,
        Meet both at length in silver-breasted Thames
        Where in greater current they conjoin:
    So I my best-beloved's am, so he is mine.

    A **dead metaphor** is a metaphor that has become so common that we no longer even notice that it is a figure of speech. Our everyday language is filled with dead metaphors, such as *foot of the bed, bone of contention,* and *mouth of the river.*

    A **mixed metaphor** is the incongruous mixture of two or more metaphors. Mixed metaphors are usually unintentional and often conjure up ludicrous images: "If you put your money on that horse, you'll be barking up the wrong tree."

See pages 214, 841, 851, 1117.

METAPHYSICAL CONCEIT See Conceit.

METAPHYSICAL POETRY **A term applied to the poetry of John Donne, Andrew Marvell, and other seventeenth-century poets who wrote in a similarly difficult and abstract style.** Metaphysical poetry, which is intellectual and detached in contrast to the Elizabethan love poetry that preceded it, is distinguished by ingenious, obscure imagery, philosophical meditation, rough-sounding meter, and verbal wit.

See pages 246, 247.

METER **A generally regular pattern of stressed and unstressed syllables in poetry.** When we want to indicate the metrical pattern of a poem, we mark the stressed syllables with the symbol ' and the unstressed syllables with the symbol ˘. Indicating the metrical pattern of a poem in this way is called **scanning** the poem, or **scansion.** Here is how to scan these lines from William Blake's "The Tyger" (Collection 8):

Tyger! Tyger! burning bright
In the forests of the night

Meter is measured in units called feet. A **foot** consists of one stressed syllable and usually one or more unstressed syllables. The basic metrical feet used in English poetry are the **iamb** (as in cŏnvínce), the **trochee** (as in bórrŏw), the **anapest** (as in cŏntrădíct), the **dactyl** (as in áccŭrăte), and the **spondee** (as in séaweéd). A poem is described as iambic, trochaic, anapestic, dactylic, or spondaic according to what kind of foot appears most often in its lines.

A complete description of a metrical line indicates both the type and number of feet the line contains. For example, a line of iambic pentameter consists of five iambs, while a line of trochaic tetrameter consists of four trochees.

See pages 216, 385, 525, 712, 807.

METONYMY **A figure of speech in which something closely related to a thing or suggested by it is substituted for the thing itself.** You are using metonymy if you call the judiciary "the bench," the king "the crown," the president (or presidential staff) "the White House," or the race track "the turf." Closely related to metonymy is **synecdoche** (si·nek′də·kē), a figure of speech in which a part stands for the whole, as in "our daily bread," meaning food.

MOCK EPIC **A comic narrative poem that parodies the epic by treating a trivial subject in a lofty, grand manner.** A mock epic uses dignified language, elaborate figures of speech, and supernatural intervention. The style of the mock epic is called **mock heroic** (and short mock epics are often called mock heroics). Alexander Pope's The Rape of the Lock (Collection 6) is considered the supreme mock epic in the English language.

See page 526.

MOOD See Atmosphere.

MOTIF **In literature, a word, character, object, image, metaphor, or idea that recurs in a work or in several works.** The rose is a motif that runs through many love poems. The motif of ill-fitting clothes appears throughout Shakespeare's Macbeth (Collection 4). It starts in Act I, Scene 3, when Macbeth asks Ross: "The Thane of Cawdor lives: why do you dress me / In borrowed robes?" This is soon followed by Banquo's observation: "New honors come upon him, / Like our strange garments, cleave not to their mold / But with the aid of use." The motif of ill-fitting clothes reaches its culmination in Act V, Scene 2, when Angus says of Macbeth: "Now does he feel his title / Hang loose about him, like a giant's robe / Upon a dwarfish thief." A motif almost always bears an important relationship to the **theme** of a work of literature.

MOTIVATION **The reasons for or forces behind the action of a character.** Motivation is revealed through a combination of the character's desires and moral nature with the circumstances in which he or she is placed. In Shakespeare's Macbeth (Collection 4), the witches' prophecy and Macbeth's overweening ambition combine to provide the motivation for his killing of the king.

See page 948.
See also Character.

MYTH **An anonymous traditional story that usually serves to explain a belief, custom, or mysterious natural phenomenon.** Most myths grew out of religious rituals, and almost all of them involve the exploits of gods and heroes. Such myths make it possible to understand and cope with things beyond human control. Every culture has its own **mythology,** but in the Western world, the most important myths have been those of ancient Greece and Rome. In twentieth-century literature, **allusions** to myths are often **ironic,** intended to reveal how diminished humanity has become in comparison with grand mythological figures.

See pages 368, 1081, 1105, 1108.

NARRATOR **One who tells, or narrates, a story.** In fiction, the narrator occupies any one of a variety of relations to the events described: from the center of the action to a distant, even objective, observer. A narrator may also be reliable or unreliable—if unreliable, the reader is made aware that the narrator's perceptions and interpretations of the action are different from those of the author. Such unreliable narrators can be deceitful or bumbling, but are often just naive characters—like Larry, the young narrator who humorously misunderstands much of the story's action in Frank O'Connor's "My Oedipus Complex" (Collection 14).

See pages 557, 714, 857, 1031.
See also Point of View.

NEOCLASSICISM **The revival of classical standards and forms during the late seventeenth and eighteenth centuries.** The neoclassicists valued the classical ideals of order, reason, balance, harmony, clarity, and restraint. In particular, they studied and tried to emulate the Latin poets Horace and Virgil. Alexander Pope (Collection 6) and John Dryden (Collection 7) were leaders of the neoclassical movement in England.

See pages 469, 580.

NOVEL **A long fictional prose narrative, usually of more than fifty thousand words.** In general, the novel uses the same basic literary elements as the short story: **plot, character, setting, theme,** and **point of view.** The novel's length usually permits these elements to be more fully developed than they are in the short story. However, this is not always true of the modern novel. Some are basically character studies, with only the barest plot structures. Others reveal little about their characters and concentrate instead on setting or tone or even the language of the novel itself.

Some of the greatest novels in English literature are *Tom Jones* by Henry Fielding, *Pride and Prejudice* by Jane Austen, *Jane Eyre* by Charlotte Brontë, *David Copperfield* and *Great Expectations* by Charles Dickens, *Middlemarch* by George Eliot, *Jude the Obscure* by Thomas Hardy, *Lord Jim* by Joseph Conrad, *Sons and Lovers* by D. H. Lawrence, and *Ulysses* by James Joyce.

See pages 482, 516, 726, 727, 795, 859, 916.

OCTAVE **An eight-line stanza or poem or the first eight lines of an Italian, or Petrarchan, sonnet.** The usual rhyme scheme of the octave in this type of sonnet is *abbaabba*. The octave, which is sometimes called the **octet,** is followed by a six-line **sestet** with the rhyme scheme *cdecde* or *cdcdcd*.

See pages 220, 838.
See also Sonnet.

ODE **A complex, generally long lyric poem on a serious subject.** In English poetry, there are basically two types of odes. One is highly formal and dignified in style and is generally written for ceremonial or public occasions. This type of ode derives from the choral odes of the classical Greek poet Pindar. John Dryden's "Song for St. Cecilia's Day" is an English version of the Pindaric ode. The other type of ode derives from those written by the Latin poet Horace, and it is much more personal and reflective. In English poetry, it is exemplified by the intimate, meditative odes of such Romantic poets as Wordsworth, Keats, and Shelley (Collections 8 and 9).

See pages 482, 672, 737.

ONOMATOPOEIA **The use of a word whose sound imitates or suggests its meaning.** Many familiar words, such as *clap, squish, sizzle,* and *wheeze,* are onomatopoeic. In poetry, onomatopoeia can reinforce meaning while creating evocative and musical effects. The following lines, from Alfred, Lord Tennyson's "Mariana," contain several imitative sounds:

> The sparrow's chirrup on the roof,
>   The slow clock ticking, and the sound
> Which to the wooing wind aloof
>   The poplar made, did all confound
> Her sense. . . .

See pages 738, 927, 1037, 1050.

OTTAVA RIMA **An eight-line stanza in iambic pentameter with the rhyme scheme *abababcc*.** The form developed in Italy and was popularized by the fourteenth-century Italian poet Giovanni Boccaccio. The most famous example of ottava rima in English poetry is Lord Byron's *Don Juan* (Collection 9). William Butler Yeats's "Sailing to Byzantium" is another notable example.

See page 714.

OXYMORON **A figure of speech that combines apparently contradictory or incongruous ideas.** "Bitter sweet," "cruel kindness," and "eloquent silence" are oxymorons. The classic oxymoron "wise fool" is almost a literal translation of the term from the Greek—*oxys* means "sharp" or "keen," and *moros* means "foolish." A famous oxymoron in literature is John Milton's description of Hell in *Paradise Lost* (Collection 5):

> No light, but rather darkness visible . . .

See page 924.

PARABLE **A short, allegorical story that teaches a moral or religious lesson about life.** The most famous parables in Western literature are those told by Jesus in the Gospels of the Bible.

See page 425.

PARADOX **An apparent contradiction that is actually true.** A paradox may be a statement or a situation; as a statement, it is a figure of speech. The metaphysical and Cavalier poets of the seventeenth century (Collection 3) made brilliant use of paradoxes, as in this famous example from John Donne's "Death Be Not Proud" (Collection 3):

> One short sleep past, we wake eternally,
> And death shall be no more; Death, thou shalt die.

The speaker in the cartoon below doesn't understand the famous series of paradoxes that open *A Tale of Two Cities* by Charles Dickens.

See pages 218, 254, 266, 318, 738.

"I wish you would make up your mind, Mr. Dickens. Was it the best of times or was it the worst of times? It could scarcely have been both."

PARALLELISM **The repetition of words, phrases, or sentences that have the same grammatical structure or that restate a similar idea.** Parallelism is often used in literature meant to be spoken aloud, such as poetry, drama, and speeches, because it can help make lines emotional, rhythmic, and memorable. It is also one of the most important techniques used in Biblical poetry. The parallelism in the following lines, from William Blake's "A Divine Image," heightens their emotional effect and sharpens their meaning:

> Cruelty has a human heart
> And Jealousy a human face;
> Terror the human form divine,
> And Secrecy the human dress.

> *See pages 405, 421, 521, 655.*

PARODY   **The imitation of a work of literature, art, or music for amusement or instruction.** Parodies usually use exaggeration or inappropriate subject matter to make a serious style seem ridiculous. Alexander Pope's *The Rape of the Lock* (Collection 6) is a parody of such serious and sweeping epics as the *Iliad* and the *Aeneid*. Richard Armour's portrayal of *Macbeth*'s famous witches (Collection 4) is a contemporary example of parody.

> *See pages 742, 920, 1155.*

PASTORAL   **A type of poem that depicts rustic life in idyllic, idealized terms.** The term *pastoral* comes from the Latin word for shepherd, and originally pastorals were about shepherds, nymphs, and rustic life. Today, the term has a looser meaning and refers to any poem that portrays an idyllic rural setting or that expresses nostalgia for an age or place of lost innocence. The most famous traditional English pastoral is Christopher Marlowe's "The Passionate Shepherd to His Love," which is satirized in Sir Walter Raleigh's "The Nymph's Reply to the Shepherd" (both in Collection 3). Examples of untraditional pastorals include William Wordsworth's "Tintern Abbey" (Collection 8), William Butler Yeats's "The Lake Isle of Innisfree" (Collection 13), and Dylan Thomas's "Fern Hill" (Collection 13).

> *See pages 233, 520, 606.*

PERSONIFICATION   **A kind of metaphor in which a nonhuman thing or quality is talked about as if it were human.** In these lines, from Percy Bysshe Shelley's "A Dirge," the speaker describes the wind as if it were capable of feeling the human emotion of grief:

> Rough wind, that moanest loud
> Grief too sad for song

> *See pages 669, 960.*
> *See also Apostrophe, Figure of Speech, Metaphor.*

PLOT   **The series of related events that make up a story or drama.** The plot is the underlying structure of a story. Most plots are built on these "bare bones": A **basic situation,** or **exposition,** introduces the characters, setting, and, usually, the story's major **conflict.** Out of this basic situation, **complications** develop that intensify the conflict. **Suspense** mounts until a **climax**—the tensest or most exciting part of the plot—is reached, where something happens to determine the outcome of the conflict. Finally, all the prob-

lems or mysteries of the plot are unraveled in the **resolution,** or **denouement.**

> *See pages 153, 388, 1069, 1098.*
> *See also Climax.*

POINT OF VIEW   **The vantage point from which a writer tells a story.** There are three main points of view: **first-person, limited third-person,** and **omniscient third-person.**

In the **first-person point of view,** the narrator is a character in the story. Using the pronoun *I,* this narrator tells us his or her own experiences but cannot reveal any other character's private thoughts. When we read a story told in the first person, we hear and see only what the narrator hears and sees. We may have to interpret what this narrator says because a first-person narrator may or may not be objective, honest, or perceptive. For example, in Frank O'Connor's "My Oedipus Complex" (Collection 14), the narrator is a young boy whose understanding and insight are limited by his age: He believes that babies are purchased for seventeen shillings.

In the **limited third-person point of view,** the narrator is outside the story—like an omniscient narrator—but tells the story from the vantage point of only one character. The narrator can enter the mind of this chosen character but cannot tell what any other characters are thinking except by observation. This narrator also can go only where the chosen character goes. For example, "In the Shadow of War" by Ben Okri (Collection 12) is told entirely from the point of view of Omovo, the main character. We experience the stupifying summer heat, the mysteriousness of the veiled woman, and the horror of the gruesome river scene through Omovo's eyes alone.

In the **omniscient** (or **"all-knowing"**) **point of view,** the person telling the story knows everything that's going on in the story. This omniscient narrator is outside the story, a godlike observer who can tell us what all the characters are thinking and feeling, as well as what is happening anywhere in the story. For example, in "The Rocking-Horse Winner" by D. H. Lawrence (Collection 13), the narrator enters into the thoughts and secrets of every character, revealing both the "hard little place" in the mother's heart and Paul's determination to "compel her attention" by being lucky.

> *See pages 646, 970, 990, 993, 1023.*
> *See also Narrator, Stream of Consciousness.*

PROTAGONIST   **The main character in fiction, drama, or narrative poetry.** The protagonist is the character we focus our attention on—the person whose conflict sets the plot in motion. (The character or force that blocks the protagonist is called the **antagonist.**) In *Beowulf* (Collection 1), the title character is the protagonist and the monster Grendel his antagonist. Most protagonists are **rounded, dynamic** characters who change in some important way by the end of the story. Whatever the protagonist's weaknesses, we still usually identify with his or her conflict and care about how it is resolved.

PUN   **A play on the multiple meanings of a word or on two words that sound alike but have different**

meanings. Many jokes and riddles are based on puns. ("Why was Cleopatra so negative? Answer: Because she was the queen of denial.") Shakespeare was one of the greatest punsters of all time. Some of his puns are humorous, but others are more serious and subtle wordplays. A sinister pun occurs in Act II, Scene 2, of *Macbeth* (Collection 4), after Macbeth has murdered Duncan:

> I'll gild the faces of the grooms withal,
> For it must seem their guilt.

Here, Lady Macbeth plays on the words *gild* (to coat something with gold leaf) and *guilt*.

See page 1037.

QUATRAIN **A four-line stanza or poem or a group of four lines unified by a rhyme scheme.** The quatrain is the most common verse unit in English poetry. This quatrain from Alfred, Lord Tennyson's *In Memoriam A.H.H.* (Collection 10) has the rhyme scheme *abba* (sometimes called the envelope stanza):

> Thy voice is on the rolling air;
> I hear thee where the waters run;
> Thou standest in the rising sun,
> And in the setting thou art fair.

See pages 96, 220.

REALISM **In literature and art, the attempt to depict people and things as they really are, without idealization.** Realism as a movement developed during the mid–nineteenth century as a reaction against Romanticism. Realist writers believed that fiction should truthfully depict the harsh, gritty reality of everyday life without beautifying, sentimentalizing, or romanticizing it. The Norwegian playwright Henrik Ibsen was among the first to introduce realism to the stage. The English novelists Charles Dickens, George Eliot, Thomas Hardy, and Joseph Conrad are all considered realists.

See pages 799, 1068.
See also Romanticism.

REFRAIN **A repeated word, phrase, line, or group of lines.** While refrains are most common in poetry and songs, they are sometimes used in prose, particularly speeches. Refrains are used to create rhythm, build suspense, or emphasize important words or ideas.

See pages 90, 96.

RESOLUTION See Plot.

RHYME **The repetition of accented vowel sounds and all sounds following them in words that are close together in a poem.** *Park* and *bark* rhyme, as do *sorrow* and *borrow*. The most common type of rhyme, **end rhyme,** occurs at the ends of lines. **Internal rhyme** occurs within lines. Both types are used throughout *The Rime of the Ancient Mariner* by Samuel Taylor Coleridge (Collection 8), contributing to the poem's bouncy, songlike rhythm:

> The fair breeze blew, the white foam flew,
> The furrow followed free;
> We were the first that ever burst
> Into that silent sea.

When words sound similar but do not rhyme exactly, they are called **approximate rhymes** (or **half rhymes, slant rhymes,** or **imperfect rhymes**). In the following stanza, from W. H. Auden's "Five Songs," *began/gun* and *flush/flash* rhyme by means of **consonance,** while *began/flash* and *flush/gun* rhyme (very loosely) by means of **assonance:**

> That night when joy began
> Our narrowest veins to flush,
> We waited for the flash
> Of morning's leveled gun.

The pattern of rhymed lines in a poem is called its **rhyme scheme.** A rhyme scheme is indicated by giving each new rhyme a new letter of the alphabet. For example, the rhyme scheme of Coleridge's lines is *abcb*. There are two interlocking rhyme schemes in Auden's stanza. The one based on consonance is *abba;* the one based on assonance is *abab*.

See pages 96, 149, 221, 683, 807, 840, 930.

RHYTHM **The alternation of stressed and unstressed syllables in language.** Rhythm occurs naturally in all forms of spoken and written language. The most obvious kind of rhythm is produced by **meter,** the regular pattern of stressed and unstressed syllables found in some poetry. But writers can also create less structured rhythms by using rhyme, repetition, pauses, and variations in line length and by balancing long and short words or phrases. (Poetry that is written without any regular meter or rhyme scheme is called **free verse.**) The rhythm of the following lines, from Gerard Manley Hopkins's "Pied Beauty" (Collection 10), reinforces their meaning. The words themselves seem dappled, as if a painter's brush has stippled them onto the page:

> All things counter, original, spare, strange;
> Whatever is fickle, freckled (who knows how?)
> With swift, slow; sweet, sour; adazzle, dim

See pages 90, 712, 1050.
See also Free Verse, Meter.

RISING ACTION See Climax.

ROMANCE **Historically, a medieval verse narrative chronicling the adventures of a brave knight or other hero who must undertake a quest and overcome great danger for love of a noble lady or high ideal.** Such a heroic character is bound by the code of **chivalry,** which emphasizes loyalty to his lord and ready service to the oppressed. He also must adhere to the philosophy of **courtly love,** an idealized view of the relationship between the sexes in which a knight performs brave deeds to win the approval of his lady.

Today, the term *romance* has come to mean any story that presents a world that is happier, more exciting, or more heroic than the real world. Characters in romances "live happily ever after" in a world where good always triumphs over evil. Many of today's most popular novels, movies, TV shows, and even cartoons are essentially romances. *Sir Gawain and the Green Knight,* Sir Thomas Malory's *Le Morte Darthur* (both in Collection 2), and Edmund Spenser's *The Faerie Queene* (Collection 3) are famous English romances.

See pages 82, 158, 167, 826.

ROMANTICISM **A literary, artistic, and philosophical movement that developed during the late eighteenth and early nineteenth centuries as a reaction against neoclassicism.** While classicism and neoclassicism emphasize reason, order, harmony, and restraint, Romanticism emphasizes emotion, imagination, intuition, freedom, personal experience, the beauty of nature, the primitive, the exotic, and even the grotesque. However, many critics feel that the traditional opposition between Romanticism and classicism is all too often forced and exaggerated.

In English literature, William Blake, Samuel Taylor Coleridge, William Wordsworth, Percy Bysshe Shelley, John Keats, Lord Byron (all in Collection 8 or 9), Mary Wollstonecraft Shelley, and Sir Walter Scott are the leading Romantic writers.

See pages 630, 635, 672.

RUN-ON LINE **A line of poetry that does not contain a pause or conclusion at the end, but rather continues on to the next line.** Run-on lines force the reader on to the next line. Only with the next line do they form a grammatical unit and thus make complete sense. Such lines are said to exhibit **enjambment** (French for "striding over"). The following lines from Margaret Atwood's "Mushrooms" (Collection 13) are run-on lines:

> Here is the handful
> of shadow I have brought back to you:
> this decay, this hope, this mouth-
> ful of dirt, this poetry.

See page 662.
See also End-stopped Line.

SARCASM **A kind of particularly cutting irony, in which praise is used tauntingly to indicate its opposite in meaning.** The speaker's tone of voice can also be an important clue in understanding this kind of irony. When a mudsoaked, windblown friend arrives for dinner, one might say sarcastically, "Why, don't you look lovely!"

See pages 501, 991.

SATIRE **A kind of writing that ridicules human weakness, vice, or folly in order to bring about social reform.** Satires often try to persuade the reader to do or believe something by showing the opposite view as absurd or—even more forcefully—vicious and inhumane. Among the most brilliant and scathing satirists in English literature are Geoffrey Chaucer, Alexander Pope, John Dryden, Jonathan Swift, Jane Austen, George Bernard Shaw, and Evelyn Waugh.

See pages 481, 495, 500, 537, 714.

SCANSION *See* Meter.

SESTET **A six-line stanza or poem or the last six lines of an Italian, or Petrarchan, sonnet.** The usual rhyme scheme of the sestet in an Italian sonnet is *cdecde* or *cdcdcd*. It follows an eight-line **octave** with the rhyme scheme *abbaabba*.

See pages 220, 838.

SETTING **The time and place of a story or play.** Usually the setting is established early in a story. It may be presented immediately through descriptive details, as in Anita Desai's "Games at Twilight" (Collection 14), or it may be revealed more gradually, as in Rudyard Kipling's "The Mark of the Beast" (Collection 11). Setting often contributes greatly to a story's emotional effect. The wild heath at the opening of Shakespeare's *Macbeth* (Collection 4) produces an atmosphere of horror, while the green valley in William Wordsworth's "Tintern Abbey" (Collection 8) creates a contemplative calm. Setting may also play a role in a story's conflict, as the fortresslike suburban houses do in Nadine Gordimer's "Once upon a Time" (Collection 15). Two of the most important functions of setting are to reveal character and to suggest a theme, as the setting of blitzed London does in Graham Greene's "The Destructors" (Collection 12).

See pages 606, 675, 948, 990, 1042.
See also Atmosphere.

SHORT STORY **A brief work of fiction.** The short story generally has a simpler plot than a **novel** and often reveals character through significant moments, or **epiphanies,** rather than through the accretion of many incidents or detailed descriptions.

See page 1068.

SIMILE **A figure of speech that makes a comparison between two seemingly unlike things by using a connective word such as *like, as, than, or resembles.*** Here is a simile from William Wordsworth's "It Is a Beauteous Evening, Calm and Free" that makes a connection between two sound images:

> The holy time is quiet as a Nun
> Breathless with adoration. . . .

An **epic simile,** also called a **Homeric simile,** is an extended simile in which many parallels are made between two dissimilar things.

See pages 247, 449, 851, 1117.
See also Figure of Speech, Metaphor.

SOLILOQUY **A long speech in which a character who is usually alone onstage expresses his or her private thoughts or feelings.** The soliloquy is an old dramatic convention that was particularly popular in Shakespeare's day. Perhaps the most famous soliloquy is the "To be or not to be" speech in Shakespeare's play *Hamlet.* Another major soliloquy occurs in Act V, Scene 5, of *Macbeth* (Collection 4), when Macbeth bewails his wife's death in the celebrated "Tomorrow, and tomorrow, and tomorrow" speech.

See page 383.

SONNET **A fourteen-line lyric poem, usually written in iambic pentameter, that has one of several rhyme schemes.** There are two major types of sonnets. The oldest sonnet form is the **Italian sonnet,** also called the **Petrarchan sonnet** (after the fourteenth-century Italian poet Petrarch, who popularized the form). The Petrarchan sonnet is divided into two parts: an eight-line **octave** with the rhyme scheme *abbaabba* and a six-line **sestet** with the rhyme scheme *cdecde* or *cdcdcd.* The octave usually presents a problem, poses a question, or expresses an idea, which the sestet, or **turn,** then resolves, answers, or drives home. John Donne's sonnets (Collection 3) and John Keats's "On First Looking into Chapman's Homer" (Collection 9) are written in the Italian form.

The other major sonnet form, which was widely used by Shakespeare, is called the **Shakespearean sonnet,** or the **English sonnet** (Collection 3). It has three four-line units, or **quatrains,** followed by a concluding two-line unit, or **couplet.** The organization of thought in the Shakespearean sonnet usually corresponds to this structure. The three quatrains often express related ideas or examples, while the couplet sums up the poet's conclusion or message. The most common rhyme scheme for the Shakespearean sonnet is *abab cdcd efef gg.*

A third type of sonnet, the **Spenserian sonnet,** was developed by Edmund Spenser (Collection 3). Like the Shakespearean sonnet, the Spenserian sonnet is divided into three quatrains and a couplet, but it uses a rhyme scheme that links the quatrains: *abab bcbc cdcd ee.*

A group of sonnets on a related theme is called a **sonnet sequence** or a **sonnet cycle.**

See pages 219, 223, 268, 672, 746, 838.

SPEAKER **The imaginary voice, or persona, assumed by the author of a poem.** This voice is often not identified immediately or directly. Rather, the reader gradually comes to understand that a unique voice is speaking and that this speaker's characteristics must be interpreted as they are revealed. This process is an especially important part of reading a **lyric poem.**

See pages 264, 635, 759, 763, 1033.

SPENSERIAN STANZA **A nine-line stanza with the rhyme scheme *ababbcbcc.*** The first eight lines of the stanza are in iambic pentameter, and the ninth line is an **alexandrine**—that is, a line of iambic hexameter. The form was created by Edmund Spenser for his long poem *The Faerie Queene* (Collection 3). Several English Romantic poets have used the Spenserian stanza, including John Keats, Percy Bysshe Shelley, Lord Byron, and Robert Burns (Collections 8 and 9).

See pages 221, 725.

SPRUNG RHYTHM **A term coined by Gerard Manley Hopkins to designate his unconventional use of poetic meter.** Instead of the regular, musical **meter** of most poetry, Hopkins uses sounds that impede smooth reading and echo the sound of Anglo-Saxon poetry, which greatly influenced him. Sprung rhythm is based on the stressed syllables in a line without regard for the number of unstressed syllables; it also makes frequent use of **alliteration** and inverted syntax.

See page 840.

STANZA **A group of consecutive lines in a poem that form a single unit.** A stanza in a poem is something like a paragraph in prose: It often expresses a unit of thought. A stanza may consist of only one line or of any number of lines beyond that. The word *stanza* is Italian for "stopping place" or "place to rest."

See page 220.

STREAM OF CONSCIOUSNESS **A writing style that tries to depict the random flow of thoughts, emotions, memories, and associations rushing through a character's mind.** The term **interior monologue** is often used interchangeably with "stream of consciousness." James Joyce (Collection 13) and Virginia Woolf (Collection 15) were among the first to experiment with the stream-of-consciousness style in their novels.

See page 993.

STYLE **The manner in which writers or speakers say what they wish to say.** An author's style simultaneously expresses an individual's ideas and his or her unique way of expressing them. Style is closely connected to **diction,** or word choice, and, depending on what the author wants to communicate, can be formal or casual, plain or ornate, abstract or concrete, as well as comic, poetic, forceful, journalistic, and so on. Sir Francis Bacon (Collection 5) and Samuel Johnson (Collection 7) are both often cited as exemplars of style.

See pages 457, 578.
See also Diction.

SUSPENSE **The uncertainty or anxiety we feel about what is going to happen next in a story.** Writers often create suspense by dropping hints or clues that something—especially something bad—is going to happen. In "The Demon Lover" by Elizabeth Bowen (Collection 13), we begin to feel suspense when Mrs. Drover receives a mysterious letter that makes her lips "go white"; our anxiety increases sharply when the flashback reveals that the letter writer is her old fiancé; and our suspense reaches a climax when she escapes into a taxi and we discover who the driver is.

See pages 332, 333.

SYMBOL **A person, place, thing, or event that stands both for itself and for something beyond itself.** Many symbols have become widely recognized: A lion is a symbol of power; a dove is a symbol of peace. These established symbols are sometimes called **public symbols.** But writers often invent new, personal symbols, whose meaning is revealed in their work. For example, the old house in Graham Greene's "The Destructors" (Collection 12) is a symbol of civilization and beauty.

See pages 167, 393, 647, 739, 982, 996, 1061.

SYMBOLISM **A literary movement that began in France during the late nineteenth century and advocated the use of highly personal symbols to suggest ideas, emotions, and moods.** The French Symbolists believed that emotions are fleeting, individual, and essentially inexpressible—and that therefore the poet is forced to suggest meaning rather than directly express it. Many twentieth-century writers were influenced by the Symbolists, including T. S. Eliot, William Butler Yeats, James Joyce, Dylan Thomas, and Virginia Woolf (Collections 12, 13, and 15).

SYNAESTHESIA **In literature, a term used for descriptions of one kind of sensation in terms of another.** For example, color may be described as sound (a "loud" yellow), sound as taste (how "sweet" the sound), odor as tangible (a "sharp" smell), and so on. These lines from John Keats's "Ode to a Nightingale" (Collection 9) describe a sip of wine as tasting of color, motion, sound, and heat:

> Tasting of Flora and the country green,
> Dance, and Provençal song, and sunburnt mirth!
>
> *See page 759.*

SYNECDOCHE See Metonymy.

TALL TALE **A type of folk literature characterized by humorous exaggeration and outlandish plot details.** Although part of the literature of many countries, it is mainly associated with Mark Twain and the American West.

See page 514.

TERCET **A triplet, or stanza of three lines, in which each line ends with the same rhyme.** It is also either of the two three-line groups forming the sestet of a **sonnet.**

See pages 525, 805.

TERZA RIMA **An interlocking, three-line stanza form with the rhyme scheme *aba bcb cdc ded* and so on.** Terza rima is an Italian verse form originally devised by Dante for *The Divine Comedy* (Collection 4). Among the many English poems that borrowed the form, Shelley's "Ode to the West Wind" (Collection 9) is one of the most famous.

See page 738.

THEME **The central idea or insight of a work of literature.** A theme is not the same as the subject of a work, which can usually be expressed in a word or two: old age, ambition, love. The theme is the idea the writer wishes to convey *about* that subject—the writer's view of the world or revelation about human nature. For example, one theme of James Joyce's "Araby" (Collection 13) might be stated this way: One of the painful aspects of growing up is that some of our dreams turn out to be illusions.

A theme may also be different from a **moral,** which is a lesson or rule about how to live. The theme of "Araby" stated above, for example, would not make sense as a moral.

While some stories, poems, and plays have themes that are directly stated, most themes are **implied.** It is up to the reader to piece together all the clues the writer has provided about the work's total meaning.

See pages 231, 959, 1116, 1147.

TONE **The attitude a writer takes toward the reader, a subject, or a character.** Tone is conveyed through the writer's choice of words and details. For example, Jonathan Swift's *A Modest Proposal* (Collection 6) is satiric in tone, while the tone of "Pied Beauty" by Gerard Manley Hopkins (Collection 10) might be described as awed.

See pages 263, 714, 849, 1096.

TRAGEDY **A play, novel, or other narrative depicting serious and important events, in which the main character comes to an unhappy end.** In a tragedy, the main character is usually dignified, courageous, and often high ranking. This character's downfall may be caused by a **tragic flaw**—an error in judgment or character weakness—or the downfall may result from forces beyond his or her control. The **tragic hero** usually wins some self-knowledge and wisdom, even though he or she suffers defeat, possibly even death. Tragedy is distinct from **comedy,** in which an ordinary character overcomes obstacles to get what he or she wants. *Beowulf* (Collection 1), Shakespeare's *Macbeth* (Collection 4), and John Milton's *Paradise Lost* (Collection 5) are all tragedies.

See pages 300, 591.
See also Comedy.

TURN See Sonnet.

TURNING POINT See Climax.

UNDERSTATEMENT **A figure of speech that consists of saying less than what is really meant or saying something with less force than is appropriate.** Understatement is the opposite of **hyperbole** and is a form of **irony.** You are using understatement if you come in from a torrential downpour and say, "It's a bit wet out there," or if you describe a Great Dane as "not exactly a small dog." Understatement can be used to create a kind of deadpan humor, but it can also function as a sustained ironic tone throughout a work, as in W. H. Auden's "The Unknown Citizen" (Collection 14).

See page 501.
See also Hyperbole, Irony.

VERNACULAR See Dialect.

VILLANELLE **A nineteen-line poem divided into five tercets (three-line stanzas), each with the rhyme scheme *aba,* and a final quatrain with the rhyme scheme *abaa.*** Line 1 is repeated entirely to form lines 6, 12, and 18, while line 3 is repeated as lines 9, 15, and 19. Thus, there are only two rhymes in the poem, and the two lines used as **refrains** (lines 1 and 3) are paired as the final couplet. The villanelle was originally used in French pastoral poetry. Dylan Thomas's "Do Not Go Gentle into That Good Night" (Collection 13) is an example of a modern villanelle.

See page 1040.

WIT **A quality of speech or writing that combines verbal cleverness with keen perception, especially of the incongruous.** The definition of *wit* has undergone dramatic changes over the centuries. In the Middle Ages, it meant "common sense"; in the Renaissance, it meant "intelligence"; and in the seventeenth century, it meant "originality of thought." The modern meaning of *wit* began to develop during the eighteenth century with the formulations of John Dryden (Collection 7) and Alexander Pope (Collection 6). In his *Essay on Criticism,* Pope said:

> True wit is Nature to advantage dressed:
> What oft was thought, but ne'er so well expressed

Perhaps the best examples of more modern wit can be found in the works of Oscar Wilde and George Bernard Shaw.

See pages 480, 533, 714.

COMMUNICATIONS HANDBOOK

ACTIVE READING STRATEGIES

Use the following reading strategies to help you discover meaning in what you read and relate that meaning to your life.

PREVIEWING AND SETTING A PURPOSE

Previewing the Text   Preview a reading assignment or a book to get an overview of its organization. Read the title and any information included about the author. If you are assigned a book, flip through the pages and look at the table of contents, the index, and any illustrations, charts, or diagrams. Note the genre of the text—novel, history, biography, short story, play, or essay—and the difficulty of the vocabulary. Finally, consider what you already know about the subject and what you'd like to find out about it.

Setting a Purpose   Before you begin to read, you should establish a clear purpose for reading. Purposes include (1) to be entertained, (2) to find out specific information, (3) to share an experience, (4) to learn about the craft of writing. You may have more than one purpose in mind as you read a particular text. Your purpose can dictate how closely you read and whether you take notes or use other study skills.

Activating Prior Knowledge   As you read, you should use your prior knowledge and experiences to look for connections with the text. For example, as you read Orwell's essay "Shooting an Elephant" (page 1139), you might review what you know about colonialism in Burma and its effects on Burma (Myanmar) even up to the present day.

Constructing a KWL Chart   To help you keep track of your prior knowledge, your purpose in reading, and your new learning, make a three-column chart and use it before, as, and after you read a work. In the first column, write what you already know (K) about the work. In the middle column, write what you want (W) to know. In the last column, record what you learned (L) as a result of your reading.

K	W	L
What I **know**	What I **want** to know	What I **learned**

READING ACTIVELY

Making and Confirming Predictions   For some texts, such as short stories and novels, you should occasionally predict what will happen. To start the process of making predictions, ask yourself questions like *Where will the plot lead? How will the character act when he begins to lose his struggle?* Your answers will be predictions about what you are going to read. For example, in the first paragraph of D. H. Lawrence's "The Rocking Horse Winner" (page 997), the narrator tells you that a woman is incapable of feeling love. At once you should begin to ask questions and make predictions about what else you will learn about this character and what will become of her and, possibly, her children.

Making Inferences   An **inference** is an educated guess. Inferences about a literary work are based on clues in the text and on your own knowledge. For instance, the title of Elizabeth Bowen's story "The Demon Lover" (page 1019) strongly suggests that something preternatural will happen to the main character. Ben Okri's title "In the Shadow of War" (page 971) suggests that the story will have to do with the violence of war.

Conclusions and generalizations are types of inferences. A **conclusion** is a judgment based on evidence in a text. You will probably conclude from the speaker's words in Wilfred Owen's "Dulce et Decorum Est" (page 929) that he is profoundly disillusioned by the patriotic slogans that mask the horror of war. A **generalization** is a broad statement based on specific examples. You might generalize from the selections in the collection of Anglo-Saxon literature that an elegiac strain is characteristic of the imaginative expressions of that period.

Noting Organization   As you read, think about the way the writer presents ideas, people, and events. **Sequential,** or **chronological, order** arranges the events in a historical account or a story in the order in which they occur. You may find words such as *first, then, next, while,* and *finally.* Some great literary works, such as Virginia Woolf's novel *Mrs. Dalloway,* present events in **nonsequential order,** thereby "fragmenting" time. **Spatial order** tells you where one person or thing is in relation to another. Factual information is usually presented in **order of importance,** either from most to least important or from least to most important. **Logical order,** a type of sequential order, organizes ideas in terms of meaning, so that one idea leads directly to the next. In an essay, an argument is best made in logical order, rather than scattering ideas so that a point in paragraph six is explained in paragraph two.

DEALING WITH DIFFICULT TEXTS

When you're having difficulty understanding a text, try one or more of these strategies:

1. **Rereading.** Stop reading and go back to the last point at which you had a grasp on the text. Reread from there.
2. **Reading on.** Keep reading to see whether context clues and/or new information clarify the text.
3. **Pausing to reflect.** Stop and think about what you've read so far. Perhaps construct a graphic organizer.
4. **Asking questions.** Ask *who, what, where, when, why,* and *how* questions about the text.
5. **Using resources.** Use a dictionary or other reference works to clarify the meaning of a passage.

MAKING SURE YOU UNDERSTAND A TEXT

Paraphrasing, outlining, and summarizing are useful strategies to make sure you understand a text. When you **paraphrase,** you restate an entire work or passage in your own words. Paraphrasing helps you to clarify anything that may have been fuzzy as you read. Here is a paraphrase of lines 1–4 of Shakespeare's Sonnet 116 (page 228):

I won't be made to find impediments, or blocks, to the union of two minds that are true to each other. Love doesn't change even when other things are changing. Love doesn't adjust or alter itself even when other things are being altered or changed.

A work of nonfiction, such as Jonathan Swift's "A Modest Proposal" (page 502), can be **outlined** by showing its **main ideas** and **supporting details,** as below:

I. Main idea
  A. Supporting detail
    1. Supporting detail
    2. Supporting detail
  B. Supporting detail
[Etc.]

A **summary** is a concise restatement of the principal ideas and details of a text (usually prose). You can do a summary in different ways—for example, in paragraph form or in a story map like the following:

Story Map

Basic situation
Setting
Main character
His or her problem
Main events or complications
Climax
Resolution

STUDY SKILLS

USING A DICTIONARY

Use a dictionary to find the precise meaning (**denotation**) and usage of words. The elements of a typical entry are explained below.

1. **Entry word.** The entry word shows how the word is spelled (capitalizing the first letter if required) and divided into syllables.
2. **Pronunciation.** Phonetic symbols, sometimes with diacritical marks above them, show how to pronounce the entry word. Accent marks indicate which syllable is stressed. A key to symbols usually appears on every other page.

3. **Part-of-speech label.** This label classifies the entry word as noun, adjective, adverb, and so forth. When a word can be used as more than one part of speech, definitions are grouped by part of speech. The sample entry that follows shows four definitions for *derive* as a transitive verb (*vt.*) and one as an intransitive verb (*vi.*).
4. **Other forms.** Some dictionaries show the spellings of plural forms of nouns, principal parts of verbs (like *-rived'* and *-riv'ing* in the sample), and comparative and superlative forms of adjectives and adverbs.
5. **Word origin.** A word's **etymology** (et'ə·mäl'ə·jē) shows its linguistic history. According to the sample entry, the word *derive* comes from the Middle English word *deriven,* which in turn comes from the Old French word

deriver, which itself comes from the Latin word *derivare,* meaning "to divert." *Derivare* was created by adding the prefix *de-,* meaning "from," to the word *rivus,* meaning "stream." The sample entry shows that additional information on etymology appears in the entry for *rival.*

6. **Definitions.** If a word has more than one meaning, the meanings are numbered or lettered.

7. **Special-usage labels.** These labels identify special meanings or special uses of the word. Here, *Chem.* indicates that the fourth definition is a meaning of *derive* used in chemistry.

8. **Synonyms and antonyms. Synonyms** (words similar in meaning) and **antonyms** (words opposite in meaning) may appear at the end of an entry. Here, **—SYN.** RISE tells you that synonyms for *derive* are given in the entry for *rise.*

9. **Related word forms.** Different forms of the entry word are listed. Usually these are created by the addition of suffixes, such as in *derivable.*

Sample Dictionary Entry

Webster's New World Dictionary of American English, Third College Edition.

USING A THESAURUS

A **thesaurus** is a collection of synonyms. You use a thesaurus to find a word with a specific meaning. There are two basic formats for a thesaurus. The first, developed by Peter Mark Roget (1779–1869), groups words in categories. To use Roget's format, follow these steps:

- In the index, look up the word that expresses the general meaning of the word you are looking for. You may be looking for a synonym of the verb *thin,* for example. Under *thin,* you find the words *dilute, rarefy,* and *weed.*
- Choose the subentry closest to the meaning you have in mind. In this case, suppose you choose *dilute.*
- Note the number that follows the subentry, and find it in the body of the text. There, you will find synonyms of *dilute.*

The second kind of thesaurus presents words in alphabetical order, as in a dictionary:

Sample Thesaurus Entry

commencement, *n.* **1.** [A beginning] —*Syn.* genesis, start, initiation; see **origin** 1, 2. [Graduation ceremony] —*Syn.* convocation, graduation, commencement exercises, services; see **celebration** 1, 2, **ceremony** 2, **graduation.**

©1997 Webster's New World Thesaurus, Third Edition.

USING STUDY GUIDES

A **study guide** works as a reader's companion by providing help in understanding a text. It can clarify points and stimulate thinking. Study guides often include a biography of the author, critical reaction to the work, and analyses of characters, themes, and other literary elements. Many study guides also include suggestions for further reading and viewing.

A study guide usually examines a text in sections. A play by Oscar Wilde, for instance, might be examined scene by scene or act by act. Besides giving a summary of the section, a study guide might include commentary, helpful information, and questions to consider.

RECOGNIZING LOGICAL FALLACIES

When you are reading a piece of writing that aims to persuade you to share an opinion or adopt a course of action, you should be alert to the ways in which the writer argues his or her points. Writers should argue their points logically. Sometimes, however, they use incorrect or fallacious reasoning. Be on the lookout for **fallacies.** They appear at first glance to be based on sound reasoning but in fact contain mistakes of logic. Here are six common fallacies; there are many more.

1. **Circular reasoning or "begging the question."** The writer restates a point just made as if it were a new conclusion. In the sentence *Alison is lazy because she doesn't like to work,* the clause after *because* just restates the opening clause and doesn't tell you why Alison is lazy. The sentence *Alison is lazy because she enjoys sitting around and daydreaming* gives you a reason for Alison's laziness.

2. **Arguing ad hominem ("to the person").** The writer attacks the person or people presenting the issue rather than dealing logically with the issue itself. In the sentence *People who oppose a lower speed limit don't care about children,* "people" who oppose lower speed limits are attacked—but reasons for lowering the speed limit are not given.

3. **Hasty generalization.** The writer draws a conclusion from insufficient evidence or from exceptional or biased evidence. In the sentence *Today's films are loaded with foul language,* the writer incorrectly categorizes all films, failing

to account for the many films that have little or no foul language.

4. **Either-or fallacy** or **false dichotomy.** The writer presents only two alternatives when there are more than two. In the sentence *We have just two choices—either go to the ballgame or sit around the house,* the writer fails to mention additional choices, like seeing a movie.

5. **False analogy.** The writer assumes that because two things are alike in some ways, they must be alike in other ways. Notice the false analogy in the sentence *Since player A and player B are the same height and fast runners, they must have similar batting averages.* The writer ignores other important reasons for a particular batting average.

6. **False cause.** This fallacy is also known as *post hoc, ergo propter hoc,* meaning "after this, therefore because of this." In this fallacy, the writer argues that because A preceded B, A caused B. For example, *Right after Jim joined the Cardinals as a bench warmer, the team began a ten-game winning streak.* The writer makes a false connection between a winning streak and a player who rarely plays.

(For more on fallacies, see page 614).

RESEARCH STRATEGIES

When you're looking for information, where should you begin? You might first create a research plan that outlines the topics you want to explore or the questions you want to answer. Then you can begin your search for print and nonprint resources that might be relevant to your plan. When doing research, do not rely solely on one source; instead, consult as many reliable sources as possible. The following research strategies can help you find resources in a library or media center or on a computer linked to the Internet.

USING A LIBRARY OR MEDIA CENTER

Library Catalogs

A library's main resources usually are printed volumes stored on shelves. More and more often, however, libraries (or, as they are sometimes called, media centers) feature holdings stored in electronic form and accessed from a computer terminal or other electronic device. To find information in a library, start by looking in the catalog. Most libraries record their holdings in an **on-line, or computer, catalog.**

On-line catalogs vary from library to library. With some, you begin by searching for resources by **title, author,** or **subject.** With others, you simply enter **key words** related to the subject you're researching. With either system, when you enter the relevant information in response to on-screen prompts, a new screen will display a list of materials or subject headings related to your request. When you find an item you want to examine, write down the title, author, and **call number,** the code of numbers and letters that shows you where in the library the item is located.

Some libraries still use **card catalogs.** A card catalog is a collection of index cards containing key information about each library holding. The cards are arranged in alphabetical order by surname of author, by the first word of title (omitting initial articles), and—for works of nonfiction—by subject.

Other Library Resources

Every library has a **reference section** containing materials you can use only in the library. Reference works include encyclopedias; yearbooks; dictionaries; directories; almanacs; atlases; and **indices,** extensive alphabetical lists (often of books or periodicals). *Books in Print* is a useful index, as is *The Reader's Catalog.* Reference works can appear in electronic or print format. Because many reference books are updated periodically, look for the most recent edition.

Electronic Databases These are large collections of information that you access at a computer terminal. Among the types of information stored on databases are statistics, biographical data, museum holdings, indices, and back issues of magazines.

There are two basic kinds of electronic databases. An **on-line database** is accessed at a computer terminal that is connected to a distant server computer that contains the database. Many computers can access the database at the same time. A **portable database** is available on magnetic tape, disk, CD-ROM, or other electronic medium not connected to a server computer. As a rule, only one person at a time can access the database.

A **CD-ROM** (compact disc–read-only memory) is a portable database stored on a disk that you access via a computer's CD-ROM drive. CD-ROMs can store not only text but also sound, images, and video clips. If you were to look up Thomas Hardy in a CD-ROM encyclopedia, you might find a clip from a film version of one of his novels.

Periodicals Most libraries hold a variety of periodicals as well as indices that help you locate information in them. To find up-to-date magazine or newspaper articles on a topic, look in an electronic index such as *InfoTrac, ProQuest,* or *EBSCO.* Some electronic indices provide summaries, or **abstracts,** of articles. Other databases allow you to access the entire text of articles, which you can read on screen or print out. The *Readers' Guide to Periodical Literature* is an excellent index to hundreds of periodicals. Back issues of periodicals may be stored in print form or on **microfilm** (a reel of film), **microfiche** (a sheet of film), CD-ROM, or other information storage-and-retrieval device.

Audiovisual Resources Most libraries hold recordings of actors or authors reading books, videotapes of movies, and CDs and DVDs. These resources are useful when preparing a multimedia project.

USING THE INTERNET

The **Internet,** or **Net,** is a worldwide electronic network that connects millions of personal computers to other personal computers and to server computers containing vast amounts of data, words, and images. On the Net you can find information on almost any topic by accessing libraries, museums, electronic newspapers, government agencies, and many other sources. **E-zines** (often called **zines**) and **e-journals** are periodicals found only on-line. You gain access to the Net via Internet service providers (ISPs). The following are some ways in which the Internet can be used for research.

E-Mail

E-mail is an electronic message sent over a computer network. On the Internet you can use e-mail to contact institutions, businesses, and individuals. This is a quick and inexpensive method of consulting experts (located 1 mile or 10,000 miles away) on a topic you're researching. You can also use e-mail to exchange messages with students around the world.

Electronic Forums

Internet forums, or **newsgroups,** enable you to discuss and debate various subjects. You can post a question in a forum and receive responses from other knowledgeable people. Be careful, however: Responses may be incorrect.

The World Wide Web

The easiest way to conduct Internet research is on the World Wide Web (WWW). On the Web, information is provided on colorful, easy-to-access files called **Web pages.** A Web page may include text, images, sounds, and even video clips.

Using a Web Browser You can view Web pages with a **Web browser,** such as Netscape's *Navigator* or Microsoft's *Internet Explorer.* Every page on the Web has its own address, called a **URL,** or Uniform Resource Locator. If you know the URL of a Web page you want to access, enter it in the *location* field of your browser. See the accompanying illustration.

Web pages are connected by **hyperlinks,** which enable you to reach relevant data quickly by jumping from one page to another. These links are indicated by underlined or colored words or by images on your computer screen. When you click on hyperlink words or images, you are automatically transferred to another Web page.

Using a Web Directory and a Search Engine With many millions of linked Web pages, how do you find the information you want? If you're looking for general information on a topic, go to a **Web directory** (such as Yahoo), a list of topics and subtopics created to help you find an appropriate Web site. A directory is like a book's index. Begin with a broad category, such as Literature. Then, work your way down through the subtopics, from perhaps English: Literature to Renaissance Literature: Authors until you find a Web page that looks promising, such as one on Francis Bacon.

Sample Web-Browser Screen (1998)

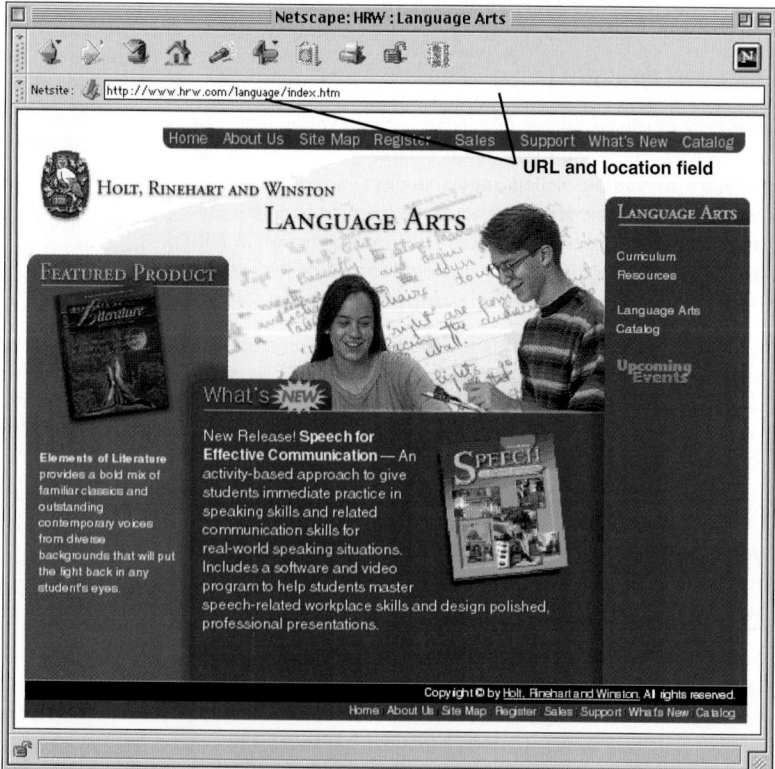

URL and location field

COMMON SEARCH OPERATORS AND WHAT THEY DO	
AND	Demands that both terms appear on the page; narrows search
+	Demands that both terms appear on the page; narrows search
OR	Yields pages that contain either term; widens search
NOT	Excludes a word from consideration; narrows search
–	Excludes a word from consideration; narrows search
NEAR	Demands that two words be in proximity; narrows search
ADJ	Demands that two words be in proximity; narrows search
" "	Demands the exact phrase; narrows search

If you are looking for more specific information, try using a **search engine,** an incredible software tool that indexes millions of Web sites. Some popular search engines are Lycos, Alta Vista, and Excite. To use a search engine, enter a **search term,** which is one or more keywords. The search engine will then list Web pages that contain your search term along with the first few lines of each page. A search term like the name *Bacon* can produce thousands of results, or **hits,** including Web pages dealing with the actor Kevin Bacon or smoked meats. If you're looking for information on the writer Francis Bacon, most hits will be irrelevant. It's important, therefore, to refine, or tailor, your search.

Refining a Keyword Search   Searches using more than one keyword generally provide more focused results. Most search engines allow you to use **search operators** to create a string of keywords. Common search operators include the capitalized terms AND, OR, NOT, ADJ (adjacent), and NEAR. Use these operators to focus your search. Here's how the operators work. Let's assume, for example, that you're looking for material on Sir Francis Bacon and his treatise *The New Atlantis.* You might use this search term:

Bacon ADJ Francis AND Atlantis

This search term yields pages that contain the names *Francis, Bacon,* and *Atlantis* but most likely nothing about movies or smoked meats. Now suppose you want to learn more about Renaissance literature. If your first search turns up words about plays, you can expand your search by using OR:

plays OR poems

Doing a Phrase Search   Exact phrases often produce better results than single words or strings of keywords. If you're looking for information on Renaissance poetry, for example, a search made with the unlinked keywords *Renaissance* and *poetry* will yield thousands of pages about the Renaissance and about poetry in general. On the other hand, a search using the exact phrase "Renaissance poetry"—signaled by quotation marks—will yield only pages containing that phrase.

Knowing Your Search Engine   Not all search engines operate in the same way. Some have rules about using uppercase and lowercase letters. Some require a plus sign or minus sign between keywords, rather than the operator AND or NOT. Some require that you enter exact phrases within quotation marks. Some provide a list of options that enable you to search by exact phrases, individual words, and so on. Because the rules governing search engines differ, read the online Help information before you begin a search.

EVALUATING THE CREDIBILITY OF SOURCES

Before you begin taking notes from any source—print or electronic or an interviewee—be sure your source provides information that is current, accurate, and free of strong bias. Evaluate both primary and secondary sources. **Primary** sources, or firsthand accounts, include letters, autobiographies, diaries, historical documents, and interviews. **Secondary sources,** which are derived from primary sources, include encyclopedias, documentary films, biographies, and historical books. To evaluate the usefulness of a source, use this 4R test.

1. **Relevant.** The source must have information *directly* related to your topic. To find out if a book is relevant, you can check its table of contents and index. For some books and for articles, skimming can help. *Book Review Digest* offers, for selected titles, useful summaries and review excerpts; videotapes and audiotapes sometimes provide written summaries of their content; and periodical indices may include summaries of articles.

2. **Reliable.** The source must be accurate. A periodical whose reputation depends on accuracy, such as *Smithsonian* or *National Geographic,* or a well-regarded authority, such as a scholar, generally can be counted on to fact-check rigorously before publication. If in doubt about the reliability of a source, consult an expert, such as a teacher or librarian.

3. **Recent.** For most topics, use sources that are as current as possible. Ongoing research findings can change perceptions, generalizations, and opinions. For example, the discovery of a poet's childhood illness can lead to a new interpretation of her or his poems about childhood. Often, long-ago political events are reinterpreted in light of newly discovered information.

4. **Representative.** If there are opposing viewpoints on your topic, you should consult sources that provide a variety of interpretations. If one interpretation is strongly favored, you should also consult another source with a different slant.

TAKING NOTES AND DOCUMENTING SOURCES

If you use another person's words or ideas without giving credit, you are **plagiarizing,** which is a serious offense. Avoid plagiarizing by acknowledging in your work the source of each quotation, paraphrase, statistic, figure, and idea that you found through research. Careful documentation starts with accurate source cards and notes.

Preparing Source Cards

As you gather information, you can save time and ensure accurate documentation by preparing source cards in the format needed for your report's **sources cited** list (see page 1213). Put each source on a 3-inch × 5-inch card, or record it in a computer file. Follow these guidelines:

1. **Assign each source a different number.** When taking notes, it will save time to write the number rather than the author and title. Place the number at the top right of the card or computer entry.

2. **Record full publication data.** Data include subtitles, translators, and volume and edition numbers. Use a shortened form of the publisher's name, deleting initial articles and the type of business organization.

3. **Note the call number or location.** This information will help you reaccess the source quickly.

Sample Source Card

```
                                              3


 Goodrich, Norma Lovve. Merlin.
 New York: Harper, 1988.


       Westbank Community Library
```

Taking Notes

After evaluating your sources and preparing source cards, you are ready to read carefully and take notes. Use the following guidelines to prepare note cards that will be easy to use when writing your paper.

GUIDELINES FOR TAKING NOTES

1. Use a 4-inch × 6-inch note card, a half sheet of paper, or a separate computer file. Never put notes from more than one source on the same card or sheet of paper or in the same electronic file.
2. In the upper right, write the number you have assigned to the source.
3. In the upper left, use a word or phrase to identify the topic or main idea.
4. In the lower right, note the page numbers from which the information is taken.
5. Reread the note to be sure it is accurate.

Your notes may be direct quotations, summaries, or paraphrases. A **direct quotation** contains the author's exact words. When quoting directly, copy the statement word for word—including punctuation, capitalization, and spelling—and enclose the passage in quotation marks. A **summary** condenses the author's ideas and facts in your own words. A **paraphrase** restates information in your own words. To summarize or paraphrase, use lists and phrases instead of complete sentences.

Using Quotations

Relevant, interesting quotations add authority and punch to your research paper. The following chart describes several ways to use quotations effectively.

GUIDELINES FOR USING QUOTATIONS

- **Quote a whole sentence, introducing it in your own words.**

  EXAMPLE   Woolf commented on Victorian conversation: "Nobody ever broke the convention. If you listened, as I did, it was like watching a game." (129).

- **Quote part of a sentence within a sentence of your own.**

  EXAMPLE   Woolf wrote that the Victorian conversational style "allows one to say a great many things which would be inaudible if one marched straight up and spoke out" (129).

- **Quote just one or a few words within a sentence of your own.**

  EXAMPLE   The essay draws attention to the lack of information on women writers and "call[s] for a history of women" (15).

- **Use an ellipsis (. . .) to indicate omissions from quotations.** Sometimes you need only a part of a quotation to make your point. Insert an ellipsis where words have been deleted.

  EXAMPLE   Judith Shakespeare has a "poet's heart . . . caught and tangled in a woman's body" (50).

- **Set off longer quotations as extract blocks.** If a quotation will be more than four typed lines, start a new line and indent the entire quotation ten spaces from the left. Double-space, and do not use quotation marks.

Formatting Electronic-Source Citations

Writing electronic-source citations for a list of sources cited can be difficult. On-line sources often change, and many do not provide all the information required. For instance, many Web pages don't identify an author. In such cases, include in your citation whatever relevant information is available.

The format for citing electronic sources depends on (1) whether the source is on-line or portable and (2) whether the source has an identical print version or stands alone.

Listed below are the elements required for the citation of various kinds of electronic sources—in the order in which they should appear. Most elements likely to be included are listed, but many actual citations will not include all possible elements. (Note: If a URL runs onto a second line, divide the address immediately *after* a slash mark or *before* a dot. Never use a hyphen to divide a URL.)

Source from a Computer Network, such as the World Wide Web, with an Identical Print Version

- author's last name, then first name
- title of poem, short story, essay, document, or similar short work, set off by quotation marks
- title of book or periodical, underlined
- name of editor of book, preceded by the abbreviation *Ed.*
- publication data for print version
- title of scholarly project, database, or professional or personal site, underlined; or, for a professional or personal site with no title, a description such as *Home page*
- volume or issue number
- number range, or total number, of any numbered pages or paragraphs
- date of electronic publication or latest revision
- name of any sponsoring institution
- date you accessed the information
- full URL, in angle brackets

EXAMPLE   Housman, A. E. A Shropshire Lad. London: K. Paul, Trench, Truebner, 1986. Project Bartleby. Jan. 1996. Columbia University. 22 Oct. 1999 <http://www.cc.columbia.edu/acis/bartleby/housman>.

Source from a Computer Network, such as the World Wide Web, with No Print Version

- author's last name, then first name
- title of poem, short story, essay, document, or similar short work, set off by quotation marks
- title of scholarly project, database, periodical, or professional or personal site, underlined; or, for a professional or personal site with no title, a description such as *Home page*
- name of editor of complete work or database, preceded by the abbreviation *Ed.*
- publication date or date of last revision
- number range or total number of any numbered sections
- name of any sponsoring organization
- volume, issue, or version number
- date you accessed the information
- the full URL, in angle brackets

EXAMPLE   Patterson, Arthur Paul. "A Frankenstein Study." Watershed Online: Resources for a Literary Imagination. 1996. Watershed Online. October 1999. <http://www.watershed.winnipeg.mb.ca/index.html>.

CD-ROM with a Print Version

- author's last name, then first name
- title of document or article, set off by quotation marks
- title of print version, underlined
- publication data for print version
- database title, underlined
- edition, release, or version number
- publication medium (CD-ROM)
- city of publication
- name of publisher of electronic version
- date of electronic publication

EXAMPLE   Miller, Arthur. <u>The Crucible.</u> New York: Bantam, 1959. <u>The Crucible.</u> CD-ROM. New York: Penguin, 1996.

CD-ROM with No Print Version

Omit the print information called for above.

EXAMPLE   "American Renaissance." <u>The History of American Literature.</u> CD-ROM. Chicago: CLEARVUE/eav, 1995.

Citing Sources

Parenthetical Citations   A short **parenthetical citation** gives source information in parentheses in the body of the text. It contains just enough information to lead a reader to the correct full entry in the sources cited list. Parenthetical citations include the author's last name and a page number, with these exceptions:

- a nonprint source such as an interview (Use name only.)
- a print source of only one page (Use name only.)
- a sentence that includes the author's name (Use page number only. See the first and fourth bulleted items in Guidelines for Using Quotations, page 1211.)
- an author with more than one entry on your list of sources cited (Add year of publication—for example: Roberts 1992, 65.)

For more information on specific kinds of parenthetical citations, see the chart below or the most recent edition of the Modern Language Association's *MLA Handbook for Writers of Research Papers.*

PARENTHETICAL CITATIONS

Works by One Author

Author's last name and page(s): (Goodrich 100)

Works by More Than One Author

All authors' last names (or first author and *et al.* if more than three) and page(s): (Radford and Swanton 78)

Multivolume Works

Author's last name, volume number, and page(s): (Vinaver 1:81–82)

Works with No Author Listed on Title Page

Full title (or a shortened version) and page(s): ("Arthurian Journey" 813)

Literary Works Published in Several Editions

Full title and any information that would help readers find the quotation in any edition, such as chapter number or act, scene, and line numbers: (<u>Macbeth</u> II:2:34–39)

Indirect Sources

Qtd. in ("quoted in") before the source and page(s): (qtd. in Goodrich 100)

More Than One Source in the Same Citation

Relevant information for each source, separated by a semicolon: (Goodrich 195; Hopkins 47)

Use the following guidelines for correctly placing parenthetical citations.

Placement of Citations

- Place the citation as close as possible to the material it documents. If possible, place it at the end of a sentence.
- Place a citation after closing quotation marks and before the end punctuation mark.
- For an extensive quotation, set as an extract block (see Guidelines for Using Quotations, page 1211), place the citation *two spaces after* the final punctuation mark.

LIST OF SOURCES CITED

The **sources cited** list, which you should include at the end of your report, contains all the sources, print and nonprint, that you credit in your paper. Other names for this list are *bibliography* and *works* or *literature cited,* but they are only appropriate if your sources are limited to books and articles.

Formatting To prepare the sources cited list, center the words *Sources Cited* on a blank sheet of paper one inch from the top of the page. Double-space between "Sources Cited" and the first entry and between all subsequent entries. Double-space within entries as well. Begin each entry on a new line, even with the left margin. If an entry runs more than one line, indent the subsequent line or lines in the entry five spaces.

As a general rule, alphabetize your sources by the author's last name. If there is no author (or editor), alphabetize by title, ignoring *A, An,* and *The* as the first word of the title. For example, *The Cambridge History of Literary Criticism* would appear under *C* rather than *T.*

Publication Information When providing publication information, use shortened forms of publishers' names, unless this would lead to confusion. Abbreviate U.S. state names and months of the year (except May, June, and July).

Page Numbers You should include page numbers only for articles in periodicals or for other works that are part of a whole work, such as one essay in a book of essays. However, page and volume numbers aren't needed if entries are alphabetized, as in an encyclopedia.

SOURCES CITED: SAMPLE ENTRIES	
STANDARD REFERENCE WORKS	
Encyclopedia	"Malory, Sir Thomas." The New Encyclopaedia Britannica: Micropaedia. 15th ed. 1988.
Biographical Reference	"Malory, Sir Thomas." Merriam-Webster's Biographical Dictionary. 1995 ed.
BOOKS	
Book with One Author	Alcock, Leslie. Arthur's Britain: History and Archaeology A.D. 367–634. London: Penguin, 1971.
Book with Two or More Authors	Radford, C. A. Ralegh, and Michael J. Swanton. Arthurian Sites in the West. Devon: U of Exeter, 1975.
Book with No Author Listed	The Cambridge History of Literary Criticism. New York: Cambridge UP, 1989.
Book with One Editor	Brengle, Richard L., ed. Arthur, King of Britain. New York: Appleton, 1964.
Book with Two or More Editors	Pickford, Cedric E., Rex Last, and C. R. Barker, eds. The Arthurian Bibliography, II: Subject Index. Cambridge: Brewer, 1983.
Translation	Niane, D. T. Sundiata: An Epic of Old Mali. Trans. G. D. Pickett. London: Longman, 1965.

SELECTIONS FROM BOOKS	
Selection from Book of Works by One Author	Tennyson, Alfred Lord. "To the Queen." The Works of Tennyson. Ed. Hallam, Lord Tennyson. London: Macmillan, 1913.
Selection from Book of Works by Several Authors	Oakeshott, W. F. "The Finding of the Manuscript." Essays on Malory. Ed. J.A.W. Bennett. Oxford: Clarendon Press, 1963. 1–6.
Selection from Collection of Longer Works	Steinbeck, John. The Acts of King Arthur and His Noble Knights: From the Winchester Manuscripts of Thomas Malory and Other Sources. Ed. Chase Horton. New York: Farrar, 1976. 51–98.
ARTICLES FROM MAGAZINES, NEWSPAPERS, AND JOURNALS	
Weekly Magazine Article	Porter, Andrew. "Purcell: King Arthur." The New Yorker 31 July 1989: 69.
Monthly or Quarterly Magazine Article	Converse, Florence. "Merlin Met Morgan-Le-Fay." Atlantic Monthly Sept. 1922: 376–377.
Article with No Author Listed	"An Arthurian Journey." Atlantic Monthly June 1980: 811–829.
Daily Newspaper Article, with Byline	Riding, Alan. "'King Arthur' Goes to Paris After 300 Years." New York Times 20 Feb. 1995, late ed.: C9+.
Daily Newspaper Article, No Byline	"Steinbeck Find Said to Be First 'Morte d'Arthur' Manuscript." New York Times 2 Jan. 1966, natl. ed.: 52.
Unsigned Daily Newspaper Editorial, No City in Title	"Supreme Injustice." Editorial. Star Ledger [Newark, NJ] 6 Oct. 1991: 17.
Scholarly Journal	Field, P.J.C. "Sir Thomas Malory, M.P." Bulletin of the Institute of Historical Research 47 (1974): 24–35.
OTHER SOURCES	
Personal Interview	Kibler, William W. Personal interview. 15 Oct. 1990.
Telephone Interview	Kibler, William W. Telephone interview. 12 Oct. 1990.
Published Interview	Campbell, Joseph. Interview with Bill Moyers. The Power of Myth. New York: Doubleday. 1988.
Radio or Television Interview	Harris, Richard. Interview with Scott Simon. Weekend Edition. Natl. Public Radio. WBUR Boston. 26 Mar. 1994.
Thesis or Dissertation	Couroux, Gerard Oliver. "Courtly Love in Malory's 'Le Morte Darthur.'" Diss. Loyola U of Chicago, 1968.
Cartoon	Stevens, Mick. Cartoon. The New Yorker Book of Lawyer Cartoons. New York: Knopf, 1994: 22.
Speech or Lecture	Bell, A.R.L. "The Road to Santiago de Compostela: The French Connection." Long Beach Ebell Club. 10 Oct. 1983.
Recording	Welcher, Dan. The Visions of Merlin. Cond. Akira Endo. LP. Louisville Orch. First Edition Records, 1989.
Film or Filmstrip	The Sword in the Stone. Dir. Wolfgang Reitherman. Walt Disney, 1963.
Videotape	Arthur the King. Dir. Clive Donner. CBS. KTBC, Austin. 26 Apr. 1985.

WRITING FOR LIFE

The writing you do now prepares you for the writing you will do in college and in your career. Your ability to write clear and effective memos, business letters, and résumés will be a major factor in your success as a professional. As a student, you will write letters of application for admission to colleges and universities, and you will write résumés to apply for jobs. As an employee, you may write interoffice memoranda and business letters.

When composing documents that others will read, follow the steps listed below. (Note: Computers and software programs make the writing process more efficient.)

1. **Prewriting.** Make notes about the key points you want to include in your document and how to present them.
2. **Writing a draft.** Compose a first draft, or version, of the document.
3. **Evaluating and revising.** Evaluate your draft closely, correcting any errors of spelling, grammar, and punctuation. Review the presentation of information and ideas for clarity and readability, and revise as necessary. Delete repetitive or irrelevant material.
4. **Preparing the final version.** Fine-tune the revised draft as necessary to prepare a final version. Make sure you proofread the document.

WRITING INTEROFFICE MEMOS

In the business world, writing is functional and is expected to be structured. One standard form of communication within a company or organization is the **memo** (or memorandum). Memos are concise messages that tell the reader *when, who, what, where, why,* and *how.* Memos contain guide words (*date, to, from, subject* or *re*) that immediately identify the date, destination, origin, and purpose of a message. Memos generally cover only one of the following categories.

- **Meeting notices.** Include the meeting date, time, place, purpose, and any other significant information, such as the agenda or the persons who will be attending.
- **Meeting summaries.** Provide a brief, factual report of discussions and decisions. Include the names and titles of individuals involved.
- **Requests for action or information.** Open by making the request, and then follow with details. If you have several requests, list them, phrasing each one similarly. Include a deadline stating when you need a response.

For more on memos, see page 1186.

WRITING EFFECTIVE BUSINESS LETTERS

Another essential form of business writing is the business letter. Whether you're writing to request information, make an offer, or register a complaint, your business letters can make a lasting impression on readers. If errors and inaccuracies or a sloppy appearance distract readers from the contents of a letter, you risk giving an impression of inefficiency or even incompetence. Keep these rules in mind:

1. Use formal, standard English.
2. Be clear.
3. Use the correct format.

Types of Business Letters

Request and Order Letters   You write a **request letter** to ask for information about a job, college, product, service, policy, or procedure. You write an **order letter** to order merchandise. When writing a request or order letter, include all important details relating to time, location, size, style, cost, and so on.

Complaint or Adjustment Letters   You write a **complaint** or **adjustment letter** when you are dissatisfied with a person, product, or service. Your letter should explain exactly what is wrong and should request a satisfactory resolution of the problem, such as a replacement of merchandise or a refund of your money. Keep the tone of your letter calm and courteous.

Letters of Application   A **letter of application** introduces you to a selection committee or a potential employer. The letter should provide the reader with enough information to determine whether you are a good candidate for a job, scholarship, college, or university. Keep the following points in mind when writing a letter of application.

1. Identify the job or situation for which you are applying, and mention how you heard about it.
2. Depending on the situation, include
   - your age, grade in school, and grade point average
   - your experience, activities, awards, and honors
   - the personal qualities that make you a good choice
   - the dates or times you are available
3. Provide references—names of two or three responsible adults, other than relatives, who agree to recommend you. Include their addresses and telephone numbers.

Sample Letter of Application, Block Style

Heading
Your address, including city, state, and ZIP code.
Your e-mail address
Date you write the letter

Inside Address
Name, title, and address of person you are writing to. Use a title (*Mr., Ms., Mrs., Dr., Esq.,* etc.) with the person's name, and put his or her business title after the name.

Salutation (greeting)
Use *Dear* followed by the person's title and last name and a colon. If the letter isn't addressed to a specific person, use a business title.

Body
Your message. If the body contains more than one paragraph, leave a blank line between paragraphs. Don't indent paragraph openings.

Closing
Use *Yours truly* or *Sincerely yours* followed by a comma.

Signature
Type or print your name, leaving space for your signature. Sign your name in ink.

Use "Enclosure" if you're including something with your letter.

1632 Garden View Drive
Anytown, PA 12345
mmanrique@ISP.com

September 23, 1999

Mr. John Lao
Director of Human Resources
XYZ Insurance Company
10 Central Avenue
Anytown, PA 12346

Dear Mr. Lao:

Are you looking for someone who carries out assignments efficiently and enjoys working with people? I have these qualities and other important business skills to bring to the position of administrative assistant you advertised in Sunday's Herald.

I am a 17-year-old senior at Jefferson High School and have completed courses in business English, word processing, and accounting. I can word-process at a rate of 50 words per minute while transcribing from recordings.

Last summer, as a receptionist at QRS Supply Company, I did filing and billing in addition to my regular duties. I feel at home in an office setting and enjoy taking on responsibility.

My résumé, which is enclosed, lists references who can tell you about my business skills and my personal strengths.

I believe that my background qualifies me for the position of administrative assistant. Please contact me by telephone at 555-1234 or by e-mail at mmanrique@ISP.com to set up an interview.

Yours truly,

Marisol Manrique

Marisol Manrique

Enclosure

WRITING A PERSONAL RÉSUMÉ

Your **résumé** (or **curriculum vitae** [CV]) summarizes who you are, what you have learned, and what you have accomplished. The information in your résumé should include skills and achievements that give a potential employer a positive overview of your qualifications. When you apply for a job, you usually include your résumé with your letter of application to potential employers.

The structure, organization, and overall appearance of your résumé will give the reader an impression of you and your abilities. Print out or type your résumé on white or ivory paper. Proofread it carefully, making sure there are no factual or typographical errors, erasures, correction fluid, or stray marks. Your goal is to get an interview. Try your best to make a good first impression.

The following **model résumé** is written in reverse chronological order; it lists the most recent work experience first.

Sample Résumé

MARISOL MANRIQUE

1632 Garden View Drive
Anytown, PA 12345
Telephone: (215) 555-1234
E-mail: mmanrique@ISP.com

EDUCATION:
Senior, Jefferson High School
Major studies: Business and foreign language courses
Grade point average: 3.0 (B)

WORK EXPERIENCE:

Summer 1999 — Receptionist
QRS Supply Company
Anytown, PA

Summer 1996 — Volunteer Office Worker
YWCA
Anytown, PA

SKILLS:

Word processing: 50 wpm

Business machines: Dictating, calculating, and copying machines; personal computers

Other languages: Spanish (fluent)

EXTRACURRICULAR ACTIVITIES:
Vice president, Future Business Leaders of America
Member, Spanish Club

REFERENCES:

Dr. Robert Robertson, Principal — (215) 555-6789
Jefferson High School
Anytown, PA

Ms. Mary Jackson, English Teacher — (215) 555-4567
Jefferson High School
Anytown, PA

Mr. Juan Ramos, Owner — (215) 555-3456
QRS Supply Company
Anytown, PA

COLLEGE ADMISSIONS

To apply to a college, you will have to complete an application. Most applications have two parts: the form and the essay.

Completing the College Application Form

Application forms usually ask for basic information about you: name, address, birth date, grade point average, extracurricular activities, and the educational background and occupations of your parents. Many colleges have adopted the Common Application form so that you need fill this form out only once and send it to all the schools you are applying to. The form can be downloaded from the Internet. It can also be sent by e-mail to many colleges. (Note: Some schools require their own forms instead of or in addition to the Common Application form.)

Be sure to ask your high school to send a copy of your **transcript** to the colleges you apply to. A transcript lists all the courses you have taken in high school and the grades you earned.

Writing the Admission Essay

Most colleges and universities ask for an admission essay because it tells them things about you that can't be gleaned from bare facts. An essay reveals how you approach a question, how you think, what is important to you, and how well your education and experience have prepared you to express yourself verbally.

Consider these points as you prepare to write your admissions essay:

1. Read the question carefully. Be sure you are answering what is asked.
2. Be yourself. Admissions staff ask for the essay because they want to get to know you. The essay is an opportunity to introduce yourself to the admissions staff. Write about something important to you. Your conviction will come across to the reader. Don't worry about what the reader might expect from you—say something you want to say.
3. Be neat. Write as many drafts as necessary. Fine-tune until your essay is the best you can make it. Then, check the revised draft carefully for any errors in spelling, grammar, and usage before you produce the final version.

PROOFREADING

Proofreading refines the mechanics of your writing. If you are using a computer to write, a spelling checker can help you with your spelling, but it cannot do everything. For example, spelling checkers will not help you determine if you should use *too*, *two*, or *to* or other homophones. A dictionary and a style book will serve as helpful reference tools when you proofread. As you review your writing, you might find this list of questions helpful: (1) Are all words spelled correctly? (2) Do subjects and verbs agree? (3) Do pronouns agree with their antecedents? (4) Are verb tenses consistent? (5) Are all proper nouns capitalized? (6) Are sentence fragments eliminated? (7) Are all punctuation marks appropriate?

As you proofread your work, use the standard proofreaders' marks listed in the chart below.

PROOFREADERS' MARKS

SYMBOL	EXAMPLE	MEANING
≡	Twenty-second street	Capitalize lowercase letter.
/	Sarah's Uncle	Lowercase capital letter.
∧	the capital Maine *of*	Insert.
ꝰ	What's the the point?	Delete.
⌢⌣	a heavy back pack	Close up space.
∿	tragedy	Change order (of letters or words). Transpose.
¶	¶"Help," he yelled.	Begin new paragraph.
⊙	Stay calm⊙	Add period.
⋀	Of course you may be wrong.	Add comma.

ANSWERING ESSAY QUESTIONS

Essay tests require you to think critically and to express your understanding of a topic clearly. Your answers to essay questions must be well organized and include details to support your generalizations. A well-written answer must contain a complete response to a question.

Scan the questions on the test before you start writing. If you have a choice of questions, identify the ones you can answer best. Budget your time so you can give adequate attention to each question.

1. Read each essay question carefully, and notice whether a question has several parts.
2. Identify the important terms in the questions. Find the key verbs, and identify the tasks you must accomplish. Identify how much evidence is required for an adequate treatment.
3. Take a few minutes to prewrite. Make notes or a simple outline on scratch paper, organize your material logically, and write a thesis statement. Write one paragraph for each point you wish to make, and end with a paragraph that summarizes or restates your main points.
4. Evaluate and revise as you write. Watch for spelling and grammatical errors. You will not have time to redraft the entire essay, but you can edit to strengthen specific parts. Keep your paper neat.

Essay questions usually ask you to perform specific tasks expressed by the verb in the question. The following chart lists the task required by some key verbs.

ESSAY TEST QUESTIONS

KEY VERB	TASK	SAMPLE QUESTION
analyze	Take something apart to see how it creates meaning.	Analyze the use of verbal music in "The Lake Isle of Innisfree."
argue	Take a stand on an issue, and give reasons supporting your opinion.	Argue whether high school students should be required to pass a skills test before they graduate.
compare/contrast	Discuss likenesses/differences. At times test makers use the verb *compare* to include "contrast."	Compare and contrast Roman Polanski's movie of *Macbeth* with Shakespeare's play.
define	Give specific details that make something unique.	Define the term *modernism* as it relates to literature.
demonstrate (also **illustrate, present, show**)	Provide examples to support a point.	Demonstrate an example of circular reasoning.
discuss	Examine in detail.	Discuss the character of Macbeth as portrayed in Polanski's movie.
explain	Clarify, expound on, or give reasons for, or a cause of, something.	Explain the function of the witches in *Macbeth*.
interpret	Discuss or explain the meaning or significance of something.	Interpret the symbolism of blood and water in *Macbeth*.
list (also **outline, trace**)	Give all steps (in order) or all details about a subject.	List the events that lead to the death of Lady Macbeth.
summarize	Give a brief overview of the main points in a piece of informative writing or of the main events in a narrative.	Summarize the plot of Coleridge's *The Rime of the Ancient Mariner*.

SPEAKING AND LISTENING

Organizing Your Materials

Gather and organize information for your speech by following the basic process for writing a paper. If you are presenting an informative speech, use reliable sources of information, and take notes on what you find. Make an outline of the major points. Then, prepare note cards.

SPEECH NOTE CARDS

1. Put only one key idea, possibly accompanied by a brief example or detail, on each card.
2. Make a special note card for material that you plan to read word for word, such as a quotation, series of dates, or list of statistics.
3. Make a special note card to indicate when you should show a visual aid, such as a chart.
4. Number completed cards to keep them in order.

Unless you are presenting a memorized speech in a competition, you don't want to memorize your speech. You want your delivery to sound fresh and natural. If you use short phrases and signal words rather than full sentences to indicate key ideas on your note cards, you will not be tempted to read or memorize your speech.

Practicing Your Speech/Audience Evaluation

Practice your speech as often as you can to achieve a smooth, effective presentation. Practice at least once before an audience to get feedback. Be sure this audience evaluates your presentation based on criteria that you have agreed on.

Using Body Language   Your body language can reinforce the impression you make on your audience. Body language includes facial expressions, eye contact, gestures, posture, and movement. Here are several tips for using body language effectively:

- Making eye contact when speaking can indicate honesty and sincerity. Make eye contact with individuals in your audience to make them feel you are talking *with* them.
- Posture conveys attitude. Stand confidently, and look alert and interested in what you are saying.

Using Your Voice   Speak clearly and loudly enough for everyone in your audience to hear what you are saying. This sounds easy, but there are different aspects of speaking that affect how you sound to others:

- **Pitch** is how high or low a sound is or the natural rise and fall of your voice. Use pitch to emphasize various ideas and to avoid a monotone.
- **Volume** is the loudness or intensity of sound. You need to be loud enough to be heard when you are speaking. You also can raise or lower your voice for emphasis.
- **Stress,** or emphasize, important words or phrases to convey a point to your audience.
- **Rate** is the speed at which you talk. Speak at a comfortable, relaxed pace, and use changes in rate to communicate emotion and drama to your listeners.

Delivering Your Speech

Focus on your purpose for speaking. Think about what you want your listeners to do, know, believe, or feel.

MODEL RESEARCH PAPER

Shakespeare's Sister: A Fable of Gender Inequality

"Let me imagine," muses Virginia Woolf, "since facts are so hard to come by, what would have happened had Shakespeare had a wonderfully gifted sister, called Judith, let us say" (Woolf, <u>Room</u> 48). Virginia Woolf, the great British novelist, essayist, and critic of the early twen-

Introductory Paragraph
Catches reader's interest.
Primary source citation.

tieth century, goes on to speculate about the destiny of Shakespeare's imaginary sister Judith. Like Shakespeare, Judith also has a genius waiting to be born. Unlike Shakespeare, however, Judith cannot attend school and is denied access to the London theater. Like other women of the sixteenth century, she is intended for an early marriage and a life confined to domestic duties. There is no opportunity for her gift to flourish. It dies, unborn, when Judith dies (Woolf, Room 49–50).

Virginia Woolf spoke of the fable of Judith in lectures she gave at two women's colleges at Cambridge University in 1928. Her talks became the well-known essay A Room of One's Own. The essay draws attention to the lack of information on women writers and "call[s] for a history of women" (Scott 15). It strongly criticizes gender discrimination. Woolf addressed her comments to an audience of young women who were experiencing inequality firsthand at Cambridge. Why, then, did Woolf not address the issue of Cambridge women directly? Why did she clothe her comments in the fable of Shakespeare's imaginary sister? The reason lies partly in the political climate of Cambridge at the time.

Two women's colleges, Girton and Newnham, were established at Cambridge by 1873, allowing female students to attend men's lectures and take degree examinations exactly as male students did (Brittain 35–36). Women were not admitted to full status, however, and did not receive degrees from Cambridge until after World War II (Bradbrook 78–79). During those intervening years, men's attitudes toward female students ranged from reluctant toleration to outright hostility. Female undergraduates were accused, for example, of everything from "distracting" men in libraries to obscuring men's views with their picture hats (McWilliams-Tullberg 193). In 1920, when a proposal to admit women was defeated, male undergraduates appeared as a "howling mob" who chanted "we won't have women" and bribed children to do the same (McWilliams-Tullberg 193). . . . [The paper continues.]

In Judith Shakespeare, Virginia Woolf may have seen a reflection of herself. Certainly, she recognized the parallel when she wrote that her fictional heroine "lives in you and me, and in many other women who are not here tonight for they are washing up the dishes and putting the children to bed" (qtd. in Gilbert and Gubar 93). Then, too, there is another parallel in the two lives. Judith Shakespeare dies, her gift wasted. In 1941, Virginia Woolf died prematurely, her gifts also lost. "Who shall measure," Woolf wrote, "the heat and violence of the poet's heart when caught and tangled in a woman's body" (Woolf, Room 50)?

Side annotations:
- Thesis statement.
- Body
- Topic sentence.
- Supporting details.
- Secondary source citation.
- Topic sentence.
- Supporting details.
- Secondary source citation.
- Conclusion

Sources Cited

Bradbrook, M. C. 'That Infidel Place': A Short History of Girton College, 1869-1969. London: Chatto, 1969.

Brittain, Vera. The Women at Oxford: A Fragment of History. New York: Macmillan, 1960.

Gilbert, Sandra M., and Susan Gubar. The War of the Words. New Haven: Yale UP, 1988, Vol. 1 of No Man's Land: The Place of the Woman Writer in the Twentieth Century. 3 vols. 1988-94.

Malcolm, Janet. "A House of One's Own." The New Yorker. 5 June 1995: 58-78.

McWilliams-Tullberg, Rita. Women at Cambridge: A Men's University--Though of a Mixed Type. London: Gollancz, 1975.

Scott, Joan Wallach. Gender and the Politics of History. New York: Columbia UP, 1988.

"Virginia Woolf." The Modern World: Ten Great Writers. Narr. Hermione Lee. London Weekend Television. London. 9 June 1988.

Woolf, Virginia. A Room of One's Own. New York: Harcourt, 1957.

[Note: This is a partial list of Sources Cited for this research paper.]

1 THE PARTS OF SPEECH

PART OF SPEECH	DEFINITION	EXAMPLES
NOUN	Names person, place, thing, or idea	writer, Ben Okri, Anglo-Saxons, family, country, Wales, poem, "My Last Duchess," Romanticism
PRONOUN	Takes the place of one or more nouns or pronouns	
Personal	Refers to one(s) speaking (first person), spoken to (second person), spoken about (third person)	I, me, my, mine, we, us, our, ours you, your, yours he, him, his, she, her, hers, it, its, they, them, their, theirs
Reflexive	Refers to subject and directs action of verb back to subject	myself, ourselves, yourself, yourselves, himself, herself, itself, themselves
Intensive	Refers to and emphasizes noun or another pronoun	(See Reflexive.)
Demonstrative	Refers to specific one(s) of group	this, that, these, those
Interrogative	Introduces question	what, which, who, whom, whose
Relative	Introduces subordinate clause and refers to noun or pronoun outside that clause	that, which, who, whom, whose
Indefinite	Refers to one(s) not specifically named	all, any, anyone, both, each, either, everybody, many, none, nothing
ADJECTIVE	Modifies noun or pronoun by telling *what kind, which one, how many,* or *how much*	**a paperback** book, **an Anglo-Saxon** law, **this** one, **the seven brave** warriors, **less** space
VERB	Shows action or state of being	
Action	Expresses physical or mental activity	describe, travel, fight, believe, consider, remember
Linking	Connects subject with word identifying or describing it	appear, be, seem, become, feel, look, smell, sound, taste
Helping (Auxiliary)	Assists another verb in expressing time, voice, or mood	be, have, may, can, shall, must, would
ADVERB	Modifies verb, adjective, or adverb by telling *how, when, where,* or *to what extent*	walks **slowly, quite** different, **somewhat** boldly, coming **here soon**
PREPOSITION	Relates noun or pronoun to another word	about, at, by, for, from, in, on, according to, along with, because of
CONJUNCTION	Joins words or word groups	
Coordinating	Joins words or word groups used in the same way	and, but, for, nor, or, so, yet

(continued)

Correlative	A pair of conjunctions that join parallel words or word groups	both . . . and, either . . . or, neither . . . nor, not only . . . but (also)
Subordinating	Begins a subordinate clause and connects it to an independent clause	although, as if, because, since, so that, unless, when, where, while
INTERJECTION	Expresses emotion	ah, wow, ugh, whew

2 AGREEMENT

AGREEMENT OF SUBJECT AND VERB

2a. **A verb should agree with its subject in number. Singular subjects take singular verbs. Plural subjects take plural verbs.**

SINGULAR   **He lives** in Camelot.
PLURAL   **They live** in Camelot.

2b. **The number of the subject is not changed by a phrase or a clause following the subject.**

EXAMPLE
The **Lilliputians,** a nation of tiny people, **capture** Gulliver.

2c. **Indefinite pronouns may be singular, plural, or either.**

(1) The following indefinite pronouns are singular: *anybody, anyone, anything, each, either, everybody, everyone, everything, neither, nobody, no one, nothing, one, somebody, someone,* and *something.*

EXAMPLE
One of the most beautiful places in England **is** the Lake District.

(2) The following indefinite pronouns are plural: *both, few, many,* and *several.*

EXAMPLE
Both of the epics **were written** by John Milton.

(3) The indefinite pronouns *all, any, most, none,* and *some* are singular when they refer to singular words and are plural when they refer to plural words.

SINGULAR   **None** of the equipment **was damaged.** [*None* refers to *equipment.*]
PLURAL   **None** of the machines **were damaged.** [*None* refers to *machines.*]

2d. **A *compound subject* may be singular, plural, or either.**

(1) Subjects joined by *and* usually take a plural verb.

EXAMPLE
After rehearsal, **Juan, Anita,** and **Marcus are going** out to dinner.

A compound subject that names only one person or thing takes a singular verb.

EXAMPLE
His **wife** and **partner** in crime **is** Lady Macbeth.

(2) Singular subjects joined by *or* or *nor* take a singular verb.

EXAMPLE
Jill or **Jorge plans** to write a character analysis of Macduff.

(3) When a singular subject and a plural subject are joined by *or* or *nor,* the verb agrees with the subject nearer the verb.

EXAMPLE
Neither the **dancers** nor the **choreographer was** pleased with the routine.

2e. **The verb agrees with its subject even when the verb precedes the subject, as in sentences beginning with *here, there,* or *where.***

SINGULAR   Where **is** [*or* where's] **Malcolm**?
PLURAL   Here **are** [*not* here's] **Malcolm** and his **brother.**

2f. **A *collective noun* (such as *audience, flock,* or *team*) is singular in form but names a group of persons or things. A collective noun takes a singular verb when the noun refers to the group as a unit and takes a plural verb when the noun refers to the parts or members of the group.**

| SINGULAR | The tour **group is** on the bus. [The group as a unit is on the bus.] |
| PLURAL | The tour **group are talking** about their plans. [The members of the group are talking to one another.] |

2g. An expression of an amount (a length of time, a statistic, or a fraction, for example) is singular when the amount is thought of as a unit or when it refers to a singular word and plural when the amount is thought of as many parts or when it refers to a plural word.

| SINGULAR | **Fifty years is** how long Beowulf rules Geatland. [one unit] |
| PLURAL | **One fourth** of the seniors **are working** on a production of *Macbeth*. [The fraction refers to *seniors*.] |

Expressions of measurement (length, weight, capacity, area) are usually singular.

EXAMPLE
Four and seven-tenths inches is the diameter of a compact disc.

2h. The title of a creative work (such as a book, song, film, or painting) or the name of an organization, a country, or a city (even if it is plural in form) takes a singular verb.

EXAMPLES
"Tears, Idle Tears" was written by Alfred, Lord Tennyson.
The **United Nations was formed** in 1945.
Has the Netherlands been flooded recently?

2i. A verb agrees with its subject, not with its predicate nominative.

| SINGULAR | The **subject** of the lecture **was** epic heroes. |
| PLURAL | **Epic heroes were** the subject of the lecture. |

AGREEMENT OF PRONOUN AND ANTECEDENT

A pronoun usually refers to a noun or another pronoun. The word to which a pronoun refers is called its *antecedent*.

2j. A pronoun agrees with its antecedent in number and gender. Singular pronouns refer to singular antecedents. A few singular pronouns also indicate gender (feminine, masculine, or neuter). Plural pronouns refer to plural antecedents.

EXAMPLES
Alfred, Lord Tennyson published *Idylls of the King* after **he** became poet laureate. [singular, masculine]
Lady Macbeth helps **her** husband. [singular, feminine]
The **Lilliputians** gave **their** captive food. [plural]

2k. Indefinite pronouns may be singular, plural, or either.

(1) Singular pronouns are used to refer to the indefinite pronouns *anybody, anyone, anything, each, either, everybody, everyone, everything, neither, nobody, no one, nothing, one, somebody, someone,* and *something.* The gender of any of these pronouns is determined by the word or words that the pronoun refers to.

EXAMPLES
Each of the **boys** has learned **his** part in *Macbeth*.
One of the **girls** has injured **herself.**

If the antecedent may be either masculine or feminine, use both the masculine and feminine pronouns to refer to it.

EXAMPLE
Anyone who is going on the field trip needs to bring **his** or **her** lunch.

(2) Plural pronouns are used to refer to the indefinite pronouns *both, few, many,* and *several.*

EXAMPLE
Many of the spectators leapt from **their** seats and cheered.

(3) Singular or plural pronouns may be used to refer to the indefinite pronouns *all, any, most, none,* and *some.* These indefinite pronouns are singular when they refer to singular words and are plural when they refer to plural words.

| SINGULAR | **None** of the renovated theater matches **its** original beauty. [*None* refers to the singular noun *theater.*] |
| PLURAL | **None** of the geese have left on **their** annual migration. [*None* refers to the plural noun *geese.*] |

2l. A plural pronoun is used to refer to two or more singular antecedents joined by *and.*

EXAMPLE
Malcolm and Donalbain left Scotland soon after **their** father was killed.

2m. A singular pronoun is used to refer to two or more singular antecedents joined by *or* or *nor.*

EXAMPLE

Neither **Malcolm nor Donalbain** felt **he** was safe.

2n. A collective noun (such as *club* or *family*) takes a singular pronoun when the noun refers to the group as a unit and takes a plural pronoun when the noun refers to the parts or members of the group.

SINGULAR The **jury** reached **its** decision less than one hour later. [The jury decided as a unit.]

PLURAL The **jury** disagree on how much importance **they** should give to one of the defendant's statements. [The members of the jury disagree.]

2o. The title of a creative work (such as a book, song, film, or painting) or the name of an organization, a country, or a city (even if it is plural in form) takes a singular pronoun.

EXAMPLES

I read ***Gulliver's Travels*** and wrote a report on **it**.
The **United Arab Emirates** generates most of **its** revenue from the sale of oil.

3 USING VERBS

THE PRINCIPAL PARTS OF VERBS

Every verb has four basic forms called the *principal parts:* the *base form,* the *present participle,* the *past,* and the *past participle.* A verb is classified as *regular* or *irregular* depending on the way it forms its past and past participle.

3a. A *regular verb* forms the past and past participle by adding *–d* or *–ed* to the base form. An *irregular verb* forms the past and the past participle in some other way.

COMMON REGULAR AND IRREGULAR VERBS

The following examples include *is* and *have* in italics to show that helping verbs (forms of *be* and *have*) are used with the present participle and past participle forms.

BASE FORM	PRESENT PARTICIPLE	PAST	PAST PARTICIPLE
REGULAR			
attack	*is* attacking	attacked	*have* attacked
drown	*is* drowning	drowned	*have* drowned
occur	*is* occurring	occurred	*have* occurred
risk	*is* risking	risked	*have* risked
try	*is* trying	tried	*have* tried
use	*is* using	used	*have* used

IRREGULAR			
be	*is* being	was, were	*have* been
bring	*is* bringing	brought	*have* brought
burst	*is* bursting	burst	*have* burst
come	*is* coming	came	*have* come
eat	*is* eating	ate	*have* eaten
go	*is* going	went	*have* gone
lead	*is* leading	led	*have* led
pay	*is* paying	paid	*have* paid
see	*is* seeing	saw	*have* seen
sing	*is* singing	sang	*have* sung
steal	*is* stealing	stole	*have* stolen
take	*is* taking	took	*have* taken
throw	*is* throwing	threw	*have* thrown

NOTE If you are not sure about the principal parts of a verb, look in a dictionary. Entries for irregular verbs give the principal parts. If no principal parts are listed, the verb is a regular verb.

TENSES AND THEIR USES

3b. The *tense* of a verb indicates the time of the action or state of being that is expressed by the verb.

(1) The ***present tense*** is used mainly to express an action or a state of being that is occurring now.

EXAMPLE

The article **compares** Beowulf with other epic heroes.

The present tense is also used

- to show a customary or habitual action or state of being
- to convey a general truth—something that is always true
- to make a historical event seem current (such use is called the **historical present**)
- to summarize the plot or subject matter of a literary work or to refer to an author's relationship to his or her work (such use is called the **literary present**)
- to express future time

EXAMPLES

Every Friday, our teacher **gives** us a vocabulary quiz. [customary action]

Reptiles **are** coldblooded. [general truth]

The Greeks **establish** separate city-states, which **war** among themselves. [historical present]

In the land of the Lilliputians, Gulliver **appears** gigantic. [literary present]

The two-week seminar on Shakespeare **begins** on Monday. [future time]

(2) The **past tense** is used to express an action or state of being that occurred in the past but did not continue into the present.

EXAMPLE

An expert on T. S. Eliot's poetry **spoke** to our class.

(3) The **future tense** (*will* or *shall* + base form) is used to express an action or a state of being that will occur.

EXAMPLE

Laurie **will play** the part of Lady Macbeth.

 NOTE *Shall* and *will* are both acceptable in forming the future tense.

(4) The **present perfect tense** (*have* or *has* + past participle) is used to express an action or a state of being that occurred at some indefinite time in the past.

EXAMPLE

Kenneth Branagh **has played** the roles of Henry V and of Iago.

The present perfect tense is also used to express an action or a state of being that began in the past and continues into the present.

EXAMPLE

Herot **has stood** empty for twelve years.

(5) The **past perfect tense** (*had* + past participle) is used to express an action or state of being completed in the past before some other past occurrence.

EXAMPLE

The kingdom **had suffered** before Beowulf arrived. [The suffering occurred before the arriving.]

Be sure to use the past perfect tense in "if" clauses that express the earlier of two past actions.

EXAMPLE

If you **had read** [*not* read *or* would have read] the article, you would have learned about Sutton Hoo.

(6) The **future perfect tense** (*will have* or *shall have* + past participle) is used to express an action or state of being that will be completed in the future before some other future occurrence.

EXAMPLE

By this time tomorrow, I **will** [*or* **shall**] **have memorized** "The Seafarer."

3c. Avoid unnecessary shifts in tense.

INCONSISTENT	Wiglaf discovered the dragon's treasure and then brings it to Beowulf. [shift from past to present tense]
CONSISTENT	Wiglaf **discovered** the dragon's treasure and then **brought** it to Beowulf. [past tense]
CONSISTENT	Wiglaf **discovers** the dragon's treasure and then **brings** it to Beowulf. [present tense]

When describing events that occur at different times, use verbs in different tenses to show the order of events.

EXAMPLE

She **taught** school for several years, but now she **works** for a publishing company. [Because she taught at a specific time in the past, the past tense *taught* is correct. Because she works at the present time, the present tense *works* is correct.]

ACTIVE VOICE AND PASSIVE VOICE

3d. *Voice* is the form a transitive verb takes to indicate whether the subject of the verb performs or receives the action.

A verb is in the **active voice** when its subject performs the action (its object receives the action).

ACTIVE VOICE	William Shakespeare **wrote** more than thirty-five plays.

A verb is in the **passive voice** whenever its subject receives the action (the verb has no object). A passive verb is always a verb phrase that includes a form of *be* and the past participle of an action verb.

PASSIVE VOICE	More than thirty-five plays **were written** by William Shakespeare.

3e. **Use the passive voice sparingly.**

In general, the passive voice is less direct and less forceful than the active voice. In some cases, the passive voice also may sound awkward.

AWKWARD PASSIVE	The sleeping grooms are smeared with King Duncan's blood by Lady Macbeth.
ACTIVE	Lady Macbeth **smears** the sleeping grooms with King Duncan's blood.

Although you generally will want to use active voice rather than passive voice, the passive voice is not less correct than the active voice. In fact, the passive voice is useful in the following situations:

1. when you do not know the performer of the action

EXAMPLE
The Globe **was built** in 1599.

2. when you do not want to reveal the performer of the action

EXAMPLE
The actor **was criticized** for his portrayal of Macbeth.

3. when you want to emphasize the receiver of the action

EXAMPLE
King Duncan **was murdered** while he was asleep.

4 USING PRONOUNS

CASE

Case is the form that a noun or a pronoun takes to indicate its use in a sentence. In English, there are three cases: *nominative, objective,* and *possessive.* Most personal pronouns have a different form for each case.

The Nominative Case

4a. **A subject of a verb is in the nominative case.**

EXAMPLES
They built the tower near the sea as **he** had requested. [*They* is the subject of the verb *built. He* is the subject of the verb *had requested.*]

4b. **A predicate nominative is in the nominative case.**

EXAMPLE
The only students who auditioned for the part of King Arthur were **he** and **Carlos.** [*He* and *Carlos* are predicate nominatives that follow the linking verb *were* and identify the subject *students.*]

PERSONAL PRONOUNS			
SINGULAR			
	NOMINATIVE	**OBJECTIVE**	**POSSESSIVE**
FIRST PERSON	I	me	my, mine
SECOND PERSON	you	you	your, yours
THIRD PERSON	he, she, it	him, her, it	his, her, hers, its
PLURAL			
	NOMINATIVE	**OBJECTIVE**	**POSSESSIVE**
FIRST PERSON	we	us	our, ours
SECOND PERSON	you	you	your, yours
THIRD PERSON	they	them	their, theirs

NOTE The form of a noun is the same for both the nominative case and the objective case. A noun changes its form for the possessive case, usually by adding an apostrophe and an s to most singular nouns and only an apostrophe to most plural nouns.

For more information about forming possessives of nouns, see page 1249.

The Objective Case

4c. **An object of a verb is in the objective case.**

EXAMPLES

The knight's answer pleases **her.** [*Her* is a direct object that tells *whom* the answer pleases.]

The Pardoner tells **them** a story about three greedy rioters. [*Them* is an indirect object that tells *to whom* the Pardoner tells a story.]

4d. **An object of a preposition is in the objective case.**

EXAMPLE

Are the Lilliputians afraid of **him**? [*Him* is the object of the preposition *of*.]

The Possessive Case

4e. **A noun or a pronoun preceding a gerund is in the possessive case.**

EXAMPLE

We were all thrilled by **Joetta's** [*or* **her**] scoring in the top 5 percent. [*Joetta's* or *her* modifies *scoring*, a gerund used as the object of the preposition *by*.]

Do not confuse a gerund with a present participle, which is a verb form that ends in *–ing* and may function as an adjective.

EXAMPLE

Macbeth found **them** [*not* their] standing around a caldron. [*Them* is modified by the participial phrase *standing around a caldron*.]

SPECIAL PRONOUN PROBLEMS

4f. **An appositive is in the same case as the noun or pronoun to which it refers.**

EXAMPLES

Duncan's sons, **Malcolm and he,** leave Scotland. [The compound appositive *Malcolm and he* refers to the subject, *sons*.]

Macduff suspects both of them, **Malcolm and him.** [The compound appositive *Malcolm and him* refers to *them*, the object of the preposition *of*.]

4g. **A pronoun following *than* or *as* in an elliptical construction is in the same case as it would be if the construction were completed.**

An **elliptical construction** is a clause from which words have been omitted.

NOMINATIVE I see him more often **than she.** [I see him more often *than she sees him*. *She* is the subject in the elliptical construction.]

OBJECTIVE I see him more often **than her.** [I see him more often *than I see her*. *Her* is the direct object in the elliptical construction.]

4h. **A pronoun ending in *–self* or *–selves* should not be used in place of a personal pronoun.**

EXAMPLE

Everyone except John and **me** [*not* myself] has read *Don Juan*.

4i. **The pronoun *who* (*whoever*) is in the nominative case. The pronoun *whom* (*whomever*) is in the objective case.**

EXAMPLES

Who wrote "Ozymandias"? [*Who* is the subject of the verb *wrote*.]

With **whom** did Wordsworth write *Lyrical Ballads*? [*Whom* is the object of the preposition *with*.]

CLEAR PRONOUN REFERENCE

The word that a pronoun stands for or refers to is called the **antecedent** of the pronoun.

4j. **A pronoun should always refer clearly to its antecedent.**

Avoid an ambiguous, a general, a weak, or an indefinite reference by

1. rephrasing the sentence, or

2. replacing the pronoun with an appropriate noun, or

3. giving the pronoun a clear antecedent.

AMBIGUOUS When the Green Knight was talking to Sir Gawain, he was holding his head in his hand. [The antecedent of *he* and *his* is unclear. Was the Green Knight holding Sir Gawain's head or his own?]

CLEAR The Green Knight was holding his head in his hand when he was talking to Sir Gawain.

GENERAL Macbeth will become king. This is one of the witches' prophecies. [*This* has no specific antecedent.]

CLEAR That Macbeth will become king is one of the witches' prophecies.

WEAK	Our dog Hank is jealous of my new baby sister. To help him get over it, I try to give him extra attention. [The antecedent of *it* is not expressed.]
CLEAR	To help our dog Hank get over his jealousy of my new baby sister, I try to give him extra attention.
INDEFINITE	In this book it includes pictures of artifacts from the Sutton Hoo ship burial. [*It* is not necessary to the meaning of the sentence.]
CLEAR	This book includes pictures of artifacts from the Sutton Hoo ship burial.

5 USING MODIFIERS

A *modifier* is a word or group of words that limits the meaning of another word or group of words. The two kinds of modifiers are *adjectives* and *adverbs*.

5a. Use an *adjective* to limit the meaning of a noun or a pronoun. Use an *adverb* to limit the meaning of a verb, an adjective, or another adverb.

COMPARISON OF MODIFIERS

5b. *Comparison* refers to the change in the form of an adjective or an adverb to show increasing or decreasing degrees in the quality the modifier expresses.

The three degrees of comparison are *positive, comparative,* and *superlative.*

1. Most one-syllable modifiers form the comparative and superlative degrees by adding *–er* and *–est.*

2. Some two-syllable modifiers form the comparative and superlative degrees by adding *–er* and *–est.* Other two-syllable modifiers form the comparative and superlative degrees by using *more* and *most.*

3. Modifiers of more than two syllables form the comparative and superlative degrees by using *more* and *most.*

4. To show a decrease in the qualities they express, all modifiers form the comparative by using *less* and the superlative by using *least.*

POSITIVE	COMPARATIVE	SUPERLATIVE
soft	softer	softest
thirsty	thirstier	thirstiest
slowly	more slowly	most slowly
skillfully	less skillfully	least skillfully

☞ For information about adding suffixes such as *–er* and *–est* to words, see page 1252.

5. Some modifiers form the comparative and superlative degrees in other ways.

POSITIVE	COMPARATIVE	SUPERLATIVE
bad (ill)	worse	worst
far	farther (further)	farthest (furthest)
good (well)	better	best
little	less	least
many (much)	more	most

5c. Use the comparative degree when comparing two things. Use the superlative degree when comparing more than two.

COMPARATIVE	After reading *King Lear* and *The Winter's Tale,* I can understand why *King Lear* is the **more popular** play. [comparison of two plays]
SUPERLATIVE	Of the three plays I saw, I think *Macbeth* was the **most powerful.** [comparison of three plays]

5d. Avoid a double comparison or a double negative. A *double comparison* is the use of two comparative forms (usually *–er* and *more* or *less*) or two superlative forms (usually *–est* and *most* or *least*) to modify the same word. A *double negative* is the use of two negative words where one is enough.

EXAMPLES

Who is the **noblest** [*not* most noblest] of King Arthur's knights?

I know **nothing** [*not* don't know nothing] about the Wars of the Roses.

5e. Include the word *other* or *else* when comparing one member of a group with the rest of the group.

ILLOGICAL Wiglaf is bolder than any of Beowulf's followers. [Wiglaf is one of Beowulf's followers. Logically, Wiglaf cannot be bolder than himself.]

LOGICAL Wiglaf is bolder than any of Beowulf's **other** followers.

5f. Avoid comparing items that cannot logically be compared.

ILLOGICAL I think Olivier's portrayal of Hamlet is more compelling than any other actor. [The sentence makes an illogical comparison between a portrayal and an actor.]

LOGICAL I think Olivier's portrayal of Hamlet is more compelling than any other actor's [portrayal]. [The sentence makes a logical comparison between portrayals.]

PLACEMENT OF MODIFIERS

5g. Avoid using a *misplaced modifier*—a modifying word, phrase, or clause that sounds awkward because it modifies the wrong word or group of words.

To correct a misplaced modifier, place the word, phrase, or clause as close as possible to the word or words you intend it to modify.

MISPLACED The old man told the three young rioters under a tree they would find Death. [What occurred under a tree: the telling or the finding?]

CLEAR The old man told the three young rioters they would find Death **under a tree.**

MISPLACED The anxious hunter watched the raging lion come charging at him as he readied his bow and arrow.

CLEAR **As he readied his bow and arrow,** the anxious hunter watched the raging lion come charging at him.

5h. Avoid using a *dangling modifier*—a modifying word, phrase, or clause that does not sensibly modify any word or words in a sentence.

You may correct a dangling modifier by

- adding a word or words that the dangling word, phrase, or clause can sensibly refer to
- adding a word or words to the dangling word, phrase, or clause
- rewording the sentence

DANGLING After becoming poet laureate, "The Charge of the Light Brigade" was written. [Who became poet laureate?]

CLEAR After becoming poet laureate, Alfred, Lord Tennyson wrote "The Charge of the Light Brigade."

CLEAR Alfred, Lord Tennyson wrote "The Charge of the Light Brigade" after he became poet laureate.

6 PHRASES

WHAT IS A PHRASE?

6a. A *phrase* is a group of related words that is used as a single part of speech and that does not contain a verb and its subject.

EXAMPLE
The Rime of the Ancient Mariner, **Coleridge's best-known poem,** was published in 1798.
[*Coleridge's best-known poem* functions as a noun, *was published* is a verb, and *in 1798* functions as an adverb.]

THE PREPOSITIONAL PHRASE

6b. A *prepositional phrase* begins with a preposition and ends with the *object of the preposition,* a word or word group that functions as a noun.

EXAMPLE
From the rafters of Herot hung one **of Grendel's arms.** [The noun *rafters* is the object of the preposition *from.* The noun *Herot* is the object of the preposition *of.* The noun *arms* is the object of the preposition *of.*]

An object of a preposition may be compound.

EXAMPLE
The three men ignored the warnings **of the tavern-knave and the publican.** [Both *tavern-knave* and *publican* are objects of the preposition *of*.]

(1) An *adjective phrase* is a prepositional phrase that modifies a noun or a pronoun. An adjective phrase tells *what kind* or *which one*.

EXAMPLE
The three rioters found eight bushels **of gold coins.** [*Of gold coins* modifies the noun *bushels*.]

An adjective phrase usually follows the word it modifies. That word may be the object of another preposition.

EXAMPLE
They told stories on their journey **to Canterbury.** [*To Canterbury* modifies *journey*, the object of the preposition *on*.]

More than one adjective phrase may modify the same word.

EXAMPLE
Chaucer's trips **to Italy on important diplomatic missions** broadened his knowledge. [The phrases *to Italy* and *on important diplomatic missions* modify the noun *trips*.]

(2) An *adverb phrase* is a prepositional phrase that modifies a verb, an adjective, or an adverb. An adverb phrase tells *how, when, where, why,* or *to what extent* (*how long* or *how far*).

As you can see in the example below, more than one adverb phrase can modify the same word. The example also shows that an adverb phrase, unlike an adjective phrase, can precede the word it modifies.

EXAMPLE
In 1799, Wordsworth returned **with his sister to the Lake District.** [Each phrase modifies the verb *returned. In 1799* tells *when*, *with his sister* tells *how*, and *to the Lake District* tells *where*.]

VERBALS AND VERBAL PHRASES

A *verbal* is a form of a verb used as a noun, an adjective, or an adverb. A *verbal phrase* consists of a verbal and its modifiers and complements.

Participles and Participial Phrases

6c. A *participle* is a verb form that is used as an adjective. A *participial phrase* consists of a participle and all the words related to the participle.

The two kinds of participles are the *present participle* and the *past participle*.

(1) *Present participles* end in *–ing*.

EXAMPLE
Sir Gawain heard the Green Knight **sharpening his ax.** [The participial phrase modifies the noun *Green Knight.* The noun *ax* is the direct object of the present participle *sharpening*.]

(2) Most *past participles* end in *–d* or *–ed*. Others are irregularly formed.

EXAMPLE
Tormented by her guilt, Lady Macbeth lost her sanity. [The participial phrase modifies the noun *Lady Macbeth.* The adverb phrase *by her guilt* modifies the past participle *tormented*.]

Gerunds and Gerund Phrases

6d. A *gerund* is a verb form ending in *–ing* that is used as a noun. A *gerund phrase* consists of a gerund and all the words related to the gerund.

EXAMPLES
For Gulliver, **living in Brobdingnag** is quite different from **living in Lilliput.** [*Living in Brobdingnag* is the subject of the verb *is. Living in Lilliput* is the object of the preposition *from.* The adverb phrases *in Brobdingnag* and *in Lilliput* modify the gerund *living*.]
The Miller enjoys **playing the bagpipes.** [*Playing the bagpipes* is the direct object of the verb *enjoys. Bagpipes* is the direct object of the gerund *playing*.]

Infinitives and Infinitive Phrases

6e. An *infinitive* is a verb form that can be used as a noun, an adjective, or an adverb. An infinitive usually begins with *to*. An *infinitive phrase* consists of an infinitive and all the words related to the infinitive.

EXAMPLES
The three rioters vow **to kill Death.** [The infinitive phrase acts as a noun and is the direct object of the verb *vow. Death* is the direct object of the infinitive *to kill*.]
She had a great desire **to visit Stratford-on-Avon.** [The infinitive phrase acts as an adjective and modifies the noun *desire. Stratford-on-Avon* is the direct object of the infinitive *to visit*.]

Macbeth goes to the witches' haunt **to talk to them.**
[The infinitive phrase acts as an adverb and modifies the verb *goes.* The adverb phrase *to them* modifies the infinitive *to talk.*]

Lady Macbeth helps her husband **become king.**
[The sign of the infinitive, *to,* is omitted. The infinitive has a subject, *husband,* making the entire construction an **infinitive clause.** The infinitive clause acts as a noun and is the direct object of the verb *helps.*]

APPOSITIVES AND APPOSITIVE PHRASES

6f. An *appositive* **is a noun or a pronoun placed beside another noun or pronoun to identify or explain it. An** *appositive phrase* **consists of an appositive and its modifiers.**

An appositive or appositive phrase usually follows the word it identifies or explains.

EXAMPLES

Have you read Coleridge's poem **"Kubla Khan"**?
[The appositive *"Kubla Khan"* identifies the noun *poem.*]

Shakespeare was born in Stratford-on-Avon, **a market town about eighty miles from London.**
[The entire appositive phrase *a market town about eighty miles from London* identifies the noun *Stratford-on-Avon.*]

For emphasis, however, an appositive or an appositive phrase may precede the word that it explains or identifies.

EXAMPLE

A riot of colorful sights, intriguing aromas, and surprising noises, a Cairo bazaar is great fun to visit. [The appositive phrase explains why a Cairo bazaar is fun to visit.]

7 CLAUSES

7a. A *clause* **is a group of words that contains a verb and its subject and that is used as part of a sentence. There are two kinds of clauses: the** *independent clause* **and the** *subordinate clause.*

THE INDEPENDENT CLAUSE

7b. An *independent* **(or** *main***)** *clause* **expresses a complete thought and can stand by itself as a sentence.**

EXAMPLE

SUBJECT   VERB
William Shakespeare wrote more than 150 sonnets. [one independent clause]

THE SUBORDINATE CLAUSE

7c. A *subordinate* **(or** *dependent***)** *clause* **does not express a complete thought and cannot stand alone as a sentence.**

EXAMPLE

SUBJECT   VERB
that **Lord Byron swam** across the Hellespont

The thought expressed by a subordinate clause becomes complete when the clause is combined with an independent clause to create a complete sentence.

EXAMPLE

I read **that Lord Byron swam across the Hellespont.**

The Adjective Clause

7d. An *adjective clause* **is a subordinate clause that modifies a noun or a pronoun.**

An adjective clause always follows the word or words that it modifies. Usually, an adjective clause begins with a **relative pronoun** (such as *that, which, who, whom, whose*). A relative pronoun both relates an adjective clause to the word or words the clause modifies and performs a function within its own clause by serving as a subject, an object of a verb, an object of a preposition, or a modifier.

EXAMPLES

Mary Shelley, **who wrote *Frankenstein,*** liked reading ghost stories with her friends. [The relative pronoun *who* relates the adjective clause to the noun *Mary Shelley* and serves as the subject of the verb *wrote.*]

The knight **for whom Sir Gawain is searching** is the Knight of the Green Chapel. [The relative pronoun *whom* relates the adjective clause to the noun *knight* and serves as the object of the preposition *for.*]

An adjective clause may begin with a *relative adverb,* such as *when* or *where.*

EXAMPLES
My uncle Robert told us about the time **when he backpacked across the island of Luzon.** [The adjective clause modifies the noun *time.*]
Malcolm flees to England, **where he raises an army to attack Macbeth.** [The adjective clause modifies the noun *England.*]

The Noun Clause

7e. A *noun clause* is a subordinate clause that may be used as a subject, a predicate nominative, a direct object, an indirect object, or an object of a preposition.

Words that are commonly used to introduce noun clauses include *how, that, what, whether, who, whoever,* and *why.*

EXAMPLES
That Fleance escapes the murderers troubles Macbeth. [subject]
Power is **what Macbeth desires.** [predicate nominative]
Banquo suspected **that Macbeth had murdered Duncan.** [direct object]
The teacher will give **whoever can recite the soliloquy** ten points. [indirect object]
The teacher will give ten points to **whoever can recite the soliloquy.** [object of a preposition]

The word that introduces a noun clause may or may not have another function in the clause.

EXAMPLES
Do you know **who wrote *Don Juan*?** [The word *who* introduces the noun clause and serves as the subject of the verb *wrote.*]

The witches predict **that Macbeth will become king.** [The word *that* introduces the noun clause but does not have any function within the noun clause.]

The Adverb Clause

7f. An *adverb clause* is a subordinate clause that modifies a verb, an adjective, or an adverb.

An adverb clause, which may come before or after the word or words it modifies, tells *how, when, where, why, to what extent,* or *under what condition.* An adverb clause is introduced by a *subordinating conjunction*—a word or word group that relates the adverb clause to the word or words the clause modifies.

EXAMPLES
He acted **as though he had seen a ghost.** [The adverb clause modifies the verb *acted,* telling *how* he acted.]
Jane is taller **than her grandmother is.** [The adverb clause modifies the adjective *taller,* telling *to what extent* Jane is tall.]
They stayed longer **than I thought they would.** [The adverb clause modifies the adverb *longer,* telling *to what extent* their stay was longer.]

The Elliptical Clause

7g. Part of a clause may be left out when the meaning can be understood from the context of the sentence. Such a clause is called an *elliptical clause.*

EXAMPLES
While [he was] **painting,** Rembrandt concentrated completely on his work.
Ken may ride with us **if he wants to** [ride with us].
This job took longer **than the last one** [took].

 For more about using pronouns in elliptical constructions, see page 1228.

8 SENTENCE STRUCTURE

SENTENCE OR FRAGMENT?

8a. A *sentence* is a group of words that has a subject and a verb and expresses a complete thought.

EXAMPLES
"My Last Duchess" is an example of a dramatic monologue.
For how many years was Winston Churchill the prime minister of Britain?
What an ambitious man Macbeth was!

Only a sentence should begin with a capital letter and end with a period, a question mark, or an exclamation point. Do not be misled by a group of words that looks like a sentence but that either does not have a subject and a verb or does not express a complete thought. Such a word group is called a **sentence fragment.**

FRAGMENT	Awakens and finds himself surrounded by people six inches tall.
SENTENCE	Gulliver awakens and finds himself surrounded by people six inches tall.

SUBJECT AND PREDICATE

8b. A sentence consists of two parts: a subject and a predicate. A *subject* tells *whom* or *what* the sentence is about. A *predicate* tells something about the subject.

In the following examples, all the words labeled *subject* make up the **complete subject,** and all the words labeled *predicate* make up the **complete predicate.**

EXAMPLES

SUBJECT	PREDICATE
My sister and I	enjoyed *Gulliver's Travels.*

PREDICATE	SUBJECT	PREDICATE
For fifty years	Beowulf	ruled Geatland.

The Simple Subject

8c. A *simple subject* is the main word or group of words that tells *whom* or *what* the sentence is about.

EXAMPLE
The first **leader** of the gang was Blackie. [The complete subject is *the first leader of the gang.*]

The Simple Predicate

8d. A *simple predicate* is a verb or verb phrase that tells something about the subject.

EXAMPLE
Have you **read** "The Seafarer"? [The complete predicate is *have read "The Seafarer."*]

The Compound Subject and the Compound Verb

8e. A *compound subject* consists of two or more subjects that are joined by

a conjunction—usually *and* or *or*—and that have the same verb.

EXAMPLE
A **nun** and three **priests** accompany the Prioress on the pilgrimage.

8f. A *compound verb* consists of two or more verbs that are joined by a conjunction—usually *and, but,* or *or*—and that have the same subject.

EXAMPLE
Truth **enlightens** the mind, **frees** the spirit, and **strengthens** the soul.

How to Find the Subject of a Sentence

8g. To find the subject of a sentence, ask *Who?* or *What?* before the verb.

(1) The subject of a sentence is never within a prepositional phrase.

EXAMPLES
A **group** of pilgrims gathered at the Tabard. [Who gathered? Group gathered. *Pilgrims* is the object of the preposition *of.*]

Out of the stillness came the loud **sound** of laughter. [What came? Sound came. *Stillness* is the object of the preposition *out of. Laughter* is the object of the preposition *of.*]

(2) The subject of a sentence expressing a command or a request is always understood to be *you,* although *you* may not appear in the sentence.

COMMAND	Name the pilgrim accompanying the Plowman. [Who is being told to name? *You* is understood.]

The subject of a command or a request is *you* even when the sentence also contains a **noun of direct address**—a word that names or identifies the one or ones spoken to.

REQUEST	Marla, [you] please read the first stanza of "To a Skylark."

(3) The subject of a sentence expressing a question usually follows the verb or a part of the verb phrase. Turning the question into a statement will often help you find the subject.

QUESTION	Have you read Lord Byron's poem "She Walks in Beauty"?
STATEMENT	**You** have read Lord Byron's poem "She Walks in Beauty." [Who has read? You have read.]

QUESTION	Were Shakespeare's plays popular during his own lifetime?
STATEMENT	Shakespeare's **plays** were popular during his own lifetime. [What were popular? Plays were popular.]

(4) The word *there* or *here* is never the subject of a sentence.

EXAMPLES

There is **Canterbury Cathedral.** [What is there? Canterbury Cathedral is there.]

Here are my **drawings** of Chaucer's pilgrims. [What are here? Drawings are here.]

COMPLEMENTS

8h. A *complement* is a word or a group of words that completes the meaning of a verb or a verbal. The four main kinds of complements are *direct objects, indirect objects, objective complements,* and *subject complements.*

The Direct Object and the Indirect Object

8i. A *direct object* is a noun, a pronoun, or a word group that functions as a noun and tells *who* or *what* receives the action of a transitive verb.

EXAMPLES

Banquo definitely suspected **him.** [Suspected whom? him]

Beethoven composed **sonatas** and **symphonies.** [Composed what? sonatas and symphonies— compound direct object]

8j. An *indirect object* is a word or word group that comes between a transitive verb and a direct object. An indirect object, which may be a noun, a pronoun, or a word group that functions as a noun, tells *to whom, to what, for whom,* or *for what* the action of the verb is done.

EXAMPLES

The Wife of Bath told the other **pilgrims** an interesting story. [Told to whom? pilgrims]

We should give **practicing for the concert** our full attention. [Should give our full attention to what? practicing for the concert]

The Objective Complement

8k. An *objective complement* is a word or word group that helps complete the meaning of a transitive verb by identifying or modifying the direct object. An objective complement, which may be a noun, a pronoun, an adjective, or a word group that functions as a noun or an adjective, usually follows the direct object.

EXAMPLES

Macduff called Malcolm **king.** [The noun *king* identifies the direct object *Malcolm.*]

He believed the money **his.** [The pronoun *his* modifies the direct object *money.*]

Everyone considered him **chivalrous.** [The adjective *chivalrous* modifies the direct object *him.*]

 NOTE A *transitive verb* is an action verb that takes an object, which tells who or what receives the action.

The Subject Complement

8l. A *subject complement* is a word or a word group that completes the meaning of a linking verb or a verbal and that identifies or modifies the subject. The two kinds of subject complements are *predicate nominatives* and *predicate adjectives.*

(1) A *predicate nominative* is a word or group of words that follows a linking verb and refers to the same person, place, thing, or idea as the subject of the verb. A predicate nominative may be a noun, a pronoun, or a word group that functions as a noun.

EXAMPLES

Of these three poets, Wordsworth was the most prolific **one.** [The pronoun *one* refers to the subject **Wordsworth.**]

The main characters are **Paul** and his **mother.** [The two nouns *Paul* and *mother* are a compound predicate nominative that refers to the subject *characters.*]

(2) A *predicate adjective* is an adjective that follows a linking verb and that modifies the subject of the verb.

EXAMPLES

Did King Hrothgar feel **powerless**? [The adjective *powerless* modifies the subject *King Hrothgar.*]

Iago is **sly** and **scheming.** [The two adjectives *sly* and *scheming* are a compound predicate adjective that modifies the subject *Iago.*]

 For a list of linking verbs, see page 1222.

SENTENCES CLASSIFIED ACCORDING TO STRUCTURE

8m. According to their structure, sentences are classified as *simple, compound, complex,* and *compound-complex.*

(1) A **simple sentence** has one independent clause and no subordinate clauses.

EXAMPLE
"Not Waving but Drowning" is one of my favorite poems.

(2) A **compound sentence** has two or more independent clauses but no subordinate clauses.

EXAMPLES
Othello is a great man, but his character is flawed.
Agatha Christie was a prolific writer; she wrote
   more than eighty books in less than sixty years.

(3) A **complex sentence** has one independent clause and at least one subordinate clause.

EXAMPLE
The poet who wrote "Ode on a Grecian Urn" is John Keats. [The independent clause is *the poet is John Keats.* The subordinate clause is *who wrote "Ode on a Grecian Urn."*]

(4) A **compound-complex** sentence has two or more independent clauses and at least one subordinate clause.

EXAMPLE
After Macbeth killed their father, Malcolm fled to England, and Donalbain escaped to Ireland. [The two independent clauses are *Malcolm fled to England* and *Donalbain escaped to Ireland.* The subordinate clause is *after Macbeth killed their father.*]

SENTENCES CLASSIFIED ACCORDING TO PURPOSE

8n. According to their purpose, sentences are classified as *declarative, interrogative, imperative,* and *exclamatory.*

(1) A **declarative sentence** makes a statement. It is followed by a period.

EXAMPLE
The lock on the front door is broken.

(2) An **interrogative sentence** asks a question. It is followed by a question mark.

EXAMPLE
Have you read Dylan Thomas's "Fern Hill"?

(3) An **imperative sentence** makes a request or gives a command. It is usually followed by a period. A very strong command, however, is followed by an exclamation point.

EXAMPLES
Please return this book to the library.
Give me the name of the warrior who succeeds
   Beowulf.
Stop making that noise!

(4) An **exclamatory sentence** expresses strong feeling or shows excitement. It is followed by an exclamation point.

EXAMPLES
What a talented writer she was!
We won!

 For more information about using end marks, see pages 1243–1244.

9 SENTENCE STYLE

WAYS TO ACHIEVE CLARITY

Coordinating Ideas

9a. To *coordinate* two or more ideas, or to give them equal emphasis, link them with a connecting word, an appropriate mark of punctuation, or both.

EXAMPLE
I read the novel *Frankenstein,* **and** then I saw the film.

Subordinating Ideas

9b. To *subordinate* an idea, or to show that one idea is related to but less important than another, use an adverb clause or an adjective clause.

EXAMPLES
Sir Gawain accepts the magic sash **because he wants it to protect him from the Green Knight.** [adverb clause]
Hrunting is the name of the sword **that Unferth gives Beowulf.** [adjective clause]

Using Parallel Structure

9c. Use the same grammatical form (*parallel structure*) to express ideas of equal importance.

(1) Use parallel structure when you link coordinate ideas.

EXAMPLE
In the winter I usually like **to ski** and **to skate**. [infinitive paired with infinitive]

(2) Use parallel structure when you compare or contrast ideas.

EXAMPLE
Einstein liked mathematical **research** more than laboratory **supervision.** [noun contrasted with noun]

(3) Use parallel structure when you link ideas with correlative conjunctions (*both . . . and, either . . . or, neither . . . nor,* or *not only . . . but also*).

EXAMPLE
Virginia Woolf was not only **a novelist** but also **an essayist.** [Note that the correlative conjunctions come directly before the parallel terms.]

When you revise for parallel structure, you may need to add an article, a preposition, or a pronoun before each of the parallel terms.

| UNCLEAR | I admire the poems of Byron more than Wordsworth. |
| CLEAR | I admire the poems of Byron more than **those of** Wordsworth. |

OBSTACLES TO CLARITY

Sentence Fragments

9d. Avoid using a *sentence fragment*— a word or word group that either does not contain a subject and a verb or does not express a complete thought.

☞ For more information about sentence fragments, see pages 1233–1234.

Here are two common ways to correct a sentence fragment.

1. Add words to make the thought complete.

| FRAGMENT | Twelve Geats around Beowulf's tower. [The verb is missing.] |
| SENTENCE | Twelve Geats **rode** around Beowulf's tower. |

2. Attach the fragment to the sentence that comes before or after it.

| FRAGMENT | A doctor and a gentlewoman see Lady Macbeth. Walking in her sleep. [participial phrase] |
| SENTENCE | A doctor and a gentlewoman see Lady Macbeth **walking in her sleep.** |

 NOTE Sentence fragments can be effective when used in expressive and creative writing and in informal writing.

Run-on Sentences

9e. Avoid using a *run-on sentence*—two or more complete thoughts that are run together as if they were one complete thought.

The two kinds of run-on sentences are *fused sentences* and *comma splices*. A **fused sentence** has no punctuation or connecting word at all between the complete thoughts. A **comma splice** has just a comma between the complete thoughts.

| FUSED SENTENCE | Wiglaf helps Beowulf the other warriors retreat in fear. |
| COMMA SPLICE | Wiglaf helps Beowulf, the other warriors retreat in fear. |

You can correct run-on sentences in several ways.

1. Make two sentences.

EXAMPLE
Wiglaf helps Beowulf. The other warriors retreat in fear.

2. Use a comma and a coordinating conjunction.

EXAMPLE
Wiglaf helps Beowulf, **but** the other warriors retreat in fear.

3. Change one of the independent clauses to a subordinate clause.

EXAMPLE
Wiglaf helps Beowulf, **while the other warriors retreat in fear.**

4. Use a semicolon.

EXAMPLE
Wiglaf helps Beowulf; the other warriors retreat in fear.

5. Use a semicolon and a conjunctive adverb.

EXAMPLE
Wiglaf helps Beowulf; **however,** the other warriors retreat in fear.

Unnecessary Shifts in Sentences

9f. *Avoid making unnecessary shifts in subject, in tense, and in voice.*

AWKWARD	Grandma goes to the farmers' market, where the freshest produce is. [shift in subject]
BETTER	**Grandma** goes to the farmers' market, where **she** finds the freshest produce.
AWKWARD	Macbeth sees Banquo's ghost, but no one else did. [shift in tense]
BETTER	Macbeth **sees** Banquo's ghost, but no one else **does.**
AWKWARD	Lyle spent four hours at the library, but no books on his research topic were found. [shift in voice]
BETTER	Lyle **spent** four hours at the library, but he **found** no books on his research topic.

REVISING FOR VARIETY

9g. **Use a variety of sentence beginnings.**

Putting the subject first in a declarative sentence is not wrong, but starting every sentence with the subject can make your writing boring. To add variety to your sentences, rearrange sentence parts to vary the beginnings. The following examples show how a writer can revise sentences to avoid beginning with the subject every time.

SUBJECT FIRST	Lady Macbeth is cunning and ruthless and goads her husband into committing murder.
SINGLE-WORD MODIFIERS FIRST	**Cunning** and **ruthless,** Lady Macbeth goads her husband into committing murder.
SUBJECT FIRST	*In Memoriam,* **which was published in 1850,** is Alfred, Lord Tennyson's elegy for his friend Arthur Hallam.
PARTICIPIAL PHRASE FIRST	**Published in 1850,** *In Memoriam* is Alfred, Lord Tennyson's elegy for his friend Arthur Hallam.
APPOSITIVE PHRASE FIRST	**An elegy for Alfred, Lord Tennyson's friend Arthur Hallam,** *In Memoriam* was published in 1850.

Varying Sentence Structure

9h. **Use a mix of simple, compound, complex, and compound-complex sentences in your writing.**

EXAMPLE

The three "weird sisters" greet Macbeth and Banquo with prophecies. [simple] According to the witches, Macbeth will become king, but Banquo will not, though his descendants will. [compound-complex] When Macbeth asks the witches to tell him more, they vanish. [complex] The subsequent conversation between Banquo and Macbeth lends insight into each man's character. [simple] That is, Banquo is skeptical of the witches' prophecies; however, Macbeth believes in them. [compound]

 For information about the four kinds of sentence structure, see page 1236.

Revising to Reduce Wordiness

9i. **Avoid using unnecessary words in your writing.**

The following guidelines suggest some ways to revise wordy sentences.

1. Take out a whole group of unnecessary words.

WORDY	Grendel's mother carried Beowulf to her home where she lived.
IMPROVED	Grendel's mother carried Beowulf to her home.

2. Replace pretentious words and expressions with straightforward ones.

WORDY	In *Lord of the Flies,* a group of males, all of whom are under thirteen years of age, is stranded on a land mass surrounded by water and totally free of inhabitants.
IMPROVED	In *Lord of the Flies,* a group of **young boys** is stranded on an **uninhabited island.**

3. Reduce a clause to a phrase.

WORDY	Sir Lancelot falls in love with Queen Guinevere, who is the wife of King Arthur.
IMPROVED	Sir Lancelot falls in love with Queen Guinevere, **King Arthur's wife.**

4. Reduce a phrase or a clause to one word.

WORDY	At that point in time, Mr. Thomas returns.
IMPROVED	**Then,** Mr. Thomas returns.

10 SENTENCE COMBINING

COMBINING BY INSERTING WORDS AND PHRASES

10a. Combine related sentences by taking a key word (or using another form of the key word) from one sentence and inserting it into another sentence.

ORIGINAL	The famous magician Harry Houdini performed impossible escapes. The escapes only seemed impossible.
COMBINED	The famous magician Harry Houdini performed **seemingly** impossible escapes. [The verb *seemed* becomes the adverb *seemingly*.]

10b. Combine related sentences by taking (or creating) a phrase from one sentence and inserting it into another.

ORIGINAL	Have you read the poem "The Hollow Men"? It was written by T. S. Eliot.
COMBINED	Have you read the poem "The Hollow Men" **by T. S. Eliot**? [prepositional phrase]

COMBINING BY COORDINATING IDEAS

10c. Combine related sentences whose ideas are equally important by using coordinating conjunctions (*and, but, or, nor, for, so, yet*) or correlative conjunctions (*both . . . and, either . . . or, neither . . . nor, not only . . . but also*).

The relationship of the ideas determines which connective will work best. When joined, the coordinate ideas form compound elements.

ORIGINAL	*Paradise Lost* was written by John Milton. *Paradise Regained* was also written by him.
COMBINED	*Paradise Lost* **and** *Paradise Regained* were written by John Milton. [compound subject]
ORIGINAL	*Adonais* is one of Shelley's best-known poems. Many critics think that *Prometheus Unbound* is his masterpiece.
COMBINED	*Adonais* is one of Shelley's best-known poems**, but** many critics think that *Prometheus Unbound* is his masterpiece. [compound sentence]

Another way to form a compound sentence is to link independent clauses with a semicolon or with a semicolon and a conjunctive adverb (such as *however, likewise,* or *therefore*) followed by a comma.

EXAMPLES
She was willing to compromise**;** he was not.
They moved to Dorsetshire**; however,** they stayed there only a few months.

COMBINING BY SUBORDINATING IDEAS

10d. Combine related sentences whose ideas are not equally important by placing the less important idea in a subordinate clause (adjective clause, adverb clause, or noun clause).

ORIGINAL	I read about the life of Queen Victoria. She ruled Great Britain from 1837 to 1901.
COMBINED	I read about the life of Queen Victoria, **who ruled Great Britain from 1837 to 1901.** [adjective clause]
	or
COMBINED	Queen Victoria, **whose life I read about,** ruled Great Britain from 1837 to 1901. [adjective clause]
ORIGINAL	Grendel's mother attacks Herot. King Hrothgar once again asks Beowulf for help.
COMBINED	**When Grendel's mother attacks Herot,** King Hrothgar once again asks Beowulf for help. [adverb clause]
ORIGINAL	They will find Death under an oak tree. An old man tells the three rioters that this will happen.
COMBINED	An old man tells the three rioters **that they will find Death under an oak tree.** [noun clause]

 For more information about subordinate clauses and subordinating ideas, see pages 1232–1233 and 1236.

11a. Capitalize the first word in every sentence.

EXAMPLE

The warrior who succeeds Beowulf as king is Wiglaf.

(1) Capitalize the first word of a sentence following a colon.

EXAMPLE

Mrs. Kelley asked me this question: **H**ow old is Beowulf when he fights Grendel?

(2) Capitalize the first word of a direct quotation.

EXAMPLE

After winning, Brian said, "**W**e couldn't have done it without the support of the good people of Raleigh."

When quoting from another writer's work, capitalize the first word of the quotation only if the writer has capitalized it in the original work.

EXAMPLE

After winning, Brian acknowledged "**t**he support of the good people of Raleigh."

(3) Traditionally, the first word of a line of poetry is capitalized.

EXAMPLES

If all the world and love were young,
And truth in every shepherd's tongue,
These pretty pleasures might me move
To live with thee and be thy love.
   —Sir Walter Raleigh, "The Nymph's
      Reply to the Shepherd"

NOTE Some writers do not follow this rule. Whenever you quote from a writer's work, always use capital letters exactly as the writer uses them.

11b. Capitalize the first word in the salutation and the closing of a letter.

EXAMPLES

Dear John,   **D**ear Sir or Madam: **S**incerely,

11c. Capitalize proper nouns and proper adjectives.

A **common noun** is a general name for a person, a place, a thing, or an idea. A **proper noun** names a particular person, place, thing, or idea. A **proper adjective** is formed from a proper noun. Common

nouns are capitalized only if they begin a sentence (also, in most cases, a line of poetry), begin a direct quotation, or are part of a title.

COMMON NOUNS	PROPER NOUNS	PROPER ADJECTIVES
dramatist	**S**hakespeare	**S**hakespearean performer
country	**R**ussia	**R**ussian diplomat
mountains	the **A**lps	**A**lpine flora

In most proper nouns made up of two or more words, do not capitalize articles (*a, an, the*), short prepositions (those with fewer than five letters, such as *at, of, for, to, with*), the mark of the infinitive (*to*), and coordinating conjunctions (*and, but, for, nor, or, so, yet*).

EXAMPLES

Speaker **of** the **H**ouse **of** **R**epresentatives
American **S**ociety **for** the **P**revention **of** **C**ruelty
   to **A**nimals

NOTE When you're not sure whether to capitalize a word, check a dictionary.

(1) Capitalize the names of most persons and animals.

GIVEN NAMES	Virginia	Geoffrey
SURNAMES	Woolf	Chaucer
ANIMALS	Lassie	Rocinante

NOTE Some names contain more than one capital letter. Usage varies in the capitalization of *van, von, du, de la,* and other parts of many multiword names. Always verify the spelling of a name with the person, or check the name in a reference source.

EXAMPLES

| La Fontaine | O'Connor | al-Khansa | McEwen |
| Van Doren | Ibn Ezra | van Gogh | de Vega |

(2) Capitalize the names of nationalities, races, and peoples.

EXAMPLES

Japanese   Caucasian   Hispanic   Celt

(3) Capitalize brand names. Notice that the noun that follows a brand name is not capitalized.

EXAMPLES

Sealtest milk   Wonder bread   Crest toothpaste

(4) Capitalize geographical names.

TYPE OF NAME	EXAMPLES	
Towns, Cities	Stratford-on-Avon Rio de Janeiro	Dublin South Bend
Counties, Townships	Marion County Brooklyn Borough	Alexandria Township Lafayette Parish
States, Territories	Oklahoma Yucatán	North Carolina Yukon Territory
Regions	the Middle East Western Hemisphere	the Lake District the Southwest
Countries	England	Costa Rica
Continents	South America	Europe
Islands	Long Island	British Isles
Mountains	Himalayas Pikes Peak	Mount Rainier Sierra Nevada
Other Landforms and Features	Cape of Good Hope Death Valley	Isthmus of Corinth Black Forest
Bodies of Water	Indian Ocean Bering Strait	Red Sea San Francisco Bay
Parks	Hawaii Volcanoes National Park Point Reyes National Seashore	
Roads, Highways, Streets	Route 42 Interstate 75	King Avenue Thirty-fourth Street

 NOTE Words such as *city, state,* and *county* are often capitalized in official documents such as proclamations. In general usage, however, these words are not capitalized.

OFFICIAL USAGE
the State of Iowa

GENERAL USAGE
the state of Iowa

 NOTE Words such as *north, western,* and *southeast* are not capitalized when they indicate direction.

EXAMPLES
north of London
heading **s**outhwest

NOTE The second word in a hyphenated number begins with a small letter.

EXAMPLE
Forty-second Street

(5) Capitalize the names of organizations, teams, business firms, institutions, buildings and other structures, and government bodies.

TYPE OF NAME	EXAMPLES
Organizations	Disabled American Veterans Professional Photographers of America
Teams	River City Eastside Bombers Harlem Globetrotters
Business Firms	Aaron's Carpets National Broadcasting Corporation
Institutions	Oxford University Southern Christian Leadership Conference
Buildings and Other Structures	Lincoln Center for the Performing Arts the Great Wall of China
Government Bodies	United States Congress House of Commons

NOTE Do not capitalize words such as *democratic, republican,* and *socialist* when they refer to principles or forms of government. Capitalize such words only when they refer to specific political parties.

EXAMPLES
The citizens demanded **d**emocratic reforms.
Who will be the **R**epublican nominee for governor?

 NOTE Do not capitalize words such as *building, hospital, theater, high school,* and *post office* unless they are part of a proper noun.

(6) Capitalize the names of historical events and periods, special events, holidays and other calendar items, and time zones.

TYPE OF NAME	EXAMPLES	
Historical Events and Periods	Middle Ages	Reign of Terror
Special Events	Super Bowl	Pan-American Games
Holidays and Other Calendar Items	Monday November	Memorial Day National Book Week
Time Zones	Eastern Daylight Time (EDT) Central Mountain Time (CMT)	

NOTE Do not capitalize the name of a season unless it is being personified or used as part of a proper noun.

EXAMPLES
We moved here last fall.
This month Fall begins painting the leaves in brilliant hues.
The Fall Festival is next week.

(7) Capitalize the names of ships, trains, aircraft, spacecraft, monuments, awards, planets and other heavenly bodies, and any other particular places and things.

TYPE OF NAME	EXAMPLES	
Ships	Merrimac	U.S.S. Nautilus
Trains	Zephyr	Hill Country Flyer
Aircraft	Enola Gay	Spruce Goose
Spacecraft	Columbia	Magellan
Monuments	Mount Rushmore National Memorial Effigy Mounds National Monument	
Awards	Nobel Prize	Medal of Freedom
Planets and Other Heavenly Bodies	Neptune Big Dipper	Polaris Cassiopeia
Other Particular Places and Things	Hurricane Alma Marshall Plan	Silk Route Union Jack

NOTE Do not capitalize the words *sun* and *moon*. Do not capitalize the word *earth* unless it is used along with the proper names of other particular places, things, or events.

EXAMPLES
The equator is an imaginary circle around the earth.
Is Mercury closer to the sun than Earth is?

☞ For more information about the names of particular places and things, see the discussion of proper nouns on page 1240.

11d. Do not capitalize the names of school subjects, except names of languages and course names followed by a number.

EXAMPLES
French   art   Algebra I

11e. Capitalize titles.

(1) Capitalize a title belonging to a particular person when it comes before the person's name.

EXAMPLES
General Patton   Dr. Sanchez   President Clinton

In general, do not capitalize a title used alone or following a name. Some titles, however, are by tradition capitalized. If you are unsure about capitalizing a title, check in a dictionary.

EXAMPLES
Who is the prime minister of Britain?
When was Ann Richards governor of Texas?
The Prince of Wales met earlier today with European leaders.

A title is usually capitalized when it is used alone in direct address.

EXAMPLE
Good afternoon, Sir [*or* sir], may I help you?

(2) Capitalize a word showing a family relationship when the word is used before or in place of a person's name, unless a possessive comes before the word.

EXAMPLES
I asked Mom if Uncle Bob is named after her uncle Roberto.

(3) Capitalize the first and last words and all important words in titles of books, periodicals, poems, stories, essays, speeches, plays, historical documents, movies, radio and television programs, works of art, musical compositions, and cartoons.

TYPE OF NAME	EXAMPLES	
Books	*A Tale of Two Cities*	*Gulliver's Travels*
Periodicals	*National Geographic*	*Time*
Poems	"She Walks in Beauty"	"To His Coy Mistress"
Stories	"The Rocking-Horse Winner"	"Games at Twilight"
Essays and Speeches	"A Modest Proposal"	the Gettysburg Address
Plays	*The Tragedy of Macbeth*	*Pygmalion*
Historical Documents	Magna Carta	Treaty of Versailles
Movies	*Robin Hood: Prince of Thieves*	*Clueless*
Radio and TV Programs	*Adventures in World Music*	*Nova*
Works of Art	*The Kiss*	*March of Humanity*
Musical Compositions	*War Requiem*	"Tears in Heaven"
Cartoons	*For Better or Worse*	*Jump Start*

NOTE Unimportant words in a title include articles (*a, an, the*), short prepositions (those with fewer than five letters, such as *of, to, in, for, from, with*), and coordinating conjunctions (*and, but, for, nor, or, so, yet*).

☞ For information about which titles should be italicized and which should be enclosed in quotation marks, see pages 1247 and 1248.

11f. Capitalize the names of religions and their followers, holy days and celebrations, holy writings, and specific deities and venerated beings.

TYPE OF NAME	EXAMPLES	
Religions and Followers	Christianity Muslim	Buddhist Judaism
Holy Days and Celebrations	Easter Passover	Ramadan Holy Week
Holy Writings	Bible Talmud	Koran I Ching
Specific Deities and Venerated Beings	Allah Dalai Lama	God Jehovah

NOTE The words *god* and *goddess* are not capitalized when they refer to mythological deities. The names of specific mythological deities are capitalized, however.

EXAMPLES
The Greek god of the sea was Poseidon.

12 PUNCTUATION

END MARKS

12a. A statement (or declarative sentence) is followed by a period.

EXAMPLE
The Ancient Mariner told an amazing tale.

12b. A question (or interrogative sentence) is followed by a question mark.

EXAMPLE
Do you know who played the leading role in the first movie version of *Hamlet*?

12c. A request or command (or imperative sentence) is followed by either a period or an exclamation point.

EXAMPLES

Turn the music down, please. [request]
Name the poet who wrote "The Lady of Shalott." [mild command]
Watch out! [strong command]

12d. An exclamation (or exclamatory sentence) is followed by an exclamation point.

EXAMPLE

What an interesting story "My Oedipus Complex" is!

TYPE OF ABBREVIATION	EXAMPLES
Personal Names	Howard G. Chua-Eoan W. H. Auden
Organizations, Companies	Co. Inc. Ltd.
Titles Used with Names	Ms. Sr. Dr.
Times of Day	A.M. (or a.m.) P.M. (or p.m.)
Years	B.C. (*written after the date*) A.D. (*written before the date*)
Addresses	St. Blvd. P. O. Box
States	S.C. Calif.

12e. An abbreviation is usually followed by a period.

If an abbreviation with a period ends a sentence, do not add another period. However, do add a question mark or an exclamation point if one is needed.

EXAMPLES

The store opens at 10 A.M.
Does the store open at 10 A.M.?

Some abbreviations, including those for most units of measurement, are written without periods.

EXAMPLES

AM/FM, CIA, CNN, PC, NASA, SOS,
cc, ft, lb, kw, ml, psi, rpm [*but* in. *for* inch]

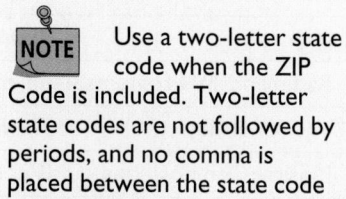

NOTE Use a two-letter state code when the ZIP Code is included. Two-letter state codes are not followed by periods, and no comma is placed between the state code and the ZIP Code.

EXAMPLE

Lexington, **KY** 40505

COMMAS

12f. Use commas to separate items in a series.

EXAMPLE

Virginia Woolf, James Joyce, and D. H. Lawrence are among the writers we are studying.

If all the items in a series are linked by *and, or,* or *nor,* do not use commas to separate them.

EXAMPLE

Byron **and** Shelley **and** Keats were contemporaries.

12g. Use a comma to separate two or more adjectives preceding a noun.

EXAMPLE

Gawain is the most gallant, honorable knight.

When the last adjective before a noun is thought of as part of the noun, the comma before the adjective is omitted.

EXAMPLE

I've finally found a decent, affordable used car. [*Used car* is thought of as one unit.]

12h. Use a comma before *and, but, or, nor, for, so,* and *yet* when they join independent clauses.

EXAMPLE

I read Seamus Heaney's "The Grauballe Man," and now I want to read more of his poems.

You may omit the comma before *and, but, or,* or *nor* if the clauses are very short and there is no chance of misunderstanding.

12i. Use commas to set off nonessential clauses and nonessential participial phrases.

A *nonessential* clause or phrase is one that can be left out without changing the meaning of the sentence.

| NONESSENTIAL CLAUSE | W. H. Auden, **who was born in York, England,** became an American citizen in 1946. |
| NONESSENTIAL PHRASE | The little blue sports car, **leaving all the others far behind,** forged into the lead. |

 For more information about phrases, see Part 6: Phrases. For more on clauses, see Part 7: Clauses.

An *essential* clause or phrase is one that cannot be left out without changing the meaning of the sentence. Essential clauses and phrases are *not* set off by commas.

| ESSENTIAL CLAUSE | The writer **who received the Nobel Prize in literature in 1923** was William Butler Yeats. |
| ESSENTIAL PHRASE | The pilgrims **riding along with the Knight** are the Squire and the Yeoman. |

12j. Use commas after certain introductory elements.

(1) Use a comma after a one-word adverb such as *first, next, yes,* or *no* or after any mild exclamation such as *well* or *why* at the beginning of a sentence.

EXAMPLE
Yes, I have read *Don Juan.*

(2) Use a comma after an introductory participial phrase.

EXAMPLE
Looking calm, Jill walked to the podium.

(3) Use a comma after two or more introductory prepositional phrases or after a single long one.

EXAMPLE
With the help of Wiglaf, he killed the dragon.

(4) Use a comma after an introductory adverb clause.

EXAMPLE
After I had locked the car door, I remembered that the keys were still in the ignition.

12k. Use commas to set off elements that interrupt a sentence.

(1) Appositives and appositive phrases are usually set off by commas.

EXAMPLES
George Bernard Shaw's first play**, *Widowers' Houses,*** was published in 1893.
Is that she**, the one holding the sunflowers**?

Sometimes an appositive is so closely related to the word or words near it that it should not be set off by commas. Such an appositive is called a **restrictive appositive.**

EXAMPLE
The poet **Edmund Spenser** died suddenly in 1599.

(2) Words used in direct address are set off by commas.

EXAMPLE
Your research paper**, Dylan,** is quite interesting.

(3) Parenthetical expressions are set off by commas.

Parenthetical expressions are remarks that add incidental information or that relate ideas to each other. Some common parenthetical expressions are *for example, I think, moreover,* and *on the other hand.*

EXAMPLE
Macbeth is superstitious and sensitive; Lady Macbeth**, on the other hand,** is logical and bold.

 NOTE A contrasting expression introduced by *not, rather than,* or a similar term is parenthetical. Set it off by commas.

EXAMPLE
Percy Bysshe Shelley**, not John Keats,** wrote "Ode to the West Wind."

12l. Use a comma in certain conventional situations.

(1) Use a comma to separate items in dates and addresses.

EXAMPLES
On April 23**,** 1616**,** William Shakespeare died.
My grandparents' address is 505 King Street**,** Austin**,** TX 78701.

(2) Use a comma after the salutation of a personal letter and after the closing of any letter.

EXAMPLES
Dear Alicia**,**   Yours truly**,**

(3) Use commas to set off abbreviations such as *Jr., Sr., RN, M.D., Ltd.,* or *Inc.*

EXAMPLES
Is Jorge Rivera**,** Jr.**,** in your class?
She is the owner of Flowers by Arthurine**,** Inc.

SEMICOLONS

12m. Use a semicolon between independent clauses that are closely related in thought and are not joined by *and, but, for, nor, or, so,* or *yet.*

EXAMPLE
The rain had finally stopped**;** a few rays of sunshine were pushing through breaks in the clouds.

12n. Use a semicolon between independent clauses joined by a conjunctive adverb or a transitional expression.

A **conjunctive adverb**—such as *furthermore, however,* or *nevertheless*—or a **transitional expression**—such as *for instance, in fact,* or *that is*—indicates the relationship of the independent clauses that it joins.

EXAMPLE

The snow made traveling difficult; **nevertheless,** we arrived home safely.

12o. Use a semicolon (rather than a comma) before a coordinating conjunction to join independent clauses that contain commas.

EXAMPLE

During the seventeenth century—the era of such distinguished prose writers as Sir Thomas Browne, John Donne, and Jeremy Taylor—the balanced compound sentence using commas and semicolons reached a high degree of perfection and popularity; but the tendency today is to use a fast-moving style with shorter sentences, fewer commas, and fewer semicolons. [commas within the clauses]

12p. Use a semicolon between items in a series if the items contain commas.

EXAMPLE

The summer reading list includes *Jude the Obscure,* by Thomas Hardy; *Lord Jim,* by Joseph Conrad; and *Lord of the Flies,* by William Golding.

COLONS

12q. Use a colon to mean "note what follows."

(1) Use a colon before a list of items, especially after expressions such as *as follows* and *the following.*

EXAMPLE

Collection 8 includes poems by the following authors: Robert Burns, William Blake, William Wordsworth, and Samuel Taylor Coleridge.

 NOTE Do not use a colon before a list that directly follows a verb or a preposition.

EXAMPLES

Collection 8 includes poems by Robert Burns, William Blake, William Wordsworth, and Samuel Taylor Coleridge. [The list directly follows the preposition *by.*]

The main characters in Charles Dickens's *A Tale of Two Cities* are Dr. Manette, Lucie Manette, Charles Darnay, and Sydney Carton. [The list directly follows the verb *are.*]

(2) Use a colon before a quotation that lacks a speaker tag such as *he said* or *she remarked.*

EXAMPLE

His father's response surprised him: "I'm proud of you, son."

 For information about punctuating quotations that do have speaker tags, see page 1247.

(3) Use a colon before a long, formal statement or quotation.

EXAMPLE

When he awoke, Gulliver found himself tied down: "I could only look upward; the sun began to grow hot, and the light offended my eyes. I heard a confused noise about me, but in the posture I lay, could see nothing except the sky."

12r. Use a colon in certain conventional situations.

EXAMPLES

12:01 A.M. [between the hour and the minute]
Mark 3:10 [between chapter and verse in referring to passages from the Bible]
To Whom It May Concern: [after the salutation of a business letter]
"A Valediction: Forbidding Mourning" [between a title and a subtitle]

13 PUNCTUATION

ITALICS

Italics are printed characters that *slant to the right like this.* To indicate italics in handwritten or typewritten work, use underlining.

13a. Use italics (underlining) for words, letters, and symbols referred to as such and for foreign words that have not been adopted into English.

EXAMPLES

The words *hiss* and *clang* are examples of onomatopoeia.
You typed *ie* instead of *ei.*
The motto *e pluribus unum* appears on all United States coins.

13b. Use italics (underlining) for titles of books, plays, long poems, periodicals, newspapers, works of art, films, television series, long musical compositions, record-ings, comic strips, computer software, court cases, trains, ships, aircraft, and spacecraft.

TYPE OF NAME	EXAMPLE	
Books	*The Canterbury Tales*	
Plays	*The Taming of the Shrew*	
Long Poems	*The Rime of the Ancient Mariner*	
Periodicals	*Sports Illustrated*	
Newspapers	*The Boston Globe*	
Works of Art	*The Persistence of Memory*	
Films	*It's a Wonderful Life*	
TV Series	*American Playhouse*	
Long Musical Compositions	*The Planets*	
Recordings	*Unforgettable*	
Comic Strips	*Doonesbury*	
Computer Software	*Lotus 1-2-3*	
Court Cases	*Marbury v. Madison*	
Trains, Ships, Aircraft, and Spacecraft	*Orient Express* *Enola Gay*	*Queen Elizabeth 2* *Apollo 13*

NOTE The article *the* before the title of a book, periodical, or newspaper is neither italicized nor capitalized unless it is part of the official title. The official title of a book appears on the book's title page. The official title of a periodical or newspaper is the name on its masthead, usually found on the editorial page.

EXAMPLES
What role does fate play in "The Seafarer"?
I found this information in *The New York Times.*
My mom looks through the *Sun-Times* every morning.

For a list of titles that are enclosed in quotation marks, see page 1248. For information about capitalizing titles, see page 1243.

QUOTATION MARKS

13c. Use quotation marks to enclose a *direct quotation*—a person's exact words.

(1) A direct quotation usually begins with a capital letter.

EXAMPLE
Sir Francis Bacon wrote, "**K**nowledge is power."

However, when the quotation is only a part of a sentence, do not begin it with a capital letter.

EXAMPLE
In Act 1, Scene 5, Lady Macbeth describes her husband's nature as "**t**oo full o' th' milk of human kindness."

Do not use quotation marks to enclose an ***indirect quotation*** (a rewording of a direct quotation).

DIRECT QUOTATION	Al said, "I'm going fishing today."
INDIRECT QUOTATION	Al said that he is going fishing today.

(2) When the expression identifying the speaker divides a quoted sentence, the second part begins with a lowercase letter.

EXAMPLE
"All good moral philosophy," according to Sir Francis Bacon, "**is** but the handmaid to religion." [Notice that each part of a divided quotation is enclosed in quotation marks.]

When the second part of a divided quotation is a new sentence, the first word begins with a capital letter.

EXAMPLE
"On his first voyage, Gulliver finds himself in Lilliput," explained Ms. Chávez. "**T**he people there are only six inches tall."

(3) When used with quotation marks, other marks of punctuation are placed according to the following rules.

- Commas and periods are always placed inside the closing quotation marks.

EXAMPLES
"Read these lines**,**" he said, "and tell me what you think they mean**.**"

- Semicolons and colons are always placed outside the closing quotation marks.

EXAMPLES

Gloria promised, "I'll go to the dance with you"; however, she said that several weeks ago.

Find examples of the following figures of speech in Wordsworth's poem "I Wandered Lonely as a Cloud": personification, metaphor, and simile.

- Question marks and exclamation points are placed inside the closing quotation marks if the quotation itself is a question or an exclamation. Otherwise, they are placed outside.

EXAMPLES

Did Keats write "Ode on a Grecian Urn"?

"What an imagination you have!" exclaimed Beth.

(4) When quoting a passage that consists of more than one paragraph, put quotation marks at the beginning of each paragraph and at the end of only the last paragraph in the passage.

EXAMPLE

"At Mr. Bowyers's, a great deal of company; some I knew, others I did not. Here we stayed upon the leads and below till it was late, expecting to see the fireworks; but they were not performed tonight. Only, the City had a light like a glory round about it, with bonfires.

"At last I went to King Street; and there sent Crockford to my father's and my house to tell them I could not come home tonight, because of the dirt and a coach could not be had."

—Samuel Pepys, *The Diary of Samuel Pepys*

(5) Use single quotation marks to enclose a quotation within a quotation.

EXAMPLE

Ms. Markham asked us, "What do you think John Donne meant when he said, 'No man is an island, entire of itself'?"

(6) When writing *dialogue* (a conversation), begin a new paragraph every time the speaker changes, and enclose each speaker's words in quotation marks.

EXAMPLE

This frighted the fellow that attended about the work; but after some pause John Hayward, recovering himself, said, "Lord, bless us! There's somebody in the cart not quite dead!"

So another called to him and said, "Who are you?"

The fellow answered, "I am the poor piper. Where am I?"

"Where are you?" says Hayward. "Why, you are in the dead-cart, and we are going to bury you."

—Daniel Defoe, *A Journal of the Plague Year*

13d. Use quotation marks to enclose titles of short works, such as short stories, poems, essays, articles, songs, episodes of television series, and chapters and other parts of books.

TYPE OF NAME	EXAMPLE
Short Stories	"The Doll's House" "Games at Twilight"
Poems	"Ode to a Nightingale" "Thoughts of Hanoi"
Essays	"Shakespeare's Sister" "The Myth of Sisyphus"
Articles	"How to Improve Your Grades"
Songs	"Wind Beneath My Wings" "Frankie and Johnny"
TV Episodes	"Tony's Surprise Party" "Inside the Earth"
Chapters of a Book	"The Age of Reform" "How Ecosystems Change"

NOTE Neither italics nor quotation marks are used for the titles of major religious texts or for the titles of historical or legal documents.

EXAMPLES

the Bible
Code of Hammurabi
Bill of Rights
Monroe Doctrine

 For a list of titles that are italicized, see page 1247.

ELLIPSIS POINTS

13e. Use three spaced periods called *ellipsis points* (. . .) to mark omissions from quoted material and pauses in a written passage.

ORIGINAL At last she spoke to me. When she addressed the first words to me I was so confused that I did not know what to answer. She asked me was I going to *Araby*. I forget whether I answered yes or no. It would be a splendid bazaar, she said; she would love to go.

—James Joyce, "Araby"

(1) If the quoted material that comes before the ellipsis points is not a complete sentence, use three ellipsis points with a space before the first point.

EXAMPLE

Of his conversation with Mangan's sister, the narrator says, "When she addressed the first words to me **. . .** I did not know what to answer."

(2) If the quoted material that comes before the ellipsis points is a complete sentence, use an end mark before the ellipsis points.

EXAMPLE

According to Mangan's sister, "It would be a splendid bazaar**. . . .**"

(3) If one sentence or more is omitted, ellipsis points follow any end mark that precedes the omitted material.

EXAMPLE

The narrator recalls his encounter with Mangan's sister: "At last she spoke to me**. . . .** She asked me was I going to *Araby.*"

(4) To show that a full line or more of poetry has been omitted, use a line of spaced periods that is as long as the line of poetry above it.

ORIGINAL   It fell about the Martinmas time,
          And a gay time it was then,
          When our goodwife got puddings to make,
          And she's boild them in the pan.
             —Traditional, "Get Up and Bar
               the Door"

ONE LINE It fell about the Martinmas time,
OMITTED . . . .
          When our goodwife got puddings to make,
          And she's boild them in the pan.

APOSTROPHES

Possessive Case

13f. The *possessive case* of a noun or a pronoun indicates ownership or relationship. Use an apostrophe in forming the possessive case of nouns and indefinite pronouns.

(1) To form the possessive of a singular noun, add an apostrophe and an *s.*

EXAMPLES

Beowulf**'s** shield   the principal**'s** office

 NOTE When forming the possessive of a singular noun that ends in an *s* sound, add only an

apostrophe if the addition of *'s* will make the noun awkward to pronounce. Otherwise, add *'s.*

EXAMPLES

Ms. Rodgers**'** class   the witness**'s** testimony

(2) To form the possessive of a plural noun ending in *s,* add only the apostrophe.

EXAMPLES

the players**'** uniforms   the volunteers**'** efforts

(3) Form the possessive of only the last word in a compound word, in the name of an organization or business, or in a word group showing joint possession.

EXAMPLES

brother-in-law**'s** car
Ralph Merrill and Company**'s** products
Macbeth and Lady Macbeth**'s** plan

 NOTE When a possessive pronoun is part of a word group showing joint possession, each noun in the word group is also possessive.

EXAMPLE

Chen**'s,** Ramona**'s,** and **my** project

(4) Form the possessive of each noun in a word group showing individual possession of similar items.

EXAMPLE

Byron**'s,** Shelley**'s,** and Keats**'s** poems

(5) Possessive forms of words indicating time, such as *minute, day, month,* and *year,* and words indicating amounts in cents or dollars require apostrophes.

EXAMPLES

four weeks**'** vacation   a dollar**'s** worth

(6) To form the possessive of an indefinite pronoun, add an apostrophe and an *s.*

EXAMPLES

no one**'s** fault   somebody else**'s** jacket

Contractions

13g. Use an apostrophe to show where letters, words, or numbers have been omitted in a contraction.

EXAMPLES

let us . . . . **let's**   she would . . . . . **she'd**
you will . . . . . **you'll**   1998 . . . . **'98**

The word *not* can be shortened to *–n't* and added to a verb, usually without changing the spelling of the verb.

EXAMPLES

do not . . . . **don't**   should not . . . **shouldn't**
EXCEPTION
will not . . . **won't**

Plurals

13h. Use an apostrophe and an *s* to form the plurals of all lowercase letters, some uppercase letters, numerals, and some words referred to as words.

EXAMPLES
There are two *c*'s and two *m*'s in *accommodate*.
Try not to use so many *I*'s in your cover letter.
[Without the apostrophe, the plural of the pronoun *I* would spell *Is*.]

NOTE You may add only an *s* to form the plurals of words, numerals, and capital letters if the plural forms will not cause misreading. However, it is never wrong to use an apostrophe in such cases and is usually a good idea to do so.

EXAMPLE
James I ruled England during the early **1600s** [*or* **1600's**].

HYPHENS

13i. Use a hyphen to divide a word at the end of a line.

● Do not divide a one-syllable word.

EXAMPLE
Did the Green Knight know that Sir Gawain had **kissed** [*not* kis-sed] his wife?

● Divide a word only between syllables.

EXAMPLE
First, Macbeth was killed; then he was **decapi-tated** [*not* decapita-ted].

● Divide an already hyphenated word at the hyphen.

EXAMPLE
Queen Elizabeth I was ruler of England for **forty-five** [*not* for-ty-five] years.

● Do not divide a word so that one letter stands alone.

EXAMPLE
Paradise Lost by John Milton is a famous English **epic** [*not* e-pic].

13j. Use a hyphen with compound numbers from twenty-one to ninety-nine and with fractions used as modifiers.

EXAMPLES
thirty-seven
a **three-fourths** majority [*but* **three fourths** of the voters]

DASHES

13k. Use dashes to set off abrupt breaks in thought.

EXAMPLE
The playwright handles her material—I should say lack of material—quite well.

13l. Use dashes to set off appositives or parenthetical expressions that contain commas.

EXAMPLE
Several of the British Romantic poets—Shelley, Keats, and Byron, for example—led fascinating lives.

13m. Use a dash to set off an introductory list or group of examples.

EXAMPLE
Alliteration, caesuras, and kennings—these are features of Anglo-Saxon poetry.

PARENTHESES

13n. Use parentheses to enclose informative or explanatory material of minor importance.

EXAMPLES
A *roman à clef* (literally, "novel with a key") is a novel about real people to whom the novelist has assigned fictitious names.
The Globe (see the drawing on page 284) was built in 1599. [The *s* in *see* is lowercase because the parenthetical sentence is within a complete sentence.]
The Globe was built in 1599. (See the drawing on page 284.) [The *S* in *See* is capitalized and a period follows *page 284* because the parenthetical sentence is not within another sentence but instead stands on its own.]

BRACKETS

13o. Use brackets to enclose an explanation within quoted or parenthetical material.

EXAMPLE
The newspaper article stated that "at the time of that Democratic National Convention [in Chicago in 1968] there were many protest groups operating in the United States."

14 SPELLING

UNDERSTANDING WORD STRUCTURE

Many English words are made up of roots and affixes (prefixes and suffixes).

Roots

The **root** of a word is the part that carries the word's core meaning.

ROOT	MEANING	EXAMPLES
–fin–	end, limit	final, infinite
–gram–	write, writing	grammar, epigram
–tract–	pull, draw	tractor, extract
–vit–	life	vitamin, vital

Prefixes

A **prefix** is one or more letters or syllables added to the beginning of a word or word part to create a new word.

PREFIX	MEANING	EXAMPLES
contra–	against	contradict, contrast
inter–	between, among	interstate, interact
mis–	not, wrongly	misfire, misspell
re–	back, again	reflect, refinance

Suffixes

A **suffix** is one or more letters or syllables added to the end of a word or word part to create a new word.

SUFFIX	MEANING	EXAMPLES
–fy	make, cause	verify, pacify
–ish	suggesting, like	smallish, childish
–ist	doer, believer	artist, humanist
–ty	quality, state	cruelty, certainty

SPELLING RULES

NOTE Always keep in mind that the best way to be sure you have spelled a word correctly is to look the word up in a dictionary.

ie and *ei*

14a. Write *ie* when the sound is long *e*, except after *c*.

EXAMPLES
relieve   chief   field   conceit   deceive
EXCEPTIONS
either   leisure   neither   seize   protein

14b. Write *ei* when the sound is not long *e*.

EXAMPLES
reign   foreign   their   sovereign   weight
EXCEPTIONS
ancient   view   friend   mischief   conscience

NOTE Rules 14a and 14b apply only when the *i* and the *e* are in the same syllable.

–cede, –ceed, and –sede

14c. The only English word ending in *–sede* is *supersede*. The only words ending in *–ceed* are *exceed, proceed,* and *succeed.* Most other words with this sound end in *–cede.*

EXAMPLES
concede   precede   recede   secede

Adding Prefixes

14d. When adding a prefix, do not change the spelling of the original word.

EXAMPLES
over + run = **over**run   mis + spell = **mis**spell

Adding Suffixes

14e. When adding the suffix *–ness* or *–ly,* do not change the spelling of the original word.

EXAMPLES
gentle + ness = gentle**ness**   final + ly = finally

EXCEPTIONS

For most words ending in *y*, change the *y* to *i* before adding –*ness* or –*ly*.

heavy + ness = heav**iness**   ready + ly = read**ily**

NOTE   One-syllable adjectives ending in *y* generally follow rule 14e.

EXAMPLES

shy + ness = shy**ness**   sly + ly = sly**ly**

14f. Drop the final silent *e* before a suffix beginning with a vowel.

EXAMPLES

awake + en = awak**en**   race + ing = rac**ing**

EXCEPTIONS

Keep the final silent *e*

- in a word ending in *ce* or *ge* before a suffix beginning with *a* or *o*
  peac**eable**   courag**eous**
- in *dye* and in *singe* before –*ing*
  dy**eing**   sing**eing**
- in *mile* before –*age*
  mil**eage**

NOTE   When adding –*ing* to words that end in *ie*, drop the *e* and change the *i* to *y*.

EXAMPLES

die + ing = d**ying**   lie + ing = l**ying**

14g. Keep the final silent *e* before a suffix beginning with a consonant.

EXAMPLES

care + less = car**eless**   sure + ty = sur**ety**

EXCEPTIONS

nine + th = nin**th**   judge + ment = judg**ment**
true + ly = tru**ly**   wise + dom = wis**dom**

14h. For words ending in *y* preceded by a consonant, change the *y* to *i* before any suffix that does not begin with *i*.

EXAMPLES

heavy + est = heav**iest**
accompany + ment = accompan**iment**
verify + ing = verif**ying**

14i. For words ending in *y* preceded by a vowel, keep the *y* when adding a suffix.

EXAMPLES

enjoy + ing = enjo**ying**   play + ed = pla**yed**

EXCEPTIONS

day + ly = da**ily**   lay + ed = la**id**
pay + ed = pa**id**   say + ed = sa**id**

14j. Double the final consonant before a suffix that begins with a vowel if the word *both* (1) has only one syllable or has the accent on the last syllable *and* (2) ends in a single consonant preceded by a single vowel.

EXAMPLES

rap + ing = ra**pping**   refer + ed = refe**rred**

EXCEPTIONS

- For words ending in *w* or *x*, do not double the final consonant.
  bow + ed = bow**ed**   tax + able = tax**able**
- For words ending in *c*, add *k* before the suffix instead of doubling the *c*.
  picnic + k + ing = picnic**king**

FORMING THE PLURALS OF NOUNS

14k. Remembering the following rules will help you spell the plural forms of nouns.

(1) For most nouns, add –*s*.

EXAMPLES

beagle**s**   senator**s**   taxi**s**   Saxon**s**

(2) For nouns ending in *s, x, z, ch,* or *sh,* add –*es*.

EXAMPLES

glass**es**   waltz**es**   brush**es**   Perez**es**

(3) For nouns ending in *y* preceded by a vowel, add –*s*.

EXAMPLES

journey**s**   decoy**s**   Saturday**s**   Kelley**s**

(4) For nouns ending in *y* preceded by a consonant, change the *y* to *i* and add –*es*.

EXAMPLES

comed**ies**   cavit**ies**   theor**ies**   sk**ies**

EXCEPTIONS

For proper nouns, add –*s*.
Gregory**s**   Kimberly**s**

(5) For some nouns ending in *f* or *fe,* add –*s*. For others, change the *f* or *fe* to *v* and add –*es*.

EXAMPLES

belief**s**   loa**ves**   giraffe**s**   wi**ves**

EXCEPTIONS

For proper nouns, add –*s*.
DeGroff**s**   Rolfe**s**

(6) For nouns ending in *o* preceded by a vowel, add –*s*.

EXAMPLES

radio**s**   cameo**s**   shampoo**s**   Matsuo**s**

(7) For nouns ending in *o* preceded by a consonant, add —es.

EXAMPLES
torpedo**es**   echo**es**   hero**es**   potato**es**

For some common nouns ending in *o* preceded by a consonant, especially those referring to music, and for proper nouns, add only an —s.

EXAMPLES
photo**s**   hairdo**s**   solo**s**   soprano**s**   Spiro**s**

(8) The plurals of a few nouns are formed in irregular ways.

EXAMPLES
geese   **men**   child**ren**   **mice**   **teeth**

(9) For a few nouns, the singular and the plural forms are the same.

EXAMPLES
deer   series   Chinese   Sioux

(10) For most compound nouns, form the plural of only the last word of the compound.

EXAMPLES
courthouse**s**   seat belt**s**   four-year-old**s**

(11) For compound nouns in which one of the words is modified by the other word or words, form the plural of the noun modified.

EXAMPLES
son**s**-in-law   passer**s**by   mountain goat**s**

(12) For some nouns borrowed from other languages, the plural is formed as in the original languages. In a few cases, two plural forms are acceptable.

EXAMPLES
analysis—analys**es**   phenomenon—phenomen**a**
or phenomenon**s**

(13) To form the plurals of figures, most uppercase letters, signs, and words referred to as words, add an —s or both an apostrophe and an —s.

EXAMPLES
1500**s** *or* 1500**'s**   B**s** *or* B**'s**
$**s** *or* $**'s**   and**s** *or* and**'s**

> **NOTE** To avoid confusion, add both an apostrophe and an —s to form the plural of all lowercase letters, certain uppercase letters, and some words used as words.

EXAMPLES
The word *fictitious* contains three *i***'s.** [Without an apostrophe, the plural of *i* could be confused with the word *is.*]
Sebastian usually makes straight A**'s.** [Without an apostrophe, the plural of *A* could be confused with the word *As.*]
Because I mistakenly thought Evelyn Waugh was a woman, I used *her***'s** instead of *his***'s** in my paragraph. [Without an apostrophe, the plural of *her* would look like the pronoun *hers* and the plural of *his* would look like the word *hiss.*]

> **NOTE** In names, **diacritical marks** (marks that show pronunciation) and capitalization are as essential to correct spelling as the letters themselves. If you're not sure about the spelling of a name, check with the person whose name it is, or consult a reference source.

EXAMPLES
François   Lagerlöf
Van Doren   van Gogh
Márquez   **Marín**
de Vega   **al-Khansa**

15 GLOSSARY OF USAGE

The Glossary of Usage is an alphabetical listing of expressions with definitions, explanations, and examples. Some of the examples are labeled *standard, nonstandard, formal,* or *informal.* The label **standard** or **formal** identifies usage that is appropriate in serious writing and speaking (such as in compositions and speeches). The label **informal** indicates standard English that is generally used in conversation and in everyday writing such as personal letters. The label **nonstandard** identifies usage that does not follow the guidelines of standard English usage.

accept, except   *Accept* is a verb meaning "to receive." *Except* may be a verb meaning "to leave out" or a preposition meaning "excluding."

EXAMPLES
Does Sir Gawain **accept** the challenge from the Green Knight? [verb]
Certain states **except** teachers from jury duty. [verb]
I have read all of *Macbeth* **except** the last act. [preposition]

affect, effect *Affect* is a verb meaning "to influence." *Effect* may be either a verb meaning "to bring about or to accomplish" or a noun meaning "the result [of an action]."

EXAMPLES

How did the murder of King Duncan **affect** Lady Macbeth? [verb]

In this dispute, management and labor should be able to **effect** a compromise. [verb]

What far-reaching **effects** did the *Brown* v. *Board of Education of Topeka* decision have? [noun]

all ready, already *All ready* means "all prepared." *Already* means "previously."

EXAMPLES

Are you **all ready** for the audition?

We have **already** read "The Seafarer."

all right *All right* means "satisfactory," "unhurt; safe," "correct," or, in reply to a question or to preface a remark, "yes." *Alright* is a misspelling.

EXAMPLES

Does this look **all right** [*not* alright]?

Oh, **all right** [*not* alright], you can go.

all the farther, all the faster Avoid using these expressions in formal situations. Use *as far as* or *as fast as*.

EXAMPLE

Is that **as fast as** [*not* all the faster] Chris can run?

all together, altogether *All together* means "everyone in the same place." *Altogether* means "entirely."

EXAMPLES

The knights were **all together** for the celebration.

Sir Gawain was not **altogether** honest with the Green Knight.

allusion, illusion An *allusion* is an indirect reference to something. An *illusion* is a mistaken idea or a misleading appearance.

EXAMPLES

The speaker made an **allusion** to Emily Brontë's *Wuthering Heights.*

Before selecting a career, he had to abandon some of his **illusions** about his own abilities.

The director chose certain colors to create an **illusion** of depth on the small stage.

a lot Avoid this expression in formal situations by using *many* or *much*.

EXAMPLE

Many [*not* a lot] of my friends work part time after school and on weekends.

already See **all ready, already.**

altogether See **all together, altogether.**

among See **between, among.**

and etc. *Etc.* stands for the Latin words *et cetera,* meaning "and others" or "and so forth." Always avoid using *and* before *etc.* In general, avoid using *etc.* in formal situations. Use one of its meanings instead.

EXAMPLE

We are comparing the main female characters in Shakespeare's tragedies: Lady Macbeth, Cleopatra, Juliet, **and others** [*or* etc. *but not* and etc.].

any one, anyone The expression *any one* specifies one member of a group. *Anyone* means "one person, no matter which."

EXAMPLES

Any one of you could win the poetry contest.

Anyone who finishes the test early may leave.

as See **like, as.**

as if See **like, as if.**

at Avoid using *at* after a construction beginning with *where*.

NONSTANDARD	Where was Beowulf at when Grendel's mother attacked?
STANDARD	**Where** was Beowulf when Grendel's mother attacked?

a while, awhile *A while* means "a period of time." *Awhile* means "for a short time."

EXAMPLES

Herot remained empty for quite **a while.**

They stayed there **awhile.**

bad, badly *Bad* is an adjective. *Badly* is an adverb. In standard English, *bad* should follow a sense verb, such as *feel, look, sound, taste,* or *smell,* or other linking verb.

EXAMPLE

The prospects for fair weather look **bad** [*not* badly].

because In formal situations, do not use the construction *reason . . . because.* Instead, use *reason . . . that.*

EXAMPLE

The **reason** Sir Gawain accepts the green sash is **that** [*not* because] he thinks it will protect him from the Green Knight.

being as, being that Avoid using either of these expressions for *since* or *because*.

EXAMPLE

Because [*not* being as *or* being that] Sir Gawain is a knight, we expect him to behave chivalrously.

beside, besides *Beside* means "by the side of" or "next to." *Besides* means "in addition to" or "other than" or "moreover."

EXAMPLES

The Geats built Beowulf's tomb **beside** the sea.
No one **besides** Wiglaf helped Beowulf battle the dragon.
I have decided that I do not want to take journalism; **besides,** I cannot fit it into my schedule.

between, among Use *between* to refer to only two items or to more than two when comparing each item individually to each of the others.

EXAMPLES

The reward money will be divided **between** Chang and Marta.
Sasha explained the difference **between** assonance, consonance, and alliteration. [Each item is compared individually to each of the others.]

Use *among* to refer to more than two items when you are not considering each item in relation to each other item individually.

EXAMPLE

The reward money will be divided **among** the four girls.

bring, take *Bring* means "to come carrying something." *Take* means "to go carrying something."

EXAMPLES

I'll **bring** my copy of *Gulliver's Travels* when I come over.
Please **take** the model of the Globe Theater to the library.

bust, busted Avoid using these words as verbs. Instead, use a form of *break* or *burst,* depending on the meaning.

EXAMPLES

The window is **broken** [*not* busted].
The water main has **burst** [*not* busted] open.

can, may Use *can* to express ability. Use *may* to express possibility.

EXAMPLES

Can you play the guitar?
It **may** rain later.

cannot (can't) help but Avoid using *but* and the infinitive form of a verb after the expression *cannot (can't) help.* Instead, use a gerund alone.

| NONSTANDARD | I can't help but laugh when I look at that photograph. |
| STANDARD | I can't help **laughing** when I look at that photograph. |

compare, contrast Used with *to, compare* means "to look for similarities between." Used with *with, compare* means "to look for both similarities and differences between." *Contrast* is always used to point out differences.

EXAMPLES

The simile at the end of the poem **compares** the eagle's fall **to** a thunderbolt.
We **compared** Shakespeare's style **with** that of Christopher Marlowe.
The tour guide also **contrasted** the two castles' provisions for defense.

could of See **of.**

double subject Avoid using an unnecessary pronoun after the subject of a sentence.

EXAMPLE

George Bernard Shaw [*not* George Bernard Shaw he] wrote *Pygmalion.*

due to Avoid using *due to* for "because of" or "owing to."

EXAMPLE

All schools were closed **because of** [*not* due to] inclement weather.

effect See **affect, effect.**

either, neither *Either* usually means "one or the other of two." In referring to more than two, use *any one* or *any* instead. *Neither* usually means "not one or the other of two." In referring to more than two, use *none* instead.

EXAMPLES

Either of the two quotations would be appropriate to use at the beginning of your speech.
You should be able to find ample information about **any one** of those four poets.
Neither of the Perez twins is in school today.
None of the seniors have voted yet.

etc. See **and etc.**

every day, everyday *Every day* means "each day." *Everyday* means "daily," "ordinary," or "usual."

EXAMPLES

Every day presents its own challenges.
The party will be casual; wear **everyday** clothes.

every one, everyone *Every one* specifies every single person or thing of those named. *Everyone* means "everybody, all of the people named."

EXAMPLES

Elizabeth Bowen wrote **every one** of these stories.
Did **everyone** read "The Demon Lover"?

except   See **accept, except.**

farther, further   Use *farther* to express physical distance. Use *further* to express abstract relationships of degree or quantity.

EXAMPLES
Your house is **farther** from school than mine is.
The United Nations members decided that **further** debate was unnecessary.

fewer, less   Use *fewer* to modify a plural noun and *less* to modify a singular noun.

EXAMPLES
Fewer students are going out for football this year.
Now I spend **less** time watching TV.

good, well   Avoid using the adjective *good* to modify an action verb. Instead, use the adverb *well,* meaning "capably" or "satisfactorily."

EXAMPLE
We did **well** [*not* good] on the exam.

Used as an adjective, *well* means "in good health" or "satisfactory in appearance or condition."

EXAMPLES
I feel **well.**
It's eight o'clock, and all is **well.**

had of   See **of.**

had ought, hadn't ought   Do not use *had* or *hadn't* with *ought.*

EXAMPLES
Your application **ought** [*not* had ought] to have been sent in earlier.
She **ought not** [*not* hadn't ought] to swim so soon after eating lunch.

illusion   See **allusion, illusion.**

imply, infer   *Imply* means "to suggest indirectly." *Infer* means "to interpret" or "to draw a conclusion."

EXAMPLES
The speaker of "To a Skylark" **implies** that the skylark is a divine being.
I **inferred** from her speech that she would support a statewide testing program.

in, in to, into   *In* generally shows location. In the construction *in to, in* is an adverb followed by the preposition *to. Into* generally shows direction.

EXAMPLES
Rudyard Kipling was born **in** Bombay.
He found the treasure and turned it **in to** his king.
Sir Gawain rode **into** the wilderness to find the Green Knight.

infer   See **imply, infer.**

irregardless, regardless   *Irregardless* is nonstandard. Use *regardless* instead.

EXAMPLE
Regardless [*not* irregardless] of the danger, he continued his journey.

its, it's   *Its* is the possessive form of *it. It's* is the contraction of *it is* or *it has.*

EXAMPLES
The community is proud of **its** school system.
It's [it is] a symbol of peace.
It's [it has] been cooler today.

kind of, sort of   In formal situations, avoid using these terms for the adverb *somewhat* or *rather.*

| INFORMAL | Macbeth appeared to be kind of worried. |
| FORMAL | Macbeth appeared to be **rather** [*or* **somewhat**] worried. |

kind of a(n), sort of a(n)   In formal situations, omit the *a(n).*

| INFORMAL | What kind of a poem is "The Passionate Shepherd to His Love"? |
| FORMAL | What **kind of** poem is "The Passionate Shepherd to His Love"? |

kind(s), sort(s), type(s)   With the singular form of each of these nouns, use *this* or *that.* With the plural form, use *these* or *those.*

EXAMPLES
This type of engine performs more economically than any of **those types.**

less   See **fewer, less.**

lie, lay   The verb *lie* means "to rest" or "to stay, to recline, or to remain in a certain state or position." Its principal parts are *lie, lying, lay,* and *lain. Lie* never takes an object. The verb *lay* means "to put [something] in a place." Its principal parts are *lay, laying, laid,* and *laid. Lay* usually takes an object.

EXAMPLES
Gulliver was **lying** on his back and could hardly move. [no object]
The Lilliputians **laid** baskets of food near Gulliver's mouth. [*Baskets* is the object of *laid.*]

like, as   In formal situations, do not use *like* for *as* to introduce a subordinate clause.

| INFORMAL | John looks like his father looked twenty years ago. |
| FORMAL | John looks **as** his father looked twenty years ago. |

like, as if   In formal situations, avoid using the preposition *like* for the compound conjunction *as if* or *as though* to introduce a subordinate clause.

INFORMAL	The heavy footsteps sounded like they were coming nearer.
FORMAL	The heavy footsteps sounded **as if** [*or* **as though**] they were coming nearer.

might of, must of   See **of.**

neither   See **either, neither.**

nor   See **or, nor.**

of   *Of* is a preposition. Do not use *of* in place of *have* after verbs such as *could, should, would, might, must,* and *ought* [*to*]. Also, do not use *had of* for *had.*

EXAMPLES

If I **had** [*not* had of] known about the shortcut, I **would have** [*not* would of] been here sooner.

Avoid using *of* after other prepositions such as *inside, off,* and *outside.*

EXAMPLE

Flimnap fell **off** [*not* off of] the tightrope.

off, off of   Do not use *off* or *off of* for *from.*

EXAMPLE

You can get a program **from** [*not* off of] the usher.

on to, onto   In the expression *on to, on* is an adverb and *to* is a preposition. *Onto* is a preposition.

EXAMPLES

The lecturer moved **on to** her next main idea.
She walked **onto** the stage.

or, nor   Use *or* with *either;* use *nor* with *neither.*

EXAMPLES

The list of authors does not include **either** James Joyce **or** [*not* nor] D. H. Lawrence.
Neither James Joyce **nor** D. H. Lawrence is on the list of authors.

ought   See **had ought, hadn't ought.**

ought to of   See **of.**

raise   See **rise, raise.**

reason . . . because   See **because.**

refer back   Since the prefix *re–* in *refer* means "back," adding *back* is generally unnecessary.

EXAMPLE

The writer is **referring** [*not* referring back] to the years when he lived in Ireland.

rise, raise   The verb *rise* means "to go up" or "to get up." Its principal parts are *rise, rising, rose,* and *risen. Rise* never takes an object. The verb *raise* means "to cause [something] to rise" or "to lift up." Its principal parts are *raise, raising, raised,* and *raised. Raise* usually takes an object.

EXAMPLES

Her blood pressure **rose** as she waited. [no object]
The Green Knight **raised** the ax above his head. [*Ax* is the object of *raised.*]

should of   See **of.**

sit, set   The verb *sit* means "to rest in an upright, seated position." Its principal parts are *sit, sitting, sat,* and *sat. Sit* seldom takes an object. The verb *set* means "to put [something] in a place." Its principal parts are *set, setting, set,* and *set. Set* usually takes an object.

EXAMPLES

Banquo's ghost **sits** in Macbeth's place. [no object]
Please **set** the groceries on the table. [*Groceries* is the object of *set.*]

some, somewhat   In formal situations, avoid using *some* to mean "to some extent." Use *somewhat.*

EXAMPLE

The Wedding Guest was somewhat shaken [*not* shaken some] by the Ancient Mariner's gaze and appearance.

sort(s)   See **kind(s), sort(s), type(s)** and **kind of a(n), sort of a(n).**

sort of   See **kind of, sort of.**

take   See **bring, take.**

than, then   *Than* is a conjunction used in comparisons. *Then* is an adverb meaning "at that time" or "next."

EXAMPLES

Is King Macbeth more superstitious **than** Lady Macbeth?
First, we will read "The Lamb"; **then,** we will read "The Tyger."

that   See **who, which, that.**

their, there, they're   *Their* is a possessive form of *they.* As an adverb, *there* means "at that place." *There* is also used to begin a sentence. *They're* is the contraction of *they are.*

EXAMPLES

They built a tomb for **their** fallen leader.
Macduff was not **there** at the time.
There is very little time left.
They're waiting for Banquo.

theirs, there's *Theirs* is a possessive form of the pronoun *they*. *There's* is the contraction of *there is*.

EXAMPLES
The treasure is **theirs** now.
There's an allusion to the Bible in the poem.

them Do not use *them* as an adjective. Use *those*.

EXAMPLE
Have you seen **those** [*not* them] murals by Judith Baca at the art museum?

then See **than, then.**

there See **their, there, they're.**

there's See **theirs, there's.**

they're See **their, there, they're.**

this here, that there Avoid using *here* or *there* after *this* or *that*.

EXAMPLE
This [*not* this here] poem was written by Robert Browning.

try and, try to Use *try to*, not *try and*.

EXAMPLE
I will **try to** [*not* try and] finish reading *The Diary of Samuel Pepys* tonight.

type, type of Avoid using the noun *type* as an adjective. Add *of* after *type*.

EXAMPLE
What **type of** [*not* type] character is the knight in "The Wife of Bath's Tale"?

type(s) See **kind(s), sort(s), type(s).**

ways Use *way*, not *ways*, when referring to distance.

EXAMPLE
Is Canterbury a long **way** [*not* ways] from the Tabard Inn?

well See **good, well.**

when, where Do not use *when* or *where* to begin a definition.

NONSTANDARD	A caesura is where you break or pause in a line of poetry.
STANDARD	A caesura is **a break or pause in a line of poetry.**

where Do not use *where* in place of *that*.

EXAMPLE
I read **that** [*not* where] you won a scholarship.

where . . . at See **at.**

who, which, that *Who* refers to persons only. *Which* refers to things only. *That* may refer to either persons or things.

EXAMPLES
Sir Gawain was the knight **who** [*or* that] accepted the Green Knight's challenge.
The Globe, **which** was built in 1599, burned down in 1613.
Is this the only poem **that** Sir Walter Raleigh ever wrote?

who's, whose *Who's* is the contraction of *who is* or *who has*. *Whose* is the possessive form of *who*.

EXAMPLES
Well, look **who's** [who is] here!
Who's [who has] read all of the play?
Whose treasure is it?

would of See **of.**

your, you're *Your* is a possessive form of *you*. *You're* is the contraction of *you are*.

EXAMPLES
Is that **your** car?
I can see that **you're** tired.

GLOSSARY

The glossary that follows is an alphabetical list of various words found in the selections in this book. Use this glossary just as you use a dictionary—to find out the meanings of unfamiliar words. (Technical, foreign, or more obscure words are not listed here but are defined instead in the footnotes that accompany each selection.)

Many words in the English language have more than one meaning. This glossary gives the meanings that apply to the words as they are used in the selections in this book. Words closely related in form and meaning are usually listed together in one entry (*agitated* and *agitation*), and the definition is given for the first form.

The following abbreviations are used:

adj., adjective	*n.,* noun	*prep.,* preposition
adv., adverb	*pl.,* plural form	*v.,* verb

Unless a word is very simple to pronounce, its pronunciation is given in parentheses. A guide to the pronunciation symbols appears at the bottom of each right-hand glossary page.

For more information about the words in this glossary or about words not listed here, consult a dictionary.

abasement (ə·bās′mənt) *n.:* humiliation.
abate (ə·bāt′) *v.:* to lessen.
abject (ab′jekt) *adj.:* degrading; humiliating.
ablution (ab·lōō′shən) *n.:* washing of the body, especially as a religious rite.
abominable (ə·bäm′ə·nə·bəl) *adj.:* disgusting; hateful.
absolution (ab′sə·lōō′shən) *n.:* forgiveness.
abstain (ab·stān′) *v.:* to refrain from; hold oneself back from.
abyss (ə·bis′) *n.:* bottomless pit.
accentuate (ak·sen′chōō·āt′) *v.:* to emphasize.
accrue (ə·krōō′) *v.:* to increase over time.
acquit (ə·kwit′) *v.:* to clear of a charge; absolve.
admonish (ad·män′ish) *v.:* to scold mildly.
adversity (ad·vur′sə·tē) *n.:* trouble; misfortune.
aesthetics (es·thet′iks) *n. pl.:* principles of beauty.
affliction (ə·flik′shən) *n.:* deep suffering.
aggrieved (ə·grēvd′) *adj.:* offended; wronged.
agitated (aj′i·tāt′id) *adj.:* disturbed; upset. —**agitation** *n.*
agog (ə·gäg′) *adj.:* in a state of excitement and anticipation.
alienate (āl′ē·ən·āt′) *v.:* to drive apart.
allege (ə·lej′) *v.:* to declare or assert, often without proof.
alleviation (ə·lē′vē·ā′shən) *n.:* something that lightens, relieves, or makes easier to bear.
allotment (ə·lät′mənt) *n.:* distribution.
alms (ämz) *n. pl.:* goods donated to the poor as charity.
altruistic (al′trōō·is′tik) *adj.:* unselfish.
ambiguous (am·big′yōō·əs) *adj.:* having more than one meaning; unclear; vague.
amiability (ā′mē·ə·bil′ə·tē) *n.:* friendliness. —**amiable** *adj.*

amorous (am′ə·res) *adj.:* full of love.
anecdote (an′ik·dōt′) *n.:* brief, little-known fact or amusing story.
anguish (aŋ′gwish) *n.:* agony.
animosity (an′ə·mäs′ə·tē) *n.:* hostility; intense hatred or resentment.
annals (an′əlz) *n. pl.:* historical records.
annihilate (ə·nī′ə·lāt′) *v.:* to destroy completely.
annul (ə·nul′) *v.:* to do away with; cancel.
aperture (ap′ər·chər) *n.:* opening.
apparition (ap′ə·rish′ən) *n.:* strange figure, like a ghost, that appears suddenly.
apprehensible (ap′rē·hen′sə·bəl) *adj.:* able to be seen or understood. —**apprehend** *v.*
approbation (ap′rə·bā′shən) *n.:* approval.
arable (ar′ə·bəl) *adj.:* suitable for growing crops.
arboreal (är·bôr′ē·əl) *adj.:* full of trees.
ardor (är′dər) *n.:* passion; enthusiasm. —**ardent** *adj.*
arrears (ə·rirz′) *n. pl.:* overdue debts.
arrest (ə·rest′) *v.:* to check or halt in motion.
assail (ə·sāl′) *v.:* to attack. —**assailable** *adj.*
assent (ə·sent′) *n.:* acceptance.
assert (ə·surt′) *v.:* to declare.
assignation (as′ig·nā′shən) *n.:* appointment; meeting.
asunder (ə·sun′dər) *adv.:* apart.
attenuate (ə·ten′yōō·āt′) *v.:* to make very slender or drawn out.
audacious (ô·dā′shəs) *adj.:* bold.
audit (ôd′it) *n.:* examination or accounting.
augment (ôg·ment′) *v.:* to increase.
avarice (av′ə·ris) *n.:* greed. —**avaricious** *adj.*
aversion (ə·vur′zhən) *n.:* dislike.
avow (ə·vou′) *v.:* to openly declare; acknowledge.

baleful (bāl′fəl) *adj.:* sinister; threatening.
baser (bās′ər) *adj.:* less valuable or worthy.
bastion (bas′chən) *n.:* fortified place; bulwark.
beguile (bē·gīl′) *v.:* 1. to pass the time in a pleasant way. 2. to charm.
benediction (ben′ə·dik′shən) *n.:* blessing.
benign (bi·nīn′) *adj.:* kind; gracious.
bequest (bē·kwest′) *n.:* gift left by means of a will.
blanch *v.:* to turn pale.
blasphemy (blas′fə·mē′) *n.:* mockery of God. —**blaspheme** *v.*
blight (blīt) *n.:* something that causes decay or withers one's hopes. —**blighted** *adj.*
botanical (bə·tan′i·kəl) *adj.:* of plants or plant life; connected to the science of botany, which is the study of plants, their structure, growth, and so on.
breach (brēch) *v.:* to break.
brevity (brev′ə·tē) *n.:* being brief.

---

fat, āpe, cär; ten, ēven; is, bīte; gō, hôrn, look, tōōl; yoo, cure; yōō, use; oil, out; up, fur; get; joy; yet; chin; she; thin; then; zh, leisure; ŋ, ring; ə for *a* in *ago*, *e* in *agent*, *i* in *sanity*, *o* in *comply*, *u* in *focus*; ′ as in *battle* (bat′'l).

---

brocade (brō·kād′) *n.*: richly woven cloth.
buffet (buf′it) *v.*: to hit or slap.
buoyancy (bɔi′ən·sē) *n.*: lightness.
burlesque (bər·lesk′) *n.*: derisive or comic spoof; satire.

cadence (kād′′ns) *n.*: rhythmic flow of sound.
cajole (kə·jōl′) *v.*: to coax with flattery.
calamitous (kə·lam′ə·təs) *adj.*: bringing great trouble.
candor (kan′dər) *n.*: honesty.
carouse (kə·rɔuz′) *v.*: to drink and celebrate noisily.
carrion (kar′ē·ən) *n.*: decaying flesh eaten by scavenging animals.
casement (kās′mənt) *n.*: window.
cavalcade (kav′əl·kād′) *n.*: parade of horses and carriages.
censure (sen′shər) *v.*: to condemn.
chaff (chaf) *n.*: 1. husks of grain. 2. anything worthless.
chalice (chal′is) *n.*: cup.
chasm (kaz′əm) *n.*: deep crack or fissure; abyss.
chasten (chās′ən) *v.*: to restrain from excess.
chastise (chas·tīz′) *v.*: to scold or punish.
circumambulate (sʉr′kəm·am′byōō·lāt′) *v.*: to walk around.
circumscribe (sʉr′kəm·skrīb′) *v.*: to limit; confine.
cistern (sis′tərn) *n.*: tank for collecting rainwater.
civility (sə·vil′ə·tē) *n.*: courtesy.
clamorous (klam′ər·əs) *adj.*: noisy.
clarion (klar′ē·ən) *n.*: clear, sharp, ringing sound.
clemency (klem′ən·sē) *n.*: compassion; mercy.
clinical (klin′i·kəl) *adj.*: detached; impersonal.
cloister (klɔis′tər) *v.*: to seclude; confine. —**cloistered** *adj.*
coalition (kō′ə·lish′ən) *n.*: temporary alliance or union for some specific purpose.
cohort (kō′hôrt′) *n.*: band of soldiers.
collateral (kə·lat′ər·əl) *adj.*: corresponding.
commiserate (kə·miz′ər·āt′) *v.*: to feel sorrow or pity for; sympathize.
commission (kə·mish′ən) *n.*: act of doing something.
companionable (kəm·pan′yən·ə·bəl) *adj.*: having the traits of a good companion; friendly.
comparatively (kəm·par′ə·tiv′lē) *adv.*: relatively; in comparison to others.
compel (kəm·pel′) *v.*: to force.
comprehensive (käm′prē·hen′siv) *adj.*: including all of the details; broad and sweeping.
concede (kən·sēd′) *v.*: to grant.
conceive (kən·sēv′) *v.*: 1. to form in the mind. 2. to cause life to begin. —**conception** *n.*
conciliate (kən·sil′ē·āt′) *v.*: to soothe the anger of; placate.
condescend (kän′di·send′) *v.*: to lower oneself; stoop.
confederate (kən·fed′ər·āt′) *v.*: to unite; form an alliance.
confiscate (kän′fis·kāt′) *v.*: to seize as a penalty.
conform (kən·fôrm′) *v.*: to become similar; adapt.
confound (kən·fɔund′) *v.*: 1. to confuse. 2. to damn.
congeal (kən·jēl′) *v.*: to thicken.
conjecture (kən·jek′chər) *v.*: to reason; guess. —**conjectural** *adj.*
conjure (kän′jər) *v.*: to summon as by a magic spell. —**conjurer** *n.*
consecrate (kän′si·krāt′) *v.*: to dedicate to sacred use.
conspicuous (kən·spik′yōō·əs) *adj.*: attracting attention by being unusual.

constancy (kän′stən·sē) *n.*: loyalty.
constellation (kän′stə·lā′shən) *n.*: group of stars, usually named after the object, animal, or mythological being its outline, or configuration, suggests.
consternation (kän′stər·nā′shən) *n.*: alarm; bewilderment.
consummate (kän′sə·māt′) *v.*: to complete; fulfill.
contagion (kən·tā′jən) *n.*: spreading of disease.
contemptuous (kən·temp′chōō·əs) *adj.*: scornful; disdainful. —**contemptuously** *adv.*
contend (kən·tend′) *v.*: to compete; struggle.
contingent (kən·tin′jənt) *n.*: group.
contortion (kən·tôr′shən) *n.*: unnatural form; distortion.
converge (kən·vʉrj′) *v.*: to come together at a point.
copious (kō′pē·əs) *adj.*: wordy; profuse.
cornice (kôr′nis) *n.*: decorative strip that runs along the top of a wall.
corporal (kôr′pə·rəl) *adj.*: bodily.
corrode (kə·rōd′) *v.*: to eat away, as by rust.
cosmopolitan (käz′mə·päl′ə·tən) *adj.*: representative of many parts of the world; not constrained by provincial habits or prejudices.
countenance (kɔun′tə·nəns) *n.*: face; appearance.
courtly (kôrt′lē) *adj.*: suitable for a royal court; with dignity or politeness. —**courtliness** *n.*
covet (kuv′it) *v.*: to long for with envy.
covetousness (kuv′ət·əs·nəs) *n.*: greed. —**covetous** *adj.*
cowed (kɔud) *adj.*: frightened by threats.
credulous (krej′ōō·ləs) *adj.*: believing too readily.
crucial (krōō′shəl) *adj.*: of the greatest importance.
crystalline (kris′təl·in) *adj.*: transparent like crystal.
crystallize (kris′təl·īz′) *v.*: to assume definite form; harden.
culinary (kul′ə·ner′ē) *adj.*: of or about cooking.
cynical (sin′i·kəl) *adj.*: mistrustful.

dapple (dap′əl) *adj.*: spotted.
daunt (dônt) *v.*: to intimidate.
debar (dē·bär′) *v.*: to exclude; hinder.
decree (dē·krē′) *v.*: to officially order or decide.
decussate (dē·kus′āt′) *v.*: to cross so as to form an X; intersect.
defer (dē·fʉr′) *v.*: to postpone.
deference (def′ər·əns) *n.*: respect; courtesy.
definitive (di·fin′ə·tiv) *adj.*: conclusive; authoritative.
degrade (di·grād′) *v.*: to corrupt; dishonor. —**degradation** *n.*
deify (dē′ə·fī′) *v.*: to make divine; glorify.
delirium (di·lir′ē·əm) *n.*: uncontrollable excitement.
delusion (di·lōō′zhən) *n.*: false belief. —**delude** *v.*
demented (dē·ment′id) *adj.*: mad; wild.
demise (dē·mīz′) *n.*: death.
denude (dē·nōōd′) *v.*: to strip; lay bare.
desolate (des′ə·lit) *adj.*: lonely; forlorn.
despondency (di·spän′dən·sē) *n.*: hopelessness.
despotic (des·pät′ik) *adj.*: tyrannical; oppressive.
deter (dē·tʉr′) *v.*: to prevent.
deviation (dē′vē·ā′shən) *n.*: a turning off from the usual or normal course.
diatribe (dī′ə·trīb′) *n.*: bitter criticism; rant.
diffusive (di·fyōō′siv) *adj.*: spread out; not concentrated. —**diffuse** *v.*

digress (di·gres′) *v.*: to wander off the subject.
diligent (dil′ə·jənt) *adj.*: patient; persistent.
diminutive (də·min′yōō·tiv) *adj.*: very small.
dire (dīr) *adj.*: dreadful.
dirge (dʉrj) *n.*: funeral hymn; lament.
discern (di·sʉrn′) *v.*: to perceive; understand.
discomfit (dis·kum′fit) *v.*: to embarrass; make uneasy.
disconcert (dis′kən·sʉrt′) *v.*: to embarrass, confuse, or fluster.
discourse (dis′kôrs′) *n.*: conversation.
discreet (di·skrēt′) *adj.*: cautious about one's words and actions.
discriminate (di·skrim′i·nāt′) *v.*: to carefully distinguish between; differentiate.
disdainful (dis·dān′fəl) *adj.*: scornful.
disparage (di·spar′ij) *v.*: to speak disrespectfully of; belittle.
dispassionate (dis·pash′ə·nət) *adj.*: without emotion; impartial.
dispel (di·spel′) *v.*: to cause to vanish.
dispirit (di·spir′it) *v.*: to make sad or apathetic.
disposed (di·spōzd′) *adj.*: having a tendency toward.
dissuasion (di·swā′zhən) *n.*: advice or persuasion against.
distemper (dis·tem′pər) *n.*: disorder; disease.
distend (di·stend′) *v.*: to expand; stretch out; swell.
distill (di·stil′) *v.*: to draw out the essence of.
distraught (di·strôt′) *adj.*: agitated.
dither (dith′ər) *n*: excited or confused condition; nervousness.
diverge (dī·vʉrj′) *v.*: to branch off; separate.
divert (də·vʉrt′) *v.*: to amuse. —**diversion** *n.*
divinity (də·vin′ə·tē) *n.*: God; sacred being.
divulge (də·vulj′) *v.*: to make known.
docile (däs′əl) *adj.*: submissive; obedient.
dogged (dôg′id) *adj.*: persistent; stubborn.
dominion (də·min′yən) *n.*: governed territory.
dregs *n. pl.*: residue.
drone (drōn) *v.*: to hum or buzz continuously.
dubious (dōō′bē·əs) *adj.*: doubtful; uncertain.
duly (dōō′lē) *adv.*: as is right or required.
dumbfound (dum′found′) *v.*: to astonish; shock.
duress (dōō·res′) *n.*: pressure; force.

eddy *n.*: little whirlpool.
edict (ē′dikt′) *n.*: official order.
efficacious (ef′i·kā′shəs) *adj.*: effective. —**efficacy** *n.*
effluvium (e·flōō′vē·əm) *n.*: flow of vapor and invisible particles.
ejaculation (ē·jak′yōō·lā′shən) *n.*: sudden impassioned utterance; exclamation.
emanate (em′ə·nāt′) *v.*: to flow; come forth.
emancipate (ē·man′sə·pāt′) *v.*: to set free.
eminent (em′ə·nənt) *adj.*: distinguished; noteworthy.
encumber (en·kum′bər) *v.*: to burden or hinder. —**encumbrance** *n.*
endeavor (en·dev′ər) *n.*: earnest attempt.

engender (en·jen′dər) *v.*: to create; produce.
entreaty (en·trēt′ē) *n.*: plea; sincere request. —**entreat** *v.*
enumerate (ē·nōō′mər·āt′) *v.*: to count; list.
epicure (ep′i·kyoor′) *n.*: one who takes great pleasure in eating fine foods.
equivocate (ē·kwiv′ə·kāt′) *v.*: to be ambiguous; deliberately evade or lie. —**equivocation** *n.*
eradicate (ē·rad′i·kāt′) *v.*: to exterminate.
exhilaration (eg·zil′ə·rā′shən) *n.*: excitement; high spirits.
exorbitant (eg·zor′bi·tənt) *adj.*: excessive.
expedient (ek·spē′dē·ənt) *n.*: convenient means to an end.
expiate (eks′pē·āt′) *v.*: to make amends for wrongdoing; atone.
extort (eks·tôrt′) *v.*: to get by threats or violence.
exult (eg·zult′) *v.*: to rejoice. —**exultation** *n.*

façade (fə·säd′) *n.*: front of a building.
fallow (fal′ō) *adj.*: unplanted; uncultivated.
fanlight (fan′līt′) *n.*: fan-shaped window over a door.
feign (fān) *v.*: to make up; invent.
feint (fānt) *v.*: to pretend to strike.
fervent (fʉr′vənt) *adj.*: passionate. —**fervor** *n.*
fetter (fet′ər) *v.*: to chain.
flag *v.*: to decline; lose strength or interest.
foment (fō·ment′) *v.*: to stir up; incite.
forbear (fôr·ber′) *v.*: to avoid; cease.
formidable (fôr′mə·də·bəl) *adj.*: difficult to handle or overcome.
fortitude (fôrt′ə·tōōd′) *n.*: courage.
fraught (frôt) *adj.*: filled.
fray *n.*: noisy quarrel; commotion.
frugal (frōō′gəl) *adj.*: thrifty.
funereal (fyōō·nir′ē·əl) *adj.*: suitable for a funeral; solemn.
futile (fyōōt′'l) *adj.*: unable to succeed; useless.

gambol (gam′bəl) *v.*: to frolic; play animatedly.
garish (gar′ish) *adj.*: too showy or gaudy.
garret (gar′it) *n.*: attic.
garrulous (gar′ə·ləs) *adj.*: talkative.
gauntlet (gônt′lit) *n.*: series of challenges.
genial (jē′nē·əl) *adj.*: 1. mild-mannered; friendly. 2. pleasantly warm and healthful.
glut *v.*: to overfill.
gnome (nōm) *n.*: in folklore, a small being who dwells in the earth.
gorge (gôrj) *v.*: to stuff completely.
grovel (gräv′əl) *v.*: to crawl with the face close to the ground.
guffaw (gu·fô′) *n.*: loud laugh.
guile (gīl) *n.*: sly dealings.

haggard (hag′ərd) *adj.*: worn or tired looking.
harbinger (här′bin·jər) *n.*: indicator of what is to come.
hinterland (hin′tər·land′) *n.*: rural area; backwoods.
homage (äm′ij) *n.*: something done or given to show respect.

---

fat, āpe, cär; ten, ēven; is, bīte; gō, hôrn, look, tōol; yōo, cure; yōō, use; oil, out; up, fʉr; get; joy; yet; chin; she; thin; then; zh, leisure; ŋ, ring; ə for *a* in *ago*, *e* in *agent*, *i* in *sanity*, *o* in *comply*, *u* in *focus*; ′ as in *battle* (bat′'l).

---

homily (häm′ə·lē) *n.*: sermon.
hospitable (häs·pit′ə·bəl) *adj.*: friendly toward guests.
hue (hyoo) *n.*: shade of color.
hysteria (hi·ster′ē·ə) *n.*: outbreak of uncontrolled emotion.
　—**hysterical** *adj.*

ichor (ī′kər) *n.*: thin, watery substance from a sore.
　—**ichorous** *adj.*
idolatrous (ī·däl′ə·trəs) *adj.*: idol-worshiping; excessively
　devoted.
ignoble (ig·nō′bəl) *adj.*: shameful; degrading.
ignominy (ig′nə·min′ē) *n.*: shame and dishonor.
immaterial (im′mə·tir′ē·əl) *adj.*: 1. not consisting of physi-
　cal matter. 2. unimportant.
impart (im·pärt′) *v.*: to share; tell.
impassive (im·pas′iv) *adj.*: calm; indifferent.
　—**impassively** *adv.*
impede (im·pēd′) *v.*: to hinder; obstruct. —**impediment** *n.*
impel (im·pel′) *v.*: to push forward.
imperceptible (im′pər·sep′tə·bəl) *adj.*: so gradual or sub-
　tle that it is not easily sensed.
imperialism (im·pir′ē·əl·iz′əm) *n.*: policy in which one
　country seeks power by conquering other countries and
　establishing colonies.
imperturbable (im′pər·tʉr′bə·bəl) *adj.*: calm; impassive.
impetuous (im·pech′oo·əs) *adj.*: sudden; uncontrolled.
impinge (im·pinj′) *v.*: to strike; touch.
impious (im′pē·əs) *adj.*: lacking reverence or respect.
implacable (im·plak′ə·bəl) *adj.*: inflexible; relentless;
　obstinate.
implore (im·plôr′) *v.*: to beg.
importune (im′pôr·toon′) *v.*: to make repeated
　demands of.
impromptu (im·prämp′too′) *adj.*: unplanned.
improvise (im′prə·vīz′) *v.*: to make for the occasion from
　whatever is handy.
impudent (im′pyoo·dənt) *adj.*: shamelessly bold or dis-
　respectful.
impute (im·pyoot′) *v.*: to attribute to or accuse another.
inadvertent (in′ad·vʉrt′′nt) *adj.*: unintentional. —**inadver-
　tently** *adv.*
inanimate (in·an′ə·mit) *adj.*: not alive.
incarnation (in′kär·nā′shən) *n.*: physical representation of
　an idea or quality; embodiment.
incendiary (in·sen′dē·er′ē) *n.*: firebomb.
incense (in·sens′) *v.*: to make angry.
incentive (in·sent′iv) *n.*: something that prompts one to
　take action or work harder.
incessant (in·ses′ənt) *adj.*: never ceasing; constant.
inclemency (in·klem′ən·sē) *n.*: harsh quality; severity.
inconsiderable (in′kən·sid′ər·ə·bəl) *adj.*: not worth con-
　sideration; unimportant.
inconstancy (in·kän′stən·sē) *n.*: unsteady loyalty;
　fickleness.
incorporeal (in′kôr·pôr′ē·əl) *adj.*: without substance.
incredulous (in·krej′oo·ləs) *adj.*: disbelieving.
indifferent (in·dif′ər·ənt) *adj.*: showing no concern or
　feeling.
indignant (in·dig′nənt) *adj.*: scornful.
indispensable (in′di·spen′sə·bəl) *adj.*: absolutely necessary.

indissoluble (in′di·säl′yoo·bəl) *adj.*: unable to be broken;
　permanent.
inevitable (in·ev′i·tə·bəl) *adj.*: certain to occur.
inference (in′fər·əns) *n.*: conclusion drawn by logical
　reasoning.
ingenious (in·jēn′yəs) *adj.*: clever.
inimitable (in·im′i·tə·bəl) *adj.*: difficult or impossible to im-
　itate.
insatiable (in·sā′shə·bəl) *adj.*: unable to be satisfied; greedy.
intemperance (in·tem′pər·əns) *n.*: lack of restraint.
inter (in·tʉr′) *v.*: to bury.
intercession (in′tər·sesh′ən) *n.*: pleading on behalf of
　another.
interim (in′tər·im) *n.*: period of time between.
intermittent (in′tər·mit′′nt) *adj.*: starting and stopping at
　intervals; periodic.
interstice (in·tʉr′stis) *n.*: small or narrow place between
　things.
intone (in·tōn′) *v.*: to chant.
intoxicate (in·täks′i·kāt′) *v.*: to cause wild excitement or
　happiness, often to a point beyond self-control.
intrepid (in·trep′id) *adj.*: fearless.
invariable (in·ver′ē·ə·bəl) *adj.*: constant; without change.
invincible (in·vin′sə·bəl) *adj.*: unconquerable.
ire (īr) *n.*: anger.
iridescent (ir′i·des′ənt) *adj.*: showing rainbowlike colors.
irreconcilable (ir·rek′ən·sīl′ə·bəl) *adj.*: cannot be brought
　into agreement.
irrelevant (ir·rel′ə·vənt) *adj.*: not related to the subject;
　not important.
itinerant (ī·tin′ər·ənt) *adj.*: traveling.

jocund (jäk′ənd) *adj.*: in good humor; cheerful.
judicious (joo·dish′əs) *adj.*: wise; prudent.

kindle (kin′dəl) *v.*: to set on fire; ignite.
knell (nel) *n.*: solemn sound of a bell.

labyrinth (lab′ə·rinth′) *n.*: maze; complex or confusing
　arrangement.
lament (lə·ment′) *n.*: cry of grief.
languish (laŋ′gwish) *v.*: to lose vitality; become weak.
laudable (lôd′ə·bəl) *adj.*: praiseworthy.
levy (lev′ē) *v.*: to impose.
lineage (lin′ē·ij) *n.*: ancestry.
livid (liv′id) *adj.*: 1. discolored by a bruise; gray blue. 2. red
　or white, as in "livid with rage." —**lividity** *n.*
loathsome (lōth′səm) *adj.*: disgusting.
lucid (loo′sid) *adj.*: clearheaded; sane. —**lucidity** *n.*
lugubrious (lə·goo′brē·əs) *adj.*: very solemn or mournful,
　especially in a way that seems exaggerated or ridiculous.
lunacy (loo′nə·sē) *n.*: madness.
luxuriate (lug·zhoor′ē·āt′) *v.*: to take enormous pleasure.

magenta (mə·jen′tə) *adj.*: purplish red.
magnanimous (mag·nan′ə·məs) *adj.*: generous in rising
　above insults.
malady (mal′ə·dē) *n.*: illness.
malevolence (mə·lev′ə·ləns) *n.*: spite; ill will.

malicious (mə·lish′əs) *adj.:* intentionally mischievous or harmful; spiteful. —**malice** *n.*

malignity (mə·lig′nə·tē) *n.:* harmful or evil thing.

maniacal (mə·nī′ə·kəl) *adj.:* crazed; wildly enthusiastic.

marauder (mə·rôd′ər) *n.:* raider; plunderer.

martyrdom (märt′ər·dəm) *n.:* prolonged suffering or self-sacrifice.

maxim (maks′im) *n.:* general truth or rule of conduct.

meager (mē′gər) *adj.:* poor in quality or small in amount.

metamorphosis (met′ə·môr′fə·sis) *n.:* change of form.

mien (mēn) *n.:* manner; bearing.

mill *v.:* to move in a circular or random pattern, as a crowd or flock.

millennium (mi·len′ē·əm) *n.:* period of a thousand years.

mimic (mim′ik) *v.:* to imitate; mock.

mirth (murth) *n.:* joyfulness.

miry (mīr′ē) *adj.:* swampy; muddy.

monotonous (mə·nät′′n·əs) *adj.:* repeating without interruption.

mortal *adj.:* fatal.

mortify (môrt′ə·fī′) *v.:* to cause to feel shame or embarrassment.

multitudinous (mul′tə·tood′′n·əs) *adj.:* numerous.

munificent (myoo·nif′ə·sənt) *adj.:* very generous.

murky (murk′ē) *adj.:* shadowy.

mute (myoot) *v.:* to muffle or soften.

myriad (mir′ē·əd) *n.:* great number of persons or things.

negligent (neg′lə·jənt) *adj.:* careless; lax.

nemesis (nem′ə·sis) *n.:* agent of retribution or punishment.

nicety (nī′sə·tē) *n.:* delicacy; elegance.

nimble (nim′bəl) *adj.:* moving quickly.

nonpareil (nän′pə·rel′) *adj.:* unrivaled; unequaled.

notorious (nō·tôr′ē·əs) *adj.:* widely but unfavorably known; famous.

noxious (näk′shəs) *adj.:* harmful.

oblique (ō·blēk′) *adj.:* slanting; indirect. —**obliquity** *n.*

obnoxious (əb·näk′shəs) *adj.:* offensive.

obscure (əb·skyoor′) *adj.:* little-known; vague. —**obscurely** *adv.*

obstinate (äb′stə·nət) *adj.:* unreasonably stubborn.

odious (ō′dē·əs) *adj.:* hateful; offensive.

officious (ə·fish′əs) *adj.:* eager to serve; obliging.

omen (ō′mən) *n.:* sign supposedly foretelling the future.

ominous (äm′ə·nəs) *adj.:* threatening.

oppressive (ə·pres′iv) *adj.:* hard to bear.

oracle (ôr′ə·kəl) *n.:* one capable of providing divine revelation or wisdom; seer.

ostentation (äs′tən·tā′shən) *n.:* showiness.

overture (ō′vər·chər) *n.:* proposal.

overwrought (ō′vər·rôt′) *adj.:* overly excited.

palliative (pal′ē·ə·tiv) *adj.:* easing; alleviating.

pallor (pal′ər) *n.:* paleness.

palpable (pal′pə·bəl) *adj.:* easily felt; tangible.

panegyric (pan′ə·jir′ik) *n.:* formal speech elaborately praising something.

parry (par′ē) *v.:* to reply evasively.

pathos (pā′thäs′) *n.:* a quality in something experienced or observed that evokes feelings of pity or sorrow.

patronize (pā′trən·īz′) *v.:* to be a customer of.

penance (pen′əns) *n.:* act of atonement for sin.

pensive (pen′siv) *adj.:* thinking deeply, often of something sad.

perceptible (pər·sep′tə·bəl) *adj.:* visible.

perfidious (pər·fid′ē·əs) *adj.:* treacherous. —**perfidy** *n.*

perfunctory (pər·funk′tə·rē) *adj.:* halfhearted; indifferent. —**perfunctorily** *adv.*

pernicious (pər·nish′əs) *adj.:* wicked; extremely harmful.

perpetual (pər·pech′oo·əl) *adj.:* continuing forever; eternal.

perplexity (pər·pleks′ə·tē) *n.:* confusion; bewilderment. —**perplexedly** *adv.*

persevere (pur′sə·vir′) *v.:* to continue in a course of action despite difficulty or opposition; persist.

personable (pur′sən·ə·bəl) *adj.:* attractive in appearance and personality.

perturb (pər·turb′) *v.:* to upset; disturb. —**perturbation** *n.*

pervade (pər·vād′) *v.:* to spread throughout.

perverse (pər·vurs′) *adj.:* disagreeable; contrary.

pestilence (pes′tə·ləns) *n.:* plague; infection. —**pestilential** *adj.*

phosphorescent (fäs′fə·res′ənt) *adj.:* luminous; glowing.

pilgrimage (pil′grim·ij) *n.:* journey made to a place of religious or historical interest.

pious (pī′əs) *adj.:* devout or virtuous; sacred.

pique (pēk) *n.:* ruffled pride; displeasure.

placid (plas′id) *adj.:* calm; peaceful.

posterity (päs·ter′ə·tē) *n.:* all succeeding generations.

potent (pōt′′nt) *adj.:* powerful; mighty. —**potency** *n.*

prate (prāt) *v.:* to talk idly; chat.

precarious (prē·ker′ē·əs) *adj.:* uncertain; insecure.

precipitate (prē·sip′ə·tit) *adj.:* sudden. —**precipitately** *adv.*

predatory (pred′ə·tôr′ē) *adj.:* living by eating other animals.

predominant (prē·däm′ə·nənt) *adj.:* having the greatest influence or control.

preoccupied (prē·äk′yoo·pīd′) *adj.:* absorbed in one's own thoughts.

prerogative (prē·räg′ə·tiv) *n.:* right or privilege.

presumptuous (prē·zump′choo·əs) *adj.:* boldly over-confident.

pretext (prē′tekst′) *n.:* excuse.

prevail (prē·vāl′) *v.:* to predominate; hold sway.

prevaricate (pri·var′i·kāt′) *v.:* to lie. —**prevarication** *n.*

pristine (pris′tēn′) *adj.:* pure; unspoiled.

procure (prō·kyoor′) *v.:* to obtain; get. —**procurement** *n.*

prodigious (prō·dij′əs) *adj.:* huge.

prodigy (präd′ə·jē) *n.:* genius.

---

f<u>a</u>t, <u>ā</u>pe, cär; t<u>e</u>n, <u>ē</u>ven; <u>i</u>s, b<u>ī</u>te; g<u>ō</u>, h<u>ô</u>rn, l<u>oo</u>k, t<u>oo</u>l; y<u>oo</u>, c<u>u</u>re; y<u>oo</u>, <u>u</u>se; <u>oi</u>l, <u>ou</u>t; <u>u</u>p, f<u>u</u>r; get; joy; yet; <u>ch</u>in; <u>sh</u>e; <u>th</u>in; <u>th</u>en; zh, leisure; ŋ, ring; ə for *a* in *ago*, e in *agent*, i in *sanity*, o in *comply*, u in *focus*; ′ as in *battle* (bat′′l).

---

profess (prō·fes′) v.: to openly declare.

proffer (präf′ər) v.: to offer; propose.

proficiency (prō·fish′ən·sē) n.: skill.

profound (prō·found′) adj.: deep.

promiscuous (prə·mis′kyoo·əs) adj.: casual; undiscriminating.

promontory (präm′ən·tôr′ē) n.: peak of land that juts into the sea.

prophetic (prō·fet′ik) adj.: foreshadowing; predicting.

propitious (prō·pish′əs) adj.: favorable.

propriety (prō·prī′ə·tē) n.: the quality of being proper or fitting.

prosaic (prō·zā′ik) adj.: ordinary; dull.

prostrate (präs′trāt′) adj.: lying face down in a show of submission or weakness. —**prostrating** v.

protract (prō·trakt′) v.: to draw out; extend.

prowess (prou′is) n.: outstanding ability or skill; bravery.

proximity (präks·im′ə·tē) n.: closeness.

prudent (prood′′nt) adj.: careful and wise.

prurient (proor′ē·ənt) adj.: lewd; offensive.

pungent (pun′jənt) adj.: sharp-smelling.

purge (purj) v.: to get rid of; expel.

putrid (pyoo′trid) adj.: decayed; foul-smelling.

quaint (kwānt) adj.: pleasantly unusual.

quell (kwel) v.: to subdue.

rancid (ran′sid) adj.: stale or foul-smelling.

rancor (raŋ′kər) n.: ill will.

rank adj.: overgrown.

ravage (rav′ij) v.: to violently destroy.

ravenous (rav′ə·nəs) adj.: extremely hungry.

rebuke (ri·byook′) v.: to blame or scold.

recapitulate (rē′kə·pich′ə·lāt′) v.: to repeat; summarize.

recess (rē′ses) n.: indentation.

reckon (rek′ən) v.: to consider; judge.

recompense (rek′əm·pens′) n.: repayment; reward.

redress (rē′dres′) n.: compensation for wrong.

reflux (rē′fluks′) n.: a flowing back; ebb.

refract (ri·frakt′) v.: to cause a ray to bend as it passes from one medium to another.

reiterate (rē·it′ə·rāt′) v.: to repeat.

remonstrate (ri·män′strāt′) v.: to protest.

renown (ri·noun′) n.: great fame.

reparation (rep′ə·rā′shən) n.: payment to compensate for wrongdoing.

repose (ri·pōz′) v.: to lie calmly or quietly.

reprisal (ri·prī′zəl) n.: punishment in return for injury.

reproachful (ri·prōch′fəl) adj.: full of or expressing blame.

reprove (ri·proov′) v.: to express disapproval; rebuke.

repulse (ri·puls′) v.: to drive away.

requite (ri·kwīt′) v.: to repay.

resigned (ri·zīnd′) adj.: showing passive acceptance.

restive (res′tiv) adj.: impatient; nervous.

reticulate (ri·tik′yə·lit) adj.: having a network of veins like the threads of a net.

retinue (ret′′n·oo) n.: string of attendants.

revelation (rev′ə·lā′shən) n.: awareness of something previously unknown; realization.

reverberate (ri·vur′bə·rāt′) v.: to echo a sound; resonate.

reverent (rev′ər·ənt) adj.: having deep respect, love, or awe, as for something sacred.

rhetoric (ret′ər·ik) n.: 1. art of speaking and writing. 2. showy but meaningless language.

rite n.: formal ceremony.

rudiments (roo′də·mənts) n. pl.: basics.

rue (roo) v.: to feel remorse; regret.

ruffian (ruf′ē·ən) n.: hoodlum; lawless person.

sacrilegious (sak′rə·lij′əs) adj.: violating something sacred.

sally n.: quick witticism or retort; quip.

sanctity (saŋk′tə·tē) n.: sacred quality; holiness.

sarcastic (sär·kas′tik) adj.: having biting irony; sneering.

saunter (sôn′tər) v.: to stroll.

score v.: to mark with a scratch or groove.

scrupulous (skroo′pyə·ləs) adj.: extremely careful and precise in deciding what is right or wrong.

scrutinize (skroot′′n·īz) v.: to examine carefully.

secular (sek′yə·lər) adj.: not related to religion.

seethe (sēth) v.: to surge; appear constantly active or violently agitated.

semblance (sem′bləns) n.: appearance of something else; resemblance.

seminar (sem′ə·när′) n.: scholarly group discussion.

senile (sē′nīl′) adj.: showing the deterioration that sometimes accompanies old age. —**senility** n.

sensibility (sen′sə·bil′ə·tē) n.: capacity for being affected emotionally.

sepulcher (sep′əl·kər) n.: vault for burial.

sepulchral (sə·pul′krəl) adj.: gloomy.

sequel (sē′kwəl) n.: 1. something that comes after. 2. consequence or result.

sequester (si·kwes′tər) v.: to separate from others; isolate.

serene (sə·rēn′) adj.: calm; peaceful.

serous (sir′əs) adj.: thin and watery. —**serosity** n.

serrate (ser′āt′) adj.: having jagged, sawlike notches along the edge.

servile (sur′vīl′) adj.: like or characteristic of a slave; humbly submissive or yielding.

shambles (sham′bəlz) n. pl.: scene of great disorder.

sheaf (shēf) n.: stalks of grain bound up in a bundle. —**sheaves** n. pl.

shoal (shōl) n.: shallow place; sandbar.

signalize (sig′nəl·īz′) v.: to draw attention to.

silt v.: to fill up with sediment or residue.

sinew (sin′yoo) n.: tendon or connective tissue.

skeptical (skep′ti·kəl) adj.: doubting.

slake v.: to satisfy or quench.

slovenly (sluv′ən·lē) adj.: untidy.

sodden (säd′′n) adj.: soaked; soggy.

solace (säl′is) n.: peace; relief.

solicit (sə·lis′it) v.: to ask or plead earnestly.

solicitous (sə·lis′ə·təs) adj.: showing care or attention.

somber (säm′bər) adj.: gloomy.

sovereign (säv′rən) adj.: superior to all others.

spare adj.: meager; thin.

spawn (spôn) v.: to bring into being.

specter (spek′tər) n.: ghost. —**spectral** adj.

squalid (skwäl′id) adj.: foul or unclean; wretched.

squeamish (skwēm′ish) adj.: easily upset.

stagnate (stag′nāt′) v.: to become inactive or sluggish.

stature (stach′ər) *n.*: height.
statute (stach′o͞ot) *n.*: law.
stealth (stelth) *n.*: secret or sly behavior.
stifle (stī′fəl) *v.*: to suppress; hold back.
stint *n.*: limitation.
stratagem (strat′ə·jəm) *n.*: trick.
strident (strīd′nt) *adj.*: harsh; sharp.
stupefy (sto͞o′pə·fī′) *v.*: to dull the mind and senses; make lethargic, as in a state of stupor.
subdue (səb·do͞o′) *v.*: to conquer; overcome.
sublime (sə·blīm′) *adj.*: awe-inspiring; majestic.
subsistence (səb·sis′təns) *n.*: existence; means of support or sustenance.
subtle (sut′′l) *adj.*: delicately suggestive; not obvious.
succumb (sə·kum′) *v.*: 1. to yield; give way. 2. to die.
suffice (sə·fīs′) *v.*: to satisfy. —**sufficient** *adj.*
sundry (sun′drē) *adj.*: various.
supercilious (so͞o′pər·sil′ē·əs) *adj.*: disdainful or scornful; haughty.
superfluity (so͞o′pər·flo͞o′ə·tē) *n.*: excess.
supplant (sə·plant′) *v.*: to replace; displace.
suppliant (sup′lē·ənt) *adj.*: requesting humbly. —**supplication** *n.*
surfeit (sur′fit) *v.*: to fill to excess.
surmise (sər·mīz′) *n.*: guess; speculation.
surmount (sər·mount′) *v.*: to rise above.
surname (sur′nām′) *n.*: last name.
sustenance (sus′tə·nəns) *n.*: food or money to support life.
swathe (swäth) *n.*: long strip of cloth; bandage.
sylvan (sil′vən) *adj.*: of the woods.
symmetry (sim′ə·trē) *n.*: similarity of form on either side of a dividing line; balance.

taut (tôt) *adj.*: stretched tight.
tedious (tē′dē·əs) *adj.*: boring.
teem *v.*: to swarm.
temerity (tə·mer′ə·tē) *n.*: foolish or rash boldness; recklessness.
temperance (tem′pər·əns) *n.*: restraint; control.
temporal (tem′pə·rəl) *adj.*: limited to this world; not spiritual.
tenacity (tə·nas′ə·tē) *n.*: persistence; steadfastness.
tentative (ten′tə·tiv) *adj.*: hesitant; uncertain.
terrestrial (tə·res′trē·əl) *adj.*: of the earth.
theological (thē′ə·läj′i·kəl) *adj.*: having to do with the study of God.
theoretical (thē′ə·ret′i·kəl) *adj.*: in the realm of ideas, as opposed to practice or application.
timorous (tim′ər·es) *adj.*: full of fear; timid.
tincture (tiŋk′chər) *v.*: to color lightly; tint.
titillate (tit′′l·āt′) *v.*: to excite; stimulate.
titter *v.*: to giggle.
traipse (trāps) *v.*: colloquial for "to wander."
tranquil (tran′kwil) *adj.*: calm; peaceful.
transcend (tran·send′) *v.*: to exceed; surpass.

transgress (trans·gres′) *v.*: to overstep a limit or break a law.
transitory (tran′sə·tôr′ē) *adj.*: temporary or fleeting.
transom (tran′səm) *n.*: small hinged window directly above a door.
tremulous (trem′yo͞o·ləs) *adj.*: trembling; quivering.
tribulation (trib′yo͞o·lā′shən) *n.*: great misery; affliction.
tribute (trib′yo͞ot) *n.*: tax paid by a vassal to a lord or ruler.
trifle (trī′fəl) *v.*: to mock; treat lightly.
trivet (triv′it) *n.*: three-legged stand for holding pots.
tumult (to͞o′mult) *n.*: uproar; commotion.
turbid (tur′bid) *adj.*: thick; dense.
tyranny (tir′ə·nē) *n.*: cruel and unjust rule. —**tyrannical** *adj.*

uncanny (un·kan′ē) *adj.*: strange; eerie; weird.
uncouth (un·ko͞oth′) *adj.*: crude; uncultured.
unfathomable (un·fath′əm·ə·bəl) *adj.*: unmeasurable; infinite.
unnerve (un·nurv′) *v.*: to cause one to lose courage or confidence.
unprecedented (un·pres′ə·den′tid) *adj.*: not done or seen before; unique.
unscrupulous (un·skro͞o′pyə·ləs) *adj.*: dishonest; unprincipled.
unwary (un·wer′ē) *adj.*: not watchful or cautious.
usurper (yo͞o·surp′ər) *n.*: one who seizes power unlawfully.
utter *adj.*: total.

vanquish (vaŋ′kwish) *v.*: to conquer.
vaulted (vôlt′id) *adj.*: arched.
vehement (vē′ə·mənt) *adj.*: passionate; forceful.
vellicate (vel′i·kāt′) *v.*: to twitch; pluck.
velocity (və·läs′ə·tē) *n.*: speed.
verisimilitude (ver′ə·si·mil′ə·to͞od′) *n.*: appearance of being real.
verity (ver′ə·tē) *n.*: truth.
vermin (vur′mən) *n.*: disease-carrying pest. —**vermin** *n. pl.*
vex *v.*: to annoy highly.
vigor (vig′ər) *n.*: strength; vitality.
viscous (vis′kəs) *adj.*: having the form of a sticky fluid.
vivacity (vī·vas′ə·tē) *n.*: liveliness; animation.
vociferate (vō·sif′ər·āt′) *v.*: to speak loudly and vehemently. —**vociferous** *adj.*
void (void) *adj.*: empty.

waggish (wag′ish) *adj.*: prankish; playful.
wan (wän) *adj.*: pale; weak with sadness.
wanton (wän′tən) *adj.*: luxurious; unrestrained.
winning (win′iŋ) *adj.*: charming.
wither (with′ər) *v.*: to decay; wilt or shrivel.
wizened (wiz′ənd) *adj.*: dried up; withered.
wrath (rath) *n.*: great anger; rage.
wrought (rôt) *adj.*: shaped; fashioned.

zeal *n.*: enthusiasm; passion.

---

f̲at, āpe, c̲är; t̲en, ēven; i̲s, bīte; gō, hôrn, l̲o̲o̲k, to̲o̲l; yo̲o̲, c̲ure; yo͞o, use; o̲il, o̲ut; up, fur; g̲et; joy; y̲et; c̲hin; s̲he; t̲hin; t̲hen; z̲h, leisure; ŋ, ring; ə for *a* in *ago*, *e* in *agent*, *i* in *sanity*, *o* in *comply*, *u* in *focus*; ′ as in *battle* (bat′′l).

ACKNOWLEDGMENTS

For permission to reprint copyrighted material, grateful acknowledgment is given to the following sources:

Agencia Literaria Mercedes Casanovas: "La guitarra" from *Obras completas* by Federico García Lorca.

The Asia Society: "Thoughts of Hanoi" by Nguyen Thi Vinh from *A Thousand Years of Vietnamese Poetry,* translated by Nguyen Ngoc Bich. Copyright © 1974 by The Asia Society.

Stephanie Bailey: "Worn Out" by Stephanie Bailey from *Legends,* vol. X, May 1992. Copyright © 1992 by Stephanie Bailey. Published by Taylorsville High School.

Bantam Books, a division of Bantam Doubleday Dell Publishing Group, Inc.: From "Give Us This Day Our Daily Bread" from *Shakespeare Alive* by Joseph Papp and Elizabeth Kirkland. Copyright © 1988 by the New York Shakespeare Festival.

Robert Bly: "The Guitar" by Federico García Lorca from *Lorca and Jiménez: Selected Poems,* chosen and translated by Robert Bly. Copyright © 1973, 1997 by Robert Bly. Published by Beacon Press, Boston, 1973, 1997.

D. S. Brewer: From "The Day of Destiny" from *The Morte Darthur: Parts Seven and Eight* by Sir Thomas Malory, edited by D. S. Brewer. Copyright © 1968 by D. S. Brewer.

Curtis Brown Ltd., London, on behalf of the Estate of Sir Winston S. Churchill: From "Speech on Dunkirk, House of Commons," June 4, 1940. Copyright 1940 by Winston S. Churchill. From page 24 (retitled "A Scream of Rage") and from "The Black Death" from *The Birth of Britain* by Winston S. Churchill. Copyright © 1956 by Winston S. Churchill.

Cambridge University Press: From "The Medieval Situation" from *The Discarded Image* by C. S. Lewis. Copyright © 1964 by Cambridge University Press.

Delacorte Press/Seymour Lawrence, a division of Bantam Doubleday Dell Publishing Group, Inc.: From *Sextet: T. S. Eliot, Truman Capote and Others* by John Malcolm Brinnin. Copyright © 1981 by John Malcolm Brinnin.

Devin-Adair, Publishers, Inc., Old Greenwich, CT 06870: From *The Book of Margery Kempe* by Margery Kempe. Copyright © 1944 and renewed © 1972 by Devin-Adair, Publishers, Inc. All rights reserved.

Doubleday, a division of Bantam Doubleday Dell Publishing Group, Inc.: "Marriage Is a Private Affair" from *Girls at War and Other Stories* by Chinua Achebe. Copyright © 1972, 1973 by Chinua Achebe. From *How the Irish Saved Civilization* by Thomas Cahill. Copyright © 1995 by Thomas Cahill. "The Cairo Rooftop" from *Palace Walk* by Naguib Mahfouz. Copyright © 1990 by American University in Cairo Press.

Rita Dove and W. W. Norton & Company, Inc.: "Sisters" from *Grace Notes* by Rita Dove. Copyright © 1989 by Rita Dove.

Dutton Signet, a division of Penguin Putnam Inc.: From the annotations from *Macbeth* by William Shakespeare. Copyright © 1963 and renewed © 1991 by Sylvan Barnet for introduction and annotations. From *Beowulf,* translated by Burton Raffel. Translation copyright © 1963 by Burton Raffel; afterword copyright © 1963 by New American Library. From "The Unfed Dervish," "Information and Knowledge," "The Elephant-Keeper," "Safety and Riches," and "The Fox and the Camels" from *The Way of the Sufi* by Idries Shah. Copyright © 1968 by Idries Shah.

Faber and Faber Limited: "Hawk Roosting" and excerpt from *Lupercal* by Ted Hughes. Copyright © 1960 by Ted Hughes.

Famous Music Publishing Companies: Lyrics by Dean Pitchford from "Holding Out for a Hero." Copyright © 1984 by Ensign Music Corporation. International copyright secured. All rights reserved.

Farrar, Straus & Giroux, Inc.: From "On Keeping a Notebook" from *Slouching Towards Bethlehem* by Joan Didion. Copyright © 1966, 1968 and renewed © 1996 by Joan Didion. "Once upon a Time" from *Jump* by Nadine Gordimer. Copyright © 1991 by Felix Licensing, B.V. "Digging" from *Poems 1965–1975* by Seamus Heaney. Copyright © 1980 by Seamus Heaney. "The Grauballe Man" from *Selected Poems: 1966–1987* by Seamus Heaney. Copyright © 1990 by Seamus Heaney. "Chaucer" from *Birthday Letters* by Ted Hughes. Copyright © 1998 by Ted Hughes. "The Mower" from *Collected Poems* by Philip Larkin. Copyright © 1988, 1989 by the Estate of Philip Larkin. Canto XXXIV from *The Inferno of Dante: A New Verse Translation* by Robert Pinsky. Copyright © 1994 by Farrar, Straus & Giroux, Inc.; translation copyright © 1994 by Robert Pinsky. From "My Muse" and from "Too Tired for Words" from *Me Again* by Stevie Smith. Copyright © 1981 by James MacGibbon. "Freedom to Breathe" and "The Bonfire and the Ants" from *Stories and Prose Poems* by Alexander Solzhenitsyn, translated by Michael Glenny. Translation copyright © 1971 by Michael Glenny. "The Virgins" from *Sea Grapes* by Derek Walcott. Copyright © 1976 by Derek Walcott.

Grove/Atlantic, Inc.: From *Waiting for Godot* by Samuel Beckett. Copyright © 1954 by Grove Press, Inc.; copyright renewed © 1982 by Samuel Beckett. From "That's All" from *Complete Plays: Three* by Harold Pinter. Copyright © 1966 by H. Pinter Ltd.

Harcourt Brace & Company: "The Hollow Men" from *Collected Poems 1909–1962* by T. S. Eliot. Copyright 1936 by Harcourt Brace & Company, copyright © 1963, 1964 by T. S. Eliot. From "Warfare and Warlords" from *The Harbrace History of England, Part I: Ancient and Medieval England, Beginnings to 1509* by J. R. Lander. Copyright © 1973 by Harcourt Brace & Company. "Shooting an Elephant" from *Shooting an Elephant and Other Essays* by George Orwell. Copyright 1950 by Sonia Brownell Orwell and renewed © 1978 by Sonia Pitt-Rivers. From "A Sketch of the Past" from *Moments of Being* by Virginia Woolf, edited by Jeanne Schulkind. Text copyright © 1976 by Quentin Bell and Angelica Garnett; introduction and editorial material copyright © 1976 by Jeanne Schulkind. From *Mrs. Dalloway* by Virginia Woolf. Copyright © 1925 by Harcourt Brace & Company; copyright renewed © 1953 by Leonard Woolf. From "Shakespeare's Sister" and from page 64 from *A Room of One's Own* by Virginia Woolf. Copyright 1929 by Harcourt Brace & Company; copyright renewed © 1957 by Leonard Woolf.

John Hawkins & Associates, Inc.: "Macbeth and the Witches" from *Twisted Tales from Shakespeare* by Richard Armour. Copyright © 1957 by Richard Armour.

Hispanic Society of America: "The Guitar" by Federico García Lorca from *Translations from Hispanic Poets,* edited by Elizabeth du Gué Trapier.

Henry Holt and Company, Inc.: "Is My Team Ploughing," "A Shropshire Lad," "To an Athlete Dying Young," and "When I Was One-and-Twenty" from *The Collected Poems of A. E. Housman.* Copyright 1939, 1940 by Henry Holt and Company, Inc.; copyright © 1967 by Robert E. Symons.

Houghton Mifflin Company: "Mushrooms" from *True Stories* from *Selected Poems II: Poems Selected and New 1976–1986* by Margaret Atwood. Copyright © 1987 by Margaret Atwood. All rights reserved. From *Gilgamesh,* translated by Herbert Mason. Copyright © 1970 by Herbert Mason. All rights reserved.

International African Institute, London: Four proverbs from *Jabo Proverbs from Liberia: Maxims in the Life of a Native Tribe* by George Herzog. Copyright © 1936 by the International African Institute. Published by Oxford University Press—London.

John Johnson Ltd.: "I Have Visited Again" from *The Bronze Horseman* by Alexander Pushkin, translated by D. M. Thomas. Translation copyright © 1982 by D. M. Thomas.

Estate of James Joyce: From *Stephen Hero* by James Joyce. Copyright © 1944, 1955, 1959, 1963 by James Joyce; copyright © by the Estate of James Joyce.

Alfred A. Knopf, Inc.: "The Demon Lover" from *The Collected Stories of Elizabeth Bowen* by Elizabeth Bowen. Copyright 1946 and renewed © 1974 by Elizabeth Bowen. "The Myth of Sisyphus" and from "An Absurd Reasoning" from *The Myth of Sisyphus and Other Essays* by Albert Camus, translated by Justin O'Brien. Copyright © 1955 by Alfred A. Knopf, Inc. From *Grendel* by John Gardner. Copyright © 1971 by John Gardner. "B. Wordsworth" from *Miguel Street* by V. S. Naipaul. Copyright © 1959 by V. S. Naipaul. "My Oedipus Complex" from *Collected Stories* by Frank O'Connor. Copyright 1950 by Frank O'Connor.

Liveright Publishing Corporation: "O sweet spontaneous" and "since feeling is first" from *Selected Poems* by E. E. Cummings. Introduction and commentary by Richard S. Kennedy. Copyright 1923, 1926, 1951, 1954, © 1991 by the Trustees for the E. E. Cummings Trust; copyright © 1976, 1985 by George James Firmage.

Arnulfo J. López: "A Poem Within a Poem" by Arnulfo J. López from *Heritage,* vol. 31, Spring 1991. Published by James Madison High School, Vienna, VA.

Macmillan General Reference USA, a division of Ahsuog, Inc.: From *Webster's New World Dictionary,* Third College Edition. Copyright © 1988, 1991, 1994, 1996, 1997 by Simon & Schuster, Inc.

Andrea D. Marzullo: "Mind" by A.D.M. from *Image,* Creative Arts Magazine, vol. 31, 1992. Copyright © 1992 by Andrea D. Marzullo. Published by Bellevue East Senior High School, Bellevue, NE.

Merlyn's Pen: The National Magazines of Student Writing: "Tu B'shvat" by Michelle Dorrien from *Merlyn's Pen,* Senior Edition, April/May 1994. Copyright © 1994 by Merlyn's Pen. First appeared in *Merlyn's Pen: The National Magazines of Student Writing.*

Melynn Minson: "Searching for a Future in the Dusk" by Melynn Minson from *Expressions,* vol. XXVII, 1992. Published by Hillcrest High School, Midvale, UT.

Edmund Morris: From "A Visit with Nadine Gordimer" by Edmund Morris from *The New York Times Book Review,* June 7, 1981. Copyright © 1981 by Edmund Morris.

New Directions Publishing Corporation: From "The Witness" from *Labyrinths* by Jorge Luis Borges, translated by James Irby. Copyright © 1962, 1964 by New Directions Publishing Corp. From *In Search of Duende* by Federico García Lorca, edited and translated by Christopher Maurer. Copyright © 1975, 1998 by the Estate of Federico García Lorca; copyright © 1975, 1998 by Christopher Maurer; copyright © 1955, 1998 by New Directions Publishing Corporation. "Dulce et Decorum Est" and from "Strange Meeting" from *The Collected Poems of Wilfred Owen.* Copyright © 1963 by Chatto & Windus, Ltd. "Not Waving but Drowning" from *Collected Poems of Stevie Smith.* Copyright © 1972 by Stevie Smith. "In my craft or sullen art" from *The Collected Poems of Dylan Thomas.* Copyright 1939, 1942, 1946 by New Directions; copyright 1952, 1953 by Dylan Thomas. "Fern Hill" and "Do Not Go Gentle into That Good Night" from *The Poems of Dylan Thomas.* Copyright © 1952 by Dylan Thomas. "Jade Flower Palace" by Tu Fu from *One Hundred Poems from the Chinese,* translated by Kenneth Rexroth. Copyright © 1971 by Kenneth Rexroth. All rights reserved.

The New York Times Company: Quote by David Ormsby Gore from *The New York Times,* October 28, 1962. Copyright © 1962 by The New York Times Company. "A Beam of Protons Illuminates Gutenberg's Genius" by Malcolm W. Browne from *The New York Times,* May 12, 1987. Copyright © 1987 by The New York Times Company. From "Scenes from a Modern Marriage" by Julia Markus from *The New York Times,* February 14, 1995. Copyright © 1995 by The New York Times Company. From "Lesson of the Bamboo Crates" by Christy Ma from *The New York Times,* April 5, 1997. Copyright © 1997 by The New York Times Company. From "A Collaboration Across 1,200 Years" by D.J.R. Bruckner from *The New York Times,* July 22, 1997. Copyright © 1997 by The New York Times Company.

North Point Press, a division of Farrar, Straus & Giroux, Inc.: From *Crow and Weasel* by Barry Lopez, illustrated by Tom Pohrt. Text copyright © 1990 by Barry Holstun Lopez; illustrations copyright © 1990 by Tom Pohrt.

W. W. Norton & Company, Inc.: "Fifth Day, Ninth Story" (retitled "Federigo's Falcon") from *The Decameron* by Giovanni Boccaccio, translated by Mark Musa and Peter Bondanella. Translation copyright © 1982 by Mark Musa and Peter Bondanella. "A Letter to My Daughter" from *The Balkan Express: Fragments from the Other Side of War* by Slavenka Drakulić, translated by Maja Soljan. Copyright © 1993 by Slavenka Drakulić; translation copyright © 1993 by Maja Soljan.

Gary P. Nunn: From lyrics to "London Homesick Blues" by Gary P. Nunn. Copyright © 1973 by Gary P. Nunn. Published by Nunn Publishing Company, BMI.

Harold Ober Associates Incorporated: From Commencement Address by Chinua Achebe, given on May 27, 1996, at Bates College. Copyright © 1996 by Chinua Achebe.

Oxford University Press, Inc.: From "The Troglodyte World" from *The Great War and Modern Memory* by Paul Fussell. Copyright © 1977 by Oxford University Press, Inc. From *Faust, Parts 1 and 2,* by Johann Wolfgang von Goethe, translated by Louis MacNeice; translation copyright 1951, 1954 by Frederick Louis MacNeice; renewed copyright © 1979 by Hedi MacNeice.

Pantheon Books, a division of Random House, Inc.: "A Clever Judge" by Chang Shih-nan and "Gold, Gold" by Lieh Tzu from *Chinese Fairy Tales and Fantasies,* translated and edited by Moss Roberts. Copyright © 1979 by Moss Roberts. "Axolotl" from *End of the Game and Other Stories* by Julio Cortázar, translated by Paul Blackburn. Copyright © 1967 by Random House, Inc.

Paulist Press: From *Julian of Norwich: Showings,* translated by Edmund Colledge, O.S.A., and James Walsh, S.J. Copyright © 1978 by The Missionary Society of St. Paul the Apostle in the State of New York.

Penguin Books Ltd.: From Introduction by Nevill Coghill, "The Prologue," "The Pardoner's Prologue and Tale," and "The Wife of Bath's Prologue and Tale" from *The Canterbury Tales* by Geoffrey Chaucer, translated by Nevill Coghill (Penguin Classics 1951, Fourth Revised Edition 1977). Copyright © 1951, 1958, 1960, 1975, 1977 by Nevill Coghill. "Night" from *The Koran,* translated by N. J. Dawood (Penguin Classics 1956, Fifth Revised Edition 1990). Copyright © 1956, 1959, 1966, 1968, 1974, 1990 by N. J. Dawood. "Question and answer among the mountains" by Li Po from *The Penguin Book of Chinese Verse,* translated by Robert Kotewall and Norman L. Smith, edited by A. R. Davis (Penguin Books, 1962). Translation copyright © 1962 by N. L. Smith and R. H. Kotewall.

Laurence Pollinger Limited and the Estate of Frieda Lawrence Ravagli: From "Letter to Rolf Gardiner, 18 December 1927," "Letter to Earl Brewster, 22 September 1922," and from "Letter to Rolf Gardiner, 17 July 1926" from *The Letters of D. H. Lawrence,* vol. IV–VI. Copyright 1932 by the Estate of D. H. Lawrence; copyright 1934 by Frieda Lawrence; copyright 1933, 1948, 1953, 1954, © 1956, 1957, 1958, 1959, 1960, 1961, 1962, 1967, 1969 by Stefano Ravagli and R. G. Seaman, executors of the Estate of Frieda Lawrence Ravagli; copyright © 1987 by the Estate of Frieda Lawrence Ravagli. Published by Cambridge University Press.

Random House, Inc.: From "Five Songs, II" [That night when joy began], "Musée des Beaux Arts," and "The Unknown Citizen" from *W. H. Auden: Collected Poems* by W. H. Auden, edited by Edward Mendelson. Copyright 1937, 1940 and renewed © 1965, 1968 by W. H. Auden. "The Ring" from *Anecdotes of Destiny* by Isak Dinesen. Copyright © 1958 by Isak Dinesen. From "Mecca" from *The Autobiography of Malcolm X* by Malcolm X with the assistance of Alex Haley. Copyright © 1964 by Alex Haley and Malcolm X; copyright © 1965 by Alex Haley and Betty Shabazz.

John Robinson for the Arthur Waley Estate: "To Tan-Ch'iu" by Li Po from *Chinese Poems,* translated by Arthur Waley. Copyright © 1946, 1961, 1983 by George Allen & Unwin (Publishers) Ltd.

Rogers, Coleridge & White Ltd., 20 Powis Mews, London W11 1JN, and Authors: From "The Seafarer" from *The Battle of Maldon and Other Old English Poems,* translated by Kevin Crossley-Holland. Copyright © 1965 by Kevin Crossley-Holland and Bruce Mitchell. From "Games at Twilight" from *Games at Twilight and Other Stories* by Anita Desai. Copyright © 1978 by Anita Desai.

St. James Press, a subsidiary of Gale Research Inc.: Quotes by Chinua Achebe and Anita Desai from *Contemporary Novelists,* Fifth Edition, edited by Lesley Henderson. Copyright © 1991 by St. James Press.

St. Martin's Press, Inc., New York, NY: From *World Within World* by Stephen Spender. Copyright © 1951 by Stephen Spender. Looking Back in 1994: A New Introduction to *World Within World.* Copyright © 1994 by Stephen Spender.

The Saturday Review: From "Black Man's Burden" by Maxwell Geismar from *The Saturday Review,* March 8, 1974. Copyright © 1974 by S. R. Publications Ltd.

Harriet O'Donovan Sheehy, c/o Joan Daves Agency as agent for the proprietor: From "After

Aughrim's Great Disaster" from *An Only Child* by Frank O'Connor. Copyright © 1958, 1959, 1960, 1961 by Frank O'Connor.

Simon & Schuster: From *In Patagonia* by Bruce Chatwin. Copyright © 1977 by Bruce Chatwin. Number 17 from Book II, numbers 15 and 21 from Book VII, and number 23 from Book XV from *The Analects of Confucius,* translated by Arthur Waley. Copyright © 1938 by George Allen & Unwin, Ltd. "No Witchcraft for Sale" and from Preface from *African Stories* by Doris Lessing. Copyright © 1951, 1953, 1954, 1957, 1958, 1962, 1963, 1964, 1965, 1972, 1981 by Doris Lessing. "No Witchcraft for Sale" from *African Stories* by Doris Lessing. Copyright © 1951, 1953, 1954, 1957, 1958, 1962, 1963, 1964, 1965, 1972, 1981 by Doris Lessing. "Death and Other Grave Matters" from *What Jane Austen Ate and Charles Dickens Knew* by Daniel Pool. Copyright © 1993 by Daniel Pool.

The Society of Authors as the Literary Representative of the Estate of Katherine Mansfield: Excerpt from "Journal: May 30 [1917]" and "To Richard Murry [June 20, 1921]" from *The Letters and Journals of Katherine Mansfield,* edited by C. K. Stead.

Wole Soyinka: "Telephone Conversation" by Wole Soyinka from *Reflections: Nigerian Prose and Verse,* edited by Frances Ademola. Copyright © 1962 by Wole Soyinka.

Time Inc.: From "Life in 999: A Grim Struggle" by Howard G. Chua-Eoan from *Time,* vol. 140, no. 27, Fall 1992. Copyright © 1992 by Time Inc.

Charles E. Tuttle Co., Inc.: "The First Principle," "The Gates of Paradise," "The Moon Cannot Be Stolen," and "Temper" from *Zen Flesh, Zen Bones: A Collection of Zen and Pre-Zen Writings,* compiled by Paul Reps. Copyright © 1957 by Charles E. Tuttle Co., Inc.

University College of Dublin: Excerpt from *Memories of the Famine* by Maire ni Grianna from *Memories of the Famine* from Main Manuscript vol. 1071, pages 279–283, in the Department of Irish Folklore, University College, Dublin.

University of California Press: From *The Diary of Samuel Pepys,* vol. I, vol. II, vol. V, and vol. VII, edited by Robert Latham and William Matthews. Copyright © 1972–1986 by The Master, Fellows and Scholars of Magdalen College, Cambridge; Robert Latham; and the Executors of William Matthews.

The University of Chicago Press: From "Sir Gawain and the Green Knight" from *The Complete Works of the Gawain-Poet,* translated by John Gardner. Copyright © 1965 by The University of Chicago. From *The Panchatantra,* translated from the Sanskrit by Arthur W. Ryder. Copyright 1925 by The University of Chicago; copyright renewed 1953 by Mary E. Ryder and Winifred Ryder.

University of Texas Press: "Sonnet 17/Soneto 17" and "Sonnet 79/Soneto 79" from *100 Love Sonnets/ Cien sonetos de amor* by Pablo Neruda, translated by Stephen Tapscott. Copyright © 1959 by Pablo Neruda and Fundacion Pablo Neruda; copyright © 1986 by University of Texas Press.

USA TODAY: From "Groundlings Get Close Look, Rowdy Adventures," by David Patrick Stearns from *USA TODAY,* June 12, 1997. Copyright © 1997 by USA TODAY.

Viking Penguin, a division of Penguin Putnam Inc.: "Top of the Food Chain" from *Without a Hero* by T. Coraghessan Boyle. Copyright © 1993 by T. Coraghessan Boyle. "The Destructors" from *Collected Stories of Graham Greene.* Copyright © 1955, 1983 by Graham Greene. "The Rocking-Horse Winner" from *Complete Short Stories of D. H.*

Lawrence. Copyright 1933 by the Estate of D. H. Lawrence; copyright renewed © 1961 by Angelo Ravagli and C. M. Weekley, Executors of the Estate of Frieda Lawrence Ravagli. "Snake" from *The Complete Poems of D. H. Lawrence* by D. H. Lawrence, edited by V. de Sola Pinto and F. W. Roberts. Copyright © 1964, 1971 by Angelo Ravagli and C. M. Weekley, Executors of the Estate of Frieda Lawrence Ravagli. "In the Shadow of War" from *Stars of the New Curfew* by Ben Okri. Copyright © 1988 by Ben Okri. "Unfortunate Coincidence" from *The Portable Dorothy Parker*, introduction by Brendan Gill. Copyright 1926 and renewed © 1954 by Dorothy Parker.

White Pine Press: "Going Home" from *Between Two Rivers: Selected Poems 1956–1984* by Maurice Kenny. Copyright © 1979, 1981, 1987 by Maurice Kenny.

Calen Wood: "Beowulf Shrinklet" by Calen Wood from *IKON, Literary-Arts Magazine*, 1994. Copyright © 1994 by Calen Wood. Published by Bakersfield High School, Bakersfield, CA.

Yale University Press: "Riddle #32: A Ship," "Riddle #33: Iceberg," "Riddle #47: Bookworm," and "The Seafarer" from *Poems from the Old English*, translated by Burton Raffel. Copyright © 1960, 1964, 1998 by Burton Raffel.

SOURCES CITED

From *How the Irish Saved Civilization* by Thomas Cahill. Published by Doubleday, New York, 1995.
From "What Lips My Lips Have Kissed" from *Collected Poems* by Edna St. Vincent Millay. Copyright 1923, 1951 by Edna St. Vincent Millay and Norma Millay Ellis. Published by HarperCollins.

From a letter to Princess Caetani from *The Collected Letters of Dylan Thomas*, edited by Paul Ferris. Letters copyright © 1957, 1966, 1985 by The Trustees for the Copyrights of Dylan Thomas.
From "A Brief Note About the River When Its Waters Rise Up Like the Sea" by Tu Fu from *An Introduction to Chinese Literature* by Liu Wu-chi. Published by Indiana University Press, Bloomington, 1966.
From "Literature and Conscientization: Interview with Chinua Achebe" by Biodun Jeyifo from *Nigeria Magazine*, Lagos, 1983.
From *A Sort of Life* by Graham Greene. Published by Simon & Schuster, New York, 1971.
From "Verse translation is a minor art . . ." from *The Translation of Verse* by Burton Raffel. Published by the University of Nebraska Press, Lincoln, 1960.

PICTURE CREDITS

The illustrations on the Contents pages are picked up from pages in the textbook. Credits for those illustrations can be found either on the textbook page on which they appear or in the listing below.

Page 1, Erich Lessing/Art Resource, NY; 2, David Parker/Science Photo Library/Photo Researchers, Inc.; 3, (bottom) Louis Jawitz/The Image Bank; 4, (middle) ©Sylvain Grandadam/Tony Stone Worldwide, (top) ©cliché Bibliothèque Nationale de France, Paris. Fr 95 fol. 173; 5, (top right) ©Meyer/Kunsthistorisches Museum, Vienna, (bottom, left to right) ©Justin Kerr; Art Resource, NY; ©Mario Corvetto/Comstock Inc.; 6, ©Farrell Grehan/Photo Researchers, Inc.; 7, Antony Edwards/The Image Bank; 8, (middle) Courtesy of Ted Spiegel; 9, Erich Lessing/Art Resource, NY; 10, (bottom) C. M. Dixon, (top) Michael Holford Photographs; 12, Ted Spiegel; 13, Werner Forman/Art Resource, NY; 14, Boltin Picture Library; 15, Art Resource, NY; 17, C. M. Dixon; 19, Werner Forman/Art Resource, NY; 20, ©Michael Holford; 22, Werner Forman/Art Resource, NY; 24, Art Resource, NY; 27, Boltin Picture Library; 28, Werner Forman/Art Resource, NY; 34, ©Michael Holford; 35, Courtesy of Ted Spiegel; 37, Erich Lessing/Art Resource, NY; 38, Werner Forman/Art Resource, NY; 39, ©Stephanie Berger; 43, Courtesy of Ted Spiegel; 44, 45, Werner Forman/Art Resource, NY; 50, The Kobal Collection; 51, Werner Forman/Art Resource, NY; 52, (top) Bridgeman Art Library, London/New York, (bottom) Giraudon/Art Resource, NY; 54, Scala/Art Resource, NY; 55, 56, 58, Cotton Coulson/Woodfin Camp & Associates; 60, Werner Forman/Art Resource, NY; 63, Boltin Picture Library; 64, Jules Zalon/The Image Bank; 65, (bottom) Art Resource, NY; 71, F. Cruz/Superstock; 72, Art Resource, NY; 74, Robert Harding Picture Library; 76, (top) Giraudon/Art Resource, NY, (bottom) Bridgeman Art Library, London/New York; 77, (top) Giraudon/Art Resource, NY, (bottom left) Bibiothèque Nationale/Archiv für Kunst und Geschichte, Berlin; 79, Photo: IndustrieFoto Hilbinger; 90, Robert Harding Picture Library; 93, Swedowsky/The Image Bank; 94, Photo AKG London; 96, Art Resource, NY; 100 (bottom), 101, Superstock, New York; 106, Bridgeman Art Library, London/New York; 113, Marvin E. Newman/The Image Bank; 125, Bridgeman Art Library, London/New York; 140, Archives G. Dagli Orti; 142, Corbis-Bettmann; 147, 151, 152 (top), Bridgeman Art Library, London/New York; 152, (bottom) Scala/Art Resource, NY; 156, Giraudon/Art Resource, NY; 160, Art Resource, NY; 166, Fine Art Photographic Library Ltd./Private Collection; 170,

173, Bridgeman Art Library, London/New York; 177, 181, Art Resource, NY; 189, F. Cruz/Superstock; 190, The Marquess of Salisbury, Hatfield House/Ted Spiegel; 192, 194 (top), Bridgeman Art Library, London/New York; 194, (bottom, left to right) Scala/Art Resource, NY; Erich Lessing/Art Resource, NY; Archiv für Kunst und Geschichte, Berlin; 195, (top and middle) Corbis-Bettmann, (bottom left) Bridgeman Art Library, London/New York, (bottom right) ©Lindsay Hebberd/Woodfin Camp & Associates; 196, 197, Bridgeman Art Library, London/New York; 198, (bottom) Archives G. Dagli Orti; 199, (top) Erich Lessing/Art Resource, NY; 202, Bridgeman Art Library, London/New York; 205, 206 (middle and right), 207, Bridgeman Art Library, London/New York; 213, Adam Woolfitt/Woodfin Camp & Associates; 218, Bridgeman Art Library, London/New York; 219, Art Resource, NY; 221, Ted Spiegel; 223, 225, 226, 228, 235, 236 (background), Bridgeman Art Library, London/New York; 239, Bridgeman/Art Resource, NY; 244, Bridgeman Art Library, London/New York; 246, 247, Art Resource, NY; 249, 250, Bridgeman Art Library, London/New York; 255, Taro Kumamoto/Photonica; 257, 258, 260, Bridgeman Art Library, London/New York; 261, Sotheby's Transparency Library, London; 263, Art Resource, NY; 264, Bridgeman Art Library, London/New York; 265, Art Resource, NY; 267, Dave Boyer/UPI/Corbis-Bettmann; 271, Bridgeman Art Library, London/New York; 281, Republic (Courtesy Kobal); 282, Bridgeman Art Library, London/New York; 283 (top right), 284, 288 (top), Walter Hodges, The Globe Restored, ©1973 by W. W. Norton & Co. By arrangement with Coward, McCann & Geohegan, Inc.; 288, (left and bottom) G. Swann/Sygma; 290, (top) Adam Woolfitt/Woodfin Camp & Associates, (bottom) Goldwyn (Courtesy Kobal); 291, (top) Ken Howard/Old Globe Theatre, (bottom) Photofest; 292, (top) Martha Swope © Time, Inc., (bottom) Paramount (Courtesy Kobal); 293, Photofest; 294, (top) ©Michal Daniel/NY Shakespeare Festival, (bottom) Two Cities (Courtesy Kobal); 295, (top) Photofest, (bottom) Sotheby's Transparency Library, London; 296, (top) Paramount (Courtesy Kobal), (middle) ©Paul Davis. Courtesy of the artist, (bottom) Photofest; 297, Photofest; 298, (top to bottom) ©Paul Davis. Courtesy of the artist; Carol Rosegg; Art Resource, NY; 299, (top) Columbia (Courtesy Kobal),

(bottom) Bridgeman Art Library, London/New York; 300, Columbia (Courtesy Kobal); 303, 306, Robert C. Ragsdale F.R.P.S./Stratford Festival, Canada; 311, Photofest; 312, Robert C. Ragsdale F.R.P.S./Stratford Festival, Canada; 315, Photofest; 320, Robert C. Ragsdale F.R.P.S./Stratford Festival, Canada; 322, Photofest; 324, 332, Robert C. Ragsdale F.R.P.S./Stratford Festival, Canada; 337, 338, Photofest; 340, Comstock; 342, Photofest; 344, 348, 352, 360, 366, 368, 370, Robert C. Ragsdale F.R.P.S./Stratford Festival, Canada; 376, Republic (Courtesy Kobal); 378, Robert C. Ragsdale F.R.P.S./Stratford Festival, Canada; 380, Photofest; 383, Robert C. Ragsdale F.R.P.S/Stratford Festival, Canada; 386, Carol Rosegg; 388, Robert C. Ragsdale F.R.P.S./Stratford Festival, Canada; 389, Photofest; 392, (top) Bridgeman Art Library, London/New York, (bottom) Scala/Art Resource, NY; 393, Fine Art Photographic Library Ltd.; 395, Art Resource, NY; 396, 399, Scala/Art Resource, NY; 401, Bridgeman/Art Resource, NY; 403, Scala/Art Resource, NY; 404, Bridgeman Art Library, London/New York; 405, 406, Archives G. Dagli Orti; 410, 413, 414 (top and bottom), Art Resource, NY; 415, 417, Scala/Art Resource, NY; 421, Art Resource, NY; 422, Foto Marburg/Art Resource, NY; 424, Corbis-Bettmann; 428, Bridgeman Art Library, London/New York; 433, (bottom) Corbis-Bettmann; 434, Boltin Picture Library; 439, Art Resource, NY; 440, Bridgeman Art Library, London/New York; 446, 448, Art Resource, NY; 462, The Cartoon Bank; 465, F. Cruz/Superstock; 466, 468, Bridgeman Art Library, London/New York; 470, (left to right) Mary Evans Picture Library; Boltin Picture Library; Bridgeman Art Library, London/New York; 471, (bottom, left to right) ©Michael Holford; Courtesy, Peabody Essex Museum, Salem, Mass.; ©Phototèque des Musées de la Ville de Paris; 472, 473, 475, 476, 477, 478, 479, Culver Pictures, Inc.; 480, Max A. Polster Archive; 481, Bridgeman Art Library, London/New York; 482, Mansell/Time, Inc.; 483, North Wind Picture Archives; 485, Bridgeman Art Library, London/New York; 487, Culver Pictures, Inc.; 489, Mary Evans Picture Library; 493, The Arthur Rackham pictures are reproduced with the kind permission of his family; 495, Mary Evans Picture Library; 498, 499, Bridgeman Art Library, London/New York; 501, Mary Evans Picture Library; 519, 520, Bridgeman Art Library, London/New York; 521, North

INDEX OF SKILLS

READING AND CRITICAL THINKING

LANGUAGE (GRAMMAR, USAGE, AND MECHANICS)

CRITICAL COMMENTS

CREATIVE PROBLEM SOLVING

INDEX OF ART

FINE ART/ILLUSTRATIONS/ CRAFTS

INDEX OF AUTHORS AND TITLES